LONDON WRITINGS

Gottfried Semper

LONDON WRITINGS

1850–1855

Edited by
Michael Gnehm, Sonja Hildebrand, Dieter Weidmann

gta Verlag

CONTENTS

General Introduction	xi
Editorial Principles	xxxiii

LONDON WRITINGS

PRIVATE SCHOOL OF ARCHITECTURE

Lessons and Recommendation as Architect	
First Version	4
Second Version	5
Third Version	6
Fourth Version	7
School of Architecture and Engineering	
First Version	8
Second Version	8
Third Version	12
Fourth Version	13
Lessons in Architecture and Drawing	
First Version	14
Second Version	14
Third Version	15
Fourth Version	15

THE GREAT EXHIBITION

Announcement	18
A Foreign Architect's Views of the Building	18
The Great Exhibition	20
Letters on the Great Exhibition	
Outline	27
Draft of First Letter	29
Draft of Second Letter	30
Notes on Exhibits	31
Outline of a Cultural-Historical Exhibition	40
Note on a Cultural-Philosophical Collection	43
Association of Artists of Various Nations	43

POLYCHROMY IN ARCHITECTURE

On the Study of Polychromy, and Its Revival	48
On the Origin of Polychromy in Architecture	61

DEPARTMENT OF PRACTICAL ART

Report on the Private Collection of Arms at Windsor Castle	76
Berlin Productions of Plastical Art, Metal Casts, Plaster Casts	80
Observations on Some of the Specimens of Metal Work	82
A Plan of Instruction for the Metal and Furniture Classes	85
First Report on the Class for Practical Construction, Architecture, and Plastic Decoration	88
Second Report on the Class for Practical Construction, Architecture, and Plastic Decoration	91

LECTURES

Prospectuses of the Lectures on Art	96
On the Relations of the Different Branches of Industrial Art to Each Other and to Architecture	
First Version	97
Second Version	101
Third Version	104

General Remarks on the Different Styles in Art	118
The Ancient Practice of Wall Coating and Tubular Construction	127
Classification of Vessels	135
On Vessel Parts	146
Influence of the Materials and Their Treatments upon the Development of Ceramic Types and Style	151
On Timber Construction, and Its Influence upon the Development of Architectural Forms	161
The Combined Action of the Four Preceding Branches of Industry in Architecture	169
On Architectural Symbols	
First Version	177
Second Version	184
On the Relation of Architectural Systems with the General Cultural Conditions	189
Explanation of the Expression of Spatial Arrangements in Architecture	201

SUPPLEMENTARY TEXTS

London *Lothar Bucher*	206
German Studio for Architects and Engineers in London *Richard Wagner*	208
Submissions for the Great Exhibition *Franz Georg Stammann*	209
List of Books for Customs *Gottfried Semper*	
First Version	210
Second Version	212
British Museum Library Call Slips *Gottfried Semper*	217
Appointment Letter from the Department of Practical Art *Walter Ruding Deverell*	226
Principles and Practice of Ornamental Art Applied to Furniture, Metals, Jewellery, and Enamels *Henry Cole*	228

CRITICAL APPARATUS

PRIVATE SCHOOL OF ARCHITECTURE

Introduction	233
Lessons and Recommendation as Architect	238
School of Architecture and Engineering	243
Lessons in Architecture and Drawing	252

THE GREAT EXHIBITION

Introduction	257
Announcement	262
A Foreign Architect's Views of the Building	263
The Great Exhibition	271
Letters on the Great Exhibition	280
Notes on Exhibits	289
Outline of a Cultural-Historical Exhibition	296
Note on a Cultural-Philosophical Collection	308
Association of Artists of Various Nations	310

POLYCHROMY IN ARCHITECTURE

Introduction	313
On the Study of Polychromy, and Its Revival	316
On the Origin of Polychromy in Architecture	321

DEPARTMENT OF PRACTICAL ART

Introduction	327
Report on the Private Collection of Arms at Windsor Castle	332
Berlin Productions of Plastical Art, Metal Casts, Plaster Casts	353
Observations on Some of the Specimens of Metal Work	357
A Plan of Instruction for the Metal and Furniture Classes	370
First Report on the Class for Practical Construction	375
Second Report on the Class for Practical Construction	385

LECTURES

Introduction	391
Prospectuses of the Lectures on Art	396
On the Relations of the Different Branches of Industrial Art	397
General Remarks on the Different Styles in Art	426
The Ancient Practice of Wall Coating and Tubular Construction	436
Classification of Vessels	454
On Vessel Parts	461
Influence of the Materials upon Ceramic Types and Style	467

On Timber Construction, and Its Influence upon Architectural Forms	477
The Combined Action of the Branches of Industry in Architecture	488
On Architectural Symbols	497
On the Relation of Architectural Systems with Cultural Conditions	515
Explanation of the Expression of Spatial Arrangements in Architecture	530

SUPPLEMENTARY TEXTS

Introduction	535
London	536
German Studio for Architects and Engineers in London	537
Submissions for the Great Exhibition	539
List of Books for Customs	541
British Museum Library Call Slips	548
Appointment Letter from the Department of Practical Art	552
Principles and Practice of Ornamental Art	553

APPENDIX

Abbreviations of Holding Sites	559
Bibliography	
Writings by Gottfried Semper	561
Writings Cited by Gottfried Semper	563
Secondary Sources	572
Index	583
Acknowledgements	593

GENERAL INTRODUCTION

Selection and Presentation of the Texts

The writings by Gottfried Semper that are gathered together here were written during his almost five-year period of exile in London. Semper's involvement in the May Uprising of 1849 in Dresden had put an abrupt end to his successful career in the capital of the Kingdom of Saxony, where he had been teaching as Professor of Architecture at the Academy of Fine Arts since 1834 and had built up an international reputation as the architect of major buildings such as the Dresden Court Theatre. Following an interlude in Paris, the 'capital of culture', Semper arrived in London, the 'capital of the Empire', in the autumn of 1850 and established a new livelihood for himself there in conditions of considerable hardship. But London also turned out to provide extremely fertile ground for his work as a writer. In the metropolis, which was about to become the venue for the first World's Fair in 1851, Semper placed the industrial arts – considered in a global perspective – at the centre of his reflections on architectural theory and history. In the writings and lecture manuscripts that he produced during the London years, Semper laid the essential foundations for his major work on architectural theory, *Der Stil in den technischen und tektonischen Künsten, oder Praktische Aesthetik* (Style in the Technical and Tectonic Arts; or, Practical Aesthetics; 1860–63), which was written in Zurich and published in two volumes. Beginning with his first public lecture delivered in May 1853, he introduced a revolutionary approach to British academic art history which was just getting acquainted with the more traditional, chronology-based, German art history as presented by Gottfried Kinkel – another political refugee – in a lecture series at University College, London, that had started only one month earlier.[1] Semper himself viewed the significance of his period in London as highly seminal.

From Zurich, where he was appointed to the Chair of Architecture at the newly founded Swiss Federal Polytechnic (today ETH) in 1855, he wrote to the publisher Eduard Vieweg in Brunswick 'that my stay in London was extremely important for the further development of my ideas'.[2]

The present edition contains a selection of the minor writings that Semper produced in London. They are related on the one hand to his teaching work – some of which was only planned, while some was actually carried out. On the other hand, they are concerned with his critical engagement with the development of the arts and of culture as a whole. The selection of texts is based on two criteria: the extent to which they refer to the conditions in which Semper was living and working in London; and the extent to which they had an influence on his British milieu. The minor writings selected are divided into six groups. The first group covers several drafts of an advertisement intended to promote Semper's project of setting up a private school of architecture, as well as a published version of it. The programme for the school can be regarded as representing a link between the educational reforms he had introduced at the Dresden Academy of Fine Arts and his proposals for the structure of the curriculum at the Department of Practical Art in London (reorganized as the Department of Science and Art in March 1853). The second group is concerned with Semper's reflections on and responses to the most important historical event during his period in London – the Great Exhibition of the Works of Industry of All Nations in 1851. This group comprises printed advertisements, published essays on the exhibition and the building housing it, notes on the exhibits, drafts for an essay in letter form on culture and philosophy, draft programmes for a cultural history exhibition, and a note referring to the latter. The third group consists of two published essays through which Semper became involved in the British debate on architectural polychromy that flared up again in the early 1850s – not least in connection with the coloured painting of the structure of the Crystal Palace. The fourth group features reports on arts and crafts objects, a planned curriculum and annual reports on the course of his teaching work, all of which Semper wrote on behalf of the Department. The fifth group combines the extant drafts of the lectures that Semper gave in the Department in 1853 and 1854. Finally, the sixth group contains texts by other authors related to text groups one, two and four, as well as book lists compiled by Semper and call slips for books that he filled in at the British Museum Library – documents that provide revealing insights into his reading.

The framework chosen for this edition made it necessary to exclude a number of texts that were written, completed or begun by Semper during his London years. These exclusions are partly due to the length of the texts concerned and partly because they were either published in Germany or not at all, and consequently did not have any reception in the British Isles, or at most only sporadically. These texts firstly consist of three longer booklets along with the accompanying substantial manuscripts: *Die vier Elemente der Baukunst* (The Four Elements of Architecture; 1851), *Wissenschaft, Industrie und Kunst* (Science, Industry, and Art; 1852) and *Ueber die bleiernen Schleudergeschosse der Alten* (On the Leaden Slingshot Bullets of the Ancients; 1859)[3] – a work that was mostly written in London but was not completed and published until Semper's period in Zurich. Secondly, the excluded texts involve the approximately 250-page manuscript of the so-called metals catalogue, written in 1852 (a fair copy of which was edited in 2007),[4] and manuscripts that belong to Semper's 'Vergleichende Baulehre' (Comparative Architecture), begun in Paris in 1849 and continued in London but never completed.[5] The third group of excluded texts consists of writings on archaeology – some of which remained unpublished, while some appeared in *Deutsches Kunstblatt* – that do not have any clear relevance to debates in England, and a polemical text on Parisian architecture that was also intended for a German audience.

The present edition makes accessible for the first time all of the manuscripts in the text groups Private School of Architecture, The Great Exhibition, Department of Practical Art and Supplementary Texts – with the exception of the short manuscript of the 'Note on a Cultural-Philosophical Collection', published before with the letter in which it was inserted, and the manuscript of the concluding part of 'Observations on Some of the Specimens of Metal Work', separately edited before in posthumous German translation in *Kleine Schriften* (Minor Writings), which Semper's sons Manfred and Hans published in 1884. Some of the manuscripts in the Lectures group were edited in posthumous German translation in *Kleine Schriften* and by Harry Francis Mallgrave in the original English versions between 1983 and 1986.[6] However, Semper's sons muddled the arrangement of them in *Kleine Schriften* in three ways. Firstly, they distributed them – interspersed with other texts – across two sections of the book instead of uniting them in their chronological order. Secondly, in two cases they combined two different manuscripts each to produce hypothetical texts – even erroneously using the manuscripts of two different lectures for the often-mentioned 'Entwurf eines Systemes der vergleichenden Stillehre' (Outline for a System of Comparative Style-Theory).[7] Thirdly, they distorted two other manuscripts by splitting them or shortening them. Mallgrave's edition fully corrected this third type of disorder.[8] However, he only partly eliminated the first and second, since he did not edit the manuscripts of all of Semper's identifiable lectures and did not recognize that the manuscripts compiled to form the 'Outline for a System of Comparative Style-Theory' belong to two different lectures.[9] The present edition uses all of the extant manuscripts to reconstruct Semper's first series of lectures in London, and also – as far as possible – the second series. It publishes the manuscripts that contain the most complete versions of the lectures in chronological order – with individual previously undiscovered pages also being added for this purpose – and supplements them in the Critical Apparatus with the most important manuscript variants. Most of the printed texts included in this edition have been available since 2014 as reprints in Semper's *Gesammelte Schriften* edited by Henrik Karge.[10] However, the Critical Apparatus in the present edition also provides these with the associated manuscripts if they have been preserved. Moreover, the Apparatus offers an overview of all the known direct textual witnesses, bibliographical references, contextualizing and explanatory comments and information about editorial emendations. It also collates – in the case of the manuscripts – the most important authorial changes made.

   This edition forms part of the research project on 'Architecture and the Globalization of Knowledge in the 19th Century: Gottfried Semper and the Discipline of Architectural History' funded by the Swiss National Science Foundation (SNSF) – a collaboration between the Institute for the History and Theory of Art and Architecture (ISA) at the Università della Svizzera italiana (Sonja Hildebrand) and the Institute for the History and Theory of Architecture (gta) at ETH Zurich (Philip Ursprung). In addition to the present volume, the research project has led to two doctoral dissertations,[11] a series of essays and an anthology of essays centred on the disciplinary context of Semper's London years.[12] The London writings, which are made accessible here for the first time in a critical edition, exemplify the way in which Semper interacted with the global context provided by London, the ways in which he responded to contemporary debates in England, what he absorbed from them and the ways in which he articulated himself in the English-speaking environment.

Writing in Exile

Semper arrived in London after an extended period of exile in Paris – the city where he had studied architecture in Franz Christian Gau's studio from late 1826 to the autumn of 1827 and from summer 1829 to summer 1830. In Paris, he made efforts to regain his footing following the events that had turned his life upside down. In 1834, the Hamburg-born architect, who had grown up in nearby Altona (which belonged to Denmark at the time), had dismissed 'white' classicism in the pamphlet *Vorläufige Bemerkungen über bemalte Architectur und Plastik bei den Alten* (Preliminary Observations on Painted Architecture and Sculpture of the Ancients).[13] In the same year, at the age of just under thirty-one, he had been appointed Professor of Architecture and head of the School of Architecture at the Academy of Fine Arts in Dresden. His Dresden Synagogue of 1840 and the buildings near the Dresden Zwinger – the Court Theatre of 1841 and the Gemäldegalerie (Picture Gallery), begun in 1847 – consolidated his international reputation. The May Uprising of 1849 in Dresden caused a decisive break.[14] As the leader of the city militia's company of sharpshooters, he directed the construction of a barricade not far from his home on Waisenhausstrasse and commanded the forces occupying it, and he was probably also responsible for reinforcement of the main barricades, such as the one on Postplatz at the entrance to Wilsdruffer Gasse. The suppression of the uprising by Prussian and Saxon troops on 9 May caused him to flee the same day; a warrant for his arrest for high treason was issued on 16 May. Leaving his wife, Bertha, and their six children behind, Semper travelled south to Zwickau and Würzburg and then via Frankfurt am Main, Heidelberg and Karlsruhe to Strasbourg. He left Strasbourg for Paris on 6 June, arriving there on 8 June – and had already formed a plan to emigrate to North America a few days after he fled.[15]

Semper found accommodation with friends from his Dresden days – three decorative painters and theatre decorators who had been involved in work on the Court Theatre: for a short time with Édouard Desplechin in Paris, then with Jules Dieterle in nearby Sèvres, and in Paris again from December 1849 with Charles Séchan. He spent the long fifteen months in Paris not only in efforts to explore other options in Europe and establish contacts in North America but also primarily working on the book project he had agreed on with Eduard Vieweg between 1843 and 1844, from which *Der Stil* (Style) later developed. The book first began to take shape in Paris, and it was there that it was first given the title 'Vergleichende Baulehre' (Comparative Architecture) – inspired by Georges Cuvier's comparative anatomy.[16] After receiving an advance from Vieweg, Semper sent him an initial section consisting of around 400 manuscript pages on the early history of non-European architecture in May 1850. From his base in Paris, Semper was able in 1849 to have his delayed book about the Dresden Court Theatre put into print[17] and to publish essays in the Leipzig journal *Zeitschrift für praktische Baukunst*.[18] In the summer of 1850, he drafted his first text on ceramics – an essay written in French on porcelain painting, which was prompted by his contacts with the porcelain manufactory in Sèvres, where Dieterle had become the chief artist.[19]

Frustrated by the failures of his many attempts to establish a new livelihood in Europe, Semper decided in the summer of 1850 to accept the offer of an office partnership made to him by a Bremen architect who had moved to New York,

Karl Gildemeister (who was later the architect of the Crystal Palace at the 1853 World's Fair in New York), and to emigrate overseas. While he was in Le Havre waiting to depart for New York, a letter from the archaeologist Emil Braun reached him on 18 September 1850 – one day before the ship was due to sail. Braun had been secretary of the Prussian Instituto di corrispondenza archeologica in Rome since the mid-1830s (during his Grand Tour, Semper had earlier become a corresponding member of the institute). Braun was acquainted with Prince Albert and ran a galvanoplastic institute in Rome where he produced electrocast copies of ancient sculptures, some of which were included in the royal collection. He also acted as an art agent for Bernhard von Lindenau, a government minister in Saxony up to 1843, with whom Semper also had dealings. Braun had heard from the London architect Edward Falkener that Semper was intending to emigrate. Braun's letter to Semper – offering nothing more than a vague if flattering prospect of an artistic field of activity 'that promises to be no less glorious than the one you have left' – persuaded Semper to stay in Europe. While a crate with his books was already on its way to New York – it was not returned to him until the autumn of 1852 (the books contained in it are recorded in a customs list; 210–17) – he returned to Paris. After a missed meeting with Braun in Paris, and on receiving clarification from Braun that the matter concerned a project for a national cemetery near London that he was involved in, Semper travelled to the British capital to meet him.[20]

Semper arrived in London on the evening of 28 September 1850 and spent the night in the German and Commercial Hotel on Leicester Square. He was visited the next day by Braun, accompanied by the sanitary reformer Edwin Chadwick, commissioner of the General Board of Health and initiator of the cemetery project, and Eduard vom Hof, a German lawyer practising in London. The Board of Health, which had been founded in 1848, was intending to purchase the Abbey Wood estate, some 10 miles south-east of London between Woolwich and Erith, as a site for the cemetery. Semper immediately started sketching numerous designs for the cemetery (pl. 7). He moved into a flat on University Street, near the British Museum, at the beginning of October (as a subtenant of Thomas Watts, a carpenter), and was able to use a desk in Falkener's architectural office on Gracechurch Street in the City of London.[21] Political and legal disputes delayed the project, and Semper's contribution was reduced to the design of a Reception House – a chapel-like building in which the coffins were to be placed before burial and the mourners were to be received. The design, which he submitted in the summer of 1851 and for which he was paid £40, was rejected, as was that of fellow competitor Edward Cresy, superintending inspector to the Board. Shortly afterwards, the Abbey Wood cemetery project was cancelled.

Private School of Architecture

Even before this, his precarious financial situation had prompted Semper to resume a project to set up a private school of architecture. In the autumn of 1849, he had already been thinking about such a project in New York in collaboration with his former student Wilhelm Heine, who had emigrated there in the summer of 1849. In London, he drafted numerous newspaper advertisements in which he recommended himself with varying degrees of emphasis as a drawing teacher or as a consulting architect and announced the founding of a private school, complete with a boarding house, in which architectural training would be combined with engineering studies (4–15; pl. 1). He presented the idea to Braun for the first time in December 1850. Braun recommended that it should be done in collaboration with a London partner and suggested George Scharf or Edward Falkener. Both older and more recent contacts of Semper's supported him in the plan. Translations into English were provided by Karoline Heusinger, a Saxon (and a friend of Semper's wife) who was living in London, and by Mary Scarlett Campbell, the daughter of the family in which Heusinger was working as a lady-companion. Rudolph Schramm, a refugee from Berlin, edited the most detailed draft that Semper made and also brought in his friend Lothar Bucher, who placed an announcement of the project in the Berlin *National-Zeitung* (207–8) – he had become the paper's London correspondent after fleeing Berlin. Through Julius Faucher, correspondent of the *Kölnische Zeitung*, contact was established with the Basel architect Leonhard Friedrich. Through Friedrich in turn, a version of the advertisement reached Richard Wagner – Semper's friend while in Dresden, who was also a refugee from the revolution – in Zurich, and it was published in the *Eidgenössische Zeitung* there with a supportive text from Wagner (13, 208–9). However, Semper's project for setting up a school of architecture did not progress beyond this initial advertising campaign.

The Great Exhibition

Semper's social life in London was only partly influenced by the German exile community. Thanks to an invitation from Schramm to attend a refugee meeting organized by Arnold Ruge at the Cranbourne Hotel in early March 1851, he had the opportunity to meet some of the notable exiles – including Bucher and Gottfried Kinkel. The politically agitating Kinkel became Semper's colleague at the Zurich Polytechnic in 1866.[22] But Semper's political involvement was limited. He did attend the meeting in the same hotel at the end of July 1851 at which Kinkel and August Willich founded the German Emigration Club, and he was elected a month later to the board of the reorganized refugee committee alongside Bucher and Oskar Reichenbach.[23] However, Bucher and Semper declared their resignation in a jointly written letter to Kinkel the very next day, specifying that they would now devote themselves 'privately to the common cause'.[24] The committee was dissolved in 1852. In July 1853, Semper applied and was admitted to the 'German Society of Benevolence and Concord', which had been established in 1817. Remarkably, there is no known evidence of a meeting between Semper and Karl Marx. Marx was an opponent of most of the refugees with whom Semper had dealings and did not attend any of the above meetings, but he noted Semper's election to Kinkel's refugee committee.[25] Both Marx and Semper frequented the British Museum Library and, surprisingly, they had the same doctor, Jonas Freund.

More important was another initiative by Schramm at the end of March 1851. He initiated the first publication of a text by Semper in England, the essay 'Die grosse Ausstellung' (The Great Exhibition), which was published in May in the German supplement of *The Illustrated London News* (20–6). In the essay, Semper set out publicly for the first time the view that, in relation to ornamental treatment, Europe had been 'defeated by our Oriental competitors' in the field of the applied arts, which was threatening to become corrupted by 'machinery'. By this time, Semper already had first-hand access to the Crystal Palace. The collaboration he had hoped for with Joseph Paxton, the architect of the exhibition building whom Semper had met at Chadwick's at the end of November 1850, had not materialized – the commission for the decoration of the Crystal Palace for which Semper had applied had already gone to Owen Jones. Instead, however, Henry Cole – a member of the executive committee of the Great Exhibition, whose acquaintance Semper had also made through Chadwick in early December – gave him the opportunity to design some of the national sections in the Exhibition. Semper arranged the Canadian section (pl. 8), the sections for the Cape of Good Hope and Nova Scotia that were grouped around it, and the sections for Sweden with Norway and for Denmark.[26] He probably also contributed to the adjacent sections for Egypt and Turkey. Financially, the work at the Crystal Palace was not particularly lucrative. Thus, Semper was still trying to acquire work three weeks after the exhibition opened. He had an advertisement, written by the Hamburg architect Franz Georg Stammann, placed in the *Hamburger Nachrichten* (209–10) and also had a French advertisement, dated 1 April 1851, printed (18). He remained on friendly terms with the commissioner of the Canadian section, Henry Houghton, who lived in London as a warehouseman; in the late summer, he received a commission from Houghton for a drawing complete with frame, remunerated at £30.

Shortly before the essay published in *The Illustrated London News* and the many varied and fragmentary preliminary stages for it, Semper wrote drafts that can be assigned to the essay on Paxton's Crystal Palace that was published in *The Edinburgh Review* in the autumn of 1851 (18–20). Edward Aubrey Moriarty, the translator of Charles Dickens's works into German and of Franz Kugler's *Geschichte Friedrichs des Grossen* into English, among other works, had translated Semper's essay (probably with Cole as an intermediary) and inserted it in his (Moriarty's) review of the last edition of the *Official Catalogue of the Great Exhibition*. In the essay, Semper gives the Crystal Palace double-edged praise as a work that the architect had brought into an 'entire unison with nature'. The building shows 'the original type of the most primitive form of architecture unwittingly realised' – adapted to the required purpose but unsuitable for progressive architecture. A 'complete revolution', Semper concludes, 'must take place in English manners before the glass roof can find adoption in private dwellings or religious edifices'.

From May to October 1851, Semper repeatedly browsed through the Crystal Palace; hurried but highly interesting notes that he took provide evidence for the routes he followed through the building (31–9; pl. 2). Most of them list exhibits from North America and Russia – contrasting the new mechanized world (represented, for example, by locomotives and McCormick's reaper) and oversophisticated applied arts. Textiles fare better, such as an embroidered blanket from Azerbaijan. There are surprising items such as shoes, artificial teeth, Palmer's prosthetic legs and Day & Newell's unpickable lock (the latter two – like the reaper – also proved interesting for Sigfried Giedion decades later). Semper took notes on raw materials and clocks and repeatedly lingered in front of American daguerreotypes. The notes provide a panorama of the interests that flowed into *Science, Industry, and Art*, the pamphlet published in 1852 in which he intervened in debates on design reform.[27] Although it was probably Henry Cole who was behind the 'private request' he mentions as his motive for writing the pamphlet, the text was to become influential mainly in Germany during the second half of the nineteenth century.

The Great Exhibition led Semper to reflect on museology. In a fragmentary epistolary essay on cultural philosophy, addressed to Lothar Bucher (27–31), he discusses the museum as a location in which 'world ideas' condense. The Great Exhibition, which expressed the 'unconsciously born idea of a genuine cultural-historical collection', provided the elements from which the 'museum of the future' and a corresponding form of architecture would be able to crystallize on the basis of a comparative methodology. These ideas are reflected in Bucher's *Kulturhistorische Skizzen aus der Industrieausstellung aller Völker* (Cultural-Historical Sketches from the Industrial Exhibition of All Nations; 1851). Between October 1851 and January 1852, Semper wrote a new introduction and a 'Prospectus' for his 'Comparative Architecture', which was published as an appendix in some copies of *Science, Industry, and Art*. As another planned supplement to the pamphlet, he also compiled a schematic list for a collection arranged according to his four basic architectural elements (40–2), along with an associated note (43) that was to be inserted at the appropriate place in the pamphlet. Both of these remained unpublished.

By including the decorative arts in an overarching cultural-historical context, Semper was revising the reforming efforts made by the German 'Prototype Movement', as seen from the 1820s onwards particularly in Peter Beuth and Karl Friedrich Schinkel's *Vorbilder für Fabrikanten und Handwerker* (Models for Manufacturers and Craftsmen).[28] Semper had already made notes on four 'Questions for Industrial Collectors' in 1834 in this connection.[29] For one of these questions – 'How can we renew and make artistic use of what was once customary'? – he sought to provide a practical answer in the form of an exhibition planned for February 1852 in the empty Crystal Palace by an 'Association of Artists of Various Nations' that he had initiated, with 'designs, drawings and models from the field of industrial art, including architecture'. He promoted the exhibition in an advertisement published at the end of December 1851 (43–4). Slightly later on, he had an opportunity to answer another of his applied art questions from 1834 – 'How did the most important historical forms arise out of their incunabula'? Around the middle of April 1852, Cole engaged Semper to write 'a kind of illustrated catalogue raisonné on the whole field of metals technology', as Semper explained to Eduard Vieweg.[30] It was to serve as 'an illustrated catalogue for a projected collection of metalworks', he added to Antonio Panizzi, then keeper of the Department of Printed Books at the Library of the British Museum[31] – where Semper was spending a great deal of time, as evidenced by the call slips that have survived for the period from March to December 1852 (217–25; pl. 12). He sent the manuscript for the catalogue to Cole in mid-August. It was entitled 'Practical Art in Metals and hard Materials; its Technology, History and Styles' and earned him £180. In it, he set out his square diagram for a 'complete and universal Collection', based in turn on his four basic elements of architecture.

Polychromy in Architecture
Shortly after arriving in London, Semper resumed his writing work and established contacts with London institutions. In October 1850, he received an admission card for the ordinary meetings of the Royal Institute of British Architects (RIBA). He had been acquainted with Thomas Leverton Donaldson, one of the founders and secretaries of RIBA, since his first visit to London in late 1838. Probably as early as the second half of October 1850, Semper started drafting the pamphlet *The Four Elements of Architecture*, the German-language manuscript of which he sent to Vieweg on 19 January 1851.[32] The occasion for this was an invitation by Falkener to contribute to his journal *The Museum of Classical*

Antiquities. Semper was planning to provide an outline of his 'Comparative Architecture' (and the subtitle of the pamphlet is in fact marked *A Contribution to Comparative Architecture*). However, the text expanded to such an extent that Semper decided to provide Falkener with a version of the sections on architectural polychromy (pl. 3) [33] – probably prompted by lectures given by Owen Jones and Matthew Digby Wyatt at RIBA in December 1850, and a topic that was focused on in the first issue of Falkener's journal, which appeared in January 1851 with texts on polychromy by Jacques Ignace Hittorff and Falkener himself. Semper's essay was published in the July issue (48–61). In it, he denied that Greek culture had an autochthonous origin by arguing that 'the Greeks borrowed from Barbarians'. He also for the first time publicly stated his revolutionary opinion that walls 'decorated with painting and other ornaments' had developed as a 'substitution' for older 'tapestry' – an opinion prepared for graphically with his lithographs for *Die Anwendung der Farben in der Architectur und Plastik* (The Use of Colour in Architecture and Sculpture) of 1836 (pl. 9). The essay made part of *The Four Elements of Architecture* available in English as a first publication – the German pamphlet did not appear until the autumn of 1851. Three years later, Semper published another adaptation of it in English, in Jones's *Apology for the Colouring of the Greek Court in the Crystal Palace* (61–73). In it, he again emphasized that architectural 'decorations [were] borrowed from the weaver's art'. In the spring of 1852, Semper offered Falkener another manuscript on an archaeological topic for publication: an essay written in French on the Erechtheum, in which – in remarks directed against Friedrich Thiersch – he attributes inscriptions found on the Acropolis not to that temple but rather to the Propylaea.[34] Despite repeated requests from Falkener, Semper dropped this publication project and did not arrange for a translation into English.

Department of Practical Art

Semper's first direct contact with the Department of Practical Art, founded in February 1852 – the central administration of the Government Schools of Design, reformed by Henry Cole – came about through the metals catalogue mentioned above. Cole apparently commissioned him to prepare the catalogue in connection with the Museum of Manufactures, which opened provisionally in Marlborough House in Westminster, the home of the Department, in mid-May. Semper's work on the metals catalogue was one in a series of efforts he made to obtain a position as professor in Cole's Department. In the end, these efforts were crowned with success. His appointment was definitively decided on 8 September 1852, and the certificate of appointment was issued shortly afterwards, on 11 September (226–7; pl. 6). On 27 September, Semper acknowledged receipt of a prospectus drawn up by Cole for the special class on the 'Principles and Practice of Ornamental Art' in the field of metalwork which he had been appointed to teach. While he would continue to be the contact person for ceramics, furniture was made part of his immediate expertise (228). Shortly afterwards, his teaching area was expanded to include architecture. The focus on ornament is expressed in the certificate for art-instruction which he designed for the Department of Science and Art (pl. 10). Thus Semper became – alongside Ralph Nicholson Wornum – one of the first permanently employed art historians in British academic life with his special focus on the applied arts and architecture. Before, art history was taught primarily in connection with museums, as in the case of Charles Eastlake (editor of the first volume of Franz Kugler's *Handbuch der Geschichte der Malerei* in English) who was offered a post as the first professor of fine arts at London University (today's University College) in the 1830s, but declined in favour of his museum work.[35] Gottfried Kinkel's appointments as lecturer in art history in Great Britain, starting in 1853, were always temporary positions.[36] Semper's annual salary of £150 – not exorbitant, but supplemented by a share of teaching fees – nevertheless allowed him to move into a new flat near Hyde Park, at Gloucester Terrace, and to bring his family to join him.

The first semester at the Department of Practical Art, which began offering courses in the autumn of 1852, was marked by a royal commission to design the carriage for the Duke of Wellington's funeral procession, which passed from St James's Park to St Paul's Cathedral on 18 November.[37] Semper was responsible for the design and execution of the wooden structure and the richly decorated cast bronze panels that encased the ponderous funeral car. He was also involved in the overall design; however, Richard Redgrave, the Department's art superintendent, claimed sole authorship. While Semper's contribution was critically noted in London, it was celebrated in Germany as early as 1854 as 'Wellington's hearse by Professor Semper', representing one of the 'not insignificant victories of German taste over English'.[38] In the 'First Report' on his teaching work (88–91), dating from early 1854, Semper mentions the funeral carriage as an example of his teaching method, in which he aimed to have students become involved in practical work from the outset and to design the educational work in the form of a studio. He elaborated on this further in a 'Plan of Instruction for the Metal and Furniture Classes' (85–8), the draft of which, dated 1 February 1853, he submitted to the Department, supplemented with the idea of a transdisciplinary approach that would encompass technology of art, physics, mineralogy, chemistry and metallurgy.

Before he started work on the Wellington carriage, Semper carried out tasks in connection with the Department's Museum of Manufactures, which opened definitively at the beginning of September 1852 and was soon renamed the

Museum of Ornamental Art. His 'Report on the Private Collection of Arms at Windsor Castle' (76–80), dated 20 September, was commissioned to investigate the possibility of obtaining loans or copies for the museum. In his expert report on arms, Semper was returning to the branch of the decorative arts whose 'practical' side he had already emphasized in his review of the Great Exhibition: in it, he argued, 'the striving for refinement and embellishment by art of the forms offered by the purpose of the object and the material used is shown in a modest way, and for that very reason satisfies the genuine sense of beauty' (23). The report is also of particular interest because Semper's English draft with Cole's corrections has been preserved (pl. 4). Semper's expertise was also in demand in other fields. On 11 October 1852, he recommended that Cole should make purchases from an offer submitted to him of 'Berlin Productions of Plastical Art' (80–2); Redgrave approved the purchase of cast iron jewellery from the offer. For the museum catalogue, Semper wrote introductory 'Observations on Some of the Specimens of Metal Work' (82–5), the first version of which was published in the catalogue of February 1853 and expanded in a new edition in May with an addition on newly acquired articles. Semper's interest in polychrome oriental ornamentation and vessel design found its way into this work. As in the case of the Berlin cast iron jewellery, most of the metal artefacts commented on by Semper can be found in today's Victoria and Albert Museum.

Between the end of 1852 and January 1853, during his first teaching-free period, Semper drafted a number of texts aimed at a German readership, including archaeological essays. Through the assistance of the painter and antiquarian Johann Karl Bähr, Semper's friend and former colleague at the Dresden Academy of Fine Arts, these were published in the Berlin *Deutsches Kunstblatt* in the spring and autumn of 1855. One of them was an essay on 'Die Restauration des Tuskischen Tempels' (The Restoration of the Tuscan Temple), a critique of Thiersch's interpretation of Vitruvius.[39] Another was a multi-part essay on 'Die neben den Propyläen aufgefundenen Inschrifttafeln' (The Inscription Panels Found next to the Propylaea), a new version of Semper's 1852 essay in French on the Erechtheum, now published as 'Briefe aus der Schweiz' (Letters from Switzerland).[40] Semper used a research trip to the porcelain manufactory in Sèvres in January 1853, commissioned by Cole, to write an essay on 'Die neuesten pariser Bauten' (The Latest Buildings in Paris), which was published the following month in Karl Gutzkow's journal *Unterhaltungen am häuslichen Herd*.[41] Gutzkow had for a short time been a dramatic advisor at the Dresden Court Theatre, until the 1849 revolution.

During preparations for his public lectures at the Department of Science and Art, the first of which Semper delivered in May 1853, he attended a RIBA meeting in early February 1853 at which a paper by the Scottish interior decorator and art theorist David Ramsay Hay on 'Proportions and Curves of the Parthenon of Athens' was presented. The optical corrections that were discussed inspired Semper to test the relationship between mathematical regularity and aesthetic perception using the plum-stone-shaped leaden slingshot bullets of the Greeks.[42] The preface to the first version of the paper is dated 20 December 1853. Before its publication in 1859, Semper had a summary of it, concerned particularly with the trigonometric part, published in the Leipzig *Annalen der Physik und Chemie* in September 1854. As stated there in the introduction, he regarded the study as 'a contribution to the comparative theory of forms'.[43] At the same time he was afraid that it might be plagiarized by the Prussian military. In contrast, however, Semper's work on the paper was already being remarked upon in Germany in early 1854 with an assumption that it had been written 'under official commission from the English government'.[44]

Lectures

On 20 May 1853, Semper gave his first public lecture in London at Marlborough House to a distinguished audience – the inaugural lecture, 'On the Relations of the Different Branches of Industrial Art to Each Other and to Architecture' (104–17). Cole considered it 'thoughtful & suggestive'.[45] The text of the lecture is found in the first of two manuscripts that researchers have previously mistaken for interchangeable variants of the lecture with which Semper opened the autumn term in 1853.[46] Two partial drafts were considered to be the only traces of the wording of the inaugural lecture (97–103).[47] In both of these fragments, Semper starts by quoting the first of the propositions by Owen Jones that the Department had decided to use as the basis for its teaching work – namely that the decorative arts originated in architecture and should accompany it appropriately (pl. 5). In the definitive version of the lecture, Semper omitted both the quotation and his reservation that it was correct only 'if taken in its true meaning'. This was probably to avoid any appearance of presumptuousness in his divergent opinion – namely 'that architecture is based upon principles and laws, which were known and practised in ornamental art'. It was only after a lengthy introduction concerning the need to regain the lost 'consciousness of the intimate connections, which exist between the different branches of knowledge and skill', that he now took a position on this. The 'history of Architecture', he nevertheless states unequivocally thereafter, 'begins with the history of practical art'. As an example, he presents for the first time in public his comparison of the Egyptian *situla* and the Greek *hydria* – two vessels in which basic elements of the corresponding forms of architecture are prefigured. The lecture combines two key modern disciplines in an exemplary way: dynamics and ethnology. Semper presents the much-cited formula that he used to illustrate his 'Doctrine of Style': a mathematical functional equation that covers an infinite number of factors that stand for the dynamical function, the multifarious variability of artistic form-finding. Functionality is not necessarily achieved here through 'science and calculation', as is proved by the 'ornamental art' of New Zealand with its 'Sort of architecture', which consists of 'nothing but richly sculptured and painted hedges and hedgepoles', and 'the Axes of the North-American Nativs'. Even in the case of the perfectly formed 'Greec Sling bullets', it remains questionable whether they are not also 'the Result of an instinctiv feeling'. The inaugural lecture ends with a forward look at five future lectures, which correspond precisely to the programme in which Semper's lectures for the autumn semester were announced (96–7).

In the course of the autumn semester, the number of Semper's public lectures expanded from five to seven. The first, which included an introduction and two sections on 'The ancient practice of wall coating' and on 'Tubular construction', was spread across two lectures. In the opening lecture, the 'General Remarks on the Different Styles in Art' (118–26), he recapitulates his inaugural lecture, making cuts and additions. He varies the mathematical formula of his 'Doctrine of Style' and falls back on his four basic architectural elements – the hearth or fireplace, the roof, the enclosure and the substructure or terrace – with the areas of practical art assigned to them: ceramics and metalwork, carpentry, the 'Craft of matmakers and hanging-manufactures' and masonry. However, he designates – as in the inaugural lecture – 'the art or ... industry of coating ... in the widest sense', including textiles, as the first class of the artistic treatment of raw materials. The reversal in the importance assigned to ceramics and textile art that was then to follow by the time of *Style* is anticipated here. As the example of Assyrian wall coverings with 'glazed bricks' shows (Semper had discovered them in the Louvre in Paris in 1850), ceramics had provided a substitute for 'the variegated original draperies'. Conversely, Assyrian reliefs in the British Museum indicated that they were 'copies in Stone of woven or embroidered tapestries'. This first autumn lecture concludes with the 'principle of Coating' – the first time that Semper uses the term, which is then translated into German in *Style* as 'Prinzip der Bekleidung' (usually translated as 'principle of dressing').[48]

The second lecture combines 'The ancient practice of wall coating' and 'Tubular construction' into one lecture (127–35). Inspired by the Great Exhibition, Semper supplements the discussion of the four basic elements of architecture with ethnological classifications of contemporary products, including those of Trinidad – with the example of the model of a Caribbean hut, which he discusses publicly here for the first time. He equates Chinese architecture with this preliminary architectural form, as he regards it, and shocks the audience by noting that at the time when Assyria and Egypt had already developed into high cultures, the Greeks were still at the level of 'the American Indians, or the New-Zealandas' of his time. The lecture concludes with examples of metals technology in the areas of furniture, weapons and doors.

Semper expanded the third planned lecture, on ceramics, into three lectures (135–60).[49] Here he describes pottery as being 'perhaps' the 'most important of all the different branches of industry for the general history of art and for artistical science'. He includes objects made of various materials in the category of ceramics; they belonged to this field because the decisive 'traditional laws of generation and ornamentation ... have been settled by potters'. As evidence of this, he again refers to the *situla* and *hydria*, with the argument accentuated by the idea of national characteristics that allow these to be read as exemplifying the 'national Genius of the Aegyptians' and the 'lucid nature of the monteneer inhabitants of Greece', respectively. He uses the second ceramics lecture to draw a distinction between two 'principles of ornamentation': one in which ornamentation symbolized the 'dynamical function' of the object associated with its construction, and another in which it represented the cultural context in the form of historicized images. In the third lecture on ceramics, he recalls the 'mortifying truth' of an 'unquestioned superiority of half barbarous nations' in the field of the applied arts and then goes on to discuss ceramic materials, techniques and the characteristics of handmade and mechanically reproduced objects.

In the following lecture, 'On Timber Construction' (161–9; pl. 11), he discusses roof constructions and coverings among the Chinese, Egyptians, Greeks and Indians, addresses Moorish, Norman and Gothic architecture and summarizes Caucasian and Etruscan architecture as well as the vernacular architecture of Tyrol, Switzerland, Sweden and Norway. The lecture illustrates engineering science with sketches for classifying construction systems ranging from flat roofs to suspension bridges and mentions the latest English iron bridges and their traditional counterparts in South America and Tibet.

There are no surviving drafts of the subsequent planned lecture on stereotomy (masonry). The series concludes with the lecture on 'The Combined Action' of the different branches of the applied arts in architecture (169–77). Here Semper explains the 'different Styles of architecture' in relation to anthropological and political implications. Observations on 'Domestic life' lead him from the 'mouveable tent ... of the Nomad tribes' to farmhouses 'in the old saxon countries', Scandinavian stave churches and the settlement architecture of the 'descendants of the German races' with their 'Strongholds and blockhouses'. As formative types, he contrasts the 'fortified camp', which multiplied into the form of towering pyramids in Assyrian architecture, with the core of the Egyptian temple, which was expanded through the constant addition of new layers.

These represent contrasting manifestations of a 'Military despotism' based on conquest and feudalism and of a 'national Monarchy' supported by an aristocratic priesthood.

With the exception of the drafts of three lectures, little more is known about the programme of lectures Semper gave in the autumn of 1854 beyond what he noted about his teaching activities in the 'Second Report' (91–3): he held 'two courses of five public lectures on the different styles of ancient architecture'. The two extant versions of the lecture 'On Architectural Symbols' (177–89) probably mark the beginning of these. He starts with the creative potential of architecture, which is 'a pure inventiv art' or 'an art of invention'. The function of nature as a model, he argues, lies solely in an analogous 'dependency on natural laws and conditions', implying that 'the history or nature of mankind' can be narrated through architecture in exactly the same way that fossilized 'shells' and 'Coraltrees' provide information about their former organic inhabitants. There is an explicit distinction here showing that 'the history of architecture does not begin at the same point with the history of housebuilding and Engineering'. He places the Caribbean hut in the latter category, while the former is marked by a sequence of those kinds of 'social revolution' with which 'the prevalence of a new principle' is associated – successive rearrangements of the combination of the four basic architectural elements, or rather the four engineering-like basic elements – and the way in which they are shaped by the applied arts, which have always affected the 'symbolical language' of architecture. He illustrates in detail the symbolization of the complex forces that are at work in architecture using the Doric cyma, in passages in which he makes use of Karl Bötticher's *Tektonik der Hellenen* (Tectonics of the Hellenes; 1844–52) without mentioning the work. Semper probably first started reading Bötticher's book in December 1852 – as indicated by the preserved call slip from the British Museum Library (pl. 12), the notes he made on the book partly in English and the absence of earlier remarks about it.[50]

In the second lecture of 1854, 'On the Relation of Architectural Systems with the General Cultural Conditions' (189–201), Semper further discusses the way in which 'architectural monuments are ... the artistical expressions of ... social political and religious institutions': from the 'patriarchal form of society' to the 'free confederation between tribes of the same origine and race'. The latter form – although it is 'the most natural and the most reasonable' – is repeatedly overthrown by absolutism and oligarchy, as seen in the cases of Assyria and Egypt. Lengthy remarks on China follow, where he argues that the traditional 'terrible revolution of nature' (flooding) corresponds to social revolutions in China to the extent that no fundamental changes occur. Chinese architecture has thus preserved an isolated juxtaposition of 'the constructiv parts and the details … in the most primitiv and material sense'. After a brief discussion of Babylon, the manuscript breaks off with a forward look at Egyptian architecture. This preview is continued in the short fragment of the following lecture, 'Explanation of the Expression of Spatial Arrangements in Architecture' (201–3), with an outline, illustrated with sketches, of the way in which Egyptian temple types served as models for Greek and Roman architecture.

The Will to Architecture

The ultimate success of Semper's period in London was clouded by the scarcity of commissions for him as a building architect. He complained that his practical work was limited to 'furniture stuff'.[51] Following the abortive adventure of the Abbey Wood cemetery project, he drew up plans for several buildings that were not implemented. In 1851, he designed a London washhouse and public baths, and later that year he was commissioned to design an extension to The Grange in Hampshire, the country seat of William Bingham Baring Ashburton, who then preferred a design by Charles Robert Cockerell. These were followed, during the period when Semper was a professor at the Department of Practical Art (later Department of Science and Art), in mid-October 1852 by a design for a telegraph kiosk for the Electric Telegraph Company, a design for a London building for emigrants in 1853 and – in a competition setting – for a pottery school in Stoke-on-Trent. During these years, the only design commission that was implemented was for the iron frame and roof of a manufactory building for the Royal Arsenal in Woolwich, arranged through the military engineer Thomas Bernard Collinson; the work was carried out to a limited extent up to mid-1854.[52] New tasks arose for the Crystal Palace when it was rebuilt in the South London suburb of Sydenham up to 1854. Semper was commissioned by Joseph Paxton to design one of the commercial exhibition spaces there, the Mixed Fabrics Court.[53] In contrast, his proposal for a Pompeian theatre in the transept of the Palace did not progress beyond the initial design stage.

From mid-March to early June 1855, Semper stayed in Paris on behalf of the Department to help set up the British section at the second World's Fair. Dissatisfied with the tasks assigned to him there, he complained in a letter to his wife, 'The English architects have snatched everything away from me.'[54] While he was in Paris, Semper started on a design for the competition for the Théâtre de la Monnaie in Brussels, which had burned down, but he apparently did not submit it.[55] The final phase of Semper's period of exile in London was marked by a highly promising commission from Prince Albert: in mid-February 1855, through Cole, he commissioned Semper to design a kind of cultural forum in

General Introduction

South Kensington – on the site of today's Royal Albert Hall – that would house the various museum sections of the Department of Science and Art in combination with a concert hall, shops and flats. Semper's design for a gigantic reinterpretation of the Crystal Palace was ready in mid-June. It delighted Prince Albert, but the Board of Trade declined to pursue it for reasons of cost.

By this time, however, Semper's life had already taken a new turn, thanks in part to Richard Wagner's mediation. Wagner had written to him in August 1854 that there was a prospect of a position in Zurich that would make Semper 'the supreme authority on building matters for the whole of Switzerland'.[56] The position in question was that of director and first professor in the Department of Architecture at the Swiss Federal Polytechnic, which was founded in 1854 and started offering courses in the autumn of 1855. After negotiations in Zurich, Semper agreed to the offer in principle on 16 November 1854. Arguments in favour of Zurich were a tenured position, a German-speaking environment and the prospect – albeit still vague – of being able to design the new building for the Polytechnic. After the appointment had been made definitive in February 1855, Semper travelled from Paris to Zurich again in March, where he took the opportunity to find a suitable rented flat for the summer. In the meantime, his family moved to Paris for a few weeks. On returning to London at the beginning of June, Semper stayed for the last three weeks of his London exile with the German engineer and industrialist Carl Wilhelm Siemens, a friend of his, in Kensington Crescent. Semper left London on 26 or 27 June 1855 and arrived in Zurich, after a stopover in Paris, on 12 July. It was not until 1863, on 8 May, that the warrant for his arrest was withdrawn by the authorities in Saxony.[57]

1   On Kinkel's 1853 lectures at University College, see Haskell 1988, 214–16; Ashton 1996; Hönes 2019; Hönes 2021. For Semper's approach compared to contemporaneous German art history, see Karge 2013. For Semper's bourgeois-democratic context among German refugees in London, see Ashton 1986, 139–87 (Semper mentioned on 54, 163–4, 176, 182, 208); Weidmann 2014. For a broader assessment of the refugee situation in mid-nineteenth-century Great Britain, see Freitag 2003.

2   Semper to Eduard Vieweg, Zurich, 25 July 1855 (Vieweg Archives, V3:1.1.3.32); cf. draft letter (gta, 20-K-1855-07-25[S]).

3   The translation of this title adopts part of Semper's own wording in his London lectures where he speaks of 'ancient Greec Sling bullets', with 'Sling bullets' replacing the deleted word 'Projectiles'.

4   'Practical Art in Metals and hard Materials; its Technology, History and Styles' [1852] (NAL, 86.FF.64); Semper 2007a.

5   All of Semper's manuscripts for 'Comparative Architecture' ed. in Luttmann 2008, 249–609. Individual chapters ed. in Herrmann 1981, 180–216 (selected Engl. trans. in Herrmann 1984, 189–218).

6   For details of these two editions, see the textual record of the individual lectures.

7   Semper 1884, 344–50, translates a compilation of MS 117 and MS 118; Semper 1884, 259–91, compiles MS 122 and MS 124 to form the source text of the translation for 'Entwurf eines Systemes der vergleichenden Stillehre'.

8   The major part of MS 129 is translated in Semper 1884, 383–94, the concluding part in Semper 1884, 90–4. In Mallgrave's edition, both parts are combined in their original sequence; see Semper 1986a. MS 144^1 is translated in Semper 1884, 351–68, without the last two pages; MS 144^2 is omitted altogether. Mallgrave has edited both manuscript parts in their entirety; see Semper 1986b.

9   The same applies to the five lectures translated into French by Jacques Soulillou (Semper 2007b, 157–222), based on Mallgrave's English edition and complemented at places by Manfred and Hans Semper's German translation.

10 Semper 2014.

11 Chestnova 2017a, revised as Chestnova 2022; Leoni 2019.

12 Gnehm/Hildebrand 2021.

13 The title of this pamphlet as translated by William Richard Hamilton in his translation of Franz Kugler's *Ueber die Polychromie der griechischen Architektur und Sculptur und ihre Grenzen* (Kugler 1835), which was published in the *Transactions of the Institute of British Architects of London* (Kugler 1836).

14 On Semper's participation in the May Uprising of 1849 in Dresden, see Heirler 1980; Herrmann 1984, 9–12 (trans. of Herrmann 1978, 10–13); Laudel 1995, 46–9; Mallgrave 1996, 165–71; Laudel 2000; Hildebrand 2020, 77–88.

15 For Semper's life and work during his exile in Paris, see Herrmann 1984, 12–29 (trans. of Herrmann 1978, 14–31); Mallgrave 1996, 171–81; Laudel 2003, 269–73; Kalinowski/Thibault 2018; Hildebrand 2020, 88–103.

16 On Semper's 'Comparative Architecture' as related to Cuvier, see Hauser 1985; Herrmann 1990, 77–8; Laudel 1991, 43–5; Eck 1994, 228–34; Mallgrave 1996, 156–9; Gnehm 2004, 29–34, 43–6, 54; Hvattum 2004a, 123–32; Luttmann 2007, 221, 227–33; Luttmann 2008, 5–10, 119–21.

17 Semper 1849a.

18 Semper 1849b–i; Semper 1850a–c. In September 1849, Semper offered his services as a French correspondent to the journal's editor, the architect Johann Andreas Romberg; see Semper to Romberg, Paris, 7 September 1849 (gta, 20-K-1849-09-07[S]).

19 Semper, '[Observations sur l'exécution de la peinture sur porcelaine]' (June 1850) (gta, 20-Ms-47); German trans. in Semper 1884, 58–75. The essay is addressed to 'Ma fille', i.e. Semper's eldest daughter, Elisabeth.

20 For Semper's life and work during his exile in London, see Herrmann 1976; Lankheit 1976; Reising 1976; Vogt 1976; Mallgrave 1983a; Herrmann 1984, 29–83 (trans. of Herrmann 1978, 32–93); Mallgrave 1996, 176, 182–227; Hildebrand 2003; Laudel 2003, 273–97; Payne 2012, 25–64; Leoni 2014; Weidmann 2014; Charitonidou 2020; Hildebrand 2020, 103–31.

21 In a draft letter of 13 October 1850 (erroneously dated 12 October), addressed to his brother Johann Carl, Semper wrote, 'I have an office in the City with the architect Falkener 61, Grace church Street. and am living in University street 27. with Mr. Watts' (pl. 7; gta, 20-K-1850-10-13[S]). For the identification of the carpenter Thomas Watts as Semper's landlord, see London Directory 1842, 421; London Directory 1851, 1052.

22 On Kinkel's relation to Semper, see Beyrodt 1979, 350–3; Ashton 1986, 163–4; Haskell 1988, 215.

23 On Kinkel's Emigration Club, see Ashton 1986, 87, 141, 164; Lattek 2006, 99–109; for Semper's membership in the Emigration Club as noted by the Saxon Secret Police, see Gross 1980, 152.

General Introduction | xxxi

24 Lothar Bucher and Gottfried Semper to Gottfried Kinkel (copy by Conrad Kinkel), London, 30 August 1851 (ULB Bonn, Kinkel bequest, S 2675 [27 S.8]).

25 Karl Marx to Friedrich Engels, London, 31 August 1851, ed. in Marx/Engels 1984, 195–8, here 195–6; cf. Quitzsch 1981, 23.

26 For a reconstruction of Semper's Canadian Court, see Leoni 2021.

27 On Semper's *Science, Industry, and Art*, see Ettlinger 1964; Diephouse 1978; Mallgrave 1996, 205–8; Arburg 2008, 313–21; Hildebrand 2020, 116–19.

28 On the differences between Gottfried Semper's thoughts on design reform and the German *Vorbilderbewegung*, see Mundt 1971; Mundt 1976.

29 Semper, 'Fragen für Industrie Sammler' (gta, 20-Ms-37, fol. 7v), cit. in Herrmann 1981, 83.

30 Semper to Eduard Vieweg, London, 20 May 1852 (ed. in Herrmann 1976, 236–7). For Semper's metals catalogue, see Herrmann 1984, 60–4 (trans. of Herrmann 1978, 66–70); Mallgrave 1996, 210–12; Hvattum 1999; Nicka 2007; Nicka/Pokorny-Nagel 2007; Squicciarino 2009, 315–25; Chestnova 2017b; Chestnova 2018. None of these studies takes into account, or identifies correctly, the different hands to be found in the metals catalogue. The version of 1852 (NAL, 86.FF.64) was written in large parts by Charles Alfred Somerset (commissioned by Semper to write a fair copy of now lost drafts), to a lesser extent by Semper himself; a few pages are by Charles Comyns. Comments in the margins are by Somerset, Semper, Cole and John Charles Robinson (who became curator of the Museum of Ornamental Art in 1853). The copy that Semper presented to today's Österreichisches Museum für angewandte Kunst (MAK) in 1867 (ed. in Semper 2007a) was written at his request to Robinson by the latter's clerk Comyns between the autumn of 1855 and the summer of 1856.

31 Semper to Antonio Panizzi, London, 22 May 1852 (gta, 20-K-1852-05-22[S]).

32 On Semper's *Four Elements of Architecture*, see Laudel 1991, 58–64; Mallgrave 1996, 177–89; Gnehm 2004, 27–34, 57–69; Hildebrand 2020, 105–8.

33 This first version (gta, 20-Ms-79), written by Semper in French and entitled 'On Tapestry & the origin of Polychronic Decoration' ('Polychronic': *Polychromic*), is not identical with the one that Falkener used for translation; its fair copy (gta, 20-Ms-80) ed. in Semper 2020, 111–33.

34 '[Aucun reste d'antiquité]' [1852] (gta, 20-Ms-99); German trans. in Semper 1884, 109–21.

35 Robertson 1978, 48–9; Kauffmann 1993, 9–10.

36 Ashton 1986, 162–3; Hönes 2021.

37 On Wellington's funeral car, see most recently Hvattum 2021.

38 Atlantis 1854, 30.

39 Semper 1855a.

40 Semper 1855b. On Semper's 'Letters from Switzerland', see Herrmann 1981, 106; Karge 2014, 19, 23–4.

41 Semper 1853.

42 Semper 1859. On Semper's work on ancient slingshot bullets, see Herrmann 1981, 116–17; Herrmann 1984, 73–4 (trans. of Herrmann 1978, 80–1); Mallgrave 1996, 222–5; Hildebrand 2015; Papapetros 2016; Hildebrand 2021.

43 Semper 1854, 297.

44 Atlantis 1854, 32.

45 Cole Diary (20 May 1853).

46 Herrmann 1981, 109–10 (on MS 122, MS 123 and MS 124); Mallgrave 1983b, 23.

47 Herrmann 1981, 108–9 (on MS 117, MS 118 and MS 119); Mallgrave 1983b, 23 n. 5.

48 On Semper's 'Prinzip der Bekleidung', see Quitzsch 1981, 86–105; Laudel 1991, 101–16; Squicciarino 1994, 103–31; Mallgrave 1996, 290–302; Rykwert 1998; Gnehm 2004, 102–17; Laudel 2007; Arburg 2008, 286–97; Gnehm 2015; Gnehm 2017a. For a contextualization of Semper's principle within modern and contemporary architecture, see most recently Moravánszky 2018.

49 On the position of ceramics in Semper, see Mallgrave 1996, 279–84; Squicciarino 2009, 331–47; Karge 2014, 35–6. On ceramics in Semper's London period, see Poerschke 2016, 61–9; Chestnova 2021.

50 An excerpt from Semper's notes on Bötticher's *Tectonics of the Hellenes* was first published as an editorial note to the posthumous German translation of this lecture (Semper 1884, 300 n. *); all of Semper's notes on Bötticher (gta, 20-Ms-150) ed. in Gnehm 2004, 202–3, 206–21. For Semper's dispute with Bötticher, see Herrmann 1984, 139–52 (trans. of Herrmann 1981, 26–40); Laudel 1991, 117–24, 129–30; Oechslin 1994, 52–69; Mallgrave 1996, 219–22; Poerschke 2016, 69–72, 83–8.

51 Semper to Carolyne Sayn-Wittgenstein, Zurich, 8 December 1857 (gta, 20-K-1857-12-08[S]). For Semper's designs for the applied arts during his London exile, see Mundt 1976; Orelli-Messerli 2010, 163–293.

52 On Semper's contribution to the Woolwich Royal Arsenal, see Guillery 2012, 164–7, and, most recently, Fraser 2021.

53 On Owen Jones's Greek Court and the context of Semper's Mixed Fabrics Court at Sydenham, see most recently Nichols 2021.

54 Semper to Bertha Semper, Paris, 8 April 1855 (gta, 20-K-1855-04-08[S]).

55 However, the Saxon Secret Police noted that Semper had travelled to Brussels in March 1855 to submit plans for the theatre; see Gross 1980, 152.

56 For Semper's move to Zurich, see Herrmann 1984, 78–83 (trans. of Herrmann 1978, 87–93); Mallgrave 1996, 225–7; Weidmann 2010, 1:318–42; Hildebrand 2020, 126–31.

57 Johann Heinrich August Behr (Ministry of Justice) to Semper, Dresden, 8 May 1863 (gta, 20-K-1863-05-08:2).

EDITORIAL PRINCIPLES

Any edition of Semper's writings is confronted with his notoriously difficult prose. Nikolaus Pevsner, who like Semper decades before him also found refuge as an exile in England, stumbled over Semper's 'literary style which can be terrible'.[1] Semper's penchant for convoluted sentences is reflected in his manuscripts. They show the architect in the very process of thinking, as it were. In his search for a sentence that will cover all the various aspects of an idea as succinctly as possible, he deletes parts, replaces them, deletes them and adds to them again, until finally sentences emerge whose syntax is not always beyond all doubt. Palimpsest-like layers of revisions are characteristic of the German-language manuscripts edited here, and also particularly of the drafts that Semper wrote in English (pls. 5, 11). As Harry Francis Mallgrave put it in the preface to one of the selected London lectures edited by him, one is confronted in these with Semper's 'awkward, sometimes failing, knowledge of English'.[2] Werner Szambien – although he proceeded from a German-language text by Semper – had a similar experience in translating what he mistook for one of Semper's London lectures into French: the text, he commented, was far from the 'French, stimulating and sparkling style' which the London lectures recalled according to Hans and Manfred Semper.[3]

Semper only acquired a more thorough grasp of English during the course of his exile, and it was in French that he initially corresponded with Edwin Chadwick, Edward Falkener and Henry Cole, among others.[4] Although he never really felt at home in English, he did still manage to put complex thoughts down on paper in a way that made them comprehensible. What his English sounded like and what the effect of his Germanizing syntax was when he was delivering his lectures in English is an open question. Some spelling mistakes can perhaps be explained by Semper's pronunciation – for example, when he uses 'curse' instead of *course*. When he writes 'Jokes' instead of *yokes*, the J merely indicates the letter's phonetic value as in the German word *Joch*. Some of the slips are obviously due to French words that he was anglicizing – sometimes in a highly associative way. It remains questionable whether Semper delivered the lectures in the same state in which they have survived in the manuscripts. They usually have so many deletions and interpolations that he would scarcely have been able to read from them fluently. However, his lectures in German were also characterized by a halting manner of delivery. Johann Rudolf Rahn, the 'father of Swiss art history', reported from his student days with Semper in Zurich that it sometimes happened 'that he just left us without the end of a sentence altogether. "Confound it, I can't finish the cursed sentence, you do it yourselves", he would growl to himself like an infuriated lion'.[5]

The edition offers a critical reading text with as little editorial intervention as possible, so that the texts are made available in the state in which they were published or written at the time. On the one hand, this preserves the form in which they circulated, and on the other – in the case of the manuscripts – Semper's peculiar diction is preserved directly. This counteracts the risk of falsifying the bent of Semper's thoughts, of corrupting his style, and robbing his words and expressions of their spirit and their immediacy.

The Apparatus refers to the critical reading text by page and line number. Individual passages that are commented on in the Explanatory Notes, Editorial Emendations, Alterations in the Manuscript and Variants are referred to by using a lemma corresponding to the reading in the critical text and set in bold sans-serif type, followed by the lemma sign]. Where a longer passage serves as a lemma, it is shortened by using a tilde or wavy dash ~ to indicate the omitted word or words. One or several wavy dashes in the comment following the lemma bracket stand for the lemma word or words that remain unchanged in an explanation, an alteration or a variant commented on.

Textual Record
The textual record lists all the known direct textual witnesses of the edited text, as well as previous editions of it – all arranged in chronological order, starting with the oldest witness. The copy-text on which the critical reading text is based is indicated by italics. The textual record contains information on the extent of the printed texts and manuscripts and on their provenance. In the case of the manuscripts, the writer's hand and the writing material, if it is not solely black ink, are indicated. All of the edited manuscripts belong to the holdings of the gta Archives at ETH Zurich, with three exceptions: the 'Outline of a Cultural-Historical Exhibition' and 'Note on a Cultural-Philosophical Collection' are

enclosed with or inserted in letters to Eduard Vieweg that are archived at the Technical University in Brunswick. The 'British Museum Library Call Slips' are held at the Saxon State and University Library (SLUB) in Dresden. The sigla and foliations of the manuscripts in the gta Archives follow the order made by Wolfgang Herrmann in the 1970s; the sigla correspond to his manuscript numbering.[6] Where different manuscript units are archived as one unit under one number, continuous foliation is assumed, but the manuscript units are distinguished from each other with sigla extended by the editors – for example, as MS 148[1], fol. 5r–v, and MS 148[2], fols. 1r–4v. They are also rearranged chronologically. In two cases, the various manuscript parts archived under one number are not assumed to be continuously foliated, due to their random order. In the case of Semper's 'Notes on Exhibits', the folios within a manuscript unit are counted, and this unit is designated by a number preceding the foliation number (e.g. as MS 96, [2]fols. 1r–2v). The 'British Museum Library Call Slips' are not numbered at all. Succinct bibliographies list the principal literature on each of the edited texts.

Variants

When a text was published in Semper's lifetime, the printed version is used as the copy-text for the critical reading text. For the manuscripts, the latest stage of revision, taking into account all changes made by Semper, is reproduced as the critical reading text; manuscripts written in other hands are treated in the same way. The texts are edited in their original languages, whether German, French or English, as appropriate. This means that all texts are reproduced in the language in which they were printed at the time or – in the case of the manuscripts – the language in which Semper wrote them or into which he translated them or had them translated. Print variants are listed in the Apparatus in relation to individual readings of the critical text. Manuscript variants – including drafts that served as the basis for translations at the time – are usually edited integrally in the Apparatus; in exceptional cases, they are treated as variant readings for individual passages of a printed version. For print or manuscript variants that are listed in relation to individual passages, parts that are missing in textual witnesses are indicated using *om.* (omitted).

Pagination and Folio Sequence

In the case of the printed texts that are edited, the original pagination or, if it is missing, the folio sequence is included as marginalia. In the case of the manuscripts, Semper's – often irregular – pagination and the folio sequence are included as marginalia, with the folio number indicating whether the text is on the recto or verso of a sheet. Manuscript pagination in someone else's hand, such as that of Wolfgang Herrmann dating from the 1970s, is not recorded. In the critical reading text itself, a new folio, i.e. a new sheet, is signalled by a vertical bar | and a new page by a broken bar ¦.

Grammar and Syntax

Grammatical and syntactical errors are not corrected in the critical reading text, and the often Germanizing syntax of Semper's English is not commented on in most cases. If the gender of an article or an adjective is incorrect in German-language manuscripts, and if the conjugation of auxiliary verbs is incorrect in German- and English-language manuscripts due to Semper's deletions and failure to adapt the text accordingly, the source of error is elucidated in the deletions documented in the Alterations in the Manuscript.

Orthography

In the critical reading text, the orthography is generally adopted as it appears in the contemporary printed or manuscript version – in contrast to Harry Francis Mallgrave's selected edition of Semper's London lectures, with its mostly silently 'corrected numerous misspellings'.[7] Our editorial decision is based on a number of considerations. In Semper's autographs, it is not possible to identify a predominant practice of any sort on which corrections could be based. Adaptations to then-contemporary practices or modern usage would lead to a standardized text that would not correspond to the tentative character of Semper's formulations. A critical apparatus that recorded these adaptations would be inflated to an impractical size. On the other hand, general rules for silent correction would not only be impossible to justify consistently but would also mean that the peculiarities of Semper's English, shaped as it is by German and French, would disappear without a direct trace. In the critical reading text, chimerical spellings such as 'Goathares' instead of *goat hair* or 'rang' instead of *rank* are thus left as they are. These cases are commented on in the Apparatus.

The simultaneous use of British spellings and what from today's point of view would be regarded as American spellings in the manuscripts is retained in the critical reading text – as in the case of 'colour' and 'color', for example. The question of whether supposedly archaizing or obsolete orthography should be adapted to the practice of the time or to today's practices cannot be answered, since archaizing or obsolete aspects of Semper's writing in English are in most cases scarcely due to the use of outdated dictionaries, but rather to his orthographic inexperience – as in the case of 'allways' (which he usually uses) and 'always' (which also occurs in his manuscripts) – or to his own anglicization of German or French words. The German letter *Eszett* (ß) and the long *s* (ſ) are not distinguished from *ss* and *s*, respectively, in the critical reading text and Apparatus.

In the case of texts printed at the time, misprints are, in a few exceptional cases, corrected in the critical reading text and listed in the Editorial Emendations – for example, when misspellings can be traced back to incorrect deciphering of the handwritten long *s* (ſ) and its confusion with *f* by the typesetter. Examples: 'follten' (from *ſollten*), 'Erfahrungswissenschasten' (with the last 's' read as *ſ* instead of *f*), 'fcheint' (from *ſcheint*). Turned letters (e.g. *ə* instead of *e*) are corrected, with the correction noted in the Editorial Emendations. Unusual or incorrect name spellings are corrected in the Explanatory Notes in a few extreme cases such as 'Blagmann' instead of *Klagmann*, 'Letaroulz' instead of *Letarouilly* or 'Ebner' instead of *Hefner*; name variants are otherwise listed in the Index.

Missing Words or Parts of Words

Parts of words and letters that are missing in the manuscripts – as in the case of 'Seurity' and 'Architure' – are not added in the critical reading text, as they can be easily deduced, but are corrected in the Explanatory Notes. In one case, in which 'trea-' immediately before a page break is not followed by 'ting' on the next page, it is augmented in the critical reading text to 'treating'; this intervention is documented in the Editorial Emendations. If there are blanks in texts printed at the time – because the typesetting was faulty or because Semper left spaces in the manuscripts for the subsequent addition of numbers or names – they are retained in the critical reading text. In the first case, the missing passage is corrected in the Apparatus with reference to parallel passages in manuscripts that include the presumed addition; in the second case, the passage missing in both print and corresponding manuscript is given in the Explanatory Notes. If words have been preserved only in fragments due to tearing or rubbing off, they are supplemented in the critical reading text and documented in the Editorial Emendations.

Capitalization

Semper's use of capitalization in English is inconsistent throughout, and it is not possible to systematize it on the basis of any predominant practice. The critical reading text also refrains from any attempt at standardization based on contemporary or modern practices. For example, Semper writes 'But Nature never fails in the Choice of its forms', where both of the capitalized words are attributable to the capitalization of German nouns and can hardly represent personification – since elsewhere he also writes of 'the laws which nature itselfs observes in the creation of its various forms' and of the human 'choice of forms' or 'Choice of forms'. Similarly, 'eastern', for example, is not corrected when *Eastern* is meant in the sense of *Oriental*, but in this case it is commented on in the Apparatus – it occurs both in texts printed at the time, such as those on polychromy, as 'eastern sky' and 'eastern climate' and also in Semper's lecture manuscripts as 'eastern countries'. Conversely, however, he also uses 'Eastern division' when describing a palace layout and 'oriental art' elsewhere.

Word Division and Hyphenation
Semper's spelling of compound words in English is inconsistent throughout. Without any distinction, he uses the same compound written as a closed compound, as an open compound made up of two separate words or as a hyphenated compound. The critical reading text does not attempt any standardization here; there is also no standardization in the texts printed at that time and edited here, where for example the attributive 'terra-cotta' is distinguished from the noun 'terra cotta', but would be treated identically in today's spelling. If a compound word is associated with a line-end hyphenation, the hyphenation is retained in the critical reading text and the line-end hyphenation is noted in the Editorial Emendations. In both the German- and English-language manuscripts, Semper sometimes separates a word at the end of a line without a hyphen. If the word cannot be unambiguously interpreted as written together, the separation is retained in the critical reading text and the line-end separation is documented in the Editorial Emendations by displaying the line break with a thin vertical bar, as in the case of 'an | other', which may appear in Semper within a line as both 'another' and 'an other'. Where a word, retained as divided due to a line-end word division without hyphen, would be completely misleading, it is written together in the critical reading text, and the adjustment is documented in the Editorial Emendations. Where two consecutive words appear as one word due to contraction, they are given without change in the critical reading text, as in the case of 'gehorheich' (*gehorche ich*; I obey) or 'fothe' (*for the*) – accompanied by loss of letters in these two cases – and commented on in the Apparatus.

Punctuation
The punctuation is adopted unchanged from the copy-text into the critical reading text. Semper's frequent practice of ending sentences with a semicolon is therefore retained. Missing full stops or commas are not added in the critical reading text and are only commented on in exceptional cases. Missing closing brackets are neither supplied nor commented on. In some cases, missing or

incorrect punctuation is explained by Semper's deletions or insertions documented in the Apparatus in the Alterations in the Manuscript. Where missing punctuation leads to complete ambiguity, it is corrected in the Explanatory Notes, with the location at which it is missing indicated by a caret ∧ in the lemma. Where a word associated with a punctuation mark in the reading of the critical text is to be found without punctuation in a variant reading, the corresponding lemma is followed after the bracket by a tilde and a caret ~∧, signalling that the only variant consists of a missing punctuation mark. Quotation marks are always reproduced in the form they have in the copy-text and thus partly diverge from the editorial text, in which single inverted commas are used. An exception is made to this in the case of the opening running quotation marks that were used for long citations in texts printed at that time. These quotation marks have been removed because the type area in the critical reading text is different and does not allow them to be placed within the quotation in a precisely corresponding way. The sequence of punctuation and quotation mark is taken unchanged from the copy-text, while in the editorial text the punctuation is placed inside the closing inverted comma only if the quotation consists of a complete sentence. Dashes are always rendered as an en dash with a space before and after, even if an em dash was used in the texts printed at that time.

Umlauts, Diacritical Marks and Dots on I and J
Missing umlauts and missing or incorrect diacritical marks are not corrected in the critical reading text but are annotated in the Explanatory Notes. Missing dots on *i* and *j* are silently added.

Underlining and Other Marking
Text that is underlined in the manuscripts is silently italicized in the critical reading text. Single, double and wavy underlining are generally not distinguished in the critical reading text. In the Alterations in the Manuscript, underlining is not typographically emphasized but is documented descriptively as *underl.* (underlined). The use of different-colour ink and of pencil is noted in the Apparatus. The use of Latin script instead of German cursive script (*Kurrent*) or – in printed texts – Gothic type (*Fraktur*) is not taken into account. Semper generally wrote his German-language manuscripts in *Kurrent* and the English- and French-language manuscripts in Latin script. In the German-language manuscripts, he often used Latin script for names or foreign words. In the English- and French-language manuscripts, however, many letters also appear in *Kurrent*; Semper did not distinguish clearly between the use of the two scripts.

Italics in the texts printed at that time, which were used for example in titles or to emphasize a word or denote its foreign origin, are adopted without change, even if italics with quotation marks or only quotation marks alone were used at the same time to indicate foreign words. Spaced-out text and words printed in bold in the running text are silently reproduced in italics in the critical reading text. Small capitals are silently given in capitals and lower-case letters. When manuscript text is written on sheets with pre-printed text, the latter is rendered in bold, as in the case of the 'British Museum Library Call Slips' or in printed letterheads. Footnote signs such as those in the sequence of asterisk *, dagger †, double dagger ‡ and section sign § in the two texts on polychromy in their original printed form could not be retained in the critical reading text due to the differences of the type area and are silently replaced with consecutive footnote numbering.

Abbreviations
Abbreviations in German- and French-language manuscripts are resolved in the Explanatory Notes.

Blank Lines
Blank lines before subheadings are taken over from the copy-text. Several consecutive blank lines are reduced to a single blank line in the critical reading text, and their approximate extent is indicated in the Editorial Emendations relative to the page size.

Headings
In most cases, titles that are set in bold sans-serif font are those of the editors. Sometimes they are the English translation of Semper's German or French titles, and occasionally they are taken from passages in the text. In the case of the Lectures, the titles are adapted from Semper's printed 'Prospectuses' and from a manuscript subheading or, if that was not possible, translated into English from the German titles given to them by Manfred and Hans Semper in their edition of *Kleine Schriften* of 1884. The editors' titles are followed by the original headings, where available. The critical reading text does not establish a typographical hierarchy among the original headings and subheadings. They are always kept in the same font size as the running text and are specially marked only when they appear in the copy-text in capital letters or emphasized with underlining.

Uncertain Readings
Uncertain readings are documented in the Explanatory Notes.

Alterations in the Manuscript

Semper's additions – interpolations, insertions, overwriting and substitutions – are incorporated into the critical reading text without further marking; they are described with reference to the corresponding lemma word in the Apparatus under Alterations in the Manuscript. Insertion marks in the manuscripts are generally not identified but are documented if they are absent. Semper usually wrote his manuscripts in two columns, using the second column for corrections. Generally, it is not noted whether the edited text is in the left or right manuscript column. In the case of interlinear additions, regardless of whether they are above or below the line, they are described using *interl.* (interlined). Additions before or after the line, or in the left or right column, are described using *inserted*. Contemporary changes to Semper's manuscripts – additions or deletions – by other hands are not incorporated into the edited manuscript; they are noted under Alterations in the Manuscript.

Semper's deletions are documented in the Alterations in the Manuscript, marked as *del.* (deleted). Deletions within a line are documented using *before del.* or *after del.*, with reference to the preceding or following word used as a lemma. When the deleted text has been replaced with an interlinear addition, it is documented with reference to the replacement serving as a lemma, using *above del.* and *below del.* Deletions of additions before or after the line, or in the left or right column, are documented using *after inserted and del.* or *before inserted and del.*, with reference to the lemma word taken from the end of the line or beginning of the line to which the addition is attached. When deletions have been replaced by an addition before or after the line, or in the left or right column, they are documented as *repl. del.*, with reference to the replacing addition taken as a lemma. The abbreviation *repl. del.* is also used when the deleted word that is to be replaced appears in a larger deleted context that is not given in all its details. In the case of Semper's manuscript of the printed 'Report on the Private Collection of Arms at Windsor Castle', which was revised by Cole and is edited in the Apparatus, the words replaced in Cole's hand are documented as *repl. by Cole's insertion*, followed by Cole's substituting words. Overwriting is documented with reference to the word which replaces the overwritten word and which is taken as a lemma, using *over*.

In exceptional cases, words that were inadvertently left as deleted by Semper after multiple revisions are restored in the critical reading text and documented in the Apparatus. Similarly, words that were inadvertently not deleted are, as an exception, omitted from the critical reading text and documented in the Apparatus as *undel.* (undeleted, i.e. not deleted). The same also applies to word duplications. Where these occur in connection with page and line breaks (as happens in the case of catchwords, but not only), the word is included once in the critical reading text, and the duplication is documented in the Editorial Emendations. When word duplications occur in connection with Semper's changes, the choice made for the critical reading text is documented in the Alterations in the Manuscript. Words in the manuscripts that Semper used as references to join up separate passages, such as 'Siehe oben' (see above), 'Folgende Seite' (following page) and on two occasions 'Here', are not incorporated into the critical reading text but are noted in the Apparatus.

Multi-layered revisions made by Semper are generally documented yet remain limited to relevant cases. In these instances the text that – after the lemma set in bold sans-serif type – documents the penultimate stage of the changes is followed by another lemma in semi-bold sans-serif referring to that stage, and that is then followed by the preceding stage of text. If another level of changes is documented, it is indicated within round brackets.

Explanatory Notes

The notes provide explanations which contextualize the text and furnish individual commentaries. In addition to the cases mentioned above, they provide bibliographical references and identify direct and – where possible – indirect citations. They provide annotations concerning relevant persons, artefacts, buildings and other particular issues. Artefacts are, whenever possible, identified with their present location, supplemented by terms for objects or geographical names that are common today. If the meaning or gist of Semper's words is opaque or ambiguous, the reader is assisted with disambiguation in an annotation. Misspelled words are, in relevant cases, identified with italicized corrections following the corresponding lemma. Literature references cited by Semper or used – to identify artefacts, for example – by the editors are usually detailed in the commentary only to the extent needed to locate them in the Bibliography. Names of ancient authors and titles of their works cited by Semper in abbreviated form are resolved using the standard practice to refer to them by the author's name, title, book and paragraph or line division. Other references cited by Semper are listed in the Bibliography with full bibliographical details.

Notes on Variants

In print and manuscript variants edited in the Apparatus, the Explanatory Notes, Editorial Emendations and Alterations in the Manuscript are assembled into one block. Editorial corrections of words are placed in inverted commas.

1 Pevsner 1972, 253. On Pevsner's misreading of a particular passage from Semper's Zurich lecture *Über die formelle Gesetzmässigkeit des Schmuckes und dessen Bedeutung als Kunstsymbol* (1856), with which he illustrates Semper's style, see Gnehm 2004, 16–17.

2 Semper 1986a, 33.

3 Szambien 1987, 153 n. 1; cf. Semper 1884, XI. Szambien translated Semper's partial adaptation of his inaugural London lecture in a manuscript written in 1856 at the earliest. This manuscript (gta, 20-Ms-179) – a fair copy by a copyist – belongs to Semper's 'Kunstformenlehre' (Theory of Art Forms), the immediate predecessor of *Der Stil* (Style). Wolfgang Herrmann, who attributed it to a distinct project which he called 'Theorie des Formell-Schönen' (Theory of Formal Beauty), edited it in Herrmann 1981, 217–37 (Engl. trans. in Herrmann 1984, 219–44; the text translated by Szambien on 235–7 and 241–4, respectively).

4 For Semper's 'broken' English, see Weidmann 2021.

5 Rahn 1920, 2. Rahn attended Semper's course on the 'History of Architecture' in the winter term of 1862–63; see Gnehm 2012, 392–4.

6 Herrmann 1981.

7 Semper 1983, 8 n. *; cf. Semper 1986b, 43.

LONDON WRITINGS

M. Gotfried Semper, late Director of the School of Architecture, and Professor of the Fine Arts at Dresden:– also Architect of the Royal Theatre at Dresden, is desirous of giving lessons in Architectural Drawing and the principles of construction, to pupils who intend to practice Architecture professionally:– He is also desirous of giving aid to Noblemen or Gentlemen who may either desire to study Architecture and the principles of construction as a branch of the Fine Arts, or wish to obtain such an insight into them as to enable them to judge of their application for the improvement of real property.

[1852 ?]

Pl. 1: Draft of advertisement for lessons in architecture and drawing, 1851 (gta, 20-DOK-undat.:51)

PRIVATE SCHOOL OF ARCHITECTURE

Lessons and Recommendation as Architect

First Version

fol. 1r

Professor G. Semper, vormals Director der Bauschule an der Akademie der bildenden Künste zu Dresden und Architect des dortigen Theaters, des Museum, der Synagoge und anderer öffentlicher und Privatgebäude beabsichtigt in den verschiedenen Fächern seiner Kunst Unterricht zu ertheilen; und zwar hauptsächlich in Folgendem:

1) Linearzeichnen, und Entwerfen von Bauplänen, verbunden mit praktischem Unterricht in der Geschichte der Baukunst.

2) Constructionslehre.

3) Zeichnen und Erfinden von Verzierungen, architectonischen Details, Möbels, Vasen Mustern aller Art.

4) Beschreibende Geometrie und Perspective.

5) Uebungen im Ausführen malerisch-architectonischer Skizzen in Bleistift und in Wasserfarben, besonders nützlich als Vorbereitung für Reisende. ¦

fol. 1v

6) Unterricht im Zeichnen von Ornamenten, Köpfen und Figuren nach der Antike oder nach Gypsen. –

7) Wenn es gewünscht wird, können Uebungen in der Französischen und Deutschen Sprache mit diesem Unterricht verbunden seyn.

Es wäre zugleich sein Wunsch, ein Atelier für junge Architecten zu gründen, und die nöthige Ausstattung desselben an Lehrmitteln zu besorgen, wenn er für dieses Unternehmen die nöthige Theilnahme fände.

Schliesslich empfiehlt er sich als Baumeister und Dekorateur. Er würde sich, behufs der Ausführung mit einem mit hiesigen Verhältnissen vollständig vertrauten Englischen Techniker in Verbindung setzen und hauptsächlich zuerst

fol. 2r

den artistischen Theil der Leitung übernehmen, aber zugleich ¦ für den Erfolg die möglichste Sicherheit gewähren.

27. University Street.
near Gower Street. London.

Second Version

Professor Gottfried Semper, (late Director of the School of Architure, of the Academy of Arts, and Architect of the Theatre, the Museum and other public and private Buildings at Dresden,) proposes to give Private Lectures on the following subjects, and hopes to meet with encouragement.

I) Perspective explained in the most comprehensible and briefest way, combined with Exercises in the finishing of pictorial-architectural sketches in pencil or water-color; particularly useful for Tourists.

II Ancient and modern history of the plastic Arts; particularly in their connexion with Architecture. These Lectures will be illustraded with drawings, engravings and well finished sketches in chalk. If desired the study of German and French can be combined.

Professor Semper likewise intends to establish an Atélier for beginners in Architecture and to furnish it with all the necessary means of study, should his undertaking meet with sufficient patronage.

Relying upon the experience of 14 years, during which he was Director of one of the first Schools of Architecture in Germany and Proprietor of a Private-Atelier, from which several distinguished Architects have come, he will direct this Institution in the most comfortable way, and unite the theoretical Instruction with progressive practical exercises.

This Institution will comprehend chiefly:

1) Drawing of lines and Civil-Construction, together with teaching the knowledge of the different styles in Architecture and the history of it.

2) The doctrine of Construction.

3) Building of Roads, Bridges and Channels, together with the necessary teaching of rational and applicative Mechanism.

4) Describing Geometry and its application to Perspective, Doctrine of shading, Lithography, etc. ¦

5) Exercises in Drawing and Composition of Ornaments, architectural details, furniture, vases and patterns of all kind.

6) Drawing of Ornaments, Vessels and Figures from Antiques and from Plaster-Casts.

He proposes to give also private Lessons in the above mentioned branches of his Art.

Lastly he introduces himself as Architect and Decorator; branches, which in harmoniously built works were always trusted to One Hand, and the separation of which has become pernicious to Architecture.

Security would be given for any Work entrusted to him, and further Information may be had at:

27. University Street,
Gower Street.

Third Version

fol. 1r

I.

Le sousigné, ancien directeur de l'ecole d'architecture et membre du conseil directeur de l'academie des beaux arts à Dresde en Saxe, architecte du théatre, du musée de la Synagogue et de beaucoup d'autres édificies publiques et privés dans la capitale citée et ailleurs en Allemagne, se recommande au public Anglais comme architecte constructeur et décorateur, branches qui dans toutes les belles époques de l'art ont été confiées à une seule main et dont la séparation a eue des suites funestes pour son developpement organique et harmonieux.

Seurity will be given for any work entrusted to him.

fol. 1v

Il est prêt aussi à repondre à des simples consultations par ¦ rapport à toutes les questions d'architecture et de decoration exterieure ou intérieure.

Il pense en même temps de fonder une école d'architecture à l'instar de celle qu'il a dirigée à Dresde, et d'ou sont sortis la plupart des architectes et constructeurs actuellement employés en Saxe.

Son système d'instruction sera principalement fondé sur les exercices journaliers et continus pratiqués dans son atélier par les élèves.

Ces exercices ambrasseront toutes les parties de l'architecture, y compris la decoration et l'art de l'ingénieur. | Ils seront autant que possible appliqués à la pratique réelle.

fol. 2r

On aura soin d'y joindre un cycle d'instruction théorique complet, renfermé dans des cours, dont le programme sera donné.

Il prendra sur lui la surveillance principale des exercices, ainsi qu'une partie des cours scientifiques tandis que pour les sciences de l'ingénieur, pour le devis etc, l'assistance d'hommes savans et expérimentés Anglais a été promise et assurée.

Il prendra des élèves en pension entiere ou partielle.

Il propose dernièrement de donner des leçons privées dans les differentes branches de son art, principalement dans ce qui suit: ¦

1) Perspective expliquée le plus comprehensiblement et brièvement dans peu de leçons et combinée avec des exercices de dessins d'architecture pittoresque en crayon, au lavis et en couleurs; particulierement utile pour des personnes, qui veulent se preparer au voyage dans les pays classiques. (particularly useful for tourists).

2) Histoire ancienne et moderne des arts, principalement dans leur connection avec l'architecture; illustrée par des dessins des ouvrages gravés., et des esquisseés improviseés à la craie blanche.

3) Exercices etc comme au programme N° 3. À la fin: Des renseignemens plus detaillés seront donnés par (suivent les noms.)

fol. 2v

Fourth Version

I.

fol. 1r

Le sousigné, ancien directeur de l'école d'architecture et membre du conseil directoir de l'academie des beaux arts à Dresde, architecte du théatre, du musée de la synagogue et de beaucoup d'autres edifices publics et privés de la capitale citée et ailleurs, se recommande au public Anglais comme architecte constructeur et décorateur, branches qui dans toutes les belles époques de l'art ont été confiées à une seule main et dont la séparation au eue des suites défavorables pour son développement organique et harmonieux.

Il est prêt aussi à repondre à des simples consultations par rapport à toutes les questions d'architecture et de décoration extérieure ou intérieure.

Des informations seront données ¦ par:

fol. 1v

suivent des noms et adresses.

Professor G. Semper
27. University Street.
near Gower Street.

le. 2 Janvier 1852

School of Architecture and Engineering

First Version

fol. 1r

II.

Professor Semper, Architect,
late Director of *l'Ecole d'architecture*, and Member of *l'Académie des Beaux Arts*, at
Dresden, and architect of the Theatre, the Museum, the Synagogue, and many
other public and private buildings of his native Country –

is desirous of establishing in the approaching Summer a School of architecture on the model of that which he directed during *fourteen jears* at Dresden, and
from which have issued the principal architects and constructors now employed
in Saxony –

His System of instruction will embrace every branch of Architecture, comprising the science of Engineering, and the principles of Decoration –

The School will be furnished with a great variety of original drawings and
sketches, both practical and artistic; the standard works on architecture, of this
Country and the Continent, and casts in plaster of ancient and modern ornaments models of construction &c, &c –

Reference may be made to –

Second Version

fol. 3r

27. University Street. Dienstag. 24 Febr 1851.

Verehrter Freund

Ich danke Ihnen für die Raschheit mit der Sie Ihre Mittel in Bewegung setzen
um mir zu helfen. So werden sie doppelt wirksam seyn.

Meine Ideen über das zu errichtende Institut müssen sich nach dem Umfange der Theilnahme modificiren, welche die ersten, desshalb etwas allgemein
zu haltenden, Aufforderungen an das Publikum bei letzterem finden werden. –

Aber setzen wir einmal voraus, was ich leider bezweifle, dass sich genügende
Theilnahme zeigte; dann hätte ich folgenden Plan:

Die Anstalt müsste dem gemeinschaftlichen Studium für Architecten und
Ingenieurs gewidmet seyn, denn nur so liesse sich der ganze Vortheil derselben

für Deutsche Studirende ans Licht stellen. Der Unterricht wäre vorzugsweise an Uebungen zu knüpfen damit mit dem Können zugleich das Wissen erlangt werde.

Bei diesen Uebungen, die möglichst ununterbrochen den Tag über zu halten wären, müsste mehr auf die enge Verwandschaft, als auf die Verschiedenheiten der beiden genannten Fächer zu sehen und nach diesem Prinzip müssten jene gemischt vorzunehmen seyn, so dass z. B. ein Schüler mit einem Hausprojecte sich beschäftigte während sein Nachbar eine Brücke entwärfe etc.

Doch ist dahin zu sehen dass diese Uebungen in steter Relation zu demjenigen stehen, was gerade Gegenstand des theoretischen Unterrichts ist, und gewissermassen die praktischen Erläuterungen und Repetitionen desselben bilden. Zu den Vorträgen würde ich die Früh- und Abendstunden bestimmen, damit die Zeit des Zeichnens möglichst wenig unterbrochen werde. ¦

Es bedürfte der Mitwirkung von Hülfslehrern und ich würde es mir angelegen seyn lassen, tüchtige Fachmänner für mein Vorhaben zu interessiren. Besonders nothwendig wäre es, einen theoretisch und praktisch gebildeten Englischen Ingenieur dafür zu gewinnen. Ich kenne deren zwei, die mir wenigstens Rath und Auskunft ertheilen könnten. *fol. 3v*

Die Anstalt wäre zugleich für externe Schüler und für Pensionairs einzurichten. Sie wäre in zwei Klassen zu theilen. Die erste, als *Bauschule* wäre die Vorbereitung für die zweite *das Atelier*, wo unter meinen Augen und unmittelbar neben meinem Arbeitskabinette für die Ausführung gearbeitet wird. So hielt ich es in Dresden, wo es mir freilich nicht an Arbeit fehlte. Die Besten unter den Schülern hatten spätere Anwartschaft auf Honorar für ihren Beistand. Solche die sich dem Ingenieurfache widmen, würden in ein gleiches Verhältniss zu meinem Collegen treten.

Programm des Unterrichts.

A. Uebungen.

    a. Bauschule.

    1) Projectionszeichnen, Schattenkonstruction, die ersten Combinationen und Elemente der schönen Baukunst.

    2) Constructionszeichnen in Stein, Holz, Eisen.

    3) Copiren Arch. Vorbilder und erste Versuche im Entwerfen von Bauplänen im Civil- und Ingenieurfache.

    4) Ornamentzeichnen nach Vorlageblättern und Gypsmodellen. Verbunden mit Uebungen in dem farbigen Ornament. ¦

    5) Perspective und freies Handzeichnen, Ausführen malerisch-architectonischer Gegenstände nach Vorlageblättern und später nach eigener Erfindung, oder nach ausgeführten Werken. Verschiedene Behandlungsweisen in Bleistift, Tusche oder Farben. *fol. 4r*

6) Ausführung grösserer Projecte.

NB. Vierwöchentlich einmal wird Conkurrenz gehalten in welcher alle Schüler die dazu hinreichend vorgerückt sind, eine gestellte Aufgabe wetteifernd zu lösen haben. Zuerst als Skizze; Dann ausgeführt.

b. Atelier.

Die Uebungen des Ateliers sind mehr praktischer Art und sollen sich an die unmittelbare Ausführung knüpfen. Doch finden auch für die Eleven des Ateliers mehrmals jährlich Conkurrenzarbeiten Statt.

Hervorzuheben ist auch noch das fortgesetzte Ueben im freien Handzeichnen nach der Antike (im Brittischen Museum) oder nach Gypsen. Vielleicht auch nach lebenden Modellen.

Ferner werden Modellirübungen gehalten in Thon Gyps und Holz.

B. Vorträge.

1) Vergleichende Baukunde, verbunden mit der Geschichte der Baukunst. (Alle Gebäudearten werden einzeln behandelt, sowohl geschichtlich wie technisch durchgeführt und nach den Verwandschaften gruppirt. Die allgemeine Kunstgeschichte als eng verbunden mit der Geschichte der Baukunst, wird daran geknüpft. Dieser Vortrag ¦ zieht sich durch mehrere Semester.

2) Constructionslehre und Lehre von den Materialien.

3) Mechanik in zwei Semestern. 1) rationelle und 2) angewandte M.

4) Wege- Brücken- und Canalbau.

5) Beschreibende Geometrie mit ihren Anwendungen auf Perspective, Steinschnitt und Zimmermannskunst.

6) Physik in besonderer Beziehung auf Baukunst, Wasserbau. etc.

7) Chemie desgleichen.

NB. Für weniger vorbereitete Schüler ist besonderer Unterricht in den mathematischen Doctrinen zu ertheilen, der aber besonders bezahlt werden muss.

Es ist nicht rathsam, ein strenges Eintrittsexamen vorzunehmen, da die Uebungen möglichst frühe beginnen müssen und dem ausgesprochenen Grundsatze nach, die Hauptsache des Unterrichts bilden.

Für die nöthigen Lehrmittel an Vorlageblättern Büchern, Modellen u. s. w. ist Sorge zu tragen.

Um die mit dem Besuche einer ähnlichen Anstalt in London verknüpften Vortheile für Deutsche ans Licht zu stellen darf nur hervorgehoben werden:

1) Die Ueberlegenheit der Engländer in allem was die Praxis und die Construction betrifft und worauf hinzuweisen, stets meine Sorge seyn wird. (Ich würde Exkursionen mit meinen Schülern unternehmen).

2) Die Gelegenheit zur Kenntniss der Englischen Sprache und der Einfluss den das praktische Englische Treiben auf junge Techniker üben muss. |

3) Der Reichthum der hiesigen National-Kunstsammlung.

4) Die Menge der schönen Gothischen Bauwerke und die Zweckmässigkeit so vieler grossartiger gemeinnütziger Anstalten.

5) Meine langjährigen Reisen und Erfahrungen als Director einer der ersten Bauakademieen Deutschlands und praktischer Baumeister, wodurch ich in den Stand gesetzt bin, meine Schüler sowohl in allen kontinentalen Bauverhältnissen zu belehren als auch sie mit der eigenthümlich sachsisch-Englischen Bauweise bekannt zu machen.

6) Die Nachbarschaft der an Monumenten so reichen Provinzen Frankreichs und Belgiens. etc etc.

———

Schwerlich dürfte sich eine Anstalt in solchem Maassstabe anlegen lassen können. Es wäre daher wünschenswerth, wenn sich vorerst nur eine Anzahl vorgerückterer junger Männer meldeten mit denen ich in mehr intimerem Umgange stehen und ein Atelier gründen könnte. Die Vorträge würden dann noch mehr in den Hintergrund treten können. Sie liessen sich durch gelegentliche Belehrung während der Arbeiten ersetzen. Den Vortrag über vergleichende Baukunde würde ich jedoch unter allen ¦ Umständen halten; dessgleichen über Construction, beschreibende Geometrie, und Wege- und Brückenbau. –

Das Weitere mündlich. Ich betrachte das Aufgeschriebene nur als einen Anknüpfungspunkt um Ihre Ansichten zu hören.

Wenn Sie Zeit haben, so komme ich morgen Mittwoch Abend 7 Uhr zu Ihnen. Sind Sie verhindert so schicken Sie mir zwei Worte.

Ganz der Ihrige GSemper.

P. S. Fälls sich Leute meldeten, würde ich erst zu Johannis anfangen können. Es wäre bis dahin noch Manches einzurichten und ausserdem ist meine ganze Bibliothek und meine Sammlung von Zeichnungen in New-York. Ich lasse die Kisten dort, bis ich bestimmt weiss ob ich hier bleibe.

Third Version

fol. 1r

Der Unterzeichnete, während vierzehn Jahren Director der Bauschule an der Akademie der bildenden Künste zu Dresden und praktischer Architect, gegenwärtig in London als Baumeister und Ingenieur etablirt hat die Absicht, eine Anzahl junger Architecten und Techniker, die sich hier theoretisch und praktisch ausbilden wollen, unter günstigen Bedingungen und selbst unter Aussichten auf späteres Verdienst in sein Atelier und zugleich in Kost und Logis aufzunehmen. Er wird persönlich die Leitung der architectonischen Uebungen und einen Theil der wissenschaftlichen Vorträge übernehmen über die ein besonderes Programm ausgestellt wird, während er für das Ingenieurfach sich einen geschickten und erfahrenen Englischen Ingemieur beigesellt hat.

Der praktische Sinn der Engländer zeigt sich von seiner glänzendsten Seite

fol. 1v

in ihren grossartigen der öffent. | Wohlfarth gewidmeten Anlagen und in der Weise wie dieselben durchgeführt werden, so dass sie hierin die Meister aller Nationen sind. –

Selbst ihre bürgerlichen Einrichtungen besonders ihre Landhäuser, fordern in ästhetischer und technischer Beziehung zu genauerem Studium auf, da sie eine reiche Ausbeute von Motiven und Comforts mit grosser Oekonomie der Mittel und ächt germanischer Ursprünglichkeit verbinden, so dass sie gewiss mit Unrecht bisher bei uns gegen andere uns fremdere Einflüsse fast unberücksichtigt geblieben sind.

Ausserdem bildet London durch seine Sammlungen und wissenschaftlichen Institute einen Hauptort für das Studium unserer Kunst, in der der Sinn für das Schöne sich am Zweckmässigen bewähren soll; und in der Mitte zwischen dem an Werken der schönen Baukunst so reichen Frankreich und Belgien und den

fol. 2r

über England zerstreuten berühmten Werken | der Ingenieurkunst ladet es zu schnell ausführbaren Exkursionen ein, welche der Unterzeichnete in regelmässigen Zwischenräumen mit seinen Schülern vorzunehmen beabsichtigt.

Wer von meinen jungen Landsleuten durch seine Theilnahme mein Unternehmen zu unterstützen geneigt ist, erfährt nähere Auskunft unter folgenden Adressen:

Mr. G. Semper 27. University Street London.
Herrn W. Semper, Apotheker, Grosse Bäckerstrasse Hamburg.
Frau Professor Semper 3. Waisenhausgasse Dresden.
————————— .

Gottfried Semper.

London d. 26 Fbr. 1851.

Fourth Version

Deutsches Atelier für Architekten und Ingenieurs in London. *347*

Der Unterzeichnete, während 14 Jahren Direktor der Bauschule an der Akademie der bildenden Künste zu Dresden und praktischer Architekt, gegenwärtig in London als Baumeister und Ingenieur etablirt, hat die Absicht, eine Anzahl junger Architekten und Techniker, die sich hier theoretisch und praktisch ausbilden wollen, unter sehr günstigen Bedingungen in sein Atelier und zugleich in Kost und Logis aufzunehmen. Er wird persönlich die Leitung der architektonischen Uebungen und einen Theil der wissenschaftlichen Vorträge übernehmen, über die ein besonderes Programm ausgestellt wird, während ¦ er für das *348* Ingenieurfach sich einen geschickten und erfahrenen Ingenieur beigesellt hat. – Der praktische Sinn der Engländer zeigt sich von seiner glänzendsten Seite in ihren grossartigen, der öffentlichen Wohlfahrt gewidmeten Anlagen, und in der Weise, wie sie dieselben technisch durchführen, so dass sie hierin die Meister aller Nationen sind. Selbst ihre bürgerlichen Einrichtungen, besonders ihre Landhäuser, fordern in technischer und auch in künstlerischer Beziehung zu genauerem Studium auf, da sie eine reiche Ausbeute an Motiven und Comforts mit grosser Einfachheit der Mittel und ächt germanischer Ursprünglichkeit verbinden, so dass dieselben gewiss mit Unrecht bisher gegen andere, uns weit fremdere Einflüsse fast unberücksichtigt geblieben sind.

Ausserdem bildet London durch seine Sammlungen und wissenschaftlichen Institute einen Hauptort für das Studium unserer Kunst, in der das Schöne sich am Zweckmässigen bewähren soll; und in der Mitte zwischen dem Reichthum Belgiens und Frankreichs an Monumenten der schönen Baukunst und den über England zerstreuten berühmten Werken des Ingenieurs gelegen, ladet es zu schnell ausführbaren Exkursionen ein, welche der Unterzeichnete in regelmässigen Zwischenräumen mit seinen Schülern vorzunehmen beabsichtigt.

Wer von meinen jungen Kunstgenossen durch seine Theilnahme mein Unternehmen zu unterstützen geneigt ist, erfährt Näheres unter folgender Adresse:

"Professor Semper. 27. University Street – London."

Gottfried Semper.

Lessons in Architecture and Drawing

First Version

fol. 1r M. Gotfried Semper, late Director of the School of Architecture, and Professor of the Fine Arts at Dresden: – also Architect of the Royal Theatre at Dresden, is desirous of giving lessons in Architectural Drawing and the principles of construction, to pupils who intend to practice Architecture professionally: – He is also desirous of giving aid to Noblemen or Gentlemen who may either desire to study Architecture and the principles of construction as a branch of the Fine Arts, or wish to obtain such an insight into them as to enable them to judge of their application for the improvement of real property.

Second Version

fol. 1r III.

Professor Semper, Architect,
late Director of *l'Académie des Beaux Arts*, and Director of *l'Ecole d'Architecture*, at Dresden, and architect of the Theatre, the Museum, the Synagogue, and many other public and private buildings in his native land – having established himself in this country as architect, and Decorator, is desirous of filling up his time in giving private instruction in the various branches of his art.

Besides the higher sciences connected with architecture, he is ready to give instruction in Perspective, Drawing, and Colouring: in the various departments of Decoration, and in the forms and composition of ornament.

His System of Instruction will be found especially useful to Tourists, and others desirous of acquiring a rapid facility of sketching, in a few lessons, whether in pencil or crayon-drawing.

Third Version

Professor Gottfried Semper, late Director of the School of Architecture at the *fol. 1r*
Academy of Arts, and Architect of the Theatre at Dresden, proposes to give
instruction in all the branches of his Art. Namely in the designing of plans, in
the construction, drawing and Composition of ornements, furniture, vases, patterns etc. – – in perspective, and in finishing landscape and architectural sketches
in pencil or water-color. – He also undertakes to give lectures on the history of
Art and to illustrate them with drawings and engravings. ¦

27, University Street. *fol. 1v*
Gower Street.

Fourth Version

III. *fol. 1r*

Professor Semper, ancien directeur de l'ecole d'architecture, membre de l'accademie et architecte à Dresde donne des leçons privées dans les différentes
branches de son art, principalement dans ce qui suit:
1) Perspective expliquée le plus comprehensiblement et brièvement dans ses
principes et ses procedés pratiques dans peu de leçons; combinée avec des exercices de dessins d'architecture pittoresque au crayon à l'ancre et en couleurs.
particulièrement utile comme étude preparatoire pour des touristes (particularly
useful for tourists.
2) – Histoire ancienne et moderne des arts, principalement dans leur connection avec l'architecture, illustrée par des dessins, des ouvrages gravés et des es-
quisses improvisées à la craie ¦ blanche *fol. 1v*
3) Exercices dans le dessin et la composition des décorations des ornamens,
des meubles outils, vases etc au crayon, à l'ancre et en couleurs après des originaux, des plâtres et la nature. Ces études peuvent, si l'on le demande, être combinées avec un cours complet et illustratif d'histoire du décor dans lequel les
differens caractères des styles seront demontrés et exercés.
Des informations ultérieures seront données par etc.

27. Univ. Street

l. 3 Mars 1851.

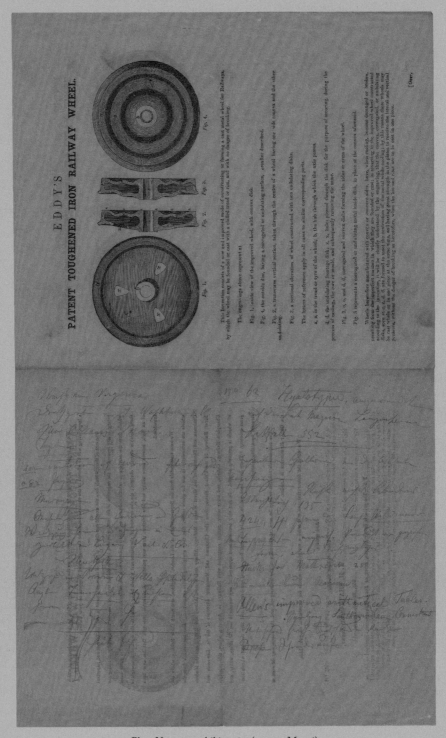

Pl. 2: Notes on exhibits, 1851 (gta, 20-Ms-96)

THE GREAT EXHIBITION

Announcement

fol. 1r

Paris, le 1er avril 1851.

AVIS.

Monsieur Semper, architecte, ancien professeur de l'Académie des Beaux-Arts à Dresde, actuellement établi à Londres, a été chargé, par la Commission exécutive de l'Exposition universelle de Londres, de l'arrangement des produits industriels et artistiques du département des Colonies anglo-américaines. Il a obtenu la même mission des commissaires de la Suède et du Danemarck, et il informe MM. les Exposants français, qu'ils peuvent s'adresser à lui pour le même objet.

Ses relations journalières avec les autorités qui dirigent l'Exposition, ainsi que ses rapports de chaque instant, comme architecte, avec les entrepreneurs et les ouvriers qui exécutent les travaux intérieurs de l'édifice, en feront un intermédiaire utile aux personnes qui s'adresseront à lui pour les renseignements et les informations à donner, et pour tous les travaux et les dispositions intérieures dans les places accordées à chaque Exposant, ainsi que pour la disposition générale des produits et des objets d'arts. Il pourrait même au besoin se charger d'en faciliter la vente.

Il informe encore MM. les Exposants, qu'il est en correspondance avec plusieurs des principaux organes de la publicité en France, en Angleterre, en Allemagne et aux États-Unis de l'Amérique du Nord; qu'il parle et écrit les langues de ces pays, ainsi que l'italien, le grec moderne et les langues anciennes.

M. Semper se chargera pour MM. les Exposants de tous les dessins à fournir pour les divers publications illustrées.

Adresser les lettres affranchies à M. Semper, architecte, à l'édifice de l'Exposition universelle, département du Canada, à Londres.

A Foreign Architect's Views of the Building

576

When the busy din around us threatens to overwhelm our senses, how gladly do we seek composure by allowing our eyes to rest on those trees, which the building still encircles with its net-work, and the axe has spared! How charming! as stimulated by the busy scene around them, they seem hastening to strip off the last cinctures that confine their blossoms, and with their fan-like forms fill out the lofty canopy of the transept, blending their verdant foliage with the bars of its airy lattice-work. What a contrast between the noisy scene below, and the majestic silence with which nature completes her works. The whole picture breathes all the youthful yet antique life and freshness of a Pompeian fresco. It does honour to the architect who has so successfully brought his work into such entire unison with nature; and, considering the character and conditions of the problem to be solved, it is hardly possible to conceive a different, not to say a better, solution – the best criterion of a happy conception. Perhaps none other than a horticultural artist could have succeeded in devising so fitting a cradle for a project whilst yet in embryo. The first suggestions of fancy are ever shapeless and gigantic; they shrink into form, and condense as they become matured, in this inverting the laws of organic development.

The simple problem was to portion off such a space from the open air, as should include a world of bazaars, and protect them from the influences of the weather; all else was vague and undecided. As yet no statistics existed to determine the relative exhibiting requirements of the several States. The building must, therefore, possess a certain degree of elastic expansibility; and consequently no limiting configuration, such as that of the circle or the square, was admissible. Instead of any compact relation among the interior members, it must offer capabilities of easy partition and be fashioned in the spirit of a huge encampment.

For the fulfilment of such a task, the artist, who had already provided for the similar requirements of his exotic plants, possessed some facilities. Structures of the latter class identify themselves in a measure with living nature; their walls and roofs invisible to the eye, and the more slender and impalpable their parts, the more suited to their purpose.

Little was needed to render this class of structure adapted to the present purpose. Here, too, no architectural embellishment must compromise the internal requirements, and consequently all conventional rules and decorations must be laid aside. Much light is needed, but sunshine injurious; a *velum* must, therefore, shroud the glassy *hypæthros*; or rather, it was necessary, in an | artistic point of view, that the latter should fall with a graceful swell within the roof; and had the glass been stronger this would have been feasible. In that case the slender columns would have become the bearers of the primitive *velum*, which would have completely harmonised with the suspended draperies and figured carpets, that hang perpendicularly between the columns and fill up the intercolumnar spaces; and thus, in our age of most complex knowledge, we should have seen in this marvellous building the original type of the most primitive form of architecture unwittingly realised. Out of the canvass stretched on poles, the Egyptian flat roof grew; and the original perpendicular partition, the suspended carpet, is the prototype of all the rich panellings, paintings, or other plastic decorations, in wood, stone, or metal, which in after times supplied the place of the original woven fabrics. The numerous trophies and ornaments suspended from the columns and girders, point to the original motives in the decoration of all columns and beams. The *velum* now wanting might be in future supplied by stained glass, and in the ornamentation of the draperies, machinery can be brought to bear with less detriment to refined taste, than has been unhappily the case in other branches of the decorative art. Who does not feel that iron arabesques and ornaments produce a feeling of disgust? and is it not perhaps a sign of a revival of better taste, that architecture ventures to exhibit the simple effects produceable by those materials, the ornamentation of which is susceptible of extension by mechanical means, and thus leaves the field open to future improvement? This primitive simplicity of the work seems to constitute its architectural importance. On the other hand, a complete revolution must take place in English manners before the glass roof can find adoption in private dwellings or religious edifices. It would lead to the introduction of courts and the Italian Palazzo style, as has long since taken place in Russia.

In conclusion, a word as to the transept, which now merely serves as a covering for trees; and the necessity for which is not sufficiently obvious from any reference to the internal economy of the building. Here must be the seat of the Areopagus that awards the prizes, the only stable point in the midst of a building elsewere subject to indefinite expansion. As to the exterior it is needless, for the reasons already assigned, to make much comment. To buildings of this character it has hitherto been found impossible to give such a configuration as can be taken in at a glance, and therefore satisfy the requirements of a strictly æsthetic feeling.

The Great Exhibition

Die grosse Ausstellung.
Die Völker von europäischer und nicht europäischer Bildung.

Selbst denen, welche die allmälige Enthüllung der das Ausstellungsgebäude füllende Gegenstände zu verfolgen Gelegenheit hatten, wird es schwerlich bereits gelungen sein, die Fülle des Gebotenen so weit zu beherrschen, als erforderlich ist, um ein allgemeines Urtheil über das noch ziemlich lückenhafte

The Great Exhibition

Ganze oder gar eine in das Einzelne gehende Critik damit zu rechtfertigen. Aber Eine Evidenz tritt bereits so deutlich hervor, dass es schon jetzt erlaubt ist, sie hervorzuheben, ehe sie von einer gewissen, dem ganzen neueren Aufschwunge abholden Partei in ihrer Weise ausgebeutet wird.

Wie sich von selbst versteht, wird in diesem grossen, nun eingeleiteten Wettkampfe die erste Palme den Werken der Urkünstlerin Natur, "der Gottheit lebendigem Kleide" verbleiben. Schon sollten die Rohprodukte in beschränkter Auffassung des Programmes einer *Industrieausstellung*, nach Einigen von letzterer ausgeschlossen bleiben; aber durch die Einsicht der kgl. Commission wurden sie in umfassendstem Masse mit in dasselbe gezogen. Auch hierin hat diese hohe Behörde, der wir für die vortreffliche Leitung und Vollendung des Ihr anvertrauten grossen Werkes unsere Bewunderung und unseren Dank aufrichtig zollen, ihr tieferes Eingehen in die Bedeutung desselben kundgegeben.

Der Preis der Natur ist in den die Bögen des Transept füllenden Laubkronen der Ulmen wunderbar glücklich symbolisirt, und wie auch künftig dieser Theil des Baues sich anders entwickeln mag, so dass er mehr geeignet ist, den Heerd aller Beziehungen des grossen (künftigen) Weltmarktes würdig zu behausen, so muss dieser symbolische Stamm durch alle folgenden Zeiten und wo immer der Gedanke ein neues Lager aufschlägt, vertreten bleiben.

Die zweite Palme, auch dieses zeigt sich schon jetzt als unzweifelhaft, gebührt der Wissenschaft in ihrer Anwendung auf das Nützliche. Sie feiert, Dank dem Architecten, der den Gedanken dazu niederlegte, Dank den erfinderischen Meistern der Technik und der Verwaltung, die ihn in so kurzer Frist zur Thatsache gestalteten, die den mächtigen, so luftigen und doch so festen Bau mit neuen von der Wissenschaft gebotenen Mitteln und unglaublich geringem Aufwande an Stoff und Arbeitskräften herrlich vollendeten, einen schönen Triumph.

Unter seinem Zeltdache füllt eine Welt von Werkzeugen, Maschinen, Apparaten und Modellen die Räume aller Nationen von europäischer Bildung, und zeugt entweder ganz neue sinnreiche Anwendungen der Theorie und der Erfahrungswissenschaften, oder bietet durch Weiterbildung des bereits Erworbenen und ausgezeichnete Vollendung der Arbeit ein reiches Feld des Prüfens und Nachdenkens.

Lang gereihet stehen sie da, gleich einer schlagfertigen Phalanx bei der Musterung, bald in bewegungsloser fast unheimlicher Ruhe, bald geräuschvoll ihre Kräfte und ihre Gewandtheit wie zum Spiele übend. Sie bieten mit ihren Hebeln und Rädern, von denen wir ahnen, dass sie die Welt erobern und umgestalten müssen, ein unenthülltes ernstes Geheimniss der Zukunft. Verwegen wäre es, über das letzte allgemeine Resultat ihres Wirkens in Beziehung auf sociale Entwicklung der menschlichen Gesellschaft Vermuthungen zu wagen. Bis jetzt gaben sie kaum mehr als ihr nächstes Wirken zu erkennen und ihre

Leistungen, deren Grösse, Vollendung und Wohlfeilheit kein menschliches Zusammenwirken, keiner Hände Fleiss und Geschicklichkeit erreicht, treten überall entgegen, wohin der Blick sich wendet. Kaum Eine von den verschiedenen Categorien des Kunstfleisses der Menschen ist frei von ihrem Einflusse geblieben.

Wenn bei ihnen, wie sich gebührt, nur ihre Bestimmung und der Stoff aus dem sie gebildet sind, und dessen zweckmässigste Gestaltung und Stärke die Wissenschaft verbunden mit der Erfahrung feststellte, formengebend auftreten, so beschämen sie gerade dadurch in ihrer unbefangenen gleichsam naturwüchsigen Zierlichkeit oft die neben ihnen aufgehäuften Producte der europäischen sogenannten Kunstindustrie oder industriellen Kunst. Sie gibt meistentheils ein unstätes und prinzipienloses Ringen nach stets neuen Mustern und Formen kund, aber bleibt in ihrer rastlosen Beweglichkeit doch in dem falschen Zirkel älterer Weisen gebannt, die desshalb ihr stetes Anrecht auf Bewunderung behaupten, weil sie der sprechende Ausdruck von Zeiten sind, die mit sich und der sie beherrschenden Idee mehr fertig waren, als es die unsrige   . Aber es sind noch die besseren Erscheinungen unserer neuesten europäischen Kunstindustrie, wo dieses treue Eingehen in alte Weisen sich zeigt, während in den meisten Fällen sich ein Durcheinander von allseits her entlehnten, mit grundsetzloser Willkür zusammengewürfelten Motiven sich für Originalität ausgibt, und mitten in dieser praktischen Zeit, den durch den Zweck und den Stoff der Gegenstände gebotenen Formen bei ihrer ornamentalen Ausstattung Nichtachtung und Trotz bietet.

Wem dies als Uebertreibung klingt, der betrachte z. B. die viel bewunderten Meisterwerke unserer neuesten Tischlerkunst genauer, an denen das Schnitzwerk überall die Formen umwuchert. Schon dass sie halb zerbrochen ausgepackt wurden, zeugt gegen sie. Zarte Lilien- und Rosenbouquets in hohler Arbeit aus Holz geschnitzt, füllen die Ecken zwischen den Füssen der Tische und Stühle und treten in leichtem Gestängel über die Ränder der Lehnen hervor, an denen man sich die Hände zerreisst, an denen die Kleider beim Niedersetzen hängen bleiben, oder die bei rascher Bewegung von letzteren mitgenommen werden. Die Geschicklichkeit des Künstlers zeigte sich in der äussersten Verachtung der Gesetze, welche ihn bei seinen Werken durch dessen Bestimmung und durch den zu behandelnden Stoff leiten sollten.

Dieselbe Styllosigkeit zeigt sich in anderen Zweigen unserer Kunstindustrie; Fussteppiche z. B. mit eingewirkten bis zur Täuschung treu nachgeahmten Goldrahmen, Kartuschen und dicken Fruchtschnuren, so dass es gefährlich scheint, auf ihnen gehen und sich gesellig bewegen zu müssen; Porzellanvasen, deren Formen nicht für die hohe Hitze des Porzellanofens berechnet waren, die daher schief und verschrumpft daraus hervorgingen, oder, wenn unsere spitzfindige Technik alle Schwierigkeiten glücklich dabei überwand, das Verdienst haben, nicht zu scheinen, was sie sind; Glasgemälde, die die Schranken der Technik, die ihnen vorgeschrieben sind, weit überschreiten und vieles dergleichen.

Nur solche Erzeugnisse unseres Kunstfleisses machen hierin eine ehrenvolle Ausnahme, bei denen der Ernst ihres Gebrauches jede unnütze Zuthat ausschliesst und die schon halb und halb in das Gebiet der Maschine hinübergreifen. Dahin gehören z. B. unsere Schiffe, unsere Wagen und Pferdegeschirre, zum Theil unsere musikalischen Instrumente und hauptsächlich unsere Waffen. An ihnen zeigt sich das Streben nach Veredlung und Ausschmückung der durch den Zweck und den Stoff gebotenen Formen durch die Kunst auf eine bescheidene und eben desshalb den echten Sinn für Schönheit befriedigende Weise. Vorzüglich gilt dies von unseren Waffen, namentlich den Schusswaffen, bei denen die eingelegte Arbeit, das Niello und das Schnitzwerk sich entsprechend den Formen anschliesst, deren Zweckmässigkeit bis zu einem Grade sich ausspricht, dass sich der Kunstsinn schon dadurch befriedigt fühlt. Noch kann an ihnen die Kunst manchen Schritt weiter gehen, ehe sie ihre Grenzen überschreitet, wie sie es früher bei uns that und wie es noch jetzt den Punjabvölkern gelingt, die unseren Kanonen von neuestem Zuschnitt schon einigen Reichthum und eine grössere Eleganz der Formen zu geben wussten. Es ist möglich, dass von den genannten und anderen, ähnlichen Schrecken unterworfenen Industriezweigen ein besseres Element der neueren industriellen Kunst ausgehen kann, das sich nach zwei Richtungen hin geltend macht, indem es das leere Stangenwerk der Techniker bereichert und der masslosen Willkür, von der oben die Rede war, Zügel anlegt.

Einstweilen wird das Maschinenwesen, indem es jede verlangte Schwierigkeit in der Verarbeitung der Stoffe spielend überwindet und seine hundert Briareusarme zu wohlfeilster Vervielfältigung jeglicher Caprice des Geschmackes willfährig leiht, jenem unklaren Walten scheinbar dienen, aber als sein geheimer Todfeind es dadurch um so sicherer und schneller in seiner Nichtigkeit blossstellen und sein Ende herbeiführen.

Es wird sich zur Evidenz herausstellen, dass wir in vielen, fast in allen Fächern der industriellen Kunst nicht bloss von denjenigen Völkern von nicht europäischer Civilisation besiegt worden sind, denen wir schon immer in dieser Beziehung manches einräumten und abborgten, von Persern, Indiern, Arabern und Türken, sondern auch von den als geschmacklos bei uns verschrienen Chinesen und selbst von den Indianern Nordamerika's.

Damit diese Behauptung nicht paradox erscheine, muss daran erinnert werden, dass der Begriff des Schönen überhaupt, und insbesondere in Beziehung auf Kunsterzeugnisse ein sehr complicirter ist.

Man kann die Künste in technische, ästhetische und phonetische eintheilen und die Schönheit eines Werkes kann, je wie dasselbe mehr in die eine oder in die andere Categorie hinüber neigt, eine mehr technische sein, das heisst eine solche, welche in geschickter Wahl eines oder mehrerer Stoffe und in deren wohlverstandener Benutzung zu einem bestimmten Zwecke begründet ist; oder eine mehr ästhetische, wenn sie direct auf sinnliches Behagen durch Wohlgeruch, Wohlgeschmack, liebliche Zusammenstellung von Formen und Farben, oder durch Rhytmik und Euphonik hinwirkt; oder drittens eine phonetische, wenn das Werk durch tiefere Bedeutung zu uns spricht und die Schönheit geistig empfunden wird. Zu dem höchsten künstlerisch Schönen erhebt sich dasjenige Werk, in welchem sich alle drei Vorzüge vereinigen.

In den bildenden Künsten kann dieses höchste Ziel nur durch die Malerei und Sculptur, und mit beider Hülfe erst durch die Architectur erreicht werden. Denjenigen Völkern, deren Industrieproducte oben mit den unserigen verglichen wurden, ist der Weg zu dieser höchsten künstlerischen Entwicklung vorerst verschlossen, wogegen wir uns einer phonetischen bildenden Kunst erfreuen, deren Sprache nicht von dem Volke verstanden wird und die, von oben herab, meistens verwirrend auf den natürlichen Schönheitssinn des letzteren einwirkt, anstatt ihn zu veredeln und zu erheben.

Sie ist nicht, wie sie es sein sollte, die natürliche Blüthe der volksthümlichen Gewerbsthätigkeit, sondern eine fremde, künstlich gezogene Pflanze. Es mag zum Theil daher rühren, dass unsere industrielle Kunst heutzutage ihre Richtung verlor und wie ein steuerloses Schiff umherschwankt. Ob sie, frei von diesen Einflüssen und sich selbst überlassen eine bestimmte, und zwar eine gute Richtung gewinnen würde, das bleibt dahin gestellt. Leider wurzelt der Ungeschmack tief in unserem Volke! Während die naiven Flechtwerke und Stickereien der Canadier durch den Styl der in ihnen herrscht, durch reizende Formen und Farben das Auge ergötzen, widern uns ähnliche Gegenstände an, die z.B. in Londons Strassen, als das Product freien Volksgeschmacks, aus Papier und Stroh, in weichen Formen und abscheulichen Farbenzusammenstellungen uns feil geboten werden.

Doch die Industrie der wilden und halbbarbarischen Völker hält stärkere Proben aus als die genannte ist. Man vergleiche nur die Teppiche des Orients, die persischen, indischen, algierischen und türkischen Fussdecken mit den Prunkstücken dieses wichtigen Industriezweiges aus den berühmten Werkstätten Europas. Dort, welche dunkle Fülle, Ruhe und Harmonie in den Farben, welcher Reichthum und doch welche Einfachheit und Zierlichkeit in den Mustern, welcher Styl in dem Ganzen, und hier, wie ist letzterer gänzlich verkannt, wie fehlt dem Ganzen Ruhe und Würde, wie ist der Inhalt der historiirten Sujets auf ihnen nichtssagend! Man werfe den Blick auf gewisse grasgrüne und rosagefärbte Glas- und Porzellan-Vasen und gehe dann nach China, um einzugestehen, dass die Chinesen das Richtige trafen, weil sie ihren Porzellan-Vasen Formen, Farben und Verzierungen gaben, die für ihre Bestimmung, sowie für die schwierige Porzellantechnik passend sind, dass sie den Porzellanstyl erfanden und dass die unbewusste richtige Schätzung dieses Umstandes (nicht etwa blosse Caprice), die Beliebtheit dieser chinesischen Formen bei uns nicht sinken lässt.

Vor Allen gebührt den Erzeugnissen des Kunstfleisses der Indier der Preis. Nichts kommt der Schönheit ihrer golddurchwirkten Stoffe gleich. Ihre Elfenbeinkästchen, von einfachster aber eleganter Form, mit vielfarbigen Mosaikmustern, gleichen alt-italienischer Arbeit. Kunstvoller noch sind ihre duftenden Sandelholzkästchen; ihre zierlichen Marmortische mit eingelegten Arabesken, ihre harmonisch bunten Lackirarbeiten bilden einen interessanten Gegensatz mit Demjenigen, was in diesen Gattungen ehemals berühmte Fabrikländer uns jetzt auftischen. Man vergleiche nur selbst. In vielen anderen Dingen, und besonders in ihren reich geschmückten Waffen sind sie unübertroffen.

Auch in den Schmuck- und Silberarbeiten müssen wir, was den Styl betrifft, einräumen, von unseren orientalischen Concurrenten besiegt zu sein.

Dabei ist es interessant zu beobachten, wie diese Völker sofort in Ungeschmack verfallen, wenn sie sich von unserer europäischen Kunst influenziren lassen, wie es dann auf einmal mit ihrer ganzen Fassung und Haltung aus ist. Soll es uns denn noch überraschen, dass es unserem Volke an Geschmack fehlt, das Jahrhunderte lang ähnlichen, ihm gänzlich fremden Einflüssen ausgesetzt war?

Der Ernst des Stoffes gebietet strengste Unparteilichkeit; gerne sei unserer europäischen Superiorität in der Auffassung der Natur und den Geheimnissen ihres Wirkens durch Wechsel von Licht, Schatten und Farbe, in der plastischen Fülle und Freiheit der Formen, in dem Sinnreichen, in der Beherrschung jeglichen Stoffes bis zum Uebermuthe noch einmal anerkannt, aber nur selten vereinigt sich bei uns hohe Künsilergabe mit gewerblicher Praxis; unsere Architecten sind mehr Gelehrte als Künstler, sind froh, wenn sie Leute finden die Etwas aus ihren dürftigen Angaben machen; kurz Werke, denen der handelnde Gedanke oder die denkende Hand das Siegel der Echtheit aufdrückte, die Styl, architektonische Schönheit und sinnvolle höhere Bedeutung in sich vereinigen, sind äusserst selten und werden von der Menge von den unechten Modestücken nicht unterschieden.

Je mehr solche Werke sprechen, das heisst die Lösung und der hohe Ausdruck einer durch Ort, specielle, oft zufällige Raumverhältnisse, Eigenheiten des Bestellers &c. modificirten Aufgabe sind, desto mehr müssen sie bluten, wenn sie aus ihrem Zusammenhange gerissen werden und unter wildfremder Umgebung in ungewohntem Lichte stehen.

Dass die meisten plastischen Kunstwerke der Exhibition, die in dem langen Mittelgange sich balgen, den Rücken zeigen und sonstige Grimassen gegen einander machen, nicht mehr Zeter schreien und aus tausend Wunden bluten, sondern sich ziemlich behaglich zu fühlen scheinen, ist gerade der grosse Vorwurf, der ihnen zu machen ist.

Ein echtes Werk von höherer phonetischer Bedeutung wird auf diesem Terrain in grossem Nachtheile stehen, und zwar nach beiden Seiten hin, einerseits gegen die naiven, rein technisch architectonischen Producte des Orientes, andererseits gegen die (kolossalen Cabinetsstücke und sonstigen) Einfälle unserer hohen Kunst.

So stehen die Sachen! Sollen wir nun wünschen, dass ein Interregnum eintretender Barbarei tabula rasa mache, damit aus frischem Keime ein neues Gewächs volksthümlicher Kunst sich dem umgewühlten Boden entwinde, oder kann Erkenntniss der Uebelstände und Fortschritt des Wissens und Könnens den angehäuften Stoff, das Erbtheil aller Länder und aller früheren ganz oder halb erstorbenen Zustände der Gesellschaft, zu neuer Einheit und Harmonie bewältigen, kann in einer grossen Völkermetamorphose die Kunst aus dem jetzigen sedimentären Zustande zu krystallklarer Selbstständigkeit zusammenschiessen? Gewiss sie kann es.

Auch die Kunst der Griechen war auf vielen Trümmern älterer, einheimischer und fremder, ihrer Wurzeln beraubter Motive erwachsen, gleich wie ihre Mythologie auf dem nicht mehr erstandenen Systeme einer uralten philosophischen Symbolik emporblühte, die ihrerseits wieder auf erstorbene fremde und einheimische Ueberlieferungen und Sagen geimpft gewesen war. Auffallende, zuweilen willkürliche und durch die Gesetze der Architectonik ungerechtfertigte Verbindungen und Verzwitterungen der verschiedenen vorgefundenen Bauelemente mussten vorhergehen, ehe die Schöpfung des griechischen Tempels vollendet ward, ehe das dorisch-ägyptische Element mit dem Jonisch- | Asiatischen, der Gegensatz des aristokratischen Priestergottes und des dynastischen Hausgottes sich bei ihnen in der höheren Idee versöhnte, und das Volk, als Priester und Dynast, in seiner Gottheit sich selbst verherrlichte.

Die Versöhnung ähnlicher Gegensätze in einer noch höheren Einheit muss auch bei uns das Ziel einer neuen Kunst werden, einer noch geistigeren und reicheren, als die Hellenische war.

Letters on the Great Exhibition

Outline

Plan des Aufsatzes.   *fol. 1r*
Briefliche Form.

1) Veranlassung zu der Absendung des Briefes. Aufgefordert den Inhalt gesprächlicher Mittheilungen zu Papier zu bringen, gehorheich diesem Winke es seinem Ermessen überlassend, ob etc etc etc etc.

2). Schwierigkeit der Wahl eines Planes zu sytematischer Musterung der Gegenstande der Ausstellung. Wäre die Aufgabe damit gelöst, wenn ein solcher Plan für jeden Gegenstand eine bestimmte Rubrik enthielte und er Uebersichtlichkeit und Ordnung hinreichend gestattete, um nichts auszulassen und jedes leicht zu klassifiziren nachzuweisen und aufzufinden so hätte sie keine Schwierigkeit. Aber ein guter Plan soll nicht bloss klassificiren, und trennen sondern auch vielmehr vergleichen und verbinden, nicht bloss das Stoffliche und die äussere Ordnung berücksichtigen, sondern mehr noch den geistigen Zusammenhang der Dinge im Auge behalten; mehr Schlüssel als Riegel seyn Er soll gewissermassen aus der Formeln konstruirt seyn, die das Gesetz der organischen Verbindung aller dieser heterogenen Gegenstände enthalten. Ein Plan der in dieser Beziehung geistiger und organischer gebildet ist, hat den Vorzug vor einem anderen, der ihn an Vielseitigkeit und Vollständigkeit übertrifft. –

Der Plan soll kein Schubkasten seyn, nach dem die Gegenstande die ohnediess schon geordnet sind, sich nur im Kopfe des Einzelnen ordnen sondern vielmehr der Schlüssel der sie offnet und den Weg der Vergleichung erleichtert. Kanon. ¦

Beispiele der ersten bloss äusserlichen Schubkastenordnung   *fol. 1v*

1tes Beispiel.

Gang durch das Exhibitionbuilding, Mittelallee Ostende bis Westende, dann zurück durch die Seitengänge und s. weiter.

2tes Beispiel Vom Mittelschiff ausgehend aber immer die betreffenden Seitenräume mitnehmend je nach den Stationen der Völker. z.B. vom Westende anfangend erst aussen die Statue des Maroketti dann England Canada und die Colonien dann Orient etc etc.

3tes Beispiel schon besser und dem Weltgedanken sich annähernd von den Rohproducten anfangend, diese vergleichend dann zu den Werkzeugen u. Maschinen übergehend und vergleichend endlich zu den Producten und vergleichend. Hat den Fehler mit der Materie anzufangen anstatt mit dem Bedürfnisse wozu die Materie und das Werkzeug die Mittel darbieten. Beispiel der Unzulänglichkeit dieses Systemes, Topf. irdener, Bronzevase Porzelanvase. Der geschichtliche Zusammenhang ist nicht ausgeschlossen aber doch auch nicht nothwendig gefolgert aus diesem Systeme.

Alle drei Wege sind höchst umfassend, man ist sicher nichts auszulassen.

Abschweifung über das unbewusste Walten des Mikrokosmus in der Weltgeschichte. D. Gottlichkeit d. menschlichen thuns bekundet sich darin am meisten dass die Weltgedanken gewissermassen als Nothwendigkeiten durchbrechen wenn die Zeit dazu reif ist, frei und unabhängig von den Erfindungen der Einzelnen deren Genie bloss den Ausdruck des in der Welt reif gewordenen Gedankens fand.

Christenthum, Gothischer Bau, Pulver, Nonius Differenzialrechnung, Teleskop. Dampfmaschine. Es lag in der Luft.

Nichts kann den Gang der Menschenidee hemmen, was sich ihr in den Weg stellt, wird umgestossen oder von ihr umwuchert und dient indirect zu reicherer Gestaltung des Gedankens, der sonst zu schematisch nackt und abstrakt und unserem Sinne unschmackhaft erschienen wäre. Der Gedanke gewinnt im Ueberwinden Stärke und Form; historische Haltung und Farbe. |

Mögen diese Ruinen stehen bleiben so lange sie nichts mehr bedeuten wollen als sie sind, wirkliche Ueberreste von Behausungen verstorbener Weltideen sind und nicht entstellende Zöpfe und dergleichen.

Die Geschichte der menschlichen Wissens und Erkennens giebt merkwürdige Beispiele ähnlicher Ideenwechsel. Jede Wissenschaft beschliesst ihr erstes Stadium damit an nichts zu zweifeln etc.

Dann folgt die Periode des Zweifelns, Scheidens Analysis, Klassification, Critik.

Vergebens treten Männer wie Baco v Verulam und Spinoza auf, die Zeiten sind nicht reif. Ihre Ideen sind Träumereien. Sie tödtet um zu forschen

Dritte Periode die des Vergleichens und Combinirens. Erforschen der höheren Idee in der sich die Gegensätze vereinigen, in denen sich die Einzelnwesen bekunden. Gesetze suchend nicht bloss Ordnung erstrebend. Sie forscht um zu beleben und neu zu schaffen, das Gesetz der Erfindung zu lehren.

1ᵗ Beispiel die Naturwissenschaften, Newton. Leibniz Laplace Cuvier, Humbold. Selbst d. Mechanik fangt an sich organisch zu beleben seitdem. ausser der Attractionskraft der Materie die Repulsionskraft der d. Wärmestoff ähnlich wirkenden Kräfte in Betracht kommen. und sonst als Axiome behandelte darauf als Lehrsatze begründet und bewiesen werden.

Zweites Beispiel die Geschichte der Sammlungen. Architectonische Anordnung der Ueberreste d. Alterthums Rumpelkammern zum Amüsement der Grossen. Dann Trennung in Gallerieen mit strenger Classification letzteres unsere Exhibition als der unbewusst geborene Gedanke der ächten Culturgeschichtlichen Sammlung. Geistreiches Wort Buchers Querdurchschnitt der Culturgeschichte.

Drittes Beispiel die Baukunst. Ging durch die beiden ersten Stadien hindurch. ¦ War schon bei den Griechen zum letzten gelangt. Der Griechische *fol. 2v* Tempel aus der Vergleichung und Erkenntniss des inneren Gesetzes fruherer Bauten d. Assyrier und Aegypter geschaffen.

Neue Architecturwissenschaft seit dem Wiederaufleben der antiken Studien und Künste. Zuerst unbefangenes und thatenkräftiges Erfassen des Stoffes, ein individuelles unkritisches Anschauen der Antike, daraus hervorgehende eigenthümliche Kunstrichtung vermischt mit Gothisch-Christlichen Elementen. Dann die Critik und Aesthetik, Regeln, Categorieen, gelehrte Sammlungen auf Papier und auf den Strassen. Schematismus und Materialismus. (siehe Einleitung zu meinem Werke.). Vergleichende Baukunde etc etc etc.

Es fehlt die architectonische Gestaltung der neuen vergleichenden ethnographischen Sammlung die folgen muss sobald dem Gedanken gewissermassen Selbstbewusstseyn erwachsen ist.

Verbindung zwischen beiden Punkten natürlich und nothwendig die vergleichende Baukunde muss die Schaffnerin Ordnerin der vergleichenden Culturgeschichte werden. Die Baugeschichte ist ein Hauptkapitel der Culturgeschichte und je mehr sie ihrer Vollendung näher tritten desto mehr werden beide in einander aufgehen.

Sammlungen und *Bibliotheken*. Letztere die Commentare zu ersteren. Gute Idee des brittischen Museum. Nicht bloss Ordnung soll die vergleichende Baukunde oder Formenkunde bringen sie soll auch zugleich das geistige Band hervorheben das die durch den Stoffliche Zeitliche und Oertliche getrennten verwandten Dinge verbindet und eine Gebrauchslehre der Sammlungen geben. Erfindungslehre, Topik. Der Willkür Einhalt thuend Styllosigkeit. Style. Gesetzlichkeit u. Angemessenheit in der Erfindung

Draft of First Letter

Lieber Freund! *fol. 10r*

Ich habe den Inhalt unserer letzten Unterredung und das Ihnen gegebene Versprechen, darüber einen Aufsatz zu schreiben, seitdem stets im Kopfe getragen und war bei meinen fast täglichen Wanderungen durch den Hyde Park-Pallast beschäftigt die Sachen nach meinem bauwissenschaftlich-vergleichenden Systeme im Geiste zu ordnen. Es schien dabei dessen vornehmlicher Werth, nämlich dass es die ideellen Verwandschaften unter dieser bunten Welt von Gegenständen als das Wesentliche hervorhebt und dem Stofflichen und Oertlichen nur eine zweite Bedeutung für die Entwickelung der Unterverzweigungen innerhalb jener von den verschiedenen Grundideen abstammenden Hauptgruppen einräumt, sich zu bewähren.

Draft of Second Letter

fol. 8r

2ter Brief.

P. P.

Was Sie neulich über die Geschichte der Sammlungen erwähnten, über das Durchgehen derselben durch drei Phasen bis zu dem vollständigen vergleichenden Museum der Zukunft, deren Ansatz Sie in dem "Crystallpalaste" sehen, fällt auffallend mit eigenen Ideen darüber zusammen; Ein Plan einer vorerst nur in Gedanken ausführbaren Organisation dieser Sammlung, den ich, wie Sie wissen, schon lange hege, ist darauf begründet und dieser hängt wieder eng zusammen mit ganz verwandten Ideen über vergleichende Baukunde, über welche ich seit Jahren meditire und worüber ein angefangenes Werk bereits in den Händen des Buchhandleres V. ist. –

Es herrscht ein von individuellem Streben unabhängiges Walten des Mikrokosmos, eine Spontaneität in der kollectiven Menschheit durch die sie sich als selbsthandelndes Individuum höherer Ordnung kund giebt. Gewisse Weltgedanken machen sich von selbst Bahn wenn die Zeit dazu reif ist, frei und unabhangig von dem Sinnen und Trachten des Einzelnmenschen, der bloss zuweilen rechtzeitig den Ausdruck dazu fand. Meistens gehen Wahrheiten nicht gleichen Schrittes mit dem gemessen fortwandelnden νοῦς der Gesellschaft. Dann sind sie keine, sondern Irrthum und Rebellion; Ihr Erfolg nur vorübergehende Zuckungen der noch in dem Schoosse der Zukunft verborgenen Menschenidee.

Dagegen kann nichts ihren Gang aufhalten, wenn sie Leben gewann. Was sich ihr in den Weg stellt, wird aus den Fugen gerissen oder von ihr umwuchert, und dient als Ruine zu reicherer Gestaltung der Zukunft.

fol. 9r

In diesem Kampfe mit dem Alten gewinnt die Idee an Stärke, Haltung und Farbe. ¦| Darum ist es nothwendig, dass die Reaction gerade in diesen Entwickelungsperioden der Menschheit am thätigsten wirkt. Ihr Widerstand dient der kreisenden Zeit als Stützpunkt. Nur die Kräfte die nach eigenem vorwitzigen Ermessen bald vorwärts bald rückwärts drängen sind unnütz und schädlich.

Wo wurde der Gothische Spitzbogenstyl erfunden, welche Nation kann sich rühmen, ihn früher als andere geübt zu haben? Er kam an vielen Orten zugleich auf. Es lag in der Luft, so und nicht anders zu bauen, sich zu tragen und zu denken wie damals geschah. Wer erfand das Pulver, die Druckmaschine das Teleskop, den Nonius, die Dampfmaschine? Alle diese Erfindungen haben mehr als einen Autor. Sie tauchten gleichzeitig an mehreren Orten zugleich auf. Wer erfand die Differenzialrechnung, Newton oder Leibnitz?

Notes on Exhibits

Wolle, sehr schlecht ausgestellt, feine Qualität.   *²fol. 2v*
Baumwolle
288. *32*. 37. 178.
Weisse Rochstofte.

Fülle von eingelegtem Holze
Marylandschrank.
Flachs Filz. Farmerhemd
Chlorkalk Chromgelb Chromgrun Talck, Leim *Salpeter* Stearin, Alaun
schwefelh. Magnesia Vitriol Zinkweiss Epsomsalz etc
Getreide Seide Papier Mehl. Holzsorten, Seife Lichter Schnupftabak.

Mineralien
Eisenerz, Kupfererz Gold Magnesia
Leder Gusseiserne Buchstaben Leinen Baumwollzeug Kufen und Eisenblech
etc
Steinkohle Granit roth. Sandstein Ziegel 3 Sorten Marmor.
Mehl von Hecker. *Croton Mills* New York. City
schlecht aufgestellt

Schinken
Gesalzenes Fleisch
Oelkuchen

Holzsorten eine schöne Sammlung aber gar nicht aufgestellt.
Schusterzwecken

Fournirholz mit Cirkularsäge

Nachzutragen
Glasmanufactur
Flintglas von grosser Reinheit Brooklyn Flint Glas Company.

Schmelztiegel von Wasserblei.

Blakes fire proof paint.

3 fol. 2v   *nᵒ 62 Hyalotypie*, angewendet auf die Lat Magica Langenheim
Bettstelle *552*

Hintere Gallerie von der Ostseite angefangen

Stühle nichts Besonderes.
Wachstuch; 135
424, sehr schöne und leichte *Wassereimer*
Orn. Teppich Boston eigenth. Product von grazioser Form, etwas ursprüng-
liches.
Stocks for Mattresses. 253
Baumwollenbaum Alabama.

Allen's improved arithmetical Tables.
Spielzeug South windham Connecticut

Unterschied zwischen Deutschland u Amerika
Schneidermuster

Wachs von Virginia

Drathproben von J. Washburn & Cᵒ
New Orleans Moos.
Tapeten
402 imitation of wood. recht gut
282. Papier

Maroquin
Sensenklingen in allen Formen und Grossen
Werkzeug Hammer und Zangen in Eins gearbeitet von *Logan, Vail & C° New York*,
Werkzeuge von Brown & Wells Philadelphia Aexte *Tomohawks. Exkursion* beste Form.

Hinter Hof.

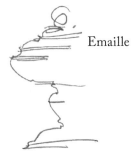 Emaille

4fol. 1r

Amerika
1) Geometrie, Dial of the seasons 2) Ruder *n° 92*. 3) Geräthe. 423.
A. M. Perkins patent Hot Water Apparatus, for warming public and private buildings Drying closets.
Perkins right and left Screw joint
Pneumatische Lokomotiven.
Die Mähmaschine mäht 15 Acker den Tag,
India rubber Ueberzug mit blättriger Textur die sich selbst darstellt. Specimen of India rubber Venering. Spielzeug Velocimeter.
Mr Hobbs, –

The Great Exhibition

5fol. 2r

Russia
Rechts unten.
Hauptallée
4 Candelaber Goldbronze
1 Louis quinze mit Blumenwerk 2 Chinesische Vasen mit schwerer Rococo-
garnitur ubereinandergestellt, auf schwer vergoldetem Unterbau. Die Garnitur
dominirt die Vasen. –
2) und 3) Arntikisirend baroker Candelaber mit Brillantfacetten an dem Schaft
und gothischem Knopfwerk.
4) Russischer Styl 3 brutale Russen in den Ecken undefinirbare Formen ohne
Feinheit des Geschmakes. Barbarischer Zopf.
1 Porphyrvase.
298. Imperial polishing manufactory Peterhoff near St Petersburg Florentiner
Arbeit stachlichter Rand; gute Zeichnung des Mosaik, ¦

5fol. 2v

Porzelanvasen im alten Zarengeschmack
Antike Vasen Warwik Wase in gehammertem Kupfer Warschau
Malachitgegenstände ohne Charakterunterschied
Official Catalogue, pa 296

Porcelan Tisch

Silberzeug, Ein Tannenbaum obenauf Blumenbouquet wie eine grossartige
Wucherpflanze
2 Style die Französisch Rokoko die Russisch Rokoko.
Ein bauchiges Gefäss von vergoldetem Silber
Ausnahme n° 11.
Ein Krug mit n° 10 bezeichnet
Dito n° 9. Ein Tannzapfen in Silber
24 Russin Sasikoff Moskau und Petersburg.
2 Hähne im barbarischen Style.

6fol. 1r

Malachit
Caucasian Sable called shahka Caucasian Daggers.
Noori Ogli Oaste Selim Molla District of Nookha
Werk in lithochromem Abdruck
gute Vorbilder im Russisch Byzantinischen Styl. Damals Byzanz wie jetzt
Paris.
Schild mit Griechischer Schilddecke
265) *Articles of furniture* von Fliz und Hasenhaar
Stickereien 276. Shirkhonin Torjok.

1 Barbarische Decke mit Papagaien oder Straussen Tigern Schlangen. Stickerei grosse Aehnlichkeit mit der der Wilden. Altbyzantinische Anklänge
Sophia Papinoff Tiflis ¦

W. Kämmerer und Saeftigen Joaillers a St Petersburg   *6fol. 1v*
5   Kaiserliche Polirfabrik in St Petersburg

———————

2 Tische. 2 Vasen von grünem Porphyr und ähnl. Malachitgegenstände /
Gold u Silbererz.
Alle Malachitgefässe mit Gold, sehr monoton
10   Parkettafeln, einige Glasscheiben, buntes Papier
die erste Querstrasse nach Clodion
290. Aga-Melik Mahomet. Hadji Ussoof Ogli. auf Gold emaillirte Becher
Knöpfe, Fingerhüte etc etc. sehr schön emaillirt
Silber im Dutzend Löffel, Messer., Becher, Dosen
15   Lithographirte Blätter bezeugen, dass die Goldarbeiterkunst einst höher stand.
Die Anmassungen mochte ich gar nicht erörtern. Germania zu den Füssen eines Helden und rechts dem gedemüthigten Frankreich.

Amerika   *7fol. 1r*
Gallerie nord) *292.* Durchsichtige Seife von Taylor. (Schlechtes Gothisches
20   Fenster von durchsichtiger Seife Spezimen von Unsinn der ausser sich ist
Fancy Soaps. von X. Bazin
Indian Rubber
Russia idem
4 weisse Schwäne Zobel Silberfuchs *Peltze*
25   Amelung & Sohn Dorpat sind so aufgehangt dass man nichts sehen kann.
Zobel und Silberfuchs 3 Pelze 2 Zobelpeltze
Gesteppte Decken.
Gestickte Decke blauer Grund, weisse Bordüre mit breiten Rothen Rändern
und Mäander, Cypressenornamente in den Ecken. Grosse Rosette in d. Mitte,
30   äusserlich weiss in der Mitte roth mit blauem Bisont von Hadji Aga Baba.
vom Gouvernt von Shemakha
Schaal von weissem Ziegenhaar aus dem Gau Orenburg.
Man erkennt das Nachtheilige der directen Leitung des Ganzen von Seiten
des Staates, vergl. die Französische Austellung ¦

35   Glaskasten II.   *7fol. 1v*
Schöne Gänsekiele Riabzewitch St Petersburg
Papierfabrik von Caluga. (Aristarkoff)

———————

Unten Südseite United States
Pendeluhr von Chauncey Jerome, Patent twelve month clock's mit einem
Pendel das horizontal sich dreht. und bald rechts bald links.
Schuhmacher 294. 410. 411. 295, 382, 471

2. sehr schöne Landcharte von der ganzen Erde nach Mercators Projection
worin die hauptsächlichsten neuen Entdeckungsreiserouten angedeutet sind.
Herausgegeben von August Mitchell Philadelph.
Drilliche, Flanelle Baumwollenzeuge von der Amoskeag manufacturing Co
Boston. Auch Vattenmuster.
Die andere Landcharte Vereinigte Staaten von A
Das Schuhwerk durch häufige Anwendung des Kautschuk influencirt.
Einfluss der Indischen Stickerei auf Luxusschuhwesen |

⁷fol. 2r Ueber den Schuhen und Uhren ein Stück Tauwerk bestehend aus 7 Strangen,
von gleicher Stärke von denen der mittelste aus gröberem Stoffe zu seyn
scheint. glanzt wie Seide
Sample of six stranded Man. Ropes manufactured from manilla on their
improved machinery

$\left.\begin{array}{l} 1 \\ 2 \end{array}\right\}$ *Untergallerie.* Tapetenproben nichts Interessantes darbietend

1 Boot aus vollem Holze geschnitten
Uhren von schlechtem Aeusserem und grober Arbeit, 1 Kinderwagen
1 eisernes Bett von schlechter Zeichnung, 1 Teppich dito. 3 Glasmalereien dito.
3te Untergalerie – Sud. siehe oben ferner.
441. Johnson Flanell von sehr feiner Qualität. 407. feine wollene Decken.
Confer Frankreich. England etc. ¦

⁷fol. 2v Auffallend die Erscheinung von Erleichterungsmitteln des Unterrichts,
Schneller hinweg kommen über das Mittel um den Zweck zu erreichen.
Deane Dray & Deane Swan Lane London bridge. Charles Howland

King William Street au pont de Londres

Silber Medaille
4. Untergallerie
1 mächtiges Vergrosserungsglass.
2 prachtvolle Aufsätze von Bronze oder vergoldetem Silber Weinlaub darstel-
lend 8 Zweige aus einem Korb sich erhebend und rothe Glasgefasse tragend.
In der Mitte ein grösseres der zweite dto von weissem Glasse. 459. in or molu |

Modell einer Brücke   7fol. 3r

Patent metallic air exhausted coffins luftdichte Metallsärge.
Susquehanna Viaduct 3800 Fuss lang und Modell einer Spannung à 180 Fuss
227. feine Miniaturmusterfabrikation dieselbe Berechtigung wie die grossen
Muster.
Modell einer schwimmenden Kirche
Chirurgische Instrumente. (Zapfenzangen)
Violinen
Notenbuchwender auf Jenny Linds Empfehlung.
Blitzableiter mit magnetischen Spitzen
Seife ¦

20. *Schlosserarbeit*   7fol. 3v
Grosse Auswahl von künstlichen Zähnen (419, 9, 350, 518. 558. 33. 47 61. 220.
63. 302)
5^t) *Untergalerie*
künstliche Beine von B. Frank. Palmer. 376 Chestnut Street. Philadelphia
4 goldene 6 silberne und 1 kupferne Medaillen
Lampen Cornelius & C° nicht besser und nicht schlechter als die unsrigen
etwas geschmackloser.
Modell einer Brücke in Amerikanischem Gitterwerk. 147.
New Brunswick Rubber Co.
Sattelzeug von Lloid in Albany State of New York. sehr gelobt von einem
Sattler. |

Besonders herauszuheben 2 Sattelzeuge. 41.   7fol. 4r
(*138*) Kassenschlosser mit veränderlichem Schlüssel, 2 goldene Medaillen.
Gekrepptes Pferdehaar Schwanenpelz, Silberfuchs (87,
6te *Gallerie* Bürsten. Uhren Sattel (476)
Perücken (133). Hüthe 130 (Castor) 232. besser als irgend wo. 303 Damenhüthe
feine Strohhüthe
Büchsen, Militärwaffen. Kinderkleider

7fol. 4v

Mittelraum, Daguerotyps.
1 *Rahmen*. 2 junge Damen, wahrsch. Schwestern in dem 2ten Rahmen. (491)
Niagarasturtz. Lords Prayer. Thy will be done on earth. Notre Dame
223) Camera Obscura und Daguerotypes 1 Fuss hoch C. C. Harrison Grösstes
Bild ¦ Geschmackvolle und einfache Kleidung
Rahmen von *Brady* New York. Schöner alter Kopf. Vortreffliche Porträts,
From life by John A. Whipple Familienstudien weniger künstlerisch aufgefasst.
1) J. E. *Mayall* 5 Rahmen Porträts, (Notre Dame)
Niagarafall 2 Stück aussen die beiden Rahmen vom Vaterunser.

Panoramatische Ansichten von Philadelphia. Talbotyp von Langenheim
do von Cincinnati Daguerotyp von Fontayne und Porter.
3 Rahmen von M. M. Lawrence Vew York.
Das Bild die 3 Zeiten die Vergangenheit jung lustig schwarz gekleidet, Gegenwart ernst Zukunft traurig gesenkten Hauptes. Porträt von Webb. u.
W. Bryant

8fol. 1r

Hinzu gekommene Sachen
Skulptur Olliver Twist ein vor Ermattung hingesunkener Knabe.
R. Bell Hughes, Boston.
Ashmead & Hurlburt's highly improved Gold Foil. und Chas. Abbey & Son
Philad.
Vorwiegende Berücksichtigung der Gesundheit und des Eigenthumes,
Robin officier de la marine France inventeur serrure avec clef avec panneton
changeant.

8fol. 1v

Day & Newell. & Mc. Gregor 298. 20 Arrowsmith ¦ ein anderes System
Der Erfinder heisst Jennings Jennigs patent rotary permutation Lock.

From the London Gallery Buffalo State of New York
Whitehursts Galleries of Premium Daguerotyps
die grösten mir bekannten Portrats
Pres. Fillmore, Honbl. A. H. H. Stuart secr. of the interior Honbl. John B.
Kerr Charge d'Affaires Bogota,
Meade Brothers. New York. ¦

Daguerotyps von Brady. *8fol. 2r*
vorzüglich ausgezeichnet 6 Porträts 6zollige General Taylor, Calhoun Gen.
Cass. Dr. Valentine Mott.
R. de Trobriand Asa Whitney, Dr Selleck. W. v. Dohm
John Kane James Perry J. A. Mac Dougal Captn Nones, 6 weibliche Porträts
vortrefflich. n° 5 alte Dame und n° 6 Kind

Linke Seite
1) Talbotyp von Langenheim
2) Daguerotyp von Cyncinati von Fontayne et Porter.
3) M. M. Lawrence New York schlecht aufgehangt 3. Rahmen.
4) London Gallery. (Evans proprietor) Buffalo.
5) from Hoggs American Dagureotype Gallery
6) J. H. Whitehurst Gallerie of premium ¦ Daguerotypes, weniger artistisch *8fol. 2v*
arrangirt und weniger harmonisch und klar, als Brady's Werke dagegen die
grössten Abdrücke
6) Meade Brothers New York.
7) Sammlung Ausgezeichneter Manner von Virginia.

---

6 Sophas und Stühle fur Kranke zum Stellen.
10 Pianos
1 transportabls Bettstelle

Whitmarsh's Patent.

Elfenbeintafeln 41 Fuss lang durch die Holyssäge hervorgebracht. by Julius
Pratt of Meriden Conn.

Outline of a Cultural-Historical Exhibition

fol. 12r

Beilage.

Plan zur Uebersicht einer kulturhistorischen Ausstellung, basirt auf den vier
Grundelementen häuslicher Niederlassung:
Heerd, Wand, Terrasse, Dach.

I.   *Heerd.* Mittelpunkt jeder Niederlassung, materiell und symbolisch.   5
    A.   *– wärmend*
       Heerd, Kamin, Ofen. (Caloricologie)
    B.   *– lichtbringend*
       Spähne, Fackeln, Candelaber, Lampen Lichter (aus Harz, Wachs,
       Talg &.) Gasflammen.   10
       Bei dieser Abtheilung wie bei allen anderen, muss die Fabrikation
       der Gegenstände vom Rohstoffe an, mit allen dazu erforderlichen
       Werkzeugen und Maschinen vom Einfachsten bis zur letzten Ver-
       vollkommung verfolgt werden. (Photologie)
    C.   – Nahrung bereitend (Culinarische Kunst).   15
       a.   Pflanzenspeisen. Feldbau mit allen seinen Verzweigungen. (Ag-
           ronomie, Oeconomie Horticultur, Mühlenbau) cet cet.
       b)   Fleischspeisen (Viehzucht, Jagd, Fischerei)
       c.   Getränke Milch, Bier, Wein etc. (Technologie ihrer Bereitung)
       d)   Gewürze, Salz, Zucker u. s. w. ¦   20

fol. 12v

       e)   Luxusgenüsse, (Café, Thee, Toback, Opium Parfums)
    C.   *Mittelpunkt der Beziehungen für den Hausrath*
       a.   Gefässe (Ceramik)
          α.   Urgefäss (Kürbiss Cocusnuss,)
          β.   Thongefäss, roh, gebrannt, gelasirt, Glas Porcelan; durch   25
              alle Sorten gebrannter Erdwaren durchzuführen (vde An-
              merkg oben)
          γ.   Metallgefässe, Metallurgie, Schmelz- und Treibekunst,
              Löthen und Schmieden, Emailliren und Ciseliren, Vergol-
              den, Galvanoplastik. (vde Anmerkung oben bis)   30
          δ.   Gefässe aus Stein und anderen Stoffen,
    D.   *Ruheplatz*
       Stühle, Tische, Möbel und Geräthe aller Art. (Tischlerkunst,
       Schnitzerei)
    E   *Sitz des Nachdenkens der Mittheilung und Unterhaltung.*   35
       a   Logik.
       b.   Redekunst, Schreibekunst Buchdruckerei.

c)   Poesie
d.   Musik
e.   Tanz
f.   Drama.
F.   *Sitz der Krankenpflege.* (Medecin)
G.   *Ort der Berathung und des Abschlusses von Verträgen.*
     Gesetzgebung, Staatskunst, Handel Rechnenkunst. (Jurisprudenz
     Politik)
H.   *Ort der religiösen Gebräuche.*
     Ahnenbilder, Bildnerei, (Theologie) Altar. |

II *Die Wand.*   *fol. 13r*

A.   Der ursprüngliche Raumesabschluss, das Pfahlgeflecht (Gitter, Bal-
     lustraden).
     a   Bast- und Binsenmatten, Pflanzenfädengeflecht, Gewebe aus
         anderen Substanzen. Muster aus farbigen Fäden aus der Textur
         entsprossen. Ornamentik, Färberei, die *Teppichwirkerei* das Ur-
         motiv der Wandverzierungen und der *Malerei.* Die *Teppich-
         stickerei* der Ursprung der Reliefkunst (China, Assyrien)
     b. Nachbildung der Teppichwände in Platten von Holz, Metall,
         Stein, Erdwaare. Mosaik, Glasmalerei, gebrannte Ziegel, Ta-
         peten. u. s. w.
     NB. Bei diesem wichtigen Abschnitte muss auf die Stylgesetze hin-
     gewiesen werden die aus dem gemeinschaftlichen Ursprunge und der
     Verschiedenheit der Stoffe die in Anwendung kommen bei jeder ein-
     zelnen Verzweigung des Motives hervorgehen.
B.   Die Wandbereitung in ihrer Anwendung auf Bekleidung.
     a   Pelz, Leder. (Schuhmacherei)
     b) Linnen
     c) Baumwolle.
     d) Wolle – (Schaafzucht)
     e) Seide
     ·   etc
     ·   etc.
     ·

     Schneiderei
     Schuhmacherei
     Spitzen, Litzen, Pasementirarbeit
     Bänder Strumpfwirker etc etc etc ¦

fol. 13v

III. *Die Terrasse.*

    A. *Erd- und Metallarbeiten*

        a. Schutz des Heerdes gegen Ueberschwemmungen (Wasserbau.)

        b) Schutz des Heerdes gegen Feinde (Schlosserarbeit Festungsbau, Waffen)

        c) Beschützung und Erleichterung des Zuganges und der Verbindung zwischen den Feuerstellen. (Wege und Brückenbau, Canalbau, Schiffarth. Telegraphie u. s. w.)

        d. Gränzbestimmung des Eigenthumes (Geometrie, Geodäsie)

        NB. Dieser wichtige Theil umfasst eine grosse Menge von theoretischen und praktischen Bethätigungen der Menschen, die sich auf verschiedene Weise innerhalb desselben ordnen lassen.

    B. *Maurerarbeiten.*

    Steinkonstruction, Ziegelkonstruction Gewölbe, (Steinschnitt.). Formen der höheren Baukunst die aus diesem Theile der Construction hervorgehen, nebst ihren von den Stoffen und anderen Umständen abhängenden Modificationen.

    (s. Anmerkung oben).

IV. *Das Dach.*

    A. *Gerüste.*

        a. Holz. technische und bildnerische Entwickelung desselben. Formen der höheren Baukunst, die diesem Ursprung angehören. Giebel, Saulenordnung. Fenster, Thüren.

        b. Metall. technische und bildnerische Entwickelung.

    B. *Dachbedeckung.* |

fol. 14r

        a) *Ueberzug,*

        Gewebe, Felle, Filz, Asphalt, Steinplatten Metall (gränzt an die Categorie von der Wand).

        b) *Schuppendach*

        Schiefer, Ziegel, Metall (gränzt an die Categorie der Maurerarbeit.).

V. *Zusammenwirken der vier Elemente.*

    Culturphilosophie. Hohe Wissenschaft. Hohe Kunst.

—————— .

Note on a Cultural-Philosophical Collection

Note.   *fol. 1v*

Es kann diesen Plan, den ich als Zugabe des obigen Schrifchens beizufügen mir
erlaube der Vorwurf treffen, dass er zu architectonisch sey und dass Manches
sich ihm nur auf ziemlich gezwungene Weise füge. Diess mag der Fall seyn,
besonders für einige Rubriken der ersten Hauptabtheilung. Aber es fragt sich,
5 ob ein anderer Plan gefunden werden könne, der in dieser Hinsicht bequemer
wäre, der jedem Gegenstände seine *nothwendige* Stelle anwiese, und der zugleich für die Erreichung des Zweckes, den der Verfasser bei *seinem* Entwurfe
im Auge hatte, und den er in der vorliegenden Schrift auseinander setzte, dieselben Vortheile böte. Es dürften übrigens die für den bezeichneten Zweck in-
10 differenten Gegenstände bei der für sie mehr oder weniger willkürlich gewähl-
ten Rubricirung an Uebersichtlichkeit nichts verlieren.

In Bezug auf die weitere Organisation der Sammlung nach dem gegebenen
Plane ist noch zu bemerken, dass jede Abtheilung so instructiv wie möglich in
15 sich gegliedert erscheinen muss. Es ist wünschenswerth die Producte in den
Haupträumen zusammenzustellen, wodurch die Vergleichung derselben und
das Studium erleichtert wird; In den korrespondirenden Nebenräumen muss
dann möglichst nahe die Technologie dieser Gegenstände, vom Rohstoffe an bis
zu der letzten Durch- | bildung desselben, mit allen dabei in Anwendung kom-   *fol. 2r*
20 menden Mitteln, Geräthen und Maschinen zu finden seyn.

Schluss der Note.

_____

Association of Artists of Various Nations

Es hat sich in London ein Verein von Künstlern verschiedener Nationen, meist   *385*
Franzosen, Engländer und Deutschen, worunter rühmlichst bekannte Namen,
25 wie *Blagmann, Dieterle, Horeau, Lienard* u. s. w. gebildet, welche im Monate Februar des künftigen Jahres gemeinsam eine Kunst-Ausstellung zu veranstalten
beabsichtigen, in der vorzugsweise Entwürfe, Zeichnungen und Modelle aus
dem Gebiete der Kunst-Industrie, incl. der Baukunst, namentlich des dekora-

tiven Theils derselben, ihren Platz finden sollen. Die Gesellschaft hat zu diesem Behufe bereits die Genehmigung zur Benutzung eines Theiles des Ausstellungs-Gebäudes erlangt, und eine nicht unbedeutende Sammlung von Zeichnungen, Modellen u.s.w. sind schon beisammen. – Es erscheint nun wünschenswerth, dass bei dieser Gelegenheit das deutsche Vaterland in geeigneter, würdiger Weise vertreten werde, und Herr *Semper* richtet an alle diejenigen Genossen, welche dem Bereiche der Kunst-Industrie angehören, die Bitte, sich an diesem Unternehmen reichhaltig zu betheiligen.

Einstweilen, und bis ein bestimmter Fonds vorhanden ist, wird die *portofreie Anmeldung* der etwa einzusendenden Gegenstände, Zeichnungen u.s.w. gewünscht, um die Räumlichkeit und das zu erwartende Material danach bemessen zu können. Diese Anmeldungen erbietet sich Herr Architekt *Semper*, 27 University-Street, London, in Empfang zu nehmen, und wird derselbe zugleich späterhin für die geschmackvolle und vortheilhafte Aufstellung der eingehenden Kunstgegenstände, der Bildhauerwerke, Gemälde, Zeichnungen, Modelle u.s.w. Sorge tragen. –

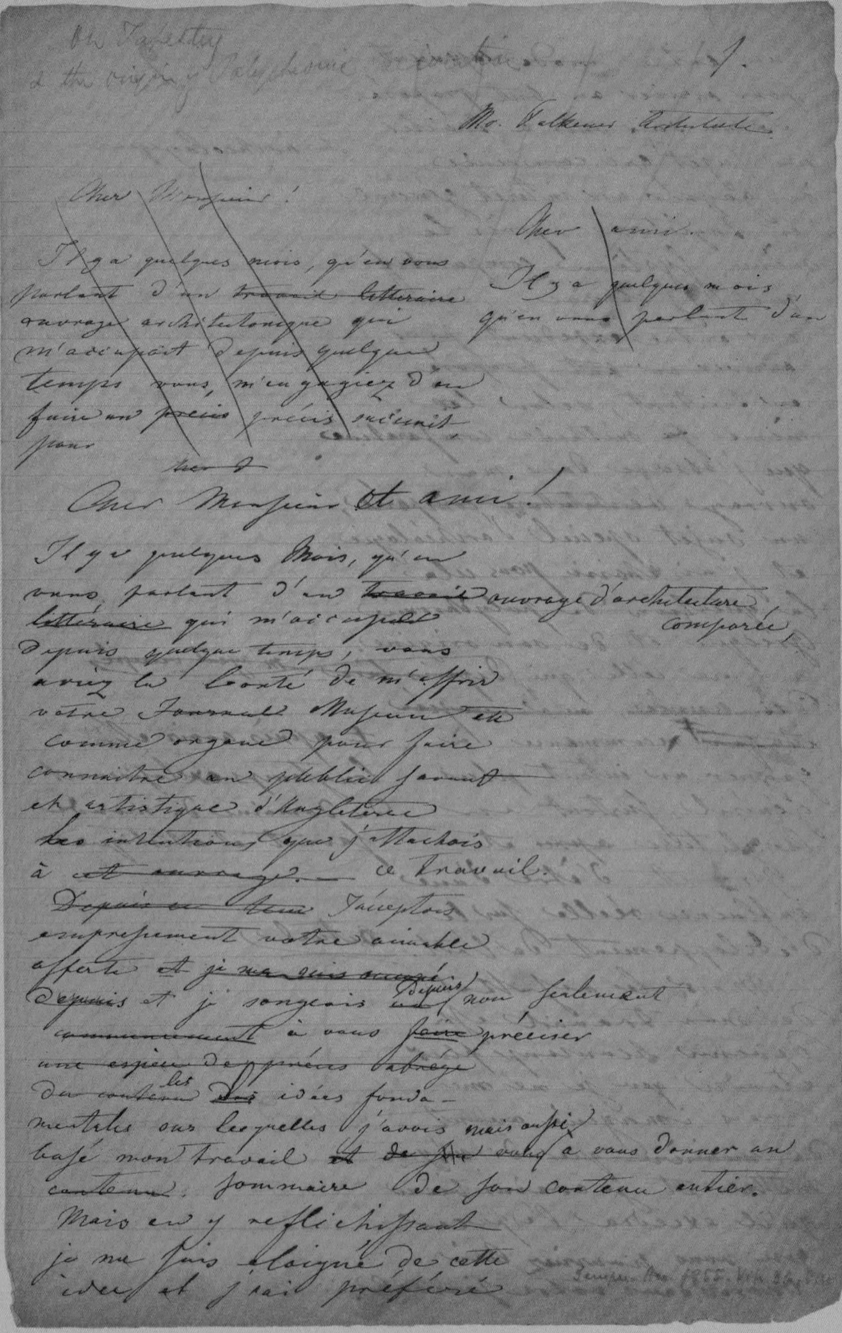

On Tapestry
& the origin of Polychromie

1.

Mr. Falkener Architecte

Cher Monsieur!

Il y a quelques mois, qu'en vous parlant d'un travail litteraire ouvrage architectonique qui m'occupait depuis quelque temps vous m'engagiez d'en faire un précis précis succinct pour

Cher ami.

Il y a quelques mois qu'en vous parlant d'un

Cher Monsieur et ami!

Il y a quelques Mois, qu'en vous parlant d'un travail ouvrage d'architecture litteraire comparée qui m'occupait depuis quelque temps, vous avez eu la bonté de m'offrir votre Journal Museum et comme organe pour faire connaitre au public savant et artistique d'Angleterre les intentions que j'attachois à cet ouvrage. ce travail. Depuis ce temps J'acceptois empressement votre aimable offerte et je me suis occupé depuis et je songeais depuis non seulement commencement à vous faire préciser une espèce de apperçus abrégé du contenu des les idées fondamentales sur lesquelles j'avois mais aussi basé mon travail et de plus à vous donner un contenu. sommaire de son contenu entier. Mais en y reflechissant je me suis eloigné de cette idee et j'ai préféré

Pl. 3: Draft of essay on tapestry and the origin of polychromic decoration, 1851 (gta, 20-Ms-79)

POLYCHROMY IN ARCHITECTURE

On the Study of Polychromy, and Its Revival

XX.
ON THE STUDY OF POLYCHROMY, AND ITS REVIVAL.[1]

Since the publication of the celebrated work by Quatremère de Quincy – *Le Jupiter Olympien* – that is to say, scarce forty years ago, the question of the polychromy of ancient monuments has not ceased to occupy the antiquarian and artistic world, without having, as yet, been determined in a satisfactory manner.

That celebrated *savant* gave us, so to say, the abstract theory of polychromy, in founding his argument on the genius and general character of ancient art. For in his time scarcely anything was known or discovered of the existence of those traces of colour in the architecture and sculpture of antiquity with which we are now acquainted. This circumstance, while | it redounds to the greater merit of the artist, detracts greatly from the value of his work, which contains but mere general ideas upon the subject in question.

The effect produced by this work was, therefore, unconvincing; for, independent of the author's having no certain points whereon to ground his theory, the influence of long-continued custom, and of modern masterpieces of art executed in conformity to it, were too deeply enrooted in the public mind to permit ideas to be received which were at once so novel, and so contrary to the tastes of the times. They were disposed to concede but very little, and that under great restrictions. It was therefore only among the younger students of art and antiquity that the revelations which it contained – opening as they did such a wide field for imagination and discovery – found some enthusiastic followers. This controversy commenced at the period of the breaking out of the Greek insurrec-

---

[1] Dr. Kugler, in his work, *Ueber die Polychromie der Griechischen Architektur und Sculptur, und ihre Grenzen*, 4to. Berlin 1835, translated by W. R. Hamilton, Esq., and published in the *Trans. Inst. B. Archts.* vol. i. part 1, 1835–6, is of opinion that the general flat surfaces of Grecian monuments retained the natural colour of the marble, and that the ornaments and details were the only portions decorated with colour.

M. Hittorff, in the paper which we published in the first number of this periodical, considers that the whole surface of these buildings was painted, and believes the more prominent flat surfaces to have been of a bright cream colour.

In the present essay, M. Semper endeavours to show that this tint was of a darker colour, more approaching to red; that, in fact, it exactly resembled the rosy hue of the glowing sunset of an eastern sky. This opinion he supports by an ingenious reasoning, but the reader must judge for himself as to the probability of such a system.

Independent of this assumption, M. Semper maintains that the whole surface was covered over with a transparent varnish, a circumstance which, if established, would in some measure tend to reconcile these several theories, in so far as the general effect of polychromized structures is concerned. – Ed.

On the Study of Polychromy, and Its Revival 49

tion from the Turkish yoke – an event which excited such temporary fanaticism in favour of the descendants of ancient Greece. This feeling developed itself in an especial manner in Germany, and particularly among such persons of distinction as patronized the arts; and it was also very generally felt in France and England.

It was under the influence of these impressions that many young artists proceeded to Sicily and Greece, in order to study those celebrated monuments which had been neglected for so long a period. They published the result of their researches in works which have since been duly appreciated; and the excavations which they effected have furnished the principal museums of Europe with masterpieces of Greek sculpture. They were subsequently enabled to put in practice the result of their studies in many important edifices, executed in the Hellenic style.

Among these travellers, there were several who devoted a particular attention to the subject under consideration. A splendid work appeared by Baron Stackelberg, containing ¦ much important material. M. Bröndsted, in his *Voyages et Récherches en Grèce*, unfolded a complete system of polychromy, of which we shall have occasion to speak hereafter. Le Duc de Luynes published his discoveries at Metapontum, and Il Duca di Serradifalco his researches in Sicily. But it was the restoration of a small temple at Selinuntum, published by M. Hittorff, which set in dispute the whole archæological world; and a controversy ensued upon all points of the question – without result, it is true, but which served to render us acquainted with all the passages from ancient authors which in any way bear upon the subject, and which interpreted them in all the various manners in which they were capable of being explained.[2]

This controversy was at its height when I returned from my travels in Italy, Sicily, and Greece. I had brought with me a portfolio of coloured drawings and restorations of Greek and Etruscan polychromy.[3] Encouraged by the reception

2   Most of the passages in ancient authors which refer to works of art are so indeterminate and equivocal, that it would sometimes be impossible even for the learning of a Herman to ascertain whether they referred to works of painting, of sculpture, or even of embroidery, or works in which all the arts were equally employed. Such passages were placed in the index as of equivocal or doubtful interpretation, but the precision and clearness of the Greek idiom would not have failed to give a distinct meaning to the different varieties of expression, had they not been considered collectively by the Greeks. It is by the assistance of these passages that we are enabled to form an idea of the general effect of a Greek monument, in which all the branches of art are collectively employed.
3   These drawings were in part the result of researches made in company with the late Jules Goury, a young French architect of great distinction, whose premature death will ever be lamented by the friends of art. After investigating the monuments of Athens, he passed into Egypt, his studies in which country were esteemed by the Egyptian savant, M. Prisse, to be superior to any hitherto executed. From Egypt he repaired to Spain, and had

Polychromy in Architecture

231 which these experienced, and by the interest which the question | excited, I published a short pamphlet,[4] which was intended to serve as introduction to a larger work, on Greek Polychromy, divided into three parts, treating separately of Greek, Etruscan and Roman, and Mediæval.

The first essays on this subject in Germany were not very promising. The different opinions of antiquaries and artists found their zealous followers among the public. Here, one saw a pale and timid style, with *seladon* (Chinese green) and rose-colour, assuming to be the true Greek style; there, appeared a blood-red building, equally arrogating to itself to be *the* style.

As the Philhellenic enthusiasm changed to Mediæval, Greek polychromy gave way to the coloured decoration of the Byzantine and the Gothic styles. This new direction was, I believe, first produced in Germany by the restoration of the Cathedral of Bamberg by Gärtner. On the occasion of the repairs, ancient mural paintings were discovered, which due care was taken to repair and to restore. Examples and models for imitation in mediæval polychromy were not wanting, especially in Italy; and the attempts to restore this style of decoration were therefore more successful than those in Greek architecture, although they rather sought to imitate the peculiarities and barbarism of the style, than to determine and follow out the great principles which they contained. The study of Greek polychromy was therefore set aside for the introduction of Gothic, which now began to be the mode. The Gothic system of colouring made especial progress in France, owing to the exertions which had been made in that country, for some ten years previously, to re-establish the architecture of the middle ages.

Several Romanesque and Gothic churches have been restored with the care and research which distinguish French artists; among others, the *Sainte Chapelle*, *232* by M. Duban, | deserves especial notice, as the most finished and perfect example of the polychromatic architecture of the early ogieval style of France. All these restorations are much more satisfactory than the attempts at Greek polychromy which had been made at various places on the Continent, the inferiority of which is to be attributed partly to the inexperience of the artists, and partly to the circumstance that, in barbaric monuments – and the works of the middle ages are so to a certain extent – we observe a grandeur of effect, and a collective harmony, obtained by a sacrifice of parts to the greater importance of the whole. But this grandeur and harmony could only be obtained, among the Greeks, by a free admixture of the elements of which the aggregate was composed, which

just completed the drawings of his magnificent work on the Alhambra, – since published by his coadjutor, Mr. Owen Jones, – when he was carried off by cholera. His portfolio of Grecian drawings contained a most complete collection of the evidences of polychromy in Attica. What has become of this collection?

4 *Bemerkungen über die vielfärbige Architectur und Sculptur bei den Alten.* Altona 1834.

allowed them a perfect and independent development, within such limits as they could not pass without disturbing the mutual correspondence of the whole. If we could form to ourselves an exact idea of this union of the free and circumscribed relation of the arts which co-operate together to the formation of a Greek monument, we should be better able to distinguish ancient art, which we are now too often in the habit of qualifying as being purely *plastic*.

It is plain that the restoration of edifices of a barbarous style is easy and satisfactory, while Greek art can only be understood in an age and nation, the character of which is distinguished by equally artistic, harmonious, and free perceptions. While on the Continent this question was discussed and agitated in the literary world, and put in practice with more or less success in various buildings, it scarcely excited attention or remark in this country – a circumstance which is the more inexplicable, that the first discoveries relative to the existence of traces of painting were made by Englishmen.[5] Among the | causes which checked the development of Gothic polychromy in England, was the unsuitableness of the usual subjects of church paintings to Protestant places of worship. It was not till after the publication of Gowry and Jones's work on the Alhambra that the people of this country began to direct their attention to the subject, which has excited more and more interest to the present time; and it is now probable that the nation may, with its usual enterprise and determination, pursue the system to its greatest extension, and apply the principle to every new and important edifice.

Much light may doubtless be thrown upon the subject of Greek polychromy by the investigations of the monuments, the paintings, and the miniatures of the first ages of the Christian era, especially in those countries which were at one time the seats of ancient civilization; and it is with great interest that we look forward to the publication of the Mosque of Santa Sophia, and other edifices of like antiquity, which have been promised to us. But what have most assisted in the investigation of ancient polychromy are the discoveries in Assyria, and the better acquaintance with the monuments of Persepolis and of Egypt; which latter now appear more closely connected with the works of other nations, instead of seeming, as formerly, to be but isolated phenomena. The monuments of Athens have also been the object of new and scrupulous research, which has led to the discovery of important principles both in form and colour, the result of which will form another valuable addition to the works of the Dilettanti Society. But the most important publication in reference to this subject

---

5 Among the earliest discoverers was Professor Donaldson; who, in the year 1830, fully proved that the whole surface of the marble temples of Athens was originally coloured. – *Trans. R. Inst. B. Archts.* i. 85, 86.

will be the work by M. Hittorff, the plates of which were obligingly shown to me by that author.

Monumental polychromy must now, therefore, be considered in a new light. It is no longer the enthusiastic speculation of a few artists or antiquaries, but the historian, the scholar, the antiquary, and the artist, all unite to support its evidence with their authority; and at length it commences to be appreciated ¦ by the public, who are becoming weary of the monotony of naked architecture.

The different opinions upon the spirit and extent of Greek polychromy may be comprehended in two general divisions, which may be subdivided in various others. In the first class may be comprehended those who regard polychromy as a means of art whereby to assist and increase the effect of sculpture and architecture, and to conceal the inferiority of materials, otherwise unsuitable to the character and dignity of the work to which they are applied. Those of the second class acknowledge no priority of importance in sculpture or architecture over painting; they deny the existence of limits between the different manifestations of Greek art, which, in their collectiveness, form but one indissoluble whole. They believe that sculpture was as much employed to increase the effect of painting, as painting was made use of to heighten the effect of sculpture or architecture; and, finally, they show that Greek polychromy is based upon ancient traditions, or rather upon the first elements of architecture, and that it was diligently cultivated by the Greeks, as favourable to the harmonious and free development of Hellenic art.

The first class may be divided into two distinct parties. The first is represented by the learned Dane, M. Bröndsted, who applies polychromy to three different purposes – the concealing or preserving the original material; the heightening the architectural and sculptural effect; and the substitution for sculpture of a cheaper process. The following is the result of his deductions, as published in his *Voyages et Recherches en Grèce*: –

"L'application des couleurs était de trois espèces –

"1. La couleur y était comme couche, et sans aucun effet d'illusion pour soutenir l'architecture proprement dite, c'est-à-dire, pour relever la teinte insignifiante et monotone de la pierre, pour réunir et rapprocher de l'œil ce qui dans l'idée de l'artiste devait se présenter ensemble, mais ce que dans l'exé- ¦ cution la distance séparait; pour faire ressortir toutes les parties correspondantes, et les mettre plus à la portée de l'œil et de l'esprit de l'observateur; en général, pour ajouter à l'effet de l'ensemble par l'aspect clair et agréable de ses parties: il ne faut pas oublier non plus l'avantage matériel que l'enduit procurait pour préserver de la décomposition des materiaux souvent poreux et veineux.

"2. La couleur servait pour produire de l'illusion dans certaines parties de la construction, c'est-à-dire pour l'effet des ombres et des jours, du relief et des

On the Study of Polychromy, and Its Revival   53

enfoncements sur un plan uni; en un mot, pour faire des veritables tableaux, et par conséquent pour *remplacer la sculpture* dans les ouvrages architectoniques.

"3. L'application s'annonce comme *achèvement des parties proprement plastiques,*"[6] &c.

He afterwards adds, "Toutefois ce même ornement en couleur, pratiqué dans l'intention de faire illusion, n'était jamais qu'une *substitution.*"[7]

The second division of the first class is composed of learned professors, and of the directors of the various museums of antiquity in Germany; and is represented by M. Kugler.

They maintain that the Greeks were induced to adopt the use of colour in their buildings solely from æsthetic principles; and they believe that the application of polychromy to sculpture consisted in little more than the occasional coloured border given to the Grecian tunic.

M. Kugler, in his work on the polychromy of Greek architecture, already cited, concludes that – "if no others, yet certainly the white marble buildings erected in the flourishing time of Greece, – that is, the greater proportion of those of Attica, – exhibited in their principal parts the material of which they were built, in its own proper colour; that painting, | therefore, is only to be referred to the subordinate details."[8] And again: "If we wish to present to ourselves the impression of the most remarkable buildings in the flourishing period of Greece Proper, we must conceive their effect to have been produced by a rich white marble in its own natural brilliancy; and, when the materials employed were of a baser description, by a coating of stucco, which in its outward appearance did not much differ from that of marble; these were then combined with appropriate ornaments, and made resplendent with gold."[9]

This opinion M. Kugler grounds chiefly upon a passage of Herodotus: –

When the Prytaneia in Siphnos shall be white,
When the Agora shall be white, &c.

"But the Agora and the Prytaneion of the Siphnians (Herodotus continues) were at this time (that is, at the fulfilment of the oracle) built (or cased) with *Parian stone.*"[10] Dr. Kugler then goes on to state: "What makes this passage so important for our purpose, is not the insulated information we get from it re-

236

---

6 Bröndsted, P. O. *Voyages dans la Grèce*, fol. Paris 1830. ii. 146.
7 *Id.* ii. 153.
8 Hamilton's *Kugler*, p. 93.
9 *Id.* p. 84.
10 Herod. iii. 57.

54   Polychromy in Architecture

specting the white edifices of the Siphnians, but the reason for which they were white."[11]

It is surprising, however, that M. Kugler, who appreciates justly the importance of the passage in Herodotus, and who is jealous that its authenticity be not questioned, has cited only a portion of the passage, in lieu of giving it in all its integrity, by which alone we shall be enabled to judge of its real meaning. Herodotus tells us: – "Those of the Samians who had fomented the war against Polycrates, when the Lacedæmonians were about to abandon them, set sail for Siphnus, for they were in want of money. The affairs of the Siphnians were at that time in a flourishing condition, and they were the richest of all the island-ers, having in the island gold and silver mines, so that | from the tenth of the money accruing from thence, a treasure is laid up at Delphi equal to the richest; and they used every year to divide the riches that accrued (from the mines). When, therefore, they established this treasure, they consulted the Oracle whether their present prosperity should continue with them for a long time, but the Pythian answered as follows: –

Ἀλλ᾽ ὅταν ἐν Σίφνῳ πρυτανήϊα λευκὰ γένηται
λεύκοφρύς τ᾽ ἀγορὴ, τότε δὴ δεῖ φράδμονος ἀνδρὸς
φράσσασθαι ξύλινόν τε λόχον κήρυκά τ᾽ ἐρυθρόν.

"When the Prytaneia in Siphnos shall be white,
And the Agora white-fronted, then there is need of a prudent man
To guard against a *wooden troop* and a *crimson herald*."

The Agora and Prytaneum of the Siphnians were then adorned (ἠσκημένα) with Parian marble. This response they were unable to comprehend, either then at the moment, or when the Samians arrived. For as soon as the Samians reached Siphnus, they sent one of their ships conveying ambassadors to the city. Former-ly all ships were painted red. And this it was of which the Pythian forewarned the Siphnians, bidding them beware of a wooden *troop*[12] and a crimson herald. These ambassadors, then, having arrived, requested the Siphnians to lend them ten talents; but when the Siphnians refused the loan, the Samians ravaged their territory. But the Siphnians having heard of it, came out to protect their property, and, having engaged, were beaten, and many of them were cut off from the

---

11 Hamilton's *Kugler*, p. 82.
12 The word is translated *ambush*: but the original seems to compare the oars of a galley to the naked feet of a compact body of infantry.

city by the Samians, and they afterwards exacted from them a hundred talents." – Cary's *Herod.* iii. 57.

Here we have reference to an oracle, the consequences of which might entail disaster, and which it was therefore their interest to provide against as much as possible.

The oracle, as usual, is involved in obscure antithesis, the coincidence of which appeared impossible. A red herald was ¦ a thing unknown among the Greeks, for white, from its purity, was always selected as the official colour for heralds. A red herald was therefore as absurd a thing as a troop of wooden soldiers. The poetical equilibrium of ancient verse requires that the antithesis of the red herald, – namely, the Agora and the Prytaneum, of a white colour, should be equally absurd in the opinion of the Greeks.

Could the oracle attach the accomplishment of its prediction to circumstances which were common and ordinary? Impossible! No doubt, therefore, that a white Agora or a white Prytaneum was in opposition to the customs of the people at the time of the utterance of the oracle. But the symmetry of oracular verse permits a yet bolder construction: –

Since red is applied to the herald, who, according to custom, should be clothed in white, is it not probable that the white colour, here so mysteriously applied to the Agora and Prytaneum, was opposed to the general custom of painting them red?

Are we to believe that, with the introduction of white marble for the construction of their buildings, such a revolution took place in the feelings of the people that they ceased altogether to paint their edifices in their former colours? or shall we not rather suppose that it was by accident that the Agora and Prytaneum of the Siphnians were of a white colour when the Samian vessels arrived off their coasts? Could the Siphnians have altogether forgotten the ancient oracle, and become perfectly indifferent and incredulous as to what they foretold, when they deliberately resolved to adorn their edifices with Parian marble? This must have been the case, if they really had the intention to let them remain of the natural colour of the stone. But this want of reverence towards ancient traditions is incompatible with the character of the Greeks; and it is probable that the two facts recorded of the history of the Siphnians were not very far apart.

It will be observed that the historian is speaking of a past time. He relates that the Agora was *then* adorned with white | marble (τοῖσι δὲ Σιφνίοσι ἦν τότε ἡ ἀγορὴ καὶ τὸ πρυτανήϊον Παρίῳ λίθῳ ἠσκημένα). Now Herodotus lived two generations after the event recorded in this history; and as the city of the Siphnians was not destroyed, but simply placed under a forced contribution, it is probable that the edifices were still standing when Herodotus read his history at Olympia; but that they were no longer in the same state, as regards colour, as when the Samians landed.

Moreover, if so radical a change had taken place in the manner of decorating buildings and in the habits of the people, is it not wonderful that no record should appear of it in history?

We are, therefore, obliged to confess that the Siphnians were surprised by fate when they had just completed their edifices in Parian marble, but before they had had time to colour them; and that in this interim, when the buildings were purely white, the oracle was fulfilled.

This explanation of the legend appears founded on a certain dramatic consequence, other than which is unworthy of the Greek historian. M. Kugler, like the Siphnians, has been deceived by the Pythia, for, not having comprehended her, he deduces a wrong conclusion: "we may thence," says he, "draw a positive inference – that what was constructed in the brilliant period of Greek art, of Parian marble, and, as a necessary consequence also, of any and every white marble, particularly, as at Athens, of Pentelic marble, was allowed to preserve essentially its external white appearance."[13] |

13   Kugler, p. 82. In Professor Faraday's *Report on the Analysis of the Colours found on the Monuments of Athens*, he states: "'Portion of coating taken from the columns of the Theseum' – I am doubtful about this surface. I do not find wax or a mineral colour, unless it be one due to a small portion of iron. *A fragrant gum appears to be present in some pieces, and a combustible substance in all.* Perhaps some vegetable substance has been used." And in answer to the question, whether the ochreous tint and glossy surface visible on the statues of the Fates in the eastern pediment were due to some foreign matter artificially applied to the surface, he replies: – "The particles you sent me seem to come from a prepared surface. Being put into a dilute acid, a portion of adhering matter is dissolved, and the principal portion is left in an untouched and cleaner state. Being then washed and dried, it is found that this consists of carbonate of lime, and a combustible substance which protects the carbonate from the acid." – *Trans. R. Inst. B. Archts.* vol. i. part 2.

Dr. Kugler maintains also that temples and other edifices represented on Greek vases of the best period are always of a white ground, and that the only ornaments introduced are capitals of a yellow colour; but on examining the vases of the British Museum, it will be found that such only of the Basilicata, and those even of a less ancient date, are so painted; and it is questionable whether the white ground was not once covered with a coloured varnish. But in all the more ancient Attic and Etruscan vases the edifices are not white, but either coloured or black, like the figures. In case xxxv. of the "Bronze Room" of the British Museum are several Attic *Lekythi* of the best period, which have the neck and base black, and the body of the vase white, with red outlines very delicately drawn. Among these there is one which shows the remains of a thick coat of enamel; but in those parts where the colour has fallen off, we perceive the original white ground, with the same delicate outlines. It is evident, therefore, that under those parts where the enamel is still perfect there exist the original lines of the drawing, which served to guide the artist who afterwards applied the enamel. And we may consequently suppose that, in all those vases which present a rude white ground, the lines of the drawing and the subsequent enamel have fallen off.

On the coloured Lekythos referred to, the tomb of Agamemnon is represented, ornamented with white eggs, and with green leaves above the cornice. The yellow ground is destroyed, but we can perceive traces of its having once existed. It is very remarkable that the use of white grounds in attic vases coincides with that of the white marble of the same

The second class of writers and controversialists may be styled the historical party, because they refuse to consider Greek polychromy in Attica as an insulated phenomenon, and explicable by the simple laws of utility and taste. They endeavour to discover the origin of the custom in its various ramifications, not only investigating what the Greeks practised and invented, but endeavouring to ascertain what the Greeks borrowed from Barbarians, receiving their customs in a more elevated sense, and refining and spiritualizing their ideas. |

M. Hittorff may be considered as the exponent of this party, and by his restoration of the Temple of Empedocles, and by the works which he has executed at Paris, he has contributed more than any other to render the science of polychromy more generally understood. His system is based principally upon a small temple in Sicily, constructed of ordinary stone, and covered with stucco; but he also refers to the white marble temples of Greece itself. His work, which we are now led to expect, will doubtless contain important documents for the history and theory of polychromy, and will furnish convincing proofs of the truthfulness of his theory.

M. Hittorff admits the greatest extension to polychromy, but he gives to the constructive portions of his buildings, as the columns, architrave, and cornices, a light cream tint, relieved by a dark but richly-decorated ground on the wall behind. Except in this particular, his system is nearly identical with that of Kugler, who supposes that the only plain surfaces of marble temples which received a general tint of colour were the two extremities of the cella.

From a careful examination of ancient monuments, and from a diligent study of ancient authors, I am led to conclude –

1. The custom of painting edifices was general among ancient nations; and it was intimately united, and almost identical, with the use of stucco.

2. The use of stucco, decorated with painting or other ornaments, was but a substitution of a still earlier *motif*, more ancient than the wall itself – tapestry.

3. Every portion of ancient edifices, from the earliest period to the time of the Romans, was covered with stucco or some other material, decorated and coloured, with the exception of the plinth or stylobate, which in the more ancient structures displayed its natural construction.[14] |

country, and that traces of colour different in its material character from what one observes elsewhere, but greatly resembling each other, are found on each. I believe that encaustic painting required a white chalk ground, as a representation of the marble or ivory for which this species of painting was invented. In the "Etruscan Room" there are two remarkable vases, No. 280 of case xii. and an adjoining one. They represent porticoes of fountains, composed of black Doric columns; the metropes and the tympana alone are white.

14 The influence of these ancient motives on the external character and appearance of their structures must have continued for a long period; and this character was that of

4. The Romans were the first to introduce a visible mural construction in their architecture, both in the exterior and interior of their buildings. This principle was confirmed at the commencement of our æra, and became constant on the substitution of the arch for the wooden ceiling.

5. The employment of marble and other hard stones is more recent than that of sun-dried or burnt bricks, or of common stone.

6. White marble was employed principally because it answered most perfectly all the requirements of a fine stucco – because it was, so to say, a natural stucco; although, without doubt, it must also have been employed from the excellence of its other qualities, as its hardness, its closeness of grain, its smoothness, – but, above all, its transparency and its whiteness, both of which latter qualities were necessary, even when it was intended to receive a complete covering of polychromy.

7. The more general employment of marble coincides with the introduction of a new application of colouring, which greatly affected the development of painting among the Greeks.[15] The ancient encaustic method which Pliny describes to us[16] was only | capable of being applied with wax on marble, or with a transparent gum on ivory. After this ancient method, opposed to the employment of melted wax, they applied coloured wax in the form of a paste, which they laid on in various colours, in the manner of a mosaic, or enamel work. This they melted afterwards with hot irons, covering the edges with a fillet of a different colour to the parts in contact.

The white marble never remained naked, not even in the parts intended to appear white; but the layer of colour by which they were covered was rendered

variously-coloured tapestry, of tabulation, or lining with slabs, and of incrustation. It continued to exert its influence, even when decoration in sculpture and painting had reached their last stage of development. The sixth book of Vitruvius is very important, as demonstrating the system of ancient mural decoration as resulting from a particular process in the execution of stucco, which, in like manner, was founded on the traditional system of mural incrustation and of constructive necessity. Compare Wiegmann, *Die Malerei der Alten.*

15 "Ceris pingere, ac picturam inuere quis excogitaverit, non constat. Quidam Aristidis inventum putant, postea consummatum a Praxitele. Sed aliquanto vetustiores encausticæ picturæ exstitere, ut Polygnoti, et Nicanoris, et Arcesilai Pariorum," &c. – Plin. *H. Nat.* xxxv. 39.

16 "Encausto pingendi duo fuisse antiquitus genera constat, cera, et in ebore, cestro, id est, viriculo, donec classes pingi cœpere. Hoc tertium accessit, resolutis igni ceris penicillo utendi, quæ pictura in navibus nec sole, nec sale, ventisque corrumpitur." – Plin. *H. Nat.* xxxv. 41.

The word cestro is supposed to be the instrument, and is considered to signify an iron *stylus*. But *cestrum* is also the name of a botanical plant. The word viriculum does not occur in other Latin authors; and it is therefore uncertain whether Pliny here speaks of an iron instrument for applying the wax, or of some resinous matter therein employed. See Faraday's Analysis, in the *Transactions of the Institute of British Architects.*

On the Study of Polychromy, and Its Revival 59

more or less transparent, to enable the white colour of the marble to appear through it. In the same manner, coloured and polished marbles, granite, ivory, gold, and other metallic portions of the edifice, were all protected by a coating of transparent colour.[17] Further proof is afforded by Egyptian monuments in granite,[18] and by many passages in ancient authors referring to this practice.

8. It is difficult to advance any general system of Greek polychromy, on account of the variations being probably ¦ greater in this flexible and changing element, than in the more fixed proportions and forms of either architecture or sculpture, even in which materials we find it very difficult to determine the normal proportions, so various do they appear. This becomes apparent, by consideration of the various dispositions of colour which have been observed in different monuments of Greek civilization. But the opposing principles of Dorism and Ionism which exist in all the institutions of Greece, in its politics, in its customs, in its poetry, and in its arts, are strikingly exhibited in the forms of architecture and sculpture. This same difference is observable with respect to ancient music, which in like manner consisted of Doric and the Ionic. Now, we know that the Doric legislators sought to found their civil institutions on the Egyptian system; while those of the Ionians based theirs on the traditions of Asia. Recent researches on the monuments of Assyria and Egypt have shown that the forms of Doric architecture were derived from Egypt,[19] while those of Ionia came from Assyria, or at least from some Asiatic country of common origin.

It may, therefore, be presumed that the different modes of music and of Greek polychromy were derived from the same sources.

The Doric style in music and in polychromy was Egyptian, as the Ionic was Asiatic. There is more in this than the mere name, for we are fully acquainted

17 "Durat et Cyzici delubrum, in quo filum aureum commissuris omnibus politi lapidis subjecit artifex, eboreum Jovem dicaturus intus, coronante eum marmoreo Apolline. *Translucet* ergo pictura tenuissimis capillamentis, lenique afflatu simulacra refovente, præter ingenium artificis, *ipsa materia, quamvis occulta*, in pretio operis intelligitur." – Plin. *H. Nat.* xxxvi. 22. The word *translucet* and the expression *ipsa materia, quamvis occulta*, prove that the gold, equally with the stone, was covered with a varnish. *Lapis politus* does not necessarily signify, as we might at first suppose, the polish given to a hard stone, but that the stone was covered with a coating, whether of stucco or colour, and then polished. Compare the following passages in Vitruvius, among many others: – "Item Halicarnassi potentissimi regis Mausoli domus, cum Proconnesio marmore omnia haberet ornata, parietes habet latere structos, qui ad hoc tempus egregiam præstant firmitatem, ita tectoriis operibus *expoliti*, ut vitri perluciditatem videantur habere." – Vitr. ii. 8. "In his vero supra podia abaci ex atramento sunt subigendi, et poliendi, cuneis silaceis seu miniaceis interpositis. ... Ipsi autem politionibus eorum ornatus proprias debent habere decoris rationes," &c. – *Id.* vii. 5.

18 See ante, p. 99.

19 See ante, p. 87.

with the Egyptian style, and we know also the harmonious music of Asiatic colouring; for Byzantine, Arab, and Gothic painting, as indeed all modern painting, are derived from it. We may observe the two different styles contrasted together on the walls of Pompeii and Herculaneum.

It would perhaps be more easy to arrive at some definite conclusion on the different characteristics of Greek polychromy by help of this hypothesis, than by the feeble traces of colour | which we observe with difficulty, and which give rise to such opposing theories. We find the same difference between the Egyptian and Hellenic polychromy,[20] as between hieroglyphics and illustrative ornament and sculpture.

9. Greek art did not reach the zenith of its perfection till the Doric influence was penetrated by the Ionic – the material by the spiritual. Those arts which are least dependent on the material, would be the first to emancipate themselves. The Ionic feeling might exert its influence on the Doric style of painting, even though the architectural forms preserved the stamp of their original extraction; and this change would most readily take place in Attica. It is, therefore, to be inferred that Attic polychromy was richer and more Asiatic than that of Sicily, or of those countries where pure Doric influence existed.

10. The following is the result of my researches and observations on polychromy, as applied to architecture: –

Colour of the Architectural Masses. – The prevailing colour of the temple burned with all the glowing beauty of the setting sun. The colour may be defined as of a yellow red, very vapoury, resembling that of the finest terra cottas. In fact, the general appearance of the temple would precisely resemble the appearance of a fine day in an eastern climate.

This yellow tint covered all portions of the order – the columns, the architrave, the cornices, and probably the triglyphs[21] and the beams. But all the flat ground members, as the walls – often decorated with paintings and ornaments – the tympana, the lacunaria, and perhaps the metopes, were of a | blue-black.[22] These colours would be laid on pretty thick, so as to obtain a sufficient body: the red would be transparent, but not the blue.

Colours of the Mouldings and Ornaments. – The prevailing colours of the mouldings and ornaments were red, blue, and green; the two former colours

---

20 "Pictura quoque non alium exitum fecit, postquam Ægyptiorum audacia tam magnæ artis compendium invenit." – Petronius, *Init.*

21 I have not been able to determine definitely what were the colours of the tryglyphs or the metopes. In my restoration of the Parthenon I have followed Vitruvius, and the Doric and Etruscan examples of Sicily and Italy, in colouring the triglyphs blue, and the metopes red; but I have reason to believe that the contrary was the fact.

22 This was of a middle tint, rather lighter than the colour of the ornaments. It was composed of black, blue, white, and a slight touch of green.

being more perfect, more brilliant, and deeper, than in those parts which served as grounds. The green is very delicate, of a bright moss colour. The details of the ornaments alternate regularly, and are united together by very delicate and projecting fillets of white, black, or gold. In the temples of Athens, I believe them to have been of gold.[23] Above the tolerably thick ground tint, may be observed thinner and transparent tints, completing the forms and subdivisions. It is difficult to tell the colour of the second tints, but they were probably of the same colour as the first. The enamels of Egypt, surrounded by golden fillets, give an idea of the appearance of the Athenian ornaments when executed in ancient encaustic. The gold with which the whole was lined, as in a spider's web, is concentrated in parts with greater effect and intenseness.

Sculpture partook of the same system of polychromy: the figures of females were almost white; those of men were of a darker tint. The use of gold was also very prevalent in sculpture.

11. Painting was not the mere filling up of the mouldings, or imitation of sculpture; but more probably the sculpture was rendered accessory to the painting.

Gottfried Semper.

On the Origin of Polychromy in Architecture

ON THE

ORIGIN OF POLYCHROMY IN ARCHITECTURE.[1]

From the time of antiquity to our own day men have sought to discover or invent the probable origin of the various systems of architecture. Besides the well known *hut* of Vitruvius, and the no less celebrated *grotto* of the Ichthyophagi or fish-eating races, (the supposed type of the Egyptian temples), the tent of the Nomad, or wandering races, occupies a very important place in our theories of the origin of styles. In the catenary formed by the fall of the drapery of a Mongol tent, has been recognised the type of Chinese and Tartar architecture.

---

23 This bordering we find in Assyrian, Egyptian, and Etruscan paintings, and is either red or black.

1 Extracted from an Essay written in 1852, and published in Germany under the title of "The Four Elements of Architecture." By Professor Gottfried Semper.

But no notice has been taken of the much more evident and less doubtful influence, which drapery itself, in its quality of a vertical wall, or partition, has exercised on certain architectural forms. Nevertheless it is the *motif* which I venture to cite, as the one on which ancient art has been principally founded.

It is well known that the nascent taste for the beautiful among those races which are in a state of social infancy, is first exercised in the manufacture of coarse tissues, which serve either as beds or as partitions.

The art of dress is less ancient than that of the manufacture of stuffs, as several examples of people to whom clothing is unknown, and who nevertheless possess an industry, more or less developed, in tissues and embroidery, may satisfy us.

The earliest woven work would seem to be the *fence*, that is, branches of trees interlaced, serving the purpose of enclosure and of partition. The most savage tribes are acquainted with this method of construction. Thus the employment of coarse tissue or woven work (which was a mere fence) as a means of securing privacy from the world outside certainly far preceded the constructed wall of stone, or of any other material; this last only became necessary at a much later period, for requirements which in their nature bear no relation whatever to space and its subdivision. The stone wall was made for greater security, longer duration, and to serve as a support for heaps of various materials and stores; in fine, for purposes foreign to the original idea; viz., that of the separation of space, and it is most important to remark, that *wherever the secondary motives did not exist, woven fabrics maintained, almost without exception, especially in southern lands, their ancient office, that of the ostensible separation of space*; and even in cases where the construction of solid walls became necessary, these last are but the internal and unseen scaffolding of the true and legitimate ¦ representatives of division, that is to say, of drapery richly varied with ornamental work, interlacings, and colours.

The difference which exists between the ostensible and principal separation, and the constructed separation, is expressed in ancient and modern languages by terms more or less significative.

In the Latin tongue, a distinction is made between *paries* and *murus*.

The Germans, in the word *wand* (of the same root with *gewand*, which means texture) recal still more directly the ancient origin and type of a wall.

New inventions soon led to different methods of replacing the primitive drapery, and every art was successively called in to contribute its part to these innovations, which may have been brought about by various reasons; such, for example, as the desire for longer endurance, for the sake of cleanliness, economy, comfort, distinction, coolness, heat, &c.

One of the most ancient and most general methods of replacing the use of drapery or tapestry is the coat of stucco or of plaster, furnished by the masons who built the walls.

Another very ancient method of replacing the original tapestry is, that of wooden panels, with which the wall was covered internally. That which proves the antiquity of this custom is, that in several ancient languages the expression which is only properly applicable to panels of wood, serves indifferently to signify every kind of flat surface (*table*) in wood, metal, ivory, or any other material.

It is thus we must explain the Greek expression πιναξ, (in Latin *tabula*) as a painting on wood, or also on marble, baked clay, &c. Plates of burnt clay, thin but of large circumference, were equally called "πινακες."

The style of mural painting at Pompeii is only to be understood by the same ancient custom of covering and inlaying the walls which they reproduced in appearance by divisions and painted draperies. See Vitruvius, on this point, in the chapter on Plastering. Wiegmann has erred in attributing the same system of ancient painting to purely technic causes.

The Ceramic art was, in its turn, called on as a means of replacing drapery. It is certain that potter's clay painted, and even glazed, served, at a very remote period, as a covering for walls. It may even be admitted, that the employment of the potter's art on the surface of walls, preceded the manufacture of burnt bricks, and that the invention of burning bricks was the result of the custom cited above.

The mural incrustations in baked clay were the precursors of brick masonry; in the same manner as the Assyrian slabs may be considered to be the forerunners of constructions in hewn stone. We shall return again to this subject.

Among the various methods of replacing the use of drapery, should be also mentioned those furnished by metallurgic processes. Vestiges of metallic coverings on walls have been found on the oldest existing monuments; and the most ancient annals of mankind are filled with recitals of buildings resplendent with gold and silver, bronze and tin respectively.

As an invention of relatively recent date, may be cited lastly, the use of slabs of marble or stone, granite, alabaster, &c., notwithstanding that we find traces of this custom, but as it were already effaced, on the most ancient monuments of the earth. (*See farther on*).

In all the cases we have named, *the character of the substitute followed* | *that of its original type*, and the painting and sculpture, or rather the two united, on wood, plaster, burnt clay, metal, stone, or ivory, was – and traditionally continued to be – an imitation, more or less faithful, of the embroideries or variegated interlacings which ornamented the antique wall-coverings.

It may be asserted that the entire system of decoration, with the art of painting and sculpture in relief, up to the period of its highest application, which is that of the tympanums of the pediments in the Greek temples, proceeded from the manufactures of the Assyrian weavers and dyers; or rather from their predecessors in human inventions. In any case, it was the Assyrians – next to the Chinese – who appear to have preserved most faithfully the antique type, even in its application to a different material. We will enter a little more explicitly on this subject.

THE ASSYRIANS.

The ancient writers often mention and praise the Assyrian tissues for the art employed in their manufacture; for the splendour and harmony of their colours, and the richness of the fanciful compositions with which they were embroidered. The mystical figures of bucentaurs, lions, dragons, unicorns, and other monsters, which the authors describe, are absolutely identical with those which we see on the bas-reliefs of Nimroud and Khorsabad. But this identity was not in the subjects alone. There is no doubt that the manner of treatment, the *style* of these subjects, was identical with that of the objects embroidered on the tissues, which ancient authors have described.

On examining somewhat attentively the Assyrian sculptures, it is easy to satisfy oneself that the art of the Assyrian sculptor moved within limits traceable from its origin, viz., embroidered work, allowance being made for certain alterations of style, caused by the requirements of a new material.

One perceives in these Assyrian sculptures, the desire on the artist's part of an attention to the truth of Nature, but that he has been hindered in his task, not – as with the Egyptians – by a regular hieroglyphic system and hieratical laws, but rather by the caprices of a method difficult, and indeed foreign to sculpture, the influence of which was still strongly felt. Thus the sculpture of this people kept itself within the bounds of a very low and flat relief, exactly similar to that of some productions of Chinese woven work, seen in the Great Exhibition of 1851, which possessed peculiar interest in the history of Art, inasmuch as they exhibited the transition of the high woof into polychromic bas-relief.

The Assyrian figures, without being embalmed mummies like those of Egypt, show, nevertheless, much stiffness and irregularity; they appear as it were imprisoned and confined within an invisible canvas. Their contours are, so to speak, tacked in with threads. One recognises in them an awkwardness and hardness arising from the contest of the artist with a material foreign to the style: whilst the Egyptian bas-reliefs evince an original, canonical, and voluntary stiffness. I am tempted to believe that all those slabs of alabaster from Assyria, with their religious, warlike, and domestic scenes, are nothing more than exact copies in stone, after originals in tissues, at that time celebrated and executed by good native artists, who worked on that material only, whilst they employed mere workmen ¦ to transfer the originals on to stone, as well as the material would allow, which explains the difference between the design and execution which these works betray. This same character is also found on the Assyrian paintings.

It is not to be doubted that the true tapesteries were employed with profusion, side by side with the stereotyped copies: and probably these last were often covered with the orignals, on the occasion of solemn ceremonies, &c., and that they were only exposed during the intervals between the *fêtes*, &c. We observe the same thing at this day in the Catholic churches, where this ancient custom, with many others, is strictly preserved. The inscriptions and their application in bands, indicate the same origin. Does it not appear as if the cuneiform characters were invented and designed for execution in needlework? In fine, the simplicity of the system of paving of the rooms, otherwise so richly ornamented, goes to prove that they were originally covered with tapestry. It is only the slabs which form the cills of the doors on which tapestry could not be placed, which indeed form an exception, being ornamented with engraved work, in imitation of tapestry. (*See* Layard.) It is thus that these last became also the types of parquetry work in mosaic.

Up to the present point, we have only considered what relates to the representations found on the Assyrian slabs. But these, in themselves, give us still more cause for reflection, and singularly justify our assertion of the importance, in an architectural point of view, of the coverings of walls.

The principle of panelling constructed work shows itself here in all its primitive simplicity. We know that almost all the lower portions of walls, within and without, were covered with thin slabs of alabaster or basalt. The same principle under another form, obtained in the upper portions of the walls; here, the walls of unbaked brick were inlaid with glazed bricks; but the plan pursued by the Assyrians in executing this incrustation differs greatly from that which we observe elsewhere, and from what we pursue at the present day.

The Assyrian bricks are only glazed on the external side, and the ornaments and other subjects which were figured on them in the glazing, bear no relation to the construction, so that the ornamental lines cross the joints of the bricks irregularly.

The enamel is very fusible and the bricks but slightly burnt, evidently with the sole intention of fixing the glazing on them, which induces me to conjecture, that the use of glazed pottery preceded and prepared the way for that of baked bricks, and that the art of pottery was already far advanced before the introduction of burnt brick-work. Other indications which would take too long to specify here, have proved to me, that the bricks received their coating placed in a horizontal position: First, they were ranged in the order which they would take when in their place, they then traced the design formed on this arrangement of unburnt bricks; next, they covered with these painted bricks – observing still the same order – the interior of the room; and lastly, they placed a fire in the room to fix the varnish which covered the walls.[2]

It results, from what I have observed, that the decoration of the wall did not depend upon the construction of the same, even when baked and glazed bricks were employed. |

The *constructive system* – after the manner of mosaic – *of decoration in enamelled bricks is a later invention*, probably a Roman one. The enamelled Assyrian bricks, should be regarded as a mural incrustation, as a covering absolutely independent of the wall itself, and even of the terra-cotta slab or tile, on which it was directly fixed.

THE PERSIANS.

The Assyrian system of panelling the lower portions of their buildings with slabs of alabaster, may be considered as the first step towards construction in hewn stone, and towards the introduction of the *"coupe de pierre"* into the number of architectural and ornamental elements.

It is only in the terraces, and the sub-basements of buildings, in the primitive ages of art, that hewn stone and its construction appeared to the eye. These parts of the buildings were the mason's oldest domain.

The Persian monuments of Murgaub and Istakir, afford us the means of observing the second step which decorative art made towards the principle of construction. They were composed, like their models in Assyria, of unbaked bricks, of which nothing remains, whilst however, the direction of the walls is still indicated by marble pillars, which originally served to strengthen the angles of the walls, and by the jambs of doors and windows and by niches, with which the walls were ornamented.

All these parts were ornamented in the Assyrian manner, and testify to the principles of which we have been speaking. But here we have no longer slabs, but hewn masses of stone of enormous dimensions, frequently monoliths. Nevertheless, in spite of their solidity, they betray their type, in a most remarkable manner, inasmuch as they form a kind of framework hollowed out internally to receive the mass of masonry in unbaked brick, which they were designed to cover and to protect, and which, in the interspaces of the pillars and jambs

---

2   The same method is to be found in some old buildings in Scotland.

THE EGYPTIANS.

above-named, were covered with slabs of marble, or more probably, with panels of cypress-wood, covered in turn by plates of gold and silver, or it may be also with richly embroidered stuffs.

The theocratic system of the Egyptians, although its origin extends beyond the horizon of history and even of tradition, is not the less based on the ruins of a social state more ancient still, and much more natural. The founders of this system, have altered the primitive style of architectural decoration in petrifying it; that is to say, in making it a style eminently adapted for stone constructions and monuments.

But amidst the hieroglyphical symbols may still be recognised the traces of its origin, obscure it is true, but unmistakeable. It has been observed by travellers in Egypt, that Egyptian art bears quite a different character in the sepulchral tombs, to that which is observed on the great temples and palace temples of the kings. It is that in these sepulchral chambers, art could move somewhat more freely than it was permitted to do in those grand monumental edifices, which were raised under the immediate influence of the priesthood.

Now it has been proved that in all the tombs, the ancient method of draping the walls, or rather of decorating them in the style of tapestry, ¦ was apparent in its greatest simplicity. It is observable, first in the character of the ornaments themselves, which consist of interlacings and gracefully varied knots, whilst these decorations borrowed from the weaver's art, are almost banished from the temples and are replaced by symbolic figures and ornament. It may be recognised, in the second place, by the fact, that the paintings in the sepulchral tombs are generally enclosed with borders, as if to indicate that they represent suspended tapestry.

Although this primitive type shows itself less positively in the temples, indications are nevertheless not wanting which remind us of it.

The contemporary artists of the French expedition have already observed – and their discovery has been since then verified – that the monuments of Egypt, including even those executed in granite, have been covered with a complete coating of colour and varnish, over the *entire surface*. That indeed might be expected, for the hewn stonework of the Egyptian constructions, in spite of the neatness of its workmanship, is not laid in regular courses, which tends to prove that this irregularity, which contrasts with the symmetrical system of the decoration on it, was hidden beneath a coating which covered the whole mass.

These monuments exhibit then the third transition step towards regular construction in hewn stone.

The construction, though massive and real, is always hidden, and does not enter yet as an ornamental motive in the compositions of the architect.

It is worthy of observation, that one of the mouldings of Egyptian architecture seems to be explained by the same ancient custom of encrusting brick buildings with stone slabs, which we have remarked on the Assyrian monuments. I allude to the torus moulding which encloses the external walls of edifices. It served to hide the joints of the slabs which covered the internal work.

It is certain that the most ancient monuments in Egypt were constructed in unbaked bricks, which must have been covered with stone slabs in the manner above indicated. The Pyramids afford us very remarkable examples of this system of panelling, which is found still perfect in the sepulchral chambers contained in them, and the traces of which are still visible on the exterior. The same observation applies to the Palace of Osirtesen at Karnak, the walls of which are panelled with slabs of polished red granite, bearing the traces of a transparent coating with which they were covered.

THE CHINESE.

China is a country where architecture has remained stationary from its early birth, and, consequently, the elementary motives of it are most distinctly preserved; they are placed side by side, without being conjoined by a general ruling idea. The external surface of the wall is still quite independent of the wall itself, and indeed is most frequently movable. The wall bears its own burden alone, and has only in view the filling up of the intervals between the wooden columns which support the third elementary want, (*i. e.*) the roof. The wall is only a screen, more or less solidly executed than others, constructed in slight brick work, covered externally with painted stucco decoration or interlaced cane work, and internally with tapestry, or its substitute, painted paper. The internal | divisions are formed by screens of the same description, and by drapery hung from the ceiling. The design of the ornament, painted and carved upon them and throughout the building, is founded on the same principle of interlacings and cane trellis-work, more or less intricate, and hardly to be recognised through the oddities of successive fashions. A polychromy, rich and brilliant, prevails, which has not been considered with that attention which it deserves in its relation with the ancient style of polychromy.

THE INDIANS.

The monuments of Oriental India, bear the impress of a settled civilisation, at least of the tertiary period. They are comparatively modern in principle and in date; but they furnish us, nevertheless, with very important hints on the history of polychromy.

The frequent use of stucco, which is better made in India than anywhere else, recals the system of the ancients, in covering their fine hewn stonework with a very fine and hard incrustation of stucco.

The Indian edifices constitute, as it were, but a scaffolding from which to hang the drapery forming divisions of their spaces, as in China, and as formerly in Assyria, Egypt, and Greece.

THE JEWS AND PHENICIANS.

At present we have only mentioned existing examples; but the ancient writings furnish us with other no less important matter. The description of the celebrated Ark of Moses, and of the Tabernacle, taken with that of the Temple of David, contains a complete history of polychromy. This curious recital of Jewish antiquities presents us with a progressive development of that elementary principle of architecture which I term "the Enclosure."

The documents and chronicles of other nations furnish us with parallels to what is contained in the holy writings. The Temple of the Slaves at Mechlenburg, according to the description of Baron von Rumohr, on the faith of ancient chroniclers; was constructed in the Oriental fashion, and richly ornamented with tapestry and gilded wood work.

THE GREEKS.

We now come to the Greeks. Hellenic art must have partaken of the composite character which is manifested in Hellenism generally, and which is so well expressed in the Grecian mythology.

As the beautiful marble, which forms the cliffs and coasts of Greece, notwithstanding its homogeneous transformation, betrays by veins, by fossils, and other indications, its sedimentary origin, so Hellenism, although it may appear homogeneous, and cast – so to speak – in one single jet, betrays, nevertheless, its secondary origin, and the sediment which constitutes its material groundwork.

It would be important to follow up these vestiges of rudimentary Hellenism, since they might enlighten us on certain phenomena in Hellenic art, which have been up to the present time inexplicable without them.

This applies especially to the polychromy of Greek edifices. Much yet remains to be done in this department of Art History, which has been generally discussed either by learned men but no artists, or artists with little learning. The vestiges of rudimentary Hellenism of which I speak, wherever visible, present the same features that we meet with in Assyria, Egypt, and China, and even among savage races; but it would appear that the Greeks, prior to treating in their peculiar manner those principles of art which they inherited, had partly forgotten their origin and their material or hieratical meaning. Thus, only, could they have had the mind free, and ready to commence them anew with an artistic and poetical feeling.

Exactly the same thing occurred in their mythology, which is only poetic fiction based on traditions and fables, partly native, partly foreign, the primitive meaning of which was no longer understood by the poets, who formed them into the groundwork of their cosmogony.

The system of Greek polychromy is the richest of all those of antiquity; but it is, apparently, based neither on a principle of construction or material as among the Assyrians, nor on a hierarchical principle as among the Egyptians. The most striking oppositions of principle are found united in it and harmonised, a more artistic and elevated, but less positive conception. Nevertheless, this applies only to the edifices of a period when art was in a state of high development among them, since the ancient Doric system appears to have had much in common with Egyptian art before it was penetrated by Ionian influence, which depended rather on Asiatic traditions.

I am convinced that the style of Doric polychromy was essentially different to that of the Ionic, which was, notwithstanding, of equal antiquity and originality.

Doric polychromy was based on the Egyptian system, whilst that of Ionia was based on Asiatic models. The first named was lapidary; the colours were detached on a whitish or yellowish ground; there was no gilding, and the use of blue was common, that being the holy colour of the Egyptians (a turquoise blue), the symbolic colour of the priesthood and aristocracy.

The second was more primitive in its nature and recalled more directly the elementary motive of *tapestry* and *embroidery*. The ground was generally of a rather deep colour, blue or red, even in the constructive portions, such as the shafts of columns, architraves, &c., a good deal of gilding and sea-green (prasinum) was used; the favourite colour of the Assyrians, the symbolic colour of absolutism and of democracy. The green is still now the holy colour of the successors of the Assyrians in Asia.

This difference of style, analogically observable in the music of these two races, explains the divergent investigations made on the temples of Sicily, and those of Athens. The monuments of Athens, Doric in their general appearance partook, nevertheless, a good deal of the Ionic character. The Ionic mind had penetrated Doric matter, and colour being the least material was that which the Ionian sentiment most easily mastered.

It would be a difficult but very interesting task to unravel the religious and political signification of certain colours in ancient times. We know that red, blue, turquoise, and sea-green, were the four colours by which the factions of the circus distinguished themselves. These were not capriciously chosen, each faction having adopted that colour, the symbolic and traditional meaning of which agreed with the political principles professed by it. |

Traces of the antique system of covering construction with tables of wood, plates of metal, or slabs of stone, representing tapestry-work, may still be perceived in the Grecian monuments, for those parts of them which were destined to be ornamented with historical paintings or painted sculpture, are executed in the Assyrian fashion; as, for example, the tympanums of the pediments, the metopes, the friezes, the parts between the columns, and round the walls of the "cella." It is thus that Grecian monuments show us the fourth path which architecture made towards stone style.

The constructive parts of the building, that is to say, those parts which constituted the entablature of the roof, and its supports, *the columns*, were painted with the colour of the Greek vases, viz., a very transparent and vaporous brown-red. The walls, inclusive of the "*antæ*," which formed only projecting parts of the walls, were of a blue, which was broken by black and a little yellow, and not very dark. This colour formed also the ground for most of the sculptures, except the metopes, which I believe had red grounds. The red in the ornamented mouldings was a very bright vermilion, differing from the red of the ground by colour and treatment.

The same is the case for the blue, which, in the ornamented mouldings, is deeper than on the large surfaces, and tinted in different shades. The *oves*, or eggs, for instance, were blue, with a darker blue tint around.

The green is a colour which occurs frequently on the Athenian temples, so on the leaves on the moulding which runs under the frieze of the opisthodome of the temple of Theseus, and between the red and blue leaves of the capitals of the antæ. The same sea-green occurs on the draperies of some sculptured figures.

The enamels of wax were frequently covered with washes of thinner colours. This has not been remarked by our restorers of antique polychromy, but is nevertheless necessary for giving softness to the general effect.

The ornaments, as I have just observed, are placed in pieces and soldered together; the solderings forming fillets slightly elevated from the surface and of another colour. I cannot say whether in gold, black, or even in some parts white. I have, for my own part, adopted the hypothesis that it was gold in the Athenian temples, but not on those of Sicily where a strict Doric character prevailed.

I have not found many traces of colour on the Ionic temple of Minerva Polias, and cannot say if the red, which I found on the columns of the Northern Portico, belonged to the ancient colouring, or was of more recent date. On the plate, in my work, which gives a panel of the temple of Theseus, is seen the design of a row of pearls, with a double range of disks.

I can guarantee the exactitude of my observations, although this extreme richness and smallness of detail in an object destined to be seen from a distance may well astonish us.

I have traced every mark on the stones themselves: and, moreover, subjects of this kind are not capable of being invented; indeed it would be a great compliment to suppose me capable of inventing these designs, which I consider charming.

In the portion which I have found in the wall with the niche (see my work), these details are not to be seen. I have also discovered traces of colour, very much effaced, on the small choragic Monument of Lysicrates, which I have carefully examined. It appears that on the ornament which surmounts ¦ the roof, there was a variety of blue and red, and that the acanthus leaves were coloured green. The tripod was not placed upon this ornament, but round it, the feet resting on the three volutes which descend from the roof, analogously to the marble tripods which are often met with in various museums of antiquities.

I will not speak of the colours of the Parthenon, which are not so well preserved as those on the Temple of Theseus, but the traces of ornament which decorated that temple are seen by the incisions still remaining. It would appear that the system of ornament there applied was similar to that on the Temple of Theseus.

Some years after my sojourn at Athens, portions of this building have been excavated, with the colours very well preserved; as well as other fragments of architecture which belong to the old Hecatompedon (destroyed by the Persians) covered with painted stucco.

I have not found very decided traces of the colours employed on the Temple of Minerva Polias; the columns appear to have been red, as at the Temple of Theseus. The ceiling of the Temple of the Caryatides had painted frets and orvolos, which I have traced; but the colour was no longer visible. Traces of painted ornaments are to be found also on the Tower of the Winds. I have not been able to get a close view of them.

As regards the sculptures, I have found some regularly encrusted with colour. I have found green (prasinum) on the tunic of one of the seated goddesses, on the frieze of the Temple of Theseus: another figure was clad in a vestment of a deep rose colour. The Caryatides of the Erectheum had blue tunics. We may see that, even on the one in the British Museum.

Mr. Bracebridge has described statues which were excavated in his presence near the Parthenon with flesh tints and painted eyes. The figures of the pediment of the Temple at Egina still retain traces of the colours with which they were decorated. The same observation applies to the metopes of the temple at Selinuntum, now at Palermo. Curious fragments of painted architecture may also be seen at the museums of Syracuse and Girgenti.

The Romans painted their white marbles, like the Greeks. The three columns of the Jupiter Stator in the Roman Forum are painted red on that portion which has remained a long while buried.

The Trajan Column, which I have examined, retains traces of colour and gilding: the entire column had been once covered with a rather thick coating of colour, in which I recognised green, blue, and yellow; but it is probable that this last was the remains of the gilding.

for annual report in Demy 8°.
— set in Bourgeois – full meas.
4 proofs Henry Cole
28 July 52

To the Superintendents
of the Department
of Practical Art.

Private

Report on the
Collection of arms at
Windsor Castle
(the property of Her Majesty
the Queen) prepared with
Her Majestys Gracious
permission, by
Gottfried Semper Professor
of Metal working in the
Department of Practical Art

The Instruments of War and
of Chase have always been considered as the most suitable
ornaments of their noble bearers
and therefore they were
early objects of decorative art
while the works of their
they permitted other decorations, the task, as confirmed
rigorously to the principal laws
of Style, fitness, and convenience

Their importance for the
Study of Ornamental art in
general and of Metalworking
especially is therefore evident.
The Test Procerts of
the Armorers and Swordsmiths
are firstly interesting 1°
for the variety and perfection
of the different Processes
occurring in the Art of Metal
working, which processes
have been applied in their
fullest development on arms
and weapons. It is certain,
that no other branch of
Metalworking, not even that
of the Goldsmiths and Jewellers,
presents greater choice,
variety and perfection of
Processes, than those which
we find in this
branch in question

They are not less
important secondly for the
Study of Style, in so far
as we understand by this
term those achievements

Pl. 4: Report on the private collection of arms at Windsor Castle, 1852 (gta, 20-Ms-107)

DEPARTMENT OF PRACTICAL ART

Report on the Private Collection of Arms at Windsor Castle

364 (B.) – Report on the Private Collection of Arms at Windsor Castle, the property of Her Majesty the Queen, prepared, with Her Majesty's gracious permission, by G. Semper, Professor of Metal Working in the Department of Practical Art.

To the Superintendents of the Department of Practical Art.

The instruments of war and of the chase have always been considered as most suitable ornaments for their noble bearers, and therefore from a very early period they were objects of decorative art, while the uses to which they were put did not permit other decorations than such as conformed rigorously to the principal laws of fitness, convenience, and style.

Their importance in the study of ornamental art in general, and of metal working especially, is therefore evident.

These products of the craft of the armourers and swordsmiths are interesting,

First, for the variety and perfection of the different processes connected with the art of metal working, which processes in their fullest development have been applied on arms and weapons. It is certain that no other branch of metal working, not even that of the goldsmith and jeweller, presents greater variety and perfection of processes than those which we find in this.

Secondly, they are not less important for the study of *style*, in so far as we understand by this term those achievements in works of art, arising from using the means artistically and observing the limits, which are contained in and defined by the task and problem in question; as well as by all the accessories, which modify the solution of it in every case. It has already been mentioned why such objects must necessarily be suitable models for studies of styles.

Thirdly, arms and weapons are interesting for the study of what might be called the history of styles, arising out of that peculiar character by which the artistic productions of different countries and ages are distinguishable from each other.

The history of ornamental art in metals cannot therefore be better illustrated than by a collection of arms and weapons; for we see at once all requisite conditions observed, what has been done, what is the most convenient for style, and what is the most pure and rich for decoration. Thus we may observe a relative elevation of art manifesting itself on arms and weapons, arising out of these very circumstances, when in the centuries of barbarism and decay the practice and science of art was otherwise almost lost.

The same results appeared when ornamental art attained its highest elevation in the ages of flourishing civilisation. The craft of the armourer has often been the seminary for artistic talents of every description, and high art did not disdain this branch of application.

A relative purity and chastity of taste and style is finally observable on arms in those luxurious periods of art when the principles of style were disregarded, and the arts followed the general direction of the age for novelties and extravagances of all kinds. |

We have happily better opportunities to pursue the study of art on arms and weapons than is afforded by any other branch of ornamental art; since many fine collections of arms are to be found in the different countries of Europe forming so many almost *unexplored* treasuries of ornamental art for artistic investigation.

The largest and most renowned armouries in Europe were in the beginning practical institutions, for they were arsenals. Some others, for instance that of Vienna, formerly at Castle Ambrass, had from its commencement a more antiquarian and historical destination.

Others partake of both of the two qualifications, such as the private collections of sovereigns, princes, and others.

Among the last is the royal collection of arms at Windsor Castle, without doubt one of the most interesting and perhaps the most valuable of all.

Besides the richness of its contents it is highly important for the artistic significance of many of the objects and their rare state of preservation.

But the artistic significance of the Windsor collection, or of any other collection of arms, has not as yet been sufficiently explored.

Some illustrated publications on arms and weapons, as, for instance, the works of Meyrick, of Tubinal on the Madrid armoury, that on the imperial collections of Russia, and Baron von Ebner's work on costumes of the middle ages, contain very useful materials, and their acquisition for the library of the Department of Practical Art is most desirable, as well as the printed catalogues of the most important collections in Europe.

But they scarcely give more than the general forms and characteristics of the weapons, and are not sufficiently detailed for practical instruction.

I therefore beg leave to recommend to the attention of the Superintendents of the Department of Practical Art the following proposals respecting the enrichment of the Museum with some specimens of arms, swords, guns, &c.

It would be difficult to provide the new establishment at once with a sufficient number of selected specimens of arms, proportionate to their importance as means of instruction. But this want of the Museum may be temporarily supplied by loans from the possessors of collections of arms.

Her Majesty the Queen has already graciously permitted the Department to borrow specimens from the rich collection in Windsor Castle.

The collection is unique for its treasures of Oriental arms, but as it appears to me that Oriental art is at present very well represented in our Museum, I reserve my proposals for other branches of the armourer's art, and mention only three objects of Eastern art, as being very instructive and interesting for the richness and originality of the processes employed in their ornamentation.

1. Burmese sword, No. 9,356, for the beauty and peculiarity of the chased hilt, &c.

2. Sword, which passes for Moorish, but which certainly is Chinese, No. 2,315, for the richness and originality of the processes employed for the decoration of its hilt and scabbard, with ornaments of various metals.

3. The breast-plates, forming part of the armour of Tippo Saib (hanging in the passage, decorated like a tent). It is remarkable as a beautiful specimen of steel-chasing and of pure simplicity of design.

Among the Western arms may be mentioned a strong Gallo-Roman sword of iron, with bronze hilt. It would appear modern and counterfeit, if it had not on the hilt some small silver rosettes, like filigree works, which once were filled up with enamel. The general form of the sword, and this ornament on it, render this specimen remarkable. The rosettes are instructive in the history and practice of the enamellers art. ¦

The collection of Rénaissance weapons is very considerable, and has perhaps the greatest interest for our modern practice.

Among the swords there are three of the first distinction.

One of them, No.   , has been attributed to Benvenuto Cellini without reason. It has some relation in style and execution with the fine shield belonging to the Queen, which is at present in the Museum, and perhaps belonged to the same panoply.

The second, No. 222, is of a somewhat later period, and inlaid with silver. The general form is very elegant, and the ornaments are of the best style.

The third, No. 276, has been executed after the same principle as the second, and shows the third step in the development of the form of the modern sword.

Another sword, probably of James II.'s time, has a hilt formed by serpents, chased in steel, and is of very good design and well executed.

Then comes the Dutch sword of the 17th century, which is decorated with fine chased medallions, with portraits of some heroes of the Dutch history.

This series may be closed for the present by mentioning one very beautiful sword of the time of Louis XVI., which in the catalogue is given as an English work. The hilt is gold, with enamel pictures in cameo on azure ground, which no doubt were done by one of the best masters of the time. I have never seen better enamel pictures.

Report on the Private Collection of Arms at Windsor Castle   79

This specimen is not only to be recommended for the beauty of its details, but also for its general form and the good taste and careful execution which pervade it.

It gives an evidence of what has been said before, that purity of style is to be found on arms and weapons even when general bad taste in art is dominant.

Among the other Occidental weapons, besides the guns, may be noticed here the beautiful halberd of the time of Henry VIII., a present of the Pope to the King, and of Italian workmanship.

Among the guns are the Oriental guns, not less distinguished by the beauty of the workmanship of the barrels than by the good taste and the richness of their ornamentation; and it is principally for the first quality that they excel our modern guns.

It may be allowable to allude here to the excellent arrangement in the Museum of Practical Geology, where the different processes (among others that of barrel-making) are shown in technological surveys, to the great profit of the students. Would it not be desirable to have similar arrangements for our Museum, with this difference, that the artistic element must predominate above the geological and the metallurgical?

Among the Occidental guns, which are altogether excellent, I remark for the present the famous Lazarino Cominazo guns, distinguished for the style of their barrels, which is, at the same time, decorative and practical. They are manufactured with the nails and the shoes of the Appenine mules.

The gun of Louis XIV., worked by Piraube, is probably the finest gun in the world. The barrel is inlaid with gold flowers, the sight is silver, the head-sight steel, carved in open work. The whole is rich and sober at the same time, and the distribution of the decorated part is perfectly well understood. The execution is also very beautiful. It is a model for ornamental art in its application on guns.

The same case contains other admirable specimens of more modern workmanship. – One Spanish gun of Joachim da Zelaja, and the fine pistols worked by Weiss at Suhl, in Germany. The same master made two guns, which are at the same place. These arms are the finest specimens of Louis XV. style: and for this reason, as well as for their fitness and for the excellent workmanship of the whole, are very interesting. |

The same case holds also the renowned Kuchenreuter guns and pistols; they *367* are the best for practical use, and the application of the ornaments on them is graceful.

These are the objects which, among so many other things exacting attention, it may be sufficient to point out for special notice.

I take this opportunity to make two other propositions, relating to the same object.

I beg leave to recommend – Firstly, that coloured drawings of the most interesting arms and weapons in the Windsor collection and at other armouries in England and elsewhere should be made. Sometimes coloured drawings are more useful than plaster casts for students.

Secondly, that plaster casts be made in such cases where this manner of reproducing the originals, is more useful; as, for instance, for répoussé works and steel carvings; and,

Thirdly, that electrotypes be made of the finest specimens of arms; such, for instance, as those at Dresden. Some electrotypes have already been reproduced of the beautiful shields which are at Dresden.

Gottfried Semper.

London, September 20, 1852.

Berlin Productions of Plastical Art, Metal Casts, Plaster Casts

fol. 2r   *1. b*   Henry Cole Esquire
Superintendent etc etc etc.

My Dear Sir

Mr D. Born, Agent for Berlin Productions of Plastical Art, Metal casts, Plaster Casts etc. proposes to the Superintendency of the Department of Practical Art to purchase for the Museum some of his articles, which partly are specified in the bygiven Catalogue.

Among the Objects it contains are two Suits of Gems and Medals, which for I beg leave to call the Attention of the Superintendents.

The first is the Collection of antique Gems, known under the name of the Stosch Collection, which forms the principal part of the Collection of gems in the Museum at Berlin. |

fol. 2v   The price of the plastercasts of this Suit of gems, (including the well known Catalogue of it, prepared by Winkelmann in the Year 1769,) ranged together in 20 neat boxes, will be, including the charges of transport etc, about 25 Liv.

Each Cast of a gem is sold separately for 2½ Silver groschen or circa 3 pens at Berlin. Hundert pieces together are sold for 6⅔ Dollars or circa one Pound.

The whole Suit contains 3444 pieces. –

In the bygiven frame are contained some specimens of this Suit. –

2° – The Collection of Cinque-cento Medals and gems, *500 pieces*, cast after the Originals of Italian and German Masters, who executed them partly in wood and Speckstone, partly in Metal. The Originals are in the Royal Museum and in the Kunstkammer at Berlin, and some other belong to private Collectors.

They originate from the Epoch between 1440 and 1640 and are the works of Pisani Sperandio, Boldu, Valerio, Leo Leone, Albrecht Durer, Heinrich Reitz, Magdeburger, Jamnitzer, and other.

This Suit is very interesting | for artists and it would be desirable, to have in the Museum some of the finest specimens of this Branch of art, in which the Italian rivalled with the German Masters of the period in question, and were not equalled since.   *2 b.   fol. 3r*

The whole Suit costs about 10 Liv. (60 Dollars at Berlin) and the single peaces are sold between 3 pens and 5 pens each.

The suit of German Medals separately is bought in London for circa 2 Liv. complete. –

Mr Born wishes to be informed before the Season of the Winter has advanced farther, the Transport from Berlin beeing afterwards interrupted by the River-ices. –

Mr Born brought me also the table with Zinc-casts of Mr Eichler's Manufacture, which had been exposed in the Exhibition of 1851. and thinks, that it would be interesting for the Museum of the Department. It will effectually be so, for the comparison with the English and Frensh productions of the same kind.

He leaves it for 18 Shillings. |

Then Mr Born recommands to the Attention of the Superintendents of the Department the cast Iron Ornaments of Devaranne at Berlin. He gives some specimens of these objects; among them The following numbers may be the most interesting for the Museum, as proofs of Skill in Casting Iron.   *fol. 3v*

The Brooch 2/6. the Bracelet 5/6. – n° 540. – Bracelet and Brooch.

Each à 4/6. – n° 126 – Bracelet and Brooch.

6./ – n° 113 – Pendants –

3/.6. – n° 558 – Brooch –

The peculiar nature of the sand into which the metal is poured, seems to be very influential for this fine industry; I therefore beg leave to recommend the proposition, to procure some quantity of this Sand, as specimen for the Museum, and perhaps for experiments, by the mediation of the Agent, Mr Born. –

The same proposes also for acquisition a Copy of the Shield of Hercules, composed and executed by Schwanthaler in Munich. This Copy is cast and ciselld in Copper or Bronze by the artist and costs 400 florins or circa 40 Livres.

82 Department of Practical Art

fol. 4r   3 b.

But I think this summ too large and believe that a Plaster copy or at the most a Electro-type Copy of the Shield will suffice, if altogether the Superintendents should | find this Subject, proposed by Mr. Born for acquisition, for the moment wanting for the Museum.

11 October 1852.

I am Dear Sir   5
Yours feathfully,
GSemper.

Observations on Some of the Specimens of Metal Work

37

OBSERVATIONS ON SOME OF THE SPECIMENS
OF METAL WORK.
By Professor Semper.   10

The comparison between the numbers M 1 and M 20 on the one hand, and number M 2 on the other, is interesting as a study of ornamental colouring. In M 1 we see how the blue and green enamel grounds stand crudely opposed to each other, without being united by a common parentage. Even the introduc-   15 tion of the ruby into the system is hardly sufficient to render them more harmonious. Even in M 20 we observe some deficiency of harmony, but here it is less violent, the green and blue tints being broken and connected together by the neutral black, which has been interposed between the two tints. These and some similar works of Oriental art stand in direct opposition to the beautiful Tulwar   20 or Sword, M 2, and such objects as M 11 and M 12, which belong to the same system of colouring and ornamentation. Here the various powerful and brilliant colours, although violent, are united by a common hue or tint, which is spread over the whole. Every colour is one shade of a general scale, to which all the others belong, passing from the green through the white to the red, which last,   25 in its special hue, is thus made the dominant colour of the whole system. The ground is formed, not by white, but by a neutral jade colour, which is very pale, but always greenish on the scabbard, where it works in unity with the green leaves and the gold rims to contrast the ruby or rather the Oriental red (sang de bœuf) of the flowers, which last are here dominated by this coalition.   30

The same alliance between the green leaves and the jade coloured base, as complementary to the red, is more fully exhibited on the lower part of the hilt of the sword, where the ground is of a somewhat darker greenish tint.

On the middle compartment of the hilt, however, the same jade coloured ground takes another hue, and enters into an alliance with the ruby against the green, making thereby the ruby the dominant colour.

Thus we observe on this beautiful specimen of Oriental art, variety and contrast most happily combined with harmony and repose, which result has been obtained, first, by a common key, upon which the whole tone of the system of colours has been tempered, and, secondly, by the system of subordination, which has been carried throughout.

The first quality, harmony, obtained by a common tone of the colours which enter into the system, is one of the great mysteries of beauty which unerringly prevail in nature and such works of men as are simple expressions of natural artistic feelings.

Such works are generally tinged by the natural hues of the materials employed, which hues form the bases and connecting links between the bright colours which enter often into the composition of their ornamentation. This may be seen in the straw and rush carpets of the Oriental, American, and African tribes; in the embroideries upon leather and wood-bark by the Canadian; in the raw-silk and cotton tissues of the Chinese; in the ornaments made with tinged rice; in coloured gutta-percha ornaments; in the terra cotta vases of the Greek, and in the jade vases of the Chinese and Indian. ‌|

Specimens of this kind are extremely interesting for the study of colouring, and are very often at the same time good examples of ornamental art in general.

The fine jade vases, M 102 and M 103, belong to this sort of ornamental industry, and are, with their inlaid stones, nearly related to the enamels in question, which seem to be quasi imitations of the natural materials which enter into the composition of these works.

The attainment of that great object of ornamental art, which consists in the due subordination of the ornamental parts to the chief impression, is not often to be found in works of early periods of art, and seldom prevails in Oriental art, which generally suffers from the absence of this principle; we see on them flowers and ornaments spread over the whole, like net-work. The above-mentioned sword forms, however, a beautiful exception, though the hierarchical principle in it seems to be neutralized by its double application.

Egyptian, and more especially Greek ornaments and implements, combine these two high qualities, and moreover excel the Oriental works in the elegance of their general forms and outlines; it will therefore be extremely useful to have a greater number of antique ornamented works for comparison with the Oriental, mediæval, and modern articles in the Museum.

The modern works in the Museum are chiefly specimens of the facility and skill of the present age in treating materials, but at the same time, some of them give evidence of danger to the true progress of art, which may arise from their study. The works of Vechte are worthy of being placed at the side of the works of Michael Angelo and Cellini; and the vases and other works of Sèvres manufacture are beautiful specimens of modern enameling.

The sword, M 55, is very well executed, but the ornamental parts of the hilt are not adapted to the principal object, and in themselves a little clumsy. The hunting knife in the style of the 15th century, manufactured by Marrel Freres, is a fine specimen of execution in metal, but seems to fail in style and character.

The amourer's art is one of those which most require to be sustained by old examples; these nevertheless have been neglected by modern armourers, because their immediate application to modern arms is not so easy, nor has it been so much required, as the imitation of old bracelets or broaches, for the copying of ecclesiastical candelabra.

The newly acquired additions to the Museum, included in the numbers M 123 to M 134, are interesting as illustrating the history of styles, while some of them are fine specimens of ornament.

Among them the cast-iron knocker, M 125, deserves the first notice. It comes, probably, from Nuremberg or Augsburg, or some other town in Middle Germany, and dates from the end of the 15th century.

In Germany the Gothic style lost its simplicity and purity at the beginning of the 15th century, or even before that time; and its early decay was partly owing to the introduction of new processes and modes of execution, both in architecture and other works of practical art.

Among the innovations of this kind which most largely occasioned this change, were those of casting metal and producing the details of architecture and of ornamental art, by casting such as before this period were usually carved or cut in hard materials, or executed in chased, hammered, and forged metal.

Architecture and ornamental forms had obtained, under the influence of the old processes, a certain conventional style, which henceforward contradicted the new means of execution.

Under these circumstances, it would have been a fault instead of a merit if the sharp angular forms of the old style had been preserved by the artists and architects of the 15th century. |

Peter Visscher's monument of St. Sebaldus is a very interesting evidence of this fact. It is indeed, as a Gothic monument, very impure in style, and contrasts strongly in this respect with the design, made by another sculptor of the time, for the same monument, whose working drawings are known to us, having been published by Heidcloff; but it would have been an error if Viet Stop's design had been adapted, suited as it is for wood carving, to be executed in cast-metal instead of that of Peter Visscher, which, although impure as a style, is admirably adapted for metal casting.

The classical (antique) style which was introduced at this time, was a happy solution of the contradiction, and had long before become necessary.

The cast-iron knocker, M 125, is a small, but very interesting specimen of this period of transition. It is one of the earliest pieces of iron casting I know, and has a special interest from being connected with the history of this specialty.

2. The small Gothic key is, in some respects, the companion to the former work, as it shows iron forging combined with the purer forms of the Gothic style.

3. Indian enamel vase. If it is Indian, it is the only example in the Museum of this kind of enameling executed by Indians. All the other Indian enamels are of the nature of Champleve's enamels: the handles look rather Chinese or Japanese; at all events it forms a fine specimen of Oriental art, and evidences the limits within which bright colours may be employed without loss of harmony. The other objects have more interest in the history of styles than as beautiful models in themselves.

G. Semper.

A Plan of Instruction for the Metal and Furniture Classes

(F.) – A Plan of Instruction for the Metal and Furniture Classes. By Professor Semper.

I. – *System of Instruction.*

Experience seems to prove that institutions for teaching practical art and art in general will be most likely to fulfil the purpose for which they are designed if established in form of ateliers rather than schools.

For this reason I may be allowed to express a wish that such a form of instruction should be adopted for these classes.

It differs in the following essential points from that of schools of design and academies: –

1. In workshops or ateliers there is no classification of the pupils or students, either as to age or as to their various progress in art. Thus, beginners learn quicker and easier by working amongst the more advanced, and by seeing them work.

2. The different subjects of instruction are not systematically arranged in daily and weekly succession, nor divided into lessons, according to a fixed order of studies, except as regards lectures, and such instruction as | requires preparation, as lighting and firing kilns, &c.; or those which the students participate in, together with other classes and under other instructors, within or out of the Department.

3. The students assist the Professor of the atelier in his practical works; and in this way they are brought into many relations with practical men, and have the best opportunity of getting practical knowledge and experience.

II. – *Subjects of Instruction.*

1. Geometrical principles of design, including perspective and projection of shadows, &c., illustrated with examples which are so chosen as at the same time to be exercises in proportion, the elementary forms of practical art and architecture, and in construction. These exercises must be combined with instruction in the geometric principles of design and in modelling. (See lectures.)

2. The principles of style illustrated by examples which are to be copied by the students. These studies should at the same time be studies of technology and of the history of practical art.

The models are either real objects of practical art, or fac similes of them, in plaster or otherwise, or finally drawings.

The usual mode of copying the models is by drawings, with or without colouring. It may however be desirable, in some circumstances, to have them done by modelling, and opportunities should be provided in the room for modelling in clay and wax. (See 4.)

3. Composition of objects of ornamental art.

That very important part of the instruction in the arts, how to cultivate invention either of objects themselves or of their ornamental details, is now too much neglected; and we daily see clever draughtsmen and modellers who are well acquainted with anatomy and able to represent truly whatever they see before them, yet have but little ability in the art of composition. The students pass the whole of their time in copying and making studies after nature, without trying their powers on productions of their own.

Those copies and those studies would have much more interest for the student, and be rewarded with much greater progress, if done in connexion with some idea which the student had in his mind, or had sketched, and which he requires to work out to completion.

The talent and spirit for composition ought to find encouragement from the beginning of the artistic education.

I therefore make the following proposition for the studies of my classes: –

Competitions between the Students.

Competitions between the students of the metal-room to take place regularly every fortnight, on Monday.

The students to spend one day composing sketches for some subject of ornamental art, to be proposed to them by the Professor in written programmes, fixed on the wall on the morning of the day of competition.

Two such programmes will be given at once, – one for beginners, the other for the more advanced students, who will be classified only according to this distinction.

The sketches might be ready *in one day*; those not delivered on the evening of the same day to be excluded from the competition.

On an early day after these competitions the Professor to give a critical review of the sketches sent in, and afterwards leave to the students themselves to point out, among others, those which merit the preference.

The sketches, with explanatory remarks, will afterwards be presented to the Superintendents of the Department for them to determine the prizes.

Small rewards and official certificates should be delivered to the two most meritorious as prizes.

Besides these small competitions, there should be twice a year competitions of finished works.

The programmes of these competitions will be given on the first Mondays of the months of April and September, or any two months in the year, and six weeks will be allowed for finishing the works.

The second competition of the year should be the so-called great prize competition. The successful candidates being rewarded by gold, silver, and bronze medals, and by official testimonials. The gold medal might be the highest prize, and only be given if one of the competitors is not only the best among the others, but has highly distinguished himself by his labours. To that medal might be attached, by the Board of Trade, certain contingent advantages to the student in the prosecution of his studies, to be hereafter determined upon. The works rewarded should be the property of the Department.

The other competition, the first in the year, is of the same nature as the former, except that no higher prize than the silver medal could be obtained.

The competitors of the second class will be advanced to the first class, if they succeed in gaining the prizes in the two great competitions, having their own programmes.

Further details as to the competitions and rewards can be given, if this plan is considered a desirable one.

4. The various Professors of the Department may be thus combined for instructional purposes: –

(*a*.) Enamelling – different processes of enamelling and enamel painting. By Mr. Simpson and P. Semper.

(*b*.) Modelling, moulding, and casting, in plaster. By Messrs. Townsend, Brucciani, and Semper.

(*c*.) Chasing and embossing. By

5. Visits to museums, workshops, and manufactories.

The Professor should, at certain intervals, visit with his pupils the public and private collections of practical art and antiquities, and give historical, statistical, and technical explanations of the objects they contain.

6. Lectures.

Public lectures on the relations of the different branches of practical art to each other, and to architecture (including characteristics of style), the history of art, and its technology.

Students lectures in the metal and furniture class. On the geometrical principles of design (including perspective, stereotomy, and other branches of study, illustrated by models, for students of the Department only.

The students might be permitted and required to follow the lectures on physics, mineralogy, chemistry, metallurgy, &c., in the Department of Practical Geology, as well as those which are delivered in Marlborough House.

G. Semper.

First Report on the Class for Practical Construction, Architecture, and Plastic Decoration

(d.)

Report of Professor Semper on the Class for Practical Construction, Architecture, and Plastic Decoration.

I have the honour to submit a report of the state and working of the class of metal-working, furniture, and practical composition, since its commencement.

The subject of *practical composition* has only been entrusted to me since the last session, but I have made practical composition in the more extended sense of the expression (as I understand it,) the foundation of my system of exposition since the opening of my class.

The want of knowledge of composition and of practice, the ignorance of the architectural principles of design, of style, and of beauty generally, the ignorance of the fact, that a high degree of artistical accomplishment is consistent with industrial art, which is absolutely even necessary for it, seem to be the principal causes why our young artists show generally little taste, and even a kind of prejudice against this interesting branch of art; they generally think it is to lower their position and their art, to apply themselves to industrial art and to utility.

Several students who frequented my class at its beginning were well advanced in the academical principles of drawing and painting, and skilful draughtsmen and modellers, but they partook a little of the prejudice which I have mentioned; but knowing by my former experience, how useless it is merely to preach against this feeling, I waited for an opportunity of introducing them at once into practice, and imparting to them experimentally as it were, the knowledge of the difficulties, means, pleasures, and profits of the practical branches of Art. This opportunity presented itself, when I was entrusted with the execution of the metal works of the funeral car of the late Duke of Wellington. Two modellers, Mr. Whittaker and Mr. Wills, executed in common with myself and after my working-drawings, the models of the ornamental posts of the car, and were afterwards employed in inspecting the operations of moulding and chasing the bronze casts. A third student of Somerset House, was afterwards employed in chasing some parts of the ornaments of the car, which for want of time would not be finished before the funeral took place. One of the students so employed, has, in consequence of his share at this work, since been appointed as modeller in one of the great industrial establishments at Sheffield.

Some other practical works, of less importance of course, have been executed in the class. For instance, besides other pieces of furniture and architectural details, a large sideboard commissioned by Sir James Emerson Tennant, which was destined to be executed in ebony wood by Indian workmen in the Isle of Ceylon. The two students who were appointed to design this piece of furniture, Mr. Cuthbert and Mr. King have thus had an opportunity of having a short but an effective course of architecture and practical composition, which I believe, will add to their abilities. Several other students have been engaged in copying some of the more interesting pieces of metal work in the Museum, connected with the Department; and two architectural students have made their elementary studies in architectural drawing and ornament.

The number of students who were under my charge in the first session of the year was eight: namely –

Messrs. Fallen, from Boston, architect; Austin, painter; Armitage, painter; Whittaker, modeller; Wills, modeller; Cuthbert and King, decorators; and Semper, architect.

At the exhibition of furniture at the Gore House, which opened last May, I superintended the copying, modelling, and moulding the details of the more important pieces which were exhibited. An interesting collection of drawings and of casts has been the result of this practical course, and several students who knew very little about architectural drawing | and proportion, and about ornament, have learned on this occasion to enter upon such kind of works.

The students who attended at Gore House were Messrs. Armitage, Cuthbert, Halgate, and Brenan, designers; Messrs. Whittaker and Wills, modellers; and Mr. Semper, architect.

Since I have been appointed the Professor of Practical Composition, in addition to the former branches; I have had to follow another system of instruction. Formerly I had to deal with students, who by their antecedent academical knowledge, were rather too much elevated by the idea of preparing for a career of high art; while, in the latter case, I am endeavouring to impart some higher direction and artistical feeling to students who generally are operatives, and devote themselves too exclusively to mere practical instruction. These students only attend for a short time, and I have therefore adopted the system of introducing them "in medias res," and of showing the principles and elements of design and composition, while they struggle with work which, in a more elaborated and systematical course of instruction, ought perhaps to come later. Some of these students had no idea of perspective drawing whatever when they commenced three months ago, but are now able to execute complicated compositions of perspective, which they would not have been able to do in the usual mode of instruction of perspective drawing. I however generally begin with a short explanation of the very first elements of designs, and the simplest notions of geometrical projection, as the preparatory school education of most of my students has been very neglected.

The number of this class of students during the last session has been seventeen.

The students who have received medals for works executed under my superintendence have been Messrs. Whittaker, Armytage, King, and Cuthbert.

The extent to which manufacturers or others have sought the assistance of myself or of my students has been already explained in part; but I must add, that I have had several private commissions besides, those mentioned, which have been executed in presence of my students and partly with their assistance. Some few applications for advice in questions of practical Art have been made to me.

The leading idea, to show the connection existing between practical application and artistical conception, has been the object of my course of lectures on the relations which exist between the different branches of practical art among each other and to architecture.

I delivered in the month of May one lecture, as an explanation of my system, which, in the course of the second session, I have been endeavouring to develop in a series of lectures.

The acquisition of some books and architectural drawings for the particular use of my class appears very necessary and urgent.

As for instance the work of "Letaroulz on Roman Architecture," which is the best collection of fine specimens of modern architecture for the use in schools of architecture. There is one copy of this work in the library of the Department, but we ought to have *one other for our special use*. I propose also, the purchase of some fine drawings of the best French ornamental and architectural designs, such as those of M. Dieterle. The material treatment of this kind of art by Frenchmen is by far the most distinguished.

My suggestion for the improvement of the studies refers principally to the locality, which, for want of daylight, is wholly unfit for a School of Design. The students ought to be altogether in one room, so as to have the benefit of a system of mutual instruction and emulation, which I have found to be the most effieca-cious in teaching Art.

Gottfried Semper, Professor.

To the Secretaries of the Department.

Second Report on the Class for Practical Construction, Architecture, and Plastic Decoration

Report of Professor Semper on Class for Practical Construction, Architecture, and Plastic Decoration.

Sir,

The following is a report of the state and general working of the class for Practical Construction, Architecture, and Plastic Decoration during the year ending 31st of December 1854.

1. I have three distinct classes of students under my instruction, each of which requires its special method of instruction, they are –

1st. The day students of my special class.

2nd. Those who attend only in the evenings.

3rd. The masters in training.

The first-named of these three divisions partly consists of students studying architecture (properly so speaking), and is the only class which enables me to apply that system of instruction which I practised for many years at the Royal Academy at Dresden, combining theory and æsthetics with immediate practice, and making the last the basis of the system. ¦

I then had the opportunity (from the number of works under my hands) of employing the students on the works in course of execution, and making my class a real *atelier* for architects.

The students were very anxious to be employed in this manner, in making copies of plans, carrying out working drawings and details after my sketches, making estimates, and surveying the works under execution, which employment they considered to be and really was a distinction.

Although my practice at present is comparatively but little, it would nevertheless afford an opportunity of pursuing the same system of teaching art here, only I have not found the same readiness and desire on the part of the students for this mode of learning which is the requisite for the successful application of the before-mentioned method.

Most of the students, attending only in the evenings, are employed during the day in some of the different crafts connected with house-building, and demand special instruction immediately applicable to their specialities, which I am endeavouring to give, and to impart to them at the same time the necessary knowledge in geometrical drawing, projection of shadows, and other elementary parts of architectural science.

The mode of instruction to be followed for the masters in training is to me a problem yet to be solved. I have thought it right to endeavour to teach them the general principles of style in architecture, (being the same which prevailed in the whole world of industrial art,) instead of entering too much into specialities. The real sense and structural meaning of the mouldings, and generally of the different decorative forms usual in architecture, as well as in many other branches of practical art, is very little known; to which circumstance may partly be attributed the failure of many modern works in architecture, pottery, furniture, &c. The explanation of these forms, and the use and application of the same at their proper places, have been one principal object which I had in view in comparing, in a series of class lectures, the different styles of ancient architecture.

2. The number of students who attended the day class during the year 1854, was 13. Two of them have since entered into practice as architects.

The number of the students attending the evening class has been 22, which makes together 35 students for the year 1854, exclusive of the masters in training, who have numbered about 50.

3. The progress of the students is satisfactory.

4. The day students have carried out several compositions of houses, after their own ideas, or after suggestions given them.

5. Five Department medals and one book have been awarded in the course of the year to the students of this class.

6. Several drawings have been carried out for manufacturers.

7. I have delivered, in the public lecture-room at Marlborough House, two courses of five public lectures on the different styles of ancient architecture, their distinctions and connexions. I further delivered a series of class lectures (one a week) on the mouldings and decorative forms, to the training masters.

I have, &c.

Henry Cole, Esq., C.B.   Gottfried Semper.

The decorative arts arise from
and should be properly be
attendant upon architecture

Pl. 5: Draft of lecture on the relations of the different branches of industrial art, 1853 (gta, 20-Ms-118)

LECTURES

Prospectuses of the Lectures on Art

Architecture.

May 20th.

On the relations of the different branches of industrial art to each other and to architecture. By Professor Semper.

_____

ON ARCHITECTURE, PRACTICAL CONSTRUCTION, AND PLASTIC ART GENERALLY.

Five Lectures. By Professor Semper.

On Friday Evenings, 11th, 18th, 25th November, and 2d and 9th December at Nine o'Clock.

LECTURE I. – *Friday Evening, 11th November*, 9 p.m.
General remarks on the influence of the primitive forms in industrial works, the materials employed, and upon the development of the different styles in art. 1. The ancient practice of wall coating, and its significance in history of architecture and art in general. 2. Tubular construction, well known by the ancients, and forming the fundamental idea of Greek architecture.

LECTURE II. – *Friday Evening, 18th November*, 9 p.m.
On the Connexion of Ceramic Art with the art of Metal casting. Its influence on architecture and the other arts.

LECTURE III. – *Friday Evening, 25th November*, 9 p.m.
On *Timber Construction*, and its influence upon the development of architectural forms. Metal works as belonging to timber construction, in opposition to other modes which belong to the tnbular construction, or to ceramic art (art of casting.)

LECTURE IV. – *Friday Evening, 2d December*, 9 p.m.
On Stereotomy, or stone construction; including the art of cutting forms out of hard masses. Its importance in the history of art. |

LECTURE V. – *Friday Evening, 9th December*, 9 p.m.
The combined action of the four preceding branches of industry in architecturc. Assyrian, Egyptian, and Grecian architecture, as examples of three different

principles of monumental art, being expressions of the political and religious differences between the three nations. Modern parallels to these examples.

Admission for registered Students of the Department, Free.
For the Public 2*s*. 6*d*. the Course, or 1*s*. each.

On the Relations of the Different Branches of Industrial Art to Each Other and to Architecture

First Version

Entwurf zu den Vorlesungen über die Beziehungen der verschiedenen Zweige der industriellen Kunst zu einander und zur Architectur. *fol. 1r*

Erste Vorlesung.

Introduction.

The decorative arts arise from and should properly be attendant upon Architecture

Dieser Satz steht an der Spitze der wenigen Grund Regeln, welche das Departement als Norm des Unterrichts aufgestellt hat. Doch jeder, der über diesen Satz nachdachte, wird sich sagen, dass er näherer Durchführung bedarf, um in der gedrängten Kürze und Allgemeinheit, wie er hingestellt ist, in seiner ganzen Consequenz erkannt und praktisch anwendbar gemacht zu werden, und zweitens auch, um falschen Consequenzen zu denen er führen konnte, vorzubeugen. ¦|

die veränderten Verhältnisse genöthigt war anzunehmen. Ich würde die Beziehungen der verschiedenen Zweige der praktischen Kunst zuerst behandeln dann auf ihr Zusammengreifen in der Baukunst, und die Wechselwirkungen zwischen letzterer und jenen kommen und zuletzt die Werke der Baukunst als die Resultate der ersteren behandeln, und sie nach dem vergleichenden Prinzipe in Arten, Geschlechter und Familien gruppiren. – . **fol. 73r*

Ich sage dieses nicht ohne Plan und Absicht – obschon es scheinen mag, als gehöre es nicht hieher. Denn es führt mich zu einer ersten wichtigen Bemerkung, die ich bezüglich und zu der Erläuterung des Prinzipes zu machen habe, mit welchem ich meinen Vortrag eröffnete.

Die Baukunst, Architectura, führt den Namen als Urkunst als erste unter den praktischen Künsten und sie ist es in der That in mehrfachen Beziehungen, die ich nicht einzeln durchzuführen brauche. Durch sie erst finden die Einzeln-künste ein äusseres Band und eine Richtung nach einem gemeinsamen Kunst-effecte und an ihr entwickelte sich die eigentliche hohe Kunst, die vorher nicht bestand, die historische Plastik und Malerei. Aber ∥ ist die Baukunst auch in so fern die erste der praktischen Künste, als vor der Entwickelung ihrer Gesetze und artistischen Elemente dieselben Gesetze und artistischen Elemente unbe-kannt waren und keine Anwendung fanden? Gewiss nicht. Welcher Einfluss ist der ältere und der wichtigere, derjenige, welchen die Baukunst auf die Ent-wickelung der übrigen Zweige der praktischen Kunst übte, oder umgekehrt derjenige, den die letzteren auf die Entstehung der konventionellen Formen und Gesetze der ersteren hatten? Gewiss der letztere. Entlehnten die übrigen Künste ihre Processe in der Behandlung des Stoffes, ihre Formen und Verzierungen von der Baukunst, oder lassen sich die Formen und Regeln der Baukunst auf die-jenigen zurückführen, die lange vorher in den spezielleren Branchen der prak-tischen Kunst geübt wurden? Sicher das letztere. –

There was a rich industrial art and Luxury dwelt in simple tents, rude strong-holds and camps through many thousand years, before the invention of archi-tectural forms and monumental art. Domestical ¦ industry, the market, trade war and robbery furnished the household of the praearchitectural centuries with articles of luxury, with carpets, hangings rich cloathings vases, tripods. cande-labras lamps arms, jewels and trinkets. So it was with the Greec even at the times of the Ionic poets, of Homer and Hesiodus, whose brillant Descriptions of rich arms, tripods vases, tapestries and other articles of hellenic industrial art, are no doubt formed upon things, they had seen before their eyes; They were allowed to exagerate the richness and the beauty of those things by their poet-ical treatement but they could not be mere inventions of their rich imagination; In this case their art would have been without effect, not being understood by their hearers. We shall have the opportunity to return to these poetical descrip-tions of old Hellenic practical art, which are highly interesting not only for the | antiquarian, but also for modern practice of art and which have since the time of the Greec till now greatly occupied the greatest talents among the artists. for instance Phidias, by working his famous shield of Minerva in the Parthenon at Athens Leonardo da Vinci who decorated a beautiful shield with his pictures, which is now in the Florentine Gallery, Mihel Angelo. in many of his powerfull compositions. Benvenuto Cellini and those, whose beautiful works are attrib-uted to the same artist whose name got a sort of mythical celebrity and absorbed the names of so many skillful artists of the same period. Under the modern artists who have worked upon the descriptions of Hesiodus and Homerus are to

On the Relations of the Different Branches of Industrial Art   99

be mentionned such names as Thorwaldson, Flaxmann Schwanthaler. in Munich, and other artists of high rang, which by this way did more for the propagation of artistical feeling and taste among the industrial branches of art, than by their more celebrated and larger works.

5   Now what are the descriptions of buildings in the same poets. They prove alltogether that state, which I alluded to before, namely no monumental architecture, ruled by its own organic laws, Luxury combined with the most primitive simplicity and crudenessness of construction, barraks, court Yards, wide Halls, without floors, with fireplaces, without Flues; all ornamental ¦ parts,   *fol. 3v*
10 consisting partly of woven or metallic coatings partly beeing nothing else but moveable furniture, are mere applications, go not out of the intrinsic and organic laws of architecture It may be allowed here to give some instances of such Homeric descriptions of dwellings, which will give for the following some interesting matter for reflexion.
15 1) The tent of Achilles
    2) The Pallace of Priamus
    3) the Pallace of the King of the Phaeaks
    4) The dwelling of Ulissees
Such was the state of relation between industrial art and architecture in the
20 times of beginning civilisation of the Greec, which by a happy fate we are able to judge of. But not only this, the influence of industrial art upon civilisation was still more general. The Greec mythology, is an ingenious and poetical creation, formed and so to speak modelled out of a formless but very plastical Mass of mythic fables, partly indigenous, partly borrowed from other countries,
25 which were no longer understood in their original significations. This creation was the work of the poets, which I alluded to before, which very probably were guided in their compositions by images borrowed from ¦ the myths pictured and   *fol. 4r*
represented upon arms, vases, tapestries clothes and utensils, for they often allude to such representations in their descriptions and we also see such an influ-
30 ence in the illustrative character of their reciets. Forms, partly foreign, partly native, by being used as ornament, melt together and are prepared for a new result. –

    But I schall try to show in one of the following lectures, how the Greec Architecture developped itself out of these antecedents by the influence of the
35 lawgiving and tempelbuilding race of Doria, in contrast with the poetical Ionians, sacrifising to their Gods on their mountain tops, and having properly speaking no tempels at all.

    Many thousand Years before we see the Greec making their first steps of national education, there existed several centerpoints of highly finished civilisa-
40 tion in Asia and Aegypt, and there we see Architecture more emancipated from

fol. 4v

the industrial Arts and following its own laws. Nevertheless we observe on the monuments of these countries undubitable traces ¦ and proofs of what I maintained that the architectural forms and ornaments are alltogether originally borrowed from the different branches of industrial art, and that architecture is based upon principles and laws, which were known and practised in ornamental art, long time before the invention of monumental architecture. It will not yet be in time to penetrate deeper in this question by analysing the different styles of architecture, but You may see at some examples of details, taken from Aegyptian temples of the elder periods, how the pure structure is veiled by ornamental applications executed in stone. This column is a pillar surrounded with cane,

**fol. 1r*

which is fastened with strings and | a piece of richly ornamented tapestry. This capital shows flowers of papyrus and Lothus, which evidently are only fastened with strings, in the same manner as it was custom by the Aegyptian ladies to put the same flowers into their hairdresses. –

I thought these introductory remarks necessary to apologize for the plan which I adopted in this essay, which may by the first view appear contradictory to the principle which I alluded to before. I hope that this appearant contradiction will find finally a satisfactory solution.

—————

As I was, some twenty Years ago, a Student at Paris, my usual walk was to the jardin des plantes or the Zoological Garden near the town, and allways I was attracted, like by some magic force, from the sunny Garden into those Rooms, where the fossil Remains of the foregone formations of the earth, together with

**fol. 1v*

the sceletons and carcasses of the species of our ¦ present creation stand ordered together in long series for comparation.

As all those antediluvian and postdeluvian organisations are but different developments of the same principles, as Nature for its infinite richness is nevertheless very sparing and simple in its elementary ideas, as we observe the same scaffolding of the sceleton differently modified and developd according to the rang which each individual occupies in the universal creation and to its conditions of existence, the same, so I told to myself, will be the case with the works of my art.

Second Version

1° Some excuses and introductory remarks, with relation to the difficulties I must feel etc.

The decorative arts arise from and should be attendant upon Architecture.
This principle, if taken in its true meaning, will bee freely subscribed to by every one who has meditated on the relations, which exist between the different manifestations of that inborn instinct, by which we endeavour in the choice of forms and colours. to give expression and beauty to the productions of our hands

Architecture is the working together of all the other branches of art to one great monumental effect and after one directing Idea.

The laws of beauty and style which we aknowledge in practical art and in art generally speaking, have first been fixed and systematically settled by architects.

The History of art seems in some points to contradict this principle, but it may be asserted Nevertheless that these points are the strongest evidences of that intimate connection by which all the branches of art are bound together. ||

A. First we find, that the practical or industrial arts had arrived to a high degree of development many centuries before the invention of architecture as an art.

Luxury dwelt in simple tents, in barracks and rude strongholds, many thousand Years before the invention of architectural forms.

So it was for instance with the Greecs downwards to the time of Homer and Hesiod and even much later. The descriptions which these old poets give of the arms of the Heros, of vases, tripods, draperies, embroideries and other objects of an early Industrual art are doubtless based upon real things. The poets by that liberty which poets take were allowed to exagerate the beauty and richness of these objects, but their art would have had no effect if their Hearers had not been acquainted with things, analogous to those which they described.

Now what are the descriptions of monuments and architectural works which the same poets lay before us?

These descriptions alltogether, prouve that immense luxury was then combined with the most primitive simplicity of construction in buildings, and of Household arrangments.

All the enrichments of the buildings were mere applications consisting of draperies or netallic incrustations, in shields, trophees, Earthen- and Metal-vases, Figures, festoons, flowers and other mouveable things, borrowed fron the industrial arts, or from Nature. ||

The same buildings, which were cowered with embossed Gold and Tinplates, had no floors, no fireplaces no flues.

1.   *fol. 1r*

2.   *fol. 2r*

3.   *fol. 3r*

A parallel might here be drawn if time allowed between the Homeric dwellings and that singular mixture of simplicity and luxury which in our own times prevails in the tents and dwellings of the Orientals nations.

I refer for this to the lively narrative relating to the Household of an Arabian Sheik, of which Mr Layard gives an account in his travels in Mesopotamia.

While the Greeks were in this stage of antearchitectural civilisation, there existed in other parts of the old world some centerpoints of very ancient culture, based upon other principles, which were, if considered under a certain point of view, more favorable for the Development of Architecture as a selfexisting art.

But what see we at the ruins of Niniveh and Thebes? The undoubted proof of what has been asserted before; that the architectural forms of the Aegyptian and Assyrian Monuments are all borrowed from the industrial arts.

The mats, and afterwards the Carpets and Draperies were the earliest materials for deviding spaces, and for making those separations of room, which men found necessary for their protection and comfort. – The same materials were employed for this service long before the invention of brick-walls and the well known Assyrian Alabasterplates are nothing but imitations of the original carpets, plastically executed in stone.

The history of wall Decoration in all its phases begins and is based upon this fundamental ¦¦ motive of carpet making.

fol. 4r   *4.*

Again if we look at the Aegyptian columns of the earlier periods of Egyptian art, we recognize square pillars, covered with cane, which is fastened with strings and a piece of richly ornamented tapestry round them, so that the square pillar remains visible at the top above the capitel. The last is formed by flowers, of the Papyrus and Lottusplant, thrust into the strings at the neck of the capital, quite in the same manner as the fair Aegyptian Ladies of the time used to fasten the same flowers into the Laces of their Hairdresses.

A great part of the forms used in Architecture thus originate from works of industrial art, and the rules and laws of beauty and style, which we aknowledge, were determined and practicised long before the existence of any *monumental* art.

The works of industrial art give therefore very often *the keys and bases for the understanding of architectural forms and principles.*

B. A second point in which the History of art seems not to be consistent with our principle is this, that the periods in which the industrial arts were hierarchically governed by architecture, were not the periods most favorable for the development of high art or of industrial art. –

fol. 5r   *5.*

In These periods the ¦¦ relation between the two manifestations of art become directly the opposite of what has been described.

For instance under the influence of the Mediaeval or so called pointed Gothic style the industrial arts became quite dependant upon the forms used in this style, which had taken its principal decorative motives from stone construction. So the reliquaries were small churches, the vases had buttresses and ogival arches amd ogee mouldings, and were covered with pointed roofs.

The arches became the fundamental motives of the surface ornamentation, and the dominant influence of architecture extended itself downwarts even to the bootsmaker and tailor's craft.

Was this a normal and sound state of things, and can we call this direction of taste in practical art a pure one?

It may perhaps appear audacious to deny it.

After the revival of the ancient principles of architecture the architectonic system upheld its influence for some time, at least in some parts of practical art, as for instance in furnitures. But this style was perhaps more accomodating then the former, and great liberty was allowed in appliing it to practical art.

At the end of this period begins the empire of an other principle; we see the industrial arts and especially furniture taking their own way, || guided by a very   6.   *fol. 6r* refined study of that which is fit and comfortable, but unhappily influenced allso by a predilection for Chinese industry, which influence upon the development of that Style which we call Rococo has not yet been sufficiently explained in our histories of art. It then happened that the monuments became pieces of furniture executed in stone, and architects adopted forms, which can be only justified if executed in Porcelaine or wood and applied to mouveable things. – .

Revolutions in architectural styles were thus allways prepared by innovations which had been introduced before in the mode of practicising Industrial art; and architecture will soon loose its dominion over the other arts, if, as at present it isolates from them itself.

Our architecture is devoid of originality and has lost its precedence over the other arts. It only will revive when more attention shall be paid to our present state of Industry by modern architects.

The Impulse to such a happy change will again go out from practical art.

In this light we may recognize the right feeling, which presides over the efforts of our Government for the progress of national education in art, by paying especial attention to the practice of industrial art.

———————

Third Version

fol. 1r *1.* Ladies and Gentlemen.

A Foreigner must naturally feel very timid and embarrassed in addressing to You a paper written in English on a Subject, which by itself is difficult, and would be so to him, if he had to treat it in his own linguage.

But knowing the kindness and forbearance toward foreigners, which distinguishes an English Audience, this is neither the only nor the principal reason of his hesitation.

It becomes an Artist to consider well and hesitate long, before he undertakes to contribute to the Mass of Writings and reflexions on art, which distinguishes the present age.

Indeed we are as rich on writings as we are poor in works of art, namely in such works, which really are our own, and which really and truly are works of Art.

This coincidence is well worthy of reflexion and leads to the supposition of a reciprocal relation betwixt these two phenomena.

They may both depend upon more intimate causes, but it is true at the same *fol. 1v* time, that we are overpowered by | the mass of learning, that we have lost our own track, and, as we say in German, we do not simetimes see the forest for trees.

The feeling of the difficulties which arise from the accumulation of learning it not new, and it is not alone in that branch of knowledge, which we are treating of, that the same has been felt, and therefore systems and classifications have been instituted for reducing into order the immense amount of learning which is our heritage of so many centuries.

We see also, arising from the same cause the Division of labor systematically instituted by lawgivers of the oldest ages, for instance by the founders of the political and religious institutions of the Egyptians and of the Indians.

But it has happened, that in this way the consciousness of the intimate connections, which exist between the different branches of knowledge and skill, has been lost. |

fol. 2r *2* It is the tendency of modern science to endeavour to find again those connections between the things, and of transforming into an organic system of comparison what was before only an exterior and more or less arbitrary system of coordination and of exterior order.

So even Chimistry for instance, the most experimental of all Sciences, begins now to be much more constructive than it was before, to separate with the Idea of combining, to search for the differences of the things with the Idea of referring them alltogether to some few elements and natural forces.

When I was a Student at Paris I went often to the *Jardin des Plantes*, and I was always attracted, as it were by a magic force, from the sunny garden into those Rooms, where the fossil Remains of the animal tribes of the primaeval World stand in long series ranged together with the sceletons and shells of the present ¦ creation. In this magnificent collection, the work of *Baron Cuvier*, we perceive the types for all the most complicated forms of the animal empire, we see progressing nature, with all its variety and immense richness, most sparing and oeconomical in its fundamental forms and Motives; we see the same sceleton repeating itself continually, but with innumerable varieties, modified by gradual developments of the Individuals and by the conditions of existence which they had to fulfill.

Here we see some parts left out, some other parts only indicated, which are exceedingly developped on other individuals.

If we observe this immense variety and richness of nature notwithstanding its simplicity may we not by Analogy assume, that it will be nearly the same which the creations of our hands, with the works of industrial art? | They are like those of nature, connected together by some few fundamental Ideas, which have their simplest expressions in *types*. But these normal forms have given and give rise to an infinite number of varieties by development and combination according to the exigencies of their specialities, according to the gradual progresses in invention and to so many other influences and circumstances which are the conditions of their embodiment.

Will it not be important to trace out some of those types of the artistical forms, and to follow them in their gradual progress from step to step up to their highest development?

A method, analogous to that which Baron Cuvier followed applied to art, and especially to architecture would at least contribute towards getting a clear insight over its whole province and perhaps also it would form the base of a doctrine of *Style*, and of a Sort of topic or Method, how to invent, which may ¦ guide us, to find out the natural way of invention which would be more than could be allowed to the great Naturalist to do for his sublime science. –

If we go through the great number of works on Art, and especially on Architecture in search of such a Guide for Artists, like the Book of Cuvier on the animal Empire and his comparing Osteology, or the Cosmus of Humboldt, which are Guides for Naturalists in so far as these books contain the full development of the Idea of a comparing system of natural History, we find nothing analogous.

Very few authors have made attempts of the kind I allude to, and these few followed the track of some speciality by which they were inconsciously led away from the aim which they had perhaps before their mind.

The Frenchman Durand in his parallels and other works on Architecture has

fol. 4r *4* perhaps | come the nearest to it, but he looses his way under the influence of the proposition which was made to him, namely to set up a sort of *"compendium artis"* for the students of the Ecole Polytechnique who were by no means artists, as well as under the influence of the general tendency of the time of Napoleon (the Great). He looses himself into tabular-formularies, he puts the things into rows and brings about a Sort of Alliance between them by mechanical ways instead of showing the organic laws by which they are connected together. many important branches of artistical knowledge which we now possess, were undiscovered at that time. It was not ripe for producing such a work, as Durand was endeavouring to execute.

In spite of this his books are remarkable for the comparing idea which they contain.

Some other attempts of more recent date have been made upon the same

fol. 4v principle, but ¦ less happily.

In return we are so much richer in specialities, and the amount of materials which increases every day, is almost overpowering.

While the publications of documents and the Engravings of Objects of art and architecture of all Periods are increasing and multiplying in England and in France, the Germans have composed their Aesthetical Science and some of the best books on the history of Art.

But in the same time we observe no proportionate progresses in the practice of art, especially in architecture and in industrial art; which seems to confirm what has been asserted before, that we have not yet arrived at that point, where all these knowledges will increase the power of artistical invention, instead of paralising it as it now seems to do.

Since the time that I first felt this want, I have had the opportunity of giving lectures on Architecture at one of the Academies of fine arts in Germany. |

fol. 5r *5* As was natural, these lectures were more or less influenced by similar reflections.

But since then my position has altered and with it the point of view, from which I now consider the same question.

At that time I payd too little attention to the relations between the other branches of practical art and architecture. Now I feel convinced more than I did before of the fact, that the history of Architecture begins with the history of practical art, and that the laws of beauty and style in Architecture have theyr paragons in those which concern Industrial art.

The laws of proportion of Symmetry and harmony, the principles and the traditionnal forms of ornamentation, and even those elements of the Architec-

fol. 5v tural forms, which we kall mouldings were partly invented and ¦ practised long time before the foundation of Architecture as a selfexisting art.

The Characters of the different architectural styles were clearly expressed in certain characteristic forms of the earliest industrial art, applied on the first necessities of life.

Let us compare for instance these two different forms of ancient vases.

The first is the holy Nile-Pail, or Situla of the Ancient Aegyptians, – the other is that beautiful Greec Vase which is called the Hydria.

Both of them relate to the same use, that of catching running water.

But the first is a drawing Vessel, for getting Water out of a Rivver, and therefore Characteristic for Egypt, the Gift of the Nile.

Two such Vessels were carried by the Egyptian Water-carriers on Jockes, so that one hung before and the other behind. | The haviest part is very properly the bottom, as a precaution to prevent spilling It is formed like a Waterdrop. We feel the fittness of this form for its use, which is the Opposite to that Greek Hydria, which is a Vessel, for catching Water, as it flows from the fountain. Hence the funnel chaped feature of the mouth and the neck, which is rigorously prescribed by the object in view.

On the other hand, the mode in carriing those vessels has led to the Idea of removing the Center of gravity of the Vessels from the bottoms towards the summits. For they were carried on the heads upright when full, lenghtways when empty, as we see on this diagram, traced from a picture which decorates to body of the Vessel.

Any one, attemting to balance a Stick on his finger, will find the ¦ feat much easier, if the heaviest end is uppermost.

This experiment explains the form of the Greec Hydria, which is completed by the Addition of two horizontal handles placed at the level of the point of Gravity.

A third Vertical handle was sometimes added afterwards, not only for the sake of variety and as a mark of distinction between the front and the back of the Vessel, but also with regard to its utility.

How strikingly is symbolised the light spiritual and lucid nature of the mountaineer inhabitants of Greece in this form, opposed to the Pail, which is a true Representative of the National Genius of the Egyptians, and of institutions the first principle of which was stability.

The two nations were certainly well aware and conscious of the high significance | of these forms, in making them national and religious Emblems.

The Nile Pail was the holy Vessel of the Aegyptians and in like manner the Hydria of the Greeks was the sacred Vase, carried by Virgins in their religious processions.

It may be added, that the fundamental features of Aegyptian Architecture seem to be contained in Embryo in the Construction of the Nile-Pail, and in the same proportion we are allowed to recognize in this Hydria the Key to the Doric Order of Greek Architecture. –

Architecture is the combining together of all the branches of industrial art and of art in general in one great general effect, and after one directing Idea. The laws and principles of Style and beauty which we aknowledge in art, have probably been the first systematically fixd by Architects, but practical Art had reached to a ¦ high degree of development long before the invention of architecture; The principles of Aesthetics in Architecture have had their first applications on objects of Industry, and the separation which exists now between the latter and between Architecture and high art is one of the principal causes. of their decai. –

In what I have sayd Allusion has frequently been made to certain laws of beauty which we recognize in Art. It may be asked here, which are those principles, what is beauty, what is style?

This question leads us to a very dangerous matter, which has been treated by Philosophers and Artists of all periods. Many Volumes have been written about it. |

I shall not risk to enter into an examination of the different definitions, and senses, which have been attached to these notions, which form the bases of the aesthetical Science. It fortunately happens that the intimate connection which exists between them allows us, to attack the matter, at what end we like, one of these notions, if pursued in its consequences leading to the understanding of the others.

I therefore take leave to point out only one of these notions, that of *Style* in art; I want for the following to explain myself clearly on the sense which I attache to this expression; but the following definition of the notion Style in art is not given with the pretention of being absolute and of general application, it is only an exposition of what *in this paper* is understood by the word Style.

This term is used for the notification of certain achievements in works of art, arising

1°) *from using artistically the means* and

2°) *from observing the limits,* which are contained in and defined by the task and problem in question, as well as by the Accessories which modify the solution of it in every case.

Every work of art is a *result*, or, using a Mathematical Term, it is a *Function* of an indefite number of quantities or powers, which are the variable coefficients of the embodiment of it.

$$U = \Phi \, x, y, z, t, v, w.$$

As soon as one or some of these coefficients vary, the Result must vary likewise, and must show in its features and general appearance a certain distinct ¦ caracter; – if this is not the case, then it fails for want of Style.

Now which are these variable coefficients which constitute the general formula of an Artistic work?

Their number is undefined and we shall only point out some of the most important, which will lead to the explanation of a plan for a course of lectures on the different branches of industrial art, to which this paper may be considered as an introduction. |

We must distinguish two different kinds of influences, which act upon the embodiment of an artistic work,

The first Class comprises the exigeancies, of the work itself and which are based upon certain laws of nature and of necessity, which are the same at all times and under every circumstance.

The second Class comprises such vehicles, which we may call outward influences acting upon the performance of a work of art.

That part of the Doctrine of Style, which treats of the first class, embraces the elementary Ideas or what the Artist calls the Motives of the things, and the early forms, in which these fundamental Ideas have been cloathed. These early forms are the Types of the Ideas. It is a satisfaction to artistic feeling, when in any work of Art its first Idea, widely as it may depart from its origin, still pervades the whole composition, like a theme in Musik; and it is certain that clearness in the conception of the fundamental Idea by the artist is most important.

The new will thus be engrafted upon the old without being its copy and will be freed from the Influence of mere fashion.

To illustrate this I may be allowed to give an example. Mattings, and afterward carpets, wether woven or embroidered were the primitive divisions of space in dwellings and were the precursors of all decorations of walls, of all Mosaiks, of | all stained Glass, and many other relative branches of Industry, which, be their direction ever so various, can always be traced to a common origin.

It is also appearant that the Ancients from the Assyrians to the Romans, and afterwards the mediaeval nations, in decorating and cloathing their walls, whether by design or not, followed the principles of tapestry. –

Fortunately this historical element of the Doctrine of Style can be carried out in the midst of our modern confused relations.

But this first part of the doctrine of Style contains an other Subdivision, which should teach, how to change old forms, consecrated by necessity and tradition, according to our new means of fabrication.

This part is unhappily more difficult of application for the present time.

An example may also here be in its place.

The Granite & Porphyr Monuments of Aegypt exert an incredible power over every mind. Whence is this Charm? Partly perhaps, because they are the neutral Ground, where the hard and resisting material and the pliant hand of man have met.

"So far shalt thou go and no farther" has been the silent linguage of these massive creations for centuries. Their majestic quietness, their sharp, flat, and angular lineaments, the Economy of labor in the treatement of the stern material and their whole appearance are beauties of Style, which to us, who can cut the hardest stone like Chalk are no longer prescribed by necessity. |

How shall we now treat Granite? It is difficult to give a satisfactory answer; The first thing to be done is to employ it only where its Durability is demanded, and this should regulate its treatement. Little attention is payd to this at our times.

The second part of the Doctrine of Style comprehends shiefly local and personal Influences. such as the climate and physical constitution of a country, the political and religious institutions of a nation, the Person or the corporation by whom a work is ordered, the place for which it is destined, and the Occasion on which it was produced. Finally also the individual personality of the Artist.

Thus we say: Chinese Style Indian Style, Style of Louis XIV. Style of Raphael, Ecclesiastical Style, Rural Style etc.

If the first practical part of the doctrine of Style is difficult to apply in our times, this part may appear almost out of question, since Speculation, supported by Capital, has taken in its hand the protection of the industrial arts.

Ready made things must naturally exclude a good part of such qualifications of Style, which are depending upon local and personal circumstances and relations.

Every market ware must be so prepared, as to be as far as possible of *universal application*. It should have no other Attributes, than such as are suggested by its use, its material and the treatement of the latter.

This we find for instance to be the case with Oriental Industry.

The Products of Oriental Industry are most in place in a Bazaar, and their greatest recommandation is that they suit all positions. |

The Persian carpets are as appropriate in a Church or in a Mosquée, as in the Boudoir of a Lady. The Ivory boxes of Lahore with their inlaid Mosaik patterns appropriately serve as Censers, Cigar Cases or work boxes, according to the Will of their owners.

But complete in themselves as they are, those Indian works, and so opposed in technical and aesthetical beauty to our European want of Style, we yet miss in them individual Expression, the *high intellectual beauty*, the *soal*.

This expression is always to be in some measure attained even in an object destined for the market;

Tritons, Nereids, Nymphs have meaning in a Fountain, Venus and the Graces upon a Mirror. Trophees and battles upon arms, whether these things be made for the market or for a particular destination. It is so easy to find such appropriate Emblems, that it is astonishing, what a want of imagination and of common sense is sometimes apparent in the application of emblematic ornaments in our modern art-manufactures.

For example we see on certain Frensch Clocks two soldiers sitting on a Cornice, playing at cards or dice, or perhaps asleep. What does the Artist mean to express by this? "Let us waste time. Let us kill time" Let us sleep away time"

These are courious inscriptions for a clock, an odd translation of Virgil's "Vivite – Venio! –

Notwithstanding all this, we possess an affluence of knowledge, a perfection of practical appliances, never surpassed, a multitude of artistic images, and a just view of nature, not to be exchanged | for even beautiful semibarbarous concep- *11* *fol. 11r* tions.

What we should learn from nations, who lack European Culture is the art of catching the simple Melodies in form and colour, which appears instinctive in the work of man in his primitive combinations and which we, with our more extended means, find it difficult to seize and retain.

We must therefore study the simplest works of man and the history of their Development as carefully as we should consider the works of nature itself. We saw for instance in the Great Exhibition of 51 that the meritorous effort to imitate nature leads aesily to mistakes, when not guided by Study of Style.

—————————— .

Among the different Vehicles, which act upon the embodiments of the Works of our hands, there is one Group, which being of the most universal application, must be specified here a little more.

These are the following:

First the use of the things.

secondly the material out of which they are done.

thirdly The modes of execution or the Processes, which come in question for their execution.

1° *The use of a thing.*

Every manufacture has a certain use and destination; it is really or at least in the Idea a means of satisfying some exigeancy of life. It is a tool, an instrument or at least an arrangement for protection or for action.

Now every tool or contrivance, no matter how simple it may be, is a ¦ Ma- *fol. 11v* chine.

What is a machine?

A Machine is a body, or a system of bodies, having the destination of receiving on the one hand, and of exercing on the other certain forces.

This definition is a Lemma taken from the Science of Mechaniks – for we have here to do with *forces*, in their state of Equilibrium or of active mouvement, and we can only arrive at the understanding of the forms of the things, (so far at least as these forms are results of the destinations of the things,) by application to the mechanical Sciences; *to the Statics*, for forms, which are the result of an Equilibrium of Forces, and to *the Dynamical Science*, for things, which are the means for exercing certain active forces upon other things, for instance knifes, weapons, axes and tools of every kind.

We may extend this to natural forms; which we can not understand without the science of Mechaniks, they being altogether necessary results of certain natural powers and forces, partly the same, which constitute the conditions of the Embodiment of a work of industrial art.

But Nature never fails in the Choice of its forms, which unfortunately is not the case with us! The more we advance in civilization and science the more it seems that that instinctiv feeling, which men followed in their first attempts in industrial art, looses its strength, while Science has not yet | attained to the point, of compensating us for this loss.

It very often happens, that we are led back by science and calculation to such forms, which were observed heretofore only by Savages, and semi-Barbarians. So for instance the Axes of the North-American Nativs, which are natural pebbles or imitations of such stones, which are ground by the continual action of water. The so chaped axes were considered the best for their fittness in the last great Exhibition.

These ancient Greec Sling bullets, which have the form of plumkernets executed in lead, would give an other instance for this. The other projectile laying by them, is a Prussian pointed musket-ball, it is a sort of incomplete imitation of the first, but it can be proved by science that the first are much more convenient for their use than their modern copies; It is questionable weither these Projectiles are the Result of an instinctiv feeling of their makers for fittness or if they are proofs of the high state of Mechanical Science with the Greecs. We know at least, that Men like Archimedes and Apollonius have applied their Mathematical knowledge to the Machineries of war for the defense of their country.

These bullets are very interesting for the illustration of the preceeding. If such a leaden bird is fliing in the air, it is surronded by an Envelop of atmospheric air, which before it is condensed and behind it is rarefied. The condensed air ¦ acts in proportion to its density opposite to the mouvement of the Bullet by its resistance, the rarified air behind acts also in proportion to its density against the resisting air before the bullet and is therefore a positive power.

Further we know that the living force or the impetus of such a bullet is increasing with the mass, – therefore, by filling up a part of this *vacuum* or imperfect *vacuum* with mass we will increase the vis viva of the bullet. So does Nature in its horror Vacui, by giving to all bodies, which have the destination of fliing or Swimming in resistent mediums. They have alltogether this form, this End being the front and the allongated tale filling up the Vacuum behind. This is the form of all the fishes; and of the birds, when we take the Ground-plans of their bodies, The same is allso evident on the falling waterdrops and on the flame, by the same reasons. The proportions of these bodies differ according to their special destinations. They are sharp and allongated if Quikness is the first aim for | a chosen form, they are rather round, like Eggs, if they have the destination of carriing great masses. ||

We know pretty well the general principles of mouvement, we know the laws of certain natural forces, for | instance that of gravitation, of fricture and others; we know the properties of the fluids and their principles of equilibrium in themselves and with swimming bodies, We have sattled some principles of mouvement in the resisting mediums, and of the action of gasses, – but one power has as yet escaped the investigations of our Dynamists – which is the power *of animal and vegetable Life*. We know only that it acts independently of gravity and often in opposition to it, and that it is a defined force.

It is by this force that Nature produces its most interesting formations – and we must add, that, the more the works of our hands have the appearance of being results of such living forces, which act against gravity and substance, the higher they stand upon the scale of artistical accomplishment.

But on this field we have no other Guides than our own natural feeling assisted by a right study of natural History and of that of art.

If we go through the History of Architecture and compare the different styles, it strikes us, that they are allmost alltogether based upon very sound principles of Statics and of Construction. But there is only one example, of a nation succeeding in giving organic life to its architectural formations and to its industrial productions in general. |

This was the case with the Greecs. The Greec temples and monuments in general are not constructed, they have grown, they are not merely ornamented by application of vegetable or organic accessories, like those of the Aegyptians for instance, their forms by themselves are such, as organic life produces, when counteracting and struggling against gravity and Substance.

We can not otherwise explain the incomparable charm of a Greek Column:

The Greeks alone attempted and succeeded in making human forms the supporters of the entablatures of their edifices – an attempt which we are right to consider as an aberration of taste, – but it gives an evidence of the fact, that the Greecs were aware and conscious of their aim in animating the architectural parts themselves instead of decorating them with ornamental applications taken from the organic nature, like the Aegyptians did.

For this the Greek Architecture and Greek art in General will allways be living, and periodically grow joung again, while all the other styles belong only to History.

I can not leave this interesting matter, without giving another observation of practical application.

Attempts have often been made to explain the Greek forms and to find out a Scheme for them by taking exact measures from the best Greec Monuments and by comparing the Geometrical projections of the forms which were carefully drown up after these measures. But these attempts will never succeed, for, if it is right in Mathematics, to ¦ consider certain surfaces as the results of revolving curves, it is not the same in Natural history and in Art. Very beautiful natural as well as artistical forms may have sections of no proportion and beauty, and beautiful sectional outlines or projections may produce by revolving them very unhappy Surfaces. Nature works not like a turner after working drawings or what they call templates., its forms are alltogether dynamical productions, and it is only by the way of that science, which treats of the mutual actions and reactions of forces, that we may hope to find the keys for some of the simplest material forms.

What is true in Nature, has its application also for artistical forms, if they are animated by organic life, like the works of the Greeks.

The well known history of Phidias Colossal bronze Figure of Athena Promachos which was misunderstood by the Amateurs while standing in the Workshop of the artist, may be quoted here as an illustration of this. ¦

We pass now to the second great Agent, to *the Materials* which we employ for the manufacture of Objects of art.

It lays not in the plan of this lecture, to give a systematical suit to this important question;

It gives rise to a great number of very important practical remarks, which will find best their places by specifiing the different branches of industrial art which I wish to be allowed to do at other occasions. −

The abstract of All the special rules of Style, so far as it depends on the material, is the following:

1° Take that material which is the most adapted for the proposition which You intend to resolve.

2°) Take all possible profits of Your material, but observe the limits which are traced by the Idea which lays in the Object to the Embodiment of which a material whatever will be employed.

3°) Take the substance not as a mere passiv *medium* but as a *means*, as a second activ power and vehicle for invention. − .

It follows as a consequence out of this, that the question on the meterials can not be separed from the question on the different processes in trea- ¦ ting them.

The importance of the material in the question of Style is so great, that some of the best Writers on art have considered it the very thing which constitutes for itself alone what we call style in Art.

So for instance Baron Rumohr, one of our best German writers on art, who gives in his Researches on Italian Art the following definition of this notion.

Style is the accomodation of the artist to the intimate demands of the material in which the sculptor really forms his objects, and the painter represents them.

The same reason has also led to that System of Classification, which we generally observe for collections of industrial Arts. |

We generally order, and divide them in different classes after the materials of which they are made.   *15*   *fol. 15r*

This mode of classification appears to be the most natural, and it is certainly that, which offers the greatest facility. With this System of classification it is not easy to mistake the place to which every thing belongs.

It will allways remain the simplest and perhaps the best for collections of works of industry which have a practical destination.

But for an ideal collection of industrial works, or rather for a revue of the Objects of art with regard to the styles to which they belong, it may be perhaps less accomodating. For instance We see here a Metal-Work, there is an other piece of industrial art, made out of the same Metal,

This Indian Coat of Mail has nothing in common with that Indian Vase, except that they are both of the same Material and done by Indians.

Now we see on the other hand this vase of Earthenware related in form and destination to that of Iron although it is made with an other material and not by Indians.

And the Coat of Mail has more relation in style with this coat of wool, than with the Indian Vase.

This example is striking, but there is a multitude of cases, where the three different Systems of arrangement which we use for collections of art, ¦ namely 1°   *fol. 15v* the historical system 2°) the ethnographical System 3°) the material System, where these three systems appear less arbitrary, but where they are in reality more injurious, by separing things, the relationship of which is less conspicoous, but not less important and interesting for the question of Style.

These are not mere subtilities, but very practical remarks; Before going farther in the matter I must return to an expression, which I have used already several times in this paper. This is the word type.

Types as we have seen, are primitive forms, prescribed by necessity, but modified after the first materials, which were used for their embodiment.

Now it has happened very often, that Changes were introduced in the material and the manner of execution of these types.

Then the secondary forms became plastic or pictorial treatements of the types;

The styles, which then resulted out of these secomdary treatements were composite styles, which partook on one hand of the *types*, and the conditions of Style, of the old materials employed for the latter, and on the other hand, they partook of the style | which suits the new selected substance and manner of treatement.

So it happens that the same material for instance Metal, if employed in a later period of development of art for different types, has to follow quite different conditions of Style. Othersides we observe, that materials of quite different qualities, if employed for representing the same types, approach to each other in style, as the representatives of identic fundamental ideas.

So we see for instance, bronze-Doors in their oldest treatement appear as thin bronze plates, with flat surface ornamentations, covering wooden Door wings. –

In their more developd forms they are hollow and penneld like wooden doors, for instance the Pantheon Doors and that of Remus in Rome which latter is quite an imitation of Cabinets makers-work. In this state of development they are ornamented on another principle.

These Bronze doors belong then after the system which I am now endeavouring to develope, to the same class as wooden doors, and have no more relation to bronze vases, than this pennypeace. has.

They are rather somewhat connected with this Coat of Mails by a common Idea, that of *Coating*. But this I hope to be able to explain elsewhere. – ¦

A system of Classification, based upon principles which I have tried to indicate will include the history of art, but it will place things close together, which are very far from each other, by distance of time and Space; for instance the Merovingian and Byzantine Style with the style of industrial art with the Assyrians and the Greecs of the Heroic age. |

The whole province of practical art may be brought, according to this comparing system, into 4 General Classes, for their relations to certain types which they have in common.

First class It comprehends all the things which have their types in the art or in the Industry of Coating.

Weawing forms one important branch of this very extensive Class, but it includes a great number of other Methods of covering or protecting things with thin surfaces.

Second Class.

Things which have their paragons in the *Ceramic* art.

Like Weaving for the first, so forms Pottery only one division of this second class, which includes many other processes having in the Ceramic art their points of contact. |

Third Class.   fol. *17v*

Manufactures which have their types in timberconstruction.

The significance of forms, which have their origines in timberconstruction is well known in the history of architecture.

Fourth Class.

Such as have their types in stone construction and in Stereotomy, or the Art of Cutting forms out of hard masses. –

Many formations are transitional, they find their places between the classes of which they partake.

For instance the Chinese Bamboo treillis, which is an important Element for industrial Art in China.

It holds the Middle between Weaving and timberconstruction and is the type for Some | higher forms in Antik and mediaeval Architecture, as well in   18   fol. *18r* the Art of working Metal.

Other formations are mixd, and of a composite Character; This is namely the case with the works of *Architecture,* which are combinations of elements, belonging for their types to the four different Classes, which I mentionned above.

A thorough illustration of the system I have briefly sketched out, is too arduous a task for me. But I shall perhaps be able to offer some usefull contributions towards this object.

This then is the extent of my ambition, and with this view I purpose to give five lectures.

as follows: |

1°) Art applied to the Industry of Coating, including textile Industry.   fol. *18v*

2°) Art applied to Ceramics in its widest meaning

3°) Art applied to timber-construction and other branches which are related to this industry.

4°) Art applied to Stone construction and other branches of industry approaching to it.

5°) Monumental Art in which the working together of the above mentioned four elements under the presiding Power of Architecture will be chown.

This frame of a course of lectures seems to permit no room for *Metalworking.* The reason for this lies near; Metal is not a primary material. | The types were   19   fol. *19r* fixed before the emploiement of metal for their execution.

Nevertheless I shall go particularly into the details of this branch of Industrial art, which is now my speciality. – .

General Remarks on the Different Styles in Art

fol. 1r   *1.*   For some months I had the honour to read in this room a paper which I then considered as the introduction to a series of lectures for which I had prepared the materials and fixed the general outlines. At that time I endeavoured to show the want of a comparing system of Technology, or more properly speaking of Artistical science, a system analogous to that which has been adopted so very successfully by our naturalists for natural history.

If we observe the great Variety and richness of nature notwithstanding its simplicity, we may by analogy assume, that it will be nearly the same with the creations of our hands, with the works of industrial art.

They are like those of nature, connected together by some few fundamental ideas, which have their simplest expressions in some *primitive forms* or *types*. But these normal forms have given and give rise to an infinite number of varieties

fol. 2r   *2*   by ¦¦ development and combination, according to the exigencies of their specialities, according to the gradual progresses in invention, and to so many other influences and circumstances, which are the conditions of their embodiment.

Will it not be important to trace out some of those types of the artistical forms and to follow them in their gradual progress from step to step up to their highest development?

Such a method would at least contribute towards getting a clear insight over the whole province of practical art, and perhaps also it would form the base of a doctrine of *Style* and of a Sort of Method how to invent, which may guide us, to find out the natural way of composition.

If we go through the great number of works on art, and especially on architecture in search of a guide for Artists, like the book of the celebrated Frensch Naturalist Baron Cuvier on the Animal Empire and his comparing osteology, or the Cosmos of Humboldt, which are Guides for naturalists in so far as these books contain the full development of a comparing system of natural history, we find nothing analogous. ¦¦

fol. 3r   *3*   I allways painfully felt this want at my lectures on architecture which I had the opportunity of giving at the Academie of fine Arts at Dresden; and it was natural, that these lectures were more or less influenced by this feeling. Although I never entertained the pretention or the hope of filling up this want; it was then my endeavour to contribute some few materials for the use of a future Cuvier in Artistical science, which materials I have laid down in different pamphlets which were published in Germany under the title of Contributions to a comparing science of architecture. (Beiträge zur vergleichenden Baukunde).

The contents of these pamphlets have suggested the principal material to the present and to the following lectures.

General Remarks on the Different Styles in Art

But when I wrote them I payd too little attention to the existing relations between the other branches of practical art and architecture. Now I feel convinced more than I did before of the fact that the history of architecture begins with the history of practical art, and that the laws of beauty and style in Architecture have their paragons in those which concern Industrial Art. The laws of proportion, of || Symmetry, of Harmony, the principles and the traditional forms of ornamentation and even those elements of the architectural forms, which we kall mouldings were partly invented and practised long time before the foundation of Architecture as a selfexisting Art.

The caracters of the different Architectural Styles were clearly expressed in certain characteristic forms of the earliest industrial Art, applied on the first necessities of life. This will be shown in the following at many instances.

So architecture is the last born of the arts, but it is the Combining together of all the branches of Industry and art in one great general effect, and after one directing Idea; The laws and principles of Style and beauty which we aknowledge in art have probably been the first fixd by Architects.

These remarks are made with the intention of apologizing for the order which in the following will be observed by considering the different branches of art and Industry, principally, but not exclusively as || attendant upon Architecture.

Every work of art is a *result*, or, using a mathematical term, it is a Function of an indefined number of *agents* or *powers*, which are the variable coefficients of the Embodiment of it.

$$Y = \Phi(x, z, t, v, w, .).$$

In this formula, Y stands for the General Result, and x, y, z, t, v, w represent as many different agents, which work to gether in a certain way which way is expressed here by the Greec letter Φ or Function

As soon as one or some of these coefficients vary, the result must vary likewise, if x becomes $(x+a)$ the result will be U, quite a different one from that, which we call now Y; but it will in the principle remain identical to the last, being connected with it by a common relation which is expressed by the letter Φ.

Likewise, if x, y, z, t cet remain the same but if Φ changes, then Y will change in an other manner than before it will be fundamentally different from what it was before the Change took place, although the coefficients x, y, z, t, v. etc have undergone no change. The new principle will only be modified by the different values which we may be induced to attribute to the letters x y z t. cet. ||

It will be said, that an artistical problem is not a mathematical one and that results in fine arts are hardly obtainable by calculation. This is very true, and I am the last to believe that mere reflexion and calculation may at any time succeed in filling the place of talent, and natural taste.

Also I only wanted this shedula as a crutch for leaning on it in explaining the subject I therefore will kindly be allowed to prosecute my proposition and to give some real attributions and values to those letters.

By the letter Φ we may understand the exigencies of the work of industry or art in itself, which are based upon certain laws of nature and of necessity which is the same at all times and under every circumstance.. A drinking cub for instance will be the same in its general feature for all nations and at all times; it will be in principle the same, if executed in wood, in Earthenware in Glass in metal or what- ¦¦ ever other material it may be. no matter.

The elementary Idea of a work of Art, which is based upon its use and destination; is independent upon fashion upon material and upon temporal and local conditions. The artists call this the motiv of an object of Art. The motives have generally their simplest and purest expression in nature itself, and in the early forms, in which they have been cloathed by men in the beginning of industrial art.

These natural and early industrial forms are called the types of the Ideas. It is a satisfaction to artistical feeling, when in any work of Art its first idea, widely as it may depart from its origin, still pervades the whole composition, like a Theme in Musik, and it is certain, that clearness in the conception of the Motive by the Artist is the first and most important condition to be observed in composition.

The new will be thus engrafted upon the old, ¦¦ without being its copy and will be freed from the influence of mere fashion.

The knowledge of the types and early forms constitutes therefore one of the principal parts of the doctrine of *style*, which word is used for the *notification of certain achievements in works of art, arising from using artistically the means and from observing the limits, which are contained in and defined by the problem in question, as well as by the accessories which modify the solution of it in every case.*

The art of catching the simple melodies in form and colour, which appear instinctive in the works of man in his primitive combinations is very difficult to us with our more extended means and knowledges, to seize and retain.

We should therefore study the simplest works of man and the history of their development as carefully as we consider the works of nature itself. Direct Imitation of nature in ornamental ¦¦ art leading easily to mistakes, when not guided by study of style.

We come now to those coefficients of our result which I signified in the general formule by the letters x, v t w etc.

Those are the different vehicles which act upon the embodiment of our hands, and modify the appearences of the Elementary ideas.

General Remarks on the Different Styles in Art

I must specify them here forthwith a little more. Their number is undefined, but they can be grouped into three distinct classes

1°) Materials and processes.

Among these agents is one group which consists of the materials and the modes of execution, or the processes which come in question for their execution. –

2°) Ethnological influences,

The second Group comprises the local and ethnological influences upon artistical performances, the influences of Clime, religious and political institutions and other national ‖ conditions.

The third Group is that, which includes all the personal influences which give an individual caracter to the works of art. The last can be of a double nature; The personal influences upon the embodiment of works of art can arise from those who are the commenders of the works, or from the artists and the practical performers of the last. –

These three different kinds of influences upon the embodiment of works of art constitute as many different significations of that important artistical notion of style.

Thus we say a work has no style, when the material has been treated in a manner, which is not convenient to the nature of the first.

We say also Aegyptian Style, Arabian Style etc, and here has this word quite an other sense, this part of the doctrine of style is the Subject of history and Ethnology of art.

Lastly we say, Style of Raphael, style of Louis XIV Style of Jesuits; The treatment of this sort ‖ of Style belongs to an other part of history of Art, which can be named Museology.

The first two only of these three significations of Style will form the programm for these lectures.

First the treatement of the materials, with respect to style.

Secondly, in an additional lecture, some general vues on the works of art, and especially of architecture, as expressions of local, circumstances and of the political and religious institutions of nations.

—————— .

The different manners of treating raw materials and transforming them into productions of industrial art, can be brought, nothwithstanding their manifoldness, into 4 general classes, for their relations to certain ‖ types which they have in common.

1° The first Class comprehends all the things which have their types in the art or in the industry of coating.

Textile art forms one important branch of this very extensive class, but it includes a great number of other methods of covering and protecting things with thin surfaces. We shall take in the following this word coating in the widest sense.

2ᵈ Class. The second Class

Things which have their paragons in the Ceramic art.

Like textile art for the first, so forms *pottery* only one division of this second class, which includes many other processes, having in the Ceramic Art their points of contact and their types.

Third Class.

Manufactures which have their paragons in timberconstruction.

Here also we must take the word in its widest sense which includes constructions which are executed in ‖ Stone, metal or any other material but after the principle of timberconstruction

The high Significance of architectural forms, which have their origines in timber-construction is well known in the history of Architecture; This is not the case with those, which are the results of textile art.

Fourth Class,

Such as have their types in stone construction and in Stereotomy or the art of cutting forms out of hard masses.

————————

These are the four general classes which permit a great number of transitional formations, which find their places between the Classes of which they partake.

For instance the basket, which is a vase executed in textil work; another instance is the Chinese bamboo treillis, which forms the transition between mattings and timber-construction and is an important element for industrial art and history of Style. It is the type for several higher forms in Antik and mediaeval Architecture.

This frame seems to permit no room ¦ for Metalworking; the reason for this lies near; Metal is not a primary meterial The types were fixed before the emploiment of metal for their execution. But we shall, to be sure, not forget this important branch of industrial art.

———————— .

Let us now proceed at once, (for the material is overpowering,) to the specification of that class, which has been mentionned the first, *the art of coating*. It may be doubtfull if it is the first by anciennity, if it is that, in which the earliest attempts of mankind in art were maid, but undoubtedly it has influenced earlier than the others did, the general artistic education, by giving the first motives for monumental decoration. We shall consider it first under this point of view and afterwards give some few observations on its emploiment for dresses and for other domestical implements.

————————

General Remarks on the Different Styles in Art   123

This branch of industrial art has supplied the first types for || one Element of   *fol. 14v*
architecture which is not the least important among the three, which constitute
the substance of all architectural performances without exception. and which
are the natural protections of the holy Symbol of settlement, civilisation and
humanity, namely the *hearth* or the fire place.

But Here I feel obliged to interrupt the course of the matter with the insertion of some short remarks on the constituent parts of architectural constructions.

They are four;

1°) the fireplace as the Center,

2°) The protecting Roof,

3°) The Enclosure.

4°) The Substruction

1° *The Hearth.* The Hearth or the fire place is the first, the moral Element of
Architecture, |

Round the hearth the first families assembled; the first elements of human   15   *fol. 15r*
society began near the vivifiing and nurrishing flame. Here it was where the
first confederations and social settlements were made and where the first religious ceremonies originated. The Altar, this early Symbol of religion was and is
still now nothing but a holy fireplace.

The hearth is the only Element of Architecture, which is selfexisting and has
a meaning, without the coexistance of other constructions, without the protection of a Roof, without being included by walls, or elevated on terraces and
basements. It therefore constitutes in itself the elementary Idea of a certain important class of edifices, namely those, which we understand under the term of
Monuments, if we take this term in its more special sense.

The hearth or the Altar, its highest expression, will form for us in the following the Cardinal-Point, whereto all the other things will relate.

Round the fireplace three other elements of ¦ Architecture are grouped,   *fol. 15v*
which form, as it were, the protecting negations of the three *Natural Elements*
which are ennemies to the flame of the fire place; These defenders of the hearth
are the *Roof,* the *Enclosure* and the *substruction* or as we may call it the *terrace.*

The combinations which result from the common employment of these protected and protecting parts of a building are manifold, and differ widely from
each other, after the special influences under which they take place. It happened
that under certain circumstances some of these constituant parts were more
developped, and others only maintained symbolically. I shall have the opportunity to come back to this at an other day.

Every one of the above mentioned constituent parts of a building may justly
be considered as the special domain of one of the different four branches of
practical art.

The ceramical and afterwards the metallotechnical arts may be grouped round the hearth, as the representative and Center of interior life. |

fol. 16r *16* Engineering and maçonry had for its speciality the substrution, and Carpentry the roof with its Appartenences.

But what technical branch was especially attached and developpd itself on   5
that part of architectural Construction which I called before the *Enclosure*?

No other than the Craft of matmakers and hanging-manufacturers.

This assertion, which perhaps will appear strange, wants justifying.

It is a fact, that the first attempts of industrial art, which have been made and which we still observe to be made by human beings, standing on the sill of civil-   10
isation, are *tresses* and *mats*. This part of industry is observed to be known even by tribes, which have no Idea of *dressing*; They employ the raw productions of textile art for their protection against the humidity of the ground and for the separation of their propriety from what does not belong to it.

As the first raw attempts of this kind may perhaps be considered the *hedges*,   15
or interlaced branches; fixed into the soil.

fol. 16v There is even one example in Ethnology, of a nation, with a ¦ pretty well developped ornamental art, which has even a Sort of architecture, but whose architectural monuments are nothing but richly sculptured and painted hedges and hedgepoles.   20

These are the New Seelanders. Their Civilization was stoppd at a very early time of its development; like we see it with the Chinese, only that the last were much more advanced when they became stagnant.

The second stepp was to make mattings out of the barches of trees; then they made the first essays in weaving with Gras and fibrous parts of plants and so on.   25

The application of hangings, or of their natural paragons, the skins of animals and the barches of trees, together with hedges, for the separation of space and for the protection against the weather or against ennemies, by far preceeded that of walls. executed in stone or in wood.

And as the interlaces and hangings were the origines of the Separations of   30
fol. 17r *17* space, it was natural, that these productions of industrial art beheld | a great part of its influence upon the outer formation and decoration of the walls, even when the last subsequently were executed in solid masses. The hangings or coatings of the walls remain the true representants of the idea of *Spaceseparation*, they are the types of the last.   35

The hangings are the visible walls; What is behind them has nothing to do with the Idea of *Separation* of Spaces; The thick stone-walls are only necessary with respect to other secundary considerations, as for instance to give strength, Stability, security, etc.

General Remarks on the Different Styles in Art 125

Where these secundary considerations had no place, there remained the hangings the only means of separation; and even, when the first became necessary, they formed only the inner scaffold of the true representatives of the walls, namely the variegated hangings and tapestries.

So it comes that the oldest ornaments in architecture are mostly deriveable from the enterlacs and tress works, which are the natural and gracefull results of the process of twisting and weaving with natural stuffs of different colours. |

We have in our German linguage a word which signifies the visible part of the wall, we call this part of the Wall, *die Wand*, a word which has a common root and is nearly the same with *Gewand* which signifies Woven stuff; The constructiv part of the wall has another name, we kall it Mauer. This is very denoting. – .

fol. 17v

The significance of the ideal representatives of the separation of space remained the same, even when the traditional mattings and hangings were set aside, and reimplaced by other coverings.

The inventive instinct of mankind has been inexhaustible in producing new means of covering the walls, and very different reasons gave rise to these innovations. At some occasions it was by oeconomy, at others by luxury; Sometimes for coolness for Durability etc. |

Every branch of Industry has been set into contribution for this.

18   *fol. 18r*

One of the most ancient and most important surrogates was suggested by the maçons, namely the Coating of the walls with Stucco. It gave rise to the development of painting as an independant Art. We shall see hereafter that Wallpainting never denied its origine with the antik Nations down to the Romans of the later periods, and that the Same was the case with the Mediaeval Wall Decoration. |

The Ceramic arts furnished an other reimplacement for the variegated original draperies. These were the glazed bricks This invention was probably owed to the genious of the Assyrians; It is even probable to me, that the desire of giving a glazing to the bricks, which generally were employed in a unbournd state, has conduced to the invention of burning bricks. I had the opportunity to examine accurately the Assyrian glazed and ornemented bricks which Mr Botta has brought from Chorsabad to Paris; I made on them the following observations.

fol. 18v

first they are very imperfectly burnt, they remain quite unburnt immediately behind the thin Glazing with whith they are covered.

secondly The Glazings on them are of a very fusible and tender kind,

thirdly The ornaments which are painted and fixed with a smooth fire, cross the joints of the tiles quite irregularly and the ornamental lines stand in no relation whatever with the construction of the wall. |

126 Lectures

fol. 19r 19   *fourdly*, The Glazing covers only one side of the bricks only, but the colour dropped at some parts round the Edges of the stone which prouves that the bricks were layd horizontally when they were painted on their outer front with Enamel colours. –

The consequence of these observations is, that the old Assyrian method of employing Glazed tiles has nothing in common with the more modern invention of forming ornaments with bricks of different colours, which last is a sort of Mosaic work. – The constructiv principle was not employed for wall decoration by the Assyrians, excepting on the basements of the buildings

The second Consequence is this that the bricks probably were burnt in their proper position, by a firing made in the room itself after they had been painted *on the Ground* before and than put in an unburnt state at their places. The same process of burning the bricks in their proper positions on the edifice has been observed at some old skotch Edifices. |

fol. 19v   Another Surrogate for draperies as a decoration of walls is the covering of the walls with wooden pannels;

To these komes an other one, which is the richest and only employed for temples and Royal edifices, the covering of the Walls with Metal plates, sometimes with Goldplates, which were fixed on the wall itself or on the wooden pannels, which I named before.

Finally may be mentionned the slates of Granite, Marble Alabaster, Porphyr. and other hard or precious stones, with which the walls of the Edifices of Assyria, Persia, Egypt and even of Greece were frequently invested.

———— |

fol. 20r 20 Such heterogeneous materials and processes, applied for wall investment and Wall-Decoration have produced naturally as much variations of Style but this variety of new Motives in art has taken place within the bounderies which were given and prescribed by the old traditional type, which was the common origine of all the new inventions;

Painting and plastical Art on Wood Stucco, Terra Cotta Metal and Stone remained dependant upon that style, which is the peculiarity of textile works and needle works.

fol. 20v   Ornamental Art and Architecture itself in its general features, | was, till down to the Romains, subject to the principle of *Coating*. An immense material for comparison lais here before us, a material, which remains quasi *untouched*, for no writer on art in general or on architecture especially has as jet paid due attention to this question. To pursue it here in all its consequences would be a task widely depassing my forces and besides., time would not permit it. –

The Ancient Practice of Wall Coating and Tubular Construction

On Friday last; I devided the constructiv elements of Architecture into four, and based the plan of my lectures on this division. An instructiv illustration of this system is to be seen on this sketch, which has been made after a Model of a Caraib cottage, exhibited in the Colonial-Division at the Great Exhibition of 52. we see here all the Elements of construction in their simplest expressions and combinations. Every Element of Construction is speaking for itself alone and has no connection with the others.

This raw and elementary construction notifies no intention whatever from the side of the builder to be an architect or a decorator, with the exception of these mats, which devide the bedroom or inner apartment from that sort of open hall, where the fireplace stands. The regular squares of these mats, made with barks of trees ¦ of different colours, show the first origine of walldecoration and of architectural Ornament. –

There is a nation which is very far advanced in industrial art and in civilisation in general, and was the same many thousand Years before the first germs of culture began to grow in Europe, whose Architecture stands still in the same state of development which You see here on this simple cottage. I mean the Chinese. – The Architecture of the Chinese remains unaltered through the ages. their imperial pallases and temples show in principle no difference from this Caraib Cottage. The Roofs have their own pillars, and have nothing to do with the walls which in most cases are mouveable shrines, or hollow-brick constructions made in imitation of shrines. The wall does not touch the Roof, there being a distance between the top of the Wall and the frame-work of the Roof, like we see it here on the Caraib Cottage. The framework of the Roof is visible inside They often make both the Roof and the columns, that support it, of precious woods; sometimes enriching them with Ornaments with inlaid ivory, brass, and mother of pearl. The columns have no capitals nor bases and are ¦ without Entasis, they are no columns but simple shafts although they are richly ornanented and varnished with deep colours mostly with purple.

In every House they have a provision of wooden leaves or sliders, two or three feet broad, and ten or twelfe feet long, which when rooms are wanted, they fasten to the floor. and ceiling and in a few hours form any number of apartment. Some of these sliders are open from the top to within four feet of the flooring and, instead of Glass, the open part is filled with very thin oister shells, sufficiently transparent to admit the light. At other cases the upper part of the folding doors is of lattice work covered with painted gase, which admits light into the room. These doors and pannels are nearly made of wood, and are richly varnished in red blue and other colours.

Instead of doors they generally take cane mats, which lit up and down occasionally to keep out rain and sunshine. The constructed walls are matted about 3 or 4 feet upwards from the pavement the rest being neatly covered either with wite or crimson or gilt paper,

We may say that Chinese Arnamental art is too much disdained by us, we may learn many things of the Chinese which are of direct practical application; But the Study of Chinese ornamental art is also very instructiv for the understanding of the state of architecture and ornamental art with the ancient nations, ¦ If we were allowed to see the ancient Babylonian Pallaces as well as the Egyptian and even the Greec monuments in their compleatness, with their Accessories of frameworks, mattings, drapperies and mouveable things, particularly with their polychromical and metallic ornamentations, they would approach under many rapports very much to Chinese architecture and ornamental art. –

We shall now proceed in showing the gradual transition of the principle of wallcovering to a more constructiv style of architecture. which transition we shall pursue on the remaining traces of Assyrian Persian Aegyptian Greec and Romain architecture.

Among these are the Aegyptian monuments without doubt the most ancient; Some of the most important Egyptian temples at Thebes and elsewhere, and many old tumbs in Aegypt, which still exist, have been built thousands of Years before the Assyrian monuments, whose ruins have been lately discovered by Botta and Layard. But the first, notwithstanding their greater antiquity belong to a later state of development, at least with respect to their constructiv elements, and we shall therefore begin with the second. |

The Assyrians remained the faithfull conservators of the old principle. Although they knew pretty well Stone Construction, they employed it only as an architectural and decorative principle for the basements of their edifices; We must mention at once, that these basements formed a very important part of the Assyrian Architecture; The Assyrian architecture is before all the others a Terrace-architecture as we shall see it in the last lecture.

But the cooperation of the maçon to produce an artistical ensemble or a monument, stopped here; his art was hidden behind a richly ornamented cover for all those parts of the construction, which form the building itself, and this inside and outside of the Walls.

The old Greec historians, Herodotus, Ctesias, Xenophon, Diodorus of Sicily and others give us descriptions of the outside decorations of the Assyrian bildings. They were entirely coverd with polychrome ornaments, executed in Terra Cotta and Metal, with Frieses, representing battles, chases and processions, analogical to those which we see now represented on the Alabasterslabs at the Brittish Museum.

Xenophon tells us, that on the days of Ceremonies these beautiful ornaments were hidden ¦ by those renomated Assyrian Tapestries, which are mentionned in the oldest records of mankind and celebrated for their richness, colours, and designs, and Skillfull execution.

5   These draperies were the true Models for the above mentionned Terra cotta ornaments, on the outer walls, as well as for these Alabaster slabs; which formed a sort of panneling, inside and outside of the buildings, about 5 to 8 feet upwards from the pavement.

   The descriptions of Dragons, Lyons, Tigers, Unicornes and other Mystic

10   Animals, which we read in the ancient records remind perfectly the ornaments and Embroideries which we observe on the Dresses of the Gods and Kings on the Assyrian Basreliefs; Even more the whole Ensemble of the last reminds us the ancient Descriptions of Similar objects, as being represented on tapestries.

   These sculptures remain within certain limits which seem not to be pre-

15   scribed by hierarchical laws, which was the case in Egypt, | but by the reaction of a treatment and of a Style of execution, which is not that of Stone sculpture. They are copies in Stone of woven or embroidered tapestries and look like that.

   There were at the Chinese Department in the Exhibition of 52 some Tapestries or Embroideries in relief, which in their style reminded perfectly these

20   basreliefs.

   Other representations, such like battles, hunting partys etc are comparable to the well known Bayeux Drapery which represents the battles between the Normans and King Harold and was made by King William the firsts Queen at the time of the Conquest.

25   Real Draperies and rich floor Carpets were combined with the sculptured and painted tapestries to a general splendid and harmonious effect.

   Very often the walls were covered with pannels of precious wood, with which at the same time the ceilings were made. This we know from notices given by Xenophon in his Cyropaedia.

30   The columns which were the supporters of the ceilings were likewise of Wood, ornamented with latticework of Cane and covered with Gold and Silver-plates. ¦

   The pannelating of the Walls with Stone slabs was the first step to stoneconstruction, –

35   The second step towards the last as an ornamental Element is visible on the Ruins of Persepolis and Pasargadae in Persia. These Ruins are better known only since the beautiful publication on Persia, made by Mrs Coste and Flandin, by order of the Frensh Government.

   As for the terraces of the old Persian Castles we see the principle of Stone

40   Construction highly developd, they are executed in immense blocks, of black marble, very regularly and at some instances evidently with the view of employing the joints of the stones as ornamental lines.

130 Lectures

Here also the maçons-cooperation as an decorator stopps; but we see a remarkable progress towards the Emancipation of the Material at the main buildings themselves. The Columns, which were of Wood and covered at times with Metal with the Assyrians, are now, with the Persians, allready executed in Stone, but they behold the entire Character of Wooden-Pillars, by their | slender proportions and details taken from wood Construction. This we shall see in the Chapter on wood Construction. But this is not the only proof of the Progress towards an other Style of Construction.

The sculptures on the remaining parts of the walls at Persepolis and Pasargadae are in general style but little different from those in Assyria, but Stone is already employed not only as a cover, but as a constructiv part.

The principal parts of the Walls, with the exception of the staircases, the Window- and Door-frames, and the Corners of the walls, were still only built of unburnt bricks; These parts of the Walls are gone, and the former only remain.

They are Stones of immense Size, a few of them forming the Corner of a wall. but they are hollowed out, so that they form some thing like a solid shell for reception and the protection of the Earthen wall, which last was covered with precious wood and Metalplates, as we know by the history of Alexander, who destroied this Royal Pallace by fire. |

We come now to Egypt, with its immense stone monuments. The manner how the Egyptians constructed their edifices is a proof, that stone construction had not yet arrived to that point where it is a selfexisting part of ornamental Architecture. The Egyptian monuments are as it were, cut out of an artificial roc; The Stones, which were set together very carefully it is true, but without consideration for linear effects of the joints, and very irregularly, first formed a very raw idea of the outer and inner features of the building, which was given only afterwards to the walls with the cisel. After the general forms of the building having been finished by the Maçon it came under the hands of the Sculptor and lastly the whole was painted over by the painter.

This only with Respect to the Buildings themselves, while on the Terraces we observe The stone construction in its own right and standing for itself like in Assyria and Persia.

On some of the oldest edifices as for instance on the Pyramids, inside and outside, and on the oldest part of the Tempel at Carnak in upper Egypt, (Theben) the pure old principle of Wall coating appears still in its purest application.

The Piramids, even those constructed of Sandstone or Limestone, were once covered with highly polished and ornamented Granit | And what is a very remarkable circumstance, these Granite slabs themselves appear to have been covered with a transparent coating of Varnish Colours.

There is a moulding in Aegyptian Architecture, which may find its explanation in the construction of platework or pannelled work It is a moulding, which our carpenters employ for hiding the joints of the boards on the Corners; I mean the Torus round the walls, the principal moulding of Egyptian Architecture.

The sculptured and painted decorations of the Egyptian monuments greatly deviate from their origine; They are not more sculptured Embroideries, they are Lapidar-inscriptions, hollowed out of the Wall and filled up with colour; They are a sort of Champlevé Enameling in a large architectural scale and style.

But this is not the case with the pictures on the walls of the Tumbs. Wall-decoration remained here true to its old principle. Most of the representations are given here like as being draperies fixed on the walls, and their frames show very beautiful patterns, executed in a ¦ pure ornamental, and not hieroglyphical style; The motives of these patterns are alltogether taken from textile ornamentation, they are interlaces, squares, Meanders etc.

Lastly The ceilings of the Aegyptian tempels represent the idea of a lofty canopy, suspended between the columns of the Hypostilium.

I shall trie to show at an other occasion, how the principle of Aegyptian architecture notwithstanding its massivity, has taken its Analoga from provisional wooden constructions and tents, like we have seen it to be the case with the Tempel of Salomon.

The fourth path was made by the Greecs. ¦

The Greeks were not much more advanced in Civilisation than the American Indians, or the New-Zealandas are now, while Assyria and Egypt were allready the seats of highly developd forms of society. It then was but natural, that the former overkame the types for their institutions and for their art partly from abroad, and at a period, when the last were not more ligible in their proper and direct significance. The Greecs remained faithfull to many of these traditional types, but they took them up in a pure artistical sense.

We first observe on the Greec monuments an organic connection between the single elements of construction, which on the Assyrian monuments and even those of Egypt, have no connection together and work each for itself on its place; ¦ The Greecs even by doing so, were not allways consistent in their principles, depassed in some cases the justifiable bounderies, in favour of some higher idea which they proposed to carry out, as is shall show at an instance here after.

Secondly there is that difference between Greec and barbarian architecture, that the ornamental parts of the last are *applications*, or at least represented like such, they are fastened round the kernet of construction which is still visible. while the construction and the ornaments of the first are one and indivisible from each other. The Greec ornaments are emanations of the constructiv forms and in the same time they are Symbols of the dynamical functions of the parts to which they belong. –

They have no other meaning than to explain the constructiv forms by analogical notions, taken from nature itself or from other branches of art, while the ornaments on the barbarian monuments find generally their | explanations in some historical, local, or religious notions, which have nothing in common with the part of the building, whereon they are applied. –

The accuracy and beauty of Greec Stoneconstruction has never been reached since, but their edifices are sculptured and not constructed in Stone. Also they did not show the stone, except on the terraces, which supported the edifices; Ewery where else the stoneconstruction was covered with a thin coating of stucco which last was painted and ornamented after the ancient principle. This was even the case for their white marble monuments, which last material was adopted principally for the reason of being indispensable for the application of a new process of Wallpainting invented by the Greecs and unknown to the Egyptans and the Assyrians. – ¦

We come now to the Romans, which are the inventors of real stone construction. or at least which made this principle of building the dominant in the whole civilised old world. The art of constructing vaults was not unknown to Assyrians and to the Egyptians, and even the Greecs were acquainted with it, as we shall see at the Chapter on Stone construction, but neither of these nations adopted this form as an element of architecture. The Romans, or the Etruskans, their ancestors by doing this, were the inventors of architecture as an selfexisting art, which may exist for itself without the assistance of the other branches of art..

It would be interesting if it was permitted by time, to pursue the history of Wallcoating farther through the mediaeval ages, where it bekame again the dominant principle of architecture, and the starting point of a new development of art in general. |

I may now be allowed to give some additional notices about some specialities of industrial art, which derive from or are connected with the principle of Coating.

1°.

On the early style of Metalconstruction and of Metaldecoration.

It is highly probable that Metal was first employed for ornament only, and in form of Metal sheeds.

Goldleaves found in large quantities on the Indians on the discovery of America by Columbus and Cortez.

Such Ornaments in Gold- Silver and Tinleaves of a very early caracter are to be seen at the Brittish Museum. They are stamped and pierced with ornaments and figures. So the process of driving bending stamping and engraving metal-shieds may appear the earliest which came in practice.

A Second step was the art of making metalthreads and filigran work, belonging to the same Cathegory of processes.

We find Wires and spiralformed ornements in the old Etruscan as well as German and Celtic Tombs; alse brass- and Gold-bracelets, and Collars in the same style. ¦

A third invention was that of Chains, first employed as ornaments, afterwards for defensive arms. The Type of the Oriental Style of defensive arms. adopted in the time of the Crusades by the western nations. –

Metal threads were also employed at an very early period for woven staffs and Embroideries.

The Pallaces of the Kings of Babylone says Philostratus were ornamented with carpets in Gold and Silverweavings instead of pictures.

Hence the Gold and Silver-embroideries the types of decoration for larger flat metalsurface Instances the Walldecorations of the temple of Jerusalem, The Brass plates in the Christian Churches. –

The arts of nielling and enameling are inventions which derive from the same origine. Enamelling is a sort of Niello with vitreous substances. An other Style of Enamelling that which derives from Jewelry and imitation of precious stones. (Emaux à Cabochon and Cloisonnés In the whole 7 different Styles of Enameling. |

Oriental art never changed its general Character; as far as our knowledge reaches in pursuing it; – oriental art is the absolute expression and the result of the more instinctive feelings and aptitude of mankind for the Embellishments of human wants; this explains the fact, that after the fall of the Roman Empire, the oriental Style or at least a style nearly approximating thereto, reappeared with all its elementary motives, even among nations, where oriental influences could not prevail.

The works of industrial art of the first centuries of the Christian Era appear in immediate conjunction with the productions of the earliest antiquity.

To this sort of style belong the gold ornaments discovered in the Tomb of Childeric near Tournay and the imperial Ornaments of Charlemagne, now at Vienna.

Furnitures and implements for domestic life
The taste for rich and splendid furniture and implements preceeded by far the want of fixed settlements. ¦

Wooden furnitures entirely covered with metal plates, belong to the earliest forms of this branch of industry.

Parts of Assyrian Specimens of this kind are at the Brittish Museum. The Same Style prevailed among the Etruscans and the Greecs of earlier times

The Egyptians seem not to have followed the same style of Metalplating. The A. furnitures bear the thin caracter of wrought or cast Metal.

The Assyrian Warcharriots were evidently executed in the former style those of Egyptians were made of Cast metal.

The same principle of construction prevailed in the early mediaeval ages in Western Europe. Such was the Chair of Charlemagne ¦

The Imperor Othon of Germany opened the Grave of Charlemagne at Aix la Chapelle In the Year 1000. He Was found sitting on a Wooden Chair covered with Goldplates and with Precious stones, in the same Style in which are executed the Imperial ornaments at Vienna. ¦

In the Life of Charlemagne written by his secertery Eginhard, is constained a list of | the valuable things, which constituted the inheritance of the Imperor, which is of great interest for the state of metalworking at that time.

Among others there are mentionned 3 driven tables, in Gold and Silver with inlaid work, representing the Map of Constantinopel and of Rome and other compositions.

The Chairs of the Archbishops in Some churches in Italy and Germany executed in Marble are executed after these wooden metalcovered types.

Application of Metal for defensiv arms.
The application of Metal plates for defensiv arms is of very early date.

The oriental Style of defensiv arms, the coat of mail, was not adopted by the Greeks and Romans.

The Greec and Roman shields, helmets and Armures show a perfect application of the principle of strenghtening thin Metal plates by corrugations and curvatures, an important moment for the ¦ history of construction.

The Greec cuirasses were modelled after and well adapted to the formation of the parts, which they were intended to secure, Interesting instances of metal applied to armury in Homers Songs, Ilias 18, 478.

The Shield of Achilles; consisting of 5 plates of different metal laid one over the other. Iron, Bronze, tin, Gold and Silver; Id has been the favorite problem for Sculptors to reproduce the form of this Chield with alle the rich ornaments and Emblems, which describes Homerus on the praecited song. There were screw Zones, Surrounding a Center representing Haeven. the Shield of Diomedes other Shields described by Greec poets. Very good Specimens of Greec armuries at the Brittish Museum.

It is more than probable that the hollow Metal construction or tubular construction has first been principially settled by Greec armurers. The same was the Case in the 15th Century after the invention of the firearms.

It was natural that the same important principle of construction was employed hereafter to other constructions, and namely for building

We have several examples to show that | it was practically carried out with the Romans, For instance the roof of the Pantheon which formerly consisted of tubular bronze spars, riveted together – The whole Vault of the Edifice was covered with brassplates, which have been taken in time of Sixte V by the Architecte Borromini for the large Baldachin in St Peters.

The antik Bronze doors give a second example of tubular construction, The history of the Brass doors is a very interesting part of general history of art. The Doors have allways been propositions for the best artists and occasions for elevating

The older forms of Brass doors were nothing else than a coat of metal nailed on wood, Such were the Silver Doors of St Peters, stripped of their valuable coat by the Saracens in the Jear 846: The silver was of the weight of 975 ℔.

This styles appeared in the same nudity in the Byzantine doors at St Peter et Paolo ¦ at Rome, which dissapeared with the destruction of that ancient Basilica by fire some 20 Years ago. –

But elder doors, in Germany made by Saxon founders at Hildesheim belong rather to the advanced Roman Style with pannels in imitation of wooden framework. in which last Style all the celebrated brass doors of the Cinque Cento are executed.

Classification of Vessels

The most important of all the different branches of industry for the general history of art and for artistical science is perhaps the potters industry, of which I shall try to give some notions in the following; – The word pottery comes from the Latin word potum, which word indicates nor the form nor the material, but the use of the object It is the latin name for a drinking cup.

Another name for the same branch of industry has been adopted from the Greek linguage, which name is less usual in English but which we shall be obliged to employ frequently to day because it gives us a more general notion of the whole empire of the branch of industry in question.

The Greec name for pottery is Keramos; It signifies nor the nature of the material, nor the use of the vessel, but the horn of an animal, which was the original form of the drinking vases, a form which has been maintained partly traditionally partly by imitation till now for the same or for analogical applications. |

fol. 1v

But the signification of the word was afterwards extended to the whole domain of the potters craft, from the unburnt brick to the finest Etruscan or Greek vase and even to the terra cotta sculptures. Thus we may be justified by taking this expression in a still wider sense and comprehending with it the whole empire of those industrial productions, which by their prototypes or by the processes of execution are related to and attendant upon pottery.

The vases of Gold, of Ivory, of Crystal and other hard stones, of Glass, amber or wood do not belong to the potters art by their materials, but they belong to it by certain natural and traditional laws of generation and ornamentation which first have been settled by potters. It is the same case with the Sculptures executed in Metal or in hard materials, they belong to ceramic art by their historical origine as well as by the fact, that all these objects of art first must be executed plastically in clay before they can be cast in metal or cut in stone. The prescriptions of the ceramic material, the clay, and of the tools belonging to its treatement are lawgiving in statuary, so that under a certain point of view we may be |

fol. 2r   2

right to place all these categories of human art under the same general division.

The productions of Ceramic art stood in a very high consideration with all the nations at all times, they have to us nearly the same interest as monumental art itself. which has been greatly influenced by the first, partly directly by application of parts *materially* belonging to pottery partly *indirectly* by adopting principles and prescriptions of beauty, proportion and ornamentation, which first were settled and applied on potters works.

The first and most general application of pottery was doubtless allways and everywhere that, which has for its object the domestical utilities; but it soon acquired a higher destination by being employed for religious and funeral services.

By this they became objects of high art and symbols and we owe to this circumstance the conservation of an immense quantity of beautiful vases, while very little of the domestical poteries have come to us. The burnt clay, even the softest and least temperd by fire, is the most durable material, much mor durable than even stone and metal, which was perhaps one of the reasons, why this material was so generally employed for funeral urns. The Terra Cotta vases, which

come from the excavations of tombs are for history ¦ of mankind, what are the
fossil remains of plants and animals for history of nature.

They are the most ancient and the most speaking documents for history of
civilization. Show me what sort of potteries a nation has produced and I shall
tell You what nation it was. – I had at an other occasion the opportunity of parallelising these two different forms of ancient vases, which both had a high religious significance. The first is the holy Nile-Pail, or Situlus of the ancient
Aegyptians. – The other is that beautiful Greec vase, which is calld the Hydria.

Both of them relate to the same destination, that of catching running water.

But the first is a drawing Vessel, for getting Water out of the Nile, and therefore Characteristic for Egypt, the Gift of the Nile. Two such Vessels were carried by the Egyptian Water-carriers on Jokes, so that one hung before, and the
other behind. as we see them on wallpictures in the Egyptian Speos or tombs.

The heaviest part is very properly the lowest, as a precaution to prevent spill-
ing. It is formed like a Waterdrop. We feel the fittness of this form | for its use,
which is the opposite to that Greek Hydria, which is a Vessel for catching Water
as it flows from a fountain.

Hence the funnel chaped feature of the mouth and the neck, which is rigorously prescribed by the object in view

On the other hand, the mode of carriing those vessels has led to the Idea of
removing the Centers of Gravity of the Vessels towards the summits. For they
were carried on the heads upright when full, lengthways when emty, as we see
on this diagramm, traced from a picture, which decorates the body of the Vessel.

Any one, attemting to balance a stick on his finger, will find the feat much
easier, if the heaviest end is uppermost.

This experiment explains the form of the Greec Hydria, which is compleated
by the addition of two handles, placed at the level of the center of Gravity.

A third handle was added, for a second person which assisted the Water-
carriing Greec woman by lifting the full Vase on the head, and down.

How strikingly is symbolised the light spiritual and lucid nature of the monteneer inhabitants of Greece in this form, opposed to the Nile Pail, which is a
true representative of the national Genius of the Aegyptians, and of institutions
the first principle of which was stability.

The two nations were certainly well aware and conscious of ¦ these forms, in
making them national and religious Emblems.

The Nilepail was the holy Vessel of the Egyptians and in like manner the
Hydria of the Greeks was the sacred Vase, carried by Virgins in their religious
processions, and perhaps the type for an architectural form, which is characteristic in Doric architecture, while the fundamental features of Aegyptian Architecture seems to be contained in Embryo in the construction of the Nile-pail;

We possede some excellent works on Ceramical art, Among which is the most important the work of Brogniard, *traité des arts ceramiques*, which is a necessary manual for every practical man in this branch of art. The history of pottery by Marriat is an other excellent guide. –

But the object has been treated in these books more from the scientifical and historical point of view rather than artistically. The | only essay in the last sense has been made by a French artist and manufacturer of potteries, Mr Ziegler, whose book Etudes Ceramiques is very interesting and usefull, although it is full of errors and paradoxes.

He gives a Sheme of the fundamental forms which occur in Ceramical art, which I reproduced here, as being usefull, allthough it gives no suggestions about the relations which exist among the forms and the real or symbolical uses and the manners of execution of the last.

He derives all the forms of the vases from two generating forms,

1 the straight line and the cube

2) The curved line and the Sphere.

From the first derive three primitive forms,

1) the Cylinder
2) the Conoid
3) the Clavoid.

He gives as a rule of proportion for vases, which partake of these forms at least three times the half diameter and at the most three times the full diameter.

From the second, namely from the Spere, derive thre other fundamental forms in pottery,

1) the Spheroid,

2) the Ovoid,

3) the Ogivoid.

The Sphere is for him an unartistical form, because it has no *sense*, that is to say it appears the same in every sense it may be taken; It is a neutral form without any proper significance, when not assisted by other forms.

The Spheroid in the contrary has already a sens, which distinguishes its elevation from its extent in the horizontal sens.

It is the same with the Ellipsoid; but both of these forms offre little expedients in the beautiful ceramic compositions.

These forms may be corrected by contrasts of straight lines. and square frames.

The Ogivoide is for the Sphere what the Conoid is for the Cylinder, and a form as important in ceramic art as in architecture; |

The Ovoid is to the Sphère, what the Clavoid is to the Cylinder; this is the inversed cone, and the first is the inversed egg.

This form is the most usual in Ceramics; In the Brittish Museum are several old Hetruscan imitations of real Austrich Eggs in white clay or marble and painted, which belong to the oldest period of Etrucsan art. –

The beautifull Panathenean Vases and their numberless imitations in old and modern times belong to the Ovoidal form.

The body of an Ovoidal vase must have the proportions of an Egg, but among hundred eggs there is one which is beautifuller than the others are, and among hundred persons there is *one* more capable then the others to feel and to distinguish this difference.

Hereafter he comes to the mixt forms, which are the following,

I. Such as derive from the Cylinder and the Sphere with the curvatures directed inside:

D 1) The Canopian form

D 2) The Napiform

D. 3) The turbiniform

E The Phoceenform

E The Lacrimiform

E The Piriform ¦

The last three are the inverse of the first three;

These forms are the most usual in Egypt. The Phocean form was the representative of upper Egypt, while the Nile pale was that of the lower Country which was called Canopus. The first form we know already as that of the Nile pale.

The Canopian vases were employed as conservatories for momies of holy animals with covers, representing Animals heads. or heads of Deities.

The varieties of these two forms, which Ziegler calls napiforms and turbiniforms are but varieties of the first.

The Phocean form derives its name from the Phoceans which adopted this form from the Egyptians. The last adopted this form for many of their architectural parts. Some Columns have the outlines of these Vases. –

6 Other mixted forms derive from the *Cylinder* and the *sphere* and have the curvatures directed outside

1) the Corolle which curvature begins at the first third of its hight from the top,

2) the Corolle which curvature begins at the Second theird of the hight, ¦ the *Campanula*, with a double curvature. –

Varieties of these three forms are the so calld tiges or *stalks*, allso in the number of three and distinguable by the same qualities.

They have their analogies in the most beautiful forms of nature, in the flowers, and are very important types for ceramical as well as architectural forms.

Another Class of mixd forms are the Crateroids and discoids used for plates and sacrificial vases.

Most of the Assyrian Metalvases, of which we shall speak hereafter are belonging to these forms. They generally are decorated only inside and the laws of proportion of their elevations given by Ziegler are unfounded, because they are not calculated to be seen from the side.

———————

The different primitiv or mixt forms, when they concur to one Ensemble, the result is a composite work, to which belong the most pompeous productions of Ceramic art and of Architecture. Nevertheless these Composite works are subjected to one or the other fundamental form which is the base of the composition. |

fol. 6v   This diagramm gives the three prncipal parts which constitute a vase mixt and those of a Composite Vase and their denominations –

But we shall now leave Mr Zieglers Theory and. consider the Ceramic forms from an other point of view – by taking these forms and their ornamentations as the results, *first* of their real or supposed uses and applications.

2°) of the Materials and the processes which come in question for their execution.

first Consideration.

Three distinct intentions preside for every preparation of vessels – which devide themselves into primitive or mixd forms according as one or more of those intentions are fulfilled by preparing them.

The first intention is that of holding a containing a fluid or a collectiv mass of substances.

The second intention is that of *dipping up* or *bailing.* We seek an Utensil capable of *catching* fluids.

The third intention is that of *emtiing.* |

fol. 7r   7.   Nature offers us many forms, which are the clear Expressions of one or the other of the foregoing three conceptions: for example the Gourd or pumpkin and the Egg, both of which are in the strictest sense conservative vessels; The horn offers us a natural bailing vessel, and when perforated at the point, it serves as a funnel or filling Vessel;

These natural forms were early comprehended and applied; man however in his early state of civilisation was guided by an instinctive Impulse, which scarcely needed these models, to direct his Choice of forms according to the laws of nature.

The Works of Ceramic art acquire no artistic Signification until the three primary intentions or at least two of them unite in the formation of a Vessel.

Strictly considered there is not a single Vessel, that does not contain all the three motives here specified, but in most instances one is predominant over the other two, or if two are evident, the third nearly dissapears. – .

Besides these fundamental motives, which operate on the construction of Vessels others also claim our notice, which may be considered as accessory; these are the following.

1° The *stand* of a Vessell

2°) The *Handles.*

3°) The *Cover.*

By connecting these accessories with the Ground forms, the latter become more animated and raise ¦ themselves to objects of art. *fol. 7v*

Still these accessory Components cannot properly be regarded as marks of distinction in the Classification of Vessels.

According to the foregoing the Vases and Wessels may be grouped in the following classes.

1ˢᵗ Class. Reservoirs, Holding or containing vessels,

The spheroidal shape with sectional outlines approaching to the circular form is the Original.

The antique Dolia are nearly pure expressions of the type for this class. The Assyrian Earthenware vessels belong mostly to this sort of forms. – . The Spanish Tinajas, which are of extraordinary size, and the Mexican Koupchines are other examples of Reservoirs

The dolia have small apertures, no necks, and no stands or feet, they are round or pointed on the lower end and want a support to stand upright. – .

Deriving forms from the Dolium are

1°) The *Amphorae*, which are dolia with high proportions wide apertures, and handles but without feet; They are allready combined formations, having a short funnelshaped neck.

2°) The *Urns* which are flat at the lower end, have in their simpler combinations no necks, and no handles.

Such are the Canopian uns of the Egyptian | and the Ash Unrs of the Greecs. *8.* *fol. 8r* There is one large Greec beautiful Bronce urn of the simplest kind in the Elgin saloon of the Brittish Museum.

Some Glass urns discovered in England are also to be seen at the Brittish Museum.

The Urns with feet, handles and necks are productions of the high Classic age, most of the beautiful Terra Cotta Vases belong to this kind of pottery.

———————— .

A third class of reservoirs are the *Crateres*, which originally were vessels for mixing wine with water. The Mouth has the widest Diameter of the Whole. They are with and without handles.

These vessels, as well as the Dolia require stands which were originally of Wood, but later, as art advanced made of metal. They were chiefly of the well known tripod form; But there is a wooden stand for an Egyptian Crater which has six feet.

The stand was often the dominant part of the whole, then it was called a Tripod

At other cases the tripod was very low and a sort of ring standing upon three feet. Beautiful Specimens of this kind of Craters are at the Brittish Museum.

These forms particularly the Craters with high feet, were most frequently used as vessels of state |

The celebrated Vase in the Villa Medicis and that in the Villa Albani, belong to this Class. The same form was adopted for small sized vases executed in precious stones and glass. for instance the Barberini Vase of Glass and the Vase of St Denis, formed of a single onyx.

The Arabian Basins belong to this Class of which there is one beautiful Specimen in the Brittish Museum.

4°) The *Tanks, tazzas* or Basins are opposite to the amphore, The last is the extreme limit in length of the Dolium, the tazza appears when the Dolium becomes very shallow.

There also three principal forms of subdivision appear

Basins convex underneath, requiring stands to rest. The whole Assyrian Metal vessels belong to this Class. They were *Emblems*, that is to say they were the inner part of an other Vessel of an other less precious material as we shall see afterwards.

A rare Vessel of this kind the Gold Patera found at Rennes, which is now in the Paris library and the celebrated Sardonyx Cup, six inches in Diameter preserved at Naples. The inside is coverd with a flat Goldplate rihly ornamented with repoussework, which can be separated from the body of the cup; This is what the ancients called an Emblem in the first sense of the word.

———————— .

When they are flat underneeth, they are called *patenae* or *paterae*. which form was used at sacrifices. | the Roman Catholic Church adopted this form also; The Holy *Graal* at Genova, is a Bazin of green Glass;

When the Tazzas are very flet and of great diameter, they are called Dishes and plates. –

When they have high stands the take the Character of Cups. They were very popular in the middleages and after the Renaissance, and only applied to secular purposes,

The Cups of Benvenuto Cellini are the most celebrated under these vessels.

Another kind of Reservoirs are the *Labra* or *Tubs*. generally of a subverted conical form and large in size, a form which has got a religious significance in Christianity as a Symbol of Baptism.

—————————— .

The second Division *Vessels* for *drawing and intercepting fluids.*.

These Vessels are divided into two distinct classes.

The first are the *pails* or *Buckets*.

The second are the *funnels*.

The Bucket of the Egyptians, the holy Situlus we know it already, but the same had also a religious significance with the Assyrians which gave to their holy Buckets ¦ very richly ornamented forms.   *fol. 9v*

Christian ornamented well Buckets are at Milan and in Pavia. in several Churches.

The ladles, Scoops and Spoons, other applications of the same type, have given rise to beautiful productions of industry in antiquity as well as in the middleages. They also numbered among the holy vessels and we have at the Brittish Museum beautiful examples of such instruments which are as many proofs of the artistic feeling of the ancients.

In the Works Le Moyen Age et la Renaissance, which is in the Library, are contained some Mediaeval spoons which are as well as the first, very instructiv for the study of Style.

As the type for the class of the intercepting vessels may be considered the funnel. but we have scarcely one example of a pure funnel treated in an artistical sense and ornamented.

This form only acquires its true signification in Connection with the Reservoir, to fill which it is so especially adapted. From this combination arises the Antique Hydria, the holy Vessel of the Greeks. |

The third Division contains the Filling or pouring *Vessels*.   *10.   fol. 10r*

In this series are comprised all such Vessels, which take their Special Character from the act of emtying or pouring out fluids, in a certain measure and a given direction.

For this purpose they require a particular construction and as it were particular organic features, distinguishing them from others.

They seem to have their natural prototypes in the horns and the shells, which two natural forms are frequently employed for symbols in ornamenting vessels of this kind.

As simply emtiing Vessels the well known Saucer may serve as a familiar Example, which has frequently been treated artistically in the mediaeval times.

But this form, like the others, becomes of more importance for Art, when in connection with other forms.

fol. 10v

An especially important combi- ¦ nation of this kind are the Lamps, which have at all times had a highly religious and symbolical meaning and are of great importance in private Life.

Ancient and modern ceramic art is excedingly rich in combinations of spouded vessels, but none of them has reached the importance and development required by the porteable Hydria with the *Spoud*. 5

By this addition the Greec National Vessel the Hydria acquired its full development.

What it lost by this connection in doric Magnitude it gained on the other hand in physionomical Expression and Ionic Elegance. 10

The Austere form, conditioned by the Potters wheel received thro' the irregularities, impressed by the single hand, without tools, freedom and life.

The form in this case does not deny its Prototype, the potters wheel, but is emancipated from it.

It was the use of this Vessel in sacrifices that gave it an especial Sanctity. 15 From this Vessel the fluid was poured into the patera, and from the latter the Libation was performed.

fol. 11r *11.*

For this reason these two Vessels are found in tombs | almost invariably together. The Christian era also adopted these Vessels among its sacred Utensils as Recipiens for the Wine in the administration of the Sacrament. 20

The Egyptians had hydrias with very projecting spouds, mentionned by the ancient writers and to be seen in a small modell in the Brittish Museum among a collection of toys for children which were found in a tomb.

The Arabian Bures used for the ceremony of Hand-washing belong to this kind of Vessels, which were also the Predilection of the Renaissance artists. 25 They produced beautiful bures in Mayolica Enamel and precious metals, maintaining the ancient prototype, but modifiing it by judiciously taking profit of the new technical means of execution, which they invented.

Other pouring Vessels are the Cans, Evers, Bottles, fieldflasks and other which it would be impossible to specify here, but which tell all their own history 30 of development.

The same is the case with the immense number of drinking Vessels with the Ancient and modern nations. The Geek Author Athenaeus gives us the name of

fol. 11v

more than hundred sorts of such vessels, and still there are many ¦ others contained in other books. 35

We encounter nearly the same variety and incertainty with the Drinking Vessels of the Middleages.

As exceptional and capricious forms are prevailing among them it would be very difficult to range them into certain classes; What has been sayd with reference to vessels in general, holds also good for this particular branch of Ceram- 40 ical art; The drinking Vessels in their Ensemble form reductions or repetitions after a smaler Scale of the different vessels which we have bespoken before, with the Exception of some peculiarities depending from their esspecial uses.

Among them however is one sort, which by its religious veneration in Christian time has been the Object of great distinction by art and ornamentation. This is the *Chalice*, a semi-ovoidal drinking Cup, without handles, standing on a high foot. It seems to be the same, which the Greeks and Etruscans took for solemnel libations on their festivals. |

I shall now give some few remarks about the laws of ornamentation of vessels. –

Every vase or ustensil whatever it may be, is, like a building, a whole which is composed out of parts, which have each to fullfill their own function while cooperating with the others to a general aim and effect.

Not only the whole of the thing, but each part of it also, must speack *out*, its function by its appearance and the choice of the ornaments must be made with the intention to increase by their application the caracteristic quality and function of every part and of the whole.

Like it is necessary for a monument to show its immouveability, the same a mouveable thing must show its mouveability.

Therefore the stands of the Ancient mouveable things are so often ornamented with feet of animals or sometimes are pure imitations of feet. This is a constant type which can not lose of its value by repetitions. There is in the Brittish Museum one Example of a Tripod standing upon Lyons feet, which are supported ⁞ by turtles, which appear to progress Stowly and insensibely. This is a refined reinforcement of the idea, which has been imitated or repeated by Peter Fisher, whose Sebaldus monument, which represents a bier, is standing upon *snails*.

The handles are other Symbols for the same function or fundamental idea; Therefore handles are not only excusable but also in many cases vanted for Vases, which by their size and Weight would impossibly be mouveable by hands –

A composite Vessel, has

1) *a body.*
2) *a Stand*
3) a neck with Lips or spouds.
4) *a cover.*
5) *handles.*

The body is containing and the ornamentation must show this function. it must avake the Idea of *Embracing* if a body is rifled, which is a natural ornamentation the rifles must go from down upwarts. |

fol. 13r 13.	In other cases, f.e. at this Aeg. Situlus, the stripes must go dounwarts, for the stripes represent here the direction of the force of gravity, which was formgiving for the vessel itself. It is a sort of bagg, executed in Clay or bronze.

In other cases the body forms a neutral Ground; then it may be ornamented by a representation the signification of which has nothing in common with the structure function of the body; Such are most of the Etruskan Vase pictures. But they are fixed on the Body with Rubans, to show that they are Attributions and belonged not to the Vase itself.

The Stand has two functions which meet in the center; which is the fulcrum of the two powers, which are activ in the stand. ¦

fol. 13v

This fulcrum must be expressd by some strong neck or ring or offset and it seems to be statically wanted to have it nearer to the beginning of the body than to the Abacus or the tablet at the bottom of the stand.

The Elastic lines of the vegetable nature are very speaking for the two activ parts of the foot, but they must be directed in opposite Senses, the holding or containing part of the *stand*, which last may be considered as a sort of Vase with foot, including an other one without foot, works upwarts and so the ornamental lines employed for this part must strenghthen this feeling. The lower part should be less developd in size, but stronger in appearance – its organization goes downwarts. Nearly the same is to be observed for the Neck and the Aperture.

The neck has also a double function, It is a funnel; but a funnel which in most of the cases, is narrowest in the middle and wider on the two ends. – a hyperboloid formed funnel.

On Vessel Parts

fol. 1r 1. a   On Friday last I had commenced to explain some of the principles of ornamentation as applied on ceramic Art;

I mentionned, the constituting parts of a composite Vessel to be the following:

1°) the body.
2°) the stand.
3) the Neck
4 the spoud.
5°) The Handles.
6) the Cover. – .

Every one of these parts has its own signification and function. Their forms and ornaments are principally attending upon their material or symbolical uses; I say principally for they are much influenced also by the materials which come in question for their fabrication, but upon this I shall call Your attention hereafter, while I am now only ¦ speaking of principles of proportion form and ornamen-   *2. a fol. 1v* tation which are independent upon the materials, so that the following finds its application for Earthenware as well as for Metalworks or others.

I must begin my specification with a general introductory remark on two different principles of ornamentation in industrial art and in art in general.

The first one of the principles which I allude to, we may call it the *constructiv* or perhaps better the *dynamical* principle; The last name is better, for the construction of a work is dependant upon the material out of which it is made, while its dynamical function remains the same for all materials.

Every part of a work as well as the Ensemble of it, must tell what dynamical function it has to fullfill, not only by its form but also by its ornaments. When the last have no other significations but that, to be symbols, taken from nature or borrowed from other arts, | with the sole intention to awake in our minds in   *3.a fol. 2r* a agreable manner a clear conception of the dynamical function of a whole or a part of a work of art, then they are ornaments and Symbols in the first sense of the word.

The beautiful Greec ornaments are mostly Symbols of this kind.

The second sort of ornaments are those which, while agreably variating the elementary form of a work or part of a work, by means of outlines and colours, are representing thinks, actions and circumstances, which are not immediately connected with the dynamical or structiv idea of a thing. Such are for instance the beautiful pictures on the Greec vases, representing Heroic battles and objects relating to the destinations of the Vases.

The more advanced the artistic feeling of a nation is, the more we observe on its productions of industrial art a strong distinction between the two principles of ornamentation while the same are confounded and pass gradually over one into the other with other nations of less artistical and perhaps more poetical and religious tendency.

Such for instance is the Egyptian art; the monumental art in Egypt shows no ornament properly speaking; every decoration is a religious or a political or a topographical Symbol, every colour employd is the same; The Egyptian ¦ Style   *4 a fol. 2v* of composition is a writing the Egyptian Style of Colouring is not a musik with colours like it was allways in oriental art, it is a prosody. –

Greec art, as I sayd before, was based upon an other principle a more artistic and a less symbolic one. The Greecs reserved their beautiful Symbols of the second kind only for the Enrichment of those parts of a work of Industrial art, including architecture, which form a neutral territory between others, which are more activ and structiv parts of it. This rule, which we may adopt without hesitation from them, is one of the most important in ornamental art.

Instances.

The Altar, to which the whole temple with all its structiv parts relates, the first object of high art. The tympanon of the pediments the triglyphs, the Frieses, etc. |

fol. 3r 5. a The body of a Vase is another such a neutral Ground on which the higher conceptions of art may find their applications.

The body of a Vase has the function to contain a fluid in a state of hydrostatic Equilibrium. There is a dynamic action and reaction from the Center to the surface and from there back to the Center; but this action neutralises itself, it goes not over to other parts of the whole; It is independant upon that of gravity, which the body has in common with the other parts of the vace and wants a support. The impression produced by a well Shaped body of a Vase must be that of repose and selfexistance which impression is so perfectly symbolized in the Eggs, the pumkins and othe natural vessels. Some of the last are rifled with a direction of the Channels from downwards, to upwards or Covered with Net-

fol. 3v 6. a work, ¦ like the Melons are;

Both natural structures are very speaking dynamical symbols or ornaments, and may under circumstances be employed very successfully; but the most perfect and most symbolical natural form of this kind is the Egg with its perfectly smooth surface. In most of the cases it will be convenient to adopt this natural symbol of a plain concentric surface; the neutral Ground for applications of painted or sculptured ornaments of the higher kind, which I may be allowed to call in the following phonetical ornaments.

This name has been introduced in England for this sort of ornaments by Mr. Fergusson who employed it in his work on Architecture. The Idea of applying these Phonetic ornaments must be symbolized by bands or frames, with the aid of which the representations are supposed to be fixed on the body. This we see generally observed on the Greec vases and those of Etruria. |

fol. 4r 7. a We come now to another part of the Vase to the *Stand*..

The stand has two functions the one part working upwards as the recipient of the body, the lower part working downwart, as supporting and counteracting against the weight of the whole.

These two activ forces meet together and find a common fulcrum towards the middle between the body of the Vase and the Abacus which is the representativ of the Ground.

This fulcrum or point d'appui is generally ornamented in a horizontal direction; very speaking symbols for it are such ornaments which remind us lacework or stripps; it is a band round the stand to strengthen it. But we may consider this fulcrum of the two forces which are activ in the stand also as a neutral Ground and make it a convenient place for application of Phonetical ornaments, or at least. such which have nothing to do with the structiv idea; for instance inlaid stones, Enamels etc.

The upper part of the stand is working upwards and holding. ¦

The elastic insinuating forms of vegetable nature, principally the Chalices of flowers, with their stalks have been frequently and successfully adopted as dynamical Symbols for this part of the stand.   *8. a fol. 4v*

The lower part of the stand is counteracting and supporting. The articulations of this part must be bolder than on the first, and going in the direction of Gravity; It must show a vegetable or animal life and not appear like a dead supporting mass only. In the same time it should remember the mouveability of the supported thing. The Ripps and Stripes of this part must naturally go from upwards downwards. – This part of the stand gives under certain circumstances room and opportunity for the application of non dynamic and phonetic ornaments as stones, Enamels pictures and sculptures, while this ¦ is seldom the case with the upper part of the stand. But we must in such cases have the working sceleton of the support well pronounced by dynamical ornamentation; between the rips of this structure are neutral parts for ornaments of the phonetic kind.   *9. a fol. 5r*

Most of the modern and many of the Oriental and even Romain vases fail with respect to this, while on Greec Vases we may exhibit scarcely one instance of contravention.

As to the proportions of the stands to the body and the other parts it will be difficult to give rules of general application. But I may say that the stand must be or a important part of the whole or a very subordinated one. The middle between these two parties will seldom Do well. But this only holds good to a certain limit, for when The stand bekomes the doninant part and the body of the vase the secundary one, then the whole goes over into the kingdom of implement and furniture; it becomes a tripod or a Candelabrum and is not more a Vase. ¦

As the stand is virtually the strongest part of the whole and should appear so, we must employ in ornamenting it darker colours than for the body When metal and other materials are employed for the Ensemble of a Vase, we must make the   *10. a fol. 5v*

Stand of Metal. When metals of different colours are employed we take the darkest in colour for the stand.

3°) *The Neck and the Spout.*
There is a near relation between the stand and that opper part of the Vase which is formed by the neck and the Aperture.

Here also two powers are working in an opposed sense. The Neck is the funnel for entering the liquid and for pouring it. It is a double funnel; It must be able to receive the liquid one side and to give it out other side. Two functions are joined in one, but the two functions are no negations one of the other, like on the stand, they | go gradually over in another and alternate in their services. The Greecs were well avare of this difference which they proved by the manner of ornamentation they adopted for the necks.

The height of the neck increases generally in the inversed proportion of the aperture of the vase at the root of the neck. A body with a large opening, an urn for instance has a short neck, a bottle in the contrary must have a high neck.

The fulcrum which we had at the Stand is not wanted on the neck. But for this we see an ornament, which works upwarts and downwarts and which we kan take in the two senses.

The juncture between the neck and the body is often indicated by a horizontally ornamented band or zone, or pictured or sculptured; It embraces the body on a part, where the sectional curve of the last becomes more inclined to the horizontal line. The part between this band and the neck properly speaking is kalld by the French the collet. In Greec it is the Hypotrachelion. The Hypotrachelium is not properly speaking a part of the neck, it has its own principle of ornamentation with descending. channels.

As there is a report between the stand and the Neck, in opposition to the body which is self existing and has no pendant, we do well to employ similar colouring etc for the neck as for the stand, which we see on the Greec Vases.

The spouts are a very important and interesting part of the wase. Nothing what caracterises them more individually and gives them more the appearance of an organic creature than this addition of the hand of the potter to the production of his wheel.

The Variety of the forms of the Spouts is without limitation; there exist some laws of fittness and some relations between the spouds necks and handles and between those parts together and the body which it is much easier to feel than to explain. ¦

The lips are the only parts where the interior of a composite Vase appears in connection with the Exterior. This gives the Occasion to beautiful transitions, which find their prototypes and symbols in those beautiful varieties of forms and colours which are exhibited by nature in the various shells.

12. a fol. 6v

The handles.

The handles are to the spouds what the neck is to the Stand; One is the pendant of the other. The position of the spoud with reference to the Vertical Axis of the whole and to the point of Gravity, prescribes in a certain degree the position of the handle. Proved by instances.

The Symbol of Ornamentation of the handls is that of branches, *ears* fingers, Serpants. and *hands*, (barbarians) Clasps, masks. |

In a great many of cases, the handles were without symbols and their forns the simple consequences of fittness and construction.

13 a fol. 7r

		Three Sorts of handles
animal parts, serpants.		the horizontal handle, (for *basins*, cubs, plates and other flat vases,) Serpants.
	plants.	*vertical handles* for Urns, and Vases with narrow openings.
twisted *strings*, bands with Meander ornaments and others of kind.		*pail handles* for pails. sometimes double, a

---

.

Influence of the Materials and Their Treatments upon the Development of Ceramic Types and Style

Influence of the materials and their treatements upon the development of Ceramic types and style.

1). fol. 1r

.

We are infinitely more advanced in the practical sciences and the knowledge of utilising the materials than it was the case with any other nation at any age; but if we look at the products of ancient pottery as well as other branches of art, if we see the unquestioned superiority of half barbarous nations, exspecially of India with her gergeous products of industry we must feel convinced, that we with our science have done but little.

The same mortifiing truth meets us, when we compare our productions with those of our own ancestors. In spite of all our progress in the invention of new processes, we are still inferior to them in the beauty and significance and even in the convenience of forms and ornaments.

Our best things are more or less exact recollections, others show a praiseworthy Endeavour to borrow immediately from nature, but how seldom are we successfull in these attempts.

One and not the least of the dangers of our modern artistical position is the superfluity of means or rather the want of power to employ ¦ artistically. Our industry wearies herself in vain to become misstress of her new inventions, while the great founders of art in times gone by received *their* materials prepared as they were by use during centuries and carried out a popular motive to its higher significance by treating it artistically.

Gradual progress in art and Science went hand in hand with the full mastery of what they had already gained and a full knowledge of its value. Bernhard Palissy spent half his life in seeking for an Enamel for his Earthenwares, which he at last succeeded in finding; Thus long experience taught him how to use what he found. *We* receive our new processes and new colours ready made from the Chemists and naturalists; before we had time to master the old and before we were seeking. for news.

We have many books on the applications of science on art, but we are wanting of a manual, which teaches the principles of beauty and style as applied to the new inventions of science and manufacture.

These remarks are particularly applicable to the present state of ceramic art which it remains to us considering to day from the technological point of view.

The proper materials for the Ceramic works are the plastic masses; We call plasticity, the quality of a ¦ material to take under the hand of the workman all forms, which he whishes to produce. The common clay is a very plastic material and that, which since the earliest periods was found to be the most convenient for plastical purposes and for pottery especially.

The qualities of this material and the processes and manipulations necessary for its treatement, had therefore a great part in the development of the first forms and types which are accepted in Ceramic art; Its influence reaches even boyond this, as I had already the opportunity to mention. to You.

Although the treatement of this material appears very simple, nevertheless the plainest piece of pottery passes through a great number of processes before its completion.

I shall only mention here the most important of these processes, chiefly respecting their importance for the artistical question.

1°) The first process *is the mixture of the pasts.* presupposing the knowledge of the nature of the materials.

2°) The *Façonage*, which includes a great many of special processes, all relating to the formation of the object in its general feature.

3°) The covering and glazing.

4°) The burning and all preparatory and accessory manipulations ¦ connected with this important part of the potters industry. *4) fol. 2v*

All of these processes should be known practically as well as theoretically by artists, who undertake to make paterns and designs for manufacturers of potteries, which unhappily is not always the case.

Both, practical knowledge and artistical skill and feeling are not more so frequently combined in one person as it was the case at Palissy's and Cellini's and even at Böttcher's time.

I° *On the materials*
I shall not be permitted for want of time to give here a consistent specification of the different pasts and plastic materials of old and modern pottery, and shall therefore be confined to speak about the influences of the proprieties | of the materials only at occasions, which will present themselves in the following. – *5). fol. 3r*
For | every speciality of pasts necessitates its own treatment and style. The antique urns and Etruscan Vases for instance, consisting of a very soft and slightly tempered past, are not fit for being executed in our modern China or Fayence pasts nor in metal; The Portland Vase, which is of Glass and cut with the Steel Wheel and cisel, is not to be imitated in Stoneware, | *4) fol. 2v*

This is a very selfunderstanding principle, it is only to be wondered, how seldom it has been followed by our manufacturers till at present. *5). fol. 3r*

2°) *The façonnage*
The tool, which is the most ancient and still now the most frequently used in pottery is the horizontal potters wheel. It is that, which is the most important for the development of the forms; It is among all the Engines that which leaves to the hand of the artisan all its power and artistical liberty; the most spirited

among all the mashines, which ought to be adopted as the Symbol and Sign of Industrial art.

But for this reason also it ought to be manipulated everwhere by intelligent hands and not as it often happens by an other machine, which knows only to turn after templets or what he has been drilled for himself. ¦¦¦

fol. 4v 7. We find potters wheels represented in the Tombs of Beni hassan and Thebes, from the 19th Century before Christ. So the Greeks, in attributing this invention to one of their contrymen, Thales, who lived only 1200 Years before Christ, were certainly wrong, but at least they knew to take from it the best possible advantages. It is sayd that one of their great philosophers glorified himself of being the inventor of an improved wheel.

It is stated that most of the beautiful Greec vases have been entirely finished on the potters wheel without being finished in the dry state on the lath, as it is believed by some antiquarians. for by their perfect accuracy they have the appearance of being finished that way.

The Romans had an other kind of pottery; made of the so calld terre sigillata which required an other mode of treatment. These Roman potteries are executed with the greatest care and knowledge of nearly all the means, which we actually employ in the most perfect fabrications. |

fol. 5r 8) The use of the wheel is constant in all the round pieces; the outlines, mouldings, bands and rifles are very regularly executed and generally with the assistance of the lath. and the basrelief ornaments on them are executed by three different means, 1°) by moulding 2°) by the roulette, a small wheel, like a spur, with the ornaments in hollow on it. 3) à *la barbotine.* application of a very liquid paste with a brosh, a sort of transition between painting and basrelief. –

It is a curious fact, that the beautiful Etruscan Vases are made free hand, without the aid of the potters wheels, which explains the liberty and richness of the Hetruscan outlines, as compared with the others. The Style of Hetrurian Vases find their explanation partly in this circumstance.

The Celts and Britons new the wheel and employd it frequently; Not so the Germans, who made their vases without wheels by the process calld Colombin; here it is not the piece of pottery which turns, but the potter who turns round the pot. Sometimes they employd for smaler pieces turning dishes like those of our Sculptors. The large Jarres of France, the Tinacas of Spane the Camucis of Bresilia and other vases of enormous size, are all made free hand.

fol. 5v 9. The *lath* or horizontal wheel is much more employed in our times, than it was with our masters in pottery. It is a rather dangerous instrument and has ¦ but little contributed to the progress of art; To the same cathegory belongs the treatment of the wedd clay by the way of templets, cutt out of Metall or wood, which process is calld in Frensh the *Calibrage.* By employing this instrument, we may give to the forms more sharpness in the mouldings and obtain some other advantages, which are impossible otherwise to obtain. It will be good to remember this for such cases, where the templets come in application. The forms then to be given to the paterns must show that sharpness in moulding and the undercutts, which are the domain of this mode of execution.

2° *Process*, the *Moulding*.

Moulding is one of those processes which by their negative influences are important elements for that what we understand under Style. I mean the imperfection of this process, is its power, The modeller must know and *submit* to these imperfections and remember, that a moulded piece of pottery can not, and must not appear like a piece which is turned on the wheel or on the lath. Moulded pieces ought to be not circular but oval or angular in their horizontal sections. A form of Circular Section is spoild by the slightest irregularity and ofset in the outlines, which are altogether impossible to evoid in the process of moulding.

These ofsets and regular irregularities which the moulded objects have and which are inevitable may be used as ornaments, or they may be hidden by mouldings, by projecting parts and by reliefs. The Henry II Vases which I shall mention hereafter, are beautiful instances of moulded potteries. |

The Moulded works have generally the destination of being multiplied frequently, whence the symbols and ornaments for the decoration of the moulded works must show a sort of Market type and be of more general application.   *10) fol. 6r*

It is a fact, that the moulded potteries, when exposed to fire, do more *shrink*, than turned potteries doe.

This circumstance is to be well observed by those who are modelling large Vases or other forms, intended to be executed in Terra Cotta or China; *Evaded forms large smoth surfaces*, circular sections undercutts, and *high projecting parts* and *ornaments*, all these things are of no use for large sized and moulded Terra Cotta forms. –

The last must be defectiv in proportion, if they shall look proportionate when burnt and finished.

It is impossible to pay too great attention to the first model of a work which is intended to be reproduced a great many of times. ¦

But the truth of this seems not generally to be accepted among our manufacturers, who pay very little for the models.   *10) fol. 6v*

The process of Casting Coulage.

The absorbing propriety of a mould in plaster reduces a liquid past of clay which has been versed into it, quickly in a State of dryness, sufficient to retain its form; in the same time the mould does not retain the dried past, so that it may easily be taken out after a few moments when arrived to a certain state of Dryness.

On this is based a certain process of execution in pottery which is partly employd for large pieces of earthenware, as columns, Water-pipes, Vases, partly for very thin theacups, the so calld Eggshells,.

This process was unknown to the Ancients. It has newly been executed at Sèvres with great successes. |

fol. 7r 11).   There is a number of other processes of Façonage, usual in pottery, which are calld the finishing processes, not less important for the practical study of Style as the former.

Potteries painting.

The painters art as applied on pottery has its own rights and its own restrictions or limits, which, it is certain, the ancients and owr ancestors knew better than we do. I shall not venture to enter deeper here in this difficult matter, which requires alone two or three lectures for itself: Nevertheless I can not pass without giving some general remarks, additional to some principles which I had the opportunity to mention occasionally.

It is evident that the painters art has depassed some of the limits which are prescribed by natural laws, in pottery as well as in Eameling. – The Progress of Chemistry has less advanced real art as first was expected; But this is not the fault of Chemistry, but owr own. The wide boundaries of our modern technical means are still too narrow for us, we depass these by employing colours and treatements of colouring, which even our advanced science and practice can not make standing in strong fire. The success of the China-manufacture of Sèvres in *fol. 7v 12)*   the Great Exhibition was partly owed to the strict observation ¦ of the stylistic limits of China painting and of Enameling; as well as to the moderated style of the representations, which are no copies of pictures having another destination, but which are composed for the purpose. My Friend, Mr Dieterle, who is the arts superintendant at Sèvres, has introduced only since a few Years this new and happy principle, which will soon be followed and perhaps depassed by others.

Among the finishing processes counts also the Garniture of a piece of Ceramic art, which consists in the application of outerworks, which properly do not belong to the piece; as handles, stands, spouds covers etc, which generally, with us, are made of the same material with the body of the vase, but which it very often happens to be borrowed from other branches of industrial art;

This style of mounting potteries is one which deserves the greatest attention; and more, than our manufacturers now pay to it, for it reconduces us to the old types and is therefore much less dangerous than many other means of decorating pottery ware. |

fol. 8r 13)   The mounting of precious potteries glasses or Stonewases with metal feet and Metal handles, spouds etc, has been practiced frequently in antiquity, and adopted by the Greeks after the conquest of Asia by Alexander of Macedonia;

Influence of the Materials upon Ceramic Types and Style 157

It was dominant also in the Mediaeval times and is very successfully practiced with the Chinese still now. The principles of ornamentation which I gave at the beginnig are applicable for such kinds of additional parts.

The process of guilding, silvering and platinizing also is to be mentionned among this series of operations, which belong to the façonage.

The guilding is a very convenient ornament for the parts which form the extremities of the vases, as such, which in their types or origines are not belonging to the real vase, and which may be supposed to be of Metal. It is also applicable for the junctures frameworks and bands, by which the Emblematic decorations ¦ are supposed to be fixed on the bodies of the vases. The dangerous instrument which unhappily is too often employd is here the Burnisher. The Gold, after having been applied in very fine powders, obtained by chemical dissolutions or by mechanical processes, with the aid of a brosh on the glazing of the Vase, shows a very agreable natural luster after the firing, which it would be impossible to obtain by artifices; but our manufacturers do not like this, and polish the whole with a burnisher; This was not the taste of the Greecs if they knew guilding of Earthenwares at all. But they probably followed an other system even for their Gold and Silver Vessels. The Oriental Guilding is likewise only a luster. At least, when the polisher must be employed, it will be advisable to follow the principle of the Venitian Painters for the distribution of light and shadow in their pictures, leaving the general Mass quiet, reserving for the brillancies only a small part of the tablet. The metallic luster has very happily been imitated or rather supplanted by a beautiful yellow glazing by the Arabian Potters of Spain and Sicily, | and afterwards, in their imitation by the Faenca potters. They knew very well the art of guilding, and they were no economists, but they disliked Guilding in pottery.

The mat guilding has been reintroduced in the China potteries of Sèvres by my Friend Mr. Dieterle.

fol. 8v

14) fol. 9r

———

These are the most important processes of those which belong to the façonage we should now speak of the remaining two important processes in Potters art, the glazing and the burning, which are like the others, lawgiving for the styles of potteriesworks.

The glazing followes sometimes immediately after the driing of the piece, before the firing, sometimes it is applied between two firings, one before, and the other after the glazing.

There are three different manners of glazing, the *Vernish*, The *Enamel*, and the *covver*

The first is a plombiferous transparent coating, which is very fusible, applied on common potteries and on fine fayences.

158 Lectures

fol. 9v 15.   The *Enamel* is a vitrifiable glazing, opaque and ¦ generally stanniferous. The discovery of the opaque Enamel was made probably first by the Arabian potters of Spain and Sicily in the tenth or eleventh Century. There was a Manufacture of opaque Enameld potteries at the Island of Majorka, which has given the name to this kind of potteries. – Luca dalla Robbia was the first who applied   5 this kind of Enameling on his beautiful Terracotta's but he was preceded by the Pesaro potters, who employd a white cover or as it is calld an Engobe which was laid as a lining overthe dry past, forming a white ground for a transparent glazing.

The opaque Enamel was also known to the Persian potters at an early time as   10 well as in China and Japan.

But the discovery reached its highest degree of development in the 16th Century between 1540 and 1560 under the protection of the Duc of Urbino at Faenza, Pesaro Gubbio and Tlorence. This Enamelig process is only applicable to a special sort of paste, a composition of clay and sand with a little marl, of a soft   15 texture; ¦

fol. 10r 16.   The style of the Faenza potteries, which we justly admire is a result of both, of the material and its opaque cover;

The façonnage of these wares is rapidly and rawly executed with the assistance of the Wheel, and by moulding. The Enamel is thick and wants a strong   20 firing, These circumstances, and principally the thick cover, are not favorable for the application of plastic ornaments, but most convenient for painting; It was for this reason principally, that this sort of pottery became at last the exclusive domain of pitterresque ornamentation. this we must remember and follow the same principle only where it is equally prescribed by the materials which come   25 in consideration and not for instance for stoneware or China.

The Frensch celebrated Palissy works are an other kind of Fayence, related to the first by the opacity of the Enamel, but treated in another way. The paste also is very different from the Italian ware and more like pipeware. The Style of this Class of potteries is somewhat extravagant and the apposite of the system fol-   30 lowed by the Italians.

Much more interesting for us are the fine potteries known under the name of Henry II potteries.

They belong not precisely to the opaque enameled potteries for they are simply glazed with an vitrious glazing, and should therefore find their places else-   35
fol. 10v where; but in style and in the paste they belong to the same group. ¦ with the Italian and Palissy ware.

_____ .

These potteries are beautifull instanes of an artistic exploitation of the means offered by the process of *moulding*. The paste is a very beautifull Fayence fine,   40

Influence of the Materials upon Ceramic Types and Style

without any trace of lime in it, and stands in the strongest fire; The piece first was made entirely smooth and without ornament, out of this past with the aid of moulding; This first layer was coverd with a cover or Engobe, not very thick, of the same paste, on which the ornaments, the masks and the Varnishes were applied. – . The Engobe is ornemented in a very convenient and constructive style; by impressions made and incrustations of Arabesks executed with differently coloured pasts. The whole pervades an Oriental feeling and conception, which appears also in this particular style of coating the Vase like a Wall with a coating of Stucco. |

Mr. Brogniard gives in his work a very good description of this interesting pottery of which only some 40 pieces are existing. now.

17). fol. 11r

_____ .

A third glazing process is that which technically is calld the *Cover*; *la couverte*. It is a vitrifiable and earthy substance, which smelts only at a very high temperature equal to that which is wanted for paste. It is employed for the potteries of hard paste, and principally for the *hard China.* and it consists of feldspath and quarz, sometimes with sometimes without gypse, but allways without lead or tin.

This glazing and cover, sspecial to the China potteries together with the Caoline paste, which is very short and less plastic than other pasts influences very much the Style of China pottery in general forms in sculptured and in painted ornaments. |

The beautifull white translucide nature of the China paste and its hardness are the first characteristic qualities of China ware; these qualities are agreable for the senses in themselfes and they are in the same time favorable for the application of different ornaments and principally of coloured ornaments on their surfaces. But on the other hand these applications have to meet with very great practical difficulties which the China-painter must be acquainted with; The heigh Temperatures which are wanted for the burning of the paste and for the glazing necessitates a great many of precautions for the application of forms, which shrink, and of colours, which will not stand. The China style is therefore a very complicated and confused style, one which it is very difficult to | difine. – .

18. fol. 11v

19. fol. 12r

The China pottery style like the others, has its *historical* types, independently from the consideration of the material and the services of the objects; These types are the *Chinese wares.* We will in our taste in China pottery be allways more or less followers of the Chinese; and I am excusing this direction for this special kind of industry, more than for any other. But the better will be that of following our own way and of taking for guides the nature of the materials, the idea of that which is to be represented, and the traditions of our own European

Pottery works, which, well applied, will allways afford good precedents, for instance this beautifull Chinawase, a piece which shows a good model of how to apply traditional forms to new materials and new processes. – ¦

fol. 12v

The English soft China is not so difficult, to be treated, artistically as well as that renomated old Sèvres Vases, which are made with a sort of artificial paste, nearly as hard but much more fusible than the hard China; and therefore the field for the application of beautifull contrasts of tints and of pictures.

—————— ¦

fol. 13r 20.

Some other important potteries have no glazing at all and belong to none of the above mentionned classes or Kethegories; among which are the Stonewares of great artistical interest. They are impermeable in themselves and have no glazing or only a plumbiferouz glazing obtained by the so called process of smearing.

The Flamish and Germans were the promotors of this beautiful branch of pottery, in the artistical as well as in the practical sense. It was the pottery of luxe in the 16th Century in the northern countries. – .

They are rich and beautiful in forms and show generally their natural gray ground, enriched by a quiet and sevère system of colouring, which speaks well out, that it had to sustain a strong fire. – .

We make pretty good Stonewares, but they are not equal in beauty of Style and even in beauty of materials to those ancient ¦ German *Canns*, or Cannettes.

fol. 13v

—————— .

I ought to mention here also the old Etruscan and Roman potteries, which have no glazing but only a Lustre, which we have not yet arrived to imitate nor even to know of what it is composed.

Assyrische Vasen
Bleche Embleme. – .
Grosser Reichthum an
(Aegypter wahrscheinlich Erfinder der Kunst, zu giessen.)

—————— .

Die Griechen zu Homers Zeiten kannten nur getriebene Vasen. Die Archaischen Statuen aus Metall meistens kolossal in Bronze. –

Es ist merkwürdig dass der Geschmack an getriebener Arbeit und an kolossalen Sculpturen wieder aufkam zur Zeit der grossen Blüthe Griechenlands.

On Timber Construction, and Its Influence upon the Development of Architectural Forms

the mechanical qualities of which are known.

The Chinese adopted the same anomaly for their less inclined roofs, not, as has been advanced by some writers on Architecture, in imitation of the tents of their ancestors, but rather in imitation of the old Wooden edifices of the first dynasties, which as we know from the Chinese records were piously imitated in their state of decai by the succeeding imperors; or perhaps also for a hydrodynamical reason.

Roofs curved in the other sense, were usual in Egypt at least at the time of the Greec dynasty, as we know by remains of houses and by representations on Mosaics and others.

The same form occurs still now in India. – .

The covering of the roofs is a question which I may mention occasionally here as being a very influential decorativ element of the first and of architecture in general.

Two kinds of coverings are to be distinguished, the covering in form of scales, and the coating or the covering in form of a continual skin. The last has only been used with the ancients for flat roofs. It is much more usual now, but it is less recommendable than the first for utility and durability, and also for the question of beauty; it gives little opportunity for ornamental development. | In return, the other scalelike mode of covering is more constructiv and most appropriate for ornamental purposes.

The tyle construction of the Hellenic buildings is one instance of the Genius which let the Greecs in their artistic exploitations of the simplest and most natural forms of construction.

The first ornamented tyles were made in burnt clay or terra cotta in imitation of the wooden shingles; last they were executed in Marble and ornamented outside and inside with beautifully sculptured ornaments and with colours. Sometimes they were made of bronze and guilt; guilt stone tiles and terra cotta Tiles were also usual for temples and other public and even private buildings.

They are most artfully constructed and have a layer of flat plates, which at some instances were visible inside and beautifully ornamented; (*see the drawing*)

fol. 2r

Over this were layd the tiles, one supporting the other and covering mutually their joints; and finally over the so protected joints was layd another row of Channelformed tyles, going from the board of the Roof to its ridge. The last ridge was finally protected with another highly ornamented layer of horizontal Saddletyles. The whole forms a kind of in clined wall, supported by a prominence in the large stones, which form the upper corniche; and the Channelformed | tyles have their own supports, in form of palmets, at other instances the boards of the roofs are formed. by richly ornamented Watercourses, with gutters in form of lyonheads or masks.

The Gothic style of covering is much simpler but not less ornamental. The German Churches, for instance the Cathedral of Wienna are beautiful examples of ornamented roofs with tyles, glazed in different colours, and disposed in a constructiv and drapery-like manner. This mode of roof ornamenting seems to be of oriental origine, the Orientals being the new inventors of the glazed tyles.

Some beautiful tyle Roofs, executed in imitation of the Saracenesk roofs in Spain and Sicily, are at Palermo. for instance that of the Gate of the Town, near the Royal Pallace.

The mode of ornamented tyles has been happily reintroduced by our modern English Architects. But one of the most meritorous promoters of this good ornamental principle is Mr Minton at Staffortshire.

The Chinese are very fond of decorating their roofs in this manner; Their tyle construction is very nearly that of the Ancients. |

fol. 2v

This for the general forms of the roofs as consequences of their destinations; I shell now have to consider the constructiv part of the question. –

The materials which may be employed in constructions, whatever they may be, resist in three different manners.

1°) The force is directed perpendicularly upon the length of the piece, and tends to break it transversally

(*Resistance by Rigidity.*)

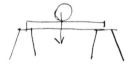

2°) They resist a force directed in the sense of the length of the piece of construction, and tending to *crush* it.

(Resistence to compression)

3°) they resist a force directed in the sense of the length tending to dilate it. (Resistence to Extension.)

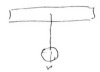

Every timber construction is composed of parts, which are affected in one or the other of these three different manners; and at many cases one part is affected by a combined action of two of the three directions of forces.

The modes of combining materials with the view of counteracting these actions and of forming a solid and durable system of resistance to them, may | be generally classified as follows.

fol. 3r

I Class.
The rigid principle is prevailing
    three subdivisions
    1°) the rigid system without any accessory system.

Examples. The Egyptian Roofs, Layers of stoneplates, which afford a multiplication of supports and explain the disposition of the Egyptian Groundplans. (See diagramm).

The Assyrian mode of protecting some parts of their edifices described by Diodorus of Sicily and explaining the narrow position of the walls. Diodor calls the Rooms which were protected by horizontal stone layers pipes, (syringes) for their allongated forms, adding that they were highly ornamented

We may consider the narrow Assyrian halls, discovered by Layard and Botta, as such pipes or Syringes.

Adoption of the same, or nearly the same principle for the Construction of the ceilings with the Greecs. The roof construction was not visible inside in the Greec temples, although formgiving for the Exterior. Greec Architecture was, as we shall see in the next lecture of a very compount caracter.

The rigid system has newly most sucessfully been adopted for bridges.

1°) the American bridges, | consisting of a treilliswork forming a rigid system supported by pillars. *Example.* the bridge over the James Rivver at Richmont in Virginia. (Diagramm).

fol. 3v

The tubular System, a rigid tube invented and successfully employed in England (Victoria bridge).

b) the Rigid system with an accessory system of compression.

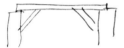

Indian roofs or ceilings, with weider distances between the pillars, than was usual in Egypt; Generally adopted for Roofs and Ceilings in the Middle Ages *in England.*

The style of inner Roof decoration which is very frequently found in England, based upon this principle is seldom at the continent;

The best instances of English Roofs of the middle Ages are collected by Raphael and Arthur Brandon in the book intitled the Open timber Roof of the middle Ages cet. London 1849.

c) the rigid system with an accessory system of extension

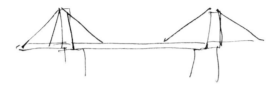

An instance of this construction is the Roman mode of covering the large theaters with Velas suspended on stringes with the aid of high Mates, towering above the highest corniches of the Walls, (Engraving.)

New adaptation of this | Construction for covering large circular rooms, like the Hippodromes at Paris, executed by Mr Hittorf. – .

II. Class.

The principle of compression is prevailing.

This Class has three subdivisions

1°) Compression without any accessory system.

The ancient tombs of the Etruscans, the Gates in the Cyclopean walls, the ceilings in the pyramids. instances of this construction of Celtic Origine in France and England. The first application of the principle which has led to the art of waulding.

The Periclean Odeon at Athens was covered with a roof, made with the mates of the Persian vessels taken in the naval Victory at Salamis, executed according to this system; the Spars acted together in one button or central piece, and were supported by a range of columns surrounding the inner Wall of the building.

2°) the compression system, with another accessory system of compression.

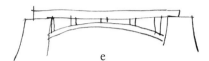

e

Examples of this in Gothic architecture and more frequently in modern times for bridges.

3°) System of compression with an accessory System of extension.

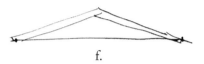

f.

This is the most important for architecture and housebuilding by its having been the types for the sacred edifices.

It seldom is employd purely but in combination with an other system, which will follow on its turn.

III. Class.

The principle of Extension is prevailing.

It has also three Subdivisions.

1°) The principle of Extension without any accessory system.

The natural Suspension bridges in Southamerica formed by wayfaring trees and plants; Suspension-Bridges in China and Tybet; The Vela of the ancients, being the types for flat ceiling decoration; The names of the single parts of the Greec temple ceilings are all borrowed from textile art, even those mighty stone beams, which we still admire on the Parthenon; and all the parts, so named, were ornamented consequently with textile ornaments. The painted ceilings at Pompea have alltogether their motives in the Vela, which they represent. This is an important remark for decorators; which will find a leader for their compositions of ceilings if they remember the Original Motive of the art of decorating flat ceilings.

fol. 4v

2° System. The Extension with another accessory system of Extension.

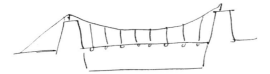

A Modern invention, applied for bridges first and best by English Ingeneers; – but still imperfect and subjected to frightfull accidents; the same also as for the artistical question.

3°) Extension with an accessory system of compression.

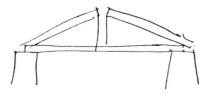

This combination contains the full development of the | *Roof* properly speaking, as an Element of outer architecture; in combination with the 3ᵈ division of the Second Class, namely the compression with an accessory system of extension.

This form is not only a decorativ one for outer architecture, it has also been at all periods and by most nations employed artistically inside;

It was introduced with the ancients, when first they undertook covering the courtyards, which formed the usual mainparts of their public edifices. Such covered courts were calld, at later times, Basilicas, which name shows that it was a construction borrowed from abroad. The inside visible roofs were only employd for rooms, which in their original Idea are supposed to be courts, all the other parts were covered with ceilings independently from the roof construction. The first example of a Greec building with an inside visible roof is the above mentionned Odeon of Pericles.

The Latin Basilicas likewise were first uncovered, then they became to be covered with large roofs, in the same style which we still see on some of the ancient Christian Basilicas at Rome, Florence and elsewhere in Italy and Sicily. Here are some instances of such ornamented roofs taken from Sicilian, Florentine and Veronese basilicas.

Some of the richly already bespoken ornamented roofs in the English Gothic style are other more recent instances of the same kind; Exemples Westminster hall, Hampton court, Windsor. an many others. They take their Ornaments from the complicated and artful construction itself, while the German and Frensh Gothic Roofs are very simple in construction, but much richer in sculptured and pictured ornamental details.

The ornamenting principle ¦ of northern woodconstruction is differing from *fol. 5v* that, which was usual in Italy by the ample application of sculptured ornaments. In the northern countries, it appears the art of cutting and Sculpturing the timbers was very old; Even Tacitus in his Germania seems to indicate that the ancient Germans sculptured their wooden huts. The Gallic woodconstructions were admired by Caesar. Here are some instances of very old wood-constructions with sculptured ornaments taken from Norvegian Churches, (9th or 10th Century) – .

In these northern countries the art of the carpenter was extending itself far beyond the roof, the carpenter was and is at some places still now the architect of the house; his art is dominant; The Gothic architecture inherited of this northern style of ornamenting the wood constructions.

We must make a distinction between two different modes of constructing wooden houses. The one is the horizontal Construction, pieces of timber disposed horizontally one over the other and joined ad their ends in a durable manner. These blockhouses are standing | on stone Substructions, which gener- *fol. 6r* ally are used for stables, and surrounded by a Gallery supported with sculptured columns; The Galleries are beautifully ornamented in a very simple manner, by cutting the boards into a regular form, which by repetition make a very harmonious Ensemble.

The Roofs are very projecting and the brackets and supports of the beams ornamented; Such were the old Colchian houses and probably those of the Etruscans, such are still now the houses of the Tyrolians and Switzer peasants; It is the usual construction also in Sueden and Norvegia.

Here is a collection of Switzer Edifices of this kind. Here is an other Example of a Tyrolian house.

The second Class of wood buildings is that with frameworks and the interstices filld up with maçonry. This kind of Woodarchitectare is most general in northern Germany, beautiful exemples of such buildings are collected by Mr Bötticher in Berlin, which we should have in our library.

To the same belong these ¦ drawings, from buildings actually existing in *fol. 6v* Normandy. – You furtherly see in this collection here the details of ornamental timber construction, systematically arranged.

I must come back here to the ancients, which also had their highly developed timber architecture; we see this on the wall pictures at Pompea which most probably were imitations of wood and metal constructions. This diagramm shows one of the slender supporters of the phantastic constructions represented on the Walls of the Greco Roman buildings.

Even the Egyptians notwithstanding their massif Stone buildings had a great predilection for Wood and Metal Construction and the same is the case

with the Assyrians, Their ceilings and tablatures of Cedar wood, are mentionned by Xenophon and other Greec authors.

We know also by the Greec and Roman authors, that the Naval architecture
of the ancients was a very ornamental one. We have very interesting and detaild
descriptions of some of them. A very remarkable application of ornamental timber construction were the Rogi or funeral piles, which are represented on some
Roman medals. The funeral piles were also objects of ornamental art with the
Greecs at least at the time of Alexander the Macedonian and his successors.

I have the Idea that the Lycian monuments, two of which are now in the
Brittish Museum, and which are made in imitation of timber construction, are
nothing | but the stone Copies of the original funeral piles of those to the mem-
ory of which the first were erected. – .

The similarity of these monuments, with the representations of funeral piles
on Roman medals is indeed very striking;

It would now be here the place of giving some details about joiners art, or
timber construction in application to doors, windows, furnitures and other
mouveable or immouveable parts of a household. But the time is nearly past, and
I am obliged to be short. The art of the joiners consist therein, to make a solid
system out of thin boards or wooden plates, and under circumstances, to execute
a leining or cover of a wall or of a part of a wall with pannels made of boards;
the art of joining boards and of employing ¦ and disposing the frameworks and
pannels, which result from the process of joining, in an artistical and ornamental manner.

The joiner's art is therefore connected with the art of wall coating and has
some of its principles in common with textile art for instance that of surface
decoration. Marquetry, a sort of Niello and Mosaico in different woods, Aegyptian and Greec Marquetries, Venitian Marquetry. Louis XV. Wood inlaid with
Brass. Louis XIV. – .

Application of Metal for Roofconstruction.
If we look at these diagramms, we observe some parts, which are affected in a
manner, which seems to require them to be of stone and metal rather than of
Wood.

for instance | for b, *the rigid system*, with an Accessory system of compression.
we may wish, for the sake of solidity, those braces of the beam made out of Stone
or Bronze or cast Iron. –

At c, in turn, we feel it necessary, to have the suspension strings here made
out of wrought metal chains or twisted wires. – .

ad d we feel this construction having more application for stones or Cast-
Metal than for wood.

this is also the case with the following system. but the System f, may best be executed entirely of metal, the compression system in Cast the extension system in wrought Metal. etc. – .

———————— .

This leads to the idea of employing for each part of the roof that material, which seemd ¦ the most proper for the mode how it is affected by forces. – – .

fol. 8v

The proper application of this simple principle is one of the most difficult questions in construction and in ornamental art;

———————— .

It is evident, that a new Material adopted for a service which was formerly done by an other one, requires many alterations in the forms and dimensions of the whole;

On the other side we are bount to observe some traditional types, if we will be artistically understood by our contemporaries. and these types are borrowed from timber-construction.

———————— .

There is an other difficulty in the artistical exploitation of the new inventions in Metal roof construction.

Metal chains or wrought

The Combined Action of the Four Preceding Branches of Industry in Architecture

I shall terminate to day this course of lectures with some remarks on the different Styles of architecture, which last we take as the result of the combining and working together of the different branches of industrial art.

1   fol. 1r

The earliest and highest symbol of civilisation and human culture is the fireplace; it is also the first and most important element and as it were the soul of every architectural work. Round it are grouped, as the protecting Negations of the three natural elements, ennemies to the flame, the three other Elements of architecture, the Roof, the Wall and the terrace. ¦

The number of possibilities how these four constituant parts can be combined in an edifice, is indefined, or at least very great; they are different according to the differences between the races and nations, to their natural genius, to their political and religious tendency and development, and chiefly to the clime and nature of the countries in which they live.

fol. 1v

Under certain circumstances it happens that one or some of these constituant parts are more developd than the others, which last take on their turn the first place in other combinations.

It wants no proof, that, where man lives in isolated groups or families, where the fireplace wants protection only against thee Injuries of the clime, where the right of property in the beginning of the national development was not existing or not easily attaked, where the form of society has grown out of a federation of single corporations families and tribes, that, I say, under circumstances similar to these | The roof must have been obtaining a very significant part in the architectural combinations, showing itself in form of a mouveable tent, or in form of a *roof* first *covering an excavation in the Ground*, and afterwards raising itself over the Ground on a basement.

The first, the mouveable tent, was and is at present the home of the Nomad tribes of herdsmen and huntsmen, the last is the original form of the houses of backwoodsmen and agricultural sattlers.

Domestic life is developping itself in these hutts, in opposition to the life in free nature full of pains and struggles. They become little worlds for themselves excluding all what does not belong to the family, with the only exception of the friendly daylight, passing through holes, left in the walls. The family and the beests take equal part of the protecting roof. They are single standing and form irregular groups in the natural scenery, mostly along the inviting banks of some rivver or brook.

In those countries of Germany, which are inhabited by a mixt population of partly German, partly Wendish Origine for instance in the Duchies of Mecklemburg and Holstein, it is easy to recognise the ¦ desendance of every place; All the German villages and towns are built in form of rows along a rivver and without walls; the slavonic sattlements in the contrary are distinguishable by concentric forms, or square or round the Marketplaces of regular disposition in their center and by fortifications. –

It is evident, that the original types and simplest expressions of this style of architecture, had to undergo with the centeries many alterations and additions according to the influences of increasing civilisation and the introduction of foreign customs; but still it maintains its principle in the countries inhabited by the descendants of the German races; The best mode of showing the differences between this principle of architecture in contrast to those, which we shall consider hereafter is to watch at the laws, how the edifices grow and develop themselfes to more artfull and complicated combinations. |

I shall follow this way here and next, for the other styles which we shall make acquantance with.

The first and simplest Roof house is consisting of one Room of an allongated rightangular form, like this diagramm shows, which gives a farmers house one

The Combined Action of the Branches of Industry in Architecture   171

of those which are general in the old saxon countries, in Westphalia, Friesland, Holstein and Schleswig, here I have a whole collection of similar buildings. The farmers houses of the Anglo Saxons in England were certainly the same. The fireplace is a low brickconstruction standing in the center without Chimney or flue, and the turfsmoke is going its way freely round the beams and rafters of the roof, coated like the walls with a brillant black coating of sutt, and ornamented with fine bakons, hams and saussages.

Before the fireplace is the thrashing floor, along it are the stables for horses, and opposite those for oxen and cows. The part of the building behind the fireplace has only at later periods been divided by glazed walls. into partitions for living rooms and bedrooms, with large Alcoves.

There is no articulation in this form, and the mode of passing from this to another more complicated form of a Saxon house is only *twofold*; the first is to juxtapose one roof to the other and to form a free and generally unsymmetrical group of roofs. ¦

Each mainpart of the building shows itself distinctly outside by having its own roof; it tells its own tale.

The same principle is observed also for more monumental edifices like Churches, showing a very pitturesque variety of roofs and being a conglomeration of parts, each of which has its own Selfexistance.

Most of the German and Scandinavian Churches built before the introduction of the pointed style, show this most happy and pitturesque arrangement and are much more congenious to our habits than the Gothic basilicas are, notwithstanding the ornaments of the last being borrowed from our northern flora, which was not the case in the same degree with the first.

(*Dahl's Churches.*).

The second mode of increasing a Saxon house is the Story construction. The first step to this is the elevation of the Stone basement, and the utilising of the suchwise gained room for the stables and cellars. Such are the Switzerhouses which I have shown in the last lecture.

This mode of construction is very | convenient for Strongholds and blockhouses, such as become necessary, when the sattlers are exposed to attacks from the part of natifs which they dislodged, or in consequence of quarrels and feuds between each other, at times when the property began to be disputed and to be the prise of the Strongest.

This is the origine of the northern towers and strongholds, a high Stone basement with a wooden house on its top. generally standing on a naturally fortified place, as for instance on the top of a rock or in a marsh. The tower is the Center of an agglomeration of other roofs, each forming a single building for itself but so combined as to form together a irregular advanced fortification round the dungeon.

fol. 3v

4   fol. 4r

The most important of these surrounding buildings is the so called pallace, (the Pfalz in German) a large hall with an open staircase being the meeting room of the guests and having, at the Grondfloor an other large room for the reception of the followers and servants of the knights. The Chapel was original-ly in the lower part of the Dungeon. Where it is a distinct building, it is of a later date than the other parts of the castle.

fol. 4v On the foot of the hill is an other circle or row of edifices ¦ the stables and barns and the houses of the clients Vassals and serfs. –

Such was the feodal Castle; very different it is true from the old Saxon Allo-dial dwellings, but allways caracterised by being an irregular conglomeration of rooms, each one protected by its own pointed and gabled roof, and taking the day-light from windows left in the outer wall and by the absence of that prin-ciple which we shall call in the following the court-style.

I should now give the descriptiond of a Northern dwelling such as it developd itself out of its original type in the towns, where the Story principle becomes naturally more important by the scarcity of room, which obliges to built one house over the other.

The English Town dwellings are alltogether of the same caracter and propar-ly speaking only the repetion of one room in three or four stories, with the necessary staircase.

fol. 5r 5. The interior arrangements of the town-dwellings in the North of Germany are much more variated | and different according to the trade or profession of the inhabitants and of more individuality. The old Merchant houses at Ham-burg for instance are aranged like the Roman houses with a covered Atrium and a skylight in the center, supported by a triple or quadruple range of columns, forming a gallery for each story and with a fine staircase on the side.

In the Southern countries of Germany and in Saxony, where the stone con-struction is prevailing, the domestic Architecture are more mingled with Italian motifs and perhaps influenced by Roman Reminiscences. The same is the case in France,

But I must conclude here this chapter in passing to an other most important principle of architecture.

This other principle of architecture, fundamentally opposed to the first, ori-ginated in the southern and more favorised countries by clime and fertility, but which wanted to be conquered from nature by a cooperating activity and great national enterprises.

fol. 5v Such lands are Egypt and Mesopotamia, wonce the seats of the earliest ¦ civilisation and inhabited by an immense population, the richest countries in the world, but now for want of the principle of centralisation of labor reconquerd by nature, and nearly what they were, first, before the foundation of the Egyptian and Assyrian political systems, brooks and deserts, inhabited by nomad Arabian and other tribes.

These countries were the native countries of strong political and religious institutions and of absolutism, the sole form of society under which such combined action of forces, which was necessary for overcoming the difficulties which nature here opposes against its exploitment. –

This explains a great part of the particularities of the Styles of Egyptian and Assyrian Architecture.

Both are, what I called before, Court styles, but very different from each other except in the community of this principle |

The prosperity of the fertil plains of Mesopotamia after having been gained from nature by a stupendous system of canalisation and of ennbankment, soon became the object of cupidity of the neighbouring tribes, against which a system of defense was necessary to be adopted,

The constructions and arrangements thus necessitated for the security of the settlements, must have been of influence upon the Style of architecture of the oldest Assyrians.

while they were successfull against their Ennemies, these influences could not alter the fundamental character of the architectural forms, which were allways allowed to develop themselves out of their natural origines.

But it was an other thing, when, as it soon happened, the same countries became the pray of conquering people of other races and of quite different political institutions.

Now an other principle grew up in the *fortified camp*, and was combined with the first.

The conquerors were sons of the desert or mountaneers, and in | their former state the inhabitants of roofed huts, similar to those described before. They built their regular camps out of hutts, and thus combined the, northern roof architecture to a new architectural Ensemble for which the first exigeancies were strength, regularity easy articulation, subordination rank and order.

The roof, as an remembrance of the earlier state of the conquering nation before the conquest, maintains its right only symbolically for the holy Edifices, while the other two elements, the terrace and the Wall, are generally prevailing.

Not the Same with the Egyptians; That difference, which prevails between a nativ and originally national Monarchy, based upon a rich and powerfull Aristocracy or priesthood one side and a System of government, which is based upon Conquest, feodality Servitude, and Military despotism, otherside the same difference shows itself in the architectural styles of the two nations. |

The prosperity and political power of a nativ dynast grows by and by, his house grows with his house-hold, partly by additional buildings, partly by a more organic development from inside of the house.

The Wealth and power of the Satrap and feodary on the other hand is a gift and donation accorded to him by his gracefull master and suddenly overcome; His house is since the beginning ready made for the position he abruptly obtained and a repetition of the Court or Pallace of his master in a smaler scale; Enlargements are only possible by the way of an outerly combination of two units of the same kind.

In the first instance is the Great a development and accomplishment of the Small; in the second instance the Small is only a copy and a crippled imitation of the Great. |

The military principle in architecture is not very favorable for the arts; but nevertheless it is of great importance for the history of the last.

It sometimes became to be gradually overpowered after having had the time of implanting some of its better elements into the conquered soil; This for instance was the case in *Assyria*; but not in *China*, which last has been arrested by a sudden torpidity, while the military principle was in its vigour.

The Chinese Architecture, is, with the exception of this Caraib Hutt, the most elementary of all. The fireplace in its higher qualification as Altar, is allmost wanting in it and in consequence there is no center of relations between the parts.

The Tartar Camp is the type of the Chinese Pallace. It remained unaltered the same, not having been fructified with the addition of older national or of foreign architectural Motivs. |

But I must leave the Chinese here and hasten to return to Egypt and Assyria, whose architectural styles have more interest for us. − .

The Egyptian Style is the only which, without being essentially disturbed by conquest or by other political revolutions, entirely grew on the nativ Ground. −

No foreigners, but a cast of inborn priests were the foundators of the Aegyptian form of Society and in consequence of Egyptian Architecture.

They judiciously observed and studied the natural and popular forms, and skillfully exploited them artistically. −

The Elementary motiv of the Egyptian temple is the Sacred Cage, the Sekos, or tabernacle, with the holy Bird or Serpant, the representative of the God of the Nomos or Village.

In the antearchitectural times the same Sacred Cage stood freely and only surrounded with a simple Wall-enclosure on the embankment of the Nile. before it stood an Altar. This Altar was the starting point and the End of the Procession of the Sacred cage, to which procession the Pilgrims of the neighbouring districts assembled. |

But the fame of the Sanctuary was increasing and now the old Enclosure prooved to be not more sufficiently large to contain the greater assembly. An

The Combined Action of the Branches of Industry in Architecture 175

additional Court or Enclosure is wanted for the meetings and the preparatory ceremonies of the holy procession. –

And while increasing by addition of new parts, some essential alterations are going on inside of the edifice.

Once, the court was covered partly with drapperies, only for the occasions at holy days; now this Ceiling made of temporary drapperies becomes a solid one executed in wood. or stone. And parts of the suchwise created tempelroom, were cutt of by walls, forming partitions for the temple treasure, for documents and other sacred stores.

The more a Sanctuary grows in reputation, the more additional courts and enclosures are wanted, the walls of the last are increasing in proportion, so that the interior wall is wholy covered by the exterior. And inside the Metamorphosis continues alike, the different parts of the building becoming gradually more and more developd and articulated. |

The first or the most interior court, which was once open but afterwards covered, in which stands the Secos and the Altar, is getting in its turn a Sanctuary, only accessible to the priests, this is the so calld *Neos*, the real temple. and the next enclosure, before the Neos, becomes to be covered, but it being much larger than the first, this operation of covering horizontally was not possible without supports or Columns.

This Court was called the Pronaos, and was the Assembly Room of the Priesthood, consisting of the descendants of the families of the nomos or district, which the first erected the Sanctuary.

The remaining thirth Court, after some time having been followed by an additional fourth one, had an similar inside development. but a more articulated one than the first three.

1°). The walls are first provisionally than solidly provided with galleries for the protection of the pious assembly against the sunshine.

2°) a Portico of higher proportions is formed traversing the whole Court Yard from the ¦ door of the Pronaos to the oppisite door leading out of the building. This portico was only covered with draperies first, and even later, as for instance at this tempel of Luxor. These columns for instance, in the large courtyard at Carnac, never had the destination of being supporters of a ceiling. They only were the pillars of a large and enormously high Canope for the protection of the Images carried on the shoulders of the priests in their religious Processions,

Some times the protecting Canope as well as the surrounding Galleries of the court, were executed in solid construction, by leaving the rest of the court Yard open; or, at other instances by covering the whole Yard, with or without a higher passage through the axe. So the principle of a covered court Yard gave rise to a great variety of combinations in Architecture, which have been typical-

fol. 10r *10* ly fixd | which were good for all periods of architecture; and whose knowledge it seems to be quite necessary for the understanding of the Aegyptian art, as well as for that of the later styles. – .

I shall not speak to day about the Egyptian architectural details and mention only that singular arrangement of the intrances, known under the name of Pylone. It was at first only single and has been only duplicated at later times. Each of them forms, like a lock of a bracelet the End and the beginnig of the Enclosure.

They are imitations of the form of the invisible Sekos or Tabernakel, and intended to be seen from far by the pilgrims and to be a tablet for inscriptions.

fol. 10v *This for Egypt.* Now let us see what became architecture in the ¦ planes of Assyria, a land similar under many reports to Egypt.

The starting point for architecture was probably the same or very similar at the two countries; but Assyria was allways the pray of foreigne Conquerors, which adopted part of the habitudes of the old inhabitants, without giving entirely up their own customs; and one period of Conquest was, after intervalls of only a few centuries, regularly followed by another; events of regular repetion like natural phenomena. The commercial and colonial relations of this country made it the meeting point of foreigners; in opposition to Egypt, which was nearly closed to foreigners.

In Egypt, the Embryo and fundamental form of the Architecture was, as we have been showing, the Pilgrims-Chappel, here in Assyria it starts from an
fol. 11r *11* other principle the fundamental form is the encampment. | a combination of the Court principle and the terrace. but The Gabled roof remains the holy Symbol of the divinity and reserved only for temples. – .

The terrace principle was the dominant in Assyria.

After what we know by Herodote and Diodoros the Pyramids of the Assyrians were nothing but Gigantic substructions of Small temples on their tops; similar to the Ionic Greec roofed tempelcellas.

But This pyramidal Terrace, with the Tempel on its top was only the last degree of still a wider system of terraces and Yards, forming the Ensemble of an Assyrian Pallace. and which was backed by the Pyramid or the family tomb of the dynasty.

The whole was standing on an immense Oblong of stone construction se-
fol. 11v cured ¦ by projecting towers, and other fortificatory details.

Inside was the first peribolus, a sort of camp with tents for the tributary hosts, guards and soldiers; On an other higher terrace then was following an other story of buildings, like the first secured by fortifications and ornamented with staircases sculptures and Enameld brick pictures. Inside was the Gymnasium and the School for the Aristocratic jouth under the instruction of their fathers.

Thirdly came an other fortified terrace with large intrance Gates, after which this whole part of the building had its name the high port, the seat of the government with the hypostyle hall for public judgements and states ceromonies.

Last came a fourth partition aequal to the first but still higher for the kings lodgings and the Serail | and over all these parts governed the Belus Pyramid with its golden tempel at the top.   *12.   fol. 12r*

The whole finally was connected with beautiful gardens, the so calld paradises, large enougf for hunting with pavillons bathhouses, fountains caskades, grotts and other Enrichments.

On Architectural Symbols

First Version

Architecture is a pure inventiv art, for it has no ready made prototypes in nature   *1.   fol. 1r*
for its forms, they are free productions of human imagination and intellect.

It would therefore, with respect to this, appear to be the freest among the different arts of design, if it was not entirely depending on the laws of nature in general and the mechanical laws of matter especially; for whatever object of architectural art we may consider, its first and original conception will have rosen from the necessity of providing for some material want, especially that of protection and shelter against injuries of clime and elements, or of other hostile powers; and as we can obtain protection of this kind only by solid combinations of matters, which nature procures, we necessarily are constrained for those constructions to the strict observance of the statical and mechanical principles

This material dependency on natural laws and conditions which remain the same everiwhere and at all times gives to the works of architecture a certain caracter of necessity and in a certain degree makes them appear to be | natural   *2.   fol. 1v*
works, but such which nature creates through the medium of reasoning and freely acting beings. The works of architecture tell the history or nature of mankind, as truly as the shells and the Coraltrees give account of the low organisations, which once inhabited them. |

The study of these works and of the history of architecture gives us evidences   *3   fol. 2r*
of the following very striking facts, relativ to the development of this art.

1°) There is no state of childhood and gradual development observable for any independant style of architecture; Every one has been born full grown out of its own principle. It was the most perfect in its first period. at least for the purity of expression of the principle which it represented, 2°) most of them died a suddenly and violent death through a great social revolution and the prevalence of a new principle.

3°) The only Greec architecture seems to make an exception whose fullest development falls not at the beginning of its existence – but this only in consequence of the final solution of the problem of reconciliating two principles which for a long time stood in opposition to each other and separed the two principal tribes of the Hellenic race. The Dorians and the Ionians. But for every one of the two Styles the Doric style and the Ionic style each considered for itself the same, what has been said at n° 1, is true, each of them had its own individual perfection at the commencement of its existence.

4°) The Greec architecture is also the only one which makes an exception to what has been said at n° 2; it had its resurrections ¦ and will never die in its principles for the reason because they are based upon nature because they are of general and absolute truth, and speak to us in a language which is comprehensible by itself in every age and at every place, that of nature alone.

I shall trie in the curse of my lectures, to give the evidences of these assertions.

As for the first of them it must be remembered, that the history of architecture does not begin at the same point with the history of house-building and Engeneering. We see nations in a state of high political and practical perfection who have no history of architecture at all.

This Caraib cottage is an instance of housebuilding which in its Ensemble as well as in its parts, answers well the purpose for which it has been constructed, and even the laws of Statics and proportion.

But each member of it works only accidentally it has not been modelled on purpose for the function it performs. The columns are trees and nothing else. The wall partitions are matts hung up between the trees.

The whole has nothing | in common with Architecture as an art and can only occupy our attention as a most elementary sheme for Roofconstruction combined with matting as the elementary sheme of vertical partitions. – .

It would appear that the next step towards architecture as an art would be the modelling and cutting natural and formless materials into regular forms, such as are prescribed by the statical and other material conditions, which each part of the whole has to perform, and their combination to a structure.

But we find no example of a Style of construction resting on this point of development, except in our days of merely practical and commercial tendency.

Of old people had probably less practical but sertainly more poetical qualifications.

They could not help giving a sort of plastical life to the blocs of marble or granite in preparing and modeling them into cylinders and prismatic beams for the use of their temples and other architectural works. ¦

They made them tell their history, the reasons for their existence, the direction and power of their action, the part which they were destined to take in the whole work, and how their relations would be to each other, they made them tell also for what destination the whole construction was made.

These tales were made in a language consisting of caracteristic forms, partly painted partly sculptured and then painted, performed on the surfaces of the naked shematical parts of the construction; and this symbolical language was found already almost perfectly prepared for this purpose by the other branches of industry, which, it must be known, had reached to a high degree of technical and even artistical perfection long before the building of monuments was thought of.

So this language was allready prepared for general understanding, so much the more, as most of the symbols employed were taken or | derived from analogies in nature and selfunderstanding for every man who has some feeling for natural forms and their dynamical significations

But there are others and some of them are very important as relating to the general feature and disposition of the monument, which are not taken from nature directly, but from reminiscencies out of the first stages of society and social establishment, or from old traditional types of construction or finally from productions of industries which in the antearchitectural times were connected with house building and house-furniture.

A third class of Symbols employed refers only to the special destination of the building, to the god of the temple or the foundator. of it.

The Greecs generally employed those symbols in a manner which wanted no special key, namely so, that they had at the same time a statical and a mystical signification ¦ for instance, they ornamented the moulding, whose statical function was symbolised generally by a wreath of leaves, with lorrel-leaves for Apollon, with wine leaves for Bacchus, with Mirth leaves for Venus. – the statical signification of the symbol remained unaltered by the special signification which was given to it.

It was not the same with the Egyptians and the Assyrians – wherefore their Symbolisme was only valeable for the duration of the social principles then prevailing – .

I shall now give a few examples of symbols used in architecture to show their meaning, their power of expression and their application.

I shall do this only here with the view of explaining the content of the foregoing, referring for a more orderly explanation of the forms, which are used | in the different styles of architecture to the comming lectures –

We shall begin with examples of traditional Symbols reminding old constructions, because they had the greatest influence on the general formation of the monuments.

———————— .

1°) *The fireplace,.*

It is the first Embryo of social settlement. Round the fireplace the first family groups assembled here it was where the first federations were made and the first religious rites were performed. The fireplace is the holy center and focus, to which, through all periods of the development of society, the different parts and divisions of an establishment relate. It is still now the center of our domestical life and in its higher significance as *altar,* that of our religious establishments. It is the symbol of civilisation and religion and an altarformed object, will be symbolised as a sacred one. By elevating a building or an object on a altar-formed pedestal or basement it signifies to be sacred. Basement of a temple. ¦

The gabled roof –

The Roof with gables is the universal Symbol for divinity and the attribute of sanctuaries, and divine dwellings. It at later times only became also the ornament of royal and imperial pallaces, when the royal or imperial persons assumed for themselves divine honours.

The only part in the Egyptian temple which is gabled is the small sekos or sanctuary which contains the holy representativ of the God; while the other parts of the building being only the outer works of the temple for the service of the priests and the worshippers as we shall see hereafter, were covered with flatt roofs.

The same is the case in Assyria where the gabled sanctuary was standing in a diminutive form on the top of the highest terrace of the Assyrian palace. –

It was after the analogy of the gabled ark of the covenant that the great temple of Salomon had a roof of the same form. |

The holy Caaba or grave of Mahomet, is gabled – It is the only temple of the Islams the Mosquees being no temples but only houses for praying and preaching.

The Gable is also the Symbol of divinity in the Greec temple, but here it appears in its fullest development, not more hidden by outworks like in Egypt, nor as a small crowning ornament on the top of an immense terracework like in Assyria; it governs its Environs, and forms the principal element of Greec architectural ordinance. –

It was in the earlier times of Greecian history defended by law to employ gabled roofs for private houses, and this ornament was only applied to other public buildings, in the supposition that they were sacred to some Divinity. It was the same with the Romans.

The Gabled roof retains part of its significance in mediaeval architecture although also employed for private buildings. – .

Some of the most important constructiv symbols in Greec architecture are taken from the most elementary composition of a wooden gabled roof.

The Greecs considered these elementary constructions as quasi natural objects and treated them in a symbolical Manner like they did with the plants and animal forms.

Another very important symbol, which takes a great part in Greecian ornament, has derived from the elementary mode of making partitions and ceilings with the aid of sails and carpets. Not only the walls and partitions but also the ceilings and suspended rafters on which the last rested, were symbolized with ornaments, reminding textile works. |

Which mode of symbolising the Idea of suspension is as significant and self-understanding as if it was taken from nature itself. In fact, it would be difficult to find any natural symbol for this idea of the same general application and value. and every other ornament on these places would have less meaning or none at all.

Symbols taken from textile art were also frequently employed for signifiing a tye, an attache of one part to another, as a symbol showing that the attached part is only an attribution and not a structural part. finally they were on their places for ornamenting the soils and floors. –

On natural symbols.

Most of the symbols, which the Greecs so frequently and so successfully employed for the decoration of the constructiv parts of their buildings, and which were the organs, expressing the functions of the first, have derived from analogical forms in nature. |

What principles did they observe in the choice and the application of such symbols?

1°) They did not transfer the Copy of the naturel object which gave the analogy to the idea which was to be represented in all its accidental details, they left out all what was not necessary for its explanation.

2°) they altered the originals in those particularities which could disturb the clearness of the meaning of the Symbol, and put parts of an organisme together which were sufficient for the expression of the Idea, finding it useless and disturbing to take the whole. Instance foot of a chair, but an foot sense upright and mouveable. Vase of Dieterle. not clear easing. Coping round. (Coffemill)

So for instance did they alter the natural colours of the objects in covering them with conventional colours, except in cases where the colour of the thing itself was the analogy which they searched for. –

since in every other case the natural colouring of the object would have permitted a double explication of its meaning.

3°) They made abstraction of the material of the originals as well as of that of the building which, it must be well understood, was entirely covered with colour. ¦ for this abstraction they were permitted to make the images of tender leaves the symbols of a conflict between two mechanical forces, and even to establish a scale for the intensity of the action of a part of construction, by the degree of curvature which the elastic line of the leave band received by the hand of the sculptor and painter. –

One of the most important symbols in architecture is the Cyma, (Κυμα, Κυματιον) which includes the ideas of ending receiving and that of a conflict between two forces.

Take (fig 1) the sheme of an upright standing leave of any sectional form taken from nature. The leave may have a strong board and a rib. in the axis. take a row of such shemes and fix or bind it with a band on the board of a free laing or uncovered part of the structure, | then this will be a Symbol for the ideas: upright standing, free finishing, A piece which has been symbolised in such manner will not otherwise be employed than as an upright standing and unburdened one.

Exemple an antique Coronation of the roof of a Doric tempel.

when we lay now a slight burden on such a row of leaves, for instance a tablet (abacus), then the bottoms of the leaves will incline a little forward (fig 3) (a) is the real, (b) the plastical formation of the leaves shown in section. (see 4 and 5) –

When more burdened, the leaves will still more bend an incline to their roots. and so on.

Sometimes two leaves were supposed standing one before the other and forming a double row; this supposition did not alter the mode of the formation of the elastic curves which resulted from their being burdened. ¦

You will understand how it was possible to establish through this simple symbol an ideal but in the same time a very accurate scale of the proportion to which a part of the construction was supposed to be burdened or to which the same was enabled, by its resisting force to oppose a burden. – It gives also the means of altering and tuning for any intended musical mode the real forces and the material proportions of the naked structural parts.

The moulding, which resulted out of the plastical ebauche of this symbol is called the Doric Cyma and although it is perhaps the most speaking among all the symbols expressing similar functions, it has not been adopted in later styles

The leaves were allways represented on this moulding as well as on every other moulding of ancient architecture in general. or painted or sculptured and then painted with conventional colours, (red blue divided with golden threads, the interstices green.) |

The curves were performed by hand after the feeling of the architect, no mechanical way of construction of the elastic Curves observable on Greec monuments is admissible.

Let us return to our burdened leaveband and see what followes, when still more burdened.

At a certain moment of increased burdening the leaves will break in the middle or at least they will take a sharp folding and the forehanging part will cover that below which is curved outward in a certain elastic line of great resisting power. This will happen so much earlier, the more the supposed leaves are burly and ripped, like the leaves of waterplants. In this state they perform that sectional form which we see on the Doric Capitals and other mouldings of the same form occurring on the Doric as well as other ancient edificies. They are or were formerly alltogether ¦ ornamented with that sort of ornament, which we very unartistically call egg and tong, whose first sheme is formed after the analogy of waterleaves, returning their broken points against the roots and forming a convex sectional curve. The Greec name for this moulding is Echinos, it symbolises a very powerfull conflict between too forces which resist each other.

It has undergone many variations in Greec and Roman times as well as in the different periods of modern architecture; most of the later modifications are made without consideration of the origine and the intended expression of the symbol.

Another variation of the same symbol. signifiing a conflict, is the so called Cyma reversa or ogee; in Greec Lesbian Cyma. It is again a double row of waterleaves of an other kind, whose broken parts form a sectional composite curve half concave and half convex, with the convex part below. The moulding which results from the plastical ebauche | of this symbol was very usual with the Ionian architects; It is much less expressiv than the two other related symbols. The leaves did never fail on mouldings of this kind as well as on the others, and where they are wanting we may be certain that they were once painted on it and have disapeared.

This at least is certainly true for Greec buildings of all periods.

Where the same curve occurs upside down, a form which we call the cyma recta, there of curse it is the plastical ebauche of an other Symbol of a quite different meaning. but, as my intention was only to day, to illustrate by some examples the mode of symbolising architectural parts, which I did, I shall not go farther and spare for the following lectures the explanation of the parts of Greec Architecture in their Ensemble and separately.

Second Version

fol. 1r   *1a*   Architecture is an art of invention that is to say, it has not, like the other arts of design, the immediate imitation of nature for its object.

Works of architecture have no prototypes in nature, they are entirely the results of imagination experience, and combining science.

This is evident not only for the general dispositions of architectural works, for their *Structural* forms in general, but also for what we use to call the *ornamental parts* of architecture, that is to say for those symbolical investments of the bare structure, with the aid of which we give higher significance, artistical expression and beauty to the last;

Architecture would therefore, with respect to this, appear to be the freest among the different arts of design if it was not entirely depending on the material laws of nature. Whatever object of architecture we may consider. (or of industrial art in general,) its first conception will have rosen from the necessity of

fol. 1v   *2a*   providing for some material want, ¦ especially that of protection and shelter against the injuries of clime elements and weather, or also against other hostile powers, and as we can obtain protection of this kind only by combinations of solid matters which nature procures, we necessarely are constrained for those constructions to the strict observance of the statical and mechanical principles, that is to say to the laws which nature itselfs observes in the creation of its various forms.

This dependency on natural laws and conditions gives to the works of architecture a certain caracter of necessity and makes them appear like natural works, but such natural works, which God created through the medium of reasoning and free acting beings.

The history of architecture forms therefore a very important part of the history of mankind. The monuments of former ages give us an account of the state of civilization and of the caracter of bygone generations, like the fossil shells and the corall-trees give us an account of the low organisations, which once in-

fol. 2r   *3a*   habited | them. – .

But in turn we can not entirely understand those remnants of architectural works without the knowledge of the history of human culture in general, and of the history of the nations, who created these works, especially. –

The general history of culture of mankind gives us evidences of the following important fact: namely that the history of architecture does not begin at the same point with the history of housebuilding and Engineering.

We see nations, in a high state of practical and political development, who have no history of architecture, whose architectural works are bare structures, occasionally enriched by furnitures, draperies, and other implements, which do not belong to the structural works themselves, but are mere applications, borrowed from the other industrial arts, like pottery, textile art, metalworking furnituremaking etc. – This is nearly the case for instance in China, and with the Arabian tribes, who live luxuriously in simple tents. ¦

This Caraib cottage is an instance of housebuilding which in its Ensemble as well as in its details answers the purpose, for which it has been constructed and the laws of statics and proportion are pretty well observed in its construction. There is even an element of ornamentation visible in the mattings, made of differently coloured natural stuffs, which they employed for their partitions. But each member of this Ensemble works only accidentally, it has not been modelled on purpose for the function it performs. The columns are trees of the bambu plant and nothing else. The wall partitions are matts hung up between these trees. The whole has nothing in common with architecture as an art and can only occupy our attention as a most elementary sheme for Roofconstruction, combined with matting as the elementary sheme for vertical partitions.

4a   fol. 2v

—————— .

The first step towords architecture as a real art would appear to be the modelling and cutting natural and formless materials into regular forms, such as are prescribed by statical | and other material conditions, which each part of the whole has to perform, and their combination to a well calculated structure.

5a   fol. 3r

But we find no exemple of a style of construction resting on this point of development, except in our own days of merely practical mechanical and commercial tendency.

Of old people had probably less practical but certainly more poetical qualifications.

They could not help giving a sort of plastical life to the blocs of wood or stone, in preparing and modelling them into prismatic beams or cylinders in order to make them fit for the construction of their temples and other architectural works.

They made them tell their history, the reason for their existence, the direction and power of their action, the role and part which ¦ they were destined to take in the whole work, and how their relations would be to each other; They made them tell also by whom and for what destination the whole construction was made.

6a   fol. 3v

These tales were made in a language consisting in certain caracteristic types, performed on the surfaces of the nacked shematical forms of the building. and this symbolical language was found already almost entirely prepared for this purpose by the other branches of industry, which, it must be known, had reached to a high degree of practical and even of artistical perfection long before the building of monuments was thought of.

So this language was already prepared for general understanding, so much the more as most of the Symbols employed were taken or derived from analogies

fol. 4r   *7a*   in nature and self understanding for every one who has some feeling | for nature and the dynamical signification of natural forms.

But among these symbols or types, are others, and some of them are very   5 important as relating to the general features of the monuments, which are by no means self understanding, being not taken from nature directly, but reminiscencies of old traditional elements of construction, or of processes, which in the antemonumental times were connected with housebuilding and housefurniture.

A third class of symbols finally refers to the special destination of the build-   10 ing or the God of the temple and the religion of the foundators. This last class of symbolical language was not intended to be of general understanding, and composed of mystical types, comprehensible only for those who were initiated into the secrets of religion. –

We observe the predominance of the two last mentionned classes of symbols   15 on the monuments of the ancient barbarian nations, as the Assyrians and Egyptians, while the Greecs generally employed such symbols in architecture which wanted no espacial key, or at least, when their symbols had a mystical sense, |

fol. 4v   *8a*   they were at the same time the expressions of some statical or mechanical function of the part of the construction, on which they were applied.   20

For instance, they took for the moulding, whose statical function, as a band or a tie, was often symbolised by a wreath of leaves, different kinds of leaves, according to the different destinations of the building, to which the moulding belonged. The lorrel leaves belonged to Apollon, wine leaves to Bacchus, Mirthleaves to Venus, etc. – The caracters of the leaves were different, but the general   25 statical significations of the symbols remained unaltered; |

fol. 5r   *9a*   It was not the same with the Assyrians and the Egyptians, whose monuments do not speak to us in a linguage which, like that of the Greek monuments, is comprehensible by itselfs in every age, and at every place, namely the linguage of nature itself. – .   30

I shall now proceed in giving some few instances of symbols used in architecture, and in showing their meaning, their power of expression and their application; I shall do this here only with the view of explaining the foregoing assertions, and refer for a more complete and systematical explanation of the symbolical forms in architecture to the comming lectures.   35

On Structural Symbols.

Most of the Symbols, which the Greecs employed for the decoration of the constructiv parts of their monuments have derived from analogical forms in nature. |

One of the most important symbols in Greec and most of the later styles,   *10a* *fol. 5v*
which more or less derived from the Greec, is the so called Cyma, (Κύμα,
Κυμάτιον)

Take a row of upright standing leaves of any sectional form; these leaves may
have strong projecting boards and ribbs in the axes. |

bind the row of leaves with a band on the board of a free laiing or uncovered   *11a* *fol. 6r*
part of structure, then this row or crown of leaves will be a Symbol of the Ideas,
upright standing and free finishing.

A piece, which has been symbolised in such a manner, will not otherwise be
on its place, than as an upright standing and unburdened part of the structure.

Examples are some coronations of the pediments of Doric temples.

When we now lay a slight burden on such a row of leaves, for instance a tablet (abacus) then the bottoms of the leaves will incline a litte forward. (fig 3).

a is the real sheme,

b is the plastical interpretation or reddition of the sheme in stone shown in
section.

When more burdened, the leaves will still more bend and incline to their
roots or to the band by which they are supposed to be fastened on the structural
part. |

You will understand how we are enabled through the aid of this simple sym-   *12a* *fol. 6v*
bol, to establish an ideal but a very speaking and accurate scale of the proportion, to which a part of the construction is supposed to be burdened or to which
the same is enabled by its resisting power, to oppose a given burden. The variation of the elastic lines formed by the bending leaves is infinite and as manni-
fold is the expression which we are enabled to give to the part on which the
ornement is applied, with respect to its statical function.

By this way we shall have the means of tuning our material proportions of
the structural parts, for any intended musical or rather architectonical mode
whatever.

Sometimes two rows of leaves are supposed standing on before the other and
forming a double order. | This supposition does not alter the mode of the forma-   *13a* *fol. 7r*
tion of the Elastic curves which result of the conflict between vital force and
gravity. These curved leaves are representatives and symbols of a conflict between two powers and applicable in architecture, where such conflicts take
place.

The moulding which results out of the plastical ebauche of this symbol is
called the Doric Cyma. Although it is perhaps the most speaking of all the
symbols expressing similar functions, it has not been adopted by later styles.

The leaves are the real shemes for the idea, the moulding is only the plastical
ebauche of the former, which never failed to be represented on the moulding, or

painted, or sculptured and then painted. This is true for every moulding of ancient architecture; Nacked mouldings without their accomplishments pepresented on them, were scarcely known with the ancients. ¦

fol. 7v   14a   The curves were performed free hand; without the assistance of compasses or other mechanical means.

Let us return now to our burdened leaveband and see what followes, when we burden it still more.

At a certain moment of increased burdening the leave will take a sharp folding in the center part, and the upper part will fall down and cover that below it, which according to the form of the leave, is curved outward in a certain elastic line of great resisting power.

This will happen so much the earlier the more the supposed leaves are burly and ripped like the leaves of waterplants. In this state they perform the sectional form of the Doric Echinos, which every where was ornamented with that sort

fol. 8r   15a   of ornament, which we commonly ¦ call Egg and tong ornanent, whose first sheme is formed as has been shown, after the Analogy of waterleaves turning their burdened points against the band or tye by which they are fastened and forming a convex sectional curve. The moulding which is the plastical ebauche of the echinos ornament is used, where a powerfull conflict between two vertical forces which resist normally each other, is to be expressed.

An other variation of the same Symbol signifiing a conflict is the so called *Cyma reversa* or ogee, in Greec Lesbian Cyma. –

It is like the Echinos, a double row of waterleaves, whose broken upper parts form a composite sectional curve, half concave and half convex with the concave part below. ¦

fol. 8v   16a   The moulding which results from the plastical ebauche of this Symbol was very usual with the Ionian Greecs. The ornamental leaves on this moulding did never fail, as is the case with the former, and where they now are wanting we may be satisfied that they formerly were painted on it and have disapeared with the time.

This at least is true for Greec buildings of all periods.

Where the same curve occurs upside down, a form which we call the Cyma recta,) there of curse it is the plastical Ebauche of an other Symbol of a quite different meaning and destination. But I shall spare the explanation of this and

fol. 9r   17a   other symbols for the following, ¦ adding only here some general remarks on the principles which the Greecs observed in the choice and application of their structural symbols.

1°) They did not transfer the copy of the natural object which suggested the analogy to the Idea which was to be represented in all its accidental details they left out all what was not necessary for its explanation.

2°) They altered the originals in those particulars which could disturb the simple meaning of the symbol, and put parts of an organism together which were sufficient for the expression of the Idea, leaving out the other parts and finding it useless and prejudicial to represent the whole thing. Instance the head and foot of an animal as a stand of a mouveable object. |

For the same reasom did they alter the natural colours of the objects, except in cases., where the colour of the thing itself was thee point of comparison and the analogy which they searched for. – since in every other case the natural colour of the object would have troubled the mere statical sense of the Symbol.

18a   fol. 9v

3°) they made abstraction of the materials of which the originals of the analogies consisted, as well as of that of the building itselfs which, it is most important to know, in Greec architecture was entirely covered with conventional colours. –

By this double abstraction they were permitted to make the images of tender | leaves the symbols of a conflict between two mechanical forces, and to establish a scale of the intensity of action between havy stones by the degree of their curvature. –

19a   fol. 10r

We shall now consider some symbols of the traditional kind, which had the greatest influence on the general formation of monuments.

1° *The fireplace.* see other paper.

On the Relation of Architectural Systems with the General Cultural Conditions

We shall not be able to understand the individual characters of the different systems of architecture, without having first gained some notice about the social, political and religious conditions of the nations or the ages, to whom the sayd architectural styles were proper.

1.   fol. 1r

For architectural monuments are in reality but the artistical expressions of the same social political and religious institutions; both, the forms of society as well as those of art, are necessary results of some absolute principle or original idea, which is older than both. |

Still less will we be able to conceive any distinct idea about specialities of a certain style of architecture, for instance of what we commonly call the ordinances and mouldings of a style, without having at least some general notions

fol. 1v

about the whole Ensemble of the monuments, to which refer these details, and of the principle of which they are the expressions.

But were are unhappily yet in a very great uncertainty just about the most essential of these general notions, not for those styles only, of whom very few remains and historical evidences are existing, but also for Greec and Roman architecture, and that of the middle ages. We do not even precisely know our own present conditions.

However this may be, I shall feel obliged to start from some such general notions in endeavouring to explain to You the different forms of architecture. |

fol. 2r   2   I give them in the hope that in every case they will give some hold to the immense material which lays before us, even if it should happen that I was mistaken in some of them.

I considered in my last lecture the fireplace as the Embryo of social forms in general and the Symbol of settlement and united volition.

The first social form aggregating itselfs round this focus of humanity is the patriarchal form of family-life, conditions similar to those which we find so poetically described in the books of the old testament and which in the same countries of Asia, to which these descriptions refer, are still existing.

In this condition of society there is yet no architecture, although it may allow some degree of progress in ornamental art and luxury, manifesting itself in the productions of pottery, woodcarving, weawing, furniture making, metalworking etc.

This patriarchal form of society suffered no essential alterations in principle by being widened into the form of confederation between the different families and tribes of the same race. ¦

fol. 2v   This political form of free confederation between tribes of the same origine and race, although it seems to be the most natural and the most reasonable, we find it everywhere overthrown by other principles availing themselves in those countries, which are the creddles of human civilization. viz. the dynastical government and absolutisme onesides, or the hierarchical government and oligarchy othersides.

We have little notice about the circumstances under which these changes took place but we see the large centers of civilization in the ancient world allready formed and modelled after one or the other of these two principles or after a mixture of both, at the very commencement of our historical knowledge.

These principles were the first, which found or received expressions in architectural art. The history of this art begins with their prevalence. The two mentionned principles were in opposition to each other although they go together in certain points, and it is the same with the edifices, which resulted out of them.

The hierarchical governments affected the maintainment of old traditions

fol. 3r   3   and the forms resulting out of this | principle of conservation would be for us comprehensible enough, if they were not partly invested and made indiscerneable for profane eyes, by that mystical symbolism which has been expressely invented by the priesterly foundators of this political system for not beeing understood by the vulgars and forming the hieratical-linguage intelligeble for the priests only,

This renders the explanation of the architectural forms of this priniple of political institutions rather douptfull and difficult for us, although the remainders of these works are more important and in better conservation than those of any other period of human development. The Egyptian monuments were resorting out of this principle as well as those of India.

The other principle the despotical one is revolutionary in its nature, and therefore the opposite to the first in its essential point; The old forms of society are entirely abolished by it and replaced by a quite different one. ¦ but the dynastical or despotical foundators of the new political form of society had less spirit of invention and were less learned than the first; which circumstance gives us more facility of seasing the meaning of the general forms as well as of the specialities of the architectural styles which resulted out of this despotical principle of society. For this reason I shall begin with the explanation of the architectural forms which are the expression of this social principle, and take as an instance the architecture of the Chinese, of the Assyrians and their followers, the Bactrans and Persians.

It is a curious fact, that all the traditions of the Asiatic nations, which since the beginning of history were governed by despots, agree together and concur in mentioning a terrible revolution of nature which destroied a great part of the ancient inhabitants of the country and drove together the survivors, who, in consequence of their common distress | felt induced to forget their old family-alliances and their inimities, in order to stop by united forces the destructiv power of the elements and to regain by great national constructions the territory which by the great revolution of nature, they had been obliged to abandon.

This aim they could not fulfill without submitting to one man's command; and subordination then became the new principle of society.

The history of China which most merveillously is ascertained to us by contemporary monuments since more than two thousand five hundert years before Christ, gives us an exemple of the influence of such an evenement on the political life of a nation. It begins with the reign of an electiv imperor, with the name Jao who was named to direct the great work of the repression of a general deluge which had overflown the whole China as far as to the western mountains near Thybet. ¦

The first minister of the Imperor and his follower on the throne was Sii; who undertook immense hydraulik works in order to give passage to the waters. an inscription executed in large letters was hewn into a Roc named Hong-Chan, where the old imperors held their annual sacrifices and thankgivings to God.

This inscription is still existing and we have true copies of it.

O our assistant and counsellor! All the great and small islands as far as to the highest points, all the couches of the beests and of the birds, all the human settlements are overflown everywhere, go at work and drive the waters back to the sea and make didges.

It is a long time that my countrimen are waiting for assistance. I am sitting on the top of the mountain Tho-lou! I have persuaded the spirits | of the people by vigilance and by activity. The heart knows no repose.

restless labour is my recreation. The mountains Hoa, Tho, Thai, Heng were the beginning and the End of my undertakings.

After having finished my work I have brought in the center of the country a Sacrifice of gratification, but my sorrows have not ended. The disturbances of natural forces have ceased, the great rivers of the South have returned to the Sea.

The dresses can now be wowen, the seads can now be prepared.

The thousand kingdoms have now peace. |

This imperor and the two after him, Chun and Ju were electiv princes after which the imperial crown had become hereditary; It is at the time of these first imperors of the Dinasty Hia that the Chinese allways look as to a golden age that of Greatniss and happiness. Every revolution in that country is made under the pretext of reviving the old insti- | tutions of the imperor Jao.

These antiquarian reactions threw allways the Chinese back to the old forms and is one of the reasons, why that land remained in the same state of culture since the deluge to our time. So for instance has the Pallace of the Imperor Jao, become the fundamental motif of Chinese architecture, in construction as well as in the general disposition. Besides, this style has been arranged and prepared for every class of the nation by invariable laws, being as old as those times of which we speak, which laws ¦ are observed rigourously till our times.

We are in the possesion of an old description of the pallace of the first imperors of China, which is the following:

Description of the Pallace of the Imperor Yao,
The roof was of Straw and clay, the rains of the summer covering it with a green coat of gras.

Behind the intrance door or triumphal port, which was laying against the South, came a large Court, where the hall of audience stood. At the opposite side of this court was a large hall, surrounded with a wall, containing the public measures and balances, for the use of the market, which was helt in this curt. Behind this hall was another court, on the northern side of which was the modest pallace of the Emperor and his family.

The hall of audience was on a terrace of three degrees, made out of | turf. There were trees planted before the doors for those who were waiting for an audience. to protect them and the Imperial servants against the sunshine.

This simple model of a pallace contains nearly all the elements of the richest and most complicated buildings of the same destination built in later times. This is true for the general dispositions of the Chinese pallaces as well as for the details of construction and singularities of that Style. So for instance we are told that the curved form of the old roof of the imperial Pallace of Jao, a consequence of its antiquity, had become hereafter the motif for that singular curved form, which is particular to the roofs in China. And the green colour of the old shingle roof of Jao's hall was the reason, why the imperial palaces are allways covered with green tiles.

A striking contrast with it makes that most splendid Pallace of the actual Imperors at Peking but still it is in imitation of the same motif.

The first and principal disposition of this Pallace is owed to the Chief of the Mongol Cublai Chan who conquered China in the 13th Century.

The description of this old Pallace is to be found in Marco Polo's travels. but his description gives us no idea of the Ensemble of it. He mentions one hall which could hold 6000 men. and says that all the walls, inside and outside were covered with Gold and ¦ ornamented with Dragons, beests, birds and other creatures.

The modern town of Peking is in itself a sort of imitation of the same principle of which we speak.

It is built in form of a rectangle and surrounded with walls. It is divided inside in two parts by a transverse wall. The eastern part is a sort of faubourg touching on the western side to the wall of the city.

The City is square formed and protected with walls and ditches.

It contains thre concentric square divisions of the same kind surrounded with walls.

The smallest square in the center is the residence of the Imperor and is called the forbidden town.

The space between this and the next circumvallation is called the imperial town It is the residence of the higher Classes of employed men |

The Space between this and the outer wall of the city is for merchants and tradespeople and is called the town simply.

The forbidden town has 4 Gates one on each side of the square.

It is impossible to give a description of the magnificence and beauty of the isoladed buildings which are symmetrically disposed and separed by richly decorated court-yards in the interior of the forbidden town. The whole Circuit is surrounded by a deep channel with parapets built of polishd Granite blocks. and between the Channel and the wall are houses which have half the height of the wall. except on the Southside where is the main intrance,

The walls are covered with glazed tiles and the way which leads to the inner courts is inlaid with mosaic parquets.

The interior is again divided into three parts separed from each other by walls the eastern, the middle and the western part. The middle part contains ¦ the imperial pallace, which is divided into a multitude of Courts, every one of which has its one destination. The lay one behind the other from the south intrane to the north gate. The eastern and western divisions, next to the Imperial Pallace, contain many Subdivisions, each of which has its own circumvallation and contains a court with pavillons and halls.

The middle pallace is an immense suit of splendid Gateways or triumphal arches, courts, galleries, Isolated buildings terraces, ballustrades, bridges etc. It contains 13 courts, at the northern end of each is standing on an elevated terrace an isolated roofed building of one or more stories and the effect is always increasing to the | last pavillon, which is called the house of the Serene heaven, and which is the highest and most splendid of all. It is the private apartment of the Emperor: There are some other buildings belonging to the private apartments behind the main buildings This is the Serail of the Imperor. Each lady has her own house surrounded with walls containing fountains cannels, flowers and shrubbs.

But on the northern Side of the private appartments begins a new suit of courts and single edifices The last, the 17th pavillon is the Van-Sie, ¦ which forms the intrance to the private imperial Garden of indescriptible beauty and richness forming a large square surrounded with a wall.

The two main divisions east and west to the Pallace contain the pallaces of the mother of the Imperor and of the princes, the privy Counsel hall, the academy of sciences, the temple of Confutsie, the library, the house of the historical society, the treasury, different tempels and Chappels, theaters; and schools for princes, imperial guorderobes, Offices for the different Courtcharges. the Chancery etc. On the Westside, of the pallace is the public Garden with large models of all the public buildings in China. A Sort of school for architects. The Garden is divided by a Serpentine Rivver with suspensionbridges and marmorbridges. On a high hill is a buddha temple in form of a bottle.

———————— |

But all these wonders are nothing as compared with the constructions, carried   9   *fol. 9r*
out by the Great Restaurator of the Chinese monarchy Tshin Chi Houang Ti,
(249 before Christ).

Before him the land had been dissolved into a great many of independant
states by the rebellion of the Satraps under the last feable imperors of the Dynasty Yu. He reconquished all the independant Vassals of the Empire and destroied the aristocratical power of the learned mandarins, who had formed a sort
of priesthood in opposition to the monarchical system.

He gave an architectonical expression to his political system in founding a
new Capital or Pallace at Hien Yong.

He made drawings of the pallaces of all the Satraps which he had vainquished and killed, and rebuild them exactly in their original forms and sizes
on the place of his new Residence, furnishing them with all their original richnesses and forcing the widows and the whole household of the deceased princes
to follow him at his pallace. These single pallaces he then united together in a
general plan of arangement, by means of ¦ galleries, walls and courts, exactly in   *fol. 9v*
the same manner as the pavillons and halls in the Pallace of Peking are united
and arranged together by the same means.

One of these courts was wide enough to contain 10000 Soldiers. –

This gigantic pallace stood on the board of a rivver and was surrounded by a
double storied colonade.

He then ordered his high functionaries to imitate his example and to build
palaces near to his own and after the same principle.

Thus he created a new capital; 70000 families were forcibly transplated from
the countries into this new residence. –

A still greater work of the same Imperor is the well known Chinese wall,
which extends | from the Gulf of the yellow sea to the eastern frontier at a   10   *fol. 10r*
length of 5 or 600 frensh lieux.

This was only the practical and architectonical execution of the Idea, laid
down by one of the first imperors, as early as 2200 Years before Christ, who divided the Empire into 6 concentric squares. The first or innerest square was the
residence of the imperor. The second was formed by the imperial dominions.
The room between the second and third square was for the high functionaries
and Vassals. Then came the so called district of peace. Hereafter that of the
penitentiaries and lastly that of the outlaws and proscribed.

Therefore the Chinese Empire is called the Empire of the Center.

One and the same Idea prevails among all these different Chinese political
and architectural forms; that ¦ of coordination and subordination of many indi-   *fol. 10v*
viduals to one great Ensemble only by outer bands. the military and despotic
system of order. There is no organic development, no growing up of an individ-

ual out of a more incomplete state of Childhood into that of adultness; E contrary, the simpler specimens of architecture are only reductions of the Imperial pallaces; The houses of the lower classes are like the pallaces are, only in a smaler scale, with reduced pavillons, reduced curts, reduced terraces and so on. –

If we look at the constructiv parts and the details of Chinese architecture, we will again encounter. the same principle. – The different elements of construction are isolated, they do not work together nor do they complete each other. Every part works for itselfs in the most primitiv and material sense. The columns are simple poles sustaining the roof; without capitals or bases. and without Entasis. |

fol. 11r   *11*   The terraces, on which these constructions stand are sometimes made out of freestones and ornamented with mouldings and rusticated work, not very much different from those usual in Greec and Roman architecture, and employed after the same principles. On these terraces only and on the parapets and staircases belonging to them, the nacked stone and the art of the Stonemaçon shows itselfs.

This is not the case with the exterior walls of the houses, which generally are of hollow brick construction, covered with Stucco, and like the columns and corniches of the roofs richly decorated with painted ornaments. The ornaments of the lower parts of the walls are real or painted imitations of bambutreillis work, which is the most original mode of making wall partitions; the higher parts of the same walls are painted in imitation of curtains and draperies, or like embroidered carpets. |

fol. 11v   The partitions inside of the houses are generally mouveable shrines or real draperies or imitations of draperies.

The outer walls have nothing to support but their own weight. They are sometimes applied on the outside of the columns; (for larger buildings) on other occasions they are placed betven two rows of columns. Thirdly they are placed behind the columns inside the house, for small pavillons.

The roof with its columns shows the same most elementary system of construction.

The covering is of slate or rather of a Stone similar to our slate or of stoned tiles of different colours; The form of these tiles and the system of covering is much like that of the Ancient Greecs and Romans.

The corniches are sometimes constructed in form of a large scotia ornamented with Dragonteeth, at other cases. but generally the sparheads are hidden by a sort of tent bordering or what the Frenschmens call a lambrequin.

The Spandrils between the columns, underneath of the frame or wall plate, are the most decorated part of the building, the right angels of the two lines being brocken by treilliswork |

The columns are standing on stone plints which project over the soils of the terraces. They are or square or polygon or round. without Entasis, basis or capitals. Sometimes they have brackets for supporting the projecting sparrheads.

The thickness of the columns stands, according to the ordinances of the architectonic policy, in proportion to their distances and their heights. A column of 2 feet diameter must have 14 feet for its hight The distances are, for large buildings, four times the diameter of a column. The size of a buildings is allways measured after the distances between the columns. So for instance they say: a house has nine distances of front and 5 distances of deepness. – ¦

Thus, in this country, the principles of beauty and proportion in art are laid down in the policeordinances and owerwatched by policemen and constablers.

Chambers describes the house of a Chinese merchant at Canton as follows,

> The plan is an oblong The groundfloor is divided by a wide passage on each side are four apartments. Each of which contains a reception room, a bad room and an office. The Elavation to the Street is covered by shops, behind which lays the staircase. The opposite elevation opens to a court, which is enriched with flowers, artificial rocks, bambu-plants, vases, fountains et.
> At the wings of the house are the kitchen, the baths and the servants-rooms.
> The upper floor is nearly a repetition of the Grondfloor. In the open Gallery is a house altar. The floors are inlaid with marble of different colours and the walls to the hight of 3 or 4 feet | are covered with bambu treillis. The rest of the wall is decorated with Silk draperies or with paperhangings The side of the hall, towards the garden is open, but the opening can be shutt up with a treilliswork of bambu. 4 Silk Lanterns are hung up at the ceiling of the hall. etc.

Such double stories are, according to other travellers, only allowed in the retired parts of the buildings. The Imperor himself is not allowed to have in the public part of his pallace, buildings of more than one stories hight.

The simple tradesmans house has only 3 distances of columns and two courts.

The professional man has 3 distances of columns and three courts allowed. The mandarin has 5 distances, the prince 7. The imperor alone has the right of giving 9 distances width to his houses.

But the distances themselfes are modified after the sizes of the columns. –
Pauthier La Chine in the univers pittoresque.
Sir William Chambers on Chinese architecture furniture etc.

——————————

fol. 13v

Assyria.

The land which shall occupy us now is that alluvial plain, watered by the Tygris
and Euphrates, which extends from the Persian Gulf to the Armenian mountains unbroken by any natural elevation of ground.

It was once, what it is to day, a marchy prairie being in the spring the common pasture ground for the neighbouring tribes but for the rest of the Year a
morass or a dry step without water.

It is the most fertile ground in the world, but its richnesses must be gained
from nature by energetic works which can only be carried out by great national
enterprises.

It was of old the great commercial Overland way between India and the
western lands.

The nation, which, as far as we know first had taken possession of this land,

fol. 14r   *14*   and gained it from | nature, belonged to the Semitic race and appears in the
oldest records as an ingenious enterprising but luxurious and somewhat overbearing nation.

Behold the land of the Chaldaeans, says Isaya, this people was not, till the
Assyrians dammed up the land for them that dwelt in the wilderniss. They
transformed the tents of the nomads into solid settlements and raised the pallaces of the land.

The first traditions of this nation are again turning about a great deluge,
which gave the first occasion for the great work of civilization.

This may be as it will, we know this land, since the beginning of history as
governed by strong military institutions founded on the right of conquest, by a
sort of military and feodal constitution. Its history is the continual repetition of
the same political event, the submission of a highly cultivated but enervated
nation by uncivilised but energetic invaders, who take possession of the land,

fol. 14v   adopt the | institutions language, dresses and habits of their new subjets and
soon fall into the same state of political and moral decline, which was the cause
of the fall of the empire which they had destroied.

There is a regular periodical regularity perceptible in the succession of such
circumstances in the history of the middle Asiatic Empires, like in natural
phaenomena.

What applies to one period, holds also good for precedent periods as well as
for those who follow.

The conquest of Assyria by the Persians is one of the later revolutions of the country, but the instructions, which Cyrus, the Persian Conqueror, gave to his satraps, gives in a few words the essence of the political form and state of the land as it was before him under other despots, and as he restored it to the advantage of his own conquering race. |

Xenophon tells us, that Cyrus, after the conquest, devided the provinces between his generals and friends, to govern the subjects, to collect the taxes and to entertain strong garrisons for the defence of the new government. *15 fol. 15r*

He recommends them to follow his exemple and to create a military nobility with their friends and the first families of the old vainquished race; to establish a rigid court ceremonial, to give regular audiences to the great proprietors of their provinces, to invite them often to large dinner- and hunting parties at their court, etc. "That, who in proportion to his revenues, he continues entertains the greatest number of vassals, horsemen and charioteers will be my best friend and the boldest support of my Empire. – . |

The camp of Cyrus, of which the same Xenophon gives a description was arranged as follows. The tents of the king with his staff were erected on an elevated Square terrace in the center. Round this highest part was another wall, covering the tents. of the friends and life guards of the king. Round this circuit was an other, formed by the cavalry men and Charotiers, then came the fourth circuit formed by the archers and the light infantry. The last circuit was formed by the Oplites and heavy infantry. – *fol. 15v*

Thus we see here like in China the military principle, that of subordination order and strength prevailing in the institutions of Assyria, and it was the same in Architecture. |

What we know about Assyrian architecture by historical traditions and the new discoveries made by Mrs Layard and Botta on the ground where once the celebrated town of Ninive stood, confirm this. *16. fol. 16r*

Herodotus on Babylone.

square

480 Stadiums each side walls unburnt brick with Asphalt. didges round. Two parts each side of the rivver Euphrates.

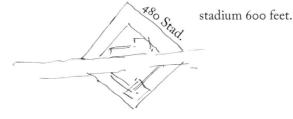

stadium 600 feet.

The walls were 400 feet high and 100 feet thick. On the tops of walls were houses containing one room only. opposite to each other, and 100 town gates gave intrance to the town the gates and frameworks of the door were of bronze.

The houses have 3 or 4 terraces and are richer in ornament than anywhere else.

The streets are regularly disposed and very wide.

Behind the outer wall was an other wall and the space between the two walls formed an open ground, occupied with the tents of the caravans, and tributary tribes comming in town to bring their contributions.

In the middle of each interior town was a royal castels. with their own circumvallations on a very elevated terrace, so that the town was entirely dominated by it – the ancient royal Castel of the Belus at the west Side contains the Sanctuary of Belus (square, two Stadiums each side). In the interior of the sanctuary is the tower of Belus square, one stadium each Side; one stadium high, 8 terraces. ¦

fol. 16v   on the top of. the highest terrae stood a tempel with the statue of Belus carried out in driven Gold.

The royal Castel was like the town itselfs, surrounded by a double wall. The Space between the walls was free and for tents. only. The second wall was circular, and enriched with glazed tiles, representing hunting parties and military scenes. (40 Stad. circumference). 100 feet hight.

Then kame a third wall forming the Acropolis or highest terrace. This wall was again richly ornamented with glazed tiles.

Three entrance doorways with Bronze pinnakels and bronze gates, which were moved with machinery. |

fol. 17r   17.   terraced gardens or paradises were connected with the Castels.

The ancients describe the most celebrated of these works, known under the name of the hanging gardens of Semiramis. as follows.

13 terraces forming a square in the groundplan, 400 feet each side; The highest terrace was about 70 feet high.

Each terrace was 32 feet wide and planted with trees and shrubbs on a floor of large slabs supported by Stone walls 22 feet thick.

On the terraces and between the plantations stood pavillons, baths and other isolated buildings, as residences for the cool Season and the nights. Besides there were fountains water basins and other enrichments.

The spaces between the stonewalls had their lights from the distances between two terraces and contained many richly ornamented and well furnished royal apartments. – .

This last circumstance is very important for us, as it gives us the explanation of the plans of Assyrian palaces which we now know by the discoveries of Mr. Layard and Botta. near Mossul on the ground of ancient Ninive. ¦

Explanation of the Groundplans.   *fol. 17v*
formerly more terraces. destroied by time.
terracework out of freestones or Cyclopic constructions.
On this ground stood other terraces with isolated buildings of which we only
know now the foundations and the lower parts of the walls. –
made out of unburnt bricks and panneld with Stone slabs or in cases only
covered with Stucco.
Explanation of these Constructions.
On columns and their uses.
On their styles as wooden and half implementary. or mouveable. |

Egypt. – .   *18.   fol. 18r*
Egyptian institutions based on an aristocratical form of society. before the monarchical power was founded by Menes the first king about. 5 or 6000 before
Christ. Priesthood in the sane time the state of the rich landsowners The whole
property in the hand of the priests and their vassals the warriors.

The greatness of a natif aristocracy grows by and by instead of the splendour
military aristocray being the result of one victory.

The difference which prevails between these two

Explanation of the Expression of Spatial Arrangements in Architecture

6 December 1854.   *fol. 18v*

I explained in the last lecture the general idea laid down in the disposition of the
Egyptian temples who appear like agglomerations round an invisible kernet.
formed by the sanctuaries of the Gods to the honour of whom they were erect-
ed. but it remains for us to show how | the Aegyptians succeeded in the same   *19   fol. 19r*
time in giving to these agglomerations of walls an organic development from
inside; and how they became, by doing so, the first inventors of almost all the
local arrangements, which we know in Architecture which still to our times are
current having only been augmented by very few new combinations since the
time of the first foundators of the Aegiptian policy religion and architecture.

In this respect the Egyptians werre superior not to the other Barbarians only
but even to the Greecs, who adapted only at later times a great part of the Egyp-

tian interior arrangements, and this only for profane buildings; the greec templestyle excluding them absolutely.

Explanation of the Expression of local arrangements.
Importance of the precinction or the fence for the history of architure. First solid buildings in the eastern countries were mere precinctions erected more for defense than for protection on terraces. The eastern countries are covered with very old constructions of this kind, which occasionally do yet the same service for which they were erected. ¦
as a shelter for the shephards and their floggs against pirates and robbers.
the protection from above is only an afterthought, and in many cases even at later times frequently only obtained by mouveable and provisional roofings, such as canevas, or wooden ceilings supported by mouveable columns.
The Different modes of covering such precinctions or fenced open courts. gave rise to the many different local arrangements which have become in their later developments as many elements of architectural.

1) The open courtyard without any part covered.

 precinctio..
presaepium
fence.

2) the wholy covered courtyard.

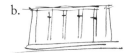 *hypostyle hall.*   οἴκημα.
cubiculum.
room.

3) the courtyard protected round the wall by colonades.

 peristyle

4) the courtyard protected only in the Center by a roof supported by colonades.

scena.

5) the combination of 4 and 5. |

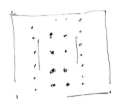

tempel of. Lucsor.

20.   *fol. 20r*

6) the basilica covered court. with lower wings.

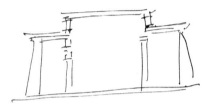

———————

Details of aegiptian style compared with the Assyrian.
   Stone Style from the Beginnig.
   Propylon. two large pillars or pyramids on each side of the door. heving the same destination as our steeples. a Signal for the pilgrims in the desert, as well as for the processions; the stations where the processions halted giving, together with the Allees of sphinxes in the same time the direction of the procession.
   large writing tables. formig a kind of lock
   Entire dependency of the parts from the ensemble no individuality even to picture and sculpture not free no action which would disturb the monumental unity.

trochleus pulley,

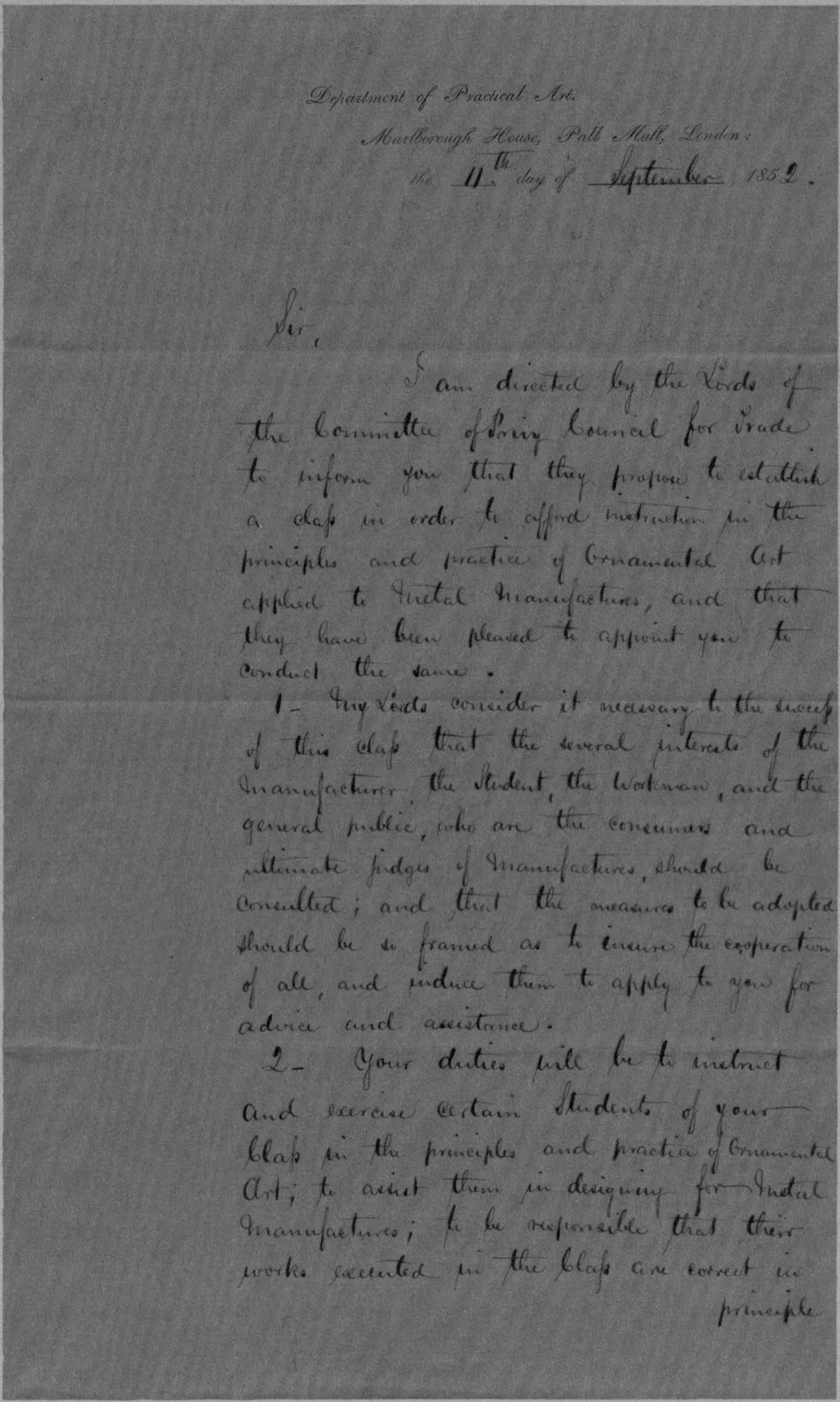

Department of Practical Art.

Marlborough House, Pall Mall, London:

the 11th day of September 1852.

Sir,

I am directed by the Lords of the Committee of Privy Council for Trade to inform you that they propose to establish a class in order to afford instruction in the principles and practice of Ornamental Art applied to Metal Manufactures, and that they have been pleased to appoint you to conduct the same.

1 — My Lords consider it necessary to the success of this Class that the several interests of the Manufacturer, the Student, the Workman, and the general public, who are the consumers and ultimate judges of Manufactures, should be consulted; and that the measures to be adopted should be so framed as to insure the co-operation of all, and induce them to apply to you for advice and assistance.

2 — Your duties will be to instruct and exercise certain Students of your Class in the principles and practice of Ornamental Art; to assist them in designing for Metal Manufactures; to be responsible that their works executed in the Class are correct in

principle

Pl. 6: Appointment letter from the Department of Practical Art, 1852 (gta, 20-K-1852-09-11)

SUPPLEMENTARY TEXTS

London
Lothar Bucher

□ *London*, 15. März. Vorgestern feierten die hier lebenden Deutschen, Flüchtlinge und Nichtflüchtlinge, den Jahrestag der Wiener Revolution, zur Erinnerung daran, dass, wenn die Hoffnungen des deutschen Volkes in den Jahren 1848 und 1849 nicht in Erfüllung gegangen, doch seine Ueberzeugungen und sein Glaube an die Zukunft durch die Erfahrung um so mehr gekräftigt sind. – Der grosse Saal der Freimaurerhalle in Queenstreet war gedrängt voll von Deutschen und von Nichtdeutschen; es fehlten natürlich nicht die edlen Frauen aller Nationen, und es erhöhten unter den Fremden die schönen Gestalten der Ungarinnen im malerischen nationalen Kostüm den künstlerischen Eindruck der geschmackvollen Anordnung. Da es allein auf die geistige Feier ankam, und da man den Unbemittelten die Theilnahme so leicht als möglich machen wollte, so war der Eintrittspreis auf eine halbe Krone (25 Sgr.) beschränkt. Das Fest selbst war öffentlich – für Alle, auch für die Spione, die man – beiläufig gesagt – hier sämmtlich kennt und zur unschuldigen Selbstergötzung oft mit den sonst auftauchenden Enthüllungen ausrüstet. Toaste fanden während des Mahles nicht statt, da der ausdrückliche Wunsch der Versammelten sich dahin erklärte, dass die Grösse und der Ernst der Feier nicht durch den Ausdruck vereinzelter Gefühle verringert werde. Als die Tafel aufgehoben, verlas der Präsidirende, General *Haug*, sechs Propositionen, deren Annahme er der Versammlung empfahl und durch welche ihr Glaube an die Zukunft, ihr Verharren in den Grundsätzen der bürgerlichen und religiösen Freiheit und ihr Abscheu vor Despotismus und Willkür ausgedrückt werden sollten. Jede der Propositionen wurde durch zwei Redner unterstützt und vertheidigt und bei der Abstimmung genehmigt. Wir heben unter den Reden, die alle ebenso leidenschaftlos und taktvoll, als der Bedeutung des Tages angemessen waren, unter den Deutschen, die von *Gottfried Kinkel* und *Arnold Ruge*, unter den andern, die von *Mazzini* und die eines Ungarn *Roley* hervor. Während Kinkel und Ruge besonders den mächtigen Einfluss der philosophischen Ideen und der Reformation auf Deutschland und ganz Europa und das Verhältniss der socialen Fragen zu denen der bürgerlichen Freiheit entwickelten, sprachen Roley und Mazzini über die Solidarität der Völker und über die Bedeutung der Völkerverbrüderung. Roley sprach ungarisch und deutsch unter dem beständigen Beifall der Anwesenden, der sich namentlich bei dem letzten lateinischen Theile seiner Rede steigerte. Mazzini's edler und einfacher Ausdruck in französischer Sprache, der um so mehr durch seinen Inhalt wirkte, als er jeden rhetorischen Schmuck vermied, musste besonders wohl denen unangenehm gewesen sein, die den grossen italienischen

Patrioten gern mit den Karrikaturzeichnungen gewisser Personen in Uebereinstimmung gebracht und gern die Erzählung von einer wilden, fanatischen Rede geliefert hätten. Mazzini's Darstellung war aber leidenschaftlos, ungeschmückt und historisch. Er zeigte, wie sich bisher die Geschichte der europäischen Knechtschaft um die beiden Angeln gedreht, welche Kaiser und Papst heissen, und dass die Bestimmung der Zukunft die sei, an die Stelle des Kaisers – das Volk zu setzen und an die Stelle des Papstes – Gott (beiläufig bemerkt, nicht "Natur" wie die Times – man weiss nicht, warum? berichten, da an jedem Ende des Saales deutlich das Wort "dieu" zu vernehmen war).

Ein Gefühl hatte wohl Jeder, der diesen Reden zuhörte – das Gefühl, dass die deutsche Emigration, die freiwillige sowohl als die unfreiwillige, nach den erduldeten Leiden und Erfahrungen, ihre Aufgabe und ihre Stellung vollkommen begreift: ihre Aufgabe, die politischen Ueberzeugungen, denen sie lebt, zu läutern und durch Studien und Thätigkeit für die Zukunft nützlich zu machen; ihre Stellung, dass sie keine Aehnlichkeit bietet mit denen, welche die Verfolgungssucht als das Arkanum der Staatsweisheit bezeichnen, und dass sie alle Verdächtigungen nur bemitleidet, welche die Demokratie mit Mord und Kommunismus d. h. Vermögenskonfiskation in Zusammenhang setzen, als ob die Demokratie nur nachzuahmen und nicht Neues zu schaffen hätte.

Ueber die Haltung und den Verlauf des Festes, an dem mindestens 6–700 Personen theilnahmen, bedarf es keiner Bemerkung, nachdem selbst das Blatt der heiligen Alliance dieselben "respektable" genannt – unbeschadet der vielfachen Entstellungen und *thatsächlichen Unrichtigkeiten*, mit denen das erwähnte Blatt seinen Bericht über den "anniversary of the German revolution" ausgestattet hat. Wir beleuchten den Spuk von der "socialen Republik", der natürlich in der "Times" nicht fehlen darf, mit der authentischen Bemerkung, dass die sehr kleine kommunistische Fraktion der Deutschen, welche hier lebt und die man auszuschliessen ganz und gar keinen Grund gehabt, ihre Betheiligung an dem Feste ausdrücklich *abgelehnt* hatte. Es fehlten ebenso die Kommunisten der andern Nationen.

Vielleicht kommt die Notiz nicht zu spät, dass die Cirkular-Depesche vom 11. Februar aus der Feder des früheren Predigers, jetzigen Geheimen Legationsraths Abeken, herrührt. Welchen Eindruck die Politik, die Moral und der Styl dieses Dokumentes hier gemacht haben, braucht nicht gesagt zu werden. Besonderes Interesse erregt es, dass England für "einen wohl zu gebrauchenden Bundesgenossen" erklärt wird. – Unser Landsmann, Professor *Semper*, steht im Begriff, hier eine *Bau-Akademie* zu gründen. Semper ist einer der wenigen Künstler, der die Gunst der Grossen nicht suchte, sondern sich von ihr suchen liess und ihr den Rücken wandte, als das Vaterland rief. Der Professor an der Akademie der Künste in Dresden, Direktor der königl. Bauschule, Erbauer des neuen Theaters, des Museums, der Synagoge, des Maternihospitals daselbst, warf im Mai 1849 Zirkel und Massstab bei Seite und errichtete – Barrikaden. Nachdem Dresden gerettet war, wandte er seinen Sinn dem demokratischen Amerika zu und hatte bereits das Schiff betreten, als das hiesige Gesundheitsamt ihn einlud, den Bau der Leichenhäuser zu übernehmen, die in der neuen Begräbnissbill vorgeschrieben sind. Die Ausführung dieser Gebäude ist aber durch umfassende Expropriationen verzögert. Semper benutzt diese unfreiwillige Musse zur Einrichtung einer Bauschule, von der sich unter seiner Leitung und am hiesigen Platze die besten Resultate versprechen lassen. Eleven vom Festlande bietet sie, neben der Gelegenheit die Sprache zu erlernen, den ausserordentlichen Vortheil, die industriellen Bauwerke Englands an Ort und Stelle zu studiren. Semper ist bereit, den Prospektus mitzutheilen; seine Wohnung 27 University-street, London. –

Die parlamentarischen Zustände werden trostlos. Vorgestern, wo die Bill wegen Zulassung der Juden eingebracht werden sollte, bestellt sich Lord John Russell selbst, wie man behauptet, ein unbeschlussfähiges Haus. Gestern äussert er eine Todesahnung wegen Baillies (nicht Ashley's, wie es in unserm gestrigen Berichte heisst) Tadelsvotum über Ceylon. Sehr gut bemerkt die "Times": er hätte am Budget, an der Protektion und an der Wahlreform sterben können; weshalb er sich Ceylon, die ferne Insel in der Südsee, als Sterbeplätzchen aussuche und noch im letzten Moment seinen Namen an den blutigen Namen Torrington knüpfen wolle, sei nicht zu begreifen.

German Studio for Architects and Engineers in London
Richard Wagner

348 Wenn der Sinn für Schönheit auch in der Architektur uns zunächst durch das Studium der Antike geweckt worden ist, so haben sich die Bauwerke, die wir in der Nachahmung der Antike konstruirten, doch nie in eine warme Wechselbeziehung zu unserm Leben und dessen natürlichen Bedürfnissen stellen können. *Semper* klärte uns, als er vor 17 Jahren aus Griechenland zurückkehrte, in seiner berühmten Schrift: "Bemerkungen über vielfarbige Architektur und Skulptur bei den Alten. Altona 1834" – über die wesentlichen Gründe jener Erscheinung auf, indem er an den hellenischen Kunstwerken selbst ein organisches Hervorgehen derselben aus den anfangs allernächsten Bedürfnissen einer Häuslichkeit und dann einer Oeffentlichkeit nachwies, wie sie bei uns eben

nicht vorhanden sind. Durch eine unmotivirte Nachahmung der Antike ist uns-
re moderne Baukunst in den Zwiespalt gerathen, dass wir der Schönheit nur in
unnützen Bauwerken – wie sie z. B. auf Anordnung des Königs Ludwig von
Baiern entstanden sind – huldigen zu können, in nützlichen dagegen sie ganz
ausser Acht lassen zu müssen glauben. Vermöge seiner gesunden künstlerischen
Anschauung erkennt nun Semper da, wo sich unser häusliches wie öffentliches
Leben am konsequentesten aus unsern Bedürfnissen entwickelt und zu so umfassender Fähigkeit ausgebildet hat wie in England, auch den gedeihlichsten
Boden für die Ausbildung einer schönen Architektur in einem heimischen und
innig verständlichen Sinne, weil dort unserm natürlichen Bedürfnisse bereits in
so zweckmässiger Fülle genügt wird, dass diese Fülle sich ganz von selbst zum
Bedürfnisse nach Schönheit gestaltet. – Wer die geniale Produktivität Sempers
aus seinen berühmten Bauwerken, namentlich dem Schauspielhause und dem –
gegenwärtig seiner Vollendung nahen – Museum zu Dresden, kennt, – wer den
ganzen Bildungsgang dieses reich begabten und hocherfahrenen Künstlers von
seinen Studien auf den Trümmern Athens an bis zu seinem Erfassen des praktischen Sinnes der Engländer beobachtet hat, der wird bezeugen müssen, dass
jungen Architekten, welche auf irgend einer Bauschule ihr theoretisches Studium beendet haben und zu ihrer praktischen Ausbildung weiter zu schreiten
gedenken, kein willkommeneres Anerbieten gemacht werden kann, als das vor-
anstehende meines Freundes, den ich mich glücklich schätze, auf das wärmste
hiermit auch meinen schweizerischen Gastfreunden empfehlen zu dürfen, und
über dessen Unternehmung Näheres mitzutheilen ich jederzeit bereit bin.

Zürich, 25. März 1851.   *Richard Wagner.*

Submissions for the Great Exhibition
Franz Georg Stammann

Hamburg, den 22sten März

* Der Architect, Professor Semper aus Dresden, welcher sich gegenwärtig in
London aufhält, ist im Auftrage der Executiv-Commission im Ausstellungsgebäude mit dem Arrangement der englischen Coloniewaaren beschäftigt und
hat unter Anderm auch für Schweden die Aufstellung der von dort eingesandten Sachen zu besorgen. – Es wird noch jetzt für manche deutsche Behörde,
Comité oder Privaten von Interesse sein, zu erfahren, dass sich dieselben in

London an diesen bekannten, zuverlässigen Landsmann wenden können, der im Gebäude selbst schon mit Arrangements beschäftigt ist, daselbst seinen steten Aufenthalt hat, die dortigen Behörden und Arbeiter kennt und also bei der Einrichtung, Decorirung &c. sowohl Einzelnen, als ganzen Landestheilen, Städten, Provinzialabtheilungen durch seine Befähigung und seine Bekanntschaften von wesentlichem Nutzen sein kann.

List of Books for Customs
Gottfried Semper

First Version

fol. 5r

93) On Dorways by Donaldson, English, publ at London, dutyfree 1. 4°

94) Greec Dictionary by Schneider 2 Vol. 4°

95) Latin   d°   by Scheller 3 Vol. 8.°

96) d°   d°   by Weber. 3 Vol. 8.°

97) Some numbers of the R. Institute of Br. Architects

98) Alderson on Steam Engineering, (dutyfree)

99) The Analysis given by Fisher 8°

100) Vieth Mathem. in their application to art and architecture. One Volume is wanting 3 Vol. 8°

101) Thibauts Analysis 1 V. 8°

102) The same pure Mathematiks 1 – 8°

103) Eulers differential Calculus.

104) Hirschs Algebra with Sax's Solutions. 2 Vol. 8°

105) Methematiks of Lorenz. 1 Vol 8.

106) Physiks by Mayer 1 Vol. 8°

107) Logarithmik tables by Vega. 1 Vol. 4°

108) Log. tables by Lalande 1 Vol. 12°

109.) Mathem. by Bezout. 7 Vol. 8°

110) Cours de Mathematiques pures by Francoeur. 2 Vol.

111) Heerens Historical works. 3 Vol. 8°

112) Volney's Travels, (German) one Vol. 8°

113) History of Poelitz. 8.

114) History of Mexico. 1 Vol. 8.

115) The old World by Bürck. 1 Vol 8.

116) Universal History by Rotteck. 2 Vol. 8.

List of Books for Customs

118) Nardi Storia di Firenze 1 Vol 4°
119) Marco Polo by Bürck. 1 Vol. 8° |
120. Homeri Ilias and Odyssea, and Prolegomena by Wolff. 5 Vol. 8. *fol. 5v*
121 Euripidis Tragoediae 3 Vol. 12°
122. Pindari Carmina 1 Vol. 8.
123 Aristophanis Opera 2 Vol. 8.
124) Herodotus 3 Vol. Tauchnitz 8.
125. Sophocles. 1 Vol. 12°
126. Aeschylus. 2 Vol. 12°
127. Plinius, letters, 1 Vol. 12°
128. Tacitus ed. Ernesti 2 Vol. 8°
129. Taciti Germania 1 Vol. 8°
130. Cicero by Ernesti. 5. V. 8.°
131. Cicero de amicitia 8°
132. Sueton 1 Vol. 8°
133. Persius & Juvenalis 1 Vol. 8°
134. Horatius 1 Vol. 8°
135. Livius not compl. (Tauchnitz Ed.) 12°
136. Virgilius 1 Vol.
137. Cornelius Nepos 1 Vol.
138. Olaus Magnus. History 1 Vol. 12°
139. Eginhartus. 1 Vol. 12°
140. Vellejus Paterculus 1 Vol. 8°
141. Seneca 5 Vol. 8°
142. Julius Caesar. 1 Vol. 8°
143. Catullus, Tibullus, Propertius 1 Vol. 12°
144. Justinus 1 Vol. 8°
145. Plautus 1 Vol. 8.
146. Sallustius 1 Vol. 8°
147. Vigerus eddt. Hermannus 1 Vol. 8.
148. Seneca Hercules furens 1 Vol. 8.
149. Homerus and Hesiodus in German, 3 Vol. 8°
150. Bröders Latin Grammar. 1 Vol.
151. Grotefend's d° Grammar 1 Vol.
152. Köppen's notes to Homerus. 3 Vol.
153. Orationes Salustii Livii & other. 1 Vol. 12°
154. Artis Latine Scribendi principia 1 Vol.
155. Wolf's Philosophy 1 Vol.

Second Version

fol. 1r

I.) Books on Art and Architecture, Engineering History of Art, Sciences applied to art and architecture.

1.	Magazin for Engineers by Böhme German 12 Vol. 8°	
2).	Eytelweins Hydrotechnics, German.	1 Vol. 4°
3)	Manuel of Hydrostatics by the same.	1 Vol. 8°
4)	Antiquities of Athens by Cckerell and other, in German. Text only	1 Vol. 8°
5)	Manuel of Mechanics by Eytelwein	1 Vol. 8°
6)	The Engeneer by Weissbach, German	1 Vol. 8°
7)	On Roofs by Linke, German	1 Vol. 8°
8)	Rondelets Art of building, German. Text only	5 Vol. 8°
9)	Eytelweins Statics, German.	3 Vol 8
10)	Milizia's Architecture 1ˢᵗ & 3ᵈ part	2 Vol 8°
11)	Burg's geometrical Drawing Text only	1 Vol. 8°
12)	Gärtner on Private dwellings German	1 Vol. 8°
13)	Lessing on beaty in Art, (Laocoon) German.	1 Vol. 8°
14)	Müller' Archaeologia of Art. Text only.	2. Vol. 8°
15)	Hirt's History of Architecture.	3 Vol. 4°
16)	Rumohr's Italian Researches. only I and III Part, second wanting	2 Vol. 8°
17)	Knochenhauer – On Vaults and their Statiks	1 Vol. 8°
18)	Meissner's on heating with hot air.	1 Vol. 8°
19)	Müllers History of the Hellenic tribes	5. Vol. 8° ¦

fol. 1v

20)	On the Art of Wallpainting with the Ancients by Wichmann.	1 Vol. 8°
21)	Weisbachs Manual of Engineering and Mechaniks German.	5 Vol. 8°
22)	Vademecum, (Manual) for Civil-Engeneers and architects.	1 Vol 8.
23)	Gilly's Manuel for rural architecture, Text only	2 Vol. 8°
24)	The Greec Theaters by Geppert.	1 Vol. 8°
25)	Aesthetiks of the Architecture by Wagner – Text only.	1 V. 8.
26)	Heeren's Ideas on the State of the arts, sciences, commerce etc with the old Nations. One Volume is wanting	5. V. 8.
27):	Humbolds Cosmus. and letters on the same	3 Vol 8°
28)	Wolfs Aesthetiks of Arch.	1 V. 8.
29)	On Perspective by Hetsch	1 V. 8.
30)	Archaeologia by Schaaf	2 Vol. 8.
31)	Heine's Architecture.	1 v. 4°

32)	The same Architectural laws	1 – 8.	
33)	The same on the same	1 – 8.	
38)	Reimers Tables.	1 – 12.	
29)	Böttigers, Archeologia	3 – 8.	
30)	On Theaters. by Weinbrenner	1 – 8.	
31)	On fascineering by Eytelwein	1 – 8	
32)	Theater at Münich	1 – 8.	
33)	Models of old German Architecture	1 – 4°	
34)	Cavellari Historical development of the arts	1 – 8.	
35)	Normand the Orders of Architecture	1 – fol.	
36)	Art of the Carpenter by Romberg Text only	1 – fol.		

88)	Magazin for Italian Art. by Jagemann	1 V. 8.	*fol. 2r*
89)	Lexicon of the artists (Künstlerlexicon) by Nagler	15 Cahiers 8°	
90)	The Railway of the lower Danube by Kreuter. (Several Copies)	4°	
91)	Instruction for Engineers by Thielke.	8°	
92)	On art and artists by Koch	12.	
93)	On Architecture by Wolff	8°	
94)	Old-Christian Art at Ravenna by Quast. German	1 – fol.	
95)	Stereotomia by Strobel	fol.	
96)	Perspective by Quaglio	1 Cah. fol.	
97)	Carpenters art by Mitterer	1 Cah. fol.	
98)	Monuments of German Style.		
99)	A Lot of Guide books and Catalogues, very usefull for history of art. in different Linguages.		
100)	A Portfolio with manuscripts and small Pamphlets on art and history of art, mathematics etc.		
101)	Description of Rome by Carlo Fea.	3. Vol. 8°	
102)	Annals and Bulletins of the Roman Institute of archeological Correspondence. without the Engravings – Some numbers only.		
103)	The Florentine Observer, giving descriptions of objects of art and monuments	8 Vol. 8	
104)	The Cathedral of Florence	1 V. 4°	
105)	Thibauts Perspective, Text only	4°	
106)	L'art de bâtir 2. Vol. by Briseux.		
107)	History of Frensh Architecture by Ramée	1 Cah. 8°	
108)	Thiersch on Greece.	2 Cah. 8°	*fol. 2v*
109)	Vallée Traité de la Science du Dessin deux Volumes.	4°	
110)	Memoires sur le pont de Jarnac. par Quénot.	4°	

111)	Traité des couleurs pour la peinture en Email.	8°	
112)	Le Vignole de Poche by Thierry.	12°	
113)	Traité de Geometrie descriptive by Hachette 1 Vol.	4°	
114)	Monumens Antiques by Millin.		
115)	Nouvel Itineraire (for builders) 2° Volume only	8°	5
116)	Dictionnaire d'Architecture par Vagnat.	8°	
117,)	La Science de l'ingenieur par Delaistre 2 Vol.	4°	
118)	La science des Ingenieurs par Belidor. 1 Vol.	4°	
119)	Architectonographie des Theatres *Text only* by Kaufmann.	8°	
120)	Perspective by Isabeau. 1 vol.	8.	10
121)	Some numbers of the Yournal: Revue Generale d'architecture bound together 1 Vol.	4°	
122)	Lettres d'un antiquaire à un Artiste. by Letronne. 1. vol	8°	
123)	Kugler's Polychromy.	4°	
124)	Semper's Polychromy, several Copies.	8°	15
125)	Nouvelle architecture pratique by Michet. second volume. only.		
126)	Etudes de Constructions by Bruères one Vol. only.	Fol.	
127)	On colours by Chevreuil. German.	12°	
128)	Annals of Antiq. Society at Dresden 1 Cahier only. Stieglitz's Architecture 2 Vol.	8° |	20

fol. 3r

129)	Description of Amsterdam by Zesel	4°	
130)	German Antiquities by Wagner.	8°	
131)	On Mineral and vegetable forms by Metzger.	8°	
132)	Plinii Historia. one Vol.	4°	
133)	Vitruvius by. Barbarus.	4°	25
134)	Pausanias, Stereotype.	3 Vol. 12°	
135)	Greec Dictionary by Schneider	2 Vol. 4°	
136)	Lat. dto by Scheller	3 vol. 8°	
	do do by Weber	2 Vol. 8°	
137).	a Collection of the most approved doorways by Donaldson. (dutifree.)	4°	30
138)	Alderson on Steam Engineering. do. (dutyfree.)	8°	
139)	Some numbers of the R. Institute of Britt. Architects.		
140)	On Analysis by Fischer	8°	
141)	Vieth's Mathematics in their applications to Art etc. One Volume is wanting. 3 Vol.	8°	35
142)	Thibaut's Analysis. and pure Mathematics.	2 Vol. 8°	
143)	Euler's differential Calculus	4 Vol. 8.	
144)	Hirsch's Algebra with Sachs Solutions of the problems given by Hirsch	2 Vol. 8°	40
145).	Mathematics by Lorenz.	8°	

146)	Physiks by Mayer	8°
147)	Logarithmes by Vega.	4°
148)	Logarithmes by Lalande	12°
149)	Mathematics by Bezout. 7 Vol.	8°
150)	Cours de Math. pures by Francoeur. 2 Vol.	8°

II. *History, Archeology, Statistics* Travels.

1)	Heeren's Statistiks.	8.
2)	Volney's Travels, (German) 2 Vol.	8.
3)	Heeren's Old History	8°
4)	Plutarchs Biographies (German) 10 Vol	8°
5)	History by Pölitz (German) 1 vol.	8
7)	Heeren's System of the Eur. Empires	8°
8)	History of Mexico.	
9)	The old world by Bürck.	8°
10)	Universal History by Rotteck. 2 Vol	8.
×11)	The war of 1809, by Valentini. 1 v.	8°
×12)	On Saxe.	8°
×13)	The battle of Leipzig 1 Cahier.	4°
×14)	History of the Fr. Revolution. 3 Vol.	4°
×15)	History of the Rev. of 1830.	12.
×16)	Histoire de Napoleon par Ségur. first. Vol. only.	12.
17)	Nardi Storia di Firenze.	4°
18)	Marco Polo translated by Burk.	8°

fol. 3v

III. *Old. Classics. and ancient linguages.*

Homeri Ilias and Odyssea. 5 Vol.	8.
Euripidis Tragödiae 3 Vol.	12.
Pindari Carmina 1 Vol.	8.
Aristophanis opera. 2 Vol.	8.
Herodotus. 3 Vol. Tauchnitz. not complete.	8.
Sophocles. 1 Vol.	12.
Aeschylus 2 vol.	8.
Plinius, Historiae naturalis libri. 1 Vol.	8°
Tacitus, 2 Vol	8°
Taciti Germania 1 Vol.	8°

Cicero with clavis Ciceroniana by Ernesti	5 Vol. 8°	
Cicero de amicitia	1 – 8°	
Sueton 1 Vol.	8°	
Persius and Juvenalis 1 Vol.	8°	
Horatius 1 Vol	8°	5
Livius. not complete (Tauchnitz Edition)	8°	
Virgilius 1 vol.	8°	
Cornelius Nepos	12°	
Olaus Magnus, Historiae. 1 Vol	8°	
Vellejus Paterculus 1 Vol.	8°	10
Catullus 1 vol.	8.	
Seneca 5 Vol.	8°	
Julius Caesar 1 Vol.	8°	
Plinius Secundus, Epistolae 1 Vol.	12°	
Justinus – historiae 1 Vol.	8°	15
Plautus 1 Vol.	12°	
Sallustius 1 Vol.	8°	
Vigerus eddt Hermannus.	8°	
Seneca Hercules Furens.	8°	
Homer and Hesiod in German. 3 Vol.	8.	20
Bröders Latin, Grammar. 1 vol.	8.	
Grotefends dito. 1 Vol.	8	
Köppens Notes to Homer 3 Vol.	8.	
Orationes Sallustii Livii Taciti etc. 1 Vol.	8.	
Apparatus Eloquentiae 1 Vol.	8.	25
Artis latine scribendi Principia 1 Vol.	8.	
Institutiones Philosoph by Wolf. 1 Vol.	8.	
Introductiones in lingua latina 1 Vol.	8.	
Buttman's Lexilogus one Volume.	8°	
Observationes Livianae.	8°	30
Eschenburg, Classic litterature 1 Vol.	8°	

fol. 4r

Modern linguages and miscellaneous books.

24 Copies of Semper's Polychromy.
6 Copies of. Kreuter's Pamphlet on Railways in Ungaria.
Italian Dictionary by Jagemann
 d° d°

35

Synonymics by Quandt. – 1 Vol. 8°
Fick's English-German Grammar. 1 Vol. 8°
Dante's divina Comedia 3 parts. Italian 3 Vol 8.°
Detmold's Sketches German
5 Molières Comédies, (Frensch) 2 Vol. 12°
Bellona a Military Yournal 36 fascicles.
Ben Johnson translated by Baudissin 2 Vol. 8°
Topiks or the Art to invent. 1 Vol. 12°
Börne's Works incomplete.
10 Some few other books of no great value and interest.

British Museum Library Call Slips
Gottfried Semper

Press Mark.	Title of the Work wanted.	Size.	Place.	Date.
196. 1263.i x55.	Description de l'Asie Mineure faite par ordre du gouvernement Francais par Charles Texier 2 Vol.	Fol.	Paris	1839.
(Date)	8th Mars 1852.	Gottfried Semper.		(Signature).

Press Mark.	Title of the Work wanted.	Size.	Place.	Date.
886.	Atlas von Vorder Asien			
(Date)				(Signature).

Press Mark.	Title of the Work wanted.	Size.	Place.	Date.
1401.K.	Academies Europe. Prussia. Berlin Ueber den protestanti schen Geist aller wahrhaften Kunst etc v. Tolken.	4°	Berlin.	1839.
(Date)	12t Mars 52	Gottfrd Semper		(Signature).

Press Mark.	Title of the Work wanted.	Size.	Place.	Date.	
786.h.23.	Rumohr (Carl Fr. von) Italienische Forschungen 3 Theile.	8°	Berlin	1827.	
(Date)	27 April 52		Gottfried Semper.	(Signature).	5

Press Mark.	Title of the Work wanted.	Size.	Place.	Date.	
791.b.10.	Rumohr. (C. F von) Drei Reisen nach Italien Erinnerungen von – C. F. v. R.	12°	Leipzig	1832.	10
(Date)	27ᵗ Apr. 52.		Gottfried Semper.	(Signature).	

Press Mark.	Title of the Work wanted.	Size.	Place.	Date.	
P.P.1898.	Sammlung fur Kunst und Historie v. C. F. v. Rumohr.	8°	Hamburg	1816–23.	15
(Date)	29 April 1852		*Gottfried Semper.*	(Signature	

Press Mark.	Title of the Work wanted.	Size.	Place.	Date.	
344.h.	Leibnitz Scriptores rerum Brunswicarum 3 Tomi	fol.	Hannover	1707–11.	20
(Date)	30. April 52		GSemper.	(Signature).	

Press Mark.	Title of the Work wanted.	Size.	Place.	Date.	
564.g.	Cicognara (Leopoldo) Storia della Scultura etc. 3 Vol.	fol.	Ven.	1813.	25
(Date)	15ᵗ May 52.		Gottfried Semper.	(Signature).	

Press Mark.	Title of the Work wanted.	Size.	Place.	Date.	
T.487.a.	Murphy James the Arabian Antiquities of Spain	fol.	Lond.	1813.	30
(Date)	15 May 52.		Gottfried Semper.	(Signature	

Press Mark.	Title of the Work wanted.	Size.	Place.	Date.
1260.e.	Pottier (A) Monumens Francais inédits etc. accompagnés d'un texte historique 2 Tom.	fol.	Paris	1839.
(Date)	21 May 1852.	Gottfried Semper.		**(Signature).**

Press Mark.	Title of the Work wanted.	Size.	Place.	Date.
556.h.	Agincourt Histoire de l'art par les monumens. *Sculpture* & peinture	Fol.	Paris	1823.
(Date)	21 May 52.	Gottfried Semper.		**(Signature).**

Press Mark.	Title of the Work wanted.	Size.	Place.	Date.
1260.2.	Pottier A. Monu- mens Francais inedits 2 Tom.	fol.	Paris	1839.
(Date)	24 May 1852.	Gottfried Semper		**(Signature).**

Press Mark.	Title of the Work wanted.	Size.	Place.	Date.
130.h.2.	Seroux d'Agincout. histoire de l'Art par les monumens 6 vol.	fol	Paris	1811.
(Date)	24 M. 52.	Gottfried Semper		**(Signature).**

Press Mark.	Title of the Work wanted.	Size.	Place.	Date.
1394.h	Vega Georg v. Tabulae Logarithmicae etc. 2 Bde.	4°	Leipzig	1812.
(Date)	28ᵗ May. 1852.	Gottfried Semper.		**(Signature).**

Press Mark.	Title of the Work wanted.	Size.	Place.	Date.	
529.e.	Lagrang. J. L. Lecons sur le calcul des fonctions.	8°	Paris	1806.	
(Date)	29 May 52		Gottfried Semper.	(Signature).	5

Press Mark.	Title of the Work wanted.	Size.	Place.	Date.	
559.e.	Serlio Seb. Architettura	fol.	Venetia	1537. 1559–62.	
(Date)	29 May 52.		Gottfried Semper.	(Signature).	

Press Mark.	Title of the Work wanted.	Size.	Place.	Date.	
559.c.	Seb. Serlio Architettura.	4°	Vicenza.	1619.	10
(Date)	29 M 52.		Gottfried Semper	(Signature).	

Press Mark.	Title of the Work wanted.	Size.	Place.	Date.	
535.g.	Newton Isaac. Phil. naturalis principia w. Commentariis illustrata Le Seour & F. Jacquier.	8°	Glasg.	1822.	15
(Date)	2 Jun. 1852		Gottfried Semper.	(Signature).	

Press Mark.	Title of the Work wanted.	Size.	Place.	Date.	
787.i.	Müller Karl Ottfrd De Minervae Poliadis Sacra et aede etc	4°	Götting	1820	20
(Date)	11 Jun. 52.		GSemper.	(Signature).	

Press Mark.	Title of the Work wanted.	Size.	Place.	Date.	
1263.c.	C. Ottfried Müller Die Alterthumer v. Athen mit Beiträgen von …	8°		1829.	25
(Date)	11 Juin 52.		G. Semper.	(Signature).	

Press Mark.	Title of the Work wanted.	Size.	Place.	Date.	
769.f.	Εφημερις αρχαιολογικη 1837–42 and following	4°	Athens	–	30
(Date)	12 June 52		G Semper.	(Signature).	

Press Mark.	Title of the Work wanted.	Size.	Place.	Date.
P.V.1926.	Revue Archeologique années 1845 et 1846.	8°	Paris.	− .
(Date)	12 June 1852.		G. Semper.	(Signature).

Press Mark.	Title of the Work wanted.	Size.	Place.	Date.
1049.f.	Fr. H. v. der Hagen Briefe in die Heimat 4 Bde.	12°	Breslau.	1818.
(Date)	28 June 1852.		Gottfried Semper.	(Signature).

Press Mark.	Title of the Work wanted.	Size.	Place.	Date.
619.g.	Zur Geschichte der Sammlungen für Wissenschaft und Kunst. in Deutschland.	8°	Zerbst.	1837.
(Date)	28 June 52		Gottfried Semper..	(Signature).

Press Mark.	Title of the Work wanted.	Size.	Place.	Date.
1310.e.	Allgemeine Culturgeschchte der Menschheit.	8°	Leipzig	1843
(Date)	28 June 52		Gottfried Semper.	(Signature).

Press Mark.	Title of the Work wanted.	Size.	Place.	Date.
350.h.	Montfaucon les monu- mens de la Monarchie Francaise 5 Tom.	fol.	Paris.	1729 −33.
(Date)	28 June 1852.		Gottfried Semper.	(Signature).

Press Mark.	Title of the Work wanted.	Size.	Place.	Date.
562.f.	Sir Samuel Rush Meyrick a Critical inquiry into ancient Armour. etc. 3 Vol.	4°	Lond.	1824.
(Date)	30 June 1852.		Gottfried Semper.	(Signature).

Press Mark.	Title of the Work wanted.	Size.	Place.	Date.
562.f –	Specimens of ancient furniture with descriptions by Sir S. R. M.	fol.	Lond	1836.
(Date)	30 June 1852	GSemper.		(Signature

Press Mark.	Title of the Work wanted.	Size.	Place.	Date.
60.h.5.	Androuet Ducerceau Jacques. Architecte de architectura opus.	fol.	Paris	1559.
(Date)	1 July 52.	Gottfried Semper		(Signature).

Press Mark.	Title of the Work wanted.	Size.	Place.	Date.
559.e.	Dieterlein Wendel. Architectura	fol.	Germ.	1593.
(Date)	1 July 52	Gottfried Semper.		(Signature).

Press Mark.	Title of the Work wanted.	Size.	Place.	Date.
1268. g. & 561.	Heideloff. Carl A. Die Ornamentik des Mittelalters. 3 Bde	4°	Nurnbg.	1843–47.
(Date)	1 July 52.	Gottfried Semper.		(Signature).

Press Mark.	Title of the Work wanted.	Size.	Place.	Date.
85.h.1.	Oeuvres de Clement Marot. 4 Vol.	4to	la. Haye	1731.
(Date)		G. Semper.		(Signature).

Press Mark.	Title of the Work wanted.	Size.	Place.	Date.
61.d.5.	Jean Marot: Recueil des plans, profils et élévations des plusieurs palais chasteaux, eglises etc. bâtis à Paris.	4°	Paris.	
(Date)	1 Jul[ ]. 1852	G Semper.		(Signature).

Press Mark.	Title of the Work wanted.	Size.	Place.	Date.
142.f.11.	Ciampinus vetera monumenta etc. 2 Vol.	fol.	Romae	1690– 1699
(Date)	2 July 52		GSemper.	(Signature).

Press Mark.	Title of the Work wanted.	Size.	Place.	Date.
143f.21.	Ciampinus De sacris aedificiis a C. M. constructis etc.	fol.	Romae	1693
(Date)	2 July 52		GSemper.	(Signature).

Press Mark.	Title of the Work wanted.	Size.	Place.	Date.
1367f.	Leo Marsicanus, Bishop of Ostia Chronica	4°	Venice	1573.
(Date)	2 July 1852		GSemper.	(Signature

Press Mark.	Title of the Work wanted.	Size.	Place.	Date.
552.g.7.	Instituto di corrispon denza archeologica	fol.	Rom. Paris	1829 & following
(Date)	2 July.		GSemper.	(Signature

Press Mark.	Title of the Work wanted.	Size.	Place.	Date.
409g & h R.R.	Archeologia. Vol. 28–32.	8°	Lond	1840– 46.
(Date)	3 July 52		GSemper.	(Signature).

Press Mark.	Title of the Work wanted.	Size.	Place.	Date.
409.h. R.R.	Index to Archeologia from Vol. 16 to Vol. 30 incl.	4°	Lond	1844.
(Date)	3 July 52		GSemper.	(Signature).

Press Mark.	Title of the Work wanted.	Size.	Place.	Date.
7955.c.	Indian Archipelago Exhibition of 1851. Articles collected by the Local Comittee of Singapore etc.	8°	Singapore	1851.
(Date)	3 July 52.		GSemper.	(Signature

Press Mark.	Title of the Work wanted.	Size.	Place.	Date.
573.e.	v. Murr Merkwürdigkeiten der Stadt Bamberg.	8°	Nurmberg	1799.
(Date)	3 July 52		GSemper.	(Signature).

Press Mark.	Title of the Work wanted.	Size.	Place.	Date.
619.e	v. Murr Beschreibung der ehemals zu Aachen aufbewahrten drei Konigl. Kronungszierden	4°	Nurnbrg	1801
(Date)	3 July 52		GSemper.	(Signature).

Press Mark.	Title of the Work wanted.	Size.	Place.	Date.
1326.g. 12.	A true description and direction of what is most worthy to be seen in all Italy Harlejan Miscellany Volume 12.	8°	L.	1808. cet.
(Date)	13 July 1852		GSemper.	(Signature).

Press Mark.	Title of the Work wanted.	Size.	Place.	Date.
819m.	Doppelmayr. J. Gabriel. Historische Nachrich von den Nurn berger Mathematicis etc. 2 Vol.	fol	Nurnb.	1730.
(Date)	13 July 1852		GSemper.	(Signature).

Press Mark.	Title of the Work wanted.	Size.	Place.	Date.
1300–a.	Nuovissima Guida dei viaggiatori in Italia 1842.	12°	Milan	1842
(Date)	13 July 52		GSemper.	(Signature).

Press Mark.	Title of the Work wanted.	Size.	Place.	Date.
560–c. 11 & 94	Museo Borbonico Vol 1–14 –	4°		1824.–37.
(Date)	3th Aug. 52.		Gottfried Semper	(Signature).

Press Mark.	Title of the Work wanted.	Size.	Place.	Date.
556.c.	Forkel Ueber die Theorie der Musik.	4°	Götting	1777
(Date)	18 Aug 52		GSemper.	(Signature).

Press Mark.	Title of the Work wanted.	Size.	Place.	Date.
7707.f.	Michel Angelo *Lanzi* Sec. Opera Cufica. acc. di un atlante in 74 tavole 3 Tomi.	4°	Parigi	1846.
(Date)	19 Aug 52		GSemper.	(Signature).

Press Mark.	Title of the Work wanted.	Size.	Place.	Date.
1263. f.	Péclet, Traité de la Chaleur 3e Ed. Avec planches en fol.	8°	Liège	1844
(Date)	19 Aug 52.		GSemper.	(Signature).

Press Mark.	Title of the Work wanted.	Size.	Place.	Date.
1260.a. 1260.d	Bötticher Carl G W Die Tektonik der Hellenen. (with 45. Eng) 2 Volumes.	4° fol.	Potsdam	1844–52.
(Date)	11 Dec.		Gottfried Semper.	(Signature).

Appointment Letter from the Department of Practical Art
Walter Ruding Deverell

fol. 1r

Department of Practical Art.
Marlborough House, Pall Mall, London:
the 11ᵗʰ day of September 1852.

Sir,

I am directed by the Lords of the Committee of Privy Council for Trade to in- 5
form you that they propose to establish a class in order to afford instruction in
the principles and practice of Ornamental Art applied to Metal Manufactures,
and that they have been pleased to appoint you to conduct the same.

1 – My Lords consider it necessary to the success of this class that the several
interests of the Manufacturer, the Student, the Workman, and the general pub- 10
lic, who are the consumers and ultimate judges of Manufactures, should be
consulted; and that the measures to be adopted should be so framed as to insure
the co-operation of all, and induce them to apply to you for advice and assistance.

2 – Your duties will be to instruct and exercise certain Students of your Class 15
in the principles and practice of Ornamental Art; to assist them in designing for
Metal Manufactures; to be responsible that their works executed in the Class

fol. 1v

are correct in ¦ principle, and to certify all those designs which you approve. –
Occasional Students Workmen and Manufacturers may probably bring or send
their works to receive the benefit of your advice, which you will afford them, as 20
you may best be able under the circumstances.

3 – You will be required to give demonstrations to your Class and occasional
public lectures, on the uses to be made of the objects in the Museum, the collection of casts, books, prints, drawings &c in the Library. When necessary, it will
be your duty to provide illustrative drawings and designs for the use of the class, 25
and it is expected that you will make yourself generally acquainted with the
information afforded by other illustrations.

4 – You will have to visit and report on Collections when required, and upon
the state of the Museum, Collection of Casts, and Library of the Department,
so far as respects Metal Manufactures and to inform the Superintendents of any 30
examples which it may appear desirable that the Museum should possess.

5 – You will be prepared to receive the instructions of the Superintendent of
Art and to make the practice of Art conform to the General principles recog-

fol. 2r

nized by the | Department, and you will be held generally responsible for the

Appointment Letter from the Department of Practical Art

success of the Class, which you will promote in every way in your power, and which, in this new experiment to afford practical instruction in Art for industrial purposes, will be chiefly dependent on your exertions.

6 – You will report annually on the progress of your Class before the 31st of December in each year.

7 – You will have to attend at Marlborough House three hours daily (except Saturdays) and register both your own attendance and that of your pupils.

8 – For these services My Lords have determined you shall receive a salary at the rate of £150 a year, together with the half of any fees which may be paid by Manufacturers, Students (not holding Scholarships, who are free) and Workmen attending your class or applying for your advice, and by the General Public attending your lectures.

You will also have the privilege of practising Ornamental Art at Marlborough House at any times when your class is not meeting, during the official hours from 10 to 4.

Your engagement commences ¦ on the 1st of September 1852, and, in the event of its being desirable to terminate it, three months notice is to be given on either side.

fol. 2v

I am, Sir,
Your Obedient Servant
WRDeverell
Secretary.

To /
Professor Semper
&c &c &c

Principles and Practice of Ornamental Art Applied to Furniture, Metals, Jewellery, and Enamels

Henry Cole

126 II. Principles and Practice of Ornamental Art applied to Furniture, Metals, Jewellery, and Enamels. – Conducted by Professor *Semper*.

Arrangements are made to supply to the manufacturer, student, designer, and workman all the advice and assistance that the Professor may be able to afford them, in improving Art applied to all kinds of Metal, Jewellery, and Enamels. Professor Semper attends daily from 10 till 1.

A class of students meet daily to practise Ornamental Art, and to become qualified as designers, or skilled workmen in the execution of works of Ornamental Art. The students may have the advantage of attending demonstrations of actual processes, such as Repoussée, Chasing, Casting, Forming, &c.

Manufacturers, Designers, &c. may consult the Professor on the execution of any works or designs originated by them, or obtain information as respects the examples in the Museum, or books, prints, &c., in the Library; also as respects the fitness of students of the Department to become designers or Art workmen, &c. |

127 Manufacturers, and others who are unable to attend personally, may send their works to receive the benefit of any suggestion from the Professor by paying the necessary postage or carriage of the same to and from Marlborough House, and transmitting the appointed fees.

Occasional lectures will be delivered by the Professor.

The *Fees*, which are to be paid in advance, are as follows: –

1. Daily students (who are required to demonstrate that they possess an adequate power of Drawing and Modelling before they are permitted to enter the class), 50*s.* a quarter, or 8*l.* a year.

2. Manufacturers, designers, or others, seeking occasional advice, 6*s.* a week, or 2*s.* each separate consultation.

3. Manufacturers and others, by subscribing annually 5*l.*, may attend themselves, or send their workmen, at any time, to receive advice and assistance in originating or executing Ornamental Designs.

———

III. Pottery, and other Manufactures.

For information on these divisions application is to be made to Professor Semper until other arrangements are made.

———

CRITICAL APPARATUS

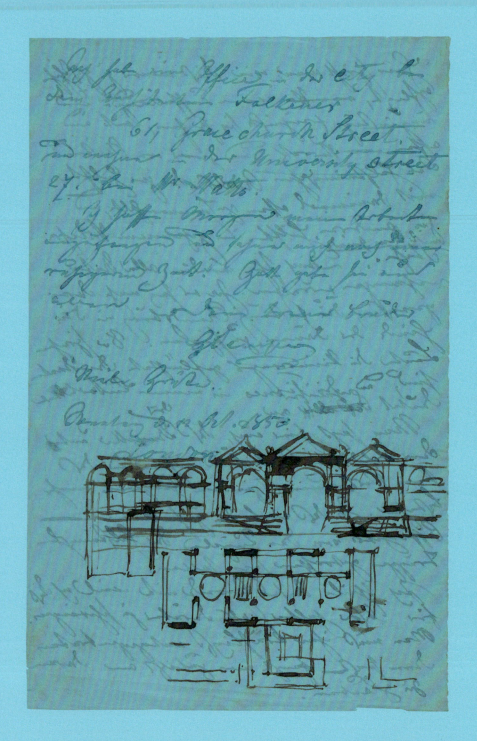

Pl. 7: Sketch of London cemetery chapel on draft letter, 1850 (gta, 20-K-1850-10-13[S])

PRIVATE SCHOOL OF ARCHITECTURE

Introduction

Between the end of December 1850 and the beginning of March 1851, Gottfried Semper was developing plans for ways of offering his services in London as a teaching, consulting, designing and executive architect. He was also planning to establish an actual private school of architecture, modelled on the architectural college that he had directed at the Academy of Fine Arts in Dresden. He started making these plans after learning at the end of November 1850 from Edwin Chadwick, commissioner of the General Board of Health, that there were to be delays in establishing the new national cemetery near Erith, London. The German archaeologist and entrepreneur Emil Braun had involved Semper in that prospective enterprise, thus prompting him to move from Paris to London instead of North America. Semper drafted newspaper advertisements that ranged from offers of architectural drawing lessons to the establishment of an architecture school for day students and pensioners. He classified five of these twenty-two, partly fragmentary, drafts using the roman numerals I, II and III – two each with 'I' and 'III' and one with 'II'. In the present edition, different versions from each of these classes are grouped together under the headings 'Lessons and Recommendation as Architect' (I), 'School of Architecture and Engineering' (II) and 'Lessons in Architecture and Drawing' (III).

Only one of these draft newspaper advertisements, from class II, made its way to publication – in the *Eidgenössische Zeitung* of 28 March 1851, under the title 'Deutsches Atelier für Architekten und Ingenieurs in London' (German Studio for Architects and Engineers in London; 13). The school of architecture is announced in the advert as being connected to a boarding house for students. The advertisement is followed by a supportive note from Richard Wagner (208–

9). The only other identified publication that included Semper's announcement of a school of architecture is an article in the Berlin newspaper *National-Zeitung* of 19 March 1851 (206–8). The plan is mentioned there in passing by the paper's London correspondent, Lothar Bucher, in a report on events in Britain. Semper had met Bucher at some time between late February and early March 1851 through Rudolph Schramm (like Semper, they were both political refugees). In the article, Bucher announced the imminent founding of an 'Academy of architecture' and the 'establishment of a school of architecture' – along with a summary of Semper's reasons for initiating the project.

A letter from Braun to Semper, dated 1 and 4 January 1851, reveals that Semper had mentioned his 'plan regarding the establishment of an architectural drawing school' on 22 December 1850 and had added the idea of a 'drawing academy in London with a well-equipped collection of plaster casts' on 23 December. Braun agreed that this might be 'a very good speculation' and recommended that Semper should look for a 'manager who could relieve you of the administrative burdens of such an institute'. He suggested the artist and later director of the National Portrait Gallery, George Scharf, with whom Semper might perhaps 'join up, to set up a drawing academy and saddle him with the business part of it'. Although Semper did contact Scharf, no specific results emerged. On 29 January 1851, Braun thereupon suggested to Semper that although he should not do without Scharf as assistant (*Famulus*), he should perhaps 'carry out the plan of setting up a large studio' in association with the architect Edward Falkener. With the help of Braun, Semper had been able to move into an office in Falkener's architecture practice at the beginning of October 1850. Through Falkener, Braun believed, 'quite a few other things for English industry could be linked' to Semper's plan. In general, Braun thought that this type of school – in connection, as he noted, with 'practical instruction in the theory of architecture' – was sure to be successful, since 'the public drawing schools are useless', so that 'the rush to join a reputable private institute would soon be very great'.

Semper did not favour Braun's suggestion that he should work with Falkener or Scharf as associates, but he was indeed planning to include an 'English engineer' as a 'colleague' for the school – as he noted in the plan, assigned to class II, that he drafted in a letter written to Rudolph Schramm on 25 February (9.16–17, 9.26). In his reply, Schramm – like Braun – also advised having an associate who would be able to support Semper organizationally and in financial matters for the school. The advertisement published in the *Eidgenössische Zeitung* states that Semper had 'engaged a skilful and experienced engineer for the field of engineering' – a claim that did not actually correspond to any specific agreement.

In addition to the two advertisements for the school of architecture that were published in German, Semper was also planning English advertisements. As he had scarcely any command of English at this point, he enlisted help from English speakers or people with a good knowledge of English. What is probably the very first draft is in English, in a calligraphic script from an unknown hand (pl. 1). It can be assigned to advertisement class III, in which Semper was intending to publicize lessons in architecture and drawing (14, First Version), and it was probably drawn up in connection with Braun's letters from the beginning and end of January 1851. It may have been formulated by Braun and copied out by his wife, Anne Braun – the daughter of James Thomson, an industrial chemist and calico printer.

It is possible that the same people were also the sources for the drafts in English that are written in Semper's hand – another version belonging to the third class (14, Second Version) and an initial version belonging to the second class about the actual school of architecture and engineering (8, First Version). These two drafts in English were probably made at about the same time, around mid-February 1851, before Semper began to cooperate with Karoline Heusinger, a Saxon friend of his wife, Bertha Semper. He visited Heusinger – a lady-companion in the family of John Campbell, the Chief Justice of the Queen's Bench – for the first time on 8 February 1851, and on 22 February he brought her a draft in German belonging to the third class of adverts (254, DOK:39). The draft was translated by Mary Scarlett Campbell, John Campbell's daughter. Heusinger sent a copy of it in her own handwriting to Semper on 24 February 1851 (15, Third Version). Previously, on 23 February, Semper had sent her an initial German version, which was never translated, from the first class of adverts (4). In the advertisements belonging to this class, Semper announced not only architecture lessons offered by the hour but also his desire to set up the architecture school. He also recommended his own services as an architect and decorator. Semper immediately followed this version with another version in German (240–1, DOK:42), the translation of which – now made by herself – Heusinger sent back on 27 February 1851 (5–6, Second Version).

At the beginning of March 1851, Semper drew up some final draft advertisements in French, such as a version belonging to the third category dated 3 March (15, Fourth Version) and a version from the first category that was probably written shortly afterwards (6–7, Third Version). They were both intended for translation into English and may have been prepared as translation material for either Edward Falkener or Thomas Leverton Donaldson. Semper had known Donaldson, the co-founder and one of the secretaries of the Royal Institute of British Architects, since December 1838, when he had travelled to London in connection with the building of the Hoftheater (Court Theatre) in Dresden. Semper corresponded with both of them in French.

Before drafting the French advertisements, Semper turned to Henry Cole, who was then a member of the Commission for the Great Exhibition and chairman of the council of the Society of Arts. He had first met Cole, introduced by Edwin Chadwick, on 5 December 1850, as Cole noted in his diary. On 25 February 1851, Semper wrote to Cole regarding his plan to offer his services 'as a teacher of drawing and architecture', mentioning that he had 'a plan to found an architecture studio modelled on the one in Dresden'. Until the plan was implemented, he would have to 'restrict himself to lessons at home', and for this purpose he asked Cole for his support and requested him to forward the programme he would shortly send to him to 'pass on to gentlemen with whom you are acquainted', in order if possible in this way to reach 'heads of families' who 'would be disposed to entrust me with the artistic education of their children'. However, it is not quite certain whether this programme was really sent to Cole.

Semper was planning to open the actual school of architecture and engineering in the summer of 1851, on Saint John's Day (i.e. 24 June 1851), as he wrote in the draft sent to Schramm. He did not tell his wife Bertha about these plans until the end of February 1851, in a letter with which he also enclosed a draft advertisement – probably the version dated 26 February 1851 (12), or a variant of it. He was planning for Bertha to play the role of 'lady of the house', who would do the honours and take care of purchasing, with their daughter Elisabeth helping out. Bertha was to contact Friedrich Krause, the headmaster of a private school in Dresden, about the advertisement and to ask for information about conditions in England. In his reply of 10 March 1851, however, Krause advised Semper against the plans for setting up a school. He argued that architecture students in Germany and France tended to choose countries other than England for their study trips, while on the other hand the English would be unwilling to study with a foreigner. Finally, with regard to establishing a boarding house, he pointed out that 'it is probably not the moment just now to rent a house for a longer period of time, since the interest rate will surely be much higher than otherwise due to the Exhibition'.

The Great Exhibition, which Krause mentioned here as a reason for potential financial obstacles, also played a part in the negative response to the school plans that Edwin Chadwick sent to Semper on 9 March 1851. Chadwick had been the intermediary in arranging a position for Semper as assistant to the architect of the Crystal Palace, Joseph Paxton, on his premises in Chatsworth, Derbyshire. In his reply to the offer of the position, Semper told Chadwick on 8 March 1851 about the advertisements he had drafted for publication in Germany and Switzerland in connection with his 'intention to found a studio for architects in London'. And he asked, 'Would it not be possible for me, for example, to have some pupils at Chatsworth who could at the same time be useful and help Mr. Paxton in his work?' This would have implied a switch from being Paxton's assistant to his partner. Chadwick's answer left no room for doubt. Firstly, he did 'not think, that an architectural class could soon be got together in England'; in addition, 'more knowledge of the habits & wants of the class of architectural students would be required' than Semper 'would be likely to obtain readily'. Secondly, he had 'no doubt, that it would be entirely impracticable to carry on such a school at Chatsworth', and, with respect to Paxton, 'that it would not meet with his views'.

Ultimately, however, the Great Exhibition provided Semper with a good reason to postpone his plans for setting up a school. Henry Cole, who had promised help on 26 February 1851 in reply to Semper's request for support ('If I can aid your views I shall be happy and will try to do so'), assisted him shortly afterwards in obtaining the commissions to set up several sections in the Great Exhibition. The school plans did not fade away completely, however. After the exhibition commissions had been completed, Semper reported on 5 May 1851 to his brother Johann Carl Semper, who was a textile manufacturer in Altona, that he had 'at least one pupil already'. He returned to the school plans just under a year later, changing the date of a third draft advertisement in French belonging to class I to 2 January 1852 (7, Fourth Version). And in a renewed effort to obtain a livelihood as a teacher, Semper also wrote to Henry Cole on 29 January 1852 to offer him his services in connection with 'the Establishment of a School for art and industry' that he had heard of. With his subsequent employment in said school, the Department of Practical Art, founded in the spring of 1852, Semper again obtained success through Cole, as in the case of the Great Exhibition.

BIBLIOGRAPHY Semper 1880, 11, 20–1; Pevsner 1940, 251; Knoepfli 1976, 264–5; Herrmann 1978, 47–50; Herrmann 1984, 43–5; Mallgrave 1996, 191–2; Lütteken 2008, 43 fig. 107, 188; Weidmann 2010, 288–93; Weidmann 2014, 8–10; Hildebrand 2020a, 108–9

Lessons and Recommendation as Architect

First Version

TEXTUAL RECORD

DOK:38   gta, 20-DOK-undat.:38, fol. 1r–v (1v blank), in Semper's hand; breaks off after number 4 in the programme of DOK:41 without having divided it into numbers
DOK:41   gta, 20-DOK-undat.:41, fols. 1r–2v (2v blank), in Semper's hand, *copy-text*

EXPLANATORY NOTES

Semper sent this draft, which was intended for an English readership but remained untranslated, to Karoline Heusinger together with a letter dated 'Sunday 22 Feb 1851'. If it was written on the Sunday, however, it would have been 23 February. It is a revised version of the draft he had taken to Heusinger on 22 February 1851 (254, DOK:39; its English translation 15, Third Version). In the letter, Semper explained the changes he had made by saying that the fifth point – 'making artistic architectural sketches' – seemed to him to be 'particularly important for ladies' and that he wanted to connect it to the preceding point on perspective drawing. Mention would also have to be made of the planned school of architecture. In her reply to Semper's letter and the enclosed programme, Heusinger wrote on 24 February that she would 'ensure that it was translated' but added that she could 'hardly advise setting up a boarding school'. However, as she had little experience in such matters, she recommended that Semper should ask her 'experienced and upright Dr Freund for advice'. Jonas Freund was to become Semper's physician; Karl Marx was among his other patients.

4.10 **Vasen∧ Mustern**] *Vasen, Mustern*   4.12–13 **5) Uebungen ~ für Reisende.**] In the letter to Karoline Heusinger accompanying this draft, Semper wrote: 'Die Nummer 5 scheint mir für Damen besonders wichtig ich werde sie mit Nummer 4 in Verbindung setzen und allemal einen Cours de perspective vorausschicken. Meine Methode Perspective zu lehren ist leicht und kurz. In 12 bis 18 Stunden muss alles Nöthige erworben seyn. Vielleicht kann so etwas hinzugefügt werden.'   4.16–17 **Uebungen in der Französischen und Deutschen Sprache**] In the above-mentioned letter, Semper wrote: 'Zu Nummer 7 habe ich ein Wort hinzugesetzt, was wichtig ist, nämlich Uebungen in der *Französischen* und Deutschen Sp. Mancher der nicht Deutsch kann, wird Französisch sprechen wollen.' This refers to the last sentence in the draft Semper brought to Karoline Heusinger on 22 February 1851 (254.7–8).   4.18–19 **ein Atelier ~ zu gründen**] In the above-mentioned letter, Semper explained this reference to the planned school of architecture: 'Besonders aber darf das Ende nicht fehlen [following the seven numbers of the programme]. Vielleicht gelingt es, einige Familienväter zu betheiligen dass sie mir ihre Söhne anvertrauen. Dann bin ich gedeckt. Mit 6 Schülern getraue ich mir die Kosten eines Ateliers zu übernehmen. Aber ohne die geringste vorherige Garantie darf ich nichts unternehmen. Eine Basis muss ich haben.' Semper similarly mentioned heads of families in his letter to Henry Cole of 25 February 1851 (236).   4.22–3 **behufs der Ausführung mit einem ~ Englischen Techniker in Verbin-**

dung setzen] In the above-mentioned letter to Heusinger, Semper added: 'Wegen der Ausführungen hat es zwar wahrscheinlich gute Wege, doch dürfte diese Andeutung, dünkt mich, auch nichts schaden können.' The word 'Ausführungen' (implementations) can refer to two points in Semper's programme: on the one hand to his recommending himself as 'Baumeister und Dekorateur', and on the other to his plan to organize his school of architecture in association with an English engineer.

ALTERATIONS IN THE MANUSCRIPT

4.2 Theaters] *interl.*   **4.4 Kunst**] *del. and underl. with dots cancelling deletion*   **4.6 und**] *interl.*   **4.12 5**] *after del.* 5) Uebungen im Ausführen landschaftlicher und architectonischer Skizzen in Bleistift und in Wasserfarben;   Uebungen im Ausführen] *above del.* Ausführung   **4.13 als Vorbereitung**] *after del.* für diejenigen   **für**] *over* zu   **Reisende.**] de. *added*   **4.14 Ornamenten,**] *altered from* ~∧   **Köpfen**] *interl.*   **4.14–15 der Antike**] *after del.* antiken und *after del.* Gypsen und Modellen   **4.16 7)**] *interl.*   **4.16–17 Wenn es gewünscht wird ~ verbunden seyn.**] *inserted on fol.* 2r *after inserted and undel.* 7)   **4.19 besorgen,**] *above del.* übernehmen,   **wenn**] *after del.* wenn es ihm gelänge die nöthige Anzahl von Theilnehmern   **4.21 Schliesslich**] *after del.*

Schliesslich empfiehlt er sich als[1] ausübender Architect.[2] Er[3] würde sich[4], behufs der Ausführung mit einem einheimischen Techniker in Verbindung setzen, und[5]

> [1] **als**] *after del.* als Architect   [2] **Architect.**] *altered from* ~∧   [3] **Er**] *above del.* und
> [4] **sich**] *after undel.* er   [5] **und**] *after del.* und für gute, schnelle und billige Ausführung einstehen

4.22 hiesigen] *above del.* den einheimischen   **4.23 Englischen**] *above del.* hiesigen   **4.24 übernehmen,**] *altered from* ~.   **aber zugleich**] *inserted*   **4.24–5 für ~ gewähren.**] *inserted*

Second Version

TEXTUAL RECORD

DOK:40   gta, 20-DOK-undat.:40, fols. 1r–2v, in Semper's hand; breaks off after number 5 of the programme of DOK:42

DOK:42   gta, 20-DOK-undat.:42, fols. 1r–2v (2v blank), in Semper's hand, German source text of English translation DOK:50

DOK:50   gta, 20-DOK-undat.:50, fol. 1r–v, in Karoline Heusinger's hand, her translation, *copy-text*

EXPLANATORY NOTES

Semper sent the German draft translated here (240–1, DOK:42) to Karoline Heusinger shortly after that of 23 February 1851 (4). In the reply of 27 February along with which Heusinger returned the translation, she wrote that she herself had translated the text, because her 'Marie' (Mary Scarlett Campbell, John Campbell's daughter, for whom Heusinger was acting as a lady-companion) was 'busy for her father'. Heusinger added that she had given the translation to an 'English governess for review', who had advised her to 'show it to an English architect', as she was unable to 'judge the correctness of some technical terms'. Heusinger mentioned three expressions that she had found 'unclear' and for which she had not been able to find 'any English words in the dictionary' – namely 'Civilbau, rationelen und architectonische Details' (see notes 5.21, 5.25). She went on to say that if Semper 'is wary of the cost of having this long programme printed', he should venture to use 'the short one' – that is, the one brought to her on 22 February 1851 (254, DOK:39), which Mary Scarlett Campbell then translated (15, Third Version); Campbell, she stated, 'has said it is sufficient'. Heusinger ended by saying that she had 'kept a copy of both the German and the English'.

5.1 **Architure**] *Architecture*   5.21 **Civil-Construction**] 'Civilbau' in the German source text, i.e. *civil engineering*   5.24 **Building of ~ Channels**] 'Canalbau' in the German source text, i.e. *canal construction*   5.25 **rational and applicative Mechanism**] 'rationalen und angewandten Mechanik' in the German source text, i.e. *rational and applied mechanics*   5.27 **Lithography**] 'Steinschnitt' in the German source text, i.e. *stonecutting* or *stereotomy*   5.30 **Vessels**] 'Köpfen' in the German source text, i.e. *heads*. The translator, Karoline Heusinger, apparently read *Töpfen* instead of 'Köpfen'.

EDITORIAL EMENDATIONS

5.1 **Architure**] Archi- | ture   5.7 **water-color**] water- | color   6.2 **at:**] *before one-half page blank*

ALTERATIONS IN THE MANUSCRIPT

5.1 **Gottfried**] *interl.*

MANUSCRIPT VARIANTS
DOK:42

fol. 1r   Professor G. Semper, vormals Director der Bauschule an der Akademie der bildenden Künste zu Dresden und Architect des dortigen Theaters, des Museum, und anderer öffentlicher und Privatgebäude beabsichtigt über folgende Gegenstände Privatvorträge zu halten und fordert zu gefälliger Theilnahme auf: 4

Lessons and Recommendation as Architect

1) Perspective, vorgetragen in fasslichster und kürzester Weise und verbunden mit Uebungen im Ausführen malerisch-architectonischer Skizzen in Bleistift und in Wasserfarben. Besonders nützliche Vorbereitung für Touristen.

2) Geschichte der bildenden Künste, besonders in ihrem Zusammenhange mit der Baukunst; Alte und neue Zeit. Erläutert durch Zeichnungen, Kupferwerke und während des Vortrages auf der schwarzen Tafel mit Kreide ausgeführte Skizzen.

Diese Vorträge können, wenn es gewünscht wird, mit Uebungen in der Französischen und Deutschen Sprache verbunden werden.

Zugleich hegt er die Absicht, ein Atelier für angehende Architecten zu gründen, und die nöthige Ausstattung desselben am Lehrmitteln aller Art zu besorgen, wenn er für dieses Unternehmen die nöthige Theilnahme findet.

Er würde, gestützt auf 14jährige Erfahrung ¦ als Director einer der ersten Bauschulen   *fol. 1v*
Deutschlands und Vorstand eines Privatateliers aus der mehrere bereits in ihrem Fache ausgezeichnete Architecten hervorgegangen sind, diese Anstalt auf die ihm am zweckmässigsten scheinende Weise einzurichten suchen, und den theoretischen Unterricht an fortlaufende praktische Uebungen knüpfen.

Letztere würden sich hauptsächlich auf folgende Lehrzweige erstrecken:

1) Linearzeichnen und Civilbau, verbunden mit Unterweisung in der Kenntniss der verschiedenen Stylarten der Baukunst und in der Geschichte derselben.

2) Constructionslehre

3) Wege Brücken und Canalbau, verbunden mit dem nöthigen Unterricht in der rationalen und angewandten Mechanik.

4) Beschreibende Geometrie und ihre Anwendung auf Perspective, Schattenlehre, Steinschnitt etc.

5) Uebungen im Zeichnen und Erfinden von Verzierungen, architectonischen Details, Möbles, Vasen, Mustern aller Art.

6) Zeichnen von Ornamenten, Köpfen ¦ und Figuren nach der Antike und nach Gypsmodel-   *fol. 2r*
len. In allen diesen Fächern wird er auch Privatunterricht ertheilen.

Schliesslich empfiehlt er sich als Baumeister und Dekorateur, Fächer, die bei harmonisch durchgebildeten Werken der Baukunst stets in einer Hand lagen und deren Trennung für letztere verderblich wurde. Er würde für den Erfolg des ihm anvertrauten Werkes die möglichste Sicherheit gewähren.

Nähere Nachweisungen über ihn sind zu geben bereit:

(Folgen die Namen der Gewährsleute.).

27. University Street. London.

241.1 **fasslichster und kürzester Weise**] *after del.* fasslicher und unterhaltender Weise
241.2 **malerisch-architectonischer**] *after del.* malerischer   241.3 **nützliche**] e *added*
241.5 **während**] *after del.* augen[b]   241.10 **am**] m *altered from* n   241.13 **bereits**] *after*
del. geschickte Architecten *after del.* bereits in ihrem F   241.15 **und**] *after del.* indem
241.17 **folgende**] f *over* F   241.18 **Civilbau**] *above del.* Entwerfen von Bauplänen *and*
underl. possibly by Karoline Heusinger   241.21 **Wege**] *before del.* und Brückenbau   **ratio-**
nalen] *after del.* Mechanik und Statik *and underl. possibly by Heusinger*   241.25 **Details**]
underl. possibly by Heusinger   241.31 **den**] en *over* ie   241.33 **Nähere**] *after del.* Nachweisungen über   **über**] *after del.* zu [ ]

242   Private School of Architecture

Third Version

TEXTUAL RECORD

DOK:44   gta, 20-DOK-undat.:44, fol. 1r–v, in Semper's hand; breaks off with 'il propose
de donner des leçons privées' (the place of this sentence corresponds roughly to
that in DOK:45 and DOK:46)

DOK:45   gta, 20-DOK-undat.:45, fols. 1r–2v, in Semper's hand; breaks off with '3) exercices dans le dessin ~ après la nature.' (see below, Explanatory Notes 7.11)

DOK:46   gta, 20-DOK-undat.:46, fols. 1r–2v, in Semper's hand, *copy-text*

EXPLANATORY NOTES

This draft in French was intended for English translation; in it, Semper was recommending
his services 'to the English public as a constructional and decorative architect'. It may have
been prompted by Karoline Heusinger's advice in her letter of 27 February 1851 to submit to
an English architect the programme that she had translated (235, 240). The draft in French
was probably written at the earliest on 3 March 1851; the reference at the end, 'comme au
programme Nº 3', is probably to the last draft in French from the third class of adverts,
marked with the roman numeral III and dated to that day (15, Fourth Version).

6.6 **l'ecole**] *l'école*   6.7 **l'academie**] *l'académie*   **théatre**] *théâtre*   6.8 **édificies**] 'ci'
uncertain reading, *édifices*   6.11 **eue**] *eu*   6.12 **pour son developpement organique et
harmonieux.**] 'developpement': *développement*; 'pour le developpement organique & harmonieux d'une conception quelconque de l'art.' DOK:44   6.13 **Seurity**] *Security*   6.14
repondre] *répondre*   6.15 **decoration exterieure**] *décoration extérieure*   6.17 **une école
d'architecture**] 'un atélier d'architectes' DOK:44   6.18 **d'ou**] *d'où*   6.19 **actuellement
employés en Saxe.**] 'de son pays.' DOK:44; 'actuellement employés dans son pays.' DOK:45
6.21 **atélier**] *atelier*   6.22 **ambrasseront**] *embrasseront*   6.23 **decoration**] *décoration*
6.31 **entiere**] *entière*
7.1 **differentes**] *différentes*   7.3 **comprehensiblement**] *compréhensiblement*   7.5 **particulierement**] *particulièrement*   7.6 **preparer**] *préparer*   7.10 **improviseés**] *improvisées*
7.11 **3) Exercices etc comme au programme Nº 3.**] '3) exercices dans le dessin et la composition des ornamens, des details d'architecture, des meubles vases etc. Les exercices se feront
au crayon à l'encre et en couleurs après des originaux, après des plâtres et après la nature.'
DOK:45   7.12 **detaillés**] *détaillés*

ALTERATIONS IN THE MANUSCRIPT

6.5 **I.**] *after underl. and del.* Premier projet de programme   6.10 **belles**] *del. and underl. with
dots cancelling deletion*   6.11 **eue**] *final* e *added*   6.31 **Il prendra des élèves en pension
entiere ou partielle.**] *interl.*
7.9 **par**] *above del.* avec   **dessins**] *before del.* et   7.11 **au programme Nº 3.**] *after del.* à
Nº 3. du pr   pr] *after del.* projet   **renseignemens**] *after del.* instructions

School of Architecture and Engineering   243

Fourth Version

TEXTUAL RECORD

DOK-1852:3   gta, 20-DOK-1852:3, fol. 1r–v, in Semper's hand, dated 2 January 1852 (altered from an earlier date, probably 2 March 1851; see below, Alterations in the Manuscript 7.28), *copy-text*

EXPLANATORY NOTES

Semper assigned this draft to the first class of advertisements by marking it with the roman numeral 'I'. It is a – probably slightly earlier – variant of DOK:46, the draft published here as the third version (6–7, Third Version). However, it does not offer the lessons advertised there but is limited to the first part of it, which ends with the recommendation of his services as a consulting architect. The special aspect of this draft is also its dating; Semper altered the first date given, probably 2 March 1851, to 2 January 1852 (the month of the first date, probably 'Mars', is scarcely decipherable due to dense crossing-out).

7.15 **l'academie**] *l'académie*   **théatre**] *théâtre*   7.16 **edifices**] *édifices*   7.19 **au eue**] *a eu*
7.21 **repondre**] *répondre*

ALTERATIONS IN THE MANUSCRIPT

7.15 **directoir**] *interl.*   7.20 **harmonieux.**] *before del.* Security will be given for any work entrusted to him.   7.22 **intérieure.**] *before inserted and del.* ‡ voyez plus bas.   7.28 **Janvier**] *above del.* [Mars]   **1852**] 2 *over* 1 *before inserted and del.* ‡. Il s'offre aussi de prendre des elèves en pension entière ou partielle   s'offre] *above del.* est prêt   ou] *after del.* et

School of Architecture and Engineering

First Version

TEXTUAL RECORD

DOK:47   gta, 20-DOK-undat.:47, fol. 1r–v (1v blank), in Semper's hand, in pencil (some alterations in black ink), *copy-text*

EXPLANATORY NOTES

This draft is the first for an advertisement devoted exclusively to the school of architecture and engineering. It was written in English in Semper's handwriting but includes two phrases in French, 'l'Ecole d'architecture' and 'l'Académie des Beaux Arts' (8.3), and a spelling mistake, 'jears' instead of years (8.7). It was probably written before the English translation of the third advertisement in the third class (15, Third Version), the German source text of which Semper had taken to Karoline Heusinger on 22 February 1851 (254, DOK:39). Before they were altered in ink by Semper, manuscript lines 2–7 of this pencil-written draft ('Professor Semper ~ native Country') corresponded almost verbatim to the same lines written in pencil, also in Semper's handwriting, in the English draft of the second advertisement in the third class, the rest of which is written in ink (14, Second Version). The two draft advertisements were thus probably created at about the same time.

ALTERATIONS IN THE MANUSCRIPT

8.1 **II.**] *inserted in pencil* 8.3 **late Director of l'Ecole d'architecture,**] *transposed by use of numbers in ink from after* Beaux Arts, *at 8.3* **late**] *in ink after undel. in ink* 1. *(indicating sequence to be altered) and both over* and **l'Ecole d'architecture,**] *before del. in ink at* Dresden, **and Member of**] *in ink after undel. in ink* 2. *(indicating sequence to be altered) and both over* late Director of 8.3–4 **at Dresden,**] *interl. in ink* 8.5 **Country**] *in pencil over erased* Land 8.6 **in the approaching Summer a School of**] *altered by deletion and superscription in ink from* in this City a School of in this City a School of] *in pencil over erased* himself in this Country as 8.11 **the science of**] *in pencil above del.* decorations and 8.12 **original**] *in pencil over erased* drawings 8.13 **standard**] *in pencil over erased* principal 8.13–14 **of this Country**] *after del. in ink* both 8.14 **casts**] *after del.* plaster **ancient**] *after del. in ink* the finest 8.14–15 **ornaments**] *before interl. and del. in pencil* and models 8.15 **models**] *after del. in ink* in the various Museums of Europe, in] *undel.* **construction**] *after del. in ink* public buildings,

Second Version

TEXTUAL RECORD

K-1851[1]   gta, 20-K-1851-02-25(S):2, fols. 1r–2v, in Semper's hand, fragmentary draft
K-1851[2]   gta, 20-K-1851-02-25(S):2, fols. 3r–5v, in Semper's hand, dated 24 February 1851 but written on 25 February 1851 (see 245, Explanatory Notes 8.17), *copy-text*

School of Architecture and Engineering

EXPLANATORY NOTES

Semper outlined this draft advertisement, along with the programme, on 25 February 1851 in reply to a letter from Rudolph Schramm with the same date. Schramm informed Semper that he had 'asked the local correspondent of the *National Zeitung in Berlin*' – i.e. Lothar Bucher – 'to do a report … on your project to establish a school of architecture'. Bucher's report appeared on 19 March 1851 (207–8). At the same time, Schramm also suggested 'doing the same for the Kölner Zeitung', for which he, Schramm, wanted to 'send in his own article, headed *Project for a German Academy of Architecture in London*'. He had 'sufficient material' for the purpose in Semper's 'previous programme'. (On the advertisement for the *Kölnische Zeitung*, see 247, 249–50.) The previous programme referred to here was possibly the first draft, written in English, on the project for an actual architecture school (8, First Version), as Schramm's further comments suggest. On the one hand, Schramm stated that he would consider it 'better to await the success of these *German* advertisements *before* publishing the *English programme*'. In the German version, on the other hand, he would want to see 'some mention of *the advantages* which staying in London would offer to those who are keen on architecture', with 'attention being drawn to the peculiar features of English dwelling houses and other peculiarities, such as the use of machines for construction'. These points are lacking in the previous draft advertisement in English but are included in the 'Teaching Programme' formulated by Semper in his letter to Schramm. An undated draft letter from Semper breaks off after about two-thirds (K-1851[1]). Important differences are listed below. Some notes, underlining and crossing out, also listed, probably originate from Hans Semper.

8.17 **Dienstag. 24 Febr 1851**] 24 February 1851 was a Monday, but the letter was written on Tuesday, 25 February 1851 in response to Rudolph Schramm's letter of the same date.   8.23 **Aufforderungen**] 'Notificationen' K-1851[1]   8.26–7 **für Architecten und Ingenieurs**] 'der Civilbaukunst und der Ingenieurwissenschaft' K-1851[1]
9.9–12 **dass diese Uebungen ~ Repetitionen desselben bilden.**] 'dass diese praktischen Uebungen in einer gewissen Relation zu den wissenschaftlichen Vorträgen stehen, die nothwendig in mehr oder minder umfassender Weise Statt haben müssen.' K-1851[1]   9.16– 17 **Englischen Ingenieur ~ Ich kenne deren zwei**] possibly William Lindley and Joseph Paxton. Lindley was the engineer who provided the first reconstruction plan following the Great Fire of Hamburg in 1842, which Semper opposed with his own scheme. Semper was in contact with Lindley again after he went into exile. Contact with Paxton, whom Semper mentioned in connection with his school plans, was made through Edwin Chadwick in November 1850 at Semper's request (236–7, 314).   9.24 **hatten**] 'hätten' K-1851[1]
9.33 **Arch.**] 'architectonischer' K-1851[1]   9.36 **Uebungen in dem farbigen Ornament.**] 'Uebungen in der Anwendung der Farbe zur Dekoration.' K-1851[1]
10.2–4 **NB. Vierwöchentlich einmal wird Conkurrenz gehalten ~ Dann ausgeführt.**] om. K-1851[1]   10.7–8 **Doch finden auch ~ Conkurrenzarbeiten Statt.**] om. K-1851[1]
10.12 **Ferner werden Modellirübungen gehalten in Thon Gyps und Holz.**] 'und das Ausführen von Ornamenten und Constructionsmodellen in Thon, Gyps. und Holz.' K-1851[1]
10.20 **angewandte M.**] 'Angewandte Mechanik (nach Belanger).' K-1851[1]; see Bélanger 1847 and Bélanger 1848   10.24 **Physik**] after deleted 'Industrielle' K-1851[1]   10.27 **Doctrinen**] 'Vorkenntnissen' K-1851[1]   10.31 **Lehrmittel an Vorlageblättern Büchern, Modellen u. s. w.**] 'Lehrmittel, Bücher, Modelle, Vorlageblätter Gypsabgüsse etc.' K-1851[1]   10.34

Um] after 'Bestimmung des Schulhonorars – .' K-1851[1]   10.35 **werden:**] K-1851[1] breaks off with 'werden, 1) meine langjährige Praxis in Deutschland, verbunden mit der Kenntniss Französischer und Englisch sachsischer Bauweise deren Eigenthümlichkeit für den Architecten des Continents grosses Interesse haben muss, und bisher dort weder gekannt noch angewendet wurde. 2) Die grosse technische'.

11.7 **sachsisch-Englischen**] *sächsisch-englischen*   11.25 **Fälls**] *Falls*   **Johannis**] Saint John's Day, i.e. 24 June 1851. Semper also mentioned this day as the opening date to his wife, Bertha Semper, in a letter at the end of February 1851 in which he reported his plans for a school of architecture to her for the first time (gta, 20-K-1851-02[S]:1): 'Nun also frisch an's Werk und rasch ohne Aufschub angefangen. Wenn ich nur 8 oder 12 Schüler habe, kann ich hier schon darauf anfangen und spätestens zu Johannis mein Atelier eröffnen.'   11.26–8 **ist meine ganze Bibliothek ~ in New-York ~ bis ich bestimmt weiss ob ich hier bleibe**] In September 1850, Semper had had a large part of his library and drawings sent to New York, to which he had been planning to emigrate before he moved to London – a plan that he only definitively abandoned in August 1852.

ALTERATIONS IN THE MANUSCRIPT

8.17 **27.**] *after probably Hans Semper's underl. note in black ink in upper left corner* VI. 01 VI] *after probably H. Semper's del. note in black ink* XII   8.19–9.1 **Ich danke Ihnen ~ ans Licht stellen. Der Unterricht wäre**] *del. in black ink probably by H. Semper*   8.24 **genügende**] *underl. in black ink probably by H. Semper*   8.26 **Architecten**] *underl. in black ink probably by H. Semper*   8.27 **Ingenieurs**] *underl. in black ink probably by H. Semper*
9.14–18 **Es bedürfte ~ Auskunft ertheilen könnten.**] *del. in black ink probably by H. Semper*
9.20 **in zwei Klassen**] *underl. in black ink probably by H. Semper*   9.21 **das Atelier**] *after del.* in dem   9.29 **a. Bauschule.**] *underl. in black ink probably by H. Semper*
10.2 **Vierwöchentlich**] *after del.* Wöchentlich   10.3 **die**] *over* ein   **eine**] *altered from* einer *after del.* nach   10.15 **Gebäudearten**] *above del.* Theile der Baukunst   **behandelt,**] *altered from* ~∧ *before del.* und   10.16 **nach**] *after del.* mit   10.20 **rationelle**] *above del.* Materielle   10.24 **Baukunst,**] *altered from* ~∧ *before del.* und   **etc.**] *interl.*   10.28 **rathsam**] *after del.* gut   **Eintrittsexamen**] *after del.* Examen   10.36 **und die**] und *interl. and* die *over* in
11.1 **hiesigen**] *before del.* grossen   11.4 **5)**] *after del.*

5) Der Umstand dass ich, durch[1] meine[2] langjährigen Reisen und praktischen Arbeiten mit allen kontinentalen Bauverhältnissen genau bekannt geworden bin und zugleich mit diesen, meine "Schüler" die[3] eigenthümlich Englisch Sächsische[4] Bauweise

> 1 **durch**] *above del.* wegen   2 **meine**] *altered from* meiner   3 **die**] *after del.* auf   4 **Englisch Sächsische**] Englisch | Sächsische

11.5 **praktischer Baumeister**] *after del.* Erbauer meh[r]   11.6 **sowohl**] *after del.* mit   11.6–7 **kontinentalen Bauverhältnissen**] *underl. in black ink probably by H. Semper*   11.7 **sachsisch-Englischen**] *underl. in black ink probably by H. Semper*   11.9 **6)**] *after del.*

School of Architecture and Engineering

6) Die Nähe Frankreichs[1] mit den herrlichen Monumenten der[2] Pikardie und Normandie

     1 **Frankreichs**] *before interl. and del.* und Belg   2 **der**] *undel.*

11.9 **so**] *interl.*   11.13 **vorerst**] *underl. in black ink probably by H. Semper*   11.13–14 **nur eine Anzahl ~ Männer**] *underl. in black ink probably by H. Semper*   11.18–19 **Construction,**] *altered from ~∧ before del.* und   11.19 **Geometrie,**] *altered from ~.*   **Wege- und Brücken-bau**] *after del.* Brückenbau   11.20 **Ich betrachte**] *after del.* Es ist mir daran gelegen

Third Version

TEXTUAL RECORD

DOK:43   gta, 20-DOK-undat.:43, fol. 1r (1v Semper's fragmentary draft letter probably to Friedrich Krause, before 26 February 1851, the putative date of the drafted note), in Semper's hand

DOK-1851:4   gta, 20-DOK-1851:4, fols. 1r–2v (2v blank), in Semper's hand, dated 26 February 1851; gives addresses of Wilhelm Semper and Bertha Semper, thus probably version of the draft Wilhelm Semper referred to in his letter to Gottfried Semper of 8 March 1851, *copy-text*

EXPLANATORY NOTES

This draft advertisement, dated 26 February 1851, takes points from the 'Teaching Programme' that Semper had formulated in his letter to Rudolph Schramm of 25 February 1851 (8–11, Second Version) but did not now explain in detail. It is the first draft of an advertisement at the end of which not only Semper himself but also other figures are listed as referees – in this case, his brother Wilhelm Semper, pharmacist in Hamburg, and his wife, Bertha Semper, in Dresden. It is therefore probably the draft of which Semper sent either a copy or a variant both to Hamburg and to Dresden. He received replies from both that can be related to this draft advertisement. The draft also probably more or less corresponds to the one that Semper sent to Rudolph Schramm for an advertisement in the *Kölnische Zeitung* (249).

Semper enclosed a version of this draft advertisement in the letter to Bertha Semper at the end of February 1851 in which he first told her of his plans to found a school of architecture in London. He wrote that he had 'made one last decisive plan for a way of keeping me here if possible' – that is, for staying in London instead of emigrating to North America. He was planning 'a boarding house [*Pensionsanstalt*], i.e. a large lodging for boarders ... for young architects who want to study here in London and whom I will teach in my studio ... and also for other German and French travellers who want to stay with me'. Regarding the advertisement, he told Bertha Semper that 'The enclosed note ... will have to be printed as quickly and as much as possible in the best German papers'. She should therefore contact

Friedrich Krause and send 'A copy … to Romberg in Meissen at once with a request to print it in the next issue of his journal' (gta, 20-K-1851-02[S]:1). However, no advertisement by Semper appeared in Johann Andreas Romberg's *Zeitschrift für praktische Baukunst*, published in Leipzig.

A fragment of a draft of this version of the advertisement is found on the back of a draft letter probably addressed to Friedrich Krause; in it, Semper was writing to his 'worthy and honourable friend', and stated that he was 'relying, for Saxony, on your support' (248.19–20). The place name and characterization match Krause, who provided support for Semper on several occasions, with the exception of his negative response to Semper's school plans of 10 March 1851 (given in the name of Bertha Semper as well; 236). Similarly, Wilhelm Semper had already expressed reservations from Hamburg on 8 March. In relation to himself and Bertha being named as referees to provide information, Wilhelm also mentioned that he lacked a precise teaching programme and details on the 'location of the institution' and the type of rooms, as well as on the 'status of the costs and the income to be hoped for'.

12.10 **Ingemieur**] *Ingenieur*   12.12 **öffent.**] *öffentlichen*   12.36 **d.**] *den*   **Fbr.**] *Februar*

MANUSCRIPT VARIANTS
DOK:43

fol. 1r

Der Unterzeichnete, wahrend 14 Jahren Director der Sächschen Bauschule an der Akademie der Künste in Dresden und gegenwärtig als Baumeister und Ingenieur in London etablirt hat die Absicht eine Anzahl junger Architecten und Techniker die sich hier theoretisch und praktisch ausbilden wollen, unter sehr günstigen Bedingungen und Aussichten in sein Atelier und zugleich in Kost und Logis aufzunehmen. Er wird persönlich den Unterricht und die Leitung der Uebungen übernehmen, wahrend er für das Ingenieurfach sich einen erfahrenen Englischen Ingenieur beigesellt hat. – Darstellung der Vortheile.

———————— · |

fol. 1v

kommt die grossartige Nationalsammlung und die Lage Londons als Mittelpunkt der Länder des Westens, wo die schönsten Werke des Mittelalters entstanden sind, Belgiens und Frankreichs einerseits, und derjenigen, wo die moderne praktisch-materielle Richtung ihre Triumphe feiert andererseits. Kurz in dieser Beziehung wäre der Aufwand durch den damit verknüpften Vortheil gewiss gerechtfertigt, und es müsste dem jungen Manne wohl zur Empfehlung gereichen, wenn er seine Vorstudien unter ähnlichen Verhältnissen machte. – Aber Leider ist der andere Punkt um so bedenklicher, und wird manchen Familienvater abhalten mir seinen Sohn anzuvertrauen, so dass ich bei mehrerem Nachdenken auch hier wieder verzagen möchte!

Dennoch will ich den Versuch machen; und ich baue, für Sachsen, dabei auf Ihre Stütze, edler und verehrter Freund!

Ich schicke Ihnen das geschriebene Programm bei und bitte Sie, vielleicht mit meiner Unterschrift eine kleine Notiz in eins der gelesensten Blätter Sachsens einzurücken, worin ich zur Theilnahme auffordere und um nähere Auskunft auf meine Adresse in London verweise

School of Architecture and Engineering   249

248.1 **Sächschen**] *'sächsischen'*   248.3–4 **die sich hier theoretisch**] *above del.* die sich unter   248.4 **und praktisch ausbilden wollen,**] *above del.* seiner persönlichen Leitung **unter sehr günstigen Bedingungen und Aussichten**] *inserted after inserted and del.* gegen Bedingungen die von den in Deutschland üblichen   248.5 **Er**] *after del.* Für die Ausbildung im Civilbaufache und für einen Theil   248.6 **Uebungen**] *after del.* Studien im praktischen   **wahrend**] *'während'*   248.7 **erfahrenen**] *before undel.* und *and both above del.* ausgezeichneten   248.8 **Darstellung der Vortheile.**] *inserted after inserted and del.* Entwick   248.10 **kommt**] *altered from* kommen   **grossartige**] *altered from* grossartigen   **Nationalsammlung**] *altered from* Nationalsammlungen   248.13 **andererseits.**] *after del.* Grossbrittanien *after del.* England   248.14 **gerechtfertigt**] *above del.* aufgewogen   248.21 **Ich ~ vielleicht**] *del.*   **mit**] *after del.* mit

Fourth Version

TEXTUAL RECORD

DOK-1851:5   gta, 20-DOK-1851:5, fols. 1r–2v (2v blank), in Semper's hand, dated 1 March 1851

DOK-1851:6   gta, 20-DOK-1851:6, fols. 1r–2v (2v blank), in Semper's hand, dated 3 March 1851

Spyri   Spyri Archives, without shelf mark, fol. 1r–v, 'Deutsches Attelier für Architekten und Ingenieurs in London', in Richard Wagner's hand

EZ   'Deutsches Atelier für Architekten und Ingenieurs in London', *Eidgenössische Zeitung* (Zurich) 7, no. 87 (28 March 1851, morning issue), 347–8 (ZB Zurich, WB 87; another copy gta, 20-DOK-1851:8), *copy-text*

Kirchmeyer 1985   'Deutsches Atelier für Architekten und Ingenieurs in London', 57–8, ed. of EZ

BIBLIOGRAPHY Knoepfli 1976, 264–5; Mallgrave 1996, 191–2; Lütteken 2008, 43 fig. 107, 188; Hildebrand 2020a, 109

EXPLANATORY NOTES

Semper revised the draft advertisement dated 26 February 1851 (12) without waiting for responses from his wife, Bertha Semper, his brother Wilhelm Semper or Friedrich Krause. He had also sent it, in this form or a variant of it, to Rudolph Schramm, who replied with suggested corrections in a letter written probably between 27 February and 1 March 1851. Schramm also reported that it would not be he himself, as stated in the letter of 25 February, but rather the England correspondent of the *Kölnische Zeitung*, Julius Faucher, who would review Semper's project – provided a payment was made for an additional advertisement, as the newspaper required (gta, 20-K-1851-02:2). Although neither the advertisement nor

Faucher's review appeared in the *Kölnische Zeitung*, some of the proposed corrections were included in the version printed in the *Eidgenössische Zeitung*, for which Schramm had also given the initial impetus.

On 26 February 1851, Schramm had written to Semper that Julius Faucher had given him the addresses of the Basel architects Leonhard Friedrich and Johannes Müller, 'since Swiss architecture enthusiasts always like to attend foreign colleges' – Switzerland did not have a public college of architecture at the time. The orientation of Semper's planned school of architecture towards Switzerland as well was also mentioned in the letter to Bertha Semper at the end of February 1851 (Semper wrote that he would forward 'an identical copy' of the advertisement version sent to Bertha 'to Hamburg and Switzerland'). On 3 March 1851, Semper sent Leonhard Friedrich a variant, now lost, of a draft advertisement with that date (251, Manuscript Variants 13.29, 13.30), with a request to have it published 'in the most widely read papers in Switzerland' by the Berne architect Ludwig Stürler and the 'conductor Wagner', who lived near Zurich. Semper had known Stürler since they studied together in Franz Christian Gau's Paris studio. Richard Wagner persuaded Johann Bernhard Spyri, the editor of the *Eidgenössische Zeitung* and later the husband of Johanna Spyri, to print the advertisement he had copied along with his supporting text (for Wagner's text, see 208–9).

In the letter to Leonhard Friedrich, Semper explained that he would 'submit a teaching programme … immediately', if desired. He estimated 'that the annual fees for board, lodging and full tuition would be 100 pounds sterling'. However, he would 'certainly allow the most favourable conditions to apply for compatriots, among whom I also include the Swiss'. Friedrich only replied on 27 April 1851: he had 'forwarded the enclosed note … soon after receipt of your letter to Mr. Stürler, as well as a copy of it to the conductor Mr. Wagner, with a request to publish your plan in an appropriate manner in accordance with your wishes' (gta, 20-K-1851-04-27). No reactions to Semper's published advertisement are so far known of. There is as yet no evidence also of whether Stürler succeeded in having the advertisement printed (perhaps in the *Berner-Zeitung*).

13.1 **Deutsches Atelier für Architekten und Ingenieurs in London.**] this title also in 1851:5 – a variant of the title 'Deutsche Bau und Ingenieurschule in London' suggested by Schramm in his letter of late February 1851 (gta, 20-K-1851-02:2, also containing Schramm's suggestions cited in the following passages)   13.6 **unter sehr günstigen Bedingungen**] Schramm suggested, with reference to the version of 26 February 1851 (12.5–6), 'unter sehr günstigen Bedingungen, und selbst *mit* Aussicht auf späteres Verdienst'.   13.18 **so dass dieselben gewiss mit Unrecht bisher**] Schramm suggested, with reference to the version of 26 February 1851 (12.18–19) and the phrase cited by Schramm as 'so dass *sie* gewiss mit Unrecht bisher bei uns', that 'statt sie ist hier deutlicher *dieselben*'.   13.20–1 **Ausserdem bildet London ~ einen Hauptort**] Schramm suggested, with reference to the version of 26 February 1851 (12.21–2), 'Ausserdem *bietet* London – einen Hauptort. Ich nahm an, dass es *bildet* heissen soll.' However, the version of 26 February 1851 has 'bildet', not 'bietet', as Schramm seems to have read the word, unless he was referring to a version differing at least in this point.   13.22–5 **und in der Mitte ~ Exkursionen ein, welche**] Schramm suggested, with reference to the version of 26 February 1851 or one differing also in this point (12.23–6): 'Den Nachsatz habe ich der Deutlichkeit wegen mit Verwandlung eines Adverbs in ein Hauptwort so formirt: "und, in der Mitte zwischen dem Reichthume Belgiens und Frankreichs an Werken der schönen Baukunst und den über England zerstreuten berühmten

School of Architecture and Engineering 251

Werken der Ingenieurkunst gelegen, ladet diese Centralstadt zu schnell ausführbaren Exkursionen ein ohne'". 13.30–1 **Semper.** —] before Richard Wagner's supporting text for Semper's 'Deutsches Atelier für Architekten und Ingenieurs in London' (208–9)

MANUSCRIPT VARIANTS

13.1 **Deutsches Atelier für Architekten und Ingenieurs in London.**] *inserted DOK-1851:5 om. DOK-1851:6* **Atelier**] Attelier *Spyri* **Architekten**] Architecten *DOK-1851:5* 13.2 **Direktor**] Director *DOK-1851:5 DOK-1851:6* 13.3 **bildenden**] *om. DOK-1851:6* **zu**] in *DOK-1851:6* **Dresden**∧] ~, *Spyri* **Architekt**] Architect *DOK-1851:5 DOK-1851:6* 13.4 **Absicht,**] ~∧ *DOK-1851:5 DOK-1851:6 Spyri* 13.5 **Architekten**] Architecten *DOK-1851:5 DOK-1851:6* 13.6 **sehr**] *interl. DOK-1851:5 om. DOK-1851:6* **Bedingungen**] *before del.* und Aussichten *DOK-1851:5 before* und Aussichten und] *after del.* und selbst unter Aussichten auf spätere Beschäftigung gegen Honor[a] *DOK-1851:6* **Atelier**∧] Attelier, *Spyri* 13.7–8 **architektonischen**] architectonischen *DOK-1851:5 DOK-1851:6* 13.9 **wird,**] ~; *Spyri* 13.10 **Ingenieur**] *after* Englischen *DOK-1851:5 DOK-1851:6* 13.12 **grossartigen,**] ~∧ *DOK-1851:5 DOK-1851:6* **Wohlfahrt**] Wohlfarth *DOK-1851:5 DOK-1851:6* **Anlagen,**] ~∧ *DOK-1851:5 DOK-1851:6* 13.13 **Weise,**] ~∧ *DOK-1851:5 DOK-1851:6 Spyri* **wie sie dieselben technisch durchführen**] wie dieselben technisch ausgeführt werden technisch] *interl.* ausgeführt] *altered from* durchgeführt *DOK-1851:5* wie dieselben durchgeführt werden *DOK-1851:6* 13.14 **sind.** ∧] ~. – *DOK-1851:5 Spyri* 13.15 **in technischer und auch in künstlerischer**] ~ ~ ~ selbst in künstlerischer *DOK-1851:5* ~ ~ ~ selbst in ästhetischer *DOK-1851:6* 13.16 **an Motiven**] von ~ *DOK-1851:5 DOK-1851:6* 13.18 **dieselben**] *above del.* sie *DOK-1851:5* sie *DOK-1851:6* **andere,**] ~∧ *DOK-1851:5 DOK-1851:6* 13.18–19 **weit fremdere**] *after del.* ferner *DOK-1851:5* 13.19 **fast**] *before* ganz *DOK-1851:6* 13.21 **unserer**] unsrer *Spyri* 13.22 **soll;**] ~, *DOK-1851:5 DOK-1851:6 altered from* sollte; *Spyri* 13.22–4 **Mitte zwischen dem Reichthum ~ und den ~ Werken des Ingenieurs gelegen,**] Mitte *before del.* zwischen dem Werken der Baukunst so reichen Frankreich und Belgien und den über England zerstreuten berühmten Werken der Ingenieurkunst, dem] *altered from* den England] *after del.* Gross-Brittanien *DOK-1851:5* ~ ~ ~ an Werken der Baukunst so reichen Frankreich und Belgien und den über Grossbritanien zerstreuten berühmten Werken der Ingenieurkunst, *DOK-1851:6* 13.25 **Exkursionen**] Excursionen *DOK-1851:5 DOK-1851:6* 13.28 **folgender Adresse**] folgenden Adressen *DOK-1851:5 DOK-1851:6* 13.29 **"Professor Semper**] ∧~ ~ *DOK-1851:5* ∧Professor G. Semper ∧Professor] *after del.* ∧Mr. G. Sem *DOK-1851:6* **University Street**] ~ street *DOK-1851:5* **– London."**] ∧ London.∧ | ...... | ...... *DOK-1851:5* ∧ Gower Street. London.∧ | P. P. v. Stürler in Bern. Bern.] *before del.* Baumeister Friedrich in Basel *DOK-1851:6* ∧ London." *Spyri* 13.30 **Gottfried Semper.**] *before* London d. 1 Marz 1851. *DOK-1851:5 before* London d. 3 März 1851. *DOK-1851:6* ~ ~∧ *Spyri*

Lessons in Architecture and Drawing

First Version

TEXTUAL RECORD

DOK:51   gta, 20-DOK-undat.:51, fols. 1r–2v (1v–2v blank), in unknown hand (pl. 1), *copy-text*

EXPLANATORY NOTES

Probably the first draft of Semper's advertisements, this is so skilfully written that Wolfgang Herrmann considered it to be an 'elegantly printed prospectus' and dated it to the beginning of March 1851 (Herrmann 1984, 272 n. 154). It was probably produced after Braun's reply to Semper's proposals for a school of architecture in early January 1851. In his letter to Semper of 29 January 1851, Braun went on to write that 'Practical instruction in the theory of architecture is likely to be very attractive even for men like Chadwick, and people like that really ought not to do without it'. This recalls the passage in the present draft advertisement in which Semper recommends himself as offering 'aid to Noblemen or Gentlemen' (14.5). Thus, the advertisement may have been formulated by Emil Braun and written out by his wife, Anne Braun, daughter of the industrialist James Thomson.

Second Version

TEXTUAL RECORD

DOK:48   gta, 20-DOK-undat.:48, fol. 1r–v (1v sketch of triangles in pencil probably by Semper), in Semper's hand, first third in pencil, rest in black ink, *copy-text*

EXPLANATORY NOTES

This is one of two draft advertisements drawn up in Semper's handwriting in English probably before the drafts that he exchanged with Karoline Heusinger starting on 22 February 1851. It was probably written at around the same time as the other draft, which belongs to class II (8, First Version; 235, 244).

Lessons in Architecture and Drawing

EDITORIAL EMENDATIONS

14.21 **crayon-drawing**] crayon- | drawing

ALTERATIONS IN THE MANUSCRIPT

14.9 **III.**] *inserted in pencil*   14.10–13 **Professor ~ native**] *in pencil*   14.13 **land**] *in ink over* country   country] *in pencil*   –] *in pencil*   14.13–21 **having ~ crayon-drawing.**] *in ink* 14.17 **Drawing**] *after del.* Drawing, whether in pencil, crayon or Colouring   or] *interl. and underl. after del.* , or water | colours   14.18 **in**] *interl.*   14.19 **of Instruction**] *interl.*   **useful**] *after del.* advantageous

Third Version

TEXTUAL RECORD

DOK:39   gta, 20-DOK-undat.:39, fol. 1r–v, in Semper's hand, German source text of English translation DOK:49
DOK:49   gta, 20-DOK-undat.:49, fol. 1r–v, in Karoline Heusinger's hand, Mary Scarlett Campbell's translation, *copy-text*

EXPLANATORY NOTES

This draft advertisement in English is the translation by Mary Scarlett Campbell that she was entrusted with by Karoline Heusinger, a lady-companion in the Campbells' home. Semper had brought the German source text to Heusinger on 22 February 1851 (254, DOK:39). Heusinger sent Semper her copy of the translation on 24 February 1851 (235, 238, 240).

15.3–4 **in the construction, drawing and Composition of ornements**] The German source text has 'in der Construction, im Zeichnen und Erfinden von Verzierungen' (254.3–4), speaking of construction on the one hand, and on the other hand of ornaments; in Heusinger's copy of Campbell's translation, the whole phrase relates to ornaments, thus speaking of the construction of ornaments.   15.7 **engravings.**] The following sentence 'If desired the study of German can be combined.' is deleted in Karoline Heusinger's hand, whereas the sentence is not deleted in the corresponding German source text (254.7–8).

ALTERATIONS IN THE MANUSCRIPT

15.1 **Gottfried Semper**] *after del.* S   **at**] *interl. after del.* on   on] *above del.* and of   15.7 **engravings.**] *before del. on fol. 1r–v* If desired the study of ¦ German can be combined.

MANUSCRIPT VARIANTS
DOK:39

fol. 1r   Professor Gottfried Semper früherer Director der Bauschule an der Kunstakademie, und Erbauer des Theaters zu Dresden beabsichtigt in allen Zweigen seiner Kunst Unterricht zu geben; Namentlich in dem Entwerfen von Bauplänen, in der Construction, im Zeichnen und Erfinden von Verzierungen, Möbeln, Vasen, Mustern etc, in der Perspective, und im Ausführen landschaftlicher und Architectonischer Skizzen in Bleistift und in Aquarell.   5
Auch übernimmt er es, Vorträge über Geschichte der Kunst zu halten und diese mit Zeich-
fol. 1v   nungen und Kupferwerken zu erläutern. Wenn es gewünscht wird ¦ kann Uebung im Deutschen damit verbunden werden.

27. University Street
Gower Street.   10

254.3 **Namentlich**] *after del.* Hauptsächlich *after del.* Hauptsächlich macht er sich ver-bindlich

Fourth Version

TEXTUAL RECORD

DOK-1851:7   gta, 20-DOK-1851:7, fol. 1r–v, in Semper's hand, dated 3 March 1851, *copy-text*

EXPLANATORY NOTES

This draft advertisement was intended for translation into English; repeating the French in English, it emphasizes benefits for travellers ('particularly useful for tourists', 15.17–18). Like the French draft from advertisement class I (6–7, Third Version), which was probably writ-ten shortly afterwards, this version may also have been prompted by Karoline Heusinger's advice in her letter of 27 February 1851 to show the advertisement she had translated to an English architect (240). It probably corresponds to the programme referred to in the French advertisement belonging to class I in the sentence 'Exercices etc comme au programme N° 3' (7.11). In comparison with other drafts belonging to advertisement class III, this version is optionally extended to include 'a complete and illustrative course on the history of decora-tion'.

15.11 **l'ecole**] *l'école*   15.11–12 **l'accademie**] *l'académie*   15.14 **comprehensiblement**] *compréhensiblement*   15.15 **procedés**] *procédés*   15.16 **l'ancre**] *l'encre*   15.17 **preparatoire**] *préparatoire*   15.22 **ornamens**] *ornements*   15.23 **l'ancre**] *l'encre*   15.26 **differens**] *différents*   **demontrés**] *démontrés*   15.29 **l. 3 Mars 1851**] *le ~ ~ ~*

EDITORIAL EMENDATIONS

15.27 **par etc.**] *before one-sixth page blank*

ALTERATIONS IN THE MANUSCRIPT

15.11 **Professor**] *after del.* Professor Semper, etc. etc. donne des leçons privées   etc. etc.] *undel.*   **l'ecole**] *after del.* l'aca   15.15 **leçons;**] *altered from ~∧ before del.* et   15.16 **au crayon**] *before del.* et   15.17 **touristes**] *after del.* personnen qui vont faire des voyages dans les pays classiques de l'ar   15.20 **l'architecture,**] *altered from ~.*   15.22 **des décorations**] *interl.*   **ornamens,**] *before del.* des détails d'architecture,   15.24 **Ces études peuvent**] *after del.*

Si l'on veut, ces etudes peuvent embrasser tout l'art du décorer et être combinées avec un cours illustratif d'histoire du[1] décor[2] dans le quel la difference des caractères des differens styles sera demontrée.

     1 **du**] *above del.* de la   2 **décor∧**] *altered from* décoration.

15.25–6 **les differens caractères**] *after del.* la difference

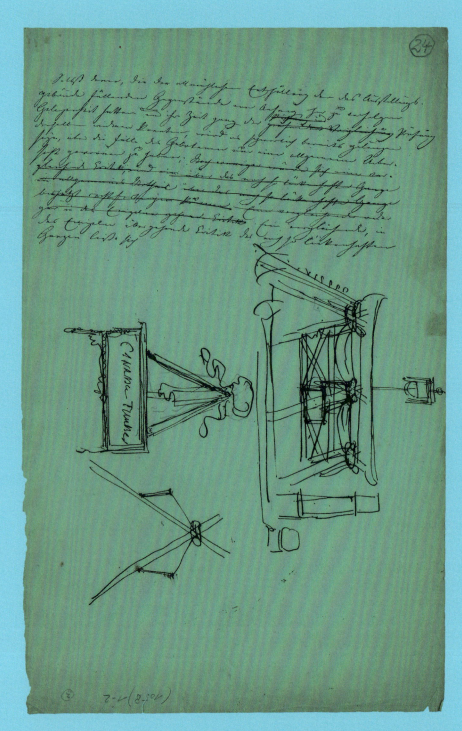

Pl. 8: Sketches of Canadian Timber Trophy, 1851 (gta, 20-Ms-94)

THE GREAT EXHIBITION

Introduction

The Great Exhibition of the Works of Industry of All Nations that was presented to the public in Joseph Paxton's Crystal Palace in Hyde Park from 1 May to 11 October 1851 marked a turning point in several respects for Gottfried Semper during his period of exile in London. The six months brought him work – and work of a type from which he was able to benefit directly in relation to architectural theory and indirectly in practical architectural work, particularly after his appointment to a professorship in architecture at the Swiss Federal Polytechnic School in Zurich in 1855.

The texts gathered together here are connected with Semper's commissions to decorate sections representing various countries in the exhibition at the Crystal Palace, on the one hand. On the other, they also belong in the context of *Wissenschaft, Industrie und Kunst* (Science, Industry, and Art), the booklet that Semper started writing shortly before the end of the Great Exhibition and completed in January 1852. In it, he extended the approach taken in his essay *Die vier Elemente der Baukunst* (The Four Elements of Architecture) – which he had started in October 1850 and completed in January 1851 – namely viewing architecture as a product of the combined industrial or applied arts. Central elements of these studies were incorporated into the two volumes of *Der Stil in den technischen und tektonischen Künsten, oder Praktische Aesthetik* (Style in the Technical and Tectonic Arts; or, Practical Aesthetics), which he wrote in Zurich and which contains several references to the London exhibition.

Semper obtained the commissions to decorate national sections for the Great Exhibition through Henry Cole, who was responsible for coordinating the arrangement of the exhibits in the Crystal Palace. Semper himself acknowledged this debt when he wrote to Cole in October 1854 to inform him that he had been offered the professorship in Zurich. He mentioned Cole's 'kind disposition' towards him, to which he owed his present 'position at Marlborough House' (the home of Cole's Department of Science and Art, which had been founded as the Department of Practical Art in early 1852). As a German draft of the letter notes, however, Semper was also indebted to Cole for his 'employment in the Exhibition building'. There is only scattered evidence of what this actually involved. When in 1860 Semper was working on the placement of exhibits in the Collection of Antiquities in the main building of the Polytechnic School in Zurich, he emphasized to the head of the canton's building department, Franz Hagenbuch, that he had 'decorated four sections (Canada, Turkey, Sweden, Denmark) at the great industrial exhibition in London'. Other letters and notes contain further information on Semper's commissions in the Crystal Palace but do not allow their exact scope to be determined.

Semper probably took on initial tasks at the beginning of March 1851. In a reply written on 8 March to Edwin Chadwick's offer of a position as Joseph Paxton's assistant in Chatsworth, Derbyshire, Semper wrote that he was hesitant to accept it immediately, as he had already agreed to 'some little jobs relating to the coming exhibition of industry'. This may have been referring to the decoration of the Canadian court, as Henry Cole sent a note to Semper on 12 March 1851 to tell him that John Lindley, superintendent of the colonial departments to which Canada belonged, wanted to see him in the Crystal Palace because 'The half counter on the east of the Canadian span, next the main aisle, *cannot* be occupied by Canadian goods.'

Cole's note hints at other matters as well. The counter to the east of the Canadian court next to the main avenue in the Crystal Palace belonged to the exhibition area for the British colonies in West Africa. Although Semper does not appear to have been involved in that section, the situation was different on the western corner of the Canadian court adjoining the main avenue. This had been assigned to the Cape of Good Hope, a British colony since 1814. On a coloured design by Semper for the Canadian court, it can be seen that he had designed a four-bayed oblong cabinet for the Cape of Good Hope's section (HfBK Dresden, Custody, B 969) as a continuation of the three temple-like glass cabinets along the west wall of the Canadian court. The cabinet was in fact constructed, in a form apparently different from the design – as a contemporary woodcut of a 'Group of Objects Selected from the Contributions of the Cape of Good Hope' published in *The Illustrated Exhibitor* of 27 December 1851 suggests. On 4 September 1851, Semper was still requesting payment for the work he had done for the Cape of Good Hope, for which he had buffalo heads suspended above the cabinet (visible in the woodcut). In the letter, which has survived in an unaddressed draft, Semper pointed out that he had carried out the work involved together with the addressee at the latter's suggestion. The individual concerned was probably William Butler Simpson, since a reply from his office for architectural decoration followed the same day.

As an advertisement of 22 March 1851 in the *Hamburger Nachrichten* shows – published by the Hamburg architect Franz Georg Stammann on Semper's behalf in order to attract exhibitors from Germany – Semper had already been commissioned in March 'among other things, also to arrange for Sweden the exhibition of items sent in from there' (209.29–30). Semper was in contact with the Swedish consul-general, Charles Tottie, who was commissioner for Sweden and Norway, which were politically allied. Work on decorating this smaller section was joined around the same time by tasks for the adjoining, similarly small exhibition from Denmark. This emerges among other things from a printed advertisement leaflet in French dated 1 April 1851. The leaflet states that Semper had been entrusted with arranging their exhibition items 'by the commissioners of Sweden and Denmark' (18.6–7). For his part, Denmark's commissioner, Regnar Westenholz, informed Semper on 29 March 1851 that 'the ship with the things from Denmark' had 'arrived on the river today', and they would 'thus very soon be able to start setting them up or at least with preparations for it'.

There is less clarity about Semper's other contributions. Friedrich Wetzler, an acquaintance of Semper's, stated in a letter of 12 April 1851 to the Leipzig publisher Otto Wigand that Semper would in addition to his employment 'as commissioner for Sweden, Denmark, Hamburg and Canada … also probably be representing Greece and another part of the United States'. Semper's involvement with the exhibition section from Hamburg never materialized. Greece had possibly come into view because it was exhibiting alongside Turkey, whose section Semper claimed to have decorated. Nothing else is known of the Turkish commission – which was similar in its spatial extent to that of Canada – apart from what is contained in reports on the exhibition (in which Semper's name is never mentioned) and in illustrations: a tented passage shared with Egypt led to a miniature mosque under a vaulted marquee. The alleged other 'part of the United States' that Semper was perhaps to have represented may have been due to confusion with the British colonies of Newfoundland, New Brunswick and Nova Scotia. Semper was probably involved in those sections – the Hamburg advertisement mentions generally that he was responsible for 'English colonial wares', while the French announcement refers to the 'Anglo-American colonies'. Semper's Timber Trophy in front of the Canadian court did in fact assemble exhibits from manufacturers from different sections – as the above-mentioned William Butler Simpson, who erected it, pointed out in a letter to Matthew Digby Wyatt of 18 September 1851 in which he requested payment for it from the Royal Commission. Accordingly, the Trophy was crowned with a canoe from Nova Scotia, as noted in Robert Hunt's *Hand-Book to the Official Catalogues*.

At the time of the opening, Semper had 'practically completed' his decoration work at the Crystal Palace, as he reported on 5 May 1851 to his brother Johann Carl Semper in Altona. The Turkish court was completed on 22 May, as was noted by a German business journalist (Scherer 1851, 175). Semper was now combing through the exhibition as a kind of independent juror. He also received visitors, particularly from Germany. In the second half of May, his brother Johann Carl came; in August, Semper was visited by his publisher Eduard Vieweg from Brunswick, the school director Friedrich Krause from Dresden, the architect Franz Georg Stammann from Hamburg and two of Bertha Semper's acquaintances from the same city. In the meantime, Semper had also obtained new work; he wrote to Johann Carl in the letter of 5 May that he had 'commissions from various journalists and I will be well paid if I write'. He did so in two published essays and drafts of additional texts, and ultimately in *Science, Industry, and Art*. The ongoing preliminary work for these included the hurried 'Notes on Exhibits' that Semper wrote as he rambled around the Crystal Palace (31–9, pl. 2).

In October 1851, the architectural critique of the Crystal Palace written by Semper between the end of March and mid-May 1851 was published anonymously in *The Edinburgh Review* ('A Foreign Architect's Views of the Building', 18–20). It was incorporated into Edward Aubrey Moriarty's anonymous review of the final edition of the *Official Catalogue of the Great Exhibition*. In the other essay, 'Die grosse Ausstellung' (The Great Exhibition), which appeared anonymously in the German supplement of *The Illustrated London News* of 17 May 1851, Semper combined his observations on the Crystal Palace with an attempt – based on the exhibits – to develop criteria for assessing the relationship between 'Peoples of European and non-European Culture', as the essay's subtitle states. He took up the approach used in his never-completed 'Vergleichende Baulehre' (Comparative Architecture), which he had been working on since the 1840s.

This approach also guided Semper's plan for a series of essays on the Great Exhibition in the form of letters to Lothar Bucher, which remained unpublished (27–31). Possibly Semper began writing them as a reaction to a suggestion made by Friedrich Wetzler to the Leipzig publisher Otto Wigand that he should publish reports on the Great Exhibition by Semper as a twelve-part weekly and then in book form. This proposal did not come to fruition, nor did Wigand's alternative suggestion that Semper should write articles for the Leipzig *Illustrirte Zeitung*. Following theoretical arguments regarding a system for classifying exhibits in his letters to Bucher, Semper attempted to organize the system into a ramified list, which he drafted as an insert for *Science, Industry, and Art* between October 1851 and January 1852 as an 'Outline of a Cultural-Historical Exhibition' (40–2), to be accompanied by a 'Note' in which he assigned the classification categories to rooms in a collection, with the products in the main rooms and the techniques and raw materials necessary for their production in the adjoining rooms (43).

The Great Exhibition, which inspired Semper to develop these plans for a collection, also provided the framework for his idea to arrange an exhibition in part of the emptied Crystal Palace in February 1852 presenting 'sketches, drawings and models from the fields of industrial art, including architecture'. The 'Association of Artists of Various Nations' that Semper initiated for the purpose appealed for contributions in the Berlin *Zeitschrift für Bauwesen* of 31 December 1851 (43–4). There is no evidence that the exhibition plan was ever implemented; Semper's ambitions might have been simply exaggerated. In a letter to Vieweg of 2 December 1851, he enclosed a draft of the essay *Science, Industry, and Art* and described it as being suitable 'to draw the attention of the English and also German audience to the purpose of this exhibition, which goes further and involves the founding of a school of industry in London'.

The fact that Semper regarded *Science, Industry, and Art* as also addressing an English audience is a reference to the English translation, the completion of which had delayed the revision of the German version, as he wrote to Vieweg in the same letter. Semper mentioned the offer to publish the essay in English for the first time in a letter of 17 October 1851 to Eduard Vieweg's son Heinrich just after having sent a first version of *Science, Industry, and Art* to Brunswick. The translation was ready for publication just a few weeks later under the title 'Remarks upon Artistic taste among the People and the means of its Development' (gta, 20-Ms-89), as Semper wrote to Vieweg on 2 and 18 December. Cole was obviously involved in the publication project: on 8 April 1852, Semper asked Cole to correct 'an erratum' in a passage of *Science, Industry, and Art* 'before printed' (the passage concerned with the Portland Vase; cf. 468–9, Explanatory Notes 153.24–5). Yet the translation was never published. Possibly Cole planned to have it serialized in *The Athenaeum*. In any case, he reported to Semper three times in February 1852 about negotiations with the editor of *The Athenaeum* regarding the publication of manuscripts, the last time on 24 February with the information 'that the Athenaeum will print your paper'.

Semper was nevertheless convinced – as he wrote to Vieweg on 20 May 1852 – that the 'little brochure "Science, Industry, and Art"', publication of the 'English version of which has so far been prevented due to a chain of unfortunate events', had 'borne fruit', as he now had a 'prospective post as professor at the drawing school here' – that is, at Cole's Department of Practical Art, which had emerged from the Government School of Design. The reform of art education proposed in *Science, Industry, and Art* (Semper 1852, 61–72) does indeed discuss elements of Cole's programme for the new school, such as the establishment of special classes according to different branches of industry, practice in workshops, a collection of manufactures and an annual exhibition organized for the purpose of encouraging mutual competition. Cole (and not Prince Albert, as often claimed) might therefore have been the person behind the 'private request' mentioned by Semper in the preface (dated 24 November 1851) of *Science, Industry, and Art* as having prompted the writing of the essay as a contribution to 'the organization of improved teaching for trainee technicians' and to the 'development of taste'.

BIBLIOGRAPHY Bucher 1879; Semper 1880, 20; Ahrens 1886a, 24–47; Ahrens 1886b; Brinckmann 1903; Leisching 1903; Mrazek 1966; Lankheit 1976; Reising 1976; Rykwert 1976, 70; Vogt 1976; Herrmann 1978, 50–4, 58–60; May 1980; Herrmann 1981, 99–101, 104; Nigro Covre 1982; Herrmann 1984, 45–8, 53–4; Mallgrave 1985b; Mallgrave 1996, 189–208; Hvattum 1999; Franz 2000; Mallgrave 2002; Hildebrand 2003; Hvattum 2004b; Hildebrand 2007; Mallgrave 2007; Arburg 2008, 311–34; Luttmann 2008, 124–39; Leoni 2014; Chestnova 2017b; Hildebrand 2020a, 110–19; Leoni 2021

Announcement

TEXTUAL RECORD

DOK-1851:9a   gta, 20-DOK-1851:9a–d and 9f–l, 'Avis', dated 1 April 1851, eleven copies with, at the foot of fol. 1r, imprint 'Paris. – IMPRIMERIE LE NORMANT, rue de Seine, 10' and, on fol. 1v, stamp 'TIMBRE cen. 1. OUDINE ET VAUTHIER. SEINE' with figure of Justitia in the centre

DOK-1851:9e   gta, 20-DOK-1851:9e, 'Avis', dated 1 April 1851, one copy with same imprint and stamp as in DOK-1851:9a, *copy-text*

BIBLIOGRAPHY Herrmann 1978, 50 n. 163; Herrmann 1984, 272 n. 159

EXPLANATORY NOTES

Semper drafted this advertisement for tasks related to the Great Exhibition after consulting, around mid-March 1851, Charles Séchan (one of the decorative painters with whom he had worked at the Court Theatre in Dresden). Through Séchan's efforts, it was printed in Paris and distributed in France but was not particularly successful (nor was the other printed advert for Hamburg; see 209–10). Between 11 April and 20 June 1851, Semper received inquiries from nine French exhibitors. A producer of wine, spirits and vinegar, a cooper, a fabric printer and a lime-burner asked for further information; a shoemaker, a glass manufacturer, a spinner and a clay manufacturer commissioned him with the arrangement of their products. Another clay manufacturer, Jean-Jacques Bouvert, requested Semper after the Exhibition had already opened to present his products to the jury for assessment – even though he had already withdrawn them. Semper made remarkably energetic efforts to promote one of Bouvert's products, a fuel material. He tried to obtain a certificate through the Canadian geologist William Edmond Logan, the commissioner responsible for exhibiting Canadian minerals, and as late as January 1852 he was still negotiating with his brother Wilhelm Semper, a pharmacist in Hamburg, regarding the distribution of Bouvert's fuel.

18.23 **divers**] *diverses* (see below, Print Variants 18.23)

PRINT VARIANTS

18.5 **Exposition**] Expédition *DOK-1851:9a*   18.23 **divers**] diverses *DOK-1851:9a*

A Foreign Architect's Views of the Building

TEXTUAL RECORD

MS 94^1 gta, 20-Ms-94, fol. 6v, in Semper's hand
MS 94^2 gta, 20-Ms-94, fol. 5r–v (5r variant of MS 94^1), in Semper's hand
MS 94^3 gta, 20-Ms-94, fol. 6r, in Semper's hand
MS 94^4 gta, 20-Ms-94, fol. 7r–v (7v blank; variant of MS 94^3), in Semper's hand
MS 94^5 gta, 20-Ms-94, fol. 3r–v (3v blank; variant of MS 94^2), in Semper's hand
MS 94^6 gta, 20-Ms-94, fol. 4r–v (4v blank; variant of MS 94^5), in Semper's hand
MS 94^7 gta, 20-Ms-94, fols. 1r–2v (1r–v variant of MS 94^6; 1v–2r variant of MS 94^2 and MS 94^4), in Semper's hand
ER   'A Foreign Architect's Views of the Building', *The Edinburgh Review* 94, no. 192 (Oct. 1851), 576–7 (BL, P.P.6199.h), Edward Aubrey Moriarty's English trans. of a missing German source text, in Moriarty 1851, *copy-text*
ERAm   'Official Catalogue of the Great Exhibition of the Works of Industry of All Nations, 1851', *The Edinburgh Review: American Edition* (New York) 94, no. 192 (Oct. 1851), 285–306, here 295–6
DN   'The Great Exhibition – The Official Catalogue', *The Daily News* (London), no. 1682 (14 Oct. 1851), 6; no. 1687 (20 Oct. 1851), 2; here no. 1682, 6
LA   'Official Catalogue of the Great Exhibition of the Works of Industry of All Nations, 1851', *Littell's Living Age* (Boston) 31, no. 393 (29 Nov. 1851), 385–400, here 392
Semper 2014 vol. 1, 411–12, Karge's reprint ed. of ER

264   The Great Exhibition

BIBLIOGRAPHY Vogt 1976, 180–9; Herrmann 1978, 54 n. 173; Herrmann 1980, 49; Herrmann 1981, 65–6, 101; Herrmann 1984, 273 n. 168; Gnehm 2015, 36

EXPLANATORY NOTES

Semper had been writing his critique of the Crystal Palace between the end of March and mid-May 1851, although it did not appear until October. Of Semper's essays on the Great Exhibition, it is the only one published in English at that time – alongside two German publications, one of which appeared in the German supplement of *The Illustrated London News* (20–6) and the other as the booklet *Science, Industry, and Art* of 1852. Although the essay was published anonymously, the translator, Edward Aubrey Moriarty, in his review of the *Official Catalogue* in which he inserted the text, alluded to Semper's authorship on several occasions. In introducing Semper's text, he wrote (Moriarty 1851, 575):

> The original Paper emanated, we have reason to believe, from the pen of a writer, himself the architect of one of the most admired of modern edifices – the late Dresden Opera-house; and its remarks on the structural peculiarities of the building are of a character sufficiently interesting to excuse our translation and insertion of them here. The unhappy political convulsions of the year 1849 proved equally fatal to the high professional position of its author, and the graceful monument of his genius. The Paper was written on the eve, and amidst all the bustle and preparation of the opening: –

Two pages before, Moriarty referred to Semper's essay and remarked that it reflected 'the opinion of one of the most distinguished foreign architects of the day'. Moriarty's authorship both of the review (it was also published anonymously) and of the translation of Semper's text is suggested on the one hand by the fact that he edited the *Amtlicher Catalog der Ausstellung der Industrie-Erzeugnisse aller Völker* (published on 21 July 1851), the German version of the *Official Catalogue*. On the other hand, Moriarty had met Henry Cole on 31 August, as well as on 9 and 27 September 1851, in connection with an article (probably the same review) for *The Edinburgh Review*, as Cole noted in his diary. As the intermediary for Semper's employment for the Great Exhibition, Cole might have known about Semper's draft texts about the Crystal Palace. The manuscript from which the English translation was made is not extant, but various fragmentary German drafts by Semper survive; they have their own interest, as they contain passages that did not make it into the translation – for example, passages on the tower of Babel and the despotism of mechanization.

18 **A Foreign Architect's Views of the Building**] title taken from header in ER, 577

PRINT VARIANTS

18.28 **spared!**] ~. *DN*   18.28–9 **as∧ stimulated**] ~, ~ *LA*
19.3 **lattice-work**] lattice work *DN*   19.4 **her works.**] ~ ~! *LA*   19.6 **honour**] honor *LA*
19.7 **and, considering**] ~∧ ~ *DN*   19.12 **into form,**] ~ ~∧ *ERAm*   19.14 **The simple problem**] *no paragraph DN*   **open air,**] ~ ~∧ *DN*   19.17 **States**] states *DN LA*   19.23 **For the fulfilment**] *no paragraph DN*   19.28 **Little was needed**] *no paragraph DN*

19.32 **artistic**] artististic *DN*   19.36 **harmonised**] harmonized *ERAm LA*   19.40 **realised**] realized *LA*   **canvass**] canvas *DN*
20.8 **refined taste,**] ~ ~∧ *DN*   20.17 **of courts**∧] ~ ~, *LA*   20.19 **In conclusion**] *no paragraph DN*   20.23 **elsewere**] elsewhere *ERAm DN LA*

MANUSCRIPT VARIANTS
MS 94[1]

Es ist eine Pracht um die beiden Bäume in der Transept des Hyde Park Palastes, wie sie   *fol. 6v*
lebensstrotzend sich eilen ihre letzten Blätterhüllen abzustreifen, gleich als sporne sie das
3   hastige rings sie umbrausende Gestaltungsdrängen.

> 265.1 **Es**] *after del.* Es ist eine Pracht um die beiden Bäume in der Transept des Hyde Park
> Pallastes, angespornt durch das hastige Treiben, was sie umgiebt,   Pracht] *after del.*
> volle *(volle above del.* wundervolle)   des Hyde Park Pallastes] *after del.* des Schaumarkt-
> gebäudes   angespornt] *after del.* wie sie, gleichsam   hastige] *repl. del.* rege   **in der**
> **Transept**] *'in dem Transept'*   265.2 **sporne**] *after del.* wäre   265.3 **rings**] *after del.* rings
> sie umschwärmende *after del.* Treiben was sie umgiebt

MS 94[2]

Es ist eine Pracht um die beiden Bäume in der Transept des Hydepark-Palastes, wie sie   *fol. 5r*
5   lebenstrotzend sich eilen ihre letzten Blätterhüllen abzustreifen, als sporne sie das hastige
Drängen nach naher Gestaltung, das sie umschwärmt. Gleich mächtigen Fächern füllen
ihre Zweige das Halbrund des Schiffes und durch ihr zartes Grün spielt anmuthig das
leichte Stangen- und Gitterwerk des luftigen Baues. Noch ist das graue Segeltuch, das den
Bau bedecken soll, über diesen Theil desselben nicht ausgebreitet und des Himmels Blau
10   mit den leichten Frühlingswolken blickt überall herrlich hindurch. Das Ganze athmet
junge Lebensfrische und jubelt dem Erbauer des Werkes ein Loblied entgegen.
Kehrt dann das Auge auf den chaotischen Werdedrang dort unten zurück, dann ängstigt
der Contrast zwischen diesem Gewirre und der majestätischen Ruhe, womit die Natur
die Entstehung ihrer Werke vollendet.
15   Wird das unter diesen tausendfältigen Hammerschlägen Geboren die Inkarnation eines
lebensfähigen Weltgedankens seyn, ¦ oder bauen wir an einem modernen, nicht die Höhe,   *fol. 5v*
sondern die Breite erstrebenden Nimrodswerke? Diese Frage drängt sich dann auf und
mahnt zu ernsten Betrachtungen, die eine beruhigende Richtung nehmen, so oft der Blick
auf jenes Bild der Eintracht des aus unbefangener Auffassung der Aufgabe hervorgegange-
20   nen Werke des Baumeisters, mit der Natur zurückkehrt.
Gewiss wir tragen zu keinem Thurme von Babel den Stoff zusammen bei dem die Völker
aus einander liefen noch ehe die Spitze des müssigen Baues erreicht war; Unser Werk hat
keine despotische Spitze wohl aber soll es einen Mittelpunkt haben, an den es sich in unbestimmter stets unbestimmter bleibender Ausdehnung mit geordneter Freiheit anfügt.

> 265.4 **in der Transept**] *'in dem Transept'*   265.5 **lebenstrotzend**] leben *altered from* lebens
> **Blätterhüllen**] *after del.* Bluth *(possibly for 'Blüthen')*   265.6 **füllen**] *above del.* gestalten
> sich   265.7 **Grün**] G *over g after del.* Frühlings- ¦   265.8 **graue**] *interl.*   265.9 **soll**]

266   The Great Exhibition

above del. wird   265.10 **den leichten Frühlingswolken**] *after del.* dem Wolkenspiel **Das Ganze**] *after del.* Es ist eine Lebensfrische in diesem Bilde, die dem Baumeister des Werkes   **Es**] *altered from* es *after del.* Wahrlich   265.11 **Loblied**] *above del.* herrliches Triumphlied   265.12 **Kehrt**] *after three del. variants:*

Weniger erquicklich ist das chaotische Treiben[1] rings um aus dem sich nur der Werdedrang nicht aber bis jetzt die künftige Gestaltung erkennen lässt.
Weniger erquicklich ist der Blick auf das Chaos dort unten, an dem sich wohl deutlich der Werdedrang, nicht aber bis jetzt die künftige Gestaltung erkennen lässt.
Kehrt dann das Auge auf den chaotischen Werdedrang dort unten zurück, so ängstigt[2] der Contrast zwischen der unruhigen Hast, mit

     1 **Treiben**] *repl. del.* Gedränge   2 **so ängstigt**] *after del.* so wünscht man dass die Gestaltung die

265.13 **Contrast**] *after del.* Abs[t]   **Gewirre**] *above del.* wirren Treiben   265.14 **die**] *above del.* das Werk ihrer   **vollendet.**] *altered from* ~ *before del.* und findet die Frage 265.15 **Wird**] *after del.* Wird unter diesen tausendfachen Hammerschlägen ein zu nachhaltigem Leben befähigter Weltgedanke geboren und *after del.* Man fragt   **das**] *above del.* dasjenige, was   **Geboren**] *'Geborene'; altered from* geboren *before del.* wird,   265.16 **lebensfähigen**] *del. and underl. with dots cancelling deletion after del.* neuen   **seyn,**] *before undel.* oder   **oder**] *after del.* bauen wir an einem neuen, nur statt nach der Höhe nach der Breite gehenden Nimrodswerke und steht uns aus ihm, statt der Lösung unserer neuen ~ Höhe] *above del.* modernen Thurm zu Babel   uns] *above del.* uns eine neue Sprachverwirrung   265.17 **Nimrodswerke?**] *altered from* ~, *before del.* und steht uns aus ihm nicht die Lösung unserer Wirren sondern die Vollendung unserer Wirren bevor? wird statt erstrebter Harmonie nur vollständige   265.19 **Bild**] *after del.* früher erwähnte früher] *after del.* oben   **des**] *altered from* dem *after del.* zwischen   265.20 **Werke**] *'Werkes'*   **Baumeisters,**] *after del.* Kun *(possibly for 'Künstlers') and altered from* ~∧ *before del.* und   265.21 **tragen**] *above del.* bauen   **zu**] *over an*   **Thurme**] *after del.* Werke despotischen Uebermuthes *after del.* Babylonischen Thurme,   **den Stoff zusammen**] *interl.*   265.22 **Baues**] *interl. before del.* Sinnbildes der Gewalt   265.23 **despotische**] *interl. after interl. and del.* Despotismus   265.24 **stets**] *interl.*

MS 94[3]

fol. 6r   Damals suchte despotischer Unsinn mit geschlossener Pyramidenform das den Elementen unerreichbare Endlose und die Völker liefen, den Wahn erkennend, aus einander, noch ehe die monarchische Spitze fertig war. Jetzt bauen wir an einem Werke, das seiner Idee nach keine festen Grenzen in den Breitenausdehnungen haben darf, sich somit jeder bildnerischen Form entziehen würde, und somit, wie jenes, nur nach entgegengesetzter Seite hin,   5 ein Unding bleiben muss, findet sich nicht noch rechtzeitig genug der wahre Mittelpunkt der Beziehungen, der Brennpunkt, dessen Attractionskraft stark genug ist, um das Auseinanderfallen der Elemente, die der erste Anstoss der Idee zusammenrüttelte, zu verhindern und sie zu einem wahren Gebäude der Zukunft dauernd zu gestalten. Hier

266.2 **aus einander**] aus | einander   266.3 **Jetzt**] *after del.* Wie damals   **seiner Idee nach**] *after del.* seinen Bestandtheilen nach keine   266.4 **Breitenausdehnungen∧**] *altered from* ~, *before del.* ja selbst keine   266.5 **wie jenes, nur**] *interl.*   266.6 **ein Unding**] *after del.* wie jener Babelsthurm   **noch rechtzeitig genug**] *above del.* zur rechten

A Foreign Architect's Views of the Building 267

Zeit   266.7 **dessen Attractionskraft**] *after del.* dessen Attractionskraft stark genug
wäre, um die variirenden und losen Elemente die der Gedanke, in seiner ersten Entwick
266.7–8 **um das Auseinanderfallen**] *after del.* um das Formlose zu einem Systeme zu
gestalten.   266.8 **zusammenrüttelte**] *above del.* vereinigte   266.9 **sie**] *above del.* ihre
bildnerische Gestaltung   **wahren**] *after del.* harmonischen   **dauernd**] *after del.* zu
gestalten.   **gestalten.**] *before del.* Seyn und nicht seyn

MS 94⁴

Damals erstrebte der mosaischen Sage nach despotischer Unsinn mit geschlossener Pyra-   *fol. 7r*
midenform eine den Elementen unerreichbare endlose Höhe und die Völker liefen, den
Wahn erkennend aus einander, noch ehe die monarchische Spitze erreicht war. Jetzt bauen
wir an einem Werke, das seinem Inhalte nach, keine festen Grenzen in den beiden Breiten-
5   ausdehnungen haben darf, sich somit jeder bestimmten bildnerischen Form entzieht und
desshalb, wie jenes, nur nach entgegengesetzter Seite hin, so lange ein Unding bleiben
muss, bis sich der wahre Mittelpunkt der Beziehungen fand, dessen Attractionskraft die
unbestimmbar variirenden in Individualitäten zerstückelten Bestandtheile des grossen
Baues zu einem Systeme vereinigt, und es möglich macht, dass bei grösster Gestaltungsfrei-
10   heit des Einzelnen, das Ganze ein harmonisches

267.1 **erstrebte**] *interl. before del.* suchte   suchte] *above del.* wollte   **der mosaischen**
Sage nach] *interl.*   267.2 **eine**] *repl. del.* die   die] *inserted before del.* endlose und *(end-*
lose *altered from* Endlose *after del.* Unendliche, den Himmel [er] *after del.* das)   267.3
erkennend] *before del.* und das Thörichte   267.4 **seinem Inhalte nach,**] *above del.* seiner
Idee nach∧   **den**] *after del.* der Ausdehnung   267.5 **bestimmten**] *after del.* Form
267.6 **wie**] *after del.* ein nach einer entgegengesetzten Seite hin und ab[handen] führt   **so**
lange] *after del.* in bildnerischer Beziehung ein Unding ist, so lange nicht ein grosser fester
und kraft   in bildnerischer] *after del.* ein Unding *after del.* ein Unsinn bleibt, so lange
Unding] *after del.* formloses   267.7 **die**] *above del.* das   267.8 **variirenden**] *inserted after*
del. Ausgedehnte aus   267.9 **und**] *after del.* einen wirklichen Bau er   **grösster**] *after del.*
möglichster   267.10 **ein**] *after del.* eine harmonische Gestaltung gewinnt

MS 94⁵

Wenn dort drüben in dem Welt-Schaumarkte der jetzt im höchsten Paroxismus begriffene   *fol. 3r*
Werdedrang mit seinem wüsten Getöse zu betäuben beginnt, und die Besonnenheit im
eigenen Walten mitten unter diesem allgemeinen Gewühle untergehen will, dann bieten
die drei letzten der Bäume des Hydeparkes die das Netzwerk des Gebäudes umspann und
15   die Axt noch verschonte, einen wundersam beruhigenden Anblick dar. Es ist eine Pracht,
wie sie, gleich wie angespornt durch die Hast die sie umschwärmt, in strotzender Lebens-
fülle sich eilen, ihre letzten Blätterhüllen abzustreifen. Gleich mächtigen Fächern füllen
ihre Zweige das Halbrund der Transept und durch ihr junges Grün spielt anmuthig das
leichte Stangen- und Gitterwerk des luftigen Baues. Noch ist das Segeltuch, das den Bau
20   bedecken wird, über diesen Theil desselben nicht ausgebreitet und des Himmels Blau mit
den eilenden Frühlingswolken blickt überall herrlich hindurch. Das Ganze athmet junge
Lebensfrische und lobt den Baumeister dessen Werk sich so harmonisch mit der Natur

268 The Great Exhibition

vermählte. Und welcher Contrast zwischen dem Gewirre dort unten und der majestätischen Ruhe, womit die Natur die Entstehung ihrer Werke vollendet! Man möchte aus jenen Zweigen ein Orakel vernehmen, eine Antwort auf die wichtige Frage, ob wir Menschlein hier unten, mit unseren tausendfachen Hammerschlägen die Geburt eines lebensfähigen Weltgedankens zu fördern berufen sind, oder ob wir an einem modernen, nicht in die   5 Höhe, aber in die Breite frevelnden Nimrodswerke den Stoff herbeitragen? Aber kein Luftzug bewegt die Zweige der gefangenen Bäume, kein Säuseln der Blätter erhebt sich, und das Orakel bleibt stumm.

> 267.11 **Welt-Schaumarkte**] *after del.* Exhibit   im] *above del.* in seinem   267.12 **zu**] *after del.* mich   **und**] *after del.* dann *after del.* dann blicke ich von Zeit zu Zeit auf   267.14 **der**] *interl.*   267.15 **noch**] *interl.*   **wundersam**] *after del.* seltsam   267.18 **der Transept**] '*des Transepts*'   267.19 **Stangen-**] *after del.* bl[ ]   267.20 **des Himmels Blau**] *before del.* blickt zuweilen durch Wolken herrlich hindurch.   blickt] *after del.* mit den 267.22 **dessen**] *after del.* an
> 268.2 **Man**] *after del.* Oft frage ich diese Bäume   frage] *after del.* suche ich   268.3 **die**] *above del.* jene   268.4 **tausendfachen**] fachen *after del.* fältigen   268.7 **Zweige**] *below del.* Blätter

MS 94[6]

fol. 4r

Wenn in dem Welt-Schaumarkte dort drüben das mich umbrausende Gewirre meine Sinne zu betäuben anfängt, dann lasse ich, um mich zu sammeln meine Blicke eine Weile auf   10 jenen drei letzten Bäumen ruhen, die das Netzwerk des Gebäudes umsponnen und die Axt noch verschont hat. Es ist eine Pracht, wie sie, gleichsam gestachelt durch die sie umschwärmende Hast, sich eilten, ihre letzten Blätterhüllen abzustreifen und nun gleich mächtigen Fächern die hohen Bogen der Transept füllen. Durch ihr junges Grün spielt anmuthig das leichte Stangen- und Gitterwerk des luftigen Baues. Noch ist das graue   15 Segeltuch, das den Bau bedecken wird, über diesen Theil desselben nicht ausgebreitet und des Himmels Blau mit den eilenden Frühlingswolken blickt überall herrlich hindurch.

Das Ganze athmet junge und zugleich antike Lebensfrische und lobt den Baumeister, dessen Werk so harmonisch sich mit der Natur vermählte. Wir glauben aus jenen lichten Zweigen leise neue Weisen zu vernehmen, die doch wie Ahnung längst verlorener alter Herrlichkeiten klingen. Sind sie ein tröstender Spruch auf die beängstigende Frage, ob wir   20 Menschlein hier unten mit unseren tausend Hammerschlägen die Geburt eines Weltgedankens zu fördern im Begriffe stehen

> 268.9 **Wenn**] *after del.*

Wenn mir in dem Welt-Schaumarkte dort drüben das wüste Getöse die Sinne zu benehmen anfängt, dann lasse ich meine Augen eine Weile

> 268.9 **in**] *after del.* mir   **meine**] *above del.* die   268.10 **betäuben**] *above del.* benehmen   **anfängt,**] *altered from* ~∧ *before del.* und die Besonnenheit mich verlassen will   **ich,**] *altered from* ~∧   **um mich zu sammeln**] *interl.*   268.13 **nun**] *interl.*   268.14 **der Transept**] '*des Transepts*'   268.15 **graue**] *after del.* Segeltuch   268.16 **den**] *after del.* sie   268.18 **Das Ganze athmet**] *after del.*

Das Ganze athmet junge und zugleich antike Lebensfrische und lobt den Baumeister, dessen Werk so harmonisch sich mit der Natur vermählte, das so neue und zugleich so alte längst verhallte anmuthige Weisen[1] singt.

1 **anmuthige Weisen**] *after del.* Lieder

268.19 **Wir**] *after del.* Neue Weisen klingen uns aus jenen Zweigen entgegen die doch. 268.20 **Ahnung**] *interl. before del.* Anklang   Anklang] *above del.* Ahnung   **alter**] *after del.* unbekannter   unbekannter] *repl. del.* nur noch geahnter *(*geahnter *after del.* in glücklichen*)*   268.21 **tröstender**] *final* r *over* s   **Spruch**] *above del.* Orakel   268.22 **die**] *after del.* einen

MS 94[7]

Wenn in dem grossen Welt-Schaumarkte dort drüben das brausende Gewirre um mich her meine Sinne zu betäuben droht, dann lasse ich, um mich zu sammeln, meine Blicke eine Weile auf jenen drei letzten Bäumen ruhen, die das Gebäude mit seinem Netzwerke umsponnen, und die Axt noch verschont hat. Es ist eine Pracht, wie sie, gleichsam gestachelt
5   von der sie umschwirrenden Hast, sich eilten, ihre letzten Blätterhüllen abzustreifen und nun fächerartig die hohen Bögen der Transept füllen.
Durch ihr junges Grün spielt anmuthig das leichte Stangen- und Gitterwerk des luftigen Baues. Noch ist das graue Segeltuch, das ihn bedecken wird, über diesen Theil desselben nicht ausgebreitet, und des Himmels Blau, mit den eilenden Frühlingswolken blickt überall
10 herrlich hindurch. Das Bild athmet junge und zugleich antike Lebensfrische und lobt den Baumeister, dessen Werk sich so harmonisch mit der Natur vermählte.
Aus jenen lichten Zweigen glauben wir leise liebe Weisen zu vernehmen, die so neu und doch wie Anklang alter längst verlorener, nur geahnter Herrlichkeiten herunter säuseln. ¦
Dann verlassen uns jene Zweifel, die uns ängstigen, während wir mitten in dem Gedränge
15 befangen sind, und das Durcheinander des bereits Erschaulichen uns wie verkörperter Wahnsinn fratzenhaft bunt entgegengrinzt.. Welcher Contrast zwischen diesem Gewirre und der majestätischen Ruhe, womit die Natur die Entstehung ihrer Werke vollendet!
Wird das unter so tausendfachen Hammerschlägen Geborene die erste Inkarnation eines wirklich lebensfähigen Weltgedankens seyn, oder tragen wir zu einem modernen, nicht in
20 die Höhe, aber in die Breite frevelnden Nimrodswerken den Stoff zusammen? – Damals erstrebte, der Mosaischen Sage nach, Despotischer Unsinn mit geschlossener Pyramidenform eine den Elementen unerreichbare, den Bergen trotzende Höhe, und die Völker liefen, den Wahn erkennend, aus einander, noch ehe die monarchische Spitze vollendet war. Jetzt bauen wir an einem Werke, das keine festen Schranken horizontaler Ausdehnung kennt, ¦
25 und aus umgekehrten Gründen so lange ein gleich unmögliches Unding bleibt, bis sich der wahre Mittelpunkt der Beziehungen findet, der Attractionskraft genug besitzt, um das Heterogene und Ungemessene zu einem lebendig gegliederten und geschlossenen Systeme zu vereinigen. Geschieht dieses nicht, sondern tritt kurzsichtiges Interesse gleich beim Anfange dem natürlichen Entwickelungsgange des internationalen Verkehres gerade bei die-
30 ser Gelegenheit auf eine Weise entgegen, die geeignet ist, den noch jungen Enthusiasmus der Völker für die Idee zu brechen, dann wird kein äusseres Band sie zusammenhalten und, wie damals wird alles mit allgemeiner Enttäuschung und Sprachverwirrung endigen. ¦

fol. 1r

fol. 1v

fol. 2r

fol. 2v

Mögen diejenigen, die Geist und Beruf dazu befähigt, sich dieses geistigen Baues mit ganzer Seele annehmen und mit allen ihnen zu Gebote stehenden Kräften das Ihrige dazu beitragen, dass er sich immer mehr gestalte und entwickele.

——————

Ein gutes Omen für sein Gedeihen ist der körperliche Ausdruck, den ihm der Baumeister   5
zu geben wusste. das beste Zeichen eines genialen Werkes. Es konnte auch nur einem Gartenkünstler gelingen den Gedanken in seiner ersten Entwickelungs-

> 269.3 **Gebäude**] *after del.* Netzwerk   **Netzwerke**] *after del.* gewaltigen   269.6 **fächerartig**] *above del.* gleich mächtigen Fächern   **der Transept**] *'des Transepts'*   269.8 **ihn**] *above del.* den Bau   269.13 **säuseln.**] *before del. on fol. 1r–v*

Dann verlassen uns jene Zweifel, die ängstigend sich aufdrängen, während wir mitten in dem Gedränge befangen sind und das bunte Allerlei des bereits Erschaulichen uns wie verkörperter Wahnsinn überall bunt und fratzenhaft entgegen grinzt.
Werden wir Menschlein hier unten berufen seyn, mit unseren tausendfachen Hammerschlägen ¦ mit unseren Tapezierarbeiten und Glaskasten, die Geburt

> 269.14 **uns ängstigen,**] *inserted after del.* ängstigend sich aufdrängen,   sich] *after del.* zurückkehren,   269.16 **Welcher**] *above del.* Welch ein   269.18 **tausendfachen**] fachen *above del.* faltigen   **erste**] *interl.*   269.21 **Despotischer**] D *over* d   269.24 **das**] *before del.* seinem Inhalte nach   **Schranken**] *repl. del.* Grenzen   269.25 **und aus umgekehrten Gründen**] *after two del. beginnings of variant on fols. 1v–2r:*

und wie jenes, nur nach entgegengesetzter Seite hin, so lange ein Unding[1] bleiben muss, bis sich der wahre Mittelpunkt der Beziehungen fand, der Attractionskraft genug besitzt um die |
und wie dort die begränzte[2] Bauform den Zweck der Erreichung des Unbegränzten unmöglich machte, so würde umgekehrt das Bestreben den an sich der Ausdehnung nach unbestimmbaren Stoff in begränzte Form zu bringen und wie dort

> 1 **Unding**] *after del.* formloses   2 **begränzte**] *after del.* bestimmte *after del.* geschlo

> 269.27 **zu einem**] *after del.* bleibend zu vereinigen und *and before del.* einträchtigen Systeme zu vereinigen.   269.27–8 **lebendig ~ vereinigen.**] *inserted*   269.28 **Geschieht dieses nicht**] *after del.*

Geschieht dieses,[1] wird der Welt-Schaumarkt erhoben zu einem Welt-Freihandelsmarkte, wird wenigstens die Anbahnung dieses letzten Zieles durch kurzsichtiges Interesse nicht gewaltsam gestört, wird wenigstens nur dem natürlichen Entwickelungsgange des internationalen Verkehres kein solches[2] Hinderniss entgegen gesetzt, das geeignet ist, die Theilnahme der Völker gleich beim Anfange zu kühlen

> 1 **dieses,**] *altered from* ~∧ *before del.* nicht,   2 **solches**] *above del.* absichtliches

> 269.30 **noch**] *interl.*   269.32 **Enttäuschung und**] *above del.* Verwirrung   **Sprachverwirrung**] *before del.* [wie in]
> 270.1 **Mögen**] *after del.*

Doch mögen dazu Befähigtere sich den geistigen Bau zu Herzen nehmen und mit allen ihnen zu Gebote stehenden Kräften dazu beitragen dass er sich immer mehr gestalte; Mir sey[1] es nur gestattet, über das, was sich bei dieser ersten Phase der Entwickelung schon jetzt als klares Resultat herausstellt, eine

[1] **sey**] *above del.* ist

270.5 **Ein gutes Omen**] *after two del. beginnings of variant:*

Ein gutes Omen für sein Gedeihen ist der Umstand, dass
Es ist ein gutes Omen dafür, dass ein wahrer und lebensfähiger Weltgedanke

270.6 **wusste.**] *before del.* Es ist nun kaum möglich, sich die Aufgabe nur anders, geschweige denn besser, gelöst zu denken, seitdem sie so und nicht anders gelöst wurde;
270.7 **Entwickelungs-**] *possibly for 'Entwickelungsphase' (see note 270.1: 'bei dieser ersten Phase der Entwickelung')*

The Great Exhibition

TEXTUAL RECORD

MS 94[8]   gta, 20-Ms-94, fol. 9v, in Semper's hand
MS 94[9]   gta, 20-Ms-94, fol. 13v, in Semper's hand
MS 94[10]   gta, 20-Ms-94, fol. 16v, in Semper's hand
MS 94[11]   gta, 20-Ms-94, fol. 16r (variant of MS 94[10]), in Semper's hand
MS 94[12]   gta, 20-Ms-94, fol. 14r–v (14v blank; variant of MS 94[11]), in Semper's hand
MS 94[13]   gta, 20-Ms-94, fols. 8r–9r, 10r–12v (8v, 10v, 11v, 12v blank; 9r variant of MS 94[8]; 10r variant of MS 94[9]; 12r variant of MS 94[12]), in Semper's hand
MS 94[14]   gta, 20-Ms-94, fol. 17r–v (17v note 'Synagoge Dresden 39' in pencil; variant of MS 94[13], fol. 8r), with three sketches of the Canadian Timber Trophy, one of them inscribed with 'Canada Timber', in Semper's hand (pl. 8)
MS 94[15]   gta, 20-Ms-94, fol. 15r–v (15v blank; variant of MS 94[13], fols. 11r, 12r), in Semper's hand
MS 94[16]   gta, 20-Ms-94, fol. 13r (variant of MS 94[13], fol. 12r), in Semper's hand
ILN Suppl. 'Die grosse Ausstellung. Die Völker von europäischer und nicht europäischer Bildung', *The Illustrated London News: Deutsches Supplement*, no. 3 (17 May 1851), 34–5 (private library), *copy-text*
May 1980   'Die grosse Ausstellung. Die Völker von europäischer und nicht europäischer Bildung', 62–6, abridged ed. of ILN Suppl.
Semper 2014 vol. 1, 369–70, Karge's reprint ed. of ILN Suppl.

BIBLIOGRAPHY Herrmann 1978, 54; May 1979; Herrmann 1980, 49, 51 n. 4; May 1980; Herrmann 1981, 65–6, 101, 104; Herrmann 1984, 48, 273 n. 168; Squicciarino 2009, 119–21; Gnehm 2015, 37; Hildebrand 2020a, 115–16; Hildebrand 2021, 110–11

272   The Great Exhibition

EXPLANATORY NOTES

The first publication of one of Semper's essays on the Great Exhibition in the German supplement of *The Illustrated London News* was initiated by Rudolph Schramm. On 26 March 1851, he asked Semper to write an article 'on the architectural style, the construction and decoration of the Crystal Palace'. While the first two of those points formed a special topic in the text that was translated for *The Edinburgh Review* ('A Foreign Architect's Views of the Building', 18.26–20.27), the last one was included in the essay for *The Illustrated London News*. The supplement's editor – a native Bohemian called Pokorny who had worked for Eduard Meyen and Julius Faucher's ephemeral Berlin *Abend-Post* (Beta 1852, 306) – invited Semper on 3 May 1851, the publication date of its first issue, to contribute to it.

20.31 **füllende**] *füllenden*
21.30 **zeugt**] *zeigt* (see 275.36)
22.16 **unsrige**] before blank until full stop, leaving space for word, thus probably *unsrige ist* (see 274.4, 274.7, 276.8, 279.3)   22.19–20 **sich ein Durcheinander ~ sich für Originalität ausgibt**] *ein Durcheinander ~ sich für Originalität ausgibt* or *sich ein Durcheinander ~ für Originalität ausgibt* (cf. 279.7–8: 'sich ein Durcheinander von allseits her entlehnten mit grundsatzloser Willkür zusammengewürfelten Motiven als Originalität gerirt')   22.19 **grundsetzloser**] *grundsatzloser* (see 279.8)   22.33 **dessen**] *deren*
24.39 **fehlt**] *fehlen*
25.24–5 **unserer europäischen**] *unsere europäische*   25.29 **Künsilergabe**] *Künstlergabe*
26.14 **kann**] *können*   26.22 **erstandenen**] *verstandenen*

EDITORIAL EMENDATIONS

21.7 **sollten**] follten *(long s [ſ] misprinted as f)*   21.30–1 **Erfahrungswissenschaften**] Erfahrungswissenschasten *(second f misprinted as long s [ſ])*   22.38 **scheint**] fcheint *(long s [ſ] misprinted as f)*   26.18 **Zustande**] Zustandǝ

MANUSCRIPT VARIANTS
MS 94⁸

fol. 9v   Schon sollte sie aus beschränkter Auffassung des Programmes einer Industrieausstellung aus ihr in ihren Rohproducten ausgeschlossen werden; Aber durch die Einsicht der die Ausstellung dirigirenden Hohen Commission, die auch hierin von ihrem tiefen Eingehen in den ihr zum Grunde liegenden noch im Werdedrange begriffenen Weltgedanken und von ihrer Befähigung für das grosse ihr anvertraute und so glücklich von ihr vollendete   5
Werk

272.1–6 **Schon ~ Werk**] *del.*   272.1 **Schon**] *after del.*

The Great Exhibition   273

die[1] schon Gefahr liefen aus beschränkter Auffassung des Programmes einer[2] Industrieausstellung aus ihr ausgeschlossen zu werden, aber durch die Einsicht der sie dirigirenden Hohen Commission, die auch hierin von ihrer Befähigung für das grosse ihr anvertraute und so glücklich von ihr vollendete Werk

   1 **die**] *inserted*   2 **einer**] *repl. del.* der

   272.1 **sollte**] *after del.* liefen   **sie**] *i.e. die Natur (nature)*   272.3 **Hohen**] *after del.* Com-
missi

MS 94 [9]

er befähigt sey, den Heerd und das Mittel aller Beziehungen des Baues zu behausen, immer   *fol. 13v*
muss der symbolische Stamm durch alle Jahrhunderte und wo immer künftig ein folgender
Weltmarkt aufgeschlagen werde, vertreten bleiben.
Die zweite Palme, auch das zeigt sich schon jetzt als unzweifelhaft, gebührt der Wissen-
5   schaft in ihrer Anwendung auf das Nützliche. Sie feiert in dem Gebäude selbst einen schönen Triumph. Preis dem Architecten, der den Gedanken dazu niederlegte, Preis den erfinderischen Baumeistern und Ingenieurs, die den mächtigen so luftigen und doch so festen
Bau mit neuen von der Wissenschaft gebotenen Mitteln und unglaublich geringem Auf-
wande an Materiale und an Arbeitskräften in so kurzer Zeit vollendeten.
10   Unabsehbare Reihen von Maschinen und Instrumenten aller Art füllen die Räume aller
Nationen von Europäischer Bildung und zeigen zum Theil, gleich jenem rein constructiven
Bauwerke, eine gewisse unbefangene und naturwüchsige Zierlichkeit und Schönheit in den
Formen, wodurch sie die

   273.1–13 **er ~ wodurch sie die**] *del.*   273.1 **er**] *above del.* er besser als jetzt   **den Heerd**]
after del. das Herz   **das Mittel**] *after del.* den   **Baues**] *above del.* Weltmarktes   273.2
Stamm] *above del.* Ulmenstamm   **ein folgender**] *above del.* der   273.3 **vertreten bleiben**] *after del.* Wiederholung finden   273.4 **auch**] *interl.*   273.4–5 **Wissenschaft**] *after
interl. and del.* Europäi   273.7 **mächtigen**] *interl.*   **doch**] *interl.*   273.9 **Materiale**]
after del. Materiellem   **vollendeten**] *after del.* und *after del.* vollendeten; Preis denen
273.10 **Art**ᴧ] *before del.* , bestimmt   273.11 **zum Theil**] *interl.*   273.12 **eine**] *after del.*
selbst *after del.* in ihren Formen.

MS 94 [10]

in den besten Fällen aus dem falschen Zirkel der studirtesten Nachbildung älterer Weisen   *fol. 16v*
15   nicht

   273.14–15 **in ~ nicht**] *del.*   273.14 **in den besten Fällen**] *inserted before del.* Doch *and after
del.* Doch aus dem falschen Zirkel des Veralteten und in seiner Wiederaufnahme in unserer Zeit   **studirtesten**] *after del.* Nachahmung des Alten das für uns

MS 94¹¹

fol. 16r   in dem falschen Zirkel der Nachahmung älterer Weisen gebannt bleibt, die desshalb mit Recht als schön und musterhaft bewundert werden, weil sie der sprechende Ausdruck von Zeiten sind, die mit sich selbst und der sie beherrschenden Idee schon mehr fertig waren, als es die unsrige ist, aber die an Werken   4

> 274.1–4 **in ~ Werken**] *del.*   274.1 **in**] *after del.*

in dem falschen Zirkel der Nachahmung älterer Weisen gebannt ist, die uns desshalb stets schön und musterhaft bleiben, weil sie die reinen Ausdrücke¹ einer² mit sich selbst mehr im Klaren befindlich

> 1 **Ausdrücke**] *before del.* ihrer Zeit sind,   2 **einer**] *after del.* von einer *after del.* einer minder unklaren

> 274.3 **fertig**] *before del.* und im Klaren   274.4 **aber**] *after del.*

aber die in ihrer verbalen Wiederholung an modernen Werken des industriellen Fleisses und der Kunst nur ein der Blutwärme¹ ermangelndes

> 1 **ein der Blutwärme**] *after del.* ein blut *after del.* als leblose Hüllen erscheinen aus denen das geistige Element und die Blutwärme des   **leblose**] *after del.* seelen *after del.* seelenlose [ ]

MS 94¹²

fol. 14r   *E.*   in dem falschen Zirkel der Nachahmung älterer Weisen gebannt bleibt, die desshalb ihr   5   ewiges Anrecht auf Bewunderung behaupten, weil sie der sprechende Ausdruck von Zeiten sind, die mit sich und der sie beherrschenden Idee mehr fertig waren, als es die unsrige ist. An den Werken unsereres modernen industriellen Fleisses, der alle Bestrebungen früherer Zeiten überflügelte, können diese einst lebensfrischen Formen nur zu larvenhafter der   10   Blutwärme ermangelnder Scheinexistenz

> 274.5 **ihr**] *after del.* mit Recht   274.8 **An**] *after del.* In ihrer verbalen   **unsereres**] *'unseres'* **der**] *del.*   **alle**] *after del.* so sehr *after del.* Dank de *after del.* in der Richtung zum Nützlichen   274.9 **können**] *after del.* erscheinen diese

MS 94¹³

fol. 8r   *A.*   Selbst denen, die den Enthüllungsprocess der das vaste Ausstellungsgebäude füllenden Schaugegenstände von Anfang zu verfolgen Gelegenheit hatten und ihre ganze Zeit und Aufmerksamkeit der prüfenden Vergleichung dieser Gegenstände widmen konnten, wird es schwerlich bereits gelungen seyn, über die Fülle des Gebotenen nur eine oberflächliche allgemeine Uebersicht gewonnen zu haben; Noch weit weniger würde sich eine ver-   15   gleichende Critik und ein darauf begründetes Urtheil über das noch so lückenhafte Ganze jetzt schon rechtfertigen. Aber Eine Thatsache tritt dennoch bereits so deutlich hervor, dass

The Great Exhibition   275

es erlaubt ist, sie hervorzuheben, ehe sie von einer gewissen dem ganzen neueren Ideenumschwunge abholden Parthei in ihrer Weise ausgebeutet wird:

Wie sich von selbst versteht, wird in diesem grossen nun eingeleiteten Wettkampfe der Natur, "der Gottheit lebendigem Kleide" die nie bestrittene erste Palme verbleiben. ‖

Schon sollte sie aus beschränkter Auffassung des Programms nach Einigen aus der Industrieausstellung in ihren Rohproducten ausgeschlossen bleiben; Aber durch die Einsicht der die Ausstellung dirigirenden hohen Commission wurden letztere in umfassendstem Maasse mit in das Programm gezogen. Diese hohe Behörde, der wir für die vortreffliche Leitung und Vollendung des Ihr anvertrauten grossen Werkes unsere Bewunderung, unsere Verehrung und unseren Dank zollen, hat auch hierin von ihrem tiefen Eingehen in die wahre Bedeutung des diesem Werke inliegenden, noch im Werdedrange begriffenen Weltgedankens Zeugniss abgelegt. –

Aus der Bekanntschaft mit den Rohproducten der Länder unseres Erdkörpers und ihrem zweckgemässen freien Austausche muss die vielchörige reichgegliederte Harmonie eines künftigen Weltverkehres und zugleich höchster materieller und geistiger Entwickelung aller Völker nach allen Richtungen hin emporwachsen, und schon jetzt wird mancher Gewerbtreibende, mancher Künstler, und zwar je der Beste unter der Menge ahnungsvoll seinen Sinn an der Betrachtung und Vergleichung der von der Natur gespendeten, hier in wohlgeordneten Proben repräsentirten Stoffen erfrischen, wenn ihn das bunte und zugleich monotone Gewirre der ihn umgebenden Erzeugnisse Europäischen Kunstfleisses ermüdete und Zweifel über Richtung und Ziel eigenen und fremden Strebens ihn ängstigen. Der Triumph der Natur ist in den die Bögen der Transept füllenden Laubkronen der Ulmen wunderbar schön symbolisirt und wie auch künftig dieser Theil des Baues sich anders entwickeln und gestalten möge, so dass ‖ er geeignet sey, den Heerd und das Mittel aller Beziehungen des grossartigen Weltmarktes würdig zu behausen, so muss dieser symbolische Stamm durch alle folgenden Zeiten und wo immer künftig ein neuer Bau von gleicher Bestimmung aufgeschlagen wird, vertreten bleiben.

Die zweite Palme, auch dieses zeigt sich schon jetzt als unzweifelhaft, gebührt der Wissenschaft in ihrer Anwendung auf das Nützliche. Sie feiert, Dank dem Architecten der den Gedanken dazu niederlegte, und Dank den erfinderischen Meistern der Technik und der Verwaltung, die ihn in so kurzer Zeit zur Thatsache gestalteten, die den mächtigen, so luftigen und doch so festen Bau mit neuen von der Wissenschaft gebotenen Mitteln und unglaublich geringem Aufwande an Stoff und Arbeitskräften herrlich vollendeten, einen schönen Triumph! –

Unter seinem Zeltdache füllt eine Welt von Werkzeugen, Maschinen, Instrumenten, Apparaten, und Modellen die Räume aller Nationen von Europäischer Bildung, und zeigt entweder ganz neue sinnreiche Anwendungen der Theorie und der Erfahrungswissenschaften oder bietet durch Weiterbildung des bereits Erworbenen, oder durch die Vollendung der Arbeit die an ihnen erscheint, ein reiches Feld des Forschens, des Prüfens und Vergleichens. ‖

Lang gereihet stehen sie da in bewegungsloser, fast unheimlicher Ruhe, gleich einer schlagfertigen Phalanx bei der Musterung vor dem Kampfe. Jetzt, da diese stummen Werkzeuge nur erst ihr nächstes materiellstes Ziel verrathen bieten sie mit ihren Hebeln und Rädern von denen wir ahnen dass sie die Welt erobern müssen, ein unenthülltes Geheimniss der Zukunft.

Wenn bei ihnen, wie sich gebührt, nur ihre Bestimmung und der Stoff aus dem sie gebildet sind, und dessen zweckmässigste Gestaltung und Stärke die Wissenschaft verbunden mit

B.   fol. 9r

C.   fol. 10r

D.   fol. 11r

276 The Great Exhibition

der Erfahrung feststellte, formengebend auftreten, so beschämen sie dennoch in ihrer unbefangenen, gleichsam naturwüchsigen Zierlichkeit, alle die neben ihnen angehäuften Producte der Europäischen sogenannten Kunstindustrie, die meistentheils ein unstätes und
prinzipienloses Ringen nach stets neuen Mustern und Formen kund giebt, aber in ihrer
rastlosen Beweglichkeit doch ¦| in dem falschen Zirkel der Nachahmung älterer Weisen   5
gebannt bleibt, die desshalb ihr ewiges Anrecht auf Bewunderung behaupten, weil sie
der sprechende Ausdruck von Zeiten sind, die mit sich und der sie beherrschenden Idee
mehr fertig waren, als es die unsrige ist, die aber nur zu larvenhafter und der Blutwärme
ermangelnder Scheinexistenz bei uns wieder aus der Vergangenheit heraufbeschworen
worden sind; Und dieses nur in den besseren Fällen; Meistens gerirt sich in unserer mo-   10
dernen Kunstindustrie ein Durcheinander von allerseits her entlehnten willkürlichst zusammengewürfelten Motiven als Originalität und wird der allgemeinen Richtung zum
Nützlichen durch gänzliche Nichtachtung des durch den Zweck Gebotenen bei der ornamentalen Ausstattung der Gegenstände Trotz geboten. Dabei ist es interessant zu verfolgen, wie das Maschinenwesen, indem es jenem unklaren Walten scheinbar dient und seine   15
tausend mächtigen Arme zu wohlfeilster Vervielfältigung seiner Einfälle willfährig leiht,
als sein geheimer Feind das bevorstehende Ende seines Reiches beschleunigt. –
Ueber diesem Theile unserer Europäischen Betriebsamkeit wird ein strenges Gericht walten; Nicht bloss von den Persern, Indern und Arabern, Völkern deren Kunstfertigkeit
und Geschmack schon früher in einigen Theilen ihrer Industrie anerkannt wurde, sondern   20
auch von den Chinesen und selbst von den Canadischen Wilden und den Hottentotten
werden wir besiegt werden.

fol. 12r   *E.* (left margin, line 5)

274.11 **Selbst**] *after two del. beginnings of variant:*

Selbst demjenigen, der seit der Eröffnung der Industrieausstellung
Selbst denen, die den Enthüllungsprocess der das vaste Ausstellungsgebäude füllenden
Schaugegenstände von Anfang zu verfolgen Gelegenheit hatten, und ihrer Vergleichung
und Prüfung ihre volle Zeit widmen konnten, wird[1] es schwerlich schon jetzt gelungen
seyn, über die Fülle des Dargebotenen nur eine oberflächliche und rein sachliche Uebersicht zu gewinnen; Noch viel weniger würden sie sich eine vergleichende Critik über das
zum Theil noch

    1 **wird**] *after del.* möchte es schwer fallen, schon jetzt eine nur oberflächliche und
    rein sachliche Uebersicht über den ganzen Reichthum des Dargebotenen

274.13 **prüfenden**] *interl.*   **Vergleichung**] *before del.* und Prüfung   274.16 **Critik**] *before*
del. über das noch so lückenhafte Ganze   über] *after del.* über das zum Theil noch un-
vollkommen, oder zum Theil noch gar nicht   275.1 **ist**] *after del.* seyn mag sie   275.4 **verbleiben.**] *before del.* In ihren Rohproducten, die
beschränkte Auf-   275.5 **Programms**] *before del.* einer Industrieausstellung   275.5–6
der Industrieausstellung] *repl. del.* letzterer   275.13 **Aus**] *after del.* Die Rohproducte
müssen die Grundtöne seyn,   der] r *over* n   **Bekanntschaft mit den**] *interl.*   275.13–
14 **und ihrem zweckgemässen freien Austausche**] *inserted*   275.15 **materieller und**]
interl.   275.16 **emporwachsen,**] *altered from* ~.   275.16–17 **und schon jetzt ~ ahnungsvoll**] *repl. del.* Mancher Gewerbtreibende, mancher Künstler, und zwar je der Beste
unter ihnen, wird   Mancher] *after del.* Mancher Industrielle, mancher Künstler, den die
Richtungslosigkeit die sich an eigenen und an Anderer Werken kund giebt, ängstigt, der
über Richtung und Ziel   275.18 **Vergleichung**] *after del.* Prüfung   275.19 **Stoffen**]
'*Stoffe*'   275.21 **Zweifel**] *after del.* ih[m] gerechte   275.22 **der Transept**] '*des Transepts*';

der *altered from* des   275.23 **anders**] *interl.*   275.24 **das Mittel**] *after del.* Mittel.   275.25 **so**] *repl. del.* immer   275.30 **Meistern**] *above del.* Männern   275.36 **Räume**] *after del.* wesentlichsten Theile der den einzelnen Nationen angewiesenen Räume   275.37 **sinnreiche Anwendungen**] *after two del. beginnings of variant:*

sinnreiche[1] Anwendungen der Mechanik[2] zu den verschiedenartigsten industriellen und wissenschaftlichen Zwecken
sinnreiche Anwendungen der Wissenschaft zu den verschiedenartigsten

    1 **sinnreiche**] *before del.* Applicationen der Kräfte zu Ersetzung menschlic   2 **Mechanik**] *before del.* zum Zwecke der Vervollkommnung und Erleichterung

275.37–8 **Erfahrungswissenschaften**] *before del.* zu industriellen   275.38 **Weiterbildung**] *after del.* Vollendung und *after inserted and del.* zweckfördernde   **oder durch**] oder *below del.* und *and* durch *interl.*   275.41 **Lang**] *after del.*

Gereihet[1] stehen sie da in bewegungsloser Ruhe, gleich einer schlagfertigen Phalanx bei der Musterung vor dem Kampfe. Ihre Hebel und Räder sollen die[2] Welt erobern; Jetzt, da diese stummen Werkzeuge nur erst ihr nächstes materiellstes Ziel erkennen[3] lassen, stehen sie wie

    1 **Gereihet**] *above del.* In langen Reihen   2 **die**] *after del.* in friedlichem Kampfe   3 **erkennen**] *after del.* dem Eingeweiheten

275.43 **verrathen**] *above del.* enthüllen, *after del.* erkennen lassen, *after del.* dem Eingeweiheten   275.45 **Zukunft.**] *altered from* ~, *before del.* das zu den ernstesten Betrachtungen und Muthmassungen über dessen endliche Lösung auffordert.
276.2 **Zierlichkeit,**] *before del.* ohne über müssiges die Form überwucherndes Beiwerk die Form überwucherndes] *after del.* ornamentales   **alle die**] *inserted after del.* ornamentales Beiwerk, die   276.3 **meistentheils**] *inserted after del.* ein rastloses prinziplos   276.4 **Mustern**] *after del.* ungewohnte   **giebt**] *above del.* geben   **aber in**] *after del.* ohne sich jemals *and before del.* dem falschen Zirkel   276.7 **Zeiten**] *before del.* und Civilisationszuständen   276.10 **Und dieses nur in den besseren Fällen;**] *repl. del.* Doch sind dieses noch die besseren Bestrebungen unserer modernen Kunstindustrie, in welcher **Meistens**] M *over* m   **gerirt sich**] *inserted*   276.10–11 **in unserer modernen Kunstindustrie**] *above del.* sich   276.12 **Originalität**] *before del.* gerirt   **wird**] *interl.*   276.14 **geboten.**] *altered from* ~∧ *before del.* wird.   276.18–19 **walten;**] *altered from* ~∧ *before del.* das wenn es auch diessmal noch mit seinem Endurtheile zurückhält, dennoch gewiss sehr bald   276.19 **Indern∧**] *altered from* ~,   **und**] *interl.*   **Arabern,**] *altered from* ~∧ *before del.* und Chinesen,   276.19–20 **Kunstfertigkeit und**] *interl.*   276.20 **Geschmack**] *before del.* in gewissen Theilen der Industrie wir   **schon**] *after del.* wir   276.22 **werden.**] *altered from* ~∧ *before del.* und zwar in F

MS 94[14]

Selbst denen, die der allmählichen Enthüllung der das Ausstellungsgebäude füllenden Gegenstände von Anfang her zu verfolgen Gelegenheit hatten und ihre Zeit ganz der Prüfung derselben widmen konnten, wird es schwerlich bereits gelungen seyn, über die Fülle des Gebotenen nur eine allgemeine Uebersicht gewonnen zu haben; Eine vergleichende, in das
5   Einzelne übergehende Critik des noch so lückenhaften Ganzen liesse sich

fol. 17r

278.1 **der allmählichen**] *'die allmähliche'*   277.2 **Prüfung**] *repl. del.* Prüfung und Vergleichung   Prüfung und] *above del.* prüfenden   277.4 **Eine**] *after two del. variants:*

Noch weniger würde sich eine vergleichende Critik,[1] über das noch so lückenhafte Ganze bisjetzt rechtfertigen können.
Eine vergleichende oder gar in das Einzelne gehende Critik

    1 **Critik,**] *before del.* und ein *before del.* über das noch so lückenhafte Ganze *before del.* ein allgemeines Urtheil

MS 94[15]

fol. 15r

Lang gereihet stehen sie da bald in bewegungsloser, unheimlicher Ruhe, gleich einer schlagfertigen Phalanx bei der Musterung, bald geräuschvoll ihre Kraft und Gewandheit vor der erstaunten Menge übend. Sie bieten mit ihren Hebeln und Rädern, von denen wir ahnen, dass sie die Welt erobern müssen, ein unenthülltes Geheimniss der Zukunft. Verwegen wäre es über das letzte allgemeine Resultate ihres Wirkens in Beziehung auf die socialen Verhältnisse des Menschengeschlechtes Vermuthungen zu wagen. Bis jetzt geben diese stummen Werkzeuge kaum mehr als ihr nächstes materielles Ziel zu erkennen und Zeugnisse ihres Wirkens, Leistungen, deren Vollendung Zweckdienlichkeit und Wohlfeilheit kein menschlicher Fleiss keine menschliche Geschicklichkeit erreicht, treten überall entgegen, wohin der Blick sich wendet. Kaum eine von den verschiedenen Kategorieen des menschlichen Kunstfleisses die in der Industrieausstellung repräsentirt sind, ist frei von ihrem Einflusse geblieben.

    278.1 **Lang**] *after four fragments of variant del. in unclear sequence:*

Als rastlos fleissige geschickte und unbedingt gehorsame Arbeiter bieten sie ihre tausend Briareusarme dienstwillig[1] jeglichem Dienste, und keine menschliche Geschicklichkeit erreicht nach langen Mühen, was sie in Augenblicken schaffen,[2] und ihre Werke
Verwegen wäre es über das letzte Resultat der socialen Umwälzungen die sie herbeiführen müssen, Vermuthungen aufzustellen
Die nächsten Ergebnisse ihres Wirkens, deren Zweckdienlichkeit, Wohlfeilheit und Vollendung keine menschlicher[3] Fleiss, keine Handgeschicklichkeit erreichen kann,
Lang gereihet stehen sie da in bewegungsloser, fast unheimlicher Ruhe, gleich einer schlagfertigen Phalanx bei der Musterung vor dem Kampfe oder sie üben ihre Kraft und Geschicklichkeit zum Schauspiele der staunenden Mengen in

    1 **dienstwillig**] *above del.* willfährig   2 **schaffen,**] *altered from* ~. *before del.* Treu ergebene Knechte   3 **menschlicher**] *altered from* menschliche *before del.* Geschicklichkeit

278.1 **unheimlicher**] *after del.* fast   278.3 **Rädern**] *above del.* Armen   278.5 **Resultate**] *'Resultat'*   278.6 **Bis jetzt**] *above del.* Jetzt   278.8 **Zeugnisse**] *after del.* ihr Wirken   **Vollendung**] *after del.* Wohlfeilheit   278.11 **ist frei**] *after del.* ist von   von] *after del.* ihrem Einflusse

The Great Exhibition 279

MS 94 [16]

in dem falschen Zirkel der Nachahmung älterer Weisen gebannt bleibt, die desshalb ihr   *E.*   *fol. 13r*
ewiges Anrecht auf Bewunderung behaupten, weil sie der sprechende Ausdruck von Zeiten
sind, die mit sich und der sie beherrschenden Idee mehr fertig waren, als es die unsrige ist,
die aber nur zu larvenhafter und der wahren Blutwärme ermangelnder Scheinexistenz an
5 Werken unserer Zeit wieder aus der Vergangenheit heraufbeschworen worden sind.
Und diess sind noch die besseren Erscheinungen unserer Europäischen Kunstindustrie, in
welcher in den meisten anderen Fällen sich ein Durcheinander von allseits her entlehnten
mit grundsatzloser Willkür zusammengewürfelten Motiven als Originalität gerirt und der
allgemeinen Richtung zum Nützlichen durch gänzliche Nichtachtung der durch den
10 Zweck gebotenen Form der Gegenstände bei ihrer ornamentalen Ausstattung Trotz geboten wird. – Dabei ist es interessant zu verfolgen, wie das Maschinenwesen, indem es jenem
Unsinne scheinbar dient und zu wohlfeiler Vervielfältigung seiner Einfälle benutzt wird,
sein ärgster Feind ist und das bevorstehende Ende seines Reiches beschleunigt

> 279.1 **desshalb**] *after del.* an alten Werken   279.5 **wieder aus der Vergangenheit**] *inserted*   **heraufbeschworen**] *after del.* wiederbel   279.6 **Und**] *after del.* Die künstlerische Gestaltung *after del.*

> Und diess sind noch die besten Erscheinungen unserer[1] Europäischen Kunstindustrie, bei
> welcher in den meisten Fällen ein Durcheinander von allseits her entlehnten heterogenen[2]
> mit grundsatzloser Willkür zusammengeworfenen und sich der allgemeinen Richtung
> zum Zweckmässigen und Nützlichen entgegen

>> 1 **unserer**] *repl. del.* der modernen   2 **heterogenen**] *before del.* Motiven

> 279.6 **besseren**] *above del.* besten   279.9 **Nichtachtung**] *before del.* des Zweckmässigen
> 279.11 **Dabei**] *after del.*

> Dabei ist es interessant[1], wie das Maschinenwesen dadurch, dass es zu wohlfeiler Vervielfältigung des ornamentalen Schmuckes benutzt wird, und jenem Unsinne dienen
> muss, dem[2] bevorstehenden Ende seines Reiches

>> 1 **interessant**] *above del.* seltsam   2 **dem**] *after del.* mit furchtbarer

> 279.11 **das**] *before interl. and del.* die Errungenschaften des Wissens er   279.12 **seiner
> Einfälle**] *interl. before del.* des ornamentalen Schmuckes   279.13 **beschleunigt**] *after del.*
> mit

Letters on the Great Exhibition

Outline

TEXTUAL RECORD

MS 95[1]   gta, 20-Ms-95, fol. 5r–v (5v blank), 'Plan des Aufsatzes', in Semper's hand, version 1

MS 95[2]   gta, 20-Ms-95, fol. 7r–v (7v blank; variant of MS 95[1]), in Semper's hand, version 1

MS 95[3]   gta, 20-Ms-95, fol. 3r (3v see 287, MS 95[10]), 'Plan des Aufsatzes', in Semper's hand, version 2

MS 95[4]   gta, 20-Ms-95, fols. 1r–2v, in Semper's hand, version 3, *copy-text*

MS 95[5]   gta, 20-Ms-95, fol. 15r–v (15v blank), in Semper's hand

MS 95[6]   gta, 20-Ms-95, fol. 11r–v (11v blank; possibly variant of MS 95[4], fol. 1v; variant of MS 95[5]), in Semper's hand

MS 95[7]   gta, 20-Ms-95, fol. 16r–v (16v blank), in Semper's hand

MS 95[8]   gta, 20-Ms-95, fol. 14r–v (14v blank; possibly variant of MS 95[4], fol. 1v; variant of MS 95[7]), in Semper's hand

BIBLIOGRAPHY Herrmann 1978, 52 n. 170; Herrmann 1981, 101, 104; Herrmann 1984, 273 n. 165; Hildebrand 2003, 263; Hildebrand 2007, 245–7; Luttmann 2008, 124, 128–32

EXPLANATORY NOTES

Semper's unpublished essay on the Great Exhibition in the form of a series of letters is extant only in numerous fragmentary drafts of an outline and of the first two letters, which have Lothar Bucher as their unnamed addressee. Semper mentions the letters as being addressed to Bucher in one of the drafts of the second letter (288.2). He was working on this essay while Bucher's series of essays on the 'Gewerbeausstellung aller Völker' (Industrial Exhibition of All Peoples) was being published in the Berlin *National-Zeitung* from May to July 1851. In speaking of 'Bucher's ingenious expression' that the Great Exhibition offered a 'cross section of cultural history' (29.1–2), he indirectly referred to Bucher's essays (published in book form as *Kulturhistorische Skizzen aus der Industrieausstellung aller Völker* by the end of 1851). Semper tried to develop, as he wrote in one of the drafts, an 'Explanation of an architectonic survey of the Exhibition's contents and results' (283.2–3). He considered ways of carrying out a 'systematic examination of the objects in the exhibition' with the aim of carrying out a classification of them reflecting the history of knowledge, modelled on 'comparative architecture' as the intellectual 'creator' and 'orderer of a comparative cultural history' (27.6–7, 27.11–14, 29.17–19). The manuscript bundle contains eight drafts of the outline, three drafts of the first letter and two of the second. Another five single manuscript sheets with drafts of passages either intended for this essay series or for *Science, Industry, and Art* are not detailed here. In *Science, Industry, and Art*, Semper referred to the idea he had had, around the time of the opening of the Great Exhibition, 'to give a comparative overview of its contents in a series of essays' (Semper 1852, 5–7). Bucher's expression 'cross section of cultural history' also made it into one of Semper's drafts of 'Comparative Architecture'

Letters on the Great Exhibition

(gta, 20-Ms-97), which he referred to in the draft of the second letter (30.15–17). It also appears in the manuscript of the catalogue of 'Practical Art in Metals and hard Materials' of 1852, in which Semper stated that 'A complete and universal Collection must give, so to speak the longitudinal Section, the transverse Section and the plan of the entire Science of Culture' (NAL, 86.FF.64, art. 1, 15; cf. Semper 2007a, 55). Similarly, one of the draft letters addresses 'the complete and comparative museum of the future' (288.5–6).

27.4 **gehorheich**] *gehorche ich*   27.6 **sytematischer**] *systematischer*   27.7 **Gegenstande**] *Gegenstände*   27.15 **der Formeln**] *den ~*   27.19 **Gegenstande**] *Gegenstände*   27.21 **offnet**] *öffnet*   27.26 **s.**] *so*   27.29 **Maroketti**] *Marochetti*
28.7 **D.**] *Die*   **Gottlichkeit**] *Göttlichkeit*   **d.**] *des*   28.27 **v**] *von*   28.33 **1**ᵗ] *1*ᵗᵉˢ   28.34
d.] *die*   **fangt**] *fängt*   28.35 **d.**] *dem*   28.37 **Lehrsatze**] *Lehrsätze*   28.39 **d.**] *des*
29.5 **fruherer**] *früherer*   29.6 **d.**] *der*   29.20 **tritten**] *treten* (cf. 282, Alterations in the Manuscript 29.20)

EDITORIAL EMENDATIONS

29.21 **in einander**] in | einander

ALTERATIONS IN THE MANUSCRIPT

27.5 **es seinem Ermessen überlassend**] *after del.* indem es frei steht *after del.* mit dem Bemerken   27.6 **zu**] *after del.* bei   **Musterung**] *after del.* Beurtheilung   27.7 **Gegenstande**] Geg *over* Exp   **Wäre**] *after two del. beginnings of variant:*

Ein guter Plan muss nicht bloss den bloss äusserlichen Erfordernissen der Ordnung Uebersichtlichkeit und
Wäre die Aufgabe damit gelöst, dass[1] er neben der Uebersichtlichkeit Symmetrie und Ordnung

> 1 **dass**] *after del.* einen Plan

27.7 **wenn**] *before del.* es einem gelang   27.7–8 **ein solcher Plan**] *after del.* nach einem bestimmten Systeme   nach ~ Systeme] *before del.* alles sich übersichtlich   27.8 **enthielte**] *before del.* und der reiche Stoff sich ausserlich   27.14 **mehr**] *after del.* mit einem Worte   27.15 **Formeln**] n *added*   27.18 **übertrifft. –**] *before del.*

Sammlungen Geschichte derselben[1], Querdurchschnitt der Culturgeschichte. Rumpelkammer

> 1 **Geschichte derselben**] *underl.*

27.25 **Ostende**] *after del.* Westende. England, Colonien   27.32–3 **u. Maschinen**] *interl.*
28.9–10 **Erfindungen der Einzelnen**] *before del.* die bloss Ausdruck   28.10 **Ausdruck des**] *before del.* Gesammt   28.16 **abstrakt**] *before del.* mangel *before del.* unvollkommen   28.22

der menschlichen Wissens] der *before del.* Wissenschaften   28.23 **beschliesst**] *after del.* beginnt   28.25 **Scheidens**] *interl.*   28.26 **Critik**] *after del.* Sammlungs   28.29 **Erforschen**] *after del.* Zurückführen der entferntesten   28.33 **Naturwissenschaften**] *after del.* Naturgeschichte *after del.* Geschichte der Sammlungen   **Newton**] *after del.* Cuvier **Leibniz**] *above del.* Cuvier   28.34 **ausser der**] *before del.* todten *before del.* nur   28.36 **Betracht**] *above del.* Rechnung   **behandelte**] *before del.* Lehrsätze   28.41 **geborene**] *after del.* entstandene

29.1 **Querdurchschnitt**] *before del.* athnographischer   29.5 **Erkenntniss**] *after del.* Combinati   29.7 **antiken Studien**] *after del.* Kuns[t]   29.8 **thatenkräftiges**] th *over* kr 29.14 **fehlt**] *altered from* führt *before del.* dieser Ordnung   dieser] *altered from* diese   29.18 **Schaffnerin**] *interl.*   29.19 **Die**] *interl. after del.* Die Baukunst ist das Haus   29.20 **tritten**] *altered from* tritt   29.22 **Bibliotheken.**] *before del.* Räumliches Wissen, Korper okulares Wissen, linguistisches Wissen,   linguistisches] *after del.* phone   29.25 **den Stoffliche**] Stoffliche *altered from* Stoff   **Zeitliche und Oertliche**] *interl.*   29.28 **u. Angemessenheit**] *interl.*

MANUSCRIPT VARIANTS
MS 95[1]

fol. 5r

Plan des Aufsatzes..

Zum erstenmale ein kulturphilosophischer Ueberblick über Vergangenheit, Gegenwart und Zukunft gestattet. und es wäre sicher nicht die unwichtigste Folge welche dieses grosse internationale Unternehmen haben könnte sollte es einem   4

282.2–4 **Zum ~ sollte es einem**] *del. in pencil*   282.2 **Zum**] Z *over* D   282.3 **gestattet.**] *before del.*

Schwierigkeit[1] Sollte es Begabteren gelingen die höheren Beziehungen zusammenzufassen und[2]

1 **Schwierigkeit**] *underl.*   2 **und**] *after del.* so würde da

MS 95[2]

fol. 7r

Wie von der Terrasse eines geschickt angelegten Belvedere dem Blicke die Herrschaft über   5 waldige Bergtriften gelingt, so gestatten vielleicht die Gallerieen des Crystallpallastes zum erstenmale einen umfassenden Ueberblick über die gesammte vergleichende Culturphilosophie und es wäre sicher nicht der geringste Gewinn, den dieses grossartige internationale Unternehmen zur Folge hätte, wenn es einem umfassenden Geiste gelänge, den überschwänglichen Reichthum des dargebotenen Stoffes einer Doctrin zu vindiziren und unter-   10 zuordnen, welche auf wahren Prinzipien begründet wäre Lebensfähigkeit genug besässe, das Nothwendigkeit Werdende aus dem Gewesenen und Seyenden zu folgern und letzteres zu zwingen sich vor dem denkenden Bewussseyn zu rechtfertigen.

282.5 **Wie]** *after del.*

Wie von der Terrasse eines geschickt angelegten Belvedere dem Blicke die Herrschaft über waldige Bergtriften gelingt, so bieten die Gallerieen des Crystallpallastes zum erstenmale einen umfassenden[1] Ueberblick über die gesammte[2] vergleichende[3] Culturphilosophie. Hiervon überzeugt sich selbst der einfache Fachmann bei der Fülle der Beobachtungen und darauf begründeten Inductionen die schon in seiner beschränkteren[4] Sphäre[5] sich ihm aufdrängen. Er muss es Befähigteren überlassen den Blick zu jenem höchsten und

      1 **umfassenden]** *above del.* weiteren vergleichenden   2 **gesammte]** *before del.* Culturphilosophie. der Menschheit   3 **vergleichende]** *interl.*   4 **beschränkteren]** *altered from* beschränkten   5 **Sphäre]** *before del.* des Beobachtens

282.6 **gestatten vielleicht]** *above del.* bieten   282.7 **einen]** *after del.* vielleicht   282.10 **einer]** *after del.* einer Doctrin zu unterwerfen, welche *after del.* in diesem Sinne der Wissenschaft zuzueignen in letzterer die   Doctrin] *underl.*   **Doctrin]** *after del.* lebendigen 282.11 **auf wahren Prinzipien begründet wäre]** *interl.*   282.12 **Nothwendigkeit]** *interl.* **Gewesenen]** wesenen *over del.* wordenen   **und Seyenden]** *interl.*   **und letzteres]** *after del.* und die Irrationalitäten Widersprüche und Unvernünftigkeiten des letzteren aus aus] *after del.* nachzuw   282.13 **Bewussseyn]** *'Bewusstsein'*

MS 95[3]

Plan des Aufsatzes.   *fol. 3r*

Endzweck. *Darlegung einer architectonischen Ueberschau über Inhalt und Ertrag der Ausstellung.*
Einleitung. Die L. Ausstellung kann als der Anfang einer neuen Aera der Culturgeschichte
betrachtet werden Die Wahrheit dieser Ansicht kann nicht in Zweifel gezogen werden aber ihre Weiterfuhrung und Verfolgung im Einzelnen kann doch nur zu mehr oder weniger scharfsinnigen Hypothesen führen, von wenig praktischem Interesse. Sie kann zweitens als der letzte Ausdruck von Zuständen gelten, die schon in das Leben getreten sind und hier zum erstenmale fasslich vor die Augen treten. Von diesem Gesichtspunkte aus betrachtet muss sie auf positivere Resultate führen und praktisches Interesse nach allen Richtungen hin bieten.
Diese Aufgabe vom höchsten kulturhistorischen internationalen politischen Standpunkte aus anzugreifen muss höheren Begabten überlassen bleiben
Aber es hat ein Jeder das Recht es von seinem engeren Standpunkte aus so zu betrachten und die Richtigkeit der Behauptung für das Feld das er zu übersehen vermag zu verfolgen. Erst Wenn diess von vielen Seiten aus geschehen ist, kann die allgemeine Auflösung erfolgen. Diess ist der Gang der Entwickelung jeglicher Materien.
Diess rechtfertige mein Vorhaben, die Bedeutung d. Sammlung von dem Standpunkte der Architecturgeschichte zu betrachten.
Die Extreme berühren sich; In diesem abgenutzten Gemeinspruch liegt eine höhere Wahrheit verborgen. Das Ende knüpft an den Anfang an in der Bahn der Himmelskörper so wie in dem Laufe der Entwickelungen menschlicher Verhältnisse Alles war schon ein-

mal da. Nur dass die durchlaufenen Bahnen keine geschlossenen Kurven sondern Spiral-
linien sind, denn sonst wäre kein Fortschritt, der doch sonst evident ist unmöglich.

Die Wissenschaften haben die Herrschaft über die Praxis erworben und sind, verbunden
mit dem Spekulationsgeiste dem Bedürfnisse vorangeschritten der Bedarf geht nicht mehr
zu Markte, sondern der Markt schafft neuen Bedarf.

> 283.2 **Inhalt und**] *above del.* den   283.4 **L.**] *'Londoner'*   **kann**] *after del.* reiht d   283.5
> **betrachtet werden**] *before undel.* und von *before del.* diesem Gesichtspunkte aus kann der
> Scharfsinn zu Hypothesen führen.   283.6 **Weiterfuhrung**] *'Weiterführung'*   283.12 **kul-**
> **turhistorischen**] *before del.* und   283.13 **höheren**] *after del.* einem   **bleiben**] *before del.*
> Aber   283.14 **hat**] *above del.* darf   **das**] *above del.* mit   283.15 **und**] *before del.* zu zeigen
> **Feld**] *after del.* eng   283.16 **Erst**] *above del.* Dadurch   **geschehen**] *altered from* ge-
> schieht *before del.* , kann es   283.18 **d.**] *'der'*   283.20 **abgenutzten**] *interl.*   283.21
> **verborgen.**] *after del.* gebo *and before del.* Die Geschichte des Fortschreitens der Be-
> wegung
> 284.2 **unmöglich**] *'möglich'*   284.3 **Wissenschaften**] *before del.* in ihrer Anwendung auf
> das Nützliche   284.4 **Spekulationsgeiste**] *before del.* und der Industrie   **der Bedarf**]
> *after del.* der Markt ist *after del.* welches sie

MS 95[5]

fol. 15r   Ordnung von eigentlich ganz zufälligen Dingen abhängig machen; Dort von der Disposition des Hauses. und dem durch sie geleiteten Zuge der Neugier, hier von dem willkürlichen Uebereinkommen bei der Vertheilung des Raumes und den fast ebenso willkurlichen
politischen Eintheilungen der Völker; Beide ermüden durch Monotonie und erschweren
das Erkennen der Unterschiede und Eigenthümlichkeiten mehr noch

> 284.6 **machen**] en *above del.* t   284.7 **Hauses.**] *before del.* und dem Raum   284.8 **fast**]
> *interl.*   **willkurlichen**] *'willkürlichen'*   284.9 **Monotonie**] *after del.* die   284.10 **das**
> **Erkennen**] *repl. del.* die Vergleichung

MS 95[6]

fol. 11r   Ordnung von eigentlich ganz zufälligen Dingen abhängig machen, dort von der Disposition, welche der Architect dem Hause gab und dem durch sie geleiteten Zuge der Neugier,
hier von willkürlichem Uebereinkommen bei der Vertheilung der Räume und den fast eben
so willkürlichen politischen Eintheilungen der Völker. Beide ermüden durch Monotonie
und erschweren die Vergleichung, die erst zuletzt, nachdem man sich durch das Ganze
durchgearbeitet und über dem Einen das Andere zum Theil vergessen hat, erfolgen kann.
Beide Pläne lassen nichts aus, auch verhindern sie keinen, der sie befolgt, in ihr Maschen-
werk ein noch so reiches und buntes Muster von Einfällen des Geistes und der Laune
hineinzusticken, aber sie leiten nicht, wie sie sollen, von selbst auf diejenigen Resultate,
worauf es hauptsächlich ankommt.

Scheinbar organischer ist das System, welches mit den Rohstoffen anfängt, dann zu den
Werkzeugen und Maschinen zu ihrer Verarbeitung übergeht, zuletzt die Fülle der Erzeugnisse unseres Kunstfleisses nach den Stoffen aus denen sie bestehen gruppirt, und nur das

Letters on the Great Exhibition

hierin Gleichartige der verschiedenen Länder zusammenhält. Es hat aber genau genommen
wenig voraus vor den beiden zuerst genannten Wegen der Vergleichung, ist eben so äusserlich und materiell und

> 284.11–12 **Ordnung ~ durch**] *first three lines of manuscript over* 6.   284.13–14 **eben so**]
> eben│so   284.14 **ermüden**] *above del.* erschweren   284.15 **zuletzt,**] *altered from* ~∧ *before*
> *del.* erfolgen kann,   284.16 **zum Theil**] *interl.*   284.17 **Beide**] *after del.* Der Plan
> **befolgt,**] *before del.* ihnen durch   284.20 **ankommt.**] *before del.* Was   284.23 **und**] *after*
> *del.* nur das hierin Gleichartige bei den verschiedenen Zusammenhälten und für die In-
> dustrie der verschiedenen Völker nach einer gewissen Anzahl von Categorieen
> 285.2 **eben**] *after del.* ebenfalls

MS 95[7]

Ein solches System der Ordnung hat seine grossen Bequemlichkeiten. Es kann alles in sich   *fol. 16r*
aufnehmen und jedem seine Zelle zutheilen, aber das Zusammenwachsen der äusserlich
zusammengehaltenen und geregelten Massen zu organischem Leben ist damit noch nicht
erreicht. Da es darauf nicht hinwirkt, ist es auch unfähig jener anarchischen Zerfahrenheit
Einhalt zu thun, von welcher oben die Rede war. – Mich dünkt, dass alle bisherigen Versuche, den in dem Hyde Park zusammengetragenen Stoff systematisch zu ordnen, an dem-
selben Gebrechen der

> 285.4–10 **Ein ~ Gebrechen der**] *del.*   285.5 **jedem**] *below del.* es ihm   285.7 **darauf nicht**
> **hinwirkt,**] *above del.* dieses nicht vermag,   285.8–9 **bisherigen Versuche**] *after del.*
> bisher befolgten Pläne,   befolgten] *above del.* beobachteten   285.10 **der**] *before undel.*
> [U]

MS 95[8]

Ein solches System der Ordnung hat seine grossen Bequemlichkeiten und Vortheile. Es   *fol. 14r*
kann alles in sich aufnehmen und es zusammenhalten, aber das Zusammenwachsen der
äusserlich verbundenen und geregelten Massen zu organischem Leben vermag es nicht zu
erzwingen. Da es dieses nicht vermag, sind aber auch alle seine Vortheile der Kollectivität
und Uebersichtlichkeit nur scheinbar und ungeachtet aller Regeln und Fächer giebt sich
jene anarchische Zerfahrenheit kund, von

> 285.13 **verbundenen**] *after del.* zusammenge *(probably for 'zusammengehaltenen'; see 285.6)*
> **Massen**] n *added*   285.14 **aber auch**] *interl.*   285.15 **ungeachtet**] *after del.* den Regeln
> und Vorschriften

Draft of First Letter

TEXTUAL RECORD

MS 95[9]   gta, 20-Ms-95, fol. 4r–v, in Semper's hand
MS 95[10]   gta, 20-Ms-95, fol. 3v (3r see 283–4, MS 95[3]; variant of MS 95[9]), in Semper's hand
MS 95[11] gta, 20-Ms-95, fol. 10r–v (10v blank; variant of MS 95[10]), in Semper's hand, *copytext*

ALTERATIONS IN THE MANUSCRIPT

29.30 **das**] *above del.* mein   **gegebene**] *altered from* gegebenes
30.1 **Es**] *above del.* Mir   30.2 **ideellen**] *after del.* geistigen   30.4–5 **innerhalb**] *after del.* in jenen grossen   30.5 **Grundideen**] ideen *above del.* motiven

MANUSCRIPT VARIANTS
MS 95[9]

fol. 4r   Lieber Freund

Ich habe das Ihnen gegebene Versprechen über den Inhalt unserer neulichen Unterhaltung einen Aufsatz zu schreiben, seitdem stets im Kopfe herumgetragen und war bei meinen täglichen Wanderungen durch den Hydeparkpalast ämsig beschäftigt, die dort angehäuften Gegenstände im Geiste nach einem Systeme zu ordnen, welches bei der grossen   5
Schwierigkeit in der Wahl eines Planes zu systematischer Musterung derselben, die jedem der ernstlich darüber nachdachte entgegen getreten seyn wird, mir noch immer als das-
fol. 4v   jenige erscheint, ¦ welches die *inneren* Verbindungsfäden dieser bunten Welt von Gegenständen am besten zusammenhält. –
Bei diesen Versuchen fügte sich alles wie von selbst zusammen, was durch Raum Zeit und   10
Stoff getrennt war, und die

> 286.1 **Lieber**] *after del.*
>
> Lieber Freund!
>
> Ich habe das Ihnen gegebene Versprechen über den Inhalt unserer neulichen Unterhaltung einen Aufsatz zu schreiben, seitdem stets im Kopfe herumgetragen und war bei meinen täglichen Wanderungen durch den Hydepark-Palast ämsig beschäftigt, die dort angehäuften Gegenstände im Geiste nach einem[1] Systeme zu ordnen, welches[2] mir bei der grossen Schwierigkeit der Wahl eines Planes zu systematischer Musterung der Gegenstände dieser Ausstellung
>
> > 1 **einem**] *altered from* meinem   2 **welches**] *after del.*
>
> Bestict mich das Gefühl der Vaterschaft oder ist es wirklich der Fall – ich finde dass bei der grossen Schwierigkeit der Wahl eines Planes zu systematischer Muste-

rung der Gegenstände dieser Ausstellung, die jedem der ernstlich darüber nachdachte, entgegen getreten seyn wird, die architectonisch vergleichende Anordnung derselben immer noch die meiste Logik enthält und wie von selbst auf die

286.8 **welches**] *after del.*

welches[1] die inneren Verbindungsfäden dieser bunten Welt von Gegenständen am besten zusammenhält und[2] ihren Zusammenhang nicht bloss von örtlichen, zeitlichen und stofflichen also bloss zufälligen und äusserlichen Bedingungen oder gar von ihrer noch zufälligeren räumlichen Vertheilung innerhalb des Gebäudes abhängig macht.

1 **welches**] *after del. on fol. 4r–v* welches nicht bloss meinem ¦ Standpunkte der Anschauung dieser Gegenstand[e] entspricht, sondern 2 **und**] *after del.* und vielleicht, später bei grösserer Entfaltung des Gedankens einer permanenten kulturhistorischen Sammlung

MS 95[10]

Lieber Freund

fol. 3v

Ich habe den Inhalt unseres neulichen Gespräches und mein Ihnen gegebenes Wort darüber einen Aufsatz zu schreiben, seitdem stets im Kopfe herumgetragen und war bei meinen fast täglichen Wanderungen durch den Hydepark Pallast beschäftigt, die Sachen auf bauwis-
5 senschaftlicher Basis im Geiste zu ordnen. Es wurde mir immer klarer, dass dieser Plan vor allen anderen den grossen Vorzug besitzt, die intimeren Verbindungsfäden dieser bunten Welt von Gegenstanden am besten zusammenzuhalten, und dass er den Blick auf gewisse unverrückbare Punkte leitet, die uns gestatten, bei der Beweglichkeit sowohl des eigenen Standpunktes der Beobachtung wie der uns umgebenden Erscheinungen deren gegenwär-
10 tige Lage und Richtung sowohl der Zeit als dem Raume nach richtig zu bemessen.

287.4 **Hydepark Pallast**] Hydepark | Pallast   **auf**] *after del.* nach   287.5–6 **vor allen anderen**] *interl.*   287.7 **Gegenstanden**] 'Gegenständen'   **und dass er**] *after del.* und dass sich aus ihm *after del.* und dass er von selbst auf gewisse unverrückbare Punkte leitet, die uns gestatten *after del.* und dass dessen Folgerungen von selbst auf dasjenige führen, was *after del.* ohne dass   **den Blick**] *after del.* wie von selbst   287.9–10 **gegenwärtige**] *repl. del.* wahre   287.10 **Richtung**] *before del.* zu bemessen.   zu bemessen.] *after del.* zu berechnen.   **sowohl**] *after del.* Dieselben Haltpunkte dienen aber auch zu der Beurtheilung früherer und entfernterer   Dieselben] *after del.* Denselben Halt gewährt er zu der Beurtheilung   **richtig**] *inserted*   **bemessen.**] *altered from ~, before del.* ein Vorzug den keine anderere Disposition   Disposition] *before three del. variant parts of next sentence:*

Dadurch zwingt er[1] uns zu der Anerkennung gewisser Thatsachen und Erscheinungen im äusseren, deren richtige Würdigung verbunden mit
Dadurch zwingt er uns gewissermassen zu der Anerkennung der Ursachen gewisser Erscheinungen in nicht[2]
Ohne diese wichtige Eigenschaft desselben, würde jeder[3] andere noch so

1 **zwingt er**] *after del.* führt er *after del.* leitet er   2 **Erscheinungen in nicht**] *each word del. separately*   3 **jeder**] *after del.* ich

288   The Great Exhibition

Draft of Second Letter

TEXTUAL RECORD

MS 95^{12} gta, 20-Ms-95, fol. 6r–v (6v blank), '2$^{ter.}$ Brief', in Semper's hand
MS 95^{13}   gta, 20-Ms-95, fols. 8r–9v (8v, 9v blank; variant of MS 95^{12}), in Semper's hand, *copy-text*

EXPLANATORY NOTES

30.8 **P. P.**] *praemissis praemittendis*; 'premising what is to be premised', 'as above', referring to the addressee: in first letter 'Lieber Freund!'   30.17 **Buchhandleres**] *Buchhändlers*   **V.**] *Vieweg*   30.21–2 **unabhangig**] *unabhängig*

ALTERATIONS IN THE MANUSCRIPT

30.9 **Sie**] *before del.* mir   30.12 **eigenen**] *after del.* meinen   **Ein**] *above del.* Mein ganzer   30.16 **Werk**] *before del.* von mir   30.28 **ihren**] *above del.* seinen   30.31 **an**] *interl.*   **Stär-keʌ**] *altered from* ~, *before del.* raschere Entwickelung   31.3 **unnütz**] *after del.* als *and before del.* zu beseitigen   31.8 **die Druckmaschine**] *interl.*

MANUSCRIPT VARIANTS
MS 95^{12}

fol. 6r   2$^{ter.}$ *Brief.*   Anfang eines
Briefes an L. Bucher. im
Lieber Freund   Jahre 1852.

Was Sie mir neulich über die Geschichte der Sammlungen sagten, über das Durchgehen derselben durch drei Phasen bis zu dem vollständigen vergleichenden Museum der Zu-   5
kunft, deren Ansatz Sie mit Recht in dem "Crystallpallaste" sehen, fällt auffallend mit meinen eigenen Ansichten zusammen; Mein ganzer Plan einer wenn auch vorerst nur im Gedanken ausführbaren Organisation dieser Sammlung, den ich wie Sie wissen schon lange hege, ist darauf begründet, und dieser hangt wieder eng zusammen mit ganz verwandten Ideen über vergleichende Baukunde über welche ich seit Jahren meditire und ein   10
halb fertiges Werk von mir bereits in den Händen des Buchhändlers V. ist. Es herrscht ein vom individuellen Streben unabhängiges Walten des Mikrokosmus eine Spontaneität in der kollectiven Menschheit durch die sie sich als denkendes selbsthandelndes Individuum hoherer Gattung kund giebt. Gewisse Weltgedanken machen sich von selbst Bahn wenn die Zeit dazu reif ist, frei und unabhängig von dem Sinnen und Trachten des Einzelnmen-   15
schen, der bloss zuweilen rechtzeitig genug den Ausdruck des reif gewordenen Weltgedankens fand, um ihm als Geburtshelfer zu dienen. Gehen Wahrheiten nicht gleichen Schrittes mit dem ruhig fortwaltenden νοῦς der Gesellschaft, so sind sie es nicht, sondern

Irrthum und krankhafte Rebellion des Gliedes gegen das Ganze, zuweilen auch Zuckungen des ungeborenen im Schoosse der Zukunft verborgenen Weltgedankens und des Marthyrerthums der Menschenretter etc. Sie verschwinden wie Phänomene

Dagegen kann nichts den Gang der Menschenidee aufhalten, was sich ihr in den Weg stellt, wird von den neuen saftigen Sprösslingen der Zeit aus den Fugen gerissen oder umwuchert, und dient zu reicherer Gestaltung das sonst eine zu schematische und unseren historisch erzogenen Sinnen nicht schmackhafte Form angenommen hätte.

Der Gedanke gewinnt in diesem Kämpfe mit dem Alten Stärke raschere Entwickelung, historische Haltung und Farbe. So wirkt die Reaction gerade in den Entwickelungsperioden des Menschenthums am thätigsten und ihr Widerstand dient der kreisenden Zeit als nothwendiger. Stützpunkt.

Nur diejenigen, die nach ihrem vorwitzigen Ermessen bald vorwärts bald rückwärts drängen, und über dem Kampfe zu stehen glauben werden sind unnütze und schädliche Kräfte.

288.1 **2**$^{ter.}$] *after* Lieber Freund *turned upside down near bottom of page* 288.1–3 **Anfang eines Briefes an L. Bucher. im Jahre 1852.**] *in pencil (in Semper's hand, probably early 1870s)* 288.1 **Anfang**] *after in pencil and del. in pencil* Angefangene 288.2 **L.**] *'Lothar'* 288.3 **1852**] *'1851'* 288.5 **dem**] *inserted before del.* der der] *after del.* ihrer ethnographisch-historischen Vollständigkeit **vergleichenden**] *after del.* Sammlung der 288.7 **eigenen**] *interl.* 288.10 **über welche**] *after del.* an welcher ich nun schon seit 288.11 **von mir**] *interl.* **bereits**] *after del.* bereit *after del.* im Schreibtische **V.**] *'Vieweg'* 288.12 **individuellen**] *after del.* menschlichen 288.13–14 **hoherer**] *'höherer'* 288.16 **der**] *above del.* dessen Genie **rechtzeitig**] *above del.* frühzeitig 288.17 **Gehen**] *altered from* Geht *after del.* Kommt er damit vor der Zeit zum Vorschein, so gilt er nicht nur als Träumer und Schwärmer, sond **Wahrheiten**] *above del.* Erfindungen Erfindungen] *after del.* letztere (letztere *above del.* das Genie mit seinen) 288.18 **es**] *after del.* nicht Gedanken nur Einfälle, und der

289.2–3 **im Schoosse ~ Phänomene**] *inserted after del.* Weltgedankens. etc etc 289.5 **wird**] *before del.* umgestossen 289.5–6 **umwuchert**] *after del.* so 289.6 **und dient**] *after del.* dass es 289.8 **Kämpfe**] *'Kampfe'* **Stärke**] *before del.* Gestaltung und Gestaltung und] *after del.* und 289.9 **Reaction**] *before del.* für für] *after del.* als nothwendige Kraft 289.9–10 **Entwickelungsperioden**] *after del.* Zeiten der 289.10 **dient**] *after del.* giebt in den Mutterwehen 289.11 **nothwendiger.**] *interl.* 289.13 **und über**] *after del.* die

Notes on Exhibits

TEXTUAL RECORD

MS 96 gta, 20-Ms-96, eight individual manuscript units with notes in pencil, in Semper's hand, *copy-text* (with the exception of the first unit)

[1]fols. 1r–4v: notes on the Salon of 1849 in Paris, with brief discussions and some sketches of works by Auguste Girardin, Pierre-Joseph Garrez, Victor Ruprich-Robert, Jules Bouchet (see Explication des ouvrages 1849)

[2]fols. 1r–2v (1r–2r printed matter): notes written on prospectus for 'Blake's Patent Mineral Fire and Water Proof Paint, or Artificial Slate'

[3] fols. 1r–2v (1r, 2r printed matter; 1v blank): notes written on prospectus for 'Eddy's Patent Toughened Iron Railway Wheel' (pl. 2)
[4] fols. 1r–2v (1v–2v blank)
[5] fols. 1r–2v (1r–v blank)
[6] fol. 1r–v
[7] fols. 1r–4v
[8] fols. 1r–2v

BIBLIOGRAPHY Herrmann 1981, 104; Hildebrand 2020a, 114–15

EXPLANATORY NOTES

These notes on exhibits, jotted down during several walks through the Crystal Palace, are part of the preliminary work for what was to become *Science, Industry, and Art*. In its preface 'To the German audience', Semper explained its larger scope: while its 'content concerns primarily only English and American conditions', he had intended to add 'some more specifics about German, Belgian and Russian industry and art' – notes he had collected during the Exhibition (Semper 1852, 1). However, the notes preserved relate mainly – as does *Science, Industry, and Art* – to exhibits from the United States and, to a lesser extent, to Russian exhibits. We have established the probable sequence of these notes by dividing the seven manuscript units into three groups, which may perhaps correspond to that number of walks through the Crystal Palace by Semper.

The first group contains notes written on two American advertising leaflets (31.12–33.8); accordingly, these notes refer exclusively to American exhibits such as textile raw materials, minerals, food products and tools (such as tomahawks). The second group comprises the largest portion of the notes (33.9–38.17); they alternate between notes on American technology and Russian luxury industry and address exhibits such as Cyrus McCormick's reaper and malachite vases and furniture from St Petersburg. The notes in the third group focus again on American exhibits (38.18–39.25), some of which, addressed as 'Hinzu gekommene Sachen' (Items added; 38.18), were apparently shown only towards the end of the Great Exhibition (among them Robert Ball Hughes's sculpture of Oliver Twist). Semper took these last notes perhaps in early October, after returning from a two-week reunion with his family in Bruges.

All in all, Semper's notes present a motley collection of brief comments on exhibits that range from fancy soap, toys, false teeth and artificial legs to the latest photographic exploits in the field of daguerreotypes, talbotypes, hyalotypes and the magic lantern. Photography was obviously intriguing for Semper, as he made notes about it in all three manuscript groups and discussed it in *Science, Industry, and Art* (Semper 1852, 10, 74–5). The large number of exhibits on which Semper made notes has led us to identify them in the list below (wherever possible) by their reference numbers in the last, probably the third, edition of the three-volume *Official Descriptive and Illustrated Catalogue* of 1852 (ODIC 1852; for the dating, see Cantor 2013, 1:xxxii), to which a supplementary volume was added. The state of this edition corresponds to that of the 'Presentation Copy' of the *Reports by the Juries* of 1852 (Rep. Jur. 1852), to which reference is also made. The smaller *Official Catalogue* is cited if the information on exhibits or exhibitors differs from that in the *Official Descriptive and Illustrated Catalogue*.

31.14 **288**] ODIC 1852, 3:1453 (no. 288)   **32**] ODIC 1852, 3:1434 (no. 32)   **37**] ODIC 1852, 3:1434–5 (no. 37)   **178**] ODIC 1852, 3:1449 (no. 178)   31.15 **Rochstofte**] uncertain reading, *Rohstoffe*   31.18–27 **Marylandschrank ~ 3 Sorten Marmor**] ODIC 1852, 3:1459 (no. 371), 1460 fig.; Rep. Jur. 1852, 151, 651–2   31.20 **Chromgrun**] *Chromgrün*   31.21 **schwefelh.**] *schwefelhaltig*   31.28 **Mehl von Hecker**] ODIC 1852, 3:1440 (no. 114)   31.30 **Schinken**] ODIC 1852, 3:1449 (no. 200), 1459 (no. 363); Rep. Jur. 1852, 65; Rodgers 1852, 24–5; Tallis/Strutt 1852, 2:87   31.32 **Oelkuchen**] ODIC 1852, 3:1467 (no. 530)

32.1 **Holzsorten ~ Sammlung**] ODIC 1852, 3:1440 (no. 115); Rep. Jur. 1852, 149; Rodgers 1852, 137–8   32.2 **Schusterzwecken**] ODIC 1852, 3:1450 (no. 211), 1462 (no. 422)   32.4 **Fournirholz mit Cirkularsäge**] probably ODIC 1852, 3:1452 (no. 244)   32.9 **Flintglas ~ Flint Glas Company**] ODIC 1852, 3:1440 (no. 113); Johnson 1852, 147; Rep. Jur. 1852, 536; Rodgers 1852, 57 and pl.   32.10 **Schmelztiegel von Wasserblei**] ODIC 1852, 3:1463 (no. 426); Rep. Jur. 1852, 585–6   32.12 **Blakes fire proof paint**] ODIC 1852, 3:1451 (no. 233); Johnson 1852, 23; Rep. Jur. 1852, 587   32.13 **n° 62 Hyalotypie ~ Lat Magica Langenheim**] 'Lat': *Laterna*; ODIC 1852, 3:1437 (no. 62); Arnoux 1851; Rep. Jur. 1852, 277; on Langenheim's magic lantern, see Semper 1852, 75   32.14 **Bettstelle 552**] ODIC 1852, 3:1468 (no. 552); Hunt 1851, 2:778   32.19 **Wachstuch; 135**] ODIC 1852, 3:1441 (no. 135)   32.20 **424 ~ Wassereimer**] ODIC 1852, 3:1462 (no. 424); Rep. Jur. 1852, 602   32.21 **Orn. Teppich**] 'Orn.': *Ornamentaler* or *Ornamentierter*; ODIC 1852, 3:1464 (no. 453); Rep. Jur. 1852, 475   **eigenth.**] *eigenthümliches*   32.23 **Stocks for Mattresses. 253**] ODIC 1852, 3:1452 (no. 253); Rep. Jur. 1852, 103   32.24 **Baumwollenbaum Alabama**] Amtl. Ber. 1852/53, 1:354   32.26 **Allen's improved arithmetical Tables**] ODIC 1852, 3:1470 (no. 591): 'Educational tables' presented by John Ellery Tyler, probably comprising those by Edwin Allen; for the latter, see Seton 1850   32.29 **Deutschland u Amerika**] *~ und ~*   32.33 **Drathproben ~ Washburn**] ODIC 1852, 3:1462 (no. 421)   32.34 **New Orleans Moos**] Off. Cat. 1851³⁻⁵, 192 (no. 559): 'Hicks, G. London. – Samples of New Orleans moss'; cf. Rep. Jur. 1851, 103; a different exhibitor for this catalogue number listed in ODIC 1852, 3:1469 (no. 559): 'Miller, John E., New York. New Orleans moss'   32.35 **Tapeten**] ODIC 1852, 3:1435 (no. 48), 1452 (no. 260)   32.36 **402 imitation of wood**] ODIC 1852, 3:1462 (no. 402)   32.37 **282. Papier**] ODIC 1852, 3:1453 (no. 282)

33.1 **Maroquin**] ODIC 1852, 3:1447 (no. 165)   33.2 **Grossen**] *Grössen*   33.3–4 **Logan, Vail & C° New York**] agents for George Vail & Co., Speedwell Iron Works, Morristown; see advertisements in *Scientific American* 6, no. 28 (29 March 1851), 223, and 7, no. 12 (6 Dec. 1851), 95. Neither Logan, Vail & Co. nor George Vail & Co. are listed as exhibitors in ODIC 1852.   33.5 **Werkzeuge ~ Brown & Wells**] ODIC 1852, 3:1452 (no. 259); Rodgers 1852, 42   **Aexte Tomohawks**] ODIC 1852, 3:1439 (no. 97), 1441 (no. 119); Johnson 1852, 136; Rep. Jur. 1852, 489–90; Rodgers 1852, 42   33.11 **Geometrie, Dial of the seasons**] ODIC 1852, 3:1452 (no. 263); Rep. Jur. 1852, 313–14   **Ruder n° 92**] ODIC 1852, 3:1439 (no. 92); Johnson 1852, 152   **Geräthe. 423**] ODIC 1852, 3:1462 (no. 423)   33.12–14 **A. M. Perkins ~ Screw joint**] ODIC 1852, 3:1468 (no. 541)   33.15 **Pneumatische Lokomotiven**] ODIC 1852, 3:1466 (no. 504)   33.16 **Mähmaschine**] ODIC 1852, 3:1437–8 (no. 73), pl. 393; ODIC Suppl. 1852, 1530–1 and pl.; ILN 1851b; Cryst. Pal. 1852, 12–13; Johnson 1852, 93–9; Rep. Jur. 1852, 231–2; Rodgers 1852, 14–16, 139; Tallis/Strutt 1852, 3:19 and pl.   33.17–18 **India rubber Ueberzug ~ Spielzeug**] ODIC 1852, 3:1461 (no. 378) and fig.; Johnson 1852, 120, 149; Rep. Jur. 1852, 594–5, 678; Rodgers 1852, 16–18; Tallis/Strutt 1852, 2:77–9   33.18 **Venering**] *veneering*   **Spielzeug**] Rep. Jur. 1852, 595; Amtl. Ber. 1852/53, 2:705: rubber toys produced by Charles Goodyear   **Velocimeter**] ODIC 1852, 3:1468 (no. 542); Rep. Jur. 1852, 253   33.19 **Mʳ Hobbs**] probably the

292 The Great Exhibition

American Alfred Charles Hobbs, agent of Day & Newell, who picked the safest English locks (by Bramah & Co. and Chubb & Son) during the Great Exhibition; see ILN 1851c; Johnson 1852, 139–43; Rodgers 1852, 66–71, 90–1; Hobbs 1853, 99–102, 115–30; Giedion 1948, 57; on Day & Newell, see note 38.26   34.5 **1 Louis quinze mit Blumenwerk**] 'i': *1)*; ODIC 1852, 3:1383–4 (no. 365), pl. 373; Cryst. Pal. 1852, 136 and fig.; Tallis/Strutt 1852, 3:33   34.5–6 **Chinesische Vasen ~ Unterbau**] ODIC 1852, 3:1377–9 (no. 323), possibly pls. 366–7; Illustrated Exhibitor 1851, no. 16 (20 Sept.), 286 and fig.; Cryst. Pal. 1852, 4 and fig., 304 fig.; Rep. Jur. 1852, 570–1. During his Dresden years, Semper himself had designed two pedestals for Russian malachite vases on behalf of Frederick Augustus II, the Saxon king; see Semper's draft letter to Heinrich Wilhelm Schulz, 9 September 1851 (gta, 20-K-1851-09-09[S]), cited in Weidmann 2010, 266 n. 5; Orelli-Messerli 2010, 75.   34.6 **ubereinandergestellt**] *übereinandergestellt*   34.8–9 **Arntikisirend baroker Candelaber mit ~ gothischem Knopfwerk**] 'Arntikisirend' uncertain reading, *Antikisierend*; ODIC 1852, 3:1376 (no. 287), pl. 353; Art-Journal Cat. 1851, 278 and fig.; Cryst. Pal. 1852, 4 and fig., 136 and fig.; Tallis/Strutt 1852, 1:127   34.10–11 **Russischer Styl ~ Barbarischer Zopf**] ODIC 1852, 3:1384 (no. 370), pl. 381; Illustrated Exhibitor 1851, no. 8 (26 July), 127 fig., 129; Cryst. Pal. 1852, 136 and fig.   34.10 **Russen︿ in den Ecken**] *Russen, in den Ecken*   34.12 **Porphyrvase**] jasper mistaken for porphyry; ODIC 1852, 3:1379–80 (no. 326), pl. 353; Cryst. Pal. 1852, 4; Rep. Jur. 1852, 566; Tallis/Strutt 1852, 1:128; see also note 35.7   34.13–14 **298 ~ Florentiner Arbeit**] ODIC 1852, 3:1376 (no. 298), pl. 355; Rep. Jur. 1852, 567   34.15–16 **Porzelanvasen ~ Antike Vasen**] ODIC 1852, 3:1376 (no. 318), pls. 359–60; Illustrated Exhibitor 1851, no. 8 (26 July), 125 fig., 128 fig., 129   34.16 **Warwik Wase ~ Warschau**] 'Warwik Wase': *Warwick Vase*; ODIC 1852, 3:1381 (no. 329) and fig.; Semper 1852, 52–3   **gehammertem**] *gehämmertem*   34.17 **Malachitgegenstände ohne Charakterunterschied**] ODIC 1852, 3:1377–9 (no. 323), pls. 363–8; Illustrated Exhibitor 1851, no. 16 (20 Sept.), 286 and fig.; Cryst. Pal. 1852, 4 and fig., 304 fig.; Rep. Jur. 1852, 569–71; Tallis/Strutt 1852, 1:127–8 and pls.   34.18 **Official Catalogue, pa 296**] 'pa': *pagina*; probably relating to the first page of the list of Russian exhibits in Off. Cat. 1851² or Off. Cat. 1851³ (the list of Russian exhibits in Off. Cat. 1851¹ comprises pages 290–5)   34.20 **Porcelan Tisch**] ODIC 1852, 3:1376 (no. 318), pl. 361   34.22–30 **Silberzeug ~ im barbarischen Style**] ODIC 1852, 3:1384 (no. 366), pls. 375–80; Rep. Jur. 1852, 515   34.22 **Tannenbaum obenauf Blumenbouquet**] ODIC 1852, 3: pl. 375; Cryst. Pal. 1852, 5, 136, 137 fig.; Tallis/Strutt 1852, 1:128; 3:33 and pl.   34.24 **die Französisch Rokoko**] 'die': either *das*, referring to 'Rokoko', or *der*, referring to *Styl*   **die Russisch Rokoko**] 'die': either *das*, referring to 'Rokoko', or *der*, referring to *Styl*   34.25 **bauchiges Gefäss von vergoldetem Silber**] ODIC 1852, 3: possibly pl. 380   34.27–8 **Krug ~ Dito n° 9**] ODIC 1852, 3: possibly pl. 380 34.28 **Tannzapfen in Silber**] ODIC 1852, 3: pl. 377   34.29 **24 Russin Sasikoff**] '24': probably *n° 24*; one of the figures of Russian women exhibited by Ignace Sazikoff; see ODIC 1852, 3:1383 fig.   34.30 **Hähne im barbarischen Style**] unverifiable; two possible meanings of 'Hähne': *roosters* or *faucets*   34.31 **Malachit**] see note 34.17   34.32 **Caucasian Sable ~ shahka**] 'Sable' derived from German *Säbel*: *sabre*; 'shahka': *shaska*; ODIC 1852, 3:1371–2 (nos. 162–3)   **Caucasian Daggers**] ODIC 1852, 3:1372 (nos. 164–5)   34.33 **Noori Ogli Oaste Selim Molla ~ Nookha**] 'Oaste': *Ooste*; ODIC 1852, 3:1372 (no. 165)   34.34 **Werk in lithochromem Abdruck**] ODIC 1852, 3:1383 (no. 362); Rep. Jur. 1852, 706   34.38 **265) Articles of furniture**] ODIC 1852, 3:1375 (no. 265); Cryst. Pal. 1852, 6; Rep. Jur. 1852, 600; Tallis/Strutt 1852, 1:129   **Fliz**] *Filz*   34.39 **Stickereien 276. Shirkhonin Torjok**] 'Shirkhonin': *Shikhonin*; ODIC 1852, 3:1375 (no. 276); Amtl. Cat. 1851, (no. 276)

Notes on Exhibits   293

35.1–3 **Barbarische Decke ~ Sophia Papinoff Tiflis**] 'Papinoff': *Popinoff*; ODIC 1852, 3:1376 (no. 310); Rep. Jur. 1852, 472, 479–80   35.4 **W. Kämmerer und Saeftigen Joaillers a St Petersburg**] 'Joaillers a': *joailliers à*; ODIC 1852, 3:1384 (no. 376), pl. 382; Cryst. Pal. 1852, 5; Rep. Jur. 1852, 515; Tallis/Strutt 1852, 1:128   35.5 **Kaiserliche Polirfabrik in St Petersburg**] ODIC 1852, 3:1376 (no. 298), pls. 355–6; Rep. Jur. 1852, 567   35.7 **Tische**] ODIC 1852, 3:1377–9 (no. 323), possibly pl. 364; Rep. Jur. 1852, 570–1; Tallis/Strutt 1852, 1:128   **Vasen von grünem Porphyr**] jasper mistaken for porphyry; ODIC 1852, 3:1380–1 (no. 327) and fig., pl. 360; see also note 34.12   **ähnl. Malachitgegenstände**] see note 34.17   35.8 **Gold u Silbererz**] ~ *und* ~; ODIC 1852, 3:1362–3 (no. 4), 1377–9 (no. 323); Rep. Jur. 1852, 34   35.9 **Malachitgefässe mit Gold**] see note 34.17   35.10 **Parkettafeln**] ODIC 1852, 3:1376 (no. 299), pls. 357–8; Cryst. Pal. 1852, 327, 328 fig.; Rep. Jur. 1852, 545   **Glasscheiben**] ODIC 1852, 3:1376 (nos. 294–5)   **buntes Papier**] ODIC 1852, 3:1375 (nos. 261–2), 1383 (no. 359) 35.11 **Clodion**] possibly the clock by Félix Chopin, for which he was inspired by the terracotta model for the monument 'The Invention of the Balloon', an allegory of the first manned balloon flight designed by the sculptor Clodion in 1784; ODIC 1852, 3:1383–4 (no. 365), pl. 374; Veillerot 1851, 182   35.12–13 **290. Aga-Melik ~ Fingerhüte**] ODIC 1852, 3:1376 (no. 290)   35.15 **Lithographirte Blätter**] ODIC 1852, 3:1383 (no. 362); Rep. Jur. 1852, 706 35.16 **mochte**] possibly *möchte*   35.16–17 **Germania ~ Frankreich**] probably ODIC 1852, 3:1381 (no. 328), pls. 368–71; commemorative plaster medallions by the sculptor Fyodor Petrovich Tolstoy showing allegories of the wars of 1812–14, among these pl. 370 representing the liberation of Berlin perhaps addressed here by Semper   35.19 **292. Durchsichtige Seife von Taylor**] ODIC 1852, 3:1453 (no. 292); Rep. Jur. 1852, 615; Rodgers 1852, 48   35.20 **der ausser sich ist**] uncertain reading   35.21 **Fancy Soaps. von X. Bazin**] ODIC 1852, 3:1434 (no. 36); Rep. Jur. 1852, 613   35.24 **weisse Schwäne**] pelicans mistaken for swans; ODIC 1852, 3:1374 (no. 244)   **Zobel Silberfuchs Peltze**] ODIC 1852, 3:1384 (no. 381); Cryst. Pal. 1852, 6; Tallis/Strutt 1852, 1:130–1   35.25 **Amelung & Sohn Dorpat**] ODIC 1852, 3:1376 (no. 296)   **aufgehangt**] *aufgehängt*   35.26 **Zobel ~ Zobelpeltze**] see note 35.24 35.28–30 **Gestickte Decke ~ Hadji Aga Baba**] ODIC 1852, 3:1375 (no. 269)   35.29 **in d. Mitte**] ~ *der* ~   35.31 **Gouvernt**] *Gouvernement*   35.32 **Schaal ~ Gau Orenburg**] ODIC 1852, 3:1375 (no. 282); Cryst. Pal. 1852, 6; Tallis/Strutt 1852, 1:131   35.34 **Austellung**] *Ausstellung*   35.36 **Gänsekiele Riabzewitch St Petersburg**] ODIC 1852, 3:1383 (no. 360) 35.37 **Papierfabrik von Caluga. (Aristarkoff)**] ODIC 1852, 3:1383 (no. 359) 36.2 **Penduluhr von Chauncey Jerome**] ODIC 1852, 3:1467 (no. 514); Hunt 1851, 2:782; ILN 1851a   36.4 **294**] ODIC 1852, 3:1453 (no. 294); Rep. Jur. 1852, 595   **410**] ODIC 1852, 3:1462 (no. 410)   **411**] ODIC 1852, 3:1462 (no. 411)   **295**] ODIC 1852, 3:1453 (no. 295)   **382**] ODIC 1852, 3:1461 (no. 382); Rep. Jur. 1852, 596   **471**] ODIC 1852, 3:1465 (no. 471)   36.6–8 **Landcharte ~ August Mitchell**] ODIC 1852, 3:1458 (no. 360)   36.9 **Drilliche ~ Amoskeag**] ODIC 1852, 3:1433 (no. 2); Rodgers 1852, 58–9   36.10 **Vattenmuster**] *Wattenmuster*   36.11 **Landcharte Vereinigte Staaten von A**] 'A': *Amerika*; probably Augustus Mitchell's map of the United States; see note 36.6–8   36.13 **Luxusschuhwesen**] ODIC 1852, 3:1441 (no. 116)   36.14–18 **Tauwerk ~ improved machinery**] ODIC 1852, 3:1465 (no. 474)   36.14 **Strangen**] *Strängen*   36.16 **glanzt**] *glänzt*   36.17 **Man.**] *Manilla*   36.20 **Tapetenproben**] ODIC 1852, 3:1435 (no. 48), 1452 (no. 260)   36.22 **Boot aus vollem Holze geschnitten**] ODIC 1852, 3:1448 (no. 174)   36.24 **eisernes Bett**] possibly ODIC 1852, 3:1470 (no. 634)   **Teppich**] Johnson 1852, 133, 155; Rep. Jur. 1852, 474   **Glasmalereien**] possibly ODIC 1852, 3:1453–4 (no. 311); another exhibitor of stained glass additionally listed in Off. Cat. 1851$^{2-5}$, 189 (no. 346)   36.25 **Sud**] *Süd*   36.26 **441. Johnson Flanell**] ODIC

1852, 3:1463 (no. 441)   **407 ~ wollene Decken**] Off. Cat. 1851$^{2-5}$, 190 (no. 407)   36.30
Deane Dray & Deane ~ London bridge] ODIC 1851, 1:389–91 (no. 180) and figs.; 2:591
(no. 6), 613–14 (no. 186) and figs.; Cryst. Pal. 1852, 12 fig., 13   **Charles Howland**] ODIC
1852, 3:1465 (no. 486); Hunt 1851, 2:775–6; Cryst. Pal. 1852, 295; Rep. Jur. 1852, 295; Rodgers
1852, 56; Tallis/Strutt 1852, 1:69   36.32 **King William Street au pont de Londres**] probably referring to gunsmiths Deane, Adams & Deane; ODIC 1851, 1:353 (no. 223); Cryst. Pal.
1852, 386 fig., 387; Rep. Jur. 1852, 220; Amtl. Ber. 1852/53, 1:679   36.36 **Vergrosserungsglass**] *Vergrösserungsglas*; ODIC 1852, 3:1433 (no. 16); Rep. Jur. 1852, 267   36.37–9 **Aufsätze ~ 459. in or molu**] ODIC 1852, 3:1464 (no. 459)   36.38 **Glasgefasse**] *Glasgefässe*
36.39 **Glasse**] *Glase*
37.1 **Modell einer Brücke**] possibly ODIC 1852, 3:1467 (no. 511); Rodgers 1852, 38–9 and pl.
37.2 **Patent metallic air exhausted coffins**] ODIC 1852, 3:1451 (no. 229); Hunt 1851, 2:779–
80; Tallis/Strutt 1852, 1:69   37.3 **Susquehanna Viaduct**] ODIC 1852, 3:1455–6 (no. 327)
37.4 **227 ~ Miniaturmusterfabrikation**] ODIC 1852, 3:1451 (no. 227)   37.6 **Modell einer
schwimmenden Kirche**] ODIC 1852, 3:1457 (no. 356), 1458 fig.   37.7 **Chirurgische Instrumente. (Zapfenzangen)**] ODIC 1852, 3:1434 (no. 26)   37.8 **Violinen**] ODIC 1852,
3:1463 (no. 442); Rep. Jur. 1852, 330; Rodgers 1852, 32–3   37.9 **Notenbuchwender**] ODIC
1852, 3:1467 (no. 527)   37.10 **Blitzableiter mit magnetischen Spitzen**] ODIC 1852, 3:1433
(no. 5); Rep. Jur. 1852, 312–13   37.12 **20. Schlosserarbeit**] ODIC 1852, 3:1434 (no. 20)
37.13 **419**] ODIC 1852, 3:1462 (no. 419)   **9**] ODIC 1852, 3:1433 (no. 9)   **350**] ODIC 1852,
3:1457 (no. 350)   **518**] ODIC 1852, 3:1467 (no. 518)   **558**] ODIC 1852, 3:1469 (no. 558)   **33**]
ODIC 1852, 3:1434 (no. 33)   **47**] ODIC 1852, 3:1435 (no. 47)   **61**] ODIC 1852, 3:1437 (no. 61)
220] ODIC 1852, 3:1450 (no. 220)   37.14 **63**] ODIC 1852, 3:1437 (no. 63)   **302**] ODIC 1852,
3:1453 (no. 302)   37.16 **künstliche Beine ~ Palmer**] ODIC 1852, 3:1435 (no. 39); Art-
Journal 1851, 211; Johnson 1852, 121; Rep. Jur. 1852, 345; Rodgers 1852, 50–1, 81–3, 121–4, 136–7;
Giedion 1948, 390–1   37.18 **Lampen Cornelius**] ODIC 1852, 3:1435 (no. 46), 1436 fig.; Illustrated Exhibitor 1851, no. 14 (6 Sept.), 255 fig., 256; Cryst. Pal. 1852, 294–5 and fig.; Rodgers
1852, 42–3; Tallis/Strutt 1852, 1:68 and pl.   37.20 **Modell einer Brücke ~ 147**] ODIC 1852,
3:1446 (no. 147); Rep. Jur. 1852, 208; Rodgers 1852, 38–9 and pl.   37.21 **New Brunswick
Rubber Co.**] ODIC 1852, 3:1469 (no. 560)   37.22 **Sattelzeug von Lloid**] ODIC 1852, 3:1438
(no. 78); Johnson 1852, 127   37.24 **Sattelzeuge. 41**] ODIC 1852, 3:1435 (no. 41); Illustrated
Exhibitor 1851, no. 29 (20 Dec.), 547, 548 fig.; Cryst. Pal. 1852, 294; Rep. Jur. 1852, 394; Tallis/
Strutt 1852, 1:68   37.25 **(138) Kassenschlosser mit veränderlichem Schlüssel**] 'Kassen-
schlosser': *Kassenschlösser*; ODIC 1852, 3:1441 (no. 138)   37.26 **Gekrepptes Pferdehaar**]
ODIC 1852, 3:1450 (no. 205); Rep. Jur. 1852, 388   **Silberfuchs (87**] ODIC 1852, 3:1438 (no.
87)   37.27 **Bürsten**] ODIC 1852, 3:1433 (no. 17), 1449 (no. 190)   **Sattel (476)**] ODIC 1852,
3:1465 (no. 476); Rep. Jur. 1852, 394   37.28 **Perücken (133)**] ODIC 1852, 3:1441 (no. 133)
Hüthe 130 (Castor)] ODIC 1852, 3:1441 (no. 130)   **232**] ODIC 1852, 3:1451 (no. 232)   **303
Damenhüthe**] ODIC 1852, 3:1453 (no. 303)   37.30 **Kinderkleider**] ODIC 1852, 3:1440 (no.
108); Johnson 1852, 135
38.2–3 **1 Rahmen ~ Notre Dame**] '1': *1.*; ODIC 1852, 3:1465 (no. 491); Arnoux 1851; Rep. Jur.
1852, 277   38.2 **wahrsch.**] *wahrscheinlich*   38.3 **Lords Prayer**] on John Edwin Mayall's
daguerreotype 'The Lord's Prayer' (1843–44), see Gernsheim 1991, 73; Hannavy 2008, 1:907
38.4 **223) ~ Harrison**] ODIC 1852, 3:1450 (no. 223); Arnoux 1851; Cryst. Pal. 1852, 295; Rep.
Jur. 1852, 275, 277; Tallis/Strutt 1852, 1:69   38.6 **Rahmen von Brady ~ Vortreffliche
Porträts**] ODIC 1852, 3:1441 (no. 137); Arnoux 1851; Rep. Jur. 1852, 277; Rodgers 1852, 19
and pl.   38.7 **From life by John A. Whipple**] ODIC 1852, 3:1464 (no. 451); Arnoux 1851;

Rep. Jur. 1852, 277; Tallis/Strutt 1852, 1:136   38.9–10 **Mayall ~ Vaterunser**] see notes
38.2–3, 38.3   38.10 **2 Stück∧ aussen**] *2 Stück, aussen*   38.12 **Panoramatische Ansich-**
ten ~ Langenheim] see note 32.13   38.13 **do von Cincinnati ~ Fontayne und Porter**]
'do': *dito*; ODIC 1852, 3:1468 (no. 550); Arnoux 1851; Rep. Jur. 1852, 277   38.14–17 **Rahmen**
von M. M. Lawrence ~ Bryant] ODIC 1852, 3:1446 (no. 151); Arnoux 1851; Rep. Jur. 1852, 277
38.14 **Vew York**] *New ~*   38.15 **Bild die 3 Zeiten**] on Martin M. Lawrence's 'Past, Present,
Future', see Semper 1852, 75. A copy of the daguerreotype is reproduced in Dinius 2012, 82
fig. 7.   38.19–20 **Skulptur Olliver Twist ~ Bell Hughes**] 'Bell': *Ball*; Hunt 1851, 2:780;
Tallis/Strutt 1852, 2:38 and pl.   38.21 **Ashmead & Hurlburt's ~ Gold Foil**] ODIC 1852,
3:1467 (no. 535)   38.21–2 **Chas. Abbey & Son Philad.**] ODIC 1852, 3:1436 (no. 54)   38.24–
5 **Robin ~ serrure avec clef avec panneton changeant**] unverifiable. None of Pierre-
Marie-Bernard Robin's locks is mentioned among the exhibits or the components of
Charles Aubin's lock trophy; on the latter, see ODIC 1851, 2:665 (no. 663); Cryst. Pal. 1852,
402; Hobbs 1853, 166–71.   38.26 **Day & Newell**] ODIC 1852, 3:1453 (no. 298); Cryst. Pal.
1852, 402 and fig.; Rep. Jur. 1852, 500; Rodgers 1852, 29–30; Giedion 1948, 58–9 and fig.; see
also note 33.19   **Mc. Gregor**] ODIC 1852, 3:1434 (no. 20)   **298**] see note 38.26 on Day &
Newell   **20**] see note 38.26 on McGregor   38.26–7 **Arrowsmith ~ permutation Lock**]
see note 37.25   38.28 **London Gallery Buffalo**] ODIC 1852, 3:1440 (no. 105); Arnoux 1851;
Rep. Jur. 1852, 277; the 'London First Premium Daguerrian Gallery' in Buffalo, run by
Oliver Benton Evans (Buffalo Directory 1851, 91)   38.29 **Whitehursts Galleries of Pre-**
mium Daguerotyps] ODIC 1852, 3:1461 (no. 377); Arnoux 1851; Rep. Jur. 1852, 277; Tallis/
Strutt 1852, 1:136   38.30 **grösten**] *grössten*   38.30–3 **Portrats ~ Meade Brothers**] 'Portrats' uncertain reading, *Porträts*; ODIC 1852, 3:1440 (no. 109); Arnoux 1851; Rep. Jur. 1852,
277; Hannavy 2008, 1:915–16   38.32 **Charge**] *chargé*
39.1–6 **Daguerotyps von Brady ~ n° 6 Kind**] see note 38.6; on Mathew Brady's portrait
photographs and the lithographs published in his *Gallery of Illustrious Americans* (1850), see
Trachtenberg 1989, 21–79; Hannavy 2008, 1:197–200   39.1 **Daguerotyps**] possibly written
as 'Daguorotyps'   39.4 **Selleck**] unidentified person   **Dohm**] uncertain reading,
unidentified person   39.9 **Talbotyp von Langenheim**] see note 32.13   39.10 **Daguero-**
typ von Cyncinati ~ Fontayne et Porter] see note 38.13   39.11 **M. M. Lawrence**] see note
38.14–17   **aufgehangt**] *aufgehängt*   39.12 **London Gallery. (Evans proprietor)**] see note
38.28   39.13 **Hoggs American Dagureotype Gallery**] 'Dagureotype': *Daguerreotype*;
Rep. Jur. 1852, 277; possibly the 'American Daguerrean Portrait Rooms' in London, run by
Robert Hogg (Ruff 1852, 219), brother of the English surgeon and photographer Jabez Hogg
39.14 **Whitehurst Gallerie of premium Daguerotypes**] see note 38.29   39.17 **Meade**
Brothers] see note 38.30–3   39.18 **Sammlung Ausgezeichneter Manner von Virginia**]
'Manner': *Männer*; ODIC 1852, 3:1452 (no. 264); Arnoux 1851; Rep. Jur. 1852, 277   39.20
Sophas und Stühle ~ zum Stellen] ODIC 1852, 3:1449 (no. 193), 1470 (no. 590); Johnson
1852, 148   **fur**] *für*   39.21 **Pianos**] ODIC 1852, 3:1437 (no. 59), 1438–9 (no. 90), 1460 (no.
374), 1463 (nos. 435, 438), 1464 (no. 458); Art-Journal Cat. 1851, 128 and fig., 252 and fig.; Hunt
1851, 2:776–7; Cryst. Pal. 1852, 42, 202, 295; Rodgers 1852, 32, 136; Tallis/Strutt 1852, 1:68
39.22–3 **transportabls Bettstelle Whitmarsh's Patent**] 'transportabls': *transportable*;
ODIC 1852, 3:1456 (no. 334); Hunt 1851, 2:778   39.24–5 **Elfenbeintafeln ~ Julius Pratt**]
ODIC 1852, 3:1469 (no. 567); Rep. Jur. 1852, 599   39.24 **Holyssäge**] probably *Hollysäge*; thus
a holly saw as used for cutting holly veneers in the manufacture of marquetry work

EDITORIAL EMENDATIONS

34.22 **obenauf**] oben | auf *(see 292, Explanatory Notes 34.22)*   37.10 **Blitzableiter**] *doubly underl.*

ALTERATIONS IN THE MANUSCRIPT

32.30 **Schneidermuster**] *after del.* Dress   32.36 **recht gut**] *after del.* schl *(possibly for 'schlecht')*

33.2 **Sensenklingen**] klingen *interl.*   33.7–8 **— Hinter**] *after undel.* Hi   33.11 **423.**] *after del.* 43.

34.5 **2**] *interl.*

35.12 **Becher**] *after del.* Ringe,   35.29 **Mäander**] *after del.* Flecht[w]   35.32 **Schaal**] *altered from* Shawl   35.35 **Glaskasten II.**] *after del. on fol.* 1r Riabzewitch Schöne Gansekiele.   Riabzewitch] *underl.*

36.6 **2.**] *above del.* Eine   **Landcharte von**] *before del.* Nord   36.7 **hauptsächlichsten**] *after del.* Reis   36.9 **manufacturing Co**] *above undel.* Manufactur.   36.37 **2**] *over* 1

37.2 **coffins**] *before del.* Särge   37.8 **Violinen**] *before undel.* J   37.13 **518. 558. 33. 47 61. 220.**] *interl.*   37.15 **5ᵗ**] *over* 4   37.17 **4**] *over* 11   37.24 **Sattelzeuge**] *before del.* in dem Glaskasten.   37.25 **(138) ~ Medaillen.**] *inserted*   37.27 **6ᵗᵉ**] 6 *over* 4   **(476)**] *interl.*   37.30 **Büchsen**] *after del.* G *(possibly for 'Gewehre')*

38.7 **From life ~ Whipple**] *above del.* Hon. David Sears   David Sears] *underl.*   38.9 **5**] *over* 4 *over* 3 *over* 2   **Porträts**] *interl.*   38.12 **Panoramatische**] *after del.* Daguerotyp by Pratt & Co 264.   **Philadelphia**] *before del.* und Cincinnati   38.18 **Hinzu**] *after del.* Oli[v] *after in ink and del. in pencil* Mein verehrter Herr Westenholz | Der Ueberbringer dieses ist der Mann von dem ich Ihnen sagte   38.24 **serrure**] *after del.* des   38.26 **Day**] *after del.* Se[r]   **& Mc. Gregor**] & *interl.*   **20**] *after del.* 216.   38.30 **die grösten mir bekannten Portrats**] *inserted*   mir bekannten Portrats] *on opposite page (fol. 2r)*

39.6 **alte Dame**] *interl.*   **Kind**] *interl.*

Outline of a Cultural-Historical Exhibition

TEXTUAL RECORD

MS 92[1]   gta, 20-Ms-92, fol. 5r–v (5v blank), in Semper's hand, fragmentary draft

MS 92[2]   gta, 20-Ms-92, fols. 6r–9v (6r variant of MS 92[1]), 'Beilage zu dem Aufsatze: Vorschläge zur Anregung nationalen Kunstgefühles', in Semper's hand, fragmentary draft

MS 92[3]   gta, 20-Ms-92, fols. 3r–4v (3v–4v blank), in Semper's hand, fragmentary draft

MS 92[4]   gta, 20-Ms-92, fols. 1r–2v (1r variant of MS 92[3]), in Semper's hand, fragmentary draft

MS 92[5]   gta, 20-Ms-92, fols. 10r–11v, 'Beilag II. Plan einer allgemeinen kulturgeschichtlichen Sammlung', in Semper's hand

MS 92[6] gta, 20-Ms-92, fols. 12r–15v (14v–15r calculations and sketches possibly for Semper 1859; 15v blank; variant of MS 92[5]), 'Beilage. Plan zur Uebersicht einer kulturhistorischen Ausstellung', in Semper's hand, probably the draft of the plan which Semper sent to Eduard Vieweg on 20 January 1852 (for the letter, see 308–9), *copy-text*

K-1855 gta, 20-K-1855-08-28(S), fols. 2r–4v (1r–v copy of Semper's letter to Lothar Bucher, 28 August 1855; 4v blank; variant of MS 92[6]), 'Plan zu der Anordnung einer culturhistorischen Sammlung', in Manfred Semper's hand, 1880, copy of appendix to Semper's letter to Lothar Bucher

BIBLIOGRAPHY Herrmann 1976, 211–12, 232–5; Herrmann 1981, 100; Hildebrand 2007, 245–50; Luttmann 2008, 124–5, 128–32, 137–9

EXPLANATORY NOTES

Semper envisaged this plan for the way in which an exhibition should be organized as an insert for *Science, Industry, and Art*. Between October 1851 and January 1852, he drafted four incomplete and three complete versions. The first complete version, which he probably sent to his publisher Eduard Vieweg on 17 October 1851, has as its header a reference to the passage in *Science, Industry, and Art* to which it refers as an enclosure: 'Beilag II. (zu Seite 4)' (302.1). Enclosure I was probably the fair copy of part of the manuscript of *Science, Industry, and Art*, enclosed with the letter to Vieweg (for the letter, see Herrmann 1976, 232). The indicated page number '4' to which the exhibition outline refers identifies it as a complement to the first chapter of *Science, Industry, and Art* where, at the beginning, Semper reported on his plan for a series of essays as a 'comparative overview' of the contents of the Great Exhibition, to be organized in an 'architectural' way (Semper 1852, 5–7).

In one of the manuscripts of *Science, Industry, and Art*, Semper added the reference 'Siehe Beilage' after the published passage in which he explained his 'architectural' exhibition plan (gta, 20-Ms-88, fol. 4v): 'The plan conceived was an architectural one, based on the elements of domestic settlement: hearth, wall, terrace, roof' (Semper 1852, 7). Correspondingly, the main headings in the plan consist of the four basic elements that Semper had developed in *The Four Elements of Architecture* of 1851. In *Science, Industry, and Art*, Semper went on to explain a fifth element, also presented in the exhibition plan: 'A fifth main section was to comprise the interaction of these four elements: the high art and, in a symbolic sense, the high science.' The plan, Semper added, was intended to 'make visible by itself the derivations of objects and forms from their original motifs and the change of their style according to the determining circumstances'. In this way, Semper's exhibition plan was a ramified visualization of 'the complete and comparative museum of the future' that he intended to discuss in his 'Letters on the Great Exhibition' (288.4–11). The idea that a list or its architectural arrangement would allow the connections of the elements exhibited to become self-explanatory, is, of course, highly idealistic. The problems associated with this are evident not least in the varying classifications of the material in the different versions, which are hardly ever free of contradictions.

Vieweg did not ultimately include Semper's exhibition plan in *Science, Industry, and Art*. Semper, however, continued to think about it. On the one hand, he drew up a truly architectural plan for it in his catalogue of 'Practical Art in Metals and hard Materials; its Tech-

298 The Great Exhibition

nology, History and Styles' of 1852: a square with each side reserved for one of the four elements, which meet in the centre of the square for interaction (NAL, 86.FF.64, art. 1, 18; cf. Hildebrand 2003, 263; Hvattum 2004b, 129; Semper 2007a, 57). On the other hand, Semper discovered his exhibition plan anew when reading Lothar Bucher's reports on the Paris Exposition universelle of 1855 (published in the Berlin *National-Zeitung*). He sent him a copy of that 'old plan for an overview of the field of cultural history' on 28 August 1855, suggesting the possibility of 'publishing or mentioning it' in the subsequent reports (Herrmann 1976, 211 n. 42). This third version of Semper's exhibition plan corresponds mostly to the second one but expands it in several details; thus it was probably not written until 1855.

40.25 **gelasirt**] *glasiert* (see 299.29, 303.4)   40.26–7 **vde Anmerkg**] *vide Anmerkung* 40.30 **vde**] *vide*   **bis**] uncertain reading; possibly in the sense of *to repeat*, referring to 'vde Anmerkg oben' (40.26–7)
41.37 **Pasementirarbeit**] *Passementierarbeit*
42.7 **Wege∧ und Brückenbau**] *Wege- und Brückenbau* (see 300.33, 304.5–6; cf. 306.45: 'Wege∧ & Brückenbau'   42.18 **s.**] *siehe*   42.23 **Saulenordnung**] *Säulenordnung*   42.34 **—**] curlicue

EDITORIAL EMENDATIONS

42.25 **B. Dachbedeckung.**] B. Dachbedeckung. | B. Dachbedeckung.

ALTERATIONS IN THE MANUSCRIPT

40.2–3 **Plan ~ Niederlassung:**] *above del.*

Plan einer Uebersicht über eine Industrieausstellung[1] basirt auf den Grundelementen häuslicher Niederlassung:

> 1 **Uebersicht über eine Industrieausstellung**] *above del.* kulturphilosophischen Sammlung   kulturphilosophischen] *after del.* allgemeinen

40.2 **zur**] *after del.* zu einer   40.5 **symbolisch.**] *before del.*

Das wärmende[1], lichtbringende, Nahrung bereitende Prinzip. Der Mittelpunkt der geselligen Beziehungen

> 1 **wärmende**] *after del.* nährende *after del.* körperlich

40.12 **Gegenstände**] *after del.* licht   40.22 **C**] *over* c   40.36 **a**] *before del.* 1) 41.14 **a**] *after del.* B.   41.22 **NB.**] *after del.* c.   41.25 **hervorgehen**] *after del.* Anwendung finden.   41.35–8 **Schneiderei ~ etc etc etc**] *in pencil*
42.2 **Erd-**] *after underl. and del.* Erdarbeiten   42.4 **(Schlosserarbeit**] *inserted*   ∧**Festungsbau**] *altered from* (~   42.19 **Dach**] *after underl. and del.* Gerüste   42.26 **Ueberzug,**] *before del.* [G]   42.27 **Metall**] *interl.*

Outline of a Cultural-Historical Exhibition

MANUSCRIPT VARIANTS
MS 92²

Beilage zu dem
Aufsatze: Vorschläge zur Anregung nationalen
Kunstgefühles.

fol. 6r

Plan

5 einer allgemeinen kulturphilosophischen Sammlung nach der Gemeinschaft des Ursprunges und den Verwandschaften der Gegenstände geordnet.

Die vier Haupteintheilungen der Sammlung entsprechen den vier Elementen der häuslichen Niederlassung:

1) Heerd, 2) Unterbau, 3) Wand. 4) Dach.

10 I^{te} *Sammlung.*

Heerd. Mittelpunkt jeder Niederlassung, materiell und symbolisch. Das körperlich nährende und wärmende, das geistig belebende und sammelnde Prinzip, welchem die drei anderen Grundbestandtheile des Hauses dienen.

    A. Der Heerd in seiner substantiellen Bedeutung.

15   a) Der Heerd als Wärmegeber.

          Caloricalogie. Dreifüsse, Kamine, Oefen, etc.

       b) Der Heerd als Nahrung bereitend.

          Culinarische Wissenschaften und Künste

          1) Pflanzenspeisen, – Feldbau mit allen seinen Verzweigungen, Oekonomie,

20   Agricultur, Mühlenbau etc.

          2) Fleischspeisen, – Viehzucht, Jagd, Fischerei.

          3) Getränke, Technologie ihrer Bereitung. |

          4) Gewürze wie oben.

fol. 6v

          5) Luxusgenüsse, Cafe, Thee, Tobak, Opium, Parfüms. etc.

25   Technologie dieser Gegenstände.

       c) *Der Heerd als Werkofen.*

          Gefässkunde. (Keramik.)

          1) Urgefäss, (Kürbisse).

          2) Thongefässe, roh, gebrannt, glasirt, Glas. Durch alle Sorten von Erd-

30   waaren durchzuführen mit Einschluss des Glases und Porcellanes.

          3) Metallgefässe, (Metallurgie) Schmelz- und Treibekunst Löthen und

             Schmieden, Ciseliren und Emailliren. Legirung. Vergoldung. Galvano-

             plastik etc etc. |

          4) Gefässe aus Stein.

fol. 7r

35   5) d° d° aus Holz und anderen Stoffen.

          Anmerkung. Diese reiche Sammlung ist stylistisch und technologisch so instructiv wie möglich zu ordnen. Sie muss die Procedur des Bereitens vom Rohstoffe an mit den dabei angewandten Werkzeugen und Maschinen vom Ursprünglichsten bis zur letzten Erfindung enthalten. Es ist wünschenswerth,

40   die Producte in einer in sich abgeschlossenen Abtheilung zusammenzustellen,

wodurch das künstlerische Studium erleichtert wird. In den korrespondirenden Nebenräumen muss dann möglichst nahe die Technologie dieser Producte zu finden seyn.

Diese Bemerkung ist für alle Sammlungen gültig.

   d.) *Der Heerd als Lichtbringer.*

      Photologie. Optik. Spähne, Fackeln, Kandelaber, Lampen, Lichter, (aus Harz, Wachs, Talg etc) Leuchter, Kronleuchter, Gasbeleuchtung.

   e) Der Heerd als Ruheplatz.

      Stühle, Tische, Möbel aller Art. Nach den Stoffen aus denen sie bereitet sind zu ordnen. ¦

fol. 7v   5) Der Heerd als Sinnbild der äusseren Reinheit

      Wasch- und *Reinigungsapparate.*

  B. Geistige Bedeutung des Heerdes.

   a) Sitz des Nachdenkens. Logik.

   b) Sitz der Mittheilung, der Belehrung und der Unterhaltung.

     1) Redekunst. (Schreibekunst – Druckerei)

     2) Poesie.

     3) Musik

     4) Geschichte

     5) Tanz,

     6) Drama.

   c) Sitz der Krankenpflege (Medecin).

   d) Ort der Verträge, Staatskunst, Gesetzgebung, Handel, Rechenkunst. etc.

   e) Ort der religiösen Gebräuche.

      Altar, Ahnenbilder, *Bildnerei. Theologie.*

   f) Sinnbild geistiger Reinheit Moral. ¦

fol. 8r   II^te Sammlung.

Der Unterbau. des Heerdes.

  A) *Erdarbeiten.*

   a) Schutz des Heerdes gegen Ueberschwemmungen. Wasserbau. Deichbau etc.

   b) Schutz des Heerdes gegen Feinde. Festungsbau, Waffen.

   c) Erleichterung des Zuganges zu dem Heerde und der Verbindung zwischen von einander entfernt liegenden Niederlassungen. Wege- und Brückenbau, Canalbau, Schiffarth. Feldmesskunst, Geometrie etc. etc. Fuhrwerke, Dampfwagen,

  B.) *Maurerarbeiten.*

     Ziegelkonstruction, Steinconstruction Gewölbe. *Steinschnitt.* Formen der höheren Baukunst die aus diesem Theile der Construction hervorgegangen sind und hervorgehen können, nebst ihren von den angewandten Stoffen abhängigen Modificationen.

     NB. Dieser wichtige Theil umfasst eine grosse Menge von theoretischen und praktischen Bethätigungen des Menschen, die sich auf verschiedene ¦ Weise innerhalb desselben ordnen lässt. Da die Arbeiten der Maurer sich am spätesten künstlerisch entwickelt haben, so sollte eigentlich diese Sammlung die vierte in der Reihenfolge seyn, überall wo es die Hauptabsicht bei der Anlage der Sammlungen ist, den Formensinn zu bilden.

fol. 8v

Outline of a Cultural-Historical Exhibition   301

III.ᵗᵉ Sammlung.

Die Wand.

A. Die Wandbereitung in ihrer Anwendung auf Raumesabschlüsse.

a) Das Pfahlgehege und das Zweiggeflecht als der ursprünglichste Raumesabschluss. (Gitter und Ballustraden).

b) Fortbildung des Motives. Bastmatten, Binsengeflecht, Pflanzenfadengewebe,
Gewebe aus animalischen Substanzen, Muster aus der Textur entsprossen.
Ornamentik, Färberei. Grundmotiv aller Wandverzierung und der Malerei in
der Teppichwirkerei zu suchen. Ursprung der Relief- | kunst in der Stickerei.
(Haute lisse, China, Assyrien)

c) Nachbildung der Teppichwände in Platten aus Holz, Stein, Metall, Erdwaare,
glasirten Ziegeln, Glas. (Mosaik)

d) Nachbildung der Teppichwände in Leder und Papier. (Tapetenmanufactur).

e) Nachbildung der Teppiche als Fenstervorhänge. (Fensterglasmalerei)

NB. Bei dieser wichtigen Abtheilung muss durch gute Anordnung der Gegenstände anschaulich gemacht werden, wie eins aus dem anderen hervorgewachsen
ist und wie sich die Wand mit dem konstructiven Prinzipe der Mauer vermischte
und wie diese Vermischung erst spätere Geltung in der höheren Baukunst erhielt.
Es muss auf die Stylveränderungen hingewiesen werden die aus den Eigenschaften
der Stoffe hervorgehen, in welchen das Motiv zur Erscheinung tritt.

B. Die Wandbereitung in ihrer Anwendung auf Bekleidung. |
Dieser Abschnitt muss die ganze wichtige Industrie der Leder- Pelz- Linnen
Baumwollen- Wollen- Seiden Filzfabrikation umfassen und in den oberen Abschnitt ergänzend eingreifen. Beide müssen von einem Mittelpunkte ausgehen und
nach zwei entgegengesetzten Seiten auslaufen.

*IV.*ᵗᵉ Sammlung.

Das Dach mit seinem Gerüste.

A. *Dachbedeckung.*

a) *Ueberzug.* Felle, Gewänder, Filze, Asphalt, Steinplatten, Holzplatten, Metallplatten. etc.
Diese Abtheilung spielt hinüber in das Gebiet der Wandbereitung; Es gilt von
ihr das Gleiche was von letzterer in Beziehung auf ihren dekorativen Einfluss
anschaulich zu machen ist.

b) *Schuppendach* Blätter, Schindeln Schiefer, Dachziegel; Gränzt an die Abtheilung der Maurerarbeiten.

fol. 9r

fol. 9v

299.6 **Gegenstände**] *before del.* in ihren   299.7 **vier Haupteintheilungen**] *after del.*
Grundeintheilu   299.9 **Heerd,**] *before del.* Wand,   299.12 **geistig**] *below del.* moralisch   299.16 **Dreifüsse,**] *interl.*   299.26 **c) Der Heerd als Werkofen.**] *after del.* c)
Der Heerd als Mittelpunkt der Beziehungen für den Hausrath.   c)] *undel.*   299.28
(Kürbisse).] *before del.* Hieran können sich die Holzgefässe Tonnen etc anschliessen.
299.30 **Porcellanes.**] *before del.* Stylistisch und technologisch so instructiv und vollständig wie möglich zu ordnen.   299.32–3 **Galvanoplastik etc etc.**] *before del. on fols. 6v–7r*

Diese reiche Abtheilung muss, die Procedur des Bereitens vom Rohstoffe an, mit den
dabei angewandten Werkzeugen und Maschinen etc. vom Einfachsten und Ursprünglichsten bis zur letzten Erfindung enthalten. Es ist wünschenswerth, die Pro-

ducte in einer | in sich geschlossenen Abtheilung zusammenzustellen, um das Formenstudium zu erleichtern. In den korrespondirenden Nebenräumen muss dann möglichst nahe die Technologie dieser Kunstproducte zu finden seyn.

299.34 **Stein**] *before del.* und anderen Stoffen   299.35 **5) ~ anderen Stoffen.**] *interl.*
299.40 **Abtheilung**] *before del.* als Hauptgegenstände
300.2 **Producte**] *after del.* Kunstpro-   300.4 **alle**] *before del.* folgenden   300.5 **d.**] *repl. del.* 3   300.7 **Gasbeleuchtung**] beleuchtung *after del.* flammen   300.8 **e**] *repl. del.* 4
300.9 **Möbel**] *before del.* und Geräthe   300.11 **Sinnbild der äusseren Reinheit**] *repl. del.* Prinzip der Reiniger.   Reiniger.] *before del.* (hier materiell)   300.14 **Logik.**] *before del.*

Philosophie, (diese Abtheilung kann die Astronomie und andere abstracte Wissenschaften enthalten.) Ist eine Bibliothek mit der Sammlung verbunden, so muss erstere eine analoge Eintheilung erhalten und jeder

300.25 **Altar,**] *above underl. and del.* Theologie,   300.28 **des Heerdes.**] *inserted*   300.34 **Schiffarth.**] *transposed by guide line from after* Dampfwagen, *at 300.34–5*   300.43 **am spätesten**] *after del.* geschichtlich   300.44 **vierte**] *above del.* letzte   300.45 **überall**] *interl.*
301.15 **muss**] *before del.* das stufenweise Wachsen der [ ]   301.17 **Wand**] *before del.* später   301.18 **wie diese Vermischung erst spätere**] *interl.*   **erhielt.**] *altered from ~,*   *before del.* nachdem die Wand vorher lange Zeit die ungemischt   301.29 **Felle, Gewänder,**] *above del.* Gewand, Fell,   **Filze**] e *added*   **Steinplatten**] *final* n *added*   **Holzplatten**] n *added*   301.29–30 **Metallplatten**] n *added*   301.31 **spielt hinüber**] *after del.* gränzt   301.34 **Blätter, Schindeln**] *interl.*   **Dachziegel**] *before del.* Schindeln

MS 92[5]

fol. 10r

Beilag II. (zu Seite 4).

Plan
einer allgemeinen kulturgeschichtlichen Sammlung, geordnet nach der Gemeinschaft des Ursprungs und den Verwandschaften der Gegenstände in ihren Motiven, basirt auf den Grundelementen häuslicher Niederlassung:
Heerd, Gehege, Terrasse, Dach.

I. *Heerd.* Mittelpunkt jeder Niederlassung, materiell und symbolisch. Das körperlich nährende und wärmende, das moralisch belebende Element, dem die drei anderen zum Schutze dienen. In seiner höchsten Bedeutung der Altar, das Symbol der höheren gesellschaftlichen Bande, der Religion.
A. Der Heerd in seiner materiellen Bedeutung.
    a. Wärmend, – Kamin, Ofen etc. Caloricologie
    b. – Nahrung bereitend. Culinarische Wissenschaften und Künste
        1) Pflanzenspeisen – Feldbau mit allen seinen Verzweigungen. Oekonomie, Kameralwissenschaft. Ackerbau, Mühlenbau u. s. w.
        2) Fleischspeisen Viehzucht, Jagd, Fischerei. Waffen.
        3) *Getränke* Milch, Bier, Wein etc. Technologie ihrer Bereitung.
        4) *Gewürze,* Salz, Zucker u. s. w. wie oben.
        5) Luxusgenüsse, Cafe, Thee, Toback, Opium Parfüms etc. etc.

Outline of a Cultural-Historical Exhibition

    c. – Mittelpunkt der Beziehungen für den Hausrath.

        1) Gefässkunst (Ceramik)

           α   Kürbiss. (Urgefäss)

           β. Thongefäss, roh, gebrannt, glasirt, Glas. Durch alle Sorten von Erd-
warren durchzuführen incl. des Glases und Porcellanes. ¦

           γ. Metallgefässe, Metallurgie. Schmelz- und Treibekunst. Löthen und   *fol. 10v*
Schmieden, Emailliren und Ciselliren. Vergolden, Galvanoplastik.

           δ.   Gefässe aus Stein und anderen Stoffen

              NB. Bei diesen Abtheilungen muss die Procedur des Bereitens vom Roh-
stoffe an mit den dabei angewendeten Werkzeugen und Maschinen etc.
vom Einfachsten Ursprünglichsten, bis zur letzten Vervollkommnung
verfolgt werden.

        3.   Der Heerd als Lichtbringer. Photologie.

             Spähne, Fackeln, Candelaber, Lampen, Lichter (aus Harz, Wachs, Talg
etc) Gasflammen (Siehe Anmerkung oben). Optik.

        4) Der Heerd als Ruheplatz.

             Stühle, Tische, Möbel und Geräthe aller Art.

  B. Moralische Bedeutung des Heerdes.

      a. Sitz des Nachdenkens. Logik.

      b. Sitz der Mittheilung und Unterhaltung.

         1) Redekunst. Schreibekunst – Druckerkunst.

         2) Poesie

         3) Musik

         4) Geschichte

         5) Tanz.

         6) Drama.

      c) Sitz der Krankenpflege. Medecin

      d) Ort der Verträge, Staatskunst, Gesetzgebung, Handel. Rechnenkunst. etc.

      e) Ort der religiösen Gebräuche, *Theologie* Ahnenbilder, Bildnerei. ¦

II. *Die Wand.*   *fol. 11r*

  A. Das Pfahlgehege oder das Zweiggeflecht der ursprünglichste Raumesabschluss.
(Gitter und Balustraden)

  B. Fortbildung des Motives: Bastmatten, Binsengeflecht, Grasgewebe, Pflanzen-
fädengewebe, Gewebe aus animalischen Substanzen. Muster aus farbigen Fäden
aus der Textur entsprossen. Ornamentik, Färbereien. Grundmotiv aller Wandverzierung und der Malerei in der Teppichwirkerei. Ursprung der Reliefkunst in der
Stickerei. (China, Assyrien.)

      Nachbildung der Teppichwände in Platten aus Holz, Stein, Metall, Erdwaare.
Mosaik, Glasmalerei, gebrannte Ziegel, Tapeten. u.s.w.

      Bei der Entwickelung des Motives muss die stufenweise Ordnung beobachtet und
zugleich auf die Stylveränderungen hingewiesen werden, die aus den Eigenschaften der Stoffe in welchen das Motiv zur Erscheinung tritt, hervorgehen.

  C. Die Wandbereitung in ihrer Anwendung auf Bekleidung.

      Dieser Abschnitt muss die ganze wichtige Industrie der Leder, Pelz, Linnen,
Baumwollen- Wollen und Seidenfabrikation umfassen und in den oberen Abschnitt ergänzend eingreifen. Beide müssen von einem Mittelpunkt ausgehen und
nach zwei entgegensetzten Seiten auslaufen.

III. Die Terrasse.
A. Erdarbeiten.
a) Schutz des Heerdes gegen Ueberschwemmung. Wasserbau.
b) Schutz des Heerdes gegen Feinde. Festungsbau. Waffen. |
c) Beschützung und Erleichterung des Zuganges zu dem Heerde. – Wege- und Brückenbau. Canalbau.
d) Feldmesskunst – (Geometrie und Geodäsie)
B. Maurerarbeiten.
Steinconstruction, Ziegelkonstruktion, Gewölbe, *Steinschnitt.* Formen der höheren Baukunst die aus diesem Theile der Construction hervorgingen, nebst ihren von den angewendeten Stoffen abhängigen Modificationen.
Dieser wichtige Theil umfasst eine grosse Menge von theoretischen und praktischen Bethätigungen der Menschen, die sich auf verschiedene Weise innerhalb desselben ordnen lässt.

IV. – Das Gerüste.
A– Holzkonstruction, technische und bildnerische Entwickelung derselben. Formen der höheren Baukunst die diesem Ursprunge angehören. *Giebeldachform, Säulenordnung. Thüren,* Fenster.
B) Eisen Metallkonstruction. technische und bildnerische Entwickelung. Schlosserarbeit.
C.) *Dachbedeckung.*
1) Ueberzug. Gewand, Fell, Filz, Asphalt, Steinplatten, etc. gränzt an die Abtheilung von der Wandbereitung
2) *Schuppendach.* Schiefer, Ziegel u. s w. gränzt an die Abtheilung von der Maurerarbeit.

V. *Zusammenwirken der vier Elemente. Culturphilosophie.* Hohe Wissenschaft. Hohe Kunst.

302.1 **Beilag**] *'Beilage'* 302.12 **Caloricologie**] *inserted with a thinner pen* 302.13
Culinarische Wissenschaften und Künste] *inserted with a thinner pen*
303.2 **1) Gefässkunst**] *altered from* 2) ~ *after del.* 1) Formen des Heerdes selbst, Kamine, Oefen Kochöfen. 303.4–5 **Erdwarren**] *'Erdwaren'* 303.6 **Metallurgie.**] *interl.*
303.13 **Photologie.**] *inserted with a thinner pen* 303.14 **Spähne**] *after del.* α) 303.15
Optik.] *inserted with a thinner pen before del.* β. 303.19 **des Nachdenkens**] *after del.*
der Erfindung und **Logik.**] *inserted with a thinner pen before del.* Philosophie Logik.
Schreibekunst – Druckerkunst. Reine Wissenschaften. Astronomie. Philosophie]
underl. Logik.] *interl.* Schreibekunst] *underl.* Druckerkunst] *underl.* 303.21
Schreibekunst – Druckerkunst.] *inserted with a thinner pen* 303.28 **Staatskunst**]
after del. Politik, 303.30 **Die Wand.**] *after underl. and del.* Gehege 303.36 **Ursprung**]
after del. Plastik 303.38 **Erdwaare**] *with a thinner pen above del.* Topfwaare 303.41–2
Eigenschaften der] *interl.* 303.42 **Stoffe**] *altered from* Stoffen **tritt,**] *before del.* und
ihren Eigenschaften 303.44 **der Leder, Pelz,**] *inserted before del.* der 303.47 **entgegensetzten**] *'entgegengesetzten'* **auslaufen.**] *before del.* Die natürliche Textur
304.2 **A. Erdarbeiten.**] *after del.*

A. Erdarbeiten. Wege und Brücken, Mittel des Fortkommens. Wasserbau, (Schutz des Heerdes gegen Ueberschwemmung)

304.4 **Feinde**] *after del.* wilde Thiere und feindliche   wilde] *after del.* feindselig
304.9 **Steinconstruction**] *after del.* Constr   304.15 **IV. – Das Gerüste.**] *above underl.*
and del. C. Dacharbeiten.   **Das Gerüste.**] *in faint ink after underl. and del.* Das
Dachgerüste   304.18 **Thüren, Fenster.**] *inserted in faint ink before inserted and del. in
faint ink* Schlosserarbeit.   304.19 **technische**] *after del.* Nach   304.19–20 **Schlosserarbeit.**] *in faint ink above del.* Letztere unmöglich.   unmöglich] *after del.* schwer
304.22 **Steinplatten**] *interl. with a thinner pen*   gränzt an] *repl. del.* fällt in   304.22–3
Abtheilung] A *over* Ca   304.24 **gränzt**] *above del.* fällt   an] a *over* i   304.24–5
Maurerarbeit.] *before interl. in faint ink and del. in faint ink* D. Thüren und Fenster
304.26 **Culturphilosophie**] *after underl. and del.* Tectonik,   304.26 **Hohe Kunst**] *after
del.* Mathematik,

K-1855

Plan zu der Anordnung einer culturhistorischen Sammlung basirt auf den vier Grundbe-   *fol. 2r*
standtheilen häuslicher Einrichtung, nämlich:
Heerd, Wand, Damm, Dach &
den Ideen welche durch dieselben symbolisirt werden.

5   I.   *Heerd* Mittelpunkt jeder Niederlassung & Embryo der Gesellschaft.
        A.   *wärme*gebend
              Kohlenpfannen, Kamine, Öfen etc (kalorische Wissenschaft)
        B.   *lichtbringend*
              Spähne, Fackeln, Kandelaber, Lampen, Leuchter (alles kleine Heerde) Leucht-
10   thürme Gaslaternen. (Photologie)
        C.   *nahrung*bereitend
              kulinarische Kunst
              a.   *Pflanzenspeise.* Feldbau in seinen Verzweigungen – Agronomie, Oeconomie
                    Horticultur, Mühlenanlage
15   b   *Fleischspeisen.* Viehzucht, Jagd, Fischerei.
              c.   *Getränke.* Wasser, Milch, Bier, Wein, geistige Getränke überhaupt.
                    Brunnenbau, Hirtenleben, Weinbau, Technologie der Bereitung der Ge-
                    tränke.
              d   *Gewürze.* Salz. Zucker. Pfeffer. (Salinen, Plantagen)
20   e   *Luxusgenüsse.* Café, Thee, Opium u. s. w. (Plantagencultur)
        D   *rauchend*
              Reinigung mit Schwefeldämpfen, Weihrauch, Parfüms, Tabak (Religiöse Be-
              deutsamkeit dieser Funktion des Heerdes. Der Dampf des Heerdes als geistigster
              Theil des Nahrungsstoffes den Göttern geweiht. (siehe unten) ⁞
25   E.   Mittelpunkt der Beziehungen für den Hausrath.   *fol. 2v*
              a   1. Gefässe. Keramik.
                    α.   *Urgefässe.* Kürbiss, Ei, hohle Hand, Horn.
                    β.   *Thongefässe.* Durch alle Sorten von Erdwaaren durchzuführen.
                    γ.   *Metallgefässe.* Metallurgie. Schmelz & Treibekunst, Löthen & Schmieden,
30   Emailliren u. Ciseliren, Vergolden, Elektrotypiren u. s. w.
                    δ.   *Gefässe aus Stein* u. anderen Stoffen
              b   *Anderer Hausrath* wie Besen, Fächer, Blasebalg etc.

F. *Ruheplatz.*
Stühle, Tische, Möbel u. Geräthe aller Art (Tischlerei, Schnitzerei u. s. w.)
G. *Sitz des Nachdenkens der Mittheilung & Unterhaltg*
    a   Logik.
    b   Redekunst, Schreibekunst, Buchdruckerei
    c. Poesie.
    d. Musik.
    e. Tanz.
    f. Drama. (Zusammenwirken der Künste
    g. Putz. (wichtiger Artikel für die Kunstfragen).
H. *Sitz der Krankenpflege.*
    Medizin, Kräuterkunde, Chemie, Botanik.
I. *Ort der Berathung & des Abschlusses v. Verträgen*
    Gesetzgebung, Staatskunst, Handeln, Rechenkunst, Politik. Jurisprudenz.
K. *Ort der religiosen Gebräuche.*
    Ahnenkultus, Bildnerei, Altar, Theologie. |

fol. 3r

II *Die Wand*
A. *Ursprünglicher Raumabschluss*
    Pfahlgeflecht.
    Bast & Binsenmatten
    Pflanzenfädengeflecht & Gewebe aus anderen natürlichen Substanzen.
    Muster aus natürlich-farbigen Naturstoffen zusammengewirkt, geben ein frühes,
    der Textur entsprossenes farbiges Ornament, das in der Baukunst grösste Bedeu-
    tung behält.
    Die *Teppichwirkerei & Stickerei.* Der Ursprung der Malerei & Reliefkunst (China,
    Assyrien) Gobelins.
    Nachbildung der Teppichwände in Platten von Holz, Metall, Stein, Erdwaaren
    (Mosaik, Glasmalerei, gebrannte Ziegel, Tapeten u. s. w.
    Anmerkung. Bei diesem wichtigen Abschnitte muss auf die Stylgesetze hingewie-
    sen werden die aus dem gemeinschaftlichen Ursprunge u. der Verschiedenheit der
    Stoffe die in Anwendung kommen bei jeder einzelnen Verzweigung des Motives
    hervorgehen.
B. *Die Wandbereitung in ihrer Anwendung auf Bekleidung.*
    a   Pelz & Leder (Kürschnerei, Schuhmacherei)
    b   Linnen.
    c. Baumwolle
    d. Wollen
    e. Seide u. s. w.

III *Der Damm.*
    Erdarbeiten. Ingenieurwissenschaft.
    a. Schutz des Heerdes gegen Überschwemmung. Wasserbau.
    b. Schutz des Heerdes gegen Feinde (Festungsbau & Waffen) |
    c. Beschützung & Erleichterung der Verbindung zwischen den verschiedenen
        Feuerstellen.
        Wege & Brückenbau. Canalbau, Schifffahrt, *Telegraphie* etc

fol. 3v

Outline of a Cultural-Historical Exhibition 307

d. Grenzbestimmung des zum Heerde gehörigen
Geometrie, Geodasie. Cameralistik
Anmerkg. Dieser Theil umfasst eine Menge v. wichtigen theoretischen sowie praktischen Bethätigungen der Menschen die sich auf unterschiedliche Weise innerhalb desselben anordnen lassen.
B. *Maurerarbeiten.*
Steinkonstruction, Ziegelconstruction, Gewölbe (Steinschnitt) Formen der höheren Baukunst die aus diesem Theil der Construction hervorgehen nebst ihren von
den Stoffen u. anderen Umständen abhängigen Modificationen.
In diese Rubrik gehören auch die Künste die sich mit der Bearbeitung harter Stoffe
auf kaltem Wege & mit der Zusammensetzung von Systemen der Construction aus
vielen kleinen harten Theilen beschäftigen z. B. Steinschneidekunst – Graviren,
selbst das Schmieden ist eine Ubergangsform & gehört *halb* hierher. Es muss bei
allen diesen Abtheilungen jedes Einzelne vom ursprünglichsten Keime u. vom ersten Stoffe, der in Frage kam, an bis zur letzten Verkörperung des Gedankens verfolgt werden. Alles zur Verkörperung des Gedankens Beitragende, der Rohstoff,
die Werkzeuge u. die Maschinen müssen zusammen bleiben.

IV *Das Dach.*
A. *Gerüste.*
a. *Holzgerüste,* technische & bildnerische Entwickelung, Formen der Baukunst
die diesem Ursprunge angehören. Giebel – Säulen, Fenster. Thüren (selbst
Geräthe)
b. *Metallgerüste* technische & bildnerische Entwickelung der Metallconstruc-
tionen. |
B. *Dachbedeckung.*   *fol. 4r*
a *Überzug.* Gewebe, Felle, Filz, Holz. Asphalt, Metall Stein (gränzt an die Categorie v. Wand)
b. *Schuppendecke.* Schiefer, Schindel Ziegel, Metall in kleinen Platten, desgleichen Stein (gränzt an die Categorie der Maurerarbeit
Hohe Bedeutung des Giebels in der Baukunst als Symbol der göttlichen Weihe des
Heerdes. Baldachin Schirm des Buddha – Aëtos der Griechen.

V. *Zusammenwirken der vier Grundbestandtheile der häuslichen Einrichtung.*
A. *Hohe Kunst.*
a Architektur
b. Drama.
B. *Hohe Wissenschaft.*
Theologie
Physiologie
Moral. –

306.3 **Unterhaltg**] *'Unterhaltung'*   306.14 **Handeln**] *'Handel'*   306.15 **religiosen**] *'religiösen'*
307.2 **Geodasie**] *'Geodäsie'*   307.3 **Anmerkg**] *'Anmerkung'*   307.13 **Ubergangsform**]
'Übergangsform'

Note on a Cultural-Philosophical Collection

TEXTUAL RECORD

Vieweg Vieweg Archives, ViS:246, fols. 1v–2r (1r, 2r Semper's letter to Eduard Vieweg, 20 January 1852, see 308–9; 2v note '1852 Janr 20 Prof Semper London' probably by Eduard Vieweg), 'Note', in Semper's hand, *copy-text*

Herrmann 1976 'Briefe Gottfried Sempers an Eduard Vieweg 1843–1852 aus dem Verlagsarchiv Vieweg: 15', 234–5, here 235, emended ed. of Vieweg

BIBLIOGRAPHY Herrmann 1976, 211–12, 234–5

EXPLANATORY NOTES

Semper conceived this note as a complement to the version of the 'Outline of a Cultural-Historical Exhibition' sent to Eduard Vieweg on 20 January 1852 (40–2). The note's divergent title reflects the fact that Semper had changed the title of the ramified plan several times and was also wavering between whether it was intended for an exhibition or a collection. Both the outline and the note were planned as addenda to *Science, Industry, and Art*. Semper included the note in his letter to Vieweg, explaining its role after having referred to an 'announcement' to be appended to *Science, Industry, and Art*. This was the prospectus of his planned 'Comparative Architecture' and was published at the end of some rare copies of *Science, Industry, and Art*. The beginning of the letter in question reads:

London 20ᵗ Jan. 1852

Verehrter Herr und Freund.

Ich schickte Ihnen gestern einen Brief mit den gewünschten Erweiterungen der Epistel die als Annonce dienen soll. – Das zweite von Ihnen zur weiteren Prüfung mitgegebene Beiblatt, (den Plan einer kulturphilosophischen Sammlung,) behielt ich zurück, glaube aber vergessen zu haben, Ihnen zu schreiben, dass der Plan mir etwas zu spekulativ vorkommt, und ich desshalb bedenklich bin ihn zu veröffentlichen. Doch beurtheilt man seine eigenen Sachen nicht immer richtig, daher appellire ich heute bei zweiter Ueberlegung an Sie und stelle es Ihnen ganz frei, ihn mitzugeben oder es zu lassen. Nur müsste im ersten Falle folgende Note unten beigedruckt werden:

Then follows the note which, like the 'Outline of a Cultural-Historical Exhibition', was not published. It provides an explanation of the spatial arrangement in Semper's plan for a 'complete and universal museum' which he drew up in his slightly later catalogue of 'Practical Art in Metals and hard Materials' (297–8). Further comments on the 'Outline of a Cultural-Historical Exhibition', interrupted by a remark concerning Theodor Kell's translation of a work on flax and cotton (Ryan 1852; cf. Herrmann 1976, 232), conclude the letter:

Noch habe ich zu bemerken, verehrter Freund, dass ich an dem beiliegenden Plane ein paarmal die Folge der Abtheilungen verändert habe; aber wenn es zu viele Umstände macht, das abzuändern, so lassen Sie es ja beim alten.

Noch eine Angelegenheit, die mich eigentlich hauptsächlich dazu bewogen hat, Ihnen diesen zweiten Brief nachzuschicken.

Herr Kell erwartet sehnlich von Ihnen eine Auskunft ich weiss nicht genau mehr über welche Anfrage über eine litterarische Arbeit die er an Sie gestellt hat. Ich habe es schon zweimal vergessen, Ihnen diess zu schreiben.

Viele Empfehlungen an die Ihrigen
Ganz der Ihrige
GSemper.

Ich wiederhole, dass ich es ganz Ihrem Ermessen überlasse, ob Sie den Plan beigeben wollen. Vielleicht kann er manchem Ordner v. Sammlungen interessant werden.

The last sentence is preceded by a deleted comment on the plan: 'Er ist nicht genug durchgebildet.' (It is not developed enough.)

43.2 **Schrifchens**] *Schriftchens*; i.e. *Wissenschaft, Industrie und Kunst* 43.7 **Gegenstände**] *Gegenstande*

ALTERATIONS IN THE MANUSCRIPT

43.1 **Note**] *after del. on fol. 1r*

… Note …[1]

Es mag in dem gegebenen Plane manche Gezwungenheit in der Rubricirung der Gegenstände, besonders in dessen erster Hauptabtheilung hervortreten, aber selbst für[2] diejenigen Gegenstände, welche sich ihm nur mehr oder weniger gezwungen fügen, würde[3] es schwer seyn, einen anderen Plan zu erdenken, der das Zusammengehörige besser vereinigte und übersichtlicher als dieser wäre, und zugleich die Eigenschaft hätte, die anderen Objecte, für welche der gegebene Plan der einzig[4]

1 … **Note** …] *ellipses by Semper* 2 **selbst für**] *interl.* 3 **würde**] *after del.* und welche und] *after del.* würden dabei in ihrer Uebersichtlichkeit 4 **der einzig**] *del. separately*

43.2 **Es**] *above del.* Man 43.2–3 **diesen Plan ~ erlaube**] *above del.* den gegebenen Plan der vielleicht nicht unverdiente Vorwurf den] n *over* m Plan] *altered from* Plane der] r *over* n unverdiente] *altered from* unverdienten 43.3 **der**] *interl.* **treffen**] *above del.* machen **sey**] *above del.* ist 43.4 **füge**] e *over* t 43.5 **einige**] *above del.* manche 43.6 **könne,**] *altered from* kann, 43.7 **der**] *above del.* alles alles] *after del.* und **anwiese,**] *altered from* ~. **und**] *after del.* Es ist **der**] *above del.* dieselben Absichten 43.8 **die**] ie *over* en **Erreichung**] *after del.* Zweck des 43.9 **auseinander setzte**] *above del.* des Weiteren darlegte des Weiteren] *after del.* darlegte, 43.10 **die für den**] *after del.* diejenigen Gegen 43.14 **instructiv**] in *over* ei 43.20 **Mitteln**] *after del.* Masch

310   The Great Exhibition

Association of Artists of Various Nations

TEXTUAL RECORD

Vieweg Vieweg Archives, V3:1.1.3.32, fols. 1v–2r (1r–v, 2r–v Semper's letter to Eduard Vieweg, 2 December 1851, with request to quickly publish *Science, Industry, and Art* as an advertisement for the planned exhibition), in Semper's hand; written on paper with letterhead 'Great Exhibition of 1851. Official Catalogue. Contractors, Spicer Brothers, Stationers, and W. Clowes & Son, Printers, City Office, 29, New Bridge Street, Blackfriars'

ZfB   'Bauwissenschaftliche und Kunst-Notizen', *Zeitschrift für Bauwesen* (Berlin) 1, no. 11/12 (31 Dec. 1851), 385 (ETH Library, P Rar 331), *copy-text*

BIBLIOGRAPHY Herrmann 1978, 58–9; Herrmann 1981, 100; Herrmann 1984, 53

EXPLANATORY NOTES

Semper developed the idea for an exhibition in part of the emptied Crystal Palace following an initial suggestion that he had made in August 1851 to Jules Dieterle (the artistic director of the Sèvres porcelain manufactory near Paris, whom he had known since their collaboration on the Court Theatre in Dresden) to 'open an office for information and advice on industrial art, including decoration and even architecture', focusing on 'ceramics, glassmaking … furniture, tapestry, wallpaper, designs for fabrics, etc., etc.' Due to reservations expressed by Dieterle, Semper turned for the 'project for an exhibition room' to Dieterle's friend Charles Séchan (who had also worked on the Dresden Theatre), who replied equally critically on 28 November 1851. Despite this, Semper continued to pursue the exhibition project further, for which – as he wrote to Eduard Vieweg on 2 December 1851 – the 'Exhibition building' had now 'been placed at our disposal'. He asked Vieweg to forward the enclosed 'letters to various notable people of my acquaintance' (311.12–13), probably including Friedrich Hitzig as a member of the editorial board of the *Zeitschrift für Bauwesen*, in which the call for entries was published (Semper was still praising Hitzig in 1860 as one of the best architects in Berlin). The letter to Vieweg contains a summary of the context and objective of the exhibition, a kind of variant of the published advertisement, of which no draft is known. So far, nothing more is known about the fate of this exhibition, which apparently did not take place.

43.23 **Es**] after introduction by journal editor:

London. Von dem Architekten Herrn *G. Semper* geht uns die nachfolgende Mittheilung zu, auf welche wir hiermit das betreffende Publikum Deutschlands aufmerksam machen:

43.24 **Deutschen**] *Deutsche*   43.25 **Blagmann**] *Klagmann*   **Lienard**] *Liénard*
44.16 **tragen. –**] before conclusion by journal editor:

Wir empfehlen diese Angelegenheit dem betheiligten deutschen Publikum hiermit auf das Wärmste.

———————

MANUSCRIPT VARIANTS
Vieweg

Eine Anzahl Französischer, Englischer und Deutscher Künstler hat sich vereinigt, im Februar eine industrielle Kunstausstellung zu veranstalten, und wir haben dazu das Exhibition building zu unserer Disposition erhalten. Natürlich werden wir nur eine einzige kleine Abtheilung davon in Anspruch nehmen. *fol. 1v*

5 Die besten Franz. Künstler werden ihre Beiträge dazu liefern, wie Dieterle, Lienard, Klagmann u. a. Der letztere Klagmann ist der ausgezeichneteste Bildhauer von denen welche die industrielle Kunst ihres Talentes nicht unwürdig halten. |

Er bildet ein Mitglied unseres Comité, welches ausserdem mich, den Arch. Horeau und den Bronzefabrikanten Matifat und einige andere Künstler und Techniker zu seinen Mitglie- *fol. 2r*

10 dern zählt.

Es liegt uns daran, die Deutschen Kunstler u. Architecten für die Ausstellung zu interessiren, wesshalb ich einige Briefe an verschiedene mir bekannte Notorietäten unter ihnen beilege, welche Sie gütigst mit der Post weiter besorgen wollen.

Diese Schrift wäre geeignet, sowohl das Engl. wie d. Deutsche Publikum auf den Zweck

15 dieser Ausstellung aufmerksam zu machen, der weiter geht und die Begründung einer Industrieschule in London betrifft.

311.2 **industrielle**] *after del.* Ausstellung industrieller Zeich **Exhibition**] E *over* g
311.5 **Lienard**] *'Liénard'* 311.6 **u. a.**] *'und andere'* **ausgezeichneteste**] *after del.* beste
von denen welche] *above del.* in der sich auf 311.9 **Bronzefabrikanten**] fabrikanten
after del. manufa 311.11 **Kunstler**] *'Künstler'* 311.14 **Diese Schrift**] *i.e. Wissenschaft,
Industrie und Kunst* **d.**] *'das'*

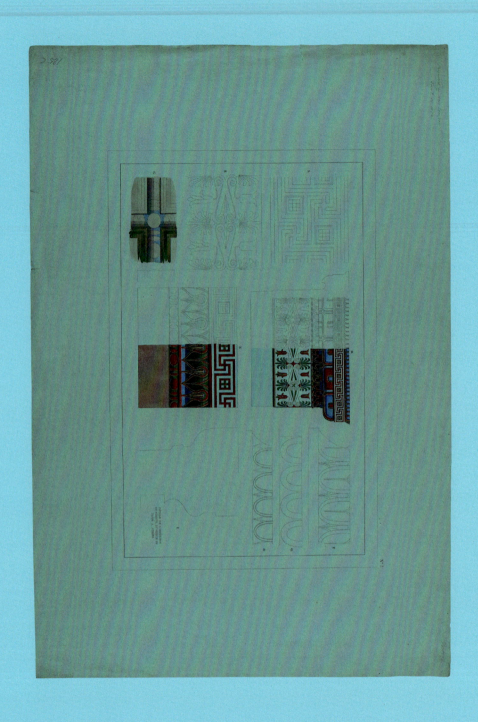

Pl. 9: Plate from *Die Anwendung der Farben in der Architectur und Plastik*, 1836 (RIBA Library)

POLYCHROMY IN ARCHITECTURE

Introduction

Semper's two essays in English on polychromy in architecture – the first of which was published in Edward Falkener's *Museum of Classical Antiquities* of 1851, the second in Owen Jones's *Apology for the Colouring of the Greek Court in the Crystal Palace* of 1854 – take up topics that he had been developing in two essays in German: in his very first booklet, published shortly before he became professor of architecture at the Academy of Fine Arts in Dresden, *Vorläufige Bemerkungen über bemalte Architectur und Plastik bei den Alten* (Preliminary Observations on Painted Architecture and Sculpture of the Ancients) of 1834, and in the booklet *Die vier Elemente der Baukunst* (The Four Elements of Architecture), published in the autumn of 1851. Semper had sent the completed manuscript of this booklet to his publisher Eduard Vieweg on 19 January 1851, explaining that it was 'actually written for England'. As a matter of fact, on 1 December 1850, Semper had learned from Rachel Chadwick that Henry Cole was trying to have the booklet published by the Society of Arts, whose council Cole chaired. And indeed, both of Semper's English essays on polychromy are variants of parts of *The Four Elements of Architecture*. The first – 'On the Study of Polychromy, and Its Revival' (48–61) – synthesizes several of its six chapters, while the second – 'On the Origin of Polychromy in Architecture' (61–73) – summarizes large parts of the fifth chapter, entitled 'Die vier Elemente' (The Four Elements).

The issue of architectural polychromy in antiquity was attracting some attention in London around this period. In the autumn of 1850, Owen Jones was commissioned to design the polychromatic interior decoration of Joseph Paxton's Crystal Palace in Hyde Park. Semper came into direct contact with the current English debate on polychromy for the first time here. In a letter of 13 November 1850, he asked Edwin Chadwick to recommend him to Paxton 'for the decoration of the Building for 1851', which was to involve the application of polychromy – as he learned at the latest from Chadwick's reply of 26 November, stating that Paxton was unable to consider Semper's 'services for the Polychrome decoration of the edifice for the new exposition' because 'the task of painting and decorating the edifice, is in the hands of Mr Owen Jones'. Jones presented his design in a paper 'On the Decorations Proposed for the Exhibition Building' that was read at the Royal Institute of British Architects (RIBA) on 16 December 1850. Shortly before this, on 2 December, Matthew Digby Wyatt had read a paper at RIBA on 'Observations on Polychromatic Decoration in Italy, from the 12th to the 16th Century'. Semper himself took part in subsequent debates on polychromy held at RIBA about a year later. On 12 January 1852, Thomas Leverton Donaldson read a paper on Jacques Ignace Hittorff's *Restitution du temple d'Empédocle à Sélinonte* of 1851. Donaldson also referred to works by Semper – as Hittorff had also done – namely to *Preliminary Observations on Painted Architecture and Sculpture of the Ancients* and to the hand-coloured lithographs in the folio work *Die Anwendung der Farben in der Architectur und Plastik* (The Use of Colour in Architecture and Sculpture) of 1836. The lithographs were displayed at the meeting, among them details from the Temple of Theseus (pl. 9) and the restoration of a part of the Parthenon. Donaldson's paper was discussed at the RIBA meetings of 26 January and 9 February 1852, again with drawings by Semper being shown. At the first of these two meetings, Semper explained the drawings and 'his colored restoration of the Parthenon' and referred to the interpretation that he had put forward in the first of his English essays on polychromy in defence of the proposed mainly red tint.

Semper's contributions in English to the debate on architectural polychromy had been prompted by yet other factors. These relate to his then still continuing work on 'Vergleichende Baulehre' (Comparative Architecture), which he had started in Dresden at the instigation of Eduard Vieweg. Semper was to have delivered the first part to him in the autumn of 1844 but did not send it until 13 May 1850, while he was in exile in Paris – a manuscript of about 400 pages containing chapters on the primal elements of architecture and the domestic architecture of Assyria, Chaldea, Media, Persia, China, India and Egypt. Shortly after Semper's arrival in London on 28 September 1850, Emil Braun – the person who had persuaded Semper to move to England instead of America – suggested that he should carry out a 'revision' in English of his 'Comparative Architecture', as Semper wrote to Vieweg on 2 October 1850. After Semper had moved into an office on Edward Falkener's premises a few days later, he took the opportunity to present an outline of the work in Falkener's journal *The Museum of Classical Antiquities*, the first issue of which was to be published in January 1851 with essays on polychromy by Jacques Ignace Hittorff and Falkener himself.

By around mid-May 1851, Semper had drafted an initial proposal for Falkener's *Museum* in French (MS 79; pl. 3), the language that he and Falkener shared. In a prefatory note to Falkener, he wrote that – instead of giving the planned 'summary' of the 'work on comparative architecture' – he had restricted himself to 'a few salient pages from its contents' and focused on a 'specialized archaeological subject', namely 'the question of Greek polychromy and its origin', which was beginning to attract 'more general interest, particularly in England'. However, the manuscript is a first adaptation and translation by Semper into French of the fifth chapter ('Die vier Elemente') of the booklet *The Four Elements of Architecture*, which primarily situates the origins of architecture in the industrial arts. It is thus an early witness to Semper's transformation of his arguments on polychromy into *A Contribution to Comparative Architecture*, as the subtitle of *The Four Elements of Architecture* reads. Falkener did not publish this manuscript but another, missing, one which he received by the end of May or the beginning of June 1851 (on 7 June 1851, he urged Semper to respond to his request of a few days earlier, namely 'to see me and examine your MS etc., etc. I need to send it to the printers'). Published as 'On the Study of Polychromy, and Its Revival', the essay centres on the polychrome debate in general and particularly on Franz Kugler's attack – published in German in 1835 and in English in 1836 – on Semper's position as expounded in *Preliminary Observations on Painted Architecture and Sculpture of the Ancients*.

Semper's first French draft (MS 79) – the summary of the fifth chapter of *The Four Elements of Architecture* – became part of the source material for the essay 'On the Origin of Polychromy in Architecture' in Owen Jones's *Apology*. Jones wrote the latter in defence of his Greek Court with its three partial, and painted, copies of the Parthenon frieze, which formed part of the Crystal Palace's Fine Arts Courts that opened on the building's new site in Sydenham on 10 June 1854. Semper had already revised the first French draft during the summer of 1851 (again in French), now giving it the title 'Second Essay. Sur l'origine de l'architecture polychrome' (MS 82). However, the English version published in Jones's *Apology* is neither a direct translation of the first French version nor of the second but a combination of the two supplemented by arguments which Semper had developed in the third chapter of *The Four Elements of Architecture*, entitled 'Der chemische Beweis' (Chemical Evidence). The manuscript of the English essay is missing.

Semper's involvement in the English debate on architectural polychromy had some lasting material effects. Semper donated some of his works on the subject to RIBA (where they are still held) – presenting a copy of *Preliminary Observations* at some time before 13 January 1851 and, on the occasion of the meeting of 12 January 1852, a copy of *The Four Elements*, as well as the five lithographs from *The Use of Colour in Architecture and Sculpture* that were shown at the meeting. A complete copy of *The Use of Colour* was incorporated into the library of the Department of Practical Art, now in the National Art Library at the Victoria and Albert Museum. Interestingly, the RIBA Library does not hold an ordinary copy of *The Four Elements* but one of the rare copies that have a different main title (the subtitle is the same) – namely *Ueber Polychromie und ihren Ursprung* (On Polychromy and Its Origin). Semper must have received some of these copies in late August 1851 when Vieweg visited the Great Exhibition, while he acknowledged the receipt of copies with the final title (upon which he decided on 9 September 1851) in mid-November 1851. Three of the variant copies survive in London; in addition to the one at RIBA, there are two copies in the library of the Victoria and Albert Museum, one of which is the one that Semper presented to Henry Cole with the autograph dedication 'H. Cole Esq. with the Authors fullest Respects May 17th 1852'. Finally, Semper referred to both of his English essays on polychromy in the first volume of *Style in the Technical and Tectonic Arts*, when discussing his 'principle of coating' (Semper 1860/63, 1:226–7).

BIBLIOGRAPHY Ettlinger 1937, 49–63, 69–78; Van Zanten 1977a, 27–9, 50–6; Van Zanten 1977b, 8–10, 41, 42a–44, 52–64, 73–4, 155, 167–9, 403–5; Herrmann 1978, 46–7, 62; Herrmann 1981, 95; Van Zanten 1982, 187, 209–15; Herrmann 1984, 42, 56; Jenkins/Middleton 1988; Pisani 2003; Hildebrand 2020a, 105–8

On the Study of Polychromy, and Its Revival

TEXTUAL RECORD

MCA	'On the Study of Polychromy, and Its Revival', *The Museum of Classical Antiquities* (London) 1, no. 3 (July 1851), 228–46 (BL, P.P.1900.b), *copy-text*
JDM	'On the Study of Polychromy', *The Journal of Design and Manufactures* (London) 6, no. 34 (Dec. 1851), 112–13; reprint of the conclusion of MCA (241–6) without the notes, introduced by Henry Cole
Semper 2014[a]	vol. 1, 371–89, Karge's reprint ed. of MCA
Semper 2014[b]	vol. 1, 390–1, Karge's reprint ed. of JDM

On the Study of Polychromy, and Its Revival   317

BIBLIOGRAPHY Reising 1976, 56 and n. 43; Van Zanten 1977a, 28; Herrmann 1978, 46–7, 62; Herrmann 1981, 95; Van Zanten 1982, 213; Herrmann 1984, 42, 56; Mallgrave 1989, 2–19; Gnehm 2004, 55–69; Weidmann 2014, 6; Gnehm 2017b

EXPLANATORY NOTES

Semper's English essay on polychromy in the July issue of Falkener's *Museum of Classical Antiquities* of 1851 is the first, partial, publication of the German version of *The Four Elements of Architecture*, which was published only in the autumn of 1851. It comprises roughly the book's first and second chapters and touches on topics developed in the fourth and fifth chapters. The essay begins with an overview of the polychromy debate (48.4–52.2), corresponding to the book's first chapter (Semper 1851b, 1–12), and then moves on – in a passage which is missing from *The Four Elements of Architecture* – to Semper's critique of Franz Kugler's only partial acknowledgement of polychromy by differentiating between two positions (52.3–53.25): the first position, in which polychromy is regarded 'as a means of art' to 'assist and increase the effect of sculpture and architecture', and the second one, in which sculpture, architecture and painting are considered to be 'one indissoluble whole' without any 'limits between the different manifestations of Greek art'. Then follows Semper's detailed critique of Kugler's position (53.26–56.15), a summary of large parts of the book's second chapter (Semper 1851b, 13–29) and a critique reiterated at the RIBA meeting of 26 January 1852. After a passage, absent in the book version, on Hittorff as a representative of the second position (57.1–22), the essay concludes with arguments for a Greek polychrome architecture in accordance with the other arts, listed in eleven points (57.23–61.17) – a concise summary not offered in the book version, in which the corresponding parallels are to be found in the fourth and fifth chapters. Henry Cole reprinted this eleven-point conclusion (without the footnotes) in his *Journal of Design and Manufactures* of December 1851, partially fulfilling his promise to have *The Four Elements of Architecture* published by the Society of Arts (see 313).

48.4–5 **Quatremère de Quincy – Le Jupiter Olympien**] Quatremère de Quincy 1815; cf. Semper 1851b, 1   48.23–4, 49.1–2 **This controversy ~ ancient Greece.**] German philhellenism underwent a major revival with the outbreak in 1821 of the Greek revolution against Ottoman rule, which led to the establishment of the Kingdom of Greece in 1832 with its first King Otto, son of King Ludwig I of Bavaria; cf. Semper 1851b, 2.   48.25–7 **Kugler ~ in the Trans. Inst. B. Archts. vol. i. part 1, 1835–6**] Franz Kugler's *Ueber die Polychromie der griechischen Architektur und Sculptur und ihre Grenzen* (1835), translated by William Richard Hamilton; for this and all further references to 'Kugler' and 'Hamilton's Kugler', see Kugler 1836   48.30 **Hittorff ~ in the first number of this periodical**] Jacques Ignace Hittorff's essay 'On the Polychromy of Greek Architecture' (Hittorff 1851b)
49.15–16 **splendid work ~ by Baron Stackelberg**] Stackelberg 1826   49.16–17 **Brøndsted, in his Voyages et Récherches en Grèce**] for this and all further references to 'Brøndsted' and his *Voyages et recherches en Grèce*, see Brøndsted 1826/30 (with 'Récherches' as *recherches*). Semper mentions Brøndsted's work 'on the sculpture of the Parthenon' in *Preliminary Observations on Painted Architecture and Sculpture of the Ancients* (Semper 1834, 5 n. **, 18).   49.18–19 **Duc de Luynes ~ discoveries at Metapontum**] Luynes/Debacq 1833
49.19 **Duca di Serradifalco ~ researches in Sicily**] Serradifalco 1834/42, referred to in

Semper 1834, 18   49.20–1 **restoration of a small temple at Selinuntum, published by M. Hittorff**] Hittorff/Zanth 1826/30, mentioned in Semper 1834, 18   49.30 **Herman**] Gottfried Hermann, a philologist Semper refers to in *Preliminary Observations* and *The Four Elements* (Semper 1834, 43, 49; Semper 1851b, 2 n. *, 52 n. *)   49.38–42, 50.36–7 **researches ~ cholera**] On his study trip of 1830–33, Semper left Rome in February 1831 together with the French architect Jules Goury. After a journey through the Alban Hills and the Lepini Mountains, they travelled to Naples and Pompeii, sailed to Sicily and then to Greece, where they arrived in October 1831. In the spring of 1832, Goury continued his journey together with Owen Jones, travelling to Constantinople, Palestine, Egypt and Granada, where Goury died of cholera in 1834 while working on his drawings of the Alhambra, which were later published by Jones (Jones 1842/45); cf. Semper 1851b, 3–4, 9, 32–3; Semper 1860/63, 1:516; 2:318 n. 1.

50.3–4 **larger work ~ Mediæval**] Semper's folio work *The Use of Colour in Architecture and Sculpture* with six hand-coloured lithographs (Semper 1836). Only the first part on Greek and Etruscan polychromy was published.   50.12–13 **restoration of the Cathedral of Bamberg by Gärtner**] The remains of the polychrome interior of Bamberg Cathedral were found during its restoration, which was intended to remove later additions to the original building. Commissioned by Ludwig I of Bavaria, the painter Friedrich Karl Rupprecht began the refurbishment process in 1829; it was continued by two architects: 1831–34 by Carl Heideloff and 1834–37 by Friedrich von Gärtner. Semper had visited Bamberg in 1833 on his return from the study trip to Italy and Greece. He refers to Heideloff's Bamberg work in *Preliminary Observations* (Semper 1834, 42) and discusses medieval polychromy with reference to Bamberg Cathedral in *The Four Elements* (Semper 1851b, 6).   50.25–6 **Sainte Chapelle, by M. Duban**] Félix Duban, assisted by Jean-Baptiste Lassus, began the restoration of the Sainte-Chapelle in Paris in 1837; Lassus took over in 1849, and Émile Boeswillwald completed it in 1857–63. In *The Four Elements*, Semper refers to the Sainte-Chapelle on account of the completeness and richness of its polychrome system (Semper 1851b, 6). In *Style in the Technical and Tectonic Arts* he mentions the Sainte-Chapelle as an example of the way in which medieval polychromy served to give calm and stability to the dynamics of the Gothic ribbed vaults and the system of slender pillars (Semper 1860/63, 1:511–12).   50.40 **Bemerkungen über die vielfärbige Architectur und Sculptur bei den Alten**] This is how the title (with 'vielfärbige' printed correctly as *vielfarbige*) appears on the engraved title page of *Preliminary Observations* (Semper 1834).

51.17–18 **Gowry and Jones's work on the Alhambra**] 'Gowry': *Goury*; see note 49.38–42, 50.36–7   51.27 **publication of the Mosque of Santa Sophia**] Fossati 1852; cf. Semper 1851b, 9 n. *   51.29 **discoveries in Assyria**] In *The Four Elements* (Semper 1851b, 10), Semper refers to 'two beautiful works' on Assyria, meaning Paul-Émile Botta and Eugène Flandin's *Monument de Ninive* (1849–50) and the first series of Austen Henry Layard's *Monuments of Nineveh* (1849/53) – both actually describing not the ruins of Nineveh but those of Khorsabad and Nimrud, respectively. Layard unearthed the remains of the actual Nineveh in a second expedition, published in the second volume of his work (1853). Semper later refers to Layard's and Botta's discoveries in his London lectures (128.22–3, 163.20, 199.26–8, 200.40–1; 447.1–2).   51.30 **monuments of Persepolis and of Egypt**] In *The Four Elements* (Semper 1851b, 10), Semper mentions Eugène Flandin and Pascal Coste's *Voyage en Perse* (1851). The monuments of Egypt had been published, for example, by Semper's Paris teacher and friend Franz Christian Gau in his *Antiquités de la Nubie* (1822).

51.32–6 **monuments of Athens ~ Dilettanti Society**] Semper refers to Francis Penrose's

Investigation of the Principles of Athenian Architecture in *The Four Elements* as a forthcoming publication of the Society of Dilettanti (Semper 1851b, 10–11). Earlier publications of the Society of Dilettanti include *Antiquities of Ionia* (1769/1840) and *The Unedited Antiquities of Attica* (1817). 51.37–9 **Donaldson ~ Trans. R. Inst. B. Archts. i. 85, 86**] Donaldson's observations on colour discovered at the Temple of Theseus in Athens date from 1820, not 1830; they were partially published in Kugler 1836, 85–6 n. ‡, and translated by Semper into German in *The Four Elements* (Semper 1851b, 31–2).

52.1–2 **work by M. Hittorff, the plates of which were obligingly shown to me by that author**] Hittorff's *Restitution du temple d'Empédocle à Sélinonte* (Hittorff 1851a); cf. Semper 1851b, 11–12. Semper had known Hittorff since his studies in Paris in 1826–27 and 1829–30; he kept in touch with him during his Parisian exile in 1849–50. 52.35 **général**] 'général' in Brøndsted 1826/30, 2:146 52.38 **materiaux**] 'matériaux' in Brøndsted 1826/30, 2:146 53.1 **des veritables**] 'de véritables' in Brøndsted 1826/30, 2:146 53.15 **if no**] 'If then no' in Kugler 1836, 84 53.24 **that of marble**] 'that marble' in Kugler 1836, 84 53.25 **made resplendent**] 'made' missing in Kugler 1836, 84 53.37 **Herod. iii. 57**] for this and all further references to 'Herod.' and 'Cary's Herod.', see Herodotus 1848, 194–5, with minor differences to the cited text

56.16 **Faraday's Report**] Michael Faraday's analysis of the Elgin Marbles of 1837, published in Hamilton 1842, 106–7; cf. Semper 1851b, 44–5; Semper 1860/63, 1:516–17

57.1–22 **The second class ~ of the cella.**] missing in Semper 1851b 57.27–8 **2. ~ tapestry.**] cf. fifth chapter in Semper 1851b, 59 57.29–32 **3. ~ construction.**] cf. fifth chapter in Semper 1851b, 66–7 57.38 **metropes**] *metopes*

58.1–4 **4. ~ ceiling.**] cf. fifth chapter in Semper 1851b, 67–8 58.5–6 **5. ~ stone.**] cf. fifth chapter in Semper 1851b, 57–9 58.6 **burnt**] *baked* 58.7–13 **6. ~ polychromy.**] cf. fourth chapter in Semper 1851b, 46–7 58.14–24, 59.1–5 **7. ~ practice.**] cf. fourth chapter in Semper 1851b, 47–8 58.27 **Vitruvius**] Semper had a copy of Daniele Barbaro's edition of Vitruvius's *Ten Books of Architecture* among his books (see 214.25), probably the Latin edition first published in 1567. 58.30–1 **Wiegmann, Die Malerei der Alten**] Wiegmann 1836 58.34–5 **Plin. H. Nat. xxxv. 39**] here and in further references Pliny's *Naturalis Historia* (Natural History); also cited in Semper 1851b, 47 n. *. Semper had one volume of it among his books (see 215.32). 58.38–9 **Plin. H. Nat. xxxv. 41**] also discussed in Semper 1851b, 48 n. *

59.4–5 **Further proof ~ granite**] together with note 18, 'See ante, p. 99' (59.42), a reference to Falkener's contribution to the debate on polychromy, 'On the Application of Polychromy to Modern Architecture' in the first issue of *The Museum of Classical Antiquities*, which discusses the decoration of the Crystal Palace; see Falkener 1851b, 99: 'Among the coloured decorations at Thebes, I was much struck with granites stained artificially with *transparent* colour approaching to yellows and reds; the felspar, mica, and quartz, being perfectly distinguishable underneath.' 59.6–26, 60.1–10 **8. ~ ornament and sculpture.**] cf. fifth chapter in Semper 1851b, 96–8 59.20 **forms of Doric architecture were derived from Egypt**] together with note 19, 'See ante, p. 87' (59.43), a reference to Falkener's paper 'On Some Egyptian-Doric Columns in the Southern Temple at Karnak' published in the first issue of *The Museum of Classical Antiquities*. Falkener's discussion of an Egyptian capital is accompanied by a woodcut (Falkener 1851a, 87) which Semper copied for the first volume of *Style* to illustrate what he calls a 'Protodoric capital' (Semper 1860/63, 1:419). 59.30–1 **Plin. H. Nat. xxxvi. 22**] In *Style*, Semper cites this passage from the edition by Jacques Daléchamps, originally published in the sixteenth century; Semper 1860/63, 1:460 n. 1; this edition is also cited in Semper 1860/63, 2:283 n. 5, 584 n. 2.

60.25 **eastern climate**] Van Zanten 1982, 272 n. 83, observes: 'In Semper's original text a small "e" is used, but this makes no sense; Semper must mean Oriental, not eastwards.' This was actually corrected in Cole's reprint of the paper (see below, Print Variants 60.25). In a parallel passage of *The Four Elements*, Semper speaks of 'southern regions', where the 'reddish vitreous coating' conferred on the marble temple a 'tonal key of colour' which made the building mass fade into the 'tone in which the lower portion of the sky glows … at high noon' (Semper 1851b, 39–40).   60.34–5 **"Pictura ~ Petronius, Init.**] a line in the beginning of Petronius's *Satyricon* where the narrator scolds the decay of rhetoric and poetry (also referred to in *The Four Elements*; Semper 1851b, 98). Semper translates the sentence in *Style* (Semper 1860/63, 1:494): 'Auch die Malerei nahm kein besseres Ende, seitdem die frechen Aegypter ein Schema dieser grossen Kunst erfanden' (Painting, too, has come to no better end since the impudent Egyptians invented a scheme for this great art).   60.36 **tryglyphs**] *triglyphs*

PRINT VARIANTS
JDM

48.1–2 **XX. On the Study of Polychromy, and its Revival.**] On the Study of Polychromy, by Gottfried Semper. *before Henry Cole's introduction:*

Already a considerable change has taken place in public taste on the subject of colouring public buildings, and a more genial feeling for colour has begun to develope itself. All nations have shewn their natural instinct towards colour, and it has been the means of completing and adorning all styles of architecture in all ages. The English were as natural in their love for colour as any other people until the Puritanic movement set in after the Reformation, and deluged the churches with whitewash. That and our transitional state, which has left us without principles of any kind in art, have helped, even to this day, to make the mass of the public sceptical about the good taste of colouring public buildings. But a better feeling is already growing, and it may be foreseen, that, in a few years, any architect will be considered as leaving his building naked and imperfect who shall fail to complete it with the charms of colour. In the "Museum of Classical Antiquities," a learned quarterly periodical, we have some condensed remarks on this subject, which convey useful information: they are by M. Gottfried Semper, the tasteful architect of the Berlin theatre, who is at present resident in this country: –

48.4–57.24, 57.33–9 **Since the publication ~ white.**] *om.*
57.30 **Romans,**] ~∧   57.40–1, 58.25–31 **The influence ~ Alten.**] *om.*
58.15 **development**] developement   58.32–5 **"Ceris ~ Plin. H. Nat. xxxv. 39.**] *om.*
58.36–44 **"Encausto ~ Architects.**] *om.*
59.2 **coloured and**] ~ or·   59.12 **civilization**] civilisation   59.19 **shown**] shewn   59.27–41 **"Durat ~ Id. vii. 5.**] *om.*   59.42 **See ante, p. 99.**] *om.*   59.43 **See ante, p. 87.**] *om.*
60.3 **painting**] paintings   60.23 **terra cottas**] terra-cottas   60.25 **eastern**] Eastern   60.34–5 **"Pictura ~ Petronius, Init.**] *om.*   60.36–9 **I have ~ fact.**] *om.*   60.40–1 **This was ~ green.**] *om.*
61.16–18 **painting. Gottfried Semper.**] painting." *before Henry Cole's conclusion:*

On the Origin of Polychromy in Architecture

Mr. Semper it was who so skilfully arranged the Canadian Court in the Great Exhibition. His knowledge both of architecture, and generally of decoration, is profound, and his taste excellent. It is men of his acquirements from whom our manufacturers would be likely to obtain great help.

61.29–30 **This bordering ~ black.**] *om.*

On the Origin of Polychromy in Architecture

TEXTUAL RECORD

MS 79   gta, 20-Ms-79, fols. 1r–25v, 'On Tapestry & the origin of Polychronic Decoration' ('Polychronic': *Polychromic*), in Semper's hand; French translation of part of a draft of the fifth chapter of *The Four Elements of Architecture*, written in German to be translated into English (gta, 20-Ms-78; Rachel Chadwick, Edwin Chadwick's wife, began the English translation on or shortly before 26 November 1850 but abandoned it in late January or early February 1851)

MS 80   gta, 20-Ms-80, fols. 1r–17v, partly in Mary Semper's hand (1r–13v, 15r–17v; emendations in Manfred Semper's hand), partly in Manfred Semper's hand (14r–v), early 1880s, copy of MS 79

MS 82   gta, 20-Ms-82, fols. 1r–17v, 'Second Essay. Sur l'origine de l'architecture polychrome', in Semper's hand, dated 2 August 1851

Apology   'On the Origin of Polychromy in Architecture', in Jones 1854a, 47–56 (BL, RB.23.a.29891), *copy-text*

Semper 2014   vol. 2, 551–60, Karge's reprint ed. of Apology

BIBLIOGRAPHY Herrmann 1981, 95–6; Mallgrave 1989, 19; Gnehm 2004, 41–2; Gnehm 2007, 64–5; Weidmann 2014, 11

EXPLANATORY NOTES

Semper's second English essay on polychromy was included in the appendix of Owen Jones's *Apology for the Colouring of the Greek Court in the Crystal Palace* (published on 12 June 1854), together with additional texts on architectural polychromy, among them George Henry Lewes and William Watkiss Lloyd's 'Historical Evidence', which discusses literary sources, and Thomas Leverton Donaldson and Michael Faraday's 'Material Evidence' concerning the polychromy of the Elgin Marbles that were examined in 1836–37, with the results published in 1842. A note to the text explains that it was 'Extracted from an Essay in 1852, and published in Germany under the title of "The Four Elements of Architecture"'. Besides the wrong date – the booklet *Die vier Elemente der Baukunst* was published in 1851 – it would be more accurate to say that the essay published in Jones's *Apology* is an adaptation of Semper's first French manuscript (MS 79) and its revision (MS 82), both of which furnish summaries of the fifth chapter of *The Four Elements of Architecture* (see 315). Both titles of these French versions point to the title of the published English essay: the first one being 'On Tapestry & the origin of Polychromic Decoration', and the other 'Second Essay. Sur l'origine de l'architecture polychrome', which contains the exact French variant of the title of the English essay. The manuscript of the latter is missing but – despite or precisely because of some French remnants – was possibly written directly in English with the assistance of Manfred Semper, Gottfried's son, who helped him in writing letters in English on other occasions. Just to mention two examples of the relations and differences between the French manuscripts and the English text: The beginning of the published essay is the same as that of MS 82; both here omit the beginning of the fifth chapter of *The Four Elements of Architecture* on the composite character of Greek culture, with which MS 79 begins in its turn. However, the English essay incorporates this passage a few pages further on (69.17–70.4). Finally, its concluding part is omitted in both French manuscripts – a condensed discussion of the colour system of the Greeks adapted from the third chapter of *The Four Elements of Architecture*, entitled 'Der chemische Beweis' (Chemical Evidence).

Hans Semper, in a biography of his father, assumed that 'On the Origin of Polychromy in Architecture' appeared 'as an appendix to the Description of the Greek Court in Samuel Sharpe's work on the "Crystal Palace"' (Semper 1880, 20) – a mistake that seems to confuse several publications issued on the occasion of the opening of the Crystal Palace at Sydenham: Jones's *Apology*, George Scharf's *Greek Court Erected in the Crystal Palace* (Scharf 1854) and Jones's *Description of the Egyptian Court*, which contains Samuel Sharpe's 'Historical Sketch of the Egyptian Buildings and Sculpture' (Jones 1854b, 35–71).

61.22–8, 62.1–64.8 **From the time ~ subject.**] cf. Semper 1851b, 56–9

63.9 **πιναξ**] πίναξ (*pinax*)   63.10 **burnt**] *baked* (see also 63.20–1, 63.37, 65.37, 66.1)
63.11 **πινακες**] πίνακες (*pinakes*, plural of *pinax*) in Semper 1851b, 58, 66; translated in Semper 1860/63, 1:293, as 'Täfelung' (panelling)   63.15–16 **Wiegmann ~ causes.**] see Wiegmann 1836, 29–30, 46–7, 79–80; see also Semper's discussion of that point, with reference to Wiegmann 1836, in 'On the Study of Polychromy, and Its Revival' (58.27–31)

64.9–66.15 **The Assyrians ~ fixed.**] cf. Semper 1851b, 59–62   64.34 **irregularity**] 'angulosité' (angularity) in MS 79 and MS 82. An equivalent word is missing in the corresponding passage of *The Four Elements of Architecture*, which describes how the rigid ('steif') posture of Assyrian sculpture is an indication for its origin in embroidery (Semper 1851b, 60).

65.8 **tapesteries**] *tapestries*   65.10 **orignals**] *originals*

66.5 **unburnt**] *unbaked*   66.5–7 **next, they covered with these painted bricks ~ the interior of the room; and lastly, they placed a fire in the room to fix the varnish which covered the walls.**] This passage differs from the French versions of MS 79 and MS 82 in that there the bricks are described as first painted in the order in which they would cover the wall of a room, then numbered and put into the furnace and fixed onto the wall only at the end. In *The Four Elements of Architecture*, the corresponding passage suggests similarly that the bricks were painted and baked ('ornamentirt und glasirt', ornamented and glazed) before being applied to the wall (Semper 1851b, 61–2).   66.21–3 **It is only in the terraces ~ the mason's oldest domain.**] cf. Semper 1851b, 67

67.4–68.13 **The Egyptians ~ covered.**] cf. Semper 1851b, 62–3   67.29 **French expedition**] Napoleon Bonaparte's invasion and occupation of Egypt in 1798–1801

On the Origin of Polychromy in Architecture   323

68.4 **torus moulding**] see the drawing in MS 82 and the corresponding woodcut in Semper 1851b, 63   68.11 **Palace of Osirtesen**] Semper addresses the structure that King Senusret I (Sesostris I) – equated with Osirtasen I in the nineteenth century – is said to have built inside the temple complex at Karnak.   68.14–31 **The Chinese ~ polychromy.**] cf. Semper 1851b, 64   68.32–69.3 **The Indians ~ Greece.**] cf. Semper 1851b, 64

69.4–10 **The Jews ~ "the Enclosure."**] cf. Semper 1851b, 64–5   69.10 **Enclosure**] one of Semper's four elements, the French word in MS 79 and MS 82 being 'l'enclos' and the German word in Semper 1851b, 55, 'die Umfriedigung'   69.12–13 **Temple of the Slaves at Mechlenburg ~ Baron von Rumohr**] 'Slaves': French for *Slavs*. The passage is missing in MS 79, MS 82 and Semper 1851b. This temple of the Slavs was the main sanctuary of a Slavic tribe that is thought to have lived, from the tenth to the twelfth century, in a region on the Baltic Sea that corresponds to Mecklenburg in north Germany; for Semper's reference to the discussion of the temple, see Rumohr 1816/23, 1:9–122.   69.17–70.4 **Hellenic art ~ cosmogony.**] Besides the remarks on polychromy, this passage corresponds to the beginning of the fifth chapter of *The Four Elements of Architecture* (Semper 1851b, 52–3); Semper concludes his essay 'Die grosse Ausstellung' with similar remarks (26.20–4) and adapts the passage in *Science, Industry, and Art* (Semper 1852, 33), in drafts of the first and third lectures that he was to give at the Department of Practical Art (99.22–32, 131.22–5) and in *Style in the Technical and Tectonic Arts* (Semper 1860/63, 1:220, 426–7). While MS 79 begins with this passage, it is missing in MS 82 in which Semper announces that 'Quant à l'ensemble de l'architecture Grecque, il sera demontré dans un autre memoire qu'elle étoit d'un caractère très composite' and then briefly discusses the four elements of architecture in connection with the use of panelling in a variant version of the corresponding passage in *The Four Elements of Architecture* (Semper 1851b, 65–7; see also note 63.11).

70.5–34 **The system ~ easily mastered.**] a passage towards the end of the fifth chapter in Semper 1851b, 97   70.35–40 **It would ~ professed by it.**] missing in MS 79, MS 80 and Semper 1851b

71.1–72.34 **Traces ~ painted eyes.**] This next to last part of the essay is a summary of the findings expounded in the third chapter ('Chemical Evidence') of *The Four Elements of Architecture* (Semper 1851b, 30–45).   71.19–20 **oves, or eggs**] part of an ornament called egg-and-dart moulding; see Semper 1851b, 23 n. *: 'mit blauen Oven am Simms'   71.22–3 **moulding ~ opisthodome of the temple of Theseus**] The opisthodomos is the rear hall of a Greek temple (see Semper 1834, 48; Semper 1851b, 32). Its moulding at the Temple of Theseus is illustrated in *The Use of Colour in Architecture and Sculpture* (pl. 9; Semper 1836, pl. 2 figs. D, E) and in *Style* (Semper 1860/63, 1: pl. IX).   71.36 **plate, in my work ~ panel of the temple of Theseus**] Semper 1836, pl. 4; see also Semper 1860/63, 1: pls. V–VI

72.5–6 **In the portion which I have found in the wall with the niche (see my work), these details are not to be seen.**] The 'portion' refers to a fragment covered with a 'glassy, enamel-like colour' which Semper had discovered – as he says in *The Four Elements of Architecture* in a citation of *Preliminary Observations on Painted Architecture and Sculpture of the Ancients* – in the 'niche between the antae of the porch which were made of fragments of the temple's ceiling during Christian times'. Semper had brought one of these fragments with him 'to the evidence ad oculos for the doubters' (Semper 1834, 48–9, cited in Semper 1851b, 30–1); it is the fragment of the ceiling of the Temple of Theseus reproduced in *The Use of Colour* (pl. 9; Semper 1836, pl. 2 fig. C). In *The Four Elements of Architecture*, in which it is depicted as a woodcut, Semper notes that it had been 'badly damaged on travelling and by touching' (Semper 1851b, 36, 38 fig.; cf. 35, 39 n. *); the fragment is also mentioned and re-

324 Polychromy in Architecture

produced as a colour plate in *Style* (Semper 1860/63, 1:523, pl. II). 72.7 **Monument of Lysicrates**] cf. Semper 1851b, 37–8. In *Style*, Semper discusses this monument only briefly with respect to colour (Semper 1860/63, 1:485) but repeatedly in connection with ceramics and tectonics (Semper 1860/63, 2:95, 115 n. 1, 242 n. 2 and fig.) and stereotomy (Semper 1860/63, 2:355, 385 fig., 468–71, 473–4). 72.18 **Some years after my sojourn at Athens**] see 318, Explanatory Notes 49.38–42, 50.36–7 72.18–20 **portions of this building ~ Hecatompedon**] This excavation of the Parthenon and parts of the Hecatompedon temple is the one that was undertaken in 1835–36, reported by Charles Holte Bracebridge (see note 72.33–4) and mentioned by Semper in *The Four Elements of Architecture* (Semper 1851b, 43). 72.25 **orvolos**] *ovolos*; the ornament in the form of carved 'oves, or eggs' of the Greek convex moulding (see note 71.19–20) 72.26 **Tower of the Winds**] In Semper 1851b, 37, this octagonal tower in Athens is called 'Tempel der Winde' (Temple of the Winds). 72.33–4 **Mr. Bracebridge ~ painted eyes.**] Charles Holte Bracebridge described these statues in a letter of 1837 which was published as part of the report on the examination of the Elgin Marbles in 1842 (Hamilton 1842, 104–5). In *The Four Elements of Architecture*, Semper paraphrases Bracebridge's whole letter in German (Semper 1851b, 42–4); most of it was reprinted in Owen Jones's *Apology* (Jones 1854, 39–40). 72.34–73.7 **The figures of the pediment ~ gilding.**] This concluding passage is not to be found in *The Four Elements of Architecture*.

73.4 **Trajan Column ~ examined**] a reference to Semper's first publication on polychromy in antiquity, 'Scoprimento d'antichi colori sulla colonna di Trajano', published in the *Bullettino* of the Prussian Instituto di corrispondenza archeologica in Rome (Semper 1833). Semper refers to this text again in *Style* (Semper 1860/63, 1:500); on Trajan's Column, see also Semper's *Preliminary Observations* (1834, 36–9).

Pl. 10: Design of certificate for art instruction at Science and Art Department, 1853 (gta, 20-0163-265C)

DEPARTMENT OF PRACTICAL ART

Introduction

From the autumn term of 1852 to the autumn term of 1854, which lasted up to the end of February 1855, Semper taught at the Department of Practical Art – the school founded by Henry Cole under this name in the wake of the Great Exhibition in early 1852 and reshaped by the Board of Trade to become the Department of Science and Art in March 1853. By then, it also included the Schools of Art (the former Government Schools of Design), the School of Science Applied to Mining and the Arts (the former School of Mines), the Museum of Ornamental Art, the Museum of Practical Geology and other institutions. Semper started teaching on 18 October 1852 at Marlborough House in Pall Mall, London – the Department's location – as the *First Report of the Department of Practical Art* records (DPA[1], 225). His subject area, as described in the appointment letter of 11 September 1852, was 'the principles and practice of Ornamental Art applied to Metal Manufactures' (226.7). However, Semper's responsibility at the Department soon underwent changes, encompassing architecture officially from the autumn of 1853.

When Semper's appointment as a professor was announced in *The Athenaeum* on 25 September 1852, his teaching area was already described against the backdrop of his architectural expertise. Along with Octavius Hudson, who was to teach 'Ornamental Art applied to woven fabrics of all kinds and to paper staining', the announcement first states that 'Prof. Semper of Berlin' (Dresden would have been the correct location) had been appointed for the field of 'Ornamental Metal Work' and then notes that 'Besides his constructive knowledge, Prof. Semper has made the treatment of metals his particular study.' Henry Cole, the superintendent of the Department, had already observed in December 1851 – in the concluding note to a partial reprint of 'On the Study of Polychromy, and Its Revival' – that Semper's 'knowledge both of architecture, and generally of decoration, is profound, and his taste excellent. It is men of his acquirements from whom our manufacturers would be likely to obtain great help' (321, Print Variants 61.16–18). Before Semper's architectural background officially came to the fore, his teaching area was specified and expanded to include jewellery, enamels and even furniture, as Cole's prospectuses for Semper's class indicate (see 228, 554). An advertisement signed by the Department's secretary, Walter Ruding Deverell, in *The Athenaeum* of 8 January 1853 (announcing the resumption of 'Special Classes for the Study of the Principles of Ornamental Art' on 10 January) already described Semper's and Octavius Hudson's subject areas as being 'Ornamental Art in Metals, Furniture, and all kinds of Woven Fabrics'.

Overall, Semper was apparently soon able to extend his subject area to include the industrial arts in general and architecture in particular. In his 'Plan of Instruction for the Metal and Furniture Classes', drafted by 1 February 1853 and published in the *First Report of the Department of Practical Art*, he proposed that the curriculum should also include lectures 'on the relations of the different branches of practical art to each other, and to architecture' (88.13–14) – which was to be the title of his first public lecture, held at the Department on 20 May 1853 (see 96.3–4, 97). A text by the art superintendent, Richard Redgrave, in the same *Report* confirms at least an intention to enlarge Semper's responsibility to also include 'architectural arrangements of surfaces' and 'architectural construction, &c.' (Redgrave 1853, 370). Semper's area of responsibility in the Department, which soon became wide-ranging, is reflected in his teaching for the autumn term of 1853, which started on 3 October and was announced in *The Athenaeum* of 10 September 1853 under the title 'Practical Construction, including Architecture, Building, and the various processes of Plastic Decoration, Furniture, and Metal Working'. This corresponds to Semper's subject area as stated in the 'Prospectus of the Central Training School of Art' for October 1853 in the *First Report of the Department of Science and Art* (DSA[1], 195). In the area of technical courses, Semper was now the only person responsible for architecture, which had been taught by Charles James Richardson under the title of 'Architectural Details and Practical Construction' from the autumn term of 1852 (DPA[1], 225, 383); Cole proposed to terminate Richardson's appointment on 23 July 1853 'to coincide with reopening of School in Autumn' (Herrmann 1984, 277 n. 247). In the autumn terms of 1853 and 1854, architecture became an integral part of Semper's special class, which, in his two reports on his teaching during 1852–54, is called the 'Class for Practical Construction, Architecture, and Plastic Decoration' (88, 91) – additionally termed as 'Plastic and Architectural Design' for the autumn term of 1854 (DSA[2], 201).

Before Semper was entrusted with teaching on the subject of metals, Cole appears to have considered him primarily as a professor of ceramics. Semper himself had drawn attention to this in a letter of 29 January 1852 in which he offered Cole his services in the context of the imminent 'Establishment of a School for art and industry' (which was to become the Department of Practical Art). As 'the head of an practical atelier for architects and artisans' in Dresden, he wrote to Cole, the 'decorative part of architecture' had been one of his particular specialities, including works in bronze, furniture and 'the exigencies of China fabrication'. To document this, he enclosed with the letter a basic treatise on painting on porcelain (in Semper's English, 'the first part of an elemental treaty on China picture') – a treatise that he had written in French in Sèvres in June 1850 (gta, 20-Ms-47). Cole – who promised on 4 February 1852 that 'If I have an opportunity I will endeavour to promote your wishes' – sent Semper to Herbert Minton's pottery factory in Stoke-on-Trent for three weeks on 20 March 1852, asking him to prepare a lecture on ceramic manufacture (Herrmann 1984, 58–60). However, shortly after Semper's return, Cole commissioned him in mid-April 1852 to 'provide a kind of illustrated catalogue raisonné for the whole field of metals technology', as Semper wrote to his publisher, Eduard Vieweg, on 20 May 1852. In the same letter, he presumed that he was awarded the commission due to the attention he had received from his booklet *Wissenschaft, Industrie und Kunst* (Science, Industry, and Art) and described it as a task that would serve as an 'introduction to more permanent official work' at the 'School of Design' (261–2).

In asking Semper to specialize in metals, Cole had apparently changed his mind after having been unable to attract Matthew Digby Wyatt to take up the post. This was despite the fact that Wyatt – who was just completing a book on *Metal-Work and its Artistic Design* (Wyatt 1852) – had told him on 18 March 1852 that he was 'willing to lecture on Metals' (Cole Diary). Yet Semper expanded his catalogue of 'Practical Art in Metals and hard Materials; its Technology, History and Styles' to include both ceramic and metal vessels (NAL, 86.FF.64, art. 3.2, 95–142; cf. Semper 2007a, 189–227). What he presents in this part of the catalogue might correspond to elements of the lecture that he was commissioned to prepare in connection with his visit to Minton. Around mid-August, Semper sent the catalogue to Cole, who began to read it on 19 August. However, Cole had prepared Semper's appointment before receiving the catalogue – as he noted in his diary, he had already 'Settled Class book in Metals for Semper' with Joseph Warner Henley, the president of the Board of Trade, on 2 July 1852. On 8 September, he arranged with Henley for Semper to be appointed to a professorship in metals, and Semper approved the conditions of employment on 10 September 1852 (Cole Diary). But in the list of the Department's prospectuses, directly after the listing for Semper's class on 'Principles and Practice of Ornamental Art applied to Furniture, Metals, Jewellery, and Enamels', Cole still continued to refer to Semper as the person to contact for information concerning 'Pottery, and other Manufactures' (228.31–3). Semper himself included pottery in the draft of his 'Plan of Instruction' (373.1).

In addition to teaching in the Department, Semper was busy with research work for its Museum of Ornamental Art, which opened provisionally in Marlborough House on 19 May 1852 and definitively on 6 September 1852. According to his terms of employment, he was obliged to 'report on Collections ... and upon the state of the Museum, Collection of Casts, and Library of the Department' and 'to inform the Superintendents of any examples which ... the Museum should possess' (226.28–31). The research included a 'Report on the Private Collection of Arms at Windsor Castle', a list of suggested purchases in relation to 'Berlin Productions of Plastical Art, Metal Casts, Plaster Casts' and 'Observations on Some of the Specimens of Metal Work' in the Museum (76–85). All of this was related to one of the central issues for which the Department was aiming to provide new foundations in art education – namely surface decoration. Semper's own objective was to convey the theoretical role of ornament in direct relation to practical concerns and to provide students with opportunities for practical collaboration in courses that were organized along the lines of the studio workshop. Semper's theoretical and practical position on ornament was expressed in his design for the school certificate of the Department of Science and Art, approved on 10 September 1853 (pl. 10): in his pencilled draft, the central inscription on one of the two vertical bands of the ornamental frame, which stands for 'Industry', bears the name 'Jacquard' – symbolizing the industrialization of the textile arts and the fundamental role that Semper assigned to textiles not only for ornaments but for the arts in general (the final version of the certificate has 'Flaxman' instead). In *Style in the Technical and Tectonic Arts*, he reproduced the lateral and central pendant triangles of the certificate when discussing tectonics (Semper 1860/63, 2:220–1).

In his 'Plan of Instruction for the Metal and Furniture Classes', Semper had already proposed that students should assist in the professor's practical work (86.7), and he referred to opportunities to carry this out in the two reports on his 'Class for Practical Construction' – opportunities including the commission to design the funeral car of the Duke of Wellington, at the beginning of the autumn term of 1852 (89.16–25), and the commission to design one of the commercial exhibition spaces in the rebuilt Crystal Palace in Sydenham in 1854, the Mixed Fabrics Court – one of Semper's rare architectural commissions during the London years, which was actually executed. The practically oriented side of Semper's teaching met with some scepticism from Henry Cole, who empha-

Introduction 331

sized in the conditions for Semper's appointment that it was a 'new experiment to afford practical instruction in Art for industrial purposes' (227.2–3).

In the autumn term of 1854 – from October 1854 to February 1855 – Semper for the last time held his class on 'Practical Construction, including Architecture, Building, and the various processes of Plastic Decoration, Furniture, and Metal Working', as it was announced in *The Athenaeum* on 9 September 1854. His presence and availability in the spring term, from 1 March to 31 July 1855, was also mentioned. However, at this point he was only sporadically active for the Department and was otherwise busy with moving to Zurich. On 16 November 1854, Semper had accepted the offer of the Chair of Architecture at the newly founded Swiss Federal Polytechnic School. Apart from a visit to Switzerland lasting around a week, he spent a considerable part of the spring term of 1855, from 21 March to 5 June, in Paris, where under Cole's supervision he was concerned with the decoration of the British section of the Exposition universelle on behalf of the Department of Science and Art.

Also during the spring term of 1855, at the command of Prince Albert, Semper designed a vast complex of buildings in part of the area of South Kensington that had gradually been purchased by the commissioners for the Exhibition of 1851. As Henry Cole noted in a memorandum of 24 May 1855, Prince Albert suggested a building that was to combine 'temporary galleries for Marlborough House Museum, Educational Museum, Patent Museum, &c.', and – like the Palais Royal in Paris – 'shops with a colonnade, and flats for residence above', all arranged around 'a large covered building suitable for the performance of Music'. Semper presented the design (reproduced in Physick 1994) to Cole on 15 June 1855; ten days later, the Board of Trade had the plans examined by a Mr Cubitt (probably the building developer Thomas Cubitt) and the engineer Samuel Morton Peto. Both of them considered 'that the scheme could not be carried out to pay' (Herrmann 1984, 79–80, 282 n. 311). On 26 or 27 June, Semper left London via Rouen and Paris for Zurich, where he arrived (with a ticket from Basel dated 11 July) on 12 July 1855.

Richard Redgrave had already noted in May 1855 that the 'loss of the valuable services of Professor Semper' had 'not … yet been adequately supplied' (DSA³, 225). The respect Semper enjoyed in London certainly contributed to his thoughts of returning there while he was experiencing professional frustration during his early period in Zurich. In mid-1856, he asked the industrialist Carl Wilhelm Siemens (who was working in London) to inquire of Cole whether he might return to the Department of Science and Art, under the condition that he would have 'a good prospect of practical work in addition to theoretical work'. Following prolonged clarifications, Cole asked Semper on 4 July 1857 to 'give me an idea of what sort of arrangement you would desire to have made with you'. In the draft of his response, Semper demanded 'architectural work or work as an artist, and not merely as a teacher'. With the approval of the Board of Education, Cole reported back to him on 1 August 1857 that he was 'authorized to offer the following terms for your consideration. I° You would have to give a course of practical instruction to a class of Students and some public lectures on Architecture .... II° The Department would give you other work connected with Architecture'. Semper negotiated with Cole in London on 4 September 1857 on the conditions of employment and discovered – as he wrote to Bertha Semper – that he was to be employed 'on extensive buildings' in South Kensington. On 30 November 1857, he tried through Siemens to persuade Cole to increase the associated salary. The effort was unsuccessful, and Semper abandoned the idea of returning to London.

BIBLIOGRAPHY Semper 1880, 20–1; Cole 1884, 1:281–9, 294–301, 305–7, 322; Leisching 1903; Ettlinger 1940; Pevsner 1940, 251–3, 255–6, 264; Ettlinger 1964; Macdonald 1970; Sheppard 1975; Herrmann 1976, 236–7; Reising 1976, 56–63; Van Zanten 1977b, 242–56; Diephouse 1978; Herrmann 1978, 62–93; Schädlich 1980; Herrmann 1984, 56–83; Physick 1994; Mallgrave 1996, 208–18; Burton 1999, 46–7, 112–13; Bonython/Burton 2003, 145–69, 172–5; Hildebrand 2003, 263–8; Squicciarino 2009, 143–8, 256–75, 288–93; Orelli-Messerli 2010, 163–293; Weidmann 2010, 341, 569–77; Bryant 2011; Hildebrand 2013; Chestnova 2014; Hildebrand 2020a, 119–31; Hvattum 2021; Nichols 2021

Report on the Private Collection of Arms at Windsor Castle

TEXTUAL RECORD

MS 108	gta, 20-Ms 108, fols. 1r–2v (2v blank), in Semper's hand
MS 109	gta, 20-Ms-109, fols. 1r–2v, in Semper's hand
MS 110	gta, 20-Ms-110, fols. 1r–4v (1v blank), in Semper's hand
MS 107	gta, 20-Ms-107, fols. 1r–11v (all versos blank), in Semper's hand (emendations in Henry Cole's hand), dated 20 September 1852
DPA¹	'Report on the Private Collection of Arms at Windsor Castle', in *First Report of the Department of Practical Art*, London: Eyre & Spottiswoode for Her Majesty's Stationery Office, 1853, 364–7 (NAL, 602.AD.0777), dated 20 September 1852, *copy-text*
Semper 1884	'Bericht über die Waffensammlung in Windsor Castle', 76–83, dated 20 September 1852, German trans. of DPA¹ (76.6–23, 76.25–80.9, 80.12–13)
Semper 2014	vol. 2, 538–41, Karge's reprint ed. of DPA¹

Report on the Private Collection of Arms at Windsor Castle 333

BIBLIOGRAPHY Herrmann 1978, 72 n. 263, 131–2; Herrmann 1981, 107; Herrmann 1984, 277 n. 247; Squicciarino 2009, 347–50

EXPLANATORY NOTES

Semper's report on the collection of arms at Windsor Castle is related to the Museum of Ornamental Art, which was established with the Department of Practical Art at Marlborough House in Pall Mall, London, and fully opened to the school and the public on 6 September 1852. Initially also known as the Museum of Manufactures, it took over holdings of the former London School of Design and was supplemented by donations and loans, as well as exhibits acquired from the Great Exhibition, to form a comprehensive collection of the decorative arts. Semper's report was the first commission from the Department of Practical Art, and its purpose was to identify arms from Queen Victoria's collection that could be recommended for loan to the museum.

On 9 September 1852, one day after Semper's appointment had been decided, Henry Cole sent him and Richard Redgrave to Windsor to inspect the royal collection of arms (Cole Diary). In addition to its content, the text is of particular interest because Semper's complete draft with Cole's emendations is extant (345–52). In his report, Semper not only points out weapons of instructive value but also discusses the artistic significance of weapons in general and recommends that the Department purchase further teaching materials from this area. In the process, he elaborates on the observations on weapons as a special field of metalwork from his catalogue of 'Practical Art in Metals and hard Materials', previously commissioned by Cole (NAL, 86.FF.64, art. 3.2, 95–142; cf. Semper 2007a, 180–4). He now more explicitly declares the weapons industry to be 'that branch of Metalworking, which affords the greatest interest for the Study of Ornamental art' (339.15–17).

Semper completed the report, as stated in the last of the four drafts and in the printed version, on 20 September 1852 (80.12, 348.27) and sent it – illustrated with three drawings of swords (347.15) – to Cole a week later. Cole revised the report, as stated at the top of the same draft and in his diary, on 28 September (348, note 345.1). When Semper's report was printed in the *First Report of the Department of Practical Art*, which appeared in the spring of 1853, it underwent further minor changes. It likely contributed to the Queen lending to the Department of Science and Art some 150 items of arms and armour in the spring of 1854. In *Style in the Technical and Tectonic Arts*, Semper refers to the report in the section on metals technology and in relation to the 'practical question of style', arguing that the 'armourer must follow the strictest laws of practicality' and 'Therefore at all times there prevailed a certain relative chastity and purity of taste in weapons' (Semper 1860/63, 2:549).

76.1 **B.**] designates the report as one of several miscellaneous texts in 'Appendix VII' of the *First Report of the Department of Practical Art*, to which also belongs Semper's 'Plan of Instruction' (85–8)   76.9–10 **principal laws of fitness, convenience, and style**] a variant of Vitruvius's three architectural principles of *firmitas, utilitas, venustas* (solidity, utility, beauty)   76.19–28 **Secondly ~ study of style ~ Thirdly ~ study of ~ the history of styles ~ distinguishable from each other**] Cole here changed the meaning of the last sentence in a not insignificant way by altering Semper's 'study of ... the *Historical Style*' (345.20–1; italics in original) to 'study of ... the history of styles'. For Semper's understand-

334   Department of Practical Art

ing of the 'term' *style* as defined by the artistic use of 'means', the 'limits' of the 'task and problem', the 'accessories' and the 'peculiar character' of works 'of the different countries and ages', see his definition and discussion of style in two of his lectures of 1853, 'On the Relations of the Different Branches of Industrial Art to Each Other and to Architecture. Third Version' (108–11) and 'General Remarks on the Different Styles in Art' (119–21). 76.29–30 **The history of ornamental art in metals cannot therefore be better illustrated than by a collection of arms and weapons**] Semper's complete draft here has 'The History of Ornamental Art can not better be summed as by a collection of Arms and Weapons' (345.23–4). Cole replaced 'summed as' with 'illustrated than' and restricted Semper's contention that weapons are representative of the history of ornamental art in general by adding 'in Metals' to 'Ornamental Art'.

77.5 **relative purity and chastity of taste and style**] Semper adopted this sentence in *Style* (Semper 1860/63, 2:549, cited above, 333) and had already put forward the corresponding view in *Science, Industry, and Art*, where he contends – when speaking of the 'confused muddle of forms or childish dalliance' of objects shown at the Great Exhibition – that 'At most, objects whose seriousness of use does not permit anything useless, such as carriages, weapons, musical instruments, and the like, sometimes show more healthiness in the decoration and refinement of the forms strictly defined by their purpose' (Semper 1852, 11–12). 77.15 **Vienna, formerly at Castle Ambrass**] In his catalogue of 'Practical Art in Metals and hard Materials', Semper refers for the former collection of Ambras Castle in Innsbruck to Primisser 1819 and Richter 1835 (Semper 2007a, 67).   77.26–8 **works of Meyrick, of Tubinal on the Madrid armoury, that on the imperial collections of Russia, and Baron von Ebner's work on costumes of the middle ages**] Semper's drafts have the name of the misprinted 'Tubinal' correctly as 'Jubinal' (340.1, 341.17, 346.24), while the error in the name of the misprinted 'Ebner' is also contained in Semper's complete draft (346.25) and in one of the fragmentary drafts (341.19); a third, fragmentary, draft has the correct name of 'Hefner' (340.5). In one of the drafts (339.26), Semper refers to the two volumes of *Engraved Illustrations of Antient Arms and Armour* that depict Samuel Rush Meyrick's collection at Goodrich Court, Herefordshire (Meyrick 1830). He had already requested Meyrick's *Critical Inquiry into Antient Armour* (Meyrick 1824) from the British Museum Library on 30 June 1852, when he was working on his catalogue of 'Practical Art in Metals and hard Materials' (221.26–31). Publication of Achille Jubinal's work on the Royal Armory at Madrid (*La Armeria real*) started in 1837 (Jubinal 1837/54). The three-volume work on the Russian imperial collection of arms at Tsarskoye Selo, near St Petersburg, with lithographs after drawings by Alois Rockstuhl, was published in 1835–53 (Gille 1835/53), and Jakob Heinrich von Hefner-Alteneck's *Trachten des christlichen Mittelalters* in three volumes from 1840 to 1854 (Hefner-Alteneck 1840/54). In one of the drafts (340.4), Semper additionally mentions the section on armoury in *Le Moyen-Âge et la Renaissance* (Saulcy 1851), which is also cited in his catalogue of 'Practical Art in Metals and hard Materials' (Semper 2007a, 107). Most of these works are referred to in *Style*: Meyrick's collection at Goodrich Court in the section on ceramics (Semper 1860/63, 2:70), his *Critical Inquiry into Antient Armour* in the section on metals technology, together with Jubinal's *Armeria real* (Semper 1860/63, 2:550). Semper also refers to the latter for examples of Moorish swords as counterparts to the 'Saracen sabre allegedly from Charlemagne's time', which was part of the imperial regalia of the Holy Roman Empire (Semper 1860/63, 2:546 n. 4). He had it sketched by an unknown person during his period in London (gta, 20-1-16), possibly for the catalogue of 'Practical Art in

Metals and hard Materials', where it is mentioned (Semper 2007a, 110, 181). Hefner's work on medieval costume is cited in *Style* particularly for illustrations of the 'bronze effigy of Emperor Louis the Bavarian' and the 'grave plate of Rudolf of Swabia ... in the Cathedral of Merseburg' (Semper 1860/63, 1:170; 2:526 n. 1).   77.28–9 **acquisition for the library of the Department of Practical Art**] In a report on the Department's library, dated 10 November 1852, Ralph Nicholson Wornum illustrates desiderata through the example of books on metalwork that are lacking and notes that 'the Library possesses neither Jubinal's great work on the "Royal Armoury of Madrid," containing beautiful illustrations of the most remarkable ornamental metal-work in existence; nor the great work of Rockstuhl on the "Imperial Armoury of Russia," containing Oriental as well as European specimens; nor does it possess even Sir J. Meyrick's "Illustrations of ancient Arms and Armour"' (DPA¹, 296). The Department purchased the second edition of Meyrick's *Critical Inquiry into Ancient Armour* in 1854 (DSA², 192; Meyrick 1842); the other books recommended for purchase by Semper – with the exception of Meyrick's *Engraved Illustrations* and Hefner's work – were also acquired by 1855 at the latest (Wornum 1855, 161).

78.13–14 **breast-plates, forming part of the armour of Tippo Saib (hanging in the passage, decorated like a tent)**] Tipu Sahib's armour, captured after his defeat and death at Seringapatam, was placed in a niche fitted up as a tent in the North Corridor of Windsor Castle (known today as the China Corridor) – then the location of the armoury.   78.22 **Rénaissance**] Two of Semper's drafts correctly have 'Renaissance' (342.45, 347.13).   78.24 **swords ~ three of the first distinction**] Two of Semper's drafts here refer to sketches of these swords (342.47, 347.15). The sketches (preserved at gta, 20-2) are drawn in Semper's hand on three individual sheets and show the hilts of two of the three swords that Semper praises as being 'of the first distinction': The first, erroneously attributed to Benvenuto Cellini (78.25), and the other with the number '222' (78.29). Semper's third example – the sword numbered '276' (78.31) – has not been identified. The third extant drawing corresponds to the 'sword of the time of Louis XVI.' (78.38).   78.25–6 **One of them ~ attributed to Benvenuto Cellini without reason**] The catalogue number of this sword is also missing in two of Semper's drafts (343.1, 347.17). The sword in question is a rapier of *c.* 1640, reputed to have belonged to John Hampden; the blade is stamped with the marks of Clemens Horn of Solingen (Laking 1904, 32–3, pl. 10 [no. 65; RCIN 62994]). One of the three drawings that Semper had attached to the draft of his report shows the hilt in all its details, with subjects from the life of King David (gta, 20-2).   78.26–7 **shield belonging to the Queen, which is at present in the Museum**] This shield with scenes from the life of Julius Caesar 'has been supposed to be the work of Cellini; another tradition regarding it is, that it was presented to Henry VIII, by Francis I' (Meyrick 1842, 3:114 n. 3); it is now believed to be of French or Belgian origin, from the mid-sixteenth century (Laking 1904, 35–7, pl. 12 [no. 71; RCIN 62978]; Norman/Eaves 2016, 277–82). The so-called Cellini Shield was exhibited at the Museum of Ornamental Art (CatM¹, 59; DPA¹, 287, 386) after it was brought as a loan from Windsor Castle on 12 May 1852 (Cole Diary).   78.29 **The second, No. 222**] a sword with an iron hilt of the first quarter of the seventeenth century. The pommel and the outer side of the guards are encrusted with flowers and leaves in silver against a blackened ground (gta, 20-2; Laking 1904, 29, pl. 9 [no. 60; RCIN 62964]).   78.33 **sword, probably of James II.'s time, has a hilt formed by serpents**] possibly the sword once believed to belong to William the Conqueror but later identified as being of French workmanship of the first quarter of the seventeenth century. Its pommel is 'shaped as four intertwined serpents', while 'numerous serpent-like shapes that coil and intercoil' form 'the knuckle-guard, the shells, the quillon and the counter-guards' (Laking 1904, 204, pl. 30 [no. 681]).   78.35–6 **Dutch sword of the 17th century ~ decorated with ~ medallions, with portraits of some heroes of the Dutch history**] possibly a sword with a hilt which is, if not identical with, then similar to that of the German sword said to have been a wedding gift on the occasion of the marriage of Frederick William of Brandenburg to Louise Henriette of Nassau. The portraits of the medallions in relief on this hilt are identified as those of the descendants of the house of Brandenburg from the late fifteenth to the early seventeenth centuries (Laking 1904, 27–8 [no. 58; RCIN 62988]). In one of the drafts, Semper has – instead of 'portraits of some heroes of the Dutch history' – 'Portraits of the time of the Dutch Revolution' (343.11). In the complete draft, he had altered 'Dutch Revolution' to 'Dutch History' (347.27).   78.38–9 **sword of the time of Louis XVI. ~ in the catalogue ~ given as an English work ~ with enamel pictures in cameo**] The hilt of this sword bears the Paris hallmark of 1786 (Laking 1904, 177, pl. 24 [no. 609]). Semper has annotated his drawing of the hilt with detailed comments on the colouring (gta, 20-2). The technique of 'enamel pictures in cameo' is referred to in Semper's drafts as 'en Camajeu' (343.13, 347.30; properly spelled *en camaïeu*, a technique that imitates cameos), altered by Cole to 'en Cameo' (350, note 347.30). The pictures are oval panels in shadings of blue and white, which are dispersed about the hilt and represent cupids, gods and goddesses, and musical and warlike trophies.

79.13–14 **arrangement in the Museum of Practical Geology**] The Museum of Practical Geology in London, established in 1835, reopened in a new building in Jermyn Street in May 1851. In addition to the fact that Semper had the opportunity to visit the institution, he had certainly also read about it in the papers, for example in the article on the Museum's inauguration published in the third issue of the German Supplement of *The Illustrated London News* on 17 May 1851 – the issue in which Semper's essay on the Great Exhibition was published (see 20–6). Another article on the Museum appeared in the fifth issue of the German Supplement of *The Illustrated London News* on 31 May 1851 (ILN Suppl. 1851). In this article, the objective of the Museum is described as being 'to demonstrate the different ways in which ores are formed and, as far as is practicable, to show the way in which mining is carried out', accompanied by 'models of the machines and hand tools used for the work' and explanations of the 'chemical process by which the various metals are obtained', as well as of their 'use … in art and manufacture'. Besides this, 'earth and clay materials … for the production of glass and porcelain' were exhibited in the context of 'giving a history of the various manufactured products', including a historically comprehensive collection of pottery, glass fabrication, building and ornamental stones from all parts of the British Empire. The 'similar arrangements' based on a predominance of the 'artistic element', which Semper suggests for the Museum of Ornamental Art (79.16–17), correspond to the concept of an ideal museum that he developed in the catalogue of 'Practical Art in Metals and hard Materials' in 1852, in which he also mentions the Museum of Practical Geology (Semper 2007a, 55–8).   79.20 **Lazarino Cominazo guns**] Lazarino Cominazzo (also Cominazo) is the name of an Italian family of gunsmiths, active in Brescia from the sixteenth century; for three pairs of flintlock pistols of the second half of the seventeenth century, stamped with the name 'Lazarino Cominazzo', see Laking 1904, 114, pl. 22 (nos. 357–8; RCIN 61065); 134 (nos. 439–40; RCIN 67158); 140 (nos. 471–2; RCIN 61606).   79.23–5 **gun of Louis XIV. ~ by Piraube ~ probably the finest gun in the world ~ head-sight steel ~ in open work**]

Report on the Private Collection of Arms at Windsor Castle

a richly ornamented hunting gun ornamented with classical scenes, made by Bertrand Piraube in 1682 for Louis XIV (Laking 1904, 129–30 [no. 425; RCIN 61115]). It has a pierced rear sight, which corresponds to the 'open work' of the part which Semper calls 'Hindsight' in the complete draft (348.5). In the same draft, Semper considers this weapon to be 'the finest gun in the world', which was altered by Cole to 'probably the finest gun in the world' (348.4; 350, note 348.4).   79.29 **Spanish gun of Joachim da Zelaja**] for the flintlock fowling piece by the gunsmith Joaquín de Zelaya, signed and dated 'Joachin de Zelaia, en Madrid. Año de 1753', see Laking 1904, 126 (no. 414; RCIN 67155)   79.29–31 **pistols ~ by Weiss at Suhl ~ two guns ~ finest specimens of Louis XV. style**] for a mid-eighteenth century pair of flintlock pistols and a flintlock rifle by Johann Georg Weiss of Suhl, Thuringia, see Laking 1904, 123–4 (no. 405; RCIN 61118); 142, pl. 23 (nos. 485–6; RCIN 61562)   79.34 **Kuchenrenter guns and pistols**] Kuchenreuter (correctly named in the complete draft, 348.14) is the name of a family of gunsmiths who were active in Regensburg from the seventeenth century onwards; for mid-eighteenth-century guns and pistols by Johann Jacob Kuchenreuter, see Laking 1904, 90 (no. 281; RCIN 61752); 123 (no. 403; RCIN 61098); 141 (nos. 479–80; RCIN 62951); 142 (nos. 487–8; RCIN 61136).

80.6 **répoussé works**] *repoussé works*; 'Repousse works' in the complete draft (348.23) 80.8–10 **that electrotypes be made ~ electrotypes ~ of the beautiful shields which are at Dresden**] Electrotypes, making use of an electro-galvanic process named after Luigi Galvani, are reproductions made of base materials, such as plaster, wax or gutta-percha, and an electrolytic coating usually of copper. In the draft before Cole's revision, Semper specifies that 'One of the Officers of the Historical Museum at Dr. is a clever Electrotypist and has allready reproduced several of the beautifull Shields which are at Dresden' (348.25–6). This 'clever' official was Gustav Büttner, Inspector of the Royal Historical Museum at Dresden, who had displayed 'Three electrotype copies of classical shields' at the Great Exhibition (ODIC 1851, 3:1113 [no. 187]). Emil Braun, Semper's mentor, had founded a galvanoplastic institute in the later 1840s and, in February 1851, tried to persuade Semper to act as an agent for him to gain market share in England, where he was in contact with Elkington, the English market leader in Birmingham (Braun to Semper, 19 February 1851, gta, 20-K-1851-02-19:1). Semper discusses Braun's collaboration with Elkington in *Science, Industry, and Art* (Semper 1852, 49) and classifies 'Galvanoplastik' as being among the ceramic arts grouped under the architectural element of the hearth in his 'Outline of a Cultural-Historical Exhibition' (40.30). He again refers to electrotypes in his recommendation of purchases for the Museum of Ornamental Art (82.2).

MANUSCRIPT VARIANTS

MS 108

The instruments of war and of Chase, notwithstanding their terrible uses and applications, have been at all times considered as the true and most worthy ornaments of man. – These two very distinct Qualifications of the arms and veapons, as ornaments and as instruments, for or against destruction, procure the greatest interest to them with respect to the 5 Study of ornamental art, its history and Style; for in no other application ornamental art is more strictly bound to observe the first principles of Style as it is the case with the Arms and Weapons. ¦

fol. 1r

Department of Practical Art

fol. 1v   The Armurers and Swordcuttlers were the conservators of the processes and traditions of the art of Metalworking through the Centuries of Barbarism, and the same observed relative purity of style in the ornamentations of their products amidst the Extravagancies of other times, when true principles and laws of ornamental art were misregarded at every other occasion.

And while thus they were so strongly resistant to Barbarism and Degeneration in the times of Decay, we find them at the Summit of high Art in the times of florishing civilisation. The masterpieces of the Italian Armurers Swordcuttlers and Gunmakers of the Period of the Renaissance, give interesting Evidences of the absolute Validity of Principles not only for

fol. 2r   ornamental art, | but for Art in General. – .

The importance of this branch of industry for the study of art, history of art, and Style has been justly appreciated in our times, while such objects, as arms, veapons and Costumes were formerly collected for their historical or ethnological interest they afforded.

Such were the original caracters of the most important wellknown armuries of Europe; but they have been long time unhappily neglected,

---

337.1 **The instruments**] *after two variant beginnings, the first one del. and the second one undel.:*

The instruments of war and Chase, the arms and weapons have been objects of decoration and[1] art since the beginning of human civilisation. They have allways been regarded as the very[2] ornaments of the warriors,[3] and
The instruments of war and of Chase were objects of Decoration and art, since the first[4] beginning of Civilisation, they having been allways considered as the most distinguished ornements of the body[5], notwithstanding their terrible and dangerous uses,[6] which last confined the

---

1 **decoration and**] *repl. del.* ornamental   ornamental] *after del.* decorative
2 **very**] *above del.* most worthy   3 **warriors,**] *before del.* notwithstanding   4 **first**]
after del. earliest   5 **the body**] *after del.* the warriors and   6 **uses,**] *altered from* ~;
before del. The last   The last] *after del.* which forcibly confined the decorative arts

---

337.1 **terrible**] *after del.* dangerous and   337.2 **have**] *after del.* were objects of Decoration and Art since the beginning of Civilisation, and   **man.**] *repl. del.* the warlike Youths.
337.3 **These two very distinct Qualifications**] *repl. del.* These double destinations
These] *altered from* This   destinations] *above del.* caracter   337.6 **strictly**] *before del.* and forcibly   **observe**] *after del.* hold and
338.1 **The Armurers**] *after del. on fol. 1r–v*

We observe[1] an early endeavour for embellishments[2] in the armurers[3] works of ¦ the times, when practice of art. was sunk into decline or allmost lost,[4] and, at[5] other times, when true principles and laws of ornamental art were misregarded and forgotten, a sort of relative purity of Style is allways to be

---

1 **observe**] *after del.* therefore   2 **an early endeavour for embellishments**] *repl. del.* a relative elevation and elegance of Style   a] *undel.*   elegance] *repl. del.* purity   3 **armurers**] *after del.* ornaments   4 **lost,**] *altered from* ~; *before del.* we see a sort of purity and sobriety of Style   5 **at**] *interl. after del.* amidst of the extravagances of

Report on the Private Collection of Arms at Windsor Castle 339

338.2–3 **relative**] *above del.* relative   relative] *after del.* the   338.5 **occasion.**] *above del.* application of ornament.   338.6 **so strongly**] *interl.*   338.7 **civilisation.**] *altered from* ~; *before del.* and their works rivalise with   338.8 **Armurers**] *before del.* and   338.9 **interesting**] *above del.* the   338.11 **The importance**] *after del.*

The importance of this Branch of industry[1] for the study of Art. has been justly appreciated in our times, while[2] before, arms[3] weapons, and Costumes were brought together and collected only by historical[4] and ethnographical Interest.
Such is[5] the caracter of all the most important armoiries of Europe,

1 **industry**] *altered from* industrial   industrial] *after del.* Metalworks *and before del.* art   2 **in our times, while**] *del. separately*   3 **arms**] *after del.* the collections of *and before del.* and   4 **historical**] *before del.* or technological   5 **is**] *after del.* are

338.13 **for**] *after del.* merely by   338.14 **were**] *above del.* are   **original**] *interl.* **wellknown**] *inserted*   **Europe;**] *altered from* ~, *before del.* which contain   338.15 **neglected,**] *before del.* and   and] *after del.* so that *after del.* even

MS 109

Report on   *fol. 1r*

The instruments of war and Chase, besides their terrible destinations have allways been considered as the glorious ornaments of their warlike bearers.
They have been among the first objects of art and Decoration, which last has always been
5   profusely applied to them, although in no other application than in that of arms and veapons ornamental Art is more strictly bound by necessity to observe the first and most important principles of Style and convemience. ⁞
Thus it comes that The Armurers and Swordcuttlers were the Conservators of the Traditions   *fol. 1v*
of the Art of Metalworking through the Centuries of Barbarism and Decay; and that the
10   same stood on the Summit of Decorative art in the florishing times of Civilisation and their Craft formed one of the Seminaries for artistical celebrities of every extraction; – and amidst the Extravagancies of Luxury, when the true principles and laws of Ornamental Art were misregarded at every other occasion, this craft has been obliged by necessity to observe a relative purity of style and taste in its productions. –
15   The works of the Armurers Swordcuttlers and gunsmiths must therefore be considered as that branch of Metalworking, which affords the greatest interest for the Study of Ornamental art and its History and style. and we have full opportunity to indulge to it, since we possess a great number of fine and rich collections of arms and veapons in Europe; which formerly were pure conservatories for arms etc. (Arsenals) and had a practical destination,
20   or which have been assembled in a interest for History and Antiquarian science. They importance for the study of art has only now been better appreciated, so that they form as much almost | inexplored shafts for artistical Inquiry. – .   *fol. 2r*
The Descriptions and works on Armuries, we possess, bear still the same Character as the Collections themselves. viz they are simple inventories with some few Dates and notes
25   about the single objects, or they are Antiquarian and Historical Essays. – Some illustrated Publications about Armuries, as the work of Meyriks on the Goodrik court Collection, that

of Jubinal on the Armury of Madrid and that which is now in Publication on the Imperial Armuries of Russia, contain good Representations of some of the most interesting pieces of Armury, although they give little more than the general Forms and Characters of the Objects. Other Specimens are given in the Moyen-Age et la Renaissance and by the Baron von Hefner in a Work on the Costumes of the Middle-Ages, which is much recommended by those who have seen it. –

fol. 2v

These and other collections of Stamps and lithographies on Arms and Weapons will be excellent means for instruction, but ¦ a small, artistically selected number of real specimens arms, and some exact Drawings of other, which have a really artistical Interest or which are instructive for history of art and Style, will be much more usefull.

There are principally three points which must be taken into consideration by selecting these Objects.

First the Knowledge of Processes, which last have always been applied in their fullest development on arms. No other productions of Metalworking not even the mere Jewellers ornaments show the same variety and concurrence of all possible processes which we observe on arms.

Secondly. The Study of practical Style, that is to say of style, in so far as it is depending upon the materials coming into consideration, and upon the Destinations and uses of the objects.

Thirdly The Study of historical Style, which last is that peculiar coin which

339.2 **allways**] *interl.* 339.3 **considered**] *before del.* at all times and everywhere **glorious**] *after del.* hon[o] *after del.* most 339.4 **They**] *after del.* Ornamental art has *after del.*

and allthough[1] the two distinct qualifications as ornaments and as instruments

1 **and allthough**] *after del.* These two distinct qualifications which occur also in many other

339.4 **among the first**] *interl.* 339.4–5 **which last ~ applied to them,**] *inserted* 339.5 **although**] *above del.* but 339.8 **Thus it comes that**] *interl. after del.* The interest, which is attached The] *after two del. beginnings of variant on fol. 1r–v:*

The arms and veapons must therefore be considered as that branch of Metalworking, which affords the greatest interest for the study of ornamental Art its History and Style. – The Armurers, Swordcuttlers, and the Gunmakers have been obliged by necssity to observe a relative purity of Style in their works amidst the Extravangancies of certain times, when the true principles and laws of ornamental Art were misregarded at every other occasion. This Craft was the conservatory of the traditions of the art of Metalworking through the Centuries of Barbarism. It was the same, which stood on the Summit of the Art[1], in the florishing times of civilisation, and which formed[2] one of the great Seminaries for artistical celebrities of every extraction. ¦ Its importance with respect to the Study of Art has justly been appreciated only in our

1 **the Art**] the *above del.* High *and* Art *altered from* art 2 **and which formed ~ extraction.**] *repl. del.* and which procured artists of the highest qualification for many

339.12 **Luxury**] *above del.* certain times 339.15–17 **The works ~ History and style.**] *inserted* 339.17 **and we have full opportunity to indulge to it, since**] *inserted before del.* Happily *and after del. on fols. 1v–2r*

Report on the Private Collection of Arms at Windsor Castle 341

Its importance[1] for the Study of art has only now been appreciated – and the existing collections of arms in Europe which are numerous and very rich, form as much allmost inexplored shafts for artistical inquiry. |

They formerly were pure Conservatories[2] for arms, (Arsenals,) and had a practical destination or they were collected together in a historical[3] or antiquarian sense; and so the existing

1 **Its importance**] *after del.* This important place, which the art of the armurers takes among the　2 **formerly were pure Conservatories**] *repl. del.* have been collected partly　3 **historical**] *after del.* mere

339.19 **destination**] *before del.* for war and Chase　339.20 **They**] *'Their'*　339.22 **shafts**] *Semper uses this word in the sense of 'wells', but he actually means 'sources'.*　339.23 **bear**] *above del.* are　**the same**] *after del.* of　339.25 **Some illustrated**] *repl. del.* The best and most important

340.2 **good**] *repl. del.* very interesting　340.3 **little**] *after del.* nothing　340.5 **which**] *after del.* which I have not yet seen, but　340.7 **Stamps**] *'prints'*　**Arms**] *after del.* Metal　340.8 **excellent**] *above del.* usefull　**instruction**] *before del.* for metalworking　**a small**] *after del. on fol. 2r–v* it is very ¦ desirable to have not only a collection of Drawings　**number**] *above del.* collection　**specimens**] *interl.*　340.9 **exact**] *interl.*　340.14 **productions**] *above del.* branch　340.14–15 **the mere Jewellers ornaments**] *repl. del.* that of the Jewellers　340.15 **show**] *repl. del.* can produce　**variety**] *after del.* Richness, *and before del.* in the Ensemble of the　Richness] *before del.* and　340.18 **and upon**] *after del.* upon instruments which　**objects.**] *before del.* It has been sayd that　340.19 **coin**] *'stamp';* *after del.* Direction of

MS 110

The Armurers, Swordcuttlers and Gunsmiths and their works take therefore perhaps the *fol. 1r* first Place in the whole Department of Metalworking and it is this branch of the last, which affords the greatest Interest for the Study of Ornamental Art, its History and Style.

Happily have we better opportunity to pursue this study on them, than on any other branch
5　of Metalworking, since we have many fine collections of Arms and veapons in Europe, which form as many almost inexplored treasuries for artistical inquiries;

The largest and most renowned Armuries in Europe were in the beginning practical institutions, as arsenals. Some other, for Instance that of Wienna, formerly at Castel Ambrass in Tyrol, had a more antiquarian and historical Destination. –
10　Other pertake of both of the two qualities; Such are the private Collections of arms of Souverains, Princes, and some healthy Private Personages.

Among the last is the Royal Collection of Arms at Windsor undoubtedly one of the most important chiefly by the artistical value and interest of the rare and beautiful Specimens, it contains.
15　But the artistical importance of the objects of this as well as of the other celebrated collections, has not yet been explored sufficiently.

Some illustrated Publications on Arms, as the Works of Meyricks, that of Jubinal on the Armury of Madrid, another collection of Lithographs on Russian and Oriental Arms in Russia, Baron v. Ebners ¦| Work on the Costumes of the Middle-Ages, contain very usefull　*fol. 2r*
20　Materials for Students, and their acquasition for the Library of the Departement of Practi-

cal Art is highly desirable; – But they give scarcely more than the General Forms and Characters of the Objects and the informations they give appear not to be sufficient for practical Instruction.

It may therefore be allowed to recommend to the High Superintendency for examination the following Propositions, respecting the Enrichment of the Museum of the Department of Practical Art, with a Collection of Specimens of Arms, weapons guns etc. – .

Those Products of Metalworking are important firstly for the Study of the Processes of Metalworking, which have been always applied in their fallest development on arms. Even the Goldsmiths and the Jewellers-works present herein not the same variety and completeness.

fol. 2v

Secondly for the Study of *Style*, in so far as we understand by Style that perfections in Works of Art, arrising from artistically using the means, which ¦ are given by a Practical Problem and by all the Accessories, which modifie the Embodiment of it.

They thirdly are of the greatest interest for the Study of the Historical Style, which is that peculiar caracter by which the artistical works of the different ages and people are distinguisheable.

———————— ¦

fol. 3r

It would be difficult and very expensive, to provide the new established Museum at once with a number of selected Specimens of Arms, proportionate to their importance for public instruction in practical art.

This Gap of the Museum may be temporarely filled out in some degree by borrowing from the rich Collections of arms, which are in England, some of their contents.

Some beautiful Pieces have already been generously lent by Her most gracious Majesty the Queen, and by some Private Gentlemen, but they are not sufficient to give any survey of the richness of this class of Arts manufacture, and it will be necessary to appeal once more to Her Majesties kindness for lending some more specimens of the rich containts of the Windsor-Castle Armury.

————————

The Windsor Collection is unique for the richness and beauty of the oriental arms it contains, – but thinking, that this branch of armury is still now better represented in our Museum, than the other, There may be pointed out only three as very instructiv for the richness

fol. 3v

and ¦ Originality of the Processes emploied in their Manufacture

1) *Burmese Sword* no 9356 remarcable for the richness and beauty of the Chased Handle etc.

2) Sword, which passes for Moorish, but which certainly is Chinese, no. 2315, for the beauty and originality of the Processes employed for Decorating the Handle and scabbord with Reliefo Ornaments in different metals.

3) The *Breast-Plates of Tippo Saib*, (in the Passage decorated as a Tent) remarcable as a Specimen of Steel-cutting and for the simplicity and purity of the ornamentation. – .

A strong Gallo Roman Iron-sword, at the same Collection with Bronze Handle would appear modern and counterfeid, if it was not decorated on its Handle with small Silver Rosaces, which once were filled up with Enamel.

These Rosaces are very interesting for the Study of the Process of the Art of Enameling and its History. – .

The Collection of Renaissance veapons is very considerable, and beautiful and the same

fol. 4r

have without contest the most interest for our practical modern. ¦ Practice. –

Among the Number of fine Swords, the three which are represented in the bygiven sketch, are distinguished.

Report on the Private Collection of Arms at Windsor Castle

The first is (falsely) attributed to Bonvenuto Cellini. It has great resemblance in Style and execution with the fine Shield which is now in the Museum of Präctical Art and belonged perhaps to the same Full-Armure. – .

The second no. *222.* is of a somewhat later Period as the first and inlaid with Silver; The General Form is very elegant and the Ornaments in the finest Style.

The third *no 276.* has been executed after the same Principle as the second, and shows the third Stepp of development of the (modern) Sword Handle form.

An other Sword, perhaps belonging to James's the II time, has a handle formed by Serpents well executed and of good invention.

The Hilt of an Dutch Sword of the 17th Century is decorated with fine chased Medallons with Portraits of the time of the Dutch Revolution. –

I shutt the series of the Swords in mentioning one very fine Sword of the Time of Louis XVI which ¦ is in Gold, with Enamel Pictures en Camajeu upon Azur Ground undoubtly exe-cuted by one of the best Masters in Enameling of the time. I newer saw better Enamel pictures.

This Sword is not only recommendable for the beauty of its Details, but also for its General Form and the good Taste and careful execution which appear on it. –

It gives an Evidence of what has been said before, that Purity of Style is to be found on arms and veapons even in the Times when generally bad taste had taken Possession of the Arts.

fol. 4v

Among the Guns are the Oriental Guns distinghed by the Richness and often by the good taste and Style of their ornamentation, but not less by the beauty of the workmanship of their barrels. It may be allowed to mention here occasionally the profit which would derive for the Institution of Practical Art, from the establishment of similar

> 341.3 **Style.**] *before in opposite column* ‡ siehe unten *before probably del. line pointing to the space between this paragraph and the next one*   341.7–16 **The largest ~ celebrated collections,**] *in opposite column after undel.*

They formerly were conservatories[1] for Arms of War and Chase, with a pure practical Destination, or they were collected together in a antiquarian or historical Interest. Other partake of both of the two qualities, as the Armuries of some Souverains, Princes and healthy Private Personages[2].

> 1 **conservatories**] *after del.* pure   2 **Personages**] *after del.* men

> 341.7 **were in the beginning**] *interl. after del.* had formerly a   **practical**] *after del.* pure   341.7–8 **institutions**] *interl. before del.* caracter   341.8 **arsenals**] *after del.* conservatories   341.10 **pertake**] *'partake'*   341.11 **healthy**] *'wealthy'*   341.13 **important**] *above del.* interesting   341.16 **has not yet been explored sufficiently**] *repl. del.* has been only occasionally mentionned by single connaisseurs and in the Guidebooks and Catalogues   has been] *after del.* They contain objects of the highest artistical Interest, which last   341.19 **contain**] *before del.* certainly   341.20 **acquasition**] *'acquisition'; altered from* acquain   342.1 **scarcely**] *above del.* little   342.2 **the informations they give**] *above del.* they will not   **appear not to be**] *inserted before undel.* be   342.4 **It**] *after del.* The *after del.*

the undersigned[1] ventures therefore[2] to Submit the following Propositions, respecting the Enrichment of the Museum of The Department of Practical Art with some selected Specimens of Arms, and Veapons, in Originals in Plastercasts, Electrotyps and in Drawings. –[3]

1 **the undersigned**] *after del.* In consideration of what has been fore-noticed,
2 **therefore**] *interl.*   3 **Drawings. –**] *before undel.* Siehe oben.

342.4 **Superintendency**] *before del.* of the Departement of Practical Art   342.5 **respecting**] *after del.* submitted with   342.7 **Those**] *altered from* those *after del.* The high
importance of   **Metalworking**] *before del.* is trifold. They   342.8 **fallest**] *'fullest'*
342.9 **herein**] *inserted*   342.9–10 **completeness.**] *altered from* ~∧ *before del.* with regard
to the means of   342.11 **Secondly**] *before del.* they are important *and after del. on fol.* 2r–v

Secondly they are important for the Study of Style, in so far as by Style is understood the
artistical treatement of a practical problem ¦ and of all inward and outward cooperative

342.12 **which**] *del. before del. on fol.* 2r–v which are given in ¦ a practical Problem, and all
which are   given] *before del.* and contained   342.15 **peculiar**] *after del.* peculiar coin
what the progressing time impresses upon the works of mankind and marks them with a
time] *after del.* age   works] *after del.* the artistical works of the centuri   **caracter**] *above
del.* coin and mark   **by which**] *after del.* which impresses upon the human works the
progressing time. The different Styles of the *after del.* which progressing ages   342.15–16
distinguisheable] *altered from* distinguished   342.18 **It**] *after inserted and del.* In considering that *after three del. beginnings of variant on fol.* 2v:

In consideration, that it would be impossible to complete[1] the Museum with a sufficient
number of Originals
In consideration, that it will be impossible to acquire for the Museum at once such a number of selected specimens of Arms, as will be necessary to give an abstract of the whole
Armurers Art, it will be very desirable:
firstly, that in order to compensate this Gap
It will be[2] impossible to acquire for the Museum at once a proportionate number of selected Specimens of arms, proportionate to the importance[3] of the object for public instruction in art, it will be very desirable
firstly to fill up partly this Gap by some originals

1 **complete**] *after del.* make the acquisition of a sufficient number of original pieces
of arms,   2 **It will be**] *after del.* In consideration that   3 **to the importance**] *after
del.* so as will be necessary to answer

342.20 **art.**] *altered from* ~, *before del.* – In this it will be desirable   342.21 **This**] *altered
from* this *after del.* firstly that   firstly] *underl.*   342.22 **contents.**] *altered from* ~∧ *before
del.* and exposing them for a time to the public   342.23 **Some**] *after four del. beginnings of
variant:*

secondly. that
None
The Royal Collection of Arms at Windsor is one of the
We have allready

342.23 **generously**] *interl.*   342.24 **and by some Private Gentlemen,**] *inserted*   any]
altered from an *before del.* abstract of the whole   342.26 **the rich**] *after del.* the *after del.*
those beautiful   **containts**] *'contents'*   342.29 **The Windsor**] *repl. del.* This   342.30
still now] *repl. del.* already   better] *repl. del.* very well   342.31 **for the richness**] *after
del.* for the Knowledge of Processes and of s *after del.* for the richness and beauty of the
342.38 **simplicity**] *inserted before del.* beauty   342.39 **A strong Gallo Roman**] *after del.*
Mediaeval [G]   342.40 **was**] *after del.* had not two small   342.41 **Rosaces,**] *inserted*

after del. Medallons, **Enamel.]** *altered from* ~∧ *before del.* which is now gone   342.45
have] *above del.* are   **the most interest]** *inserted before undel.* the most interesting
interest] *after del.* practical   **practical modern.]** *inserted*   342.46 **bygiven]** by- | given
derived from German 'beigeben': 'enclosed'
343.3 **Full-Armure]** *'full armour'*   343.6 **the second]** *after undel.* the   **shows]** *repl. del.*
forms   343.7 **Stepp]** *after del.* Development   **development of the]** *inserted*   343.8
has] *after del.* is intersting for the   **formed]** *after del.* decoration. wi[t]   343.10 **Hilt]**
above del. Handle   343.12 **I shutt]** *after del.* The Halbard   343.13 **Enamel]** *after del.* Azur
Enamel   **en Camajeu]** *'en camaïeu'*   343.17 **careful]** *after del.* good execution   343.18
gives] *after del.* shows   343.21 **distinghed]** *'distinguished'*   343.23 **barrels]** *after del.*
Cannons   **It may]** *after del.* At this Occa *after del.* It will perhaps be recommendable to
give a survey of th   **allowed]** *after del.* occasionally mentionne[d]   343.24 **from the**
establishment] *inserted*   **of similar]** *before del.* colle *and inserted after del.* of practical
of practical] *after del.* if there were in the Collection some

MS 107

To the Superintendency of the Departement of Practical Art.   *1*   *fol. 1r*

Report on the Collection of arms at Windsor Castle etc.

The Instruments of War and of Chase have always been considered as the most suitable
ornements of their proud bearers, and therefore, they were very early objects of ornamental
5   art, while, by their serious applications and uses they permit no other Decorations, than
such, as answered rigorously to the principal laws of Style, fittness and convenience.
Their importance for the Study of Ornamental Art in general and of Metalworking especially is therefore evident. These Products of the Armurers and Swordsmiths-craft are firstly interesting for the variety and perfection of the different Processes occurring in the Art
10   of Metal-working, which processes have been applied in their fullest development on arms
and veapons. It is certain, that no other branch of Metalworking, not even that of the Goldsmiths and Jewellers, presents the same choice, variety and perfection of Processes, as we
find on the branch in question.
But they are not less important secondly for the Study of *Style*, in so far as we understand by
15   this term those perfections ‖ in works of art, arrising from artistically using the means and   *2*   *fol. 2r*
observing the limits, which are contained in and defined by the Task and Problem which is
in question, as well as by all the Accessories, which modify the Solution of it in every cases.
It has already been mentionned why the objects in question must necessarily be suitable
models for Stylistical studies. –
20   Arms and veapons are thirdly interesting for the study of what might be called the *Historical*
Style, which is that peculiar character, by which the artictical productions of the Different
countries and ages are distinguishable from each other.
The History of Ornamental Art can not better be summed as by a collection of Arms and
veapons; For we see at all conditions on them, what has been done the most convenient for
25   Style and the most pure and rich for decoration. So we observe a relative elevation of art
manifesting itself on the Arms and veapons of the very circumstances, when everywhere
else the Practice and science of Art was allmost lost, in the centuries of Barbarism and
Decay.

346   Department of Practical Art

fol. 3r   *3*   The same appeared at the Summits of Ornamental Art in the Ages of florishing ¦| Civilisa-
tion; The Craft of the Armurers has often been the Seminary for artistical Talents of every
direction, and High art did not disdain this branch of Application.

A relative purity and Chastity of Taste and style is finally observeable on arms in those
luxurious periods of Art, when the principles of style were misregarded, and the Arts fol-   5
lowed the general Direction of the Age for Novelties and Extravagancies of all kind.

We have happily a greater opportunity to pursue the before mentionned studies on the
Arms and Veapons, than is given in any other Branch of Ornamental Art; since many fine
collections of Arms are restant or new established in the Different countries of Europe,
which form as many allmost *inexplored* treasuries for Ornamental art and for artistical in-   10
vestigations.

The largest and most renowned Armuries in Europe were in the beginning practical institutions, they were Arsenals. – Some other, for instance that of Wienna, formerly at Castle
Ambrass, had since the beginning a more Antiquarian and Historical Destination ¦|

fol. 4r   *4*   Other pertake of both of the two qualifications; such as the Private Collections of Souve-   15
rains, Princes, and other healthy Private Personages.

Among the last is the Royal Collection of Arms at Castle Windsor without doubt one of the
most interesting and perhaps the most valuable of all.

Besides the Richness of its containts, it is highly important for the artistical significance of
many of the Objects and their rare conservation.   20

But the artistical Significance neither of the Windsor Collection nor of any other Collection of Arms has as yet been sufficiently explored.

Some illustrated Publications on arms and veapons, as for instances the Works of Meyricks,
that of Jubinal on the Madrid Armury, an other Publication on the Imperial Collections of
Russia, Baron von Ebner's Work on Costumes of the Middle Ages, contain very usefull   25
Materials, and their acquisition for the Library of the Departement of Practical Art is most
desirable, as well as that of the printed Catalogues of some of the most important Collec-
tions in Europe. ¦|

fol. 5r   *5*   But they give scarcely more than the general Forms and Caracters of the Objects and are not
sufficient for practical Instruction.   30

It may therefore be allowed to recommend moreover to the attention of the High Superintendency the following Propositions, respecting the Enrichment of the Museum of the
Department for Practical Art with some Specimens of Arms, swords, guns etc.

It would be difficult to provide the new Establishment at once with a sufficient number of
selected Specimens of arms, proportionate to their importance as means of Instruction; But   35
this blanc of the Museum may be temporarely filled out with the contributions of the Possessors of Collections of Arms, who will kindly favor the new Institution with their patri-
otical Sympathy, and lend some specimens of the contents of their collections.

Some beautiful pieces have already been generously lent by Her Majesty the Queen and by
some Private Gentlemen, but it will be necessary to appeal once more to Her Majesties   40

fol. 6r   *6*   Grace for some more Specimens ¦| of the Rich Windsor-Caste Collection of Arms.

The last is unique for its Treasures of oriental Arms, – but thinking, that Oriental Art is still
now very well represented in our Museum, I spare my propositions for other branches of the
armurerers art and mention here only three objects as very instructive and interesting for the
Richness and Originality of the Processes, employed in their ornamentation.   45

Report on the Private Collection of Arms at Windsor Castle

347

I.) Burmese Sword n° 9356 for the beauty and Peculiarity of the Chased hilt etc.

2) Sword, which passes for Moorish, but which certainly is Chinese. n° 2315. for the Richness and Originality of the Processes employed for the Decoration of its Hilt and Scabbard with Ornaments of Various Metals,

3) The Breast-Plates, forming part of the Armurs of Tippo Saib. (hanging in the Passage, decorated like a Tent.). It is remarcable as a beautiful Specimen of Steel-chasing and of pure Simplicity of Design.

Among the Western arms may firstly be mentionned a strong Gallo Roman Sword of Iron, with Bronze Hilt. It || would appear modern and counterfeid, if it had not on the hilt some small Silver Rosaces, like filigranworks, which once were filled up with Enamel. The General Form of the Sword and this Ornament on it, render this specimen interesting. The Rosaces are instructive for the History and practice of the Enamellers art.

The collection of Renaissance veapons is very considerable; The same have perhaps the most interest for our modern practice.

Among the Swords, the three, which are given in the bylaid Sketches, are of first distinction.

One of them n°   has been attributed to B. Cellini without reason. It has some relation in Style and Execution with the fine Shield which is at present in the Museum and perhaps belonged to the same Panoplie.

The second, n° 222 is of a somewhat later period, and inlaid with Silver.

The general Form is very elegant and the Ornaments are of the best Style.

The third n° 276 has been executed after the same Principle as the Second, and shows the third stepp of the Developpment of the Modern Swordform. ||

Another Sword, probably of James's the II. time, has a Hilt formed by Serpents, chased in Steel, and is of very good invention and well executed.

The comes the Dutch Sword of the 17th Century, which is decorated with fine Chased Medallons with Portraits of some Heroes of the Dutch History.

This Series may be shutt in mentionning one very beautiful Sword of the time of Louis XVI, which in the Catalogue is given as an English work. The Hilt is Gold, with Enamel-Pictures en Camajeu on Azur Ground which no doubt are done by one of the best masters of the time. I newer saw better Enamel-pictures.

This specimen is not only recommendable for the beauty of its Details, but also for its general Form and the good taste and carefull Execution which appear on it.

It gives an Evidence of what has been said before, that Purity of Style is to be found on arms and veapons even when generally bad taste is dominant in Art.

Among the other Occidental veapons, except the guns, it must be noticed here for attention the beautifull Halbard of the Time of Henry 8th a Présent of the Pope to the || King, and of Italian Workman-ship. –

Among the Guns are the Oriental Guns not less distinguished by the beauty of the Workmanship of the barrels, than by the good taste and the Richness of their ornamentation, and it is principally for the first quality that they excell our modern guns.

It may be allowed to allude here occasionally to the excellent arangement in the Museum of Practical Geology, where the different Processes, (among the other also that of Barrelmaking) are shown in Technological surveys, to the greatest profit of the Students. Should it not be desirable to have similar Arrangements for our Museum? with the Difference, that the artistical element must predomine above the geological and the metallurgical. –

348 Department of Practical Art

Among the Occidental Guns, which are alltogether excellent, I distinguish only the famous Lazarino Cominazo Guns, for the Style of their Barrels, which is in the same time Decorative and practical. They are manufactured with the nails and the shoes of the Appenin-Mules. The Gun of Louis XIV, worked by Piraube, is the finest gun in the world. The Barrel is ||

fol. 10r   *10*   inlaid with Gold-flowers, the Sight is Silver, the Hindsight Steel corved in open work. The   5
whole is rich and sober in the same time, and the distribution of the decorated part is perfectly well understood. The execution is also very beautifull. It is a modell for ornamental Art in its application on Guns.

The same Case contains admirable other specimens of more modern workmanship. One Spanish Gun of Joachim da Zelaja, and the fine Pistols, worked by Weiss at Suhl in Germany. The same Master made two Guns which are at the same spot. These arms are the   10
finest specimens of Louis XV Style, and for this reason, as well as for their fittness and for the excellent workman-ship of the whole, very interesting.

The same case holds also the renommated Kuchenreuter Guns and Pistols, they are the best for practical use, and the application of the Ornaments on them is gracefull.   15

These are the Objects which, among so many other things which call to attention, may be sufficient to point out for special notice. –

It may be allowed now to make two other propositions, relating to the same object. ||

fol. 11r   *11*   Firstly to collect colour drawings of the most interesting armours and veapons to be seen at the Windsor Collection and at other Armuries in England and elsewhere. Sometimes   20
colour drawings are more usefull then plaster casts for Students.

Secondly to collect plastercasts for such cases, where this manner of reproducing the Originals is more usefull, as for instance for Repousse works. and Steel-carvings.

Thirdly to order Electrotypes to be made of the finest specimens of armures, for instance those at Dresden. One of the Officers of the Historical Museum at Dr. is a clever Electro-   25
typist and has allready reproduced several of the beautifull Shields which are at Dresden.

London 20 Sptber 1852.

                               Gottfried Semper.

         345.1 **To**] *after Henry Cole's insertion in top margin:*

         for annual report in Demy 8°.
         –
         set in Bourgeois – full measure.
         4 proofs,
         Henry Cole

         ————————————

         28 Sep: '52

         345.1 **Superintendency**] cy *altered by Cole to* ts   345.2 **Report**] *doubly underl. by Cole*
on the] *before interl. by Cole* Private   Private] *above inserted and del. by Cole* Royal   **Collection of arms**] *doubly underl. by Cole*   etc.] *repl. by Cole's insertion* the property of Her
Majesty the Queen, prepared with Her Majesty's gracious permission, by G Semper Professor of Metalworking in the Department of Practical Art   G Semper Professor]
underl. by Cole   G] *altered by Cole from* Gotfried   345.3 **Chase**] *after interl. by Cole* the
the] *del. by Cole*   345.4 **ornements**] *first* e *altered by Cole to* a   of] *repl. by Cole's insertion*
for   **proud**] *repl. by Cole's insertion* noble   **therefore**] *before interl. by Cole* from a very
early period   **very early**] *del. by Cole*   **ornamental**] *repl. by Cole's insertion* decorative
345.5 **by their serious applications and uses they**] *repl. by Cole's insertion* the uses to

which they were put did not   no] *del. by Cole*   345.6 **answered]** *repl. by Cole's insertion*
conformed   **Style]** *altered by Cole to* & Style   & Style] *transposed by Cole's guide line to*
after convenience *at 345.6 (cf. 76.10)*   and] *del. by Cole*   345.7 **for]** *repl. by Cole's insertion*
in   345.8 **Armurers]** *altered by Cole to* Armourers   Armourers] *after interl. by Cole* craft
of the   **Swordsmiths-craft]** Swordsmiths-|craft   craft] *del. by Cole*   345.8–9 **firstly]**
del. by Cole   345.9 **interesting]** *before inserted by Cole* 1°   345.10 **Metal-working]**
Metal-|working   **have been applied]** *transposed by Cole's guide line to after* development
at 345.10 (cf. 76.15)   345.12 **the same choice,]** *repl. by Cole's insertion* greater
as] *repl. by Cole's insertion* than those which   345.13 **on]** o *altered by Cole to* i   **the]**
e *altered by Cole to* is   **branch in question]** *del. by Cole*   345.14 **But they]** *altered by Cole*
to They   **secondly]** *transposed by Cole's guide line to before* But they *at 345.14 (cf. 76.19)*
345.15 **perfections]** *repl. by Cole's insertion* achievements   **arrising]** *second* r *del. by Cole*
artistically] *transposed by Cole's guide line to after* means *at 345.15 (cf. 76.21)*   345.17 **cases]**
es *altered by Cole to* e   345.19 **Stylistical]** *del. by Cole*   **studies. –]** *altered by Cole to* ~. of
Styles   345.20 **thirdly]** *transposed by Cole's guide line to before* Arms *at 345.20 (cf. 76.25)*
345.20–1 **Historical Style]** *repl. by Cole's insertion* History of Styles   345.21 **artictical]**
'*artistical*'   345.23 **Art]** *before interl. by Cole* in Metals   **can not]** can|not   summed
as] *repl. by Cole's insertion* illustrated than   345.24 **at]** *before interl. by Cole* once   **them,]**
altered by Cole to ~∧ observed;   **done∧]** *altered by Cole to* ~; what is   345.25 **Style and]**
before del. by Semper princip *and before interl. by Cole* what is   **observe]** *after interl. by*
Cole may   345.26 **of]** *after interl. by Cole* arising out
346.1 **same]** *before interl. by Cole* results   **at the Summits of]** *del. by Cole after interl. by*
Cole when   **Art]** *before interl. by Cole* attained its highest Elevation   346.1–2 **Civilisa-**
tion;] *altered by Cole to* ~.   346.2 **Armurers]** *altered by Cole to* Armourers   346.4
observeable] *altered by Cole to* observable   346.5 **misregarded]** m *altered by Cole to* d
346.7 **a greater]** *del. by Cole before interl. by Cole* better   **opportunity]** y *altered by Cole to*
ies   346.7–8 **the Arms]** the *del. by Cole*   346.8 **given in]** *repl. by Cole's insertion* afforded
by   346.9 **restant or new established]** *repl. by Cole's insertion* established   **restant]**
'*extant*'   346.10 **as]** *repl. by Cole's insertion* so   346.12 **Armuries]** u *altered by Cole to* o
346.13 **they]** *after inserted by Cole* for   **other]** *altered by Cole to* others   **Wienna]** W
altered by Cole to V   346.14 **since the]** *repl. by Cole's insertion* from its   346.15 **Other]**
altered by Cole to Others   **pertake]** *first* e *altered by Cole to* a   346.16 **other]** *altered by*
Cole to others   **healthy Private Personages]** *del. by Cole*   346.17 **Castle]** *transposed by*
Cole's guide line to after Windsor *at 346.17 (cf. 77.19)*   346.19 **containts]** ai *altered by Cole*
to e   346.20 **rare]** *before interl. by Cole* state of   **conservation.]** *altered by Semper from* ~∧
before del. by Semper and beauty. *and con altered by Cole to* pre   346.21 **neither]** *del. by*
nor] *repl. by Cole's insertion* or   346.22 **has]** *before interl. by Cole* not   **explored.]** *before*
Cole's line connecting explored. *and* Some *at 346.23 (cf. 77.25), thus deleting paragraph*   346.23
instances] es *altered by Cole to* e   **Meyricks]** s *del. by Cole*   346.24 **that]** *del. by Cole*
an other Publication] *repl. by Cole's insertion* that   346.25 **Russia,]** *altered by Cole to* ~∧ &
346.25–7 **of the Middle Ages ~ desirable]** *marked to the left, possibly by Cole, by a vertical*
double line in pencil   346.29 **Caracters]** *altered by Cole to* Characteristics   346.30 **suffi-**
cient] *altered by Cole to* sufficiently   sufficiently] *before interl. by Cole* detailed   **Instruc-**
tion.] *inserted by Semper after del. by Semper* institution. –   346.31 **It may therefore be**
allowed to] *repl. by Cole's insertion* I therefore beg leave to   **moreover]** *del. by Cole*
High] *del. by Cole*   346.31–2 **Superintendency]** *altered by Cole to* Superintendents *before*
interl. by Cole of the Department of Practical Art   346.32–3 **of the Department for**
Practical Art] *del. by Cole*   346.36 **blanc]** c *altered by Cole to* t *(*blanc *can be misread as*
'*Wanc' which consequently was altered by Cole to 'Want'; see 77.38: 'want')*   **filled out with**
the contributions of] *repl. by Cole's insertion* supplied by loans from   346.37–8 **who will**
kindly ~ contents of their collections] *del. by Cole*   346.39 **Some beautiful pieces**
have already been generously lent by] *del. by Cole*   346.39–41 **and by some Private**
Gentlemen ~ for some more] *del. by Cole*   346.41 **Specimens]** *after inserted by Cole* has
already graciously permitted the Department to borrow   **of]** *altered by Cole to* from
Windsor-Caste] '*Windsor Castle'; after inserted by Cole* in *and both transposed by Cole's guide*

line to after Collection of Arms. *at 346.41 (cf. 78.2)*   346.41 **of Arms.**] *del. by Cole*   346.42 **last**] *repl. by Cole's insertion* collection   **thinking**] *repl. by Cole's insertion* as it appears to me   346.42–3 **still now**] *repl. by Cole's insertion* at present   346.43 **spare**] *repl. by Cole's insertion* reserve   **propositions**] *altered by Cole to* proposals   346.44 **armurerers**] u *altered by Cole to* o *(*armurerers *can be misread as 'armuurers' which would have been altered to 'armourers'; see 78.5: 'armourer's')*   **objects**] *before interl. by Cole* of Eastern art   **as**] *before inserted by Cole* being

347.4 **Ornaments**] *after del. by Semper* Reliefo   347.5 **Armurs**] urs *altered by Cole to* our   347.6 **remarcable**] c *altered by Cole to* k   347.8 **firstly**] *del. by Cole*   **mentionned**] second n *del. by Cole*   347.9 **counterfeid**] d *altered by Cole to* t   347.10 **Rosaces**] *repl. by Cole's insertion* rosettes   **filigranworks**] an *altered by Cole to* ee   347.11 **interesting**] *repl. by Cole's insertion* remarkable   347.12 **Rosaces**] aces *altered by Cole to* ettes   **for**] *repl. by Cole's insertion* in   347.13 **The same have**] *repl. by Cole's insertion* and has   **most**] *repl. by Cole's insertion* greatest   347.15 **the three**] the *altered by Cole to* there are   **which are given in the bylaid Sketches, are**] *del. by Cole*   **bylaid**] *derived from German 'beilegen': 'enclosed'*   **of**] *before interl. by Cole* the   347.17 **n°**] *before blank left for number (see 335, Explanatory Notes 78.25–6)*   **B.**] *before interl. by Cole* envenuto   347.18 **Shield**] *before inserted by Cole* belonging to the Queen   347.19 **Panoplie**] ie *altered by Cole to* y   347.20 **Silver.**] *before Cole's line connecting* Silver. *and* The general Form *at 347.21 (cf. 78.29–30), thus deleting paragraph*   347.23 **stepp of**] of *repl. by Cole's insertion* in   **Modern**] *after interl. by Cole* form of the   **Swordform**] form *del. by Cole*   347.25 **invention**] *repl. by Cole's insertion* design   347.26 **The**] *altered by Cole to* Then   347.27 **History**] *after del. by Semper* Revolution   347.28 **shutt**] *repl. by Cole's insertion* closed   **closed**] *before interl. by Cole* for the present   347.30 **Camajeu**] ajeu *altered by Cole to* eo   **Azur**] *altered by Cole to* Azure   **are**] *repl. by Cole's insertion* were   347.31 **newer**] 'never'; *after interl. by Cole* have   **saw**] *repl. by Cole's insertion* seen   **Enamel-pictures.**] *before Cole's line connecting* Enamel-pictures. *and* This specimen *at 347.32 (cf. 79.1), thus deleting paragraph*   347.32 **recom-mendable**] *altered by Cole to* recommended *after inserted by Cole* to be   347.33 **appear on**] *repl. by Cole's insertion* pervade   347.35 **generally**] ly *del. by Cole*   **in Art.**] *transposed by Cole's guide line to after* bad taste *at 347.35 (cf. 79.5)*   347.36 **Occidental**] *above del. by Semper* Modern   **except**] *after del. by Semper* is specially *and repl. by Cole's insertion* besides   **it**] *del. by Cole*   **for attention**] *del. by Cole*   347.38 **Workman-ship**] Workman- | ship   347.42 **allowed**] ed *repl. by Cole's insertion* able   **occasionally**] *del. by Cole*   347.45 **Arrangements**] *after del. by Semper* Groups of   347.46 **predomine**] *final* e *altered by Cole to* ate

348.1 **distinguish only**] *repl. by Cole's insertion* remark for the present   348.2 **for**] *after interl. by Cole* distinguished   **in**] *altered by Cole to* at   348.3 **nails**] *before del. by Semper* of the Italian   **shoes**] *altered by Semper from* Horseshoes   348.4 **is the finest**] is *before interl. by Cole* probably   348.5 **Hindsight**] 'rear sight'   **corved**] 'carved'   348.6 **in**] *altered by Cole to* at   348.11 **spot**] *repl. by Cole's insertion* place   348.13 **workman-ship**] workman- | ship   **whole,**] *before interl. by Cole* are   348.14 **renommated**] ommated *repl. by Cole's insertion* owned   348.16 **which call to**] *repl. by Cole's insertion* exacting   **may**] *after interl. by Cole* it   348.18 **It may be allowed now**] *repl. by Cole's insertion* I take this opportunity to   348.19 **Firstly to collect**] *repl. by Cole's insertion* I beg leave to recommend 1° that   **to be seen**] *del. by Cole*   348.20 **at the**] at *repl. by Cole's insertion* in   **elsewhere.**] *before inserted by Cole* should be made   348.21 **then**] 'than'   **plaster casts**] plaster | casts   348.22 **Secondly**] *underl. by Cole*   **to collect**] *repl. by Cole's insertion* that   **plastercasts**] *before interl. by Cole* be made   **for**] *repl. by Cole's insertion* in   348.23 **Steel-carvings.**] *before inserted by Cole* And   348.24 **Thirdly**] *underl. by Cole*   **to order**] *repl. by Cole's insertion* that   **to be**] to *del. by Cole*   **armures**] 'armours'   **for**] *repl. by Cole's insertion* such for   **instance**] *before interl. by Cole* as   348.25 **One of the Officers of the Historical Museum at Dr. is a clever**] *repl. by Cole's insertion* Some   **Dr.**] 'Dresden'   348.25–6 **Electrotypist**] ist *altered by Cole to* es   348.26 **and**] *del. by Cole*   **has**] s *altered by Cole to* ve   **reproduced**] *after interl. by Cole* been   **several**] *del. by Cole*

MS 107

WITH HENRY COLE'S EMENDATIONS

76.1 **(B.)–Report**] Report   **Windsor Castle,**] ~ ~∧   76.2 **prepared,**] ~∧   76.3 **G. Sem-per,**] ~∧ ~∧   **Metal Working**] Metalworking   76.3–4 **Practical Art.**] ~ ~∧   76.5 **To the Superintendents of the Department of Practical Art.**] *before title, with* 'Department' *as* Departement   76.7 **period**∧] ~,   76.8 **while**∧] ~,   76.9 **decorations**∧] Decorations, such∧] ~,   76.10 **of**∧ **fitness,**] ~, fittness∧   **convenience,**] ~∧   **and style**] & Style 76.11 **in general,**] ~ ~∧   76.11–12 **metal working**] Metalworking   76.12 **especially,**] ~∧ 76.13 **interesting,**] ~∧   76.14 **First,**] 1°   **connected with**] occurring in   76.15 **metal working**] Metal- | working   76.16 **weapons**] veapons   **certain**∧] ~,   76.16–17 **metal working**] Metalworking   76.17 **goldsmith**] Goldsmiths   **jeweller**] Jewellers   76.18 **processes**∧] Processes,   76.19 **Secondly, they**] secondly∧ They   76.22 **problem in question;**] Problem which is in question,   76.23 **mentioned**] mentionned   76.23–4 **such objects**] the objects in question   76.24 **necessarily**] necessarly   76.25 **Thirdly,**] thirdly∧   **weapons**] veapons   76.26 **arising out of**] which is   **character**∧] ~,   76.27 **artistic**] artictical   **different**] the Different   76.29 **cannot**] can | not   **therefore be better**] better be   76.30 **weapons; for**] veapons; For   **requisite**] *om.*   76.30–1 **conditions**] ~ on them   76.31 **observed,**] ~;   **done,**] ~;   **style,**] Style∧   76.32 **Thus**] So 76.33 **arms and weapons**] the Arms and veapons   **these**] the   76.34–5 **in the centuries of barbarism and decay the practice and science of art was otherwise almost lost.**] everywhere else the Practice and science of Art was allmost lost, in the centuries of Barbarism and Decay.

77.2 **flourishing**] florishing   **armourer**] Armourers   77.3 **artistic**] artistical   **description**] direction   77.6 **art**∧] Art,   77.7–8 **extravagances**] Extravagancies   77.8 **kinds**] kind   77.9–10 **study of art on arms and weapons**∧] before mentioned studies on Arms and Veapons,   77.11 **to be found**] established   **Europe**∧] ~,   **forming**] which form 77.12 **almost unexplored**] allmost inexplored   **treasuries of**] ~ for   **for artistic investigation**] and for artistical investigations   77.13 **armouries**] Armories   77.14 **arsenals.** ∧] Arsenals. –   77.15 **commencement**] beginning   77.16 **destination.**] Destination∧   77.17 **qualifications,**] ~;   77.18 **sovereigns**] Souverains   77.19 **Windsor Castle,**] ~ ~∧   77.21 **contents**∧] ~,   **artistic**] artistical   77.23 **artistic**] artistical **collection,**] Collection∧   77.24 **arms,**] Arms∧   77.25 **weapons**] veapons   **as, for instance,**] ~∧ ~ ~∧   77.26 **Tubinal**] Jubinal   **armoury**] Armury   77.27 **Russia, and**] ~∧ &   77.27–8 **middle ages**] Middle Ages   77.28 **useful**] usefull   77.29 **Department**] Departement   **the printed catalogues**] that of the printed Catalogues of some   77.31 **scarcely give**] give scarcely   77.32 **weapons,**] Objects∧   77.34 **proposals**∧] Propositions,   77.35 **&c.**] etc.   77.38 **instruction.**] Instruction;   **want**] blant *(cf. 349, note 346.36)*   **temporarily**] temporarely   77.39 **arms**∧.] Arms,.

78.2 **Windsor Castle.**] ~-Caste∧   78.3 **Oriental arms,** ∧] oriental Arms, –   78.4 **me**∧] ~, 78.5 **armourer's art,**] armorerers art∧ *(cf. 350, note 346.44)*   **only**] here ~   78.6 **Eastern art,**] ~ ~∧   78.7 **processes**∧] Processes,   78.8 **1.**] I.)   **Burmese sword, No. 9,356,**] ~ Sword∧ n° 9356∧   78.9 **&c.**] etc.   78.10 **2.**] 2)   78.10–11 **Chinese, No. 2,315,**] ~. n° 2315. 78.12 **scabbard,**] Scabbard∧   **various metals.**] Various Metals,   78.13 **3.**] 3)   **Tippo Saib**∧] ~ ~.   78.14 **tent**∧] Tent.   78.18 **filigree works**] filigreeworks   78.19 **sword,**] Sword∧   78.22 **Rénaissance weapons**] Renaissance veapons   **considerable,**] ~; 78.24 **swords**∧ **there are three**∧] Swords, ~ ~ ~,   78.25 **them, No.**   ,] them∧ n°   ∧

Benvenuto] B.envenuto   78.27 **Queen,**] ~ʌ   **Museum,**] ~ʌ   78.29 **No. 222,**] nᵒ ~ʌ 78.30 **elegant,**] ~ʌ   78.31 **third, No. 276,**] ~ʌ nᵒ ~ʌ   78.32 **step**] stepp   **development**] Developpment   78.33 **James II.'s**] James's the II.   78.36 **medallions,**] Medallonsʌ 78.37 **by mentioning**] in mentionning   78.38 **Louis XVI.**] ~ ~ʌ   78.39 **enamel pictures**] Enamel-Pictures   **in cameo**] en Cameo   **azure ground,**] Azure Groundʌ   78.40 **never**] newer   78.41 **enamel pictures**] Enamel-pictures
79.2 **careful**] carefull   79.5 **weapons**] veapons   **artʌ**] Art.   **dominant.**] ~ʌ   79.6 **weapons**] veapons   **may**] must   79.7 **beautiful halberd**] beautifull Halbard   **Henry VIII.,**] ~ 8ᵗʰʌ   **present**] Présent   79.8 **workmanship. ʌ**] Workman- | ship. –   79.9 **Oriental guns,**] ~ Gunsʌ   **distinguished**] destinguished   79.10 **barrelsʌ**] ~,   79.11 **ornamentation;**] ~,   **excel**] excell   79.13 **arrangement**] arangement   79.14 **pro-cessesʌ**] Processes,   **others**] the other also   79.15 **barrel-making**] Barrelmaking **great**] greatest   79.16 **Would**] Should   79.16–17 **Museum,**] ~?   79.17 **this difference**] the Difference   **artistic**] artistical   79.18 **metallurgical? ʌ**] ~. –   79.19 **altogether**] alltogether   79.21 **which is,**] ~ ~ʌ   **time,**] ~ʌ   79.22 **Appenine mules**] Appenin-Mules 79.23 **Louis XIV.**] ~ ~ʌ   79.24 **gold flowers**] Gold-flowers   **head-sight**] Hindsight 79.25 **steel, carved**] Steelʌ corved   79.27 **beautiful**] beautifull   **model**] modell   79.28 **other admirable**] admirable other   79.28–9 **workmanship. –**] ~. ʌ   79.29 **pistolsʌ**] Pistols,   79.30 **Suhl,**] ~ʌ   **guns,**] Gunsʌ   79.31 **Louis XV. style:**] ~ ~ʌ Style,   79.32 **fitness**] fittness   **workmanship**] workman- | ship   79.34 **Kuchenrenter**] Kuchenreuter **pistols;**] Pistols,   79.36 **graceful**] gracefull   79.38 **notice. ʌ**] ~. –   79.39 **to make**] to to make
80.1 **– Firstly,**] ʌ 1ᵒʌ   **coloured**] colourd   80.2 **arms and weapons**] armours ~ veapons **armouries**] Armuries   80.3 **elsewhereʌ**] ~.   **made.**] ~ʌ   **coloured**] colourd   80.4 **useful than**] usefull then   80.5 **Secondly,**] ~ʌ   **plaster casts**] plastercasts   **casesʌ**] ~,   80.6 **originals,**] Originalsʌ   **useful;**] usefull,   **as, for instance,**] ~ʌ ~ ~ʌ **répoussé worksʌ**] Repousse ~.   80.7 **steel carvings; and,**] Steel-carvings. Andʌ   80.8 **Thirdly,**] ~ʌ   **arms;**] armures,   80.8–9 **such, for instance,**] ~ʌ ~ ~ʌ   80.9 **already**] allready   80.10 **beautiful**] beautifull   80.11–12 **Gottfried Semper. London, Septem-ber 20, 1852.**] Londonʌ 20ʌ Sptberʌ 1852. Gottfried Semper.

Berlin Productions of Plastical Art, Metal Casts, Plaster Casts

TEXTUAL RECORD

MS 112[1]   gta, 20-Ms-112, fol. 5r–v (5r, beside and below the text, calculations and sketches in black ink and pencil; 5v calculation and sketch in pencil), in Semper's hand

MS 112[2]   gta, 20-Ms-112, fols. 1r–4v (1r notes by Hans and Manfred Semper, early 1880s, see 355–6, Alterations in the Manuscript 80.14; 1v, 4v blank), in Semper's hand, dated 11 October 1852, *copy-text*

K-1852   gta, 20-K-1852-10-11(S), fols. 1r–4v (receipt forms for Semper's fees for the Vienna Hofmuseen and Hofburgtheater on all versos), in Manfred Semper's hand, early 1880s, copy of MS 112[2]

BIBLIOGRAPHY Herrmann 1978, 131–2; Herrmann 1981, 108; Mallgrave 1996, 213

EXPLANATORY NOTES

When Semper submitted the report on the collection of arms at Windsor Castle to Henry Cole on 27 September 1852, he also informed him about a visit from an 'Importer of Berlin Metal works etc.' two days earlier – a certain 'Mr. Born, Southampton Street Strand' (probably the German David Born). Semper promised he would deliver a report as soon as he saw the catalogue. In the completed report, dated 11 October 1852 and published here, he presents Born's offer of plaster casts and metal casts from historical and modern objects of the applied arts – jewellery in renowned royal collections, and some private collections, in Berlin, such as engraved gems, medallions, brooches and bracelets, and a shield manufactured by the recently deceased Munich artist Ludwig von Schwanthaler. Semper makes recommendations for purchases for the Museum of Ornamental Art, which already had a considerable collection of casts and whose curator was Ralph Nicholson Wornum, later secretary of the National Gallery of London. The museum's catalogue records six items 'Purchased of Mr. D. Born' in 1852 'as examples of fine casting in metal' (CatM[4], 40; DPA[1], 265; CatM[5], 56; CatM[6], 35–6). These metal castings correspond to those offered by Born as being 'cast Iron Ornaments of Devaranne at Berlin' and were recommended by Semper 'as proofs of Skill in Casting Iron' (81.26–9). Richard Redgrave agreed to these suggestions in a note at the bottom of Semper's manuscript and added some further comments (356, Alterations in the Manuscript 82.7). The cast iron jewellery acquired can be identified with some certainty with items held in the Victoria and Albert Museum (see below), although only three of them are attributed to Siméon Pierre Devaranne, one of the foremost artists of fashionable Berlin iron jewellery around 1850.

80.14 **Henry Cole Esquire**] preceded by a contemporaneous sheet with notes by Hans and Manfred Semper from the 1880s, which describe the manuscript's contents and the decision (in Manfred's hand), 'Not to be included because of too little general interest' (355–6, Alterations in the Manuscript 80.14) – that is, Hans and Manfred decided not to translate the report for Gottfried Semper's *Kleine Schriften* (Semper 1884). 80.19 **Museum**] the Department's Museum of Ornamental Art at Marlborough House, Pall Mall, London 80.20 **bygiven**] derived from German *beigeben: enclosed* (see also 81.2) 80.24–5 **Stosch Collection ~ Museum at Berlin**] Philipp von Stosch's collection of antiquities (mostly engraved gems) was acquired by the Prussian King Frederick the Great in 1764; in Semper's time, it was kept in the Königliches Museum (Royal Museum) in Berlin, as Karl Friedrich Schinkel's Altes Museum of 1830 was originally called. 80.27 **Catalogue ~ by Winkelmann in ~ 1769**] This catalogue, established by Johann Joachim Winckelmann after Stosch's death, was published in 1760 (Winckelmann 1760). 80.29 **pens**] *pence* 80.30 **Hundert**] German for *Hundred*

81.1 **3444 pieces**] the complete number of engraved gems in the Stosch collection 81.5 **Speckstone**] derived from German *Speckstein: soapstone* **Royal Museum**] see note 80.24–5 81.6 **Kunstkammer**] The Royal Kunstkammer was housed in the Berlin Stadtschloss (converted by Andreas Schlüter around 1700) up to 1855, when it was transferred to Friedrich August Stüler's Neues Museum. 81.8–9 **Pisani ~ Jamnitzer**] 'Pisani': *Pisanello*. All of these artists were working as medallists; for identification of their names, see Index. 81.14 **peaces**] *pieces* 81.15 **pens**] *pence* 81.21–2 **table with Zinc-casts of Mr Eichler's Manufacture ~ exposed in the Exhibition of 1851**] The Berlin publisher Gustav Eichler had founded 'G. Eichler's Kunstanstalt für plastische Arbeiten' in 1841; among other things, he had on offer plaster casts of the engraved gems in the Stosch collection. If Eichler's 'table with Zinc-casts' (referred to by Richard Redgrave in his comment added to Semper's manuscript as 'frame of Zinc Castings'; 356, Alterations in the Manuscript 82.7) was shown at the Great Exhibition, then it was probably not a collection of zinc casts but rather the collection of plaster casts described as 'Tableaux with 52 portraits and medallions, cast in plaster of Paris, after sculptures of German artists of the 16th century' (ODIC 1851, 3:1064 [no. 272]). 81.26 **recommands**] *recommends* 81.27 **cast Iron Ornaments of Devaranne at Berlin**] Berlin cast iron jewellery, invented as a patriotic substitute for jewellery made of precious metals at the time of the Napoleonic wars, had become highly fashionable during the first half of the nineteenth century; Siméon Pierre Devaranne was appreciated for his original designs. All of the cast iron jewellery by Devaranne that Semper recommended was purchased by the Museum of Ornamental Art and listed in its catalogue, indicating its provenance from 'D. Born'. The items are identified below by their purchase price and description in the museum catalogue with the numbers there and – by comparing the purchase price – in the inventory of the South Kensington Museum of 1868 (Inventory 1868, acquisitions of 1852), from which the museum numbers in the Victoria and Albert Museum were derived and where the items can be located with some certainty. 81.30 **Brooch 2/6.**] CatM^5, 56: 'M 112. – Cast iron brooch from Berlin. Purchased of Mr. D. Born'; Inventory 1868 (1852), 5: 'Brooch. Cast-iron filigree work. German (Berlin), modern'; V&A, 935-1852, attributed to Devaranne **Bracelet 5/6. – n° 540**] CatM^5, 56: 'M 113. – Cast iron bracelet from Berlin. Purchased of Mr. D. Born'; Inventory 1868 (1852), 5: 'Bracelet. Cast-iron filigree work. German (Berlin), modern'; V&A, 937-1852, attributed to Devaranne 81.31 **Each à 4/6. – n° 126 – Bracelet and Brooch**] CatM^5, 56: 'M 110. – Cast iron brooch from Berlin. Purchased of Mr. D. Born'; Inventory 1868 (1852), 5: 'Brooch. Cast-iron filigree work. German (Berlin), modern'; V&A, 934-1852, tentatively attributed to Johann Conrad Geiss who, besides Devaranne, dominated the production of Berlin iron jewellery in the first half of the nineteenth century; CatM^5, 56: 'M 111. – Cast iron bracelet from Berlin. Purchased of Mr. D. Born'; Inventory 1868 (1852), 5: 'Bracelet. Cast-iron filigree work. Ger-

Berlin Productions of Plastical Art, Metal Casts, Plaster Casts

man (Berlin), modern'; V&A, 936-1852, registered as a work of an unknown artist   81.32
6./ – n° 113 – Pendants] CatM⁵, 56: 'M 114. – Pair of cast iron ear[r]ings from Berlin. Purchased of Mr. D. Born'; Inventory 1868 (1852), 8: 'Ear pendants, a pair. Cast-iron filigree
work. German (Berlin), modern'; V&A, 922-1852, attributed to Devaranne   81.33 **3/.6. –
n° 558 – Brooch**] CatM⁵, 56: 'M 115. – Cast iron brooch from Berlin. Purchased of Mr. D.
Born'; Inventory 1868 (1852), 5: 'Brooch. Cast-iron filigree work. German (Berlin), modern';
V&A, 938-1852, registered as a work of an unknown artist   81.38–40 **Copy of the Shield
of Hercules ~ by Schwanthaler in Munich ~ cast and ciselld in Copper or Bronze by
the artist**] 'ciselld': *chiselled*. Ludwig von Schwanthaler was a most successful Munich
sculptor with many commissions from Ludwig I, the Bavarian king. His Shield of Hercules,
which Schwanthaler designed and modelled after Hesiod's description, was a bronze cast
manufactured in several copies by the Königliche Erzgiesserei (Royal Bronze Foundry) at
Munich starting in 1841. In the second half of the 1840s, there were already several copies in
collections in Germany and England, including the collection of the Duke of Devonshire
in Chatsworth. In the first draft of his first lecture at the Department, 'On the Relations of
the Different Branches of Industrial Art to Each Other and to Architecture', Semper mentions Schwanthaler as one of the modern artists who had worked according to Hesiod's and
Homer's description of works of industrial art (99.1).
82.2 **Electro-type Copy of the Shield**] In 1841, the director of the Königliche Erzgiesserei
(Royal Bronze Foundry) at Munich, Johann Baptist Stiglmaier, had already announced the
manufacture of electrotype copies of Schwanthaler's shield. In his comment added to Semper's manuscript, Redgrave recommends postponing the purchase of a reproduction of the
shield 'until the success of the repetition of Her Majestys is seen' (356, Alterations in the
Manuscript 82.7). This refers to the shield attributed to Benvenuto Cellini, which Semper
mentions in his 'Report on the Private Collection of Arms at Windsor Castle' (78.26–7) and
which was brought to London on 12 May 1852 after Prince Albert agreed to lend it 'to be
electrotyped' (Cole Diary). The shield was shown at Gore House during the exhibition of
students' works there in May 1854, together with an electrotype copy prepared by Elkington
from Birmingham, the intention being to have electrotype copies of choice objects produced
for purchase both by the Schools of Art connected with the Department and also by the
general public (DSA², 166, 202; Spectator 1854). An electrotype copy of the shield is also
listed in the exhibition catalogue of a selection from the Museum of Ornamental Art,
which circulated in the provincial schools of art from 1855 (Robinson 1856, 71 [no. 310]).
82.6 **feathfully**] *faithfully*

EDITORIAL EMENDATIONS

81.3 **Cinque-cento**] Cinque- | cento   81.21 **Zinc-casts**] Zinc- | casts   82.1 **summ**] m
geminated by upper horizontal stroke   82.2 **Electro-type**] Electro- | type

ALTERATIONS IN THE MANUSCRIPT

80.14 **Henry Cole Esquire**] *after Hans and Manfred Semper's notes on fol. 1r:*

III. e.[1]
Brief an H. Cole
Vorschläge[2] für Ankäufe für das Marlborough-house[3] Mus. – an Henry Cole
complet.
(1 Blatt; Entwurf dazu)
1[1] Oct. 1852.
Nicht[4] aufzunehmen, weil zu wenig allgemeines Interesse.

> 1 **III. e. ~ H. Cole**] *in black ink by H. Semper*   2 **Vorschläge ~ 1852.**] *in violet ink by H. Semper, with correction in black ink by M. Semper*   3 **Marlborough-house**] *inserted in black ink by M. Semper before del. in black ink by M. Semper* Kens.   4 **Nicht ~ Interesse.**] *in pencil by M. Semper*

80.19 **Museum**] M *over* Co   **specified**] *after del.* contained   80.27 **ranged**] *after del.* and 80.28 **of transport**] *after del.* for   80.30 **pieces**] ie *over* ea   81.12 **Italian**] *before del.* Masters   81.19 **from Berlin**] *before del.* of the Commands   81.22 **thinks**] th *over* is   81.23–4 **for the comparison**] *after del.* as a mean   81.24 **with**] *after del.* between   81.27 **gives**] i *over* a *and* s *added*   81.29 **Skill in Casting**] *after del.* skilfull castings   81.30 **The Brooch 2/6. the Bracelet 5/6. –**] *inserted in red ink*   **2**] *over* 5   81.31 **Each à 4/6. –**] *inserted in red ink*   81.32 **6./ –**] *inserted in red ink*   81.33 **3/.6. –**] *inserted in red ink*   81.34 **peculiar**] *above del.* particuliar   **seems**] se *over* is   81.35 **I therefore**] *after del.* so that I   81.36 **Museum**] *after del.* collection   81.37 **by the mediation**] *after del.* and 82.1 **large**] *repl. del.* much   82.2 **suffice**] *after del.* as well   82.5 **11 October 1852.**] *inserted* 82.7 **GSemper.**] *before Richard Redgrave's note in black ink:*

Order the 2[1] bracelets & Brooches pendants

–

The frame of Zinc Castings

–

perhaps 2 frames Casts of Medals – from £2 to 3£

–

Casts of Cinque Cento medals to the same amount –
Sand for Berlin casting –
Shield had better be left until the success of the repetition of Her Majestys is seen –

Rich[d] Redgrave

> 1 **2**] *above del.* 4

MANUSCRIPT VARIANTS

MS 112[1]

fol. 5r   *4b*   The German Medals, which are extremely interesting for the beauty of their execution are alltogether to be bought for 2 liv. Sterling.
It would be very desirable, to have together with the German Masters, some of the finest Italian Medals, for their comparison.

4

Observations on Some of the Specimens of Metal Work 357

If the Superintendency agrees to purchase some of these articles, it will be good to commend them instantly, for in the winter season the water communication is sometimes interrupted.

4 Mr. Born proposed also to

> 356.3 **It**] *altered from* it *after del.* But   356.4 **comparison.**] *before del.* The last are more Grand in Style, but less finished and true as the first. –
> 357.1 **some**] *after del.* those arti   357.1–2 **commend**] *'order'*   357.2 **season**] *interl.*

Observations on Some of the Specimens of Metal Work

TEXTUAL RECORD

MS 111[1]	gta, 20-Ms-111, fols. 5r–6v (6r–v blank), in Semper's hand, draft of CatM[4]
MS 111[2]	gta, 20-Ms-111, fols. 1r–4v (4r and all versos blank), in Semper's hand, draft of CatM[4]
MS 111[3]	gta, 20-Ms-111, fols. 7r–8v (8r–v blank), in Semper's hand, draft of CatM[4]
CatM[4]	'Observations on Some of the Specimens of Metal Work', in *A Catalogue of the Articles of Ornamental Art, in the Museum of the Department*, 4th ed. (Feb. 1853), London: Eyre & Spottiswoode for Her Majesty's Stationery Office, 1853, 22–3
DPA[1]	'Observations on Some of the Specimens of Metal Work', in *First Report of the Department of Practical Art*, London: Eyre & Spottiswoode for Her Majesty's Stationery Office, 1853, 248–9
MS 113[1]	gta, 20-Ms-113, fols. 3r–4v, in Semper's hand, draft of second part of CatM[5]
MS 113[2]	gta, 20-Ms-113, fols. 1r–2v (2v blank), in Semper's hand, dated March 1853, draft of second part of CatM[5]
CatM[5]	'Observations on Some of the Specimens of Metal Work', in *A Catalogue of the Museum of Ornamental Art, at Marlborough House, Pall Mall*, 5th ed. (May 1853), London: Eyre & Spottiswoode for Her Majesty's Stationery Office, 1853, 37–9 (NAL, V.1853.003), *copy-text*
CatM[6]	'Observations on Some of the Specimens of Metal Work, Enamels, &c.', in *A Catalogue of the Museum of Ornamental Art, at Marlborough House, Pall Mall*, 6th ed. (March 1854), London: Eyre & Spottiswoode for Her Majesty's Stationery Office, 1854, 18–20, revised and abridged ed. of CatM[5]
Semper 1884[a]	'Bemerkungen über einige Gegenstände der Metallotechnik', 86–9, German trans. of DPA[1]; omits the last part of the concluding sentence (DPA[1], 249.36–8, corresponding to CatM[5], 84.11–13)
Semper 1884[b]	'Kritik von Ankäufen für das Museum of practical art', 84–5, dated March 1853, German trans. of MS 113[2]
Semper 2014[a]	vol. 2, 516–17, Karge's reprint ed. of DPA[1]
Semper 2014[b]	vol. 2, 545–7, Karge's reprint ed. of CatM[5]

BIBLIOGRAPHY Herrmann 1978, 82 n. 308, 132–3; Herrmann 1981, 107–8; Wainwright 1994; Mallgrave 1996, 213

EXPLANATORY NOTES

Semper's introductory remarks to the division on metalwork in *A Catalogue of the Museum of Ornamental Art* discuss a selection of items acquired from the Great Exhibition in 1851 and 1852, which was supplemented by further purchases in 1852 and early 1853. The first selection was made by a purchasing committee consisting of Henry Cole, Richard Redgrave, Owen Jones and Augustus Welby Northmore Pugin for the former School of Design. Semper wrote the first part of his 'Observations' (82.12–84.13) until February 1853, when it was published in the fourth edition of the museum catalogue and reprinted in the *First Report of the Department of Practical Art*. The second part of the 'Observations' discusses 'The newly acquired additions to the Museum' (84.14) and was published together with the almost unchanged first part in the fifth edition of the museum catalogue of May 1853, reprinted with some revisions and substantial abridgements in the sixth edition (see 364).

The first part of the 'Observations' focuses on three metal objects indicated in the earlier print variants with the subheading 'On M 1, M 20, M 2' (CatM[4], DPA[1]; also in two fragmentary drafts, see 364.3, 365.7). The three numbers designate Indian metalwork – two bracelets and a sword – among which Semper devotes most space to the sword (M 20). He mainly discusses here the way in which enamel colours are used, thus pursuing his general interest in questions of polychromy (in *Style in the Technical and Tectonic Arts*, he refers to his 'Observations' – citing the fifth edition of the catalogue – when discussing colours in textile work; Semper 1860/63, 1:52 n. 1). The other objects are alluded to in a cursory way, often without giving a catalogue number. Among the new objects added by early 1853, Semper highlights a few specimens of objects wrought and chased in metal – a technique that he introduced towards the end of the first part with works particularly by Antoine Vechte and now discusses in relation to architectural issues.

The extant fragmentary drafts of both the first and second parts of Semper's 'Observations' contain some interesting differences from the printed versions – apart from the fact that they were not revised like the latter, probably by Cole or Redgrave. One of the drafts of the second part mentions a 'Chinese Censor' (367.32), which is omitted in Semper's printed text (listed in CatM[5], 58, as 'M 129. – Bronze tripod incense burner. Purchased of Hewett & Co. ... Rosewood stand and cover, and carved soapstone handle'; Inventory 1868 [1852], 23: 'Incense burner. Bronze. Standing on three legs, rosewood base and cover. Chinese'; V&A, 1566-1852). The printed text also omits the concluding sentence of the second draft, which provocatively states that 'Some of the Emblems etc. appear to me not interesting eno[ugh], to [keep] their places in the Museum' (369.22–3). Semper's discussion of the metalwork objects mostly differs in content from the short descriptive texts that were included with their listing in the museum catalogue. They were not provided by him but probably by members of the purchasing committee, as is fairly obvious in the case of the items from the Great Exhibition, which are described in a text that remains almost unchanged starting from the first edition of the museum catalogue, the introduction of which – signed by Henry Cole, Owen Jones and Richard Redgrave – is dated 17 May 1852 (CatM[1], iii–v). Most of the metal objects discussed are still preserved at the Victoria and Albert Museum; they are located by

Observations on Some of the Specimens of Metal Work   359

comparing the list of metal objects in *A Catalogue of the Museum of Ornamental Art* with the list of acquisitions from 1852 and 1853 in the inventory of the South Kensington Museum of 1868 (Inventory 1868), from which the Victoria and Albert Museum numbers were derived.

82.12 **M 1**] CatM⁵, 41: 'M 1. – Dagger, with enameled sheath and handle. Manufactured at Scinde'; Inventory 1868 (1852), 25: 'Knife, or Dagger. Steel. With gold enamelled sheath. Indian (Scinde), modern'; V&A, 109-1852; cf. Wainwright 1994, 362 and fig. 22   **M 20**] CatM⁵, 44: 'M 20. – Drinking cup, silver-gilt and enameled. Manufactured at Kangra'; Inventory 1868 (1852), 7 (129-1852): 'Cup. Silver gilt, inlaid with floriated ornament in champlevé translucent enamel. Indian (Kangra), modern'; missing from V&A today   82.13 **M 2**] CatM⁵, 41: 'M 2. – Thulwar or sword, with enameled hilt, point, and scabbard. Manufactured at Kotah, in Rajpootana'; Inventory 1868 (1852), 40: 'Sword ("Thulwar.") Steel, mounted in enamelled gold. In crimson velvet scabbard also mounted, and green velvet sword belt with two gold enamelled buckles. Indian (Kotah in Rajpootana), modern'; V&A, 110-1852   82.14–17 **blue and green enamel grounds ~ without being united by a common parentage ~ more harmonious**] The description in the catalogue characterizes the sheath of M 1 as 'a perfect illustration of the principle ever adopted by Eastern nations of always decorating their construction, and never constructing decoration' (CatM⁵, 41). This observation corresponds to Pugin's dictum in his *True Principles of Pointed or Christian Architecture* of 1841, 'that all ornament should consist of enrichment of the essential construction of the building' and should not be 'actually constructed, instead of forming the decoration of construction'. Semper would not have shared this apodictic opinion because of its reductive simplification of the relation between ornament and object. Accordingly, he comments only on the lack of colour harmony, which could not be compensated for by introducing ruby colour, and thus gives an alternative reading of the judgement in the catalogue list, which states that the sheath 'suffers a little from the absence of ruby colour, which would have made it more harmonious' (CatM⁵, 41).   82.17–19 **Even in M 20 ~ deficiency of harmony ~ less violent, the green and blue tints being broken and connected together by the neutral black**] In contrast, the catalogue list observes about this drinking cup that 'the colour is imperfect, requiring purple to balance the green' (CatM⁵, 44; CatM¹, 33, having 'to well balance the green').   82.20–2 **Tulwar or Sword, M 2, and ~ M 11 and M 12 ~ same system of colouring and ornamentation**] M 11 and M 12 are enamel bracelets; see CatM⁵, 42: 'M 11. – Bungaree or bracelet, enameled, and set with diamonds and rubies. Manufactured at Dholepore, in Rajpootana'; Inventory 1868 (1852), 4: 'Bracelet. Gold, enamelled and set with diamonds and rubies. Indian (Dholepore in Rajpootana), modern'; V&A, 119-1852; CatM⁵, 42: 'M 12. – Bungaree or bracelet, enameled, and set with diamonds. Manufactured at Dholepore, in Rajpootana'; Inventory 1868 (1852), 4: 'Bracelet. Gold, enamelled and set with diamonds. Indian (Dholepore in Rajpootana), modern'; V&A, 120-1852. The observations in the catalogue list praise the sword M 2 for its 'arrangement of form, and harmony of colour' and point to its hilt and scabbard as specimens of Indian art which is 'adapting the ornament to the form or space to be ornamented'; the concluding sentence, however, reverses this relationship between ornament and form when it says that 'The lines of the ornament ... seem to suggest the general form, rather than to have been suggested by it' (CatM⁵, 41; CatM¹, 26, having 'adapting the ornament so perfectly to the form or space to be ornamented'). Semper does not discuss this relationship but focuses on the way in which the distribution of colours results in 'variety and contrast ... combined with harmony and repose' due to 'a common key' of 'the whole tone of the system of colours' and to 'the system of subordination' (83.4–7). However, Semper's fragmentary drafts differ from the printed text in one major point. Whereas the latter – speaking of the colours used for the bracelets M 11 and 12, as well as for the sword – states that 'a common hue or tint' is 'passing from the green through the white to the red, which last ... is thus made the dominant colour of the whole system' (82.23–6), the drafts do not mention white or red as belonging to the 'general hue or tint', nor do they identify red as dominating the colour system generally but only refer to 'a neutral Jade Colour, which is the base and the key of the whole System' (365.20–1; similarly at 364.15–16).   82.28 **greenish on the scabbard, where**] The version in the sixth edition of the catalogue changes the sentence to 'greenish. On the scabbard' (CatM^6, 18), thus erroneously claiming that the neutral jade colour of the bracelets is green (it is blue on the actual bracelets, combined with red, green and white) – which is, according to Semper, the dominant colour only of the scabbard and the lower part of the hilt.

83.20 **jade vases of the Chinese and Indian**] Matthew Digby Wyatt's monumental work on *The Industrial Arts of the Nineteenth Century* has two corresponding plates with a 'Group of crystal vases, and Indian jewellery' (Wyatt 1851/53, 1: pl. 40) and 'Chinese vases in jade stone' (Wyatt 1851/53, 2: pl. 118).   83.23 **jade vases, M 102 and M 103**] M 102 is not a vase but a box; see CatM^5, 55: 'M 102. – Jade box and lid, inlaid with rubies. Manufactured at Lahore'; Inventory 1868 (1852), 4: 'Box. Green jade. Oblong, octagonal; with cover inlaid with gold and rubies. Indian (Lahore), modern'; V&A, 1627-1852. For M 103, see CatM^5, 55: 'M 103. – Jade cup, inlaid with rubies and emeralds. Manufactured at Lahore'; Inventory 1868 (1852), 56: 'Vase. White jade, inlaid with gold and with rubies and emeralds. Indian (Lahore), modern'; V&A, 1625-1852. It is the vase illustrated to the left of the plate with Indian jewellery in Wyatt 1851/53, 1: pl. 40.

84.2–3 **works of Vechte ~ worthy of being placed at the side of the works of Michael Angelo and Cellini**] The French goldsmith and jeweller Antoine Vechte was exiled in London from 1848. Two of his works purchased from the Great Exhibition are listed in *A Catalogue of the Museum of Ornamental Art*: the shield with subjects from Italian poets, which he designed and executed in iron repoussé for the Parisian gunmaker Le Page Moutier (M 63 in CatM^5, 49; Inventory 1868 [1852], 39; V&A, 1482-1851), and 'A large rosewater dish (suitable for a sideboard, centre ornament), representing a battle of Amazons', first being identified as a copy of 'The original ascribed to Cellini, but (? by Vechté)', and then of 'The original at Berlin, in iron, by Antoine Vechté' (M 91 in CatM^4, 38; CatM^5, 54). In *Science, Industry, and Art*, Semper refers to the electrotype copy of this dish exhibited by Elkington, Mason & Co. at the Great Exhibition (illustrated in Wyatt 1851/53, 2: pl. 138) – the original of which was bought for the Royal Kunstkammer in Berlin in the early 1840s – as Vechte's 'well-known dish in the Berlin Museum ...', which was purchased as an old-Italian work after drawings by Raphael' (Semper 1852, 48–9). He cites Elkington as an example of the growing quality of English manufacture, also praising the Cellini-like quality of a shield and vase by Vechte, namely the 'date-shaped vase with the battles of the Titans and the shield with the apotheosis of Shakespeare, Milton and Newton', 'of which Benvenuto had no need to be ashamed' (Semper 1852, 48). Vechte made them in silver repoussé for the jewellers and silversmiths Hunt & Roskell, who had shown them at the Great Exhibition (ODIC 1851, 2:686–8 [no. 97], here 686; Rep. Jur. 1852, 513, 736). Digby Wyatt, who illustrated them (Wyatt 1851/53, 1: pl. 27; 2: pl. 117), referred to 'the marvellous grace and refinement of the modelling and chasing' of Vechte's 'exquisite vase and unfinished shield' as proof that there

was 'ample room for improvement in English silversmith's work of the highest class' in his lecture of 1852 on the results of the Great Exhibition (Wyatt 1853, 241). Digby Wyatt's and Semper's praise stand in contrast to the position of A. W. N. Pugin, who – as a proponent of the Gothic style – was opposed to the plans of the purchasing committee to acquire one of Vechte's shields. This was probably the shield with the apotheosis of Shakespeare, Milton and Newton, of which only the Milton section was complete. Hunt & Roskell loaned the shield and vase to the Museum in 1852 (DPA[1], 287, 386), and the Museum appears eventually to have acquired the apotheosis shield (Cole 1884, 1:294). Vechte's Italian Poets Shield was shown (together with the Queen's 'Cellini Shield') with an initial specimen of a commercializable electrotype copy at Gore House during the exhibition of students' works there in May 1854 (DSA[2], 166, 202; Spectator 1854). Semper suggested Vechte as a teacher in the Department in a draft of his 'Plan of Instruction for the Metal and Furniture Classes' (372, Explanatory Notes 88.7; 374.26).   84.3–4 **vases and other works of Sèvres manufacture are beautiful specimens of modern enameling**] Semper had a special affinity to the royal porcelain manufactory at Sèvres through his friend Jules Dieterle, its principal designer, whom he had known since their collaboration on the Dresden Court Theatre. The Department took advantage of this contact in early January 1853, when Semper was sent to Paris to obtain technical information on porcelain painting from the directors of the Sèvres manufactory. On 9 January 1853, he reported to Henry Cole that 'Since I am at Sèvres, I have taken practical instructions in Enameling'. Three of the Sèvres enamels listed in the museum catalogue are illustrated in Matthew Digby Wyatt's work on the industrial arts with the plate of a 'Group of enamels from the royal manufactory at Sèvres' (Wyatt 1851/53, 1: pl. 51): In the foreground and background 'M 67. – Tazza and ewer, in enamel, on blue ground' (CatM[5], 50), listed in Inventory 1868 (1852), 21, as 'Ewer and Stand or Plateau. Enamel on copper. In imitation of Limoges painted enamel. French (Sèvres), modern' (V&A, 549-1852, ewer dated 1850; 550-1852, stand); in the middle of Wyatt's illustration 'M 68. – Large ewer, in enamel, on blue ground' (CatM[5], 50), listed in Inventory 1868 (1852), 21 (60-1852) as 'Ewer. Enamel on copper, mounted in ormolu. Imitation of Limoges painted enamel; in front an oval medallion with a group of Venus and two cupids. French (Sèvres). 1849'. The Sèvres vase with lid to the left of Wyatt's plate is the vase of which Semper had sketched the silhouette as an illustration of 'Emaille' in his 'Notes on the Great Exhibition' (33.9). Semper discusses Sèvres porcelain and enamels at some length in his Department lecture on the 'Influence of the Materials and Their Treatments upon the Development of Ceramic Types and Style' (156–8).   84.5 **sword, M 55**] CatM[5], 48: 'M 55. – Sword. Manufactured by Froment Meurice, 52, Faubourg St. Honoré, Paris … a copy of the sword presented to General Changarnier by the City of Paris'; maybe another copy in Inventory 1868 (1854), 29, as it was bought for a different price in 1854: 'Sword. Steel scabbard, oxydised silver hilt, with figure of the Archangel Michael; a copy of a sword presented to General Changarnier by the municipality of Paris. French. Made by Froment Meurice. Dated June 13, 1849'; V&A, 164-1854
84.7 **hunting knife in the style of the 15th century, manufactured by Marrel Freres**] The version of CatM[6], 19, also has 'in the style of the 15th century', while that in CatM[4], 23 (also DPA[1], 249), has 'in the style of the thirteenth century', in accordance with the catalogue lists in CatM[4], 31; DPA[1], 256; CatM[5], 47: 'M 50. – Hunting knife, representing the legend of St. Hubert. Style of the 13th century. Manufactured by Marrel Frères, 27, Rue Choiseul, Paris' (in the list of CatM[6], 26, the dating is omitted altogether); Inventory 1868 (1852), 40: 'Sword. Steel. A hunting sword ("couteau de chasse") with hilt and sheath in chiselled silver, representing subjects from the legend of St. Hubert, and various attributes of the chase. French,

362   Department of Practical Art

modern. (Marrel, Frères, Paris.)'; V&A, 159-1851.   84.9 **amourer's**] this misprint of *armourer's* also in CatM[4], DPA[1] and CatM[6]   84.12 **for the copying**] The earlier and later print variants all correctly have 'or the copying' (CatM[4], DPA[1], CatM[6]).   84.14–15 **newly acquired additions to the Museum, included in the numbers M 123 to M 134**] In contrast to this scope of new acquisitions by the Museum of Ornamental Art from early 1853, the fifth edition of the catalogue, in which Semper's supplementary text was first published, lists three additional numbers following M 121 – the last number for metalwork objects in the fourth edition of February 1853 (CatM[4], 41; CatM[5], 57–8): M 122 ('A series of medals in commemoration of the late Duke of Wellington'), M 135 ('Gold necklace') and M 136 ('An antique bronze jug'). The sixth edition of March 1854, which replaces some of the acquisitions of 1853, lists eight additional objects, M 137–M 144 (CatM[6], 37–8), while the list of the objects purchased for the museum during 1853 in the *First Report of the Department of Science and Art* of 1854 has forty-one additions, M 122–M 162 (DSA[1], 239–41).   84.17–19 **cast-iron knocker, M 125 ~ from the end of the 15th century**] This door knocker, together with the Gothic key (85.6), was purchased from A. W. N. Pugin's collection of ancient objects sold at auction by Sotheby's on 12 February 1853. Pugin lent the knocker to an exhibition which took place at the Society of Arts in 1850; it is described in the catalogue of this exhibition as having 'probably belonged to some religious house dedicated to St. John the Baptist, as it presents the subject of his decollation; a curious example of the transition from Gothic to Renaissance' (Wainwright 1994, 358 and fig. 16). In one of the drafts, Semper similarly states in a deleted passage that 'It shows the first traces of Renaissance elements, introduced into the Gothic Style' (367-8, note 367.2), and later he calls it a 'very inter[e]sting specimen of this period of transition' (367.22). Semper's mistake of identifying this door knocker as being cast was corrected in the sixth edition of the catalogue, where the sentence stating that 'It is one of the earliest pieces of iron casting I know' was deleted and the knocker explicitly listed as 'Wrought iron knocker' (CatM[6], 36). The knocker with plate and hammer is now said to be a composition assembled in the early nineteenth century from parts dating from the sixteenth century. See CatM[5], 57 (M 125): 'Iron Knocker. Purchased at the sale of Mr. Pugin's property'; CatM[6], 36 (M 125): 'Wrought iron Knocker, (Date, early part of 16th Century.)'; DSA[1], 239 (M 125): 'Ancient iron knocker wrought and chased'; Inventory 1868 (1853), 42: 'Knocker. Wrought iron. In form of a canopy; male and female figures in full relief on the columns; straight projecting hammer, on which is a kneeling figure under a canopy. German. About 1520'; V&A, 1221-1853.   84.34–8 **Peter Visscher's monument of St. Sebaldus ~ contrasts ~ with the design, made by another sculptor of the time ~ published by Heidcloff**] The bronze founder Peter Vischer cast the large shrine of St Sebaldus in St Sebaldus Church, Nuremberg, in 1507–19. The alternative design 'by another sculptor', dated 1488, had been attributed to Veit Stoss by Carl Heideloff in his *Ornamentik des Mittelalters*, where he had published it in three fascicles (Heideloff 1843/52, fasc. 6: pl. 3; fasc. 9: pls. 5–6; fasc. 10: pls. 2–4). The misprint of the author's name – correctly stated in the drafts (367.15, 369.3) – is corrected in CatM[6]. Semper had requested Heideloff's work from the British Museum Library as early as 1 July 1852, when he was working on his catalogue of 'Practical Art in Metals and hard Materials' (222.16–21).   84.38–9 **it would have been an error if Viet Stop's design had been adapted, suited as it is for wood carving, to be executed in cast-metal**] Both of Semper's drafts have the correct name of the woodcarver Veit Stoss. The misprint (also in CatM[6]) apparently was the result of a misreading of the manuscript. In the extant drafts, Semper has written the *ss* in *Stoss* as a German *ß* which looks similar to *p* (367.17, 369.4). The letter sequence *ei* in *Veit* is difficult to read in Semper's

Observations on Some of the Specimens of Metal Work 363

manuscripts, not least because the dot on the *i* is placed between the two letters. Heideloff's attribution of the first design of 1488 with Gothic pinnacles and much higher, spire-like, roofing to Veit Stoss is no longer upheld, which somewhat weakens Semper's argument that it follows the logic of wood construction instead of metal casting. Semper similarly argued in his catalogue of 'Practical Art in Metals and hard Materials' that Vischer's shrine 'was intended to be executed in a so called pure Gothical Style after the wooden Models of Veit Stoss who was a Wood-carver …, the Actual monument of Peter Visher, if less pure in its Architectural parts, is nevertheless better adapted to Metal Casting than it would have been the Case, if the bronze Sculptor had followed the prescriptions of his Wood Carving Competitor' (Semper 2007a, 240–1). Digby Wyatt had discussed Vischer's shrine with reference to Heideloff in his *Metal-Work and Its Artistic Design* of 1852, describing it as 'in that style which is generally known as the German Renaissance' (Wyatt 1852, 63). In the *First Report of the Department of Practical Art*, where the first part of Semper's 'Observations' was reprinted, a brief text on the 'Shrine of St. Sebaldus, at Nuremberg' by the architect Sydney Smirke (dated 6 December 1852) suggests obtaining for 'the School of Practical Art a perfect cast of this fine work' (DPA[1], 375; see the plaster cast of *c.* 1869 in V&A, REPRO.1869-14). Semper also refers to Vischer's Sebaldus shrine in his lecture 'Classification of Vessels' (145.25–8) and discusses it in the section on metals technology in *Style in the Technical and Tectonic Arts* as an example of the appropriation of the Italian Renaissance style in Germany and of 'a genuine cast-metal style … in comparison to the purer toreutic forms of the design prepared by Veit Stoss' (Semper 1860/63, 2:539, 586–7 n. 1).

85.6 **small Gothic key**] CatM[5], 57 (M 126): 'Gothic Key. Purchased at the sale of Mr. Pugin's property'; CatM[6], 36: 'Gothic key'; DSA[1], 239: 'Gothic key in chiselled iron'; Inventory 1868 (1853), 42: 'Key. Steel. Triangular head pierced with Gothic ornament, and transverse perforated tube on the stem. 15th cent[y]'; V&A, 900-1853   85.9–12 **Indian enamel vase ~ only example in the Museum ~ All the other Indian enamels are of the nature of Champleve's enamels ~ handles look rather Chinese or Japanese ~ a fine specimen of Oriental art**] This vase, which is tentatively identified here for the first time, seems to be missing from later inventories of the South Kensington Museum, as well as from V&A; the passage is omitted in the print variant of the sixth edition of the catalogue. The vase is listed as 'M 123. – An enameled Indian vase. Purchased of Mr. Heigham, at 7*s.* 6*d.* 1853' in the edition of the museum catalogue, in which Semper's text was first published (CatM[5], 57), while the next edition of the museum catalogue corrects the attribution from Indian to Chinese, apparently due to Semper's critique (CatM[6], 36, and DSA[1], 239, both have 'An enamelled Chinese vase'). Semper challenges the first attribution on formal grounds, saying of its handles that they 'look rather Chinese or Japanese', and adds technical reasons for distinguishing the enamels of the allegedly Indian vase from champlevé enamels (not 'Champleve's enamels', as misprinted in the catalogue; correctly written in the drafts: 367.29, 369.16) – the technique in which he says that all the other Indian enamel objects in the Museum are executed. His expert opinion on the vase under scrutiny as not being done in champlevé and thus not being Indian left its mark in a review of the Museum of Ornamental Art in *The Illustrated London News* of January 1854, where what is probably the same vase is illustrated – a small slender vase with six vertical bow handles at its short neck – and is described in Semper's words, together with the misprint, as being 'of Oriental (perhaps Japanese or Chinese) manufacture; and the only example in the Museum of this kind of enamelling executed in that part of the world; all the others being of the nature of Champleve's enamels' (ILN 1854, 60).

PRINT VARIANTS

82.9 **Metal Work.**] ~ ~, Enamels, &c. *CatM⁶*   82.10–11 **Semper. —**] *before subheading* On M 1, M 20, M 2. *CatM⁴ DPA¹*   82.16 **system**] ~ of arrangement *CatM⁶*   82.27–8 **pale, but always greenish on the scabbard, where**] pale, but always greenish. On the scabbard *CatM⁶*

83.15 **enter often**] often enter *CatM⁶*   83.20 **Chinese and Indian.**] ~ ~ Indians. *CatM⁶*   83.22 **in general.**] also. *CatM⁶*   83.23 **jade vases, M 102 and M 103,**] jade vases∧ M 102 and M 103∧ *CatM⁴ DPA¹*

84.2–4 **The works of Vechte ~ enameling.**] *om. CatM⁶*   84.5 **sword, M 55,**] sword∧ M 55∧ *CatM⁴ DPA¹*   84.7 **15th century**] thirteenth ~ *CatM⁴ DPA¹*   84.12 **required**] called for *CatM⁶*   **for the copying**] or ~ ~ *CatM⁴ DPA¹ CatM⁶*   84.13 **candelabra.**] candelabras. *CatM⁴ DPA¹*   84.14–85.15 **The newly acquired additions ~ models in themselves.**] *om. CatM⁴ DPA¹*   84.17 **cast-iron**] iron *CatM⁶*   84.38 **Heidcloff**] Heideloff *CatM⁶*

85.1 **classical (antique) style**] revived classical style *CatM⁶*   85.3 **cast-iron**] iron *CatM⁶*   85.4–5 **It is one of the earliest ~ specialty.**] *om. CatM⁶*   85.9–15 **3. Indian enamel vase ~ models in themselves.**] *om. CatM⁶*

MANUSCRIPT VARIANTS
MS 111[1]

fol. 5r   *1 a*   Observations on the Examples of Metal-Work in the Museum of the Department etc. etc. by GSemper.

To *M. 1, M. 20, and M. 2.*

The comparison of the two numbers M 1 and M 20 with the nunber M. 2 is very instructive for the Study of the use of colours in ornamental art.   5

We see at n° 1 hov the blue and green enamel-grounds stand crudely one against the other without being bound together and harmonized by a common tint. Even the introduction of Ruby or Purple colours into the system would hardly be sufficient for rendering it harmonious.

In M' 20 we observe the same deficiency of harmony but less evidently, because the green   10 and blue tints are broken and bound together by black.

In opposition to these and some similar Works of Indian art stand the beautiful Thulwar or

fol. 5v   sword n° 2. Here are the different brillant colours connected together by a general hue ¦ or tint, which is spread over the whole. Every colour is one shade of the scale to which all the other belong, and the Ground is formed by a Neutral Jade Colour, which forms the base of   15 the whole system.

This base is very pale greenish on the Scabbard; here it works together with the green leaves and gold rims, in opposition with the ruby or rather Sang de beuf flowers, which last are here governed by this combination.

The same "Alliance" between the Green of the leaves and the base or the Jade Ground   20 against the Red is more expressively pronounced on the lower part of the hilt, where the Jade ground assumes a darker greenish tint.

Observations on Some of the Specimens of Metal Work   365

On the middle part of the hilt. on the contrary we see the Base or Ground entering into an alliance with the Red, and so putting the Green into the Minority and Opposition.

3 So we observe here two accomplishments of orna-

> 364.6 **hov**] *'how'*   **enamel-grounds**] s *added*   364.7 **being bound**] *after del.* reliance tog
> 364.10 **In**] *after del.* The same deficiency is visible but less   364.13 **n° 2.**] *altered from* ~ ~,
> *before del.* with   364.14 **is one**] *is repl. del.* forms a step upon the   **to**] *above del.* by
> 364.15 **belong,**] *altered from* ~. *before del.* The Red is mixd with   364.18 **beuf**] *'bœuf'*
> 364.19 **here**] *after del.* in   364.22 **the**] *above del.* an   **assumes**] *above del.* takes

MS 111²

Few Observations on the Examples of Metal-Work, exhibited in the Museum for Practical   *2 a*   *fol. 1r*

5 Art.

by G Semper.

To M 1. M. 20. M. 2.

The comparison between the numbers M 1 and M 20 and the number M 2 is very interesting for the Study of ornamental color.

10 We see at n° 1 how the blue and green Enamel Grounds stand crudely one against another without beeing bound together and harmonized by a common parenty. The introduction of Ruby or Purple into the System as it is, will hardly be sufficient for rendering it more harmonious.

In M. 20 we observe some deficiency of harmony, but here less evidently because the green

15 and blue tints are broken and bound together by black.

In Opposition to these and some similar Works of Indian art stand the beautiful Thalwar or Sword n° 2 with some other || Objects of the same Style, as for instance the bracelets M 11   *3 a*   *fol. 2r*
and M 12.; Here are the different brillant colours connected together by a general hue or tint, which is spread over the whole. Every colour is one shade of the Scale to which all the

20 other belong, and the Ground is formed by a neutral Jade Colour, which is the base and the key of the whole System.

This base is very pale, but greenish on the scabbard, here it works with the green leaves and the Gold rims against the ruby or rather against the Sang De boeuf flowers, which last are here governed by this combination.

25 This alliance between the green leaves and the Jade-coloured base against the Red is more powerful on the lower part of the hilt, where the Ground assumes a darker greenish tint.

On the middle part of the hilt, we see the Base or Ground || entering into an alliance with   *4 a*   *fol. 3r*
the Red and so putting the Green into the Minority and Opposition. The two principles of ornamental colouring are here most happily combined, viz variety and opposition, – har-

30 mony and repose, and this result has been obtained by observing the common relations between the colours and by the system of hierarchy, which has been adopted for them.

> 365.4 **Few**] *interl.*   365.8 **and the**] *and repl. del.* with   365.9 **color**] *after del.* Col *after del.*
> Colorit   365.11 **parenty**] *after del.* tint   365.14 **some**] *inserted before del.* the Same
> 365.27 **Ground**] *before del.* entirely   365.28 **The**] *inserted*   **two**] t *over* T   365.29 **most**
> **happily**] *repl. del.* happily   365.30 **observing**] *repl. del.* holding

MS 111[3]

fol. 7r

of colours has been tempered, as well as by the hierarchical principle, which has been carried throw the whole. –

The first quality, the harmony obtained by a common base or tune of the colours which enter into the system, is one of the great mysteries of beauty, which prevail unerring throughout the whole nature, and such works of men, which are simple expressions of natural artistical instinct.

They are generally very harmonious in colours, which result has been obtained by the natural hue of the materials which were employed for their confection, which hue forms the base and the ligament between the lively colours, which enter sometimes into their compositions.

So for instance the Straw and rush carpets of the Oriental, American, and African people, so the Embroideries upon Leather and Wood-barks of the Canadians, so the Raw-Silk and Cotton Tissues of the Chinese and the wool Shawls of the Persians. So also the Terra Cotta works of the Ancients, and the Jade vases of the Indian and Chinese.

Specimens of these and other objects of primitive ornamental art are extremely necessary for the Museum, and their utility will be increased by the juxtaposition of such things,

fol. 7v

which give occa- ¦ sions for comparison and explication. So for Instance will it be perhaps good to place the Jade Vases, nᵒ 102 and nᵒ 103, near the Enamels, which I mentionned before, the last being quasi imitations of the inlaid Stones upon the neutral ground of the natural materials. –

The accomplishment of an object of ornamental art, which arises from the due subordination of the ornamental parts under one main impression, is not often to be found on objects of early periods of art, and seldom prevails in oriental art, which generally suffers from the Absence of this principle. We see flowers and Ornaments spread over the whole forms like net-works. So most of the Vases, the pieces of armour and several other Objets of Oriental Art. The above mentionned Sword forms, herein a beautiful exception, though the hierarchical principle in it seems to be neutralized by its double application.

Herein the Egyptian, Greec and Renaissance works are far more instructiv

366.1 **of colours**] *inserted*   366.2 **throw**] *'through'*   366.3 **harmony**] *before del.* of colours   366.4 **beauty**] *above del.* art   **prevail**] *above del.* we find   **unerring**] *'unerringly'; inserted*   366.9 **their**] ir *added*   366.9–10 **compositions**] *after del.* systems of   systems] *final* s *added*   366.11 **Oriental, American,**] *repl. del.* Indians   366.12 **Raw-Silk**] *after del.* Yellow   366.14 **and the Jade vases**] *after del.* and of some   366.15 **Specimens of**] *inserted*   **these**] t *over* T   366.17 **perhaps**] *after del.* very   366.18 **which**] *before del.* are   366.19 **quasi imitations of**] *after del.* a sort of imitation of   366.21 **accomplishment**] *after del.* second   366.27 **it seems**] *after del.* it appears not so effectfully as it is only

MS 113[1]

fol. 3r   5.a

The objects, which have been newly acquired for the Museum (from nᵒ 123 – nᵒ 134) are alltogether more or less interesting for history of style, and some of them are very fine specimens of ornamental art.

Among the last are to be named

Observations on Some of the Specimens of Metal Work   367

a) the Iron knocker, coming probably from Nurnberg or Augsburg and dating from the End
of the 15th or the Beginning of the 16th Century. –
The Gothic style in Germany had lost all its simplicity and purity with the beginnig of the
15th century and before and this early decay of the Gothic style was owed partly to the introduction of new processes in executing the objects of architecture and practical art.
One of the most influential innovations of this kind was that of casting objects, in metal;
which before ¦ were used to be cut or built in stone or other hard materials, or to be executed in chased, hammered, and forged Metal. – ......
The objects had obtained under the influence of the old processes a certain conventional
style, which now became contradictional to the new manner of execution, and its conservation therefore would have been a fault from the part of the artist instead of being a merit.
Peter Vishers Monument of St. Sebald forms one great and very interesting evidence of this
fact. It is very impure in style as a Gothical monument, and contrasts in this respect very
much with the plan for the same monument, which had been made by Veit Stoss, an other
great Sculptor; who's working drawings have been published by Heydeloff in its ornanental
art.
Now it would have been a great fault if Veit Stoss's project had been executed, instead of that
impur but for Metal-casting better adapted plan of Peter Fisher. –
The classical (antique forms | and practical art in General, which first became at this time
to be introduced in architecture and practical arts, was therefore a happy solution of contradictions, which longtime before was felt
The Cast Iron knocker is a small but very intersting specimen of this period of transition. It
is one of the earliest known Iron-Casts, and has therefore a special Interest for the Study of
processes. –
The small Gothic key is in some regard of companion to the first. as it shows Iron forging in
combination with the purer forms of Gothic style. –
3) The Indian Enamel Vase if it is Indian, is the only example at the Musium which shows,
that this kind of processes. in Enameling is known by the Indian Artisans. All the others
are Champlévé Enamels or some-thing near to it. The handles look rather Chinese.
At all Events it forms a fine Specimen of Oriental Art and gives an evidence of the limits in
employing bright colours without disharmony.
The Chinese Censor is a beautiful Specimen of old China Casting ¦ The other Objects have
more interest for the history of art. than for themselves.

fol. 3v (right margin, line 7)

6 a   fol. 4r (right margin, line 19)

fol. 4v (right margin, line 31)

> 366.29 **The objects**] *after two del. variant beginnings:*
>
> Some² new¹ acquisitions for the Museum of practical Art are fine specimens³ of
> Some of the new acquisitions for the Museum are fine Specimens of practical art, and all
> of them have Interest for
>
> > 1 **Some new ~ Interest for**] *accompanied by sketch of what is possibly a plan of houses
> > and streets*   2 **Some**] *repl. del.* Among the   the] *undel.*   3 **fine specimens**] *after
> > del.* some   some] *before del.* very interesting, as well for
>
> 366.29 **n° 123**] n° *interl.*   **n° 134**] n° *interl.*   366.30 **style**] *after del.* ornamental art and
> ornamental art] *repl. del.* art   **very**] *interl.*
> 367.1 **probably from**] *inserted before del.* without doubt from   **Nurnberg or Augsburg**]
> *repl. del.* Germany,   367.2 **15th**] *before del.* century.   **Century. –**] *before del.* It shows the

368   Department of Practical Art

first traces of Renaissance elements, introduced into the Gothic Style.   367.3 **simplicity**]
after del. purit   367.4 **before**] *after del.* even   367.4–5 **introduction**] *after del.* progresses
and before del. of new processes, by which the objects of prac[t]   processes,] *altered from*
~∧ *before del.* in art   367.6 **that**] *after del.* the more general employment of Cast meta
more] *after del.* intr   **objects,**] *before del.* which before   367.7 **were**] *after del.* had taken [t]
used to be] *above del.* usually   **or other hard materials**] *interl.*   367.9 **The**] *after del.*
The influence of the old processes in executing them had given to these objects a certain
conventional style, and this style, allthough   and] *after del.* which was not more necessary
of the old] *repl. del.* of these   367.10 **and**] *after del.* and by this conflict, purity of forms
could not well be   367.12 **Vishers**] V *over* F   **great and**] *interl.*   **this**] t *over* I *after*
del. what   367.13 **and**] *after del.* and if the Models in wood   367.14 **plan**] *above del.*
working drawings   working drawings] *before del.* of another arti   **an other**] an | other
367.15 **who's**] *after del.* which   **its**] *'his'*   367.18 **Metal-casting**] Metal- | casting *after*
del. casti   **Fisher**] *'Vischer'*   367.19 **The**] *after del.* This *and before del.* introduction of
forms] *before del. on fol. 4r* in the forms of Architecture   **first**] *interl.*   **became**] *insert-*
ed before inserted and del. reknown *and repl. del.* took place   367.20 **to be introduced** ~
practical arts,] *inserted*   a] *after del.* long wished for and   367.21 **was**] as *over* ere
367.22 **Cast Iron**] *after del.* Iron   367.23 **known**] *inserted after del.* Cast-Iron specimens
and before del. which I kn[o]   Cast-Iron] *underl.*   **Iron-Casts,**] *before del.* as metal-
Casting which I know,   as] *after del.* as Iron-Casting.   367.25 **in some regard**] *repl. del.*
so to speak   **of companion**] *after del.* a sort *(see 369.12: 'the companion')*   367.26 **style.**]
altered from ~, *before del.* which   367.27 **if it is Indian**] Indian *after del.* true   **at the**
Musium] *'at the Museum'; interl.*   367.27–8 **which shows, that**] *inserted before del.* of Indian Enamels of   of Indian] *after del.* of that process of Enameling   Enamels] *before del.*
of the third   367.29 **some-thing**] some- *altered from* ~∧ *and* thing *after del.* kind   367.30
At] *after del.* This   in] *after del.* which   367.32 **Censor**] *'censer'*   367.33 **the**] *after del.* s[t]

MS 113²

fol. 1r   The Objects, which have been newly acquired for the Museum (from n° 123 – to n° 134) are,
allmost all, very interesting for history of style and some of them are fine specimens of or-
nament. – .
Among the last takes the first place the Iron knocker, which comes very probably from
Nürenberg or Augsburg, or some other town of Middle-Germany. It dates from the End of   5
the 15ᵗʰ Century. –
The Gothic Style in Germany had lost all its simplicity and purity with the beginning of the
15ᵗʰ Century and even before. and the early decay of the Goth. Style was owed partly to the
Introduction of new Processes in executing the Objects of Architecture and Practical Art.
One of the most influential innovations of this kind was that of Casting metal and of form-   10
ing objects of architecture and ornamental art by casting them, which were used before to
be cut or built in hard materials or to be executed in chased, hammered and forged metal. |
fol. 1v   The architectural and ornamental forms had obtained under the influence of the old processes a certain conventional style, which now became contradictory to the new manner of
execution. –   15
Under these circumstances it would have been a fault, instead of being a merit, if the strong
forms of the old style were conserved by the artists and architects of the 15ᵗʰ century.
Peter Visher's Monument of St. Sebaldus forms a great and very interesting Evidence of this
fact.

Observations on Some of the Specimens of Metal Work   369

It is indeed very impure in style as a Gothical Monument and contrasts in this respect very much with the plan, which was made by another Sculptor of the time, Veit Stoss. for the same Monument, who's working Drawings have been published by Heideloff.

Now I maintain that it would have been a great fault, if Veit Stoss's Wood-carved Models had been executed in Cast-Metal instead of that impur but for Metal-casting admirably adapted plan of Peter Visher.

The Classical, (antique) style, which at this time became to be introduced, was therefore a happy solution of these contradictions, which long before was waited for. |

The Cast-Iron Knocker is a small, but very interesting specimen of this Period of Transition. It is one of the earliest *Iron-Casts* I know, and has a special Interest for the history of this speciality.

2° The Small Gothic key is in some respect the companion to the first, as it shows Iron-forging in combination with the purer forms of Gothic style.

3°) Indian Enamel Vase.

If it is Indian, then it is the only Example at the Museum of this kind of Enameling execut-ed by Indians. All the other Indian Enamels being Champlevé enamels or something of the kind.

The Handles look rather Chinese or Japonese.

At all Events it forms a fine Specimen of Oriental Art and gives an evidence of the limits in employing bright colours without disharmony.

The other objects have more Interest for history of Style than they are beautiful models for themselves. Some of the Emblems etc. appear to me not interesting enow, to behold their places in the Museum.

GSemper
March, 1853.

fol. 2r

368.2 **allmost all, very**] *repl. del.* alltogether more or less   **fine**] *after del.* very   368.17 **were**] *after del.* would   **and architects**] *inserted*
369.2 **Veit Stoss.**] *inserted*   369.7 **style**] *above del.* forms   **therefore**] fore *added*
369.12–13 **Iron-forging**] Iron- | forging   369.15–16 **executed**] *repl. del.* used   369.16 **being**] *repl. del.* are   369.21 **more**] *repl. del.* only   369.22 **appear**] *after del.* are not very
behold] *derived from German* 'behalten': 'keep'

A Plan of Instruction for the Metal and Furniture Classes

TEXTUAL RECORD

MS 114   gta, 20-Ms-114, fols. 1r–10v (9r, 10r and all versos blank), in Semper's hand, dated 1 February 1853

DPA[1]   'A Plan of Instruction for the Metal and Furniture Classes', in *First Report of the Department of Practical Art*, London: Eyre & Spottiswoode for Her Majesty's Stationery Office, 1853, 372–4 (NAL, 602.AD.0777), *copy-text*

Semper 1884   'Unterrichtsplan für die Abteilung für die Metall- und Möbeltechnik', 100–4, German trans. of DPA[1] (85.20–87.33, 87.37–8, 88.8–21)

Wingler 1966   'Unterrichtsplan für die Abteilung für Metall- und Möbeltechnik am Department of Practical Art', 83–6, ed. of Semper 1884

Semper 2014   vol. 2, 542–4, Karge's reprint ed. of DPA[1]

BIBLIOGRAPHY Pevsner 1940, 251–3, 255–6, 264; Reising 1976, 60; Herrmann 1978, 65, 73–4, 129; Herrmann 1981, 108; Herrmann 1984, 59, 66–7; Mallgrave 1996, 212; Squicciarino 2009, 263–6

EXPLANATORY NOTES

Semper's explanation of his plans for teaching in the Department of Practical Art outlines his own input into the reform of education in the decorative and applied arts that Henry Cole was seeking to achieve through the founding of the successor organization of the Government Schools of Design. The latter were primarily concerned with teaching the basics of drawing and the mastery of ornamental forms. Semper's proposals correspond to the ideas for the new Department that Cole set out also in the *First Report of the Department of Practical Art* – namely, systematically combining into special classes instruction on the theories and principles of ornamental design and its stylistic history on the one hand, and the technical side of the various fields of manufacture on the other (DPA[1], 18–19). Yet Semper went beyond this for his special class on metalworking, furniture and jewellery by proposing new solutions to the never fully implemented objective of the Schools of Design, which was 'the direct practical application of the arts to manufactures' (DPA[1], 22).

Semper's proposals were only novel and revolutionary in England, as he was adopting the teaching system that he had already used in the Dresden Academy of Fine Arts, consisting of courses organized as studio workshops in which students at all levels worked together and were involved in the professor's private commissions, thus continually being in direct contact with practical work in manufacturing and architecture. Although Cole approved of this in principle, he called for 'much caution' and emphasized the experimental character of this kind of practical teaching (DPA[1], 22, 28) – a point explicitly highlighted as a 'new experiment' in Semper's appointment conditions (227.2). Cole's reservations may also be reflected in certain differences between the published text and Semper's extant draft – differences that arose due to revisions, possibly by Cole, not only of language but also content. Semper had also outlined his teaching principles in *Science, Industry, and Art* in terms of courses

A Plan of Instruction for the Metal and Furniture Classes

conceived as practical studio workshops and against the backdrop of collections, lectures and competitions (Semper 1852, 62–72) – in a manner similar to his teaching plan for the Department of Practical Art and Cole's intentions. Cole may therefore have been the person at whose 'private request' *Science, Industry, and Art* was written (see 262).

85.18 **F.**] designates the text as one of several miscellaneous texts in 'Appendix VII' of the *First Report of the Department of Practical Art*, to which Semper's 'Report on the Private Collection of Arms at Windsor Castle' (76–80) also belongs   85.26–7 **It differs in the following essential points from that of schools of design and academies**] Semper here defines three 'essential points' – joint studio workshops for students of all levels, subjects of instruction according to the interests of the students, participation in work for which the professor has been commissioned – that correspond to the basic elements of his method of teaching architecture at the Dresden Academy of Fine Arts. He refers to this in the draft at the end of the third point, where he addresses 'practical knowledge and experience' (86.9); the draft here mentions an 'Apendix on the School of architects at Dresden' (373.15). The appendix must have largely corresponded to Semper's report on his Dresden teaching programme, of which Hans Semper published a German version (Semper 1880, 10–11). This programme specifies the three 'essential points' of Semper's London 'Plan of Instruction' and says of the second point that 'The exercises took place in no particular order on the principle that each work was to be continued uninterruptedly until it was completed, although each person was free to take on another work in-between for a change'. Semper had already referred to his Dresden system of instruction in his plans for a private school of architecture. In one of them, he says of the 'System of instruction' that it 'will embrace every branch of Architecture, comprising the science of Engineering, and the principles of Decoration' (8.10–11). In the most elaborate school programme given in a German draft, Semper differentiates between the preparatory 'Bauschule' (school of architecture) and the 'Atelier' (studio) 'where the work is carried out in front of my eyes and right next to my working cabinet' (9.20–2). Cole was aware of the practical side of this teaching method, as Semper wrote to him about his school plans and probably sent the programme to him in March 1851 (see 236). When he wrote to Cole on 8 April 1852 – the letter is dated 'Thursday 9 April 1852' but written on Thursday, 8 April 1852 – during his visit to Herbert Minton's pottery factory in Stoke-on-Trent, he also sketched out his Dresden method as a reference point for reversing the relationship between the teaching of details and the overall context of a practical work, from which 'higher instruction in the Schools of Design ought to go out': 'I used to go this way with my pupils, which, after some short preparing exercises in the first use of drawing utensils, in projections etc, soonly tried to set upon paper some part of a building in conformity to modern practice in domestic disposition and construction, and then afterwards to put together a whole cottage etc, in working out, as well as possible, the whole inner & outer parts of the building. It was only when they wanted leaves, flowers, figures etc for some decorative parts of their compositions, that they were let to draw such objects, and to make studies after casts or after nature, which they could use for the purpose they actually intended' (Semper to Cole, 8 April 1852). Semper again refers to his Dresden 'system of instruction' in his 'Second Report on the Class for Practical Construction, Architecture, and Plastic Decoration' (92.3–5).

86.25–30 **Composition of objects of ornamental art ~ art of composition**] Semper's draft instead speaks of 'Instruction how to invent objects of ornamental art' and of the 'talent and spirit for composition' (373.26, 373.30).   86.33–6 **Those copies ~ work out to**

completion.] Semper's draft formulates a sharper critique of the traditional adherence to the task of copying after models and nature (373.31–2): 'Many good talent has been spoild by having been too long time engaged with copiing and studiing from models and even from nature.'

87.28–30 **To that medal might be attached, by the Board of Trade ~ advantages ~ to be ~ determined upon**] a cautious reformulation of the costly proposal in the draft, where Semper suggests a travel scholarship of three to four years, following the example of academies of art (374.15–16)

88.1–6 **Professors of the Department ~ combined for instructional purposes ~ Simpson ~ Townsend, Brucciani, and Semper**] In the *First Report of the Department of Practical Art*, Richard Redgrave similarly suggested ways of combining the special classes into 'a systematic course of instruction' intended to 'bring the various professors of those classes into more united action'. Semper is included there along with John Simpson, Domenico Brucciani and Henry James Townsend, with somewhat different responsibilities in the field of the 'Constructive and Plastic Art', where 'The instruction ... would belong to Professor Semper, conjoined with Mr. Townsend, for artistic anatomy, and the study of the figure by drawing, modelling, painting, &c.; with Mr. Richardson for geometrical &c. drawing, &c.; with Mr. Simpson for enamelling, and, assisted by Mr. Brucciani, for moulding, casting, and cast making.' While Semper does not name the architect Charles James Richardson, Redgrave in turn names Semper in the following group responsible for the 'Decoration of Surfaces', where 'The instruction ... would be entrusted to Mr. O. Hudson, conjoined with Mr. Simpson for enamels and the surface treatment of china, and with Professor Semper for architectural arrangements of surfaces' (Redgrave 1853, 369–70). Redgrave thus indirectly anticipated Richardson's replacement by Semper (see 328). 88.7 **Chasing and embossing. By**] The blank left for a name is filled with that of Antoine Vechte in Semper's draft (374.26). Henry Cole had already 'agreed to allow Vechte to teach Repousee' on 19 October 1852 (Cole Diary). However, further evidence of efforts made to employ Vechte in the Department is as yet lacking. Semper refers to Vechte in his 'Observations on Some of the Specimens of Metal Work' (84.2) and discusses some of his works in *Science, Industry, and Art* (Semper 1852, 48–9). 88.13–14 **on the relations of the different branches of practical art to each other, and to architecture**] This became the title of Semper's first public lecture at the Department of Practical Art given on 20 May 1853, of which he says in his 'First Report' that it had as its objective the explanation of his system, which he was developing in the following lectures (91.1–3; see section 'Lectures'). 88.20–1 **Department of Practical Geology**] for the application of geological museology to teaching of the arts and crafts, see 'Report on the Private Collection of Arms at Windsor Castle', 79.13–18

A Plan of Instruction for the Metal and Furniture Classes   373

MANUSCRIPT VARIANTS
MS 114

Scheme of Instruction for the Metal, – Furniture, – (and Pottery).   *1.*   *fol. 1r*
division conducted by Professor Semper

I. *Method of Instruction.*
It has been proved by experiences, that for teaching practical art the form of the *work-shops*
5   or *Ateliers* answers the best, which I propose to adopt for this class.
It differs essentially from that of classes or schools by a less systematical mode of instruction. In the workshops are
1° no divisions by classes of the Pupils or Students after their Ages and progresses in Art. –
2°) no strong divisions of the time for teaching after a Plan of Studies, except for lectures
10   and such instructions, which the students will have ¦| in common with other classes and by   *2*   *fol. 2r*
other Professors.
3) The Pupils or Students assist the Patron of the Atelier in his profession, and being brought
by this way into contacts with the practice and with the different crafts, they will have the
best opportunity of getting practical knowledge.
15   (See Apendix on the School of architects at Dresden.).

II. Subjects of Instruction.
a. *Geometrical principles of Design*, including Perspective and shadow-construction, illustrated with examples, which are taken so as to be in the same time exercises in proportions and
the elementary forms of practical Art and Architecture. (See Lectures.) ¦|
20   b) *The principles of Style*, illustrated with examples, which are to be copied by the students.   *3.*   *fol. 3r*
These exercises must be in the same time courses of technology and history of practical art.
The models are either real objects of practical Art, or facsimiles of them, or finally drawings.
The most usual mode of copiing is by drawings with or without colours. But it will be in
many circumstances desirable, to have them done by modelling, and therefore opportunities
25   are given in the Rooom for modelling in clay and wax.
C) Instruction how to invent objects of ornamental art.
This essential part of the instruction in art is the most neglected. The Students pess the
whole of their time in copiing and making studies after nature, without triing their forces ¦|
on their own creations.   *4*   *fol. 4r*
30   The talent and spirit for composition ought to find encouragement from the beginning of
the artistical education – Many good talent has been spoild by having been too long time
engaged with copiing and studiing from models and even from nature.
I therefore make for my class, the following proposition.

Competitions
35   Competitions between the students will take place, regularly every fortnight on Monday.
The Students must then spend one day by composing sketches for any objects of ornamental
art, which have been proposed in written Programms fixed on the wall, the morning of the
same Day, by the Professor.
Two such Programms will be given at the same time, one for the beginners and one for the
40   more advanced Students. ¦| which will be classified only by this distinction.   *5*   *fol. 5r*
The sketches must be ready *in one day*. Those who are not delivered the same day, are out of
competition.

The Professor will hold the next, or one of the next days a critical review of the delivered sketches and point out, together with his students, which of the sketches are the best. Small Rewards and official Certificates will be delivered to the compositors of the two best sketches.

—————————

Great Prices.

Besides these small competitions there will be twice a Year competitions of finished works. (concours rendus)

The Programms of these compositions will be given at the first Mondays of the Month's April, and September. The time allowed for the works is 6 weeks.

The competition of the Month of September |‖ will be the so called great price competition. Then the winners will be rewarded by golden, Silver and Brass Medals, and by Certificates. – The Great golden Medal is the highest price, which will only be given in such cases when one of the competitors was not only the best relating to the other, but did absolutely well; This great medal procures to the winner the pension, for travelling three, (or four) Years for finishing his artistical education;

The other competition takes place the same way as the former, except that no higher prices than the Silver Medal will be given.

The works of the Pensionairs are proprieties of the Department.

The works which have gained medals or certificates will in cases be acquired by the Departement.

Further Details about these competitions must be given in a special Programm. |‖

D. *Different Processes.*

1) *Enameling*, different processes of Enameling by M$^{rs.}$ Simpson and Semper.

2). Modelling, forming and casting (in plaster) by Mrs Townsend, Semper and Brucciani.

3) Chasing and embossing by Mr. Wechte.

E. *Lectures.*

1) on the relations of the different branches of practical art between each other and to architecture. (including notions on Style and history of art.).

Public lectures.

2). On the geometrical principles of Design, including Perspective and Shadow Construction.

For Students only.

Lecture prepared for following Semesters, on |‖

1. *Technology*, especially with regard to metalworking furniture, decoration etc. Public.

2. *Construction.* Private.

—————————

1^r February 1853.

Gottfried Semper

373.4 **for teaching**] *after del.* for institutions   **work-shops**] work- | shops   373.8 **1°**] *accompanied in opposite column by del.* note. As conditions for intrance   note.] *underl.* 373.16 **Instruction.**] *altered from* ~∧ *before del.* within the Atelier.   373.27 **pess**] *'pass'* 373.28 **without**] with | out   373.31 **Many**] *altered from* many *after del.* On the other hand 373.34 **Competitions**] *in left margin* 374.6 **Great Prices.**] *in left margin*   374.7 **twice**] *above del.* 3 times   374.8 **rendus**] *after del.* de   374.10 **April**] *above del.* January, May   374.11 **September**] *below del.* October 374.19 **proprieties**] *'the property' (see 87.31)*   374.20 **will**] *after del.* will occasionally be

374.24 **Mʳˢ·**] *'Messrs'*   374.25 **Mʳˢ**] *'Messrs'*   374.26 **Wechte**] *'Vechte'*   374.27 **E.**] *after del.* 4)   374.34 **Lecture**] *altered from* Lectures   374.35 **metalworking furniture, decoration etc.**] *repl. del.* the different productions of ornamental and practical art.   **furniture**] *after del.* and

First Report on the Class for Practical Construction, Architecture, and Plastic Decoration

TEXTUAL RECORD

MS 115¹   gta, 20-Ms-115, fols. 1r–2v (on blueish paper), in Semper's hand

MS 159   gta, 20-Ms-159, *fol. 147r–v (on thin greyish paper, in a manuscript relating to Semper 1859), in Semper's hand

MS 115²   gta, 20-Ms-115, fol. 3r–v (on thick brownish paper), in Semper's hand, continuation of MS 159

DSA¹   'Report of Professor Semper on the Class for Practical Construction, Architecture, and Plastic Decoration', in *First Report of the Department of Science and Art*, London: Eyre & Spottiswoode for Her Majesty's Stationery Office, 1854, 210–11 (NAL, 97.PP.83), *copy-text*

Semper 1884   'Bericht über die Abteilung für Architektur-, Metall- und Möbeltechnik und praktisches Entwerfen', 95–9, German trans. of DSA¹ (88.27–89.36, 90.1–6, 90.10–27, 90.32–91.17)

Wingler 1966   'Bericht über die Abteilung für Architektur-, Metall- und Möbeltechnik und praktisches Entwerfen', 87–90, ed. of Semper 1884

Semper 2014   vol. 2, 561–2, Karge's reprint ed. of DSA¹

BIBLIOGRAPHY Ettlinger 1940; Reising 1976, 60–1; Herrmann 1978, 74–5, 80; Herrmann 1981, 108; Herrmann 1984, 67–9, 73; Mallgrave 1996, 214–15; Bonython/Burton 2003, 152–3; Squicciarino 2009, 268–71; Orelli-Messerli 2010, 210–36, 250–2; Hvattum 2021

EXPLANATORY NOTES

Semper's first report on his 'Class for Practical Construction' at the Department of Practical Art and its successor organization, the Department of Science and Art, is an important document – despite its brevity. It encompasses many of the topics that Semper addresses in his 'Plan of Instruction for the Metal and Furniture Classes' and gives information about two commissions with which he was able to put into practice the idea of organizing his teaching according to the concept of studio workshops – Wellington's funeral car, as a work connected to Semper's metal class, which he spent a great deal of energy on; and a sideboard for the Secretary of the Board of Trade, James Emerson Tennent, as a work related to his instruction in furniture, to which Semper attached less importance. Three fragmentary

376   Department of Practical Art

drafts are extant; the first part of the most complete one is identified here for the first time (MS 159, with MS 115[2] as its already known continuation), preserved in a folder with notes for another text on which Semper was working at the time – his essay *Ueber die bleiernen Schleudergeschosse der Alten* (On the Leaden Slingshot Bullets of the Ancients). On 24 January 1854, Henry Cole reminded Semper that 'We have not yet received your Annual Report, will you send it as soon as possible – as we are waiting to send it to the Printers'. Cole, or perhaps Richard Redgrave, must have revised Semper's definite manuscript – probably also with changes to the content in the places where the differences between the existing drafts and the printed text are particularly striking (see, for example, notes 88.28, 89.14).

88.24 **d.**] denotes Semper's report as the first of the 'Reports on Technical Instruction in Art' (DSA[1], 210), which include the reports on 'Textile Classes for Surface Decoration' (e), 'Mechanical Drawing' (f), 'Wood Engraving' (g), 'Lithography' (h) and 'Porcelain Painting' (i) 88.28 **practical composition**] The term 'practical composition', possibly an amendment by Henry Cole, generalizes the term 'practical construction' named both in the title of Semper's report on his special class and in the drafts, which here also have 'practical construction' or 'practical construction in general' (381.2–3, 381.20, 383.2). Equally, Semper's drafts have – instead of 'subject of *practical composition*' in the next sentence (88.29) – 'practical instruction' (with 'instruction' preceded by deleted 'ar', for 'architecture'; 381.4), 'practical construction and the principles of architecture' (in a parallel variant; 382, note 381.2) or, again, 'practical construction' (381.27, 383.3). One sentence later, the same amendment led from 'practical construction, as I understand this expression' (383.4–5) to 'practical composition in the more extended sense of the expression (as I understand it,)' (88.30–1). Semper apparently had in mind construction as a general term covering the foundations not only of architecture but also of other arts, including metalworking and furniture making, for which he was primarily responsible. The change from 'construction' to 'composition' was also made in the title of his position as 'professor of practical construction', as he wrote in one of the drafts (384.10–11), which was amended to 'Professor of Practical Composition' (90.10). In contrast, Semper's 'Second Report' refers to his 'class for Practical Construction' (91.24–5). If the amendments from 'construction' to 'composition' are due to Cole, they may have resulted from the criticism the Board of Trade had expressed against the proposal of 'a class for architectural details and practical construction' (Cole 1884, 1:299) – the class with which Charles James Richardson was entrusted in 1852.   **since its commencement**] Semper's drafts have 'in the Year 1853', 'during the Year 1843' and 'in the Year 1852' (381.3, 381.20, 383.2). While '1843' is obviously a misspelling of *1853*, which applies to the spring and autumn of 1853, '1852' applies to the beginning of Semper's teaching in the Department from the autumn of 1852.   88.29–30 **subject of practical composition ~ entrusted to me since the last session**] Apart from 'practical composition' amended from 'practical construction' (see note 88.28), two fragments in one of Semper's drafts have, instead of 'since the last session', 'since the last six months' or 'since the last 6 Months' (381.4, 381.28; cf. 383.4). This roughly corresponds to the date of Semper's first public lecture held on 20 May 1853, while 'the last session' refers to the term that began in the autumn of 1853 (see 328).   88.31 **the foundation of my system of exposition**] Semper's drafts have 'instruction' instead of 'exposition' (381.5, 381.29, 383.5); for Semper's system, see his 'Plan of Instruction' (85–8). 89.1–2 **The want of knowledge of composition and of practice, the ignorance of the architectural principles of design, of style, and of beauty generally**] Some of Semper's drafts emphasize architecture to a greater extent: one version speaks of the 'want of ac-

First Report on the Class for Practical Construction 377

quaintan[c]e with the architectural and ornamental principles of beauty and stile and with practical construction' (381.9–10), another mentions 'the want of knowledge of the difficulties which are connected with the practice of ornamental art' (381.30–1), and a third refers to the 'want of constructiv knowledge, the ignorance of the architectonical principles of beauty and style' (383.6–7). **89.14 experimentally as it were**] This emphasis on the experimental character of the practical studio workshop as an essential part of Semper's teaching method is missing in the second draft, in which Semper stresses the importance that the students make 'their own experiences' (383.16). It was apparently amended by Cole, as it is a concession to the latter's reservations about this point (330–1, 370–1). **89.17–18 funeral car of the late Duke of Wellington**] When Arthur Wellesley, the first Duke of Wellington, died on 14 September 1852, the Department of Practical Art was asked by Brownlow Cecil, the Lord Chamberlain, after a delay of more than a month, 'to suggest a design for a triumphal car and superintend its execution', as Henry Cole reported (Cole 1853, 29). Cole seized the opportunity to demonstrate the practical benefits of the Department's special classes, to which he assigned the work after the Board of Trade permitted the Department's assistance with the reservation 'that it was to be viewed as a private transaction' (DPA[1], 29). He states of the 'general design of the car' that it was 'chiefly suggested' by Richard Redgrave, while 'the successful realisation of the structure, with its ornamental details, was due to the ability of Professor Semper' who, as the head of the metal class, was particularly in charge of the lower parts of the carriage, which were cast and chased in bronze. Octavius Hudson, professor of the class for woven fabrics, superintended the textile decorations (Cole 1853, 31). The funeral procession through London took place on 18 November 1852 and ended in St Paul's Cathedral, where the car was subsequently kept in the crypt; today, it is at Stratfield Saye, Wellington's estate in Hampshire. The question of whether Redgrave or Semper can be credited with the greater part of the overall design is a controversial one, and was so already in 1852. Designs by Redgrave and Semper were presented to Prince Albert on 23 October 1852 (sketches of the car by Redgrave and one drawing by Semper, inscribed 'Redgrave design', at V&A; further drawings by Semper in Hamburg, Kunstgewerbemuseum, and at ETH Zurich, gta Archives). Cole wrote to Semper a day later that 'The Prince liked many parts of your design'. Semper, together with Octavius Hudson, Norman Macdonald, comptroller of the Lord Chamberlain's office, and William Banting, the royal undertaker, held a conference about the funeral car at Marlborough House on 25 October (Cole Diary). On 6 November 1852, *The Illustrated London News* reported the Queen's approval of the design for the funeral car and spoke of 'Mr. Semper's splendid design' (ILN 1852a), while *The Builder*, on the same day, knew of 'Some dissatisfaction … at the fact that the design for the car was intrusted to Professor Semper, the Berlin architect' (Builder 1852). The car was included by Manfred Semper in an initial fascicle of engravings of Gottfried Semper's works in 1881 (Semper 1881, pl. 49) – in a form similar to the actual car, except for two major differences. In the executed car, the bier and the coffin on top of the carriage superstructure were covered by a canopy supported by four halberds. In the version published in 1881, the canopy is missing and, instead of the halberds, four candelabra surround the superstructure. Apart from the candelabra, this comes close to the illustration in *The Illustrated London News* of the car as executed, which was published after the funeral procession had taken place. The magazine now asserted that the 'design of the Car … was given by … Mr. Redgrave', but it stated that the canopy was omitted in the woodcut 'by the wish of Professor Semper' (ILN 1852b). Afterwards, *The Illustrated London News* apologized for the omission, saying that the engraving was drawn by students at Marlborough House 'by especial arrangement with

Mr. Cole' (ILN 1852c). However, two of Semper's early sketches (in Hamburg) also show the funeral car with a canopy, although carried by six Nikes instead of the halberds, and with the corners of the carriage (with four wheels, instead of the six as executed) adorned by candelabra. This roughly corresponds to the description of Alexander the Great's funeral car that Semper discusses in *Style in the Technical and Tectonic Arts*, in connection with which he refers to Wellington's funeral car in stating that he had 'the opportunity to carry out a work for the corpse of the second greatest commander of our century, which was similar in purpose' (Semper 1860/63, 1:317–18 and 11. 2). In the obituary for Semper, Thomas Leverton Donaldson wrote that Semper 'also designed the Wellington Car' and that 'it was conceived in the spirit of the Imperial Carpentum on the Roman coins' (Donaldson 1879, 234). However, Semper had less a chariot (*carpentum*) in mind than a triumphal car in the form of a Roman funeral pyre, such as he discusses and illustrates in *Style* with reference to the funeral monuments depicted on Roman medals. (In his example, the monument is surmounted by a chariot; Semper 1860/63, 1:315 fig.) The pyre's terraced, pyramidal form is best expressed in one of Semper's drawings of the funeral car without the canopy (gta, 20-108-1). Finally, Semper concludes the second volume of *Style*, at the end of the section on metals technology, with a woodcut showing the prow of the Wellington funeral car in a variant with two personifications of victory and fame instead of the lions as supporters of the coat of arms, stating that it was 'executed differently due to lack of time' (Semper 1860/63, 2:589). 89.18 **Mr. Whittaker and Mr. Wills**] C. H. Whitaker held a scholarship at the Department of Practical Art for 1852–53 as a student of artistic anatomy and metals (DPA[1] 297); he resigned from it in January 1853 (Cole Diary). During the same period, the student William J. Wills was appointed master of the modelling class (DPA[1] 210, 216; DSA[1], 167). *The Illustrated London News* reported that Whitaker and Wills had modelled 'Some beautifully-designed figures of Victory, introduced on the bronze ornaments' of the Wellington funeral car (ILN 1852a). They were probably also involved in the manufacturing of the 'Bronze Wheel of the Wellington Funeral Car. Manufactured by Tylor and Son, London. Designed by Professor Semper, Marlborough House', which, in 1858, was shown in an exhibition of students' works of art manufacture done in connection with the Department (Cat. DSA 1858, 43). Whitaker, to whom Semper refers as a medal winner for work done under his supervision (90.31), is mentioned as having been awarded a book for a work exhibited in May 1853 (DSA[1], 358). He possibly was the Charles Henry Whitaker who went bankrupt as a designer of art manufactures in Birmingham in the early 1860s (London Gazette 1862a, 3241; London Gazette 1862b, 3562). 89.19 **models of the ornamental posts**] One of the drafts has 'Models for the bronce ornaments' (381.15–16), another has 'details of the ornamental parts' (383.21). 89.20–1 **employed in inspecting ~ the bronze casts**] One of the drafts says of the two students that 'they have even been directing the moulding and chasing of the casts' (381.17), while another names 'Whitacker' as the only student who had 'been sent to the casters, for surveilling the operations of moulding and chasing' (383.21–2). 89.21 **A third student of Somerset House**] Both of Semper's drafts contain a blank at the place where this student was to be named (381.18, 383.23). Somerset House in the Strand, London, is a large neoclassical palace dating from the last quarter of the eighteenth century, where the Government School of Design was established in 1837. 89.23–5 **One of the students ~ appointed ~ in one of the great industrial establishments at Sheffield.**] A deleted passage in one of Semper's drafts names 'Whitacker' to be this student (384, note 383.24[2]). 89.28–9 **sideboard commissioned by Sir James Emerson Tennant ~ in ebony wood**] James Emerson Tennent (in one of Semper's drafts 'Charles Emerson Tennant'; 383.28) was colonial

First Report on the Class for Practical Construction

secretary of Ceylon (today Sri Lanka) 1845–50 and secretary to the Board of Trade 1852–67. He commissioned the ebony sideboard for his dining room after having contacted Henry Cole, and sent sketches to Richard Redgrave and Semper on 20 November 1852, accompanied by an issue of *The Art-Journal* with reference objects. The sideboard, as Tennent explained, was to have cupboards on each side, which were to frame a recessing central part with shelves, the whole carrying a buffet at the back with further shelves between two niches, crowned by a canopy done in open carved work. He suggested oriental ornaments such as elephant heads, alligators, serpents, Indian fruits and plants. Semper had drawn a first perspective sketch of the sideboard on the sheet containing one of the explanatory drawings sent by Tennent to Redgrave (gta, 20-K[DD]-1852-11-20:1) and delivered two variant proposals for the sideboard, of which Tennent reported to Redgrave on 5 February 1853 that he was 'greatly pleased with the designs' but suggested a combination of elements of both variants (gta, 20-K[DD]-1853-02-05). Tennent's sideboard was shown in 1858 at the exhibition of students' works of art manufacture done in connection with the Department (Cat. DSA 1858, 68). A review of the exhibition gave 'special notice and commendation' of the sideboard and highlighted the oriental subjects of 'elephants' heads, peacocks, &c.' and 'an error', namely that 'the upper parts of the two side mirrors are framed in Saracenic arches, whilst those of the larger mirrors in the centre are bounded by low elliptic arches: the combination is incongruous' (ILN 1858). The sideboard passed to the family of Ethel Sarah and Charles Arthur Langham in 1893 and was auctioned in 2004 (Jones 2006, fig. 8). 89.30 **The two students who were appointed to design this piece of furniture**] One of the drafts has 'The two skillfull artists who were appointed to execute this piece of furniture' (383.29–30). 89.31 **Mr. Cuthbert and Mr. King**] John S. Cuthbert and John Lewis King held scholarships at the Department of Practical Art for 1852–53 as students of artistic anatomy and furniture (DPA^1, 297); Semper refers to them further below as 'decorators' and as having been awarded medals for work done under his supervision (89.40 and 90.31). However, only King is listed for medals awarded in May 1853 (DSA^1, 357). Cuthbert is the illustrator of John Marshall's *Anatomy for Artists* (Marshall 1878). The catalogue of the 1858 exhibition of students' works of art manufacture records the sideboard without reference to Semper but as being designed by Cuthbert, while King assisted him in the working drawings (Cat. DSA 1858, 68). One exhibition review, which credited Semper as the designer, doubted that improvements in English manufacture were due to English students from the schools of design, arguing that students had played only a minor role in the design of the outstanding exhibits, as in the case of the sideboard, for which 'the drawings of the design were enlarged ... by a student' (Literary Gazette 1858, 57). 89.32 **course of architecture and practical composition**] One draft has 'course of architecture and practical construction' (383.31; see also note 88.28). 89.39 **Fallen**] Charles Follen, whose full name was Charles Christopher Follen, was born in Boston as the son of the abolitionists Charles Theodore Christian and Eliza Lee Follen. He continued to study with Semper in 1854 (386, Explanatory Notes 91.29) and became an architect, practising in Boston until 1867. In a draft letter to Edward Falkener probably dating from 1851, Semper called Follen his 'Ami et elève'. Follen was possibly the person Semper had succeeded in recruiting as a pupil in early 1851, perhaps through Rachel Chadwick, who wrote to Semper at the time about a 'young acquaintance' who 'wished to receive instruction from you' (see 237). In any case, Follen wrote to Semper in a letter, probably also dating from 1851, that 'Le mardi prochain, il ne me sera pas possible de prendre une leçon.' As late as 1867, Semper remembered Follen as his 'former student' in a letter to Heinrich Mölling, his son-in-law. **Austin ~ Armitage**] Walter

Austin and Charles Armytage held scholarships in the Department of Practical Art for 1852–53 as students of artistic anatomy and metals (DPA¹, 297). Both are mentioned as medal winners for works exhibited in May 1853 (DSA¹, 356). Armytage, who resigned from the scholarship in January 1853 (Cole Diary), is mentioned by Semper as having been awarded a medal for work done under his supervision (90.31).   89.41 **Semper, architect**] Manfred Semper; see also 90.9. Manfred continued to study with his father in 1854 (386, Explanatory Notes 91.29).

90.1–4 At the exhibition of furniture at the Gore House ~ I superintended ~ practical course] Gore House was a Georgian mansion dating from the 1750s on the estate in Kensington on which the Royal Albert Hall was built in 1867–71. It was purchased, together with the whole estate, by the Royal Commission for the Exhibition of 1851 in 1852 and served as an exhibition space for the Department of Science and Art starting in the spring of 1853 until its demolition in 1857. The exhibition of cabinet work in May 1853 consisted of specimens of furniture from the fifteenth to the nineteenth centuries, which were lent to the Department by the Queen and other persons. This exhibition was accompanied by student works to 'illustrate the progress of the Schools of Art'; Semper and Octavius Hudson held classes in the exhibition (DSA¹, 299–300; cf. 384.3–9). Semper refers to the cabinet work exhibited and photographs taken from it in 1853 as a basis for the woodcut illustrations in the section on tectonics and metals technology in *Style* (Semper 1860/63, 2:347 n. 1, 560).   90.8 **Halgate, and Brenan**] Edward Holgate, from York School, and John J. Brenan, from Cork School, held metropolitan scholarships as students of drawing ('Shading from the round'; DPA¹, 297). John J. Brenan, who became a painter principally of backgrounds to portraits by his brother James Butler Brenan, was probably the student elsewhere called John Joseph Brennan who won a medal for work done in Semper's special class for 'Plastic and Architectural Design' (387, Explanatory Notes 93.3).   90.10 **Since I have been appointed the Professor of Practical Composition**] One of the drafts has 'professor of practical construction' (see note 88.28) and mentions 'the second session of the year' as the moment of appointment (384.10–11) – that is, the term starting in the autumn of 1853 (see 328).

91.1–3 **one lecture, as an explanation of my system ~ a series of lectures**] The dates of eight lectures up to the end of 1853 were listed in the *First Report of the Department of Science and Art* (DSA¹, 223), after the 'Prospectuses of the Lectures on Art' gave an outline of six lectures only (96–7). Semper's first lecture at the Department, in which he explained his system, took place on 20 May 1853 and was announced under the title of 'On the relations of the different branches of industrial art to each other and to architecture' (see 96.3–4 and, for the draft variants, 97–117) – a title to which Semper also refers in his 'Plan of Instruction' (88.13–14).   91.6 **Letaroulz on Roman Architecture**] Letarouilly started the publication of his *Édifices de Rome moderne* in 1825; in 1854, the Department purchased the edition published in 1840–54; an additional fascicle was published in 1857 (DSA¹, 339; Letarouilly 1840/57).   91.11 **Dieterle**] see 310; 361, Explanatory Notes 84.3–4   91.14–16 **locality ~ unfit for a School of Design ~ students ought to be altogether in one room ~ benefit of a system of mutual instruction and emulation**] This critique of the classrooms takes up the suggestion in Semper's 'Plan of Instruction' to establish 'workshops or ateliers' with 'no classification of the pupils or students' (85.28).

First Report on the Class for Practical Construction
MANUSCRIPT VARIANTS
MS 115[1]

To the Superintendents of the Department of Practical art. *fol. 1r*

I have the Honour to submit a report of the state and activity of the Class for practical construction, metal working and furniture, in the Year *1853*..
I am only intrusted with the latter part of practical instruction since the last six months, but
5 I made it since the beginning of my appointment the base of my system of instruction.
The students who frequented my Class next after its first opening were partly well advanced in design and prepared for higher artistical education, but they had little ¦ taste and a Sort *fol. 1v* of prejudice against the application of art to usefull things.
I knew by experience that the reason of this was only their want of acquaintane with the
10 architectural and ornamental principles of beauty and stile and with practical construction. and that it would be other when the occasion should be given to introduce them at wonce into practical Art.
A first occasion of this kind presented itself, when I was intrusted at the beginnig of the Year, with the execution of the funeral Car of the late Duke of Wellington. –
15 Two students of the Sculpture Class, Mr. Whitake and Mr   have executed the Models for the bronce ornaments jointly with me and after my working drawings. and afterwarts they have even been directing the moulding and chasing of the casts. An other ¦ student of *fol. 2r* the Somersethouse Mr.

I have the honour to submit a report of the state and the activity of the Class of metalwork-
20 ing, furniture and practical construction in general, during the Year 1843.
The Students who frequented my Class soon after its opening were good designers and modellers, they had received a preparatory education for what is generaly understood under high Art, they had little taste and a sort of prejudice against the application of art to industry and to material utility.
25 This was not the first time that I met with these prejudices, which generally prevail among youthfull artists, and which ¦

The latter part of my division, namely the teaching of practical construction, has only been *fol. 2v* intrusted to me since the last 6 Months – nevertheless I made it since the beginnig of my courses the base of my system of instruction.
30 For the want of knowledge of the difficulties which are connected with the practice of ornamental art, and the ignorance of the fact, that a high degree of artistical accomplishment is wanted for the execution of objects of ornamental art, is the principal reason of the prejudices, which prevail among the students of our academies against the application of their talent to industry and material utility.
35 The first students which frequented my Class since its opening had made their preparatory studies for what is generally calld high art, they

381.2 **I have the Honour**] *after del.* Having been appointed *after undel. in opposite column*

I have the Honour to submit a report. of the activity and progress of the Class for metalworking furniture and practical construction.

Although[1] being only commissioned first only with the former two branches of technical art, I considered[2] the last, namely practical construction and the principles of architecture allways the

> 1 **Although**] *after five del. beginnings of variant:*
>
> Although it is
> Although the last of these three branches has only been expressly
> Although I am only commisioned with the last of these three branches of practical art, namely practical construction
> Although the last of these three branches, that of practical construction, I am only commissoned with since the last six months I made it
> I was only commissioned
>
> 2 **considered**] *above del.* made

381.2 **activity**] *after del.* progress of t[h]   **Class**] *after del.* practical Class of met   of] *undel.*   381.4 **I am only intrusted**] *after del.*

The special object[1] of the class for metalworking and furniture has with the beginning of the Year 1853[2] been successfully furthered by several not unimportant works of practical art which have been executed by the Department and partly under the superintendance of the undersigned Professor and

> 1 **The special object**] *after del.* Since my appointment   2 **beginning of the Year 1853**] *the term beginning in the autumn of 1852*

381.4 **instruction**] *after del.* ar   381.6–7 **The students ~ had little**] *accompanied in left column by inserted and undel.* I observed that they   381.6 **next**] *after del.* at its   381.10 **architectural**] *after del.* more   **stile**] *'style'*   381.11 **at wonce**] *'at once'*   381.15 **Two students**] *after del.* The *after del.*

The two Sculptors, which jointly with the undersigned have executed the models and

> 381.15 **and Mr**] *before blank left for* Wills *(89.18)*   381.16 **afterwarts**] *above del.* not only this,   381.17 **directing**] *after del.* sent, for   **moulding**] *after del.* c[a] *after del.* execution 381.19 **Class**] *after del.* class of practic[a]   381.20 **during**] *after del.* to which I am appointed in the   **1843**] *'1853'*   381.21 **The Students**] *after two del. variants:*
>
> The Students who frequented my Class soon after the opening of the last were good designers and had made their preparativ
> The students who, at the opening of my Class, frequented my instructions, had received their preparatory education for the exertion of what is generally calld high art, they were well advanced in design but

381.21 **frequented**] *after del.* followed my   381.22 **they**] *after del.* but they   for] *after del.* for entering into the career of   381.25 **This**] *after del.* I knew by experience that this prejudice. (generally prevailing among youthfull artists, di *after del.* This was not the first time that I met with such prejudices and   381.26 **artists,**] *before del.* being consequences of the   **which**] *before del.* may only   381.27 **The latter part**] *after del.* Being only intrusted with the instruction of   381.29 **base**] *after del.* starting point   **instruction.**] *altered from ~, before del.* being convinced and   381.30 **For the want**] *after inserted and undel. in opposite column*

First Report on the Class for Practical Construction 383

For the want of knowledge of the difficulties[1] which are connected with the practice of every branch[2] of ornamental art[3] and of the resources and means which arise from the same[4]

1 **difficulties**] *before del.* and resources, which arise   2 **of every branch**] *inserted without insertion mark*   3 **of ornamental art**] *before del.* in general,   4 **the same**] *after del.* them for the deve

381.31 **accomplishment**] *after del.* talent and perfec   381.33 **students**] *after del.* juouthfull and

MS 159   MS 115[2]

I have the honour to submit a report of the state and activity of the Class for metalworking furniture and practical construction, in the Year 1852. **fol. 147r*

The latter part of my division, namely the practical construction, has only been intrusted to me since the last Session, – nevertheless I made the practical construction, as I understand this expression, the foundation of my system of instruction since the opening of my Class.

5 The want of constructiv knowledge, the ignorance of the architectonical principles of beauty and style, the ignorance of the fact, that a high degree of artistical accomplishment is consistent with industrial art and even more that it is absolutely wanted for it, is the reason, why our jouthfull artists show little taste and a kind of prejudice against this sort of application

10 of their talent, and generally believe that in applying themselves for this branch they lower their position.

The students who frequented my Class soon after its opening were well advanced in the academical principles of design and skillfull drawtsmen and modellers, but they partoke a little of the same prejudice knowing by precedent experiences that it would be useless to

15 preach against this feeling, I waited for an opportunity of introducing them at once into practice and imparting them by their own experiences with the difficulties means pleasures and profits of the practical branch of art.

This opportunity presented itself when, at the beginnig of the Year, I was intrusted with the execution of the ¦ Metalworks of the funeral Car of the late Duke of Wellington. **fol. 147v*

20 Two Sculptors, Mr. Whitacker and Mr.   have executed in common with me and after my working drawings the details of the ornamental parts of the car, and Mr Whitacker has been sent to the casters, for surveilling the operations of moulding and chasing. A third ancient student of the Somerset House, Mr – has been employed afterwards for chasing those parts of the ornaments, which could not be finished before. – One of these Students,

25 has in consequence of his share of the work since been placed in one of the great industrial establishments at Sheffield.

After this came some other practical works of less importance, for instance a piece of furniture, commended by Sir Charles Emerson Tennant, destined for being executed in Ebony wood at Ceilan by Indian workmen. The two skillfull artists who were appointed to execute

30 this piece of furniture, Mr. Cuthbert and Mr. – ¦ have made at this occasion a short but *fol. 3r* effective course of architecture and practical construction which I believe vill add to the abilities by which they distinguish themselves.

Several other students for architecture were occupied in the same time their special studies in architectural drawing and ornament. Some Copies of pieces of metalworking, belonging

384   Department of Practical Art

to the Meseum connected with the Department. have been made by Mr. Amentage and Austin.

At the Exhibition of furniture at the Gorehouse which opened last spring I was appointed as the intendant of the Atelier, established near the collection for copiing modelling and casting the Ensembles and the Details of the most important pieces of the Exhibition

An interesting collection of drawings of Models and of Casts has been the result of this practical course, and several students, who knew little about architectural drawing, mouldings proportions, ornament and colouring, have learned at this occasion to manage such kind of works..

With the second session of the year when I was appointed as professor of practical construction, together with the above mentioned branches, I had to follow an other system of instruction: Formerly I had to deal with Students, who by their academical instruction were rather to much mounted by the Idea of executing high Art, while I now am endeavouring of comporting some higher direction and artistical feeling to the students in the same time with the practical knowledges which they exclusively reclaim and with the first elementary instructions of geometrical design of which they are ignorant, their school instruction beeing generally very much neglected

To Show the connection between practical application and Artistical conception has been the leading Idea of my course of lectures on the relations which exist between the different branches of practical Art among each other and to architecture.

383.2 in] *after del.* which   383.3 **The latter part]** *after del.* Since my   383.4 **Session]** *after del.* 6 [M]   383.5 **foundation]** *above del.* basse   basse] *after del.* fund[a]   383.6 **constructiv knowledge]** *after del.* knowledge of the constructiv laws of bea   **architectonical]** *after del.* more   383.8 **industrial art]** *after del.* practical industry   383.9 **jouthfull]** *'youthful'*   **show]** *after del.* generally   383.10 **believe]** *below del.* think   **that]** *after del.* they abase their position in   383.12 **soon]** *interl.*   383.13 **drawtsmen]** *'draughtsmen'*   **partoke]** *'partook'*   383.13–14 **a little]** *interl.*   383.14 **prejudice]** *before del.* and had but littl taste for   383.18 **beginnig of the Year]** *the term beginning in the autumn of 1852*   383.19–30 **Metalworks ~ Mr. Cuthbert and Mr. –]** *accompanied by note written upside down on the same sheet:*

Name Stanley Bird[1].
Age 16 [ ]   *nᵒ 1.*
38 Edgeware Road   D[ ] [ ]
Articled to a builder   Freytag.

    1 **Stanley Bird]** *Stanley George Bird, later colonel and president of the Central Association of Master Builders of London, born in 1837 as the son of the builder George Bird of Edgware Road, Marylebone, London*

383.20 **Sculptors]** *after del.* students of th   **Whitacker]** *'Whitaker' (see also 383.21)*   **and Mr.]** *before blank left for* Wills *(89.18)*   383.21 **details]** *after del.* whole   **ornamental parts]** *after del.* car   **Mr Whitacker]** *interl.*   **has]** *altered from* have   383.22 **casters]** *after del.* different   383.24 **before. –]** *before del.*

This practical course[1], I trust, has not been without consequence[2] for them.

    1 **This practical course]** *after del.* I believe that they have had profit   2 **consequence]** *after del.* utility for them and one at least of them, Mr. Whitacker, has since

Second Report on the Class for Practical Construction 385

383.24 **Students,**] *before del.* who had little taste for the application of his art for technical taste] *after del.* application and the] *undel.* application] *after del.* technical applicat 383.25 **since**] *after del.* rece[i] **the**] *above del.* our 383.27 **less**] *after del.* smaler 383.28 **commended**] *'ordered'* 383.30 **Mr. –**] *dash as placeholder for* King *(89.31)* **made**] *after del.* doubtless 383.31 **vill**] *'will'* 383.33 **Several**] *after del.* At the Exhibition of furnitures I was appointed as the surintendend **were occupied**] *above del.* have made 384.1 **Meseum**] *'Museum'* **Amentage**] *'Armytage'* 384.4 **of the Atelier**] *after del.* of the modelling casting and copiing Atelier eastablished there 384.5 **Exhibition**] *after del.* Collection. 384.10 **when**] *after del.* the general princ[i] 384.11 **together**] *after del.* in *after del.* united **an other**] *after del.* an oppos[i] 384.11–12 **instruction:**] *altered from ~, before del.* for the *before del.* public [o] 384.12 **deal**] *above del.* do do] *after del.* complain 384.13 **to**] *'too'* **mounted**] *uncertain reading (cf. 90.13: 'elevated')* **high Art,**] *before del.* and had little taste for practical 384.14 **comporting**] *'imparting'* **to the students**] *after del.* to those *after del.* to the joung Gentlemen 384.16 **are**] *after del.* generally 384.18 **To Show the connection between**] *above del.* The combination of combination] *after del.* same 384.20 **architecture.**] *before del. on fol. 3v* The students who The] *after del.* Several of my students have employed their time by

Second Report on the Class for Practical Construction, Architecture, and Plastic Decoration

TEXTUAL RECORD

MS 116 gta, 20-Ms-116, fols. 1r–2v (1v, 2v blank), in Semper's hand
DSA² 'Report of Professor Semper on Class for Practical Construction, Architecture, and Plastic Decoration', in *Second Report of the Department of Science and Art*, London: Eyre & Spottiswoode for Her Majesty's Stationery Office, 1855, 147–8 (NAL, 97.PP.83), *copy-text*
Semper 2014 vol. 2, 563–4, Karge's reprint ed. of DSA²

BIBLIOGRAPHY Herrmann 1978, 74 and n. 268, 80–3; Herrmann 1981, 108; Herrmann 1984, 67, 73–6, 277 n. 251; Mallgrave 1996, 214–15; Hildebrand 2003, 265; Nerdinger/Oechslin 2003, 285–7; Piggott 2004, 68, 129

EXPLANATORY NOTES

Two fragmentary drafts on separate sheets of the same paper quality are extant for Semper's second report on his special class at the Department, the first in German and the second in English (see 388). The English draft starts on the same sheet as the German draft and continues on the second sheet with reformulations of the first paragraph left unfinished, yet undeleted, on the first sheet. The German draft and the English draft variants contain information that is not retained in the printed text, such as the names of students. Both the German and English drafts refer, in relation to the 'System of instruction', to Semper's

'First Report' (covering the period from the autumn of 1852 to the end of 1853 and printed in 1854), in which he explains his system of instruction as focusing on introducing the students 'in medias res', to the 'principles and elements of design and composition' (90.18–19) – that is, when they already had to work on some practical task. Semper explained that this practice-oriented method accommodated the students' short attendance period – a point that he mentions critically in the German draft of his 'Second Report': 'Short stay of the pupils disadvantageous and makes work more difficult' (388.1–2). He now adds that the short period of study made it impossible to generally apply the teaching system that he used in the Dresden Academy of Fine Arts, which consisted of 'combining theory and æsthetics with immediate practice' (92.3–5). Whereas in the 'First Report' he implied that this practical teaching was particularly directed at the 'operatives' (90.15), he now limits it to the day students in his architecture class (92.1–2). The evening students, who 'are employed during the day in … crafts connected with house-building' (92.18–19), are said to have been taught the basics of construction drawing – a specification of the field of 'geometrical projection' generally noted in the 'First Report' (90.20–7). Semper's German draft of his 'Second Report' contains one particularly important piece of information – namely the involvement of his students in the design and construction of the Mixed Fabrics Court in the rebuilt Crystal Palace in Sydenham.

91.29 **The day students of my special class**] In the German draft, Semper names Alexander Pilbeam, Charles Follen and Manfred Semper as the day students (388.12) and also mentions Pilbeam as the only student with perseverance, who – like Follen – 'has since taken on private work as an architect' (388.3–6). Pilbeam and Follen are the students of whom Semper says in the printed report that they 'have since entered into practice as architects' (92.36); on Follen, see 379, Explanatory Notes 89.39.   91.30 **Those who attend only in the evenings**] In the German draft, Semper says that these students were 'Handwerker' (craftsmen) who had learned to copy construction parts (388.13) – a narrower definition of the subject of 'geometrical drawing' as specified in the printed report (92.22–3).   91.31 **The masters in training**] In the German draft, Semper notes 'descriptive geometry' and the columnar 'orders' as subjects of the lessons for the training masters – the students who were to become teachers of drawing for the Schools of Art (388.14). In the printed text, this is replaced by a brief discussion of the importance of teaching 'the general principles of style in architecture' as 'being the same which prevailed in the whole world of industrial art' (92.25–7) – a summary that reflects Semper's contention as discussed in the drafts of his first lecture held in the Department on 20 May 1853 (see section 'Lectures').

92.3–4 **system of instruction ~ at the Royal Academy at Dresden**] see 371, Explanatory Notes 85.26–7   92.6–8 **opportunity ~ of employing the students on the works in course of execution, and making my class a real atelier for architects**] The German draft describes this opportunity as having been the 'work in Sydenham, in which I involved those students who agreed to participate', as it 'gave the opportunity for practical work' (388.9–10). This practical work was related to the redesigning of the Crystal Palace at its new location in Sydenham in south-east London, where it was rebuilt in a modified form after it had been dismantled at the close of the Great Exhibition in Hyde Park. Semper was commissioned through Joseph Paxton to design one of seven 'Industrial Courts' in Sydenham's Crystal Palace, namely the Mixed Fabrics Court, a commercial exhibition space for the presentation of textile samples. Semper discussed the involvement of the Department with Henry Cole on 21 January 1854 (Cole Diary) and received the contract from the Crystal

Palace Company with a letter from the Company's secretary, George Grove, dated 4 February 1854. At the opening of the new Crystal Palace on 10 June 1854, work on Semper's Court was still in progress; it was completed only towards the end of 1854 with the help of Semper's Paris friends Charles Séchan and Jules Dieterle. Despite these delays, Semper's contribution to the new Sydenham Crystal Palace was described in detail at the time of the opening, even in relation to elements not yet completed – apparently because Semper had provided detailed information. In the case of *Routledge's Guide to the Crystal Palace and Park at Sydenham*, its author, Edward MacDermott, had asked Semper on 2 May 1854 whether he would 'oblige me with the description of your Court for Printed Fabrics in the course of the present week' (gta, 20-K-1854-05-02:2). Although Semper's work is confused here with that of Charles Barry Junior and Robert Richardson Banks, who were responsible for the Printed Fabrics Court, the description of the 'Court for Woollen and Mixed Fabrics' in MacDermott's *Guide* possibly reflects Semper's description (MacDermott 1854, 157–8). Other details concerning the organization and decoration of the exhibition space divided into two parts (an open entrance part and a covered rear part) are omitted in the text but are present in the description of Semper's 'Mixed Fabrics Court' in the Company's concurrent official *Guide to the Crystal Palace and Park* – including objects that were still waiting to be executed, such as 'On the roof of the covered portion … a fountain, composed of Majolica ware, at the angles of which are placed small figures of boys on sheep' (Phillips 1854, 117). In any case, the general descriptions correspond neatly to Semper's extant drawings of the court's plan, elevation and templates for ornaments (Nerdinger/Oechslin 2003, 286–7 figs. 71.1–3).

93.3 **Five Department medals and one book have been awarded**] The *Second Report of the Department of Science and Art* lists six students who attended Semper's special class for 'Plastic and Architectural Design' as having been awarded medals for works shown in the student exhibition at Gore House in May 1854: John Joseph Brennan (probably the student elsewhere properly spelled Brenan; see 380, Explanatory Notes 90.8), Arthur Crux, Charles Follen, Alexander Pilbeam, Manfred Semper and George Andrew Stubbs (DSA[2], 204–6). The exhibition presented 114 works by Semper's students, the results of his 'instruction in architectural construction and details in plastic relief ornament, and in the scientific projection of shadows' (DSA[2], 201). It probably included 'a valuable series of studies from the ancient furniture exhibited last year' (DSA[2], 209–10; for the 1853 furniture exhibition, see 90.1–6; 380, Explanatory Notes 90.1–4). In a review of the exhibition, *The Builder* judged that 'The *architectural* works of the metropolitan normal school (under M. Semper), are very unsatisfactory. It would have been wiser to have kept them out of sight altogether' (Builder 1854a). In a reply signed by the students, who felt 'bound in gratitude to do justice to Professor Semper', a request was made to take into account the fact that the drawings were the result of a period of instruction of 'averaging only six months', in which 'the whole of our class', which 'understood nothing about architecture before they came here', had 'been taught perspective, shadow-construction, tinting, and the principal laws of architecture' (Builder 1854b).   93.6–7 **two courses of five public lectures**] Semper apparently gave both courses in the autumn of 1854; see 393–4.

388   Department of Practical Art

MANUSCRIPT VARIANTS
MS 116

fol. 1r   I. Bezug auf den Rapport v. 1854. Kurzer Aufenthalt der Schüler nachtheilig und erschwert
die Arbeit.
Pilbeam der einzige der Ausdauer gezeigt hat und wirklich in kurzer Zeit bedeutende
Fortschritte machte. Er war ganz ohne alle Kenntnisse und verliess die Schule nach 1½
Aufenthalt mit Kenntniss der Composition und Verhältnisse so dass er seitdem als Archi-   5
tect Privatarbeiten übernommen hat. Desgleichen der Amerikaner. Follen. – .
Die Abendschüler gehören meistens der arbeitenden Klasse an und beschäftigen sich fast
ausschliesslich mit Kopiren der Constructions-Theile. –
Die Arbeiten in Sydenham bei denen ich diejenigen Schüler welche dazu sich bereit
erklärten betheiligte, gaben Gelegenheit zu Praktischem.   10
3) Klassen. Tagesschüler, Abendschüler, Trainingmasters.
1) Klasse. – . Pilbeam, Follen, Semper.
2. Klasse. – . Handwerker. Kopiren von Constructionstheilen.
3 Klasse. – . Trainingmasters Descriptive Geometrie, Ordnungen. zu sehr beschäftigt.
Trockenheit des Stoffes, zu weit vorgerückt in den übrigen Theilen der Kunst und zu weit   15
zurück in den materiellen Kenntnissen..

Sir.

The System of instruction pursued this Year in 1°). the class for practical construction,
Architecture and plastic Decoration was based on the principles noticed in my report fothe
Year 1854 and has undergone since then only some modifications according to circum-   20
stances. and to the different classes of Students which ¦|

fol. 2r   The System of instruction pursued this Year in the Class for practical construction remained
generally that specified in my report for the Year 1853 but with some modifications according to the special applications of the students. I have three distinct classes of students under
my instruction each of which requires its own method of instruction.   25
1° the day students 2°) those who attend only the Evenings. 3°) the training masters.
Of these three classes the first named only which consists of Students of architecture properly speaking enables me to apply in some degree that method of instruction which I practised for many years past at the Royal Academy at Dresden, combining theoretical and
aesthetical instruction with real practice, that is to say with the employment of the Students   30
for copiing plans of buildings and other architectural works in curse of execution, making
estimates for carriing out details and working drawings etc. That time I had full opportunity of carring out

> 388.1 **1854.**] *before del.* Fortsetzung desselben Systemes Unmöglichkeit   **Kurzer Aufent-**
> **halt**] *after del.* Wunsch eines systematischen Kurses.   Wunsch eines] *undel. after del.*
> Einige Schüler haben.   388.4 **1½**] '*1½-jährigem*'; *above del.* einjahrigem   388.10 **bethei-**
> **ligte**] *after del.* beschaf   388.14 **Descriptive**] *after del.* Construc *after del.* Perspective
> 388.15 **zu weit vorgerückt**] *after del.* vorgerücktes Geschicklichsein   388.16 **Kenntnis-**
> **sen**] *after del.* Theilen   388.17 **Sir.**] *after del.*

Second Report on the Class for Practical Construction　　　389

Sir. – In making my report on the state and general working of the Class for Practical construction, architecture and plastic Decoration I refer to the

388.18 **this Year**] *interl. before del.* by myself　**1°).**] *inserted*　388.19 **was based**] *after del.* has been explained in my report of the Year　**principles**] *after del.* same *and before del.* which I had the honour to explain to　**noticed**] *after del.* I　**fothe**] *'for the'*　388.21 **and**] *after del.* The course of instruction　**to**] *interl.*　388.22 **The System**] *after two del. variant beginnings:*

The system instruction[1] pursued this Year in the class for practical construction was based on the same principles noticed[2] in my report for the Year 1853[3] (mit Ausnahmen)
The system of instruction pursued this year in the class for practical construction was generally. based on the same priniples[4] specified in my report for the Year 1853.[5] I have three[6] distinct[7] classes of students under my instruction, 1° the day students 2°· those who attend only in the Evening 3° the training masters.
It was only[8]

> 1 **system instruction**] system *above del.* system of　2 **noticed**] *after del.* which I had laid before　3 **1853**] 3 *over* 4　4 **priniples**] *'principles'*　5 **1853.**] *altered from* ~∧ *before del.* with some modifications according to circumstances.　6 **I have three**] *after del.* The *after del.* As for the method　7 **distinct**] *above del.* different 8 **It was only**] *after del.* Of these

388.24 **special**] *altered from* specialities　**applications**] *interl. after interl. and del.* and **the students.**] *altered from* ~ ~∧ *before del.* who attended my class. They　388.25 **method**] *after del.* treatement　388.26 **1°**] *after del.* 1° the Day students who are generally studiing architecture as an art. and　architecture] *before del.* as their speciality and　388.29 **combining**] *after del.* consisting of a combination of theoretical and practical　**theoretical**] *after del.* practical　388.30 **real practice**] *after del.* practice and making the last the base of the system. I had then a great　and] *undel. after del.* and introducing the students as early as possible into the　the last] the *undel.*　388.31 **curse**] *'course'*　388.31–2 **making estimates**] *interl.*　388.32 **etc.**] *before del.* which I had the　the] *after del.* full　**That time I had**] *after del.* That time I had *after del.* I then had *after del.* This system　388.33 **carring**] *'carrying'*

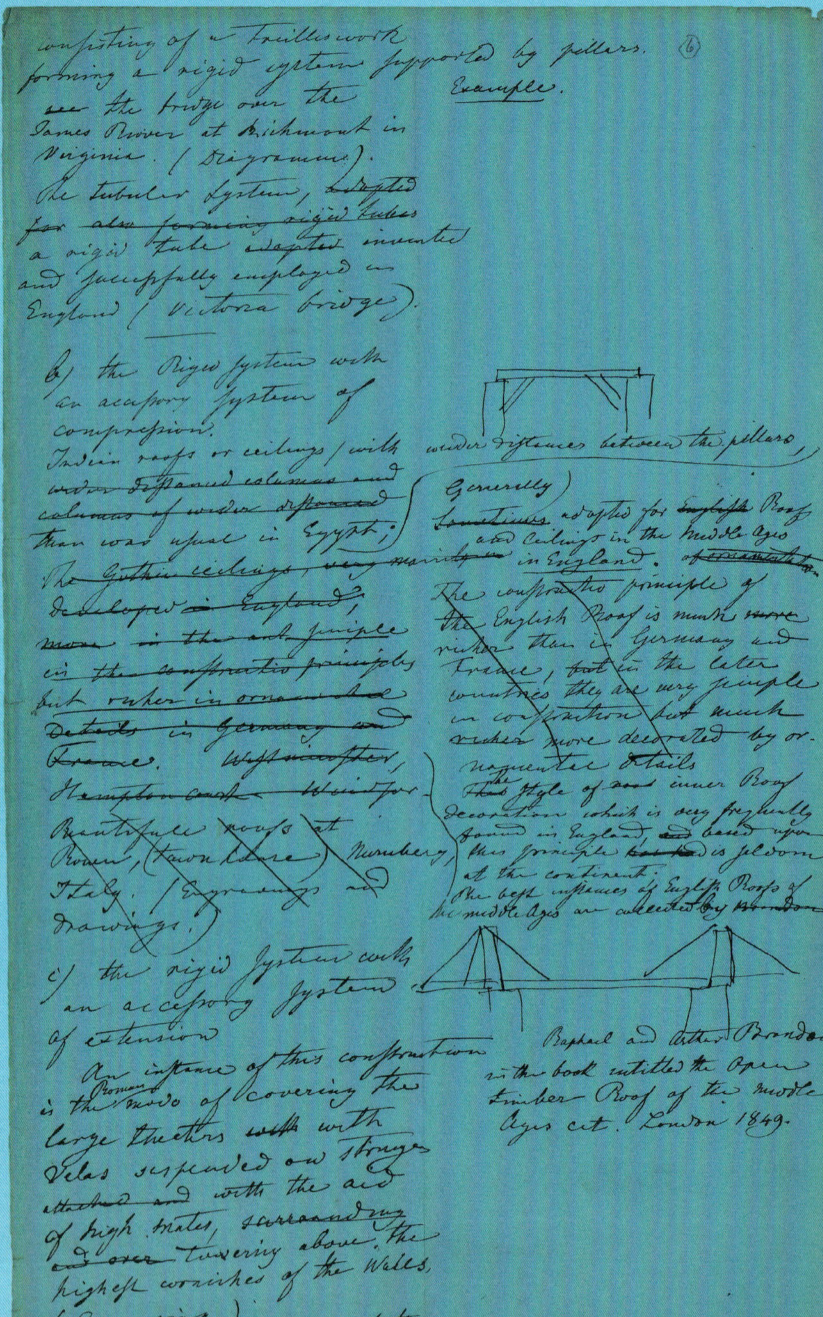

(6)

consisting of a Trelliswork forming a rigid system supported by pillars. Example. ~~see~~ the bridge over the James River at Richmond in Virginia. (Diagramme).

The tubular System, ~~adopted for also forming rigid tubes~~ a rigid tube ~~adopted~~ invented and successfully employed in England (Victoria bridge).

b) the Rigid system with an accessory System of compression.

Indian roofs or ceilings (with wider distances between the pillars, ~~wider distanced columns and columns of wider distanced~~ than was usual in Egypt;

~~The Gothic ceilings, very mainly~~ Generally ~~Sometimes~~ adopted for ~~English~~ Roofs and Ceilings in the Middle Ages in England. ~~of ornamentation~~ ~~developed in England, more in the art principle in the construction principles but richer in ornamental details in Germany and France. Westminster, Hampton court, Windsor.~~

The construction principle of the English Roof is much ~~more~~ richer than in Germany and France, but in the later countries they are very simple in construction but much ~~richer~~ more decorated by ornamental details

The style of ~~roof~~ inner Roof decoration which is very frequently found in England, ~~and~~ based upon this principle ~~[illegible]~~ is seldom at the continent.

The best instances of English Roofs of the middle Ages are collected by ~~Brandon~~ Raphael and Arthur Brandon in the book entitled the Open timber Roof of the middle Ages cet. London 1849.

~~Beautifull roofs at Rouen, (town hall) Nuremberg, Italy. (Engravings and drawings.)~~

c) the rigid System with an accessory System of extension

An instance of this construction is the Roman mode of covering the large theatres ~~with~~ with Velas suspended on strings ~~attached and~~ with the aid of high masts, ~~surrounding and over~~ towering above the highest cornices of the Walls. (Engraving.)

New adaptation of this

Pl. 11: Draft of lecture on timber construction, 1853 (gta, 20-Ms-136)

LECTURES

Introduction

In the lectures he gave at the Department of Science and Art, the successor of the Department of Practical Art, Semper combined two perspectives involving the history and theory of architecture. On the one hand, he was following up on the essay *Die vier Elemente der Baukunst* (The Four Elements of Architecture) of 1851, in which he had condensed his project of a 'Vergleichende Baulehre' (Comparative Architecture), ongoing since the early 1840s; on the other hand, he was reformulating the latter's global approach through his experiences at the Great Exhibition, from which he developed his booklet *Wissenschaft, Industrie und Kunst* (Science, Industry, and Art). All of this was finally incorporated into the two volumes of *Der Stil in den technischen und tektonischen Künsten, oder Praktische Aesthetik* (Style in the Technical and Tectonic Arts; or, Practical Aesthetics) of 1860–63.

Semper's letter of appointment from the Department of Practical Art, dated 11 September 1852, lists under point 3 the lectures he would be obliged to give in connection with his class on 'the principles and practice of Ornamental Art applied to Metal Manufactures' (226.7). The lectures were to include 'occasional public lectures, on the uses to be made of the objects in the Museum, the collection of casts, books, prints, drawings &c in the Library' (226.22–4). During his time at the Department, Semper gave public lecture series in the autumn terms of 1853 and 1854. The lectures indicate that his initial subject area – metal manufactures – rapidly expanded to include the relationship of the industrial arts to architecture.

As was also announced in an advertisement by Henry Cole of 4 March 1853 (which was published several times in *The Athenaeum*), Semper gave the first of his public lectures in London – his inaugural lecture – at Marlborough House on the evening of 20 May 1853. It was entitled 'On the Relations of the Different Branches of Industrial Art to Each Other and to Architecture'. Starting from 11 November 1853, according to the original schedule – which was published on the same date in *The Journal of the Society of Arts* and was announced again in *The Athenaeum* on 12 and 19 November 1853 – five further public lectures were to follow. Both there and in the 'Prospectuses of the Lectures on Art' published in the Department's *Report*, the dates were listed under the general title 'On Architecture, Practical Construction, and Plastic Art Generally'. Lectures were scheduled for the Friday evenings of 11, 18 and 25 November and of 2 and 9 December 1853 (96–7).

In his inaugural lecture on 20 May 1853, Semper announced the programme of the five public lectures planned for the autumn term of 1853 (117.24–39). The stated structure of the public lectures corresponds to that of the detailed version of the programme in the 'Prospectuses of the Lectures on Art': it follows the five-part discussion of architecture tracing the elements of industrial art that Semper had used in 1851 in *The Four Elements of Architecture* (Semper 1851b, 54–6): textile art, ceramic art (including metallurgical works), timber construction (later termed 'tectonics'), stone construction or stereotomy and the combination of these industrial arts in architecture. Semper used the same lecture structure in connection with his proposed reform of art education in *Science, Industry, and Art*, completed in January 1852 (Semper 1852, 67–8). In the draft of the English translation, the structure reads (gta, 20-Ms-89; see also 261): '1. Art applied to ceramics in its widest meaning. 2. Art applied to Textile Industry 3. Art applied to Carpentry. 4 Art applied to Masonry and Engineering. 5. Comparative Architecture in which the working together of the above mentioned four elements under the Presiding power of Architecture must be shewn.'

Following the printing of the lecture programme for the autumn term of 1853, Semper's public lectures were additionally scheduled for 16 and 23 December, as noted in a table listing the 'Lectures delivered in the course of the year 1853', dated 30 December 1853, in the *First Report of the Department of Science and Art* (DSA[1], 222–3). As the same *Report* records, these were the dates planned for two public lectures by Octavius Hudson 'On Surface Decoration' (DSA[1], 221). Another table in the *Report* on the public lectures delivered 'during the Autumn and Winter Session of 1853–4' shows that Hudson gave two public lectures 'On Surface Decoration' on 20 and 27 January 1854, as well as two additional public lectures 'On the Varieties of Lace' on 4 and 11 January 1854 (DSA[1], 198–9).

There is no programme detailing the additional two lectures and thus the total of seven lectures of the autumn term of 1853. In the *First Report of the Department of Science and Art*, Semper himself sums up his lecturing activity by stating that he 'delivered in the month of May one lecture, as an explanation of my system, which, in the course of the second session', he had 'been endeavouring to develop in a series of lectures' (91.1–3). On the basis of the dates mentioned and the drafts of Semper's lectures that are held in the gta Archives at ETH Zurich, the following programme can be hypothesized (the titles are taken from the printed prospectuses, except for the lectures of 25 November and 2 December, the titles of which are translated from those given by Manfred and Hans Semper in *Kleine Schriften*, and except for the lecture of 9 December, the manuscript of which includes the title):

20 May 1853   On the Relations of the Different Branches of Industrial Art to Each Other and to Architecture (MS 122, with a rejected draft in two versions, MS 118 and MS 117)

11 November 1853 General Remarks on the Different Styles in Art (MS 124)

18 November 1853 The Ancient Practice of Wall Coating and Tubular Construction (MS 129)

25 November 1853 Classification of Vessels (MS 133)

2 December 1853   On Vessel Parts (MS 134)

9 December 1853   Influence of the Materials and Their Treatments upon the Development of Ceramic Types and Style (MS 135)

16 December 1853 On Timber Construction, and Its Influence upon the Development of Architectural Forms (MS 136)

23 December 1853 The Combined Action of the Four Preceding Branches of Industry in Architecture (MS 138)

This structure shows some divergences from the original programme for the autumn term, which was restricted to five lectures. The lecture initially planned for 11 November 1853, devoted to textile art, would have been divided into two lectures, while the one on ceramic art would have been expanded to three lectures. The lecture on timber construction would have been held as the sixth instead of the third, while the lecture on stone construction originally planned as the fourth would have been omitted. Semper does in fact already discuss stone construction at some length in what was to have been the second lecture, on 'Wall Coating'. The final seventh lecture corresponds to the last, fifth lecture in the original programme.

The programme for Semper's public lectures in 1854 is less clear. The prospectus for instruction in art at the Department of Science and Art in the spring term, from 1 March to 31 July 1854, published in *The Athenaeum* starting on 11 February 1854, mentions class lectures but no public lectures relating to his field of teaching. Accordingly, a list of public 'Lectures delivered at Marlborough House from October 1, 1853 to October 1, 1854', dated December 1854 and printed in the *Second Report of the Department of Science and Art*, does not include any lectures given by Semper in the spring term of 1854 (DSA², 162–3). The prospectus for art instruction in the next two terms, from 1 October 1854 to 28 February and from 1 March to 31 July 1855, published in *The Athenaeum* on 9 September 1854 (and reprinted in the Department's *Second Report*; DSA², 123–5), says that Semper would give public lectures 'On Architecture and Plastic Decoration' in each term. However, travels to France and Switzerland, due to his departmental work for the British section at the Exposition universelle in Paris and his prospective professorship in Zurich, most probably prevented him from giving the spring lectures of 1855.

Semper himself notes in his 'Second Report on the Class for Practical Construction, Architecture, and Plastic Decoration' that, in 1854, he 'delivered, in the public lecture-room at Marlborough House, two courses of five public lectures on the different styles of ancient architecture, their distinctions and connexions' (93.6–8). However, drafts of only three lectures for this period are extant in the gta Archives. In accordance with the above-mentioned records of public lectures then given by Semper, they are clearly identifiable for the autumn term of 1854: The draft of the last of these lectures is dated 6 December 1854 (201.19), a Wednesday, and the two other draft lectures (the first of which exists in two versions) directly precede it in terms of content – a connection confirmed by corresponding cross-references. Henry Cole's diary reveals that Semper was staying on the Continent at least from 7 to 13 November and gave a lecture on 22 November 1854 – apparently the date of his first public lecture in the autumn of 1854. This fits in with a weekly lecture rhythm for the extant drafts of these public lectures (the titles of the first two lectures are translated from those given by Manfred and Hans Semper in *Kleine Schriften* and derived from Semper's draft in the case of the third lecture):

22 November 1854 On Architectural Symbols (in two versions, MS 141 and MS 142)

29 November 1854 On the Relation of Architectural Systems with the General Cultural Conditions (MS 144¹)

6 December 1854 Explanation of the Expression of Spatial Arrangements in Architecture (MS 144²)

The term's remaining weeks in December 1854 would have allowed two more lectures (possibly adding – as promised in both drafts of the first of these lectures – a more extensive discussion of Greek architecture), so that one course of five lectures would have been completed. This suggests, in relation to Semper's two courses of five public lectures, that he gave the same course twice – possibly, as other professors did, in the morning and evening of the same days.

Semper's drafts of the London lectures scarcely reflect the textual state in which they were given. They are mostly so heavily revised that it would hardly have been possible for him to read from the manuscript while giving the lectures. Several draft lectures have survived only in fragmentary form. Semper most probably revised the drafts not only during the first writing of them but also after the lectures had been held – perhaps with a view to publication. Wolfgang Herrmann has interpreted a list by Semper (gta, 20-Ms-151), possibly drawn up while he was still in London, in this sense – as representing variant titles for a new work. The list includes 'Tectonologische Studien' (Tectonological Studies), 'Vorträge über Baukunst und die in ihr zusammenwirkenden technischen Künste' (Lectures on Architecture and the Technical Arts Combined in It), 'Culturgeschichtliche und kunsttechnische Studien über Baukunst mit Holzschnitten und farbigen Tafeln illustrirt' (Cultural-Historical and Art-Technological Studies on Architecture, Illustrated with Woodcuts and Coloured Plates) and a 'Handbuch der Tectonologie' (Handbook of Tectonology). These titles may perhaps also reflect an attempt by Semper to organize the lecture material in accordance with his project for the book 'Comparative Architecture', regarding which he resumed contact with his publisher Eduard Vieweg in summer 1855, after he had already settled in Zurich. Semper wrote to him that 'I held lectures in the Department of Science and Art on comparative theory of forms, emphasizing specific aspects of industrial art'.

One of the most intriguing issues in Semper's London lectures concerns the relationship between architecture and the arts of Western peoples and the rest of the world. He made it a special topic in his first published essay – in German – on 'The Great Exhibition', in which this topic is addressed with the subtitle 'The peoples of European and non-European culture' (20.29). Semper is genuinely committed to doing justice to the particularities of non-European peoples as he sees them expressed in their artistic production. With regard to the handling of ornament in the industrial arts, he speaks in *Science, Industry, and Art* of 'the recognized victory which the semi-barbarian peoples, above all the Indians, had over us in some points of their magnificent industries of art', compared to which 'we have as yet achieved little on these points with our science' (Semper 1852, 11). However, as becomes evident here and in his lectures, this superiority of non-Europeans is at most a partial one. For Semper, it is left to European science and culture to assemble the fragmentary elements scattered across the world into a higher unity with a global scope.

BIBLIOGRAPHY Pevsner 1972, 260–2; Herrmann 1978, 78–80; Herrmann 1984, 71–3; Mallgrave 1996, 216–18

396   Lectures

Prospectuses of the Lectures on Art

TEXTUAL RECORD

DSA¹   'Appendix F.III.(j.)', in *First Report of the Department of Science and Art*, London: Eyre & Spottiswoode for Her Majesty's Stationery Office, 1854, 218–21, here 220–1 (NAL, 97.PP.83), *copy-text*

BIBLIOGRAPHY Herrmann 1978, 78 nn. 287–8; Herrmann 1981, 108–9, 111–12; Herrmann 1984, 278 n. 267, 279 n. 269

EXPLANATORY NOTES

Under the title 'Prospectuses of the Lectures on Art', 'Appendix F' to the *First Report of the Department of Science and Art* lists several of the public lectures planned for the period between April 1853 and January 1854, including six lectures by Semper. The details given for Semper's lectures certainly derive from Semper himself. A draft by Semper for the first public lecture of 20 May 1853 has a German title (97.6–7) that corresponds precisely to the English title given in the 'Prospectuses of the Lectures on Art'. In an advertisement dated 4 March 1853, Henry Cole announced Semper's inaugural lecture under this title (printed in *The Athenaeum* on 9, 16 and 23 April 1853): 'May 20. – A Lecture on the Relations of the different Branches of Industrial Art to each other and to Architecture, will be delivered by Professor Semper.' An advertisement in *The Athenaeum* on 14 May also indicates the time for the start of the lecture (6 p.m.). In a table of 'Lectures delivered in the course of the year 1853' dated 30 December 1853 that was printed in the same 'Appendix F' (DSA¹, 223), this lecture is listed under the title 'On architecture and its relation to industrial arts'. The details of the five other lectures given by Semper were probably published in a separate brochure. In newspaper advertisements, only the general title of Semper's lecture series was given along with the dates, as in *The Journal of the Society of Arts*, which announced on 11 November 1853 – the day the series started – that Semper would be giving five lectures 'on Architecture, Practical Construction, and Plastic Art Generally' on Friday evenings from 11 November to 9 December. This information was repeated in *The Athenaeum* on 12 and 19 November. As explained in the introductory section (392–3), the lecture programme for the autumn term of 1853 that is given in 'Appendix F' differs from the actual series, with its two additional lecture dates.

96 **Prospectuses of the Lectures on Art**] title taken from DSA¹, vi, 218   96.1 **Architecture.**] subtitle taken from left margin in DSA¹, 220; see next note   96.3–4 **On the relations ~ to architecture. By Professor Semper.**] accompanied in left margin by 'Professor Semper. Architecture.'   96.6–8 **On Architecture ~ Five Lectures. By Professor Semper.**] accompanied in left margin by 'Professor Semper. Architecture, &c.'   96.23 **tnbular**] *tubular*   96.28–97.2 **Lecture V. ~ these examples.**] accompanied in right margin by 'Appendix F. — Prospectus of Lectures on Art. — Architecture. &c.'   96.29 **architecturc**] *architecture*

On the Relations of the Different Branches of Industrial Art to Each Other and to Architecture

First Version

TEXTUAL RECORD

MS 118 gta, 20-Ms-118, fols. 1r–4v, 'Entwurf zu den Vorlesungen über die Beziehungen der verschiedenen Zweige der industriellen Kunst zu einander und zur Architectur' (1v calculations and sketches probably for Semper 1859), in Semper's hand, *copy-text (97.6–19, 98.6–100.11)*

MS 161 gta, 20-Ms-161 (Konv. 7), *fol. 73r–v (one preceding sheet missing at least; 72r–v, 73v calculations and sketch probably for Semper 1859; in a manuscript relating to Semper 1859), in Semper's hand, *copy-text (97.20–98.6)*

MS 123¹ gta, 20-Ms-123, **fols. 1r–2v (2r–v blank), in Semper's hand, *copy-text (100.11–32)*

MS 121 gta, 20-Ms-121, fols. 1r–11v (all versos except 3v blank), partly in Hans Semper's hand (1r–2r, 4r–11r; two emendations in Manfred Semper's hand), partly in Manfred Semper's hand (3r–v), early 1880s, Hans and Manfred Semper's German trans. of MS 118, fols. 2r–4r (additional sections: German trans. of MS 117; see 403), published in Semper 1884; see Herrmann 1981, 109

Semper 1884 'Ueber das Verhältnis der dekorativen Künste zur Architektur', 344–50, German trans. of MS 118, fols. 2r–4r (additional sections: German trans. of MS 117; see 403); for details of this composite translation, see Herrmann 1981, 168–70

BIBLIOGRAPHY Herrmann 1978, 78–80; Herrmann 1981, 108–10, 169; Herrmann 1984, 71–3; Mallgrave 1996, 217; Hildebrand 2021, 116 fig. 7, 117

EXPLANATORY NOTES

Manfred and Hans Semper combined parts of manuscripts MS 118 and MS 117, which correspond to the first and second versions of Semper's inaugural lecture, into a single text, the German translation of which they published in *Kleine Schriften* under the title 'Ueber das Verhältnis der dekorativen Künste zur Architektur', describing it as a 'Lecture, given in London in 1854' (Semper 1884, 344 n. *). Wolfgang Herrmann correctly assumed that these two manuscripts refer to the lecture Semper gave on 20 May 1853 (Herrmann 1981, 108). However, he did not notice that manuscript MS 122 represents a third version of the same lecture – namely the one that Semper actually delivered (see 410, 426).

The first version (MS 118) is clearly identifiable from the fact that the first third of it is written in German. Its title, 'Entwurf zu den Vorlesungen über die Beziehungen der verschiedenen Zweige der industriellen Kunst zu einander und zur Architectur', corresponds to the English title of the lecture given on 20 May 1853 that appeared in the 'Prospectuses of the

Lectures on Art' (see 96.3–4). The subtitle 'Erste Vorlesung' (First Lecture) indicates that Semper regarded this lecture and the lectures given in the autumn term of 1853 as a coherent series. The first version is fragmentary: it includes only an incompletely preserved introduction (97.10–100.18) and two paragraphs of the main part (100.20–32). In addition, three manuscript pages archived in other document bundles can also be assigned to it, whose connection with it was not yet recognized by Herrmann (97.20–98.6, 100.11–32; see Herrmann 1981, 109).

Semper begins the introduction to the first version of his lecture with the principle established by Owen Jones and adopted by the Department of Science and Art that 'The decorative arts arise from and should properly be attendant upon Architecture' (97.11–14; see below, Explanatory Notes 97.11–12, 97.13–14). He takes up a position critical of this principle: even if 'the individual arts' could find 'an external bond and a route towards a common artistic effect' through architecture (98.3–5), it would nevertheless be the case – as he demonstrates on the basis of descriptions in Homer and Hesiod of early Hellenic industrial works of art and buildings (98.23–30, 99.5–18) – that 'the forms and rules of architecture' can be traced back to 'those practised long before in the more specialised branches of practical art' (98.15–17). He therefore states that the plan of his lecture course is to discuss 'the relations of the different branches of practical art' first and then 'their combination in architecture' (97.20–2). Semper abandoned this draft after two paragraphs of the main part. Apart from the fact that he needed to draft the entire lecture in English, he may have felt that the firmness with which he stated that his view 'may ... appear contradictory to the principle' set out by Owen Jones (100.16–17) was too provocative.

97.11–12 **The decorative arts ~ upon Architecture**] With a few divergences in orthography and punctuation, this principle corresponds to the first of thirty-four propositions that Owen Jones discussed on 3 and 7 June 1852 in a lecture – given twice – on the collection of the Museum of Ornamental Art (see CatM[1], 10). In a printed summary of the lecture, the proposition reads (Jones 1852b, 1): 'The Decorative Arts arise from, and should properly be attendant upon, Architecture.' Jones had already presented propositions 11 and 14–34 to the Society of Arts on 28 April 1852 (Jones 1852a, 7–12), and he repeated most of them in *The Grammar of Ornament* (Jones 1856, 4–6). The Department of Science and Art in turn printed propositions 1–11 and 14–33 in 'Appendix D' of the fifth and sixth editions of the catalogue of the Museum of Ornamental Art (CatM[5], 118–20; CatM[6], 96–8). 97.13–14 **Dieser Satz steht an der Spitze der ~ Grund Regeln, welche das Departement ~ aufgestellt hat.**] In a deleted passage in the second version (MS 117), Semper describes Owen Jones's principle as 'the first of those who are fixed on the walls of the Marlborough-House' (404, Alterations in the Manuscript 101.4). These principles probably corresponded to those printed by the Department of Science and Art in 1854 under the title 'General Principles of Decorative Art' in 'Appendix B' of its *First Report* (DSA[1], 22–4). 97.13 **Grund Regeln**] *Grundregeln* 97.15 **nachdachte**] *nachdächte* 97.18 **konnte**] *könnte* 97.24–5 **sie nach dem vergleichenden Prinzipe in Arten, Geschlechter und Familien gruppiren**] This grouping resembles zoological classification and is probably inspired by Georges Cuvier's comparative anatomy, which Semper regarded as a model for comparative architecture (see 105.26–37, 118.19–28).

98.18–23 **There was a rich industrial art ~ before the invention of architectural forms ~ Domestical industry ~ furnished ~ trinkets.**] cf. Semper 1852, 31 98.24–6 **Homer and Hesiodus, whose brillant Descriptions ~ are ~ formed upon things, they had seen**

On the Relations of the Different Branches of Industrial Art   399

before their eyes] cf. Semper 1860/63, 1:130, 161 n. 1, 234, 275–6, 287, 304 n. 1; 2:76, 487 n. 2, 576 n. 2   **98.36 Mihel Angelo**] *Michelangelo*

99.1 Thorwaldson] In 1830, during his first study visit to Rome, Semper lived 'in via Gregoriana no. 17, near Thorwaldson' (gta, 20-K-1830-12-03[S]), and he probably also became acquainted with the Danish sculptor during the stay. In 1857, there was a portrait of (or a reproduction of a work by) Bertel Thorvaldsen hanging in Semper's study in Zurich (gta, 20-K-1857-12-08[S]; see 545, Explanatory Notes 213.16).   **Flaxmann**] cf. Semper 1852, 54–5, 62; Semper 1860/63, 1:XIII   **Schwanthaler**] Semper informed Henry Cole on 11 October 1852 that he had been offered 'a Copy of the Shield of Hercules, composed and executed by Schwanthaler in Munich' (81.38–9).   **99.2 rang**] derived from German *Rang*: *rank* (see also 100.30)   **99.9 with fireplaces**] The two manuscripts of the first version (MS 117, MS 119), in which the discrepancy between the luxury of the industrial arts and primitive architecture is also discussed, state the opposite: 'no fireplaces' (101.37, 406.27).   **99.15 tent of Achilles**] cf. Homer, *Iliad*, 24.448–56   **99.16 Pallace of Priamus**] cf. Homer, *Iliad*, 6.242–50   **99.17 Pallace of the King of the Phaeaks**] 'Phaeaks': *Phaeacians*; i.e. Alcinous's palace; cf. Homer, *Odyssey*, 7.78–133; Semper 1860/63, 1:302 n. 1   **99.18 dwelling of Ulissees**] 'Ulissees': *Ulysses*; cf. Homer, *Odyssey*, 17.264–71   **99.30 reciets**] possibly Semper's anglicization of French *récits* or a misspelling of English *recites* (obsolete by the end of the eighteenth century), which both mean *narratives*; cf. 401, Alterations in the Manuscript 99.30

100.10–14 This column ~ shows flowers ~ in the same manner as ~ hairdresses.] cf. Semper 1860/63, 1:211, 420–1   **100.20–32 As I was ~ a Student at Paris, my usual walk was to the jardin des plantes ~ the same ~ will be the case with the works of my art.**] Semper revised and enlarged this reference to Georges Cuvier's Cabinet d'Anatomie comparée in the third version of his inaugural lecture (105.1–31).

ALTERATIONS IN THE MANUSCRIPT

97.13 Dieser Satz] *after five del. beginnings of variant:*

This principle, which forms the
Dieser Satz[1], der an der Spitze der Grundprincipien[2] steht, welche das Departement der praktischen Kunst
Dieser Satz[3] der an der Spitze der[4] für das Department aufgesetzten Grundprincipien der praktischen Kunst, steht,[5] veranlasste[6] mich,[7] zu diesem Versuche, den ich den verehrten Hörern in dem Laufe weniger Vorlesungen mitzutheilen veranlasst worden bin – Nur die Zuversicht, die ich auf Ihre gastfreundliche Nachsicht setzte, konnte mir den Muth geben, Dieses Prinzip[8] ist Ihnen wohlbekannt, es steht
Sie wissen, meine Herren.[9]

> 1 **Dieser Satz**] *after del.* So   2 **Grundprincipien**] *after del.* für das Departement als Norm des   3 **Satz**] *after del.* erste *and before del.* in den   4 **der an der Spitze der**] *inserted*   5 **steht,**] *inserted*   6 **veranlasste**] *after del.* erweckte in mir den Gedanken, dasjenige, *after del.* gab mir die erste Veranlassung, die folgenden [ ]   7 **mich,**] *before del.* das folgende   **das folgende**] *after del.* dasjenige,   8 **Dieses Prinzip ~ steht**] *inserted in opposite column*   9 **Sie wissen, meine Herren.**] *inserted in opposite column after inserted and del.* Sie

97.13 **wenigen Grund Regeln**] *repl. del.* Grundprincipien   Grundprincipien] *after inserted and del.* Grund-   **Grund**] *interl.*   97.14 **Doch jeder**] *after del.* Doch fühlt *after del.*

Er[1] bedarf, in der gedrängten Kürze und Allgemeinheit wie er hingestellt ist, naherer Durchführung um in seinem ganzen Inhalte verstanden und anwendbar gemacht zu werden, und freilich auch um zu verhindern, dass

    1 **Er**] *repl. del.* Er ist sehr inhaltreich und   Er] *after del.* Er ist so inhaltreich

97.16 **in seiner**] *after del.* erstens   97.17 **Consequenz**] *after del.* Ausdehnung   **praktisch anwendbar**] *after del.* für die Anwendung   97.18 **zu denen er führen**] *after del.* zu denen er bei nicht hinreichend   nicht] *after del.* absoluter   97.22 **dann**] *repl. del.* und zuletzt **auf**] *interl.*   97.23 **die Werke**] *after del.* das so entstandene Resultat,   97.23–4 **als die**] *repl. del.* als   als] *after del.* unter sich.   97.24 **behandeln**] *after del.* unter sich vergleichen und ihre Verwandschaften und Unterschiede   97.27 **ersten**] *inserted* 98.1 **Die Baukunst**] *after del.*

nämlich[1] dass die Baukunst wohl ihrem Namen nach und in vieler Beziehung auch der Sache nach die erste der Künste, die Urkunst ist, dass sie aber unter allen Künsten.

    1 **nämlich**] *after del.* Ich meine

98.1 **als Urkunst**] *after del.* und ist auch in der That   98.2 **Beziehungen,**] *before del.* besonders in der   98.3 **brauche.**] *before del.* Dazu gehört   **finden**] *repl. del.* fanden   98.5 **eigentliche**] *below del.* höchste [K]   98.6 **ist die Baukunst**] *after del.* sind die Werke der hoheren Baukunst des *after undel. on *fol. 73r* ist   98.7 **praktischen Künste**] *after del.* Künste   98.8 **und artistischen Elemente**] *after del.* und Formen, dieselben Gesetze 98.11 **der übrigen Zweige**] *after del.* der Formen und Verzierungen, auf die Behandlung der Stoffe   98.13 **Entlehnten die übrigen Künste**] *after del.* Entlehnte die Baukunst ihre Processe der Behandlung ihrer Stoffe, ihre Formen und Ornamente von   Behandlung] *after del.* stoffliche   98.17 **Sicher das letztere. –**] *before del.*

Dieses in speziellen Beispielen[1] nachzuweisen, wo immer sich spätere Gelegenheit dazu darbietet, behalte ich mir vor – halte[2] diese Aufgabe für die wichtigste die ich mir stelle –

    1 **Dieses in speziellen Beispielen**] *repl. del.* Dieses   Dieses] *after del.* So weit es die Zeit *after del.* Dieses *after del.* Dieses im Einzelnen nachzuweisen und die Elemente der Baukunst   2 **halte**] *after undel.* ihre *after del.* es *after del.* ich halte diess für eine der wichtigsten Aufgaben *after del.* es wird zu

98.18 **There was a rich industrial art and**] *inserted*   98.19 **the invention**] *after del.* monumental Architecture and   monumental] *after del.* architecture as a monu   98.24 **the Ionic poets**] *after del.* Homer, whose descriptions of the tent the   whose] *after del.* so it was   descriptions] *after del.* practical   **brillant Descriptions**] *after del.* descriptions of the camps baracks   descriptions] *after del.* well   98.25 **hellenic**] *above del.* art   **industrial art,**] *before del.* howerver poetically th   98.26 **no doubt**] *above del.* certainly   **eyes;**] *altered from* ~, *before del.* and   and] *after del.* although embellishe *after del.* however   98.28 **be mere**] *above del.* invent   **inventions of their rich imagination**] *above del.* them en-

On the Relations of the Different Branches of Industrial Art   401

tirely   98.29 **In this case**] *after del.* they would not have been understood by their hearers. **art**] *repl. del.* artful inventions   98.32 **modern**] *inserted after del.* the   **practice**] *before del.* of our times   **of art**] *interl.*   98.33 **Greec**] *repl. del.* Renaissance   **occupied**] *below del.* influenced   **the greatest talents**] *after del.* these artists who were the most powerfull 98.34–5 **Phidias ~ at Athens**] *inserted with caret erroneously placed after* the artists *(98.33)* 98.34 **Parthenon**] *after del.* Acr[o]   98.35 **Leonardo da Vinci**] *before del.* Michel Angelo **who decorated**] *after del.* who painted a beautiful shie   98.36–7 **in many of his powerfull compositions.**] *inserted*   98.37–8 **are attributed to**] *repl. del.* go under the name of 98.38 **whose**] se *added*   **name got**] *inserted after del.* got 99.1 **Schwanthaler.**] *after del.* and   99.2 **did more**] *after del.* tried and succeeded to introduce *after del.* succeeded to influence greatly the   99.5 **buildings**] *above del.* architectural works   99.6 **state**] *before del.* of architecture   **no**] *repl. del.* the absence of   99.6–7 **monumental architecture**] *before interl. and del.* at all   99.7 **organic laws,**] *before undel.* barraks, court-Yards, Halls,   Halls] *after del.* coarse   99.7–9 **Luxury ~ ornamental**] *inserted*   99.8 **barraks**] *after del.* all ornamental parts,   99.9 **with**] *after del.* and   99.10 **partly of**] partly *above del.* greatly   99.11 **moveable**] *interl.*   99.13 **give**] *after del.* be usefull   99.14 **matter for**] *after del.* stuff of   **reflexion**] *after del.* contemplation   99.20 **of the Greec**] *interl.*   99.22 **The**] *inserted*   **Greec mythology**] *after del.* The Ionic poets, the foundators of the   foundators] *merged from Italian 'fondatori' and English 'founders'* **an**] n *added*   **ingenious**] *inserted before del.* compound of   99.23 **and so to speak ~ plastical**] *repl. del.* out of a dead   99.24 **borrowed from**] *after del.* introduced from t[h] 99.29 **representations**] *repl. del.* objects   99.30 **reciets**] *after del.* compositions   99.33 **But**] *after del.* It would conduce to for if I would *and before del.* We shall see in one of the to for] *'too far'* in one of the] *after del.* toward the end of o[n]   99.38 **Many thousand Years before we see**] *inserted*   **the Greec**] *after del.* While   **making their first steps**] *repl. del.* were in the infance   99.39 **national**] *after del.* their 100.1 **following its**] *after del.* forming their   **Nevertheless**] *after del.* However it mey be, 100.3–4 **originally borrowed from**] *after del.* originating from   100.4 **industrial art,**] *altered from ~ ~. before del.*

It will not yet be in time to give[1] the caracteristics of the different styles in architecture[2] but You may see[3] here by some details taken from Egyptian monuments of the eldest periods, that the ornaments are mere applications and based[4]

> 1 **give**] *above del.* explain   2 **of the different styles in architecture**] *repl. del.* of Egyptian Assyrian and Chinese art, or to   3 **You may see**] *after del.* as an illustrative example 4 **and based**] *after del.* hiding the *after del.* fixed on t[h]

100.5 **ornamental**] *repl. del.* practical   100.7 **to**] *del.*   **penetrate deeper in this question by analysing**] *repl. del.* give   **analysing**] *above del.* giving   100.7–8 **the different styles of architecture**] *inserted after del.* the caracteristics of   the] *undel.* caracteristics] *after del.* different *and before del.* of Aegyptian, Assyrian and other styles   of] *inserted* 100.9 **pure structure**] *repl. del.* construction   **is**] *del. before del.* only   only] *before del.* forms, given by constructiv parts are   **veiled by**] *after del.* disguided b   100.12 **evidently**] *interl.*   **only**] *after del.* not   100.15 **I thought**] *after five del. beginnings of variant:*

402 Lectures

It may be possible to
As I was a Student at Paris it
This for apologizing for the system which I adopted for this paper
These remarks wer
I thought these few Remarks necessary for the apology of the plan[1] which I adopted by treating the difficult and rich material which forms

> 1 **plan**] *repl. del.* System and the order   System and the order] *after del.* order *after del.* System which I adopted

100.17 **I alluded to**] *after del.* I have placed on the head of   100.20 **my usual walk**] *after del.* I used to walk   I used] *after del.* it was my   100.22 **like**] *above del.* as   100.23 **foregone formations of the earth**] *repl. undel.* animals   animals] *above del.* vorweltlichen Thiere *(*vorweltlichen Thiere *repl. del.* Vorwelt*)*   **together**] *after del.* are ordered   100.24 **carcasses of**] *before del.* Stone   **species**] *above del.* creatures   **stand**] *repl. del.* are 100.25 **comparation.**] *before del.* by the celebrated inventor of the comparing Osteology, Cuvier   by ~ Cuvier] *after del.* as all these various formations *and before del.* are but different variations and developments of some few *(*as *after del.* Like *and before del.* in*)*   100.26 **As all**] *after del.*

As all[1] those antedeluvial and postdiluvial organic formations are but different developments of the same principles, as[2] Nature, for its[3] infinite rihness[4] variety and originality of[5] creations, is nevertheless very sparing and simple in its elementary forms,[6] from[7] which the different species are derived so the same.

> 1 **all**] *after del.* the infinite variety of   2 **as**] *after del.*

> as Nature for the infinite richness is very simple and sparing in its elementary forms

>> richness] *before del.* in creating *before undel.* millions of different species, *(*millions of different species *repl. del.* new forms*)*   forms] *after del.* ideas,

>> 3 **its**] *above del.* the   4 **rihness**] *'richness'*   5 **of**] *repl. del.* in its   6 **forms,**] *before del.* so I sayd to myself, the same   the same] *after del.* there must be some anological   7 **from**] *repl. del.* to

100.26 **organisations**] *altered from* organic *before del.* formations   100.28 **ideas,**] *before del.* the same, will be the case with our human creations   same,] *before del.* I told to myself **observe**] *above del.* see   100.28–9 **the same scaffolding**] *after del.* in all the most different *after del.* the same sceleton *after del.* a repetition of   100.30 **rang**] *after del.* gradual **which**] *above del.* of   of] *after undel.* of the *after del.* which the imdividuals possess in the *(*second the *undel. and* imdividuals *after del.* creatures o*)*   **universal creation**] *after del.* scale of gradual progress   100.32 **my**] *above del.* human

On the Relations of the Different Branches of Industrial Art   403

Second Version

TEXTUAL RECORD

MS 119 gta, 20-Ms-119, fols. 4r–5v, 1r–3v (all versos with calculations and sketches possibly for Semper 1859), in Semper's hand

MS 117 gta, 20-Ms-117, fols. 1r–6v (all versos blank; 2r, 3r, 4r, 5r variant of MS 119, fols. 5r, 1r, 2r, 3r; 6r variant of MS 119, fols. 4r, 5r), in Semper's hand, *copytext*

MS 120 gta, 20-Ms-120, fols. 1r–6v (5v–6v blank), in J. Ruston Palen's hand (emendations in Manfred Semper's hand), 1880, copy of MS 117

MS 121 gta, 20-Ms-121, fols. 1r–11v (all versos except 3v blank), partly in Hans Semper's hand (1r–2r, 4r–11r; two emendations in Manfred Semper's hand), partly in Manfred Semper's hand (3r–v), early 1880s, Hans and Manfred Semper's German trans. of MS 117, fols. 1r–6r (additional sections: German trans. of MS 118; see 397), published in Semper 1884; see Herrmann 1981, 109

Semper 1884 'Ueber das Verhältnis der dekorativen Künste zur Architektur', 344–50, German trans. of MS 117, fols. 1r–6r (additional sections: German trans. of MS 118; see 397); for details of this composite translation, see Herrmann 1981, 168–70

BIBLIOGRAPHY Herrmann 1981, 108–9, 168–70; Mallgrave 1996, 217; Squicciarino 2009, 401–3; Gnehm 2020, 30–2

EXPLANATORY NOTES

The second version of Semper's inaugural lecture is not complete in itself, as Wolfgang Herrmann thought (Herrmann 1981, 109), but is limited to the introduction. With several modifications, it takes over from the first version only the part referring to Egyptian, Assyrian and early Hellenic architecture as described by Homer and Hesiod (101.18–37, 102.6–12, 102.21–31). In the second version, Semper again starts from Owen Jones's principle that 'The decorative arts arise from and should be attendant upon Architecture' (101.3; cf. 398, Explanatory Notes 97.11–12). As in the first version, he takes up a critical position towards this principle by insisting on 'its true meaning', on the correct interpretation of it (101.4–5). Whereas in the first version he confines himself to the remark that architecture gave the various arts 'an external bond and a route towards a common artistic effect' (98.4–5), in the second version he adds to this view that 'The laws of beauty and style which we aknowledge in practical art and in art generally speaking, have first been fixed and systematically settled by architects' (101.10–11). But this contradicts the statement implying the priority of the industrial arts, that 'the rules and laws of beauty and style … were determined and practised long before the existence of any monumental art' (102.29–31). This contradiction reflects Semper's diagnosis that architecture – as the second version concludes – had lost its

404   Lectures

supremacy, which could be regained only by giving renewed attention to the 'present state of Industry', that is, to 'practical art' that needs to be reformed (103.28–31). Semper's rejection of this second version as well may be explained by the fact that he now regarded even a direct reference to the Department's principle as being too provocative.

Another fragmentary manuscript of the second version has been preserved (MS 119; 406–7). It corresponds almost exactly to three-quarters of the later manuscript (MS 117) but is structured differently: the first three parts (406.1–10) correspond to the end of MS 117 (103.24–34), while the rest (406.11–407.34) appears at an earlier point in MS 117 (101.18–103.14).

101.1–2 **1° Some excuses ~ etc.**] This shortened heading may be a relic of a lecture 'On the present state of practical art', the fragmentary draft of which (gta, 20-Ms-93) starts with the crossed-out words 'Some excuses and introductory remarks, first relative to the difficulty I must feel to read an English paper' and continues with the following sentences in their place: 'I. Some Excuses relative to the ambarrassement I must feel to read a paper in English before the high committe. 2°) Some introductory remarks about the plan and aim of the intended exhibition.' If 'the intended exhibition' refers to the furniture exhibition that the Department of Science and Art held in Gore House in 1853, which is probable (see 411), then the reference to 'the high committe' is to the Royal Commission for the Great Exhibition.
101.3 **The decorative arts ~ upon Architecture.**] see 398, Explanatory Notes 97.11–12. This sentence differs from the corresponding one in the first version (97.11–12) in that 'should properly be' is reduced to 'should be'. 101.4 **bee**] *be* 101.18–19 **Luxury dwelt in simple tents ~ before the invention of architectural forms.**] see 398, Explanatory Notes 98.18–23 101.21–3 **The descriptions ~ are ~ based upon real things.**] see 398–9, Explanatory Notes 98.24–6 101.36 **cowered**] *covered* 101.37 **no fireplaces**] see 399, Explanatory Notes 99.9

102.1–2 **Homeric dwellings**] see 399, Explanatory Notes 99.15, 99.16, 99.17, 99.18 102.4–5 **I refer for this to ~ Mr Layard ~ in his travels in Mesopotamia.**] cf. Layard 1851, 69–71 102.14 **devideng**] *dividing* 102.21–7 **Again if we look at the Aegyptian columns ~ we recognize ~ flowers ~ in the same manner as ~ Hairdresses.**] see 399, Explanatory Notes 100.10–14

103.14 **then**] *than* 103.16–23 **At the end ~ things. – .**] crossed out in thin pencil probably by Hans Semper or Wolfgang Herrmann and omitted in Semper 1884, 350; cf. Herrmann 1981, 170 103.26 **loose**] *lose*

EDITORIAL EMENDATIONS

101.2 **etc.**] *before one-quarter page blank*

ALTERATIONS IN THE MANUSCRIPT

101.2 **feel**] *before del. of* of] *over* to 101.4 **This principle,**] *before del. in ink over pencil* which is the first of those who are fixed on the walls of the Marlborough-House, **bee**] *transposed by guide line in ink over pencil from after* freely *at 101.4* 101.5 **relations,**] *repl. del.* intimate connections 101.6–7 **in the choice of forms and colours.**] *transposed by guide*

On the Relations of the Different Branches of Industrial Art   405

line in ink over pencil from after hands *at 101.7*   101.6 **in the**] *in pencil repl. del. in pencil* by
101.10 **in art**] *after del.* generally   101.11 **first**] *after del.* the   **fixed**] *before del.* and settled
101.12 **The**] T *in pencil over* t   **seems**] *after del.* gives us   101.13 **Nevertheless**] *transposed*
by guide line in pencil from before The History *at 101.12*   101.15 **A.**] *inserted*   **First we find**]
after del. First we find that the periods in which the arts in general and the so called industrial arts especially had arrived to a high degree of Development,   101.20 **Homer**] *altered*
in pencil from Homeros   101.21 **Hesiod**] *altered in pencil from* Hesiodos   101.23 **based**]
above del. traced   101.23–4 **by that liberty which poets take**] *transposed by guide line in*
pencil from after richness of these objects, *at 101.24–5*   101.25 **but**] *after del. in pencil* and
have,   **had no**] *in pencil above del. in pencil* been   **effect**] *after del. in pencil* without *and*
both *above del.* effectless   101.29 **alltogether,**] *transposed by guide line in pencil from after*
prouve *at 101.29*   101.31 **arrangments.**] *before del.* Architecture had not yet reached to that
state, where it stands as an independant art for itself.
102.1 **might here be drawn if time allowed**] *interl.*   102.2 **which**] *before del. in pencil* still
own] *interl. in pencil*   102.3 **Orientals**] *before del.* would be here on its place if it was permitted by time   **nations**] *interl.*   102.5 **of**] *interl. in pencil*   **an account**] *interl. in*
pencil   **his travels**] *after del. in pencil* the report on   102.6 **Greeks**] k *in pencil over* c
were in this stage] *in pencil repl. del. in pencil* stood on that step   102.7 **ancient**] *repl. del.*
old   102.10 **Thebes**] s *in pencil over* n   **undoubted**] *above del.* doubtless   102.13–14
materials for ~ room,] *repl. del.* Divisions of space,   102.15 **for their**] *after del.* to make
102.19 **history**] *above del.* system   system] *after del.* whole   **begins and**] *inserted*
102.20 **motive**] ve *in pencil above del. in pencil* f   102.21 **Again**] *inserted in pencil*   **if**] i *in*
pencil over I   102.25 **Lottusplant**] *first* t *added*   **thrust**] *in pencil repl. del. in pencil* stick
stick] *altered in ink from* stickt   **capital**] *second* a *over* e   102.28 **A great part**] *after del.* A
great part of the forms used in Architecture, took origine in the works *after del.* A part
Architecture,] *before del.* and the laws of beauty and proportion   origine] *after del.* their
thus] *after del.* are   **originate**] *altered from* originating   102.30 **determined and**] *insert-*
ed   **practicised**] *repl. del.* practised   **long**] *before del.* time   102.34 **B.**] *inserted*   102.35
that the periods] *after del.* that it shows   102.37 **or**] *above del.* and   **industrial**] *in pencil*
above del. in pencil practical   102.38 **In**] *inserted*   **relation**] *altered from* relations *after del.*
on fols. 4r and 5r state || of   state] *del. in ink*   of] *del. in pencil*   102.39 **directly the**
opposite of what has been described] *repl. del.* to be the inverse of the first
103.1 **pointed**] *transposed by guide line from after* Gothic *at 103.1*   103.2 **dependant**] ant
above del. ing   103.3 **decorative motives**] *above del.* motifs of decoration   103.3–4 **con-**
struction.] *altered from* ~∧ *before del.* more than   103.5 **ogee**] *in pencil above del. in pencil*
gargussed   103.6 **became**] *before del.* even   **motives**] ves *above del.* fs   103.7–8 **the**
dominant influence ~ downwarts even to the] *repl. del.* the pointed style governs even
the   even] *undel.*   the] *before del.* arts of the   103.7 **dominant**] *in pencil above del. in*
pencil hierarchical   103.8 **bootsmaker**] *altered in pencil from* bootsmaker's   103.12 **archi-**
tectonic] *altered from* architectonical   103.13 **upheld**] *above del.* beheld   103.14 **furni-**
tures] *altered from* furniture *after del.* Arc[h]   103.15 **to**] *in pencil repl. del. in pencil* for
103.16–23 **At the end ~ things. – .**] *crossed out in thin pencil probably by Hans Semper or Wolf-*
gang Herrmann (cf. 404, Explanatory Notes 103.16–23)   103.16 **the empire**] *after del.* an
other principle to be   **we see**] *after del.* which is   103.17 **and especially**] *repl. del.*
namely   namely] *after del. in pencil* and   **guided**] *after del.* in wich it was *and before del.*
only *and repl. del. on fol. 5r* influenced only   103.19 **allso**] *interl.*   103.22 **stone,**] *altered*

from ~∧ before del. and plaster **and architects adopted forms, which]** *accompanied by probably Semper's own note in ink* ✕ **forms, which]** *before del.* were first intended to be executed in Porcelain **can]** *after del.* can be justified if ex 103.24 **Revolutions]** *altered from* revolutions *after del.* We see that We] *altered from* we *after del.* So **thus]** *interl. in pencil* 103.25 **mode]** *repl. del.* manner 103.26 **dominion]** *repl. del.* hierarchy **over]** *above del.* upon 103.28 **over]** *above del.* upon 103.29 **shall]** *above del.* will 103.31 **practical]** *after del. in pencil* the **art]** *altered in pencil from* arts 103.32 **In this light we may]** *in pencil above del. in pencil* Therefore we may praise and **right feeling]** *after del. in pencil* skill and 103.32–3 **efforts]** *after del. in pencil* generous

MANUSCRIPT VARIANTS
MS 119

fol. 4r

 thirdly that revolutions in the architectural styles were allways prepared by innovations which had been introduced before in the manner of practicising Industrial art, which has for its object the embellishment of the necessities of life.

 Fourdly That our architecture is devoyd of originality and has lost its influence upon the other arts. That it will only revive when more attention will be payd to our present state of 5 Industry by modern architects and that the impulsion to such a change will again go out from the practical arts. ‖

fol. 5r

 That therefore lastly we may recognise the skill and right feeling, which presides the generous efforts of our government for the artistical education of the nation, by paying especial attention to the practice of the industrial arts. – . 10

 Luxury dwelt in simple tents, in baracks and in rude strong-holds many thousand Years before the invention of architecture and of architectural forms. So it was for instance with the Greecs downwards to the time of Homeros and Hesiodos. and even much later. The descriptions which these old Greec poets give of the arms of the heros, of tripods, vases, draperies embroideries and other objects of practical art are without doubt traced upon real 15 things; they were allowed to exagerate the beauty and richness of these things, by that liberty which poets take and have, but their art would have been effectless, if their hearers were not acquainted with things analogous to those which they describe. Now what are the descriptions of monuments and architectural works which the same poets lay before us? These descriptions proouve, that an immense luxury was then combined with the most primitive 20 simplicity of construction in buildings. Architecture had not yet reached to that state, where it stands as an independent art for itself. ‖

fol. 1r

 All the embellishments of the barracks of the heros, as well as those of the more solid dynastical Halls and Court Yards were mere applications consisting in draperies or metallic incrustations, in shields, trophees, Metalfigures, festoons, flowers and other mouveable 25 things, borrowed from the industrial arts, or from natare. The same buildings, which were covered with Gold and tinplates, had no floors, no fireplaces no flues.

 A parallel between the Homeric dwellings and that singular mixture of luxury and simplicity which still in our times prevails in the interiors of the Orientals, would be here on its place if it was permitted by time. 30

 I must refer for this to the lively description which gives Mr Layard in his report on his travels in Mesopotamia of a tent of an Arabian Cheik.

On the Relations of the Different Branches of Industrial Art   407

But while the Greecs stood in that state of antearchitectural civilization, there existed in other parts of the old world some centerpoints of very old culture, based upon other principles, which were, if considered under a certain point of view more favorable for the development of architecture as a selfexisting art.

5 But what see we on the monuments of Niniveh and Theben? The doubtless proofs of the same what has been advanced before; the architectural forms and motifs of the Aegyptian and Assyrian Monuments are all borrowed from the industrial arts.

Mats, and afterwards carpets and draperies || were the earliest divisions of space they were   *fol. 2r* employed for this service long time before the construction of walls with bricks was invent-

10 ed, and the well known Alabasterplates with which the earthwalls of the Assyrian Pallaces were covered, are nothing but imitations of the original carpets, plastically executed in stone.

If we look at the Aegyptian columns of the earlier periods, we recognize square pillars, covered with cane, which is fastened with strings and a piece of ornamented tapestry round

15 it, so that the square pillar remains visible at the top above the capital. the last is formed by flowers, or knops of the Papyrus and Lothus plant, stickt into the strings by which the ornamental cover of the column is supposed to be fastened, quite in the same manner as the fair Egyptian Ladies of the time used to stick the same flowers into the Laces of their hairdresses.

20 A great part of the forms, used in architecture, as well as the laws of beauty and proportion, have their origine in the works of industrial art, which last practiced the same laws long time before the existance of any monumental art.

The works of industrial art give therefore very often || the veritable keys for the understand-   *fol. 3r* ing of the architectural forms and rules.

25 But in other periods of art, the state of relations betveen the two manifestations of art became to be the inverse of the first mentionned.

Under the influence of the so cald Gothicalstyle for instance the forms of the industrial arts became quite depending upon those which prevailed then in architecture. The reliquaries were small houses, the vases had buttresses ogival arches, mouldings with gargusses, and

30 covers like roofs. the arches became even the principal motifs of the surface ornamentations. The pointed style was introduced even in the art of the bootsmaker and tailor. Was this a normal and sound state of things? I believe not.

The architectonical System of decoration beheld its influence a long time after the revival of the antik principles of art, at least for some parts of practical art, for instance for furniture.

    406.1 **thirdly**] *after del.*

    thirdly, that periods of revolutions in architectural styles were allways prepared by innovations which before had taken place in the manner of practicising the practical arts, and that probably an improvement of the present state of architecture, which is devoyd of originality, will begin with improvements and new

    406.2 **Industrial**] *repl. del.* that   406.3 **life**.] *altered from ~, before del.*

    and that probably the first impulsion for an improvement of the present state of architecture, which is devoyd of originality, will go out from progresses in practical art; that therefore the attempts which

406.4 **Fourdly**] *'Fourthly'*   406.5 **only**] *interl.*   **revive**] *before del.* only under the condition that our architects will pay more attention to the   406.8 **That therefore lastly**]
after del. on fol. 4r

that therefore finally[1] the generous care[2] with which our government watches[3] over the
education of national taste and artistical feeling

> [1] **that therefore finally ~ feeling**] *repl. del.* that therefore finally the generous at-
> tempts which we see of the government, to forward and improve the   [2] **care**]
> *above del.* attempts   [3] **watches**] *after del.* is endeavouring to forward and   for-
> ward] *before del.* the education of

406.9 **for**] *after del.* in *after del.* in spending   406.11 **strong-holds**] strong- | holds
406.12 **forms.**] *before del.* Domestical Industry, trade war and robbery furnished the household   406.14 **heros**] *'heroes' (see also 406.23)*   406.15–16 **real things**] real *interl. and*
things *before del.* they had seen before   406.17–22 **their art ~ for itself.**] *inserted after del.*

would not[1] have been understood by their hearers, if the last had never[2] seen some analogical things before them. Theyr artful descriptions would have been without effect.

> [1] **would not**] *after del.* these exaggerated descriptions   [2] **had never**] *after del.* were
> not acquainted with the view of some analogical things

406.19–20 **These descriptions**] *above del.* They   406.20 **proouve**] *altered from prove*
406.23 **heros**] *after del.* warr[ ]   406.25 **incrustations**] *after del.* wall   406.26 **natare**]
'nature'   406.27 **no flues**] no *above del.* and   406.32 **Cheik**] *'sheikh'*
407.8 **Mats, and afterwards**] *inserted*   **carpets**] *after del.* The   407.9–10 **invented,**]
repl. del. known,   407.15 **the last**] *after del.* And   **is formed by**] *above del.* are   407.16
stickt] *'stuck'*   407.23 **give**] *above del.* are   407.25 **state of relations**] *after del.* relation
407.27 **Under**] *after del.* This may be shortly shown by one example; that of Gothical art.
In the   cald] *'called'*   407.28 **The reliquaries**] *after del.* The details of the vases and
even their ornaments were small imitations of ogival arches and   407.29 **the vases**] *after*
del. and even the vases borrowed their forms from the ogival arches   **gargusses**] *after*
del. water   407.30 **became**] *repl. del.* were   **even**] *before del.* introduced as   **motifs**]
f *over* v   407.32 **I believe not**] *after del.* It is perhaps not yet   not yet] *after del.* audacious
407.33 **beheld**] *derived from German 'behalten': 'retained'*   **revival**] *after del.* introduction
of the   407.34 **antik**] *'antique'*   **furniture.**] *before del.* But the Greec forms of Architecture were perhaps for this more accomodating.   Architecture] *before del.* with the (the
after del. their)

On the Relations of the Different Branches of Industrial Art 409

Third Version

TEXTUAL RECORD

MS 123² gta, 20-Ms 123, fols. 3r–4v (4v calculations possibly for Semper 1859), in Semper's hand

MS 123³ gta, 20-Ms-123, fols. 6r–v, 5r–v, 8r–v, 7r–v (between 5v and 8r one sheet missing at least), in Semper's hand

MS 123⁴ gta, 20-Ms-123, fol. 9r–v, in Semper's hand; continuation of del. passage in MS 122, fol. 16v (see 418–20, Alterations in the Manuscript 116.29)

MS 122 gta, 20-Ms-122, fols. 1r–23v (19v–23v blank; 2v–3v variant of MS 123²; 3r–8r variant of MS 123³; 17v–18v variant of MS 123⁴), in Semper's hand, *copy-text*

MS 125 gta, 20-Ms-125, fols. 1r–22v (21v–22v blank), in J. Ruston Palen's hand (additions and emendations in Manfred Semper's hand), 1880, copy of MS 122

MS 147¹ gta, 20-Ms-147, fols. 13v, 14v (1r–13r, 14r, 15r–22v see 515, MS 147²), in unknown hand (emendations in Hans and Manfred Semper's hands), early 1880s, Manfred Semper's del. German trans. of MS 122, fols. 8r–9r, 11r–v

MS 127 gta, 20-Ms-127, fols. 1r–39v (2v, 3v, 4v, 5v, 6v, 7v, 8v, 9v, 10v, 11v, 12v, 13v, 20v, 21v, 24v and all following versos blank; 14v, 15v, 16v, 19v, 22v, 23v notes relating to Semper's new Dresden Court Theatre; 17v three del. words), 'Entwurf eines Systemes der vergleichenden Stillehre', partly in unknown hand (1r–13r, 17r, 18r–v, 20r–22r, 23v–38r; emendations in Hans and Manfred Semper's hands), partly in Manfred Semper's hand (1r, 8r, 11r, 13r–14r, 15r, 16r, 18r, 19r, 22r, 23r, 37r–39r; one emendation in Hans Semper's hand), early 1880s, Manfred Semper's German trans. of MS 122, fols. 1r–8r, 9r–18r (additional sections: German trans. of MS 124; see 426), published in Semper 1884; see Herrmann 1981, 110

Semper 1884 'Entwurf eines Systemes der vergleichenden Stillehre', 259–91, German trans. of MS 122, fols. 1r–8r, 9r–18r (additional sections: German trans. of MS 124; see 426); for details of this composite translation, see Herrmann 1981, 159–66

Semper 1983 'London Lecture of November 11, 1853', 5–22, here 8–17, Mallgrave's ed. of MS 122

BIBLIOGRAPHY Semper 1880, 21; Rykwert 1976, 74–5; Vogt 1976, 191, 193–4; Herrmann 1978, 79–80; Herrmann 1981, 109–10, 114, 159–66; Mallgrave 1983b; Rykwert 1983, 6 fig.; Herrmann 1984, 73; Hauser 1985; Herrmann 1990, 76, 78, 80; Laudel 1991, 9, 43–5; Waenerberg 1992, 60–4, 143; Mallgrave 1996, 217–18; Gnehm 2004, 32; Arburg 2008, 271–2; Squicciarino 2009, 359–61; Poerschke 2012; Hildebrand 2014, 9–10; Papapetros 2016, 55; Poerschke 2016, 75, 82–3; Hildebrand 2020b, 67–8; Hildebrand 2021, 114–16, 119 and fig. 11

EXPLANATORY NOTES

This manuscript (MS 122), identified here as the third, definitive version of the inaugural lecture of 20 May 1853, was previously considered to be a variant of another manuscript (MS 124), with which it has certain similarities. Manfred and Hans Semper combined parts of MS 122 and MS 124 into a single text, the German translation of which they published in *Kleine Schriften* under the title 'Entwurf eines Systemes der vergleichenden Stillehre', describing it as a 'Lecture, given in London in 1853' (Semper 1884, 259 n. *). Wolfgang Herrmann and Harry Francis Mallgrave believed that MS 122 corresponded to the lecture Semper gave on 11 November 1853 and that MS 124 was a preliminary version of it (Herrmann 1981, 109–10; Mallgrave 1983b, 23). However, the connections between the content of MS 122 and the first and second versions of the inaugural lecture (MS 118 and MS 117) and – even more obviously – its references to the planned lecture series reveal that it is the definitive version of the lecture Semper gave on 20 May 1853. It mentions 'a plan for a course of lectures on the different branches of industrial art, to which this paper may be considered as an introduction' (109.4–6), and explains the plan by outlining the contents of five subsequent lectures (117.27–34). This list of contents corresponds precisely to that given in the 'Prospectuses of the Lectures on Art', originally limited to five public lectures in the autumn term of 1853 (see 96–7), which then started on 11 November with MS 124, 'General Remarks on the Different Styles in Architecture'. The 'Remarks' in turn refer to the lecture of 'some months' ago – the inaugural lecture – as an 'introduction to a series of lectures' (118.1–2).

The third version of the inaugural lecture, which is preserved in full, no longer starts with Owen Jones's principle, supported by the Department of Science and Art, like the first and second versions, but rather – appropriately for an inaugural lecture – with an address to the audience, followed by an admission of the difficulty for a foreigner of discussing a topic in English which in itself is already difficult (104.1–10). However, Jones's principle still reverberates in a paragraph of the main part on the relationship between architecture and the industrial arts (108.3–11). The contradiction latent in the second version (see 403) persists. On the one hand, 'The laws and principles of Style and beauty which we aknowledge in art, have probably been the first systematically fixd by Architects' (108.4–6), while on the other, 'The principles of Aesthetics in Architecture have had their first applications on objects of Industry' (108.8–9). In addition to the admission of his difficulty with English mentioned above, the detailed remarks on the division of the sciences caused by 'the immense amount of learning' (104.23) and on the few attempts that had been made to overcome this division through a comparative or unifying approach can be regarded as providing the introduction to the lecture (104.1–106.26). Most of these remarks are taken from a prospectus for 'Comparative Architecture' published in 1852, which in turn is based on a letter that Semper wrote to the publisher Eduard Vieweg on 26 September 1843 (see Herrmann 1976, 211, 215–18). As in the last two paragraphs of the first version (100.20–32), the third version also refers to the Cabinet d'Anatomie comparée established by Georges Cuvier in the Jardin des Plantes in Paris (105.1–22). However, it arrives at the remarkable suggestion that Cuvier's comparative approach should be transferred to the arts to obtain 'a Sort of topic or Method, how to invent' (105.26–31).

Semper begins the main part (106.27–117.20) with a second admission: he confesses that in his Dresden lectures he had paid 'too little' attention to the relationship between architecture and 'the other branches of practical art' – that is, the industrial arts (106.33–4). It was only in 1851, in *The Four Elements of Architecture*, that he had connected each architectural

On the Relations of the Different Branches of Industrial Art   411

element to a specific 'original technique' and investigated the connection between the element of enclosure and tapestry (Semper 1851b, 56–68). Despite the lecture's promising title, Semper does not discuss the relationships in question in the first London lecture systematically but only on the basis of examples and with constant reference to the explanation of his concept of style. The explanation starts with a provisional representation of a work of art as a mathematical function with variable coefficients that determine its style (108.35–41), runs through the rest of the main part and makes use of several of Semper's writings: *The Four Elements of Architecture, Science, Industry, and Art*, 'Practical Art in Metals and hard Materials' and the first draft of a treatise *Ueber die bleiernen Schleudergeschosse der Alten* (On the Leaden Slingshot Bullets of the Ancients). The main part concludes by developing the programme for further lectures planned for the autumn term of 1853 on the basis of a classification of the practical arts (116.30–117.39). Henry Cole, who attended Semper's inaugural lecture – among an audience of 90 (DSA[1], 223) – described it in his diary entry of 20 May 1853 as 'thoughtful & suggestive' (Cole Diary).

The material state of MS 122 indicates that Semper replaced the front and back parts (104.1–108.17, 116.30–117.39) and therefore wrote them after the middle part (108.18–116.29). The pages of the front and back parts are much smaller than those in the middle, and a manuscript fragment preserved in the gta Archives (MS 123[4]) originally continued the middle part of MS 122 (see 418–20, Alterations in the Manuscript 116.29). This means it must be assumed that another, partly lost stage of the drafts existed between the second and third versions.

Wolfgang Herrmann assigned the second half of another manuscript (gta, 20-Ms-93) to the manuscripts that are here classified as the third version (Herrmann 1981, 100, 110). Although this fragment corresponds fairly precisely to two passages in MS 122 (111.11–112.23, 113.10–20), Herrmann's assignment is not plausible, since the second half of the manuscript in question is materially connected (with the same paper sheets) with the first half, entitled 'On the present state of practical art', and thus most likely refers to the same event, namely 'the intended exhibition'. Herrmann's assumption that this refers to the art exhibition planned for February 1852 in the Crystal Palace (Herrmann 1981, 100; cf. 43.23–44.4) cannot be correct, as the manuscript contains reflections on 'the power of animal and vegetable life', which Semper began to make only after he had attended the presentation of a paper on 'Proportions and Curves of the Parthenon of Athens' by David Ramsay Hay at the Royal Institute of British Architects on 7 February 1853. The manuscript probably refers to the furniture exhibition that the Department of Science and Art held at Gore House from May to September 1853 (DSA[1], liii–liv, 329; see 404, Explanatory Notes 101.1–2).

104.18 **simetimes**] *sometimes*   104.21 **it not new**] *is ~ ~*

105.16 **which**] *with*   105.29 **a Sort of topic or Method, how to invent**] The word 'topic' is altered from 'topics', which would be closer to what Semper was wishing to express (see 414, Alterations in the Manuscript 105.29). In two fragmentary manuscripts of the inaugural lecture (MS 123[3], MS 123[2]), the corresponding phrase is 'a sort of topic or science of invention' (422.1) or 'a science how to invent' (420.26; cf. 421, note 420.25). It is therefore similar to the title of a book written by Christian August Lebrecht Kästner that Semper apparently owned: *Topik, oder Erfindungswissenschaft* (Kästner 1816; see 216.8). When Semper returned to the subject in the lecture 'General Remarks on the Different Styles in Art' (MS 124), he shortened the phrase used in the inaugural lecture to 'a Sort of Method how to invent' (118.21). On 26 September 1843, he had already written to Eduard Vieweg: 'es wird …

möglich seyn, eine architectonische Erfindungslehre ... zu begründen, welche den Weg der Natur lehrt' (it will ... be possible to found ... a theory of architectural invention that teaches the path of nature). The words 'Topik oder' are deleted before 'Erfindungslehre' in the letter (Vieweg Archives, V1S:246; cf. Herrmann 1976, 217). In the 'Outline' of the 'Letters on the Great Exhibition', by contrast, Semper left the words 'Erfindungslehre, Topik' in place (29.27). On Semper's relation to topics, see Gnehm 2004, 30–4, 45–8.   105.33–4 **Book of Cuvier on the animal Empire and his comparing Osteology**] Cuvier 1812, Cuvier 1817   105.34 **Cosmus of Humboldt**] Humboldt 1845/62. Only three of five volumes of Alexander von Humboldt's *Kosmos* had been published when Semper gave his inaugural lecture. He owned two of them but had not read them by the summer of 1852 (see 212.32; 541–2; 544, Explanatory Notes 212.32).

106.1 **Durand in his parallels and other works on Architecture**] Durand 1800/01, Durand 1802/05, Durand 1821   106.2 **looses**] *loses* (see also 106.6, 112.16)

107.4–108.2 **Let us compare ~ Greek Architecture.**] Semper repeated the comparison between the Egyptian *situla* and the Greek *hydria* almost verbatim in the first lecture on ceramic art (137.5–40); see 454.   107.10 **Jockes**] *yokes*   107.15 **chaped**] *shaped* (see also 112.22) 107.21 **to**] *the*

108.36 **indefite**] *indefinite*; cf. 414, Alterations in the Manuscript 108.36   108.38 **U = Φ x, y, z, t, v, w.**] Mallgrave has 'U = C x, y, z, t, v, w.' (Semper 1983, 11). In the 'Kunstformenlehre' (Theory of Art Forms), the predecessor of *Style*, Semper also represented a work of art as a mathematical function, there using the equation 'U = Φ (x, y, z, t, v, w, ...)' (Vieweg Archives, V3:1.1.3.32, sect. 'Introduction', 34).

109.3 **undefined**] Wolfgang Herrmann translates this word as 'unbestimmbar' (Herrmann 1981, 161). In fact, Semper himself used the word 'unbestimmbar' (undefinable) in the corresponding sentence of the 'Theory of Art Forms' (Vieweg Archives, V3:1.1.3.32, sect. 'Introduction', 35).   109.14–110.11 **That part of the Doctrine of Style ~ at our times.**] cf. Semper 1852, 16–18   109.24 **wether**] *whether*

110.12 **shiefly**] *chiefly*   110.25–111.21 **Every morket ware ~ Study of Style.**] cf. Semper 1852, 24–6 and n. **   110.25 **morket**] *market*   110.30 **recommandation**] French for *recommendation*   110.37 **soal**] *soul*

111.21 **aesily**] *easily*   111.39 **exercing**] *exerting* (see also 112.7)

112.24–5 **Sling bullets, which have the form of plumkernets executed in lead**] In *On the Leaden Slingshot Bullets of the Ancients*, bullets of this type are illustrated and described as 'slingshot bullets made of lead in the shape of almonds or plum kernels (hence called *balanoi* among the Greeks and *glandes* among the Romans)' (Semper 1859, frontispiece figs. 1, 3–4; 6).   112.25 **laying**] *lying*   112.26 **Prussian pointed musket-ball**] cf. Semper 1859, frontispiece fig. 5; 416, Alterations in the Manuscript 112.26   112.28–30 **It is questionable weither these Projectiles are the Result of an instinctiv feeling ~ or ~ proofs of the high state of Mechanical Science with the Greecs.**] 'weither': *whether*. Semper still does not resolve this question even in *On the Leaden Slingshot Bullets of the Ancients* of 1859, where he remarks that evidence might 'perhaps' be found to show 'that the leaden almond projectiles of the ancients were shaped in accordance with strictly scientific principles' (Semper 1859, 12). In 'Practical Art in Metals and hard Materials' in 1852, by contrast, Semper does apparently exclude the first alternative, as he admires ancient slingshot bullets 'for their well calculated general forms' (Semper 2007a, 227).   112.33 **preceeding**] *preceding*   112.33–8 **If such a leaden bird is fliing ~ positive power.**] 'fliing': *flying* (see also 113.1); cf. Semper 1859, 14–15   112.41–113.6 **So does Nature ~ by the same reasons.**] cf. Semper 1859, 11

113.3 **allongated**] derived from French *allonger*: *elongated* (see also 113.7)   **tale**] *tail*
113.10–114.3 **We know pretty well ~ only to History.**] cf. Semper 1859, 3–5   113.11 **fric-
ture**] *friction*; cf. Semper's draft of a report 'On the present state of practical art' (gta, 20-
Ms-93, fol. 4v): 'the laws of certain natural forces, for instance that of gravity; the friction
and others'   113.13 **sattled**] *settled*

114.2 **joung**] *young*   114.6–9 **Attempts have often been made to explain the Greek
forms and to find out a Scheme for them ~ by comparing the Geometrical projections ~ after these measures.**] Two such attempts of which Semper was evidently aware
are Francis Cranmer Penrose's *Investigation of the Principles of Athenian Architecture* (Penrose
1851; see Semper 1851, 10–11) and David Ramsay Hay's paper 'An Attempt to Develope the
Principle which Governs the Proportions and Curves of the Parthenon of Athens'. This
paper, read by Penrose at the Royal Institute of British Architects on 7 February 1853,
prompted Semper to plan the book *On the Leaden Slingshot Bullets of the Ancients* (see Semper
1859, 1–7). Shortly before Semper's inaugural lecture, Hay published an expanded version of
his paper under the title *The Orthographic Beauty of the Parthenon Referred to a Law of Nature*
(Hay 1853).   114.9 **drown**] *drawn*   114.12 **artistical**] Mallgrave has 'artificial' (Semper
1983, 14).   114.26 **lays**] *lies* (see also 114.36)   **give a systematical suit to**] derived from
French *donner systématiquement suite à*: *systematically pursue*   114.41 **separed**] derived from
French *séparer*: *separated*

115.6–7 **Style ~ represents them.**] In his *Italienische Forschungen*, Carl Friedrich von
Rumohr wrote (Rumohr 1827/31, 1:87; italics in original): 'We shall therefore not be diverging substantially either from the word's usage or from the true intentions of the best artists
of this [recent] period if we define style *as a compliance, which has become habitual, with the
inner requirements of the material in which the sculptor shapes his figures in reality and the painter
makes them appear.*'   115.17 **revue**] French for *review*   115.32 **separing**] *separating*; cf. 418,
Alterations in the Manuscript 115.32

116.10 **Othersides**] derived from German *anderseits*: *On the other hand*. Mallgrave has
'Otherwise' (Semper 1983, 16).   116.16 **penneld**] *panelled*   116.17 **Pantheon Doors and
that of Remus in Rome**] cf. Donaldson 1833/36, 1:41–4, pls. 17–20; Semper 1860/63, 1:367–9
116.22 **pennypeace**] *penny piece*

117.16 **Antik**] *antique*   117.21–3 **A thorough illustration ~ towards this object.**] Semper
expressed similar reservations to Eduard Vieweg on 26 September 1843 in relation to the
planned 'Comparative Architecture' (Vieweg Archives, VIS:246; cf. Herrmann 1976, 217): 'I
repeat that I do not feel equal to the task of creating a pure theory of architecture in this
sense; however, I do believe that I am able to make occasional contributions to it from what
I have thought, observed and collected in the context of my work as a teacher and practising
architect.' This passage, with slight changes, was included in the printed prospectus for
'Comparative Architecture' in 1852.   117.24 **purpose**] Mallgrave has 'propose' (Semper
1983, 17).   117.34 **chown**] *shown*

414 Lectures

EDITORIAL EMENDATIONS

104.17 **overpowered by]** overpowered by ¦ by   106.6 **tabular-formularies]** tabular- | for-
mularies   113.4 **Ground-plans]** Ground- | plans   114.41 **treating]** trea- ¦ *(ting missing)*
116.18 **Cabinets makers-work]** Cabinets makers- | work   117.29 **timber-construction]**
timber- | construction

ALTERATIONS IN THE MANUSCRIPT

104.3 **English]** *after inserted and del.* broken   104.12 **are our own]** *above del.* belong to us
104.22 **and classifications]** and *above del.* of   104.23 **instituted]** *after del.* made   104.26
ages,] *after del.* times,   104.32 **things,]** *before del.* which we no longer   104.34 **coordin-
ation]** *after del.* comparison.   104.35–6 **Sciences, begins now to be much]** *accompanied
by probably Semper's own note ?*   104.36 **more constructive than it was before,]** *accompanied by probably Semper's own note?*   **constructive]** *below del.* spirited   104.38 **natural]**
altered from nature. *after del.* laws of   **forces.]** *inserted*
105.4 **the present]** *after del.* our   105.6 **empire,]** *after del.* world,   105.26 **which]** *after del.*
by   105.29 **topic]** *altered from* topics   105.34 **Empire]** *above del.* world
106.8 **many]** *after del.* And *after del.* And finally at his time the amount of   106.9 **which
we now possess,]** *inserted*   106.10 **time]** *before del.* for instance that of mediaeval art
for instance] *after del.* which was not yet prepared for   **as Durand]** *after del.* as he intended
to execute.   106.15 **less]** *after del.* with *and before del.* fortune.   **happily.]** *inserted*
106.16 **the amount]** *after del.* very precious   106.19 **England]** *after del.* France   106.22
But] *after del.* But all these works are evidences of what   106.24 **at]** *after del.* to   106.25
all these knowledges] *repl. del.* knowledge   106.37 **paragons in]** *after del.* types in   **Industrial art.]** *after del.* practical art.   106.38 **The laws]** *after del.* The laws of proportion, of
Symmetry and harmony, the principles the traditional forms which are current in the letter,
principles] *before del.* of ornamentation the special forms which occur by tradition   letter]
'latter'
107.13 **Greek]** k *over* c   107.20 **traced]** *repl. del.* taken
108.2 **Greek]** k *over* c   108.4 **in one]** in *above del.* to   108.5 **aknowledge]** *after del.* recognize   108.10 **causes.]** *repl. del.* reasons   108.18 **I shall]** *after undel.* been treated by
philosophers and artists of all periods. Many Volumes. have been written about it;   treated]
in pencil above del. in pencil treatened   Volumes.] *repl. del.* books   it;] *altered from* ~, *before
del.* without bringing certainty in the   **and]** *interl. before del.* which have been made of the
aesth   108.19 **senses]** *inserted before del.* and notions   108.20 **connection]** *before del.*
between these notions   **which]** *over* is   108.21 **them]** *altered from* these *before del.* notions
108.22 **pursued]** *after del.* well defined and   108.24–6 **I therefore ~ expression; but the]**
inserted   108.24 **to]** *after del.* for   **that of Style]** *after del.* that which will be sufficient for
108.25 **for the following]** *inserted on fol. 7v*   **sense]** *after del.* sense of this word for the
following [ ]   108.26 **expression;]** *altered from* ~∧ *before del.* in t   **but the]** *before del.*
definition   **following]** *after del.* The   108.27 **absolute and of]** *repl. del.* of   108.29
This] is *over* e   **term]** *before del.* style   108.35 **using]** *after del. in ink over pencil* for
108.36 **indefite]** te *in pencil over hyphen of* indefi- | ned   indefined] ned *del. in pencil*
108.39 **coefficients]** *before del.* of   **vary]** *in pencil below del. in pencil* variate   variate]
above del. vary   108.39–40 **likewise]** *in pencil above del. in pencil* the same   108.40 **fea-
tures]** s *added in pencil*

109.3 **Their number**] *after four del. beginnings of variant:*

Their[1] number is undefined and we shall point out[2] only some of the most influentials[3], such, which will lead us to the explanation of that System of classification of the objects of industrial art

Their number is undefined and we shall only point out here some of them, such, which are of the most[4] influentials, and which will lead to the explanation of the order which I adopted[5] for a course of lectures on the industrial arts,[6] which I have prepared on

Their number is undefined, and we shall only point out here some of them, which are of the most general influence; for it lays[7] not in the plan of this lecture to give a systematical Suit[8] to this important question

Their number is undefined, and we shall only point out here some of the[9] most important, for it lays[7] not in the plan of this lecture to give to the question a systematical Suit[8] and to give more specialities as will be necessary for the explanation of a plan for a suit[10] of lectures which has been prepared by the reader

> 1 **Their**] *after del.* Bef   2 **point out**] *repl. del.* take out of their rang   3 **influentials**]
> s *added*   4 **of them, such, which are of the most**] *repl. del.* of the most   5 **I adopted**]
> *after del.* has been adopted for the   6 **on the industrial arts,**] *inserted*   7 **lays**] *'lies'*
> 8 **give a systematical Suit**] *'systematically pursue' (see 413, Explanatory Notes 114.26)*
> 9 **the**] *after del.* them, such as may be considered as   10 **suit**] *'course'*

109.4 **course**] *in pencil above del. in pencil* suit   109.7 **We must distinguish**] *after four del. beginnings of variant on fols. 8v–9r:*

But before giving some specification, we may devide[1] |
But before
We may devide[1] the agents, which are acting upon [t]
We may divide them into two distinct Classes

> 1 **devide**] *'divide'*

109.9 **of the**] *in pencil above del. in pencil* which lay in the   lay] *'lie'*   109.10 **laws of na-**
ture] *after del.* natural   **all**] *in pencil above del. in pencil* every   109.11 **circumstance**] e *in*
pencil above del. in pencil es   109.13 **a work of art**] *after del.* an artistic   109.14 **treats**] *in*
pencil repl. del. in pencil treatens   **of**] *in pencil above del. in pencil* on   **embraces**] *in pencil*
repl. del. in pencil embrasses   109.15 **the elementary Ideas**] *after inserted and del.* 1°)
109.16 **cloathed.**] *before del.* ‡   ‡] *accompanied by del.* ‡ 2°. the   109.23 **Mattings**] *after del.*
Watting   109.31 **principles**] s *added*   109.32 **historical element**] *above del.* part
109.34–5 **But this first part ~ should teach,**] *repl. del.* But the second division contains
another part, which we commonly call the practical part, which should teach,   109.37 **of**]
in pencil above del. in pencil to   109.38 **in**] *in pencil above del. in pencil* at
110.13 **climate**] *in pencil above del. in pencil* clime   **country,**] *after del.* Land,   110.19 **the**
doctrine of] *inserted*   110.27 **latter**] *in pencil above del. in pencil* last   110.31 **the**] *in pencil*
repl. del. in pencil a   110.33 **appropriately**] *inserted in pencil*   110.38 **even**] *interl.*
111.1 **the**] *in pencil above del. in pencil* a   111.3 **sense**] *in pencil above del. in pencil* thought
111.5 **soldiers**] *in pencil repl. del.* armed Fellows   armed] *del. in pencil*   Fellows] *del. in ink*
over pencil   111.11 **appliances**] *after del.* sciences   111.23 **different**] *interl.*   111.24 **uni-**

versal] *repl. del.* general   111.27 **the things]** the *over* a *and* things *altered from* thing
111.33 **Idea]** *after del.* fundamental   **of satisfying]** *in ink over pencil repl. del. in pencil* for
contenting   **It is]** *repl. inserted in pencil and del. in ink* suffice it to be   suffice it to be] *repl.
del. in ink over pencil* It is   111.34 **or]** *above del.* and   111.35 **no matter]** *inserted in ink over
pencil*   111.39 **on the one hand]** *above del. in ink over pencil* onesides *and accompanied in
opposite column by undel. identical insertion in pencil*   **on the other]** *above del. in ink over
pencil* othersides *and accompanied in opposite column by undel. identical insertion in pencil*
112.3 **arrive at]** at *above del. in ink over pencil* to *and accompanied in opposite column by undel.
identical insertion in pencil*   112.9 **natural forms]** *after del. in pencil* the   112.13 **never
fails]** *in ink over pencil repl. del. in pencil* fails never   112.14 **case]** *after del. in pencil* Same.
the more] more *after del.* less we   112.14–15 **it seems]** *repl. del.* we seem to loose   loose]
'lose'   112.16 **strength]** *before del. in pencil* and sharpness   **attained to the]** *in pencil repl.
del. in pencil on fols. 11v–12r* arrived to | that   112.17 **this]** is *over* e   **loss]** *before del.* of
instinctiv feeling.   112.18 **led]** *in ink over pencil above del. in pencil* conduced   112.19 **were]**
above del. are   **heretofore]** *repl. del. in pencil* till now *and accompanied in opposite column by
undel. identical insertion in pencil*   **semi-]** *in pencil repl. del. in pencil* half   112.20–1 **peb-
bles]** *in pencil repl. del. in pencil* Galenas   112.21 **ground]** *repl. del. in ink* ground   ground]
in pencil above del. in ink over pencil grinded   112.24 **ancient]** *interl. in ink over pencil*
Sling bullets] *above del.* Projectiles *and accompanied in opposite column by undel. identical
insertion in pencil*   112.26 **a]** *after del.* one of the *and both above del.* a   **musket-]** *inserted*
ball,] *altered from* balls, *before del.* which they shot into the window of my sitting Room in
the Year 1849;   112.28 **It]** *altered from* it *after del.* But   112.30 **of Mechanical]** *after del.* of
Greec M   112.32 **knowledge]** *altered in pencil from* knowledges   **for the defense]** *after
del.* for defending their   112.33–113.9 **These bullets ~ great masses.]** *inserted in left column of fol. 12r, in right column of fol. 12v and in left column of fol. 13r*   112.33 **bullets]** *above
del.* forms   **preceeding.]** *altered from* ~∧ *before del.* assertions.   112.34 **an]** n *added*   **En-
velop]** *above del.* nymbus   112.35–6 **The condensed air]** *after del.* Now *after del.* Now
nature   112.36 **in proportion to its density]** *interl.*   112.37 **also in proportion to its
density]** *interl.*   112.39 **Further]** *repl. del.* Secondly   Secondly] *repl. del.* Now   112.40
therefore,] *altered from* ~∧ *after del.* it will *and before del.* be reasonable to   **by]** *interl.*
filling] ing *added*   **vacuum]** *after del.* room   112.41 **we]** *interl.*   **will]** *after del.* and to
increase by this way the living force of the bullet which *and before del.* diminue the vacuum
and   diminue] *derived from French 'diminuer': 'diminish'*
113.2 **form,]** *before del.* with sharp   **this]** *altered from* the *before del.* thik   113.3 **filling up]**
after del. forming   113.4 **the]** *interl.*   **and of]** *above del.* all   113.4–5 **their bodies,]** *before
del.* have the same form.   113.5 **The same is]** *repl. del.* It is   **evident on the]** *above del.*
the form of the   **on the flame]** on *above del.* of   113.9 **masses.]** *before* siehe oben. *(indicating continuation on fol. 12r; see 113.10)*   113.10 **We know]** *after del.* If we go   **principles]**
above del. laws   113.11 **instance that]** *interl.*   113.14 **gasses]** *in pencil above del. in pencil*
gazes   113.15 **the investigations]** *after del.* to our science   113.16 **of]** *above del. in pencil*
from *and accompanied by undel. identical insertion in pencil*   113.17 **it,]** *altered from* ~.   **and
that it is a defined force.]** *inserted*   113.28 **industrial]** *repl. del.* artistical   113.31 **appli-
cation]** *over* acc *(for 'accessories')*   **accessories,]** *repl. del.* forms,   **Aegyptians]** *before
del.* and   113.34 **Greek]** k *in pencil over* c   113.35 **Greeks]** ks *in pencil over* cs   113.36
entablatures] en *added in pencil*   113.38 **aware and]** *interl.*
114.1 **Greek Architecture]** k *in pencil over* c   **Greek art]** k *in pencil over* c   114.6 **Greek]**
k *in pencil over* c   114.11–12 **natural]** *before del.* forms   114.12 **and]** *above del.* of   114.15

On the Relations of the Different Branches of Industrial Art   417

or what they call templates.] *inserted below inserted in pencil and del. in ink* (templates)
114.16 **treats**] *altered in ink over pencil from* treatens   **of**] *altered in ink over pencil from* on
114.17 **simplest**] *after del.* most   114.19 **in**] *in ink over pencil above del. in pencil* for   114.20
Greeks] *altered in pencil from* Greecs *before del. in pencil* are   114.24 **We pass now**] *after del.*
on fol. 13v

We pass now to the materials[1]. –
The general principles of Style, in so far as depends[2] on[3] the substance are the following:
1°) Take that material which is the most adapted for the proposition, which You intend to
resolve.

     1 **materials**] *after del.* second   2 **depends**] *after del. in pencil* it   3 **on**] *after del.* upon

114.24 **we employ**] *after del.* come into consideration for the   114.26–7 **this important
question;**] this *altered from* the and question; *altered from* questions, *before del.* and   114.31
The abstract of] *inserted*   114.32 **is**] *after del.* may be   114.34 **You**] *interl.*   **intend**]
altered from intended *after del.* is   **resolve.**] *before inserted and del. in opposite column*

The choice of the best[1] material is a very important question, for instance Modelling Vax or
Clay, *Choice of the Paper for drawings*[2] and[3] of the other drawing materials a condition of
Style which we feel every day.

     1 **best**] *interl.*   2 **drawings**] *before del.* is a very   3 **and**] *after del.* Choice of the best
pencils or co   co] *undel. after del.* br[ ]

114.35 **but observe**] *after del.* which lay within the limits of the   lay] *'lie'; after del.* may be
114.36 **a**] *above del.* the   114.37 **whatever**] *repl. del.* in question   **will**] *after del.* comes
115.1 **The importance**] *after del.* The importance of the material in the question of Style is
so great, that some of the best writers – .   115.2 **it**] *repl. del.* it   it] *after del.* the manner of
treatement of the materials   115.10 **We generally order**] *after del.*

We generally order them after the materials of which they are made.
We devide[1] them in different classes

     1 **devide**] *'divide'*

115.13 **facility.**] *altered from* ~∧ *before del.* for their arrangement.   115.14 **mistake**] *in ink
over pencil above del. in ink over pencil* fail   **belongs.**] *before del.*

But is it in the same time the most accomodating for[1] study of Style?
This leads to some remarks with which I may be allowed to conclude this introductory lecture.

     1 **for**] *after del.* for comparisons and

115.15–19 **It will ~ For instance**] *inserted*   115.15 **allways**] *after del.* therefore   **the simplest**] *after del.* the best for museums   **perhaps**] *interl.*   115.17 **But for an ideal collection**] *after del.* But is it in the same time the most accomodating for study of Style? *after del.*

But for *after del.* But it will appear that for   **or rather**] *after del.* it may perhaps be less
115.18 **may**] *after del.* will   **be**] *above del.* appear   115.19 **accomodating.**] *altered from* ~∧
before del. as it is under   is] *after del.* appears to be   115.22 **Indians.**] *repl. del.* the same
people.   115.23 **related**] *after del.* very   115.24 **not by**] *after del.* by   115.29 **Systems of
arrangement**] *repl. del.* modes,   **for collections of art**] *below del.* to observe   115.32
separing] ing *above del.* ating   **conspicoous**] *second* o *over* u   115.33 **not less**] *after del.*
very   **and interesting**] *after del.* to be made conspicoous.   115.34 **Before**] *after del.* We
must *after del.* but   115.35 **have**] *interl. in pencil*   115.36 **this paper**] *after del.* the course of
115.37 ∧ **as we have seen,**] *above del.* , as You know,   115.40 **types.**] *before del.* In the
116.1 **plastic**] *altered in pencil from* plastical   116.4 **of the types**] of *above del.* with   116.5
latter] *in pencil repl. del. in pencil* last   116.6 **of the style**] of *above del.* with   116.8 **happens**] *in pencil above del. in pencil* comes,   **material**] *repl. del.* stuff   116.11 **qualities,**]
before del. for instance, Leather, Wowen stuffs, Wood and Metal,   116.14 **with flat surface
ornamentations,**] *inserted in pencil*   116.17 **Remus**] *in pencil over* R *and blank space*   **in
Rome**] *interl. in ink over pencil*   116.18–19 **In this state ~ principle.**] *inserted in pencil*
116.19 **another**] *above del.* the   116.21–2 **have no more relation**] *in pencil repl. del. in pencil*
are not at all relating   116.22 **than**] *after del. in pencil* not more *and before del. in pencil* to
has.] has *inserted in pencil and full stop inserted in ink*   116.23 **Mails**] s *added*   116.24 **elsewhere. –**] *in pencil repl. del. in pencil* occasionally.   occasionally.] *altered from* occasion.
after del. on an other   116.25 **A system of Classification**] *after del. on fol. 16r–v*

The impressions[1] which are produced by forms and colours upon our minds are partly based
upon conventional or traditional signs or symbols, like[2] as[3] is the case in Musik and in
Speech; which[4] we are not free to neglect or to change, ¦ if we wish to be understood[5].
Art in its highest progress enriched by all the discoveries which science has made,[6] cannot
and indeed should not,[7] entirely free itself from this influence.
This is[8] one of the first rules of Style which we have to observe.

> 1 **The impressions ~ influence.**] *del. in pencil*   2 **like**] *after del.* like in Musik   3 **as**] *in
> pencil below interl. in ink and del. in pencil* it   4 **which**] *after del.* These are even the Types,
> (a type is a letter, a Character.)   5 **understood**] *before del. in pencil* and to act upon the
> minds   6 **made,**] *altered from* ~∧ *before del.* since   7 **cannot and indeed should not,**]
> *in ink repl. del. in ink* cannot and indeed should not   cannot and indeed should not] *in
> pencil above del. in pencil* can and must not (not *del. in ink*)   8 **This is ~ observe.**] *del. in
> ink*

116.25–6 **to indicate**] *before del.* as well as I was allowed to   116.26 **close**] *above del.* near
116.27 **Space;**] *repl. del.* room,   116.29 **Heroic age.**] *before del. on MS 122, fol. 16v, and undel. on MS 123[4], fol. 9r–v*

The[1] whole Province of practical art may be[2] brought according to such a system, into
4 General Classes, for their relations[3] to certain types, which they have in common.
The *first Class* comprehends all the things which have their types in the art or in the *industry
of* Coating.[4] *Weawing* forms.[5] one important branch of this very extensive and important
Class, but it includes a great number of other methods of[6] covering or protecting things
with thin[7] surfaces.
Second Class. Things which have their types[8] in the ceramic art;[9] ¦
Third Class. Manufactures, which have their types in Woodconstruction

On the Relations of the Different Branches of Industrial Art   419

Fourth Class Such as have their types in Stone Construction or maçonry[10].

Fifth Class. Monumental Art, the combining of the special branches of Art. – .

Many formations[11], are transitional, they may find their places between the classes of which they partake. For.. instance the Chinese Bamboo treillis, which is an important element for industrial art in China. It[12] is the transition from *weaving* toward[13] *wood construction*, and the type for some higher forms in Antik[14] and mediaeval Architecture.[15] |

A thorough illustration[16] of the system I have briefly sketched out, is too arduous a task for me. But I shall perhaps be able to offer some usefull contributions towards this object;[17] This then is the extent of my ambition; and with this view I purpose to give five lectures. as follows.

1°) on the Industry of Coating.

2°) On ceramic Art.

3°) on woodconstruction

4°) On Stone construction

5°) On monumental Art.

> 1 **The**] *altered from* the *after del.* It seems that   2 **may be**] *repl. del.* can be   3 **relations**] *after del.* common   4 **Coating.**] *above inserted in pencil and del. in ink* coating   coating] *repl. underl. in ink and del. in pencil* Coat-making.   5 **Weawing forms.**] *repl. del.* Weaving forms   Weaving] *altered in pencil from* Weavery (Weavery *above del.* The Art of Weaving)   6 **methods of**] *above del. in ink* methods of   methods of] *in pencil repl. del. in pencil* contrivances, which consist in   7 **thin**] *after del. in pencil* the aid of *and before del. in ink* and generally pliable   8 **types**] *after del.* fundamental   9 **art;**] *before del.* if we take this word in its more general sense, where it   10 **maçonry**] *merged from French 'maçonnerie' and English 'masonry'*   11 **Many formations**] *after three del. beginnings of variant:*
>
> There are many transitional formations, and others, which are composite,
> Many transitional formations,
> Many formations are transitional and stand at the boundary
>
> > There are ~ composite,] *accompanied in opposite column by del.* for instance the Chinese Bamboo treillis, which form an important motiv for housebuilding in Ch and others] *after del.* which may have theyr places
>
> 12 **It**] *after del.* It is the type for some higher forms in Antik and modern European Architecture. This treilllisworck is evidently a transition from the   It is] *after del.* It is a transition from Weaving to *and before del.* also   higher] *after del.* important   Antik] *'antique'*   13 **weaving toward**] *repl. del.* the art of weaving to   14 **Antik**] *'antique'*   15 **Architecture.**] *before del.* Others are composite, which then more or less   16 **A thorough illustration ~ monumental Art.**] *in right column after four del. beginnings of variant in left column:*
>
> A thorough illustration of the System, I have here briefly sketched out, is scarcely possible in the present state of artistic knowledge – it is too arduous a task for me to hope to grapple with on it entirely, but I flatter mysel
> A thorough illustration of the System I have here briefly sketched out, is too arduous a task for me
> A thorough illustration of the system I have here briefly sketched out is too arduou
> A thorough illustration of the System I have here briefly sketched out is scarcely possible in the present

too arduou] *after del.* is scarcely possible in [t]

17 **this object;**] *before del.* and   and] *after del.* and the artisti[c]

116.33 **First**] *altered from* first *after del.* The   **It**] *interl.*   116.35 **extensive**] *before del.* and important   116.36 **or**] *repl. del.* and   116.39 **Ceramic**] *before del.* or rather in the plastic plastic] *underl.*

117.1 **first**] *before del.* Class   **Pottery**] *before del.* for this class   117.2 **Ceramic**] *after del.* plastic   117.5 **in timberconstruction.**] *repl. del.* in Woodconstruction   117.6 **their origines**] *repl. del.* their types   117.11 **Many formations**] *after underl. and del.* Fifth Class. *after del.* Many formations   117.16 **as well**] *repl. del.* and   117.18 **Other**] *repl. del.* Many Many] *repl. del.* Other   117.19 **elements,**] *repl. del.* formes,   117.20 **which I mentionned above.**] *after del.* which I named before.   117.26 **as follows:**] *after del.* Each of the first four of them would treat of one of the four Classes o   of one] of *interl.*   117.27 **1°) Art**] *after del.* 1°) On the Industry of coating   117.36 **material.**] *altered from* ~∧ *before del.* on fol. *19r* for industrial art.   117.38–9 **Industrial art,**] *repl. del.* execution,

MANUSCRIPT VARIANTS
MS 123²

fol. 3r   This beautiful collection is the work of the celebrated inventor of the comparing system of Zoology, Mr Cuvier who showed, that all those antediluvian and postdiluvian creatures were and are but different developments of principles, which are common to all. Nature for its infinite richness is nevertheless very sparing and simple in its elementary ideas. For instance the Same scaffolding of the sceleton, goes threw the whole of that part of animal   5 creation which has bones but it is more and less developd and thousandfoldly modified according to the rangs and gradual progresses of the individuals and their conditions of existance. Some inferior animals have the elementary spina dorsalis without any extremities, others are nothing but head, like the fish, called Orthagoriscus Mola, other are nothing but tail, like the Myxine glutinosa. – The Kenguru has short forefeet but very long and well   10 developped hind feet, with the zeal it is the opposite case its hindfeet are nothing but indications of feet, they are the transitions to fins. With the birds we see the forefeets transformed into wings and some of them, have no wings at all, as for instance the Australian Ostrich. But even these beheld some slight indications of the non developped articulations,

fol. 3v   like symbols – They are all related together by one and the same fundamental ¦ principle. –   15 When I was observing this variety of nature in its oeconomy and simplicity I very often sayd to myself – The same as in nature There exist similar fundamental laws for the creations of my art, and a comparing method of contemplating them, analogous to that of Cuvier for natural history, will enable us to find out the elementary forms and the principles, of which all millions appearances in art are but as much different modifications. It may be of conse-   20 quence to search out these fundamental forms of architecture, and to follow them from the simplest to their highest expressions and even to their state of misformation Verkrüppelung – ¦

fol. 4r   By this way we will be able to get a wide survey over the history of art the knowledge of the principles of beauty, of style and construction, and far more, it will enable us, to make this   25 system the base of a science how to invent architectural compositions, which is more than it was allowed to the naturalist in his department. –

On the Relations of the Different Branches of Industrial Art   421

The man of Genius it is true knows no laws, he will half inconsciously succeed in its creations, he wants no instruction how to invent, no matter, it may always be a worthy proposition, to explore the dominion of the arts upon this way and to pursue thereby the porticular aim of fixing some chalons and starting points for invention for his own use and for other.
5 He will meet with the greatest difficulties and in the best case obtain a Result full of errors and voids, but by this endeavour being obliged to

> 420.1 **This**] *after del.* All those   420.5 **sceleton,**] *before del.* more or less developd and modified   **threw**] *'through'*   420.6 **thousandfoldly**] *above del.* differently   420.7 **rangs**] *derived from German 'Rang': 'ranks'*   **and gradual progresses**] *inserted*   **individuals**] *before del.* which they occupy in the   420.9 **Orthagoriscus Mola**] *scientific name for 'sunfish'*   420.10 **Myxine glutinosa**] *scientific name for 'hagfish'*   **Kenguru**] *derived from German 'Känguru': 'kangaroo'*   420.11 **zeal**] *'seal'*   420.11–12 **indications**] *before del.* and Symbols   420.13 **some of them**] *before del.* behelt only some short indications of wings, like useless symbols as for instance the Australian Ostrich.   420.14 **beheld**] *derived from German 'behalten': 'retained'*   420.15 **related**] *above del.* bound   420.16 **When**] *after four del. beginnings of variant:*

When I observed this
By observing[1] all these different variations of th
By making such comparisons I told to myself that
When I observed[2] this variety of Nature in its simplicity I very often thought by muself[3], that it may be possible to reduce the creations of man, and especially the works of architecture to certain normal and elementary forms, which, may[4]

> 1 **observing**] *after del.* following   2 **When I observed ~ forms, which, may**] *undel. in opposite column*   3 **muself**] *'myself'*   4 **may**] *inserted before del.* although the same by their general ideas, may permit an infinite variety of apparitions

> 420.16 **variety**] *after del.* beautiful   420.17 **The same as in nature**] *interl.*   **exist**] *above del.* must be   420.18 **method of contemplating them**] *above del.* system   420.20 **all millions**] *above del.* every   **appearances**] es *over* e   **are**] *over* is   420.21 **follow**] *above del.* pursue   420.21–3 **them ~ Verkrüppelung –**] *repl. del.* their gradual developments and embranchements from the Origins to their accomplishments and   accomplishments] *after del.* highest   420.22 **state**] *after del.* starved and *after del.* miscreat 420.24 **By**] *after del. on fol. 3v* It may be possible by this way, not only to find a good base for   **wide**] *interl.*   **survey**] *after del.* good base for   good] *above del.* real   420.24–5 **the principles of beauty**] *after del.* styles   420.25 **far**] *above del.* what is   **enable us**] *above del.* be possible   **to make**] *after del.* to base upon this system an architectural Topic or art to invent   **this**] *above del.* such a   420.27 **the naturalist**] *after del.* Cuvier **department. –**] *before del.*

I tried to give consequence to these speculations, in gradually working out a system which[1] I explained in my lectures which I helt annually as Professor of architecture at the academey of fine arts at Dresden. Some essays on architecture, which I have published in Germany were.

> 1 **system which**] *before del.* formed afterwards the base of

422   Lectures

421.1 **The**] *after del.* The Genius will succeed in his creations without the knowledge of rul[e] succeed] *after del.* not want **man of**] *interl.* **it is true**] *interl.* **its**] *'his'* 421.2 **may**] *above del.* will 421.3 **dominion**] *above del.* territory 421.4 **chalons**] *derived from French 'jalons': 'range poles' probably in the sense of 'reference points'* 421.5 **and**] *after del.* and in the best case he will in this aim

MS 123[3]

fol. 6r not only that, – it may be the base of a sort of topic or science of invention, which may enable us to find the natural way of composition and may hold equally distant from Schematism without individuality and from arbitrariness without thoughts. And This will be more than what was possible for the great Naturalist to do upon his field. ¦

fol. 6v These reflections I made at. an early period of my life, and since that time I was investigating 5 in the works on art and esspecially on architecture in search of a guide for artists analogous

fol. 5r to the book on the animal world of Cuvier or the Cosmus of Humboldt | which are guides for naturalists and will be more effectif for the progress of that science than are all the Volumns which were written before them on the same matter.

Very few among the great number of writers on art have made attempts of the kind I allude 10 to, and these few followed the track of some special preference they felt for one or the other branch of art or style of art, by which they were unconsciously distracted far from the aim which they had perhaps before their mind. The Frenchman Durand in his works on architecture has perhaps comen the nearest to that aim, but he looses his way under the influence of the proposition which was maid to him, namely to set up a sort of compendium of art for 15 the pupils of the ecole polytechnique, which were by no means artists, as well as under the influence of the general tendency of the time of Napoleon; He looses himself into the domain of schematism, he puts the things into rows and brings about a sort of alliance between them by the mechanical way instead of showing the organic laws by which they are connected together. Nevertheless, and in spite of these defects, his books, and namely his 20 paralels, are remarcable and important for the comparing principle which they contain. ¦

fol. 5v Some new attempts have been made upon the same principle but with less fortune. On the other hand we are so much richer in specialities and the mass of materials which increases every day, is allmost overpowering. while these publications of matters of fact and of representations of real objects of art of all periods were multiplying in France and England, the speculative Germen on the other side were the inventors of that abstract science of 25 taste, which they call Aesthetic, and the history of Art was the first treatened by them on a more critical system. But all these publications are nothing but evidences of what I mentionned before, that we have not yet arrived to that point where knowledge will increase the power of artistical invention in art instead of paralizing it as it now does. – . Since the time that the reader first felt this want, he had the opportunity of giving frequent 30 lectures on architecture at one of the first schools for Architects in Germany, and it needs not to be added, that these lectures were more or less influenced by the same impressions. But since then his position has altered, and the point of view, out of which he now considers the same question | 35

fol. 8r Let us compare for instance those two forms of ancient vases. The first is the holy Nile pail or Situlus of the ancient Egyptians, the other is that beautiful Greec Vase which is kalld the hydria.

On the Relations of the Different Branches of Industrial Art   423

Both forms relate to the same use, that of intercepting water. But the first is a drawing vessel, for intercepting water out of a river, and therefore caracteristic for Egypt; – Two of these Vessels were carried and ballanced on bars or Jokes so that one hung before and the other behind. The haviest part is very properly the bottom, as a precaution to prevent spilling. this form which is prescribed by use and fittness, is calld the canopic form. It forms a very significant contrast to the Greec Hydria, which was a *well-Vessel.*, for intercepting water which runs from fountains. Hence the funnel chaped feature of the neck and mouth which was rigourously described by the object in view, and the mode in carriing them naturally led to the Idea of removing the heavy part of the vessel towards the summit. For they were carried on the heads, upright when full, and lenghtways, when empty. (as is to be seen on a pictore at one hydria of the Brittish Museum.) ¦

Any one attempting to balance a stick on his finger will find the feat much easier if the heaviest end is uppermost.

This explains the form of the Greec Hydria, which by the Addition of two horizontal Handles placed in the high of the point of Gravity was completed, tho' a third vertical handle was often added, not only for the sake of variety, and as a mark of distinction between the front and back of the Vessel but also with respect to its utility.

How striking symbolical appears the light spiritual and lucid Sense of the Greecs in this structure, opposed to the Sytulus of the Egyptian, in whose Genius the physical Laws of Gravity found a corresponding expression. And the two nations were well conscious of the significance of these forms, – in making them to national and religious emblems. The Nilepail was the holy vessel of the Egyptians, and in like manner the hydria of the Greecs was the sacred Vessel carried by Virgins in religious processions.

It may be added, that the fundamental features of Egyptian architecture seem to be contained in Embryo in the Construction of the Nile-pail ¦

And in the same manner we are allowed to recognise in the Hydria of the Greecs the Key to the Doric order of Hellenic Architecture.

———————

No doubt, The history of architecture and of art in general is based upon that of practical art; The laws of beauty and style in architecture have their Analogs and parallels, and it may be added their origines and keys in the principles of Style in practical art. The separation which now exists between both of them, has shown itself as one of the principal reasons of their decay.

But it may be asked here, which are those principles of beauty and what is style?

This question leads us to a very dangerous matter, which has been treatened by philosophers and artists of all ages; Many books in folio and in 8° have been written about it. the result of which for practice was not very great.

I shall not enter into an examination of the different definitions which have been made of such notions, as Beauty and beautiful ¦ It luckily happens, that all the notions which constitute the aesthical science, are such, that you be allowed to attack the matter where You like one of these notions if well defined and pursued in its consequences leading to the understanding of the others.

I shall therefore restrict myself in explaining how I wish to be understood in using here in this paper the word style. in this paper I say, for I have not the pretention of giving a definition of general application and valeur.

By the term style I mean those achievements in works of art, arising
1° from using artistically the means and

fol. 8v

fol. 7r

fol. 7v

2° from observing the limits which are contained in and defined by the task and problem in question, as well as by the accessories which modify the solution of it in every case.

Every work of art is a result or for using a Mathematical term, it is a function of a indefined number of quantities or powers,

4

> 422.1 **it may be**] *repl. del.* we may be able to make it   be able] *after del.* by this way   to] *undel.*   **topic**] *'topics' (see 411–12, Explanatory Notes 105.29)*   422.3 **individuality**] *above del.* Character   **And**] *inserted*   422.4 **possible**] *after del.* was allowed to   422.5 **These**] *after del. on fol. 6r–v*

A fundamental form, the simple expression of an Idea, will, in its application undergo a great variety of modifications Now one of the greatest secrets[1] of art will consist first in making prevail and showing the fundamental forms and Idea through these modifications, secondly in making evident the reasons and what we kall the motifs of the variations of the fundamental forms which we altered. So we will have a work which will be consistent with itself and with ¦ what it is surrounded.

The Genius[2] may and will find the true way[3] by itself and half inconsciously but it may allways be a worthy proposition for an architect, to investigate on the field of his art after those simple relations which I alluded to before. This I thought[4] then w

---

> 1 **secrets**] *after del.* mysteries   2 **Genius**] *after del.* force of   3 **the true way**] *above del.* this natural way of inventi   4 **This I thought**] *after del.* He will encounter in this way the greatest difficulties and in the best case have a result full of errors and deficiencies, but he will at least fixe although it may be to great a proposition for one man   fixe] *before del.* some of the most conspicoous   to] *'too'*

> 422.5 **investigating**] *before del.* in vain after a guiding   422.8 **progress**] *repl. del.* development   422.11 **special**] *before del.* direction,   422.11–12 **preference ~ art,**] *inserted*   422.12 **branch**] *after del.* special   far] *after inserted and del.* very   422.13 **mind.**] *altered from ~, before del.* but we are rich in materials collected and even   **The**] *after del.* One remarcable work has been   422.14 **looses**] *'loses' (see also 422.17)*   422.15 **maid**] *'made'*   422.17 **Napoleon**] *after del.* the great *after del.* the Frensh Empire   422.18 **alliance**] *after del.* unity by the mechanical way,   422.21 **principle**] *after del.* Idea which   422.23 **materials**] *before del.* collected in beautifull editions   **which**] *after del.* increases every day and is allmost impossible to be overlooked   422.25 **real objects**] *repl. del.* objects   422.26 **Germen**] *'Germans'*   **were**] *after del.* gave their contributions on their way   422.26–7 **science of taste**] *after del.* art   422.27 **treatened**] *'treated' (see also 423.35)*   422.28 **But**] *after del.* But all these publications belong to that critical period of the sciences, what I mentionned before. –   critical period] *after del.* second period of   I] *repl. del.* we have   422.30 **artistical**] *interl. before interl. and del.* skill   422.31 **the reader**] *above del.* I   **felt this want**] *repl. del.* felt the want for instruction   he] *above del.* I   **frequent**] *interl.*   422.32 **first**] *above del.* largest   422.33 **the**] *after del.* ideas similar to the impressions of my *after del.* the same idea which I laid before You   422.34 **his**] *above del.* my   **the point of view**] *after del.* my ideas on art, which then were   he] *above del.* I   **considers**] *final* s *added*   422.35 **question**] *before del.* has in the same time undergone   422.36 **Let**] *after del.* If we take for instance a parallel between two very expressif forms of ancient vases, between the Egyptian Situlus or Nile Bucket and the beautiful Hydria of the Greecs, that *after del.* It may be allowed to illustrate this by an example.   422.37 **holy**] *interl.*   **pail**] *above del.* bucket   423.1 **Both**] *after del.*

On the Relations of the Different Branches of Industrial Art   425

Both forms relate to[1] the same use, that of intercepting[2] water. Both are in the same time symbolical and National emblems, they had a religious and mystical signification.
the first[3] of these formes contains the fundamental features of Egyptian Archtecture[4], in Embryo.[5] The second is the key to the Doric Order of Hellenic Architecture.

> 1 **relate to**] *repl. del.* are founded upon   2 **intercepting**] *repl. del.* collecting
> 3 **the first**] *after del.* In *after del.* The first form gives us evidently the fundamental
> features *after del.* And in the same time   4 **Archtecture**] Arch- | tecture   5 **in**
> **Embryo.**] *repl. del.* it seems to be the Embryo of Egyptian Archi   Archi] *undel.*

423.3 **Jokes**] 'yokes'   423.4 **part**] *before del.* of these vessels   423.6 **which**] *after del.* which was used for intercepting water from springs,   **well-Vessel**] 'spring water vessel'   423.7 **chaped**] 'shaped'   423.8 **bescribed**] 'prescribed'   423.9 **part**] *above del.* point   423.10 **pictore**] *after del.* representation   423.15 **high**] 'height'   423.19 **Egyptian**] *altered from* Egyptians   423.20 **And the two nations**] *after del.* How *after del.* How caracteristic are the[ ]   caracteristic] *after del.* speaking   423.21 **in making**] *after del.* for they made them to their national and religious Emblems.   423.29 **No doubt,**] *inserted*   **The**] *altered from* the *after del.* This is only one instance out of many others, which show the assertion, that   423.30 **art;**] *altered from* ~∧ *before del.* and that   **The**] T *over* t   423.34 **But**] *after del.*

But what are these laws of beauty[1] and what is style?
This question[2] may be

> 1 **beauty**] *before del.* which I alluded to at several times   2 **This question**] *after del.*
> Here it would seem

423.35 **This question**] *after del.*

This question leads us to a dangerous matter[1], which has already filld up many books in folio, and[2] octavo, without bringing[3] any great practical.

> 1 **matter**] *above del.* chapter   2 **folio, and**] *before undel.* and   3 **without bringing**]
> *after del.* without being carried to any

423.35 **has been treatened**] *after del.* has occupied many *and before del.* so often since the **philosophers**] *after del.* many   423.36 **ages;**] *altered from* ~, *before del.* and filld up 423.37 **great.**] *repl. del.* large.   423.38 **enter**] *before del.* here   423.39 **such**] *above del.* these   **as Beauty and beautiful**] *inserted before del.* and   **It**] *after del.* in restricting myself only in the explanation of what I understand under the word style.   in restricting] *after del.* in confining *after del.* confine   explanation] *after del.* question   style] *underl.* 423.40 **aesthical**] 'aesthetical'   423.40–2 **are such ~ others.**] *repl. del.* are such, that one of them includes all the other; you be allowed to attack the matter where You like.   in- cludes] *above del.* contains   423.41 **one of these notions**] *after del.* one of them, if pur- sued consistently leading   consistely] 'consistently'   423.44 **in this paper**] *after del.* This definition has no way the pretention of general application and I say here   **I say**] *interl.* **I have**] *after del.* it has not the pretention of a *after del.* I give it not   423.45 **valeur**] *French for 'value', here misused for 'validity'   423.46 **mean**] *repl. underl. and del.* understand **arising**] *before del.* from using the means artistically and 424.2 **case.**] *before del.* Style is the artistical treatement of some fundamental Idea in a work of our hands, –   424.3 **Every**] *repl. del.* A   A] *over a after del.* We may consider **is**] *above del.* as   **for**] *after del.* as a function (if it is allowed to   424.4 **number**] *after del.* quantity of   **quantities**] *after del.* variable

General Remarks on the Different Styles in Art

TEXTUAL RECORD

MS 124	gta, 20-Ms-124, fols. 1r–21v (1v, 2v, 3v, 4v, 5v, 6v, 7v, 8v, 9v, 10v, 11v, 21r blank; 21v notes and sketch), in Semper's hand, *copy-text*
MS 126	gta, 20-Ms-126, fols. 1r–14v (14r–v blank), in J. Ruston Palen's hand (emendations in Manfred Semper's hand), 1880, copy of MS 124
MS 128	gta, 20-Ms-128, fols. 1r–7v, 'Vergleichende Technologie', in Hans Semper's hand (five emendations in Manfred Semper's hand), early 1880s, Hans Semper's German trans. of MS 124, fols. 1r–14v; see Herrmann 1981, 111
MS 127	gta, 20-Ms-127, fols. 1r–39v (2v, 3v, 4v, 5v, 6v, 7v, 8v, 9v, 10v, 11v, 12v, 13v, 20v, 21v, 24v and all following versos blank; 14v, 15v, 16v, 19v, 22v, 23v notes relating to Semper's new Dresden Court Theatre; 17v three del. words), 'Entwurf eines Systemes der vergleichenden Stillehre', partly in unknown hand (1r–13r, 17r, 18r–v, 20r–22r, 23v–38r; emendations in Hans and Manfred Semper's hands), partly in Manfred Semper's hand (1r, 8r, 11r, 13r–14r, 15r, 16r, 18r, 19r, 22r, 23r, 37r–39r; one emendation in Hans Semper's hand), early 1880s, Manfred Semper's German trans. of MS 124, fols. 3r–7r, 9r–14v (additional sections: German trans. of MS 122; see 409), published in Semper 1884; see Herrmann 1981, 110
Semper 1884	'Entwurf eines Systemes der vergleichenden Stillehre', 259–91, German trans. of MS 124, fols. 3r–7r, 9r–20v (additional sections: German trans. of MS 122; see 409); for details of this composite translation, see Herrmann 1981, 159–66
Semper 1983	'London Lecture of November 11, 1853', 5–22, here 18–22, Mallgrave's ed. of MS 124, fols. 5r–11r, 13v, 14v–20v (119.21–120.23, 120.37–121.26, 122.34–126.38)

BIBLIOGRAPHY Vogt 1976, 191, 193–4; Herrmann 1981, 109–11, 159–66; Mallgrave 1983b; Herrmann 1990, 80; Mallgrave 1996, 217–18; Gnehm 2004, 45–6; Poerschke 2012; Poerschke 2016, 79–82; Hildebrand 2020b, 67, 69–70; Hildebrand 2021, 114, 118 fig. 10

EXPLANATORY NOTES

Wolfgang Herrmann and Harry Francis Mallgrave assumed that manuscripts MS 122 and MS 124 relate to one and the same lecture – the first lecture in the 1853 autumn series, held on 11 November – and that MS 124 was written before MS 122 (Herrmann 1981, 109–10; Mallgrave 1983b, 23). Both of these assumptions are incorrect, since MS 122 is obviously the manuscript of the inaugural lecture given on 20 May 1853 (see 410). The fact that MS 124 actually relates to the lecture of 11 November 1853 is evident from the first paragraph (118.1–6), which refers to MS 122.

The first assumption by Herrmann and Mallgrave is understandable to the extent that, in the first half of the lecture of 11 November 1853, Semper discusses topics that he had already dealt with in the inaugural lecture: the lack of comparative books on architectural history,

General Remarks on the Different Styles in Art 427

his own view of the relationship between architecture and the industrial arts, and the representation of a work of art as a mathematical function with variable coefficients, which is used to explain his concept of style. In the inaugural lecture, Semper implicitly assigned the requirements of use to the coefficients of this function (109.1–13). Now he explicitly assigns them to the function sign Φ (120.4–6). This assignment means that he is making a fundamental distinction between the motif and type of the work of art and its material, ethnological and personal stylistic influences (cf. Mallgrave 1983b, 28).

In the second half of the lecture, Semper discusses part of the topic announced in the 'Prospectuses of the Lectures on Art' under number 1, 'The ancient practice of wall coating, and its significance in history of architecture and art in general' (96.14–15). He regards the use of hedges, fences, skins and mats for spatial separation as being the origin of this practice. Quite briefly, he explains the way in which these methods were replaced due to secondary needs by solid walls, the coverings of which – regardless of their material quality – reveal their descent from meshes and textiles, 'the true representants of the idea of *Space-separation*' (124.34). Semper discusses only one example in greater detail, that of glazed brick walls (125.27–126.14). Finally, he concludes that 'the principle of *Coating*' dominated ornamental art and architecture throughout the whole of antiquity (126.33–4). This is the first time that he mentions this principle, for which he provides detailed evidence in the first volume of *Style in the Technical and Tectonic Arts* in 1860 (Semper 1860/63, 1:217–513).

Semper based his explanations of wall covering closely on *The Four Elements of Architecture* (Semper 1851b, 54–9, 61–2) – in accordance with his remark that 'the principal material to the present and to the following lectures' was based on his 'pamphlets' that had been published in Germany (118.37–8). However, his claim that he had already had 'different pamphlets' published 'under the title of Contributions to a comparing science of architecture' (118.34–6) is overstated: only one of his books, *The Four Elements of Architecture*, had been published with a similar subtitle.

118.1 **For some months**] *Some months ago*   118.6 **our naturalists**] This non-specific wording has been changed from 'our great naturalist' (see 429, Alterations in the Manuscript 118.6), a phrase that repeats 'the great Naturalist' from the inaugural lecture (105.31) almost verbatim. A fragmentary manuscript of the inaugural lecture (MS 123²) shows that the great naturalist being referred to is Georges Cuvier: it includes the words 'the naturalist' following the deleted name 'Cuvier' (420.27; 421, note 420.27).   118.21 **a Sort of Method how to invent**] see 411–12, Explanatory Notes 105.29   118.34–6 **different pamphlets ~ published in Germany under the title of Contributions to a comparing science of architecture**] These 'pamphlets' can only be *Preliminary Observations on Painted Architecture and Sculpture of the Ancients* (1834), which does not have a subtitle, and *The Four Elements of Architecture* (1851), which has the subtitle *Ein Beitrag zur vergleichenden Baukunde* (A Contribution to Comparative Architecture). Semper's other books – *Ueber den Bau evangelischer Kirchen* (On Protestant Church Building, 1845), *Das königliche Hoftheater zu Dresden* (The Royal Court Theatre in Dresden, 1849) and *Science, Industry, and Art* (1852) – can scarcely be regarded as 'Contributions to a comparing science of architecture'.

119.15–16 **The laws and principles ~ fixd by Architects.**] cf. the similar passage in the definitive version of the inaugural lecture (108.4–6)   119.18–19 **considering ~ art and Industry ~ as attendant upon Architecture**] an echo of Owen Jones's principle that 'The Decorative Arts arise from, and should properly be attendant upon, Architecture' (see 398, Explanatory Notes 97.11–12)   119.24 **Y = Φ (x, z, t, v, w, .).**] Mallgrave has 'Y = C (x, y, z, t, v, w, …)' (Semper 1983, 18); he has 'C' wherever 'Φ' stands in the following text. For the reading of 'Φ', see 119.27: 'the Greec letter Φ or Function'. Accordingly, Manfred Semper noted on fol. 3r of MS 128, Hans Semper's partial German translation of MS 124, where 'ε' stands instead of 'Φ': 'In mathematics, φ (phi) is used as an indication of the expression "function". Therefore, I have corrected all ε by replacing them with φ.' Gottfried Semper did in fact write the capital letter phi (Φ) like an oversized small phi (φ). In *Kleine Schriften*, however, the Greek letter φ is replaced by the Latin letter F (Semper 1884, 267–9).   119.26 **to gether**] *together*   119.32 **cet**] *etc.* (see also 119.36)   119.33 **before**ʌ] ~,

120.1 **shedula**] *schedule*, here misused for *formula*; see 119.25, 120.38; cf. 430, Alterations in the Manuscript 120.1–2¹, 120.2–3²   120.6 **cub**] *cup*   120.38 **formule**] French for *formula* 121.9 **Clime**] *climate*   121.14 **commenders**] *commanders*, here misused for *establishers* or *purchasers*   121.30 **vues**] French for *views*

122.27 **Antik**] *antique* (see also 125.24)   122.37 **maid**] *made*

123.7–13 **constituent parts ~ fireplace ~ Roof ~ Enclosure ~ Substruction**] These parts correspond to the architectural elements distinguished in *The Four Elements of Architecture*: 'Feuerstätte' or 'Herd', 'Dach', 'Umfriedigung' and 'Erdaufwurf' or 'Terrasse' (Semper 1851b, 54–5, 55 n. *). However, the word 'Substruction' translates neither 'Erdaufwurf' nor 'Terrasse'. It refers to a substructure consisting of solid material, which – in contrast to 'Erdaufwurf' or 'Terrasse' – is a part of the building rather than of the terrain.

124.3 **maçonry**] merged from French *maçonnerie* and English *masonry*   **substruction**] *substruction*   124.4 **Appartenences**] *appurtenances*   124.11 **tresses**] French for *plaits*. Mallgrave has 'dresses' (Semper 1983, 21).   124.14 **propriety**] *property*   124.21 **New Seelanders**] merged from German *Neuseeländer* and English *New Zealanders*   124.24 **barches of trees**] *barks ~ ~*, here *inner barks*; cf. Semper 1884, 287: 'Baumbast'. Mallgrave has 'branches of trees' (Semper 1983, 21).   124.27 **barches of trees**] *barks ~ ~*, here *outer barks*; cf. Semper 1884, 287: 'Baumrinde'. Mallgrave has 'branches of trees' (Semper 1983, 21).   124.28 **preceeded**] *preceded*   124.30 **interlaces**] *wattles*   124.31 **beheld**] derived from German *behalten*: *retained*

125.6 **enterlacs and tress works**] 'enterlacs' derived from French *entrelacs*: *wattlework*; 'tress works': *plaitwork* (see note 124.11). Mallgrave has 'interlaced and trellis works' (Semper 1983, 21).   125.15 **reimplaced**] *replaced*   125.22 **maçons**] French for *masons*   125.27 **reimplacement**] *replacement*   125.30 **unbournd**] *unburned*, here misused for *unbaked* 125.31 **burning**] *baking* (see also 125.35, 126.10, 126.13)   125.35 **unburnt**] *unbaked* (see also 126.12)   125.36 **whith**] *which*

126.1 **fourdly**] *fourthly*   126.7 **last**] *latter*   126.12 **than**] *then*   126.34 **Romains**] French for *Romans*   126.35 **lais**] *lies*   126.36 **jet**] *yet*   126.38 **depassing**] derived from French *dépasser*: *exceeding* (cf. 435, Alterations in the Manuscript 126.38). Mallgrave has 'surpassing' (Semper 1983, 22).   **permit it. –**] This is followed by a deleted passage first stating that the Assyrians were 'the most faithful adhearants of the principle in question' – i.e. of the principle of wall covering – and then discussing 'Assyrian tapestries' (435–6, Alterations in the Manuscript 126.38). Semper takes the content of this passage, which is borrowed from *The Four Elements of Architecture* (Semper 1851b, 59–60), over into manuscripts MS 129 and MS 131 for the lecture 'The Ancient Practice of Wall Coating and Tubular Construction' (see 128.26, 129.2–4, 129.9–11, 448.26, 448.28–32).

General Remarks on the Different Styles in Art

429

EDITORIAL EMENDATIONS

122.16 **timber-construction**] timber- | construction   122.26 **timber-construction**] timber- | construction   124.37 **stone-walls**] stone- | walls

ALTERATIONS IN THE MANUSCRIPT

118.2 **series of**] *after del.* suite of   **for which**] *before inserted and del.* since long   118.2–3 **prepared the materials**] *after del.* collected and   collected] *before del.* the materials and 118.3 **outlines**] *repl. del.* plan   plan] *after del.* outlines   **At that time**] *after del.* In *after del.* I then *after del.* I endeavoured to prove in the paper I allude to, *after del.* In *after del.* It was to   118.4 **want of a**] *after del.* utility of a *after del.* necessity of t   **Technology**] *after del.* art   118.5–6 **so very successfully**] *above del.* since   since] *after del.* since by our   118.6 **naturalists**] *altered from* naturalist *after del.* great   118.8 **we**] *interl. in black ink*   **may**] *before del. in black ink* we not   **will**] *above del.* may   118.9 **art.**] *altered from* ~?   118.22 **composition.**] *in black ink below del. in black ink* invention   invention] *before del.* which would be more   118.24 **a guide**] *after del. in red ink* such   118.26 **Cosmos**] *second* o *over* u 118.29 **I always painfully felt this want**] *repl. del.* I felt this want at an early time of my I felt ~ my] *repl. del.* Since the time that I first felt this want, *(*Since *after del.* I do not entertain the pretention to *after del.* I felt this want at an early*)*   **allways**] *in pencil below del. in red ink* very often   118.29–30 **at my lectures ~ opportunity of giving at**] *in red ink repl. del. in red ink* and having had the opportunity of giving lectures on Architecture at one of lectures on Architecture at one] *undel.*   118.30 **Academie**] *altered in red ink from* Academies   **at Dresden;**] *in red ink above del. in red ink* in Germany.   **and**] *interl. in red ink* it was] *after del.* As   118.31 **that**] *interl.*   **by this feeling.**] *above del.* by similar reflections; *and accompanied in opposite column by del.* by the desire of parallelising the   by the desire of parallelising the] *above del.* by the desire of parallelising between *(*by *undel.)* 118.31–2 **Although**] *repl. del.* but   118.32 **pretention**] *before del.* of giving a   **filling up**] *after del.* succeeding in givi   **want;**] *altered from* ~∧ *before del.* by   118.33 **it was then**] *inserted in red ink*   **my**] *in red ink above del. in red ink* My   My] *after del.* I only was endeavouring of prepar   **to contribute**] *after del. in red ink* was then only   118.34 **have**] *inserted*   **laid down**] *after del.* collected and published in severa   118.35 **were published**] *repl. del.* I wrote on the subject   **in Germany**] *interl.*   118.37–8 **The contents ~ lectures.**] *in red ink repl. inserted and del. in red ink* These publications will form the frames to this and to my following lectures.   These publications] *repl. del.* They *(*They *after del.* The contents of these essays form the esse *after del.* The content of my*)*   118.37 **have**] *in pencil above del. in pencil* will   **suggested**] ed *added in pencil* 119.1 **But**] *inserted before del.* at that time   at] a *over* A   **when I wrote them**] *interl.* **existing**] *interl. in pencil*   119.12 **This will be shown ~ instances.**] *repl. del.* Instances of this will be given in the course of these lectures   119.13–16 **So architecture ~ Architects.**] *in pencil repl. del. in pencil*

So[1] Architecture is certainly[2] the last born[3] of the[4] arts, but it is the combining to gether[5] of all the branches of industrial art and of art in general in one great general[6] effect and after one directing Idea; The laws and principles of Style and beauty which we aknowledge in art have probably been the first systematically fixd by Architects

1 **So**] *inserted after del.* But in the same time it can not be denied that architecture is the com   But ~ com] *after del.* But in the same time Practical art had reached to a high degree of development long before   2 **certainly**] *interl.*   3 **last born**] *above del.* joungest joungest] *'youngest'*   4 **the**] *above del.* her sister-   5 **to gether**] *'together'*   6 **general**] *after del.* com[ ]

119.17 **apologizing**] *after del.* just *after del.* explaining or of   119.18–19 **by considering ~ art and Industry,**] *repl. del.* in materials by considering them mai[n]   in] *undel. before del.* producing the   119.21 **a result**] *after del.* the   119.24 **x,**] *before del. in red ink* y,   119.25 **formula,**] *before del.* where   and] *inserted*   119.26 **which way**] *repl. del.* which   119.27 **here**] *interl. in pencil*   119.29 **(x + a)**] *before del.* or z   **U,**] *interl.*   119.30 **in the principle**] *repl. del.* in the same time   in the same time] *after interl. and del.* remain   **principle**] *altered in pencil from* principles   119.30–1 **remain identical to the last, being**] *inserted* 119.30 **identical**] *after del.* principally   119.33 **change ~ fundamentally**] *repl. del.* change again and will be principally   principally] *underl.*   **than before**] *in red ink repl. del. in red ink* than   than] *'then'*   119.34 **the Change took place**] *interl. in red ink*   119.35 **have**] *after del.* remain   **The**] *altered in pencil from* This   119.37–40 **It will be said ~ taste.**] *repl. del.*

I know what objection will[1] be made[2] against this, it will be said[3] that an artistical Problem is not a mathematical one and that artistical results are hardly obtainable[4] by calculation This is very true and I certainly am the last to[5] believe,[6] that the creating force[7] of artistical genius[8] may[9] be obtainable by the way of mere reflexion and knowledge.

1 **objection will**] *above del.* You may object   2 **be made**] *inserted and del. in pencil*   3 **it will be said**] *above del.* You will say   4 **are hardly obtainable**] *del. in pencil but repl. del.* can not be obtained   5 **to**] *interl.*   6 **believe,**] *after del.* of those who may pretend this. 7 **the creating force**] *del. in pencil but repl. del.* creations   creations] *above del.* works 8 **genius**] *after del.* skill and   9 **may**] *above del.* could

119.37 **It**] *altered in red ink from* it *after del. in red ink* I know what objection will be made against this argumentation;   119.38 **results**] *after del.* the   119.39 **mere reflexion**] *after del.* genius   119.40 **talent**] *after del.* genius   and] *interl. in pencil*   taste] *before del. in pencil* and genius 120.1–2 **Also I only wanted ~ subject**] *repl. del. in pencil*

I only wanted this general shedula[1] as[2] a crutch[3] for leaning on it in explaning[4] a subject which otherwise it would be difficult[5] for me to explain as shortly and clearly in a language which I know but little.

1 **shedula**] *repl. del.* formula   2 **as**] *after del.* for facilitating   3 **crutch**] *before del.* for the explanation   4 **explaning**] *interl.*   5 **difficult**] *after del.* more

120.1–2 **this shedula ~ subject**] *inserted in pencil*   120.2–3 **I therefore ~ letters.**] *repl. del. in pencil*

Let us therefore[1] give some attributions and values to those letters.[2]

1 **Let us therefore**] *del. in ink after del. in ink* Besides there will be   2 **letters.**] *altered from* ~∧ *before del.* which constitute the sheme which I layd before You.   sheme] *'scheme'*

120.2 **I**] *in pencil above del. in pencil* You   **be**] *inserted in pencil*   **allowed**] *altered in pencil from* allow me   **my proposition**] *after del.* the theme which I   120.3 **real attributions and values to those letters.**] *inserted in pencil*   120.5 **in**] *interl.*   **which are**] *after del.* the use and destination   120.7 **for all nations**] *after del.* every where and at every times, when   120.8 **in principle**] *above del.* principally   120.9 **no matter.**] *interl.*   120.10 **The elementary Idea**] *after del.* The fun *(for 'function') after del.* The elementary idea, prescribed by the use of a thing, may this use be materially or symbolically understood, no matter,   a thing] *after del.* the symbolical   no matter] *after del.* nor   120.10–11 **destination;**] *altered from* ~, *before del.* (may the last be materially or symbolically understood, no matter,)   120.11 **upon material and upon**] *interl.*   120.12 **conditions.**] *accompanied in opposite column by del.* And this is the case,   **this**] *altered in pencil over red ink from* these *before del. in pencil* elementary idea   idea] *altered in pencil over red ink from* ideas   **motiv**] *altered in pencil from* motives   120.19 **Motive**] *after del.* fundamental   120.20 **observed∧**] *altered from* ~.   120.20–1 **in composition.**] *inserted in red ink*   120.23 **fashion.**] *before del.* Consistency and clearness in expressing the elementary idea in a work of art is the first and most important qualification of an artist, which he may acquire only by incessant study of nature and of the works of early art.   120.30 **works**] s *added in pencil*   120.33 **consider**] *after del.* should **Direct**] *interl.*   120.34 **art**] *inserted in red ink*   **leading**] *repl. del.* leads   120.37 **those coefficients**] *after del.* the qualification of   120.38 **x,**] *before del.* y   120.39 **Those**] o *over* e   121.1 **I must specify them here forthwith**] *repl. del.* They must be specified here   **undefined,**] *before del. in red ink*

and I[1] shall only point out some of the most important which will lead to the explanation of my plan[2]

> 1 **I**] *interl. and undel.*   2 **plan**] *before del. in black ink* for this course of lectures.   lectures.] *altered from* ~∧ *before del.* on the different branches of industrial art.

121.2 **but**] *inserted in red ink*   **they**] t *in red ink over* T   121.3 **1°) Materials and processes.**] *inserted*   121.7 **2°) Ethnological influences,**] *inserted*   121.8 **comprises**] *altered from* comprehends   121.10 **conditions.**] *altered from* ~∧ *before del.* which have influenced and will allways influence the productions of human skill; the history   121.11 **includes**] *after del.* comprehends *and both above del.* comprises   **personal**] *before del.* and individual   121.13 **arise**] *repl. del.* come   121.14–15 **and the practical performers**] *after del.* and manufa   121.16 **different**] *above del.* groups   121.17 **significations**] *after del.* notions of that   **important artistical**] *inserted after del.* general   121.18 **of**] *above del.* which we call   121.19 **Thus we say**] *after del.* The first signification is   first] *before del.* and most   **when**] *above del.* if   **treated**] *before interl. in ink and del. in pencil* by the maker   121.25 **of Style**] *inserted in red ink*   **can**] *in pencil repl. del. in pencil* could   could] *after del.* may be   121.27 **The first two**] *after del.*

The[1] first two[2] of these three significations of style[3] will be taken up as the general proposition of the following:
First[4] The[5] treatement of the materials, principally[6] as influencing the[7] style of the works of art[8] and secondly, in an additional lecture, some general remarks on the historical notion of Style.

1 **The**] *after del.* The Specification of that what constitutes the notion style will be the first object of the following, but only as   2 **two**] *interl.*   3 **of style**] *interl.*   4 **First**] *inserted and altered from* Firstly *and del. in red ink*   5 **The**] *del. in red ink*   6 **principally**] *above del.* mainly   7 **the**] *above del.* upon   8 **of the works of art**] *interl.*

121.29 **with respect**] *after del.* chiefly   **style**] *after del.* its influencing the   **its**] *after del.* the development of *(*development *after del.* modification*)*   121.30 **on the works of art,**] *repl. del.* on art,   121.30–1 **and especially of architecture**] *inserted*   121.31 **expressions of**] *above del.* influenced by   121.31–2 **of the ~ institutions**] *of repl. del.* by   121.34–6 **The different manners ~ certain**] *repl. del. on fols. 11r and 12r*

The manners[1] of treating raw materials and of transforming them to productions of industrial art[2] are so manifold that it will appear[3] almost impossible to[4] || classify them in a manner that every one of them finds its right place.

1 **manners**] *after del.* different   2 **industrial art**] *after del.* industry and art   3 **it will appear**] *after del.* at the first sight they   4 **to**] *del. before del.* bring them into classifications so [t]

121.36 **types**] *after undel.* certain   121.37 **common.**] *altered in pencil from* ~, *before del. in pencil* according to our comparing system.
122.3 **word coating**] *after del.* branch of industry in the widest   122.7 **pottery**] *underl. in red ink*   122.13 **Stone,**] *inserted in red ink*   122.16–17 **This is ~ textile art.**] *inserted*
122.22 **These are**] *after del.*

These are the four classes which will be specified[1] in this and the following lectures[2] as far as time

1 **specified**] *before del.* as far as it may be allowed for   as far] as *undel.*   2 **lectures**] *undel.*

122.22 **transitional**] *after del.* trad   122.23 **find**] *after del.* belong to   122.26 **is**] *above del.* forms   122.29–123.20 **for Metalworking ~ fireplace.**] *repl. del. on fol. 14r*

for Metalworking[1]. The reason for this lies near; Metal is not a primary material. The types were fixed before the emploiment of metal for their execution. But we shall not forget this branch of industrial art to be sure.

———————

These different branches of industrial art find their common application[2] and act together in the works of architecture,[3] and[4] Each[5] of the 4 classes of industry has[6] given the type to one of the constituent[7] elements of architectural construction.
Which are these constituent elements of architectural construction?
The earliest[8] Symbol of Settlement[9] is the arrangement of a fire place, and the lighting of a warming, vivifiing and nurrishing flame; The first groups of men, forming the germs of association[10] and civilisation met round the hearth, on which the first alliances[11] were concluded and the first religious[12]

General Remarks on the Different Styles in Art

1 **for Metalworking**] *after undel. on fol. 13r* for   2 **application**] *before del.* in the works of architecture and every one of the four classes is represented by the four principal   is represented] *after del.* found so to speak. *after del.* has given   3 **architecture,**] *altered from* ~.   4 **and**] *interl.*   5 **Each**] *above del.* Every one   6 **has**] *after del.* is the   7 **constituent**] *after del.* most   8 **earliest**] *above del.* first   9 **Settlement**] *before del.* the first beginning is now   10 **association**] *after del.* human   11 **alliances**] *after del.* pledges were   12 **religious**] *before one-sixth page blank*

122.29 **for Metalworking**] *after inserted and del. on fol. 12v* for metal working, The re   122.35 **been mentionned**] *after del. in red ink* here   122.35–8 **It may be doubtfull ~ education,**] *in black ink repl. del. in black ink*

It may be doubtful, if it is that in which the[1] earliest[2] attempts of mankind in artistical productions were maid[3], if it is the first by anciennity – but undoubtedly it has had the greatest influence upon the general development of art,

1 **the**] *after del.* artistical skill began to   2 **earliest**] *above del.* first   3 **maid**] *'made'*

122.37 **earlier**] *before interl. and del.* and stron   122.38 **by giving**] *after del.* by its early application on [a]   **first**] *repl. del.* earliest   122.41 **other**] *interl.*
123.1 **one Element**] *after del.* one of *after del.* one of the three principle elements of   principle] *'principal'*   123.3 **substance**] *after del.* material   **all**] *above del.* every   123.4 **settlement**] *after del.* humanity and civili   123.6–15 **But Here ~ Architecture,**] *repl. del.*

The hearth[1] is the first, and the most important, the moral element of architecture. It forms the center to which all the other parts of the building relate and it is the only element of architecture which is selfexisting[2] and has[3] a meaning without the coexistance of other constructions, without the protection of a roof, without beeing included by walls, or elevated on basements and terraces. It therefore constitutes in itself the elementary[4] idea of a great number of edifices, of those namely which we comprise under the term of monuments, if we take this term in its special sense.

1 **The hearth**] *after del.* The lighting of a *after del.* The Hearth is the   2 **is selfexisting**] *after del.* by itself   3 **and has**] *after del.* and forms an   4 **elementary**] *after del.* fun *(for 'fundamental')*

123.6 **But**] *inserted*   123.7 **constituent parts**] *after del.* constructiv elements   123.13 **Substruction**] *before del.* or the   123.17 **near**] *repl. del.* at   at] *repl. del.* round   123.19 **The Altar**] *after del.*

The fireplace forms,[1] Through all the Phases of social development the[2] holy focus,[3] the center of relations for[4] all the other formal expressions of society.

1 **The fireplace forms,**] *interl.*   2 **the**] *after del.* the fireplace formed   3 **focus,**] *before del.* round which the whole   4 **for**] *above del.* of

123.19 **this early Symbol**] *after del.* this highest Symbol *after del.* the Symbol of spiritual live and   123.21 **The hearth**] *repl. del.* It   123.24–5 **certain important class**] *above del.* num-

434 Lectures

ber   123.25 **edifices**] *after del.* important   123.28 **will relate.**] *after del.* relate.   123.30
form] *after del.* are   123.31–2 **These defenders of the hearth are**] *repl. del.* namely   123.33
these] *altered from* the   123.33–4 **protected and protecting parts**] *repl. del.* four above
mentioned constituant parts   123.35 **take place.**] *repl. del.* grew up   grew up] *repl. del.*
developed themselves;   **happened**] *after interl. and del.* generally   123.37–41 **I shall ~**
practical art.] *inserted after inserted and del.* I Shall explain this   I Shall explain this] *before*
del.

At[1] the same time they became the centers for the division of labor. The different krafts[2] of
industry were grouped around them;

1 **At**] *after del.* In the same time they became at an very early time   2 **krafts**] *'crafts'*

124.2 **representative**] tive *above del.* nt   124.3–4 **Engineering ~ Appartenences.**] *after*
del. The art of Engineering a *and repl. del.* The Engineering and Maçonry round the Terrace,
the Carpenters kraft round the Roof and its appertences;   Maçonry] *'masonry' (see 428,*
Explanatory Notes 124.3)   kraft] *'craft'*   appertenences] *'appurtenances'*   124.7 **of mat-**
makers] *after del.* of Coatmakers,   124.8 **appear**] *above del.* seem   **strange,**] *altered from*
~∧ *before del.* to You, at the first t *(for 'time')*   **wants justifying.**] *repl. del.* wants to be
motivated. here.   124.10 **sill**] *after del.* first treshold of   124.12 **tribes,**] *above del.* people
124.15 **As the first raw attempts of this kind**] *repl. del.* As The first raw motive for separation of space   As] *inserted*   **perhaps**] *before del.* with some right   124.17 **of a**] *repl. del.*
that shows a   **with**] *above del.* which possesses   124.18 **has**] *above del.* knows   **a Sort**
of] *inserted*   124.19 **nothing**] *before del.* else   124.25 **fibrous**] *after del.* other   124.26
hangings] *after del.* such   124.28 **by far preceeded**] *after del.* preceded far   124.29
walls.] *after del.* stone walls or even that of wooden   124.31 **beheld**] *after del.* became
124.32 **part of its**] *interl.*   124.34 **remain**] *repl. del.* were   124.35 **are**] *above del.* were
124.36 **walls;**] *above del.* Separations;   124.38 **to give**] *inserted after del.* to be supporters of
haevy   to] *inserted after underl. and del.* Security, *and before del.* Stability, Durability etc.
125.1 **Where**] *after del.* Every where else, except on   125.2 **means of**] *inserted*   **separ-**
ation] *altered from* separations   **when**] *above del.* where   125.3 **they**] *after del.* there
125.8 **the visible part**] *after del.* the outer part,   the] *undel.*   125.9 **has**] *after del.* is derived
125.10 **root**] *above del.* racine   125.10–11 **The constructiv part of**] *after del.* The inner part
o *after del.* It   125.13 **The significance of the**] *repl. del.* These relations between the
space] *before del.* and the material walls,   125.14 **were**] *after del.* became   125.16 **new**]
above del. such   125.19 **coolness**] *above del.* freshness   freshness] *before del.* or   **Dur-**
ability etc.] *inserted before del. on fol. 18r*

better conservation and durability.
One of the most ancient and most generally adopted surrogates was suggested by the
maçons[1]; the coating of the walls with stucco. The[2] painting on Stucco and the style of
wall-decoration[3] with the antik[4] nations down to the late Romans never denied its origine.
The[5] same is the case with the mediaeval Walldecorations, for instance with those well
known decorations in the Church of Francesco di Assisi which have been modelled upon
Drapperies and which even in their historied parts show[6] the caracter and Style of Embroideries
The Wall decorations of Pompeia[7] suggest[8] the same

General Remarks on the Different Styles in Art   435

1 **maçons**] *French for 'masons'*   2 **The**] *altered from* the *after del.* We shall later see that later] *undel.*   3 **and the style of wall-decoration**] *inserted*   4 **antik**] *'antique'*   5 **The**] *after inserted and del.* We see the proofs of this   6 **show**] *after del.* belong to   7 **Pompeia**] *'Pompeii'*   8 **suggest**] *after del.* give a

125.20 **Every branch of Industry**] *after del.* Every branch of industry has been set into requisition.   has been] *repl. del.* was *(was after del.* took its part *after del.* contributed one or more   requisition.] *altered from* ~∧ *before del.* for suppliing new   125.23 **of painting**] *after del.* of the art   125.23–4 **Wall-painting**] *repl. del.* it   125.28 **the glazed bricks**] *repl. del.* the Glaced tyles   **This invention**] *after del.* which seem to be invented by the Assyrians to   125.29 **probable**] *after del.* more than   125.30 **glazing**] *after del.* colou   **bricks**] *above del.* tiles   125.31 **bricks.**] *repl. del.* the tiles.   125.32 **glazed**] *after del.* paint   **bricks**] *above del.* tyles   125.35 **quite**] *repl. inserted and del.* perfectly   **unburnt**] *after del.* in a quite *and before del.* state   125.36 **Glazing**] *after del.* cover of   125.37 **Glazings**] *before del.* or Enamelings   125.38 **fixed**] *before del.* on these tyles   **smooth fire**] *after del.* soft fire   125.39 **ornamental**] *after del.* archite
126.1 **bricks only**] only *interl.*   126.7 **ornaments**] *repl. del.* different patterns   126.8 **work**] *interl. before del.* in colourd bricks   126.9 **excepting on the basements of the buildings**] *repl. del.* even at instances where the raw materials appeared and were only covered with a thin coating of Colours.   **excepting on**] *above del.* except on   126.10 **bricks**] *above del.* tiles   126.12 **put**] *repl. del.* placed   126.13 **process**] *repl. del.* method   **bricks**] *repl. del.* tiles   126.18 **Metal plates**] *after del.* thin   126.18–19 **sometimes with Goldplates,**] *inserted*   126.21 **Finally may be mentionned**] *repl. del.* As the last of Surrogate may be mentionned   the last] *after interl. and del.* one of   126.22 **stones,**] *before del.* which we find on the remains   **with which the walls**] *inserted*   126.23 **were frequently invested.**] *inserted*   126.25 **Such heterogeneous**] *after del. on fols. 19v–20r*

These[1] different materials and processes applied to Wall decoration, must have produced naturally results[2], very different from the old[3], – but this variety of Artistical inventions and improvements was bount together by a common relation; | Painting amd plastical Art, on Wood, Stucco, Terra Cotta, Metal or Stone remained perhaps inconsciously dependant upon that Style, which is peculiar[4] to Embroidery and tabestry. Ornamental Art and Architecture in its general features[5] down to the Romains[6] remained subject to the same principle of *Coating.* Polychromy[7], the mode of covering the entire edifices even those of Marble, with Colours, t[8]

---

1 **These**] *after del. in opposite column* The Character wich was observed for the treatement of the new employed stuffs, was [b]   2 **results**] *after del.* great changes in the   3 **the old**] *after undel.* the   4 **peculiar**] *after del.* particular   5 **in its general features**] *repl. del.* never entirely   6 **Romains**] *French for 'Romans'*   7 **Polychromy**] *after del.* Antik polychromy   Antik] *'Antique'; after del.* That System of *(of undel.)*   8 **t**] *after del.* is

126.33 **was**] *after del. on fol. 20r–v* remained, ¦ lengtime dependant upon that Style, which is peculiar   lengtime] *'for a long time'*   126.38 **depassing**] *repl. del.* exceding   **besides.**] *repl. del.* apart   **permit it. –**] *before del.*

By[2] passing[1] through the history of art[3] and by examination[4] of the remaining traces of ancient architecture we must feel convinced, that the Assyrians[5] have been the most faithful adhearants of the principle in question.

The Assyrian tapestries are mentionned and celebrated in the oldest records of mankind, for the richness of their colours and the art[6] with which they were ornamented. The descriptions of Dragons[7], Lyons[8], Tigers unicorns and other mystic animals which we read, accord perfectly with what we

1 **By passing**] *above del.* If we pass   lf] *after del.* One remark *after del.* But one remark must   2 **By**] *over* In   3 **art**] *above del.* architecture   4 **by examination**] *after del.* examine the remnants of the oldest edifices,   5 **the Assyrians**] *after del.* there *after del.* among the nations of the old civilised world   6 **art**] *before del.* of the repres   7 **Dragons**] *after del.* mystic animals,   8 **Lyons**] *'lions'*

The Ancient Practice of Wall Coating
and Tubular Construction

TEXTUAL RECORD

MS 131	gta, 20-Ms-131, fols. 1r–6v (6v blank), in Semper's hand
MS 130[1]	gta, 20-Ms-130, fols. 1r–3v (3r–v blank), in Semper's hand
MS 130[2]	gta, 20-Ms-130, fol. 4r–v, in Semper's hand
MS 129	gta, 20-Ms-129, fols. 1r–18v (13r–18v blank; 1v–6v variant of MS 131, fols. 1r, 2v–6r; 7r–8r variant of MS 130[1]; 9r–v variant of MS 130[2]), in Semper's hand, *copy-text*
MS 132	gta, 20-Ms-132, fols. 1r–31v (all versos blank), 'Entwickelung der Wand- und Mauerconstruction bei den antiken Völkern', in Hans Semper's hand (one emendation in Manfred Semper's hand), early 1880s, Hans Semper's German trans. of MS 131, fols. 1r–3r, 6r, and of MS 129, fols. 1r–8v, partly published in Semper 1884[a]; see Herrmann 1981, 111
Semper 1884[a]	'Entwickelung der Wand- und Mauerkonstruktion bei den antiken Völkern', 383–94, German trans. of MS 131, fols. 1r–2v, 6r, and of MS 129, fols. 1r–8v; for details of this composite translation, see Herrmann 1981, 175–7
Semper 1884[b]	'Ueber den frühesten Stil der Metallkonstruktion und Metalldekoration', 90–4, German trans. of MS 129, fols. 9r–12v; for details of this translation, see Herrmann 1981, 159
Semper 1986a	'London Lecture of November 18, 1853', 33–42, here 33–9, 41, Mallgrave's ed. of MS 129

BIBLIOGRAPHY Herrmann 1981, 32, 36, 55, 58, 111, 159, 175–7; Herrmann, 1984, 144, 148, 167, 169; Squicciarino 2009, 351–4; Gnehm 2020, 37

EXPLANATORY NOTES

On 18 November 1853, Semper concluded the topic he had started on in the second half of the lecture of 11 November (122.34–126.38) – namely the ancient practice of wall covering. Using the example of a hut on the Caribbean island of Trinidad, a model of which had attracted his attention in the Great Exhibition, he illustrates the four elements of architecture that he had distinguished on 11 November (123.6–13). He evidently regards the hut, to which he returns in two later lectures (174.16, 178.24–32, 185.5–15), as providing evidence of the origin of architecture as described in *The Four Elements of Architecture* (Semper 1851b, 54–5) and also of the phenomenon mentioned on 11 November that 'the oldest ornaments in architecture' can in most cases be traced back to 'the process of twisting and weaving with natural stuffs of different colours' (125.5–7). He places Chinese architecture, which has remained unchanged for thousands of years (127.18–20), at the same elementary level of development but recognizes in it two changes directly affecting the topic: firstly, the transition from wattled or woven walls to covered wooden panels and brick walls (127.21–2, 127.37–8), and secondly, the covering of another element, the wooden supports and beams of the roof, with small ornamental laminae and coloured paint (127.25–9). Starting from contemporary Chinese architecture, the ornamentation of which appears to him to provide a key to the understanding of ancient ornaments and buildings (128.7–9), he sets out to trace 'the gradual transition of the principle of wallcovering to a more constructiv style' in the architecture of the Assyrians, Persians, Egyptians, Greeks and Romans (128.15–18).

In his explanations, Semper goes beyond *The Four Elements of Architecture* in many places. In discussing Greek architecture, for example, he emphasizes two aspects that are not mentioned in the book: firstly, 'an organic connection between the single elements of construction' (131.27–8), and secondly, the inseparable connection between the constructive parts and the ornaments (131.37–8). The emphasis on this second aspect can be regarded as a way of distancing himself from Karl Bötticher, whose *Tektonik der Hellenen* Semper borrowed and made excerpts from in December 1852 (see 225.27–32, 499). In contrast to Bötticher, Semper does not recognize in Greek monuments any applied ornamentation that is distinguishable from the constructive parts but does see this in 'barbarian architecture', which for him includes Assyrian, Persian and Egyptian architecture (131.34–6). Whereas Semper discusses Assyria, Persia, Egypt and Greece in more or less equivalent detail, he deals with Rome in a single paragraph (132.15–22) and dispenses with any explicit discussion of the Roman use of wall coverings. He expects the members of his audience themselves to be able to interpret, in relation to the principle of covering, his remarks that the Romans were 'the inventors of real stone construction' (132.15–16) and, through their inclusion of vaulting among architectural forms, that they were also 'the inventors of architecture as an selfexisting art' (132.20–1). When Semper describes the Romans as 'the inventors of real stone construction', he is implying that – in contrast to the Assyrians, Persians, Egyptians and Greeks – they used uncovered stone construction, designed in accordance with its own rules, not only in the element of substructure but also in the elements of enclosure and roof. The description of the Romans as 'the inventors of architecture as an selfexisting art' is scarcely understandable, as the Romans developed their wall and vault architecture from one of the industrial arts, stereotomy. Semper expresses himself more cautiously and comprehensibly in *The Four Elements of Architecture*: under the Romans, he explains there, stone wall construction attained a 'higher artistic validity' and extended its dominance 'into the area of the roof' (Semper 1851b, 99).

In partial fulfilment of his earlier promises that he would not ignore metalworking, which had been excluded from the four general classes of industrial arts (117.38–9, 122.31–2), Semper supplements his remarks on the principle of covering with a few comments – closely modelled on 'Practical Art in Metals and hard Materials' – concerning metal objects: ornaments and insignia, furniture and weapons, roofs and doors (132.32–135.26; cf. Semper 2007a, especially 104–13, 115–17, 120, 148–9). He describes the procedure used to reinforce thin sheet metal in Greek and Roman protective armour 'by corrugations and curvatures' as being 'an important moment for the history of construction' (134.26–8). In the lecture, Semper does not explain that the procedure appears to be important to him because tubular construction is also based on it (cf. Semper 1860/63, 1:366–7). The subject announced in the 'Prospectuses of the Lectures on Art' under number 2 – 'Tubular construction, well known by the ancients, and forming the fundamental idea of Greek architecture' (96.15–16) – is dealt with in a few sentences (135.1–15), in which Semper hints only vaguely at the influence of tubular construction on Greek architecture (135.5–6).

Three additional drafts of the lecture 'The Ancient Practice of Wall Coating and Tubular Construction' have survived. The first (MS 131), which – in contrast to what Wolfgang Herrmann assumed (Herrmann 1981, 111) – is probably complete, does not begin with the explanation of a Caribbean hut but rather, after a brief introduction, with the description of two Israelite buildings (447.6–448.6): the Mosaic Tabernacle and the Temple of Solomon, to which Semper inadvertently still makes a reference in the final draft of the lecture (131.17–18). This description, which takes up about one-third of the entire draft, would involve Semper having to postpone discussion of the principle of covering in Greek and Roman architecture – and consequently also the treatment of the second topic, tubular construction – until the following lecture (see 449.34–6). The second, fragmentary draft (MS 130¹) is concerned with Greek architecture and, in contrast to the definitive draft, deals with individual parts of temples – for example, the entablature of the Parthenon (451.15–23). The third draft, also fragmentary (MS 130²), contains a few remarks 'On the early style of Metalconstruction and of Metalornamentation' (453.3–15).

127.1–2 **On Friday last ~ division.**] Wolfgang Herrmann's assumption that this sentence refers to MS 122 (Herrmann 1981, 111) is not correct. Semper did not draw a distinction between the four elements of architecture in MS 122 but rather in MS 124 (123.10–13). However, his claim that he had based the plan for his lectures on this distinction on the previous Friday, i.e. on 11 November 1853, is inaccurate. On that date, he only hinted at the plan in connection with the three groups of stylistic influences (121.27–32), whereas in his inaugural lecture on 20 May 1853 he derived it from the classification of the practical arts (117.24–34).
127.1 **devided**] *divided* (see also 127.10)   127.4 **Caraib**] derived from French *caraïbe*: *Caribbean* (see also 127.20, 127.24)   127.5 **52**] *1851*   127.19 **pallases**] *palaces*   127.21 **shrines**] *screens* (see also 127.22); cf. 518, Explanatory Notes 196.25; Semper 1986a, 34 n. *
127.33–4 **of the flooring**] *off* ~ ~   127.35–7 **At other cases ~ room.**] cf. Chambers 1757, 8
127.36 **gase**] *gauze*; cf. 443, Alterations in the Manuscript 127.36; Chambers 1757, 8; Mallgrave 1986a, 34 n. 3
128.1 **lit up and down**] *open and close*. Mallgrave has 'lift up and down' (Semper 1986a, 34). William Chambers, whose *Designs of Chinese Buildings* Semper uses for support on some points, describes the typical house of a Cantonese merchant as having a saloon that is open on the courtyard side, 'having only a cane-mat, which lets down occasionally to keep out

The Ancient Practice of Wall Coating and Tubular Construction   439

rain or sun-shine' (Chambers 1757, 8).   128.4 **gilt paper**] Mallgrave has 'yellow paper' (Semper 1986a, 34).   128.5 **Arnamental**] *ornamental*   128.13 **rapports**] *respects*   128.18 **Romain**] French for *Roman*   128.21 **tumbs**] *tombs* (see also 131.7)   128.26 **The Assyrians ~ old principle.**] see 428, Explanatory Notes 126.38   128.30–1 **The Assyrian architecture ~ as we shall see it in the last lecture.**] see 176.26–177.6   128.32 **maçon**] French for *mason* (see also 130.1, 130.29)   **artistical**] Mallgrave has 'architectural' (Semper 1986a, 35).   128.39 **Frieses**] *friezes*

129.2–4 **those renomated Assyrian Tapestries ~ Skillfull execution**] 'renomated': *renowned*; see 428, Explanatory Notes 126.38   129.9–11 **The descriptions ~ Embroideries which we**] see 428, Explanatory Notes 126.38   129.18 **52**] *1851*   129.23 **Queen**] *wife* 129.33 **pannelating**] *panelling*   129.37 **beautiful publication on Persia, made by Mrs Coste and Flandin**] 'Mrs': *Messrs*; Flandin/Coste 1851; cf. 449.7–8   129.40–1 **in immense blocks, of black marble**] In *Kleine Schriften*, this phrase is translated without comment as 'von ungeheuren Blöcken weissen Marmors', and thus the colour is expressed as white, not black (Semper 1884, 390).

130.1 **stopps**] *stops*. Mallgrave has 'steps (forward)' (Semper 1986a, 36).   130.5 **behold**] derived from German *behalten*: *retain*   130.6–7 **This we shall see in the Chapter on wood Construction.**] This sentence refers to the lecture 'On Timber Construction, and Its Influence upon the Development of Architectural Forms'. However, in the two fragmentary manuscripts for that lecture (MS 136, MS 137), Semper does not touch on Persian stone columns derived from wooden columns. If he did actually include them in the lecture, he would have had to discuss them before roof forms and roofing tiles (161.2–162.23).   130.14 **unburnt**] *unbaked*   130.25 **roc**] French for *rock*   130.28 **cisel**] merged from French *ciseau* and English *chisel*

131.2 **Torus**] see 323, Explanatory Notes 68.4   131.6 **Champlevé Enameling**] Champlevé enamels are produced by pouring liquid enamel into troughs gouged out of a metal base. Semper addresses champlevé enamelling in his 'Observations on Some of the Specimens of Metal Work' (85.11) and mentions its technique as being known to the Egyptians in *Style* (Semper 1860/63, 1:425), where he also gives a definition of it when discussing enamels in the chapter on metals technology (Semper 1860/63, 2:566).   131.12 **interlaces**] *plaits*   131.16 **massivity**] Mallgrave has 'majesty' (Semper 1986a, 37).   131.17–18 **like we have seen ~ Tempel of Salomon**] an inadvertent reference to a passage in the abandoned manuscript MS 131; see 447.6–448.6   131.23 **overkame**] *overcame*, here misused for *received*; cf. Semper 1884, 393: 'empfingen'. In the corresponding passage of a rejected draft (MS 130[1]), Semper uses two verbs: 'took up and overkame' (451.3). He apparently writes 'took up' for *adopted* and 'overkame' for *received* there (not for *overcame*, as the next sentence reveals). An equivalent passage in *The Four Elements of Architecture* reads (Semper 1851b, 52): 'Hellenic culture could only have arisen on the humus ... of foreign motifs ... brought over from abroad'. The question of who brought over the motifs remains unexplained. In 'On the Origin of Polychromy in Architecture', Semper states that the Greeks 'inherited' foreign artistic principles (69.34).   131.31 **depassed**] derived from French *dépasser*: *overstepped*; cf. Semper 1986a, 38 n. 11   131.32 **is**] *I*   131.36 **kernet**] *kernel*, here misused for *core* 132.9 **Ewery where**] *everywhere*   132.35 **sheeds**] *sheets*. Mallgrave has 'shields' (Semper 1986a, 39).   132.38–133.1 **Ornaments in Gold- Silver and Tinleaves ~ at the Brittish Museum ~ stamped and pierced with ornaments and figures**] In 'Practical Art in Metals and hard Materials', Semper mentions 'Gold, Silver and tin leaves, with stamped

440   Lectures

and pierced figures and Ornaments' preserved in the British Museum (Semper 2007a, 105).
133.1–2 **metalshieds**] *metal sheets*. Mallgrave has 'metal shields' (Semper 1986a, 39).   133.3
metalthreads and filigran work] cf. Semper 1860/63, 2:490–5   133.4 **processes**] Mallgrave has 'principles' (Semper 1986a, 39).   133.6 **alse**] *also*   133.8 **Chains**] cf. Semper
1860/63, 2:497–500   133.11–12 **woven staffs and Embroideries**] 'staffs': *stuffs*; cf. Semper
1860/63, 1:160–5; 2:495   133.13–14 **The Pallaces of the Kings of Babylone ~ were ornamented with carpets in Gold and Silverweavings instead of pictures.**] cf. Semper
1860/63, 1:364. In 'Practical Art in Metals and hard Materials', Semper describes the same
sentence as being a quotation from Philostratus's 'life of Apollonius of Tyane' (Semper
2007a, 107). However, the relevant passage in Giovanni Francesco Salvemini's French
translation, *Vie d'Apollonius de Tyane*, to which Semper is probably referring, reads differently (Philostratus 1774, 2:148): 'Les maisons royales sont couvertes de cuivre qui leur donne un
certain éclat; les chambres des hommes & des femmes, les portiques & les colonnades sont,
au lieu de peintures, ornés de tapisseries tissues d'argent & d'or, & même d'or massif.'
133.15–16 **Gold and Silver-embroideries ~ Walldecorations of the temple of Jerusalem**] In 'Practical Art in Metals and hard Materials', Semper mentions 'The Wall decorations of the Temple of Soloman, consisting in Wooden pannels, covered with Gold Plates
and representing Palm Trees, Cherubim &c (Book of "the Kings", Flavius Josephus Jewish
Antiquities)' (Semper 2007, 108). While Josephus does not specify these coverings, they
are described in the biblical Books of Kings in a passage Semper refers to in *Style* (1 Kings
6:29–30; cf. Semper 1860/63, 1:402–3): 'And he [i.e. Solomon] carved all the walls of the
house round about with carved figures of cherubims and palm trees and open flowers,
within and without. And the floor of the house he overlaid with gold, within and without.'
Semper's 'Gold and Silver-embroideries' are an interpolation possibly derived from the
Books of Chronicles (also cited in *Style*) – with 'cieled' for *covered* or *coated* (2 Chronicles
3:5–7): 'And the greater house he cieled with fir tree, which he overlaid with fine gold, and
set thereon palm trees and chains. ... He overlaid also the house, the beams, the posts, and
the walls thereof, and the doors thereof, with gold; and graved cherubims on the walls.'
Semper might have had in mind also Aloys Hirt's discussion of Solomon's Temple in the
work he had in his library (Hirt 1821/27, 1:124): 'The walls ... were thoroughly panelled with
planks of cedar, with carvings of flowers, palms and cherubs.'   133.18–19 **The arts of nielling and enameling ~ derive from the same origine.**] In 'Practical Art in Metals and
hard Materials', Semper claims that 'The Art of Nielling is derived from Tattoo' (Semper
2007a, 105).   133.18 **nielling and enameling**] cf. Semper 1860/63, 2:564–74. In 'Practical
Art in Metals and hard Materials', Semper defines *niello* as 'Engraved Ornaments and
Figures filled out with black or dark Mastick', while in *Style* he defines it as 'a fluid metal
compound with which engraved indentations in a heated sheet are filled' (Semper 1860/63,
2:564; Semper 2007a, 100).   133.21 **Emaux ~ Cloisonnés**] In *Style*, Semper defines *émaux
cloisonnés* as 'thin gold threads that are soldered onto a metal surface, with the spaces between them being filled with enamel' (Semper 1860/63, 1:425).   133.21–2 **7 different Styles
of Enameling**] These seven styles are described in 'Practical Art in Metals and hard Materials' (Semper 2007a, 97–9).   133.23–31 **Oriental art ~ antiquity.**] These sentences are
taken over almost verbatim from 'Practical Art in Metals and hard Materials' (Semper
2007a, 108–9).   133.25 **instinctive**] Mallgrave has 'intuitive' (Semper 1986a, 39).   133.32–3
gold ornaments ~ in the Tomb of Childeric] In 'Practical Art in Metals and hard Materials', Semper describes these ornaments as 'A sort of filigran Work with transparent

The Ancient Practice of Wall Coating and Tubular Construction   441

Enamels', referring to the 'Magazin pittoresque year 34, p 272' and to a 'Work of Mont-faucon' (Semper 2007a, 109; cf. Semper 1860/63, 2:518 n. 1). The ornaments are described and illustrated in Bernard de Montfaucon's *Monumens de la monarchie françoise* (Montfaucon 1729/33, 1:10–16, pls. 4–6) and in the nineteenth volume of *Le Magasin pittoresque* (Magasin pittoresque 1851b) but not in the second volume of the journal, published in 1834.   133.33 **imperial Ornaments of Charlemagne**] In 'Practical Art in Metals and hard Materials', Semper mentions '*The Crown and Sword of Charlemagne* at Present at Vienna', referring to 'Arneths Monography relative to the Gold and Silver Works of the Cabinet in Vienna' and to 'Willemin' (Semper 2007a, 110; italics in original). The ornaments are described and illustrated in Nicolas-Xavier Willemin and André Pottier's *Monuments français inédits* (Willemin/Pottier 1839, 1:12–14, pls. 19–20), but not in Joseph Arneth's catalogue *Die an-tiken Gold- und Silber-Monumente des k. k. Münz- und Antiken-Cabinettes in Wien* (Arneth 1850), which also includes a few post-classical objects.   133.37–8 **The taste for rich ~ im-plements preceeded ~ the want of fixed settlements.**] 'preceeded': *preceded*. This sentence is taken over almost verbatim from 'Practical Art in Metals and hard Materials' (Semper 2007a, 111); cf. 98.18–20, 101.18–19.

134.3–4 **The Egyptians ~ Metal.**] These sentences are taken over almost verbatim from 'Practical Art in Metals and hard Materials' (Semper 2007a, 112).   134.4 **A.**] *Aegyptian* 134.5–6 **The Assyrian Warcharriots ~ in the former style those of Egyptians ~ of Cast metal.**] cf. Semper 1860/63, 2:375–6   134.10–11 **Wooden Chair covered with Goldplates and with Precious stones**] In 'Practical Art in Metals and hard Materials', Semper de-scribes this chair as 'gold Covered Wood … richly ornamented with stones, gems and enamels', referring to 'v Murr. The Imperial Ornaments at Aix la Chapelle' (Semper 2007a, 113; cf. Semper 1860/63, 2:274 n. 2). However, Christoph Gottlieb von Murr's *Beschreibung der ehemals zu Aachen aufbewahrten drey kaiserlichen Krönungs-Zierden* does not refer to the chair but to three other items owned by Charlemagne: a book of Gospels, a sabre and a reliquary known today as St Stephen's Purse. Both the book's cover – which was only made around 1500 – and the reliquary have wooden cores, which according to Murr's details are 'covered with gold foil and set with jewels' or 'covered with gold foil' and 'set with pearls and very many uncut jewels' (Murr 1801, 10, 25; cf. pl. 1 figs. 1, 3).   134.13–18 **In the Life of Charlemagne ~ other compositions.**] Chapter 33 of Einhard's *Vita Caroli Magni* cites a codicil of Charlemagne, which names the 'valuable things' that Semper mentions. Semper also refers to the codicil in *Style*, although he incorrectly assigns it to Chapter 27 (Semper 1860/63, 2:525 and n. 3). He listed a duodecimo edition of the *Vita Caroli Magni* in the inven-tory of his Dresden library (see 211.22).   134.13 **secretery**] *secretary*   **constained**] *con-tained*   134.22 **Application of Metal for defensiv arms**] cf. Semper 1860/63, 2:485–90 134.24–8 **The oriental Style of defensiv arms ~ not adopted by the Greeks and Romans ~ the principle of strenghtening thin Metal plates by corrugations and curvatures**] In 'Practical Art in Metals and hard Materials', the corresponding passage reads (Semper 2007a, 120): 'The Oriental Style of Defensive Arms, a sort of Wire texture (coat of Mail) not adopted by the Greeks and Romans. Greek and Roman Shields, helmets and Armures, show a perfect Application of the principle of strengthening thin metal plates by corrugations & curvations, thus combining strength with lightness.'   134.26 **Armures**] French for *armours*   134.27–8 **principle of strenghtening ~ by corrugations and curva-tures**] 'strengh | tening': *strengthening*. Mallgrave has 'strength (by) tensing' (Semper 1986a, 41). When Semper explains the historical significance of this principle in *Style*, he also clarifies the principle itself more precisely: it is based on the fact 'that curved and pleated metal sheets enclosing a space of suitable stereometric shape as an envelope achieve the greatest solidity and stability with the least material expense' (Semper 1860/63, 1:366). 134.34 **Id**] *id*: Latin for *it* 134.35 **Chield**] *shield* **alle**] German for *all* 134.36–7 **screw Zones**] Mallgrave has 'seven doves (?)' (Semper 1986a, 41). 134.37 **Haeven**] *heaven* 135.8–9 **roof of the Pantheon which formerly consisted of tubular bronze spars, riveted together**] 'spars': *rafters*; cf. Semper 1860/63, 1:368, 369 fig.; Semper 2007a, 149 135.10–11 **brassplates ~ taken in time of Sixte V by ~ Borromini for the large Baldachin in St Peters**] This claim is doubly incorrect: the baldachin in St Peter's was in fact created during the reign of Pope Urban VIII, and it was based on a design by Gian Lorenzo Bernini. In 'Practical Art in Metals and hard Materials' and in *Style*, Semper attributes the baldachin correctly to Bernini, without mentioning the reigning pope (Semper 1860/63, 1:368; Semper 2007a, 149). 135.12 **antik Bronze doors ~ a second example of tubular construction**] 'antik': *antique*. In 'Practical Art in Metals and hard Materials', Semper describes 'the Splendid doors of the Pantheon, which consist of two Cast bronze panels separated by a space, and only connected by the Cross panels, at the four edges' as being examples of 'the Tubular Style' (Semper 2007a, 148; cf. Semper 1860/63, 1:368 and fig., 369 figs.). 135.18–19 **Such were the Silver Doors of St Peters ~ 975 ℔.**] '℔': abbreviation of Latin *librae* (pounds); cf. Semper 2007a, 116–17 135.19 **Jear**] *year* 135.20–2 **This styles appeared ~ in the Byzantine doors at St Peter et Paolo at Rome, which dissapeared ~ some 20 Years ago.**] 'et': French and Latin for *and*. In 'Practical Art in Metals and hard Materials', Semper notes under 'Specimens of Metal Coated Doors' (Semper 2007a, 117): 'Door of St Pauls, Donation of Gregory VII. flat, with inlaid figures in Silver and Damascen Work. It was covered with brass on the outside, No longer existing, XIII. (D'Agincourt Sculpture)'; cf. Agincourt 1823, sect. 'Sculpture', 2:48; 3:13–17; 4: pls. 13–20. In *Kleine Schriften*, Manfred and Hans Semper note on this (Semper 1884, 94 n. *): 'Fragments of them, packed into chests, were found by Piper in the monastery of St Paul several years ago.' 135.23–5 **But elder doors, in Germany ~ belong rather to the advanced Roman Style with pannels in imitation of wooden framework.**] cf. Semper 2007a, 117, 150 135.25 **brass doors of the Cinque Cento**] cf. Semper 2007a, 151–2

EDITORIAL EMENDATIONS

127.23 **frame-work**] frame- | work 130.13 **Door-frames**] Door- | frames 130.17 **some thing**] some | thing 133.6 **Gold-bracelets**] Gold- | bracelets 133.15 **Silver-embroideries**] Silver- | embroideries

ALTERATIONS IN THE MANUSCRIPT

127.1–3 **On Friday last ~ sketch, which**] *repl. del.*

On Friday last I endeavoured[1] to demonstrate the development of the principle[2] of wall-covering on the tabernakle[3] of Covenant of the ancient Israelites and of the Temple of Sa-

The Ancient Practice of Wall Coating and Tubular Construction   443

lomon, which are known only by the records of the sacred[4] scriptures. We[5] shall now pursue the gradual development of this principle on actual existing buildings or remnants of buildings.
An[6] interesting example of primitive[7] housebuilding is this cottage; This sketch[8]

> 1 **endeavoured**] *after del.* mentionned the   2 **principle**] *after del.* important   3 **the tabernakle**] *after del.* the descriptions of   4 **the sacred**] *after del.* sacred and profane   5 **We**] *over* I   1] *after del.* But it will be   6 **An**] *after del.* One   7 **primitive**] *after del.* a construction, where all the elements   8 **This sketch**] *after del.* This drawing has been made

127.2 **based**] *after del.* made this division the base of   **plan**] *above del.* order   order] *before del.* which I thought to observe by triing to give a   **of**] *in black ink repl. undel.* for   **on**] *in black ink repl. del. in black ink* upon   **An instructiv**] *after del.* Here is one   127.4 **exhibited**] *after del. in black ink* which was   127.5 **we**] *after del.* Here   **here**] *interl.*   **construction**] *after del.* housebuilding *and before interl. in brown ink and del. in black ink* exhibited   **expressions**] *final* s *added in black ink*   127.6 **combinations**] s *added in black ink*   **Every**] *altered from* every *after del.*

Every Element stands for itself without being connected together with the other by any intention from the side of the builder
You see here

127.6 **is**] *interl.*   **alone**] *before del.* and protecting the fireplace which stands in the center. 127.6–7 **and has no connection with the others.**] *inserted*   127.8 **This**] *after del.* There is no architectural or decorativ intention to be *after del.* There is no intention to be seen, from the side of the builder. *after del.* You observe   127.10 **which devide**] *after del.* which are employed here as the divisions of the inner localities   inner] *after del.* roo   127.12 **barks of trees**] *before del. on fol. 1v* and Coconut bones   **first**] *after del.* very   127.14 **There is a nation**] *after del.* There is a nation which stands on a high step of industrial   127.19 **ages.**] *altered from* ~∧ *before del.* and   **their**] *altered from* the   **imperial pallases**] *after del.* house of the Imperor of China   127.20 **pillars,**] *before del.* which are simple beams, regularly round   127.21 **mouveable**] *after del.* simple   127.25 **inside**] *before del.* and richly ornamented.   127.27 **are**] *before del.* generally of Wood; even for   127.28 **Entasis,**] *before del.* and Canne *(for 'Cannelures')*   127.35 **At other cases the**] *above del.* The bottom   The] *after del.* All the   127.36 **gase**] *accompanied in opposite column by probably Hans Semper's note in pencil* gaze?   gaze] *French for 'gauze'*   127.37 **wood,**] *before del.* have several caracters and figures on them
128.4 **paper,**] *before del.* and instead of pictures they   128.5–7 **We may say ~ is also very**] *repl. del.* These details are very   These details are very] *inserted before del.* There is nothing more   128.5 **Chinese**] *after del.* the Study of   **is**] *repl. del.* has been   **disdained**] *after del.* neglected   128.8–9 **nations,**] *before del. on fol. 2v* than the actual Chinese   128.10 **compleatness**] *altered from* compleatedness   compleatedness] *above del.* true appearances   128.11 **frameworks,**] *altered from* ~∧ *before del.* and mouveables,   **mouveable**] *altered from* mouveables   **things**] *interl.*   128.12–13 **approach**] *after del.* seem to us as   128.15–23 **We shall now proceed ~ Botta and Layard.**] *repl. del.*

The Aegyptian[1] monuments are without doubt the most ancient[2]; Some[3] of them, and the most important, have been built many thousand Years before the Assyrian[4] monuments, which have been discovered[5] since a few Years by Mrs[6] Layard and Botta.

> 1 **The Aegyptian**] *after del.* Among the rest of ancient Architecture and ornamental Art
> on the Egyptian   2 **ancient**] *before del.* documents of human art which exist   art which]
> *undel.*   3 **Some**] *after del.* they are many thou-   4 **Assyrian**] *after del.* most ancient
> 5 **have been discovered**] *after del.* we know only since a few Years   only] *after del.* now
> 6 **Mrs**] 'Messrs'

128.15 **proceed in**] *above del.* try to   **showing**] ing *added*   128.23 **greater**] *interl.*   128.27
Construction,] *altered from* ~. *before del.* and had also made some progress towards   128.29
mention at once,] *repl. del.* add   128.30 **Architecture;**] *before del.* That element of architecture which we called the terrace, was even the dominant and Characteristic constructiv
element   128.32 **the cooperation**] *after del.* the stone construction and   the] *undel.*
128.40 **analogical to**] *above del.* like
129.2 **renomated**] *above del.* celebrated   129.3 **richness,**] *altered from* ~∧ *before del.* of
colours] *after del.* Colouring and   129.3–4 **and designs,**] *interl.*   129.6 **ornaments**]
after del. representatio[n]   **on the outer walls,**] *interl.*   **as well as for**] *repl. del.* and
likewise they were the models for   for] *undel.*   129.7 **about 5 to 8 feet**] *after del.* 5 to 6 feet
high from the   129.8 **pavement.**] *altered from* ~; *before del.* and for the whole inner
Wall-decoration in general.   129.10 **the ornaments**] *after del.* those well known Assyrian
Basreliefs at the Brittish museum,   Basreliefs] *after del.* Repre   129.13 **ancient**] *inserted*
Descriptions] *before del.* of Daniel and Herodote   129.15 **but by the reaction**] *after del.*
the sculpture *after del. on fol. 3v* but by the reaction of certain laws of execution and of
processes upon sculpture   129.27 **Very often**] *after del.* The ceilings and at many occasions
t *after del.* Thus the Assyrian dwellings show the first step towards stone Construction, the
pannelating   pannelating] 'panelling'   129.31 **and covered**] *after del.* and richly gilt o
and] *undel.*   129.40–1 **of black marble**] *after del.* freestones   129.41 **very regularly**] *after*
del. very regularly although not allways s   view] *above del.* intention   129.41–2 **employing**] *repl. del.* taking
130.13 **only built**] *after del.* constructed   130.16 **a few**] *after del.* one or t[w]   **Corner**]
after del. lower   130.18 **covered**] *after del.* probably   130.19 **by the history**] *after del.* by
the circumstance, that this building has been destroid   130.25 **The**] *above del.* The masses
of   130.26 **first formed**] *after del.* became afterwards not only scuptured,   130.34 **On
some**] *after del.* We shall   130.36 **appears**] *above del.* remains
131.1 **employ**] *before del.* still   **Corners;**] *altered from* ~, *before del.* where it would look
131.2 **Torus**] *after del.* round   **walls**] *after del.* Egyptian   131.3 **The sculptured**] *after del.*
The principle of Walldecoration by picture   **greatly**] *inserted after del.* have lost a great
part of their original typical   131.4 **origine;**] *altered from* ~∧ *before del.* being transformed
into   131.9 **like**] *inserted*   **as being**] *after del.* in the frame of t   131.10 **patterns, executed in a**] *repl. del.* examples of   131.13 **Lastly**] *interl.*   131.13–14 **The ceilings ~ Hypostilium.**] *inserted before del.* The fourth path towards the constructiv   131.15 **I shall trie**]
after del. We shall see at the   **principle**] *after del.* whole   131.16 **has taken its Analoga**]
after del. is related and derivable   131.19 **by the Greecs.**] *before del.*

While[1] the Architectural styles of the Barbarians were the simple expressions of one condition[2] of social life, the Architecture of the Greeks was of a very compount caracter.[3]

The Ancient Practice of Wall Coating and Tubular Construction 445

1 **While**] *altered from* while *after two del. beginnings of variant:*

We shall see in one of the following lectures that,
Greec Architecture was not a simple combination;

combination;] *altered from* ~, *before del.* like the other barbarian

2 **condition**] *above del.* principle   3 **caracter.**] *altered from* ~∧ *before del.* and contained in itself the whole   whole] *before del.* All the

131.20 **The Greeks**] *after del.*

the roofs.
2°) the ornamental parts are one and indivisible with the constructiv parts.
3°) the

131.26 **pure artistical sense.**] *after del.* higher symbolical sense;   131.27 **We first observe on the Greec monuments**] *after del.* On t[h] *after del.*

We see on the Assyrian and Aegyptian monuments the ornamental parts being real applications or atleast[1] being represented like such; This was not the case with

1 **atleast**] *'at least'*

131.30 **The Greecs**] *after inserted and del. on fol. 7r*

We will see[1] that the Greecs, by carriing out their conceptions felt even in some cases obliged to be[2] inconsistent in their principles of construction.

1 **We will see ~ construction.**] *repl. del.* We will see that the Greecs in certain cases felt obliged to sacrifice for the embodiment of a   sacrifice] *after del.* depass the bounderies of *(depass derived from French 'dépasser': 'overstep')*   2 **be**] *after del.* tr[ ] *after del.* sacrifice the consistency of their construction

131.30–1 **by doing so ~ principles,**] *repl. del.* herein   131.32 **idea**] *inserted after del.* intention   131.34 **architecture**] *above del.* art   131.37 **are one**] *after del.* are organically grown together and both   131.39 **functions**] *over expr (for 'expressions')*
132.1 **They**] *inserted after del.* The Greec ornaments, with the Exception of the historical representations   **explain**] *before del.* and to support the artistical effect of the   **constructiv** *interl.*   **forms**] *before del.* to which they belong   132.3 **on**] *repl. del.* of   132.6 **The accuracy**] *after del.* The principle of coating, led the Greecs first to the Idea of tubular Construction. It appears that the   It appears that the] the *after del.* hollow construction
132.14 **Assyrians. –**] *before del.* The Stone, as a selfrepresenting material, was only entirely The Stone ~ entirely] *after del.* The new principle of Stone construction *after del.* The last step to the emancipation of the Stone as a   selfrepresenting] *after del.* selfexisting
132.16–17 **in the whole civilised old world**] *after del.* in Euro   132.17 **The art**] *after del.* Perhaps   132.18 **were acquainted**] *after del.* knew   132.19 **adopted**] *repl. del.* accepted
132.20 **this form**] *after del.* the vaults   **element of architecture.**] *after del.* artistic one.

132.22 **exist**] *repl. del.* stand   **art..**] *before del.* The stone   132.24 **It would be interesting**] *after del.* After the fall of the Western Roman Empire *after del.* It is   **pursue**] *above del.* follow   132.25 **again**] *after del.* once   132.26–7 **and the starting point ~ in general.**] *inserted before del.*

The[1] swaddling cloths of the arts, the variegated hangings and carpets, became in the dark centuries of the bas Empire[2], as it were the winding sheets of the first.[3]

> 1 **The**] *after del.* In the dark time of centeries of the bas   2 **bas Empire**] *derived from French 'Bas-Empire': 'late Roman Empire'*   3 **first.**] *altered from ~∧ before del.* and the modern o   the modern] *after del.* the same were the

132.29 **which**] *after del.* or art   132.32 **On the early style ~ Metal decoration.**] *accompanied by Manfred Semper's underl. note in pencil* NB
133.6 **Gold-bracelets,**] *before del.* Arm   133.8 **Chains**] *before del.* and coats of mails
133.10 **in**] *above del.* at   133.11 **Metal threads**] *after del.* A very old application of Metal threads was also that for w   133.16 **Jerusalem,**] *altered from ~.*   133.18 **The arts of nielling**] *after del.* Othersides the inlaid stones,   133.20 **precious**] *after del.* inserted   133.21 **(Emaux à Cabochon and Cloisonnés**] *inserted*   133.24 **oriental art**] *after del.* The Character of   133.31 **productions of the earliest antiquity.**] *after del.* earlier oriental productions. *after del.* original and far more ancient productions of the   133.36 **Furnitures**] s *added*   133.39 **Wooden furnitures**] *after del.* The most ancient specimens of furniture on which metal is employed
134.2 **earlier**] ier *in black ink over* y   **times**] s *added in black ink*   134.7 **in the early mediaeval ages**] *after del.* under the Frankish Kings in France and Germany   134.9–12 **The Imperor Othon ~ Vienna.**] *inserted in black ink on fol. 10r after underl.* Folgende Seite.
134.13–14 **In the Life ~ list of**] *in black ink*   134.14 **Imperor,**] *before del.* Eginhard Eginhard] *after del.* He mentions   134.16 **others**] *altered from* other *before del.* things of valu
134.29 **after**] *after del.* afther the forms of the Breast   134.30 **Interesting**] *after del.* Insta[n] *and both above del.* One of the earliest   134.33–7 **consisting ~ Haeven.**] *inserted*   134.33 **plates of**] *interl.*   134.35 **reproduce the**] *after del.* represent the   134.36 **the praecited**] *after del.* the given
135.1 **hollow Metal construction**] *after del.* principle of   135.1–2 **tubular construction**] *after undel.* of   135.7 **have**] *above del.* know   135.8 **the roof**] *before del.* and the waults
135.11 **for the large**] *after del.* and smelted *and before del.* and ugly   135.12 **The antik Bronze doors**] *before del.* of the later Roman ti *(for 'time')*   **construction,**] *before del.* but which
135.14 **propositions**] *after del.* objects   135.18 **Silver**] *above del.* Golden   **stripped of their valuable coat**] *repl. del.* taken away   135.19 **The silver**] *after del.* These doors were
135.20 **This**] is *over* e   135.21 **destruction**] *after del.* great   135.23 **Hildesheim**] *before del.* and Augsburgs.

The Ancient Practice of Wall Coating and Tubular Construction

MANUSCRIPT VARIANTS
MS 131

Since the important discoveries of Layard and Botta at the Ground which once was the Seat of the Assyrian Capital, and since we are, by recent publications, better informed about the Art of the ancient Persians, the materials of a complete history of the pannelated Style of Wall construction lais before us. We can now follow it from the beginning to its final tran-
5 sition to an other principle of more constructiv Style of Decoration and Architecture. –
The records of the holy scripture, and Josephus book on the Jewish Antiquities contain very important details about this subject, which are completely intelligible only now, since the abovementionned discoveries at Nimrud and Chorsabad.
Who knows not the celebrated description of the tabernakle of covenant in the Exodus! It
10 was the Original type to the magnificent tempel of Jerusalem, which was built meny centuries afterwards by Salomon.
The Tabernakel was a mouvea- ¦ ble edifice, a Sort of richly decorated hut, it remained the only sacred Edifice of the nation, down to the time of Salomon, throw 592 Years. Its construction and richness are testimonies of a very advanced state of practical Art with the
15 Yews in that early time. They had learnt it from the Aegyptians.
The Hutt was 30 Yards long, 10 Yards wide and had the same hight.
The Walls were executed in wooden frameworks and pannels, The pannels fixed one next the other in the Ground, by means of silver shoes on their bottom. Outerly of the wooden Walls were rings, 5 on each Pannel, one over the other, which contained as many transversal
20 beams, for fastening the pannels one to the other. A Sort of Construction very similar to our Shopshutters.
Inside the room was divided into two, by 4 Pillars, which were the holders of precious draperies. which formed the division of the Room. –
The smaler division on the bottom of the hut was the Sanctuary containing the ark of the
25 Covenant. The intrance was on the East Side, and here also were hangings for the only Separation of space, attached | on wooden Pillars with Silverbases, and golden Capitels;
The wood on all these Pannels, Pillars and transverse beams inside and Outside of the building, was *covered with Goldplates.*
Four Carpets, one over the other, formed the roof of the Hutt; The lowest carpet, that which
30 appeared inside, was a rich woven Staff of Cotton. The Second was of Wool or Goathares, the third was of read Leather and the fourth of skins.
The whole was surrounded by a Peribolus 100 Yards long 50 Yards wide.
It was enclosed by hangings fastened on stringes between pillars, similar to those of the Hutt, but mounted only with bronze on the bottom. –
35 The entrance to the Peribolus was, like that of the tabernakel shut by drapperies. – .
The Tempel of Salomon was a treatement of this given type in an higher style; it was not a large building, only twice de size of its Original, 60 Yards to 20, and 30 Yards high. We Shall not give here all the Details of it; it is sufficient to say that the walls were constucted in stone but covered with Metal. The Cealing was of Cedarwood with a Roof of the same
40 material. The Roof was outerly covered with Goldplates, and on the Gables of the Roof were Golden Acroteries. ¦
The inner decoration of the tempel was magnificent; the *walls were entirely* covered with Cedarwood, which was sculptured in the Style of Draperies, with flowers, Palm-leaves and Winged Lyons. But these covering Sculptures were covered on their side with Goldplates,
45 so applied on the basreliefs, that the forms of the sculptured wood appeared.

The wooden Doors were decorated after the same Style and plated with Gold. The ceilings and even the floors were covered with Goldplates.

This the Description of the temple so far as it belongs to our present object. We see the Strong walls of the building hidden behind a rich cover of Wood and Gold, being the Stone Scaffolds of the last, which itself was the Representetiv of the former Tapestries of the Tabernakel.

———————

fol. 3r   *3*   Very interesting for our Question are also the Chinese buildings, as they are Still now They give the striking example | of an Architecture, whose elements have remained unaltered through the ages, The Roof has its own pillars, and has nothing to do with the walls, which are only shrines, or hollow brick Constructions made in imitation of the shrines. The wall does not touch the Roof there is a distance between the top of the Wall and the frame of the Roof. Bamboo hedges and treillis are very often employed on the stead of the walls, and the principal motif of Decoration is taken from this simplest production of textile Art. Tapestry has in China the same significance which it had of old with the Assyrians. The *Stucco* Surrogates for the Corpets and the paper hangings, a Chinese Invention, are very usual in China; Polychromy in architecture and Sculpture was the natural consequence of this manner of Construction, as it was the Same in Antiquity, with the Assyrians, Egyptians, and Greeks. ¦

fol. 3v   But still more interesting are the Antiquities of Assyria Aegept Greece and Rome, for the study of the gradual progress to an other more constructiv Style of Architecture.

We feel convinced, that the Assyrian monuments are the most primitives in style and principle, although they have been built thousand of Years after the monuments of Egypt; Notwithstanding their higher antiquity the last belong to a later state of Development, but this is true only respecting the *constructive* elements of Aegyptian Architecture

The Assyrians remained the faithfull Adhaerants, of this principle, although they knew very well Stone-Construction and had also maid even one Step towards the last even for the interior of their houses by pannelating them with Stoneslabs; on the place of those Assyrian tapestries, which are mentionned in the oldest records of Mankind, and celebrated for their richness of colours and skillfull Execution. |

fol. 4r   *4*   The Description of Dragons, Lyons, Tigers, Unicornes and other Mystic Animals, which we read in the ancient books, accord perfectly with what we now see at the Brittish Museum, with the representations on Dresses of the Gods and Kings and other Personages.

But even more, the whole ensemble of the Assyrian Basreliefs reminds us the Description of Similar Objects as being represented on tapestries. It is little doubt that the last were the Originals for the first.

These Sculptures remain within certain limits which seem not to be prescribed by hierarchical laws, which was the case in Aegypt.) but by the reaction of laws of execution, which belong not to Stone sculpture.

They are copies in stone of woven or embroidered Tapestries, and look like that. We have seen in the Great Exhibition of 51 certain Chinese Hautelisse figures which reminded perfectly those basreliefs.

fol. 4v   These figures are, as it were shakled but they are not mere types or ¦ hieroglyphs like the Egyptian figures are.

Other representations such like battles, hunting partys etc, remind very much the well known Bayeux drapery with the battles between the Normans and the English.

The Ancient Practice of Wall Coating and Tubular Construction 449

The edifices which were decorated with these Plates stood on a large artificial hill, on which the mighty freestones, were arranged in an ornamental manner.

Real Draperies and rich floor carpets were combined with the sculptured and painted tapestries to a splendid general effect.

5 ————————

The second stepp towards an other principle of Construction is visible on the Ruins of Persepolis and Pasargadae, in Persia. They are better known since the publication of Coste's work. Here are the same imposing foundations | but in a better State of Conservation, and   5   *fol. 5r* better executed. The Sculptures are neorly the same in general Style, but Stone is already 10 employed not only as a Cover, but also as a Constructiv part.

For inst. the beautiful Columns in white marble, instead of the Wooden or bronze-covered columns of the Assyrians.

Very interesting are the Morble Doors and the marble blocks at the corners of the former walls, which exist no more because they were only of unburnt bricks. They are Stones of 15 immense size, one or two of them forming one Corner of the Wall. but they are hollowed out, so that they form some thing like a solid shell for the protection of the angels of the Earthenwalls.

The Stone began to be constructively employed, but not yet as a selfrepresenting material.

We pass now to Egypt, whose Monuments show the third stepp of progress towards stone 20 Construction.

The Aegyptian temples are Stonebuildings the old type of Wallconstruction is not more very distinguishable on them. ¦ Nevertheless the *constructiv* principle of decoration was not   *fol. 5v* yet adopted. These Masses are no *Stoneconstructions*, they are cutt out of an artificial rock; The joints are not regular on them, and must not have been calculated to be seen.

25 On some of the oldest edifices, as for instance on the *Pyramids* and in the oldest part of the temple of Karnac the principle of *Coating* remains visible, The Sandstones are covered with Coatings of Granite.

There is a moulding in Aeg. Architecture, one of the two which the Aegyptians knew, which seems to me to be a reminiscence of the oldest Style. I mean the Slab round the angels 30 of the walls, which may have originally had the destination to cover the joints of the covering slates. Our carpenters emploi the same moulding | on similar occasions.   6.   *fol. 6r*

The columns of the Aegyptians have partly the appearance of reed bunds, fastened together with an envelopping carpet and surrounding the pillar;

The forth path of development of the constructiv principle was made by the Greeks; we shall 35 see next what they made out of the panneld style, and how the constructiv principle of ornamental Art and Architecture was carried out. under the Romans.

447.2–3 **and since ~ Persians,**] *inserted*   447.3 **pannelated**] *'panelled' (see also 448.28)*
447.4 **lais**] *'lies'*   **it**] *inserted before del.* the   **the**] *after del.* on the rests of the monuments
after del. the   447.6–7 **The records ~ and Josephus book ~ contain ~ details about
this subject**] *see the descriptions of Solomon's Temple and Palace in the Books of Kings (1 Kings
6–7), the Books of Chronicles (2 Chronicles 3–4) and Flavius Josephus, Antiquities of the Jews,
8.61–94, 8.130–40; cf. 440, Explanatory Notes 133.15–16*   447.7 **details**] *repl. del.* revelations
447.12 **mouveable**] mouvea- ¦ (ble *missing)*   **hut**] *after del.* barr[a] *(for 'barrack')*   447.13
throw] *'through'*   447.14 **are testimonies**] *after del.* shows the progress in art, which
447.15 **Yews**] *'Jews'*   447.17 **wooden**] *after del.* panneld   447.22 **precious**] *after del.*
beautiful   447.30 **Staff**] *'stuff'*   **Goathares**] *'goat hair'*   447.31 **read**] *'red'*   447.33

stringes] *'strings'*   447.35 **drapperies**] *after del.* mouveable   447.37 **de**] *'the'*   447.39
covered] *after del.* entirely   **Cealing**] *'ceiling'; repl. del.* Roof   447.43 **sculptured**] *after
del.* hidden   **Palm-leaves**] Palm-|leaves   447.44 **Winged Lyons**] *'winged lions'; after
del.* Cherubims or
448.1 **plated**] *after del.* guilt   448.8 **Very interesting**] *after del.* Another living illustration of   448.10 **The Roof**] *after del.* Each of the Elements th[ ] *after del.* and have never
been combined and stand isolated toget   448.11 **shrines**] *'screens' (cf. 518, Explanatory
Notes 196.25)*   **hollow**] *after del.* feable   448.12 **Wall**] *altered from* Wan *(for 'Wand')*
448.17 **Polychromy in architecture and Sculpture**] *repl. del.* A System of Polychromy,
probably very related to that of the Antik nations,   Antik] *'antique'*   448.26–32 **The
Assyrians ~ accord perfectly with what we**] *cf. deleted passage at the end of MS 124 (435–
6, Alterations in the Manuscript 126.38)*   448.27 **maid**] *'made'*   448.28–9 **Assyrian tapestries**] *after del.* celebrated   448.31 **Lyons**] *'lions'*   448.45–6 **Other representations ~
English.**] *repl. del.*

The[1] Appearanceces[2] of other subjects[3] on Assyrian Slates such like battles, Hunting parties Ceremonies,[4] look still more like embroideries than these large figures do. They are
treated in the same Style as the celebrated Bayeux drappery with the battles between the
English

> 1 **The**] *after del.* The fact of being sculptured imitations of Tapestries   2 **Appear-
> anceces**] ces *added*   3 **subjects**] *repl. del.* representations   4 **Ceremonies,**] *be-
> fore del.* and others

449.1 **Plates**] *in pencil repl. del. in pencil* Slabs   Slabs] *above del.* Stones,   449.2 **freestones,**] *before del.* which   449.6 **The second**] *after del.* We will see now   449.9 **general Style**] *after del.* style   449.11 **For inst.**] *accompanied in opposite column by probably
Hans Semper's note in ink* For instance   **bronze-covered**] bronze-|covered   449.13 **are**]
after del. is   **the Morble Doors and the**] *inserted before del.* the appearence of the   of
the] *before interl. and undel.* D   449.14 **unburnt**] *'unbaked'*   449.16 **some thing**] some|
thing   **angels**] *'angles' (see also 449.29)*   449.18 **constructively**] *after del.* more   449.21
the old type] *after del.* the old type has been bannished substantially, not more   449.22
on them.] *inserted before del.* on fol. 5v but nevertheless it shows itself at many parts.
449.23 **These Masses**] *after del.* The Stone walls are   **rock;**] *altered from* ~, *before del.*
prepared for this purpose bef   449.29 **angels**] *after del.* corners   449.32 **bunds**] *'bundles'*
449.33 **an envelopping**] *after del.* strings and   **pillar;**] *after del.* constructiv *and before del.*
Other indices of this transitional State of Aeg. Architecture are visible in the tumbs
tumbs] *'tombs'*   449.34 **The forth path**] *after two del. beginnings of variant:*

The fourth path toward the Emancipation of the matter[1] in construction and decoration[2]
was made in Greece; but their Architecture was under this point of vieuw little more advanced than the Aegyptian was.

———————

The fourth path towards the Emancipation of the Mate[r]

> 1 **matter**] *after del.* constructiv   2 **in construction and decoration**] *inserted*

449.34 **forth**] *'fourth'*   449.35 **next**] *before del. in pencil* time   **panneld style**] *repl. del.*
principle   principle] *before del. in* question   449.36 **was**] *after del.* only was invented by
the Romans. and carried out in   **out.**] *in pencil repl. del. in pencil* out only

The Ancient Practice of Wall Coating and Tubular Construction 451

MS 130[1]

The Greecs were a heap of tribes, not much distant in civilisation from the condition of the *fol. 1r*
American Indians, while Assyria and Egypt were already the seats of highly developped
forms of society. So it was natural that The former took up and overkame the types for their
institutions and for their art at a period, when the last were not more understood in their
proper and material sense. The Greecs remained faithfull to these traditional types, but they
took them up in a higher symbolical sense. ¦
The accuracy and beauty of Greec Stoneconstruction has never been reached since, but their *fol. 1v*
edifices are sculptured, and not constructed in stone.
Also they did not show the stone in its natural appearance; it was generally coverd with a
thin coating of Stucco which last was painted and ornamented after the ancient principle;
This was even the case for white marble monuments, which last material was adopted principally for the reason, because the marble surface was favorable and indispensable for a new
invented process that of Encaustic painting, unknown to the Aegyptians and to the Assyrians;
Many parts of the Greec buildings chiefly those which from the beginning have the destination to be ornamented with sculptured and painted subjects, show the antique slab construction. Such are for instance the tympanons or fields ¦ of the pediments, the opaea, which *fol. 2r*
in the oldest types of Doric architecture were Apertures between the Triglyphs, the friezes,
which turn round the outer walls of the Doric temples, forming a rich bandeau of sculptured
represantations, finally the slabs which formed a sort of sculptured parapet between the
Columns like those on the Egyptian temples, all these parts remember the old style of
Slabconstruction; and the same is even visible on the more constructiv parts of the building
which are hollowed out, as we see here on this section of the Parthenon entablement.
These instances show that the ancient principle was in reality not entirely laid aside with the
Greecs, but they took it up in a higher symbolical sense. – ¦
By examining the Assyrian and Egyptian monuments we observe the following. *fol. 2v*
1°) The elements of construction are not very much more connected together than on the
Chinese buildings
2°) the ornamental parts are as it were fastened round the kernet of construction, they are
mere applications
3°) The ornamental Symbols have a historical or a political or a religious sense, but they have
no relation to the constructiv and dynamical function of that part of the building whereto it
is applied.
On the Greec monuments in the contrary we observe
1°) an intimate connection of all the different elements of construction, which even in some
cases are combined in a not quite justifiable manner to a general Ensemble. Instances the
walls supporters of

> 451.1 **The Greecs**] *after seven del. beginnings of variant:*
>
> Religious[1] and political principles, which
> Like in nature, th
> They Greecs have borrowed or inherited the old forms from the barbarians of earlier[2]
> civilisation, and by

Like[3] nature produced its most perfect[4] creation, *mankind*, after having fixd the types for all the qualities which are united in the man
Like nature created its
like it was the case with their religious and political institutions.
They

> 1 **Religious]** *after del.* principles of   2 **earlier]** *above del.* older   3 **Like]** L *over* l
> 4 **most perfect]** *after del.* best

451.3 **So it was natural that]** *interl.*   **overkame]** *'overcame', here misused for 'received' (see 439, Explanatory Notes 131.23)*   451.4 **art]** *before del.* ready made but   451.5–6 **proper and material sense ~ symbolical sense.]** *inserted after del.* first meaning. But they took them up in a new form and with a new idea, by taking   took them up in a] *inserted before del.* combined those elements in a   451.5 **proper]** *above del.* original   **faithfull]** *before del.* observers of the   451.6 **sense.]** *before del.* This is true for the General Character of their architecture, which will be shown in one of the following lectures, but it is also true for 451.7 **The accuracy]** *after del.* on fol. 1r

Thus we observe the Stone constructed buildings of the Greecs materially not very progressed towards the new principle as compared with Aegyptian architecture. Although[1] the Accuracy of workmanship of Stonecutting

> 1 **Although]** *after del.* The constructiv elements of the building are more

451.7 **reached since,]** *before del.* it is true,   451.7–8 **but ~ stone.]** *repl. del.*

but nevertheless this material was not yet entirely[1] emancipated with the Greecs. Their monuments[2] are Sculptured but not constructed in stone.

> 1 **yet entirely]** *repl. del.* more   more] *after del.* yet   2 **with the Greecs. Their monuments]** *repl. del.* with the Greecs than it was under the Aegyptians. The tempels

451.9 **Also ~ generally]** *inserted after del.* The stones were *after del.* A great *after del.* All the *after del.*

The stones[1], and even the white marble of the Athenian temples were covered with coatings of picture and ornamented[2] with motivs[3], which mostly[4] take their origines from the art of weaving.

> 1 **The stones]** *after del.* They   2 **ornamented]** *after del.* over and over   3 **motivs]** *after del.* painte   4 **mostly]** *below del.* altogether

451.13 **that of Encaustic painting]** *repl. del.* of Wall-painting   Wall-painting] Wall- | painting   451.17 **opaea]** *repl. del.* triglyphs and frieses   frieses] '*friezes*'   451.18 **Triglyphs,]** *before del.* which last formed the supports of the frame-work of the roofs; the frame-work] frame- | work   frieses] '*friezes*'   451.19 **rich]** *above del.* richly ornamented 451.23 **are]** *after del.* general   **entablement]** '*entablature*'   451.24 **principle]** *repl. del.* mode of construction   451.25 **they took]** *after del.* now it remains to be proved that 451.29 **round]** *after del.* only   **kernet]** '*kernel*', here misused for '*core*'   451.31 **3°)]** *after del.* 3°) the sense of the ornamental-symbols has no relation to the constructiv or dynamical function of the part of the building, whereto they are applied, they give historical, polit-

The Ancient Practice of Wall Coating and Tubular Construction

453

ical, religious and other notices, which have nothing to do with artistical feeling   orna-
mental-symbols] ornamental- | symbols *(ornamental- inserted)*   451.32 **and dynamical**]
inserted before del. or historical   451.34 **On**] *after del.* We observe the opposite of all this
on   451.36–7 **in a not quite justifiable manner ~ supporters of**] *inserted after del.* in a
manner, which is not justifiable before   451.36 **general**] *after del.* common

MS 130[2]

I may now be allowed to give some additional notices about the different specialities of in-   *fol. 4r*
dustrial art, which derive from and are connected with the same principle of coating.

On the early style of Metalconstruction and of Metalornamentation.
Man in his material state is more anxious about ornament than the habiliments of his body.
5   and the earliest attempts in the art of decorating and ornamenting are made on things
which have no practical utility
Goldleaves employed as ornaments by the Indians on the discovery of America by Columbus and Cortez.
Such Ornaments in Gold- Silver- and Tinleaves with stamped and pierced ornaments and
10   figures have been found in Aegyptian and Etruscan tombs. Br. M. ¦
So the processes of Stamping and engraving metalsheeds and bending the sheeds into cer-   *fol. 4v*
tain forms was probably the first treatment of Metal Afterwards the Art of enchasing cabochon stones and the filigran work came into application. Very early Egyptian ornaments
with inlaid Stones and pearls are at the Brittish Museum.
15   The inlaid stones lead to the invention of artificial stones and of the process of Enameling.

453.1 **I**] *above del.* We   **additional**] *above del.* Short   453.3 **On ~ Metalornamentation.**]
repl. underl. and del. On Dresses and ornaments.   453.5 **earliest**] *above del.* first   **made**]
after del. independant from the u   453.7 **Goldleaves**] *after del.* Metall employed *after
three del. beginnings of variant:*

I shall therefore begin with the ornaments as being connected with the question about
textile art[1] and such arts which derive from the last –[2]
I shall omitt the feather and teath[3] ornaments of the Savages and begin with the Metallic
ornaments.
I shall only speek of metallic and stone ornaments, as [ ]

1 **textile art**] *after del.* dresses and   2 **last –**] *before del.* Metalsheeds are the earliest
and most simple orna   Metalsheeds] *'Metal sheets'*   3 **teath**] *'teeth'*

453.10 **Br. M.**] *'British Museum'*   453.11 **metalsheeds**] *'metal sheets'*   **sheeds**] *'sheets'*
453.12–13 **cabochon**] *after inserted and del.* coloured   453.13 **the**] *after del.* that of   453.15
lead] *'led'; after del.* let *after del.* were replaced

454   Lectures

Classification of Vessels

TEXTUAL RECORD

MS 133   gta, 20-Ms-133, fols. 1r–14v (14r–v blank), in Semper's hand, *copy-text*
Semper 1884   'Klassifikation der Gefässe', 18–34, German trans. of MS 133; for details of
               this translation, see Herrmann 1981, 156–7

BIBLIOGRAPHY Van Zanten 1977b, 249–50; Herrmann 1981, 33, 111, 156–7; Herrmann
1984, 145–6; Hauser 1985, 105–6; Waenerberg 1992, 64–5; Mallgrave 1996, 216–17; Gnehm
2004, 218–21; Squicciarino 2009, 339–42; Poerschke 2016, 61–4, 66, 69–70, 77; Chestnova
2021, 125–6, 128–30

EXPLANATORY NOTES

In discussing ceramic art, Semper diverges considerably from the initial intentions expressed in the 'Prospectuses of the Lectures on Art' (96.17–19). Firstly, he devotes not one
but three lectures to the subject (see 393); and secondly, he scarcely discusses the topics
announced in the spring of 1853, 'On the Connexion of Ceramic Art with the art of Metal
casting' and 'Its influence on architecture and the other arts'. He mentions metal casting
explicitly only once (136.22) and touches only faintly on the influence of ceramic art (136.16–
31, 137.36–40). The first divergence can probably be explained by the fact that Semper
considers that ceramic art is the most important of all the industrial arts 'for the general
history of art and for artistical science' (135.27–8), since he regards it as having major significance 'with all the nations at all times' and strong direct and indirect influences on monumental, architectural art (136.26–31). The fact that he nevertheless places ceramic art in the
second class of industrial arts (116.38–9, 122.5–6) and discusses it in second place in the
lecture series may therefore seem inconsistent. But the contradiction can be resolved by
Semper's remark that the art of covering, 'by giving the first motives for monumental decoration', had an earlier influence on 'the general artistic education' than the other industrial
arts (122.37–9). The second divergence is more difficult to explain than the first. It may be
due to the fact that the topics 'On the Connexion of Ceramic Art with the art of Metal
casting' and 'Its influence on architecture and the other arts' would have required too much
involvement with material questions, which Semper considered secondary, and with tectonics, which he intended to discuss in a later lecture.
None of Semper's other lectures was structured more systematically than the three on
ceramic art. This was probably one reason why large parts of the lecture manuscripts on
ceramics were later incorporated into his 'Kunstformenlehre' (Theory of Art Forms) and
Style in the Technical and Tectonic Arts. Semper starts the first lecture with an etymological
explanation of the words 'pottery' and 'ceramic' and with remarks on the historical significance of ceramic art, returning to the comparison of the Egyptian *situla* – which he now
calls *situlus* – with the Greek *hydria* (137.5–40). He had already discussed this comparison in
the inaugural lecture and had mentioned it for the first time in 'Practical Art in Metals and
hard Materials' (107.4–108.2; NAL, 86.FF.64, art. 3.2, 117, 119–20; cf. Semper 2007a, 210,

Classification of Vessels
455

212–13). After a few remarks on bibliographic matters, and with support from Jules Ziegler's *Études céramiques* (Ziegler 1850), he explains the basic forms of ceramic vessels and the combined forms derived from them (138.1–140.14). From this geometrically descriptive explanation – illustrated with a few examples – Semper moves on to distinguishing the functions that determine the shapes of vessels: storing, scooping and pouring (140.21–28). Following these functions and a fourth, hybrid function, drinking, he divides the vessels into four classes, which he discusses and provides examples of in detail (141.16–145.8). He closely follows the corresponding sections of 'Practical Art in Metals and hard Materials' (NAL, 86.FF.64, art. 3.2, 98–142; cf. Semper 2007a, 191–227). Finally, he explains a few rules related to the ornamentation of the individual parts of vessels (145.9–146.24). The mechanical justification provided for these recalls the definition of the craft product as a machine, as mentioned in the inaugural lecture (111.32–112.8).

135.29–31 **The word pottery ~ drinking cup.**] These sentences are translated almost verbatim from Alexandre Brongniart's *Traité des arts céramiques ou des poteries* (Brongniart 1844, 1:3), which Semper follows closely, particularly in the third lecture on ceramics (see 468).
136.5–9 **The Greec name for pottery ~ analogical applications.**] These sentences are also translated almost verbatim from Brongniart's *Traité* (Brongniart 1844, 1:3). In *Kleine Schriften*, they are replaced with a sentence that has the opposite meaning (Semper 1884, 18): 'The Greek word for pot is κέραμος, which originally referred merely to clay, i.e. the material of the vessel.' In his 'Theory of Art Forms', Semper himself had implicitly rejected Brongniart's derivation of the word 'ceramic' by translating κέραμος as 'the clay, the plastic earth' (Vieweg Archives, V3:1.1.3.32, sect. 'Ceramics', 2); and in *Style* he explained that the word 'ceramic' 'in the first place suggests only the material to be handled, namely the clay (κέραμος)' (Semper 1860/63, 2:1).   136.8–9 **applications.**] This is followed by a deleted passage on the *rhyton* (see 458, Alterations in the Manuscript 136.8–9), which possibly borrows from Brongniart's *Traité* and Joseph Marryat's *Collections towards a History of Pottery and Porcelain* (Brongniart 1844, 1:3–4; Marryat 1850, 285).   136.10–12 **But the signification ~ was afterwards extended ~ even to the terra cotta sculptures.**] cf. Brongniart 1844, 1:4; Marryat 1850, 260   136.11 **unburnt**] *unbaked*   136.16–19 **The vases of Gold ~ settled by potters.**] cf. Semper 2007a, 190   136.38 **burnt**] *fired*   136.39 **mor**] *more*
137.5–40 **I had at an other occasion the opportunity ~ Nile-pail;**] cf. 107.4–108.2   137.12 **Jokes**] *yokes*   137.18 **chaped**] *shaped*   137.30–1 **monteneer inhabitants**] *mountaineers*
138.1 **possede**] derived from French *posséder: possess*   138.2 **work of Brogniard, traité des arts ceramiques**] Brongniart 1844   138.3–4 **history of pottery by Marriat**] Marryat 1850
138.7–8 **Ziegler ~ Etudes Ceramiques**] Ziegler 1850   138.10–11 **He gives a Sheme ~ which I reproduced here**] The scheme is presented in Jules Ziegler's *Études céramiques* under the heading 'Classification et nomenclature' (Ziegler 1850, 40–2). Semper attached a copy of the same illustrated scheme to 'Practical Art in Metals and hard Materials' (Semper 2007a, 227), and he also reproduced the scheme in *Style* (Semper 1860/63, 2:80–1). In contrast to Semper, Thomas Delf – under the pseudonym Charles Martel – printed Ziegler's illustrated scheme in his *Principles of Form in Ornamental Art* in 1856 without naming its author (Martel 1856, frontispiece, ix–x).   138.18 **Cylinder**] cf. Ziegler 1850, 71–8   138.19 **Conoid**] cf. Ziegler 1850, 79–85   138.20 **Clavoid**] cf. Ziegler 1850, 91–7   138.23 **Spere**] uncertain reading, *sphere*   **thre**] *three*   138.25 **Spheroid**] cf. Ziegler 1850, 98–101   138.26 **Ovoid**] cf. Ziegler 1850, 109–13   138.27 **Ogivoid**] cf. Ziegler 1850, 102–8. In a deleted passage, Semper oddly enough describes the pineapple not as a spheroid, but as 'an Ogivoide of great

beauty by its general form and by its natural ornamentation' (see 459, Alterations in the Manuscript 138.40). In *Style*, he replaces 'Ogivoid' with 'Umgekehrtes Ovoïd' (inverted ovoid; Semper 1860/63, 2:81).

139.2 **Austrich**] derived from French *autruche*: *ostrich*; cf. 459, Alterations in the Manuscript 139.2   139.14 **Canopian form**] cf. Ziegler 1850, 114–16, 118–20   139.17 **Phoceenform**] *Phocaean form*; cf. Ziegler 1850, 114, 117–20   139.21–3 **The Phocean form ~ of upper Egypt, ~ the Nile pale ~ of the lower Country ~ called Canopus.**] 'pale': *pail* (see also 139.24). This sentence suggests that the Nile pail had a Canopic form, but Hans Semper correctly noted in MS 133 that the Nile pail corresponded to the Phocaean form (see 459, Alterations in the Manuscript 139.21–3). In *Kleine Schriften*, 'the Nile pale' is accordingly replaced with 'die kanopische Form' (Semper 1884, 23). Semper himself confirms in the next sentence of the draft lecture that the shape of the Nile pail was Phocaean (139.23–4).   139.25 **momies**] French for *mummies*   139.34 **Corolle ~ first third of its hight**] cf. Ziegler 1850, 120   139.36 **Corolle ~ Second theird of the hight**] cf. Ziegler 1850, 120   139.37 **Campanula**] cf. Ziegler 1850, 120–1   139.38 **tiges**] cf. Ziegler 1850, 121   139.39 **distinguable**] French for *distinguishable*

140.1 **Crateroids and discoids**] cf. Ziegler 1850, 121–3   140.13–14 **This diagramm ~ denominations**] cf. Ziegler 1850, 125   140.13 **vase mixt**] *vase of mixed form*; cf. Ziegler 1850, 125 and fig.: 'un vase de forme mixte'   140.14 **Composite Vase**] cf. Ziegler 1850, 125 fig.: 'un vase composite'   140.20 **first Consideration**] In *Kleine Schriften*, Manfred and Hans Semper note that Semper dealt with the second consideration in a separate 'treatise' (Semper 1884, 25 n. *). The 'treatise' referred to is the lecture 'Influence of the Materials and Their Treatments upon the Development of Ceramic Types and Style' (151–60).   140.21 **distinct**] Poerschke 2016, 63, has 'different'.   **devide**] *divide*   140.24 **holding a containing**] ~ *or* ~ (cf. 141.16, 146.16–17). Poerschke 2016, 63, has 'holding or containing'.

141.31 **uns**] *urns*   **Unrs**] *urns*

142.13 **vessels of state**] In *Kleine Schriften*, this phrase is translated as 'Prachtgefässe' (Semper 1884, 27).   142.28 **Gold Patera found at Rennes**] cf. Semper 2007a, 201   142.29 **Sardonyx Cup**] In 'Practical Art in Metals and hard Materials', Semper notes under '*Basins with convex bottoms requiring a stand to rest upon*' (2007b, 198–9; italics in original): 'A rare Vessel of this kind is the Costly Sardonyx Cup, six inches in diamater, richly ornamented on both sides, preserved at Naples, perforated in the centre by an unskillful Artist, and originally intended of stand upon a golden Tripod.' With the exception of the diameter, this description matches the Tazza Farnese (Farnese Cup), which is today held in the National Archeological Museum of Naples – known as the Real Museo Borbonico in Semper's time.   142.30–2 **The inside is coverd with a flat Goldplate ~ which can be separated from the body of the cup ~ an Emblem in the first sense of the word.**] These sentences are inserted beside the text column without any mark indicating their position in the text (see 460, Alterations in the Manuscript 142.30–2). In *Kleine Schriften*, the corresponding sentences precede the remarks on the sardonyx bowl and thus relate to the Patera of Rennes (Semper 1884, 28). This relation is confirmed by the fact that Semper notes in 'Practical Art in Metals and hard Materials', concerning the '*Gold-Patera* discovered at Rennes' (2007b, 201; italics in original): 'the bottom is ornamented with a Composition in repousse Work which can be separated from the body of the Cup. This is what the Ancients called an *Emblem* in the first Material sense of the Word … see Magazin pittoresque 1851'. The implied report, which appeared with three illustrations in the nineteenth volume of *Le Magasin pittoresque*, contains three sentences that were evidently misunderstood by Semper (Magasin pittoresque 1851a, 199; italics in original): 'La patère a été fondue tout unie. Le fond est orné d'une composition exécutée au repoussé qui se détache de la coupe: c'est ce que les anciens appelaient l'*emblêma.*' These sentences mean that the Patera of Rennes was cast as a single unit and that the base, whose inside is decorated with repoussé, differs from the rest of the bowl artistically.   142.30 **rihly**] *richly*   142.36 **Holy Graal at Genova**] 'Graal': French for *Grail*; the so-called Sacro Catino in the Cathedral of San Lorenzo at Genoa   142.37 **flet**] *flat* 142.39 **the take**] *they ~*

143.2 **subverted**] *inverted*   143.20 **Le Moyen Age et la Renaissance**] Lacroix/Seré 1848/51   143.21 **Mediaeval spoons**] cf. Lacroix/Seré 1848/51, 3: four unnumbered coloured plates under the titles 'Orfèvrerie religieuse' and 'Orfèvrerie civile'

144.4–5 **spouded**] *spouted*   144.6 **Spoud**] *spout* (see also 144.21, 145.35)   144.24 **Bures**] derived from French *buire*: ewers (see also 144.26); cf. Semper 1860/63, 2:62–4   144.26 **Mayolicaʌ Enamel**] probably *maiolica, enamel*; cf. Semper 1884, 31   144.29 **Evers**] *ewers* 144.33 **Geek**] *Greek*

145.2 **bespoken**] derived from German *besprechen: discussed*   145.8 **solemnel**] merged from French *solennel* and English *solemn*   145.9–10 **remarks about the laws of ornamentation of vessels**] Semper borrows points in these remarks from Karl Bötticher's *Tektonik der Hellenen.* Under the heading 'Abstecher von den Geräthen', he had taken excerpts from Bötticher's remarks on vessels and candelabras in the British Museum Library in 1852 (gta, 20-Ms-150c, ed. in Gnehm 2004, 218–21; cf. Bötticher 1844/52, 1:42–57).   145.11–15 **Every vase ~ appearance**] cf. Bötticher 1844/52, 1:42   145.19–20 **Like it is necessary ~ mouveability.**] cf. Bötticher 1844/52, 1:42. Wolfgang Herrmann incorrectly claimed that Semper emphasized the fundamental difference between utensil and monument 'for the first time in "Die Theorie des Formell-Schönen"' (Herrmann 1984, 145), i.e. in the introduction to the 'Theory of Art Forms'.   145.25 **Stowly**] *slowly*   145.27 **Fisher**] *Vischer*   **Sebaldus monument**] cf. 84.34–41; 362, Explanatory Notes 84.34–8   145.30 **vanted**] *wanted* 145.32–7 **A composite Vessel, has ~ handles.**] cf. Bötticher 1844/52, 1:43   145.39 **rifled**] derived from German *riffeln: grooved*   145.40 **rifles**] derived from German *Riffel: grooves* 146.1 **f.e.**] *for example*   146.6 **structive**] *structural*   146.7 **Rubans**] *rubans*: French for *ribbons*

EDITORIAL EMENDATIONS

141.10 **Ground forms**] Ground | forms   144.24 **Hand-washing**] Hand- | washing   145.6 **semi-ovoidal**] semi- | ovoidal

ALTERATIONS IN THE MANUSCRIPT

135.27–8 **The most important ~ industry**] *above del.* Among the different branches of industry the most important   Among ~ important] *accompanied in opposite column by del.*

Among[1] the different branches of practical art the[2] most important for the history of art and for artistical[3] science is the Ceramic art, of which I shall try to give some notions in the following. –
The potters art is after the[4] textile art[5] and that of manufacturing veapons that, which has been cultivated by men the first.[6]

1 **Among**] *after del.* There is no other branch of practical art   2 **the**] *after del.* there is none which   3 **artistical**] *after del.* science is   4 **the**] *inserted*   5 **textile art**] *after del.* the art of cloating   the] *undel.*   cloating] *'clothing'*   6 **first.**] *altered from* ~∧ *before del.* and which has been everywhere the first

135.27 **general**] *interl.*   135.28 **perhaps**] *interl.*   135.31 **object**] *altered from* objects *before del.* which were understood. with it   with it] *interl. (with repl. del. by)*
136.1 **Another name**] *after del.* Another name for this branch of art is taken from the Greecs, *after del.* There is another Word, the   this branch of art] *above del.* potteries   136.6 **but the horn of an animal**] *underl. in pencil probably by Manfred Semper and accompanied in opposite column by Manfred Semper's note in pencil* Κέρας Siehe Styl, II Bd. pag 1.   **Κέρας**] *'κέρας': Greek for 'horn'*   136.7 **has been**] *after inserted and del.* occasionally *and before del.* maintained its antique right   136.8–9 **applications.**] *before del.*

This[1] form was very usual with the ancients even at the time of their highest artistical development. It then became ornamented with heads of Lyons[2], eagles[3], dogs, stags and other sculptures, and garnished with precious stones and gems. In this later period the horn-shaped drinking cup, that original wessel, was calld Rhiton.

1 **This**] *after del.* In the *after del.* The Greecs called their horn shaped drinking vassel   vassel] *'vessel'*   2 **Lyons**] *'lions'*   3 **eagles**] *after del.* birds

136.10 **But**] *after five del. beginnings of variant in opposite column:*

Thus we are fully justified when we take the expression[1] Ceramic[2] art and even that of pottery in a wider sense in understanding with it all the
But the proper sense
This word, *ceramic art*, comprehends all the productions of the potter, from the brick and the tile

---

Thus we are fully justified by taking the expression ceramic art in our own sense, and
Afterwards the entire domain of the potters craft, from the brick to the finest[3] earthen Vase and even to the terra Cotta sculptures were comprehended, at[4] their precedence by the

1 **expression**] *above del.* word   2 **Ceramic**] *after del.* pott   3 **finest**] *before del.* and richest ornamented   4 **at**] *after del.* by the Greecks and

136.10 **the**] *after del.* her   her] *referring to female German noun 'Töpferei' (pottery): 'its'*
signification] *after del.* first   136.14 **or**] *above del.* and   136.17 **wood**] *above del.* other precious materials   136.18 **natural and traditional laws of generation and**] *after del.* traditional and natural laws of formation and   136.24 **in statuary**] *after del.* for   136.25 **division.**] *before del.* But the first consideration must be paid to the products of pottery properly speaking.   pottery] *underl.*   136.29 **parts**] *after del.* ornamen   **materially**] *inserted*   **adopting**] *above del.* assuming   136.30 **ornamentation**] *repl. del.* eurithmy 136.31 **and**] *repl. del.* by potters and   136.32 **pottery**] *above del.* the potters art   136.37 **conservation**] con *above del.* pre   136.38 **The burnt clay**] *after del.* The material *after del.* The softest *after del.* These fragil works

137.4 **Show me]** *after del.* Show me some Urns which bel[o]   137.5 **tell]** *after del.* be able to
137.6 **forms]** *after del.* kinds   137.10 **of the Nile,]** *after del.* of a River,   137.11 **Gift of the
Nile.]** *before del.* They have no running fountains in the Valley of the Nile.   137.14 **lowest,]**
repl. del. bottom   137.24 **feat]** *after del.* task   137.28–9 **a second person ~ woman]** *repl.
del.* assistance   137.37 **sacred]** *after del.* Secondary   137.38 **type for]** *repl. del.* model of
137.39 **in]** *repl. del.* for
138.1 **some]** *above del.* many   many] *above del.* some   **Ceramical art,]** *before del.* and rich
collections of engravings but the material has at yet been treated technically and historically rather than artistically.   technically] *after del.* more by scientifical men and by arc[h]
(probably for 'archaeologists') **which]** *above del.* the first   138.8 **Etudes Ceramiques]** *inserted in opposite column without insertion mark beside the manuscript line* artist and manufacturer *at 138.7*   138.10 **He gives a Sheme]** *after del.*

He gives an Classification of[1] the works of Ceramic art after the fundamental forms to
which they belong, which I shall reproduce here as being usefull, allthough it shows not the
relations which exist between the forms and the destinations of the things and the material
which is employed.

> 1 **of]** *del. after del.* of the different forms which occur in *and before del.* the Ceramic w   w]
> *after del.* forms o[f]

138.11 **gives]** *after del.* shows not the relations which   138.12 **among]** *repl. del.* between
138.14 **He derives]** *after del.* He classifies   138.17 **From the first derive]** *after del.* From
these he de[r]   138.30 **it appears]** *after del.* it has no direction towards a certain upper and
lower part, no   138.34 **Ellipsoid;]** *after del.* Spheroid,   138.39 **architecture;]** *altered from*
~, *before del.* where it forms the   138.40 **The Ovoid]** *after del.* The pineappel is an Ogivoide
of great beauty by its general form and by its natural ornamentation; the Eggs and the Flam
(for 'Flames')
139.2 **Austrich]** s *inserted*   **clay or marble and]** *inserted after del.* Stone and   139.3 **the]**
above del. a very   **oldest]** est *added*   139.12–13 **I. Such ~ inside:]** *inserted*   139.21–3 **The
Phocean form ~ Canopus.]** *accompanied in opposite column by Hans Semper's notes in ink ?
and* (Die phokäische Form entspricht nach Stil II p. 80 E. 1. dem Nileimer.)   phokäische]
underl.   139.21 **Phocean]** *above del.* Canopian   139.22 **upper Egypt,]** *after del.* lower
Egypt,   **while the Nile pale]** *underl. in black ink probably by Hans Semper*   **the lower
Country]** *after del.* Lower   139.31 **Some]** *above del.* The   **Columns]** *before del.* themselves   139.41 **are very important]** *after del.* form without accessories very beautiful
form] *above del.* are applicable
140.1 **are the Crateroids]** *after del.* are those which derive   are] *undel.*   140.4 **inside
and]** *before del.* have no   140.10 **Nevertheless]** *repl. del.* But   140.13 **three prncipal]**
above del. different   140.16 **by taking these forms and their ornamentations as]** *repl.
del.* Their forms and ornaments   Their forms and ornaments] *repl. del.* first from the point
of   140.17 **supposed uses]** *after del.* symbolical uses,   140.18 **come]** *after del.* are
140.21 **preside]** *after del.* direct   140.22 **as]** *after del.* to
141.1 **Vessel,]** *altered from* ~∧ *before del.* invented   141.10 **By connecting]** *after del.* The
most ancient Vessels are without feet   **Ground forms]** *after del.* original   141.12 **accessory Components]** *after del.* Accessories   141.20–2 **The Spanish Tinajas ~ Reser-
voirs]** *inserted in opposite column without insertion mark, starting alongside the manuscript line*

antique Dolia are nearly *at 141.19* 141.23 **The**] *after del.* An Egyp **dolia**] *after del.* oldest
141.23–4 **small apertures ~ lower end and**] *repl. undel.* no feet, feet,] *altered from ~∧*
before del. and 141.23 **no necks,**] *before del.* no handles 141.25 **Deriving forms**] *after del.*
When the orifices of the Dolia become wider, they take the character of Amphorae and
141.26 **dolia**] *after del.* small **high**] *after del.* higher 141.30 **no necks,**] *before del.* wide
openings and 141.36 **The Urns with feet**] *after del.* In the high Classic Age these urns
became low feet; became] *derived from German 'bekommen': 'obtained'*
142.1 **class**] *after del.* derived for[m] 142.8 **whole**] *after del.* Crater 142.13 **vessels**] *after*
del. first 142.14 **Villa Albani,**] *before del.* The vase of the Museum Barberini 142.15
Class.] *altered from ~∧ before del.* of Craters. Craters] *underl.* 142.20 **Tanks,**] *altered*
from ~∧ before del. or **or Basins**] *inserted* 142.23 **There**] *after del.* They are convex on
the lower part 142.24 **rest**] *before del.* upon 142.28 **the Gold Patera ~ now**] *repl. del.* is
a Gold Basin Gold] *after del.* Silv 142.30–2 **The inside ~ word.**] *inserted in opposite*
column without insertion mark, starting alongside the manuscript line Paris library and the celebrated *at 142.29 (cf. 456–7, Explanatory Notes 142.30–2)* 142.30 **inside**] *above del.* outside
coverd] *above del.* ornamented 142.31 **separated**] *after del.* taken 142.35 **sacrifices.**]
altered from ~∧ before del. with the pagants, pagants,] *altered from ~∧ before del.* and
the] *inserted after del.* on *fol. 8v* adopted in the **form**] *before del.* which is one of the sacred
for 142.37 **flet**] *before del.* and low
143.1 **Cups**] s *added* **are**] *after del.* in Silver is 143.4 **Christianity**] *after del.* our 143.6
Division] *above del.* Class of **for**] *after del.* are such, which 143.11 **religious**] *after del.*
very 143.16 **antiquity**] *after del.* old 143.17 **numbered**] *after del.* were 143.18 **are as**
many] *repl. del.* schow the 143.19 **proofs**] *after del.* artfull feeling 143.21 **Mediaeval**
spoons] *after del.* Silver 143.23 **As the type for the**] *repl. del.* As The second As] *in-*
serted after del. We scarcely possede an Example of an antique funnel as a selfstanding Vase
and **considered**] *above del.* mentionned 143.26 **signification**] tion *over* nce 143.29
Division contains] *repl. del.* types are types] *after del.* great division 143.39 **medi-**
aeval times.] *before del.* An especially important kind of Vessels, nearly related to this division are the lamps which have had at all times a highly religious and Symbolical meaning
and are of considerable importance even in private life. lamps] *underl.* 143.40 **this**
form,] *before del.* the pouring form **Art**] *after del.* fine
144.4 **Ancient and modern**] *after del.* The richness and beauty of forms, which the ancient
lamps show – is **combinations**] *after del.* other *and before del.* where the 144.21 **The**
Egyptians] *after del.* The old 144.21–2 **the ancient writers**] *after del.* Apulejus and
144.22 **a small modell in**] *repl. del.* a small collection of small Egyptian 144.24–5 **The**
Arabian Bures ~ Vessels, which] *inserted* 144.25 **were also**] *above del.* This form was
144.27 **judiciously**] *after del.* an judicious use of new technical and use] *after del.* conception of the 144.30 **tell**] *repl. del.* have
145.3 **esspecial**] *altered from* special *after del.* pecul 145.6 **without**] out *inserted* 145.8
festivals.] *before del.* on *fols. 11v–12r* They were in the Earlier centuries of Christianity con-
stantly ornamented with | precious stones. 145.14 **whole∧**] *altered from* ~, **of the thing**]
of *inserted* 145.16 **caracteristic**] *after del.* significance o[f] 145.21 **Ancient**] *altered from*
Ancients **mouveable things**] *inserted* 145.24 **standing upon**] *repl. del.* whose feet are
which] *before del.* themselv 145.26 **reinforcement**] *after del.* increaseme idea] *after del.*
intented 145.29 **The handles**] *after del.* The tripod vases 145.31 **hands**] s *over full stop*
145.32 **A composite Vessel,**] *after del.* A Vessel of the composite *and before del.* such as most
of the artistical forms A Vessel of the composite] *after del.* Every Vessel [h] 145.40

upwarts.] *altered from* ~, *before del.* on fol. *13r* but the Middlepart of the body can be considered as a neutral [G] *(for 'Ground')* Middlepart] *after del.* Center
146.1 **other**] *after del.* many 146.1–2 **for the stripes**] *after del.* for this is a sort of 146.4 **Ground;**] *altered from* ~, *before del.* where the acting forces ar 146.5 **a**] *inserted* **representation**] *altered from* representations **the**] *inserted before del.* which have their **of which has nothing**] *inserted* **in common with**] *above del.* not in 146.6 **body;**] *before del.* but o[n] 146.7 **to show that**] *above del.* as if **are**] *above del.* were **Attributions**] *repl. undel.* applications applications] *after del.* embroyderies fastened *(*fastened *after del.* fixed*)* 146.8 **Vase itself.**] *before inserted and del.* The same is the case with the Attributions inside of the Assyrian 146.10 **center;**] *before del.* The lower Part works downwarts, works] *after del.* develop 146.12 **and it**] *after del.* generally it 146.13 **seems to be**] *repl. del.* is 146.17 **may be considered as**] *repl. del.* is 146.19–20 **should be**] *repl. del.* is 146.23–4 **a hyperboloid formed funnel.**] *repl. del.* it is equally it] *inserted after del.* The hyperboloidal form of a funnel is] *undel. before del.* the most

On Vessel Parts

TEXTUAL RECORD

MS 149   gta, 20-Ms-149, fol. 25r–v (25v blank), in Semper's hand
MS 134   gta, 20-Ms-134, fols. 1r–7v (6r variant of MS 149; 7r–v see 472, Alterations in the Manuscript 154.6), in Semper's hand, *copy-text*
Semper 1884   'Ueber die Gefässteile', 35–42, German trans. of MS 134, fols. 1r–7r; for details of this translation, see Herrmann 1981, 157–8

BIBLIOGRAPHY Herrmann 1981, 33, 111–12, 157–8; Herrmann 1984, 145–6; Gnehm 2004, 141–3; Poerschke 2016, 61–3, 66–7, 83–5; Chestnova 2021, 125–6, 131–3

EXPLANATORY NOTES

In his second lecture on ceramic art, Semper delves into the topic he already touched on at the end of the first lecture (145.9–146.24): the ornamentation of the individual parts of the vessel. Following a few introductory remarks, some of which refer to the first and third lectures (146.25–147.7), he draws a distinction between two principles of ornamentation, which he also applies to the other industrial arts and to architecture (147.8–148.7). He calls the first one 'the *dynamical* principle' (147.11), and here – in contrast to the mechanical considerations he discussed earlier (112.1–8) – he ignores static force relationships. This principle consists of the artist using 'ornaments … in the first sense of the word', ornaments proper, to clearly express the dynamic mode of action of the work of art and its parts (147.14–20). Semper does not describe the second principle directly but expresses it as the principle of applying ornaments whose expression does 'not immediately' affect – one might add: or does not affect at all – the dynamic mode of action of the work of art (147.22–5). With reference to James Fergusson, he calls ornaments of this type, which can be executed in free sculpture or painting, 'phonetical ornaments' (148.24–8; see 463, Explanatory Notes 148.27–8). Semper regards the extent to which these two principles are distinguished as being a measure of the development of the artistic sense (147.28–32), and he illustrates this by comparing Egyptian and Greek monuments. He does not recognize any ornaments proper among the Egyptian ones, only phonetic ornaments, whereas in Greek monuments he finds that phonetic ornaments are restricted to areas that are scarcely effective dynamically (147.33–5, 147.38–148.2). He regards this restriction as representing one of the most important rules of ornamentation and also recommends it to his contemporaries (148.2–3). Applied to vessels, it means that phonetic ornaments may be applied only to the body and, to a small extent, to the neutral fields of the stand (148.8–9, 148.24–6, 149.1–3).

Semper discusses the body, stand, neck, spout and handles of a vessel, taking into account the mechanical preconditions for them and explaining not only the ornamentation but also the relationships and proportions of the parts to one other (148.10–151.18). He concludes the discussion of handles in the form of keywords in the manuscript (151.19–27); and one of the vessel parts that he mentions, the cover (145.36, 146.34), is not discussed at all. Wolfgang Herrmann concluded from this that the manuscript of the second lecture on ceramics (MS 134) was fragmentary (Herrmann 1981, 111). This conclusion is incorrect, at least in the material sense, since the manuscript does not break off after the keywords for handles but continues – under the title 'Influence of the Material upon Style. in Ceramic art' – to the beginning of the third ceramics lecture (472, Alterations in the Manuscript 154.6).

146.31–2 **3) the Neck 4 the spoud**] 'spoud': *spout* (see also 151.2, 151.11–12). Following on from the manuscript of the first lecture on ceramics (145.35), Semper initially wrote '3) the Neck with the Lip and the spoud' (see 464, Alterations in the Manuscript 146.31, 146.32). It is possible that he only divided this number 3 into numbers 3 and 4 in the Zurich period, when he was drafting the 'Kunstformenlehre' (Theory of Art Forms). Indications at least suggesting this are the facts that he used the title '3°) *The Neck and the Spout*' in the second half of the lecture (150.4) and that he distinguished the neck and the spout as numbers 3 and 4 in his 'Theory of Art Forms' (Vieweg Archives, V3:1.1.3.32, sect. 'Ceramics', 66) – as in *Style* as well (Semper 1860/63, 2:78).

147.4 **upon this I shall call Your attention hereafter**] This remark refers to the corresponding section of the lecture 'Influence of the Materials and Their Treatments upon the Development of Ceramic Types and Style' (153.16–27). 147.5–6 **I am now only speaking of principles ~ which are independent upon the materials**] In contrast to Wolfgang Herrmann's assertion (Herrmann 1981, 33), the discussion of these principles, which occupies the whole of the remaining lecture, does not show any clear influence of Karl Bötticher's *Tektonik der Hellenen*. 147.22 **variating**] *varying* 147.24 **thinks**] In *Kleine Schriften*, the word is translated as 'Gedanken' (thoughts; Semper 1884, 36). However, three alterations in the manuscript of the lecture confirm that Semper must have meant *things* here (464, 466, Alterations in the Manuscript 147.13, 147.15–16, 149.14). 147.25 **structiv**] *structural* (see also 148.2, 148.5, 149.4) 147.37 **like it was allways in oriental art**] This phrase is inserted beside the text column without any mark indicating its position in the text (see 464–5, Alterations in the Manuscript 147.37). In *Kleine Schriften*, the corresponding phrase follows the word 'Prosodie' (prosody) and thus twists the sense of the whole sentence by saying that Oriental art was also composed prosodically (Semper 1884, 37). In *The Four Elements of Architecture*, Semper himself declares the opposite (Semper 1851b, 78): 'Just as the forms of Egyptian art were arrested as hieroglyphic characters, the colour music of its poly-chromy was not allowed to become more than a colour language, and had to assume a measured and distinct colour prosody instead of the melodic oriental colour play.'

148.7 **Frieses**] *friezes*   148.17 **othe**] *other*   **rifled**] derived from German *riffeln*: *grooved*   148.18 **direction of the Channels from downwards, to upwards**] cf. Bötticher 1844/52, 1:43   148.27–8 **This name has been introduced ~ by Mr. Fergusson ~ in his work on Architecture.**] In the book indicated, *An Historical Inquiry into the True Principles of Beauty in Art, More Especially with Reference to Architecture*, James Fergusson does not use the expression 'phonetical ornaments'. He divides the 'Anthropic Arts' into 'Technic Arts' (mechanical), 'Æsthetic Arts' (sensory) and 'Phonetic Arts' (intellectual) and assigns ranks to these three classes in ascending order (Fergusson 1849, 72–124).   148.36–8 **These two activ forces ~ Ground.**] accompanied in the left column by a trigonometric equation with figures   148.37–8 **representativ**] *representative*. Poerschke 2016, 62, has 'representation'.

149.7 **insinuating**] *sinuate*   149.14 **Ripps**] *ribs*   149.20 **rips**] *ribs*   149.21 **Romain**] French for *Roman*

150.9 **one side**] derived from German *einerseits*: *on the one hand*. Poerschke 2016, 62, has '[on] one side'.   **give it out**] Poerschke 2016, 62, has 'give it [out]'.   **other side**] derived from German *anderseits*: *on the other hand*. Poerschke 2016, 62, has 'on the other side'.   150.14–16 **The height of the neck ~ high neck.**] These sentences are inserted beside the text column without any mark indicating their position in the text (see 466, Alterations in the Manuscript 150.14–16). In *Kleine Schriften*, the corresponding sentences follow the remarks on the fulcrum and an ornament with upward and downward effects (Semper 1884, 41).   150.27 **report**] *relation*   150.28 **pendant**] French for *counterpart* (see also 151.11)

151.15 **handls**] *handles*   **branches, ears**] cf. Bötticher 1844/52, 1:50   151.17 **forns**] *forms*   151.21 **cubs**] *cups*

EDITORIAL EMENDATIONS

150.14 **increases**] increa | es (*first* s *missing due to upper fourth of left margin torn off*)

ALTERATIONS IN THE MANUSCRIPT

146.25 **On Friday last**] *after two del. variant beginnings:*

On last Friday ad[1] the End of my lecture I was demonstrating[2] some of the principles of ornamentation applied on Ceramic art, when I
On Friday last the time was passd, when I began to demonstrate some principles of orna-mentation applied on Ceramic art;[3] It will be allowed to recommence this matter to day from the beginning

    1 **ad**] *Latin for 'at'; over* I   2 **demonstrating**] *after del.* mentionning   3 **art;**] *altered from* ~, *before del.* arising from the   arising] *after del.* as far as they

464   Lectures

146.25 **I had commenced**] *after del.* the time was passd, when   the] *undel. after del.* I interrupted   146.26 **ceramic Art;**] *before del.* It may be allowed, for the sake of connection and
clearness, to recommence this matter from the beginning to day.   clearness] *before del.* in
what I proposed to explain   146.27 **I mentionned,**] *inserted*   the] t *over* T   **to be**] *repl.*
del. are, as we have seen,   146.31 **Neck**] *before del.* with the Lip and   146.32 **4**] *inserted*
146.33 **5°)**] 5 *repl. del.* 4   146.34 **6)**] 6 *repl. del.* 5
147.1 **function.**] *altered from* ~∧ *before del.* and   and] *after del.* and the appearances of each
Their] T *over* t   147.2 **attending**] *repl. del.* depending   147.3 **they**] *repl. del.* their forms
and ornaments   their forms and ornaments] *above del.* they   147.4 **hereafter,**] *altered*
from ~.   147.5 **while I am now only**] *inserted before four del. beginnings of variant on fol. 1r–v:*

Before specifiing[1] each of the 5 uppermentioned constituent parts of a Vessel[2] with respect
to the
Before specifiing the 5 constituent parts of a vessel for themselves and for their proportions[3]
to each other, I must |
I speak now only from their forms and ornaments in as much they are results of th
I speak[4] now independently of the material so that the following may find its application for
Earthenware as well as for Metalwork; – but before specifiing the above mentionned 5 con-
stituent parts of a Vase under this point of vue[5], I must give a general introductory notice
about the two different principles of ornamentation which come in

> 1 **specifiing**] *above del.* taking   2 **each of the 5 uppermentioned constituent parts of**
> **a Vessel**] *repl. del.* each part aside, and explaining   3 **proportions**] *repl. del.* relations
> 4 **I speak**] *after del.* I must introduce the specification   5 **vue**] *French for 'view'; after del.*
> sight

147.5 **speaking**] *after del.* I am now   147.6 **finds**] *altered from* find *after del.* may   147.8 **on**]
above del. about   147.9 **principles of ornamentation**] *before del.* which come in application wherever we may be   come] *after del.* I find   in application] *above del.* into question
wherever] *after del.* at nearly *after del.* every   **industrial**] *above del.* ornamental   147.10
one of the] *interl.*   **principles**] s *added*   147.11–12 **construction**] *after del.* word
147.12–13 **while its**] *above del.* but the   147.13 **function**] *before del.* of a think   think] *'thing'*
remains] *after del.* is independant u[p]   147.14 **part**] *after del.* for[m]   **tell**] *after del.* be
what] *before del.* destination   **dynamical**] *above inserted and del.* or   147.15 **function**]
inserted   **to fullfill**] *interl.*   **ornaments**] s *above del.* ation   147.15–16 **When the last**]
after del. The last can speak out the destination of the think or of a part of it by a sort of
think] *'thing'*   147.16 **significations**] *altered from* signification   signification] *repl. del.*
significance   **symbols**] *before del.* or Analogies   147.17 **with the sole intention**] *after*
del. on fol. 1v with the intention to support and to strenghthen the f[u]   with the intention]
after del. to strenghthen the impression of what the   147.18 **a clear**] *after del.* a strong
147.20 **word.**] *after del.* work.   147.23 **outlines**] out *added*   147.24 **representing**] *above*
del. symbolizing   **thinks, actions**] *above del.* relations   147.25 **connected**] *after del.*
depend *after del.* attending   147.27 **the destinations**] *after del.* their persons to which they
were   **Vases**] *after del.* object   147.28 **observe**] *after del.* find the   147.29 **strong**] *after*
del. sharp   147.33 **shows**] *above del.* knows   147.35 **topographical**] *after del.* geogra
147.36–7 **with colours**] *after del.* with colours, which it is   147.37 **like it was allways in**
oriental art] *inserted in opposite column without insertion mark, starting alongside the manu-*

script line is not a musik *at 147.36*   **allways**] *interl. before del.* the case *(cf. 462–3, Explanatory Notes 147.37)*   **prosody. –**] *before eight del. beginnings of variant:*

It would be easy to find[1] other parallels for this[2] in mediaeval and recent art, but we shall not be able to follow them here for want of time.
It would be easy to find other parallels to this in mediaeval and recent ages[3], but we shall be obliged to confind ourselves here with
It would be easy to find other parallels to this in mediaeval and recent art to show the difference of the two ornamental principles. but I must confine myself
I must confine myself to this
I would be a interesting matter of seaking[4] other parallels to this in mediaeval and recent – But
It is[5] easy to find parallels to this in mediaeval and recent ages, and[6]
It[7] would be a interesting matter of seaking[4] the bounderies –

---

1 **It would be easy to find**] *repl. del.* We find   We] *after del.* But this asides   2 **for this**] *repl. del.* of the kind   3 **ages**] *after del.* ti *(for 'times')*   4 **seaking**] *'seeking'*   5 **is**] *above del.* would be   6 **and**] *after del.* but I   7 **It**] I *over* i

147.38 Greec art] *after del.* The Greecs, as I sayd before were less rich of   **147.40 the Enrichment of**] *interl. in ink and* Enrichment *accompanied in opposite column by probably Wolfgang Herrmann's note in pencil* enrichment
148.2 activ] *after del.* acting   **148.4–7 Instances ~ Frieses, etc.**] *inserted before two del. variants on fol. 3r:*

I hope to be able to explain[1] this by some more instances in the next following.
but it will be better[2] to explain this at once at instances given.

---

1 **to explain**] *after del.* in the next following   2 **it will be better**] *above del.* I shall be able

148.5 temple] *above del.* building   **the**] *repl. del.* one of [t]   **148.8 The body**] *after del.*

The body of a Vase is another[1] such a neutral Ground on which the higher conceptions of art may find their application.
The body of a Vase has the function to contain a fluid; The hydrodynamic action[2] of the fluid which it contains neutralizes itself; Thus[3] The structiv[5] Idea[4] which[6] a well shaped Body of a Vessel is a complete Equilibrium of action and reaction of forces from

1 **another**] *interl.*   2 **The hydrodynamic action**] *inserted before del.* The Equilibrium   3 **Thus**] *inserted*   4 **The structiv Idea ~ Vessel**] *inserted before del.* there   there] *after del.* there is no other direction of forces but from the center of   5 **structiv**] *'structural'; del. after del.* dyn *and both above del.* dynamical   6 **which**] *'of'*

148.13 upon] *above del.* of   **148.15 impression produced by**] *above del.* feeling of   **148.16 impression**] *after del.* feeling   **148.17 pumkins**] *altered from* pumpkins   **148.20 or**] *above del.* and   **148.22–3 perfectly smooth**] *after del.* smooth   **148.23 In**] *after del.* The *after del.*

We do allways well to adopt   148.24 **plain**] *after del.* smooth   148.25 **ornaments**] *repl. del.* objects   148.27 **introduced in England for**] *repl. del.* given to   148.28 **Idea of applying**] *above del.* Application of   Application] *underl.*   **applying**] *after del.* fixing and 148.30–1 **This we see ~ Etruria.**] *repl. del.* This was allways or at least generally the Case with the Gree[c]   148.33 **part**] *interl.*   148.36 **activ forces**] *above del.* functions   148.39 **This fulcrum**] *after del.* This fulcrum or knobb between the two opposed   **is generally**] *repl. del.* must be

149.1 **it is**] *after del.* quasi   149.3 **ornaments,**] *altered from* ~∧   149.3–4 **or at least.**] *repl. del.* and   149.5 **Enamels etc.**] *before del.* The principle of ornamentation   149.7 **nature,**] *altered from* ~∧ *before del.* are the most   149.9 **the stand.**] *before del.* At other cases the stands remind those   At other cases] *above del.* Very often   149.11 **bolder than on the first,**] *repl. del.* stronger, than the first,   149.12 **Gravity;**] *altered from* ~, *before del.* with strong expression of   **It must show**] *after del.* It must show in its appearance that it is not a dead support,   dead] *above del.* mere   support] *repl. del.* medium (medium *after del.* trans *after del.* trans)   149.13 **mouveability**] u *interl.*   149.14 **thing**] g *over* k   149.16 **and phonetic**] *interl. and* phonetic *after del.* even   149.17 **pictures**] *after del.* or Phonetical seldom] *above del.* never   149.18 **working**] *repl. del.* supporting   149.19 **support**] *below del.* Stand   149.22 **exhibit**] *after del.* sh   149.25 **As to**] *after del.* I shall conclude these observations about the stands with   **proportions**] *after del.* relations   it] *after del.* no general rule may hold   will] *above del.* may   149.26 **application.**] *before del.* The center of gravity of the whole should be in all cases lower than the half of the whole elevation of the Axis.   center] *repl. del.* point   **But I may say**] *after del.* I believe that   149.26–7 **must be**] *before del.* one of the two,   149.27 **subordinated**] *after del.* unimpor   149.28–9 **But this ~ for when**] *inserted after del.* When   149.34 **ornamenting**] *above del.* colouring 150.1 **Stand**] *above del.* foot   150.14–16 **The height ~ high neck.**] *inserted in opposite column without insertion mark, starting alongside the manuscript line* ornamentation they adopted *at 150.13*   150.14 **The height of the neck**] *after del.* The proportion of a neck's hight is generally   150.15 **body with a large opening**] *after del.* large Vase   150.17 **neck.**] *altered from* ~∧ *before del.* although here also there must be shown the double   150.20–9 **The juncture ~ Greec Vases.**] *inserted in opposite column*   150.20 **juncture**] *below del.* join   join] *above del.* junctures   **is often**] *above del.* must be   150.21 **embraces**] *after del.* mostly 150.26 **descending.**] *above del.* vegetable   150.30 **The spouts**] *after del.* The Spouts are for the Vases what the faces are for the   **very**] *above del.* most   **the wase**] *after del.* the wh *after del.* the whole vase *after del.* a Ceramic 151.1 **limitation;**] *altered from* ~, *before del.* but   151.5 **The lips**] *after del. on fol. 6r–v*

The symbols employed for the lips or spouts of the Vessels are often taken from animal ¦ nature.[1] The[2] Shells show

> 1 **nature.**] *undel. before del.* These are the only parts where the interior of the vase is visible,
> 2 **The**] *after del.* Such natural forms like shells for   Such] *altered from* such *after undel.* and

151.6 **This gives**] *after del.* Excellent types and Symbols for these parts of the Vases are the Shells   **transitions**] *repl. undel.* contrasts   151.12 **Vertical**] *after del.* line of the   151.15 **Symbol**] *above del.* Style   151.15–16 **fingers, Serpants.**] *inserted in opposite column without insertion mark*   151.16 **barbarians**] s *added*   **Clasps, masks.**] *inserted in opposite column*

Influence of the Materials upon Ceramic Types and Style 467

without insertion mark before del. on fol. 7r The Greecs adopted sometimes the constructiv principle of ornamentation, Clasps, Masks,   sometimes] *interl.*   the] *repl. del.* a more ornamentation,] *inserted*   Clasps] *underl.*   151.17 **In a great many**] *after del.* Generally such *after del.* Sometimes   **forns**] *after del.* beauty was   was] *after del.* consisted in the 151.25 **bands**] *after del.* laces,   151.27–8 **kind. — .**] *before variant beginning of lecture 'Influence of the Materials and Their Treatments upon the Development of Ceramic Types and Style'; see 472, Alterations in the Manuscript 154.6*

MANUSCRIPT VARIANTS
MS 149

We have here on the neck also a neutral part towards the center, but there is no fulcrum   *fol. 25r* wanted; Therefore we see, with the Greecs at least here an other principle of ornamentation

3   adopted, such as this, which partakes of the two senses, in which the neck may be taken,

467.1 **We**] *after del.* But here the force *after del.* The Centerpart of the neck belongs no **towards**] *above del.* in   **center**] *after del.* neck   467.2 **see, with the Greecs at least**] *repl. del.* want   467.3 **senses,**] *after del.* sensens. *after del.* directions.   **neck**] *repl. del.* funnel   **taken,**] *before del.* as a recipient or as a   recipient] *after del.* funnel or as a

Influence of the Materials and Their Treatments upon the Development of Ceramic Types and Style

TEXTUAL RECORD

MS 135   gta, 20-Ms-135, fols. 1r–13v (1r–2v variant of MS 134, fol. 7r–v), in Semper's hand, *copy-text*

Semper 1884   'Einfluss der Materialien und ihrer Behandlung auf die Entwickelung keramischer Typen und Stile', 43–57, German trans. of MS 135; for details of this translation, see Herrmann 1981, 158–9

BIBLIOGRAPHY Herrmann 1981, 112, 158–9; Chestnova 2021, 125–6, 134–7

EXPLANATORY NOTES

Semper starts the third lecture on ceramics with a critique of the contemporary European industrial arts in general and ceramic art in particular, drawn largely from *Science, Industry, and Art* or from an English translation of the book (151.32–152.28; cf. Semper 1852, 7–8, 11–12; gta, 20-Ms-89). He notes a discrepancy between the dearth of truly artistic works and the wealth of technological and scientific resources. In the latter, however, he recognizes a second deficiency (he had described a first one in two earlier lectures; see 105.32–7, 118.23–8): 'we are wanting of a manual, which teaches the principles of beauty and style as applied to the new inventions of science and manufacture' (152.24–6). A manual of this type was probably what he had in mind when he wrote the 'Kunstformenlehre' (Theory of Art Forms) and *Style in the Technical and Tectonic Arts* a few years later.

Semper introduces the main part of the lecture with a few remarks on ceramic materials and a list of the most important methods of processing them. He discusses the first process, 'the mixture of the past[e]s' (153.3), only in relation to the pastes themselves and, 'for want of time', only briefly (153.16–27). He discusses the second process in detail – the method of shaping designated by the French word *façonnage*, referring here frequently to a work he had mentioned in the first ceramics lecture: the *Traité des arts céramiques ou des poteries* by Alexandre Brongniart, the former director of the porcelain manufactory in Sèvres (Brongniart 1844; see 138.2). Following Brongniart, Semper distinguishes three types of shaping: turning, pressing and casting. He does not name turning explicitly but describes it by explaining the use of the potter's wheel and the lathe (153.29–155.4); and he only hints at an explanation of the difference between pressing, which he calls 'moulding', and casting (155.5–156.5). However, the process of 'moulding' is not self-evident. It involves filling a paste into a mould and then pressing it manually or mechanically into a finished shape. Semper also includes the mounting of the stand, handles, spout and cover as part of the shaping process (156.29–157.3), as well as the painting and gilding of the finished form (156.9–28, 157.4–28), diverging here from Brongniart (cf. Brongniart 1844, 1:118–170). With regard to the artistic mastery of painting and gilding, he praises his friend Jules Dieterle, 'the arts superintendant' of the porcelain manufactory in Sèvres (156.22–8, 157.27–8). Semper discusses the process of glazing in almost as much detail as he does the process of shaping (157.34–160.24), again drawing on Brongniart for technical matters. In the only surviving manuscript of the third lecture on ceramics (MS 135), he does not keep his promise that he will discuss the process of firing (157.31–2) – he ends the draft with a few keywords and sentences that do not refer directly to ceramic art but rather to metal vases and statues and possibly to the topic announced in the 'Prospectuses of the Lectures on Art': 'On the Connexion of Ceramic Art with the art of Metal casting' (96.18).

152.8 **recollections**] *replications*   152.13 **herself**] referring to female German noun *Industrie* (industry): *itself*   **her**] *its*; see previous note   152.18–19 **Bernhard Palissy**] cf. Brongniart 1844, 2:61–9   152.22 **the old**] ~ ~ *ones*   152.23 **news**] *new ones*   152.31 **whishes**] *wishes*

153.3–9 **1°) The first process ~ potters industry.**] This division corresponds to chapters 2–5 in the first volume of Alexandre Brongniart's *Traité des arts céramiques ou des poteries*, which Semper draws on many times in the main part of the lecture. The titles of chapters 2–5 in Brongniart's *Traité* are: 'Formation des pâtes céramiques', 'Façonnage des pièces', 'Des glaçures ou enduits vitreux' and 'Cuisson des pâtes céramiques' (Brongniart 1844, 1:33, 118, 171, 184).   153.3 **pasts**] *pastes* (see also 153.18, 153.21, 153.23–4, 155.35, 155.37, 158.8, 159.2, 159.7, 159.20)   153.5 **Façonage**] *façonnage*: French for *shaping* (see also 156.6, 157.5, 157.30)   153.8 **burning**] *firing*   153.15 **Böttcher's**] *Böttger's*   153.19 **proprieties**] *properties*   153.24–5 **The Portland Vase ~ is not to be imitated in Stoneware**] In *Science, Industry, and Art*, Semper claims that the Portland Vase consists of 'hard stone' (Semper 1852, 52–3). This ancient Roman glass vase entered the British Museum in 1810 as a loan from William Henry

Bentinck, 4th Duke of Portland.   153.25 **cisel**] merged from French *ciseau* and English *chisel*   153.26 **selfunderstanding**] *self-explaining*   153.30 **horizontal potters wheel**] cf. Brongniart 1844, 1:119–24; 3:36–7, pl. VIII figs. 1, 3–4, pl. IX figs. 2, 4

154.3–5 **But for this reason ~ or what he has been drilled for himself.**] The corresponding sentence in the 'Theory of Art Forms' reads (Vieweg Archives, V3:1.1.3.32, sect. 'Ceramics', 101): 'But precisely for this reason, it [i.e. the wheel] should everywhere be operated by intelligent hands and not by other, less tractable machines which can only turn after templates for which they are drilled.' This suggests that the male pronouns 'he' and 'himself' refer to 'an other machine' (154.4) and thus should read *it* and *itself*; cf. 472, Alterations in the Manuscript 154.4–5 [2].   154.6 **potters wheels represented in the Tombs of Beni hassan and Thebes**] cf. Brongniart 1844, 1:507; 3:34, pl. III figs. 4–5   154.10 **one of their great philosophers**] i.e. the Scythian Anacharsis; see 473, Alterations in the Manuscript 154.7– 11 [2]; cf. Brongniart 1844, 1:20   154.13 **lath**] *lathe* (see also 154.22, 154.36, 155.10)   154.16 **terre**] *terra*: Latin for *earth*   154.21 **rifles**] derived from German *Riffel*: *grooves*   154.24 **à la barbotine**] Alexandre Brongniart refers to this type of ornamentation as 'Relief en trochisque ou Pastillage' and describes it as follows (Brongniart 1844, 1:24; cf. 1:425; italics in original): 'Il consiste à faire des ornements en relief au moyen d'une *barbotine* épaisse déposée sur la surface des Poteries, comme les confiseurs font les pastilles.' Brongniart defines the material called 'barbotine' as a 'pâte délayée en consistance de bouillie épaisse' (Brongniart 1844, 1:169).   154.25 **brosh**] *brush* (see also 157.13)   154.30 **new**] *knew*   154.31 **Germans**] *Germanic peoples*; cf. Semper 1884, 47: 'Germanen'   **process calld Colombin**] Brongniart describes this process as 'le procédé du *Colombin* et du façonnage à la main sur le plateau' (Brongniart 1844, 1:21; italics in original). It consists of shaping 'au moyen de *colombins* ou *boudins*, c'est-à-dire de longs cylindres de pâte que l'ouvrier place successivement l'un sur l'autre et qu'il lie ensemble avec les mains' (Brongniart 1844, 1:124; italics in original).   154.32–3 **here it is not the piece ~ but the potter who turns round the pot**] cf. Brongniart 1844, 1:21   154.34 **Jarres of France**] cf. Brongniart 1844, 1:391: *'Jarres et Cuviers*, en France'   **Tinacas of Spane**] ~ ~ *Spain*; cf. Brongniart 1844, 1:391: '*Tinajas*, qu'on prononce *tinacas*, en Espagne'   154.34–5 **Camucis of Bresilia**] ~ ~ *Brazil*; cf. Brongniart 1844, 1:391: '*Camucis*, au Brésil'   154.36 **lath or horizontal wheel**] *lathe ~ vertical ~.* If the tool in question shall be called a wheel, it must be called a vertical wheel since its axle is horizontal. It is used for finishing the raw shape made with the horizontal wheel; cf. Brongniart 1844, 1:120, 159–60; 3:36, pl. VIII fig. 2. Hans Semper added the note '? vedi p. 5' to the word 'lath' in the manuscript of the lecture (see 474, Alterations in the Manuscript 154.36) to refer to the passage in which 'the horizontal potters wheel' is discussed (153.29– 154.15).   154.39 **wedd**] *wet*   154.40 **Calibrage**] cf. Brongniart 1844, 1:125–6

155.5 **2° Process, the Moulding**] cf. Brongniart 1844, 1:126–47   155.13 **evoid**] *avoid*   155.22 **doe**] *do*   155.24 **Evaded**] derived from French *évaser*: *expanded*. Expansion probably relates to one specific vessel part, the rim.   155.25 **smoth**] *smooth*   **undercutts**] In *Kleine Schriften*, the word is translated as 'Unterscheidungen' (distinctions; Semper 1884, 49), but Wolfgang Herrmann correctly recognizes it as a 'Druckfehler für "Unterschneidungen"' (printing error for 'undercuttings'; Herrmann 1981, 159).   155.29 **burnt**] *fired* (see also 157.32, 159.29)   155.34 **The process of Casting Coulage**] cf. Brongniart 1844, 1:147–58. Semper may also have based his remarks on this process on handwritten 'Notes sur le procédé du Coulage appliqué au Façonnage des pièces de Porcelaine dure' dated 29 April 1850 (gta, 20-Ms-49a), which Wolfgang Herrmann believes he received from a member of staff in the porcelain manufactory in Sèvres 'as documentation for his essay on porcelain painting'

470 Lectures

(Herrmann 1981, 85). 155.35 **propriety**] *property* 155.36 **versed**] derived from French *verser*: *poured*

156.9 **Potteries painting**] In June 1850, while in exile in Paris, Semper wrote the first of three parts of an essay on porcelain and enamel painting addressed to his daughter Elisabeth (gta, 20-Ms-47; cf. Semper 1884, 58–75). In it, he made use of insights obtained during visits to the porcelain manufactory in Sèvres, arranged by Jules Dieterle. 156.11 **owr**] *our* (see also 156.19) 156.16 **depassed**] derived from French *dépasser*: *overstepped* (see also 156.20) 156.17 **Eameling**] *enamelling* 156.28 **depassed**] derived from French *dépasser*: *surpassed* 156.29 **Garniture**] cf. Brongniart 1844, 1:165–70 156.30 **outerworks**] *outer parts* 156.31 **spouds**] *spouts* (see also 156.39) 156.35 **reconduces**] *reconducts* 156.38 **Stonewases**] *stone vases*

157.4 **guilding**] *gilding* (see also 157.6, 157.17–18, 157.25–7) 157.20 **Venitian**] merged from French *vénitien* and English *Venetian* 157.24 **Faenca**] *Faenza* 157.33 **potteriesworks**] *potters' works* or *works of pottery* 157.34–158.1 **The glazing ~ stanniferous.**] cf. Brongniart 1844, 1:171

158.7 **Engobe**] cf. Brongniart 1844, 2:627–32 158.8 **overthe**] *over the* 158.12–14 **But the discovery reached its highest degree of development ~ at Faenza, Pesaro Gubbio and Tlorence.**] cf. Brongniart 1844, 2:58–9 158.13 **Duc**] *duc*: French for *duke* 158.14 **Pesaro⋀ Gubbio**] ~, ~ **Tlorence**] *Florence* 158.24 **pitterresque**] derived from French *pittoresque*: *picturesque* 158.29 **pipeware**] *pipeclay ware* 158.30 **apposite**] *opposite* 158.39 **instanes**] *instances* 158.40 **Fayence fine**] *faïence fine*: French for *fine earthenware*; cf. Marryat 1850, 49

159.10–11 **Mr. Brogniard gives ~ a very good description ~ now.**] see Brongniart 1844, 2:175–9; cf. Marryat 1850, 49–55 159.13–16 **A third glazing process ~ hard China.**] cf. Brongniart 1844, 1:171 159.14 **smelts**] *melts* 159.17 **gypse**] French for *gypsum* 159.20 **Caoline**] *kaolin* 159.23 **translucide**] French for *translucid*. Herrmann 1981, 159, has 'translucent'. 159.32–3 **difine**] *define*

160.2 **Chinawase**] uncertain reading, *china vase*. Herrmann 1981, 159, has 'Chinoisan'. 160.5 **renomated**] *renowned* 160.20 **ancient German**] *old German*; cf. Semper 1884, 57: 'altdeutschen' **Canns**] derived from German *Kanne*: *jugs* **Cannettes**] *canettes*: French for *small jugs*

EDITORIAL EMENDATIONS

153.27 **has**] ha *(s missing due to upper sixth of right margin torn off)* **manufacturers**] man *(ufacturers missing due to upper sixth of right margin torn off; cf. Semper 1884, 46: 'Industriellen')* 156.22 **China-manufacture**] China- | manufacture 159.4 **the same paste**] the | the same paste

ALTERATIONS IN THE MANUSCRIPT

151.32 **We are infinitely more advanced**] *accompanied in opposite column by del.* We considered on last Friday the 151.33 **any other nation**] *after del.* those nations, whose productions in pottery as well as in other branches of Art we still admire and can not desist of copiing; not] *undel.*

Influence of the Materials upon Ceramic Types and Style   471

152.1 **see**] *after del.* look   152.3 **little.**] *altered from* ~∧ *before del.* with respect to   152.18 **knowledge**] *above del.* mastery   152.19 **Enamel**] *after del.* opaque   152.20 **how**] *after del.* better   152.22 **before**] *after del.* and   **had time**] *after del.* are ready with the old   152.24 **We have**] *after del.* it would be Under such circumstances of the greatest utility to have Under such circumstances] *transposed by guide line from before* it would be   **but**] *after del.* it would be a very usefull one   152.25 **the principles**] *after del.* the artistical application of the] *undel.*   **style**] *repl. del.* art   **as applied**] *inserted*   152.27 **applicable**] *above del.* true with respect   respect] *above del.* applicable   **ceramic art**] *before del.* and furniture. 152.28 **which ~ view.**] *inserted after inserted and del.* whose techni   **to day**] *interl.*   **point of view.**] *after del.* side.   152.30 **plasticity,**] *before del.* what   152.36 **Ceramic art**] *after del.* the entire domain of   152.37 **to You.**] *inserted*   152.38 **Although**] *after del.* Every piece of Ceramic art   **appears**] *above del.* is   **nevertheless**] *before del.* every piece   152.39 **plainest**] *above del.* simplest   **pottery**] *repl. del.* ceramic Art   **passes**] *altered from* pass *after del.* must

153.1–2 **respecting their**] *after del.* with respect to their   153.6 **formation**] *after del.* general 153.10 **theoretically**] *after del.* artistically   153.16 **I° On the materials**] *inserted*   153.17–21 **I shall ~ For every speciality**] *inserted in left column of fols. 2v–3r after del. on fol. 2v*

As for the Nature[1] of the materials, I will not be permitted to enter here into the specification of their differences and special applications as I wished to be able to do; for[2]

> 1 **As for the Nature ~ do; for**] *inserted after del.* As for the materials and their nature I can not here as I desired, enter into the specification of the different pasts of ancient and modern potteries; Perhaps shall I find the t[i]

>> **pasts**] *'pastes'*   Perhaps] *after del.* I only shall point out for the moment that one great distinction between potteries properly speaking and Ceramic

> 2 **for**] *intended to be continued by 'Every Speciality' (see note 153.21)*

153.18 **plastic**] *below del.* other   153.19 **speak**] *above del.* insert one or the other observations   **influences**] *after del.* stylistic   153.21 **every speciality**] *before undel.* etc   **of pasts**] *after undel.* Every Speciality *(cf. note 153.17–21[2])*   153.23 **Fayence**] *above del.* Parian 153.25 **Stoneware,**] *altered from* Stone *after del.* Gr *after del.* Wedgewood   153.26 **principle**] *repl. del.* remark   153.27 **at present.**] *before del.*

I regret that it will not be permitted[1] by want of time to enter into a detaild specification of the different pasts[2] and materials of old and modern potteries, at least shall I for the moment leave this object and spare[3] some remarks respecting to the Stylistic influences of the different pasts[2] which were employd in Ceramic art, for the following.

> 1 **permitted**] *above del.* allowed   2 **pasts**] *'pastes'*   3 **spare**] *'save'*

153.29 **frequently**] *after del.* usual   153.31 **for the development of the forms**] *accompanied in opposite column by del.* folgende Seite *(referring to 'Here' on fol. 4r and 'Here' on fol. 4v; see notes 154.6[28], 154.6[34])*   **Engines**] *after del.* mashines and   153.32 **hand**] *after del.* feeling 154.3 **everwhere**] *repl. del.* only   154.4–5 **which knows ~ for himself.**] *repl. del.*

which knows[1] nothing but what he[2] was teached by his master and to turn[3] his objects after templets.

> 1 **knows**] *after del.* lerned 2 **he**] *above del.* it 3 **to turn**] *after del.* what th

154.6 **We find potters wheels**] *after undel. on MS 134, fol. 7r–v, and del. on MS 135, fol. 4r–v (cf. 467, Alterations in the Manuscript 151.27–8)*

Influence of the Material upon Style. in Ceramic art. –

The[1] proper materials for the Ceramic works are the plastic masses; We call plasticity the quality, which have certain soft materials, to take under the hand of the workman all the forms which he whishes[2] to produce. The common clay is a very plastic material ¦ and[3] that which since the earliest times was found to be the most convenient for the production of vessels. The[4] qualities of this material and the processes and manipulations necessary for it, had therefore a great part[5] in the first development of the traditional forms which are accepted in that branch of industrial art, which I understood under the general expression of Ceramic art. We are infinitely more advanced in the practical sciences and the knowledge of utilising the materials, than it was the case with those nations, whose productions in pottery we Still admire and can not desist of copiing; but still our knowledge is very deficient with respect to that great secret of utilising all our means artistically.

Every piece[6] of Ceramic art must pass through a great number of different processes, before its completion.[7]

First the *mixture and formation of the pasts*[8], presupposing the knowledge of the natural[9] materials and their qualities.

2°) the *Façonnage*.

3°) *the* covering and glazing.

4°) the firing and all preparatory and accessory manipulations,[10] connected with this important process.

All[11] of them should be known practically as well as theoretically by those who undertake to make designs for manifacturers of potteries, which unhappily is not allways the case. Practical knowledge[12] and artistical skill and feeling are not more so often combined in one person as it was[13] ¦ once the case, at Palissy's and Cellini's time.[14]

As for the materials and their nature I can not enter here as I desired,[15] into the specification of the different pasts[16] which were and are employd for potteries; I only shall point out[17] that[18] one great distinction between potteries[19] properly speaking and Ceramic[20] products executed in other materials principally in *Metal*.

But I must at least give this general observation,[21] that every speciality of pasts[8] necessitates[22] its own treatement and style,[23] and that for instance the antique urns and Etrurian Vases, consisting of a very soft, slighly tempered clay,[24] are not fit for being executed in our modern China- or Gray-pasts[25], nor[26] in metal.

Some remarks, respecting to[27] the stylistic influences of the different pasts[8], may perhaps occasionally find their place.

The[29] *façonnage.*[28]

a) The *Wheel* and the *lath.*[30]

The tool which is the most ancient and still now the most usual,[31] in pottery[32] that which is[33] the most important for the development of the forms, ¦ is the potters wheel;[34]

Influence of the Materials upon Ceramic Types and Style   473

1 **The**] *after four del. beginnings of variant:*

We shall first o
The Forms which belon
The productions of Ceramic Art
The proper material of the productions of Ceramic art is that plastic mass which is called clay. The well known properties of this material were

productions of Ceramic Art] *after del.* Ceramic

2 **whishes**] *'wishes'*   3 **and**] *after del.* which quality has been *after del.* and therefore it has been taken   4 **The**] *after del.* The specialities of the manipulation of the clay   5 **a great part ~ artistically.**] *inserted before del.* vice versa a great influence on the forms of the vessels; although the last may originate and derive from natural or other forms. –
6 **Every piece ~ completion.**] *repl. del.* There is a great number of different processes wanted through which every piece of Ceramic art must pass before it is complete;   is complete] *after del.* becomes. fit for being   7 **completion.**] *after del.* completedness.
8 **pasts**] *'pastes'*   9 **natural**] *after del.* elements   10 **preparatory and accessory mani- pulations,**] *repl. del.* the processes   11 **All**] *after del.* All these different processes
12 **Practical knowledge ~ as it was**] *inserted after del.* It is very very seldom   It] *after del.*
Those who have artistical skill   13 **was**] *before del.* in   14 **once the case, at Palissy's and Cellini's time.**] *repl. del.* the case of old, at the time when Palissy, the French potter wrote his book on Potteries   at the time] *after del.* The Bernhard Palissy's and Cellinis
15 **as I desired,**] *inserted*   16 **pasts**] *'pastes'; after del.* earth   17 **shall point out**] *repl. del.* make   18 **that**] *after del.* the general di   19 **potteries**] *above del.* Ceramic works
20 **Ceramic**] *after del.* between Metalwases and such other   21 **at least give this gen- eral observation,**] *above del.* remind you   22 **necessitates**] *after del.* necessary must have   23 **and style,**] *inserted*   24 **consisting of a very soft, slighly tempered clay,**] *inserted*   25 **Gray-pasts**] Gray- | pasts: *'grey pastes'; after del.* Eart   26 **nor**] *after del.* or
27 **respecting to**] *after del.* belonging to   28 **The façonnage.**] *accompanied by* Hier (cf. notes 153.31, 154.6³⁴)   29 **The**] *after del.* We shall   30 **a) The Wheel and the lath.**] lath: *'lathe'; inserted*   31 **usual,**] *altered from* ~∧ *before del.* in plastic art, and   32 **in pottery**] *interl.*   33 **that which is**] *inserted*   34 **is the potters wheel;**] *accompanied by doubly underl.* Hier (cf. notes 153.31, 154.6²⁸)

154.7–11 **So the Greeks ~ wheel.**] *repl. del.*

So the Greeks in attributing[1] this invention to one of their countrimen, Thales, who lived 1200 Years before Christ;[2] were certainly wrong, but although they[3] were[4] not the inventors of the wheel they at least knew to take from it the best possible advantages.

1 **So the Greeks in attributing**] *repl. del.* The Greeks attributed   2 **Christ;**] *before del.* and the Scythian Philosopher Anacharsis is told to be the inventor of a new wheel;
3 **were certainly wrong, but although they**] *inserted*   4 **were**] *after del.* If the Greec
If] *altered from* if *after del.* But

154.9 **certainly**] *interl.*   154.10 **sayd**] *after del.* even   154.10–11 **being the inventor**] *after del.* the introd[u]   154.14 **for**] *above del.* but   154.15 **of being finished that way.**] *after del.* of the last.   154.16–17 **The Romans ~ treatment.**] *repl. del.*

The Roman Potteries[1] are of an other paste than the more ancient vases are,[2] which is able to be burnished and to take a lustre, which last is given with the aid of[3] the lath[4].

1 **The Roman Potteries**] *undel. before del.* have been made on the Wheel; but stamped and finished afterwards with the aid of other processes. – The Roman vases   2 **than the more ancient vases are,**] *interl.*   3 **is given with the aid of**] *repl. del.* they received on 4 **lath**] *'lathe'*

154.16 **made of**] *interl.*   154.17 **which**] *after del.* which is able to be burnished   which] *undel.*   **required**] *above del.* wanted   **mode of**] *repl. del.* kind of   154.26 **a curious fact, that**] *after del.* curious that   154.27 **aid**] *repl. del.* application   154.28–9 **The Style ~ circumstance.**] *inserted*   154.32 **potter**] *above del.* man   154.33 **the pot.**] *after del.* it. 154.33–5 **Sometimes ~ hand.**] *inserted before del.* Other instrument was the turning table; 154.36 **lath**] *accompanied by Hans Semper's note in pencil ?* vedi p. 5. *(cf. 469, Explanatory Notes 154.36)*   154.37 **rather**] *above del.* very   154.39 **templets**] *repl. del.* paterns   paterns] *after del.* forms cutt o   154.40–155.4 **By employing ~ execution.**] *inserted*   154.40 **may**] *over* can   154.41 **give to the forms**] *above del.* obtain   **obtain**] *interl.*

155.3 **paterns**] *above del.* objects,   155.6–7 **important**] *before del.* for artistical producti[ ] 155.8 **submit**] *below del.* obei   155.9 **and remember**] and *interl. after del.* and he must   he] *after del.* observe the   155.11 **ought to be**] *repl. del.* should always be   **not circular**] *after del.* more ornamented with reliefs and not spheri   **or angular**] *interl.*   155.12 **A form**] *after del.* An interrupted and imperfect Spheroid makes   interrupted] *before del.* Spheroid   **Circular**] *after del.* regular   155.14–17 **These ofsets ~ potteries.**] *inserted*   155.14 **regular**] *interl.*   **which**] *above del.* of   **have**] *after del.* never   155.15 **they may be hidden**] *after del.* at least   at least] *before del.* hidden   155.18–19 **frequently**] *above del.* often 155.20 **more**] *above del.* a   **application**] *altered from* applications   155.21 **potteries, when**] *after del.* forms, w   155.22 **turned**] *before del.* or cast   155.24 **intended**] *after del.* who are destined   **China**] *after del.* generally in   155.25 **high**] *after del.* haut   155.26 **for**] *after del.* for being cast and   155.28 **must**] *above del.* want to   155.29 **burnt**] *after underl. and del.* executed   155.30 **great**] *above del.* much   **work**] *after del.* vase, and every   vase] *above del.* pottery work   155.32 **generally**] *repl. del.* always   **accepted**] *after del.* felt 155.33 **who pay very little for the models.**] *repl. del.* which often are afraid of the costs for models, and find it more convenient to copy   which] *after del.* which are afraid to spend money for their models,   155.34 **Coulage.**] *in opposite column*   155.37 **mould**] *above del.* cast

156.1 **On this**] *after del.* These circumstances have given rise   **pottery**] *after del.* cast **partly**] *interl.*   156.2 **pieces of earthenware, as columns, Water-pipes,**] *inserted* **Vases**] *before del.* and for others   156.2–3 **partly ~ Eggshells,**] *inserted before del.* which in the contrary are very thin and fragile   156.4 **Ancients. It**] *after del.* Grecs; it   **executed**] *repl. del.* applied   156.9 **Potteries painting.**] *in opposite column*   156.10 **applied**] *above del.* emploied   156.11 **the ancients and owr ancestors**] *inserted*   **knew**] *above del.* have been   156.11–12 **than we do.**] *above del.* known by   known by] *before del.* the ancients and our own forefathers than by us.   156.12 **I shall ~ which**] *inserted before del.* This matter 156.14 **some principles**] some *above del.* those   156.18 **less**] *after del.* evidently done   **advanced**] *altered from* advant   156.19 **The wide boundaries**] *after four del. beginnings of variant:*

And we try even to depass[1] the wide boundaries[2] of modern
We are even not satisfied o[ ]
Although the means are very great, we
Although the fabrication[3] of standing colours.

Influence of the Materials upon Ceramic Types and Style

1 **depass**] *derived from French 'dépasser': 'overstep'*   2 **boundaries**] *after del.* field   3 **fabrication**] *after del.* knowledge of

156.19 **wide**] *after del.* limit   156.20 **depass**] *after del.* must   156.23 **to the strict observation**] *after del.* to the influence of my   156.23–4 **of the stylistic limits**] *after del. on fol. 7r–v* of the limits prescribed by the materials and processes ¦ as well as by the fundamental forms and ideas, which   156.24 **and**] *inserted before del.* and China ornamenting, and   156.24–6 **as well as ~ purpose.**] *inserted*   156.24 **moderated style**] *after del.* moderation in the employement of colours   156.29 **counts**] *after del.* there is one which I   **Garniture**] *after del.* Garnissage   156.31 **piece;**] *altered from ~, before del.* but are parts   156.31–3 **as handles ~ happens to be**] *inserted*   156.33 **art;**] *altered from ~, before del.* for instance Metal ornaments, precious stones pearls and smalts.   156.34 **mounting**] *repl. del.* decorating   156.35 **our manufacturers**] *inserted after del.* we may be   **pay**] *after del.* able to 156.36 **dangerous**] *before del.* and abusiv   156.38 **precious potteries**] *after del.* beautiful Vases in   **glasses**] *interl.*   156.39 **has**] *before del.* not only   **frequently**] *inserted before del.* in the most [ ]

157.1 **It was dominant also**] *after del.* It has been also adopted or   **is**] *before del.* a   **successfully**] *y added*   **practiced**] *repl. del.* mode of treating Chinavases   157.4 **guilding,**] *altered from ~∧ before del.* and   **silvering and platinizing**] *below inserted and del.* applying metallic   157.5 **façonage.**] *before del.* They are employed with the brosh or in powder or in chemical dissolutions   **brosh**] *'brush'*   157.6 **The guilding**] *after del.* The guilding should be employed only for   157.7 **extremities**] *after del.* outer   157.9 **junctures**] *before del.* or mouldings which indi   157.9–10 **decorations**] *over orna*   157.10 **vases.**] *before del.* There is a distinction to be made between the metallic lustre and the   **There**] *after del.* It seems n   157.11 **Gold**] *after del.* metal   157.13 **glazing**] *before del.* and   157.14 **shows a**] *repl. del.* becomes a   **very agreable natural luster**] *after del.* mat luster   157.16 **Greecs**] *before del.* and it is the same now   it is the same now] *inserted before del.* which gave only a polish to some   157.17 **knew**] *repl. del.* employd   **Earthenwares**] *after del.* Stonewa   157.17–18 **But they ~ Vessels.**] *inserted*   157.17 **followed**] *above del.* had   157.19–20 **it will be advisable to**] *inserted after del.* we must   we must] *repl. del.* we should   157.20 **follow the**] *after del.* reserve t[h]   **Venitian Painters**] *after del.* good   **distribution**] *after del.* light in the pictures, and   157.21 **for**] *inserted*   157.21–2 **brillancies**] *repl. del.* brillant parts brillant parts] *repl. del.* polish   157.22 **only**] *after del.* only for   157.34 **followes sometimes**] *after del.* is given in some cases   157.39 **transparent**] *inserted*   **coating**] *after del.* Glazing or varnish
158.1 **glazing,**] *after del.* covering,   **generally stanniferous.**] *after del.*

generally stanniferous.
The opaque Pottery-Enamel[1]

1 **The opaque Pottery-Enamel**] *inserted and undel. after del.* These Enamels were known to the Arabian potters in the 11th Century and afterwards adopted by Luca della Robbia, ot the beginning of the fifteenth century. It obtained its

Robbia,] *before del.* the Faenza potters and   ot] *'at'; repl. inserted and del.* in

158.8 **past,**] *altered from* ~∧   **forming**] *repl. del.* and formed   158.14 **Enamelig**] ig *added*
158.15 **paste,**] *altered from* ~∧ *after del.* grosse pottery or   **a composition ~ marl,**] *inserted*
158.17 **the Faenza potteries**] *after del.* decorat   158.18 **its opaque cover;**] *before del.* The
plastic element is not prevailing for this s   The] *after del.* The painter is *after del.* It bor-
rowes its greatest beauty   158.19–21 **The façonnage ~ These circumstances**] *inserted*
before del. Both of them   Both] *after del.* Both are not very favorable   158.20 **Enamel**]
after del. liquid   **wants**] *after del.* covers   158.22 **but most convenient for painting**]
after del. the painter has the greatest part of the decoration   158.22–4 **It was ~ ornamentation.**] *inserted*   158.26 **China.**] *before del.*

A third process[2] of glazing[1] is that which is technically calld the *cover. la couverte*. It is a
vitrifiable and earthy Substance, which smelts[3] only at a very high temperature, equal to
that which is wanted for the burning of the paste. It is that which is employed for hard
China and some Stonewares.
Many of the[5] Specialities[4] which show the fine old[6] Gray[7] or Stonewares, for instance the
old Flamish and German drinking vessels, as well as those of the better Chinas are evidently consequences

> 1 **A third process of glazing ~ some Stonewares.**] *cf. 159.13–16*   2 **process**] *after del.*
> class is   3 **smelts**] *'melts'*   4 **Many of the Specialities ~ consequences**] *cf. 160.13–18;*
> *notes 160.9, 160.16*   5 **Many of the**] *inserted before del.* The difficulties which   The]
> *altered from* the *after del.* It is evident that   6 **fine old**] *inserted after del.* better   7 **Gray**]
> *after del.* productions of

158.27–36 **The Frensch ~ group.**] *in opposite column*   158.28 **treated**] *after del.* this last
being less thick and   158.29 **like pipeware**] *after del.* fin   158.34 **belong**] *after del.* relate
158.36 **group.**] *altered from* ~∧ *before del.* which
159.3 **moulding**] *altered from* moulds   **cover**] *after del.* lining of   159.4 **ornaments**] *before*
del. were placed   159.5 **The Engobe**] *after del.* Mr Brogn   159.6 **made**] *interl.*   with]
repl. del. in   159.7 **pasts.**] *altered from* ~∧ *before del.* of different   **The whole**] *after del.*
The style is not only Arabian in the   **Oriental feeling**] *repl. del.* Arabian feeling   159.8
which] *before del.* feeling   159.11 **40**] 4 *over* 2   159.19 **This glazing**] *after del.* The paste of
the China's is short and effor   159.20 **less**] *after del.* much   **pasts**] *after del.* clays,
159.24–5 **agreable for the**] *after del.* precious for the   159.25–6 **application**] *above del.*
exhibition   159.27 **But**] *after del.* The white China's are engaging *after del.* The practical
difficulties which *after del.* But   159.29 **heigh**] *above del.* great degree of   **Tempera-
tures**] s *added*   159.30 **necessitates**] *after del.* makes   **precautions**] *after del.* observation   159.34 **pottery**] *interl.*   159.36 **wares.**] *altered from* ~, *before del.* and we shall perhaps
will] *before del.* depend   **in China pottery**] in *above del.* of   **be allways**] *after del.* allways
a little from the   159.37 **and I**] *after del.* and these are not the less happ   **am excusing**]
repl. del. see no wrong in   159.38 **industry,**] *altered from* ~. *before del.* Perhaps it is a better
way than that   159.40 **own**] *inserted*
160.1 **well**] *after del.* although   160.2 **a good model of**] *inserted before del.* a Greec Style
applied on China   Style] *above del.* Character   China] *underl.*   160.5 **renomated**]
accompanied in opposite column by Hans Semper's note in ink renomated   160.6 **more fusible**]
after del. softer in fire   China] *after del.* Po[r]   160.9 **Some other**] *after del.* Among the
Gla. *after del.* on fol. 12v*

On Timber Construction, and Its Influence upon Architectural Forms 477

Among the other potteries are to be mentionned as artistically interesting the Stonewares, which have sometimes[1] no glazing[2] and at other times[3] are glazed only by the process of *smearing* but[4] are impermeable[5] by themselfes. Those who have the best developd this sort of pottery, technically as well as artistically are the Flamish and the Germans. beautiful Stonewares also in Italia in China Japon

> 1 **sometimes**] *interl.*   2 **glazing**] *before del.* at all but form a very hard   3 **and at other times ~ smearing**] *interl.*   4 **but**] *after undel.* all   5 **impermeable**] im- | permeable; im *altered from* in *and* permeable *after del.* penetrable by them

160.9 **important**] *interl.*   160.14 **It was**] *after del.* The forms of the German *after del.* They are   160.16 **They are rich**] *after del.*

They show generally their[1] gray natural ground surfaces[2] ornemented with[3] deep and quiet colours,[4]

> 1 **They show generally their**] *inserted after del.* This Style of the old Stonewares with their 2 **ground surfaces**] *repl. del.* grounds   3 **ornemented with**] *above del.* and the   4 **colours,**] *inserted before del.* Style of colouring on this ground   ground] *undel.*

160.16 **forms**] *above del.* colours   160.18 **sustain**] *repl. del.* pass throw   throw] *'through'* **fire.**] *altered from* ~∧ *before del.* and h   160.22 **mention**] *above del.* remenber   160.24 **composed.**] *before del.* The   160.25–7 **Assyrische Vasen ~ Reichthum an**] *in left column* 160.27 **Grosser Reichthum an**] *inserted after del.* Style   Style] *after underl. and del.* Griechisce Metallvasen (Griechisce: 'Griechische')   160.28–33 **(Aegypter ~ Griechenlands.**] *in right column, starting alongside the manuscript line* Bleche Embleme. – . *at 160.26* 160.28 **der**] *after del.* of   160.30–1 **Die Archaischen**] *repl. del.* Die

On Timber Construction, and Its Influence upon the Development of Architectural Forms

TEXTUAL RECORD

MS 137   gta, 20-Ms-137, fols. 1r–4v (1r–v, 4v blank), in Semper's hand
MS 136   gta, 20-Ms-136, fols. 1r–8v (2v–5r variant of MS 137), in Semper's hand, *copytext*

BIBLIOGRAPHY Herrmann 1981, 112

478 Lectures

EXPLANATORY NOTES

Only a fragment of the manuscript of this lecture (MS 136) is preserved: it lacks the original beginning and the original end, as can be seen from the fact that both the start and the end are in the middle of sentences. Thematically, the fragment is divided into four parts. The first part (161.2–162.23) is concerned with concavely and convexly curving roof forms, on the one hand, and on the other with a field that is not directly related to wooden construction, namely the external covering of the roof. In the second part (162.24–166.9), Semper uses sketches, which he probably transferred to a blackboard in the auditorium, to explain – by means of specific examples – the three elementary and six most common combined static systems for spanning horizontal distances. In the process, he makes use of his own practical experience as a professional architect, as well as the knowledge of bridge construction that he had taught his students in Dresden in the 1840s (see 479, Explanatory Notes 162.24). Yet he describes one of the most important combined systems from an architectural point of view – the extension system 'with an accessory system of compression' – in an incorrect way (166.5–9), since in a roof construction corresponding to the sketch the main system consists of rafters that resist compression and carry a vertical accessory extension system, a king-post (which in turn carries a horizontal accessory extension system; cf. 165.8–13).

On the basis of this combined system, Semper in the third part (166.10–167.8) discusses the ancient and medieval use of wooden gabled roof construction in Europe, focusing only on the structure visible from the interior, without a ceiling cover. He justifies this construction – which is actually against his own preference for concealing the supporting structure and the symbolic translation of the spatial enclosure – by the fact that it was used to cover public spaces, which due to their origin were not regarded as interiors but rather as exteriors, as courtyards. In the fourth part (167.9–168.28), Semper deals firstly with what represented the opposite of Roman wall and vault architecture, namely the constructively varied wooden architecture encompassing walls and roof in northern and central Europe, and its earliest Mediterranean antecedents, which can be deduced only from illustrations and descriptions. Secondly, he touches on three areas peripheral to wooden construction: ships, funeral piles, which he examines more closely in *Style in the Technical and Tectonic Arts* (Semper 1860/63, 1:314–17), and carpentry products. In the fifth part (168.29–169.18), which is concerned with the secondary theme announced in the 'Prospectuses of the Lectures on Art' – 'Metal works as belonging to timber construction, in opposition to other modes which belong to the t[u]bular construction, or to ceramic art' (96.22–4) – Semper concludes by considering the elements of the various roof constructions for which cast or forged metal could be used. Here he makes no secret of the difficulty for him of overcoming the conflict between adapting to the specific properties of materials, on the one hand, and following traditional types of wooden construction on the other.

Semper had long been sceptical about the use of iron in architecture. In 1842, in an expert opinion provided for a church project in Saxony, his view was that previous attempts to give iron 'a significant and leading role in serious, great architecture' had failed because 'iron, due to its peculiar lack of volume, eludes the gaze even from a short distance, when it appears in its legitimate strength and shape' (gta, 20-Ms-7, fols. 4v–5r; cf. 485, Alterations in the Manuscript 169.15). In 1849, in his essay 'Der Wintergarten zu Paris' (The Winter Garden in Paris), Semper did not take a more favourable view of the contemporary use of iron but did mention one way of overcoming the conflict involved – namely, tubular formation of all construction elements that are exposed to deflection or compression (Semper 1849h, 521–2).

On Timber Construction, and Its Influence upon Architectural Forms

A second, shorter manuscript for the lecture 'On Timber Construction, and Its Influence upon the Development of Architectural Forms' is preserved, with the title 'On the Modes of resistance of the materials' (MS 137). It corresponds approximately to the second part of MS 136, the longer manuscript (162.24–166.16), and deals with the same elementary and combined static systems but describes three of them more succinctly than MS 136. Only the 'System of compression with an accessory system of extension', which is described as 'the most interesting in architecture as an art', is illustrated in greater detail. It concludes with the remark that Semper will return to this system 'hereafter' (486.8–16; cf. 165.8–13). In his last lecture in the autumn series of 1853, Semper did touch on the system concerned, on which the gabled roof is based, but only in passing (173.31–2, 176.24–5). He discussed it in more detail in the lecture 'On Architectural Symbols' in the autumn term of 1854 (180.15–181.4).

161.2–4 **The Chinese adopted the same anomaly ~ not ~ in imitation of the tents of their ancestors**] The words 'anomaly' and 'ancestors' refer to the concave curvature of the roof shape and the Mongols, respectively (cf. 482, Alterations in the Manuscript 161.3–4). In the essay 'On the Origin of Polychromy in Architecture', which was published in the appendix of *An Apology for the Colouring of the Greek Court in the Crystal Palace* (Jones 1854a), Semper did not contradict the view that the shape of the Chinese roof was derived from the shape of the Mongolian tent (61.27–8), whereas in *Style* he made a more critical assessment of it again (Semper 1860/63, 1:2). 161.15–16 **Two kinds of coverings ~ scales ~ skin.**] The same distinction appears in the 'Outline of a Cultural-Historical Exhibition' (42.25–31, 301.28–35, 304.21–5, 307.25–9). 161.23 **let**] *led* 161.25 **burnt**] *baked* 161.28 **guilt**] *gilt* 162.3 **board**] *eaves* (see also 162.8) 162.5 **in clined**] *inclined* 162.6 **corniche**] French for *cornice* (see also 164.13) 162.8 **Watercourses**] *gutters* 162.9 **gutters**] *gargoyles* **lyonheads**] *lions' heads* 162.11 **Wienna**] merged from German *Wien* and English *Vienna* 162.20 **Mr Minton at Staffortshire**] On 8 April 1852, during a three-week visit to Herbert Minton's ceramics factory (see 329), Semper wrote to Henry Cole (Herrmann 1978, 129): 'The glazed roof tiles of Mr. Minton are less perfect with regard to practical service than his floortiles, and it will perhaps be difficult to overwhelm all the obstacles which our clime opposes to their emploiment.' In *Science, Industry, and Art*, Semper mentions 'Minton's beautiful faiences' (Semper 1852, 52), and in *Style* he refers to Minton's 'imitations of the Arabian glazed tiles' with which Owen Jones coated his Alhambra Court at Sydenham Palace (Semper 1860/63, 2:123). 162.21–2 **The Chinese ~ tyle construction is ~ that of the Ancients.**] Semper is here apparently assuming fired and glazed clay tiles, whereas in the lecture 'On the Relation of Architectural Systems with the General Cultural Conditions' he refers to 'stoned [i.e. stone] tiles of different colours' whose style of shaping and joining reminds him of ancient Greek and Roman roofs (196.33–5). 162.24 **I shell now ~ consider the constructiv part of the question.**] 'shell': *shall*. Two lecture notebooks preserved in Zurich show that in 1841 and 1842 Semper lectured on ancient and modern bridge-building at the Academy of Arts in Dresden (gta, 20-Ms-26, 237–86; 20-Ms-28, 33–41, 43–4). Shortly before his flight from Dresden, he was also intensively concerned with the construction of the iron roof framework of the Gemäldegalerie in Dresden. 162.29 **Resistance by Rigidity**] This expression is not analogous to the expressions assigned to the second and third types of load, 'Resistence to compression' (162.32) and 'Resistence to Extension' (163.2), since it does not designate the potential deformation (namely deflection) but rather the property of the system that reduces or prevents it.

480 Lectures

163.17–19 **Diodor calls the Rooms ~ pipes ~ adding that they were highly ornamented**] cf. Semper 1851b, 82   163.19 **allongated**] derived from French *allonger*: *elongated*   163.24–5 **Greec Architecture was, as we shall see in the next lecture of a very compount caracter.**] In the two surviving manuscripts for the lecture 'The Combined Action of the Four Preceding Branches of Industry in Architecture' (MS 138, MS 139), Semper does not fulfil his promise to explain the 'compount caracter' of Greek architecture (see 169–77, 496). 163.28–9 **bridge over the James Rivver ~ in Virginia**] This wooden bridge for the Richmond and Petersburg Railroad was built in 1836–38 under the direction of Moncure Robinson.   163.30–1 **tubular System ~ employed in England (Victoria bridge)**] The use of a purely tubular system is seen only in Wales and Canada and not in England. Three famous iron railway bridges were constructed using this system, under the direction of Robert Stephenson: the Conway Bridge over the River Conway in Wales (1846–49), the Britannia Bridge across the Menai Straits in Wales (1846–50) and a bridge over the St Lawrence River near Montreal in Canada (1854–59), which at the time of Semper's lecture was already being called the Victoria Bridge. As the latter bridge was only in planning at the time, it can be assumed that Semper was referring to the larger bridge in Wales, the Britannia Bridge. 164.2 **weider**] merged from German *weiter* and English *wider*   164.8–9 **book intitled the Open timber Roof of the middle Ages cet. London 1849**] 'cet.': *etc.*; Brandon/Brandon 1849   164.11–12 **Roman mode of covering the large theaters with Velas suspended on stringes with the aid of high Mates**] 'stringes': *strings*; 'Mates': *masts* (see also 164.26). Semper himself used the ancient motif of a suspended *velum* in 1858 in his design for a theatre in Rio de Janeiro.   164.15 **Hippodromes at Paris ~ by Mr Hittorf**] cf. Semper 1853, 296. This refers to Jacques Ignace Hittorff's Cirque d'Été (1841–43) and Cirque d'Hiver (1852), although their roofs were not constructed according to 'the rigid system with an accessory system of extension' (164.10). Hittorff used this combined system only in the Panorama building (1838–39) on the Champs-Élysées in Paris.   164.24 **waulding**] *vaulting* 165.10–11 **This is the most important ~ by its having been the types for the sacred edifices.**] Semper explains the significance of this roof system more precisely in the lecture 'On Architectural Symbols' when he discusses 'The gabled roof' (180.15–181.7).   165.12–13 **in combination with an other system, which will follow on its turn**] This refers to the vertical extension system, the combination of which with a horizontal extension system and an oblique compression system Semper discusses under the title 'Extension with an accessory system of compression' (166.5–9).   165.18 **wayfaring trees**] These are bushes of the genus *Viburnum*, but Semper probably means *vines* growing from one brook bank or gorge slope to the other.   165.24 **Pompea**] *Pompeii* (see also 167.35) 166.3 **frightfull accidents**] For example, two smaller suspension bridges in England and two larger ones in France collapsed due to structural flaws: one over the River Irwell near Broughton, north-west of Manchester, in 1831 (opened in 1826); one over the River Bure near Great Yarmouth, east of Norwich, in 1845 (opened in 1829); one over the River Maine in Angers in 1850 (opened in 1838); and one over the River Vilaine near La Roche-Bernard, north of Saint-Nazaire, in 1852 (opened in 1839). Over 300 people died in the disasters. 166.12–14 **It was introduced with the ancients ~ Basilicas**] cf. Semper 1851b, 74–8, 95 n. * 166.18–19 **the above mentionned Odeon of Pericles**] see 164.25–165.3   166.25–6 **the richly already bespoken ornamented roofs in the English Gothic style**] 'bespoken' derived from German *besprechen*: *discussed*. Semper hints at this type of roof only in the second section of the first class of static systems (164.5–6). Perhaps he discussed it in front of the audience, using examples from the book *The Open Timber Roofs of the Middle Ages* (164.7–9;

On Timber Construction, and Its Influence upon Architectural Forms   481

Brandon/Brandon 1849).   166.26–7 **Westminster hall, Hampton court, Windsor**] Semper apparently refers to the Great Hall at Westminster Palace (usually called Westminster Hall), the Great Hall at Hampton Court Palace and St George's Hall at Windsor Castle. Their gable roofs are examples of the varied constructions gathered together under the term 'Hammer-Beam Roofs' in the book by the Brandon brothers (Brandon/Brandon 1849, 20–5). In an initial, abandoned approach, Semper incorrectly places them in the second section of the first class of static systems, i.e. under 'the Rigid system with an accessory system of compression' (164.1; see 482, Alterations in the Manuscript 164.3–9).   166.27 **an**] *and* 166.27–30 **They take their Ornaments from the ~ construction itself, while the German and Frensh Gothic Roofs are ~ much richer in ~ ornamental details.**] In two initial, abandoned approaches, Semper adds a similar remark to the second section of the first class of static systems (see 482–3, Alterations in the Manuscript 164.3–9, 164.4).

167.4 **Tacitus in his Germania**] Semper's private reference library in Dresden included a copy of Tacitus's *Germania* (see 211.12, 215.34).   167.6–8 **instances ~ Norvegian Churches, (9th or 10th Century)**] This probably refers to plates in Johan Christian Clausen Dahl's book *Denkmale einer sehr ausgebildeten Holzbaukunst* (Dahl 1837), which Semper mentioned in the next lecture (171.26).   167.11–12 **The Gothic architecture inherited of this northern style of ornamenting the wood constructions.**] This is followed in the manuscript by two deleted sentences referring to unnamed books on Gothic wood constructions and to drawings that Semper himself had made 'at Rouens and elsewhere in Normandy' (see 483, Alterations in the Manuscript 167.12). Another deleted passage referring to the second section of the first class of static systems mentions 'Engravings and drawings' of 'Beautifull roofs at Rouen, (town house) Nurnberg, Italy' (see 483, Alterations in the Manuscript 164.3–9). Semper illustrates two corresponding 'gabled houses in Rouen' in *Style* (Semper 1860/63, 2:305), where he also mentions a book of plates that may have been one of those unnamed books on Gothic wood constructions: Augustus Welby Northmore Pugin's *Details of Antient Timber Houses of the 15th & 16th Centuries*, published in London in 1837 (Pugin 1837).   167.15 **ad**] Latin for *at* (see also 168.38)   167.16 **blockhouses**] *log houses* 167.22–3 **Such were the old Colchian houses ~ such are still now the houses of the Tyrolians and Switzer peasants**] cf. Semper 1860/63, 2:306–16. In *Style*, Semper classifies Tyrolean houses not as log houses, but as timber-framed houses.   167.24 **Sueden**] merged from French *Suède* and English *Sweden*   **Norvegia**] Italian for *Norway*   167.25 **collection of Switzer Edifices**] This refers to the plates in Adolf von Graffenried and Ludwig Stürler's book *Architecture suisse* (Graffenried/Stürler 1844). Stürler, a former fellow student of Semper's in the studio of Franz Christian Gau in Paris (see 250), presented the book to Semper in 1850 (Stürler to Semper, 11 May 1850, 23 June 1850, 7 July 1850, gta, 20-K-1850-05-11, 20-K-1850-06-23:1, 20-K-1850-07-07:1).   167.28 **maçonry**] merged from French *maçonnerie* and English *masonry*   167.29–30 **beautiful exemples ~ by Mr Bötticher in Berlin**] see Bötticher 1842   167.31–2 **drawings, from buildings ~ in Normandy**] see note 167.11–12; 483, Alterations in the Manuscript 167.12   167.39 **massif**] *massive*

168.1 **tablatures**] *wall panels*   168.6–7 **Rogi or funeral piles ~ represented on some Roman medals**] cf. Semper 1860/63, 1:314–17   168.9–12 **I have the Idea that the Lycian monuments ~ are nothing but the stone Copies of the original funeral piles ~ erected.**] cf. Semper 1860/63, 1:229–30, 430–1   168.20 **leining**] *lining*   168.26 **Niello**] see 440, Explanatory Notes 133.18   168.27 **Venitian**] merged from French *vénitien* and English *Venetian*   168.30 **these diagramms**] the nine diagrams illustrating the individual sections of the three classes of static systems; see 163–6

169.10–15 **It is evident, that a new Material ~ requires many alterations ~ On the other side we are bount to observe some traditional types ~ borrowed from timber-construction.**] cf. Semper 1849h, 521–2; Semper 1860/63, 2:263–6

EDITORIAL EMENDATIONS

162.7 **palmets,**] palme *(ts, on fol. 3r)*   162.8 **ornamented**] ornamente *(d on fol. 3r)*   162.13 **drapery-like**] drapery- | like   167.6–7 **wood-constructions**] wood- | constructions 167.12 **wood constructions**] wood | constructions

ALTERATIONS IN THE MANUSCRIPT

161.2 **less**] *after del.* more   **roofs,**] *before del.* perhaps in imitation of the old buildings of 161.3–4 **tents of their ancestors**] *after del.* Mon *(for 'Mongol')*   161.4 **Wooden**] *after del.* holy edifices   161.6–7 **hydrodynamical**] *repl. del.* mechanical   161.12 **The covering**] *after del.* One important   161.18 **also**] *above del.* secondly   161.19 **opportunity**] *repl. del.* occasion   161.20–1 **appropriate**] *after del.* happy for or[n]   161.22 **The**] *altered from* the *after underl. and del.* Instances   **the Hellenic buildings**] *repl. del.* the Greecs,   **is**] *above del.* a happy   161.29 **usual**] *after del.* very   161.30 **constructedʌ**] *altered from* ~, *before inserted and del.* so as to form a sort of inclined wall, one stone covering the other and securing the joints against the introduction of water. The   161.31 **(see the drawing)**] *after del.* here are parts [o]

162.1 **were**] *above del.* was   was] *after del.* layer   162.2 **row of**] *interl.*   162.3 **Channel-formed tyles**] *repl. del.* tyles in form of a Channel   tyles] s *added*   162.3–4 **The last ridge was finally protected with**] *repl. del.* On the Ridge was   162.4 **ridge**] *interl.*   162.5 **Saddletyles**] *after del.* Channel-tyles   162.8 **roofs**] *after del.* Sides of the   162.14 **new**] *interl.*   162.15 **executed in imitation**] *after del.* in the Oriental Style or in im[i]   **Saracenesk roofs**] *after del.* oriental roofs   162.18 **tyles**] *after del.* roofs   162.19 **good**] *after del.* resuscitation of a   162.19–20 **ornamental**] *inserted*   162.21 **tyle**] *after del.* mode of 163.4 **cases**] *after del.* circumsta   163.6 **with the view of**] *above del.* to   **counteracting**] ing *added*   163.7 **of**] *above del.* to   **forming**] ing *added*   163.11 **three**] *after del.* 1°) 163.13–14 **a multiplication**] *after del.* narrow   163.15 **diagramm).**] *after del.* figure). 163.16 **some parts of**] *interl.*   163.18 **protected**] *after del.* underneath   163.19 **adding**] *repl. del.* and says   163.22 **the Construction**] *after del.* temple   163.24 **formgiving**] *after del.* they were   163.26 **newly**] *after del.* in the new   163.27 **bridges,**] *below del.* System, 163.28 **supported by pillars.**] *inserted*   **Example.**] *repl. del.* see   163.30 **a rigid tube**] *after del.* also forming rigid tubes   **invented**] *after del.* adopted 164.2 **weider distances between the pillars,**] *inserted before* columns of wider   columns of wider] *after del.* wider distanced columns and *and before del.* distanced   164.3–9 **Generally adopted ~ London 1849.**] *inserted before del.*

The Gothic ceilings, mainly in[1] England, more simple in the constructiv principles but richer in ornamental details in Germany and France. Westminster, Hampton court – Windsor.

On Timber Construction, and Its Influence upon Architectural Forms 483

Beautifull roofs at Rouen, (town house) Nurnberg, Italy. (Engravings and drawings.)

  1 **mainly in**] *repl. del.* very developed in

164.3 **Generally**] *above del.* Sometimes 164.4 **in England.**] *before del.*

The constructiv principle[1] of the English Roof is much richer than in Germany and France, in[2] the later[3] countries they are very simple in construction but much more[4] decorated by ornamental details

  1 **principle**] *before interl. and del.* of ornamentation 2 **in**] *after del.* but 3 **later**] *'latter'*
  4 **more**] *after del.* richer

164.11 **Roman**] *interl.* 164.12 **with the aid**] *after del.* attached and 164.12–13 **towering above**] *after del.* surrounding and over 164.14 **circular**] *inserted* 164.22 **instances**] *after del.* Celtic 164.23 **the principle**] *after del.* the principle of stone vaults 164.25–165.3 **The Periclean Odeon ~ building.**] *inserted* 164.26 **Persian**] *interl.*
165.4 **another**] *repl. del.* an 165.12 **It seldom**] *after del.* it only 165.25 **which will find a leader**] *after del.* which will not be embarrassed *after del.* which will not fail if they remind this origine 165.26 **if they remember**] *repl. del.* in
166.2 **applied**] *after del.* the best the] *undel.* **first and best**] *interl.* 166.11 **all**] *above del.* many **most**] *above del.* many 166.12 **introduced**] *above del.* taken 166.13 **courtyards**] *after del.* usual **formed**] *above del.* were **usual**] *interl.* 166.15 **abroad.**] *after del.* the barbarians. **inside**] *interl.* 166.17 **independently**] ly *added* 166.20 **likewise**] *interl.* **first**] *before del.* like 166.23 **roofs**] *after del.* basilica 166.25–30 **Some ~ details.**] *inserted* 166.25 **Some of the richly ~ ornamented**] *repl. del.* The The] *after del.* The English Churches and the roofed halls remi **already bespoken**] *interl.* **roofs**] *altered from* roofed *before del.* halls
167.1–3 **of northern woodconstruction ~ countries,**] *repl. del.* of roofs was different from this in the northern countries, where of] *undel. after del.* was altered in the time *and before del.* Gothic architecture, when the wood sculpture was for such 167.3 **cutting and**] *inserted* 167.4 **timbers**] *after del.* wood and 167.9–11 **In these northern countries ~ dominant;**] *inserted* 167.11 **The Gothic architecture**] *after del.* In this book is a collection of 167.12 **wood constructions.**] *before del.* Here are several books, containing such Gothic woodconstructions. These drawings I made at Rouens and elsewhere in Normandy.
167.13 **We must make a distinction**] *after del.* Two distinct styles of wooden house constructions are visible *after del.* But I must speak here a little more systemati *after del.* Two sor
167.14 **pieces**] *after del.* beams 167.14–15 **disposed**] *above del.* laid 167.15 **joined**] *repl. del.* engrafted 167.17 **are used for**] *repl. del.* form the 167.18 **beautifully**] *after del.* simply and 167.20 **Ensemble.**] *repl. del.* effect. 167.22 **Such were the old Colchian houses**] *after del.* Such houses are commonly seen in Switzerland 167.25 **collection**] *after del.* book containing 167.26 **house.**] *after del.* building. 167.29 **Germany,**] *before del.* where 167.31 **drawings**] *after del. on fol. 6r* Buildings drawn by Buildings] *after del.* N
actually existing] *interl. without insertion mark* 167.32–3 **You furtherly see ~ arranged.**] *inserted* 167.32 **You furtherly see in this collection here**] *above del.* In this collection you will see collection] *after del.* book 167.36 **wood and metal**] *repl. del.* such light light] *above del.* mouveable 167.36–168.2 **This diagramm ~ authors.**] *inserted* 167.37 **support-**

ers] *after del. in pencil* columns which form the **phantastic]** *after del.* lofty combinations **constructions]** *in pencil above del. in pencil* buildings 167.39 **notwithstanding]** *repl. del.* had on the side of
168.1 **Assyrians,]** *before del.* which had only wooden columns and whose houses had had] *after del.* were ornamented **Their]** *interl.* 168.1–2 **are mentionned]** *above del.* as we know 168.4 **and detaild]** *interl. in pencil* 168.5 **some of them]** *before del. in pencil* which I whished to be permitted to communcate here whished] *'wished'* 168.7 **The funeral piles]** *after del.* Alexanders 168.9 **I have the Idea]** *after del.* The woodconstructions had a high relig 168.11 **original]** *inserted* **piles]** *before del.* which the dead who w[e] 168.12 **erected. – .]** *before del. in ink over pencil*

I shall finally have to spend[1] only some few minutes to[2] metal-construction as typically connected with the first. –

---

1 **have to spend]** *repl. del.* spend 2 **to]** *after del.* to the application of this constructiv principle of] *undel. before del.* the timbercons

168.13 **monuments,]** *before del.* comp[a] 168.14 **striking;]** *before del.* and thus the singular idea, of a ra[ ] 168.15 **of]** *above del.* telling some **giving]** *altered from* give *after del.* to 168.18 **am obliged]** *after del.* must *after del.* shall **The art of the joiners]** *after del.* The joiners art belongs more or less to surface decoration 168.20 **a wall or]** *after del.* pannelled bo[a] 168.24 **has]** *after del.* belongs to the same Class and 168.26 **Marquetry]** *after del.* Inlaid wood. 168.26–7 **Aegyptian]** *after del.* Inventio 168.29 **Metal]** *after del.* other Materials, **Roofconstruction]** *after del.* timber 168.30 **If we look at these diagramms]** *after del.*

If we look at these Diagramms, we observe some parts of the constructions, which belong more to the domain of[1]

---

1 **belong more to the domain of]** *repl. del.* claim for an other material claim] *after del.* seem to demand

168.30 **affected]** *above del.* acted upon 168.31 **which seems ~ rather]** *repl. del.* as to be better of Metal as] *above del.* so **stone and]** *interl.* 168.32 **Wood]** *over* St *(for 'Stone')* **Wood.]** *altered from* ~∧ *before del.* or any other Material. or any other Material.] *before inserted and del.* Others are best executed of Stone or any other rigid substance. 168.33 **for instance]** *after del.* This is evident 168.34 **we]** *after del.* Here **may]** *interl.* 168.34–5 **Stone or Bronze or cast Iron]** *after del.* cast Iron or 168.36 **At c, in turn]** *after del.*

at c we want[1] the extension or suspension strings being[2] of wrought[3] metal,[4] rather than of any other material

---

1 **want]** *above del.* whish in tur[n] whish] *'wish'* 2 **being]** *interl.* 3 **wrought]** *above del.* metal, 4 **metal,]** *inserted after inserted and del.* cast or w

168.37 **chains]** *after del.* pieces *after del.* str 168.38 **feel]** *before del.* it to be better **application]** *after del.* aptetute aptetute] *'aptitude'*

On Timber Construction, and Its Influence upon Architectural Forms   485

169.1 **this is also**] *after underl. and del.* at e   **may best be**] *after del.* we observe   169.3
Metal] *after del.* thin   169.5 **This leads**] *repl. del.* The Architects were therefore soon let
let] *'led'*   **roof**] *repl. del.* ceiling   169.7 **The**] *above del.* A   A] *after del.* The Theory
169.10 **adopted**] *repl. del.* employed   employed] *after del.* must not   169.11 **one**] *above del.*
material   **requires**] *repl. del.* will afford   **many**] *after del.* other   169.13 **On the other**
side] *after del.* and nevertheless we are bount to old   nevertheless] *before del.* I   **trad-**
itional] *before del.* and typical   169.15 **timber-construction.**] *before del.*

Meantime it is evident that Metal[1] chains or wrought and cast Metal constructions have[2]
the inconveniance of being rather an invisible Meterial for elevations[3] like the inner Roofs
of Churches, halls, etc,

> [1] **Metal**] *after del.* the application of thin   [2] **have**] ve *over* s   [3] **elevations**] *repl. del.*
> such distances

MANUSCRIPT VARIANTS
MS 137

On the Modes of resistance of the materials.   *fol. 2r*

The Meterial which can be employed in constructions can resist in three different manners:
1) To a force, which is directed perpendicularly on the length of the piece of construction,
and which tends to break it transversally. (*Resistance by Rigidity*)
2°) To a force, which is directed in the sens of de length of the piece of construction, and
which tends to *crush* it. (*Resistance to compression*)
3°) To a force directed in the sens of the length and which tends to dilate it (Resistance to
Extension).
Every timber construction, is composed of parts, which are affected in one or the other of
these three different manners; and at many circumstance one part is affected by a combined
action of two of the three manifestations of forces; The modes in which the materials are
employed to counteract these forces and to form a solid system of resistance are very mani-
fold, but they may be classified as followes: |

I. Class. (*The rigid principle prevailing*)   *fol. 2v*
a) The rigid system without any accessory system.
The tubular system Pantheon, baths of Caracalla.
Egyptian roofs. The narrow Standing and multiplied supporters and columns are natural
consequences of the adoption of this system of protecting edifices.).
b) The rigid system with an accessory system of compression.
Indian roofs. (Gothic ceilings. The columns and supports may be placed in wider distances.
(see the Indian temples.).
c) The rigid system with an accessory system of extension. |
A kind of instance of this system employed by the ancients are the vela employed for the   *fol. 3r*
Amphitheaters and Theaters of the *Romans*.. Suspension of the Vela on Strings which were
sustained by mates or poles standing round the upper story of the Edifice. Modern imitation
of this idea by Mr Hittorf, who employed it for supporting the roofs of his large hippodromes..

II. Class.

The principle of compression is prevailing.

1°) a System of compression without any accessory system

The old Etruscan Tombs, the doors in the Cyclopean valls, the roofs of the inner roorms of the Pyranids. Origine of the vaults. – . Celtic buildings.

2°) System of compression with an accessory system of compression.

Gothic ceilings.

3°) System of compression with an accessory system of extension.

This system is the most interesting in architecture as an art, not only by the artistical development of it in the different periods of architecture but also and principally by its having been the type for the sacred edifices of all nations. *The Egyptian* Sekos or Sanctuaries, The Assyrian temples standing on the tops of the moles or Pyramids (Tower of Babel) Herodot gives us the description of the Tempel of Belus which stood on the top of that edifice which probably was identic with ¦ the Babel tower of the bible. The Caaba at Mecca the holy sanctuary of the Moslem is a roofed building. This roof the caracteristicon of Greec temples and Grec style in general. but I shall come back to this hereafter.

III. System.

1 *The principle of Extension is prevailing.*

1°) The system of Extension without any accessory system.

The natural suspension bridges, formed by wayfaring trees, in South America. Bridges usual in China, the Original suspension bridges. The Vela of the Greecs and ancients, being the types for ceiling decoration, the inner ceilings of the Greec temples stood in no constructiv rapport with the Roof, which was only formgiving for the outer architecture. (Importance of this remark for ornamental art. The velum the type for flat ceilings.

The names of the single parts of the Greec ceilings, the stone beams, the plates pierced by holes, which were coverd with other stones all taken from textile art, and ornamented consequently with textile ornaments.

2°) The system of Extension with another accessory system of Extension.

A modern invention which has been most happily developd by the English Engeneers – but still imperfect, chiefly for the artistical question.

3°) The system of Extension with an accessory system of compression.

The full development of the Roof construction. Antique Roof introduced when the wide courts of the buildings became to be covered. Basilicas. This is also one of the important ¦ circumstances in history of art, all the wide rooms typically are uncovered courts, and have maintained the appearances of outer architecture through the whole history of architecture. Antique Roof, about a third of the amplitude.

485.1 **On the Modes]** *after Hans Semper's note on fol. 1r:*

II. e.

On the modes of resistance of the materials

---

4 Seiten. Englisch.

485.4 **tends**] *after del.* works   **transversally**] *after del.* hor   **(Resistance by Rigidity)**] *before sketch resembling one in MS 136, fol. 2v (162, upper sketch)*   485.5 **in the sens**] *after del.* perpendicularly   **de**] *'the'*   485.6 **crush it**] *after del.* break it   **(Resistance to compression)**] *before sketch resembling one in MS 136, fol. 2v (162, lower sketch)*   485.7–8 **(Resistance to Extension).**] *before sketch resembling one in MS 136, fol. 2v (163, upper sketch)*   485.9 **is composed of**] *after del.* or construction composed out of   485.11 **manifestations**] *after del.* different modes of   **forces;**] *before del.* The different combinations which arise from the static equilibrium of   485.12 **these**] se *added*   **forces**] *before del.* in question   **form**] *after del.* maintain   485.14 **I. Class.**] *after del. on fol. 2r–v*

I Class,[1]
The mode of protecting edifices with The Aegyptians, only by large horizontal layers of stone plates. (*narrow*[2] (*system of supports and Columns*). ¦

IId Class
1°) The[4] system[3] resisting to compression without[5] an additional or accessory system of resistance[6]
The old Etruscan Tombs, the Doors in the Cyclopean Walls, the Pelasgic or old Hellenic Edifices, The Pyramids; The elementary principle of arches and vaults. –
2°)[7] The system[8] resisting to compression, with an accessory system resisting to

---

1 **I Class,**] *inserted after del.* (The rigid system without suspension.) *and before sketch resembling one in MS 136, fol. 3r (163, lower sketch)*   (The rigid system without suspension.)] *after del.* 1°)   2 **(narrow**] *inserted before sketch resembling one in MS 136, fol. 4r (164, lower sketch)*   3 **1°) The system ~ resistance**] 4 **The**] *above del.* Suspension   5 **without**] *above del.* with   6 **of resistance**] *above del.* of suspension   7 **2°)**] *after del.* 2°) The system resisting to compression with an accessory system of suspension, or extension *and del. sketch resembling one in MS 136, fol. 4r (165, middle sketch), and del. sketch of suspended beam*   8 **system**] *after del.* principal

---

485.14 **principle**] *above underl. and del.* system   485.15 **a) The rigid system without any accessory system.**] *before sketch resembling one in MS 136, fol. 3r (163, lower sketch)*   485.17 **Egyptian roofs**] *after del.* Egyptian roofs.. Old Galic monuments, (This system necessitates arrangements of supporting the roofs, which are characteristiques for styles which Egyptian roofs] *underl.*   **Standing**] *interl.*   485.19 **b) The rigid system with an accessory system of compression.**] *before sketch resembling one in MS 136, fol. 3v (164, upper sketch)*   485.22 **c) The rigid system with an accessory system of extension.**] *before sketch resembling one in MS 136, fol. 3v (164, middle sketch)*   485.23 **A kind**] *after del.* We have no notices of this system having been known to the ancients. Modern examples of bridges executed in this system. Adopted by Mr Hittorf Architect for two Hippodromes executed in Paris   485.25 **mates**] *'masts'*   485.25–7 **Modern imitation ~ by Mr Hittorf ~ hippodromes**] *see 480, Explanatory Notes 164.15*   485.26–7 **hippodromes..**] *before del.* 3°) A Rigid system with an accessory system of exte[n]   486.3 **1°) a System of compression without any accessory system**] *before sketch resembling one in MS 136, fol. 4r (164, lower sketch)*   486.4 **roofs**] *after del.* inner   **roorms**] *'rooms'*   486.6 **2°) System of compression with an accessory system of compression.**] *before sketch resembling one in MS 136, fol. 4r (165, upper sketch)*   486.8 **3°) System of compression with an accessory system of extension.**] *before sketch of tied arch and sketch resembling one in MS 136, fol. 4r (165, middle sketch)*   486.12 **moles**] *below del.* tombs   486.14 **identic**] *altered from* identical   **bible**] *after del.* holy   486.17 **III. System.**] *after del.* 4°   486.19 **1°) The system of Extension without any accessory system.**] *before sketch resembling one in MS 136, fol. 4r (165, lower sketch)*   486.20 **wayfaring trees**] *'vines'* *(see 480, Explanatory Notes 165.18)*   486.22 **stood in**] *above del.* had   **no**] *after del.* nothing   486.23 **rapport**] *'connection'*   **Roof**] *before del.* architecture   486.23–4 **(Importance ~ ceilings.**] *inserted*   486.24 **ceilings**] *above del.* roofs)   486.25 **The**] *after del.* 2°)   [ ]   **names of the**] *interl.*   486.28 **2°) The system of Extension with another accessory system of Extension.**] *before sketch resembling one in MS 136, fol. 4v (166, upper sketch)*   486.31 **3°) The system of Extension with an accessory system of compression.**] *before sketch resembling one in MS 136, fol. 4v (166, lower sketch)*   486.34 **all**] *after del.* that   486.36 **Antique**] *after del.* Even the inner of   inner] *after del.* Gothic Cathed[r]   **amplitude**] *after del.* width

The Combined Action of the Four Preceding Branches of Industry in Architecture

TEXTUAL RECORD

MS 139   gta, 20-Ms-139, fols. 1r–2v (2r–v blank), in Semper's hand
MS 138   gta, 20-Ms-138, fols. 1r–16v (12v–16v blank; 1r calculations and sketch of superposed triangles; 8r–v variant of MS 139), in Semper's hand, *copy-text*
MS 140   gta, 20-Ms-140, fols. 1r–8v (3v, 4v G. Völckers's letter probably to Manfred Semper, 1 October 1880), in Manfred Semper's hand, early 1880s, copy of MS 138
Semper 1884   'Ueber den Ursprung einiger Architekturstile', 369–82, German trans. of MS 138; for details of this translation, see Herrmann 1981, 172–4
Semper 1985a   'London Lecture of December 1853', 53–60, here 53, 55–60, Mallgrave's ed. of MS 138

BIBLIOGRAPHY Herrmann 1981, 112–13, 172–4; Mallgrave 1985a, 74, 76–7; Luttmann 2008, 145–7; Gnehm 2020, 36

EXPLANATORY NOTES

This concluding lecture of Semper's 1853 public course 'On Architecture, Practical Construction, and Plastic Art Generally' provides – as Semper announces in its first paragraph – 'some remarks on the different Styles of architecture' (169.20–1) in their relation to various combinations of the four architectural elements of the hearth (fireplace), the roof, the enclosure (wall) and the terrace. According to the prospectus, this would have included 'Assyrian, Egyptian, and Grecian architecture, as examples of three different principles of monumental art, being expressions of the political and religious differences between the three nations' – all of which would have been concluded with 'Modern parallels to these examples' (96.30–97.2). However, after having dealt with Egyptian architecture, the lecture breaks off with the Assyrian pyramid; Greek architecture is mentioned only in passing

The Combined Action of the Branches of Industry in Architecture   489

comparisons. Instead, Semper starts his discussion of architectural styles with an excursus on the Germanic farmhouse and multistorey constructions from fortificatory towers and castles to urban residential buildings. These constructions and their irregular grouping in settlements form instances of an architecture determined by the architectural type of the hut with the roof and the terrace as its dominating elements. Opposed to this is the 'court-style' (172.13) – that is, an architectural type dominated by the element of the wall enclosing a courtyard – which Semper discusses on the basis of the architecture of Egypt and Assyria. His aim is to define different architectural developments in terms of the genesis of social and political orders. On the one hand, there are the individual and the domestic family related to the hut and to Germanic peoples, and on the other hand the two different socio-politically collective organizations of Assyria and Egypt: the first characterized by conquests and revolutions and architecturally expressed in the regular military camp (combined with terrace works) and its monotone (mechanical) multiplication of units under the rule of des-potism, the other by an autochthonous society architecturally expressed in a hierarchical but organic development built around a kernel connected to the idea of priesthood. The lecture reproduces essentially the ideas developed in *The Four Elements of Architecture*, some-times in literal translations (Semper 1851b, 54–5, 69–83).

169.23–170.3 **The earliest and highest symbol ~ other combinations.**] cf. Semper 1851b, 55   169.29 **indefined**] *infinite*   169.31 **clime**] *climate* (see also 170.5, 172.34)
170.4–29 **It wants no proof ~ fortifications.**] cf. Semper 1851b, 69–70 and n. *   170.5 **thee**] *the*   170.15 **sattlers**] *settlers* (see also 171.32)   170.40 **allongated**] derived from French *allonger*: *elongated*   170.41 **rightangular**] *rectangular*   170.41–171.3 **diagramm ~ which gives a farmers house ~ in the old saxon countries, in Westphalia, Friesland, Holstein and Schleswig ~ England**] In 1849, Semper had Oswald Winkler from Altona make drawings of the plan, section and perspective of 'a Holstein farmhouse in the old Saxon style' for his 'Comparative Architecture' (Winkler to Eduard Vieweg, 17 November 1849, gta, 20-K[DD]-1849-11-17). The three drawings are extant in the gta Archives (20-0163-387, 20-0163-388), and the plan and section are reproduced in Semper 1884, 371. In *The Four Elements of Architecture*, Semper associates 'the Saxon settlements' with those 'in Northern Germany, Holland, Belgium, England and North America' (Semper 1851a, 70–1). 171.6 **sutt**] *soot*   171.8 **thrashing**] *threshing*; cf. 492, Alterations in the Manuscript 171.8 171.13–17 **the first is to juxtapose one roof to the other ~ unsymmetrical group of roofs ~ Each mainpart ~ having its own roof**] cf. Semper 1851b, 70: 'The roofs are actually joined to one another in free and asymmetrical groups, where each main part keeps its own roof'.   171.18–26 **The same principle ~ (Dahl's Churches.)**] 'Dahl's churches' refers to Norwegian churches described and illustrated in Johan Christian Clausen Dahl's *Denkmale einer sehr ausgebildeten Holzbaukunst* (Dahl 1837). In a manuscript on 'Comparative Archi-tecture', Semper had compared the roof construction of Norwegian wooden churches and imperial Chinese garden pavilions, known as *tai* (gta, 20-Ms-66, 89, ed. in Luttmann 2008, 488): 'The picturesque roof combination in this *tai* shows the greatest possible similarity to the assembled roofs of the Norwegian wooden churches published by Dahl. The wooden architecture of the North also shows strong affinity with Chinese motifs in other parts. Is this sufficiently explained by the generally applicable laws of wood construction, or does it indicate early relations between the Aesir, the oldest inhabitants of Scandinavia, and the East Asians? I cannot venture to judge.'   171.23 **congenious**] *congenial*   171.27 **The sec-ond mode of increasing a Saxon house is the Story construction.**] cf. Semper 1851b, 70:

'secondly, multistorey building emerges' 171.29–30 **Switzerhouses which I have shown in the last lecture**] see 167.25; 481, Explanatory Notes 167.25   171.35 **prise**] *prize*

172.13 **court-style**] at another point called 'Court principle' (176.24); cf. Semper 1851b, 71: 'constructions which, as the opposite of hut building, may be called court building'   172.19 **repetion**] *repetition* (see also 176.17)   172.22 **variated**] *varied*   172.33–6 **This other principle of architecture ~ national enterprises.**] cf. Semper 1851b, 71   172.34 **favorised**] derived from French *favoriser*: *favoured*

173.4–5 **the sole form of society under which such combined action of forces**] The German translation in *Kleine Schriften* emends the incomplete sentence by adding 'denkbar ist' (is conceivable; Semper 1884, 375).   173.11–176.3 **The prosperity of the fertil plains of Mesopotamia ~ later styles.**] cf. Semper 1851b, 71–6   173.22 **pray**] *prey* (see also 176.14) 173.36 **one side**] derived from German *einerseits*: *on the one hand*   173.37–8 **despotism, otherside∧ the same difference**] ~∧ ~, ~ ~ ~; cf. 493, Alterations in the Manuscript 173.37 173.37 **otherside**] derived from German *anderseits*: *on the other hand*

174.1–2 **The Wealth and power of the Satrap and feodary ~ is a gift ~ and suddenly overcome**] 'suddenly overcome': probably *arises suddenly*. In *The Four Elements of Architecture*, the corresponding sentence reads (Semper 1851b, 72): 'The power of the satrap and the vassal, on the contrary, is a gift of favour and arises suddenly.'   174.5 **outerly**] *outer* 174.14–15 **China ~ has been arrested by a sudden torpidity, while the military principle was in its vigour**] cf. Semper 1851b, 73   174.16–17 **The Chinese Architecture, is, with the exception of this Caraib Hutt, the most elementary of all.**] 'Caraib' derived from French *caraïbe*: *Caribbean*. In this translation of the corresponding passage in *The Four Elements of Architecture* (Semper 1851b, 73), 'Caraib Hutt' replaces 'Hütte des Wilden' (hut of the savage).   174.20–1 **It remained unaltered the same**] Mallgrave has 'It remained unaltered the house' (Semper 1985a, 58). For Chinese architecture as remaining unaltered through history – and therein comparable to the Caribbean hut – see the lecture 'The Ancient Practice of Wall Coating and Tubular Construction' (127.18–20): 'The Architecture of the Chinese remains unaltered through the ages. their imperial pallases and temples show in principle no difference from this Caraib Cottage.' Semper also states in 'On the Origin of Polychromy in Architecture', in a passage similarly adapted from *The Four Elements of Architecture*, that Chinese architecture 'has remained stationary from its early birth, and, consequently, the elementary motives of it are most distinctly preserved' (68.15–17).   174.27 **cast of inborn priests**] *caste ~ native ~*. In *The Four Elements of Architecture*, Semper speaks with respect to Egypt of the 'system of a native aristocracy' (Semper 1851b, 78).   **foundators**] merged from Italian *fondatori* and English *founders*

175.8 **cutt of**] *cut off*   175.12 **wholy**] *wholly*   175.24 **thirth**] *third*   175.27 **than**] *then* 175.34 **Canope**] *canopy* (see also 175.36)   175.39 **axe**] French for *axis*

176.11 **planes**] *plains*   176.12 **under many reports**] derived from French *sous plusieurs rapports*: *in many respects*   176.13–177.9 **The starting point ~ Enrichments.**] cf. Semper 1851b, 78–83   176.40 **jouth**] *youth*

177.1–3 **large intrance Gates, after which this whole part ~ had its name the high port, the seat of the government**] 'high port': *High Porte*. In *The Four Elements of Architecture*, Semper speaks of 'significant gates guarded by mystical colossal beasts', adding in a footnote (Semper 1851b, 81 and n. *): 'αἱ πύλαι, the gates, had the same meaning as now with the Turks. They meant the ruler's residence and seat of government.' In relation to Turkey, the French term *Sublime Porte* was usual at Semper's time.

The Combined Action of the Branches of Industry in Architecture

EDITORIAL EMENDATIONS

172.12 **day-light**] day-|light   172.13 **court-style**] court-|style   172.21 **town-dwellings**] town-|dwellings   173.40 **house-hold**] house-|hold   174.35 **Wall-enclosure**] Wall-|enclosure

ALTERATIONS IN THE MANUSCRIPT

169.20 **I shall terminate**] *after del.*

I shall terminate to day the[1] cours of my lectures with some[2] remarks on the combined action of the different manifestations of industrial art in architecture, and

> 1 **I shall terminate to day the**] *repl. del.* I promised to terminate the |promised] *after del.* I promised to speak at the End of the cours of my lectures *after del.* This my last lecture shall be devoted to   2 **some**] *repl. del.* general

169.21 **architecture,**] *altered from* ~∧ *before del.* as an art   **which last we take as the**] *repl. del.* which art is the   **result**] *after del.* combin   169.23 **The earliest and highest symbol**] *after five del. beginnings of variant:*

The kindling of the nurrishing
We have seen
The earliest[1] symbol of sattlement
The highest[2] earliest symbol of civilisation is the fireplace, it is the first[3] and most important element and as it were[4] the soul of
The high

> 1 **earliest**] *above del.* first   2 **The highest**] *repl. del.* The center of every settlement and the   3 **the first**] *after del.* in the same time   4 **and as it were**] *repl. del.* and so to speak

169.23 **human culture**] *after del.* cult   169.24 **element**] *before del.* of archite   169.25 **as the protecting Negations**] *after del.* as I endeavoured to show, the three other elements, 169.28 **The number of possibilities**] *after two del. beginnings of variant:*

The combinations of these four elements
There is an infinity of possibilities how

169.28 **parts**] *before del.* of every edifice   169.29 **or**] *repl. del.* and   169.30 **natural genius,**] *after del.* specialities, natural genius,   169.31 **political and religious tendency and development,**] *inserted after del.* education
170.4 **It wants no proof**] *after del.* It wants no proof, that where man lives in isolated groups or families, and the sattlements have no other Ennemies than   170.7 **has grown out of**] *inserted after del.* since the beginning   170.8–9 **similar to these**] *inserted*   170.9 **The roof must**] *after del. in opposite column* the Roof must obtain the dominant Element of architecture   obtain] *above del.* be   170.11 **first**] *interl.*   **an**] n *added*   **excavation**] *after del.* excavated *after del.* hole or a   **Ground,**] *altered from* ~.   170.11–12 **and afterwards** ~

basement.] *inserted and* basement *after del.* Eart 170.16–17 **life in free nature]** *after del.* free 170.19 **holes]** *before interl. and del.* and windows 170.20 **are single standing]** *after del.* stand 170.26 **form of rows]** *after del.* long rows 170.28 **concentric forms]** *after del.* their **or square or round]** *inserted* **Marketplaces of regular disposition]** *after del.* regular 170.30 **It is evident]** *after del.* But the original forms are soon altered by circumstances 170.32–3 **the introduction of foreign customs]** *after del.* to that of external 170.33 **principle]** *after del.* full 170.33–4 **inhabited by the descendants of the German races]** *after del.* of German 170.34 **races;]** *altered from* ~, *before del.* which is chiefly evident and **The best mode]** *after del.* This principle appears in contrast in] *after del.* in cons *after del.* in its cons **differences]** *repl. del.* character 170.35 **between]** *above del.* of 170.36 **laws]** *after del.* laws according to which each of them is the 170.40 **The first]** *after del.* When such *after del.* The

171.1–2 **in Westphalia, Friesland, Holstein and Schleswig,]** *inserted* 171.2–3 **The farmers houses of the Anglo Saxons]** *after del.* The houses of the Saxon Conquerors 171.4 **is a low brickconstruction]** *inserted after undel.* is 171.4–5 **or flue, and]** *inserted* 171.5 **the turfsmoke]** *after del.* the smoke goes its 171.6 **coated like the walls with]** *above del.* brillant of **a brillant black coating of sutt,]** *repl. del.* Sutt *and* coating *after del.* colour 171.8 **thrashing]** a *over* e 171.10 **has only at later periods been]** *above del.* is **by glazed walls.]** *inserted* **partitions]** *after interl. and del.* glazed 171.12 **mode]** *after del.* only 171.13 **is only twofold; the first is]** *repl. del.* is 171.17 **it tells]** *after del.* and 171.19 **showing]** *repl. del.* which shows **being]** *above del.* are 171.22 **show this]** *repl. del.* are distinguishd by the 171.23 **Gothic]** *after del.* pointed 171.24 **the ornaments]** *after del.* the principle followed by followed by] *after del.* observed by 171.27 **The second mode]** *after del.* Another mode of growing became introducted mode] *above del.* way **increasing]** *after del.* passing 171.28 **elevation]** *after del.* higher 171.31 **This mode]** *after del.* It has been more 171.32 **become]** o *over* a **necessary,]** *altered from* ~∧ *before del.* at the time, 171.33 **quarrels]** *after del.* subsequent 171.34 **times]** *after del.* later 171.36 **This]** *after del.* So the loafty towers 171.37 **top.]** *altered from* ~∧ 171.37–8 **generally ~ marsh.]** *inserted* **naturally fortified place]** *after del.* place fortified by nature 171.38 **The tower is]** *interl.* 171.40 **combined]** *above del.* arranged **irregular]** *after del.* cercle *and before del.* fortification

172.1 **The most important]** *after del.* Among the surrounding parts was the pallace the principal 172.3 **and having]** *repl. del.* and under this 172.6 **castle]** *above del.* building 172.7 **hill]** *before interl. and del.* or rock **edifices]** *before del. on fol. 4v* for 172.9 **feodal]** *after del.* allodial 172.10 **caracterised by]** *above del.* showing that specific caracter, of showing] *before del.* the irregular combination of single roofed houses, of (irregular *after del.* particularities of *and* single *after del.* different) 172.11 **one]** *below del.* of which is of which is] *above del.* being **and taking the]** *above del.* and by the intrance of 172.12 **windows]** *above del.* holes **outer]** *interl.* 172.14 **I should now give]** *after del.* I should complete this chapter with the I] *undel.* this chapter] *repl. del.* this description of a Northern house 172.16 **by]** *above del.* for 172.19 **stories,]** *before del.* devided only in the opper devided] '*divided*' 172.21 **The]** *before del.* variety **interior arrangements]** *interl. after interl. and undel.* in the 172.22 **are]** *above del.* is **more variated]** *after del.* greater, although they are not less *and before del.* than here 172.23 **individuality.]** *altered from* ~, *before del.* because they are generally the possession of 172.24 **are aranged]** *after del.* have a very fine 172.27 **In the Southern]** *after del.* But I must finish here 172.28 **are more mingled with]** *repl. del.* has been influenced greatly by 172.29 **motifs]** *repl. del.*

The Combined Action of the Branches of Industry in Architecture 493

influences **influenced**] *inserted* 172.31 **conclude**] *before del.* this important chapter **this chapter**] *interl.* **an other**] *before del.* principle of architecture, **most**] st *over* re 172.33 **This other principle**] *after del.* In such lands, which can only be conquered for which] *above del.* whose richness 172.34 **southern**] *after del.* Climes of Climes of] *after del.* more favorised (favorised *derived from French 'favoriser': 'favoured')* **by clime and**] *before del.* position. 172.35 **activity**] *before del.* of national national] *after del.* natural **great**] *interl.* 172.37 **Such lands**] *after del.* The richness of the country wanted to 172.38 **inhabited by**] *above del.* of **the richest countries**] *after del.* rich by agriculture and commerce 172.39 **labor∧**] *altered from* ~, *before del.* and of hands, 172.40 **nearly**] *interl.* 173.3 **These countries**] *after del.* In these countries, the seats of thick populations, and the *after del.* They were gained from the water an *after del.* For these countries, rich and fertile as they are wanted to be conquered populations, and the] the *inserted before del.* the craddles of the (the craddles *after del.* of) **strong**] *repl. del.* centralising strongly certain centralising strongly] *inserted after del.* the protecting system of politics 173.4 **society**] *after del.* human 173.6 **here**] *interl.* 173.7 **This explains**] *after del.* This observation *after del.* This remark is *after del.* In these countries 173.11 **prosperity**] *above interl. and del.* richness **of the**] *interl.* 173.12 **from nature**] *interl.* **a stupendous system**] *after del.* asthonishing works **soon**] *interl.* 173.15 **constructions**] *after interl. and del.* defensiv 173.16 **must have been**] *after del.* had 173.16–17 **of the oldest Assyrians**] *repl. del.* adopted in the country 173.18 **while**] *after del.* But *after del.* But As long as the first founders of the Assyrian civilisation were successfull against their warlike and But As] But *above del.* But and As *altered from* as 173.18–19 **could not alter**] *after del.* could not be of a subversing 173.20 **develop**] *after del.* follow their original 173.24 **Now an other principle**] *after del.* Now a second principle was prevailing over the first, but so as to combine itself prevailing] *undel. after del.* added and mingled [ ] 173.26 **sons of the desert or mountaneers,**] *before del.* and both people, 173.27 **They built**] *after del.* While they ranged themselves round [t] 173.28 **northern**] *interl.* 173.29 **to a new**] *repl. del.* to an to an] *after del.* with **first**] *after del.* funda[m] **exigeancies**] *repl. del.* rules 173.31 **The roof**] *after del.* Thus the Roof remains the Symbol only for the *after del.* The roofed ho[u] **remembrance**] *repl. del.* reminiscence 173.33 **generally prevailing**] *after del.* prevailing for the mass of the building mass] *after del.* other 173.34 **Egyptians**] *altered from* Egyptian *before del.* architecture **That**] *repl. del.* The same 173.34–5 **a nativ and originally national Monarchy,**] *repl. del.* a rich national Monarchical institution national] *interl.* 173.35 **nativ and**] *interl.* **and powerfull**] *interl.* 173.37 **Conquest,**] *altered from* ~∧ *before del.* and a feodal System **feodality**] *inserted* **otherside**] *inserted* 173.38 **styles of**] *after del.* productions of Styles of **the two nations.**] *before three del. beginnings of variant on fols. 6v–7r:*

This difference is chiefly evident in the | laws[1] of increasing their edifices particular to each of them.
This difference is also here the most evident in the transitions of one
The power and

      1 **laws ~ each of them.**] *after del. on fol. 6v* laws, how the two styles, which I am comparing laws ~ comparing] *repl. del. on fol. 7r* mode, how the Assyrian *(mode after del. on fol. 6v* mode how each of the two Styles)*

173.41 **from inside**] *after del.* of the formerly existing *after del.* of the interior parts.
174.1 **hand**] *above del.* side   **gift**] *after del.* gracefull   174.5 **the way**] *after del.* addition
after del. additional parts   174.7–8 **of the Small**] ll *over* ler   174.10 **The military principle**] *after two del. beginnings of variant on fol. 7r:*

But where not, like it was the case in China, a sudden torpidity
But[1] it happened some-times[2], that by superannuation the[3] military principle became to be
overpowered after having had the time of depositing[4] some

> 1 **But**] *after del.* When   2 **some-times**] some- | times   3 **the**] *interl. after del.* this gen-
> erally unfavorable   generally] *above del.* utterly   4 **depositing**] *repl. del.* giving

174.10–22 **in architecture ~ Motivs.**] *repl. del. in opposite column*

is generally[1] a very sterile one[2] for the arts[3], but where it was overpowered by superannuation after having had the time of depositing some of its better elements, like it was the case
in Assyria, there it is of great importance for the history of art.
This was not the case in China, which has been arrested by a sudden torpidity in the florishing[4] of that unfavorable period of military and feodal construction.
The Chinese style of[5] Architecture is, with the exception of this Caraib[6] Hutt, the most
primitive of all. Each of[7] The three Elements of architecture is[8] quite independently working for itself,[9] the fireplace, in its higher qualification as Altar, is allmost wanting[10] and with
it the center of relation between the other elements.
Grown out of the Tartar camp, this style had no opportunity of[11] being[12] fructified with
foreign motivs; It stands since 5 or 6000 years at the same state. Description[13] of an Chinese
house

> 1 **generally**] *before del.* speaking   2 **sterile one**] *after del.* unfavorable one   3 **arts**] *after
> del.* deve   4 **florishing**] *above del.* middle   5 **style of**] *interl.*   6 **Caraib**] *derived from
> French 'caraïbe': 'Caribbean'*   7 **Each of**] *interl.*   8 **is**] *above del.* are   are] *after del.* are
> standing in the strongest separation from one another   9 **itself,**] *altered from ~∧ before
> del.* and not bound   10 **is allmost wanting**] *after del.* forms no centr[ ] *and before del.* and
> gives no point of   11 **of**] *above del.* to   to] *before del.* mingle itself with other   12 **being**]
> ing *added*   13 **Description**] *after del.* Large Courts surrounded with Galleries, and
> Large Courts] *before del.* on the End   and] *undel.*

174.10 **arts**] *after del.* development   174.12 **It sometimes**] *after del.* Under circumstances
after del. In some   **overpowered**] *before del.* by natura   natura] *after del.* more   174.13
soil;] *before del.* in the same manner, as the political form of feodality had   had] *after del.*
looses its   174.15 **torpidity,**] *altered from ~∧ before del.* in the middle of the domination and
vigou[r]   **was in its vigour**] *after del.* was behel   174.17 **qualification**] *after del.* signi-
174.18 **in it**] *interl.*   174.20 **The Tartar Camp**] *after del.* Grown and   **Pallace.**] *altered
from ~, before del.* and it had no opportunity of being fructified and   174.21 **of older**] *after
del.* of new Motivs and by a   174.23 **But I must**] *after del.* But I leave the Chinese style here
returning to the Egyptians and Assyrians. *after del.* But I hasten now to the m[o]   return-
ing] *above del.* and hasten   **here**] *interl.*   174.26 **nativ**] *inserted*   174.27 **a cast of**] *above
del.* the   **priests**] *altered from* priesthood   174.29 **They judiciously observed**] *after del.*
They were the judicious observators of popular and natural motivs, and not less s[k]   judi-

cious] *above del.* skillfull   motivs] *before del.* which they exploited   174.35 **embanke-
ment**] *after del.* hig   174.36 **stood**] s *over* a *(for 'altar') after del.* a stone   174.40 **greater**]
after del. increas

175.1 **is wanted**] *above del.* was made,   175.3 **some essential alterations**] *after del.* the
construction undergoes also *and before del.* inside of it   175.6 **now**] *after del.* now they executed the linnen ceilings in wood and made woo   **Ceiling made of temporary drapperies becomes**] *repl. del.* drapery Ceiling becomes   becomes] *undel.*   175.7 **wood.**] *altered
from* ~∧ *before del.* and supported by wooden columns.   **or stone.**] *inserted*   **tempelroom**] *after del.* inner   175.8 **walls**] *after del.* compartments   **for the temple treasure,
for**] *inserted*   **documents**] *after del.* for stores, treasures and other   175.10 **Sanctuary**]
after del. temple   175.11 **increasing**] *after del.* highe   175.12 **wall**] *interl.*   **exterior**] *before del.* wall   175.13 **gradually**] *interl.*   175.16 **stands**] *final* s *added*   **getting**] *after del.*
soon   175.17 **the real temple.**] *after del.* or tempel.   tempel] *underl.*   175.18 **covered,**]
before del. like the first,   175.19 **was not**] *after del.* could not be   175.21 **This Court**] *after
del.* While this alteration is going on in the Second court, an other arrangement   an other]
an │ other   arrangement] *after del.* one was   175.22–3 **district**] *after del.* village   175.23
which] *after del.* where the Sanctuary first was erected. *and before del.* erected   175.24 **after
some time**] *after del.* soo[n] *and both above del.* often   175.29 **a Portico**] *after del.* There is
and Portico *after del.* higher   **of higher proportions**] *interl.*   **is formed**] *inserted before
del.* established   175.30 **door of the Pronaos**] *after del.* inner   **out of the**] *after del.* to the
175.31 **later**] *after del.* at *and before del.* times   175.32 **These columns**] *after del.* You See
175.32–3 **at Carnac**] *interl.*   175.33 **never had the destination of being**] *repl. del.* they are
columns which never were   **supporters**] ers *over* ing   **of a ceiling.**] *repl. del.* any roofs.
175.33–4 **They only were the pillars**] *after del.* They were supporters of Lyonsphinxes,
which in their turn were the holders of draperies.   Lyonsphinxes] *'lion sphinxes'*   175.34–
5 **the Images**] *after del.* the passing and   the] *undel. before del.* Procession   175.35 **on the
shoulders**] *after del.* by high   **Processions**] P *over* C *(for 'Ceremonies')*   175.38–9 **with
or without a higher passage through the axe.**] *inserted*   175.40 **combinations**] *after del.*
inside

176.1 **architecture;**] *before del.* It seems to be quite as necessary and pehaps more necessary,
for the understanding of history of architecture, to study the general   for the understant-
ing of] *del. separately*   176.1–3 **and whose knowledge ~ styles. – .**] *inserted and* whose
knowledge *above del.* which   176.4 **I shall not**] *after del.*

I shall not speak here of any details of the Eg.[1] buildings, except of the Pilones[2], at the En-
trances. which are[3] repetitions of the form of the Sekos,[4] and in the older Combinations
very simple and have been only made double

  1 **Eg.**] *'Egyptian'*   2 **Pilones**] *'pylons'; after del.* Pilones which form the flanks of the
  3 **are**] *del. separately*   4 **Sekos,**] *before del.* which is the true   is] *after del.* is invisible

176.4 **speak to day**] *repl. del.* give any more details   **architectural details**] *above del.* arch.
176.5 **arrangement**] *above del.* decoration   **of the intrances, known**] *below del.* of the
doors, known   **under**] *del.*   176.10 **tablet**] *after del.* monumental   176.11 **became**] *repl.
del.* fate hat the   hat] *'had'*   176.12 **similar**] *after del.* nearly   176.13 **starting point for
architecture**] *above del.* beginning   **or very similar**] *interl.*   176.14 **allways**] *after del.*
since the oldest ti   176.18 **colonial**] *repl. del.* political   **country**] *above del.* people

176.21 **Embryo and fundamental form**] *repl. del.* fundamental Idea　　**Architecture**]
altered from Architectural *before del.* form　　176.23 **a combination**] *after del.* with a very
developd system of terraces　　with ~ terraces] *accompanied in opposite column by del.* the
principle of Courtstyle　　176.24 **but**] *inserted*　　**The Gabled roof**] *after del.* But the Roof
was only a symbol for the holy　　176.25 **divinity**] *altered from* divine　　176.26 **The terrace**]
after del. The Assyrian Pyramids, were th[e]　　were] *after del.* standing on the　　**principle**]
after del. System　　176.28 **substructions**] *repl. del.* Bases　　**Small**] *after del.* very　　176.29
similar] *after del.* which last was in form　　176.30 **But**] *inserted*　　**pyramidal**] *altered from*
pyramide *after del.* Terrace　　**Terrace,**] *inserted*　　**only**] *interl.*　　176.31 **still**] *below del.* an
extremely　　an] *undel.*　　**a wider system**] *above del.* complication　　complication] *altered
from* complex　　**Yards,**] *before del.* succeeding each other.　　176.32 **and**] *above del.* and the
point of　　176.34 **Oblong**] *repl. del.* Rightangel　　Rightangel] *'rectangle'*　　176.35 **towers,**]
before del. groves　　**details.**] *altered from* ~∧ *before del.* and accessible on beautifuly ornamented bridges and staircases.　　and accessible] *after del.* as pinacles and bea　　176.36 **a
sort of**] *above del.* the　　**with tents for the**] *repl. del.* for　　176.37 **guards and soldiers**]
after del. and soldiers servants, and the followers of the　　the followers] *after del.* low
177.1 **fortified terrace**] *after del.* terrace with walls and　　177.3 **states**] *final* s *added*　　177.5
Belus Pyramid] *after del.* Pyramidal　　177.7 **connected**] *before del.* and woven　　**with**]
repl. del. by　　177.7–8 **paradises,**] *before del.* hunting woo *(for 'woods')*

MANUSCRIPT VARIANTS
MS 139

fol. 1r　　It is only possible to give more importance of one pallace before the others by the addition
of new courts, of new terraces, and of new pavillons, each of these parts being repetitions of
one uniform motif.

But this besides – we better pay now a little more attention to the Egyptian Style and that
of Assyria.　　　　　　　　　　　　　　　　　　　　　　　　　　　　　　　　　　　　　5

The Egyptian style is the only which grew undisturbed on the nativ ground. It has been fixd
not by foreigners, but by a cast of inborn priests, the skillfull exploiters of popular and natural motivs, of which they were the judicious observators.

The sacred cage, with the holy bird or Serpant, the representative of the God of the nomos
or district was standing with the Altar, in a very simple Wall-enclosure. on the bank of the　　10
Nile.. it was the starting point and the end of the procession, to which the pilgrims of the
neighbouring districts assembled.

fol. 1v　　The fame of the Sanctuary was growing, and the Mass of the Pilgrims increasing. | An new
Court or enclosure was made, in addition to the first, for containing the pious assembly and
for the use of preparing the procession.　　　　　　　　　　　　　　　　　　　　　　　15

At the same time the service of the God, with the increesing of his dignity, required new
arrangements inside of the enclosures.

Principally the inner court was covered for the occasion of a holy day and divine service only
with drapperies or tended sails; hereafter it received a solid roof and partitions were made
for the stores and treasures of the Sanctuary;　　　　　　　　　　　　　　　　　　　20

496.1 **It is only possible to give**] *accompanied by note in pencil* ad 8. *(referring to MS 138, fol.
8r with page number 8; 174.23–38)*　　ad 8.] ad: *Latin for 'to'; after underl. and del.* ad 7.

On Architectural Symbols

give more] *repl. del.* elevate the   496.4 **But**] *after del.* But we shall now give a little more [o]   give] *above del.* speak   a] *undel.*   **pay**] *repl. del.* give   496.6 **The Egyptian style**] *after two del. beginnings of variant:*

The Egyptian Style is that, which shows the organic development of
The Egyptian style is the only, which has grown[1] undisturbed out of the nativ ground, and monumentally arranged

  1 **grown**] *above del.* developd itself

496.6 **fixd**] *before del.* under the judicious legislation of   496.7 **not by foreigners, but**] *inserted*   **cast**] *'caste'*   **inborn**] *'native'*   **the skillfull**] *after del.* the observators and artfull exploiters of the natural motivs tenderd by popular and natural   496.8 **of**] *insert-ed*   **were**] *after del.* judiciously observated and maintained.   496.10 **in a**] *after del.* first first] *before interl. and del.* surrounded with   **Wall-enclosure**] Wall- *inserted*   **bank**] *after del.* dike of the ter   496.11 **it**] *above del.* Here   **starting point**] *above del.* com-mencement   496.13 **An**] *after del. on fol. 1r–v* It became necessary ¦ to make   **new**] *above del.* additional   496.14 **pious**] *after del.* devoti   496.16 **increesing**] *'increase'* 496.17 **inside**] *below del.* in the interior   496.18 **inner**] *interl.*   **covered**] *before del.* only 496.19 **tended**] *'tensed'*   **and**] *after del.* and the suchwise covered part was devided   de-vided] *'divided'*   496.20 **Sanctuary;**] *before undel.* [ ]

On Architectural Symbols

First Version

TEXTUAL RECORD

MS 143[1]	gta, 20-Ms-143, fols. 1r–2v (2r–v blank), in Semper's hand
MS 161	gta, 20-Ms-161 (Konv. 7), *fol. 157r–v (157v calculations possibly for Semper 1859; in a manuscript relating to Semper 1859), in Semper's hand, continu-ation of MS 143[1], fol. 1v
MS 143[2]	gta, 20-Ms-143, fol. 6r–v (6v blank; variant of MS 143[1], fol. 1v, and MS 161, *fol. 157r), in Semper's hand
MS 143[3]	gta, 20-Ms-143, fols. 3r–5v (5v blank; 3r, 4r variant of MS 143[2]), in Semper's hand
MS 141	gta, 20-Ms-141, fols. 1r–12v (10v–11v, 12v blank; 12r sketch of human head, possibly by Hans Semper; 1r–v variant of MS 143[1], fol. 1r–v; 2v–5r variant of MS 143[3]), in Semper's hand, *copy-text*
MS 141a	gta, 20-Ms-141a, fol. 1r–v (1v blank), in Hans Semper's hand, early 1880s, Hans Semper's German trans. of MS 141, fols. 7v–8r; see Herrmann 1981, 113
Semper 1884	'Ueber architektonische Symbole', 292–303, German trans. of MS 141; for details of this translation, see Herrmann 1981, 166–8
Wingler 1966	'Architektur', 104, ed. of Semper 1884, 292

Semper 1985b 'London Lecture of Autumn 1854', 61–7, here 61–2, 66–7 (additional sections: ed. of MS 142; see 511), Mallgrave's ed. of MS 141, fols. 2r–v, 5r–6v (177.28–178.19, 180.6–181.26)

BIBLIOGRAPHY Herrmann 1981, 27, 32–3, 38, 50–1, 58–60, 113, 166–8; Herrmann 1984, 140, 145, 150, 163, 169, 171–2; Waenerberg 1992, 64–5, 144–5; Mallgrave 1996, 217; Gnehm 2003, 318–19; Gnehm 2004, 210–17; Mallgrave 2004, 40; Arburg 2008, 271–3; Poerschke 2016, 68, 77; Gnehm 2020, 36

EXPLANATORY NOTES

This is the first of two drafts of the same lecture that was apparently the opening one in Semper's five-part course of public lectures 'on the different styles of ancient architecture, their distinctions and connexions' (93.7–8), held on 22 November 1854 (see 394). The second version (184–9), though incomplete – it refers for its missing concluding part to a section of the first version – provides linguistic improvements, some rearrangement of material and a few omissions and additions. Apart from that, both versions address the same broad range of topics, which is only partially (though to a large part) covered by the title 'On Architectural Symbols', taken from the German translation of the first version in *Kleine Schriften* (Semper 1884, 292). Both versions, which begin with the programmatic juxtaposition of an inventiveness of architecture independent of the imitation of nature and its simultaneous dependence on the 'laws of nature' and 'matter', refer to later lectures with respect to the comparison of different architectural styles.

In the first version, Semper promises elucidations of his revolutionary, anti-evolutionist understanding of the history of architectural styles and his contention that Greek architecture formed a certain exception among these (178.18–19). The respective section (177.28–178.17) is omitted in the second version but inserted by Harry Francis Mallgrave in his edition of the latter (Semper 1985b, 61–2). Semper then puts off until later 'a more orderly explanation of the forms ... used in the different styles of architecture' (179.40–1) and, finally, 'the explanation of the parts of Greec architecture in their Ensemble and separately' (183.38–9). Greek architecture in particular is only a marginal topic in the remaining drafts of the two following lectures (189–201, 201–3); it is therefore plausible that Semper planned to discuss it in another two lectures in December 1854, thus completing his course of five lectures.

Architectural symbols are generally important in Semper's argumentation in so far as they belong to his assertion that architectural components 'tell their history', etc. (179.4, 185.30). This 'language' of architecture leads to the two sections on 'traditional Symbols reminding old constructions' (Semper's four elements of architecture) and 'On natural symbols'. The latter section, which concludes the first version (it is transferred to another place in the second version, there headed 'On Structural Symbols'), discusses architectural symbolism by means of variations of one ornamental element in Greek architecture, the cyma. This frieze-like moulding with abstractly rendered leaves serves as an illustration of the Greeks' way of dealing symbolically with the conflict between free development and the (gravitational) 'laws of nature'. The somewhat surprising attention paid to one moulding is consistent with the fact that Semper was not simply supposed to deal with architectural styles in general but especially with 'Architecture and Plastic Decoration', as the departmental

On Architectural Symbols 499

announcements of his 1854 public lectures stated. Semper's characterizations of the Greek cyma closely follow Karl Bötticher's *Tektonik der Hellenen* in an often paraphrasing, sometimes literal, translation of passages from the section 'Symbolik des Tragens und Stützens im Konflikte' (Bötticher 1844/52, 1:28–37) – albeit without acknowledging the source. Semper, who had studied the book for the first time in the British Museum Library in 1852 (225.27–32), had previously translated into English excerpts from the same section under the heading of its German title (gta, 20-Ms-150b, ed. in Gnehm 2004, 210–15), there accompanied by sketches after Bötticher's plates with which his references to figures in this lecture can also be identified.

177.10–13 **Architecture is a pure inventiv art ~ the freest among the different arts of design**] Architecture, which is 'not an imitativ' art, as a deleted insertion says (502, Alterations in the Manuscript 177.10), is here seen as 'an art of invention' – as the draft of the second version reformulates it (184.1) – because it is not subject to the doctrine of imitation of nature to the same extent as painting and sculpture – in the words of the second version (184.1–2): 'it has not, like the other arts of design, the immediate imitation of nature for its object.' This ties in with positions in German idealism. In England, John Soane similarly described architecture as 'an Art purely of Invention' in the seventh of his Royal Academy lectures, first held in 1815 (Soane 1929, 119). Together with Semper's following contention that architecture is, despite its independence from nature, dependent on the 'laws of nature', this has a parallel in a fragmentary manuscript from the context of his 'Letters on the Great Exhibition' (gta, 20-Ms-95, fol. 12r): 'Architecture, and with it a considerable part of the technical arts, also produces original creations that are not absolutely determined by models in nature, although in accordance with the same incontrovertible laws that the latter follows in its works; they are called organic if they are the expression of a true idea and bear the impression of an inner lawfulness and necessity, like those of nature. Such natural creativity is very common among the technical arts in their infancy; hence the great importance of these beginnings of industry – which are, as it were, still fused together with nature like coral – for the [history of civilization]'. A similar passage appears in Semper's 'Comparative Architecture', preceded by the following sentences (gta, 20-Ms-55, 9–11, trans. in Herrmann 1984, 193–4): 'Although architecture produces original formations and is not an imitative art like painting and sculpture, it has over the centuries created its own store of forms from which it borrows the types for new creations; by using these types, architecture remains legible and comprehensible for everyone.'   177.16 **rosen**] *risen*   177.17 **clime**] *climate*   177.25–7 **The works of architecture ~ once inhabited them.**] Semper here applies his reference to Georges Cuvier and the study of 'fossil Remains' in the drafts of his inaugural lecture in 1853 (100.23, 105.3); cf. the parallel passage in the second version of the lecture 'On Architectural Symbols' (184.26–9), the comparison of 'The Terra Cotta vases' with 'the fossil remains of plants and animals' in the lecture 'Classification of Vessels' (136.41–137.2) and Semper's elaboration on 'the ancient monuments as the fossil shells of extinct social organisms' in *Ueber Baustyle* (On Architectural Styles; Semper 1869, 10).   177.26 **Coraltrees**] These are bushes of the genus *Erythrina*, but Semper obviously means *coral skeletons* formed like trees. 177.30–178.19 **1°) There is no state of childhood ~ I shall trie in the curse of my lectures, to give the evidences of these assertions.**] Semper omits this section in the second version. However, in the following lecture 'On the Relation of Architectural Systems with the General Cultural Conditions', he uses Chinese architecture to exemplify his contention that 'There is no state of childhood and gradual development observable for any independant style of architecture': It presents 'no organic development, no growing up of an individual out of a more incomplete state of Childhood into adultness' (195.40–196.1). In 'Comparative Architecture', Semper similarly says of Assyrian-Chaldean architecture that 'it had to come into the world fully armed, finished and closed in itself' (gta, 20-Ms-58, 80, ed. in Luttmann 2008, 399). Similarly, he says in another chapter of 'Comparative Architecture' that 'the first great centres of civilization in Asia and Egypt … were shaken together by floods and earthquakes. Not in slow development, but like Athena in full armour, they were born to the world violently by the iron hammer of distress' (gta, 20-Ms-66, 163, ed. in Luttmann 2008, 463). In contrast, when speaking in 'Comparative Architecture' not generally of Egyptian civilization but of its architecture, he contends that 'the composition of the parts of an Egyptian sanctuary can impossibly have been born in full equipment, like Minerva, from the head of a legislative priest', since it bears 'the clearest signs of a gradual emergence and expansion' (gta, 20-Ms-68, 15, ed. in Luttmann 2008, 528). However, in his 'Kunstformenlehre' (Theory of Art Forms) – a manuscript which directly preceded his work on *Style* – he generally suggests again that 'We cannot help but assume that the Egyptian temple palace, the Assyrian royal castle, the Hindu rock temple, the Doric gable-crowned building so to say suddenly emerged as finished types and, like Pallas Athena, fully armed' (Vieweg Archives, V3:1.1.3.32, sect. 'Prologue', 3). In *Style*, Semper refutes theories that the 'Hellenic columnar style' had as its 'model' the 'wooden utilitarian construction' or – criticizing Bötticher's *Tektonik der Hellenen* – that it 'emerged from stone construction finished and armed like Athena from the head of Zeus' and contends instead that it had elementary antecedents in the Asiatic 'pegma' – in carpentry work, which architecture has in common with furnishings and implements, i.e. with the industrial arts (Semper 1860/63, 1:436; cf. 2:210).

178.2–3 **suddenly**] *sudden*   178.8 **separed**] *separated*   178.18 **curse**] *course*   178.22–3 **We see nations ~ who have no history of architecture at all.**] In the second version, Semper places the Chinese and Arabian peoples close to such nations (184.36–185.4), thus implying that their buildings are related to the Caribbean hut in principle. For the comparison of the Caribbean hut with Chinese architecture, which remained 'unaltered' through history, see the lectures 'The Ancient Practice of Wall Coating and Tubular Construction' (127.18–20) and 'The Combined Action of the Four Preceding Branches of Industry in Architecture' (174.16–22).   178.24 **Caraib**] derived from French *caraïbe*: *Caribbean*   178.29 **matts**] *mats*   178.31 **sheme**] *scheme* (see also 178.32, 182.13, 182.15, 183.16)   178.33–6 **It would appear that the next step ~ would be ~ forms, such as are prescribed by ~ conditions, which each part of the whole has to perform, and their combination to a structure.**] This confusing sentence, which also occurs in the second version (185.17–20), results from Semper writing 'conditions' instead of 'functions' as in another draft (509.6). In *Kleine Schriften*, the corresponding sentence resolves the confusion by translating 'perform' as 'berücksichtigen' (take into account) and by relating 'their' to 'each part' (Semper 1884, 295).

179.1 **blocs**] *blocks*   179.26 **foundator**] merged from Italian *fondatore* and English *founder*   179.30 **lorrel-leaves**] *laurel leaves*   179.31 **Mirth**] derived from German *Myrthe*: *myrtle*   179.35 **valeable**] *valuable*, here misused for *valid*

180.1–2 **traditional Symbols reminding old constructions**] The elements of 'old constructions' mentioned in the following – fireplace, roof and wall – correspond to three of the four elements which Semper elaborates on in *The Four Elements of Architecture* (Semper 1851b, 54–6) and which he recapitulates in the first and last lectures of the autumn term 1853 (123.6–32, 169.23–7). Now, the 'terrace' as the fourth element is mentioned only in passing (180.26, 180.34).   180.5–6 **The fireplace ~ the first Embryo of social settlement**] In a draft of the 'Outline of a Cultural-Historical Exhibition', Semper similarly calls the 'Heerd' (hearth) the 'Mittelpunkt jeder Niederlassung & Embryo der Gesellschaft' (centre of every settlement & embryo of society; 305.5).   180.27 **the gabled ark of the covenant**] As in the following instance of the Kaaba, it is unlikely that Semper had in mind any source which actually describes the Ark of the Covenant as 'gabled'.   180.29 **The holy Caaba or grave of Mahomet, is gabled**] Mallgrave has 'The holy *Graba*' (Semper 1985b, 67; italics in original). The sentence contains two confusions: On the one hand, Muhammad's grave is in Medina, not in the Kaaba in Mecca; on the other hand, the Kaaba does not have a gable. Semper may have misinterpreted, or overinterpreted, descriptions such as in Edward Gibbon's *History of the Decline and Fall of the Roman Empire*, according to which the Kaaba was 'a square chapel' with a 'double roof … supported by three pillars of wood' (Gibbon 1776/88, 5:191). In any case, Semper repeatedly conflated 'gabled' and 'roofed' in relation to the Kaaba from his time in London onwards. In *The Four Elements of Architecture*, he relates 'the gable roof of the hut' with 'the holy Kaaba' (Semper 1851b, 73 and n. *). In a draft of one of his lectures given in 1853, 'On Timber Construction, and Its Influence upon the Development of Architectural Forms', he vaguely calls the Kaaba 'a roofed building' but does so below the sketch of a gable corresponding to the roof of 'Greec temples' mentioned just after the Kaaba (486.14–16). In *Style*, 'the Kaaba of the Mussulmans' is referred to as 'a hut with a *roof*' and subsumed, together with the Temple of Solomon and the Greek temple, under the 'type' of 'the gable roof with its supports' as the 'symbol of the *sanctuary*', which was adopted by the 'Christian church' (Semper 1860/63, 2:209 and n. 1; italics in original). Even in the early 1870s, in the draft of the introduction to the planned third volume of *Style*, he still places the 'Arabian Kaaba' in a series with the 'timbered roof' of the Israelite and Christian tabernacles (gta, 20-Ms-283, 21–2, ed. in Herrmann 1981, 255; cf. Semper 1869, 13).   180.37 **defended**] derived from French *défendre*: *prohibited*

181.13–14 **selfunderstanding**] *self-explaining*   181.19 **tye**] *tie*   **attache**] French for *attachment*   181.21 **soils and floors**] *exterior and interior floors*   181.22–183.39 **On natural symbols ~ separately.**] see the parallel section headed 'On Structural Symbols' in the second version (186.36–189.19)   181.35–6 **Instance foot of a chair, but an foot sense upright and mouveable. Vase of Dieterle. not clear easing. Coping round.**] 'but an', 'easing' and 'Coping round' uncertain readings. Herrmann 1981, 167, has 'hat and', 'eating' and 'loping round'; cf. the emending translation in *Kleine Schriften* (Semper 1884, 299) and the parallel passage in the second version of the lecture 'On Architectural Symbols' (189.4–5).

182.8 **leave**] *leaf* (see also 182.13–14)   182.10–12 **One of the most important symbols ~ is the Cyma ~ which includes the ideas of ending ~ and ~ of a conflict between two forces.**] From here to the end of the draft, Semper relies without acknowledgement on the section 'Symbolik des Tragens und Stützens im Konflikte' in Karl Bötticher's *Tektonik der Hellenen* with partly literal translations, as in the case of this paragraph (cf. Bötticher 1844/52, 1:28). Semper's 'ideas … of a conflict between two forces' reads in Bötticher 'Begriff … des *Konfliktes* zwischen Existenz gebenden und Existenz gewinnenden Theilen' (italics in original). The German translation here acknowledges in a note the parallels to Bötticher in the case of the cyma (Semper 1884, 300 n. *) and cites Semper's critique from another manuscript, headed 'Ueber Böttichers Tektonik. etc' (gta, 20-Ms-150a, ed. in Gnehm 2004, 206–9). In the final draft of his 1853 inaugural lecture 'On the Relations of the Different Branches of Industrial Art to Each Other and to Architecture', Semper notes on behalf of 'the power *of animal and vegetable Life*' (113.15–16; italics in original) that 'the more the works of our hands have the appearance of being results of such living forces, which act against gravity and substance, the higher they stand upon the scale of artistical accomplishment' (113.19–21).   182.13–17 **Take (fig 1) ~ free finishing**] This is another quite literal translation from Bötticher (Bötticher 1844/52, 1:28). The reference to 'fig 1' as well as the following references to figures and other mouldings that are only described can be identified with plates from Bötticher's *Tektonik der Hellenen*; for 'fig 1', see Bötticher 1844/52, 3: pl. 1 fig. 1.   182.14 **board**] derived from French *bord*: *edge* (see also 182.15)   182.15 **free laing**] *free-lying*, derived from German *freiliegen*: *exposed*   182.17 **free finishing**] *free-ending*; cf. Bötticher 1844/52, 1:28: 'a symbol for the concept of an … unladen end'   182.20 **Coronation of the roof of a Doric tempel**] the *sima* running along the eaves and the gables; cf. Bötticher 1844/52, 1:28; 3: pl. 1 fig. 2   182.21–6 **when we lay ~ and so on.**] another quite literal translation from Bötticher; cf. Bötticher 1844/52, 1:29; 3: pl. 1 figs. 3–5   182.25 **an**] *and*   182.27–8 **Sometimes two leaves ~ forming a double row**] cf. Bötticher 1844/52, 1:29; 3: pl. 2 fig. 1   182.36 **ebauche**] derived from French *ébauche*: *raw shape* (see also 183.28, 183.35). Semper uses 'ebauche' in place of Bötticher's 'Realisation' or 'Darstellung' (Bötticher 1844/52, 1:29–30). In *Kleine Schriften*, 'ebauche' is translated as 'Ausbildung' (formation; Semper 1884, 301).

183.6 **leaveband**] *leaf band*   183.9 **forehanging**] *overhanging*   183.10–11 **which is curved outward in a certain elastic line of great resisting power**] accompanied in the right column by a tiny, rather undefined, sketch of a curved leaf tip in ink   183.12 **ripped**] *ribbed*   183.14 **edificies**] uncertain reading, *edifices*   183.16 **egg and tong**] ~ ~ *tongue*; cf. Bötticher 1844/52, 1:32; 3: pl. 2 figs. 3–7   183.18 **Echinos**] cf. Bötticher 1844/52, 1:33; 3: pl. 4 figs. 1, 3   183.19 **too**] *two*   183.25 **Lesbian Cyma**] cf. Bötticher 1844/52, 1:34; 3: pl. 2 figs. 8–9   183.35 **of curse**] ~ *course*   183.38 **spare**] *save*

EDITORIAL EMENDATIONS

178.21 **house-building**] house- | building   179.24 **house-furniture**] house- | furniture 180.13 **altar-formed**] altar- | formed

ALTERATIONS IN THE MANUSCRIPT

177.10 **inventiv**] *before inserted in ink and del. in pencil and not an imitativ*   **ready made**] *in pencil repl. del. in pencil direct*   **prototypes**] *after del. in pencil models or*   **nature**] *before del. for imitation,*   177.11 **for its forms, they are**] *in pencil repl. del. in pencil its forms are* **imagination**] *after del. genius*   **genius**] *repl. del. inventiv power*   177.12 **would**] *in pencil above del. in pencil may*   177.13 **design,**] *altered in pencil from ~.*   **if it was not**] *in pencil repl. del. in pencil But othersides it is,*   177.14 **object**] *after del. special*   177.19–20 **for those constructions**] *inserted*   177.20 **observance**] *after del. obedience*   **principles**] *after del. laws of the last*   177.21 **on natural laws and conditions**] *inserted*   **natural laws and**] *above del. everlasting*   177.21–2 **which remain ~ at all times**] *inserted*   177.22 **architecture**] *after del. nat*   177.23 **necessity and**] *inserted before del. homogeneity which* 177.23–4 **natural works,**] *repl. del. works of nature itself,*   177.24 **creates**] s *over* d   177.25 **freely acting**] *above del. perfectible and freely altered in pencil from free*   **or**] r *in pencil over* f   177.27 **them.**] *before three del. beginnings of variant in opposite columns:*

On Architectural Symbols   503

Notwithstanding this,[1] there is[2] a caracter of individuality[3] and independency visible even on the most elementary works of man, for instance on this Caraib[4] Hut, erected out of Bambu trees and Palm leaves.[5]

Every part of it does well its function and speaks it out in a very intelligent[6] manner.[7] but it evidently works[8] only accidentally, it has not been made for the function it performes, and much less is it a self speaking[9] vivid personification of those functions.[10]

The junctures between the different members

There is only this difference that the monuments[11] speak their own history in an articulated language invented by the men who built them, they[12] live historically as long as they last, while the shells are dead impressions

This is the difference between the

> 1 **Notwithstanding this,**] *above del.* Nevertheless   2 **is**] *after del.* exists   3 **individuality**] *repl. del.* free action   4 **Caraib**] *derived from French 'caraïbe': 'Caribbean'*   5 **leaves.**] *altered from ~∧ before del.* on a low didge of earth.   didge] *'mound'*   6 **intelligent**] *before del.* though unartistical   7 **manner.**] *before del.* The same caracter of independency from independency] *before del.* which prevailes in this   8 **but it evidently works**] *repl. del.* It works   9 **self speaking**] *after del.* living personification of   10 **functions.**] *altered from ~∧ before del.* as are the same parts in their artistical investments on the Greec monuments.   11 **monuments**] *above del.* works of man   12 **they**] *after del.* while the shells and coraltrees are   coraltrees] *'coral skeletons' (see 499, Explanatory notes 177.26)*

177.28 **these**] *altered from* the   **works and of the**] *above del.* remains of archite   177.29 **very striking facts**] *after del.* two   **this art**] *after del.* architec[t]   177.30 **state of childhood**] *after del.* childhood   **and gradual development**] *inserted*   178.1 **in its first period.**] *inserted*   **period**] *altered from* periods   178.2 **represented,**] *altered in pencil from* represents,   represents,] *altered from ~∧ before del.* in the beginning   **2°) most of them**] *inserted and* 2°) *above inserted and del.* and   178.5 **seems to make**] *repl. del.* makes   **exception**] *before del.* among   178.7 **solution**] *after del.* co[m]   **of reconciliating**] *after del.* of combining   of] *undel.*   178.8 **for a long time stood**] *after del.* prevailed at the same time   at] *after del.* since   178.9 **tribes**] *above del.* races   **race.**] *accompanied by probably Hans Semper's T-shaped sign in pencil*   178.9–10 **every one ~ Ionic style**] *repl. del.* every style   178.10 **each**] *above del.* as   178.12 **commencement of**] *after del.* beginning of   178.13 **an exception**] *after del.* in a certain   178.14–15 **in its principles**] *repl. del.* entirely   its] *after del.* some of   178.15 **nature**] *before del.* because they are of general and everlasting truth; and comprehensible by themselves   178.15–16 **are of general and absolute truth,**] *repl. del.* are absolutely true   178.16 **speak to**] *after del.* therefore spe and *before del.* every   178.18 **shall**] *before del.* perhaps   178.20 **it must be remembered,**] *repl. del.* it is a fact,   178.22 **We see nations**] *after del.* There were nations   **perfection**] *after del.* accomplish   178.23 **at all.**] *accompanied by probably Hans Semper's slash in pencil, referring to beginning of MS 143² (508; cf. 508, note 508.1)*   178.24 **cottage**] *above del.* hut   178.29 **The wall partitions ~ trees.**] *inserted*   178.34 **modelling**] *after del.* working out of   178.36 **and their combination to a**] *after del.* and the assembling of them to a   assembling] *after del.* scientific   178.37 **Style of construction**] *after del.* constr   179.1 **marble**] *after del.* tim   179.10 **naked shematical parts**] *repl. del.* shematical forms   forms] *after del.* bodies   179.11 **found**] *inserted after del.* also   179.23 **productions**] *after del.* industrial   179.25 **A third class of Symbols**] *repl. del.* There are thirdly symbols   There are thirdly symbols] *after del.* There were thirdly symbols employed which had their

504   Lectures

key not in the constructiv functions of the parts nor *(constructiv after del.* structur *and* parts *after del.* house) **employed**] *before del.* of a mere hieratic caracter a mere] *after del.* an externa **refers only**] *repl. del.* referring only 179.26 **building,**] *altered from* ~∧ *before del.* the keys of which were the keys] *after del.* and not of general **of it.**] *inserted* 179.27 **generally**] *interl.* 179.28–9 **they had ~ signification**] *inserted* 179.28 **at the same time a**] *above del.* a 179.31–2 **the statical signification**] *after del.* but 179.35 **the duration**] *after del.* the time of *and before del.* of the existence the existence] the *above del.* their special **social**] *interl.* 179.37 **a few**] *repl. del.* some 179.40–1 **in the different styles**] *after del.* and characteristic for the d 179.41 **comming**] *after del.* next 180.1 **examples of traditional**] *repl. del.* the 180.1–2 **reminding old constructions**] *repl. del.* taken from reminiscencies of the first stages of social establishment of the] *after del.* but **constructions**] *altered from* constructiv *before del.* parts, 180.2–3 **had the greatest influence ~ monuments**] *repl. del.* do mostly refer to the whole feature of the buildings 180.8 **to**] *repl. del.* round 180.9–10 **parts and divisions**] *repl. del.* members 180.12 **the symbol**] *after del.* therefore **object,**] *altered from* ~∧ *before del.* will be the symbol of an holy place in general. will be] *undel. before del.* symbolised as an holy object 180.12–14 **will be symbolised ~ temple.**] *inserted after inserted and del.* employed as [a] 180.15 **gabled roof**] *after del.* Gableroof. 180.16 **The Roof with gables is**] *before del.* for every style of architecture 180.16–19 **the universal Symbol ~ honours.**] *repl. del.* the Symbol of divinity. the Symbol] *undel. before del.* of a divine house. *(house. altered from* ~, *before del.* probably because tribes, which in their) of divinity] *after del.* of the im 180.16 **universal**] *above del.* general 180.17 **divine dwellings.**] *after del.* the houses of God. **also**] *interl.* 180.21 **God;**] *altered from* ~, *before del.* the Serpent, the hawk or any other **while the**] *repl. del.* The 180.22 **being**] *repl. del.* are 180.23–4 **were covered with flatt roofs.**] *inserted before del.* the only gabled part of the whole was the house of the god. part of the whole] *repl. del.* sanctuary house] *after del.* temple 180.25 **The same is the case**] *after three del. beginnings of variant in opposite columns:*

The same form is visible in a diminute state in proportion to the who
The same Symbol crowns the highest terrace of the Assyrian
The same is the case in Assyria.
A Small chapel with a gable stands on the top of the tower

180.26 **Assyrian palace**] *after del.* immense 180.27 **It was**] *after del.* The gabled ark of the covenant was symbolically carried out in the great 180.29 **Caaba**] C *over* g *(C resembling* 'G' *due to undel. descender of* g) 180.29–30 **It is the only temple of the Islams**] *inserted* 180.30 **Mosquees**] *before del.* of the Islams 180.33 **like in Egypt**] *inserted* 180.34–5 **like in Assyria**] *inserted* 180.35 **it governs**] *after del.* but **the principal**] *after del.* a striking 180.36 **ordinance**] i *over* o 180.37 **of Greecian history**] *inserted*
181.1 **Gabled**] d *added* **part of its**] *repl. del.* its whole 181.3–7 **Some ~ forms.**] *inserted* 181.3 **constructiv**] *after del.* struct **in Greec architecture are**] *repl. del.* employed for the Greec entablatures are 181.4 **gabled**] *interl.* 181.5–7 **as quasi natural objects ~ plants and animal forms.**] *repl. del.* quasi as natural symbols because seized from antearchitectural forms. forms.] *before del.* They had the principle not. 181.6 **and treated them**] *after del.* and did not hesitate to take them as prototypes or analogies for further symbolical 181.6–7 **and animal**] *after del.* and organic 181.9 **has derived from**] *repl. del.* has been taken from **making partitions**] *after del.* wall 181.10 **sails**] *after del.* te[x] 181.16–17

On Architectural Symbols

and every other ornament ~ none at all.] *inserted*   181.16 **meaning**] *above del.* significance   181.18 **signifiing**] *after del.* ornamenting   181.19 **an attache**] *after del.* a member
one part to another] *after del.* two differ   181.19–20 **as a symbol ~ structural part.**] *inserted*   181.22–6 **On natural symbols ~ nature.**] *after del.*

instances. –
I shall now give an example of a symbol taken from natural analogies, one of those which
the Greecs so frequently and successfully

181.22 **On natural symbols.**] *accompanied by possibly Hans Semper's note in pencil* ✕   181.25
have] *before interl. and del.* been   181.27–8 **What principles ~ such symbols?**] *repl. del.*
How did they employ natural forms for such artistical symbols? *after del. on fol. 6v* The principal law which prevailed in the   181.31 **was not necessary for**] *after del.* did not belong
t[o]   **its**] *repl. del.* the   **explanation.**] *altered from ~∧ before del.* of the Idea which was to
be symbolised;   181.32 **2°**] *after del.*

they[1] gave on purpose[2] conventional colours to their leaves and flowers when[3] the natural
colours of the original was[4] out of question and[5] not that

  1 **they**] *after del.* for they had for their artistical creations   2 **on purpose**] *inserted*
  3 **when**] *above del.* because   4 **was**] *after del.* were no   5 **and**] *after del.* and not necessary
  to

181.32 **altered**] *after del.* even   181.33 **Symbol,**] *altered from* ~.   181.33–6 **and put ~ (Coffemill)**] *inserted*   181.38 **colours**] *after del.* for[m]   181.39 **searched for.**] *after del.* wanted.
182.1–2 **permitted**] *repl. del.* admitted   admitted] *after del.* left doubts   182.3 **made**] *before
del.* also   **originals**] s *added*   182.3–4 **of the building**] *after del.* of the material   of]
undel.   182.5 **for this abstraction**] *after del. on fol. 7r* It was only by this abstract view of
the   view] *above del.* mode of   182.6 **forces,**] *before del.* and give, through the elastic
curve which the leaves performed by the supposed pression,   182.8 **degree**] *above del.* form
182.9 **painter. –**] *before del.* The simple blocs in their pure static forms would never have
given to the eyes even of practical men   blocs] *'blocks'*   given to] *after del.* permitted to
eyes] *before del.* a clearear   182.10 **Cyma**] *after del.* symbol   182.13 **of any**] *after del.* after
any real *and before del.* real   **sectional**] *inserted*   182.14 **rib.**] *repl. del.* ripp   **in**] *del.*
take] *above del.* Imagine   182.18 **as an upright**] *after del.* as a crowning upright   crowning] *before del.* piece.   182.21 **when**] *above del.* if   if] *after del.* Now   182.25 **When**] *above
del.* If   **the**] *inserted*   **leaves**] *after del.* the wreath or row of   the] *undel. before del.* leave
threa   182.26 **on.**] *altered from* ~, *before del.* until they take a   182.27 **standing**] *above del.*
laying   laying] *'lying'*   **before**] *after del.* over   182.30 **You will understand**] *after del.*
on fol. 8r You will easily understand how it was possible to establish a very accurate scale to
the dynamical and artistical feeling   to the dynamical] *after del.* for   182.31 **an ideal but
in the same time**] *inserted*   **accurate**] *after del.* significant   182.32–3 **the same**] *after del.*
an upright   182.34 **of altering and**] *inserted after del.* of strenghtening or moderating the
for any intended musical mode] *inserted*   **any**] *above del.* every   182.35 **parts.**] *altered
from* ~∧ *before del.* so as to answer to any special   answer] *after del.* respond   182.37
speaking] *inserted before inserted and undel.* and   and] *before del.* expressiv   182.38 **expressing**] *repl. del.* which express   182.40 **in general.**] *inserted*

506 Lectures

183.5 **admissible.**] *before del.* They had no established shemes and rules vale[ ] estab-
lished] *after del.* rules but that of their *(that after del.* their es*)* shemes] *'schemes'* 183.9
they will] *interl.* 183.10 **below**] *repl. del.* part which is below, 183.10–11 **resisting**] *after*
del. inner 183.11 **leaves**] *after del.* plan *(for 'plants') after del.* vegetable 183.15 **ornament-**
ed with] *after del.* painted or sculptured and then painted w **that**] *above del.* the same
183.16 **very unartistically**] *inserted* **tong,**] *altered from* ~∧ 183.16–18 **whose first**
sheme ~ sectional curve.] *repl. del.* and in its first sheme reminds of a broken leave.
first] *undel.* sheme] *'scheme'; after del.* for *(for 'form') after del.* signif reminds] *before del.*
the analogy of a broken leave.] leave*: 'leaf'; undel.* and leave. *altered from* ~∧ *before del.*
which turns 183.21 **periods**] *after del.* stage 183.23 **symbol.**] *after del.* for[m] 183.24
symbol.] *before del.* of 183.26 **whose**] *after del.* covering with 183.28 **results from the**]
repl. del. gives the **from**] *above del.* of 183.29 **architects;**] *altered from* ~, *before del.* who
employed it sometimes **It is**] *after del.* We shall see 183.30 **leaves**] *after del.* orna- |
ment which w orna-] *undel.* 183.33 **true**] *repl. del.* the case 183.34 **upside down,**]
before del. as for instance at the bottom of the wall of the Cella of the temple of Theseos,
183.34–5 **a form which we call the cyma recta,**] *inserted* 183.36 **meaning.**] *altered from*
~∧ *before del.* and **only**] *after del.* here *and before del.* to **to day, to**] *inserted* **illus-**
trate] *after del.* give an example of the mode how the Greec knew [t] 183.36–7 **by some**
examples] *inserted* 183.38 **lectures**] *inserted* 183.38–9 **of the parts of Greec Architec-**
ture] *repl. del.* of the Greec ornamental forms 183.39 **separately**] *after del.* in the

MANUSCRIPT VARIANTS
MS 143[1] MS 161

fol. 1r

Architecture is a pure inventiv art, for it has no prototypes in nature for imitation and its
forms are free productions of human intellect and inventiv power. With respect to this, it
may appear to be the freest among all the arts who speek to us through the medium of sight.
But on the other hand it is the most dependant upon the laws of nature in general, and the
mechanical laws of matter especially, for, whatever special object of this art we may con-   5
sider, we will find that its first and original conception has arisen from the want of providing
for some necessity of private or social life, essentially that of protection and shelter against
the injuries of the elements or of other hostile powers. – and as we can obtain this protection
only by combination of dead natural materials to strong systems of construction we are
constrained to the strict observation of the statical and mechanical laws of nature.   10

fol. 1v

Thus the monuments of the different ages of human civilisation ¦ are as it were works of
nature itself, but works which nature had created through the medium of mankind, in that
position of its social development, on which it stood at the time when these works were
erected; in a certain degree comparable to the shells and corail trees, which give us an account of the nature of the organizations which once inhabited them.   15
Notwithstanding this dependency from necessity and mechanical laws of nature there is a
caracter of independency and free action visible even in the most elementary works of man,
which makes it to a work of his own. Such for instance as this Caraib hut, erected out of
trees of bambou and palmleaves on a low didge of ground. Every part of it does well its
function and speaks it out in a very intelligent manner, there is even some element of decor-   20
ation visible on the matts, which form the walls and partitions between the pillars. and the

fol. 157r

whole forms an Ensemble which is not wanting of unity and proportion. | But still it is far

On Architectural Symbols

from being a work of architectural art and can not give any further occasion to us for observations.

We shall start fron a point, where we allready see a higher intention acting and influencing upon the constructions of

> 506.1 **Architecture is a pure inventiv**] *accompanied by note in pencil* ad. 1. *(referring to MS 141, fol. 1r with page number 1; 177.10–23)* ad] *Latin for 'to'* 506.2 **With**] *above del.* In this **to this,**] *inserted* 506.2–3 **it may appear to be**] *repl. del.* it is 506.3 **among**] *repl. del.* of 506.4 **But**] *after del.*

But on the other side it is more dependant than any other on nature in general and matter[1] for its objects are, in their first conceptions at least,

> 1 **matter**] *before del.* especially.

> 506.4 **dependant**] *before del.* among all the sister-arts **the laws of**] *interl.* **in general,**] *before del.* and human condition of life 506.4–5 **and the mechanical laws of**] *inserted before del.* and 506.7 **necessity**] *after del.* essential **essentially**] *repl. del.* generally 506.8 **injuries of the**] *inserted* **of other hostile powers**] of *repl. del.* against 506.9 **dead**] *interl.* **to strong**] *repl. del.* to some **systems**] *final* s *added* **we**] *after del.* we must form **form**] *above del.* follow in the mechanical cheme of our work the cheme] *'scheme'* 506.10 **the statical and mechanical laws**] the *above del.* those **of nature.**] *repl. del.* which govern the universal material world. 506.11 **Thus**] *above del.* So we may consider **are**] *after del.* as works of nature 506.12 **mankind**] kind *added* 506.14 **comparable**] *above del.* similar **corail trees**] *'coral skeletons' (see 499, Explanatory Notes 177.26)* 506.15 **the nature of the**] *repl. del.* that 506.16 **Notwithstanding ~ laws of nature**] *repl. del.* But 506.17 **visible**] *inserted* **man**] *after del.* arch *(for 'architect')* 506.18 **Caraib**] *derived from French 'caraïbe': 'Caribbean'* **erected**] *above del.* made 506.19 **didge**] *'mound'* 506.21 **matts**] *altered from* mats 506.21–2 **and the whole forms**] *after del.* but this is not 506.22–507.4 **But still it is ~ constructions of**] *in right column of MS 161, *fol. 157r, after four del. variants in left column of MS 143[1], fol. 1v, in left column of MS 161, *fol. 157r, and in right column of MS 143[1], fol. 1v:*

But this is not yet a work of architecture. This art begins only, where we see the dead cheme[1] of mecanical construction first becoming animated through the genius of art, where the different parts of the construction | are personifications of the functions[2] which they fullfill in the whole combination[3]
But this is not yet a work of architecture. This art begins first with the poetical idea or intention of the builder to personify his work
But the man of higher organization becomes soon dissatisfied with this mere technical sheme[4] |
But still it is far from being a work of architectural art. This art begins only with the intention of the builder of[5] giving[6] higher expression and meaning to his work, of[7] animating[8] its parts and to elevate[9] the dead sheme[4] of construction[10]

> 1 **cheme**] *'scheme'* 2 **functions**] *after del.* natural forces, 3 **combination**] *before del.* of the activ and passiv 4 **sheme**] *'scheme'* 5 **of**] *inserted after del.* to 6 **giving**] *altered from* give 7 **of**] *inserted after del.* to 8 **animating**] *altered from* animate 9 **elevate**] *above del.* transform 10 **construction**] *before del.* into a

> 507.3 **a point**] *after del.* a higher **allready**] *interl.* **a higher**] *after del.* the activ influence of 507.4 **of**] *before mathematical calculations*

508   Lectures

MS 143²

fol. 6r   This cottage considered as a whole does well its function and every part of it speeks it out
clearly enough but evidently works only accidentally it has not been made and modelled on
pourpose for the function it performes, and much less is it a self speaking and living personification of the last, as are the very same parts with their artistical investments on the Greec
monuments.   5
Art only begins 1°) where we perceive the material worked out to artificial forms, which are
prescribed only by the statical and other material functions which each part has to perform
and 2°) where the material shemes which are obtained by this way, become to be still more
expressive through a poetical and ornamental

> 508.1 **This cottage considered as a whole**] *inserted after del.* The whole cottage and Every
> part of it,   The whole cottage and] *inserted*   Every part of it,] it, *repl. del.* this cottage *and*
> Every part *after two del. variant continuations of missing manuscript part:*
>
> are nothing but material ties, there is not the slightest indication¹ of those² swelling forms
> or contractions with the aid of which nature prepares and indicates³ its articulations and
> which the Greecs
> are nothing but common strings there is not the slightest indication visible of the wish for
> preparing and mediating the transition from the part which supports to that which is
> supported, nothing of those swelling forms or contractions with the aid of which nature
> prepares the articulations of
>
> > 1 **not the slightest indication**] *above del.* no idea   2 **those**] *inserted before del.* that
> > articulation with which nature symbolises its   3 **indicates**] *before inserted and*
> > *undel.* of its creatures the places   places] *del.*
>
> 508.1 **This cottage**] *accompanied by note in pencil* Ad 4. *(referring to MS 141, fol. 2v with page
> number 4; 178.14–30; cf. 503, Alterations in the Manuscript 178.23)*   Ad] '*ad': Latin for 'to'*
> **and every part of it**] *inserted after del.* and   508.2 **evidently**] *after del.* it   508.2–3 **on**
> **pourpose**] *inserted*   508.4 **with**] *above del.* in   **on**] n *(o missing due to lower left margin
> torn off)*   508.6 **1°)**] *interl.*   508.6–9 **we perceive ~ poetical and ornamental**] *inserted
> before undel.* the material shemes of construction apparent in the general form as well as on
> each part of the building   shemes] '*schemes*'   in the] the *(in missing due to lower left
> margin torn off)*   well] ll *(we missing due to lower left margin torn off)*   the building]
> building *(the missing due to lower left margin torn off)*   508.6 **perceive**] *after del.* see   **to**
> **artificial forms**] *repl. del.* in such a manner   **are**] *above del.* is   508.7 **only**] *interl.*
> **material**] *interl.*   508.8 **shemes**] '*schemes*'

MS 143³

fol. 3r   The history of architecture begins not at the same point with the history of housebuilding   10
and Engineering; they are more two different things there is a wide distance between the
two and there are nations who have no history of architecture at all.
This Caraib cottage for instance, in its ensemble as well as every part of it, does well its
function, but each member of it works only accidentally, it has not been modelled on purpose for the function it performs;   15

On Architectural Symbols 509

It therefore has nothing in common with architecture as an art and can only occupy our attention as a most elementary scheme for Roof construction. combined with matting as the elementary sheme of vertical partitions.

The first step to architecture as an art would appear to be the working out of the materials to artificial regular forms such as are prescribed only by the statical and other material functions which each part has to perform.

But we find no example of an art standing and resting on this point of development except perhaps in our own times of merely practical and commercial tendency. ‖

Of old people had probably less practical but certainly much more poetical qualifications *fol. 4r* They could not help giving a sort of plastical life to the blocs of timber, of marble and granite, in preparing and modelling them into cylinders and prismatic beams for the use of their temples and other architectural works. They made them tell the reasons for their existance, the direction and power of their action, the part which they would take in the whole work, and how their relation would be to each other.

These tales were made in a linguage consisting of symbols and caracteristic forms which were partly to be painted only, partly to be carried out plastically, and then painted; on the surface of the Schemes; This symbolical language was found almost ready prepared for this purpose by the other branches of industry which, it must be known had reached to a high degree of technical and artistical perfection long ere the building of monuments was thought of.

So this language was already prepared for general understanding, ¦ and so much the more *fol. 4v* as most of its symbols are taken or at least derived from analogies in nature, and self-understanding for every man who has the slightest feeling for natural forms and their dynamical significations.

But there are others, (and some of them are very important as relating to the general features and dispositions of the monuments) which are not taken from nature directly but from reminiscences out of the first stages of society and social establishment, from old traditional types of construction or from processes formerly prevailing in some branch of industry connected with the housebuilding or housefurniture. –

Before going farther, I want to give you some examples of symbols used in architecture to show their tendencies. their expressiv power and their application. I shall do this with the only view of explaining the containt of the foregoing, referring for a more systematical development of the forms used in the different styles of architecture, to the comming lectures. ¦

1°) Symbols taken from reminiscences out of the first stages of social establishment. *fol. 5r*
The *fireplace*

> 508.10–12 **The history ~ at all.**] *inserted*   508.10 **begins**] *after del.* begins not with the
> beginning and first has   508.11 **they are**] *above del.* not   **more**] *before del.* than history
> of painting   **two different things**] *interl. before interl. and del.* which   508.12 **nations**]
> *after del.* many   508.13 **Caraib**] *derived from French 'caraïbe': 'Caribbean'; interl.*   **for in-**
> **stance**] *interl.*   508.15 **performs;**] *altered from ~, before del.* and there is much less any
> 509.1 **in common**] *repl. del.* to do   **only**] *repl. del.* not further   509.3 **sheme**] *'scheme'*
> 509.4 **The first step**] *after del.*

The first indications of art appear only where[1] the materials are[2] worked out to artificial regular forms such as are prescribed only by the statical and other material functions which each part has to perform.[3]

1 **where**] *before del.* we perceive   2 **are**] *inserted*   3 **each part has to perform.**] *undel.*

509.4 **first**] *above del.* next   **appear to**] *inserted*   509.7 **and resting**] *interl.*   509.7–8 **except perhaps in our own times**] *repl. del.* except in the times and under conditions similar to ours   509.8 **perhaps**] *interl.*   **of**] *after del.* where practical science has entirely absorbed artistical feeling   509.9–11 **Of old ~ preparing and**] *accompanied in opposite column by Hans Semper's note in pencil* Wiederholg v. 5 unten, u 6 – *(referring to MS 141, fol. 3r–v with page numbers 5 and 6; 178.39–179.16)*   509.9 **Of old**] *after undel.* on fol. 3v The symbolic language in architecture *after three del. beginnings of variant on fol. 3r–v:*

In the times[1] of the first development of architecture
Of old[2] mankind had a more vivid imagination ¦
Of old people had[3] perhaps less practical but certainly much more poetical qualifications.[4]
They could not model their blocs[5] of granite and marble which they employed for building,[6] into cylinders and prismatic beams without giving to them a sort of plastical life.
They personified them and[7] made them tell the reasons for their existence, the direction and measure of their action,[8] in what manner they make part of the whole to which they were destined,[9] and how they would relate to each other, when on their places.[10]
For this they wanted a language – a symbolic language[11] consisting of certain caracteristic forms partly painted only partly plastically executed and then painted which they found almost ready prepared by the other branches of practical industry and art, which, it most[12] be known, had reached to a high degree of technical as well as artistical perfection long before the building of monumental works was thought of.

---

1 **In the times**] *accompanied in opposite column by Hans Semper's note in pencil* Wiederholung von 4 u 5. *(referring to MS 141, fols. 2v–3r with page numbers 4 and 5; 178.14–179.3)*   2 **Of old**] *repl. del.* In those times in which fell the development of architectural forms   3 **Of old people had**] *repl. del.* Formerly people had   Formerly] *after del.* it was much less practical perhaps than   people had] *inserted before del.* it was   4 **qualifications.**] *inserted before del.* than we are now.   5 **blocs**] 'blocks'   6 **which they employed for building,**] *inserted*   7 **They personified them and**] *repl. del.* They   They] *after del.* and making them parts of *after del.* and personifing their future functions in them by giving to them certain   8 **the direction and measure of their action,**] *inserted after del.* and   9 **they were destined,**] *repl. del.* they belong,   10 **each other, when on their places.**] *repl. del.* their neighbours.   11 **a symbolic language ~ plastically executed and then painted**] *inserted*   12 **most**] 'must'

509.9 **probably**] *repl. del.* perhaps   509.10 **blocs**] 'blocks'   509.12 **They made them**] *accompanied in opposite column by Hans Semper's note in pencil* 6 – *(referring to MS 141, fol. 3v with page number 6; 179.4–16)*   509.13 **would take**] *repl. del.* took   509.16–17 **on the surface of the Schemes; This**] *inserted after del.* which   509.17 **was**] *repl. del.* they   509.22 **So this language ~ understanding,**] *repl. del. on fol. 4r–v* By this reason this language was generally ¦ understood   reason] *above del.* circumstance   **and so much**] *accompanied in opposite column by Hans Semper's note in pencil* zu 6. u 7 *(referring to MS 141, fols. 3v–4r with page numbers 6 and 7; 179.4–29)*   509.23 **or at least derived**] *inserted* and] *after del.* which every one who has the slightest degree of feeling for natural   509.23–4 **selfunderstanding**] 'self-explaining'   509.26 **(and**] *altered from* ∧~   509.26–7 **general features and dispositions of the monuments)**] *repl. del.* Edifice as an Ensemble,   509.28–9 **reminiscences ~ or from**] *repl. del.* old traditional types of houseconstruction and   509.28 **of society**] *after del.* of the formation   509.29–30 **processes ~**

On Architectural Symbols 511

housefurniture. –] *repl. del.* processes of some branch of industrial art related to architecture and from 509.29 **prevailing**] *after del.* used 509.31 **Before going farther, I want to give you**] *repl. del.* I shall give **some**] *after del.* for an explanation of the foregoing *and before del.* few 509.33 **containt**] *'content'* 509.34 **development**] *after del.* explanation **the comming**] *after del.* my 509.37 **The fireplace**] *after underl. and del.* The altar.

Second Version

TEXTUAL RECORD

MS 142 gta, 20-Ms-142, fols. 1r–10v (10v blank), in Semper's hand, *copy-text*
Semper 1985b 'London Lecture of Autumn 1854', 61–7, here 61–6 (additional sections: ed. of MS 141; see 498), Mallgrave's ed. of MS 142

BIBLIOGRAPHY Herrmann 1981, 33, 113, 166–7; Herrmann 1984, 145; Mallgrave 1996, 221; Gnehm 2004, 113, 210–17

EXPLANATORY NOTES

The second version of the lecture 'On Architectural Symbols', which reformulates the programmatic first sentence as 'Architecture is an art of invention', generally revises the first version in terms of language, arrangement of the material and clarification of content. On the one hand, the section on natural symbols – now headed 'On Structural Symbols' (186.36), again with the Greek cyma as an example adapted without acknowledgement from Bötticher's *Tektonik der Hellenen* – does not conclude the draft, as in the first version, but precedes the section on 'symbols of the traditional kind', which forms the new conclusion (189.18–20). However, instead of writing out the latter, the second version refers to the 'other paper' (189.20) – that is, to the corresponding section of the first version on traditional symbols with its discussion of the fireplace, the roof and the walls (180.5–181.21). On the other hand, the second version contains clarifying additions. A first, longer one is provided with the third paragraph and the distinction between the 'Structural forms in general' and the 'ornamental parts', with the latter as the 'symbolical investments of the bare structure' of architecture (184.5–9). A second addition, associated with this, concerns 'nations … who have no history of architecture': their buildings – Semper now refers to China and the 'Arabian tribes' – consist of 'bare structures' with only externally applied enrichments derived from the 'industrial arts' (184.36–185.4). Finally, the second version omits the developmental assertions on the fully fledged emergence and violent death of most independent architectural styles, with the exception of those of the Greeks (177.30–178.17). While the reference to later lectures for elucidations of these assertions is also omitted (178.18–19), the other two references in the first version (179.40–1, 183.37–9) are retained with some modifications, here

512 Lectures

announcing 'a more complete and systematical explanation of the symbolical forms in architecture' (186.34–5) and the explanation of the 'Cyma recta' and 'other symbols' in Greek architecture (188.32–5).

184.1–11 **Architecture is an art of invention ~ the freest among the different arts of design**] see 499, Explanatory Notes 177.10–13   184.13 **rosen**] *risen*   184.15 **clime**] *climate*   184.26–9 **The monuments of former ages ~ once inhabited them.**] see 499, Explanatory Notes 177.25–7   184.28 **corall-trees**] *coral skeletons*; see 499, Explanatory Notes 177.26   185.5 **Caraib**] derived from French *caraïbe*: *Caribbean*   185.12 **matts**] *mats*   185.14 **sheme**] *scheme* (see also 185.15, 187.14–15, 187.39, 188.16)   185.17–20 **The first step ~ would appear to be ~ forms, such as are prescribed by ~ conditions, which each part of the whole has to perform, and their combination to a well calculated structure.**] see 500, Explanatory Notes 178.33–6   185.21–3 **But we find no example of a style ~ resting on this point ~ except in our own days of merely practical ~ tendency.**] In a deleted passage, however, 'the Chinese style' is described as such an example; see 513, Alterations in the Manuscript 185.21.   185.26 **blocs**] *blocks*   185.36 **nacked**] merged from German *nackt* and English *naked* (see also 188.2)

186.7 **self understanding**] *self-explaining*   186.11 **foundators**] merged from Italian *fondatori* and English *founders*   186.18 **espacial**] *especial*   186.24 **lorrel**] *laurel*   186.24–5 **Mirth-leaves**] *myrtle leaves*; see 500, Explanatory Notes 179.31   186.36–189.17 **On Structural Symbols ~ curvature. –**] see parallel section headed 'On natural symbols' in the first version (181.22–183.36)

187.1–188.31 **One of the most important symbols ~ the so called Cyma ~ Greec buildings of all periods.**] As in the first version, Semper here adapts corresponding passages from Karl Bötticher's *Tektonik der Hellenen*; see 501–2, Explanatory Notes 182.10–12, and – for the subsequent parallel passages – the explanations thereafter.   187.5 **boards**] derived from French *bord*: *edges* (see also 187.6)   187.6 **free laiing**] *free-lying*, derived from German *freiliegen*: *exposed*   187.8 **free finishing**] *free-ending*; see 502, Explanatory Notes 182.17   187.14 **sheme**] *scheme* (see also 187.15, 187.39, 188.16)   187.15 **reddition**] *rendition*. Mallgrave has 'reduction' (Semper 1985b, 64).   187.30 **on**] *one*   187.36 **ebauche**] derived from French *ébauche*: *raw shape* (see also 187.40, 188.18, 188.26, 188.33); cf. 502, Explanatory Notes 182.36

188.2–3 **pepresented**] *represented*   188.6 **leaveband**] *leaf band*   188.8 **leave**] *leaf* (see also 188.10)   188.13 **ripped**] *ribbed*   188.15 **tong**] *tongue*   188.17 **tye**] *tie*   188.33 **of curse**] *~ course*   188.34 **spare**] *save*   188.35–7 **adding ~ some general remarks on the principles ~ of their structural symbols**] Beside the end of this passage, Hans Semper noted in pencil 'Bis hierher Manuscr. A.', referring to the first version of the lecture (177–83), which is translated in *Kleine Schriften* (Semper 1884, 292–303). The passage provides a transition to the last formulated part of the second version (188.38–189.19) – a part which is a reformulation of a passage in the first version (181.29–182.9), serving there as an introduction to the discussion of the Greek *cyma*.

189.7 **thee**] *the*   189.20 **1° The fireplace. see other paper.**] The reference to the 'other paper' means the section on traditional symbols in the first version of the lecture, which begins with '1°) The fireplace' and ends with 'Symbols taken from textile art' (180.5–181.21).

On Architectural Symbols   513

EDITORIAL EMENDATIONS

184.28 **corall-trees**] corall- | trees   186.24–5 **Mirth-leaves**] Mirth- | leaves

ALTERATIONS IN THE MANUSCRIPT

184.1 **Architecture is an art of invention**] *after del.*

Architecture is an art[1] of pure invention – not finding[2] any adaequate prototypes or paragons in the natural forms

---

     1 **art**∧] *altered from* ~, *before del.* which   2 **finding**] *after del.* having

184.2 **design,**] *before del.* to its disposition the world of real natural forms, which it may take for models, for expressing its ideas and conceptions.   to its disposition] *after del.* for the expression of its conceptions   **the immediate imitation of nature for its object.**] *insert-ed*   184.3 **Works of architecture have**] *repl. del.* The architects have   The architects have] *repl. del.* The last have   184.3–4 **no prototypes ~ science.**] *repl. del.* no prototypes in nature for immediate imitation they are entirely the results of human imagination and intellect.   184.3 **nature,**] *altered from* ~∧ *before del.* for their ideas and conceptions, which **they**] *inserted*   184.4 **experience,**] *altered from* ~. *after del.* and combination   184.6 **Structural**] al *over* e   **forms**] *interl.*   184.8 **bare**] *above del.* naked   **significance,**] *altered from* ~∧ *before del.* to our works and   **artistical**] *inserted*   184.10–12 **Architec-ture ~ consider.**] *repl. del.* The first conception of every object of architecture,   184.11–12 **material**] *interl.*   184.13 **its first conception will have rosen**] *above del.* arises   184.15 **elements**] *interl.*   184.18 **principles**] *after del.* laws   184.19 **itselfs**] *inserted*   184.25 **The history**] *after del.* The study of *after del.* As long as we   **forms**] *above del.* is   **a very important**] *above del.* an essential   184.26 **of mankind**] *after del.* of nature   184.27 **gen-erations**] *before del.* of mankind   **fossil**] *inserted*   184.30 **But in turn**] *after del.* But in turn, we want the knowledge of human nature as it still   **remnants**] *after del.* historical 184.31 **human culture**] *after del.* culture   184.32 **these works,**] *before del.* whose remains 184.33 **general**] *interl.*   184.34 **important**] *interl.*   184.37 **whose**] *after del.* or at least, **architectural**] al *over* e   **works are**] *inserted before del.* is   **bare structures**] *after del.* nothing but ornamented structures of the simplest   ornamented] *after del.* an   struc-tures] *final* s *added*   184.38 **furnitures**] *altered from* furniture *before del.* works   **imple-ments,**] *after del.* outer works,
185.1 **works themselves,**] *repl. del.* work itself,   185.2 **textile art**] *after del.* weaving   185.3 **and with**] *after del.* as we shall   185.7 **in its construction**] *interl.*   185.8–9 **There is ~ partitions.**] *inserted*   185.8 **an**] n *added*   **element**] *above del.* beginning   **in the mat-tings**] *after del.* in the application of variated   185.9 **partitions**] *after del.* w *(for 'walls')* 185.10 **this Ensemble**] *above del.* it   185.12 **wall partitions are**] *after del.* walls are   185.21 **But we find**] *after del.*

But we find no[1] example of a style of construction resting on this point of development, excepting perhaps the Chinese style, although it is not entirely devoid[2] of symbols.

1 no] *above del.* only one   2 **devoid**] *after del.* without

185.27–8 **in order to**] *after del.* for the use of their   185.35 **types**] *above del.* forms
186.5 **types,**] *before del.* which perform the elements of the   186.7 **not**] *after del.* partly
186.7–8 **reminiscencies of**] *above del.* from   186.8 **elements**] *repl. del.* types   **of processes**] of *above del.* from   186.9 **housefurniture.**] *altered from* ~, *before del.* or finally
being mystical symbols of a mere conventional kind, as for instance most of the   symbols]
above del. types   186.10–14 **A third class ~ religion. –**] *repl. del.*

A third class of symbols refers finally to the special destination of the building, to the God
of the temple and the religion of the worshippers and founders[1], which last class of symbols is generally of a mystical[2] character, which[3] never were intended to be of general understanding

> 1 **founders**] *merged from Italian 'fondatori' and English 'founders'*   2 **mystical**] *after
> inserted and del.* voluntary and   3 **which**] *after del.* the understanding of which was al-
> ways the privilege of,   was] *after del.* is only possible with the aid of a key

186.12–13 **and composed**] *after del.* but purposely   186.16–17 **as the Assyrians and Egyptians,**] *interl.*   186.17 **such**] *interl.*   186.19 **they were at the same time**] *after del.* they
answered in the same time a certain staticcal or dynamical   answered] *above del.* fulfilled
186.21 **For instance**] *after del.* For instance, they ornamented the moulding, which represents a tie or a band, and which   which represents] *after del.* whose statical function is the
binding together of two   186.22 **often**] *above del.* generally   186.23 **according**] *after del.*
for the different Gods   186.25 **The caracters of the leaves were different,**] *inserted*
186.26 **unaltered;**] *altered from* ~∧ *before del.* by the special applications which were given to
it.   186.27–8 **whose monuments**] *after del.* wherefore their symbolisme is not of general
but only of special   186.32–3 **and in showing ~ application;**] *inserted*   186.33 **I shall**]
after del. only with the intention of expl[a]   186.33–4 **the foregoing assertions**] *after del.*
the meaning *after del.* what I   186.36 **Structural**] *above del.* natural   186.38–9 **analogical forms in nature.**] *before del. on fol. 5r–v*

What principles did they ¦ observe in the choice of such natural forms and how did they
apply them?
1°) they did not transfer the copy of the natural object which gave the analogy to the Idea
which was to be represented in all its accidental details, they left out all what was not necessary for its explanation.
2°) they altered the originals in those

187.2–3 **(Κύμα, Κυμάτιον)**] *inserted before del.* which includes the ideas of ending or crowning, that of receiving, and that of a conflict between two forces.   187.4 **Take**] *after del.*
Take (fig 1.) as the sheme of   sheme] *'scheme'*   187.11 **coronations**] *after del.* antique
187.18 **on**] *above del.* to   **structural**] *altered from* structure *before del. on fol. 6v* and so on,
until the heads of the leaves will entirely cover the lower part of it, and their points touch
the band.   187.19 **part.**] *inserted*   187.27 **By this way we shall**] *repl. del.* We   187.34 **in
architecture**] *after del.* every ¦ where   187.35 **place.**] *altered from* ~∧ *before del.* between two
187.37 **speaking**] *repl. del.* expressiv   187.40 **moulding,**] *altered from* ~.   187.40–188.1 **or
painted, or sculptured and then painted.**] *inserted*

On the Relation of Architectural Systems with Cultural Conditions 515

188.2 **architecture;**] *altered from* ~, *before del.* which contained the   188.6 **leaveband**] *altered from* leave band   leave] *'leaf'*   188.18 **curve**] *before del.* of powerfull resisting expression   188.21 **variation**] *after del.* conflict   188.23 **Echinos**] *above del.* first   **water-leaves**] *before del.* of another caracter   188.35 **following,**] *altered from* ~.   **adding only here**] *after del.* What principles did the *after del.* and   188.36 **observed**] *after del.* seem to 188.36–7 **of their structural symbols.**] *accompanied in opposite column by Hans Semper's note in pencil* Bis hierher Manuscr. A. *(cf. 512, Explanatory Notes 188.35–7)* 189.3 **sufficient**] *before del.* and wanted only   **leaving out the other parts and**] *inserted* 189.4 **to represent the whole thing.**] *repl. del.* to take the whole complexe of the natural object.   whole] *after del.* real   189.9 **troubled**] *after del.* permitted a double sense of the Symbol *after inserted and del.* left a doubt, if it was   189.17 **their curvature. –**] *repl. del.* curvature which the hand of the sculptor gave to a moulding which   which the hand] *after del.* which the elastic line of a tender leave wreath received   leave] *'leaf'*   189.18 **which had**] *after del.* because they are

On the Relation of Architectural Systems with the General Cultural Conditions

TEXTUAL RECORD

MS 145	gta, 20-Ms-145, fols. 1r–6v (4r–6v blank), in Semper's hand
MS 144¹	gta, 20-Ms-144, fols. 1r–18r, in Semper's hand, *copy-text*
MS 146¹	gta, 20-Ms-146, fols. 1r–12r, in H. T. Wegener's hand (emendations in Manfred Semper's hand), 1880 or 1881, copy of MS 144¹
MS 147²	gta, 20-Ms-147, fols. 1r–13r, 14r, 15r–22v (1v, 2v, 3v, 6v, 9v, 10v, 17v, 18v, 19v, 20v, 22v blank; 4v, 5v, 7v, 8v, 11v, 12v, 21v del. notes relating to Manfred Semper's architectural works, among them 'a new stable building for Mr Theodor Wegener in Ottensen'; 13v, 14v see 409, MS 147¹), 'Über den Zusammenhang der architektonischen Systeme mit allgemeinen Kulturzuständen', partly in unknown hand (1r–4r, 5r, 6r–7r, 8r, 9r–11r, 12r, 13r, 14r, 15r–21r, 22r; emendations in Hans and Manfred Semper's hands), partly in Manfred Semper's hand (8r), early 1880s, Manfred Semper's German trans. of MS 144¹, fols. 1r–16v, published in Semper 1884; see Herrmann 1981, 114
Semper 1884	'Ueber den Zusammenhang der architektonischen Systeme mit allgemeinen Kulturzuständen', 351–68, German trans. of MS 144¹, fols. 1r–17r; for details of this translation, see Herrmann 1981, 170–2
Semper 1986b	'London Lecture of November 29, 1854', 43–53, here 43–51 (additional sections: ed. of MS 144²; see 530), Mallgrave's ed. of MS 144¹

BIBLIOGRAPHY Herrmann 1981, 113–14, 170–2; Luttmann 2008, 147–9

516 Lectures

EXPLANATORY NOTES

This lecture, which can be dated 29 November 1854, discusses – as announced in the first two paragraphs – 'architectural styles' as 'the artistical expressions of … social political and religious institutions'. Semper's main example is the architecture of China, followed by a shorter section on that of Assyria and Chaldea and brief notes on Egyptian architecture. He alludes to his responsibility for teaching 'Architecture, and Plastic Decoration' (see 91.22, 91.25) when pointing out that 'the ordinances and mouldings of a style' can be understood only in the broader historical and social context of the architectural monuments to which they belong (189.29–190.2). After referring back to the embryonic role of the fireplace as discussed in the preceding lecture 'On Architectural Symbols' (190.13–14; cf. 180.6), Semper applies the cultural-historical approach of his 'Comparative Architecture', in which the much more extensive discussion of China, Assyria and Chaldea provides the basis for his present account (for the chapters on China in 'Comparative Architecture', see gta, 20-Ms-66, 149–97, ed. in Luttmann 2008, 455–90; for those on Assyria and Chaldea, see gta, 20-Ms-58, 38–121, ed. in Luttmann 2008, 372–417). The importance Semper attributes to China is due to his identification of primeval architectural elements in an advanced yet politically 'petrified Chinese civilisation' corresponding to a mechanistic, material-bound architecture that was 'never elevated from its common reality to higher symbolism and to the field of art' (as Greek architecture was), so that 'we may recognize in the buildings of the Chinese the wooden architecture of primeval times': 'The roof is an umbrella for the rain, the columns are supports, the supports are vertically standing trees, planed and painted' (gta, 20-Ms-66, after 189, ed. in Luttmann 2008, 604). This likens the Chinese house to Semper's Caribbean hut, in which – as he says in the previous lecture – 'The columns are trees and nothing else' (178.28). However, despite his contention, advanced in 1853, that Chinese architecture was 'arrested by a sudden torpidity' and thus became 'most elementary', comparable to the Caribbean hut (174.14–17), it is precisely this elementary perspective that leads him to say in 'Comparative Architecture' that 'the Chinese still remain our teachers in many things closely related to architecture, even when it comes to its formal aspects' (gta, 20-Ms-66, 152, ed. in Luttmann 2008, 456).

The exact sources for Semper's discussion of the relation between Chinese society and architecture are difficult to establish. He relies particularly on Guillaume Pauthier's *Chine* (Pauthier 1839) and William Chambers's *Designs of Chinese Buildings* (Chambers 1757), to both of which he refers in 'Comparative Architecture' and in the lecture (198.2–3). Further information is taken from other sources, some of which were included in a second volume by Pauthier, his *Chine moderne* (Pauthier 1853). As it would be speculative to try to identify these sources, we broadly refrain from mentioning possible works. All in all, Semper apparently proceeded directly from the draft of his 'Comparative Architecture', as some passages in the lecture that are translated literally from it suggest. Misspellings in the naming of persons and places also suggest that Semper used a fair copy (gta, 20-Ms-72) of his original manuscript (gta, 20-Ms-66), which he had received from Germany in 1851 and which contains the same misspellings. The notes on Egypt with which the draft lecture breaks off cover only part of the lecture as apparently intended to be held, since at the beginning of the next lecture Semper writes that he had 'explained in the last lecture the general idea laid down in the disposition of the Egyptian temples' (201.20–1).

190.3 **were**] *we*   190.11 **lays**] *lies* (see also 197.19)   190.13–14 **I considered in my last lecture the fireplace as the Embryo of social forms ~ and the Symbol of ~ united vol-**

On the Relation of Architectural Systems with Cultural Conditions   517

ition.] see 180.5–14   190.13 **social**] uncertain reading   190.29 **creddles**] *cradles*   190.30 **onesides**] derived from German *einerseits: on the one hand*   190.31 **othersides**] derived from German *anderseits: on the other hand*

191.2 **foundators**] merged from Italian *fondatori* and English *founders* (see also 191.13)   191.5 **priniple**] *principle*   191.8–9 **resorting**] *resulting*   191.15 **seasing**] *seizing*   191.19–20 **Bactrans**] *Bactrians*   191.26 **inimities**] derived from French *inimitié: enmities*   191.31 **merveillously**] merged from French *merveilleusement* and English *marvellously*   191.32 **hundert**] German for *hundred*   191.33 **evenement**] derived from French *événement: event.* Mallgrave has a blank and notes the word as illegible (Semper 1986b, 44 and n. 1). In *Kleine Schriften*, 'of such an evenement' is translated as 'eines derartigen Alleinherrschers' (of such an autocrat; Semper 1884, 354).   191.34–5 **electiv imperor ~ Jao**] Pauthier 1839, 35: 'Yao'   191.38 **Sii**] Pauthier 1839, 42, 45, 47, 52: 'Yu' (cf. 192.18: 'Ju')   191.40 **Roc named Hong-Chan**] 'Roc' derived from French *roc: rock*; actually a rock of the mountain 'Heng-chan' (Pauthier 1839, 53)

192.2–17 **O our assistant ~ peace.**] cf. Pauthier 1839, 53–4, and Semper's German translation in 'Comparative Architecture' (gta, 20-Ms-66, 165, ed. in Luttmann 2008, 465–6)   192.5 **didges**] *dykes*; cf. Pauthier 1839, 53: 'digues'. Mallgrave has 'ridges' (Semper 1986b, 45). On a later occasion in this lecture, Semper uses 'didges' for *ditches* (199.31).   192.7 **Tho-lou**] Pauthier 1839, 53: 'Yo-lou'   192.10 **Tho**] Pauthier 1839, 53: 'Yo'   **Thai**] Pauthier 1839, 53: 'Taï'   192.13 **but my sorrows have not ended**] In Semper's source, the sorrows have ended (Pauthier 1839, 53): '(Mon) affliction a cessé', translated by Semper into German in his 'Comparative Architecture' as 'Betrübniss hat aufgehört' (gta, 20-Ms-66, 165, ed. in Luttmann 2008, 465).   192.14 **disturbances of natural forces**] Semper first had 'revolution' instead of 'disturbances' (522, Alterations in the Manuscript 192.14). This corresponds to his contention that 'the Asiatic nations ... felt induced ... to regain by great national constructions the t[e]rritory which by the great revolution of nature, they had been obliged to abandon' (191.21–8). This 'revolution of nature' is counterbalanced by a social revolution in China, where 'Every revolution ... is made under the pretext of reviving the old institutions' (192.21–2).   192.16 **seads**] *seeds*   192.17 **peace.**] The deleted continuation of this sentence, 'and can enjoy' (see 522, Alterations in the Manuscript 192.17), is the beginning of the translation of 'et pourront se livrer éternellement à la joie' (Pauthier 1839, 54).   192.32–193.6 **Description of the Pallace ~ sunshine.**] cf. Pauthier 1839, 54 n. *, and Semper's German translation in 'Comparative Architecture' (gta, 20-Ms-66, 168, ed. in Luttmann 2008, 467)   192.35 **port**] *portal*   **laying**] *lying*

193.1 **curt**] *court* (see also 196.4)   193.19 **Mongol**] *Mongols*   193.20 **Marco Polo's travels**] Semper owned the German translation by August Bürck (Polo 1845); see 211.2, 215.23.   193.31 **thre**] *three*

194.2 **separed**] *separated* (see also 194.9)   194.12 **one**] *own*   **The**] *They*   **lay**] *lie*   194.12–13 **intrane**] *entrance*   194.16 **suit**] *suite* (see also 194.26)   194.24 **cannels**] *canals*   194.27 **Van-Sie**] 'Van-Sui' in Semper's 'Comparative Architecture' (gta, 20-Ms-66, 173, ed. in Luttmann 2008, 471)   194.28 **indescriptible**] French for *indescribable*   194.32 **Confutsie**] *Confucius*   194.34 **guorderobes**] *garderobes.* Mallgrave has 'barracks' (Semper 1986b, 46).   **Offices for the different Courtcharges**] This is Semper's translation of 'Intendanz des Hofes' and 'Hofintendanz' (gta, 20-Ms-66, 174, ed. in Luttmann 2008, 472), which he translated first as 'Court intendances' (see 523, Alterations in the Manuscript 194.34).   194.37–8 **marmorbridges**] joined from German *Marmor* (here with minuscule) and English *bridges: marble bridges*   194.38 **On a high hill is a buddha temple in form of a bottle.**] In his 'Comparative Architecture', Semper similarly describes a monument on an island in a lake of Beijing (gta, 20-Ms-66, 175, ed. in Luttmann 2008, 473): 'A white obelisk in the shape of a bottle, called Pai-tha, stands on the summit.' This corresponds – with the exception of the words 'in the shape of a bottle' – to a passage in Pauthier's *Chine moderne*: 'le sommet est couronné par un obélisque blanc appelé *paï-tha*' (Pauthier 1853, 21; italics in original). Semper apparently identified the 'buddha temple' with a 'Ta' as described and depicted in the anonymous 'Essai sur l'architecture chinoise' – an eighteenth-century manuscript held in the Bibliothèque nationale in Paris, to which he refers in his 'Comparative Architecture' and later in *Style* (gta, 20-Ms-66, 176, 189, 192, ed. in Luttmann 2008, 474, 484, 487; Semper 1860/63, 1:244). In that manuscript, the 'Ta' are described as 'les espêces de Piramides dediées à Foë & aux Esprits'; the form particularly of the first of the visualized 'Ta' can be interpreted as that of a bottle (BnF, RESERVE OE-13-PET FOL, 1: unpag., pl. 125).

195.2 **Tshin Chi Houang Ti**] 'Thsin-chi-hoang-Ti' or 'Thsin-Chi-Hoang-Ti' in Semper's 'Comparative Architecture' (gta, 20-Ms-66, 160, 179, ed. in Luttmann 2008, 461, 476), 'Thsin-chi-hoang-ti' in Pauthier's *Chine* (Pauthier 1839, especially 213–15)   195.4 **dissolved**] Mallgrave has 'dispersed' (Semper 1986b, 46).   195.6 **Yu**] *Zhou*   **reconquished**] *reconquered*   195.10 **Hien Yong**] 'Hien-Yang' in Semper's 'Comparative Architecture' (gta, 20-Ms-66, 180, ed. in Luttmann 2008, 477), 'Hien-yang' in Pauthier's *Chine* (Pauthier 1839, especially 215–16)   195.12 **rebuild**] *rebuilt*   195.20 **board**] derived from French *bord*: *bank*   195.24 **created**] Mallgrave has 'erected' (Semper 1986b, 47).   **transplated**] *transplanted*   195.28 **frensh**] *French*   **lieux**] *lieues*: French for *leagues*; cf. Pauthier 1839, 10   195.31 **innerest**] *innermost*

196.1 **adultness**] *adulthood*   196.1–2 **E contrary**] derived from Latin *e contrario*: *on the contrary*. Mallgrave has 'and contrary' (Semper 1986b, 47).   196.16 **nacked**] merged from German *nackt* and English *naked*   **Stonemaçon**] joined from English *stone* (here with majuscule) and French *maçon*: *stonemason*   196.20 **corniches**] French for *cornices* (see also 196.36)   196.25 **mouveable shrines**] *movable screens*; cf. Semper 1986b, 48 n. 5. In the essay 'On the Origin of Polychromy in Architecture', Semper says of Chinese architecture that 'The wall is only a screen' (68.21–2). In 'Comparative Architecture', he calls the walls in question at one point 'jene beweglichen Tapetenwände' (those movable paper walls) – he first wrote 'jene Charnierwände' (those hinged walls) – and at another point 'bewegliche Scheidewände' (movable partitions; gta, 20-Ms-66, 187, 191, ed. in Luttmann 2008, 482, 486). In the lecture 'The Ancient Practice of Wall Coating and Tubular Construction', he also describes the walls of the Caribbean hut as 'mouveable shrines' (127.21).   196.33 **stoned**] *stone*   196.37 **Dragonteeth**] In 'Comparative Architecture', Semper mentions 'an ornament difficult to understand, comparable to dragons' teeth' (gta, 20-Ms-66, 190, ed. in Luttmann 2008, 485; cf. Semper 1860/63, 1:254–5).   **sparheads**] *rafter heads*; cf. 'Comparative Architecture' and *Style* (gta, 20-Ms-66, 189–90, ed. in Luttmann 2008, 485; Semper 1860/63, 1:254): 'Sparrenköpfe'

197.2 **angels**] *angles*   197.5 **polygon**] *polygonal*   197.6 **sparheads**] *rafter heads*; see note 196.37   197.15–30 **Chambers describes the house of a Chinese merchant at Canton as follows ~ hall. etc.**] Semper here refers to the section 'Of the houses of the Chinese' in William Chambers's *Designs of Chinese Buildings* with its corresponding plates (Chambers 1757, 7–11, pls. 8–11) but retranslates into English most of his German digest from his 'Comparative Architecture' (gta, 20-Ms-66, 191–2, ed. in Luttmann 2008, 486–7).   197.15 **describes**] Mallgrave has 'depicts' (Semper 1986b, 48).   197.18 **bad room**] *bedroom*   **Elavation**] *elevation*   197.21 **et.**] *etc.*

On the Relation of Architectural Systems with Cultural Conditions 519

198.9 **marchy**] *marshy*   198.11 **step**] *steppe*   198.17–18 **The nation ~ belonged to the Semitic race**] In 'Comparative Architecture', Semper differentiates the racial attribution of this first 'nation' of Mesopotamia as a 'people' belonging to the 'Syrian Semitic tribe', which was 'certainly mixed with other tribes from early on'. In a later revision, he replaced 'other tribes' with 'Arian and even Turanian (Mongol) and Cushitic (Ethiopian) elements' (gta, 20-Ms-58, 41–2, ed. in Luttmann 2008, 373).   198.21–4 **Behold the land of the Chaldaeans ~ pallaces of the land.**] In a first variant of this quotation of Isaiah, 23:13, Semper cites the English translation, which is also found in Layard's *Nineveh and its Remains*: 'Behold the land of the Chaldeans, says Isaiah, this people was not, till the Assyrians founded it for them that dwelt in the wilderness, They set up the towers thereof, they raised up towers thereof' (529, note 528.9–11; the second 'towers' is written erroneously instead of 'the palaces'; cf. Layard 1849, 2:238 n. ||). However, he subsequently adapted this translation for consistency with the German translation by Johann David Michaelis, which he also cites in his 'Comparative Architecture' (gta, 20-Ms-58, 43, ed. in Luttmann 2008, 374) and in *The Four Elements of Architecture* (Semper 1851b, 71 n. *). He most likely knew Michaelis's translation through Arnold Heeren's *Ideen über die Politik, den Verkehr und den Handel der vornehmsten Völker der alten Welt* (Heeren 1824/26, 2:157; see 212.30–1).   198.32 **subjets**] *subjects*   199.6 **devided**] *divided*   199.16–22 **The camp of Cyrus ~ Xenophon ~ heavy infantry.**] cf. Xenophon, *Cyropaedia*, 8.5.2–14, and 'Comparative Architecture' (gta, 20-Ms-58, 32–3; 20-Ms-62, 80, ed. in Luttmann 2008, 310, 577).   199.20 **Charotiers**] *charioteers*   199.22 **Oplites**] *hoplites*   199.27–8 **new discoveries made by Mrs Layard and Botta on the ground where ~ Ninive stood**] 'Mrs': *Messrs*; for the respective publications, see 318, Explanatory Notes 51.29   199.31 **480 Stadiums each side**] *120 stadiums* ~ ~ (see also 199.33); cf. Herodotus on Babylon in *Histories*, 1.178, quoted by Semper in 'Comparative Architecture' (gta, 20-Ms-58, 45, ed. in Luttmann 2008, 375): 'The city … has 120 stades on each side. For it is square. Therefore, it has a circumference of 480 stades.'   **unburnt**] *unbaked* (see also 201.6)   **didges**] *ditches*; cf. Herodotus on Babylon in *Histories*, 1.178, quoted by Semper in 'Comparative Architecture' (gta, 20-Ms-58, 45, ed. in Luttmann 2008, 375): 'In the first place, a deep and wide ditch flows around it, which is always full of water.'   200.10 **castels**] *castle*   200.16 **terrae**] *terrace*   200.22 **kame**] *came*   200.24 **pinnakels**] *pinnacles*. Mallgrave has 'periwinkles' (Semper 1986b, 50).   200.26 **terraced gardens or paradises**] Mallgrave has 'Terraced garden. Paradises' (Semper 1986b, 50). Semper deleted 'or' by mistake in a sequence of alterations of the sentence which first read 'The hanging gardens or paradises were terrace works' (see 527, Alterations in the Manuscript 200.26). In the last lecture of the autumn term 1853, he similarly says of the Assyrian pyramid that it 'was connected with beautiful gardens, the so calld paradises' (177.7–8).   200.40–1 **discoveries of Mr. Layard and Botta ~ on the ground of ancient Ninive**] see note 199.27–8   201.14 **sane**] *same*   201.16–17 **splendour military aristocray**] ~ *of* ~ *aristocracy*. Mallgrave has 'splendrous military aristocracy' (Semper 1986b, 51).

EDITORIAL EMENDATIONS

191.3 **hieratical-linguage**] hieratical- | linguage   191.25–6 **family-alliances**] family- | alliances   191.32 **years**] years | years   194.3 **court-yards**] court- | yards   195.21 **double storied**] double | storied   195.26 **well known**] well | known   197.18 **bad room**] bad |

room   197.27 **bambu treillis**] bambu | treillis   199.20 **an other**] an | other   201.10
mouveable.] *before one-quarter page blank*   201.18 **two**] *before one-half page blank*

ALTERATIONS IN THE MANUSCRIPT

189.21 **We shall not be able**] *after two del. variant beginnings in opposite columns:*

As every style of architecture is the artistical expression of the social[1], political and religious
condition of that nation or that age which invented the same style,
We will not be able to conceive[2] any clear idea[3] about the individual character by which the
different styles of architecture

        1 **social**] *after del.* whole   2 **conceive**] *repl. del.* make us   make us] *above del.* have
        3 **idea**] *above del.* notice

189.21 **shall**] *above del.* will   **understand the**] *in pencil repl. del. in pencil* conceive the idea
and   **characters**] s *added in pencil*   189.22 **systems**] *in pencil repl. del. in pencil* styles
having first gained] *repl. del.* having   having] *after del.* knowing   189.23–4 **to whom the
sayd architectural styles were**] *after del.* by whom those architectural forms were   189.25
For architectural monuments] *after del.*

For architectural monuments,[1] are in reality nothing but the artistical expressions of[2] the
same Idea which was underlaiing[3] to those social political and religious institutions

        1 **architectural monuments,**] *after del.* all the *and before del.* which are so   which are so]
        after del. of which we know   2 **of**] *after del.* of the idea out of which resulted a certain
        out of which] *repl. del.* on which every society   3 **underlaiing**] 'underlying'

189.26 **same social**] *above inserted and del.* state of a nation   **institutions;**] *altered from* ~∧
before del. of a nation   189.26–8 **both ~ older than both.**] *repl. del.* and both together the
results of some social Idea.   Idea.] *altered from* ~∧ *before del.* based upon   189.27 **some
absolute**] *above del.* some principle   principle] *before inserted in pencil and undel.* of social
order. *(of social order. repl. del. in pencil* which under certain conditions of higher necessity
was just governing.)   189.29 **any**] *above del.* some   189.30–1 **ordinances**] *after del.* proportions of   189.31 **of a style,**] *repl. del.* of the different architectural styles,   189.31–190.1
notions about the] *repl. del.* idea of the
190.2 **principle**] *above del.* Idea   190.3 **But we are unhappily yet in a very great uncertainty**] *repl. del.* But we are alltogether the learned as well as the unlearned, in a very great
darkness   darkness] *undel.*   190.3–4 **just about the most essential of these general
notions**] *repl. del.* just about this most important subject   just about] *undel.*   190.4–5 **of
whom very few remains**] *after del.* who belong to the remote antiquity and   antiquity]
repl. del. ages   190.5 **and historical evidences**] *inserted*   existing] *after del.* still
also] *above del.* even   190.6 **precisely**] *interl.*   190.7 **present**] *interl.*   190.8–9 **However ~ architecture.**] *repl. del.* Nevertheless we must start from that point, and shall endeavour to explain the parts out of the whole feature of an Ensemble.   190.8 **However
this may be, I shall feel**] *repl. del.* However this may be, I feel   However this may be,]

On the Relation of Architectural Systems with Cultural Conditions   521

undel. I feel] *above del.* we are   190.9 **the different forms**] *after del.* some of the forms
after del. the caracters of the   190.10–12 **I give ~ some of them.**] *inserted after inserted and*
del. My conceptions about this subject *after inserted and del.* Even a fealure *after del.* on fols.
1v–2r

The following general conceptions about the different barbarian Styles of antiquity | are of
my own and somewhat different from the views usually given about the same Subjects. –

190.10 **in every case**] *repl. del.* even where they fail,   **some hold**] *after del.* at least   190.11
immense] *interl.*   **happen**] *above del.* be   190.13 **considered**] *above del.* mentionned
social] *accompanied by H. T. Wegener's note in pencil* social *(cf. 517, Explanatory Notes 190.13)*
190.15 **The first social form**] *after del.* The simple familiar constitution *after del.* The first
social form was the family under partriarchical   **aggregating itselfs round this focus of**
humanity] *interl.*   190.18 **existing.**] *after del.* to be found.   190.19–20 **it may allow**
some degree of progress in] *inserted*   190.20 **ornamental art∧**] *altered from ~ ~, after del.*
there may be a certain development of ar[t]   a] *after del.* great luxury   **and luxury,**] *in-*
serted   190.23 **suffered no essential**] *repl. del.* was undergoing no   190.24 **the different**]
inserted   190.26–8 **This political form ~ everywhere**] *repl. del.* This political form of
confederation, although it is the most natural and the most reasonable of states, we find it
everywhere   of states ~ everywhere] *undel.*   190.28 **overthrown**] *after del.* extinguished
or *after del.* abolished and at a very early stage of history   190.29 **are the**] *after del.* form the
190.33 **the large centers**] *after del.* all   **civilization**] *after del.* human   190.35 **very**] *in-*
serted   **our**] *interl.*   190.36 **These principles**] *after del.* The hierarchical principle
190.37–9 **The two mentionned principles ~ out of them.**] *inserted*   190.40 **old**] *after del.*
the *and before del.* feder   190.41 **conservation**] *before del.* of certain traditional forms of
society   190.42 **comprehensible enough,**] *repl. del.* the easiest to understand   **were**
not] *after del.* were not stamped and   **partly invested**] *repl. del.* invested   invested]
before del. with

191.1 **which has been**] *after del.* which was a pure invention of the priests and [o]   191.2 **by**
the priesterly foundators of this political system] *inserted*   191.5 **renders**] *above del.*
makes   **the explanation of**] *inserted*   191.6 **rather**] *inserted*   **douptfull**] *after del.* very
aenigmatical   aenigmaṭical] *after del.* difficult for explaining f[ ]   **although**] *after del.*
out of the ruined remains of the   191.6–7 **the remainders**] *repl. del.* we have more testimonies   testimonies] *after del.* remainders *(*remainders *altered from* remaining*)*   191.7
are more important] *inserted*   191.8–9 **The Egyptian monuments ~ India.**] *inserted*
191.10 **the despotical one**] *interl.*   191.11 **therefore**] *interl.*   **its**] *repl. del.* several
point;] *altered from* points.   191.11–12 **The old forms ~ different one.**] *inserted before in-*
serted and del. But this last is easy to be understood by itselfs and the   191.12 **entirely**]
above del. whole   191.12–13 **but the dynastical**] *after del.* but it is less inventi *after del.* on
fol. 3r Othersides it is less inventiv and therefore it comes that, although it retained but little
of those general forms [ ]   general] *repl. del.* social   191.13 **of the new political form of**
society] *repl. del.* of it   191.14 **circumstance**] *interl.*   191.15–17 **the meaning ~ prin-**
ciple of society.] *repl. del.* it..   it..] *altered from* ~∧∧ *before del.* and in the same time we
find the oldest traditions of elements of architecture put together in a   191.17 **architec-**
tural] *inserted*   191.19 **Chinese, of the**] *inserted*   191.21 **traditions**] *altered from* tradition
after del. old   191.22–3 **agree together and concur in mentioning a**] *repl. del.* begin with
the remembrance of some   191.24 **drove together**] *after del.* shaked   191.24–5 **in conse-**

quence of their common distress] *below del.* forcibly   191.25–6 **family-alliances]** *after del.* hostilities an   191.26 **inimities]** *before del.* and submit to one man's command   command] *after del.* order   **to stop]** *repl. del.* to face   191.28 **by the great revolution of nature,]** *inserted*   191.29 **submitting to one man's command;]** *inserted after del.* great order   191.30 **subordination]** *before del.* which   **became]** *above del.* was   191.31–4 **The history of China ~ nation.]** *after five del. beginnings of variant in opposite columns:*

But instead of developing farther
The[1] state of things which[2] an general revolution
I shall give You an example out of the old history of China which is authentically wittnessed by contemporary documents since more than three thousand Years before Christ,
The result of such a revolution for
In order to show[3] the result which must follow out of such a revolution for the form of society I shall give You an exemple out of the history of China, which last, most merveillously[4], is ascertained

> 1 **The]** T *over* t   2 **which]** *before del.* must result out of such   3 **show]** *before del.* by an exemple   4 **merveillously]** *merged from French 'merveilleusement' and English 'marvellously'*

191.34 **It]** *above del.* and   **reign]** *repl. del.* narrative   191.35 **Jao]** *repl. del.* Hoang Te   **general]** *above del.* great   191.36 **overflown the whole China]** *repl. del.* invaded China *and* overflown *above del.* submerged   191.39–40 **an inscription]** *after del.* There is still   191.40 **executed]** *after del.* existing   **was hewn into a Roc]** *repl. del.* on the Roc   **named]** *interl.*   **Hong-Chan]** *before del.* was remembering his works   **was]** *inserted*   192.2–17 **O our assistant ~ peace.]** *inserted in right column of fol. 4v and in left column of fol. 5r*   192.4 **overflown]** *above del.* submerged   **everywhere]** *after del.* as far as our   192.5 **back]** *altered from* backward   192.10 **restless]** *after del.* The   192.14 **disturbances]** *after del.* revolution   192.17 **peace.]** *altered from* ~∧ *before del.* and can enjoy [ ]   192.18 **Chun and Ju]** *interl.*   192.19 **imperial crown]** *after del.* government   192.20 **of the Dinasty Hia]** *interl.*   **a golden age]** *interl.*   192.21 **Every]** *after del.* All the institutions which were introduced at that time   **revolution]** *after del.* restaurat   192.22 **Jao.]** *before del.* We must confess, that never greater things have been undertaken and fullfilled than by those three imperors. But the high Genius of these great Lawgivers has for all   192.23 **These antiquarian reactions]** *after del.* These endless reactions and antiquarian   192.24 **one of the]** *above del.* the   **reasons]** *final* s *added*   192.25 **So for instance has the]** *above del.* The   **Jao,]** *before del.* whose description we have,   192.26 **become]** *repl. del.* is   **fundamental motif]** *before del.* of every building in its   192.27 **style]** *after del.* arch **arranged]** *repl. del.* fixed   192.28 **invariable]** *inserted*   192.30–1 **We are ~ following:]** *inserted*   192.30 **an old]** *repl. del.* the   192.32 **Yao,]** *before underl. and del.* the model Palace for all the later works of house building in China.   192.33–4 **the rains ~ coat of gras.]** *accompanied in opposite column by note in cursive script* Ursprung der gebogenen Form der Chin Dächer Grün die Farbe des Kaiserdaches.   **Chin]** *'Chinesischen'*   192.35 **triumphal]** *after del.* arch   192.36–7 **opposite side]** *repl. del.* western End   192.37 **hall, surrounded with a wall, containing the public]** *repl. del.* building or Saloon, where they held the   193.1 **balances]** *repl. del.* wages   **wages]** *derived from German 'Waage': 'balances'; after del.* weights   193.2 **hall]** *above del.* Saloon   **northern side of]** *repl. del.* western side of   193.5–6 **an audience]** *after del.* attend[a]   193.7 **model of a pallace]** *repl. del.* pallace

193.8–15 **This is true ~ tiles.**] *inserted*   193.10–11 **we are told that**] *interl.*   193.12 **antiquity**] *after del.* state of   193.13–14 **shingle**] *interl.*   193.14 **of Jao's hall**] *interl.*   193.16 **A striking contrast**] *after del.* The form of   **makes**] *after del.* is given   193.18–19 **of the Mongol Cublai Chan**] *after del.* Mongol Chan   193.19 **13ᵗʰ**] 13 *over* 10   193.20 **travels.**] *after del.* boo *(for 'book') and before del.* he says: he says:] *before del.* This pallace is the largest which has ever been seen, The roofs are exceedingly high. (roofs *after del.* ceil*)* 193.21 **the Ensemble**] *after del.* its arran   193.28 **transverse**] *inserted*   193.29 **to**] *above del.* on   193.30 **The City**] *after del.* It has a large street in the center conducing from the outer Door to the Gates of the City.   the outer] *above del.* one   Gates] *after del.* inner **City**] *over* in   193.36 **It is the residence ~ men**] *inserted*   193.39 **4**] *after del.* 1 194.4 **built**] *interl. after interl. and del.* made   194.8 **parquets**] *after del.* floo   194.9 **again**] *interl.*   194.12 **from**] *after del.* increasing gradually in hight by terraces from   in] *undel.* 194.14 **many**] *after del.* square   194.15 **halls.**] *altered from* ~, *before del.* for different   different] *after del.* government.   194.16 **an immense**] *repl. del.* a   **Gateways or**] *inserted* 194.17 **terraces,**] *altered from* ~∧ *after del.* standing on high *and before del.* of white marble. **ballustrades, bridges etc.**] *inserted*   194.17–18 **It contains**] *after del.* The effect   194.18 **13**] *over* 11   **northern**] *over* eas *(for 'eastern')*   **on an elevated terrace**] *interl.*   194.20 **last pavillon,**] *after del. on fol.* 7v end,   194.21 **all**] *above del.* the whole   **apartment**] *after del.* hab   194.23–4 **Each lady has her own house**] *inserted after del.* These buildings are   These] *after del.* In   194.24 **flowers**] *after del.* and garden arrangements *after del.* flower   194.26 **But on the northern Side**] *after del.*

The Pallace for the mother of the imperor is in the western main division.[1] the Eastern division[2] contains[3] the pallaces for the princes.
Behind the private appartments of the Imperor is a forteenth division with a very large hall and then comes the last, over the northern Gateway of the Pallace. The houses[4] On the other Side of the Street belong to the imperial town and not more to the Pallace. but there is a large bridge of marble communicating with the pallace and the imperial Garden outside the wall. of the Imperial town.

> 1 **division.**] *altered from* ~∧ *before del.* which   2 **the Eastern division**] *interl.*   3 **contains**] *before del.* also   4 **The houses**] *interl.*

194.27 **pavillon**] *after del.* main edifice   194.28 **private**] *interl.*   **richness∧**] *altered from* ~.   194.29 **forming a large square surrounded with a wall.**] *inserted*   194.30 **east**] *after del.* right   **Pallace**] *before interl. and del.* are quite of   194.33 **theaters;**] *after del.* pallaces belonging to the imperial Service.   **and**] *after del.* Each of these singel parts is enclosed by walls *and before del.* surrounded with fine gardens.   194.34 **Offices for the different Courtcharges**] *after del.* Court intendances   194.34–5 **the Chancery etc.**] *inserted before del.* etc etc.   194.35 **Westside,**] *altered from* ~∧ *before inserted and del.* corresponding to the eastern division   **of the pallace**] *repl. del.* of this waste ensemble   waste] *'vast'*   **large**] *interl.*   194.38–9 **bottle. —**] *before del.*

Very great monotony exterior military order.
Existing laws[1] for three things, the number of courts, the height, depth and length of the dwellings, the form of the walls and roofs. Every Stand[2] and grade has to observe the rule prescribed for him[3]
Tchao-Ting[4] *shreen*[5].

524 Lectures

1 **Existing laws ~ Tchao-Ting shreen.**] *cf. Semper's 'Comparative Architecture' (gta, 20-Ms-66, 176, ed. in Luttmann 2008, 474–5): 'The laws distinguish between three things in the dwellings: the number of courtyards, the height, length and depth of the buildings, and the shape and colour of the roofs and walls. The hierarchy of the classes is combined and arranged in accordance with these, from the citizen to the scholar, from the scholar to the mandarin, through all of the grades up to the Emperor. This gradation is so clearly expressed that one can see from a building who lives in it. However, since degradations, promotions and the awarding of new degrees of rank would make the observance of this law very difficult ... an attempt has been made to circumvent it by devising the so-called Tchao-Ping or Tchao-Hiang. These are isolated screen walls that are erected at a certain distance in front of the main entrance door.'* 2 **Stand**] *German for 'class'* 3 **him**] *referring to male German nouns 'Stand' (class) and 'Grad' (grade): 'it'* 4 **Tchao-Ting**] *'Tchao-Ping'* 5 **shreen**] *'screen'*

195.1 **constructions,**] *after del.* architec *and before del.* which were 195.5 **under the**] *above del.* of the **last feable**] *repl. del.* feable 195.11 **He made**] *after del.* This Pallace was composed out of as many **made**] *repl. del.* ordered to make **drawings**] *above del.* copies 195.12 **rebuild**] *after del.* to 195.13 **furnishing them**] *after del.* to furnish them with all the richnesses which they contained and all ~ and] *undel.* 195.14 **forcing**] *above del.* ordering 195.16 **courts**] *after del.* court-arrangement 195.17 **as**] *interl. after del.* how we have seen **are**] *interl.* 195.20 **on**] *after del.* along 195.22 **He**] *after del.* The same Imperor ordered his 195.23 **principle.**] *before del.* The plan which he followed was an imitation of the constellation of heaven; Each Pallace was a Star 195.25 **into**] *after del.* to 195.27 **which**] *after del.* an undertaking **from the Gulf**] *after del. on fols. 9v–10r* round the frontier | of China **the yellow sea**] *after del.* Liao-Tung 195.29 **This was only**] *after del.* This was only an extension of the same principle of despotic architecture, which we have of the same principle] *of undel.* **of the Idea**] *after del.* of an Idea owed to one of the first imperors, of the Year bef. Chr. 2200, who divided to one ~ who divided] *undel.* 195.31 **concentric squares.**] *after del.* circles. or 195.32 **imperial**] *after del.* Roy 195.33 **between the second and**] *accompanied by possibly Hans Semper's note in ink* + **for**] *after del.* filled up by 195.35 **outlaws**] *after del.* Exi 195.37 **One and the same Idea prevails**] *after del.* The same principle is **Chinese**] *repl. del.* manifestations of Chinese 195.39 **bands.**] *altered from ~∧ before del.* without any organic and [ ] 195.39–40 **the military and despotic system of order.**] *inserted* 195.40 **development,**] *altered from ~∧ before del.* of the greater individuals out of the smaler and simpler unites; unites] *'units'* 195.40–196.1 **no growing up ~ adultness;**] *inserted*
196.1 **of Childhood**] *after del.* into that of completedness 196.2 **simpler**] *repl. del.* simplest simplest] st *over* r **specimens**] *after del.* units **of architecture**] *interl.* 196.3 **pallaces;**] *altered from ~∧ before del.* and follow the 196.3–4 **The houses ~ scale, with**] *inserted* 196.6 **If we look at**] *after del.*

If[1] we look to the constructiv parts and the details of Chinese architecture, we find the same individualising[2] principle[3], bound together by exterior[4] order and

1 **If**] *after del.* But there is one great principle of individuali *after del.* Vice versa are the 2 **individualising**] *interl.* 3 **principle**] *before del.* of indivi- | duals duals] *undel.* 4 **exterior**] *after del.* outer

196.7 **again encounter.**] *repl. del.* find **principle. –**] *altered from ~∧ ∧ before del.* of individua of] *after del.* again 196.9 **primitiv and material sense.**] *accompanied in opposite column by inserted and del.* But the whole forms an aggregation of 196.10 **roof;**] *altered from*

On the Relation of Architectural Systems with Cultural Conditions

~, *before del.* which has nothing in common wit[h]   196.10–11 **without capitals or bases. and without Entasis.**] *inserted*   196.12 **The terraces**] *after del.* The walls are mostly mouveable partitions or at least do they represent such partitions; Stone which is generally hollow. – . *and before del.* only   partitions;] *altered from* ~, *before del.* even where they are constructed out of brickwork.   **these constructions**] *after del.* the woo   **stand**] *repl. del.* are placed   **sometimes**] *repl. del.* generally   196.13 **mouldings∧**] *altered from* ~, **and rusticated work,**] *inserted*   196.13–14 **very much different**] *after del.* d[i]   196.14 **Greec and Roman**] *after del.* Roman   196.16 **nacked stone and the**] *inserted*   196.17 **shows itselfs.**] *repl. del.* showed itselfs;   itselfs;] *altered from* ~∧ *before del.* which never 196.18 **are**] *before del.* made   196.19 **hollow brick**] *after del.* bric[k]   **construction, covered with Stucco,**] *repl. del.* and covered with painted ornaments imitating   painted] *after del.* coloured   196.21 **are real or painted**] *repl. del.* are   196.21–2 **bambutreillis work**] *after del.* treillis work of bambu   196.23 **and**] *above del.* or   **draperies,**] *altered from* ~∧ *before del.* with Embroideries.   **or like**] *inserted*   196.24 **embroidered carpets**] *after del.* and   196.27–30 **The outer walls ~ pavillons.**] *inserted*   196.29 **placed between**] *after del.* fixed between the walls   196.30 **for small pavillons**] *after del.* which takes   takes] *after del.* is the case   196.31 **The roof**] *before del.* shows the   196.33 **The covering is of**] *after del.* The tyles are of   **rather**] *interl.*   196.34 **colours;**] *altered from* ~, *before del.* which are   **The form of**] *after del.* The mode of co *after del.* Every condition of life has   196.35 **Ancient Greecs and Romans.**] *after del.* Greecs.   196.36 **corniches are**] *after del.* columns have   196.37 **at other cases.**] *inserted*

197.4 **on stone**] *repl. del.* on   197.5 **terraces.**] *altered from* ~∧ *before del.* of the building. 197.7 **The thickness**] *after three del. beginnings of variant:*

Every Story has its own system of columns and f[1]
When there are different Stories
A[2] house which has more[3] than one story,

> 1 **f**] *undel. after del.* nat[ ]   2 **A**] *over a after del.* In   3 **more**] *after del.* different

197.8 **policy**] *after del.* laws   **A**] *above del.* Every   197.13 **Thus, in this country**] *after del. on fol. 12r*

Thus all is settled by law,[1] in this country[2] where the maintenance of[3] the principles of beauty and aesthetics is[4] overwatched by[5] police-men[6] and constablers

> 1 **law,**] *before del.* for every sort of construction has its own proportions; the aesthetical laws of the   2 **in this country ~ constablers**] *inserted*   3 **the maintenance of**] *inserted* 4 **is**] *above del.* are   5 **overwatched by**] *del. separately after del.* prescribed by w[ ] *after del.* prescribed by policemen   6 **police-men**] police- | men

197.13 **the principles**] *after del.* all is   197.16–17 **on each side**] *after del.* into   197.19 **staircase.**] *altered from* ~∧ *before del.* for the ups   197.20–1 **bambuplants**] *after del.* and   197.21 **vases,**] *inserted*   197.24 **Grondfloor**] *after del.* lower floor   197.26 **walls**] *before del.* are 197.32 **buildings.**] *altered from* ~∧ *before del.* which lay   197.34 **tradesmans**] *final* s *added* house] *interl.*   columns] *before del.* allowed for his house. he   197.35 **professional**] *after del.* learned   197.36–7 **of giving**] *repl. del.* of

198.2 **pittoresque.**] *altered from* ~∧ *before del.* tome   198.9 **in**] *before del.* sum *(for 'summer')*
spring] *after del.* early time of the   198.10 **ground**] *interl.*   **for the neighbouring tribes**]
after del. of the   198.13 **energetic**] *before del.* preparatory   198.15 **It**] *altered from* it *after*
del. Besides its richness of ground   **of old**] *interl. after interl. and del.* before the   198.16
lands.] *before inserted and del.* Being   198.27 **know**] *repl. del.* see   **of history**] *interl.*
198.28 **conquest,**] *altered from* ~. *altered from* ~∧   **by a**] *above del.* A   A] *over* a *after del.*
and   198.29 **military and**] *inserted*   198.32 **language, dresses and habits**] *repl. del.*
languages and manners   languages] *interl.*   198.33 **was the cause**] *after del.* had brought
their   198.38 **period,**] *altered from* ~∧ *before del.* of the history

199.1 **conquest of**] *after del.* Persian *and before del.* the Assyrian plane   plane] *'plain'*
Assyria by the Persians] *inserted*   199.10 **families of the old**] *inserted*   **vainquished**
race] *after del.* inhabitants of the con[q]   199.14 **of vassals,**] *repl. del.* of curtisans,
curtisans] *derived from French 'courtisan': 'courtiers'*   199.16–17 **The camp of Cyrus ~ fol-**
lows.] *repl. del. on fol. 15r–v* To this we must at once add the description which the same
Greec writer, Xenophon, ¦ gives of the Camp of Cyrus. It was, according to him,   199.17
arranged as] *after del.* ordered as   **staff**] *before del.* and the silver armed guards   **were**
erected] *after del.* formed an elevated Square   199.18 **terrace**] *inserted*   199.19 **life**
guards] *after del.* silver armed   199.20 **men**] *inserted*   199.21 **last**] *before del.* and st
199.23 **Thus**] *after del.* And the architectural   **principle,**] *altered from* ~∧   199.23–4 **that**
of subordination order and strength] *inserted*   199.25 **Architecture.**] *altered from* ~∧
before four del. beginnings of variant:

only with that difference [b]
with¹ the p[ ]
But the Assyrians; being more exposed to invasions than the isolated Chinese, were induced
to make fortresses² of great strength out of their houses.
But the inhabitants of Assyria were more warelike³ than the Chinese and [ ]

> 1 **with**] *before del.* the difference that   2 **fortresses ~ houses.**] *repl. del.* stronghold out
> of their houses   3 **warelike**] *'warlike'*

199.27 **new discoveries**] *after del.* newly discovered remains of some   of] *undel. after del.*
confirm   199.29 **Herodotus on Babylone.**] *after del.* Herodotus on Babylone.   199.31
unburnt] un *interl.*
200.1–3 **The walls ~ bronze.**] *inserted in opposite column without insertion mark, starting*
alongside the manuscript line Asphalt. didges round. *at 199.31*   200.1 **were**] *repl. del.* had
400 feet] *after del.* 200 Yar *(for 'Yards')*   **tops of**] *interl.*   200.2 **town gates**] *above del.*
doors   200.3 **and frameworks of the door**] *interl.*   200.7 **Behind**] *above del.* Between
an other wall] *before del.* of less hight.   200.8 **occupied with the tents of the**] *above del.*
for   **caravans,**] *before del.* foreigners. and tents   200.10 **castels**] *final* s *added*   200.11–
12 **on a very elevated terrace ~ dominated by it –**] *inserted in opposite column after del.* very
elevated over the   very elevated over the] *inserted in opposite column without insertion mark*
beside the manuscript line town was a royal castels. *at 200.10*   200.11 **town**] *after del.* nev
nev] *'new'; above del.* whole   200.12 **ancient**] *above del.* old   **Belus**] *after del.* old   **con-**
tains] *above del.* with   200.13 **Sanctuary of Belus**] *before del.* (tower of Babylone).
200.14 **tower of Belus**] *before del.* (known   200.14–15 **square ~ terraces.**] *repl. del.* one
stadium high and one each side of the square   200.16 **top of. the**] *after del.* highest *and*
before del. terrace   **the statue**] *repl. del.* the coloss   200.18 **The royal Castel**] *after del.*

On the Relation of Architectural Systems with Cultural Conditions

Ninive was build[1] in the same system and nearly of the same extent[2].

It was built by Ninus, who called the richest inhabitants of the country together to live therein.

His queen[3] build[1] the tomb of the king at the end of the pallace, which was of the same form with that at Babylone.

1 **build**] *'built'* 2 **extent**] *before del.* with Babylone 3 **queen**] *'widow'; i.e. Semiramis*

200.19 **The second wall**] *after del.* 60 Stadium 200.25 **moved**] *after del.* op 200.26 **terraced gardens**] *repl. del.* hanging gardens hanging gardens] *after del.* The **or**] *del.* **paradises**] *after del.* paradysos **were**] *before del.* terrace works 200.30 **70**] *above del.* 100 200.31 **Each terrace**] *after del.* The substructions of *after del.* The whole was like an amphitheater **32 feet**] *after del.* only 200.33–5 **On the terraces ~ enrichments.**] *inserted* 200.36 **The spaces**] *after del.* The light 200.40 **plans**] *after del.* very 201.4 **with isolated buildings**] *after del.* of sma of] *above del.* with 201.12 **Egyptian institutions**] *after del.* The same difference [ ] **before**] *after del.* long *after del.* Pri 201.12–14 **the monarchical power ~ Christ.**] *inserted* 201.12–13 **monarchical**] *interl.* 201.13 **power**] *before del.* of the kings **5 or**] *inserted* 201.16 **splendour**] *interl.* 201.18 **The difference**] *after del.* The same difference is visible in the development of styles. is] *undel.*

MANUSCRIPT VARIANTS
MS 145

want of invention; no organic life   *fol. 1r*

The same in the constructiv parts. No symbols but realities. Symbols only relating to the caracter of the inhabitant, not to the function of the parts of the construction. details of a house, the different elements not working together. Each for itself no columns but only
5   supports. Antique mode of covering the roof.

Great Restaurator of the Monarchy of China, Tshin Chi-Houang Ti. (249 bef. Christ.).

The land had been dissolved into many independent states, He vainquished all the independant Vassals of the Empire and destroied the aristocratical power of the learned men a sort of priesthood, which made opposition to his system. He gave an architectural expres-
10   sion to his Idea, in the foundation of a new capital or Pallace Hien-Yong. He ordered to make copies of the pallaces of all the independent vassals of the Empire which he had vainquished and killed and to rebuild them on the place of his Residence, and to furnish them with all the furnitures and richnesses they contained. and to unite them in a general place with Galleries and courts. In one of these courts was place for 10000 Soldiers. He
15   destroied the old town to give place for his new work, (like Nero did after him,) so the whole became one immense pallace. ¦

The land whose monumental remains will occupy us now is that vast alluvial plain, watered   *fol. 1v* by the Tygris and Euphrates, which extends from the Persian Gulf to the foot of the Armenian hills, unbroken by any single eminence.
20   It was once, what it is to day, a marshy prairie, being for a short time the common pasture ground for the tribes of the neighbouring montains and for Arabs, but for the rest of the year a morass, or a dry desert without water.

528   Lectures

It is the most fertile ground in the world but its richnesses must be gained from nature by
energetic preparatory works, which can not be carried out except by great national Enter-
prises. |

fol. 2r   Besides its great fertility it is, or it was the great commercial Overland way between India
and the western seats of ancient culture, the two rivvers affording the means of easy and   5
expeditious. communication. – The nation, which, as far as we know, first had taken possession of this land and gained it from nature, belonged to the Semitic Race; It appears in the
oldest records as an enterprising luxurious and somewhat overbearing nation.
Behold the land of the Chaldaeans, this people was not till the Assyrians dammed up the
land for them, that dwelt in the wilderness; They transformed the tents of the nomads into   10
solid settlements and raised the pallaces of the land.
The first records of this nation are again, like in China, speaking of a great deluge which
gave the Occasion for the great work of civilization; they mention a certain Xithurus and his
followers as the foundators of the Assyrian Empire, whose history closely ressembles to that
of Noah. – ¦   15

fol. 2v   This may be as it will, we see the land since the beginning as one governed by military institutions founded on the right of conquest.
Its history is the continual repetition of the same political event, the submission of a highly
cultivated but luxurious and enervated nation by uncivilised but energetic invaders, who
take possession of the land, adopt a great part of the institutions of their new subjects, and   20

fol. 3r   soon fall into the same state of political and moral relaxation, which | them.
There is a certain periodical regularity perceptible in the succession of such events for the
history of the contries in question, like in that of certain natural phaenomena; and they
fullfill their regular curse in the same manner. What applies to one period of the history of
the land holds also good for the precedent periods as well as for the followig   25
The Persian conquest for instance is one of the later revolutions of the country, but the instructions, which Cyrus, the Persian conqueror gave to his satraps, contain in a few words

fol. 3v   the essence of the political state of the land as it was ¦ before him under former despots and
as he restored it to the advantage of his own conquering race.
He devides the provinces between his generals and relations; to govern the subjects, to col-   30
lect the taxes, to pay the Garrisons etc.
He recommends them to follow his exemple, and to create a military nobility with their
friends and the first inhabitants of the province;
To establish a rigid court-ceremonial, to give regular audiences to the great proprietors and
houseowners, to invite them to large dinner- and hunting parties – a. s. on. and so on. –   35
Who in proportion to his fortune, he continues, entertains te greatest number of courtisans,
horsemen and charioteers, will be my best friend and the boldest support of my empire.

> 527.1 **want of invention; no organic life**] *accompanied by note in pencil* ad. 9. *(referring to
> MS 144¹, fol. 9r with page number 9; 195.1–16)*   ad] *Latin for 'to'*   **want**] *after del.* con-
> glomeration of the same elements wi   527.2 **but**] *after del.* except such as have no relation
> to the ornamented part but.   ornamented] *after del.* structural   527.3 **caracter**] *after del.*
> dignity   **function**] *after del.* structural   **details**] *after del.* Description of the   527.4
> **the different elements not working together**] *cf. 127.20–3*   527.4–5 **no columns but
> only supports**] *cf. 127.27–9*   527.5 **Antique mode of covering the roof**] *cf. 162.21–2*
> 527.6 **Restaurator**] *German for 'restorer'*   **Tshin Chi-Houang Ti**] *see 518, Explanatory
> Notes 195.2*   527.7 **many**] *above del.* feudal   **He**] *after del.* each in consequence of the
> abno   in] *undel.*   527.8 **Empire**] *after del.* kinddom   kinddom] 'kingdom'   527.9

On the Relation of Architectural Systems with Cultural Conditions   529

made] *above del.* was in   **He**] *after del.* He was a g[   ]   527.10 **Hien-Yong**] *see 518, Explanatory Notes 195.10; after del.* at   527.12–13 **and to furnish them**] *interl.*   527.13–14 **a general place**] *before del.* extending to an immense d[   ]   527.14 **Soldiers**] *after del.* men 527.17 **The land**] *after del.* W *after del.* The land, whose monumental antiquities will occupy us to day, is an immense *after del.* Assyri *after one-eighth page blank*   527.18 **Persian Gulf**] *after del.* road Sea   road] *'Red'*   527.20 **It was once**] *after del.*

It was once what it is to day,. a marchy[1] prairie, being covered wholeover for a short time of the Year with luxuriant grass, then being the common pasture ground for the mountaineer and Arabian tribes of the neighbourhood, but for the rest of the Year

      1 **marchy**] *'marshy'*

527.20 **time**] *before del.* of the Year   527.21 **montains**] *'mountains'*
528.1 **most fertile**] *after del.* richest and   **but**] *after del.* but nature wants to be   528.2 **except**] *after del.* by single families hand and afford a great national   528.4 **is, or it was**] *inserted before del.* is very favorably situated for commerce, being   **commercial**] *inserted* **India**] *after del.* Eastern Asi[a]   528.5 **ancient**] *after del.* civil   **culture,**] *repl. del.* civilisation,   528.6 **communication. –**] *altered from* ~∧ ∧ *before del.* between   528.7 **gained**] *after del.* founded   **nature**] *before del.* by its energy   its energy] *after del.* great canalization and great   528.7–8 **It appears ~ nation.**] *inserted*   528.9–11 **Behold ~ land.**] *inserted after one undel. variant and two inserted and del. beginnings of variant:*

Behold the land of the Chaldeans, says Isaiah, this people was not, till the Assyrians founded it for them that dwelt in the wilderness, They set up the towers thereof, they raised up towers thereof. –
Behold the land of the Chaldaeans, this nation[1], which not long ago was not a nation,
Behold the land of the Chaldaeans, this people was not, till the Assyrians dammed up[2] the land,[3]

      1 **nation**] *above del.* people   2 **dammed up**] *after del.* secured the   3 **land,**] *before del.* and gave it to the inhabitants of the

528.12 **The first records ~ speaking**] *del. and then underl. with dots cancelling deletion* **The first records**] *after interl. and del.* It is remarkable *after interl. and del.* Here, like in China,   528.13 **great**] *after del.* people who   528.13–15 **they mention a certain Xithurus ~ whose history closely ressembles to that of Noah**] *cf. Layard 1851, 342 n. †* 528.13 **Xithurus**] *usually spelled 'Xisuthrus'*   528.14 **foundators**] *merged from Italian 'fondatori' and English 'founders'*   528.16 **This**] *after del. on fol. 2r* To whatever origine th *after del.* Whatever origine *after del.* This land has been the *after del.* Whatever   **beginning**] *before del.* of history   528.18 **Its history is the**] *inserted after seven del. beginnings of variant:*

The history[1] of it is a continual repetition[2] of conquests
Its favorabl
Its position and high culture [   ]
Its fertility high culture and happy position as the main commercial road maid[3] it the aim for the uncivilised tribes which dwelt around it, and its history is a continual record of conquests which last had their regular
It allways was the aim for

_____

One conques
The history of it[4] is a

1 **history**] *after del.* whole   2 **a continual repetition**] *after del.* nothing but the Chronicle of c[o]   3 **maid**] *'made'*   4 **it**] *over* A *(for 'Assyria')*

528.18 **political**] *after del.* occur   528.20 **land,**] *altered from* ~∧ *before del.* and having no elements of   **adopt**] *altered from* adopted *after del.* adopted most of the institutions adopted most of the institutions] *repl. del.* adopted the institutions. the language and the vices   528.21 **which**] *'with'; before del.* had   528.22 **There**] *after del.* The succession of such political events is a regular as certain natural phanomena, which   The] *repl. del.* The regularity in the   a] *'as'*   528.24 **fullfill**] *above del.* make   **curse**] *'course'*   528.26 **The Persian conquest**] *after del.*

The Persian Conquest for instance was one of the later revolutions[1] of the country[2] – nevertheless the constitution[3] which Cyrus, the Persian Conqueror, gave to his empire, and which the Greec author Xenophon

1 **was one of the later revolutions**] *repl. del.* was one of the later periods   2 **of the country**] *after del.* of the history   3 **constitution**] *after del.* principle of Cyrus in constituting

528.26–7 **instructions**] *after del.* order *after del.* following   528.27 **contain**] *after del.* is the true [ ]   528.28 **essence of the**] *above del.* whole   528.29 **conquering race.**] *after del.* race.   528.30 **devides**] *'divides'*   **provinces**] *after del.* land   **between his**] *after del.* among his   528.32 **create**] *above del.* form   **a military nobility with**] *repl. del.* a cortege out of   528.33 **province**] *after del.* country   528.34 **To**] *after del.* To call the first of the p **rigid**] *repl. del.* regular   528.35 **a. s. on.**] *interl.*   **and so on**] *after del.* to *after del.* in a word to   528.36–7 **Who ~ empire.**] *accompanied in opposite column by del.* I shall consider that of my servants the   528.36 **te**] *'the'*   **courtisans**] *French for 'courtiers'*   528.37 **will**] *above del.* may

Explanation of the Expression of Spatial Arrangements in Architecture

TEXTUAL RECORD

MS 144²   gta, 20-Ms-144, fols. 18v–30v (20v–30r blank; 30v sketches of plan of Babylon and of elevations and sections of Belus pyramid in pencil, calculations in pencil), in Semper's hand, dated 6 December 1854, *copy-text*

MS 146²   gta, 20-Ms-146, fols. 12r–14v (14r–v blank), in H. T. Wegener's hand (emendations in Manfred Semper's hand), 1880 or 1881, copy of MS 144²

Semper 1986b   'London Lecture of November 29, 1854', 43–53, here 51, 53 (additional sections: ed. of MS 144'; see 515), Mallgrave's ed. of MS 144²

BIBLIOGRAPHY Herrmann 1981, 38, 113–14, 172; Herrmann 1984, 150

Explanation of the Expression of Spatial Arrangements in Architecture

531

EXPLANATORY NOTES

Dated 6 December 1854, this draft lecture provides the reference point for the dates of Semper's lectures in the autumn term of 1854. It refers to the previous lecture in relation to 'the general idea ... of the Egyptian temples' (201.20–1), and it starts on the same manuscript sheet on which the draft of that lecture ends. Our lecture title is derived from a misleading phrase in the draft: 'Explanation of the Expression of local arrangements' (202.3). The context reveals that the word 'local' should read *spatial* here. Semper's overview of Egyptian temple types – from the simple, uncovered courtyard enclosure to the many-layered basilica – is concerned with a developmental quality in Egyptian architecture which he mentions in the last of the lectures given in 1853 (174.34–176.10) – borrowing from his discussion in *The Four Elements of Architecture* (Semper 1851b, 74–8) and in 'Comparative Architecture' (gta, 20-Ms-68, 15–28, ed. in Luttmann 2008, 528–35). In the latter, he contends that 'an Egyptian sanctuary' bears 'the clearest signs of a gradual emergence and expansion' (gta, 20-Ms-68, 15; see 499–500, Explanatory Notes 177.30–178.19). This leads up to a declaration of the importance of the last of the Egyptian temple types, the basilica, as 'the actual key for the entire history of architecture' (gta, 20-Ms-68, 28; cf. Semper 1851b, 103): 'Almost no new internal combination is possible since the Egyptian hypostyle basilica became the richest architectural form. Only it could take shape more freely, where the material and the external constraints no longer set the same narrow limits. This happened under the Greeks and Romans, but especially in the Christian basilica. Later on we will have to say what is necessary about the striking kinship between the fully developed Gothic basilica and the Egyptian temple complexes in terms of the idea and its general expressions.'

201.21 **kernet**] *kernel*, here misused for *core*   201.22–3 **erected**] Mallgrave has 'created' (Semper 1986b, 51).   201.26 **local**] *spatial* (see also 202.3, 202.14)   201.28 **foundators**] merged from Italian *fondatori* and English *founders*   **policy ∧ religion**] ~, ~. Mallgrave has 'policy in religion' (Semper 1986b, 51).   201.30 **adapted**] Mallgrave has 'adopted' (Semper 1986b, 51).

202.4 **precinction**] for Semper's understanding of 'precinction' as *enclosure*, see 202.5 ('mere precinctions'), 202.13 ('precinctions or fenced open courts'), 202.17–19 (a series of synonyms: 'precinctio', 'presaepium', 'fence'); cf. Semper 1986b, 51 n. 9   **architure**] uncertain reading, *architecture*; cf. 533, Alterations in the Manuscript 202.4   202.5 **solid**] Mallgrave has 'Jewish' (Semper 1986b, 51).   **eastern**] *Eastern* (see also 202.6)   **mere**] Mallgrave has 'new' (Semper 1986b, 51).   202.6 **protection on terraces**] 'on' uncertain reading. Mallgrave has 'protection or terraces' (Semper 1986b, 51). The phrase can be seen in relation to a preceding alteration in which Semper first wrote 'mere precinctions of terr' (for 'terraces') and then deleted 'of terr' (see 533, Alterations in the Manuscript 202.5). In his theory, the protective enclosure and the terrace are two of four distinct architectural elements – the enclosure is not built as a terrace but on a terrace (Semper 1851b, 54–5, 55 n. *).   202.7 **yet**] Mallgrave has 'get' (Semper 1986b, 51).   202.9 **floggs**] *flocks*   202.11 **obtained**] Mallgrave has 'attained' (Semper 1986b, 51).   202.12 **canevas**] French for *canvases*   202.13 **such**] Mallgrave has 'each' (Semper 1986b, 51).   202.15 **architectural**] *architecture*. Mallgrave has 'architectural (planning)' (Semper 1986b, 51).   202.17 **precinctio**] *precinct*; cf. note 202.4. In Vitruvius, *De architectura*, 5.3.4, 5.6.2, 5.7.2, the Latin word *praecinctio* denotes a diazoma – a horizontal, semicircular gangway that separates an upper from a lower block of seats in a theatre.   202.18 **presaepium**] *praesaepium*: Latin for *enclosure*   202.20 **wholy**] *wholly*

202.21 **οἴκημα**] *οἴκημα (oikema)*: Greek for *room* or *house*, here used in the first sense. Mall-grave has 'oiazns' (Semper 1986b, 53).   202.22 **cubiculum**] Latin for *room* or *chamber*
202.25 **peristyle**] H. T. Wegener, who copied MS 144 for Manfred Semper (see 515, 530), noted 'Webster' below the word 'peristyle' (see 533, Alterations in the Manuscript 202.25). In a letter dated 13 December 1880 (gta, 21-K-1880-12-13), he wrote to Manfred Semper: 'I would like to draw your attention to the fact that some words in the manuscript are not spelt as prescribed by "Webster's Dictionary" (recognized as the standard dictionary in England and America), and I have therefore taken the liberty of making a few changes in this respect, e.g. temple for tempel, tabernacle for tabernacel, constructive for constructiv, lions for lyons, through for throu, etc.'
203.1–2 **combination of 4 and 5. tempel of. Lucsor**] 'Lucsor': *Luxor*. Semper's sketch suggests a combination of the types 3 and 4 in one spatial unit. However, the plates in the multivolume work *Description de l'Égypte*, which Semper knew – he listed it in 'Practical Art in Metals and hard Materials' (Semper 2007a, 77; cf. Semper 1860/63, 2:187) – show, starting from the entrance, a sequence of the types 3, 4, 3, 2b, 1 and, in the rearmost area, a dense cluster of the types 2a and 2b (Description de l'Égypte 1809/22, sect. 'Antiquités' 7: pls. 5, 7–10).   203.7 **heving**] *having*   203.11 **large writing tables. formig a kind of lock**] Mall-grave has 'A large writing tablet, forming a kind of book' (Semper 1986b, 53). Semper first wrote 'A large writing table' and altered it to 'large writing tables' (see 533, Alterations in the Manuscript 203.11). Treating Egyptian architecture in the last lecture of the autumn term 1853, he says that the two pylons framing the entrance formed 'like a lock of a bracelet the End and the beginni[n]g of the Enclosure' and were 'intended ... to be a tablet for inscriptions' (176.4–10).   203.15 **trochleus pulley**] The Latin word *trochlea* means *winch* or, as translated by Semper, *pulley*.

ALTERATIONS IN THE MANUSCRIPT

201.20 **I explained**] *after two variant beginnings del. in ink and pencil, respectively:*

I explained in the last lecture how[1] the Egyptian temples affected in their general disposition to be works grown

------

I explained in the last lecture the idea[2] laid down in the general[3] disposition of the Egyptian temples by their founders[4], who affected to make their work[5] appear like aglomerations[6] round an invisible cernet[7] gradually grown up on the ground[8] itself where it stood and[9] as being still capable of indefinite ingrandisment[10];
But[11] it remains now for us[12] to show how they succeeded in the same time to give a high degree of organic deve

------

1 **how**] *after del.* how the disposition of the Groundplan of a   disposition] *after del.* Egyptian temples affected in their   2 **idea**] *after del.* general disposition and idea followed by the   3 **general**] *interl.*   4 **foundators**] *merged from Italian* 'fondatori' *and English* 'founders'   5 **their work**] *above del.* them   6 **like aglomerations ~ cernet**] *repl. del.* as a work   as] *undel.*   7 **cernet**] 'kernel', *here misused for* 'core'   8 **on the ground**] *after del.* out of a small and *after del.* round an *after del.* gro   9 **and**] *after del.* and quasi like a

Explanation of the Expression of Spatial Arrangements in Architecture   533

peace of Aegyptian nature.   peace] *'piece'*   10 **ingrandisment**] *merged from French 'agrandissement' and Italian 'ingrandimento': 'enlargement'*   11 **But**] *after del.* While *after del.* It remains now to give an explanati[o]   12 **for us**] *interl.*

201.20 **general**] *interl.*   **disposition**] *after underl. and del.* general   201.21 **who**] *interl. in pencil after del. in pencil* whose foundators made them   foundators] *merged from Italian 'fondatori' and English 'founders'*   them] *above del.* their works   201.22 **sanctuaries**] ies *above del.* y   **Gods**] *altered from* God *after del.* Divinity   **to the honour**] *after del.* which were *after del.* to whose honour it was e   201.23 **the Aegyptians**] *in pencil repl. del. in pencil on fol. 18v* they   **succeeded**] *after del. on fol. 18v* succeeded in the same time in giving to them a highly developped   in giving] *after del.* in giving a truly organic inner development to these works, and in *(to undel.)*   201.24 **giving to these agglomerations**] *after del.* organizing them   **of walls**] *interl. in pencil*   **an**] n *added in pencil*   **organic**] *after del. in pencil* more   201.25 **first inventors of**] *after del.* inventors of   **almost**] *interl.*   201.26 **which still**] *after del.* and   201.27 **having**] *in pencil repl. del. in pencil* and which have **augmented**] *after del.* since the time of the Aegyptians   201.28 **architecture.**] *before del.* And we must add that they have only been de   that] *before del.* the made Explanation of the expression lecal arrangenent *(lecal arrangenent: 'spatial arrangement'; underl.)*   201.30 **who adapted**] *after del.* how had not the same richnesses   how] *'who'; after del.* who knew not and

202.1 **arrangements,**] *before del.* which were grown in the temple architecture of this n[a] which] *after del.* and called them wit[h]   the] *undel.*   202.1–2 **the greec templestyle**] *after del.* the Greec temple architecture being much less rich in such   202.4 **for**] *over* in **architure**] *altered from* architer   202.5 **precinctions**] *before del.* of terr   202.6 **The eastern countries are**] *after del.* The countries of Morea a *after del.* Still now the   202.8 **for which**] *after del.* which they did   202.10 **the**] *after del.* Seco[n]   **protection**] *above del.* Cover   **is only**] *after interl. and del.* the roofing   **afterthought,**] *before del.* with the exception of the Sanctuary which we shall now not consider.   202.11 **obtained**] *after del.* carri *after del.* mouveable and provisional   202.12 **or wooden ceilings**] *after del.* blanckets blanckets] *before del.* supported by wooden columns,   202.13 **The**] *inserted*   202.14 **gave**] *after del.* with   202.21 **hypostyle**] *second* y *in pencil over* i   202.24 **protected**] *after del.* covered with   202.25 **peristyle**] *accompanied by H. T. Wegener's note in pencil* Webster *(cf. 532, Explanatory Notes 202.25)*   202.26 **a roof**] *after del.* an allee or a

203.1 **the combination**] *after del.* the courtyard protected both by.   203.6 **Stone Style**] *after del.* the two   **Beginnig.**] *before del.* the   203.8 **steeples**] *after del.* Church   203.9 **stations**] *after del.* places or   203.11 **large**] *after del.* A   **tables**] s *added*   203.12 **Entire dependency**] *after del.* General caracter of the   **ensemble no individuality**] *above del.* general idea

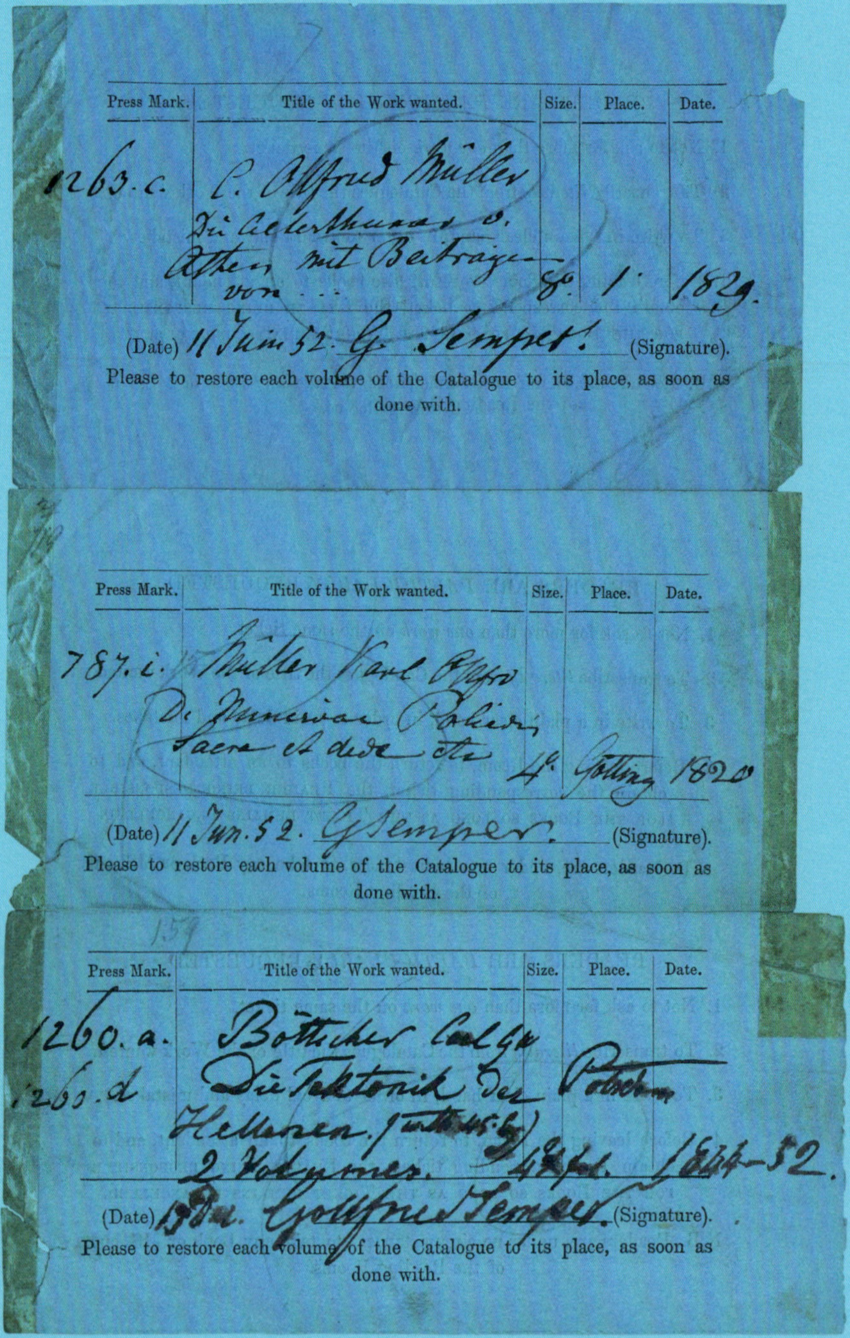

Press Mark.	Title of the Work wanted.	Size.	Place.	Date.
1263. c.	C. Otfried Müller Die Alterthümer v. Athen mit Beiträgen von …	8°	1	1829.

(Date) 11 Jun 52. G. Semper. (Signature).
Please to restore each volume of the Catalogue to its place, as soon as done with.

Press Mark.	Title of the Work wanted.	Size.	Place.	Date.
787. i. 15	Müller Karl Otfr. De Minervae Poliadis sacra et aede etc	4°	Götting	1820

(Date) 11 Jun. 52. G Semper. (Signature).
Please to restore each volume of the Catalogue to its place, as soon as done with.

Press Mark.	Title of the Work wanted.	Size.	Place.	Date.
1260. a. 1260. d	Bötticher Carl Gu Die Tektonik der Hellenen. 2 Volumes.	4 & fol.		1844–52.

(Date) 13 Ju. Gottfried Semper. (Signature).
Please to restore each volume of the Catalogue to its place, as soon as done with.

Pl. 12: British Museum Library call slips, 1852 (SLUB, Mscr. Dresd. t 3584)

SUPPLEMENTARY TEXTS

Introduction

This section assembles various additional pieces from the context of Semper's exile in London. On the one hand, it includes three newspaper articles from March 1851, written by friends of Semper's to support his attempts to make a living in London: either regarding his plans for a private school of architecture, for which Lothar Bucher, the London correspondent of the Berlin *National-Zeitung*, placed an announcement in that newspaper (206–8) and Richard Wagner, the composer and conductor, published a recommendation in the Zurich *Eidgenössische Zeitung* (208–9); or in connection with Semper's work for the Great Exhibition – namely an advertisement by the Hamburg architect Franz Georg Stammann, saying that Semper would accept further commissions for arranging exhibitions from private or official clients in the Crystal Palace (209–10). On the other hand, there are two sets of manuscript texts by Semper: two lists of books in his private Dresden reference library, written in 1852 for British customs after the library had been returned from New York, where he had had it sent in view of his planned emigration to North America (210–17), and his call slips from the British Museum Library for the period from March to December 1852 (217–25). Two other supplementary texts belong to Semper's early period at the Department of Practical Art: the letter of appointment (226–7) and the official description of the first course he gave there (228).

536 Supplementary Texts

London
Lothar Bucher

TEXTUAL RECORD

NZ 'Grossbritannien. London, 15. März', *National-Zeitung* (Berlin) 4, no. 132 (19 March 1851, evening issue), [3] (ULB Bonn, Ztg 219), *copy-text*

BIBLIOGRAPHY Studt 1992, 105 n. 9; Hildebrand 2020a, 109

EXPLANATORY NOTES

Lothar Bucher – another German political refugee in London – included an announcement of Semper's plan for a private school of architecture in his newspaper article on British events (206–8), published in the liberal Berlin *National-Zeitung*. Bucher was asked by Rudolph Schramm – a German journalist exiled in London – to report on Semper's school plans, as Schramm wrote to Semper on 25 February 1851 (see 245). Bucher became the 'dear friend' to whom Semper addressed his 'Letters on the Great Exhibition' some weeks later (27–31, 260–1, 280–9). We publish Bucher's entire report here, as it makes it possible to situate Semper's school plans within the British political climate of the day, particularly among German emigrants and political refugees. Among the individuals whose speeches on the occasion of the third anniversary of the Vienna Revolution of March 1848 Bucher refers to, special mention should be made of the German Gottfried Kinkel. He was one of the founders of a short-lived refugee committee, to the board of which Semper was elected in summer 1851 (Bucher was another member of the board). Kinkel was also to become a colleague of Semper's at the Swiss Federal Polytechnic School in Zurich in 1866 as professor of archaeology and art history. Bucher's article abruptly switches from politics to Semper's school plans (207.36–208.13) but gives a politically tinged biographical sketch, including a characterization of Semper – in relation to the reasons for him becoming a refugee – as 'one of the few artists who did not seek out the favour of the nobility, but instead let their favour seek him out, and turned his back on it when the Fatherland called' (207.37–9).

206.2 **Jahrestag der Wiener Revolution**] The Vienna Revolution broke out on 13 March 1848. It led to the resignation of Klemens von Metternich as foreign minister and state chancellor of Austria on the same day and ultimately also to the abdication of the Austrian Emperor Ferdinand I on 2 December 1848.   206.27 **Roley**] *Rónay* (see also 206.30–1)
207.40–208.1 **Erbauer des neuen Theaters, des Museums, der Synagoge, des Materni-hospitals**] Semper's first Hoftheater (Court Theatre) at Dresden, built in 1838–41, was destroyed by fire in 1869 and rebuilt following a different design in 1871–78. The second building in turn was bombed in 1945 and restored as the 'Semperoper' in 1977–85. The Dresden Gemäldegalerie (Picture Gallery), which Semper had been designing since 1838, was constructed in 1847–55, i.e. partly during his London exile. It opened in the autumn of 1855, shortly after he moved to Zurich. The Dresden Synagogue – the only religious building

by Semper that was completed – was built in 1838–40 and burnt down during the Reichs-kristallnacht in 1938. The Maternihospital, constructed in 1836–38, was completely destroyed during the bombing of Dresden in 1945.

208.2 **errichtete – Barrikaden**] Semper's participation in the Dresden Uprising of May 1849 on the side of the democrats was given particular mention in a contemporary Prussian report that noted the possibly unprecedented solidity of the barricades he had erected.

208.3 **Nachdem Dresden gerettet war**] an ironic comment on the suppression of the Dresden Uprising on 9 May 1849 by Saxon government troops supported by Prussian units

208.4–6 **als das hiesige Gesundheitsamt ihn einlud, den Bau der Leichenhäuser zu übernehmen, die in der neuen Begräbnissbill vorgeschrieben sind**] It was not the General Board of Health in London but rather Emil Braun who prevented Semper from emigrating to America (see 233). He explained to him on 22 September 1850 (gta, 20-K-1850-09-22): 'The Board of Health has just pushed through a major regulation and decided on the construction of several large graveyards, which you might be able to transform into classical necropolises.' Semper received more information about the Board's decision on 29 September 1850, one day after his arrival in London, from Braun and Edwin Chadwick, commissioners of the Board of Health. At their suggestion, he immediately started to design a Reception House (a building in which the dead and the mourners were to be received prior to interments) for the planned national cemetery in Abbey Wood near Erith, south-east of London, on the south bank of the River Thames (pl. 7). The Board of Health received Semper's design, which also included a chapel, in the second half of May 1851 but rejected it on 16 June 1851.

German Studio for Architects and Engineers in London
Richard Wagner

TEXTUAL RECORD

Spyri	Spyri Archives, without shelf mark, fol. IV, supportive note for Semper's advertisement 'Deutsches Attelier für Architekten und Ingenieurs in London' (see 249), in Richard Wagner's hand, dated 25 March 1851
EZ	supportive note for Semper's advertisement 'Deutsches Atelier für Architekten und Ingenieurs in London' (see 13, 249), *Eidgenössische Zeitung* (Zurich) 7, no. 87 (28 March 1851, morning issue), 348 (ZB Zurich, WB 87; another copy gta, 20-DOK-1851:8), *copy-text*
Kirchmeyer 1985	supportive note for Semper's advertisement 'Deutsches Atelier für Architekten und Ingenieurs in London' (see 249), 58–9, ed. of EZ

BIBLIOGRAPHY Knoepfli 1976, 264–5, 271–2; Mallgrave 1996, 191–2; Lütteken 2008, 43 fig. 107, 188; Weidmann 2010, 290–1, 293 n. 163

538 Supplementary Texts

EXPLANATORY NOTES

Richard Wagner was the most prominent personality to support Semper in his plans to establish a private school of architecture in London. He had been a long-standing friend of Semper's since their time together in Dresden. Wagner had staged his musical works in Semper's Royal Court Theatre at Dresden, completed in 1841, and Semper had attended preparatory meetings for the 1849 May Uprising in Wagner's Dresden home. During his exile in Zurich, Wagner arranged for the publication of Semper's advertising text for his 'Deutsches Atelier für Architekten und Ingenieurs in London' (German Studio for Architects and Engineers in London; 13) in the *Eidgenössische Zeitung* – a Zurich daily newspaper edited by Wagner's friend Johann Bernhard Spyri, later the husband of Johanna Spyri, who gained fame with her *Heidi* books. Wagner's recommendation for the school – actually a brief essay on Semper's view of architecture – was published in the same issue as a supportive note (without a title of its own) for Semper's advertisement (for the context of Wagner's involvement, see 249–50). Wagner later tried – albeit unsuccessfully – to recruit Swiss students for Semper's private tuition, as he wrote to him on 24 February 1853 (Wagner 1993, 203): 'I can't help you with any "young Swiss" at the moment: no one has shown up since the first inquiry; but I shall certainly think of advertising.' In the end, Semper's plans for a private school never materialized. However, Wagner also played a mediating role in getting Semper from London to Zurich: On 14 August 1854, he wrote to Semper that he had been asked 'whether you would accept the position of Professor of Architecture at the new Federal Polytechnic School that is to be established' (ETH Library, University Archives, HS 09:6). Further networks of politicians, academics and architects finally led to Semper's appointment to the chair in Zurich by the Swiss Federal Council on 7 February 1855.

209.2–4 **in unnützen Bauwerken ~ auf Anordnung des Königs Ludwig von Baiern**]
These 'useless buildings' must include those by the two most important architects in Munich during the reign of Ludwig I of Bavaria: Leo von Klenze, the court architect, and Friedrich von Gärtner.   209.13–14 **aus ~ dem Schauspielhause und dem ~ Museum zu Dresden**] see 536–7, Explanatory Notes 207.40–208.1

MANUSCRIPT VARIANTS
Spyri

208.26 **unserm**] unsrem   208.28 **Schrift: ∧**] ~∧ –   208.29 **Altona∧**] ~, **1834∧**] ~.
209.4 **Baiern**] Bayern   209.7 **unsern**] unsrn   209.8 **hat∧**] ~,   209.10 **unserm**] unsrem
209.16 **Athens**] Athen's   209.21 **Freundes,**] *altered from* ~∧ *before del.* und Schicksalsgenossen,   **schätze,**] ~∧   **wärmste**] Wärmste   209.23 **Näheres**] N *over* n
209.24 **25.**] ~∧

Submissions for the Great Exhibition
Franz Georg Stammann

TEXTUAL RECORD

K(DD)-1851 gta, 20-K(DD)-1851-03-20, fol. 1r–v, 'Nachricht in Betreff der Einsendungen aus Deutschland, zur allgemeinen Industrie Ausstellung in London',
in Franz Georg Stammann's hand, dated 20 March 1851

HN 'Tagesbericht. Hamburg, den 22sten März', *Hamburger Nachrichten*, no. 70
(22 March 1851), [3] (CB Hamburg, Safe Holdings, S/934), *copy-text*

KöZ 'Nachricht in Betreff der Einsendungen zur allgemeinen Industrie-Ausstellung in London', *Kölnische Zeitung*, no. 71 (23 March 1851, morning
issue), [6]

MüB 'Miszellen. Hamburg, 20. März', *Münchener Blätter für Handel, Industrie,
Gewerbe und Landwirthschaft*, no. 26 (30 March 1851), 102

BIBLIOGRAPHY Lankheit 1976, 34; Herrmann 1978, 50 n. 163; Herrmann 1984, 272
n. 159

EXPLANATORY NOTES

Semper's Hamburg connections were behind the advertisement recommending him for services involving submissions for the Great Exhibition. A letter written on 20 March 1851 by
the Hamburg architect Franz Georg Stammann – with whom Semper had been friends
since their studies together in Franz Christian Gau's studio in Paris – contains the draft of
the published announcement (540–1). Semper's brother Wilhelm, who ran a pharmacy in
Hamburg, can be inferred as the addressee of the letter through his mediation between
Semper and Stammann on another occasion, as evidenced by two letters of 8 and 9 March
1851 concerning Semper's plans for a private architectural school (gta, 20-K-1851-03-08, 20-
K[DD]-1851-03-09:2). It is therefore plausible that Wilhelm, on Semper's behalf, discussed
with Stammann the possibility of advertising Semper's availability for services in the Crystal Palace in a newspaper and that Stammann then drafted an advertisement that he published, with Wilhelm's consent, in the *Hamburger Nachrichten* on 22 March. With minor
differences, the advertisement also appeared in the *Kölnische Zeitung* on 23 March and in the
Münchener Blätter für Handel, Industrie, Gewerbe und Landwirthschaft on 30 March. The
only known direct response to it came from a certain George William Lüders of Hamburg,
who applied for 'a minor post' as a bookkeeper on 30 March 1851 (gta, 20-K-1851-03-30:2).
Another inquiry possibly prompted by the advertisement followed from Hamburg on 25
April 1851: The lawyer Wilhelm August Kramer, the secretary of the Hamburg Society for
the Promotion of the Arts and Useful Industries, which was coordinating contributions
from the North German states to the Great Exhibition, asked his friend Semper whether
he – along with two others – would like to represent these states in the official juries for the
prizes to be awarded (gta, 20-K-1851-04-25). Although Semper accepted and was indeed
appointed a juror, he did not receive the promised certificate of appointment by 12 May,
when the juries started their work. This is evidenced by a letter he sent to his brother Johann

Carl Semper on 5 May and by another letter his sister Elise Semper sent to him on 9 June (gta, 20-K-1851-05-05[S]:1, 20-K-1851-06-09).

209.27–8 **ist ~ mit dem Arrangement der englischen Coloniewaaren beschäftigt**] This is an overstatement, as Semper was responsible for the arrangement of exhibits only for some of the British colonies, namely Canada and the Cape of Good Hope. He was possibly also involved in the sections for Newfoundland, New Brunswick and Nova Scotia (see 258– 60). 209.29–30 **hat unter Anderm auch für Schweden die Aufstellung ~ zu besorgen**] see 259

PRINT VARIANTS

209.25 **Hamburg, den 22sten März**ʌ] *omitted KöZ* ~, 20. März. *MüB* 209.26 **Der Architect,**] ~ ~ʌ *no paragraph MüB* 209.26–7 **welcher sich gegenwärtig in London aufhält**] gegenwärtig in London *KöZ MüB* 209.27 **Executiv-Commission**] Executivkommission *MüB* 209.27–8 **im Ausstellungsgebäude**] ~ Aufstellungsgebäude *KöZ* der grossen Industrieausstellung *MüB* 209.28 **englischen Coloniewaaren**] Waaren aus den englischen Colonieen *KöZ MüB* 209.29 **Anderm**] Andern *KöZ* 209.30 **besorgen. –**] ~. ʌ *KöZ MüB* **Es**] *paragraph KöZ* 209.31 **Comité**] Comite *KöZ* 210.1 **diesen bekannten,**] einen ~, *KöZ* einen ~ʌ *MüB* 210.3 **kennt**ʌ] ~, *MüB* 210.4 **Decorirung &c.**] ~ und darauf bezüglichen Auskunft *KöZ* Dekorirung und darauf bezügliche Auskunft *MüB* 210.4–5 **Einzelnen, als ganzen Landestheilen, Städten, Provinzialabtheilungen**] für Einzelne, wie auch für ganze Landestheile, Städte u. s. w. *KöZ MüB* 210.5–6 **seine Bekanntschaften**] Bekanntschaften *KöZ MüB*

MANUSCRIPT VARIANTS
K(DD)-1851

fol. 1r

Nachricht
in Betreff der Einsendungen aus Deutschland, zur
allgemeinen
Industrie Ausstellung
in London. 5

Der Architect, Professor Semper aus Dresden, gegenwärtig in London, ist, im Auftrage der Executiv-Commission, im Ausstellungsgebäude mit dem Arrangement der englischen Coloniewaaren beschäftigt & hat, unter Andern, auch für Schweden die Aufstellung der von dort eingesandten Sachen zu besorgen. 10
Es wird noch jetzt für manche deutsche Behörde, Comite od. Privaten von Interesse sein zu erfahren, dass sich dieselben in London an einen bekannten, zuverlässigen Landsmann wenden können, der im Gebäude selbst schon mit Arrangements beschäftigt ist, daselbst seinen steten Aufenthalt hat, die dortigen Behörden & Arbeiter kennt & also bei der Einrichtung, Decorirung & darauf bezüglicher Auskunft, sowohl für Einzelne, wie für ganze 15
Landestheile, Städte, Provinzialabtheilungen u. s. w., durch seine Befähigung & Bekanntschaften von wesentlichem Nutzen sein kann. |

Vorstehend den Entwurf. *fol. 1v*
Correspondent, Allg. Augs. Zeitung, Bremer, Berliner, Winerblätter etc scheinen mir,
wenn es bekannt werden soll, zweckmässig. Für Hamb. Nachricht werde ich, wenn Sie es
wollen? sorgen.

5   20 März 51 FGeoStammann

> 540.3 **allgemeinen**] a *over* A   540.7 **Professor**] *interl.*   **gegenwärtig**] *after del.* welcher
> sich   **in London**] *before del.* aufhält   540.15 **& darauf bezüglicher Auskunft**] *above
> del.* etc.
> 541.2 **Allg.**] *'Allgemeine'*   **Augs.**] *'Augsburger'*   **Winerblätter**] *'Wiener Blätter'*   541.3
> **Hamb.**] *'Hamburger'*   **Sie**] *i.e. Wilhelm Semper*

List of Books for Customs
Gottfried Semper

First Version

TEXTUAL RECORD

MS 148¹   gta, 20-Ms-148, fol. 5r–v, in Semper's hand, *copy-text*

BIBLIOGRAPHY Herrmann 1981, 114; Laudel 1991, 42; Weidmann 2021, 88–9

EXPLANATORY NOTES

The two lists edited here under the title 'List of Books for Customs' represent a partial inventory of Semper's private Dresden reference library. The first list, which is very fragmentary, records the books without any order, while the second, which is more detailed, ar-
ranges them according to four subject areas: art and architecture, general history, classical
philology and modern philology (including miscellaneous writings). Semper's numbering
indicates that the second list is also a fragment: it is probably lacking one sheet with 51 book
titles from the field of art and architecture (see 213.11–12). The fact that the lists are written
in English and Semper's note on the only two English-language books, published in London, that they were duty-free (210.7, 210.12, 214.30–2) indicate that the lists were intended for
British customs. With his planned emigration to North America in mind, Semper had his
library sent by his wife from Dresden to Altona in August 1850 to his brother Johann Carl,
who then had it shipped from Hamburg to New York in September 1850. In February 1851,
when Semper was sending Rudolph Schramm a draft programme for his private architectural school (see 8–11, Second Version; 245), he mentioned that 'my whole library and my
collection of drawings is in New York. I am leaving the boxes there until I know for certain

whether I will be staying here' (11.26–8). Although he was still not certain about this three months later, he had the boxes sent from New York to London by his brother Johann Carl in May 1851 (gta, 20-K[DD]-1851-05-13). However, the books were still in storage in a bonded warehouse in London in August 1852, as can be seen from a letter to his wife Bertha in which Semper writes that 'My box of books … is still at the warehouse and has not been cleared through customs. I've only managed to get my drawings out, by special concession' (gta, 20-K-1852-08[S]). The first version of the list contains only two works that do not also appear in the second version: one by Einhard – almost certainly his *Life of Charlemagne* – and one by Arnold Heeren (210.26, 211.22). Apart from these two works, the titles are listed here only from the second version, with additional details in the first version being consulted for further identification. With a few exceptions – for example, if the format or number of volumes indicates a later edition – the works are listed only in their first editions. If it is unclear whether the reference is to a German translation, the edition in the original language is given. Titles that cannot be identified with a high degree of probability are generally not annotated.

210.7 **On Dorways**] ~ *doorways*; cf. 214.30–1   210.8 **Greec Dictionary**] cf. 214.27   210.9 **Latin d°**] cf. 214.28   210.10 **d° d°**] cf. 214.29   210.11 **Some numbers of the R. Institute of Br. Architects**] cf. 214.33   210.12 **on Steam Engineering**] cf. 214.32   210.13 **The Analysis**] cf. 214.34   210.14 **Mathem. in their application to art and architecture**] cf. 214.35–6   210.16 **Analysis**] cf. 214.37   210.17 **pure Mathematiks**] cf. 214.37   210.18 **differential Calculus**] cf. 214.38   210.19 **Algebra with ~ Solutions**] cf. 214.39–40   210.20 **Methematiks**] cf. 214.41   210.21 **Physiks**] cf. 215.1   210.22 **Logarithmik tables**] cf. 215.2   210.23 **Log. tables**] cf. 215.3   210.24 **Mathem.**] cf. 215.4   210.25 **Cours de Mathematiques pures**] cf. 215.5   210.26 **Historical works**] probably the first three volumes, published as *Vermischte historische Schriften* (Heeren 1821), of Arnold Heeren's collected *Historische Werke*   210.27 **Travels**] cf. 215.8   210.28 **History**] cf. 215.11   210.29 **History of Mexico**] cf. 215.13   210.30 **The old World**] cf. 215.14   210.31 **Universal History**] cf. 215.15

211.1 **Storia di Firenze**] cf. 215.22   211.2 **Marco Polo**] cf. 215.23   211.3 **Homeri Ilias and Odyssea, and Prolegomena**] cf. 215.25   **Wolff**] *Wolf*   211.4 **Euripidis Tragoediae**] cf. 215.26   211.5 **Pindari Carmina**] cf. 215.27   211.6 **Aristophanis Opera**] cf. 215.28   211.7 **Herodotus**] cf. 215.29   211.8 **Sophocles**] cf. 215.30   211.9 **Aeschylus**] cf. 215.31   211.10 **Plinius, letters**] cf. 216.14   211.11 **Tacitus**] cf. 215.33   211.12 **Taciti Germania**] cf. 215.34   211.13 **Cicero**] cf. 216.1   211.14 **Cicero de amicitia**] cf. 216.2   211.15 **Sueton**] cf. 216.3   211.16 **Persius & Juvenalis**] cf. 216.4   211.17 **Horatius**] cf. 216.5   211.18 **Livius**] cf. 216.6   211.19 **Virgilius**] cf. 216.7   211.20 **Cornelius Nepos**] cf. 216.8   211.21 **History**] cf. 216.9   211.22 **Eginhartus**] Semper cites Einhard's *Vita Caroli Magni* in his lecture 'The Ancient Practice of Wall Coating and Tubular Construction' (134.13).   211.23 **Vellejus Paterculus**] cf. 216.10   211.24 **Seneca**] cf. 216.12   211.25 **Julius Caesar**] cf. 216.13   211.26 **Catullus, Tibullus, Propertius**] cf. 216.11   211.27 **Justinus**] cf. 216.15   211.28 **Plautus**] cf. 216.16   211.29 **Sallustius**] cf. 216.17   211.30 **Vigerus**] cf. 216.18   211.31 **Seneca Hercules furens**] cf. 216.19   211.32 **Homerus and Hesiodus**] cf. 216.20   211.33 **Latin Grammar**] cf. 216.21   211.34 **d° Grammar**] cf. 216.22   211.35 **notes to Homerus**] cf. 216.23   211.36 **Orationes Salustii Livii & other**] cf. 216.24   211.37 **Artis Latine Scribendi principia**] cf. 216.26   211.38 **Wolf's**] *Wolff's*   **Philosophy**] cf. 216.27

ALTERATIONS IN THE MANUSCRIPT

210.8 **2**] *over* 3   210.16 **101)**] 01 *over* 11   210.21 **Mayer**] *after del.* Loren   210.26 **Historical**] *after del.* Statis

211.1 **118)**] *after del.* 117) The war of 1809 by Valentini 1. Vol. 8.   211.3 **120.**] *inserted after del. on fol. 5r*

120) On Saxe
121) The Battle of Leipzig

211.4 **121**] *inserted*   211.5 **122.**] *inserted*   211.6 **123**] *inserted*   211.7 **124)**] *inserted*   211.8 **125.**] *inserted*   211.9 **126.**] *inserted*   **12°**] 1 *over* 8   211.10 **127.**] *inserted*   211.11 **128.**] *inserted*   **8°**] 8 *over* 1   211.12 **129.**] *inserted*   211.13 **130.**] *inserted*   211.14 **131.**] *inserted*   211.15 **132.**] *inserted*   211.16 **133.**] *inserted*   211.17 **134.**] *inserted*   211.18 **135.**] *inserted*   211.19 **136.**] *inserted*   **Vol.**] *underl. in pencil by unknown hand*   211.20 **137.**] *inserted*   211.21 **138.**] *inserted*   211.22 **139.**] *inserted*   211.23 **140.**] *inserted*   211.24 **141.**] *inserted*   211.25 **142.**] *inserted*   211.26 **143.**] *inserted*   **Tibullus**] *after del.* 1 Vo[l]   211.27 **144.**] *inserted*   211.28 **145.**] *inserted*   211.29 **146.**] *inserted*   211.30 **147.**] *inserted*   211.31 **148.**] *inserted*   211.32 **149.**] *inserted*   **Hesiodus in German**] *underl. in pencil by unknown hand*   211.33 **150.**] *inserted*   **Latin**] *interl.*   211.34 **151.**] *inserted*   **d°**] *interl.*   211.35 **152.**] *inserted*   211.36 **153.**] *inserted*   211.37 **154.**] *inserted*   211.38 **155.**] *inserted*   **Wolf's**] *after del.* Inscriptiones

Second Version

TEXTUAL RECORD

MS 148² gta, 20-Ms-148, fols. 1r–4v (4v blank), in Semper's hand, *copy-text*

BIBLIOGRAPHY Herrmann 1981, 114; Laudel 1991, 42; Gnehm 2004, 32, 37 n. 30, 47 n. 73, 119 n. 72; Weidmann 2021, 88–9

EXPLANATORY NOTES

212.3 **Magazin for Engineers**] Böhm/Hauf 1777/95   212.4 **Hydrotechnics**] probably all four fascicles of Gilly/Eytelwein 1802/08, bound in one volume   212.5 **Manuel of Hydrostatics**] Eytelwein 1826   212.6 **Antiquities of Athens**] the third volume of Stuart/Revett 1829/33   **Cckerell**] 'c' uncertain reading, *Cockerell*   212.8 **Manuel of Mechanics**] Eytelwein 1801   212.9 **The Engeneer**] Weisbach 1848   212.10 **On Roofs**] probably Linke 1840, the second, enlarged edition of Gustav Linke's *Bau der Dorn'schen Lehmdächer* (1837)

212.11 **Art of building**] Rondelet 1833/36   212.12 **Statics**] Eytelwein 1808   212.13 **Architecture**] the first and third volumes of Milizia 1781   212.14 **geometrical Drawing**] probably the first volume of Burg 1822, which is about 'General Geometric Drawing' (the second volume is about 'Drawing and Recording Artillery Objects')   212.15 **on Private dwellings**] Gärtner 1837   212.16 **on beaty in Art, (Laocoon)**] 'beaty': *beauty*; Lessing 1766   212.17 **Archaeologia of Art**] Müller 1830, divided into two volumes   212.18 **History of Architecture**] Hirt 1821/27   212.19 **Italian Researches**] the first and third volumes of Rumohr 1827/31. The part here listed as 'wanting' must be the volume Semper had lent to Friedrich Wilhelm Meinert, his Dresden lawyer. In 1849, he asked his wife, Bertha Semper, twice to claim it back (gta, 20-K-1849-07[S], 20-K-1849-12-09[S]).   212.21 **On Vaults and their Statiks**] Knochenhauer 1842   212.22 **on heating with hot air**] Meissner 1821   212.23. **History of the Hellenic tribes**] Müller 1820/24, its second and third volumes divided into two volumes each   212.24 **On the Art of Wallpainting with the Ancients**] Wiegmann 1836   212.25 **Manual of Engineering and Mechaniks**] probably three different works: Weisbach 1835/36, Weisbach 1845/46 and Weisbach 1849 (though the third work does not discuss mechanics but its mathematical basis). On 21 September 1849, Semper advised his wife, Bertha Semper, to sell 'various expensive books that I've never even read yet ... e.g., von Humboldt's *Cosmos* 2 parts and an incomplete work on mechanics by the professor in Freiberg, I've forgotten his name' (gta, 20-K-1849-09-21[S]). The professor concerned, Julius Weisbach, did not complete his *Lehrbuch der Ingenieur- und Maschinen-Mechanik*, begun in 1845, until 1860.   212.26 **Vademecum, (Manual) for Civil-Engeneers and architects**] possibly Delaistre 1825a or Pernot 1844, the third, enlarged edition of Louis-Théodore Pernot's *Dictionnaire du bâtiment* (1826). A third book with a similar title – *Vademecum für den praktischen Ingenieur und Baumeister* (Schubert et al. 1850) – appeared in the year after Semper's flight from Dresden and is therefore not a candidate.   212.27 **Manuel for rural architecture**] Gilly 1805   212.28 **The Greec Theaters**] Geppert 1843   212.29 **Aesthetiks of the Architecture**] Wagner 1838   212.30–1 **Ideas on the State of the arts ~ with the old Nations**] five volumes of Heeren 1824/26; cf. note 215.7   212.32 **Cosmus. and letters on the same**] the first two volumes of Humboldt 1845/62 and Cotta 1848; cf. note 212.25   212.33 **Aesthetiks of Arch.**] Wolff 1834   212.34 **On Perspective**] Hetsch 1840   212.35 **Archaeologia**] probably Schaaff 1806/08   212.36 **Architecture**] probably Heine 1842, the second, enlarged edition of Gustav Heine's *Kurzer Unterricht in der bürgerlichen und Land-Baukunst* (1836), though it is in large octavo. Heine's *Handbuch der landwirthschaftlichen Baukunde* (Heine 1838) is in quarto but does not discuss what Semper understood by architecture. Heine, professor for architectural drawing at the Academy of Fine Arts in Dresden, was a former colleague of Semper's.

213.1 **Architectural laws**] Heine 1846   213.2 **33)**] nearly written as '37)'; hence the erratic number '38)' at 213.3   213.3 **Tables**] Reimer 1782   213.4 **Archeologia**] Böttiger 1837/38   213.5 **On Theaters**] Weinbrenner 1809   213.6 **On fascineering**] Eytelwein 1800   213.7 **Theater at Münich**] Meiser 1840   213.8 **Models of old German Architecture**] probably Heideloff 1838/43   213.9 **Historical development of the arts**] Cavallari 1847   213.10 **the Orders of Architecture**] Normand 1819   213.11 **Art of the Carpenter**] Romberg 1831/33   213.12 **Magazin for Italian Art**] one volume of Magazin 1780/85   213.13 **Lexicon of the artists (Künstlerlexicon)**] probably the first fifteen fascicles of Nagler 1835/52   213.14 **The Railway of the lower Danube**] Kreuter 1848; cf. 216.34, where Semper lists '6 Copies'. The Bavarian architect and engineer Franz Kreuter wrote to Semper in 1842 about the use of asphalt for roofs, and Semper was in contact with him during his period in London between

1850 and 1852.   213.15 **Instruction for Engineers**] Tielcke 1769   213.16 **On art and artists**] probably Koch 1834. Semper owned a portrait of (or a reproduction of a work by) the Austrian landscape painter Joseph Anton Koch, which he mentioned in 1857, in a letter to Carolyne Sayn-Wittgenstein, as hanging in his Zurich study with portraits of (or reproductions of works by) Bertel Thorvaldsen, Friedrich Overbeck, Peter Cornelius and Johann Christian Reinhart (gta, 20-K-1857-12-08[S]).   213.17 **On Architecture**] Wolff 1831 213.18 **Old-Christian Art at Ravenna**] Quast 1842   213.19 **Stereotomia**] Strobel 1819 213.20 **Perspective**] Quaglio 1811   213.21 **Carpenters art**] Mitterer 1817   213.22 **Monuments of German Style**] probably some fascicles of Moller/Gladbach 1815–51   213.27 **Description of Rome**] Fèa 1820   213.28–9 **Annals and Bulletins of the Roman Institute of archeological Correspondence**] some numbers of Annali 1829/85 and Bullettino 1829/85. Semper had his article on the polychromy of Trajan's column published in the *Bullettino dell'Instituto di corrispondenza archeologica* (Semper 1833).   213.31 **The Florentine Observer**] Lastri 1797/99 (the first edition, published in 1776–78, has only six volumes) 213.33 **The Cathedral of Florence**] possibly Richa 1757 or Molini 1820   213.34 **Perspective**] Thibault 1827   213.35 **L'art de bâtir**] probably Briseux 1743   213.36 **History of Frensh Architecture**] Ramée 1846   213.37 **on Greece**] probably two fascicles of Thiersch 1816/25, though they are in quarto. The second edition, published in 1829, is in octavo but did not appear in fascicles. Friedrich Thiersch's *De l'état actuel de la Grèce et des moyens d'arriver à sa restauration* (Thiersch 1833), a two-volume work in octavo, discusses politics only.   213.38 **Traité de la Science du Dessin**] Vallée 1821   213.39 **Memoires sur le pont de Jarnac**] Quénot 1828

214.1 **Traité des couleurs pour la peinture en Email**] Arclais de Montamy 1765   214.2 **Le Vignole de Poche**] Thierry 1823   214.3 **Traité de Geometrie descriptive**] Hachette 1822 214.4 **Monumens Antiques**] probably Millin 1802/06   214.6 **Dictionnaire d'Architecture**] Vagnat 1827   214.7 **La Science de l'ingenieur**] Delaistre 1825b   214.8 **La science des Ingenieurs**] Belidor 1729   214.9 **Architectonographie des Theatres**] one volume of Donnet/Kaufmann 1837/40. Semper had known the native Cologne architect Jacques-Auguste Kaufmann since his student years in Paris. In 1839, he used his acquaintance with him to get in touch 'with the most skilled *peintres en batimens, mouleurs*, etc.' in Paris, in view of the decoration of the Dresden Court Theatre (gta, 20-K-1839-01-02[S]).   214.10 **Perspective**] Isabeau 1827   214.11 **Revue Generale d'architecture**] some numbers of Revue générale 1840/90, bound in one volume   214.13 **Lettres d'un antiquaire à un Artiste**] Letronne 1835   214.14 **Polychromy**] Kugler 1835   214.15 **Polychromy**] Semper 1834; cf. 216.33, where Semper lists '24 Copies'   214.16 **Nouvelle architecture pratique**] the second volume of Miché 1825 (the first edition, published in 1812, has only one volume)   214.17 **Etudes de Constructions**] one volume of Bruyère 1823/28   214.18 **On colours**] Chevreul 1840   214.19 **Annals of Antiq. Society at Dresden**] one volume of Mittheilungen 1835/63 214.20 **Architecture**] probably Stieglitz 1834   214.21 **Description of Amsterdam**] Zesen 1664   214.22 **German Antiquities**] probably Wagner 1833   214.23 **On Mineral and vegetable forms**] Metzger 1835   214.25 **Vitruvius**] probably Daniele Barbaro's Latin quarto edition (Vitruvius 1567)   214.27 **Greec Dictionary**] Schneider 1805/06 (the first edition, published in 1797–98, is in octavo)   214.28 **Lat. dto**] Scheller 1788 (the first edition, published in 1783, has only one volume)   214.29 **d° d°**] the first two volumes of Weber 1770 (the first and second editions, published in 1734 and 1745, have only one volume each). In the first version, Semper lists three volumes instead of two (210.10), possibly including the German-Latin dictionary mentioned on the title page of the first volume.   214.30 **a Col-**

lection of the most approved doorways] probably the first volume of Donaldson 1833/36. In the first version, Semper lists one volume (210.7). He refers to the first volume, which presents examples from antiquity, in *Style* (Semper 1860/63, 2:277 n. 2, 281 n. 2).   214.32 **on Steam Engineering**] Alderson 1834   214.33 **Some numbers of the R. Institute of Britt. Architects**] probably some papers read between late 1841 and early 1849, when RIBA did not publish any transactions in volumes   214.34 **On Analysis**] Fischer 1808   214.35 **Mathematics in their applications to Art etc.**] probably three volumes of Vieth 1796/1821   214.37 **Analysis. and pure Mathematics**] Thibaut 1809 and Thibaut 1801. Semper attended Bernhard Friedrich Thibaut's 'Lectures on … Analysis, Differential and Integral Calculation, Introduction to Practical Geometry, … Applied Mathematics' at the University of Göttingen in 1823–25 (gta, 20-DOK-1825:1).   214.38 **differential Calculus**] Euler 1790/93 and Grüson 1798. Semper bought the second and third volumes of Leonhard Euler's work and its supplement from the Göttingen bookshop of Vandenhoeck & Ruprecht in January 1825, as two receipts prove (gta, 20-DOK-1824:4, 20-DOK-1825:5).   214.39 **Algebra with ~ Solutions of the problems**] Hirsch 1804 and Sachs 1810   214.41 **Mathematics**] one volume of Lorenz 1785/86

215.1 **Physiks**] Mayer 1801   215.2 **Logarithmes**] In the first version, Semper lists Georg von Vega's work as 'Logarithmik tables' (210.22), which might indicate the two-volume work *Logarithmisch-trigonometrische Tafeln* (Vega 1812) – the work he requested from the British Museum Library on 28 May 1852 (see 219.25–31), while his own book was still being held back by British customs. In the first and second versions, however, he lists a one-volume work, probably *Logarithmisch-trigonometrisches Handbuch* (Vega 1793), which also consists mainly of logarithmic tables.   215.3 **Logarithmes**] Lalande 1802   215.4 **Mathematics**] probably an incomplete collection of two works: the six-volume work *Cours de mathématiques, à l'usage des gardes du pavillon et de la marine* (Bézout 1764/69) and the four-volume work *Cours de mathématiques, à l'usage du corps royal de l'artillerie* (Bézout 1770/72)   215.5 **Cours de Math. pures**] Francœur 1809. Semper bought the two volumes of Louis-Benjamin Francœur's work from the Göttingen bookshop of Vandenhoeck & Ruprecht in January 1825, as two receipts prove (gta, 20-DOK-1824:3, 20-DOK-1825:5).   215.7 **Statistiks**] probably one volume of Heeren 1824/26, listed as 'wanting' at 212.31. Semper attended Arnold Heeren's 'Lectures on … Ancient History, History of the European State System, Statistics' at the University of Göttingen in 1823–25 (gta, 20-DOK-1825:1). Heeren gave lectures on statistics in each autumn term between 1805/06 and 1839/40 (Becker-Schaum 1993, 227), but he never published them. However, his *Ideen über die Politik, den Verkehr und den Handel der vornehmsten Völker der alten Welt*, which Semper incorrectly lists as 'Ideas on the State of the arts, sciences, commerce etc with the old Nations' in the first group of books (212.30–1), contain many statistical elements.   215.8 **Travels**] probably the first two volumes of Volney 1788/1800. In the first version, Semper lists only one volume (210.27).   215.9 **Old History**] Heeren 1799; cf. note 215.7   215.11 **History**] probably Pölitz 1808   215.12 **System of the Eur. Empires**] Heeren 1809; cf. note 215.7   215.14 **The old world**] Bürck 1844   215.15 **Universal History**] probably two volumes of Rotteck 1835, the eleventh, three-volume edition of Carl von Rotteck's *Allgemeine Geschichte vom Anfang der historischen Kenntniss bis auf unsere Zeiten* (all earlier editions have nine volumes)   215.16 **The war of 1809**] Valentini 1812   215.17 **Saxe**] French for *Saxony*   215.21 **Histoire de Napoleon**] the first volume of Ségur 1825 (all earlier editions are in octavo)   215.22 **Storia di Firenze**] Nardi 1582   215.23 **Marco Polo**] Polo 1845   215.25 **Homeri Ilias and Odyssea**] probably Homer 1784 (divided into two volumes), Homer 1785 (divided into two volumes) and Wolf

1795. In the first version, Semper lists five volumes comprising the *Iliad*, *Odyssey* and Friedrich August Wolf's *Prolegomena ad Homerum* (211.3). Hence, he probably owned Wolf's editions of Homer's *Iliad* and *Odyssey*.   215.33 **Tacitus**] Tacitus 1752. In the first version, Semper lists Johann August Ernesti's edition of Tacitus's works (211.11).

216.1 **Cicero with clavis Ciceroniana**] Cicero 1737 and Ernesti 1739   216.9 **Historiae**] Olaus Magnus's *Historia de gentibus septentrionalibus* was first published in folio (Magnus 1555), but Semper lists an octavo edition in the second version and a duodecimo edition in the first version (211.21), respectively. This points to a small octavo edition, for example the Antwerp edition of 1558 or the Frankfurt edition of 1618.   216.11 **Catullus**] In the first version, Semper lists a duodecimo volume containing works of Catullus, Tibullus and Propertius (211.26).   216.18 **Vigerus**] Viger 1802   216.21 **Latin, Grammar**] probably Bröder 1787   216.22 **dito**] probably Grotefend 1822   216.23 **Notes to Homer**] probably three volumes of Köppen 1787/92   216.25 **Apparatus Eloquentiae**] Schönsleder 1630   216.26 **Artis latine scribendi Principia**] probably Beck 1801   216.27 **Institutiones Philosoph**] possibly Friedrich Christian Baumeister's or Johann Heinrich Winckler's adaptations of Christian Wolff's philosophy (Baumeister 1735, Winckler 1735)   216.28 **Introductiones in lingua latina**] possibly Reimmann 1718 or Harless 1764   216.29 **Lexilogus**] one volume of Buttmann 1818/25   216.31 **Classic litterature**] Eschenburg 1783   216.33 **Polychromy**] see note 214.15   216.34 **Pamphlet on Railways in Ungaria**] see note 213.14   216.35 **Italian Dictionary**] the first volume of Jagemann 1790/91   216.36 **d° d°**] the second volume of Jagemann 1790/91

217.1 **Synonymics**] Quandt 1838   217.2 **English-German Grammar**] Fick 1793   217.4 **Sketches**] Detmold 1844   217.6 **Bellona a Military Yournal**] 36 fascicles of Bellona 1781/87   217.7 **Ben Johnson**] Baudissin 1836. In late 1835 or early 1836, Semper had reconstructed one elevation, two sections and one plan of the Elizabethan Fortune Playhouse to illustrate the description of this edifice in the first volume of Wolf von Baudissin's *Ben Jonson und seine Schule* (Baudissin 1836, I:XXXVII–XXXVIII and pl.; cf. Nerdinger/Oechslin 2003, 135 and fig., 171–2).   217.8 **Topiks or the Art to invent**] Kästner 1816   217.9 **Works**] some volumes of Börne 1829/34

ALTERATIONS IN THE MANUSCRIPT

212.1 **I.)**] *inserted*   212.2 **architecture.**] *altered from* ~, *before del.* Mathematical etc.   212.9 **1**] *before del.* 5   212.11 **Art**] *after del.* Architec   **5**] *before del.* 5   **5**] *over* [4]   212.13 **1ˢᵗ**] *after del.* first and third   third] *after del.* sec   **3ᵈ**] 3 *over* 2   212.14 **1 Vol.**] 1 *over* 2   212.17 **2.**] 2 *over* 1   212.23 **5.**] 5 *over* 1   212.24 **20)**] *after del.* Eros   212.26 **Manual**] *above del.* Handbook   212.27 **Manuel**] *after del.* Handb   212.28 **Theaters**] s *added*   212.30 **State**] *after del.* arts   **of**] *inserted*   212.35 **2 Vol.**] *inserted before del.* 1 v.   212.36 **Architecture**] *after del.* on

213.8 **33)**] *after del.* 33) Homer in German 2 – 8.   Homer] *after del.* Homer and   **Models**] *after del.* Old Germ   213.13 **Lexicon**] *after del.* Artists dict   **Cahiers**] *above del.* Vol.   213.31–2 **of art**] *after del.* and   213.33 **Cathedral**] *after del.* Do   213.37 **108)**] 10 *inserted and* 8 *over* 7   213.38 **109)**] 10 *inserted and* 9 *over* 8   213.39 **110)**] 11 *inserted and* 0 *over* 9   214.1 **111)**] *first* 1 *inserted and third* 1 *over* 0   214.5 **builders**] b *over* a   214.11 **Some numbers**] *after del.* 1 Number   214.14 **4°**] 4 *over* 8   214.16 **Nouvelle architecture**] *after del.* Lettres d'un Antiquaire à un artiste   214.19 **Annals**] *after del.* Ant   214.20 **Stieglitz's**

Architecture 2 Vol. 8°] *inserted*   214.21 **129)**] *inserted*   214.24 **Plinii**] P *over* [H] *after del.* The   214.28 **Scheller**] *above del.* Schaller   Schaller] Sc *over* [Br]   214.29 **d° d° by Weber 2 Vol. 8°**] *inserted*   214.30 **doorways**] *second* o *over* r   214.31 **dutifree**] i *above del.* y   214.32 **dutyfree**] y *over* i   214.34 **On Analysis**] *after del.* Old Hist   214.35 **applications**] s *added*   214.37 **and pure Mathematics. 2 Vol.**] *inserted*   214.39 **Solutions**] *after del.* 145)

215.1 **146)**] 4 *over* 0   215.5 **Cours**] *after del.* M   215.6 **II.**] *over inserted* 2)   **Archeology**] *after underl. and del.* and   **Travels.**] *after underl. and del.* etc   215.11 **by**] *over* of   215.12 **7)**] *after del.* 6) Archeologia by Schaaf. 2 vol. 8.   215.15 **8.**] *over* 1   1] *over* [2.]   215.16 **×**] *inserted*   215.17 **×**] *inserted*   **Saxe**] S *over* [t]   215.18 **×**] *inserted*   **1 Cahier.**] *below del.* 2 Vol. with   2] *over* 1   215.19 **×**] *inserted*   215.20 **×**] *inserted*   **12.**] 1 *over* [8]   215.21 **×**] *inserted*   215.23 **18) Marco Polo ~ 8°**] *inserted*   215.24 **ancient**] *above del.* Modern   **linguages**] *above del.* Authors   215.28 **Aristophanis opera**] *after del.* Euripidis Tragoediae   215.29 **not complete.**] *inserted*   **8.**] *after del.* 8   8] *over* 1[2]

216.10 **Vellejus**] *above del.* Valerius   216.16 **Plautus**] *after del.* Herodotus. 3 Vol. not complete 8°   8°] *undel.*   216.24 **Orationes**] *after del.* Selected   216.30 **Observationes**] *after del.* Vigerus

217.6 **fascicles**] *after del.* parts   217.9 **incomplete**] *after del.* very

British Museum Library Call Slips

Gottfried Semper

TEXTUAL RECORD

Mscr. Dresd.   SLUB, Mscr. Dresd. t 3584, fifty slips with printed text (edited in bold) and with orders in Semper's hand, all but two slips dated between 8 March and 11 December 1852, *copy-text*

BIBLIOGRAPHY Herrmann 1978, 68 and n. 239; Herrmann 1981, 27 and n. 12; Herrmann 1984, 62, 140, 276 n. 226, 290 n. 12; Hildebrand 2021, 107–8, 114–15

EXPLANATORY NOTES

Fifty call slips, preserved in Dresden, which Semper completed to request books in the British Museum Library between March and December 1852 provide evidence for the wide range of his reading in the same year in which he successfully applied for a post in the Department of Practical Art. The great majority of the books ordered are connected with his work on the metals catalogue, which he compiled at the request of Henry Cole from mid-April to mid-August 1852 (see 329). Work on the catalogue brought him into contact with leading figures at the British Museum and other institutions. On 16 April, Samuel Birch,

British Museum Library Call Slips   549

the assistant keeper of the Department of Antiquities at the British Museum, assisted him in obtaining access to 'any works upon the Moyen age' in the holdings of the Archaeological Institute. Birch also asked the Institute's secretary, Albert Way, to help Semper in his research (gta, 20-K[DD]-1852-04-16). On 22 May, Semper himself asked Antonio Panizzi, the keeper of the Department of Printed Books at the British Museum Library, for permission 'to make some tracings of several ingravings; for instance of some, contained in the works of Agincourt and of Willemin', which he was intending to use for his 'illustrated catalogue for a projected collection of metalworks' (gta, 20-K-1852-05-22[S]). The day before, he had borrowed *Histoire de l'art par les monumens* by Louis Georges Séroux d'Agincourt and *Monuments français inédits*, illustrated by Nicolas-Xavier Willemin, and he borrowed them again on 24 May, when his request was granted (see 219.1–24). Probably intending to make a tracing of the 'drawing of the bronze roof truss of the vestibule of the Pantheon in Serlio', to which Emil Braun had drawn his attention (gta, 20-K-1852-05-04), he consulted Sebastiano Serlio's books on architecture in various editions (220.6–12). Semper's mirror-inverted copy of the relevant woodcut (Serlio 1619, 52 verso) was ultimately included in *Style in the Technical and Tectonic Arts* (Semper 1860/63, 1:369). Again for the metals catalogue – out of interest in museology and its connections with ethnology – Semper also borrowed books by Gustav Klemm (221.11–20), a Dresden historian of culture, while he used several other works for his book project on 'Vergleichende Baulehre' (Comparative Architecture) – for example, the first book requested, Charles Texier's *Description de l'Asie Mineure* (217.11–17). The final call slip deserves particular attention. Semper used it on 11 December 1852 to order Karl Bötticher's *Tektonik der Hellenen* (225.27–32), to study it probably for the first time.
Wolfgang Herrmann was the first to draw attention to the existence of these call slips. When we consulted them in 2014, they were stored in a folder with the inscription 'Wolfgang Herrmann, London 9. 11. 1972' and were affixed to five sheets of paper using adhesive tape, without any recognizable order. We present them here in chronological sequence and have placed the only two undated slips (217.18–21, 222.22–5) alongside others to which they are related either by topic or by author. Works for which today's library shelf marks can be traced to the pressmarks used by Semper are indicated in the holdings of the British Library, the successor of the British Museum Library.
The following is printed at the bottom of each call slip:

> Please to restore each volume of the Catalogue to its place, as soon as done with.

The following is printed on the back of each call slip:

> READERS ARE *PARTICULARLY* REQUESTED
> 1. Not to ask for more than *one work* on the same ticket.
> 2. To transcribe *literally* from the Catalogues the title of the Work wanted.
> 3. To write in a plain clear hand, in order to avoid delay and mistakes.
> 4. Before leaving the Room, to return the books to an attendant, and to obtain the corresponding ticket, the *Reader being responsible for the Books so long as the Ticket remains uncancelled.*
> N.B. Readers are, under no circumstances, to take any Book or MS. out of the Reading Rooms.

217.12–13 **Description de l'Asie Mineure**] two volumes of Texier 1839/49. Semper excerpted passages from the first volume of the work in French on eight manuscript pages, the first of which is headed 'Brittish Museum 8th. Mars. 1852' – the date when he requested the book from the library (gta, 20-Ms-149, fols. 8–13; covering parts of Texier 1839/49, 1:I–III, XI–XII, XIV, 11 n. 2, 23, 82, 209, 211).   217.12 **1839**] *1839–49*   217.19–20 **Atlas von Vorder Asien**] a map series, published in individual fascicles, accompanying Carl Ritter's *Erdkunde im Verhältniss zur Natur und zur Geschichte des Menschen* (Ritter 1817/52)   217.25–7 **Ueber den protestantischen Geist aller wahrhaften Kunst**] Toelken 1839 (BL, 1401.k.37)

218.2 **1827**] *1827–31*   218.3 **Italienische Forschungen**] Rumohr 1827/31 (BL, 786.h.23). Semper's own – incomplete – copy of the work (see 212.19–20) was held back by British customs.   218.8 **Drei Reisen nach Italien**] Rumohr 1832 (BL, 791.b.17)   218.13–14 **Sammlung fur Kunst und Historie**] Rumohr 1816/23 (BL, P.P.1898)   218.19–20 **Scriptores rerum Brunswicarum**] Leibniz 1707/11   218.24 **1813**] *1813–18*   218.25 **Storia della Scultura**] Cicognara 1813/18   218.29 **1813**] The engraved title page has the year 1813, whereas the imprint below it says: 'London. Published by Cadell & Davies. June 1st 1815.'   218.30–1 **the Arabian Antiquities of Spain**] Murphy 1815 (BL, Tab.487.a)

219.3–4 **Monumens Francais inédits**] Willemin/Pottier 1839 (BL, 74/558*.g.2); cf. 219.14–18   219.9–11 **Histoire de l'art par les monumens**] probably the second to sixth volumes of Agincourt 1823 (the first volume is only concerned with architecture); cf. 219.19–24   219.15–16 **Monumens Francais inedits**] see note 219.3–4   219.20 **1811**] *1811–23*   219.21–2 histoire de l'Art par les monumens] Agincourt 1823 (BL, 130.h.2–7); cf. 219.8–13   219.24 **M.**] probably *May*   219.27 **Tabulae Logarithmicae**] Vega 1812 (BL, 1394.h.2). Semper owned a similar book by Georg von Vega (see 210.22, 215.2), which was held back by British customs.

220.3–4 **Lecons sur le calcul des fonctions**] Lagrange 1806 (BL, 529.e.8)   220.7 **Architettura**] Serlio 1559/62 (BL, 559*.e.2). The other date mentioned, 1537, refers to Sebastiano Serlio's *Regole generali di architetura* (Serlio 1537), the first of his books on architecture to be published, which finally became the fourth book.   220.11 **Architettura**] Serlio 1619 (BL, 559*.c.8)   **Vicenza**] This corresponds to the place of publication to be found on the title pages of most of the individual books assembled in this edition, while the main title page has 'Venetia'.   220.12 **M**] probably *May*   220.14–15 **Phil. naturalis principia**] Newton 1822 (BL, 535.g.10–11)   220.21–2 **De Minervae Poliadis Sacra et aede**] Müller 1820 (BL, 787.i.15)   220.26–7 **Die Alterthumer v. Athen**] Müller 1831   220.31 **Εφημερις αρχαιολογικη**] probably the first 27 numbers, published from October 1837 to June 1843, of *Ephemeris archaiologike*

221.2 **Revue Archeologique**] the second and third volumes of *Revue archéologique* (BL, P.P.1926)   221.6 **1818**] *1818–21*   221.7 **Briefe in die Heimat**] Hagen 1818/21 (BL, 1049.f.22,21)   221.12–15 **Zur Geschichte der Sammlungen ~ in Deutschland**] Klemm 1837 (BL, 619.g.11)   221.18–19 **Allgemeine Culturgeschchte der Menschheit**] 'Culturgeschchte': *Culturgeschichte*; probably the first nine volumes of Klemm 1843/52 (BL, 1310.e.12–16). The tenth volume was published after 28 June 1852 (its preface is dated 15 September 1852).   221.18 **1843**] probably *1843–51*   221.22–4 **les monumens de la Monarchie Francaise**] Montfaucon 1729/33   221.28–30 **a Critical inquiry into ancient Armour**] Meyrick 1824 (BL, 562*.f.3–5)

222.2–3 **Specimens of ancient furniture**] Shaw/Meyrick 1836 (BL, 562*.f.8)   222.10 **de architectura opus**] Androuet du Cerceau 1559 (BL, 60.h.5.[2])   222.14 **Architectura**] the first volume of Dietterlin 1593/94 (BL, 559*.e.5)   222.18–19 **Die Ornamentik des Mittelalters**] the first three volumes of Heideloff 1843/52 (BL, 1268.g.5)   222.23 **Oeuvres**] Marot 1731 (BL, 85.h.1–4). Semper may have filled in this call slip erroneously, confusing the father

of the poet Clément Marot, Jean Marot, with the architect of the same name (see next note).
222.28–30 **Recueil des plans ~ des plusieurs palais ~ à Paris**] Marot 1659 (BL, 61.d.5)
223.2–3 **vetera monumenta**] Ciampini 1690/99 (BL, 142.f.11, 142.f.12)   223.8–9 **De sacris aedificiis a C. M. constructis**] Ciampini 1693 (BL, 143.f.21)   223.13 **1573**] *1513*   223.14 **Chronica**] Leo Marsicanus 1513 (BL, 1367.f.13)   223.17–18 **Instituto di corrispondenza archeologica**] the first four volumes of Monumenti inediti 1829/85   223.19 **2 July**] The year, omitted by Semper, is almost certainly 1852, as with the other call slips.   223.21 **Archeologia**] the 28th to 32nd volumes of *Archaeologia*   223.25 **Index to Archeologia**] Carlisle 1844

224.2–3 **Indian Archipelago Exhibition of 1851**] Indian Archipelago 1851 (BL, D-7955.c.34. [3])   224.9 **Nurmberg**] *Nuremberg*   224.10–11 **Merkwürdigkeiten der Stadt Bamberg**] Murr 1799 (BL, 573.e.18)   224.15–18 **Beschreibung der ~ Konigl. Kronungszierden**] Murr 1801 (BL, 619.e.23.[6])   224.21–5 **A true description ~ Harlejan Miscellany**] Anonymous 1811 (BL, 1326.g.1–12)   224.30–2 **Historische Nachrich von den Nurnberger Mathematicis**] 'Nachrich': *Nachricht*; Doppelmayr 1730 (BL, 819.m.2)

225.2–4 **Nuovissima Guida dei viaggiatori in Italia**] Nuovissima guida 1842 (BL, 1300.a.3)
225.7 **Museo Borbonico**] the first fourteen fascicles, published in 1824–27, or the first fourteen volumes, published in 1824–52, of Real Museo Borbonico 1824/57. An advertisement in the Augsburg *Allgemeine Zeitung*, no. 223 (10 August 1852), 3568, indicates that the 56th fascicle, which concluded the fourteenth volume of the work, had just been published. Whether Semper would have been able to consult this volume on 3 August 1852 is uncertain.
1824.–37.] *1824–27* or *1824–52*   225.11–13 **Ueber die Theorie der Musik**] Forkel 1777 (BL, 556.c.14)   225.16 **1846**] *1845–46*   225.17 **Sec. Opera Cufica**] Lanci 1845/46 (BL, J/7707.f.20)
225.23–4 **Traité de la Chaleur**] Péclet 1844. Semper excerpted passages from the second chapter of the work in French on two manuscript pages, headed 'Auszug aus Peclet: über Kamine' (Excerpt from Peclet: on chimneys) and concerned with the air needed for and the gas caused by the combustion of different fuels (gta, 20-Ms-149, fols. 14–15; covering parts of Péclet 1844, 52–4 [par. 10: arts. 242, 244, 246–54, 256, 258–60]).   225.29–30 **Die Tektonik der Hellenen**] Bötticher 1844/52. Semper excerpted passages from the preface and the introduction of the work in English and German (gta, 20-Ms-150, ed. in Gnehm 2004, 202–3, 206–21; cf. Herrmann 1981, 114–15).   225.32 **11 Dec.**] The year, omitted by Semper, is almost certainly 1852, as with the other call slips.

ALTERATIONS IN THE MANUSCRIPT

217.28 **(Date)**] *after in pencil by unknown hand* 127   **12ᵗ**] *2 over 1*
218.1 **Title**] *after in pencil by unknown hand* 48   218.5 **27**] *above del.* 29   218.6 **Press Mark**] *after in pencil by unknown hand* 2⅛   218.11 **27ᵗ**] *7 over 9*   218.12 **Press Mark**] *above in pencil by unknown hand* 40   218.29 **T.487.a.**] *altered in pencil by unknown hand to* Tab487.a. Tab487.a.] *above in pencil by unknown hand* Table
219.1 **Title**] *below in pencil by unknown hand* 140   219.8 **wanted**] *below in pencil by unknown hand* 45   219.15 **fol.**] *below del.* Par.   219.25 **Title**] *below in pencil by unknown hand* 32
220.1 **wanted**] *below in pencil by unknown hand* 189   220.7 **Architettura**] *above del.* 5 Lib. [ ]   **fol.**] *below del.* 155[9]   220.10 **Work wanted**] *below in pencil by unknown hand* 190   220.13 **Press Mark**] *below in pencil by unknown hand* 10[9]   220.18 **Jun.**] *altered from* M[ ]   220.19 **Press Mark**] *after in pencil by unknown hand* 2[1]/79   220.20 **787.i.**] *before in pencil by*

unknown hand 15 220.24 **Title**] *below in pencil by unknown hand* 7 220.25 **1829**] *after undel. in 'Place' column* 1[ ] 220.30 **wanted**] *below in pencil by unknown hand* 10[7] 221.4 **(Date)**] *above in pencil by unknown hand* 29 **June**] *altered from* Juin 221.11 **Press**] *below in pencil by unknown hand* 2/155 221.12 **619.g.**] *above in pencil by unknown hand* 11 221.17 **Press Mark**] *before in pencil by unknown hand* 11/(7)7 221.26 **Title**] *below in pencil by unknown hand* 16 221.27 **4°**] *above del.* fol.

222.1 **Title**] *below in pencil by unknown hand* 17 222.3 **with**] *before del.* des 222.5 **M.**] *before del.* f 222.7 **Date**] *below in pencil by unknown hand* 9[2] 222.11 **July**] *after del.* M[a] 222.12 **Date**] *below in pencil by unknown hand* 93 222.16 **Date**] *below in pencil by unknown hand* 107 222.31 **Paris.**] *before del.* etc.

223.1 **Date**] *below in pencil by unknown hand* 152 223.6 **Date**] *below in pencil by unknown hand* 15[3] 223.12 **Press**] *after in pencil by unknown hand* 39 223.16 **Press**] *below in pencil by unknown hand* 91 223.17 **552.g.7.**] *below del.* 742.d. 223.21 **8°**] 8 *over* 1

224.1 **Press Mark**] *below in pencil by unknown hand* 44 224.8 **Mark. Title**] *below in pencil by unknown hand* 117 224.13 **Size**] *below in pencil by unknown hand* 159 224.14 **619.e**] *above del.* 6 224.20 **Place. Date**] *below in pencil by unknown hand* 1[2] 224.26 **Volume 12.**] *above del.* Vol12. 224.28 **Place. Date**] *below in pencil by unknown hand* 180

225.1 **Date**] *below in pencil by unknown hand* 11 225.10 **Title**] *below in pencil by unknown hand* 11/152 225.11 **1777**] *second* 7 *over* 1 225.15 **Press Mark**] *below in pencil by unknown hand* 24/33 225.22 **Date**] *below in pencil by unknown hand* 22[9] 225.27 **Mark**] *below in pencil by unknown hand* 159

Appointment Letter from the Department of Practical Art
Walter Ruding Deverell

TEXTUAL RECORD

K-1852   gta, 20-K-1852-09-11, fols. 1r–2v, one folded sheet with printed letterhead (edited in bold) and with letter in Walter Ruding Deverell's hand, dated 11 September 1852, *copy-text*

BIBLIOGRAPHY Herrmann 1978, 70–1; Herrmann 1984, 64

EXPLANATORY NOTES

As Henry Cole, the general superintendent of the Department of Practical Art, noted in his diary, he reached verbal agreements with Semper and with the textile designer Octavius Hudson on 10 September 1852 on their professorial appointments: 'Semper & Hudson approved of the conditions of their appointment.' The same evening, Cole was busy 'writing appointments to them', and the Department's secretary, Walter Ruding Deverell, con-

Principles and Practice of Ornamental Art

firmed Semper's appointment in an official letter on 11 September. Together with Joseph Warner Henley, the president of the Board of Trade, Cole had already agreed on the 'Class book in Metals for Semper' on 2 July 1852 (Cole Diary). During their discussion, he had also mentioned Semper's status as a foreigner and a refugee, but Henley did not regard this as any disadvantage, as Cole's diary shows: 'He did not object to his being a foreigner, if he were fit, not … his being a political refugee, not if he had "hoofs & horns"'. Henley and Cole had finally settled the 'professorships of Metal & Printed fabrics' for Semper and Hudson on 8 September (Cole Diary). The 'Superintendents' mentioned in the letter of appointment (226.30, 226.32–3) – Cole and Richard Redgrave, the 'Superintendent of Art' – were to become Semper's most important contacts in the Department. A particularly notable point is what is explicitly referred to in the letter as a 'new experiment to afford practical instruction in Art for industrial purposes' (227.2–3) – a venture in which the Department was relying on Semper's teaching experience in Dresden, although with some reservations (see 330–1, 370–1; 377, Explanatory Notes 89.14).

EDITORIAL EMENDATIONS

226.18 **principle,**] principle∧ ¦ principle, *(catchword on fol. 1r repeating first word of fol. 1v)*
227.16 **on**] on ¦ on *(catchword on fol. 2r repeating first word of fol. 2v)*

ALTERATIONS IN THE MANUSCRIPT

227.3 **dependent**] *third* e *over* a

Principles and Practice of Ornamental Art Applied to Furniture, Metals, Jewellery, and Enamels
Henry Cole

TEXTUAL RECORD

Prospectus	'II. Principles and Practice of Ornamental Art Applied to Metals, Jewellery, and Enamels. III. Pottery and Other Manufactures', in *Department of Practical Art: 1. A Brief Statement of the Contents of the Museum. 2. Prospectus of the Department* (separately paginated appendix to CatM[3]), London: Eyre & Spottiswoode for Her Majesty's Stationery Office, 1852, 13
DPA[1]	'II. Principles and Practice of Ornamental Art Applied to Metals, Jewellery, and Enamels. III. Pottery, Furniture, and Other Manufactures', in *First Report of the Department of Practical Art*, London: Eyre & Spottiswoode for Her Majesty's Stationery Office, 1853, 380–1

CatM⁵   'II. Principles and Practice of Ornamental Art Applied to Furniture, Metals, Jewellery, and Enamels. III. Pottery, and Other Manufactures', in *A Catalogue of the Museum of Ornamental Art, at Marlborough House, Pall Mall*, 5th ed. (May 1853), London: Eyre & Spottiswoode for Her Majesty's Stationery Office, 1853, 126–7 (NAL, V.1853.003), *copy-text*

BIBLIOGRAPHY Herrmann 1978, 131–2

EXPLANATORY NOTES

After Semper had been appointed professor for 'the principles and practice of Ornamental Art applied to Metal Manufactures' (226.7), Henry Cole drafted the programme of Semper's first class, to be included in the prospectus of the Department of Practical Art as part of the information about all the special classes meeting at Marlborough House. He had the programme delivered to Semper by John Matthias Dodd, the clerk of the Department's Museum of Ornamental Art. Semper returned it to Cole on 27 September 1852 with the following comment, included in the letter with which he sent Cole the 'Report on the Private Collection of Arms at Windsor Castle' (76–80), and told him about 'Berlin Metal works etc.' offered for purchase (NAL, 55.BB Box 10; cf. 80–2):

> Mr. Dodd has communicated to me the Prospectus of my special Class which I return with the sole remark, that perhaps at the first article it will appear sufficient to set: 'A Class of Students meet daily to practice ornamental art in metal. They have the advantage of attending demonstrations of actual processes, and of their expedients, value and means for ornamental art.' –
> It will be the most important to instruct the Students in those specialities of Style which arise from the different processes and to introduce them in the full possession of the 'resources' of each Process. This must be indicated in a few words. –

It is probable that Cole hardly changed his draft following these proposals. In particular, he did not adopt Semper's suggestion regarding the 'specialities of Style'. In relation to metals, Semper already addresses this point, which was very important to him, in his 'Report on the Private Collection of Arms at Windsor Castle' (see 76.14–23), and he more generally discusses the consequences of 'the different processes in treating [materials]' for 'the question of Style' in his inaugural lecture of 20 May 1853 (see 114.24–115.33).

The different printings of the prospectus reflect changes in the areas of teaching for which Semper was responsible. The first printing of 1852 mentions 'Principles and Practice of Ornamental Art applied to Metals, Jewellery, and Enamels' and adds in the next section 'Pottery and other Manufactures' as belonging to his provisional areas (for Cole's first apparent intention to employ Semper for ceramics, see 329). The second printing, published in April 1853 in the Department's *First Report*, adds 'Furniture' to the latter section, while the third printing of May 1853, included in *A Catalogue of the Museum of Ornamental Art*, moves 'Furniture' to be part of Semper's regular special class. In fact, furniture – to which Semper refers in his 'Plan of Instruction' (see 85.18) – became one of his teaching areas starting in January 1853 at the latest and remained so until his last term of teaching at the Department in the autumn of 1854 (see 328, 331).

PRINT VARIANTS

228.1 **Furniture, Metals,**] Metals, *Prospectus DPA¹*   228.2 **Enamels. –**] ~. ∧ *Prospectus*
Conducted] *paragraph Prospectus*   228.3 **student,**] ~∧ *Prospectus*   228.6 **Professor**]
paragraph Prospectus   **daily**] ~ at Marlborough House (except Saturdays) *Prospectus*
228.9 **may have**] have *Prospectus DPA¹*   228.11 **Designers**] designers *Prospectus DPA¹*
&c.∧] ~., *Prospectus DPA¹*   228.21 **Fees**] fees *no italics Prospectus*   228.24 **class),**] ~)∧
Prospectus DPA¹   228.29 **Designs**] Design *Prospectus*   228.31 **Pottery,**] ~∧ *Prospectus* ~,
Furniture, *DPA¹*

APPENDIX

ABBREVIATIONS OF HOLDING SITES

BL	British Library, London
BnF	Bibliothèque nationale de France, Paris
CB Hamburg	Commerzbibliothek, Stiftung Hanseatisches Wirtschaftsarchiv, Hamburg
ETH Library	Library of the Eidgenössische Technische Hochschule, Zurich
gta	gta Archives, Institute for the History and Theory of Architecture, Eidgenössische Technische Hochschule, Zurich
HfBK Dresden	Hochschule für Bildende Künste, Dresden
Spyri Archives	Johanna Spyri Archives, Zentralbibliothek, Zurich
NAL	National Art Library, Victoria and Albert Museum, London
RCIN	Royal Collection Inventory Number, Royal Collection Trust, London
RIBA Library	Library of the Royal Institute of British Architects, London
SLUB	Sächsische Landesbibliothek – Staats- und Universitätsbibliothek, Dresden
ULB Bonn	Universitäts- und Landesbibliothek, Bonn
V&A	Victoria and Albert Museum, London
Vieweg Archives	Vieweg Archives, University Library, Technische Universität, Brunswick
ZB Zurich	Zentralbibliothek, Zurich

BIBLIOGRAPHY

The three-part bibliography, starting with Semper's writings, lists all titles referred to in the editorial material. Texts edited in this volume are not listed here. Manuscripts referred to but not edited in this volume are specified only in the editorial material, together with their archival places. Writings cited by Semper are grouped in the second section. Writings whose use by Semper cannot be ascertained completely are listed among the third section, the secondary sources. Ancient authors are omitted from the bibliography in cases where they can be cited independently from a particular edition or where the use of a particular edition by Semper cannot be inferred.

Writings by Gottfried Semper

Semper 1833 'Scoprimento d'antichi colori sulla colonna di Trajano: Al dott. Kellermann' (10 July 1833), *Bullettino dell'Instituto di corrispondenza archeologica*, no. 7 (July 1833), 92–3.

Semper 1834 *Vorläufige Bemerkungen über bemalte Architectur und Plastik bei den Alten*, Altona: Hammerich, 1834.

Semper 1836 *Die Anwendung der Farben in der Architectur und Plastik: In einer Sammlung von Beispielen aus den Zeiten des Alterthums und des Mittelalters*, Dresden: Auf Kosten des Herausgebers, 1836. (Only 1 fasc. with 6 pls. on 'Dorisch-Griechische Kunst' published.)

Semper 1845 *Ueber den Bau evangelischer Kirchen: Mit besonderer Beziehung auf die gegenwärtige Frage über die Art des Neubaues der Nikolaikirche in Hamburg und auf ein dafür entworfenes Project*, Leipzig: Teubner, 1845.

Semper 1849a *Das königliche Hoftheater zu Dresden*, Brunswick: Vieweg, 1849.

Semper 1849b 'Thor in Harlem', *Zeitschrift für praktische Baukunst* 9 (1849), 457–8, pl. 40.

Semper 1849c 'Die Kunst unter der französischen Republik', *Zeitschrift für praktische Baukunst* 9 (1849), 481–4.

Semper 1849d 'Reise nach Belgien im Monat October 1849', *Zeitschrift für praktische Baukunst* 9 (1849), 501–6, pl. 50. (With an editorial addendum on Amiens Cathedral, 506–14.)

Semper 1849e 'Gebäude der alten Münze zu Caen', *Zeitschrift für praktische Baukunst* 9 (1849), 513–14, pls. 48–50.

Semper 1849f 'Glockenthurm in Brügge', *Zeitschrift für praktische Baukunst* 9 (1849), 515–16, pls. 51–2.

Semper 1849g 'Thor in Brügge', *Zeitschrift für praktische Baukunst* 9 (1849), 515–16, pl. 53.

Semper 1849h 'Der Wintergarten zu Paris', *Zeitschrift für praktische Baukunst* 9 (1849), 515–26, pl. 54.

Semper 1849i 'Farbiges Erdpech', *Zeitschrift für praktische Baukunst* 9 (1849), 525–8, pl. 54.

Semper 1850a 'Wohnhaus in Paris in der Rue St. George', *Zeitschrift für praktische Baukunst* 10 (1850), 9–10, pls. 1–3.

Semper 1850b 'Hof eines alten Holzhauses in Rouen', *Zeitschrift für praktische Baukunst* 10 (1850), 9–10, pl. 4.

Semper 1850c 'Wasserzuleitung für Locomotiven auf der Station zu Gent', *Zeitschrift für praktische Baukunst* 10 (1850), 23–4, pl. 7.

Semper 1851a *Ueber Polychromie und ihren Ursprung: Ein Beitrag zur vergleichenden Baukunde*, Brunswick: Vieweg, 1851. (Pre-edition of Semper 1851b with different title.)

Semper 1851b *Die vier Elemente der Baukunst: Ein Beitrag zur vergleichenden Baukunde*, Brunswick: Vieweg, 1851.

Semper 1852 *Wissenschaft, Industrie und Kunst: Vorschläge zur Anregung nationalen Kunstgefühles, bei dem Schlusse der Londoner Industrie-Ausstellung*, Brunswick: Vieweg, 1852.

Semper 1853 'Die neuesten pariser Bauten', *Unterhaltungen am häuslichen Herd* 1, no. 19 ([Feb.] 1853), 296–8.

Semper 1854 'Von der Form der Körper, die mit geringster Resistenz in widerstehenden Mitteln sich bewegen', ed. Benjamin Witzschel, *Annalen der Physik und Chemie* 93, no. 10 ([18 Sept.] 1854), 297–305, pl. 3 figs. 17–18.

Semper 1855a 'Die Restauration des Tuskischen Tempels', *Deutsches Kunstblatt: Zeitschrift für bildende Kunst, Baukunst und Kunstgewerbe* 6, no. 9 (1 March 1855), 75–9 and pl.

Semper 1855b 'Briefe aus der Schweiz: Die neben den Propyläen aufgefundenen Inschrifttafeln (geschrieben in London, Ende 1852)', *Deutsches Kunstblatt: Zeitschrift für bildende Kunst, Baukunst und Kunstgewerbe* 6, nos. 38, 42–6 (20 Sept.; 18 and 25 Oct.; 1, 8 and 15 Nov. 1855), 332–3, 370–1, 377–81, 388–90, 397–8, 404–7.

Semper 1856 *Über die formelle Gesetzmässigkeit des Schmuckes und dessen Bedeutung als Kunstsymbol*, Zurich: Meyer & Zeller, 1856. (Offprint from *Monatsschrift des Wissenschaftlichen Vereins in Zürich* 1 [1856], 101–30.)

Semper 1859 *Ueber die bleiernen Schleudergeschosse der Alten und über zweckmässige Gestaltung der Wurfkörper im Allgemeinen: Ein Versuch, die dynamische Entstehung gewisser Formen in der Natur und in der Kunst nachzuweisen*, Frankfurt am Main: Verlag für Kunst und Wissenschaft, 1859.

Semper 1860/63 *Der Stil in den technischen und tektonischen Künsten, oder Praktische Aesthetik: Ein Handbuch für Techniker, Künstler und Kunstfreunde*, vol. 1, Frankfurt am Main: Verlag für Kunst und Wissenschaft, 1860; vol. 2, Munich: Bruckmann, 1863.

Semper 1869 *Ueber Baustyle: Ein Vortrag gehalten auf dem Rathhaus in Zürich am 4. März 1869*, Zurich: Schulthess, 1869.

Semper 1881 *Die Bauten, Entwürfe und Skizzen von Gottfried Semper*, ed. Manfred Semper, Leipzig: Knapp, [1881]. (Only 1 fasc. with 4 pls. published.)

Semper 1884 *Kleine Schriften*, ed. Manfred Semper and Hans Semper, Berlin: Spemann, 1884.

Semper 1983 'London Lecture of November 11, 1853', ed. Harry Francis Mallgrave, *RES: Anthropology and Aesthetics*, no. 6 (Fall 1983), 5–22.

Semper 1985a 'London Lecture of December 1853: "On the Origin of Some Architectural Styles"', ed. Harry Francis Mallgrave, *RES: Anthropology and Aesthetics*, no. 9 (Spring 1985), 53–60.

Semper 1985b 'London Lecture of Autumn 1854: "On Architectural Symbols"', ed. Harry Francis Mallgrave, *RES: Anthropology and Aesthetics*, no. 9 (Spring 1985), 61–7.

Semper 1986a 'London Lecture of November 18, 1853: "The Development of the Wall and Wall Construction in Antiquity"', ed. Harry Francis Mallgrave, *RES: Anthropology and Aesthetics*, no. 11 (Spring 1986), 33–42.

Semper 1986b 'London Lecture of November 29, 1854: "On the Relation of Architectural Systems with the General Cultural Conditions"', ed. Harry Francis Mallgrave, *RES: Anthropology and Aesthetics*, no. 11 (Spring 1986), 43–53.

Semper 1989 *The Four Elements of Architecture and Other Writings*, trans. Harry Francis Mallgrave and Wolfgang Herrmann, Cambridge: Cambridge University Press, 1989.

Semper 2004 *Style in the Technical and Tectonic Arts; or, Practical Aesthetics*, trans. Harry Francis Mallgrave and Michael Robinson, Los Angeles: Getty Research Institute, 2004.

Semper 2007a *The Ideal Museum: Practical Art in Metals and Hard Materials*, ed. Peter Noever, Vienna: Schlebrügge, 2007.

Semper 2007b *Du style et de l'architecture: Écrits, 1834–1869*, trans. Jacques Soulillou and Nathalie Neumann, Marseille: Parenthèses, 2007.

Semper 2014 *Wissenschaftliche Abhandlungen und Streit-schriften*, reprint ed. Henrik Karge, 2 vols., Gesammelte Schriften 1.1–2, Hildesheim: Olms-Weidmann, 2014.

Semper 2020 *Écrits sur l'architecture*, ed. Anne-Marie Châtelet, trans. Léo Biétry, Gollion: Infolio, 2020.

Writings Cited by Gottfried Semper

Agincourt 1823 Jean Baptiste Louis Georges Séroux (Seroux) d'Agincourt, *Histoire de l'art par les monumens, depuis sa décadence au IVᵉ siècle jusqu'à son renouvellement au XVIᵉ*, 6 vols. (vols. 1–3, text; vols. 4–6, plates), Paris: Treuttel & Würtz, 1823.

Alderson 1834 M. A. Alderson, *An Essay on the Nature and Application of Steam, with an Historical Notice of the Rise and Progressive Improvement of the Steam-Engine: Being the Prize Essay on this Subject at the London Mechanics' Institution in the Year 1833*, London: Sherwood, Gilbert & Piper, 1834.

Androuet du Cerceau 1559 Jacques Androuet du Cerceau, *De architectura opus*, Paris: Prévost, 1559.

Annali 1829/85 *Annali dell'Instituto di corrispondenza archeologica*, 57 vols., Rome, 1829–85.

Anonymous 1811 'A True Description and Direction of What Is Most Worthy to Be Seen in All Italy', in John Malham (ed.), *The Harleian Miscellany; or, A Collection of Scarce, Curious, and Entertaining Pamphlets and Tracts, as well in Manuscript as in Print, Found in the Late Earl of Oxford's Library*, vol. 12, London: Dutton, 1811, 73–130.

Antiquities of Ionia 1769/1840 Society of Dilettanti, *Antiquities of Ionia*, 3 vols., London: Spilsbury & Haskell; Bulmer; Nicol, 1769–1840. (Vol. 1 entitled *Ionian Antiquities*.)

Archaeologia *Archaeologia; or, Miscellaneous Tracts Relating to Antiquity*, ed. Society of Antiquaries of London, London, since 1770.

Arclais de Montamy 1765 Didier-François d'Arclais de Montamy, *Traité des couleurs pour la peinture en émail et sur la porcelaine, précédé de l'art de peindre sur l'émail*, Paris: Cavelier, 1765.

Arneth 1850 Joseph Arneth, *Die antiken Gold- und Silber-Monumente des k. k. Münz- und Antiken-Cabinettes in Wien*, Vienna: Braumüller, 1850.

Baudissin 1836 Wolf von Baudissin, *Ben Jonson und seine Schule, dargestellt in einer Auswahl von Lustspielen und Tragödien*, 2 vols., Leipzig: Brockhaus, 1836.

Beck 1801 Christian Daniel Beck, *Artis Latine scribendi praecepta*, Leipzig: Leupold, 1801.

Bélanger 1847 Jean-Baptiste Bélanger, *Cours de mécanique, ou Résumé de leçons sur la dynamique, la statique, et leurs applications à l'art de l'ingénieur*, Paris: Carilian-Gœury & Dalmont; Mathias, 1847.

Bélanger 1848 Jean-Baptiste Bélanger, *Lehrbuch der Mechanik und ihrer Anwendungen auf das Ingenieurwesen*, trans. Bernhard Gugler, Ludwigsburg: Neubert, 1848.

Belidor 1729 Bernard Forest de Belidor, *La science des ingénieurs dans la conduite des travaux de fortification et d'architecture civile*, Paris: Jombert, 1729.

Bellona 1781/87 *Bellona: Ein militärisches Journal*, ed. Karl von Seidel, 20 vols., Dresden, 1781–87.

Bézout 1764/69 Étienne Bézout, *Cours de mathématiques, à l'usage des gardes du pavillon et de la marine*, 6 vols., Paris: Musier, 1764–69.

Bézout 1770/72 Étienne Bézout, *Cours de mathématiques, à l'usage du corps royal de l'artillerie*, 4 vols., Paris: Imprimerie royale, 1770–72.

Böhm/Hauf 1777/95 Andreas Böhm and Johann Carl Friedrich Hauf (eds.), *Magazin für Ingenieur und Artilleristen*, 12 vols., Giessen: Krieger, 1777–95. (Vols. 1–11 edited by Böhm; vol. 12, entitled *Magazin für Ingenieure und Artilleristen*, edited by Hauf.)

Börne 1829/34 Ludwig Börne, *Gesammelte Schriften*, vols. 1–10, Hamburg: Hoffmann & Campe, 1829–32; vols. 11–12, Offenbach: Brunet, 1833; vols. 13–14, Paris: Brunet, 1834.

Botta/Flandin 1849/50 Paul Émile Botta and Eugène Flandin, *Monument de Ninive*, 5 vols., Paris: Imprimerie nationale, 1849–50.

Bötticher 1842 Karl Bötticher, *Die Holzarchitectur des Mittelalters: Mit Anschluss der schönsten in dieser Epoche entwickelten Produkte der gewerblichen Industrie*, 4 fascs., Berlin: Schenk & Gerstäcker, 1842.

Bötticher 1844/52   Karl Bötticher, *Die Tektonik der Hellenen*, 3 vols. (vols. 1–2, text; vol. 3, plates), Potsdam: Riegel, 1844–52.

Böttiger 1837/38   Carl August Böttiger, *Kleine Schriften archäologischen und antiquarischen Inhalts*, ed. Julius Sillig, 3 vols., Dresden: Arnold, 1837–38.

Brandon/Brandon 1849   Raphael Brandon and Joshua Arthur Brandon, *The Open Timber Roofs of the Middle Ages*, London: Bogue, 1849.

Briseux 1743   Charles-Étienne Briseux, *L'art de bâtir des maisons de campagne où l'on traite de leur distribution, de leur construction, & de leur décoration*, 2 vols., Paris: Prault, 1743.

Bröder 1787   Christian Gottlob Bröder, *Practische Grammatik der lateinischen Sprache*, Leipzig: Crusius, 1787.

Brøndsted 1826/30   Peter Oluf Brøndsted (Bröndsted), *Voyages dans la Grèce accompagnés de recherches archéologiques*, 2 vols., Paris: Didot, 1826–30.

Brongniart 1844   Alexandre Brongniart, *Traité des arts céramiques ou des poteries, considérées dans leur histoire, leur pratique et leur théorie*, 3 vols. (vols. 1–2, text; vol. 3, plates), Paris: Béchet; Mathias, 1844.

Bruyère 1823/28   Louis Bruyère, *Études relatives à l'art des constructions*, 2 vols., Paris: Bance, 1823–28.

Bullettino 1829/85   *Bullettino dell'Instituto di corrispondenza archeologica*, 57 vols., Rome, 1829–85. (Vol. 1 entitled *Bullettino degli annali dell'Instituto di corrispondenza archeologica*.)

Bürck 1844   August Bürck, *Allgemeine Geschichte der Reisen und Entdeckungen zu Land und Meer: Die alte Welt*, Magdeburg: Heinrichshofen, 1844.

Burg 1822   Meno Burg, *Die geometrische Zeichnenkunst, oder Vollständige Anweisung zum Linearzeichnen, zum Tuschen und zur Construktion der Schatten*, 2 vols., Berlin: Duncker & Humblot, 1822.

Buttmann 1818/25   Philipp Buttmann, *Lexilogus, oder Beiträge zur griechischen Wort-Erklärung, hauptsächlich für Homer und Hesiod*, 2 vols., Berlin: Mylius, 1818–25.

Carlisle 1844   Nicholas Carlisle, *An Index to Archaeologia; or, Miscellaneous Tracts, Relating to Antiquity, from Volume XVI to Volume XXX Inclusive*, London: Nichols, 1844.

Cavallari 1847   Saverio Cavallari, *Zur historischen Entwicklung der Künste nach der Theilung des römischen Reichs*, Göttingen: Vandenhoeck & Ruprecht, 1847.

Chambers 1757   William Chambers, *Designs of Chinese Buildings, Furniture, Dresses, Machines, and Utensils*, London: Published for the Author, 1757.

Chevreul 1840   Michel Eugène Chevreul, *Die Farbenharmonie*, Stuttgart: Neff, 1840.

Ciampini 1690/99   Giovanni Ciampini, *Vetera monimenta, in quibus praecipuè musiva opera sacrarum, profanarumque aedium structura, ac nonnulli antiqui ritus, dissertationibus, iconibusque illustrantur*, 2 vols., Rome: Komarek; Bernabò, 1690–99.

Ciampini 1693   Giovanni Ciampini, *De sacris aedificiis a Constantino Magno constructis: Synopsis historica*, Rome: Komarek, 1693.

Cicero 1737   Marcus Tullius Cicero, *Opera omnia ex recensione Iacobi Gronovii*, ed. Johann August Ernesti, 5 vols., Leipzig: Martin, 1737.

Cicognara 1813/18   Leopoldo Cicognara, *Storia della scultura*, 3 vols., Venice: Picotti, 1813–18.

Cotta 1848   Bernhard Cotta, *Briefe über Alexander von Humboldt's Kosmos: Ein Commentar zu diesem Werke für gebildete Laien*, Leipzig: Weigel, 1848.

Cuvier 1812   Georges Cuvier, *Recherches sur les ossemens fossiles de quadrupèdes, où l'on rétablit les caractères de plusieurs espèces d'animaux que les révolutions du globe paroissent avoir détruites*, 4 vols., Paris: Deterville, 1812.

Cuvier 1817   Georges Cuvier, *Le règne animal distribué d'après son organisation, pour servir de base à l'histoire naturelle des animaux et d'introduction à l'anatomie comparée*, 4 vols., Paris: Deterville, 1817.

Dahl 1837   Johan Christian Clausen Dahl, *Denkmale einer sehr ausgebildeten Holzbaukunst aus den frühesten Jahrhunderten in den innern Landschaften Norwegens*, Dresden: [Zöllner], 1837.

Delaistre 1825b   J.-R. Delaistre, *La science de l'ingénieur, divisée en trois parties où l'on traite des chemins, des ponts, des canaux et des aqueducs*, 2 vols., Lyon: Brunet, 1825.

Description de l'Égypte 1809/22   *Description de l'Égypte, ou Recueil des observations et des recherches qui ont été faites en Égypte pendant l'expédition de l'armée française*, sect. 'Antiquités', 11 vols. (vols. 1–4, text; vols. 5–11, plates); sect. 'État moderne', 6 vols. (vols. 1–3, text; vols. 4–6, plates); sect. 'Histoire naturelle', 5 vols. (vols. 1–2, text; vols. 3–5, plates), Paris: Imprimerie impériale; Imprimerie royale, 1809–22.

Detmold 1844   Johann Hermann Detmold, *Randzeichnungen*, Brunswick: Vieweg, 1844.

Dietterlin 1593/94   Wendel Dietterlin (Dietterlein), *Architectura*, vol. 1, Stuttgart: s.n., 1593; vol. 2, Strasbourg: Jobin, 1594. (Vol. 1 entitled *Architectura vnd Aus-stheilung der V Seüln*; vol. 2 entitled *Architectur von Portalen vnnd Thürgerichten, mancherley arten*.)

Donaldson 1833/36   Thomas Leverton Donaldson, *A Collection of the Most Approved Examples of Doorways*, 2 vols., London: Bossange, Barthès & Lowell; Weale, 1833–36.

Donnet/Kaufmann 1837/40   Alexis Donnet and Jacques-Auguste Kaufmann, *Architectonographie des théâtres, ou Parallèle historique et critique de ces édifices, considérés sous le rapport de l'architecture et de la décoration*, 2 vols., Paris: Mathias, 1837–40. (Vol. 1 by Donnet and Kaufmann; vol. 2 by Kaufmann.)

Doppelmayr 1730   Johann Gabriel Doppelmayr, *Historische Nachricht von den Nürnbergischen Mathematicis und Künstlern*, 2 vols., Nuremberg: Monath, 1730.

Durand 1800/01   Jean-Nicolas-Louis Durand, *Recueil et parallèle des édifices de tout genre, anciens et modernes: Avec un texte extrait de L'histoire générale de l'architecture, par J. G. Legrand*, 2 vols. (vol. 1, text; vol. 2, plates), Paris: Gillé, 1800–01.

Durand 1802/05   Jean-Nicolas-Louis Durand, *Précis des leçons d'architecture données à l'École polytechnique*, 2 vols., Paris: Bernard, 1802–05.

Durand 1821   Jean-Nicolas-Louis Durand, *Partie graphique des cours d'architecture faits à l'École royale polytechnique depuis sa réorganisation*, Paris: Chez l'auteur, 1821.

Ephemeris archaiologike   Ἐφημερὶς ἀρχαιολογική *(Ephemeris archaiologike)*, ed. Archaeological Society at Athens, Athens, since 1837.

Ernesti 1739   Johann August Ernesti, *Clavis Ciceroniana, sive Indices rerum et verborum philologico-critici in opera Ciceronis*, Leipzig: Martin, 1739.

Eschenburg 1783   Johann Joachim Eschenburg, *Handbuch der klassischen Literatur*, Berlin: Nicolai, 1783.

Euler 1790/93   Leonhard Euler, *Vollständige Anleitung zur Differenzial-Rechnung*, trans. Johann Andreas Christian Michelsen, 3 vols., Berlin: Lagarde, 1790–93.

Eytelwein 1800   Johann Albert Eytelwein, *Praktische Anweisung zur Konstrukzion der Faschinenwerke und den dazu gehörigen Anlagen an Flüssen und Strömen; nebst einer Anleitung zur Veranschlagung dieser Baue*, Berlin: Maurer, 1800.

Eytelwein 1801   Johann Albert Eytelwein, *Handbuch der Mechanik fester Körper und der Hydraulik: Mit vorzüglicher Rücksicht auf ihre Anwendung in der Architektur*, Berlin: Lagarde, 1801.

Eytelwein 1808   Johann Albert Eytelwein, *Handbuch der Statik fester Körper: Mit vorzüglicher Rücksicht auf ihre Anwendung in der Architektur*, 3 vols., Berlin: Realschulbuchhandlung, 1808.

Eytelwein 1826   Johann Albert Eytelwein, *Handbuch der Hydrostatik: Mit vorzüglicher Rücksicht auf ihre Anwendung in der Architektur*, Berlin: Reimer, 1826.

Falkener 1851a   Edward Falkener, 'On Some Egyptian-Doric Columns in the Southern Temple at Karnak', *The Museum of Classical Antiquities* 1, no. 1 (Jan. 1851), 87–92.

Falkener 1851b   Edward Falkener, 'On the Application of Polychromy to Modern Architecture, as Exemplified in the Decoration of the Exhibition Building in Hyde Park', *The Museum of Classical Antiquities* 1, no. 1 (Jan. 1851), 98–102.

Fèa 1820   Carlo Fèa, *Nuova descrizione di Roma antica e moderna e de' suoi contorni, sue rarità specialmente dopo le nuove scoperte cogli scavi*, ed. Angiolo Bonelli, 3 vols., Rome: Puccinelli, 1820.

Fergusson 1849   James Fergusson, *An Historical Inquiry into the True Principles of Beauty in Art, More Especially with Reference to Architecture*, London: Longman, Brown, Green & Longmans, 1849.

Fick 1793   Johann Christian Fick, *Praktische englische Sprachlehre für Deutsche beyderley Geschlechts*, Erlangen: Walther, 1793.

Fischer 1808   Ernst Gottfried Fischer, *Untersuchung über den eigentlichen Sinn der höheren Analysis; nebst einer idealischen Übersicht der Mathematik und Naturkunde nach ihrem ganzen Umfang*, Berlin: Weiss, 1808.

Flandin/Coste 1851   Eugène Flandin and Pascal Coste, *Voyage en Perse pendant les années 1840 et 1841*, 8 vols. (vols. 1–3, text; vols. 4–8, plates), Paris: Gide & Baudry, 1851.

Forkel 1777   Johann Nicolaus Forkel, *Ueber die Theorie der Musik, insofern sie Liebhabern und Kennern nothwendig und nützlich ist: Eine Einladungsschrift zu musikalischen Vorlesungen*, Göttingen: Vandenhoeck, 1777.

Fossati 1852   Gaspare Fossati, *Aya Sofia, Constantinople, as Recently Restored by Order of H. M. the Sultan Abdul Medjid*, London: Colnaghi, 1852.

Francœur 1809   Louis-Benjamin Francœur, *Cours complet de mathématiques pures*, 2 vols., Paris: Courcier, 1809.

Gärtner 1837   Julius Gärtner, *Über die Mängel der Privat-Wohnhäuser in Städten, sowohl in Hinsicht der baulichen Beschaffenheit, als der zweckmässigen Einrichtung der Wohnungen*, Hamburg: Meissner, 1837.

Gau 1822   Franz Christian Gau, *Antiquités de la Nubie, ou Monumens inédits des bords du Nil, situés entre la première et la seconde cataracte*, Stuttgart: Cotta; Paris: Didot, 1822.

Geppert 1843   Carl Eduard Geppert, *Die altgriechische Bühne*, Leipzig: Weigel, 1843.

Gille 1835/53   Floriant Gille, *Musée de Tzarskoe-Selo, ou Collection d'armes de Sa Majesté l'Empereur de toutes les Russies*, 3 vols., St Petersburg: Velten, 1835–53.

Gilly 1805   David Gilly, *Handbuch der Land-Bau-Kunst, vorzüglich in Rücksicht auf die Konstruktion der Wohn- und Wirthschaftsgebäude, für angehende Kameral-Baumeister und Oekonomen*, 3rd ed., 2 vols., Brunswick: Vieweg, 1805.

Gilly/Eytelwein 1802/08   David Gilly and Johann Albert Eytelwein (eds.), *Praktische Anweisung zur Wasserbaukunst, welche eine Anleitung zur Entwerfung, Veranschlagung und Ausführung der am gewöhnlichsten vorkommenden Wasserbaue enthält*, 4 fascs., Berlin: Realschulbuchhandlung, 1802–08. (Fascs. 1–2 edited by Gilly and Eytelwein; fascs. 3–4 edited by Eytelwein.)

Graffenried/Stürler 1844   Adolf von Graffenried and Ludwig Stürler, *Architecture suisse, ou Choix de maisons rustiques des Alpes du canton de Berne*, Berne: Burgdorfer, 1844.

Grotefend 1822   Georg Friedrich Grotefend, *Kleine lateinische Grammatik für Schulen*, Frankfurt am Main: Warrentrapp, 1822.

Grüson 1798   Johann Philipp Grüson, *Supplement zu L. Eulers Differenzialrechnung*, Berlin: Lagarde, 1798.

Hachette 1822   Jean-Nicolas-Pierre Hachette, *Traité de géométrie descriptive, comprenant les applications de cette géométrie aux ombres, à la perspective et à la stéréotomie*, Paris: Corby; Guillaume, 1822.

Hagen 1818/21   Friedrich Heinrich von der Hagen, *Briefe in die Heimat aus Deutschland, der Schweiz und Italien*, 4 vols., Breslau (Wrocław): Max, 1818–21.

Hamilton 1842   William Richard Hamilton, 'Report of the Committee Appointed to Examine the Elgin Marbles, in Order to Ascertain whether Any Evidences Remain as to the Employment of Color in the Decoration of the Architecture or Sculpture' (24 July 1837), *Transactions of the Royal Institute of British Architects of London, [Sessions 1837–41]* (1842), 102–8.

Heeren 1799   Arnold Hermann Ludwig Heeren, *Handbuch der Geschichte der Staaten des Alterthums: Mit besonderer Rücksicht auf ihre Verfassungen, ihren Handel und ihre Colonieen*, Göttingen: Rosenbusch, 1799.

Heeren 1809   Arnold Hermann Ludwig Heeren, *Handbuch der Geschichte des europäischen Staatensystems und seiner Colonien, von der Entdeckung beyder Indien bis zur Errichtung des französischen Kayserthrons*, Göttingen: Röwer, 1809.

Heeren 1821   Arnold Hermann Ludwig Heeren, *Vermischte historische Schriften*, 3 vols., Historische Werke 1–3, Göttingen: Röwer, 1821.

Heeren 1824/26   Arnold Hermann Ludwig Heeren, *Ideen über die Politik, den Verkehr und den Handel der vornehmsten Völker der alten Welt*, 4th ed., 6 vols., Historische Werke 10–15, Göttingen: Vandenhoeck & Ruprecht, 1824–26.

Hefner-Alteneck 1840/54   Jakob Heinrich von Hefner-Alteneck, *Trachten des christlichen Mittelalters: Nach gleichzeitigen Kunstdenkmalen*, 3 vols., Frankfurt am Main: Keller; Darmstadt: Beyerle, 1840–54.

Heideloff 1838/43   Carl Heideloff, *Nürnbergs Baudenkmale der Vorzeit, oder Musterbuch der altdeutschen Baukunst für Architekten und Gewerbschulen*, 2 fascs., Nuremberg: Campe, 1838–43.

Heideloff 1843/52   Carl Heideloff, *Die Ornamentik des Mittelalters: Eine Sammlung auserwählter Verzierungen und Profile byzantinischer und deutscher Architektur*, 4 vols., Nuremberg: Stein; Geiger, 1843–52.

Heine 1842   Gustav Heine, *Darstellung der allgemeinen Baukunde*, 2nd ed., Dresden: Arnold, 1842.

Heine 1846   Gustav Heine, *Das im Königreiche Sachsen geltende Baurecht: Die das Bauwesen betreffenden Rechtsmaterien*, Dresden: Arnold, 1846.

Herodotus 1848   *Herodotus: A New and Literal Version from the Text of Baehr*, trans. Henry Cary, London: Bohn, 1848.

Hetsch 1840   Gustav Friederich Hetsch, *Leitfaden zu dem Studium und der Anwendung der Perspective*, Copenhagen: Gyldendal, 1840.

Hirsch 1804   Meier Hirsch, *Sammlung von Beyspielen, Formeln und Aufgaben aus der Buchstabenrechnung und Algebra*, Berlin: Frölich, 1804.

Hirt 1821/27   Aloys Hirt, *Die Geschichte der Baukunst bei den Alten*, 3 vols., Berlin: Reimer, 1821–27.

Hittorff 1851a   Jacques Ignace Hittorff, *Restitution du temple d'Empédocle à Sélinonte, ou L'architecture polychrôme chez les Grecs*, 2 vols. (vol. 1, text; vol. 2, plates), Paris: Didot, 1851.

Hittorff 1851b   Jacques Ignace Hittorff, 'On the Polychromy of Greek Architecture', *The Museum of Classical Antiquities* 1, no. 1 (Jan. 1851), 20–34.

Hittorff/Zanth 1826/30   Jacques Ignace Hittorff and Ludwig Zanth, *Architecture antique de la Sicile, ou Recueil des plus intéressans monumens d'architecture des villes et des lieux les plus remarquables de la Sicile ancienne*, 8 fascs., Paris: Renouard; Bance, [1827].

Homer 1784   Homer, *Odyssea; cum Batrachomyomachia hymnis ceterisque poematiis Homero vulgo tributis etiam nuper reperto hymno in Cererem*, ed. Friedrich August Wolf, Halle: Waisenhaus, 1784.

Homer 1785   Homer, *Ilias*, ed. Friedrich August Wolf, Halle: Waisenhaus, 1785.

Humboldt 1845/62   Alexander von Humboldt, *Kosmos: Entwurf einer physischen Weltbeschreibung*, 5 vols., Stuttgart: Cotta, 1845–62.

Indian Archipelago 1851   *Indian Archipelago: Articles Collected by the Local Committee of Singapore for the Exhibition of Arts and Industry of All Nations*, [Singapore]: s.n., [1851].

Isabeau 1827   Alexandre Isabeau, *Perspective pratique, comprenant la perspective linéaire et aérienne, et les notions du dessin linéaire, à l'usage des ouvriers*, Paris: Malher, 1827.

Jagemann 1790/91   Christian Joseph Jagemann, *Italienisch-deutsches und deutsch-italienisches Wörterbuch*, 2 vols., Leipzig: Severin, 1790–91.

Jones 1842/45   Owen Jones, *Plans, Elevations, Sections, and Details of the Alhambra*, 2 vols., London: Jones, 1842–45.

Jubinal 1837/54   Achille Jubinal, *La Armeria real, ou Collection des principales pièces de la Galerie d'armes anciennes de Madrid*, 3 vols., Paris: Didron, 1837–54.

Kästner 1816   Christian August Lebrecht Kästner, *Topik, oder Erfindungswissenschaft, aufs Neue erläutert und in ihrer vielfachen Anwendung auf die Bildung des menschlichen Geistes und auf den mündlichen Vortrag gezeigt*, Leipzig: Kummer, 1816.

Klemm 1837   Gustav Klemm, *Zur Geschichte der Sammlungen für Wissenschaft und Kunst in Deutschland*, Zerbst: Kummer, 1837.

Klemm 1843/52   Gustav Klemm, *Allgemeine Cultur-Geschichte der Menschheit*, 10 vols., Leipzig: Teubner, 1843–52.

Knochenhauer 1842   Karl Wilhelm Knochenhauer, *Die Statik der Gewölbe mit Rücksicht auf ihre Anwendung*, Berlin: Reimer, 1842.

Koch 1834   Joseph Anton Koch, *Moderne Kunstchronik: Briefe zweier Freunde in Rom und der Tartarei über das moderne Kunstleben und Treiben; oder Die Rumfordische Suppe*, Karlsruhe: Velten, 1834.

Köppen 1787/92   Johann Heinrich Justus Köppen, *Erklärende Anmerkungen zum Homer*, 5 vols., Hanover: Schmidt, 1787–92.

Kreuter 1848   Franz Jakob Kreuter, *Die Verbindung der untern Donau mit dem Adriatischen Meere durch eine Eisenbahn von Semlin nach Fiume*, Vienna: Gerold, 1848.

Kugler 1835   Franz Kugler, *Ueber die Polychromie der griechischen Architektur und Sculptur und ihre Grenzen*, Berlin: Gropius, 1835.

Kugler 1836   Franz Kugler, 'On the Polychromy of Greek Architecture', trans. William Richard Hamilton, *Transactions of the Institute of British Architects of London, Sessions 1835–36* (1836), 73–99.

Lacroix/Seré 1848/51   Paul Lacroix and Ferdinand Seré (eds.), *Le Moyen-Âge et la Renaissance: Histoire et description des mœurs et usages, du commerce et de l'industrie, des sciences, des arts, des littératures et des beaux-arts en Europe*, 5 vols., Paris: Plon, 1848–51.

Lagrange 1806   Joseph-Louis Lagrange, *Leçons sur le calcul des fonctions*, new ed., Paris: Courcier, 1806.

Lalande 1802   Jérôme de Lalande (La Lande), *Tables de logaritmes pour les nombres et pour les sinus*, Paris: Didot, 1802.

Lanci 1845/46   Michelangelo Lanci, *Trattato delle simboliche rappresentanze arabiche e della varia generazione de' musulmani caratteri sopra differenti materie operati: Seconda opera cufica*, 3 vols., Paris: Dondey-Dupré, 1845–46.

Lastri 1797/99   Marco Lastri, *L'osservatore fiorentino sugli edifizj della sua patria*, 2nd ed., 8 vols., Florence: Pagani, 1797–99.

Layard 1849   Austen Henry Layard, *Nineveh and its Remains: With an Account of a Visit to the Chaldaean Christians of Kurdistan, and the Yezidis, or Devil-Worshippers, and an Enquiry into the Manners and Arts of the Ancient Assyrians*, 2 vols., London: Murray, 1849.

Layard 1849/53   Austen Henry Layard, *The Monuments of Nineveh*, 2 vols., London: Murray, 1849–53.

Layard 1851   Austen Henry Layard, *A Popular Account of Discoveries at Nineveh*, London: Murray, 1851.

Leibniz 1707/11   Gottfried Wilhelm Leibniz, *Scriptores rerum Brunsvicensium*, 3 vols., Hanover: Förster, 1707–11.

Leo Marsicanus 1513   Leo Marsicanus, *Chronica sacri Casinensis coenobii nuper impressoriae arti tradita, ac nunquam alias impressa*, ed. Lorenzo Vicentino, Venice: de' Soardi, 1513.

Lessing 1766 Gotthold Ephraim Lessing, *Laokoon, oder Über die Grenzen der Mahlerey und Poesie: Mit beyläufigen Erläuterungen verschiedener Punkte der alten Kunstgeschichte*, Berlin: Voss, 1766.

Letarouilly 1840/57 Paul Letarouilly, *Édifices de Rome moderne, ou Recueil des palais, maisons, églises, couvents, et autres monuments publics et particuliers les plus remarquables de la ville de Rome*, 6 vols. (vols. 1–3, text; vols. 4–6, plates), Paris: Didot; Bance, 1840–57.

Letronne 1835 Antoine Jean Letronne, *Lettres d'un antiquaire à un artiste sur l'emploi de la peinture historique murale dans la décoration des temples et des autres édifices publics ou particuliers chez les Grecs et les Romains*, Paris: Heideloff & Campé, 1835.

Linke 1840 Gustav Linke, *Der Bau der flachen Dächer unter Benutzung des Lehms, der Lehmplatten, der verschiedenen Mastic-Compositionen, der Harzplatten, der Pappe, des Asphalts, der künstlichen Erdharze und des Oel-Cements*, 2nd ed., Brunswick: Vieweg, 1840.

Lorenz 1785/86 Johann Friedrich Lorenz, *Die Elemente der Mathematik in sechs Büchern*, 2 vols., Leipzig: Müller, 1785–86.

Luynes/Debacq 1833 Honoré Théodoric d'Albert de Luynes and Frédéric Joseph Debacq, *Métaponte*, Paris: Renouard, 1833.

Magasin pittoresque 1851a 'Orfévrerie antique: Patère d'or de Rennes', *Le Magasin pittoresque* 19, no. 25 (June 1851), 199–200.

Magasin pittoresque 1851b 'Tombeau de Childéric Ier', *Le Magasin pittoresque* 19, no. 34 (Aug. 1851), 271–2.

Magazin 1780/85 *Magazin der italienischen Litteratur und Künste*, ed. Christian Joseph Jagemann, 8 vols., Weimar, 1780–85.

Marot 1659 Jean Marot, *Recueil des plans, profils et eleuations des plusieurs palais, chasteaux, eglises, sepultures, grotes et hostels, bâtis dans Paris, et aux enuirons*, [Paris]: s.n., [c. 1659].

Marot 1731 Clément Marot, *Œuvres: Avec les ouvrages de Jean Marot son pere, ceux de Michel Marot son fils, & les piéces du different de Clement avec François Sagon*, 4 vols., The Hague: Gosse & Neaulme, 1731.

Marryat 1850 Joseph Marryat, *Collections towards a History of Pottery and Porcelain, in the 15th, 16th, 17th, and 18th Centuries: With a Description of the Manufacture, a Glossary, and a List of Monograms*, London: Murray, 1850.

Mayer 1801 Johann Tobias Mayer, *Anfangsgründe der Naturlehre zum Behuf der Vorlesungen über die Experimental-Physik*, Göttingen: Dieterich, 1801.

Meiser 1840 Franz Meiser, *Das königliche neue Hof- und Nationaltheater-Gebäude zu München, seine innere Einrichtung, Maschinerie und die angeordneten Feuer-Sicherheitsmassregeln*, Munich: Franz, 1840.

Meissner 1821 Paul Traugott Meissner, *Die Heitzung mit erwärmter Luft als das wohlfeilste, bequemste und zugleich die Feuersgefahr am meisten entfernende Mittel zur Erwärmung grösserer Räume, als: der öffentlichen Gebäude, der Herrschaftswohnungen, Fabriken &c.*, Vienna: Gerold, 1821.

Metzger 1835 Johann Metzger, *Gesetze der Pflanzen- und Mineralienbildung, angewendet auf altdeutschen Baustyl*, Stuttgart: Schweizerbart, 1835.

Meyrick 1824 Samuel Rush Meyrick, *A Critical Inquiry into Antient Armour, as it Existed in Europe, but Particularly in England, from the Norman Conquest to the Reign of King Charles II*, 1st ed., 3 vols., London: Jennings, 1824.

Meyrick 1830 Samuel Rush Meyrick, *Engraved Illustrations of Antient Arms and Armour, from the Collection of Llewelyn Meyrick at Goodrich Court, Herefordshire*, ed. Joseph Skelton, 2 vols., London: Schulze, 1830.

Meyrick 1842 Samuel Rush Meyrick, *A Critical Inquiry into Ancient Armour, as it Existed in Europe, Particularly in Great Britain, from the Norman Conquest to the Reign of King Charles II*, 2nd ed., 3 vols., London: Bohn, 1842.

Miché 1825 Alexandre Miché, *Nouvelle architecture pratique, ou Bullet rectifié et entièrement refondu*, ed. Adolphe François Marie Jaÿ, 2nd ed., 2 vols., Paris: Villet, 1825.

Milizia 1781 Francesco Milizia, *Principj di architettura civile*, 3 vols., Finale Ligure: de' Rossi, 1781.

Millin 1802/06 Aubin-Louis Millin, *Monumens antiques, inédits ou nouvellement expliqués: Collection de statues, bas-reliefs, bustes, peintures, mosaïques, gravures, vases, inscriptions, médailles, et instrumens*, 2 vols., Paris: Imprimerie impériale, 1802–06.

Mitterer 1817 Hermann Mitterer, *Die deutsche Zimmerwerks-Kunst als Fortsetzung der bürgerlichen Baukunst und Bauzeichnung*, Munich: Lithographische Kunst-Anstalt bey der Feyertags-Schule, 1817.

Mittheilungen 1835/63 *Mittheilungen des Königlich Sächsischen Vereins für Erforschung und Erhaltung vaterländischer Alterthümer*, 13 vols., Dresden, 1835–63. (Vols. 1–3 entitled *Mittheilungen des Königl. Sächs. Vereins für Erforschung und Erhaltung der vaterländischen Alterthümer*.)

Moller/Gladbach 1815/51 Georg Moller and Ernst Gladbach, *Denkmähler der deutschen Baukunst: Beiträge zur Kenntniss der deutschen Baukunst des Mittelalters, enthaltend eine chronologisch geordnete Reihe von Werken*, *aus dem Zeitraume vom achten bis zum sechszehnten Jahrhundert*, 3 vols., Darmstadt: Heyer & Leske, 1815–51. (Vols. 1–2 by Moller; vol. 3, entitled *Denkmäler der deutschen Baukunst*, by Gladbach.)

Montfaucon 1729/33   Bernard de Montfaucon, *Les monumens de la monarchie françoise, qui comprennent l'histoire de France*, 5 vols., Paris: Gandouin; Giffart, 1729–33.

Monumenti inediti 1829/85   Instituto di corrispondenza archeologica, *Monumenti inediti*, 12 vols., Rome: A spese dell'Instituto di corrispondenza archeologica, 1829–85.

Müller 1820   Karl Otfried Müller, *Minervae Poliadis sacra et aedem in arce Athenarum: Adiecta est interpretatio inscriptionis Atticae quae ad architecturam aedis huius pertinet*, Göttingen: Röwer, 1820.

Müller 1820/24   Karl Otfried Müller, *Geschichten hellenischer Stämme und Städte*, 3 vols., Breslau (Wrocław): Max, 1820–24.

Müller 1830   Karl Otfried Müller, *Handbuch der Archäologie der Kunst*, Breslau (Wrocław): Max, 1830.

Müller 1831   Karl Otfried Müller, 'Ueber die erhobenen Bildwerke in den Metopen und am Friese des Parthenons, besonders in Rücksicht auf ihre Composition', in Stuart/Revett 1829/33, vol. 2, 657–96.

Murphy 1815   James Cavanah Murphy, *The Arabian Antiquities of Spain*, London: Cadell & Davies, 1815.

Murr 1799   Christoph Gottlieb von Murr, *Merkwürdigkeiten der fürstbischöflichen Residenzstadt Bamberg*, Nuremberg: Grattenauer, 1799.

Murr 1801   Christoph Gottlieb von Murr, *Beschreibung der ehemals zu Aachen aufbewahrten drey kaiserlichen Krönungs-Zierden, des lateinischen Evangelienbuches, des arabischen Säbels Karls des Grossen, und der Capsul mit der Erde, worauf das Blut des heiligen Stephans soll geflossen seyn*, Nuremberg: Monath & Kussler, 1801.

Nagler 1835/52   Georg Kaspar Nagler, *Neues allgemeines Künstler-Lexicon*, 22 vols., Munich: Fleischmann, 1835–52.

Nardi 1582   Jacopo Nardi, *Le historie della città di Fiorenza*, Lyon: Ancelin, 1582.

Newton 1822   Isaac Newton, *Philosophiae naturalis principia mathematica; perpetuis commentariis illustrata, communi studio PP. Thomae Le Seur et Francisci Jacquier*, new ed., 4 vols., Glasgow: Duncan, 1822.

Normand 1819   Charles Normand, *Nouveau parallèle des ordres d'architecture des Grecs, des Romains, et des auteurs modernes*, Paris: Didot, 1819.

Nuovissima guida 1842   *Nuovissima guida dei viaggiatori in Italia*, Milan: Artaria, 1842.

Pauthier 1839   Guillaume Pauthier, *Chine, ou Description historique, géographique et littéraire de ce vaste empire, d'après des documents chinois*, L'Univers, ou Histoire et description de tous les peuples, de leurs religions, mœurs, coutumes, etc., Paris: Didot, 1839. (Series entitled 'L'Univers pittoresque' on cover.)

Pauthier 1853   Guillaume Pauthier, 'Géographie, organisation politique et administrative de la Chine, langues, philosophie', in Guillaume Pauthier and Antoine-Pierre-Louis Bazin, *Chine moderne, ou Description historique, géographique et littéraire de ce vaste empire, d'après des documents chinois*, L'Univers, ou Histoire et description de tous les peuples, de leurs religions, mœurs, coutumes, etc., Paris: Didot, 1853, 1–390. (Series entitled 'L'Univers pittoresque' on cover.)

Péclet 1844   Eugène Péclet, *Traité de la chaleur, considérée dans ses applications*, 3rd ed., Liège: Avanzo, 1844.

Penrose 1851   Francis Cranmer Penrose, *An Investigation of the Principles of Athenian Architecture, or The Results of a Recent Survey Conducted Chiefly with Reference to the Optical Refinements Exhibited in the Construction of the Ancient Buildings at Athens*, London: Longman; Murray, 1851.

Philostratus 1774   Flavius Philostratus, *Vie d'Apollonius de Tyane*, trans. Giovanni Francesco Salvemini, 4 vols., Berlin: Decker, 1774.

Pölitz 1808   Karl Heinrich Ludwig Pölitz, *Kleine Weltgeschichte, oder Compendiarische Darstellung der Universalgeschichte für höhere und niedere Lehrinstitute*, Leipzig: Hinrichs, 1808.

Polo 1845   *Die Reisen des Venezianers Marco Polo im dreizehnten Jahrhundert*, trans. August Bürck, Leipzig: Teubner, 1845.

Primisser 1819   Alois Primisser, *Die kaiserlich-königliche Ambraser-Sammlung*, Vienna: Heubner, 1819.

Pugin 1837   Augustus Welby Northmore Pugin, *Details of Antient Timber Houses of the 15th & 16th Centuries, Selected from Those Existing at Rouen, Caen, Beauvais, Gisors, Abbeville, Strasbourg, etc.*, London: Ackermann, 1837.

Quaglio 1811   Johann Maria von Quaglio, *Praktische Anleitung zur Perspektiv mit Anwendungen auf die Baukunst*, Munich: Lithographische Kunst-Anstalt, 1811.

Quandt 1838   Johann Gottlob von Quandt, *Kleines A-B-C-Buch für Anfänger im Lesen und Schreiben: Synonymen und Homonymen*, Leipzig: Brockhaus, 1838.

Quast 1842   Alexander Ferdinand von Quast, *Die altchristlichen Bauwerke von Ravenna vom fünften bis zum neunten Jahrhundert*, Berlin: Reimer, 1842.

Quatremère de Quincy 1815   Antoine Chrysostome Quatremère de Quincy, *Le Jupiter olympien, ou L'art de la sculpture antique considéré sous un nouveau point de vue*, Paris: de Bure, 1815.

Quénot 1828   Jacques-Pierre Quénot, *Mémoire sur le pont suspendu en fil de fer, construit sur la Charente, à Jarnac, et détails de sa construction*, Paris: Bachelier; Carilian-Gœury, 1828.

Ramée 1846   Daniel Ramée, *Histoire de l'architecture en France, depuis les Romains jusqu'au seizième siècle*, Paris: Franck, 1846.

Real Museo Borbonico 1824/57   Antonio Niccolini, Fausto Niccolini and Felice Niccolini (eds.), *Real Museo Borbonico*, 16 vols., Naples: Stamperia reale, 1824–57. (Vols. 1–13 edited by Antonio Niccolini; vols. 14–16 edited by Fausto Niccolini and Felice Niccolini.)

Reimer 1782   Johann Reimer, *Holz-Tafeln nebst Abhandlung von der Art, Holz zu messen*, Hamburg: Meyn, 1782.

Revue archéologique   *Revue archéologique, ou Recueil de documents et de mémoires relatifs à l'étude des monuments et à la philologie de l'Antiquité et du Moyen Âge*, Paris, since 1844.

Revue générale 1840/90   *Revue générale de l'architecture et des travaux publics*, ed. César Daly, 45 vols., Paris, 1840–90.

Richter 1835   Adolph Friedrich Richter, *Neueste Darstellung der kaiserl. königl. Ambraser-Sammlung im Belvedere in Wien*, Vienna: Haas, 1835.

Romberg 1831/33   Johann Andreas Romberg, *Die Zimmerwerks-Baukunst in allen ihren Theilen*, 10 fascs., Augsburg: Zanna, 1831–33.

Rondelet 1833/36   Jean Rondelet, *Theoretisch-praktische Anleitung zur Kunst zu bauen*, trans. Carl Heinrich Distelbarth and Johannes Hess, 5 vols., Leipzig: Leske, 1833–36.

Rotteck 1835   Carl von Rotteck, *Allgemeine Geschichte vom Anfang der historischen Kenntniss bis auf unsere Zeiten*, 11th ed., 3 vols., Freiburg im Breisgau: Herder, 1835.

Rumohr 1816/23   Carl Friedrich von Rumohr, *Sammlung für Kunst und Historie*, 2 vols., Hamburg: Perthes & Besser, 1816–23.

Rumohr 1827/31   Carl Friedrich von Rumohr, *Italienische Forschungen*, 3 vols., Berlin: Nicolai, 1827–31.

Rumohr 1832   Carl Friedrich von Rumohr, *Drey Reisen nach Italien: Erinnerungen*, Leipzig: Brockhaus, 1832.

Ryan 1852   John Ryan, *Die Zubereitung von Flachs, Flachsbaumwolle und Flachswolle nach dem Claussen'schen Verfahren*, trans. Theodor Kell, Brunswick: Vieweg, 1852.

Sachs 1810   Salomo Sachs, *Auflösungen der in Meier Hirsch's Sammlung von Beispielen &c. enthaltenen Gleichungen und Aufgaben*, Berlin: Braunes, 1810.

Saulcy 1851   Félicien de Saulcy, 'Armurerie', in Lacroix/Seré 1848/51, vol. 4, unpag.

Schaaff 1806/08   Johann Christian Ludwig Schaaff, *Encyclopädie der classischen Alterthumskunde: Ein Lehrbuch für die oberen Classen gelehrter Schulen*, 2 vols., Magdeburg: Keil; Heinrichshofen, 1806–08.

Scheller 1788   Immanuel Johann Gerhard Scheller, *Ausführliches und möglichst vollständiges lateinisch-deutsches Lexicon oder Wörterbuch zum Behufe der Erklärung der Alten und Übung in der lateinischen Sprache*, 2nd ed., 3 vols., Leipzig: Fritsch, 1788.

Schneider 1805/06   Johann Gottlob Schneider, *Kritisches griechisch-deutsches Wörterbuch, beym Lesen der griechischen profanen Scribenten zu gebrauchen*, 2nd ed., 2 vols., Jena: Frommann, 1805–06.

Schönsleder 1630   Wolfgang Schönsleder, *Apparatus eloquentiae, in quo Latinae linguae opes, ex antiquis probisque scriptoribus depromptae, & in locos communes digestae, ad orationem ornandam, variandam amplificandámque repraesentantur*, Munich: Heinrich, 1630.

Ségur 1825   Paul-Philippe de Ségur, *Histoire de Napoléon et de la grande-armée pendant l'année 1812*, 5th ed., 2 vols., Paris: Baudouin, 1825.

Serlio 1537   Sebastiano Serlio, *Regole generali di architetura sopra le cinque maniere de gli edifici*, Venice: Marcolini da Forli, 1537.

Serlio 1559/62   Sebastiano Serlio, *Libri d'architettura*, 5 vols., Venice: Sessa; Rampazetto, 1559–62. (Each vol. with its own title; vol. 4 undated.)

Serlio 1619   Sebastiano Serlio, *Tutte l'opere d'architettura, et prospetiva, diviso in sette libri*, Venice: de' Franceschi, 1619.

Serradifalco 1834/42   Domenico Lo Faso Pietrasanta di Serradifalco, *Le antichità della Sicilia*, 5 vols., Palermo: Tipografia del Giornale letterario et al., 1834–42.

Shaw/Meyrick 1836   Henry Shaw and Samuel Rush Meyrick, *Specimens of Ancient Furniture*, London: Pickering, 1836.

Stackelberg 1826   Otto Magnus von Stackelberg, *Der Apollotempel zu Bassae in Arcadien und die daselbst ausgegrabenen Bildwerke*, Rome: s.n., 1826.

Stieglitz 1834   Christian Ludwig Stieglitz, *Beiträge zur Geschichte der Ausbildung der Baukunst*, Leipzig: Schaarschmidt, 1834.

Writings Cited by Gottfried Semper

Strobel 1819   Georg Strobel, *Practisches Lehrbuch des Steinschnitts der Bögen, Gewölbe und Treppen*, Heidelberg: Oswald, 1819.

Stuart/Revett 1829/33   James Stuart and Nicholas Revett, *Die Alterthümer von Athen*, 3 vols., trans. Karl Wagner and Friedrich Osann, Darmstadt: Leske, 1829–33. (Vol. 3, entitled *Alterthümer von Athen und andern Orten Griechenlands, Siciliens und Kleinasiens*, by Charles Robert Cockerell et al.)

Tacitus 1752   Cornelius Tacitus, *Opera*, ed. Johann August Ernesti, 2 vols., Leipzig: Weidmann, 1752.

Texier 1839/49   Charles Texier, *Description de l'Asie Mineure faite par ordre du gouvernement français, de 1833 à 1837*, 3 vols., Paris: Didot, 1839–49.

Thibault 1827   Jean-Thomas Thibault, *Application de la perspective linéaire aux arts du dessin*, ed. Nicolas Chapuis, Paris: Thibault et al., 1827.

Thibaut 1801   Bernhard Friedrich Thibaut, *Grundriss der reinen Mathematik, zum Gebrauch bey academischen Vorlesungen*, Göttingen: Schröder, 1801.

Thibaut 1809   Bernhard Friedrich Thibaut, *Grundriss der allgemeinen Arithmetik oder Analysis, zum Gebrauch bey academischen Vorlesungen*, Göttingen: Dieterich, 1809.

Thierry 1823   Jules-Denis Thierry, *Le Vignole de poche, ou Mémorial des artistes, des propriétaires et des ouvriers, contenant les règles des cinq ordres d'architecture*, Paris: Audot, 1823.

Thiersch 1816/25   Friedrich Thiersch, *Ueber die Epochen der bildenden Kunst unter den Griechen*, 3 fascs., Munich: Lindauer, [1816–25].

Tielcke 1769   Johann Gottlieb Tielcke, *Unterricht für die Officiers, die sich zu Feld-Ingenieurs bilden, oder doch den Feldzügen mit Nutzen beywohnen wollen*, Dresden: Gerlach, 1769.

Toelken 1839   Ernst Heinrich Toelken, *Über den protestantischen Geist aller wahrhaften Kunst und deren neuere Entwickelung in Deutschland: Ein Vortrag gehalten in der öffentlichen Sitzung der Königlichen Akademie der Künste am 3ten August 1839*, Berlin: Druckerei der Königlichen Akademie der Wissenschaften, 1839.

Unedited Antiquities of Attica 1817   Society of Dilettanti, *The Unedited Antiquities of Attica: Comprising the Architectural Remains of Eleusis, Rhamnus, Sunium, and Thoricus*, London: Longman, Hurst, Rees, Orme & Brown; Murray, 1817.

Vagnat 1827   Joseph-Marie Vagnat, *Dictionnaire d'architecture contenant les noms et termes dont cette science exige la connaissance, et des autres arts accessoires*, Grenoble: Baratier, 1827.

Valentini 1812   Georg Wilhelm von Valentini, *Versuch einer Geschichte des Feldzugs von 1809 an der Donau*, Berlin: Nikolai, 1812.

Vallée 1821   Louis Léger Vallée, *Traité de la science du dessin*, 2 vols. (vol. 1, text; vol. 2, plates), Paris: Courcier, 1821.

Vega 1793   Georg von Vega, *Logarithmisch-trigonometrisches Handbuch, anstatt der kleinen Vlackischen, Wolfischen, und andern dergleichen, meistens sehr fehlerhaften, logarithmisch-trigonometrischen Tafeln*, Leipzig: Weidmann, 1793.

Vega 1812   Georg von Vega, *Logarithmisch-trigonometrische Tafeln; nebst andern zum Gebrauch der Mathematik eingerichteten Tafeln und Formeln*, 3rd ed., 2 vols., Leipzig: Weidmann, 1812.

Vieth 1796/1821   Gerhard Ulrich Anton Vieth, *Anfangsgründe der Mathematik*, 4 vols., Leipzig: Barth, 1796–1821.

Viger 1802   François Viger, *De praecipuis Graecae dictionis idiotismis liber*, ed. Gottfried Hermann, Leipzig: Fritschi, 1802.

Vitruvius 1567   Vitruvius, *De architectura libri decem, cum commentariis Danielis Barbari*, Venice: de' Franceschi & Chrieger, 1567.

Volney 1788/1800   Constantin-François Volney, *Reise nach Syrien und Aegypten in den Jahren 1783, 1784, 1785*, 3 vols., Jena: Mauke, 1788–1800.

Wagner 1833   Friedrich August Wagner, *Aegypten in Deutschland, oder Die germanisch-slavischen, wo nicht rein germanischen Alterthümer an der schwarzen Elster*, Leipzig: Hartmann, 1833.

Wagner 1838   Georg Wagner, *Die Aesthetik der Baukunst: Ein Leitfaden zum Selbstunterricht und Handgebrauche für Architekten, Maurer-, Zimmer-, Steinmetz-Meister und Freunde der Baukunst*, Dresden: Arnold, 1838.

Weber 1770   Johann Adam Weber, *Lexicon encyclion, oder Kurzgefasstes lateinischdeutsches und deutschlateinisches Universal-Wörterbuch*, ed. Johann Daniel Heyde, 3rd ed., 3 vols., Dresden: Walther, 1770.

Weinbrenner 1809   Friedrich Weinbrenner, *Über Theater in architektonischer Hinsicht mit Beziehung auf Plan und Ausführung des neuen Hoftheaters zu Carlsruhe*, Tübingen: Cotta, 1809.

Weisbach 1835/36   Julius Weisbach, *Handbuch der Bergmaschinenmechanik*, 2 vols., Leipzig: Weidmann, 1835–36.

Weisbach 1845/46   Julius Weisbach, *Lehrbuch der Ingenieur- und Maschinen-Mechanik*, 2 vols., Brunswick: Vieweg, 1845–46.

Weisbach 1848   Julius Weisbach, *Der Ingenieur: Sammlung von Tafeln, Formeln und Regeln der Arithmetik, Geometrie und Mechanik*, Brunswick: Vieweg, 1848.

Weisbach 1849   Julius Weisbach, *Die ersten Grundlehren der höhern Analysis oder Differenzial- und Integralrechnung*, Brunswick: Vieweg, 1849.

Wiegmann 1836   Rudolf Wiegmann, *Die Malerei der Alten in ihrer Anwendung und Technik, insbesondere als Decorationsmalerei; nebst einer Vorrede vom Hofrathe K. O. Müller in Göttingen*, Hanover: Hahn, 1836.

Willemin/Pottier 1839   Nicolas-Xavier Willemin and André Pottier, *Monuments français inédits pour servir à l'histoire des arts depuis le VIᵉ siècle jusqu'au commencement du XVIIᵉ: Choix de costumes civils et militaires, d'armes, armures, instruments de musique, meubles de toute espèce, et de décorations intérieures et extérieures des maisons*, 2 vols., Paris: Willemin, 1839.

Winckelmann 1760   Johann Joachim Winckelmann, *Description des pierres gravées du feu baron de Stosch*, Florence: Bonducci, 1760.

Wolf 1795   Friedrich August Wolf, *Prolegomena ad Homerum*, Halle: Waisenhaus, 1795.

Wolff 1831   Johann Heinrich Wolff, *Ueber Plan und Methode bei dem Studium der Architectur*, Leipzig: Leske, 1831.

Wolff 1834   Johann Heinrich Wolff, *Beiträge zur Aesthetik der Baukunst, oder Die Grundgesetze der plastischen Form, nachgewiesen an den Haupttheilen der griechischen Architectur*, Leipzig: Leske, 1834.

Zesen 1664   Philipp von Zesen, *Beschreibung der Stadt Amsterdam*, Amsterdam: Nosch, 1664.

Ziegler 1850   Jules Ziegler, *Études céramiques: Recherche des principes du beau dans l'architecture, l'art céramique et la forme en général*, Paris: Mathias; Paulin, 1850.

Secondary Sources

Ahrens 1886a   Jürgen Friedrich Ahrens, *Die Reform des Kunstgewerbes in ihrem geschichtlichen Entwickelungsgange*, Berlin: Habel, 1886. (Offprint from *Deutsche Zeit- und Streit-Fragen: Flugschriften zur Kenntniss der Gegenwart*, new ser., 1, no. 9/10 [1886], 333–96.)

Ahrens 1886b   Jürgen Friedrich Ahrens, 'Gottfried Semper's Antheil an der Reform des Kunstgewerbes', *Hamburgischer Correspondent*, no. 56 (25 Feb. 1886, evening issue), 4–6; no. 58 (27 Feb. 1886, evening issue), 5–6; no. 60 (1 March 1886, evening issue), 4–5; no. 61 (2 March 1886, evening issue), 5; no. 62 (3 March 1886, evening issue), 5–6.

Amtl. Ber. 1852/53   *Amtlicher Bericht über die Industrie-Ausstellung aller Völker zu London im Jahre 1851, von der Berichterstattungs-Kommission der Deutschen Zollvereins-Regierungen*, 3 vols., Berlin: Decker, 1852–53.

Amtl. Cat. 1851   *Amtlicher Catalog der Ausstellung der Industrie-Erzeugnisse aller Völker, 1851*, trans. Edward Aubrey Moriarty, London: Spicer; Clowes, [1851].

Arburg 2008   Hans Georg von Arburg, *Alles Fassade: 'Oberfläche' in der deutschsprachigen Architektur- und Literaturästhetik 1770–1870*, Munich: Fink, 2008.

Arnoux 1851   Jean-Jacques Arnoux, 'Exposition universelle' (19 June 1851), *La Lumière: Beaux-arts, héliographie, sciences* 1, no. 21 (29 June 1851), 82.

Art-Journal 1851   'The United States in the Great Exhibition', *The Art-Journal*, new ser., 3, no. 8 (1 Aug. 1851), 208–12.

Art-Journal Cat. 1851   *The Industry of All Nations 1851: The Art-Journal Illustrated Catalogue*, London: Virtue, [1851].

Ashton 1986   Rosemary Ashton, *Little Germany: Exile and Asylum in Victorian England*, Oxford: Oxford University Press, 1986.

Ashton 1996   Rosemary Ashton, 'Gottfried Kinkel and University College London', in Peter Alter and Rudolf Muhs (eds.), *Exilanten und andere Deutsche in Fontanes London*, Stuttgart: Heinz, 1996, 23–40.

Atlantis 1854   'Die Deutschen in London (Zweiter Artikel)', *Atlantis: Zeitschrift für Leben und Literatur in England und Amerika* 2, no. 2 (15 Jan. 1854), 29–39.

Baumeister 1735   Friedrich Christian Baumeister, *Institutiones philosophiae rationalis methodo Wolfii conscriptae*, Wittenberg: Ahlfeld, 1735.

Secondary Sources

Becker-Schaum 1993   Christoph Becker-Schaum, *Arnold Herrmann Ludwig Heeren: Ein Beitrag zur Geschichte der Geschichtswissenschaft zwischen Aufklärung und Historismus*, Frankfurt am Main: Lang, 1993.

Beta 1852   [Heinrich Beta], 'Literatur-Briefe über England im Jahre 1852: Fünfter Monatsbericht' (June [1852]), *Magazin für die Literatur des Auslandes* 41–2, nos. 76–9 (24, 26 and 29 June; 1 July 1852), 301–2, 306–7, 309–11, 314–15.

Beyrodt 1979   Wolfgang Beyrodt, *Gottfried Kinkel als Kunsthistoriker: Darstellung und Briefwechsel*, Bonn: Röhrscheid, 1979.

Bonython/Burton 2003   Elizabeth Bonython and Anthony Burton, *The Great Exhibitor: The Life and Work of Henry Cole*, London: V&A Publications, 2003.

Brinckmann 1903   Justus Brinckmann, 'Gottfried Semper und das Kunstgewerbe', *Hamburger Nachrichten*, no. 603 (25 Dec. 1903, morning issue), unpag.

Bryant 2011   Julius Bryant (ed.), *Art and Design for All: The Victoria and Albert Museum*, London: V&A Publishing, 2011.

Bucher 1851   Lothar Bucher, *Kulturhistorische Skizzen aus der Industrieausstellung aller Völker*, Frankfurt am Main: Lizius, 1851.

Bucher 1879   Bruno Bucher, 'Gottfried Semper als Begründer der kunstgewerblichen Reform', *Die Gegenwart: Wochenschrift für Literatur, Kunst und öffentliches Leben* 16, nos. 47–8 (22 and 29 Nov. 1879), 324–8, 344–5.

Buffalo Directory 1851   *The Commercial Advertiser Directory, for the City of Buffalo, 1851–1852*, [Buffalo]: Jewett & Thomas, 1851.

Builder 1852   'The Duke's Funeral', *The Builder* 10, no. 509 (6 Nov. 1852), 709.

Builder 1854a   'Exhibition of Students' Works at Gore House', *The Builder* 12, no. 590 (27 May 1854), 281.

Builder 1854b   'The Architectural Class in the Government Department of Art', *The Builder* 12, no. 592 (10 June 1854), 309.

Burton 1999   Anthony Burton, *Vision & Accident: The Story of the Victoria and Albert Museum*, London: V&A Publications, 1999.

Cantor 2013   Geoffrey Cantor (ed.), *The Great Exhibition: A Documentary History*, 4 vols., London: Pickering & Chatto, 2013.

Cat. DSA 1858   *Catalogue of the Exhibition of Works of Art-Manufacture, Designed or Executed by Students of the Schools of Art in Connexion with the Science and Art De-* *partment of the Committee of Council on Education, South Kensington, London*, London: Eyre & Spottiswoode for Her Majesty's Stationery Office, 1858.

CatM[1]   *A Catalogue of the Articles of Ornamental Art, Selected from the Exhibition of the Works of Industry of All Nations in 1851, and Purchased by the Government*, 1st ed., London: Chapman & Hall, [1852].

CatM[2]   *A Catalogue of the Articles of Ornamental Art, in the Museum of the Department*, 2nd ed., London: Eyre & Spottiswoode for Her Majesty's Stationery Office, 1852.

CatM[3]   *A Catalogue of the Articles of Ornamental Art, in the Museum of the Department*, 3rd ed., London: Eyre & Spottiswoode for Her Majesty's Stationery Office, 1852.

CatM[4]   *A Catalogue of the Articles of Ornamental Art, in the Museum of the Department*, 4th ed. (Feb. 1853), London: Eyre & Spottiswoode for Her Majesty's Stationery Office, 1853.

CatM[5]   *A Catalogue of the Museum of Ornamental Art, at Marlborough House, Pall Mall*, 5th ed. (May 1853), London: Eyre & Spottiswoode for Her Majesty's Stationery Office, 1853.

CatM[6]   *A Catalogue of the Museum of Ornamental Art, at Marlborough House, Pall Mall*, 6th ed. (March 1854), London: Eyre & Spottiswoode for Her Majesty's Stationery Office, 1854.

Charitonidou 2020   Marianna Charitonidou, 'Gottfried Semper's Perplexity before the Crystal Palace: *Stoffwechsel* as Osmosis between Decorative Objects and Architecture', *Faces*, no. 77 (Spring 2020), 63–5.

Chestnova 2014   Elena Chestnova, '"Ornamental Design Is … a Kind of Practical Science": Theories of Ornament at the London School of Design and Department of Science and Art', *Journal of Art Historiography*, no. 11 (Dec. 2014) (https://arthistoriography.files. wordpress.com/2014/11/chestnova.pdf).

Chestnova 2017a   Elena Chestnova, 'History in Things: Gottfried Semper and Popularization of the Arts in London 1850–55', doctoral diss., Mendrisio: Università della Svizzera italiana, 2017.

Chestnova 2017b   Elena Chestnova, 'The House That Semper Built', *Architectural Theory Review* 21, no. 1 (2017), 44–61.

Chestnova 2018   Elena Chestnova, 'Substantial Differences: Semper's *Stoffwechsel* and Truth to Materials', in Sonja Hildebrand, Daniela Mondini and Roberta Grignolo (eds.), *Architecture and Knowledge*, Mendrisio: Mendrisio Academy Press; Cinisello Balsamo: Silvana Editoriale, 2018, 112–25.

Chestnova 2021 Elena Chestnova, 'Vessels of Character', in Gnehm/Hildebrand 2021, 124–41.

Chestnova 2022 Elena Chestnova, *Material Theories and Objects: Gottfried Semper and the Mid-Nineteenth Century*, London: Routledge, 2022.

Cole 1853 Henry Cole, 'An Introductory Lecture on the Facilities Afforded by the Department of Practical Art, to All Classes of the Community for Obtaining Education in Art' (24 Nov. 1852), in *Addresses of the Superintendents of the Department of Practical Art, Delivered at Marlborough House*, London: Chapman & Hall, 1853, 3–38.

Cole 1884 Henry Cole, *Fifty Years of Public Work of Sir Henry Cole*, ed. Alan S. Cole and Henrietta Cole, 2 vols., London: Bell, 1884.

Cole Diary Henry Cole, Diary of the years 1850–54, transcribed by Elizabeth Bonython (NAL, 45.C.112–16).

Cryst. Pal. 1852 *The Crystal Palace, and its Contents: Being an Illustrated Cyclopaedia of the Great Exhibition of the Industry of All Nations, 1851*, London: Clark, 1852.

Delaistre 1825a J.-R. Delaistre (Delaitre), *Manuel de l'architecte et de l'ingénieur: Ouvrage utile aux entrepreneurs, conducteurs de travaux, maitres maçons, charpentiers, contre-maitres, etc., etc.*, Paris: Persan, 1825.

Diephouse 1978 David J. Diephouse, 'Science, Industry and Art: Gottfried Semper's Search for the *Juste Milieu*', *The Journal of the Rutgers University Libraries* 40, no. 1 (1978), 14–31.

Dinius 2012 Marcy J. Dinius, *The Camera and the Press: American Visual and Print Culture in the Age of the Daguerreotype*, Philadelphia: University of Pennsylvania Press, 2012.

Donaldson 1879 Thomas Leverton Donaldson, 'The Late Gottfried Semper of Vienna, Honorary and Corresponding Member', *Royal Institute of British Architects: The Transactions, Session 1878–79* (1879), 233–5.

DPA¹ *First Report of the Department of Practical Art*, London: Eyre & Spottiswoode for Her Majesty's Stationery Office, 1853.

DSA¹ *First Report of the Department of Science and Art*, London: Eyre & Spottiswoode for Her Majesty's Stationery Office, 1854.

DSA² *Second Report of the Department of Science and Art*, London: Eyre & Spottiswoode for Her Majesty's Stationery Office, 1855.

DSA³ *Third Report of the Department of Science and Art*, London: Eyre & Spottiswoode for Her Majesty's Stationery Office, 1856.

DSA⁴ *Fourth Report of the Department of Science and Art*, London: Eyre & Spottiswoode for Her Majesty's Stationery Office, 1857.

DSA⁵ *Fifth Report of the Science and Art Department of the Committee of Council on Education*, London: Eyre & Spottiswoode for Her Majesty's Stationery Office, 1858.

Eck 1994 Caroline van Eck, *Organicism in Nineteenth-Century Architecture: An Inquiry into Its Theoretical and Philosophical Background*, Amsterdam: Architectura & Natura Press, 1994.

Ettlinger 1937 Leopold Ettlinger, *Gottfried Semper und die Antike: Beiträge zur Kunstanschauung des deutschen Klassizismus* (doctoral diss., Halle: Martin-Luther-Universität, 1937), Bleicherode am Harz: Nieft, [1937].

Ettlinger 1940 Leopold Ettlinger, 'The Duke of Wellington's Funeral Car', *Journal of the Warburg and Courtauld Institutes* 3, no. 3/4 (April/July 1940), 254–9.

Ettlinger 1964 Leopold Ettlinger, 'On Science, Industry and Art: Some Theories of Gottfried Semper', *The Architectural Review* 136, no. 809 (July 1964), 57–60.

Explication des ouvrages 1849 *Explication des ouvrages de peinture, sculpture, architecture, gravure et lithographie des artistes vivants, exposés au Palais des Tuileries le 15 Juin 1849*, Paris: Vinchon, 1849.

Franz 2000 Rainald Franz, 'Das System Gottfried Sempers: Reform des Kunstgewerbes und Grundlagen für ein Museum für Kunst und Industrie in ihren Auswirkungen auf das Österreichische Museum', in Peter Noever (ed.), *Kunst und Industrie: Die Anfänge des Museums für angewandte Kunst in Wien*, Ostfildern-Ruit: Hatje Cantz, 2000, 41–51.

Franz/Nierhaus 2007 Rainald Franz and Andreas Nierhaus (eds.), *Gottfried Semper und Wien: Die Wirkung des Architekten auf 'Wissenschaft, Industrie und Kunst'*, Vienna: Böhlau, 2007.

Fraser 2021 Murray Fraser, 'Gottfried Semper and the Globalizing of the London Building World in the 1850s', in Gnehm/Hildebrand 2021, 14–37.

Freitag 2003 Sabine Freitag (ed.), *Exiles from European Revolutions: Refugees in Mid-Victorian England*, New York: Berghahn, 2003.

Gernsheim 1991 Helmut Gernsheim, *Creative Photography: Aesthetic Trends, 1839–1960*, New York: Dover, 1991.

Gibbon 1776/88 Edward Gibbon, *The History of the Decline and Fall of the Roman Empire*, 6 vols., London: Strahan; Cadell, 1776–88.

Giedion 1948   Sigfried Giedion, *Mechanization Takes Command: A Contribution to Anonymous History*, New York: Oxford University Press, 1948.

Gnehm 2003   Michael Gnehm, '"Kritik gegenwärtiger Zustände" als Ursprungskritik – zum dritten Band des Stil', in Nerdinger/Oechslin 2003, 314–20.

Gnehm 2004   Michael Gnehm, *Stumme Poesie: Architektur und Sprache bei Gottfried Semper*, Zurich: gta Verlag, 2004.

Gnehm 2007   Michael Gnehm, '"L'origine secondaire": Semper et Viollet-le-Duc sur les traces d'une histoire culturelle de l'architecture', *eaV: Revue de l'école d'architecture de Versailles*, no. 12 (2007), 62–71.

Gnehm 2012   Michael Gnehm, 'Das Nachleben der Ornamente: Kunstgeschichte aus dem Geist der Gegenwart bei Rahn und Gantner', *Zeitschrift für Schweizerische Archäologie und Kunstgeschichte* 69, no. 3/4 (2012), 391–402.

Gnehm 2015   Michael Gnehm, 'Bekleidungstheorie', *ARCH+* 48, no. 221 (Winter 2015), 33–9.

Gnehm 2017a   Michael Gnehm, 'Gottfried Semper et le métabolisme du revêtement architectural', *Gradhiva: Revue d'anthropologie et d'histoire des arts*, no. 25 (2017), 106–23.

Gnehm 2017b   Michael Gnehm, 'Gottfried Semper et le "sens divinatoire de l'artiste"', *Revue germanique internationale*, no. 26 (2017), 143–57.

Gnehm 2020   Michael Gnehm, 'A Spiraling History of Architecture', in Robin Schuldenfrei (ed.), *Iteration: Episodes in the Mediation of Art and Architecture*, London: Routledge, 2020, 25–48.

Gnehm/Hildebrand 2021   Michael Gnehm and Sonja Hildebrand (eds.), *Architectural History and Globalized Knowledge: Gottfried Semper in London*, Mendrisio: Mendrisio Academy Press; Zurich: gta Verlag, 2021.

Gross 1980   Reiner Gross, 'Gottfried Semper und seine Beziehungen zu Sachsen vom Juni 1849 bis Ende 1870', in Semper-Kolloquium 1980, 151–8.

Guillery 2012   Peter Guillery (ed.), *Woolwich*, Survey of London 48, New Haven: Yale University Press, 2012.

Hannavy 2008   John Hannavy (ed.), *Encyclopedia of Nineteenth-Century Photography*, 2 vols., New York: Routledge, 2008.

Harless 1764   Gottlieb Christoph Harless, *Introductio in historiam linguae Latinae*, Bremen: Foerster, 1764.

Haskell 1988   Francis Haskell, 'The Growth of British Art History and Its Debts to Europe', *Proceedings of the British Academy* 74 (1988), 203–14.

Hauser 1985   Andreas Hauser, 'Der "Cuvier der Kunstwissenschaft": Klassifizierungsprobleme in Gottfried Sempers "Vergleichender Baulehre"', in Thomas Bolt et al. (eds.), *Grenzbereiche der Architektur*, Basel: Birkhäuser, 1985, 97–114.

Hay 1853   David Ramsay Hay, *The Orthographic Beauty of the Parthenon Referred to a Law of Nature*, Edinburgh: Blackwood, 1853.

Heine 1838   Gustav Heine, *Handbuch der landwirthschaftlichen Baukunde*, Dresden: Arnold, 1838.

Heirler 1980   Manfred Heirler, 'Gottfried Semper, Künstler, Lehrer und Studenten Dresdens in der Revolution von 1848/49', in Semper-Kolloquium 1980, 145–51.

Herrmann 1976   Wolfgang Herrmann, 'Semper und Eduard Vieweg', in Vogt/Reble/Fröhlich 1976, 199–237.

Herrmann 1978   Wolfgang Herrmann, *Gottfried Semper im Exil: Paris, London 1849–1855. Zur Entstehung des 'Stil' 1840–1877*, Basel: Birkhäuser, 1978.

Herrmann 1980   Wolfgang Herrmann, 'Stellung Sempers zum Baustoff Eisen', in Semper-Kolloquium 1980, 46–52.

Herrmann 1981   Wolfgang Herrmann, *Gottfried Semper: Theoretischer Nachlass an der ETH Zürich; Katalog und Kommentare*, Basel: Birkhäuser, 1981.

Herrmann 1984   Wolfgang Herrmann, *Gottfried Semper: In Search of Architecture*, Cambridge, MA: MIT Press, 1984.

Herrmann 1990   Wolfgang Herrmann, 'Sempers Weg von der Mathematik zur vergleichenden Baulehre', in Beat Wyss (ed.), *Bildfälle: Die Moderne im Zwielicht*, Zurich: Artemis, 1990, 73–81.

Hildebrand 2003   Sonja Hildebrand, '"… grossartigere Umgebungen" – Gottfried Semper in London', in Nerdinger/Oechslin 2003, 260–8.

Hildebrand 2007   Sonja Hildebrand, '"nach einem Systeme zu ordnen, welches die inneren Verbindungsfäden dieser bunten Welt am besten zusammenhält": Kulturgeschichtliche Modelle bei Gottfried Semper und Gustav Klemm', in Karge 2007, 237–50.

Hildebrand 2013   Sonja Hildebrand, 'Totalità dell'architettura: Modelli formativi e del sapere in Gottfried Semper', in Christoph Frank and Bruno Pedretti (eds.), *L'architetto generalista*, Mendrisio: Mendrisio Academy Press; Cinisello Balsamo: Silvana Editoriale, 2013, 145–61.

Hildebrand 2014 Sonja Hildebrand, 'Concepts of Creation: Historiography and Design in Gottfried Semper', *Journal of Art Historiography*, no. 11 (Dec. 2014) (https://arthistoriography.files.wordpress.com/2014/11/hildebrand.pdf).

Hildebrand 2015 Sonja Hildebrand, 'Towards an Expanded Concept of Form: Gottfried Semper on Ancient Projectiles', in Sonja Hildebrand and Elisabeth Bergmann (eds.), *Form-Finding, Form-Shaping, Designing Architecture: Experimental, Aesthetical, and Ethical Approaches to Form in Recent and Postwar Architecture*, Mendrisio: Mendrisio Academy Press; Cinisello Balsamo: Silvana Editoriale, 2015, 130–43.

Hildebrand 2020a Sonja Hildebrand, *Gottfried Semper: Architekt und Revolutionär*, Darmstadt: wbg Theiss, 2020.

Hildebrand 2020b Sonja Hildebrand, 'Mathematische Kurven in der Architekturtheorie um 1850: Gottfried Semper, David Ramsay Hay und die Ästhetik der *invisible curves* des Parthenon', *Figurationen: Gender, Literatur, Kultur* 21, no. 2 (2020), 57–76.

Hildebrand 2021 Sonja Hildebrand, 'Gottfried Semper on Architectural Curvilinearity', in Gnehm/Hildebrand 2021, 106–23.

Hobbs 1853 Alfred Charles Hobbs, *Rudimentary Treatise on the Construction of Locks*, ed. Charles Tomlinson, London: Weale, 1853.

Hönes 2019 Hans Christian Hönes, 'Seductive Foreignness: Gottfried Kinkel at University College London', in Maria Teresa Costa and Hans Christian Hönes (eds.), *Migrating Histories of Art: Self-Translations of a Discipline*, Berlin: De Gruyter, 2019, 149–64.

Hönes 2021 Hans Christian Hönes, 'Untranslatable: Gottfried Kinkel, *Kulturgeschichte*, and British Art Historiography', *Zeitschrift für Kunstgeschichte* 84, no. 2 (2021), 248–68.

Hunt 1851 Robert Hunt, *Hand-Book to the Official Catalogues: An Explanatory Guide to the Natural Productions and Manufactures of the Great Exhibition of the Industry of All Nations, 1851*, 2 vols., London: Spicer; Clowes, [1851].

Hvattum 1999 Mari Hvattum, '"A Complete and Universal Collection": Gottfried Semper and the Great Exhibition', *Mac Journal*, no. 4 (1999), 33–45.

Hvattum 2004a Mari Hvattum, *Gottfried Semper and the Problem of Historicism*, Cambridge: Cambridge University Press, 2004.

Hvattum 2004b Mari Hvattum, '"A Complete and Universal Collection": Gottfried Semper and the Great Exhibition', in Mari Hvattum and Christian Hermansen (eds.), *Tracing Modernity: Manifestations of the Modern in Architecture and the City*, London: Routledge, 2004, 124–36.

Hvattum 2021 Mari Hvattum, '"A Triumph in Ink": Gottfried Semper, "The Illustrated London News", and the Duke of Wellington's Funeral Car', in Gnehm/Hildebrand 2021, 64–85.

Illustrated Exhibitor 1851 *The Illustrated Exhibitor: A Tribute to the World's Industrial Jubilee*, London: Cassell, [1851].

ILN 1851a 'The Great Exhibition: Horological Section (Second Notice)', *The Illustrated London News* 18, no. 496 (21 June 1851), 600–1.

ILN 1851b 'The Great Exhibition: American Reaping Machine', *The Illustrated London News* 19, no. 503 (19 July 1851), 89–90.

ILN 1851c 'Locks and Lock-Picking', *The Illustrated London News* 19, no. 506 (2 Aug. 1851), 141–2; no. 508 (9 Aug. 1851), 182; no. 514 (6 Sept. 1851), 274–5.

ILN 1852a 'Funeral of the Duke of Wellington: The Funeral Car', *The Illustrated London News* 21, no. 588 (6 Nov. 1852), 383.

ILN 1852b 'Official Account of the Funeral Car of the Duke of Wellington', *The Illustrated London News* 21, no. 591 (20 Nov. 1852), 439–40.

ILN 1852c 'The Wellington Funeral Car', *The Illustrated London News* 21, no. 593 (27 Nov. 1852), 463.

ILN 1854 'The Museum of Ornamental Art', *The Illustrated London News* 24, no. 664 (21 Jan. 1854), 60–1.

ILN 1858 'Exhibition of Works of Art-Manufacture', *The Illustrated London News* 33, no. 932 (21 Aug. 1858), 180.

ILN Suppl. 1851 'Das Museum für practische Geologie', *The Illustrated London News: Deutsches Supplement*, no. 5 (31 May 1851), 73–4.

Inventory 1868 *Inventory of the Objects in the Art Division of the Museum at South Kensington, Arranged According to the Dates of Their Acquisition: For the Years 1852 to the End of 1867*, London: Eyre & Spottiswoode for Her Majesty's Stationery Office, 1868.

Jenkins/Middleton 1988 Ian D. Jenkins and Andrew P. Middleton, 'Paint on the Parthenon Sculptures', *The Annual of the British School at Athens* 83 (1988), 183–207.

Johnson 1852 Benjamin Pierce Johnson, *Report of Benj. P. Johnson, Agent of the State of New-York, Appointed to Attend the Exhibition of the Industry of All Nations, Held in London, 1851*, Albany: Van Benthuysen, 1852.

Secondary Sources

Jones 1852a   Owen Jones, *An Attempt to Define the Principles Which Should Regulate the Employment of Colour in the Decorative Arts, with a Few Words on the Present Necessity of an Architectural Education on the Part of the Public: Read before the Society of Arts, April 28, 1852*, London: Barclay, 1852.

Jones 1852b   Owen Jones, *Lectures on the Articles in the Museum of the Department*, London: Eyre & Spottis-woode for Her Majesty's Stationery Office, 1852.

Jones 1854a   Owen Jones, *An Apology for the Colouring of the Greek Court in the Crystal Palace*, London: Crystal Palace Library; Bradbury & Evans, 1854.

Jones 1854b   Owen Jones, *Description of the Egyptian Court, Erected in the Crystal Palace: With an Historical Notice of the Monuments of Egypt, by Samuel Sharpe*, London: Crystal Palace Library; Bradbury & Evans, 1854.

Jones 1856   Owen Jones, *The Grammar of Ornament*, London: Day, 1856.

Jones 2006   Robin Jones, 'An Englishman Abroad: Sir James Emerson Tennent in Ceylon, 1845–50', *Apollo: The International Magazine of Art and Antiques* 164, no. 537 (Nov. 2006), 36–43.

Kalinowski/Thibault 2018   Isabelle Kalinowski and Estelle Thibault, 'Gottfried Semper, chroniques parisiennes 1849–1850: Contributions à une architecture comparée', *Les Cahiers de la recherche architecturale urbaine et paysagère*, no. 2 (2018) (https://doi.org/10.4000/craup.713).

Karge 2007   Henrik Karge (ed.), *Gottfried Semper – Dresden und Europa: Die moderne Renaissance der Künste*, Munich: Deutscher Kunstverlag, 2007.

Karge 2013   Henrik Karge, 'Projecting the Future in German Art Historiography of the Nineteenth Century: Franz Kugler, Karl Schnaase, and Gottfried Semper', *Journal of Art Historiography*, no. 9 (Dec. 2013) (https://arthistoriography.files.wordpress.com/2013/12/karge.pdf).

Karge 2014   Henrik Karge, 'Einleitung', in Semper 2014, vol. 1, 7–59.

Kauffmann 1993   Georg Kauffmann, *Die Entstehung der Kunstgeschichte im 19. Jahrhundert*, Opladen: West-deutscher Verlag, 1993.

Kirchmeyer 1985   Helmut Kirchmeyer, *Das zeitgenössische Wagner-Bild: Dokumente 1851–1852*, Situationsgeschichte der Musikkritik und des musikalischen Pressewesens in Deutschland 4.6.1, Regensburg: Bosse, 1985.

Knoepfli 1976   Albert Knoepfli, 'Zu Tische in der Aula des Semperschen Polytechnikumgebäudes: Zu den Zürcher Kreisen der frühen Semperzeit', in Vogt/Reble/Fröhlich 1976, 255–74.

Laking 1904   Guy Francis Laking, *The Armoury of Windsor Castle: European Section*, London: Bradbury & Agnew, 1904.

Lankheit 1976   Klaus Lankheit, 'Gottfried Semper und die Weltausstellung London 1851', in Vogt/Reble/Fröhlich 1976, 23–47.

Lattek 2006   Christine Lattek, *Revolutionary Refugees: German Socialism in Britain, 1840–1860*, London: Routledge, 2006.

Laudel 1991   Heidrun Laudel, *Gottfried Semper: Architektur und Stil*, Dresden: Verlag der Kunst, 1991.

Laudel 1995   Heidrun Laudel, 'Gottfried Sempers Ringen um eine repräsentative Demokratie', *Dresdner Hefte: Beiträge zur Kulturgeschichte* 13, no. 43 (March 1995), 46–55.

Laudel 2000   Heidrun Laudel, 'Was trieb Gottfried Semper auf die Dresdner Barrikaden?', in Karin Jeschke and Gunda Ulbricht (eds.), *Dresden, Mai 1849: Tagungsband*, Dresden: ddp Goldenbogen, 2000, 83–91.

Laudel 2003   Heidrun Laudel, 'Werkverzeichnis: 59–76', in Nerdinger/Oechslin 2003, 269–97.

Laudel 2007   Heidrun Laudel, 'Das Bekleidungsprinzip – Sempers künstlerisches Credo', in Franz/Nierhaus 2007, 17–37.

Leisching 1903   Julius Leisching, *Gottfried Semper und die Museen*, Brünn (Brno): Burkart, 1903. (Offprint from *Mitteilungen des Mährischen Gewerbe-Museums* 21, no. 24 [Dec. 1903], 185–92.)

Leoni 2014   Claudio Leoni, 'Art, Production and Market Conditions: Gottfried Semper's Historical Perspective on Commodities and the Role of Museums', *Journal of Art Historiography*, no. 11 (Dec. 2014) (https://arthistoriography.files.wordpress.com/2014/11/leoni.pdf).

Leoni 2019   Claudio Leoni, 'Exhibition and Cognition: Gottfried Semper's Strolls in the Crystal Palace', doctoral diss., London: University College, 2019.

Leoni 2021   Claudio Leoni, 'Staging Canada: Gottfried Semper's Contribution to the Great Exhibition of 1851', in Gnehm/Hildebrand 2021, 38–55.

Literary Gazette 1858   'The Exhibition of the Works of Art-Manufacture, Designed or Executed by Students of the Schools of Art in Connexion with the Science and Art-Department, South Kensington', *The Literary Gazette: A Weekly Journal of Literature, Science, and The Fine Arts*, new ser., 1, no. 2 (10 July 1858), 57–9.

London Directory 1842   *The Small Edition of the Post Office London Directory, 1843*, London: Kelly, [1842].

London Directory 1851   *The Small Edition of the Post Office London Directory, 1852*, London: Kelly, [1851].

London Gazette 1862a   'The Bankruptcy Act, 1861. Notice of Adjudications and First Meeting of Creditors', *The London Gazette*, no. 22637 (24 June 1862), 3237–45.

London Gazette 1862b   'The Bankruptcy Act, 1861. Notice of Sittings for Last Examination', *The London Gazette*, no. 22644 (15 July 1862), 3560–5.

Lütteken 2008   Laurenz Lütteken (ed.), *Kunstwerk der Zukunft: Richard Wagner und Zürich (1849–1858)*, Zurich: Verlag Neue Zürcher Zeitung, 2008.

Luttmann 2007   Susanne Luttmann, 'Von der Methodik des Erfindens – Gottfried Sempers "Vergleichende Baulehre"', in Karge 2007, 221–36.

Luttmann 2008   Susanne Luttmann, 'Gottfried Sempers "Vergleichende Baulehre": Eine quellenkritische Rekonstruktion', doctoral diss., Zurich: Eidgenössische Technische Hochschule, 2008.

MacDermott 1854   Edward MacDermott, *Routledge's Guide to the Crystal Palace and Park at Sydenham*, London: Routledge, 1854.

Macdonald 1970   Stuart Macdonald, *The History and Philosophy of Art Education*, London: University of London Press, 1970.

Magnus 1555   Olaus Magnus [Olof Månsson], *Historia de gentibus septentrionalibus*, Rome: Viotti, 1555.

Mallgrave 1983a   Harry Francis Mallgrave, 'The Idea of Style: Gottfried Semper in London', doctoral diss., Philadelphia: University of Pennsylvania, 1983.

Mallgrave 1983b   Harry Francis Mallgrave, 'A Commentary on Semper's November Lecture', *RES: Anthropology and Aesthetics*, no. 6 (Fall 1983), 23–31.

Mallgrave 1985a   Harry Francis Mallgrave, 'Gustav Klemm and Gottfried Semper: The Meeting of Ethnological and Architectural Theory', *Res: Anthropology and Aesthetics*, no. 9 (Spring 1985), 68–79.

Mallgrave 1985b   Harry Francis Mallgrave, 'Gottfried Semper: Architecture and the Primitive Hut', *Reflections: The Journal of the School of Architecture, University of Illinois* 3, no. 1 (Fall 1985), 60–71.

Mallgrave 1989   Harry Francis Mallgrave, 'Introduction', in Semper 1989, 1–44.

Mallgrave 1996   Harry Francis Mallgrave, *Gottfried Semper: Architect of the Nineteenth Century*, New Haven: Yale University Press, 1996.

Mallgrave 2002   Harry Francis Mallgrave, 'Gottfried Semper and the Great Exhibition', in Franz Bosbach and John R. Davis (eds.), *Die Weltausstellung von 1851 und ihre Folgen*, Munich: Saur, 2002, 305–14.

Mallgrave 2004   Harry Francis Mallgrave, 'Introduction', in Semper 2004, 1–67.

Mallgrave 2007   Harry Francis Mallgrave, 'Introduction', in Semper 2007a, 8–12.

Marshall 1878   John Marshall, *Anatomy for Artists*, London: Smith & Elder, 1878.

Martel 1856   Charles Martel [Thomas Delf], *The Principles of Form in Ornamental Art*, London: Winsor & Newton, 1856.

Marx/Engels 1984   Karl Marx and Friedrich Engels, *Briefwechsel Januar bis Dezember 1851*, ed. Maija Kotschetkowa et al., Gesamtausgabe (MEGA) 3.4.1, Berlin: Dietz, 1984.

May 1979   Walter May, 'The Illustrated London News, Volume 18. Deutsches Supplement Nr. 1–8, 1851', in *Gottfried Semper zum 100. Todestag: Ausstellung im Albertinum zu Dresden vom 15. Mai bis 29. August 1979*, Dresden: Staatliche Kunstsammlungen Dresden, [1979], 130.

May 1980   Walter May, '"Die grosse Ausstellung": Ein Aufsatz Gottfried Sempers über die Weltausstellung 1851', in Semper-Kolloquium 1980, 53–66.

Molini 1820   Giuseppe Molini (ed.), *La metropolitana fiorentina illustrata*, Florence: Molini, 1820.

Moravánszky 2018   Ákos Moravánszky, *Metamorphism: Material Change in Architecture*, Basel: Birkhäuser, 2018.

Moriarty 1851   [Edward Aubrey Moriarty], Review of Off. Cat. 1851⁵, *The Edinburgh Review* 94, no. 192 (Oct. 1851), 557–98.

Mrazek 1966   Wilhelm Mrazek, 'Gottfried Semper und die museal-wissenschaftliche Reformbewegung des 19. Jahrhunderts', in Wingler 1966, 113–19.

Mundt 1971   Barbara Mundt, 'Theorien zum Kunstgewerbe des Historismus in Deutschland', in Helmut Koopmann and Josef Adolf Schmoll gen. Eisenwerth (eds.), *Beiträge zur Theorie der Künste im 19. Jahrhundert*, vol. 1, Frankfurt am Main: Klostermann, 1971, 317–36.

Mundt 1976   Barbara Mundt, 'Das Verhältnis einiger kunsthandwerklicher Entwürfe Sempers zum historischen Kunstgewerbe', in Vogt/Reble/Fröhlich 1976, 315–27.

Nerdinger/Oechslin 2003   Winfried Nerdinger and Werner Oechslin (eds.), *Gottfried Semper 1803–1879: Architektur und Wissenschaft*, Munich: Prestel; Zurich: gta Verlag, 2003.

Nichols 2021 Kate Nichols, 'Remaking Ancient Athens in 1850s London: Owen Jones, Gottfried Semper and the Crystal Palace at Sydenham', in Gnehm/Hildebrand 2021, 142–57.

Nicka 2007 Isabella Nicka, '"Even the Question of Material Is a Secondary One …": Eine Abschrift des Manuskripts *Practical Art in Metals and Hard Materials* im Wiener MAK', in Franz/Nierhaus 2007, 51–8.

Nicka/Pokorny-Nagel 2007 Isabelle Nicka and Kathrin Pokorny-Nagel, 'Preliminary Remarks', in Semper 2007a, 21–2.

Nigro Covre 1982 Jolanda Nigro Covre, 'Babele nel "vuoto coperto di vetro": Gottfried Semper e la grande esposizione di Londra nel 1851', *Ricerche di storia dell'arte*, no. 18 (1982), 5–20.

Norman/Eaves 2016 Alexander Vesey Bethune Norman and Ian Eaves, *Arms & Armour in the Collection of Her Majesty the Queen: European Armour*, London: Royal Collection Trust, 2016.

ODIC 1851 *Great Exhibition of the Works of Industry of All Nations, 1851: Official Descriptive and Illustrated Catalogue*, 3 vols., London: Spicer; Clowes, 1851. (Reference copy: ETH Library, Rar 4777.)

ODIC 1852 *Great Exhibition of the Works of Industry of All Nations, 1851: Official Descriptive and Illustrated Catalogue*, 3 vols., London: Spicer; Clowes, [1852]. (Reference copy: NAL, EX.1851.74–6.)

ODIC Suppl. 1852 *Great Exhibition of the Works of Industry of All Nations, 1851: Official Descriptive and Illustrated Catalogue*, suppl. vol., London: Spicer; Clowes, [1852]. (Reference copy: ETH Library, Rar 4777.)

Oechslin 1994 Werner Oechslin, *Stilhülse und Kern: Otto Wagner, Adolf Loos und der evolutionäre Weg zur modernen Architektur*, Zurich: gta Verlag; Berlin: Ernst, 1994.

Off. Cat. 1851[1] *Official Catalogue of the Great Exhibition of the Works of Industry of All Nations, 1851* [1 May 1851], London: Spicer; Clowes, [1851].

Off. Cat. 1851[2] *Official Catalogue of the Great Exhibition of the Works of Industry of All Nations, 1851: Corrected Edition* [31 May 1851], London: Spicer; Clowes, [1851].

Off. Cat. 1851[3] *Official Catalogue of the Great Exhibition of the Works of Industry of All Nations, 1851: Second Corrected and Improved Edition* (1 July 1851), London: Spicer; Clowes, [1851].

Off. Cat. 1851[4] *Official Catalogue of the Great Exhibition of the Works of Industry of All Nations, 1851: Third Corrected and Improved Edition* (1 Aug. 1851), London: Spicer; Clowes, [1851].

Off. Cat. 1851[5] *Official Catalogue of the Great Exhibition of the Works of Industry of All Nations, 1851: Fourth Corrected and Improved Edition* (15 Sept. 1851), London: Spicer; Clowes, [1851].

Orelli-Messerli 2010 Barbara von Orelli-Messerli, *Gottfried Semper (1803–1879): Die Entwürfe zur dekorativen Kunst*, Petersberg: Imhof, 2010.

Papapetros 2016 Spyros Papapetros, 'Ornament as Weapon: Ballistics, Politics, and Architectural Adornment in Semper's Treatise on Ancient Projectiles', in Gülru Necipoğlu and Alina Payne (eds.), *Histories of Ornament: From Global to Local*, Princeton, NJ: Princeton University Press, 2016, 46–61.

Payne 2012 Alina Payne, *From Ornament to Object: Genealogies of Architectural Modernism*, New Haven: Yale University Press, 2012.

Pernot 1844 Louis-Théodore Pernot, *Dictionnaire du constructeur, ou Vade mecum des architectes, propriétaires, entrepreneurs de maçonnerie, charpente, serrurerie, couverture, etc.*, 3rd ed., Paris: Mathias, 1844.

Pevsner 1940 Nikolaus Pevsner, *Academies of Art: Past and Present*, Cambridge: Cambridge University Press, 1940.

Pevsner 1972 Nikolaus Pevsner, *Some Architectural Writers of the Nineteenth Century*, Oxford: Clarendon Press, 1972.

Phillips 1854 Samuel Phillips, *Guide to the Crystal Palace and Park*, London: Crystal Palace Library; Bradbury & Evans, 1854.

Physick 1994 John Physick, 'Early Albertopolis: The Contribution of Gottfried Semper', *The Victorian Society Annual* (1994), 28–36.

Piggott 2004 Jan R. Piggott, *Palace of the People: The Crystal Palace at Sydenham 1854–1936*, London: Hurst, 2004.

Pisani 2003 Salvatore Pisani, '"Die Monumente sind durch Barbarei monochrom geworden": Zu den theoretischen Leitmaximen in Sempers *Vorläufige Bemerkungen über bemalte Architectur und Plastik bei den Alten*', in Nerdinger/Oechslin 2003, 109–15.

Poerschke 2012 Ute Poerschke, 'Architecture as a Mathematical Function: Reflections on Gottfried Semper', *Nexus Network Journal* 14, no. 1 (2012), 119–34.

Poerschke 2016 Ute Poerschke, *Architectural Theory of Modernism: Relating Functions and Forms*, New York: Routledge, 2016.

Pugin 1841   Augustus Welby Northmore Pugin, *The True Principles of Pointed or Christian Architecture: Set Forth in Two Lectures Delivered at St Marie's, Oscott*, London: Weale, 1841.

Quitzsch 1981   Heinz Quitzsch, *Gottfried Semper – Praktische Ästhetik und politischer Kampf. Im Anhang: Die vier Elemente der Baukunst*, Brunswick: Vieweg, 1981.

Rahn 1920   Johann Rudolf Rahn, 'Erinnerungen aus den ersten 22 Jahren meines Lebens (Schluss)', *Zürcher Taschenbuch*, new ser., 41 (1920), 1–90.

Redgrave 1853   Richard Redgrave, 'Suggestions for a Course of Instruction for Those Holding Scholarships and Others in the Department of Practical Art', in DPA[1], 369–71.

Reimmann 1718   Jacob Friedrich Reimmann, *Introductio in historiam vocabulorum linguae Latinae*, Halle: Renger, 1718.

Reising 1976   Gert Reising, 'Kunst, Industrie und Gesellschaft: Gottfried Semper in England', in Vogt/Reble/Fröhlich 1976, 49–66.

Rep. Jur. 1852   *Exhibition of the Works of Industry of All Nations, 1851: Reports by the Juries on the Subjects in the Thirty Classes into Which the Exhibition Was Divided. Presentation Copy*, London: Clowes for the Royal Commission, 1852.

Richa 1757   Giuseppe Richa, *Della chiesa metropolitana di Santa Maria del Fiore*, Notizie istoriche delle chiese fiorentine 6, Florence: Viviani, 1757.

Ritter 1817/52   Carl Ritter, *Die Erdkunde im Verhältniss zur Natur und zur Geschichte des Menschen, oder Allgemeine, vergleichende Geographie*, 21 vols., Berlin: Reimer, 1817–52.

Robertson 1978   David Robertson, *Sir Charles Eastlake and the Victorian Art World*, Princeton, NJ: Princeton University Press, 1978.

Robinson 1856   John Charles Robinson, *Catalogue of a Collection of Works of Decorative Art: Being a Selection from the Museum at Marlborough House Circulated for Exhibition in Provincial Schools of Art*, 5th ed. (Nov. 1856), London: Eyre & Spottiswoode for Her Majesty's Stationery Office, 1856.

Rodgers 1852   Charles T. Rodgers, *American Superiority at the World's Fair: Designed to Accompany a Chromo-Lithographic Picture, Illustrative of Prizes Awarded to American Citizens, at the Great Exhibition*, Philadelphia: Hawkins, 1852.

Ruff 1852   William Ruff, *Guide to the Turf; or, Pocket Racing Companion for 1852*, London: Ackermann, 1852.

Rykwert 1976   Joseph Rykwert, 'Semper and the Conception of Style', in Vogt/Reble/Fröhlich 1976, 67–81.

Rykwert 1983   Joseph Rykwert, 'Preface', in Semper 1983, 5–7.

Rykwert 1998   Joseph Rykwert, 'Architecture Is All on the Surface: Semper and *Bekleidung*', *Rassegna* 20, no. 73 (Jan. 1998), 20–9.

Schädlich 1980   Christian Schädlich, 'Gottfried Sempers kunstpädagogische Grundsätze', in Semper-Kolloquium 1980, 40–5.

Scharf 1854   George Scharf, *The Greek Court Erected in the Crystal Palace, by Owen Jones*, London: Crystal Palace Library; Bradbury & Evans, 1854.

Scherer 1851   Hermann Scherer, *Londoner Briefe über die Weltausstellung*, Leipzig: Schultze, 1851.

Schubert et al. 1850   Friedrich Schubert et al., *Vademecum für den praktischen Ingenieur und Baumeister*, Stuttgart: Müller, 1850.

Semper 1880   Hans Semper, *Gottfried Semper: Ein Bild seines Lebens und Wirkens; mit Benutzung der Familienpapiere*, Berlin: Calvary, 1880. (Offprint from *Biographisches Jahrbuch für Alterthumskunde* 2 [1880], 49–83.)

Semper-Kolloquium 1980   *Gottfried Semper 1803–1879: Sein Wirken als Architekt, Theoretiker und revolutionärer Demokrat und die schöpferische Aneignung seines progressiven Erbes. Wissenschaftliches Kolloquium im Rahmen der Semper-Ehrung der DDR, Technische Universität Dresden, 15. und 16. Mai 1979*, Dresden: Technische Universität, 1980.

Seton 1850   Samuel Waddington Seton, 'Allen's Alphabetical, Spelling, Reading and Arithmetical Table', *Scientific American* 5, no. 21 (9 Feb. 1850), 161.

Sheppard 1975   Francis Henry Wollaston Sheppard (ed.), *The Museums Area of South Kensington and Westminster*, Survey of London 38, London: Athlone Press, 1975.

Soane 1929   John Soane, *Lectures on Architecture: As Delivered to the Students of the Royal Academy from 1809 to 1836 in Two Courses of Six Lectures Each*, ed. Arthur T. Bolton, London: Sir John Soane's Museum, 1929.

Spectator 1854   'The Department of Science and Art', *The Spectator: A Weekly Review of Politics, Literature, Theology, and Art* 27, no. 1351 (20 May 1854), 544.

Squicciarino 1994   Nicola Squicciarino, *Arte e ornamento in Gottfried Semper*, Venice: Cardo, 1994.

Squicciarino 2009   Nicola Squicciarino, *Utilità e bellezza: Formazione artistica ed arti applicate in Gottfried Semper*, Rome: Armando, 2009.

Secondary Sources

Studt 1992 Christoph Studt, *Lothar Bucher (1817–1892): Ein politisches Leben zwischen Revolution und Staatsdienst*, Göttingen: Vandenhoeck & Ruprecht, 1992.

Szambien 1987 Werner Szambien, 'Les variables du style dans une conférence de Gottfried Semper', in Jacques Guillerme (ed.), *Le droguier du fonctionnalisme*, Amphion 1, Paris: Picard, 1987, 153–9.

Tallis/Strutt 1852 John Tallis and Jacob George Strutt (eds.), *History and Description of the Crystal Palace, and the Exhibition of the World's Industry in 1851*, 3 vols., London: Tallis; London Printing and Publishing Company, [1852]. (Vol. 1 edited by John Tallis; vols. 2–3 edited by Jacob George Strutt.)

Thiersch 1833 Friedrich Thiersch, *De l'état actuel de la Grèce et des moyens d'arriver à sa restauration*, 2 vols., Leipzig: Brockhaus, 1833.

Trachtenberg 1989 Alan Trachtenberg, *Reading American Photographs: Images as History, Mathew Brady to Walker Evans*, New York: Hill and Wang, 1989.

Van Zanten 1977a David Van Zanten, 'Introduction and Overview, 1976', in *The Architectural Polychromy of the 1830's*, New York: Garland, 1977.

Van Zanten 1977b David Van Zanten, 'The Architectural Polychromy of the 1830's' (doctoral diss., Cambridge, MA: Harvard University, 1970), in *The Architectural Polychromy of the 1830's*, New York: Garland, 1977.

Van Zanten 1982 David Van Zanten, 'Architectural Polychromy: Life in Architecture', in Robin Middleton (ed.), *The Beaux-Arts and Nineteenth-Century French Architecture*, London: Thames & Hudson, 1982, 196–215.

Veillerot 1851 Veillerot, 'Revue de l'exposition de Londres. II: Joaillerie russe', *Le Palais de cristal: Journal illustré de l'exposition de 1851 et du progrès des arts industriels*, no. 12 (26 July 1851), 179, 182.

Vogt 1976 Adolf Max Vogt, 'Gottfried Semper und Joseph Paxton', in Vogt/Reble/Fröhlich 1976, 175–97.

Vogt/Reble/Fröhlich 1976 Adolf Max Vogt, Christina Reble and Martin Fröhlich (eds.), *Gottfried Semper und die Mitte des 19. Jahrhunderts: Symposion vom 2. bis 6. Dezember 1974, veranstaltet durch das Institut für Geschichte und Theorie der Architektur an der Eidgenössischen Technischen Hochschule Zürich*, Basel: Birkhäuser, 1976.

Waenerberg 1992 Annika Waenerberg, *Urpflanze und Ornament: Pflanzenmorphologische Anregungen in der Kunsttheorie und Kunst von Goethe bis zum Jugendstil*, Helsinki: Societas Scientiarum Fennica, 1992.

Wagner 1993 Richard Wagner, *Briefe September 1852 – Januar 1854*, ed. Gertrud Strobel and Werner Wolf, Sämtliche Briefe 5, Leipzig: Deutscher Verlag für Musik, 1993.

Wainwright 1994 Clive Wainwright, 'Principles True and False: Pugin and the Foundation of the Museum of Manufactures', *The Burlington Magazine* 136, no. 1095 (June 1994), 357–64.

Weidmann 2010 Dieter Weidmann, 'Gottfried Sempers "Polytechnikum" in Zürich: Ein Heiligtum der Wissenschaften und Künste', 2 vols., doctoral diss., Zurich: Eidgenössische Technische Hochschule, 2010.

Weidmann 2014 Dieter Weidmann, 'Through the Stable Door to Prince Albert? On Gottfried Semper's London Connections', *Journal of Art Historiography*, no. 11 (Dec. 2014) (https://arthistoriography.files.wordpress.com/2014/11/weidmann.pdf).

Weidmann 2021 Dieter Weidmann, 'Gottfried Semper's "Broken English"', in Gnehm/Hildebrand 2021, 86–105.

Winckler 1735 Johann Heinrich Winckler, *Institutiones philosophiae Wolfianae utriusque contemplativae et activae usibus academicis accommodatae*, Leipzig: Fritsch, 1735.

Wingler 1966 Gottfried Semper, *Wissenschaft, Industrie und Kunst und andere Schriften über Architektur, Kunsthandwerk und Kunstunterricht*, ed. Hans Maria Wingler, Mainz: Kupferberg, 1966.

Wornum 1855 Ralph Nicholson Wornum, *An Account of the Library of the Division of Art at Marlborough House: With a Catalogue of the Principal Works*, London: Eyre & Spottiswoode for Her Majesty's Stationery Office, 1855.

Wyatt 1851/53 Matthew Digby Wyatt, *The Industrial Arts of the Nineteenth Century: A Series of Illustrations of the Choicest Specimens Produced by Every Nation at the Great Exhibition of Works of Industry, 1851*, 2 vols., London: Day, 1851–53.

Wyatt 1852 Matthew Digby Wyatt, *Metal-Work and Its Artistic Design*, London: Day, 1852.

Wyatt 1853 Matthew Digby Wyatt, 'An Attempt to Define the Principles Which Should Determine Form in the Decorative Arts' (21 April 1852), in *Lectures on the Results of the Great Exhibition of 1851, Delivered before the Society of Arts, Manufactures, and Commerce*, vol. 2, London: Bogue, 1853, 213–51.

INDEX

Abbey & Son [Charles Abbey] 38

Abeken, Heinrich 207

Achilles 99, 134

Aeschylus 211, 215

Aga-Melik-Mahomet-Hadji-Ussoof-Ogli 35

Agincourt *see* Séroux d'Agincourt

Albert, prince of Saxe-Coburg and Gotha xvi, xxviii–xxix, 262, 331, 355, 377

Albert de Luynes, Honoré Théodoric d' 49

Alcinous, mythical king of Phaeacia 99, 399

Alderson, M. A. 210, 214

Alexander III (the Great), king of Macedonia 130, 156, 168, 378, 484

Allen, Edwin 32, 291

Ameloung & Son 35

Amelung & Sohn [Carl Philipp Amelung] *see* Ameloung & Son

Anacharsis 469, 473

Androuet du Cerceau, Jacques Snr 222

Apollo 179, 186

Apollon *see* Apollo

Apollonius of Perga 112

Apollonius of Tyana 440

Apuleius of Madauros 460

Archimedes 112

Aristarkhoff 35

Aristophanes 211, 215

Armytage, Charles 89–90, 380, 384–5

Arneth, Joseph 441

Arrowsmith, George A. 38

Ashburton *see* Baring

Ashley *see* Ashley-Cooper

Ashley-Cooper, Anthony, 7th Earl Shaftesbury 208

Ashmead & Hurlburt [James H. Ashmead, Edmund Hurlburt] 38

Athena 114, 500; *see also* Minerva

Athenaeus of Naucratis 144

Aubin, Charles 295

Austin, Walter 89, 379–80, 384

Bacchus 179, 186

Baco von Verulam *see* Bacon

Bacon, Francis, 1st Baron Verulam 28

Bähr, Johann Karl xxiii

Baillie, Henry James 208

Banks, Robert Richardson 387

Banting, William 377

Barbaro, Daniele Matteo Alvise 214, 319, 545

Barbarus *see* Barbaro

Baring, William Bingham, 2nd Baron Ashburton xxviii

Barry, Charles Jnr 387

Baudissin, Wolf Heinrich von 217, 547

Bazin, Xavier 35

Behr, Johann Heinrich August xxxii n. 57

Bélanger, Jean-Baptiste 245

Belidor, Bernard Forest de 214

Belli, Valerio 81

Belus (Baal) 177, 200, 486, 530

Belus, mythical Assyrian king 200

Bentinck, William Henry, 4th Duke of Portland 468–9

Bernini, Gian Lorenzo 442

Beuth, Peter xx

Bézout, Étienne 210, 215

Birch, Samuel 548–9

Bird, George 384

Bird, Stanley George 384

Blake, William 32, 289

Boeswillwald, Émile 318

Böhm, Andreas 212

Boldù, Giovanni 81

Bonaparte, Napoleon *see* Napoleon I

Born, David 80–2, 353–5, 357

Börne, Ludwig 217

Borromini, Francesco 135

Botta, Paul-Émile 125, 128, 163, 199–200, 318, 444, 447

Böttger, Johann Friedrich 153, 468

Bötticher, Karl Gottlieb Wilhelm xxvii, xxxii n. 50, 167, 225, 437, 457, 462, 499–502, 511–12, 549

Böttiger, Carl August 213

Bouchet, Jules 289

Bouvert, Jean-Jacques 263

Bracebridge, Charles Holte 72, 324

Brady, Mathew B. 38–9, 295

Bramah & Co. [Joseph Bramah] 292

Brandon, Joshua Arthur 164, 481

Brandon, Raphael 164, 481

Braun, Anne, née Thomson 235, 252

Braun, Emil xvi–xvii, 233–5, 252, 314, 337, 537, 549

Brenan, James Butler 380

Brenan, John Joseph 90, 380, 387

Briseux, Charles-Étienne 213

Bröder, Christian Gottlob 211, 216

Bröndsted *see* Brøndsted

Brøndsted, Peter Oluf 49, 52, 53 n. 6, 317

Brongniart, Alexandre 138, 159, 455, 468–9, 476

Brown & Wells 33

Brucciani, Domenico 88, 372, 374

Bruyère, Louis 214

Bryant, William Cullen 38

Bucher, Lothar xvii, xix, xxxi n. 24, 29, 234, 245, 260, 280, 288, 297–8, 535–6

Bürck, August 210–11, 215, 517

Burg, Meno 212

Buttmann, Philipp 216

Büttner, Gustav 337

Byng, George, 7th Viscount Torrington 208

Cadell & Davies [Thomas Cadell Jnr, William Davies] 550

Caesar, Gaius Julius 167, 211, 216, 335

Calhoun, John Caldwell 39

Campbell, John, 1st Baron Campbell 235, 240

Campbell, Mary Scarlett xvii, 235, 240, 253

Caracalla, Roman emperor 485

Carolus Magnus *see* Charlemagne

Cary, Henry 55, 319

Cass, Lewis 39

Catullus, Gaius Valerius 211, 216, 547

Cavallari, Francesco Saverio 213

Cavendish, William George Spencer, 6th Duke of Devonshire 355

Cecil, Brownlow, 2nd Marquess of Exeter 377

Cellini, Benvenuto 78, 84, 98, 143, 153, 335, 343, 347, 355, 360–1, 472–3

Chadwick, Edwin xvi, xviii, xxxiii, 233, 236–7, 245, 252, 258, 314, 321, 537

Chadwick, Rachel, née Kennedy 313, 321, 379

Chambers, William 197–8, 439, 516, 518

Changarnier, Nicolas 361

Charlemagne, Frankish king and emperor 133–4, 334, 441, 542

Chevreul, Michel Eugène 214

Chopin, Félix 293

Chubb & Son [Charles Chubb] 292

Chun *see* Shun

Ciampini, Giovanni 223

Ciampinus *see* Ciampini

Cicero, Marcus Tullius 211, 216

Cicognara, Leopoldo 218

Clodion (Claude Michel) 35, 293

Clowes & Son [William Clowes Snr] 310

Cockerell, Charles Robert xxviii, 212, 543

Cole, Henry xviii–xxiv, xxix, xxxi n. 30, xxxiii, xli, 80, 93, 236–8, 257–8, 261–2, 264, 313, 316–17, 320, 327–34, 336–7, 348–50, 353, 356, 358, 361, 370–2, 376–9, 386, 391, 394, 396, 399, 411, 479, 548, 552–4

Collinson, Thomas Bernard xxviii

Columbus, Christopher 132, 453

Cominazo *see* Cominazzo

Cominazzo, Lazarino 79, 336, 348

Comyns, Charles xxxi n. 30

Confucius 194, 517

Cornelius, Peter Joseph von 545

Cornelius & Co. [Robert Cornelius] 37

Cortés, Hernán 132, 453

Cortez *see* Cortés

Coste, Pascal 129, 318, 449

Cresy, Edward xvi

Crux, Arthur 387

Ctesias of Cnidus 128

Cubitt, Thomas 331

Cublai Chan *see* Kublai Khan

Cuthbert, John S. 89–90, 379, 383

Cuvier, Georges xv, xxx n. 16, 28, 105, 118, 282, 398–9, 402, 410, 420–2, 427, 499

Cyrus II (the Great), king of Persia 199, 526, 528, 530

Index

Dahl, Johan Christian Clausen 171, 481, 489

Daléchamps, Jacques 319

Dalla Robbia *see* Della Robbia

Daniel, Hebrew prophet 444

Dante Alighieri 217

David, king of Israel 69, 335

Day & Newell [Samuel S. Day Snr, Robert Newell] xix, 38, 292

Deane, Adams & Deane [George Deane, Robert Adams, John Deane] 294

Deane, Dray & Deane [George Deane, William Dray, John Deane] 36

Delaistre, J.-R. 214

Delf, Thomas 455

Della Robbia, Luca 158, 475

Della Rovere, Guidobaldo II, duke of Urbino 158

Desplechin, Édouard xv

Detmold, Johann Hermann 217

Devaranne, Siméon Pierre 81, 353–5

Deverell, Walter Ruding 227, 328, 552

Devonshire *see* Cavendish

Dickens, Charles xix

Dieterle, Jules Pierre Michel xv, 43, 91, 156–7, 181, 310–11, 361, 387, 468, 470

Dieterlein *see* Dietterlin

Dietterlin, Wendel Snr 222

Diodor *see* Diodorus of Sicily

Diodoros *see* Diodorus of Sicily

Diodorus of Sicily 128, 163, 176

Diomedes, mythical king of Argos 134

Dodd, John Matthias 554

Dohm, W. von 39

Donaldson, Thomas Leverton xx, 51 n. 5, 210, 214, 235, 314, 319, 321, 378

Doppelmayr, Johann Gabriel 224

Duban, Félix 50, 318

Durand, Jean-Nicolas-Louis 106, 422

Dürer, Albrecht 81

Eastlake, Charles Lock xxii

Eddy & Co. [George Washington Eddy] 290

Eginhard *see* Einhard

Eginhartus *see* Einhard

Eichler, Gustav 81, 354

Einhard 134, 211, 441, 446, 542

Elkington, Mason & Co. [George Richards Elkington, Henry Elkington, Josiah Mason] 337, 355, 360

Emerson Tennent, James 89, 375, 378–9, 383

Engels, Friedrich xxxi n. 25

Ernesti, Johann August 211, 216, 547

Eschenburg, Johann Joachim 216

Euler, Leonhard 210, 214, 546

Euripides 211, 215, 548

Evans, Oliver Benton 39, 295

Eytelwein, Johann Albert 212–13

Falkener, Edward xvi–xvii, xx–xxi, xxx n. 21, xxxi n. 33, xxxiii, 234–5, 313–15, 317, 319, 379

Faraday, Michael 56 n. 13, 58 n. 16, 319, 321

Faucher, Julius xvii, 249–50, 272

Fèa, Carlo 213

Ferdinand I, emperor of Austria 536

Fergusson, James 148, 462–3

Fick, Johann Christian 217

Fillmore, Millard 38

Fischer, Ernst Gottfried 210, 214

Flandin, Eugène 129, 318

Flaxman, John Jnr 99, 330

Flaxmann *see* Flaxman

Follen, Charles Christopher 89, 379, 386–8

Follen, Charles Theodore Christian 379

Follen, Eliza Lee, née Cabot 379

Fontayne & Porter [Charles H. Fontayne, William S. Porter] 38–9

Forkel, Johann Nicolaus 225

Francesco di Assisi *see* Francis of Assisi

Francis I, king of France 335

Francis of Assisi 434

Francœur, Louis-Benjamin 210, 215, 546

Frederick II (the Great), king of Prussia xix, 354

Frederick Augustus II, king of Saxony 292

Frederick William, elector of Brandenburg and duke of Prussia 336

Freund, Jonas Charles Hermann xviii, 238

Friedrich, Leonhard xvii, 250–1

Froment-Meurice, François-Désiré 361

Galvani, Luigi 337

Garrez, Pierre-Joseph 289

Gärtner, Friedrich von 50, 318, 538

Gärtner, Julius 212

Gau, Franz Christian xiv, 250, 318, 481, 539

Geiss, Johann Conrad 354

Geppert, Carl Eduard 212

Gibbon, Edward 501

Giedion, Sigfried xix

Gildemeister, Karl xvi

Gilly, David 212

Index

Girardin, Auguste 289

Goodyear, Charles 291

Goury, Jules 49 n. 3, 51, 318

Graffenried, Adolf von 481

Gregory VII, pope 442

Grotefend, Georg Friedrich 211, 216

Grove, George 387

Gutzkow, Karl xxiii

Hachette, Jean-Nicolas-Pierre 214

Hadji-Aga-Baba 35

Hagen, Friedrich Heinrich von der 221

Hagenbuch, Franz 258

Hamilton, William Richard xxx n. 13, 48 n. 1, 53 n. 8, 54 n. 11, 317

Hampden, John 335

Harold II, king of England 129

Harrison, Charles C. 38

Haug, Ernst 206

Hay, David Ramsay xxiv, 411, 413

Hecker, George Valentine 31

Heeren, Arnold Hermann Ludwig 210, 212, 215, 519, 542, 546

Hefner-Alteneck, Jakob Heinrich von xxxvii, 77, 334–5, 340–1, 346

Heideloff, Carl Alexander 84, 222, 318, 362–4, 367, 369

Heigham, Thomas George 363

Heine, Gustav 212, 544

Heine, Wilhelm xvii

Henley, Joseph Warner 329, 553

Henry II, king of England 155, 158

Henry VIII, king of England 79, 335, 347

Hercules 81, 211, 216, 355, 399

Hermann, Johann Gottfried Jakob 49 n. 2, 211, 216, 318

Hermannus *see* Hermann

Hérodote *see* Herodotus

Herodotus 53–5 and n. 10, 128, 176, 199, 211, 215, 319, 444, 486, 519, 526, 548

Herrmann, Wolfgang xxxv–xxxvi, xliii n. 3, 252, 395, 397–8, 403–5, 410–12, 426, 438, 457, 462, 465, 469, 549

Hesiod 98, 101, 211, 216, 355, 398, 403, 405–6

Hesiodos *see* Hesiod

Hesiodus *see* Hesiod

Hetsch, Gustav Friederich 212

Heusinger, Karoline xvii, 235, 238–42, 244, 252–4

Hewett & Co. [William Hewett] 358

Heydeloff *see* Heideloff

Hia *see* Xia

Hicks, George 291

Hirsch, Meier 210, 214

Hirt, Aloys 212, 440

Hittorff, Jacques Ignace xxi, 48 n. 1, 49, 52, 57, 164, 314–15, 317, 319, 480, 485, 487

Hitzig, Friedrich 310

Hobbs, Alfred Charles 33, 292

Hof, Eduard vom xvi

Hogg, Jabez 295

Hogg, Robert 39, 295

Holgate, Edward 90, 380

Homer 98–9, 101–2, 134, 160, 211, 215–6, 355, 398–400, 403, 405–6, 547

Homeros *see* Homer

Homerus *see* Homer

Horace 211, 216

Horatius *see* Horace

Horeau, Hector 43, 311

Horn, Clemens 335

Houghton, Henry xviii

Howland, Charles 36

Hudson, Octavius 327–8, 372, 377, 380, 392, 552–3

Hughes, Robert Ball 38, 290, 295

Humboldt, Alexander von 105, 118, 212, 412, 422, 544

Hunt, Robert 260

Hunt & Roskell [John Samuel Hunt, Robert Roskell] 360–1

Isabeau, Alexandre 214

Isaiah, Hebrew prophet 198, 519, 529

Jacquier, François 220

Jagemann, Christian Joseph 213, 216

James II, king of England 78, 343, 347

Jamnitzer, Wenzel 81

Jao *see* Yao

Jennings, Lewis 38

Jerome, Chauncey 36

Johnson, Sewall & Co. [James Johnson, William Sewall] 36

Jones, Owen xviii, xxi, xxiv, xxxii n. 53, 50 n. 3, 51, 313–15, 318, 321–2, 324, 358, 398, 403, 410, 427, 479

Jonson, Ben 217, 547

Josephus, Flavius 440, 447, 449

Ju *see* Yu

Jubinal, Achille 77, 334–5, 340–1, 346

Jupiter 73

Jupiter (Zeus) 48

Justinus, Marcus Junianus 211, 216

Justitia 262

Juvenal 211, 216

Juvenalis *see* Juvenal

Kaemmerer & Zeftigen 35

Kämmerer & Saefftigen [Heinrich Wilhelm Kämmerer, Constantin Ferdinand Saefftigen] *see* Kaemmerer & Zeftigen

Kane, John Kintzing 39

Karge, Henrik xiv

Kästner, Christian August Lebrecht 411

Kaufmann, Jacques-Auguste 214, 545

Kell, Theodor 308–9

Kérédern de Trobriand, Philippe Régis Denis de 39

Kerr, John Bozman Snr 38

King, John Lewis 89–90, 379, 385

Kinkel, Conrad xxxi n. 24

Kinkel, Gottfried xi, xvii–xviii, xxii, xxix n. 1, xxx nn. 22–3, xxxi n. 24, 206, 536

Klagmann, Jean Baptiste Jules xxxvii, 43, 310–11

Klemm, Gustav Friedrich 549

Knochenhauer, Karl Wilhelm 212

Koch, Joseph Anton 213, 545

Köppen, Johann Heinrich Justus 211, 216

Kramer, Wilhelm August 539

Krause, Friedrich 236, 247–9, 260

Kreuter, Franz Jakob 213, 216, 544

Kublai Khan, emperor of Mongolia and China 193, 523

Kuchenreuter, Johann Jacob 79, 337, 348

Kugler, Franz xix, xxii, xxx n. 13, 48 n. 1, 53–4 and nn. 8, 11, 56–7 and n. 13, 214, 315, 317

Lagrange, Joseph-Louis 220

Lalande, Jérôme de 210, 215

Lanci, Michelangelo 225

Langenheim, Frederick 32, 38–9, 291

Langenheim, William 32, 38–9, 291

Langham, Charles Arthur 379

Langham, Ethel Sarah, née Emerson Tennent 379

Laocoon, mythical priest 212

Laplace, Pierre-Simon 28

Lassus, Jean-Baptiste 318

Lawrence, Martin M. 38–9, 295

Layard, Austen Henry 65, 102, 128, 163, 199–200, 318, 406, 444, 447, 519

Le Normant, Jean-Baptiste-Victor 262

Le Page Moutier [Henri Le Page, Louis Moutier] 360

Le Seur, Thomas 220

Leibnitz *see* Leibniz

Leibniz, Gottfried Wilhelm 28, 31, 218

Leo Marsicanus 223

Leonardo da Vinci 98

Leone *see* Leoni

Leoni, Leone 81

Lessing, Gotthold Ephraim 212

Letarouilly, Paul Marie xxxvii, 91, 380

Letronne, Antoine Jean 214

Lewes, George Henry 321

Liénard, Michel Joseph Napoléon 43, 310–11

Lind, Jenny 37

Lindenau, Bernhard von xvi

Lindley, John 258

Lindley, William 245

Linke, Gustav 212, 543

Livius *see* Livy

Livy 211, 216

Lloyd, Lyman John 37

Lloyd, William Watkiss 321

Lo Faso Pietrasanta di Serradifalco, Domenico 49

Logan, William Edmond 263

Logan, Vail & Co. [Dorastus B. Logan, George Vail] 33, 291

Lorenz, Johann Friedrich 210, 214, 543

Louis IV (the Bavarian), German-Roman emperor 335

Louis XIV, king of France 79, 110, 121, 168, 337, 348

Louis XV, king of France 34, 79, 168, 348

Louis XVI, king of France 78, 335, 343, 347

Louise Henriette, countess of Nassau and electress of Brandenburg 336

Lüders, George William 539

Ludwig I, king of Bavaria 209, 317–18, 355, 538

Luynes *see* Albert de Luynes

Lysicrates 72

McCormick, Cyrus Hall xix, 290

MacDermott, Edward 387

Macdonald, Norman Hilton 377

McDougall, James Alexander 39

McGregor & Lee [George McGregor, Robert Lee] 38

Magdeburger, Hieronymus 81

Magnus, Olaus 211, 216, 547

Mahomet *see* Muhammad

Mallgrave, Harry Francis xiii, xxx nn. 8–9, xxxiii, xxxvi, 410, 426, 498

Marochetti, Carlo 27, 281

Marot, Clément 222, 551

Marot, Jean, architect 222, 551

Marot, Jean, poet 551

Marrel Brothers [Antoine-Benoît-Roch Marrel, Jean-Pierre-Nazaire Marrel] 84, 361–2

Marrel Frères *see* Marrel Brothers

Marryat, Joseph 138, 455

Marshall, John 379

Martel, Charles *see* Delf, Thomas

Marx, Karl xviii, xxxi n. 25, 238

Matifat, Charles Stanislas 311

Matilda of Flanders, duchess of Normandy and queen of England 129

Mayall, John Edwin 38, 294

Mayer, Johann Tobias 210, 215

Mazzini, Giuseppe 206–7

Meade Brothers [Charles Richard Meade, Henry William Mathew Meade] 38–9

Meinert, Friedrich Wilhelm 544

Meissner, Paul Traugott 212

Menes, king of Egypt 201

Mercator, Gerardus 36

Metternich, Klemens Wenzel Lothar von 536

Metzger, Johann 214

Meyen, Eduard 272

Meyrick, Samuel Rush 77, 221, 334–5, 339, 341, 346

Michael (the Archangel) 361

Michael Angelo *see* Michelangelo Buonarroti

Michaelis, Johann David 519

Miché, Alexandre 214

Michelangelo Buonarroti 84, 98, 399, 401

Milizia, Francesco 212

Miller, John E. 291

Millin, Aubin-Louis 214

Milton, John 360–1

Minerva (Athena) 71–2, 98, 220, 500

Minton, Herbert Jnr 162, 329, 371, 479

Mitchell, Samuel Augustus Snr 36, 293

Mitterer, Hermann 213

Molière (Jean-Baptiste Poquelin) 217

Mölling, Heinrich 379

Montfaucon, Bernard de 221, 441

Moriarty, Edward Aubrey xviii–xix, 260, 263–4

Moses, Hebrew prophet 69

Mott, Valentine 39

Muhammad 180, 501

Müller, Johannes 250

Müller, Karl Otfried 212, 220

Murphy, James Cavanah 218

Murr, Christoph Gottlieb von 224, 441

Nagler, Georg Kaspar 213

Napoleon I (the Great), emperor of France 106, 215, 322, 354, 422

Nardi, Jacopo 211, 215

Nepos, Cornelius 211, 216

Nero, Roman emperor 527

Newton, Isaac 28, 31, 220, 360–1

Ninus, mythical Assyrian king 527

Noah, Hebrew patriarch 528

Nones, Henry Benjamin 39

Noori Ogli Ooste Selim Molla *see* Ooste-Selim-Molla-Noori-Ogli

Normand, Charles 213

Odysseus, mythical king of Ithaca 99, 399

Ooste-Selim-Molla-Noori-Ogli 34

Osirtasen I *see* Senusret I

Othon *see* Otto III

Otto III, German-Roman emperor 134

Otto, king of Greece 317

Oudiné & Vauthier [Eugène-André Oudiné, André Vauthier-Galle] 262

Overbeck, Johann Friedrich 545

Palen, J. Ruston 403, 409, 426

Palissy, Bernard 152–3, 158, 472–3

Pallas Athena *see* Athena

Palmer, Benjamin Franklin xix, 37

Panizzi, Antonio xx, xxxi n. 31, 549

Pausanias 214

Pauthier, Jean Pierre Guillaume 198, 516, 518

Paxton, Joseph xviii, xxviii, 236–7, 245, 257–8, 313–14, 386

Péclet, Eugène 225, 551

Penrose, Francis Cranmer 318, 413

Pericles 164, 166

Perkins, Angier March 33

Perry, James Franklin 39

Persius Flaccus, Aulus 211, 216

Peto, Samuel Morton 331

Petronius 60 n. 20, 320

Pevsner, Nikolaus xxxiii, xliii n. 1

Phidias 98, 114

Philostratus, Flavius 133, 440

Pilbeam, Alexander 386–8

Pindar 211, 215

Pindarus *see* Pindar

Piraube, Bertrand 79, 337, 348

Pisanello (Antonio di Puccio Pisano) 81, 354

Plautus, Titus Maccius 211, 216

Plinius *see* Pliny the Elder, Pliny the Younger

Index

589

Plinius Secundus *see* Pliny the Younger

Pliny the Elder 58 and nn. 15–16, 59 n. 17, 214–15, 319

Pliny the Younger 211, 216

Plutarch 215

Pokorny 272

Pölitz, Karl Heinrich Ludwig 210, 215

Polo, Marco 193, 211, 215

Popinoff, Sophia 35, 293

Portland *see* Bentinck

Pottier, André 219, 441

Pratt & Co. [Julius Pratt], combmaker 39

Pratt & Co. [William Abbott Pratt], photographer 296

Priam, mythical king of Troy 99

Priamus *see* Priam

Prisse d'Avennes, Achille Constant Théodore Émile 49 n. 3

Propertius, Sextus 211, 547

Pugin, Augustus Welby Northmore 358–9, 361–3, 481

Pythia, mythical priestess 54, 56

Qin Shi Huang, emperor of China 195, 518, 522, 527

Quaglio, Johann Maria von 213

Quandt, Johann Gottlob von 217

Quast, Alexander Ferdinand von 213

Quatremère de Quincy, Antoine Chrysostome 48

Quénot, Jacques-Pierre 213

Rahn, Johann Rudolf xxxiv, xliii n. 5

Ramée, Daniel 213

Raphael (Raffaello Santi) 110, 121, 360

Redgrave, Richard xxii–xxiii, 328, 331, 333, 353–6, 358, 372, 376–7, 379, 553

Reichenbach, Oskar xvii

Reimer, Johann 213

Reinhart, Hans Snr 81

Reinhart, Johann Christian 545

Reitz, Heinrich *see* Reinhart, Hans Snr

Riabzevitch 35, 296

Richardson, Charles James 328, 372, 376

Ritter, Carl 550

Robin, Pierre-Marie-Bernard 38, 295

Robinson, John Charles xxxi n. 30

Robinson, Moncure 480

Rockstuhl, Alois Gustav 334–5

Romberg, Johann Andreas xxx n. 18, 213, 248

Rónay, Jáczint János 206, 536

Rondelet, Jean 212

Rotteck, Carl von 210, 215, 546

Rudolf of Rheinfelden, duke of Swabia 335

Rudolf of Swabia *see* Rudolf of Rheinfelden

Ruge, Arnold xvii, 206

Rumohr, Carl Friedrich von 69, 115, 212, 218, 413

Rupprecht, Friedrich Karl 318

Ruprich-Robert, Victor Marie Charles 289

Russell, John 208

Sachs, Salomo 210, 214

St John (the Baptist) 362

St Sebald *see* St Sebaldus

St Sebaldus 84, 145, 362–3, 367–8

St Stephen 441

Sallust 211, 216

Sallustius *see* Sallust

Salomon *see* Solomon

Salvemini, Giovanni Francesco 440

Savelli, Sperandio 81

Sayn-Wittgenstein, Carolyne xxxii n. 51, 545

Sazikoff, Ignace 34, 292

Schaaff, Johann Christian Ludwig 212, 548

Scharf, George Jnr xvii, 234, 322

Scheller, Immanuel Johann Gerhard 210, 214, 548

Schinkel, Karl Friedrich xx, 354

Schlüter, Andreas Jnr 354

Schneider, Johann Gottlob 210, 214

Schramm, Rudolph xvii–xviii, 234, 236, 245, 247, 249–50, 272, 536, 541

Schulz, Heinrich Wilhelm 292

Schwanthaler, Ludwig Michael von 81, 99, 353, 355, 399

Sears, David Jnr 296

Sebaldus *see* St Sebaldus

Séchan, Charles Polycarpe xv, 262, 310, 387

Ségur, Paul-Philippe de 215

Selleck 39

Semiramis, mythical Assyrian queen 200, 527

Semper, Bertha, née Thimmig xv, xvii, xxviii, xxxii n. 54, 235–6, 246–50, 260, 332, 541–2, 544

Semper, Elisabeth xxx n. 19, 236, 470

Semper, Elise 540

Semper, Hans xiii, xxx n. 9, xxxiii, xl, 245–7, 322, 353, 355–6, 371, 393–4, 397, 403–5, 409–10, 426, 428, 436, 442–3, 450, 456, 459, 469, 474, 476, 486, 497, 503, 505, 510, 512, 515, 524

Semper, Johann Carl xxx n. 21, 237, 260, 539–42

Semper, Manfred xiii, xxx n. 9, xxxiii, xl, 89–90, 297, 321–2, 353, 355–6, 377, 380, 386–8, 393–4, 397, 403, 409–10, 426, 428, 436, 442, 446, 456, 458, 488, 515, 530, 532

Semper, Mary, née Lange 321

Semper, Wilhelm 247–9, 263, 539, 541

Seneca the Younger 211, 216

Senusret I, king of Egypt 68, 323

Serlio, Sebastiano 220, 549–50

Séroux d'Agincourt, Jean Baptiste Louis Georges 219, 442, 549

Serradifalco see Lo Faso Pietrasanta di Serradifalco

Sesostris I see Senusret I

Shakespeare, William 360–1

Sharpe, Samuel 322

Shekhonin 34, 292

Shikhonin see Shekhonin

Shun, emperor of China 192

Siemens, Carl Wilhelm xxix, 331–2

Simpson, John 88, 372, 374

Simpson, William Butler 259

Sixte V see Sixtus V

Sixtus V, pope 135

Smirke, Sidney 363

Soane, John 499

Solomon, king of Israel 131, 180, 438, 440, 442–3, 447, 449, 501

Somerset, Charles Alfred xxxi n. 30

Sophocles 211, 215

Soulillou, Jacques xxx n. 9

Sperandio see Savelli

Spicer Brothers [Henry Spicer, James Spicer, William Revell Spicer] 310

Spinoza, Benedict de 28

Spyri, Johann Bernhard 250, 538

Spyri, Johanna Louise, née Heusser 250, 538

Stackelberg, Otto Magnus von 49

Stammann, Franz Georg xviii, 259–60, 535, 539, 541

Stephenson, Robert 480

Stieglitz, Christian Ludwig 214

Stiglmaier, Johann Baptist 355

Stosch, Philipp von 80, 354

Stoss, Veit 84, 362–3, 367, 369

Strobel, Georg 213

Stuart, Alexander Hugh Holmes 38

Stubbs, George Andrew 387

Stüler, Friedrich August 354

Stürler, Ludwig 250–1, 481

Sueton see Suetonius Tranquillus

Suetonius Tranquillus, Gaius 211, 216

Szambien, Werner xxxiii, xliii n. 3

Tacitus, Cornelius 167, 211, 215–16, 481, 547

Tauchnitz, Karl Christoph Traugott 211, 215–16

Taylor, Henry P. 35

Taylor, William C. 35

Taylor, Zachary 39

Tennent see Emerson Tennent

Texier, Charles 217, 549

Thales of Miletus 154, 473

Theseus, mythical king of Athens 71–2, 314, 319, 323

Thibault, Jean-Thomas 213

Thibaut, Bernhard Friedrich 210, 214, 546

Thierry, Jules-Denis 214

Thiersch, Friedrich Wilhelm xxi, xxiii, 213

Thomson, James 235, 252

Thorvaldsen, Bertel 99, 399, 545

Thorwaldson see Thorvaldsen

Thsin-Chi-Hoang-Ti see Qin Shi Huang

Tibullus, Albius 211, 547

Tielcke, Johann Gottlieb 213

Tippo Saib see Tipu Sahib

Tipu Sahib, sultan of Mysore 78, 335, 342, 347

Toelken, Ernst Heinrich 217

Tolstoy, Fyodor Petrovich 293

Torrington see Byng

Tottie, Charles 259

Townsend, Henry James 88, 372, 374

Trajan, Roman emperor 73, 324, 545

Trobriand see Kérédern de Trobriand

Twist, Oliver 38, 290

Tyler, John Ellery 291

Tylor & Son [Joseph Tylor] 378

Ulysses see Odysseus

Urban VIII, pope 442

Urbino see Della Rovere

Vagnat, Joseph-Marie 214

Vail & Co. [George Vail] 291

Valentini, Georg Wilhelm von 215, 543

Valerio see Belli

Valerius see Velleius Paterculus

Vallée, Louis Léger 213

Vandenhoeck & Ruprecht [Anna Vandenhoeck, née Parry, Carl Friedrich Günther Ruprecht] 546

Vechte, Antoine 84, 358, 360–1, 372, 374–5

Index

591

Vega, Georg von 210, 215, 219, 546, 550

Velleius Paterculus 211, 216, 548

Venus 110, 179, 186, 361

Victoria, queen of Great Britain and Ireland 76, 78, 235, 333, 342, 346, 348, 350, 355–6, 361, 377, 380

Vieth, Gerhard Ulrich Anton 210, 214

Vieweg, Eduard xii, xv, xx, xxix n. 2, xxxi n. 30, xxxv, 260–1, 288–9, 297, 308, 310, 313–14, 316, 329, 395, 410–11, 413, 489

Vieweg, Heinrich 261

Viger, François 211, 216, 548

Vigerus see Viger

Vignola (Giacomo Barozzi) 214

Vignole see Vignola

Virgil iii, 211, 216

Virgilius see Virgil

Vischer, Peter 84, 145, 362–3, 367–9, 457

Visscher see Vischer

Vitruvius xxiii, 58 n. 14, 59 n. 17, 60 n. 21, 61, 63, 214, 319, 333, 531

Völckers, G. 488

Volney, Constantin-François 210, 215

Wagner, Friedrich August 214

Wagner, Georg 212

Wagner, Richard xvii, xxix, 209, 233, 249–51, 535, 537–8

Washburn & Co. [Ichabod Washburn] 32

Watts, Thomas xvi, xxx n. 21

Way, Albert 549

Webb, James Watson 38

Weber, Johann Adam 210, 214

Wedgwood, Josiah 471

Wegener, H. T. 515, 521, 530, 532–3

Wegener, Theodor 515

Weinbrenner, Friedrich 213

Weisbach, Julius 212, 544

Weiss, Johann Georg 79, 337, 348

Wellesley, Arthur, 1st Duke of Wellington xxii, xxxi n. 37, 89, 330, 362, 375, 377–8, 381, 383

Wellington see Wellesley

Westenholz, Regnar 259, 296

Wetzler, Friedrich 259–60

Whipple, John Adams 38

Whitaker, C. H. 89–90, 378, 381, 383–4

Whitaker, Charles Henry 378

Whitehurst, Jesse Harrison 38–9

Whitmarsh, Samuel 39

Whitney, Asa 39

Wiegmann, Rudolf 58 n. 14, 63, 212

Wigand, Otto Friedrich 259–60

Willemin, Nicolas-Xavier 441, 549

William I (the Conqueror), king of England 129, 335

Willich, August xvii

Wills, William J. 89–90, 378, 382, 384

Winckelmann, Johann Joachim 80, 354

Winckler, Johann Heinrich 547

Winkelmann see Winckelmann

Winkler, Oswald 489

Wolf, Friedrich August 211, 542, 547

Wolff, Christian 211, 216, 542, 547

Wolff, Johann Heinrich 212–13

Wornum, Ralph Nicholson xxii, 335, 353

Wyatt, Matthew Digby xxi, 259, 314, 329, 360–1, 363

Xenophon 128–9, 168, 199, 519, 526, 530

Xia, Chinese dynasty 192

Xisuthrus see Ziusudra

Xithurus see Ziusudra

Yao, emperor of China 191–3, 517

Yu (the Great), emperor of China 191–2, 517

Zelaia see Zelaya

Zelaya, Joaquín de 79, 337, 348

Zesen, Philipp von 214

Zeus 500; see also Jupiter

Zhou, Chinese dynasty 195

Ziegler, Jules 138–40, 455

Ziusudra, mythical Sumerian king 528–9

ACKNOWLEDGEMENTS

This book would not have materialized without broad support. We are particularly indebted to the following persons: to Philip Ursprung for his unfailing endorsement as our partner at the gta Institute, ETH Zurich, in the collaborative Swiss National Science Foundation (SNSF) research project 'Architecture and the Globalization of Knowledge in the 19th Century: Gottfried Semper and the Discipline of Architectural History'; to Elena Chestnova and Claudio Leoni, who collaborated as researchers on that project and provided information and documentation from hard-to-access sources; to Bruno Maurer, Daniel Weiss and the staff of the gta Archives – Ziu Bruckmann, Marco Cascianelli, Almut Grunewald, Afra Häni, Muriel Pérez, Filine Wagner and Alex Winiger – for facilitating access to the materials of the Semper estate; to our team from the SNSF research project on the critical digital edition of Semper's *Style* – Carmen Aus der Au, Céline Berberat, Oliver Camenzind, Elena Chestnova, Raphael Germann and Tanja Kevic – for supporting us in numerous respects; to Veronika Darius and Moritz Gleich, the former and the current director of the gta Verlag, and its sales director, Ursula Bein, for their confidence and support in the realization of the book; to Michael Robertson, Christopher Davey and Jennifer Bartmess for their essential contribution to the linguistic shape of the book; to Murray Fraser, Abigail Grater, Henrik Karge and Thomas Skelton-Robinson for their commitment; and last but not least to Philippe Mouthon for his unwavering dedication to the graphic implementation of the complex structure of the book.